Dedication

To Zac, Shira, and Jacob

The Ultimate Jewish Teacher's Handbook

Edited by Nachama Skolnik Moskowitz

A.R.E. Publishing, Inc.

Denver, Colorado

Published by:
A.R.E. Publishing, Inc.

Library of Congress Control Number: 2003106050
ISBN 0-86705-084-5

Acknowledgements

It was an awesome privilege to be asked to edit this edition, *The Ultimate Jewish Teacher's Handbook*. Through the book's development, I read each chapter an average of five times. As editor, I have been pushed in my thinking by each of the incredible authors who lent their expertise to this volume. I thank them for their work, the manner in which they tackled my questions, and their patience with the project's duration. They wrote with attention to an audience of readers that spans the religious movements, that teaches in both formal and informal settings, and that works with a variety of ages. Clearly, their accomplishments are amazing!

I also offer my deepest appreciation to Steve Brodsky, President of A.R.E. Publishing, Inc., and Audrey Friedman Marcus and Rabbi Raymond A. Zwerin, Senior Editors, all of whom offered great behind-the-scenes assistance and gentle nudges that helped me stay on track with the book.

My children also deserve a mention on these pages, as they "lost" their mom at times to the editing of this handbook. I thank them for their support and for their back rubs when I sat at the computer for too long!

Contents

INTRODUCTION   xi

PART I: IN THE BEGINNNG

1. Beyond Apples and Honey: The Editor's Soapbox   1
   Nachama Skolnik Moskowitz

2. Quick Guide to Starting in a New School   13
   Sylvia F. Abrams

PART II: THE BIG PICTURE

3. Jewish Education in the Twenty-First Century: Framing a Vision   29
   Jonathan S. Woocher

4. A *Reform*ation in Jewish Education   35
   Jan Katzew

5. Conservative Jewish Education: Walking Purposefully toward God's Holy Mountain   44
   Robert Abramson and Serene Victor

6. Training and Developing Reconstructionist Jewish Teachers   49
   Jeffrey Schein and Linda Holtzman

7. Orthodox Jewish Education   55
   Leonard A. Matanky

8. Teaching in a Jewish Community School   66
   Marc N. Kramer

9. Connections and Journeys: A New Vocabulary for Understanding American Jewish Identity   74
   Bethamie Horowitz

10. Ethics and the Jewish Teacher   80
    Zena Sulkes

PART III: WHO WE TEACH

11. Developmental Psychology   85
    Roberta Louis Goodman

12. Jewish Early Childhood Education   109
    Maxine Segal Handelman

13. Creating Programs That Captivate Jewish Teens   127
    Debbie Findling

14. Teaching Jewish Adults   140
     Diane Tickton Schuster and Lisa D. Grant

15. Family Education   164
     Jo Kay

16. Special Needs Students   177
     Ellen Fishman

17. Dealing with Children at Risk   187
     Steven Bayar and Francine Hirschman

PART IV: WHERE WE TEACH

18. Creating a Learning Environment   202
     Rivkah Dahan and Nachama Skolnik Moskowitz

19. Building a Classroom Community through Thoughtful Classroom Management   215
     Marilyn A. Gootman

20. Advancing through Retreating   227
     Judith S. Schiller

21. Beyond the Classroom — Reaching and Teaching in the Home   241
     Enid C. Lader

22. Jewish Learning in the Digital World   250
     Caren N. Levine

23. Summer Camping: Teaching in Your Pajamas   269
     Gerard W. Kaye

PART V: CURRICULUM CONSIDERATIONS

24. Curriculum Planning: A Model for Understanding   278
     Nachama Skolnik Moskowitz

25. Applying 4MAT To Jewish Curriculum and Instruction   292
     Cynthia Dolgin, Bernice McCarthy, and Marcey Wagner

26. Studying Curriculum Materials: A Strategy for Improving Teaching   311
     Gail Zaiman Dorph

PART VI: ORGANIZING FOR INSTRUCTION

27. Multiple Intelligences   323
     Renee Frank Holtz and Barbara Lapetina

28. Empowering the Learner: A Look at Constructivism   334
    Nachama Skolnik Moskowitz

29. Learning Centers   340
    Marci Rogozen and Ronna Fox

30. Cooperative or Collaborative Learning   351
    Carol K. Ingall

PART VII: PEDAGOGIC CONTENT KNOWLEDGE

31. Teaching about God and Spirituality   363
    Sherry H. Blumberg

32. Teaching Texts   374
    Betsy Dolgin Katz

33. Teaching Torah   388
    Joel Lurie Grishaver

34. Teaching Midrash and Rashi   403
    Joel Lurie Grishaver

35. Teaching about Prayer   413
    Rachel Raviv

36. Teaching Jewish History   424
    Julia C. Phillips and Lauren B. Granite

37. Engaging with Israel   440
    Sally Klein-Katz and Paul Liptz

38. Teaching Mitzvot, Values, and Middot   453
    Steven Bayar

39. Teaching Life Cycle   461
    Bruce Kadden

40. Teaching Jewish Holidays   472
    Nachama Skolnik Moskowitz

41. Integrating Social Justice into Jewish Curriculum   481
    Sharon Morton

42. Teaching Hebrew Reading   495
    Dina Maiben

43. Teaching Hebrew Language   516
    Bunnie R. Piltch

PART VIII: ENRICHING INSTRUCTION

44. Teacher, May I . . . and Other Classroom Questions   529
    Janice P. Alper and Shayna Friedman

45. Active Learning   542
    Melissa Bailin Bernstein

46. Enriching Instruction with Art   552
    Eileen Ettinger

47. Enriching Instruction with Drama   570
    Gabrielle Kaplan-Mayer

48. Enriching Instruction with Music   580
    Julie Jaslow Auerbach

49. Enriching Instruction with Dance and Movement   592
    Ofra Arieli Backenroth

50. Enriching Instruction with Stories and Storytelling   608
    Meryl Wassner

51. Enriching Instruction with Games   620
    Susan Arias Weinman

PART IX: WORKING WITH COLLEAGUES

52. The Teacher/Principal Relationship   637
    Jody Rosenbloom

53. Partnering with a Mentor   653
    Judy Aronson

54. Collaborative Curriculum Development   662
    Rhonda Rosenheck

55. Working with Teen Assistants   675
    Patti Kroll

REFERENCE

Resources for Jewish Educators   689

Contributors   701

Commentators   711

Index   713

Introduction

How well I remember my first teaching position in the Jewish community. As a young college student, I was hired to teach an *Alef* (first year) Hebrew class. When I think now about what I did not know then, I am amazed I made it successfully through the year! That I did "well enough," and that I became a professional Jewish educator, was due to the support given me by the school director. She mentored me, modeled good classroom practice, made sure I had the appropriate resources, and held my hand.

But I did not always work in situations where a wise colleague could mentor me. Thank goodness that early in my career, A.R.E. Publishing, Inc. came out with *The Jewish Teacher's Handbook*, Vol. I, edited by Audrey Friedman Marcus. Veteran Jewish educators from across the nation came into my living room through the pages of my lovingly used copy of the Handbook, which still sits on my shelf. These experts, and those that followed in later editions, sat on my shoulder and whispered into my ear, offering their assistance.

PURPOSE

The Ultimate Jewish Teacher's Handbook is a freshly written resource for all teachers, whether new to the classroom or veteran, whether teachers of young children, high schoolers, or adults, whether in a preschool, day school, supplementary school, or informal setting, and whether in a liberal or more traditional setting.

This volume has been crafted with a vision of what makes for effective Jewish education. Those who know me professionally, know that I advocate for:

- moving beyond teaching activities that are fun, but empty of content.

- focusing on the "big ideas" of Judaism, rather than a myriad of facts about history, Bible, holidays, etc.

- taking the time to develop curriculum, instead of depending on textbooks to guide classroom teaching.

- empowering students as learners, which means shifting our roles from providers of information, to facilitators of the learning process.

- reflecting on our practice as educators.

The chapters in this handbook aim toward these understandings of our profession. The authors were chosen because they, too, see Jewish education through one or more of these lenses.

To draw you (the reader and my educational colleague) into the chapters, most authors included vignettes that bring to life their narrative. Many have also ended their chapters with "Teaching Considerations," a listing of the key ideas they want readers to take with them. Annotated bibliographies complete the chapters, each offering recommended readings to push beyond the ideas explored by the author.

Added to this volume are exciting "Teacher Comments" — reflections by both veteran and novice teachers that give first-hand "been-there-done-that" advice. Contributors bring to life the issues that are part of the day-to-day adventure of teaching.

ORGANIZATION OF THE BOOK

For ease of use, *The Ultimate Jewish Teacher's Handbook* has been divided into nine parts, each containing several chapters grouped thematically. Each of these is described below.

Part I: In the Beginning

The two chapters in this section provide a starting point – one philosophical and one practical. Chapter 1, "Beyond Apples and Honey," offers the editor's vision for Jewish education, with a delineation of the foci that will help shift our current practice to one that truly engages and empowers Jewish learners. It was through this lens that the other Handbook authors were chosen. Chapter 2, "Quick Guide to Starting in a New School" was designed to help newly hired teachers who may be overwhelmed by the preparations for opening day, but do not yet have the time to read through the rest of this book. It offers practical advice, along with the kinds of questions a new teacher should be asking of his or her school director.

Part II: The Big Picture

Each of us teaches within a setting influenced by a Jewish educational philosophy that goes beyond the particular institution. In this section, opened by a broad overview of the goals of Jewish education, authors lay out their thoughts on teaching from the perspective of the major Jewish movements in North America. So, whether in a day school, supplementary school, youth group, or camp, educators can better understand the philosophical implications of their institution. Part II concludes with an important overview of Jewish identity research, as well as thoughts on teacher ethics, a topic often swept under the carpet.

Part III: Who We Teach

Education is not about the brilliance of our teaching, but rather our understanding of the learning process through the perspective of our students. This section offers a broad overview of developmental psychology, written from the perspective of Jewish education, and then takes a closer look at the characteristics of the various populations within our institutions, including early childhood, adolescents, adults, families, special needs students, and those at risk.

Part IV: Where We Teach

The nuances of what we do as educators are influenced by the settings in which we meet our students. Part IV opens with a chapter on creating physical classroom space that is conducive to learning. It is followed by a chapter on developing the psychological space that opens students to education, particularly on building community. It is this second chapter that incorporates strategies for classroom management, within the context of a respectful community. However, Jewish education is not limited to the classroom; it also takes place in a variety of other settings, each of which have dedicated chapters in this section: retreats, home, the Internet, and summer camp.

Part V: Curriculum Considerations

Three separate chapters provide complementary information on curriculum design. The first two make applications of popular research-based models for curriculum design to a Jewish context: one offers an overview on the use of *Understanding by Design* by Grant Wiggins and Jay McTighe, and the other provides an overview of Bernice McCarthy's 4MAT system. The concluding chapter in this section offers a way for educators to improve their teaching through a study process of curriculum materials.

Part VI: Organizing for Instruction

In the process of curriculum design, there are choices an educator needs to make about the organization of the learning tasks. This section looks at four of those: multiple intelligences, constructivist philosophy, learning centers, and cooperative learning.

Part VII: Pedagogic Content Knowledge

Prior to this volume, the chapters in the A.R.E. teaching handbooks have generically fit issues surrounding the learning process. However, "Pedagogic Content Knowledge" in the title of this section means that there are certain pedagogies that best fit specific content areas. Here, then, are thoughts from expert educators on how to teach specific subject areas that are the staples of Jewish education: God and spirituality; texts; Torah; Midrash and Rashi; prayer; Jewish history; Israel; Mitzvot, Values, and Middot; life cycle; Jewish holidays; social justice; Hebrew reading; and Hebrew language.

Part VIII: Enriching Instruction

Only a fraction of the population learns best by listening, and so this section offers a variety of ways to engage learners, including the use of good questioning and active learning techniques, as well as through various media (art, drama, music, dance and movement, stories, and games).

Part IX: Working with Colleagues

The job of a teacher, whether in a classroom environment or on the lawns of a summer camp, can be isolating — just the teacher and his/her students working together. In this section, the joys and challenges of collaborating are presented. The authors focus on the teacher-principal relationship, mentors, collaborative curriculum development, and working with teen assistants.

Reference

The final section of this Handbook features a comprehensive list of resources for Jewish educators, including a list of publishers/distributors of Jewish educational materials, distributors of Jewish audiovisual materials, biographies of contributors of chapters and of commentaries, and a useful index.

HOW TO USE THIS BOOK

Some books, like novels, are designed to be read from cover to cover. They often gather dust on bookshelves after completion. Others are picked up once, referenced, and also find their way to the bookshelf. But still others, like *The Ultimate Jewish Teacher's Handbook,* are accessed for different kinds of information again, and again, and again.

Newcomers to the field of teaching should probably start with Chapter 2, "Quick Guide to Starting in a New School" by Dr. Sylvia Abrams, and then proceed to other chapters of interest, including Chapter 19, "Building a Classroom Community" by Dr. Marilyn Gootman, which offers wonderful tips for setting up a respectful environment for learning.

Those who have been in the field for a while might check out the chapters that touch on their specific teaching settings (philosophical and physical), age levels, or content. Part V, "Curriculum Considerations" and Part VI, "Organizing for Instruction" offer information on creating high level, engaging learning.

No matter where a teacher starts in the book, she or he will find something of interest and use.

CONCLUSION

So, get a cup of tea or a mug of coffee, and curl up on a favorite sofa in your home or teacher's lounge. Find a chapter that grabs your attention and enjoy the whisperings in your ear of the talented authors of this, *The Ultimate Jewish Teacher's Handbook.*

CHAPTER 1

Beyond Apples and Honey: The Editor's Soapbox

Nachama Skolnik Moskowitz

Note: This chapter represents what I have come to believe are important changes for Jewish education. The ideas in this chapter formed the content of the Handbook, and all authors were asked to write chapters that supported this philosophy of education, whether or not they read in advance this specific "soapbox." May it not only frame your reading of the rest of the Handbook, but also inspire you to make changes in your practice, regardless of the Jewish education setting in which you do your holy work on behalf of the Jewish people . . . and of our future.

WHAT TO TEACH AND HOW TO TEACH IT

The field of Jewish education has grown and changed over the last 50 years. Textbooks are now produced with beautiful color pictures, family education is more the norm than the exception, teachers are the focus of major research projects, the Internet offers a new learning modality, and incredible funding is pumped into Israel programs for older students. Our Jewish adolescents have been the focus of a number of studies in the last decade,[1] and new ways of discussing adult Jewish identity have been suggested by recent research.[2]

Yet, as it is often said, "The more things change, the more they stay the same." The core of what we do and how we do it has shifted little over time. Jewish educators (as do many secular educators) often see themselves as providers of informa-

tion, whose task is to pour important learning into the heads of their students. Our curriculum is jammed with topics that educators feel must be covered before students exit schools in large numbers at age 13 (Bar or Bat Mitzvah) or 16 (Confirmation). Supplementary school teachers structure their year-long courses to cover a different topic each session ("if it's February 25th, it must be time to teach about the sweatshops on the Lower East Side of New York at the turn of the twentieth century, so that next week we can cover Jewish women in the suffrage movement."). Our days can be filled with "fun, hands-on, experiential" projects that skim the surface of important information, such as taking three weeks of Sundays to create a *kibbutz* out of cereal boxes.

Nationally, the Jewish community is pouring tremendous financial resources into the structural aspects of Jewish education. Our central Jewish education agencies, synagogues, and national organizations are supporting more family learning activities, informal educational opportunities (such as retreats and camping), salary supplements, teacher education opportunities, Israel trips, and the like. Yet, the core of our enterprise, the decisions we make about what to teach and the ways in which we teach, remain untouched, with but a few exceptions.[3]

Unless we seriously define and address this problem, all the structural shifts in the magic bags of Jewish educators and policy makers, will not affect the educational needs of the Jewish commu-

---

[1] Adolescent studies include the Brandeis University's Cohen Center Study on Jewish Adolescents (www.brandeis.edu/ije.Inquiry.html), and the United Synagogue of Conservative Judaism's Four Up (www.jtsa.edu/academics/pubs/fourup/index.shtml).

[2] Horowitz, Bethamie. *Connections and Journeys: Assessing Critical Opportunities for Enhancing Jewish Identity*. (New York: UJA-Federation of New York, 2000).

[3] The issue is not only endemic to Jewish education: "It seems that no matter how radical restructuring talk may otherwise be, it almost never touches on the curriculum itself . . . How is it that we can claim to speak of school reform without addressing the centerpiece of schools, the curriculum?" James Beane, "Middle School: The Natural Home of Integrated Curriculum," *Educational Leadership* (October, 1991): 9-13.

nity. This chapter sets the tone for *The Ultimate Jewish Teachers Handbook,* and offers a challenge to teachers in Jewish settings nationwide to change the basic nature of what and how we teach our students, no matter what their age. There are four issues in relation to this problem, each of which is discussed below: teaching about apples, incongruence with general studies education, wasting time teaching non-core knowledge, and teaching them everything before they leave.

TEACHING ABOUT APPLES

In the late 1980s, Harvard University's Graduate School of Education embarked on a six-year collaborative project between researchers at the Harvard Graduate School of Education and a select group of reflective Massachusetts school teachers.[4] Together they developed a pedagogy of understanding, one documented in numerous articles and several books. Their work, built on the foundations laid by Dewey, Bruner, and others[5] set the backdrop for *Understanding by Design*, a curricular framework developed by Grant Wiggins and Jay McTighe, which was published a decade later.[6] UbD, as it is affectionately known, is a "backwards design process," building curriculum upon enduring understandings, the big ideas that remain with us when all the little details disappear from our memories.

In the beginning of *Understanding by Design*, the book that outlines the UbD process, the authors describe a general studies unit on apples. The students do fun, hands-on, experiential activities similar to the following:

- Individually create maps that show where apples are grown in the United States.

- Learn about Johnny Appleseed.

- Visit an orchard.

- Make apple dolls or apple prints.

- Identify apples according to their variety.

- Create flow charts showing how applesauce is made.

When all is said and done, Wiggins and McTighe ask, what have students learned? Apples! And what will they remember? Not much.

The authors make the case that all activity-based teaching, in whatever discipline, shares the weakness of the unit on apples:

> . . . there is no real depth because there is no enduring learning for the students to derive. The work is hands on without being "minds on," because students do not need to extract sophisticated ideas. They don't have to work at understanding; they need only experience.[7]

We consistently teach "apples" in Jewish schools, focusing an enormous amount of energy imparting bits of information and creating hands-on, experiential, fun learning projects. The following examples can be found in most any supplementary religious school, and in many day schools:

- In the lower grades, for the High Holy Days, teachers often make apple print New Years' cards and honey pots; the big ideas of the new year get some mention, but not full focus.

- Students read about Jonah and spend time making elaborate big fish with a man inside.

- In the middle grades, students study the stories in the Bible, learning the details from retold tales of the biblical characters. In classes across North America, they participate in activity-based projects to create Abraham's family tree, write letters to God, act out short plays of the weekly Torah portion, and draw murals of the Israelites crossing the desert.

- In the preadolescent years, information on the history of Jews in the U.S. or Israeli society is presented via textbooks, videos, or "teacher-talk," and the follow-up activities (like making the Western Wall out of grocery sacks stuffed with newspapers) do not always reinforce understanding.

- Family education programs are filled with

---

[4]Wiske, Martha Stone, ed., *Teaching for Understanding: Linking Research with Practice* (San Francisco, CA: Jossey-Bass, 1998), 5.

[5]Ibid, 13ff.

[6]Wiggins, Grant and Jay McTighe, *Understanding by Design* (Alexandria, VA: Association for Supervision and Curriculum Development, 1998).

[7]Ibid., 21.

parent-child projects in which children dabble with an art project while the parents help.

"Apples" are seductive, for they encourage the teaching of surface knowledge – a mile wide and an inch deep. It's no wonder that numbers of our students claim they do not learn much from our Jewish schools.

INCONGRUENCE WITH GENERAL STUDIES EDUCATION

Our issues do not stop with "apples." The problem becomes compounded when teachers make assumptions about educational theory or developmentally appropriate practice that are incongruent with what our students learn in their general studies classrooms. This author has witnessed:

- A second grade teacher asking her students to tell her the time difference between Israel and their city ("If it's 10 a.m. here," she would ask, "what time is it in Israel?" She was not expecting an answer like "late afternoon," but rather one like "4:00 p.m.") Yet, in their general studies math classes, these students were just getting comfortable telling time to the minute.

- A third grade teacher asking her students to use a map scale to determine through multi-digit multiplication (inches on the map times the scale indication of miles/inch), the distance between their city and Israel. Yet, in their general studies classes, these students were just learning their basic multiplication facts (3 x 9 = 27).

- A third grade teacher in a liberal setting asking her students to read a section from the Bible and identify the metaphors. (This is generally is a skill students solidify in the sixth grade.)

- A sixth grade teacher covering all of American Jewish history in 25 sessions of religious school; students at this age might spend five weeks (25 general studies sessions) on one specific period of American history.

- A seventh grade supplementary school teacher spending two weeks on the histori-

cal causes leading up to World War II in a semester-long Holocaust course. "Cause and effect" history is more generally taught in the high school years.

It's important to note that when our students don't yet have the requisite general studies skills, teachers must work doubly hard to deal with the skill, before even attempting the Jewish concept. Students frustrated at not quite "getting" the assignments can be turned off to Jewish education.

WASTING TIME TEACHING NON-CORE KNOWLEDGE

If one reexamines the non-developmentally appropriate practice listed in the section above, another pattern emerges: teachers can lose sight of the important Jewish learning, focusing instead on tertiary information that at best has some Jewish connection (e.g., spending 20 minutes figuring out the distance between Cleveland and Israel), and at worst does not contribute to a student's understanding of important Jewish ideas (in reality, this lesson was mathematically focused).

None of these teaching examples in the sections above are intrinsically bad, and most are potentially engaging. But in each of our educational settings, the issue of time and focus comes sharply into play:

- Supplementary schools have approximately 30 regular teaching sessions with class times of 45 to 60 minutes each.

- Day school teachers have broad educational mandates, splitting time between Judaics and general studies.

- Informal educational settings, whether camps or youth groups, devote minimal time to the Jewish parts of their total programs, keeping the social aspects at the fore.

TEACHING THEM EVERYTHING BEFORE THEY LEAVE

With 40-50% of students leaving Jewish supplementary schools between seventh and ninth grade, those making curricular decisions worry about not teaching some "important" aspects of Judaism before the "exodus." And so many schools have courses with a goal to impart as much information as possible to the students in the upper elementary and middle school years. These include surveys of Jewish history, overviews of the life cycle, an introduction to Jewish heroes, a look at the various cultures that make up Israeli society, a semester of Holocaust history, etc.

All these are noble and worthwhile subjects. Yet, we need to remember that *what we teach* is not necessarily *what students will learn*, for a wide variety of reasons. Consider, for instance, the example of a year-long survey of Jewish history in sixth or seventh grade in which students spend a week or two (at most) covering a specific period of history or a historical event. Teachers may think students learn what is taught (and even offer proof from student quizzes or classwork), but in most cases, the information makes little sense beyond the imparting of discrete stories of our people, and thus is soon forgotten. This format of studying history is antithetical to general studies practice, for in these same grade classrooms, students may spend five weeks (25 sessions) on one specific period of history, whether an ancient culture (e.g., Greece or Rome) or a window in time (such as the American Revolution). A full survey of history waits until the high school years, on which students spend over 150 hours (by contrast, a full survey course in Jewish history taught in seventh grade would be allotted 20 to 25 contact hours of teaching time). Logically, then, our students would do better waiting to study a full survey of Jewish history until the high school years when they have at least completed a year of general studies history; our "story" could fit in the context of previous learning and historical discipline-based skills.

Yet, there are many educators who feel that there is danger in waiting to teach some specific Jewish content areas until the high school years (or even college), for we have lost many students by that time. These educators argue that if we do not include it in our curricula prior to Bar or Bat Mitzvah, then our youth may never be exposed to the specific ideas. But the counterargument is that if we taught Judaism in developmentally challenging ways that are intellectually appropriate to their age and understanding, maybe we would hold onto them beyond their Bar/Bat Mitzvah. This position takes courage, for it means thinking quite differently about what we teach, and when.[8]

SUMMARY OF THE PROBLEM

The four issues just delineated are part of the status quo in both formal and informal Jewish educational settings (and in general studies ones, as well). Each, in and of itself, points to a weakened foundation upon which all other initiatives rest:

- the preponderance of "apples" in the curriculum

- the at-times incongruence between students' general studies education and the Jewish setting

- the tendency to teach non-core Jewish knowledge and activities

- a desire to cram into the heads of pre-13-year-olds "all" of Jewish history, knowledge, belief, and practice

Abundantly found in our supplementary schools, day schools, and informal education settings (e.g., camp and Israel trips), these issues hold us back from truly educating young Jews. Regardless of Jewish education's innovations and new structures, unless we strongly address the core of our educational enterprise (the curriculum), no real and lasting impact will result from our intense efforts on behalf of "continuity," "renewal," or "renaissance."

If the foundation of our work in Jewish education — the learning process — is not sound, then all that we build on top is in danger of crumbling. This foundation rests solidly in the hands of those who plan curriculum and those who teach.

A HYPOTHESIS

To create a strong educational foundation for our Jewish schools and community initiatives, Jewish educators must begin paying close attention (1) to curriculum and instruction, and (2) to the interplay

---

[8]One school in which this has taken place is Bet Limmud, the weekday program of B'nai Jeshurun Congregation in Cleveland, Ohio. With the assistance of Project Curriculum Renewal of the Jewish Education Center of Cleveland, Bet Limmud developed a problem-based learning curriculum for Grades 4 through 7. Student learning and engagement has increased over the four years of its use in the school. For more information on the development of this project and underlying assumptions, see "On the Edge, Ready to Leap" by Nachama Skolnik Moskowitz, in *Jewish Education News*, Summer, 1997.

between teacher and student(s), and students and subject matter.

The following hypothesis is put forth as guiding principles for educating committed Jews, steeped in their tradition, and knowledgeable about the resources available to further their own learning once out of the formal school years.

For Jewish education to be effective:

1. Learning must be developmentally appropriate.

2. The curriculum must be built upon the "big ideas" of Judaism, not disparate facts.

3. The focus must shift from "teaching" to "learning."

4. Students must be emotionally "engaged" in the learning process, individually and with his or her peers.

The following section explores each of these concepts.

Learning Must Be Developmentally Appropriate

With so little time in our Jewish educational settings, it seems quite obvious that to teach in non-appropriate ways takes up precious time and in the end fuels drop-outs. Students who are frustrated, confused, overwhelmed, or bored can make cogent arguments to their parents for not returning to this voluntary educational system.

What does it mean to teach Judaism in developmentally appropriate ways?

-   We must pay attention to what we ask students to do, not creating lessons based upon skills that students have not yet mastered in their general studies settings. While we could teach these skills before or during a Jewishly-focused lesson, most teachers of Judaica (whether in supplementary or day schools) are not educated in general studies pedagogy, meaning that the chosen teaching techniques will most likely not be efficient, and/or perhaps not even appropriate.

-   We must pay attention to the difference between what we think is important, and what is meaningful to our students. For example, we may think that it is important

for sixth graders to differentiate between the messages of the different biblical prophets, identifying the subtle nuances of each. Yet, for most 12-year-olds, this is not-meaningful information and, like most not-meaningful details taken in by the brain, it is soon forgotten. On the other hand, students would more likely identify with the inner courage needed by prophets to bring God's message to the world.

-   We must pay attention to the kinds of materials we use with students, finding those that match their reading levels and conceptual abilities. So much is available to us on the Internet, yet it is not all written in language accessible to those in elementary or middle school.

We must remember that when we translate learning that inspired us as adults (e.g., a great course on Bible, a lecture, a mentor's work), we must filter it for those younger than we. We come to our own education with years of experience and education. Our students generally have less experience in life, and so what we find compelling may make no sense to them.

The Curriculum Must Be Built upon the "Big Ideas" of Judaism, Not Disparate Facts

This chapter began with a description of an "apples curriculum," learning that may be activity-based and fun, but soon forgotten because of its fragmentation. The research is quite clear on the danger of "apples."

> . . . cognitive psychologists assert that a focus on discrete skills exaggerates differences in student ability and that many students are never able to fuse these skills into some kind of coherent whole. Learning needs to be focused on large concepts, patterns, and themes, with knowledge integrated across the curriculum.

> . . . Fragmented curricula do not easily connect with a learner's schemas; learners cannot find relationships and vital linking patterns among disparate bits of information that cannot be seen as readily coherent based on their own experience.[9]

_____

[9]Lambert, Linda. et al. *The Constructivist Leader.* (New York: Teachers College Press, Columbia University, 1995), 23.

Consider for a moment two different Sukkot units for the younger grades. One unit is built upon a well-crafted objective: Students will be able to explain and perform the *mitzvah* of sitting in the *sukkah*. In the lessons prior to the holiday, a fifth grade teacher might do the following to achieve this objective: read some stories about the *sukkah*, talk specifically about the *mitzvah* of sitting in the *sukkah*, teach the blessing for sitting in the *sukkah*, have students plan a party in the *sukkah*. Students might also create decorations for the *sukkah* and have a snack there, beginning with the appropriate "sitting" and food blessings. (And dare we doubt that students have done all these activities in previous years?)

The other unit is built upon a well crafted big idea (what the *Understanding by Design* authors call an enduring understanding): when we perform *mitzvot*, our actions strengthen our relationship to God and the Jewish people. Suddenly, our unit takes on quite a different dimension, for the *mitzvah* of sitting in the *sukkah* has a purpose behind it and the fifth grade unit would take on a different form. The teacher might ask students to read the section in the Torah describing Sukkot (Leviticus 23:33-43) and consider why God might have commanded us to sit in the *sukkah*. What did God want us to experience there? The students could develop a survey to determine the connections others feel to God or to other Jews as they perform the *mitzvah* of sitting in the *sukkah*. The students could learn about *Ushpizin* (the biblical guests we "welcome" to our *sukkah*), and then spend some time working in small groups to read material the teacher gathered about one of the individuals (one "guest" per group). With the help of focus questions, the groups each would begin to consider why this particular person is invited into our *sukkah* each year and create a poster or collage illustrating the reason. (This could then be laminated and posted in the *sukkah*.) Finally, while sitting in the *sukkah*, students could each recite the blessing individually and then say how sitting in the *sukkah* helps them feel a connection to God and/or the Jewish people.

Note the difference in the units. In each case, the activities relate specifically to the guiding statement. Yet, as compared to the one built on a finite objective or a goal, there is a richness of learning in the one built coherently around a big idea that is threaded through the learning activities.

Imagine the vibrancy of teaching units created with any of the following enduring understandings as the focal point:

- When we perform *mitzvot* (commandments), our actions strengthen our relationship to God and the Jewish People.

- Pesach is a lens through which the Jewish People view world events.

- The *Brit* (Covenant) contracted between God and the Jews through the Torah, has the power to engage and shape our lives as Jews.

- The Jewish role in the development of American music mirrors the status and comfort of Jews in American society.

There are huge implications for the field of Jewish education to move to teaching that is focused from enduring understandings:

1. *As a teacher, you must understand the big idea, which means having a sophisticated knowledge of your subject matter.* It is relatively easy to create units based on disparate facts, to read and discuss a chapter, to show a video, to do an art project, and play *Jewish Jeopardy* as the summarizing activity. But to think about the enduring understandings of Judaism and create developmentally appropriate units of study that engage students in the big idea takes a deep Jewish knowledge base and an ability to think abstractly. Many teachers in the supplementary school system, and counselors in Jewish camps, have little more than surface knowledge of Judaism, making this a difficult goal to attain.

What you can do:

- Find opportunities to deepen your understanding of Jewish thought and content

- Spend time with others talking about the "big ideas" of your units; just having the conversation will help deepen your understanding of Judaism. (This is an important process for the concrete thinkers among us.)

- Write out some enduring understandings for your units and develop learning activities to help students focus on these big ideas. (See Chapter 24, "Curriculum Planning: A Model for Understanding" by Nachama Skolnik Moskowitz, pp. 278-291 in this Handbook.)

2. *You must be sophisticated planners of learning activities.* It is critical to engage students in the enduring understanding through developmentally appropriate learning activities. Guide students to "uncover" important ideas with you, rather than "cover" a lot of discrete pieces of information. This means having a broad repertoire of learning activity formats, and the ability to match understandings with an appropriate activity. It also means advocating for longer class periods, as in-depth learning cannot be accomplished in 45 minutes.

What you can do:

- Try to gain pedagogic content knowledge, the understanding of the specific pedagogy needed for a particular content area. What are the ways that history is learned most successfully? How is that different from the way one might teach prayer? (Check out Part VII of this Handbook, "Pedagogic Content Knowledge"; it offers pedagogic approaches to a variety of content areas.)

- Broaden your repertoire of learning activities, especially ones that empower students in their learning by encouraging student-to-student interaction (e.g., cooperative learning groups). (See Part VIII of this Handbook, "Enriching Instruction"; it offers a large number of ways to enrich learning.)

- Advocate for (and then jealously guard) larger and longer blocks of learning time. While challenging to plan for at first, the in-depth learning results are worth the initial issues.

3. *Learn to focus on an enduring understanding, avoiding the temptation to include learning activities or content that you love, but that in reality have no direct relation to the big idea you wish students to learn.* A Bible class not focused on big Jewish ideas might spend two weeks building a large Noah's ark that becomes a school-wide collection receptacle for stuffed animals donated to children in need. It is cute and the end result promotes a Jewish value, but if this project does not develop a chosen enduring understanding around the story of Noah, it really does not belong in this particular unit.

What you can do:

- Work with your school director or co-teachers to plan units that coherently focus on "enduring understandings." Be "critical colleagues," carefully considering whether the learning activities really do match the big ideas of the units.

- Be open to your director, who may wish to talk about your lesson planning, help you focus learning on the big ideas, and/or offer alternatives to favorite projects.

4. *Look for materials developed with big ideas in mind.* It is rare to find a teacher, even in day schools, who brings *each* of the following to the classrooms: a sophisticated knowledge of Judaism, a broad repertoire of learning activities, an ability to keep the focus on big ideas, professional education, years of experience, and large blocks of time to devote to lesson preparation.

   All of these ingredients are key to developing learning settings that open the door to deep understanding by students. It is important that teachers have access to curriculum and teaching materials that support this conception of education.[10]

What you can do:

- Be critical of the materials you use in your teaching. Just because a textbook is nicely bound or has color photographs does not mean that it supports teaching the big ideas of Judaism. A great looking book can be very shallow, skimming the surface of Judaism, or filled with activities that do not help build a big Jewish idea. Where material falls short, try to fill in the gaps. Or, look around for another curricular piece or textbook that better fits this "non-apples" conception of education.

- If you need something to complement your teaching, ask. It is possible that your director or librarian can locate it for you, a parent can make it for you, or some kind colleague can share an idea or materials with you.

---

[10]The National Council of Teachers of Mathematics (NCTM) was able to push its agenda because publishers created materials to support the standards, which in their own way are the big ideas of math.

The Focus Must Shift from "Teaching" To "Learning"

When we teach, we can be animated, brilliant, and captivating, but that does not mean that our students have necessarily learned. Our focus in the classroom must be on our students, necessitating a change in teacher role from teacher-as-provider-of-information to teacher-as-facilitator-of-learning. Some call this moving from the image of teacher as "sage on the stage" to "guide on the side."

When students are empowered as learners, the understandings, knowledge, and information becomes theirs.

> . . . subject-matter never can be got in to the child from without. Learning is active. It involves reaching out of the mind. It involves organic assimilation starting from within. Literally, we must take our stand with the child and our departure from him. It is he and not the subject matter which determines both quality and quantity of learning.[11]

Their worth as Jews, their Jewish understandings, no longer remain dependent on an outside source, but on themselves, for Judaism takes on a different value in their lives when students think independently, know how to look something up, to find an answer, and to draw a conclusion.

Is it any wonder that when students leave the artificial world of school, with its textbooks, art projects, and teacher-led discussions, that they have little idea of how to behave Jewishly? Is it also any wonder that Jewish identity is enhanced when students are empowered as learners to find personal meaning and understandings on Israel trips, at summer camps, with youth groups, and in college?[12]

What you can do:

- Focus on student learning, and less so on your teaching. What can you do to empower students as learners? Consider doing more work in small groups and pairs, offering students primary sources (Judaic texts, photos that tell sto-

ries, etc.) from which to develop and test hypotheses.

- Be open to professional development opportunities, including coaching, that help shift traditional roles.

Students Must Be Emotionally "Engaged"

In the traditional educational model, still found in schools across the nation, the student *receives* information. Recent attention, however, has again been placed on a constructivist philosophy of education, which "place(s) in students' hands the exhilarating power to follow trails of interest, to make connections, to reformulate ideas, and to reach unique conclusions."[13]

In constructivist classrooms, students are active participants in the learning process as they reshape and internalize information by "constructing" knowledge . . . In constructivist classrooms, students often work with primary sources . . . They collaborate to gain a deeper understanding of the material studied. They are encouraged to ask questions of the material and of each other.[14]

Note the differences in student empowerment in figure 1 on page 9.

Constructivist philosophy engages learners in their studies, offering engaging and usually deep paths of learning, such as those described on the right side of figure 1 below. Many of these learning examples need larger blocks of learning time than are available, and most of them require access to a wide variety of resources, including people. They also require teachers willing to facilitate student learning and explanation, rather than giving them direct information.

This segment of the hypothesis focuses not only on student engagement in their learning, but their connections with guiding adults *and* with their peers. When offering her thoughts on the success of Jewish youth groups, Jewish college activities, Jewish camps, and trips to Israel, Dr. Bethamie Horowitz posits that these experiences work because they:

---

[11]Dewey, John, "The Child and the Curriculum," in *John Dewey on Education* (Chicago, IL: University of Chicago Press, 1964), 343.

[12]Horowitz (2000).

[13]Jacqueline Grannon Brooks, and Martin G. Brooks, *The Case for Constructivist Classrooms* (Alexandria, VA: Association for Supervision and Curriculum Development, 1999), 22.

[14]Moskowitz, Nachama Skolnik, "Bringing Authentic Learning Experiences into the Classroom," *Jewish Education News* (Winter 1996), 23-25.

Traditional model	Constructivist model
The teacher tells students about the parts of a traditional Jewish wedding and shows a video.	In small groups, students are given a box with the following items: an invitation written in Hebrew and English, four photographs of different stages of a wedding ceremony, a broken glass (safely encased), a *ketubah*, and a copy of the wedding blessings. Students are asked to determine what the symbols from a wedding tell the bride, groom, and their family about the important ideas of life as a married Jewish person. They compare ideas as a class, then watch a video to see what they might have missed.
The teacher has students read a chapter in their textbook on the connections between the Jews in Palestine and the Jews of America in the early twentieth century. They answer the questions at the back of the chapter and write a letter to one historical person of their choice.	Students are given a photograph found in the synagogue's basement by an office worker. At the bottom of the photograph is the title, "Hebrew Cultural Gardens," and the following people are labeled: Rabbi Abba Hillel Silver, Chaim Weizmann, City Manager William Hopkins, Leo Weidenthal, and a Dr. Zwick. They are told that their task is to figure out who the people are and why they are standing with shovels. To begin their work, they are given a chart that asks them what they know for sure, what they think they know, what they need to find out to solve the questions asked, and where they might go for information.
The teacher explains Judaism's emphasis on study and wisdom, illustrating her point with stories of some famous Rabbis.	Students are given blessings from the daily prayer book that emphasize learning, study, or wisdom, and are asked to analyze them in small groups using a chart provided by the teacher. They discover four different ideas about wisdom through this process, one more than the teacher anticipated.
The teacher shows students a map of Israel and points out cities and basic geographic features (mountains, desert, bodies of water, etc.).	Students work in small groups, each studying postcards from a specific geographic region in Israel and drawing conclusions about the climate. They also note any specific human interactions with the geographical features of the land.
In the midst of a unit on Shabbat, a student stumbles across the word "*eruv*."[15] When he asks the teacher, "What's an *eruv*?" she launches into an explanation.	When the student asks, "What's an *eruv*?" the teacher asks the students to figure out where they might go to find an answer to the question. After some brainstorming, the student calls one of the community's Orthodox synagogues and is directed to one of the Rabbis in charge of the city's *eruv*. The class is invited to meet the Rabbi for a "tour" and explanation.

Figure 1

---

[15]An *eruv* is a physical boundary that encircles a Jewish area of a city, creating a legal fiction that the area within the *eruv* is private domain. This permits Jews who observe *halachah* to carry items (such as a diaper bag, housekey, etc.) out from their home on Shabbat.

- enhance the formation of close relationships with other Jewish peers.

- encourage interactions with leadership-individuals who are "seen authentically as Jewish and come to represent a 'lived' Jewish life."[16]

Looking at these two bullet points one at a time begs some interesting questions: Would we attain the same results if our supplementary schools forged close relationships between Jewish children? In how many of our schools do students come from ten or more different public/private schools? In how many of our schools do students go through days on end without a meaningful conversation with another student? In how many of our schools do we keep students focused "front and center"? Indeed, could we tap into some of the positive results Dr. Horowitz reports by helping students get to know each other at the beginning of the school year and by using more cooperative learning techniques?

Studies of Jewish teachers indicate their passion for Judaism. What else needs to be done to encourage interactions with (teachers) who are "seen authentically as Jewish and come to represent a lived Jewish life"? Our students slip into classrooms late and leave early for a myriad of reasons excused by their parents. How do we open the gates to deeper (but still teacher-student appropriate) relationships?

What you can do:

- Empower students by asking questions and then waiting for their answers. Probe and press them to think, offering evidence to support their ideas.

- Find ways for students to work together. Two heads are, indeed, better than one, and the social benefit of students interacting is the building of close relationships that keep them connected to each other and to their Judaism.

- Consider your role as an authentic Jew, representing to your students a "lived Jewish life." What do they learn about the importance of being Jewish via their interactions with you?

CONCLUSION

Consider figure 2 on page 11, which illustrates the dynamic between the teacher, student, content, and the educational initiatives that affect their work together.

One may look at the diagram and consider each element alone: the teacher, the student, the subject matter and the "formats" the Jewish community has brought forth to address issues of continuity. Or, one can see the dynamics between the elements as played out in each initiative: how the teacher interacts with the subject matter, how the students interact with each other, how the students interact with the subject matter, and how the teacher thinks about the content.

Until we place greater emphasis on the core of our educational enterprise, the "what" and "how" we teach, teachable moments and teachable individuals will be lost. The conclusion seems logical — that for Jewish education to be effective:

- learning must be developmentally appropriate.

- the curriculum must be built on the "big ideas" of Judaism, not disparate facts.

- the focus must shift from "teaching" to "learning."

- students must be emotionally "engaged" in the learning process, individually and with their peers.

The challenge before us is to focus on the core of our work, to educate ourselves to the elements of powerful education, and to put them into practice. May you, the teachers of our future, go from strength to strength as you do this holy work.

---

[16]Bethamie Horowitz, vii and 191-2.

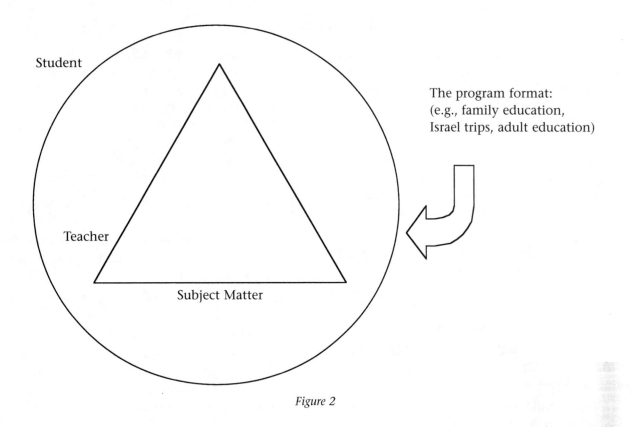

Student

The program format:
(e.g., family education,
Israel trips, adult education)

Teacher

Subject Matter

Figure 2

BIBLIOGRAPHY

Brooks, Jacqueline Grannon, and Martin G. Brooks *The Case for Constructivist Classrooms*. Alexandria, VA: Association for Supervision and Curriculum Development, 1999.

> A short, engaging book with a good, basic overview of constructivist philosophy. (Segments are quoted on the web site: http://www.adcd.org in the Professional Development section; check the "Tutorials," scroll down to the bottom of the page, then click on "Constructivism.")

Dewey, John. *John Dewey on Education*. Chicago, IL: University of Chicago Press, 1964.

> A collection of essays by John Dewey, the educator whose philosophies are the foundation of progressive educational thinking.

Eisner, Elliott W. *The Educational Imagination: On the Design and Evaluation of School Programs*. Upper Saddle River, NJ: Prentice Hall, 1985.

> A thoughtful book that helps readers understand major approaches to curriculum planning and the formation of educational goals.

Horowitz, Bethamie. *Connections and Journeys: Assessing Critical Opportunities for Enhancing Jewish Identity*. New York: UJA-Federation of New York, 2000.

> A study that offers a way of defining Jewish identity different from that of past research, one that acknowledges the journey of life and the various ways Jews connect into their heritage over time. See also Chapter 9 in this volume, "Connections and Journeys: A New Vocabulary for Understanding American Jewish Identity" by the same author, which describes this research.

Kadushin, Charles; Shaul Kelner; and Leonard Saxe. *Being a Jewish Teenager in America: Trying to Make It*. Waltham, MA: Brandeis University, Cohen Center for Modern Jewish Studies, 2000. (http://www. brandeis.edu/ije/Inquiry.html)

> A comprehensive, contemporary, study of Jewish teens and their parents representing a wide spectrum of Jewish observance and connections.

Kosmin, Barry, and Ariela Keysar. *The High School Years, 1995-1999: The Jewish Identity Development of the B'nai Mitzvah Class of 5755*. New York: The Jewish Theological Seminary, Rather Center for Conservative Judaism, 2001. (http://www.jtsa.edu/ academics/pubs/fourup/index.shtml)

> A longitudinal study of teens affiliated with the Conservative Movement.

Lambert, Linda. *The Constructivist Leader*. New York: Teachers College Press, Columbia University, 1995.

> Lambert takes the principles of constructivism, which empowers learners, and applies them to educational leadership.

Moskowitz, Nachama. "Bringing Authentic Learning Experiences into the Classroom." *Jewish Education News*, Winter 1996.

> This introduction to constructivism within a Jewish framework has been reprinted in this Handbook in Chapter 28, "Empowering the Learner: A Look at Constructivism," pp. 334-339.

_____. "On the Edge, Ready to Leap." *Jewish Education News,* Summer 1997.

> A summary of the first year's planning efforts to guide a supplementary school to a constructivist philosophy in its Grades 3-7 classrooms.

Sarason, Seymour. *The Culture of the School and the Problem of Change*. Boston, MA: Allyn & Bacon, 1982.

> A classic book in the field of education, which discusses issues of change in the school setting.

Wiggins, Grant, and Jay McTighe. *Understanding by Design*. Alexandria, VA: Association for Supervision and Curriculum Development, 1998.

> A book (and also a handbook, and a video) that guides educators through a curriculum development process, which leads to understandings of the big ideas in life.

Wiske, Martha Stone, ed. *Teaching for Understanding: Linking Research with Practice*. San Francisco, CA: Jossey-Bass, 1998.

> This book describes the Harvard University, Project Zero's Teaching for Understanding (TfU) project. It offers the philosophy and research principles of TfU, opening a window into curriculum development using this process.

CHAPTER 2

Quick Guide to Starting in a New School

Sylvia F. Abrams

Judy Klein walked out of Dr. Robbins' office giddy with excitement. She had done it — signed her first teaching contract! With a brand new Bachelor's Degree in elementary education and plans to earn a Master's Degree sometime in her future, Judy had just become the Buber Community Day School's (BCDS) new second grade teacher of both Judaic and general studies. Of course, her formal college level training fitted her for the general studies assignment, causing only minor butterflies in her tummy. It was the offer to teach Judaic studies as well that had her head reeling. Little had Judy known that her years as a day school student in the greater New York area would make her such a desirable commodity in the Midwest. And that year of volunteering in Israel hadn't been a waste! Her fluent Hebrew had locked in the offer. Now all Judy had to do was prepare to teach a double load over the next eight weeks. Where to begin?

The purpose of this chapter is to take Judy and any beginning teacher through the steps involved in opening school and starting the year successfully. While Judy is a day school teacher, the curricular and structural decisions that will chart her course for the balance of the year are applicable to teachers in any setting (day, supplementary, preschool, adult education). Judy will consider such broad topics as her goals as a Jewish educator, and such practical items as where to keep supplies. Thinking and planning for the first weeks and months of teaching will allow Judy to anticipate difficulties, minimize obstacles, and increase the probability of a wonderful first year.

SETTING GOALS

Judy spent the first day after signing her contract looking at the goals of BCDS. Such goals are sometimes rather daunting. Placed upon the shoulders of classroom teachers are responsibility for Jewish continuity, Jewish identity formation, as well as the preparation of a cadre of students who will qualify for admittance to Harvard and be Olympic athletes. Judy wondered how she could sort out her goals for second grade in a community day school from all the rhetoric of renaissance and renewal, active learning, independent thinking, lifelong learning, subject matter competency, and mastery of learning. Judy recalled the "What is a good Jew?" exercise in which she had participated as part of an Introduction to Jewish Teaching program.[1] She had tried to identify certain basic beliefs, behaviors, and attitudes that contribute to Jewish identity. Her top choices were accepting being a Jew and not hiding it, and leading an ethical and moral life. She is unsure how these lofty ideas will be transmitted into her classroom.

Goals of the School

Judy doesn't have to figure out her goals alone. The Buber Community Day School has a philosophy of education statement. Judy received this in a packet that accompanied her contract. Judy also remembered that the school's philosophy was posted on its web site. It was reassuring to read that the BCDS philosophy included integration of Judaic and general studies, community service, and the creation of active, independent learners.

- Does your school have a goal statement? Is it called its philosophy of education? Who receives this statement?

- Does your school have a web site? What kind of information is posted there that might be helpful to learning more about your new employer?

---

[1]The "Good Jew" exercise is based upon work of Steven Huberman, 1981, and is used in the Introduction to Jewish Teaching program at the Jewish Education Center of Cleveland.

Jewish Religious Movement

BCDS is not affiliated with a religious stream within Judaism. It is a member of the Jewish Community Day School Network (known by its Hebrew acronym, RAVSAK) and the Independent Schools Association (ISACS). Judy questioned if the associations promoted particular goals for their member schools. She checked their web sites for information.

- Is your school part of a one of the religious movements: Reform, Conservative, Reconstructionist, Orthodox, Lubavitch? Ask your principal for the goals of the movement.

- Does your school favor an approach to teaching: Montessori, Problem-based Learning, constructivism, essentialism? Ask your principal for information on the goals of these approaches. Find out how much this approach must guide your teaching. Does your school provide professional development for its approach to education?

Community Norms

Judy was thrilled to be relocating to *Yehofitzville*, a Midwest town with a moderate sized Jewish community and an affordable standard of living for a first year teacher. She had asked her principal during the interview process if there were any communal expectations for the teachers at BCDS that she should know about. As the only school in town, BCDS expected its teachers to maintain *kashrut* in public and to avoid activities that could be considered *chillul Shabbat* (desecration of the Sabbath). Judy was willing to abide by these norms and understood that a goal of her school was for teachers to serve as role models.

- Does your school have any norms to which you are expected to adhere? It's best to ask about such expectations during the interview process before a contract is signed. If you don't, you might be surprised.

Individual Goals

Judy has some personal goals for her first teaching

assignment. These include being prepared and finding time to investigate graduate studies. Judy believes in meeting the varied needs of students in a heterogeneous classroom. She likes the idea of flexible scheduling and being in charge of managing the students' time. BCDS's philosophy of independent active learning melds with Judy's personal goals.

- Do you have personal goals you want to incorporate into your teaching? Are they related to your professional time or to the balance of your week?

Group Goals

Judy is not the only second grade teacher at BCDS. She and her colleague, Ava Cohen, are part of the elementary division of BCDS. Judy will report directly to Jim Silver, the elementary assistant principal. Her division regularly holds its own staff meetings, she has learned. The elementary division has its own prayer services. There may be interclass group projects as well. Judy speculates about her ability to integrate the group's goals and her strong personal goals for teaching. It certainly will be a balancing act.

- Are you to be part of a team? Is there more than one teacher at your grade level?

- Who is responsible for group goals?

- How often will your class join other groups?

Cognitive (Knowledge) Goals

Buber Community Day School is required by state law to administer proficiency tests in general studies. One of Judy's goals is to prepare her second grade students to pass cognitively the third grade reading and math tests. In her recent university studies, Judy had learned about developing enduring understandings.[2] She hopes that successful preparation for the proficiency exams will not interfere with her desire to teach toward this goal. Judy is troubled by the apparent lack of formulated cognitive goals in Jewish studies. She plans to schedule time with the other second grade teacher to learn more about the goals for Hebrew language.

---

[2]Grant Wiggins and Jay McTighe, *Understanding by Design* (Alexandria, VA: Association for Supervision and Curriculum Development, 1998).

- Do you have a goals statement for your division or grade? How specific are they?

- What is the balance between cognitive and affective goals in your school?

- What do you think should be the balance between cognitive and affective goals in your classroom?

Affective (Socio-Emotional) Goals

Dr. Robbins had mentioned the importance of the whole child at BCDS. In fact, this is what had convinced Judy that BCDS was the place to begin her career. Her student teaching experience had only reinforced her view that the emotional domain was as important as content knowledge. Judy was certain that her affective goals for second graders would be in consonance with the philosophy at BCDS. She cherished her Jewish values and had been proud to be able to act upon them during her volunteer year in Israel.

- What more should Judy learn about the affective goals at BCDS?

- Do your school's goals include the child's emotional well-being?

- Does your teaching assignment include ways to act upon Jewish values?

THE CURRICULUM

Armed with knowledge of her school's philosophy and goals in broad strokes, Judy returned to BCDS to obtain her curriculum and books. Luckily for her, she had not been handed these materials with her contract; she would have been overwhelmed. There are many institutions that give the beginning teacher the curriculum and supporting materials at the same time as the contract is signed. This is more common in a congregational or supplementary school setting in which employees are usually part-time. Let's turn to what Judy can reasonably expect to receive.

Curriculum Guide

The curriculum guide may vary in its details. Usually the curriculum will provide specific instructional objectives for the particular grade, sometimes broken down into units. In some places, the curriculum will even provide objectives by lesson. This is more common in part-time programs that may be staffed by avocational or volunteer teachers.

The curriculum guide will likely provide an overview of the subject area in addition to the objectives. Some curricula also include suggested teaching activities and methods of assessment or evaluation. Judy received curriculum guides for each of the general studies areas she is to teach: language arts, mathematics, science, and social studies. For her Judaic studies subjects, Hebrew language arts and Tanach, Judy was instructed to consult the teacher guides that would be issued with the student texts.

Some schools rely upon the commercial guides prepared by textbook publishers and do not prepare school-specific curriculum guides. BCDS has invested time in writing its own curriculum guides for the general studies in order to provide guidance about how to integrate Judaic and general studies.

- Did you receive curriculum guides produced by the school?

- Were these grade-specific or general overviews of the objectives and outcomes for the learner?

Student Texts

BCDS has chosen basic texts for all the subjects Judy will teach. These include student workbooks for both English and Hebrew language arts and mathematics. Judy learns that the second graders will use a children's Tanach for Bible study. She checks the publication dates for the textbook series. She notes that most are from five to seven years old and makes a mental note to research material to update the social studies materials.

It is not uncommon for Jewish schools to use texts that are combination text and workbook. Often such texts are purchased by the student (and kept), rather than issued to them like a textbook (and returned at the end of the school year) to be used until the publisher prepares a new edition.

- Find out what texts your students will use and obtain copies in advance in order to prepare for teaching.

- If students use a textbook series, check the condition of the books.

Teacher Guides

Although Judy received a curriculum guide, she also was issued the teacher guides prepared by the publishers of each of the student texts. Such guides usually include overarching goals for the series of which this text is a part, general objectives for the particular text and suggested teaching activities. Rarely does a teacher guide include lesson plans, though they are filled with teaching and enrichment ideas.

> When my students come into class, there is a worksheet waiting for them on their desks or an assignment is written on the board. They all settle down and begin to work and get focused on the day's learning. This gives me time to collect homework, speak to children privately, and get the day under control. When students have finished the assigned task, we get right to work with no wasted time.
>
> With younger children I provide assignment sheets that are returned at the next class, signed by the parents who also indicate if there were any problems or issues that I need to know about. As I collect these, I quickly scan for these messages. If we have done anything special or unusual that day, or if there is any special information the parents need to know, I put it at the top of the homework sheet. Also, since the assignment sheet is prepared before class, when a child leaves early I just hand it to him/her to take home. When a child is absent, I put the sheet in the mail. Parents appreciate that they don't have to phone me for the work, and they have come to expect its arrival a day or two after their child's absence.
>
> *(Cheryl Cash-Linietsky, Philadelphia, Pennsylvania)*

Several Jewish publishing houses assume that instructors who utilize the teacher guide are novices.[3] These guides include model games and methods of evaluation. They also provide a summary of the content in the student text. Some congregational schools can afford to purchase only one copy of the teacher guide, which may then sit on a shelf in the principal's office.

- Find out if your student text has a teacher guide.

- Ask your principal to provide you with your own copy of any teacher guides for your student materials.

Auxiliary Teaching Materials

After Judy was issued her curriculum guides, student texts and workbooks, and teacher guides, she took several days reading them over and discovered that other types of teaching materials had been prepared for a number of her subject areas. The teacher's guide for the Hebrew language textbook referred to a classroom library, flash cards, game boards, and computer software. The social studies guides mentioned maps, videotapes, and Internet sites. The English language arts teacher's guide also included references to classroom readers and computer software.

Consequently, Judy returned to BCDS to find out what auxiliary teaching materials were available to help her prepare for the opening of school. She had made an appointment with Jim Silver, the elementary division principal who directed her to the BCDS learning center (library). From the teacher's section she borrowed flash cards and approximately 50 reading books to create an in-class library in a section of her room. Mrs. Greenberg, the media specialist, explained that the other auxiliary materials mentioned in the various teacher guides are beyond the budget of even a well supplied school like BCDS. However, Judy learned of a regional media center that loans to private schools maps, videotapes, and computer software for the general studies subjects. She was still in a quandary about where to find professional auxiliary materials for Hebrew language and Tanach.

- Plan to read your teacher guides immediately to ascertain if there are auxiliary materials available from the publisher. Find out how to obtain any that might be useful.

- Ask your school director where to obtain Judaic and Hebrew resources, perhaps through a local central agency for Jewish education.

---

[3]For sample teacher guides, consult those published by any of the major Jewish publishers.

CREATING A REALISTIC PLAN

All too often the beginning teacher can be overwhelmed by the amount of material with which to plan for the opening of the school year. In her zeal to prepare adequately, Judy has accumulated more information than she could manage. Her curriculum assignment is part of the child's total Jewish education; everything does not need to be taught in one year. Recent studies indicate the need for clear planning in order to produce measurable results.[4]

Planning Cycles

One way to approach planning for the year is to think of planning cycles, i.e., the time periods into which the school year logically breaks. These may be linked to the semester, the quarter, the school reporting-to-parents cycle, the Jewish holidays, or to units. If the planning cycle is from lesson to lesson, then material tends to be presented in a linear fashion. Some topics lend themselves to initial presentations and then to reinforcement and review by returning to them periodically. A graphical organizer such as a Gantt chart[5] is a helpful way to think of material that overlaps in this fashion (see figure 1 below).

Notice that the material represented by > is taught daily in the first week, reinforced three times in the second week, and reviewed twice in weeks three and four. In week two, the concept represented by * (and dependent upon the first material) is introduced. In week three, the next new idea that builds on the first is introduced,

while the two previous concepts continue to be part of the teaching. Judy has found this way of planning to be useful in thinking about the Tanach analysis skills she wants to introduce to her students.

- Does your course of study lend itself to a particular planning cycle?

- Find out if you are expected to plan for celebration of the Jewish holidays in your class.

- Are there other special activities or events that will affect the planning cycle this year? Sometimes these can be such things as the installation of a new Rabbi, the dedication of a Torah, the celebration of a community milestone.

Units of Instruction

How much to plan in advance is a dilemma when starting a new school year. One view is to outline the entire year by units with objectives and then to plan the first month in detail.[6] This will allow for sufficient flexibility to adjust lessons to the realities of the actual classroom while providing adequate lead time for ordering auxiliary materials and other supplies. Judy decides to outline the entire year by the big ideas that she feels will connect across her subject areas. She contemplates using this yearly map as a way to identify opportunities for integration of Judaic and general studies, particularly in social studies and language arts.[7] Unit plans may last from one week to six weeks depending upon

Week One	Week Two	Week Three	Week Four	Week Five	Week Six
>>>>>	>>>	>>	>>	>	>
*****	***	**	**	*
+++++	+++	++	++	

Figure 1

---

[4]See Mike Schmoker, *Results: The Key To Continuous School Improvement*, 2d ed. (Alexandria, VA: Association for Supervision and Curriculum Development, 1999), and *The Results Fieldbook: Practical Strategies for Dramatically Improved Schools* (Alexandria, VA: Association for Supervision and Curriculum Development, 2001).

[5]A Gantt chart is a horizontal bar chart developed as a production control tool in 1917 by Henry L. Gantt, an American engineer and social scientist. Frequently used in project management,

a Gantt chart provides a graphical illustration of a schedule that helps to plan, coordinate, and track specific tasks in a project. Gantt charts may be simple versions created on graph paper or more complex automated versions created using project management applications such as Microsoft Project or Excel.

[6]Adapted from Jeri A. Carroll, Donna L. Beveridge, and Dianne L. McCune, *The Welcome Back To School Book* (Carthage, IL: Good Apple Publishing, 1987).

their complexity. Judy's plan gives her a general sense of the flow of her units.

> There are a variety of ways to start the year. I know the value of establishing rules, of introducing the curriculum, of providing some kind of set induction that gets the students curious about what we will be studying throughout the year. One other essential ingredient is to include something that students regard as fun. This might be a game, a riddle, a funny story, or making something similar. Hopefully, students will leave class with a feeling that this might be an enjoyable place to come to for the next 25 to 30 weeks.
>
> *(Michael Fixler, Syracuse, New York)*

Lesson Plans[8]

With a basic outline of the year and an overview of the first units done, Judy has to decide how many actual lessons it is realistic to plan in advance. No matter what the setting (day school, preschool or congregational school), writing out the first month's lesson plans can provide security to the new teacher. Some schools supply lesson plan formats, while others issue plan books that include grids of each week of instruction. When no curriculum guides are available, developing lesson plans based upon planning cycles and units is crucial. The World Wide Web includes a number of sites with model lesson plans for particular subjects.

- Find out if your school uses a standard lesson plan format.

- Prepare a notebook to keep teacher-made units and lesson plans with dividers for each subject taught.

Supplies

Based upon her outline of the year and detailed plans for the first month, Judy prepares a list of needed consumable supplies. Her next step is to ascertain which she would like students to purchase, whether these supplies are available at her school, and how to obtain those that are not. BCDS has a requisition system, a common practice in many schools. With sufficient notice, the supply room coordinator will process Judy's order and place the needed items in a designated place for pickup.

> School or synagogue libraries can be an excellent source for resources, whether you're looking for books to read to the children, books for your edification, or for books that the students can read independently. I display books related to a unit of study along the blackboard's chalk ledge and on top of cubbies and bookcases in order to create a stimulating and attractive learning environment. I like to make resources for research accessible so that during or after a lesson students can look for answers to their questions. Although the Internet can be a powerful tool, today's students need to experience the extraordinary value of books.
>
> *(Diane Schon Wirtschafter, Berkeley, California)*

Many schools have only standard consumable supplies such as colored paper and scissors. Students are expected to supply their own crayons, paints, markers, and rulers.

- Find out if there is a consumable supply allowance, and how you access it.

- Are students expected to purchase their own consumable supplies? Is there a limit to the amount you may reasonably expect them to buy?

SETTING UP THE PHYSICAL SPACE FOR SUCCESS[9]

While Judy has been concentrating on preparing for teaching, Dr. Robbins, the head of BCDS, has been overseeing the preparation of the school and its grounds for opening day. Luckily for Judy, classrooms at BCDS are painted, windows washed, and

---

[7]See chapter on "Integration and Interaction in the Jewish Day School" by Michael Zeldin in *The Jewish Educational Leaders' Handbook,* edited by Robert E. Tornberg (Denver, CO: A.R.E. Publishing, Inc., 1998), 579-590.

[8]Consult Lesson Plans at www.lessonplans.com.

[9]For more information, see Chapter 18, "Creating a Learning Environment" by Rivkah Dahan and Nachama Skolnik Moskowitz, pp. 202-214 in this Handbook.

floors waxed over the summer. Judy also has the good fortune to be the only teacher using her classroom.[10] Her unit supervisor, Jim Silver, has scheduled room setup days as part of the back to school orientation. This is a useful time to consult with more experienced colleagues on the various ways to set up the classroom. In many schools, a custodian sets class furnishings with no teacher consultation.

- Find out if you may set up your room in advance and if you will be sharing space with anyone.

- When may you co-plan the room setup with those sharing the space?

- Who needs to know of your room needs in order to assure its correct setup?

The Room Arrangement

The size of the classroom and placement of permanent items such as chalkboards, bulletin boards, and electrical outlets influence the possibilities for furniture placement. Nevertheless, instructional objectives and management should govern the room's arrangement.[11] Classrooms for young learners are often equipped with small tables and chairs for group seating, while students in the second or third grades are often provided with individual desks and chairs. Some congregational schools utilize tablet armchairs because various age students use the classrooms over the course of a week. Day school classrooms often include low bookshelves and carpets for reading time. Some classrooms also have Internet connections and computer stations. Fortunate young learners will have access to a sink and to their own bathroom facilities.

Judy pondered how to devise a room arrangement that will serve the various subjects. Both English and Hebrew language arts will be taught using reading groups. Mathematics will require manipulatives and social studies instruction will include student-researched projects.

- Think about what you will teach. How might you arrange the furniture to facilitate instruction?

- Do you anticipate any classroom management issues? Check that your planned room arrangement provides you with clear sight lines to all students. Check that students will be able to see the chalkboards.

The Teacher's Work Space

Beginning teachers often feel like "pack animals" as they tote teaching preparation materials and student work from home to school. The fortunate few are able to keep a duplicate set of preparation materials at their residences. Yet, teacher work space in the classroom is usually a desk with a few drawers. Sometimes a teacher may have shelves or a file cabinet for storage.

The placement of the teacher's workspace depends upon how the teacher's role is conceptualized. In a student-directed classroom, the teacher desk might be in the back of the room, while in a class requiring more teacher management, it might be near the entrance at the front. In either case, the beginning teacher needs to make explicit who has access to the teacher's workspace.

- Do you have your own workspace? Will you be sharing with anyone?

- Where do you intend to place the teacher's desk?

Student Lockers or Cubbies

Students also require space of their own to keep materials and store coats and book bags or backpacks. Students have little private space in school. Typically, there are open shelves inside the room for younger students. Some schools have supply "pockets" that fit over the backs of student chairs. Older students often use closed lockers located in hallways. When such storage is not secured, students tend to carry their supplies and coats with them from class to class.

- Where are students expected to store coats, books, and supplies?

- Do students have private space of their own, either in a locker, cubby, or desk?

---

[10]See "Creating Learning Centers" by Sylvia Abrams in *Pedagogic Reporter* 41, no. 2 (Winter/Spring 1991), co-authored by Madeline Rothbard, for a discussion of the difficulties of shared classrooms.

[11]See Virginia Richardson-Koehler, "Allocating Time and Space Resources," in *Learning to Teach* by Richard I. Arends (New York: Random House, 1988), 123-156.

- How do other teachers solve the space/storage issues, including rules for students getting materials stored away from their desks?

Bulletin Boards

A typical classroom, whether in a day school, preschool, or congregational school, includes bulletin boards. Sometimes there are also hallway bulletin boards assigned to particular classes or grade clusters. A welcome-back-to-school themed bulletin board can provide an intriguing way to involve students. Judy has planned to incorporate photos of her students on this board.

> Most other years, I have begun the first day of school with an art project, such as decorating a *kipah* to wear during Judaic Studies class or during *Tefilah*. This year, I decided to plunge into my Judaic Studies curriculum on the first day. In the beginning week of school, my students received a taste of a variety of subjects we will cover this year: Torah, Jewish law, and ethical dilemmas. By Friday, the kids were excited about class and enthusiastic about the curriculum. I found this to be my easiest first week of school ever.
>
> *(Maura Pollak, Tulsa, Oklahoma)*

Another bulletin board (if your class has more than one) might contain information to introduce the first unit. When a teacher has responsibility for several subjects, as Judy does, the bulletin boards can be used to focus student attention. This way, a day dreaming student will still learn even if his/her mind has wandered from the daily lesson.

A way to assure fresh bulletin boards is to assign them to students. At BCDS, the responsibility for hall bulletin boards rotates among the teachers on a particular hallway.

- Does your classroom have display space?

- Figure out how to make portable bulletin boards from foam core or another sturdy material if you lack adequate display space.

- Include the date to take down your "welcome back" bulletin boards in your planning book.

Summary of Organizing the Physical Space[12]

- Arrange the student furniture based upon room activities.

- Provide an extra desk and chair for a new student.

- Set up the classroom so you can monitor students.

- Be sure each student can see the teacher.

- Allow adequate space between student furniture.

- Arrange the room so students can see the chalkboard, any maps and audiovisual screens.

- If your room is not "perfect," figure out how to adapt your surroundings.

- Keep an extra powerstrip in your room to accommodate student computers.

- High student traffic areas, such as drinking fountains, should be kept clear.

- Clear paths must be maintained to the exit doors, in case of emergency.

- Arrange for sufficient storage for jackets, lunches, and backpacks.

- Devise in-room storage for extra paper, poster board, and sentence strips.

- Keep small supplies, such as extra pencils and erasers, in covered cans or boxes.

- Color code charts and maps and hang these in a closet for easy access.

- Lock cleaning supplies under a sink (if you have one).

- Be prepared to alter your room arrangement when it is no longer practical.

COMMON PROCEDURAL EXPECTATIONS

For novice teachers like Judy, or for experienced

---

[12]Adapted from Bonnie Williamson, *A First Year Teacher's Guidebook for Success: A Step-by-Step Educational Recipe Book from* *September To June* (Sacramento, CA: Dynamic Teaching Company, 1988), 18.

teachers who have accepted a new assignment, common procedures may be expected in most educational settings. The changes in general community climate regarding the safety of the North American Jewish community have affected these procedures. Most educational settings have made provisions for student and teacher behavior in case of security breaches or natural disasters.

Security

Buber Community Day School is located on a community campus that houses the Jewish Community Center, the local Federation office, and a senior citizen's housing complex. Such consolidation of Jewish community resources is increasingly common. Admission to the common parking area is monitored by a guardhouse and controlled by an electronic gate. Judy is issued a key card to raise and lower the gate, and a hangtag to post in her vehicle.

The BCDS facility is housed in one end of the same building as the JCC. This allows for shared use of physical education facilities and a combined commissary. However, the arrangement complicates internal security. Dr. Robbins has scheduled a security briefing for all employees as part of the back to school meetings. Judy is issued a second hangtag, this one to be worn whenever she is on the premises. The school doors are locked except at the beginning and ending of school. Judy is informed of the procedures for early dismissal of a student. She learns that building visitors are expected to wear a guest pass. She further learns of the procedures for using the JCC physical education area.

- How is security handled in your educational setting?

Safety

School safety today includes more than the stereotypical crossing guard. There are designated accident reporting procedures, and there should be standard provisions for treatment of children with severe allergies, such as to peanuts. Security issues, the requirement for seat belts and (in the case of young children) of car seats, may affect school field trips. Playground safety is usually in the hands of teachers and some teaching assistants.

- Where is the first aid kit located in your setting?

- Are you expected to know CPR? universal precautions for dealing with bodily fluids? Are you expected to know how to treat anaphylactic shock or to be able to perform procedures, such as the Heimlich Maneuver, in medical emergencies?

- Who in your class has special medical needs? What emergency procedures do you need to know? What supplies do you need to keep in your room?

- What are the school policies for students who need to take medicine during class? What is your role as teacher in reminding or dispensing?

Bells and Other Strange Noises

Various educational settings use different methods to manage movement. Many schools have loudspeaker systems for announcements. State law requires a distinctive sound for emergencies (whether drill, or real). Schools ring bells to signal the start of the day and for dismissal. Some schools do not believe in the use of bells and buzzers beyond those mandated. Instead the teacher is expected to regulate time internally. Nevertheless, students need to be on time for gym class, lunch, or an assembly.

Judy learns from Jim Silver that the elementary division only uses bells for emergencies and dismissal. She discovered as part of checking her classroom that the wall mounted clock did not keep accurate time, and so has purchased a wristwatch with alarms she can set.

- Learn the sound and meaning of any bells or buzzers.

- Know what you need to do if an alarm sounds (fire, tornado, security breach). Walk through the procedure yourself, and make sure your class knows clearly what to do.

Passing in Halls, Assemblies, Fire Dills, Dismissal

Student movement may be self-regulated or in lines with partners. Typically, as students move through the grades, they have more individual freedom to go from place to place in the school on their own.

At BCDS, students begin going to assemblies in the lower grades with student monitors at the beginning and end of a line. By eighth grade, students are expected to check themselves in at morning services and report to their first period classes independent of adult supervision. Ava Cohen, Judy's second grade colleague, explains that the school philosophy is to foster self-reliance and to have minimal adult supervision of procedures like hall movement and lunch.

ADMINISTRATIVE PROCEDURES

Basic administrative procedures are part of the daily expectations of any educational setting. A number of these are discussed below.

> A teacher I worked with had a fabulous exercise she did with her students the first day of the year. She asked them to write on a piece of paper what they wanted to learn and what they thought they would learn in the coming year. These writings were folded and placed inside a bottle and sealed. At the end of the year, the class opened the bottle and read everyone's thoughts. It was a great way for the students to remember where they had started and to recognize how far they had come.
>
> (Amy Appelman, West Bloomfield, Michigan)

Attendance

Anxious to start teaching, some educators forget to take attendance. However, state law mandates official attendance figures in any Jewish day school. Even congregational and preschools may be eligible for certain kinds of financial incentives from the community based upon attendance. Most schools require that attendance be reported to the office by a particular time each session. There may be an attendance officer who phones parents of absentees.

Tzedakah

Congregational schools usually collect *tzedakah*. Many day and preschools also participate in a similar collection, either each session or once a week. These funds are usually turned in to the school office with the attendance report. Some classes

make decisions about the *tzedakah* disbursement, while in other settings, a student council decides for the school.

Communications with Parents

Announcements and other written parent communications are often sent home with students. With the advent of the Internet, some schools use e-mail for these types of materials. Most institutions have specific policies about communication with parents. Judy is expected to document in writing any phone calls she makes to parents and to notify her unit supervisor if she schedules a parent meeting outside of the regular reporting cycle.

- Find out the school administration's attitudes toward communicating with parents.

- Do you need to document parent contacts?

Ava, Judy's mentor, alerts her to anticipate early parent conferences. Judy knows she will need a system for recording student strengths and weaknesses in preparation for this important facet of parent communication.

- Learn about reporting student progress to parents in your institution.

- Are you expected to give grades?

Issuing or Selling Texts and Other Items

Distribution of texts and other student materials is an opening the year routine that can take over the first session of school. Increasingly, schools conduct book sales before the start of school so that the classroom teacher does not have to be a financial wizard. Some schools also sell book bags and other school insignia items.

- What is your role in the distribution of textbooks and other student materials?

- May students write in their books?

The Library

Judy, the BCDS second grade teacher, has already visited the learning center for teacher materials. Her school has regular administrative procedures for student use of the library. Judy's second grade class will visit the library weekly. Not all Jewish schools are equipped with a full-time librarian or media specialist. Teachers may need to assist with the loaning of materials.

- Does your school have a library or media center?

- What are your school's expectations about student use of such a center?

Internet Use

Increasingly, Jewish institutions have web sites. Many schools have a local Intranet and provide teachers with e-mail addresses. Some classrooms have Internet hookups and specific policies about student access. Most students also have computers in their homes and a general familiarity with their operation.

- Find out if your institution will issue you an e-mail address.

- Learn about the ways technology may be incorporated into your teaching and into communication with students and parents.

- Ask what the Internet Use Policy is for your students, and be prepared to enforce it.

MEETING COLLEAGUES

Just as new students sometimes find it hard to make friends, the new teacher may also be reticent. Judy is fortunate that the large staff at BCDS is organized into divisions. In addition to Jim Silver (the elementary division principal) and Ava Cohen (the other second grade teacher), there are six other teachers and four assistants in her group. Until the back to school orientation the week before school opened, Judy had met only Jim, Ava, Dr. Robbins (the head of school) and the media specialist. Dr. Robbins uses the orientation, not only for room setup and procedural matters, but also to begin the integration of new staff into the BCDS professional community. At her contract signing, Judy had received a calendar and had rearranged her summer to assure her presence at all back-to-school meetings. She sensed the importance of meeting colleagues at this time.

- Does your school hold an opening orientation?

- Find out how to meet other teachers assigned to your grade or group of students before school opens.

Teacher's Lounge

The congregating area for teachers to exchange information and enjoy some "downtime" is the teacher's room. In schools with limited space, this may take place in the school office where a corner has been set aside for coffee, and a copy machine is available for teacher use. Most day schools and preschools try to provide a separate teacher's lounge for breaks and preparation time. It is an ideal place for the new staff member to get acquainted with other colleagues.

Finding a Mentor

Support for a good start to the year is more than summer preparation. Teachers early in their careers can benefit greatly from having a mentor.[13] Judy has a natural mentor in Ava Cohen, the other second grade teacher. Ava has been trained in mentoring through a staff development program. Some communities provide mentors for beginning teachers through the local central agency for Jewish education.[14]

- Learn how to find a mentor to support your teaching.

DRESS FOR SUCCESS

The same advice that applies to any new position applies to teaching. Know the amount of formality expected in a particular educational setting. Students have indicated that the appearance of the teacher is an indication of respect for them as learners. Those hired to teach in synagogues also need to ascertain if they will be worshiping with the congregation as part of their teaching assignment. Employment in an Orthodox setting usually requires modest dress for women. Judy, as a new college graduate, is aware that she will need to invest

---

[13]Sharon Feiman Nemser, *Helping Novices Learn to Teach: Lessons from an Experiences Support Teacher* (East Lansing, MI: National Center for Research on Teacher Learning, Michigan State University, February, 1992).

[14]If you are in a small community, you may find a mentor through CAJE (Coalition for the Advancement of Jewish Education), which provides mentoring to college students and other beginning educators.

in some appropriate garb for BCDS. She is able to ask Ava about the dress expectations at BCDS.

- Check the faculty handbook for a dress code.
- Talk to colleagues about how they generally dress for school.

THE FIRST WEEK OF TEACHING

Judy is eager to begin teaching. She has prepared for the first week by setting up her classroom, sending welcome letters to students and parents, participating in the back to school orientation, and talking extensively with her co-teacher and mentor, Ava. Judy has worked all summer to be ready for the opening of school. Judy is aware of the research that shows that the beginning teacher's greatest difficulties are usually in classroom management and planning sufficient activities in lesson plans.

> I am really slow in learning names and connecting them with faces! Each year I say to myself "Next year, I'll buy a Polaroid camera and bring it to school." I would like to take pictures of each child, and label them immediately with English and Hebrew names. Then I would take them home and use them as flashcards! With children who are not yet reading fluently, I would take two pictures — one for me, and one to label their cubbie or pocket in the classroom. That way, they would be independent in locating their supplies and/or announcements to take home.
>
> *(Anne Johnston, New Haven, Connecticut)*

A Great First Day of Teaching

Judy knows that the first day of teaching will set the tone for the year. She wants the day to be exciting and also to teach some new material. She intends to create a friendly atmosphere while being clear about behavioral expectations. Judy has thought about how she will introduce herself. Her introduction will be simple, but include the name she wishes to be called by the children and some personal information about her interests. She

wants to communicate how happy she is to be teaching second grade at BCDS.

Judy has also thought about a back to school activity for the children. She has borrowed her family's digital camera and plans to photograph the students both for the classroom and for future student web site projects. She intends to integrate general and Judaic studies through the creation of a class tree utilizing students' Hebrew and English names.

It is important for the first day to include serious work that sets learning expectations. In addition to outlining the daily schedule and procedures, Judy anticipates telling an exciting story and beginning student journals. The children will either write or draw their thoughts about this story, allowing Judy to assess their listening and comprehension skills. Her first day will include a tour of the second grade wing of the school and a visit to the playground.

Judy will pace the introduction of the array of subjects to be taught throughout the first week. She plans to start with both English and Hebrew language arts, and math the first day.

- Plan opening day activities for your assignment.

Student Interest Inventory

A good way to learn about your students is to conduct a student interest inventory. In the upper grades, students might share with a partner their most unusual happening, favorite television program, or the Jewish personality they most admire.[15]

Teachers can build a file card box of student interests during the first month of instruction that can be referred to in constructing future teaching and learning.

The Remaining First Week of School

Judy intends to introduce the balance of subjects gradually over the first week. She has found a number of assessment activities through which she plans to review skills learned the previous year. Some teachers may find that this assessment and review may take up to two weeks. In higher grades, these assessments may be formal. Teachers in part-time religious schools may find that much has

---

[15]Harriet Arnold, *Succeeding in the Secondary Classroom* (Thousand Oaks, CA: Corwin Press, 2001), 26-34. The suggested

activities can be adapted to a Jewish setting.

been forgotten over the summer.

The second grade team has prepared a special Kabbalat Shabbat (welcoming Shabbat ceremony) for the first Friday. Judy will use this occasion to introduce the study of Rashi to the weekly *Parashah* (Torah portion). This is part of the BCDS philosophy of "review and move forward."

- Ask colleagues about formal and informal assessment techniques for the opening weeks of school.

- What other testing and assessment does the school expect of you?

Over-Preparation

At the end of the first week, Judy is amazed at the number of activities that she did not accomplish. Most beginning teachers find it hard to anticipate the number of learning activities and experiences that their students can accomplish. Over-preparation provides additional activities that can be utilized in case a particular task either takes less time or turns out to be inappropriate.

- How long is your first lesson? Devise at least two additional learning activities to be ready in reserve.

THE HOLIDAYS AND YOUR TEACHING ASSIGNMENT

The Jewish yearly cycle is celebrated in every Jewish school. Within that framework, many beginning teachers feel that they must take responsibility for teaching the holidays, even if they are not part of their specific assignments. Judy's day school has developed a scope and sequence of content, concepts, and skills for each holiday to deepen understandings and prevent repetition.

- Learn about your role in the teaching of, and celebration of holidays.

- What did your students learn in previous years? What will they learn next year?

CONCLUSION

Judy Klein prepared to start her school year from the moment she signed her contract. While not all teachers may be engaged to teach in as resource rich an institution as the Buber Community Day School, any new hire may replicate the steps Judy took to prepare for a successful start to the year. (For a summary calendar of the steps involved in getting ready to teach, see the Appendix on the next page.)

APPENDIX

Summary Calendar of Getting Ready to Teach[16]

May - Sign contract.

June - Obtain all teaching materials.

- Study curriculum.

July - Plan curriculum.

- Order consumable supplies.

- Visit classroom.

- Meet with other teachers, if possible.

August - Write first month's lesson plans

- Design the physical layout of classroom.

- Prepare welcome letter to parents or conduct home visits.

- Order media resources for first month.

- Attend school orientation for new teachers.

- Find a mentor.[17]

September - Plan opening day activities

- Decorate room for opening day.

- Assess and review previously learned material.

- Set expectations and procedures.

---

[16]Check lists for opening school can be found in *The Teacher's Classroom Companion: A Handbook for Primary Teachers* by Mary Coons (San Raphael, CA: Teachers Handbooks, 1996); *Keys To the Classroom: A Teacher's Guide To the first Month of School* by Carol Moran (Thousand Oaks, CA: Corwin Press, 1992); *Succeeding in the Secondary Classroom: Strategies for Middle and High School Teachers* (Thousand Oaks, CA: Corwin Press, 2001), and *A First-Year Teacher's Guidebook for Success: A Step-by Step Recipe Book from September To June* by Bonnie Williamson (Sacramento, CA: Dynamic Teaching Co, 1988).

[17]See Chapter 53, "Partnering with a Mentor" by Judy Aronson, pp. 653-661 in this Handbook.

BIBLIOGRAPHY

Arends, Richard I. *Learning to Teach*. New York: Random House, 1988.

> Undergraduate text for basic management and lesson planning based upon research.

Arnold, Harriet. *Succeeding in the Secondary Classroom: Strategies for Middle and High School Teachers*. Thousand Oaks, CA: Corwin Press, 2001.

> Manual for beginning, middle, and high school teachers that includes: strategies from planning classroom design to dressing for success; handling the first week of school; planning for classroom instruction; student record keeping; and finding a balance between work, home, and colleagues.

Coons, Mary. *The Teacher's Classroom Companion: A Handbook for Primary Teachers*. San Raphael, CA: Teachers' Handbooks, 1993.

> Step-by-step handbook takes the primary school teacher through setting up classroom's physical layout, planning the year's curriculum, and the first day of school.

Moran, Carol, et al. *Keys To the Classroom: A Teacher's Guide To the First Month of School*. Thousand Oaks, CA: Corwin Press, 2000.

> Practical, easy to use workbook provides lesson plans, classroom management strategies, student assessments, and special aids for teaching bilingual students.

Marazano, Robert J., et al. *Classroom Instruction That Works: Research Based Strategies for Increasing Student Achievement*. Alexandria, VA: Association for Supervision and Curriculum Development, 2001.

> Distills the results of nine teaching strategies that have positive effects on student learning.

———. *A Handbook for Classroom Instruction That Works*. Alexandria, VA: Association for Supervision and Curriculum Development, 2001.

> A guide to facilitating study groups on the nine teaching strategies that have positive effects on student learning.

Saphier, Jon, and Robert Gower. *The Skillful Teacher: Building Your Teaching Skills*. Acton, MA: Research for Better Teaching, 1997.

> Comprehensive textbook built on the pyramid of teaching with units on management, instruction, and curriculum; includes good introduction to assessment.

Schmoker, Mike. *Results: The Key To Continuous School Improvement*. 2d ed. Alexandria, VA: Association for Supervision and Curriculum Development, 2001.

———. *The Results Fieldbook: Practical Strategies for Dramatically Improved Schools*. Alexandria, VA: Association for Supervision and Curriculum Development, 2001.

> These two books provide a foundation for improvement: informed, effective teamwork; goal setting; and the use of performance data.

Williamson, Bonnie. *A First Year Teacher's Guidebook for Success: An Educational Recipe Book for Success*. 2d ed. Sacramento, CA: Dynamic Teaching Company, 1998.

> Many helpful tips from an expert teacher's class, including several classroom layouts for the arrangement of desks.

Wong, Harry K., and Rosemary Tripi Wong. *The First Days of School: How to Be an Effective Teacher*. Mountain View, CA: Harry K. Wong Publications, Inc., 1998.

> A manual of ideas for new teachers organized around the teacher, expectations, classroom management, lesson mastery, and becoming a professional.

Newsletters/Magazines

DeBruyn, Robert L. *The Master Teacher*. May be ordered from The Master Teacher, Leadership Lane, PO Box 1207, Manhattan, KS 66505, www.masterteacher.com.

> Weekly newsletter of teaching tips.

Instructor Magazine

> Practical activities, insights, and resources for teachers K-8. Published by Scholastic Press, http://teacher.scholastic.com/products/instructor.htm.

"Off To a Good Start: Launching the School Year." Excerpts from the *Responsive Classroom Newsletter*. Northeast Foundation for Children, 1997.

> Suggestions for the K-8 classroom that focus on

the first six weeks of school, establishing rules, building the group, and caring for materials.

Web Sites

http://www.bjeny.org/erc_NewSchoolYear.asp?dept=
Educational%20Resources
Bureau of Jewish Education of Greater New York

This page of the BJE site provides creative ideas for the start of the school year.

www.jecc.org/edres/medtech/bested.htm
Jewish Education Center of Cleveland

This site offers a section of links to lesson plans from the following sources: A to Z Teacher Stuff, AskERIC Lesson Plans, Ask Jeeves for Teachers, Busy Teacher Web site, The Discovery Channel, Newsweek Education Program, TeacherVision, Teachers Helping Teachers, Technology & Learning — Curriculum Resources, The Gateway To Educational Materials, The Lesson Plans Page, Time for Kids.

www.lessonplanspage.com
Lesson Plans Page

This site features over 1,000 lesson plans, searchable by age or subject. The lesson plans are very basic, but there are some good ideas. With so many available, you really have to search to find the one you can adapt/use in your class. Well worth looking at, however.

www.socialstudies.com/c/@4FN357V8S2oKQ/Pages/
pro.html
Social Studies School Service

Lesson plans on current events and controversial issues, plus online lesson plans using the Internet.

http://www.hcc.hawaii.edu/intranet/committees/
FacDevCom/guidebk/teachtip/teachtip.htm#top
Teaching Tips

Tips for teaching older students, including a section on the first day.

CHAPTER 3

Jewish Education in the Twenty-First Century: Framing a Vision

Jonathan S. Woocher

For North American Jewish education, the twenty-first century has dawned brightly. Never has Jewish education been higher on the collective agenda. Never has it enjoyed greater opportunities to shape a Jewish culture and the Jewish community's response to a host of critical issues. Under the banner of "Jewish Renaissance," there is a reengagement underway with Jewish learning and teaching that transcends the lines of age, setting, and religious ideology. The promise of a twenty-first century "golden age" for North American Jewish education is real, but there is no guarantee that this promise will be realized.

The other side of the coin is that there remains an enormous gap between what Jewish education today might and could be — and in a few places is — and the experience of Jewish education, both learning and teaching, that a large proportion of American Jews have on a day-to-day basis. The twentieth century left us a mixed legacy. On the one hand, its achievements were considerable:

- The modernization and Americanization of Jewish education. In many instances, Jewish education has literally been lifted out of dark basements into well lit modern classrooms. Content, teaching methods, materials, environment have all been vastly improved over the course of a century, to the point where most observers agree that, qualitatively and on the whole, Jewish education in America is better today than it has ever been before.

- The persistence of Jewish schooling as a Jewish norm. The fact that 70 percent or more of all Jewish children receive some form of Jewish schooling today is itself a signal achievement, given the fact that such participation is not only entirely voluntary, but likely to cost the family thousands, if not tens of thousands, of dollars.

- The reemergence of intensive, all-day Jewish schooling. If there is one dimension of end-of-century American Jewish education that is most improbable from an historical standpoint, it is surely the growth of Jewish day schools. Though the reasons for this growth are complex and not all benign, and though the quality of the education available is inconsistent, the fact that approximately 200,000 Jewish young people are studying in all-day Jewish schools of diverse ideological bents today cannot be considered as anything other than a triumph for Jewish education.

- The creation of a Jewish educational "counterculture": camps, youth movements, Israel programs. American Jews did not stop with creating (or continuing) Jewish schools. During the twentieth century, they also built a number of additional, in some cases historically unprecedented, educational institutions, formats, and programs. What is more, these have often proven to be strikingly effective.

- The move beyond children: family education and adult Jewish learning. In recent years especially, American Jewish education has begun to broaden its reach. Family education has become almost normative as a complement to the schooling of young children. After many decades of decline, serious adult Jewish learning appears to be expanding again in America today, and not only among traditional Jews.

On the other hand, the twentieth century has also bequeathed to us a number of apparently intractable, or at least extraordinarily difficult, challenges to confront:

- Unclear (and often unrealistic) goals that our institutions and programs must attempt to fulfill. Are we educating for identity, for cultural literacy, for specific knowledge and skills, for ideological commitment, for affective sentiments, for community involvement, for all of the above? How can we define each of these in detail, and how can we possibly realize serious goals and objectives in the time that Jewish education is typically allotted?

- A continuing pediatric focus. Despite our best efforts, most Jewish education is still Jewish education for children. Young people continue to drop out of Jewish education before they really have a chance to appreciate Judaism's richness, subtleties, and sophisticated joys and challenges.

- Fragmentation of educational efforts, making smooth handoffs, synergies, and multiplier effects difficult to achieve. Our educational system is no system at all. It is an agglomeration of individual institutions whose relationships to one another are tenuous, and even competitive. At a time when we appreciate more than ever the need to link formal and informal educational experiences, to build knowledge sequentially, and to attract and retain quality educators, the structure of our educational system makes these aspirations nearly impossible.

- Limited time allocations for Jewish learning, in terms of hours per week, weeks during the year, and years during the lifetime. For most Jews, Jewish education is still very much a part-time, leisure time pursuit. Education must compete for "shelf space" in a highly competitive environment.

- The growing shortage of quality personnel in every educational setting at every level. There can be no great education without great teachers and educators. Yet, after decades of talking about a "personnel crisis," we are hardly closer to a solution to the problem of how to recruit, prepare, retain, and reward outstanding Jewish educators than we were at mid-century.

- The isolation of Jewish education from "real living." Too much Jewish education still takes place in "bubbles" detached from the settings in which it is ostensibly located, the larger Jewish and general communities whose activity it is supposed to inform, and the real-life concerns and experiences of its students. Such education is a ritual, not a real force in shaping Jewish living.

The balance sheet of Jewish education today is thus cause for both hope and concern. Our assets are considerable, but so are our liabilities. So, the question becomes: How shall we move forward? Is there a vision that can guide us — and especially those on the front lines — as we try to fulfill the promise of the present moment, and overcome the disabilities that we have inherited from the recent past?

I believe what we do in a Jewish classroom is *holy* work. We are another link in the chain of Jewish tradition. We need to teach content, so that the students see that Judaism is a serious tradition with intellectual depth. But we also need to touch hearts and spirits so our students will continue to be connected to our people and continue in its path. We need to be passionate and serious about being Jewish.

One of the best compliments I have ever gotten was from a group of ninth graders. They were complaining about a teacher who went on and on about not interdating, not intermarrying, and not giving Hitler a posthumous victory. I said that I felt the same way about interdating and intermarriage because of the imperative that the Jewish people survive. I told the students that I was sure I was just as passionate about it as this other teacher. My students replied, "Yes, you are and we know it. But you don't preach and you don't impose. And, you try and give us the positives about living as Jews and choices about how to do so."

It is a delicate balance, to be passionate, yet not impose, and to convey the eternal truths of our tradition and yet to let the students develop their own ideas and thinking.

It's a huge responsibility today to be a Jewish educator. Our numbers are shrinking and, sometimes, I feel like the little Dutch boy with my finger in the dike. But is there any other choice?

(Cheryl Cash-Linietsky, *Philadelphia, Pennsylvania*)

I believe that over the last several years just such a vision has emerged. It has — as the best visions do — come out of a combination of practice and reflection. We have been doing some wonderful things in Jewish education, and as we look at what we have been doing, we can see patterns emerging that point a way forward. These patterns are taking shape against a backdrop of unprecedented diversity in Jewish life today. That diversity makes it impossible for any single formula for educating Jews to carry us where we wish to go. There are no magic bullets in Jewish education: not day school, nor Israel trips, nor Jewish camping, nor family education — though each of these and many other things that we do are extraordinarily powerful for some Jews and immensely important in the overall scheme of what Jewish education can and should be. Jewish education will need to remain multifarious and multidimensional, and that means difficult to organize and consolidate. There will be no master plan imposed from above; only guidelines, at best, that suggest directions.

On the other hand, all is not chaos and disorder. Certain fundamental truths remain:

- Jews (like other human beings) continue to seek meaning in their lives, intimate connections with other human beings, and to do well the things they decide are important in their lives (whether these be their professions, their hobbies, or their family roles).

- What matters most is what happens on the front lines, in the concrete educational encounters of teachers and students. Everything else only acquires significance through its impact on these encounters.

- We have no choice in the end but to trust people. Ultimately, we cannot make people do anything, but we can provide the stimuli and the opportunities to induce them to embark on courses that will lead them in directions they will embrace and we, hopefully, will wish to applaud.

- There are no final, once-and-for-all answers. We can continually do better, if we're willing to keep learning.

In the face of these realities, both chastening and encouraging, I see four fundamental elements of an emerging vision for Jewish education in the twenty-first century: creating and populating high impact pathways, "just in time" Jewish education, personalizing the nexus between learning and life, and creating communities of Jewish learning and living. Each of these is explained below.

CREATING AND POPULATING HIGH IMPACT PATHWAYS

While we cannot predict the life course of a single individual, and while we should anticipate that American Jews in the twenty-first century will indeed travel on many different Jewish journeys, we can recognize some patterns that give a measure of coherence to the diversity we encounter. The more and better quality Jewish education an individual is exposed to, and the longer the period of time in which she or he is so engaged, the more likely he or she is to be impacted by that education. This does not mean that such a learner will turn out exactly as her/his educators may have intended — education is not a stamping machine. But, the more we can construct pathways of Jewish educational experiences that are characterized by extensivity, intensivity, and high quality, and the more Jews we can induce to enter and travel along those pathways, the better off we will be.

This means that maximizing participation in educational settings and activities that work — making day schools, summer camps, Israel experiences, etc., accessible, attractive, and affordable — is very much a sound, even if unoriginal, strategy (sometimes the conventional wisdom turns out to be just that). But we need to go a step further. We need to think less in terms of programs, and more in terms of pathways. Attending to the connections between and among various programs and settings to create those smooth handoffs and synergies that are so often lacking today is the next frontier for Jewish education. There is a law of increasing returns in education: each experience an individual has enhances the impact of next. But, for this to work, we need to allow the momentum for change and growth to build over time and not be stopped short by barriers that the community itself erects. We also need to be serious about quality. There are few mysteries about what makes the difference between an excellent and a mediocre educational experience. The research is quite consistent, whether what is being studied is at a school, an Israel experience, an adult learning program, or a youth group. A clear educational vision, good personnel, attention to detail, involvement of the learners — these are what make a difference. The challenge is to apply what we know consistently, and to make the investments necessary to do what we know is right.

"JUST IN TIME" JEWISH EDUCATION

Creating powerful educational pathways is the place to start, but it will not be enough for a viable twenty-first century educational strategy. The reality is that, despite our best efforts, too many Jews will not enter our pathways, or will leave along the way, or will want to join at a point we have not anticipated.

This recognition points us toward the second element of my educational vision: building a much more flexible system of what might be termed "just in time" Jewish education. A number of years ago, Delta Airlines had a slogan that we would do well to adapt: "Delta is ready when you are." Jewish education, too, needs to be ready whenever and wherever the learner is. This is especially true if our goal is to educate not just children, but adults as well. Some moments of likely readiness are predictable: We know that families as a whole take Jewish education more seriously when their child is ready to enter school and around the time of Bar/Bat Mitzvah. Other moments can be anticipated, if not predicted: when a parent dies, when an individual moves. Some others can be neither predicted nor anticipated; they are serendipitous, even idiosyncratic, but they do occur. The question in each case is whether the Jewish educational apparatus is geared up to respond at the moment of need or opportunity.

In practical terms, a strategy of "just in time" Jewish education also translates into a number of familiar tactical steps: more family education; more adult learning opportunities, including in unusual venues; better publicity for existing programs that too often remain unknown to their prospective target audiences; more extensive use of educational technology allowing individuals to learn what, when, and where they want. Even traditional Jewish educational forms like the supplementary school can be nudged in the direction of greater flexibility and diversity in time frames, content emphases, methodologies, and types of teachers. We could (and in some instances already do) have family schools that meet on Shabbat and for regular retreats, magnet schools for achieving Hebrew fluency, afternoon programs that combine Jewish learning with recreation and school homework, and programs that emphasize community service and build a learning agenda around such activities and internships.

Above all, bringing Jewish education to the people means adopting a new mind-set, cultivating a special alertness to individual's personal needs and to where they are on their own journeys. It may also mean supporting new kinds of educators, what some have called "Jewish personal trainers," who are not bound to classes and time schedules. In St. Louis, family educators go into people's homes to help them create a Jewish lifestyle they feel comfortable with. We live in a "both/and" world, not one of "either/or." In such a world, we will need great Jewish educational institutions and programs, and we will also need education *outside* of institutions and programs, in which educators function as guides and facilitators and learning carries the student where it will.

PERSONALIZING THE NEXUS BETWEEN LEARNING AND LIFE

The personalization of Jewish education needs to extend beyond matters of venue and delivery system. Content, too, will need to be personalized and linked more directly to the learner's life concerns and experiences. Decades ago, Franz Rosenzweig argued that for the modern Jew, the path of Torah begins not with the text, but with life. Only from that starting point, from real questions and concerns that animate a search for answers, can one come to the tradition not just as an interested spectator, but as someone ready to enter its world, move around within it, and eventually be absorbed into it in an organic way. I am not talking simply about making Jewish education relevant by addressing current issues like ecology or by highlighting Judaism's mystical or meditative dimensions for a spiritually oriented constituency. Rather, it is an entire orientation to Jewish learning as inherently dialogical (in Buber's terms) that needs to be embraced. The outcome of genuinely dialogical learning is open-ended: not only the learner and her/his life, but the tradition itself may be transformed in the process (we have seen this happen with feminist studies of biblical and Rabbinic texts).

If the primary driving forces of Jewish identity today are the quests for meaning, intimate community, and mastery (and I believe they are), then Jewish education must support these quests or it will almost inevitably be ineffectual. Because these quests are pursued today in highly individualized ways, we need to offer Jewish education that is itself highly diverse, that provides the student with multiple options for engaging with the tradition (and other Jews), and that allows the learner to feel that she or he is deriving real benefit from it in the form of new knowledge, skills, and self-understanding. This is an incredibly difficult challenge, but not an impossible one to begin to address. Already, we see adult learning programs that have succeeded in blending transmission of sophisticated content with sensitivity to the underlying personal motivations that bring students to the classroom (or the computer screen) in the first place. And, we have examples of programs for adolescents (for example, Brandeis University's Genesis summer program) that help participants build bridges between their diverse interests and concerns as teens, their images of what constitutes serious learning, and Jewish sources and issues. The question is: can we make this connection stronger throughout Jewish education?

CREATING COMMUNITIES OF JEWISH LEARNING AND LIVING

Here, too, though, we need to affirm a "both/and." Personalization of Jewish education must be accompanied by a "re-communalization" of education as well. A vision for Jewish education in the twenty-first century must be a vision of learning *communities*, not just learning individuals.

There are at least two reasons why this is so. The first is a classic sociological one: to be maximally effective in transmitting values, beliefs, and norms, education needs what Peter Berger calls "plausibility structures." There must be settings in which what is "taught" can also be "caught" — i.e., encountered as lived experience. The well attested educational impact of day schools, summer camps, extended visits to Israel, and youth movements is directly linked to their being communities in which the explicit learning that is taking place finds repeated reinforcement in daily collective behavior. Indeed, what is learned *implicitly* through observation of and participation in the community may be far more important than what is being explicitly taught. Plausibility structures alone are not enough to guarantee educational effectiveness, but the lack of such structures seriously cripples any educational endeavor. The recognition that Jewish education must, therefore, simultaneously be about community building has become almost commonplace in the last few years, though we are still far from knowing how to do it well in the multitude of settings where it must be attempted.

There is also a Jewish reason for emphasizing the building of learning and living communities. At least, as I read our tradition, Judaism is about how to be a covenantal community, one that embraces a shared mission that can only be fulfilled through collective action. The current climate of religious personalism in the Jewish community and in our culture as a whole poses a challenge to this vision. For Jewish education to be faithful to its ideological underpinnings, it needs to provide a counterweight to the pull toward hyper-individualism that characterizes much of our society today. Happily, Jews do continue to seek community (albeit not always in traditional terms). This provides Jewish education with an opportunity to tap into this desire. Jewish education must create or link up with settings in which Jews can experience the satisfactions of being part of a larger whole that supports and sustains them in the here and now, one to which they can contribute some of their talents and energies, and one that may even help them to transcend the inexorable limits of time and space.

For the Jewish teacher, this is a vision for Jewish education that can be both daunting and empowering. For the not-so-secret truth is: policy makers and institutional leaders may prescribe what ought to be done, but none of this will happen unless Jewish teachers make it so. A Jewish education that is comprised of a rich chain of interlinked high impact experiences, that is at the same time attuned to individual's unique place in time and space, that builds a dialogue between life and Torah, and that also builds compelling communities of Jewish learning and living — such an education will not, cannot, happen without Jewish teachers who embrace this vision and make it come alive in their day-to-day work. What happens on the front lines *is* what ultimately matters, because it is specific teachers and concrete experiences that constitute the compelling, inspiring face of Jewish education that we would wish every Jew to encounter.

For teachers to be able to provide the kind of Jewish education they yearn to, there is so much that they in turn must receive — first-rate preparation, recognition, remuneration. This is what we, the community, owe them — and we have not delivered what we owe.

Still, the vision is there, whether in the form in which I have framed it, or some other, better one. And, it is what is driving Jewish education today. We feel the possibilities. We know that, given an opportunity, Jewish learning and Jewish teaching can change lives. We have seen the evidence that this is so, not only in our own lives, but in those of others, some of whom little suspected that this could be so. We know that Jewish education can set individuals on pathways that will carry them through their life's journey with joy and responsibility. We know that Jewish education can illuminate moments in our lives and transform them, can open individuals to a wisdom tested through the ages that nevertheless speaks to us here and now in profound and surprising ways. And, we know that Jewish education can bind people together in shared commitment, can make learning a celebration of community, and can point us toward the ultimate horizons of our existence, the hows, the whys, and the mysteries that help us touch the Transcendent.

Because Jewish education can do these things, we learn and we teach. We gratefully accept the progress that has been made; and we continue to struggle with the legacy of challenges we have inherited. It is worth it, because Torah is our life and the length of our days, in this new century, as in all that have come before it.

CHAPTER 4

A *Reformation* in Jewish Education

Jan Katzew

INTRODUCTION

The fundamental challenge we face in Jewish life in general and in Jewish education in particular transcends any single movement. How can we help episodic Jews (who live Judaism from time to time) live fully as Jews who live Judaism all the time? How can we nurture Jews by Choice, who knowingly, passionately, and joyfully identify as Jews? In the Reform Movement, this "episodic Judaism" phenomenon is frequently manifest at a Bar or Bat Mitzvah celebration. Rather than recognize Bar/Bat Mitzvah as a process and a lifelong status that begins at age 13, all too often Bar/Bat Mitzvah is treated as an event, a wedding without a marriage. Consequently, the educational mission we have consciously adopted has increasingly focused on that which distinguishes Judaism — language, ethics, ritual, memory, and vision. Rather than become part of an undifferentiated mass of American culture, education in Reform synagogues assumes the role of advocating for distinctively Jewish perspectives on life. Accepting the premise that we live in an age defined by choice, how can we raise up a generation who will consciously choose to learn and live as Jews?

Implications for Teaching

Teachers need allies, partners who share the same goals, or else we put the educational enterprise at risk. We need to cultivate coalitions of Jewish learning among faculty colleagues, parents of our students, education committee members, and congregational leaders. It takes a congregation to rear a Jew.

We need to help our students connect the dots, the highlights of the Jewish life cycle. The subject *manner* is often as important as the subject *matter*. The relationships we foster with and between our students may prove to be more enduring than the explicit lessons we teach. We want Jewish learning to constitute an inviting, engaging, and positive experience, and that will not happen by accident. How can we heighten the probability that our students will not just learn *about* Judaism from us, but also internalize the values and rituals of Judaism itself?

REFORMING JUDAISM: A WORK IN PROGRESS

Reform Judaism began when Judaism began. Rather than finding its origins in the social contract of John Locke or even the rationalism of Moses Mendelssohn, Reform Judaism hearkens to the voice of the Book of Deuteronomy, a second telling of the early history of the Jewish people. Judaism, as any living entity, has evolved. Just as Passover observance changed between Exodus and Deuteronomy, Jewish practice has continued to adapt to historical exigencies and cultural norms. Just as the dialogical web of the Talmud yielded the logical code of the *Mishneh Torah*, Jewish thought has stretched to fit the spirit of each generation. A Talmudic legend[1] recounts Moses appearing in a class taught by Rabbi Akiva (even though Moses lived over 1300 years before Rabbi Akiva). Moses was confounded, if not dumbfounded, by the discussion until a student asked the Rabbi where he had learned a certain teaching. Akiva replied that Moses had received the teaching on Mount Sinai. The teaching that was unrecognizable to Moses was the same one he had received, but in the 1300 intervening years, it had taken on a life of its own. Jews differ about the pace and content of change in Jewish life. Reform Jews can be conservative when it comes to making changes in music or liturgy, and orthodox in reference to the "right way" to observe holidays. However, in general, Reform Judaism seeks to embrace Jewish tradition and Reform innovation, searching to find harmony

---

[1] *Menachot* 29b.

between past expressions of Jewish life and contemporary attitudes, values, and knowledge. Just as Reform Jews celebrate the freedom to make identity choices and to live with their consequences, so we welcome the freedom to confirm the present rather than be bound to conform to the past.

The process of defining and determining Jewish identity is a prime example in which the Reform Movement has endeavored to balance tradition and innovation. In the Torah, Jewish identity (an anachronism, since the term "Jewish" does not appear in the Torah) is patrilineal. In the Talmud, it is matrilineal. In 1983, the Reform Rabbinate, and soon thereafter its volunteer leadership, affirmed parental descent, by which a child, one of whose parents is Jewish and who exclusively and publicly expresses a Jewish identity, is presumed to be a Jew.[2] Similarly, with respect to conversion, the Reform Movement has sought to welcome prospective proselytes rather than seek to dissuade them, as was Rabbinic custom, and to encourage ritual immersion and circumcision rather then require them. The overall thrust of these decisions is centrifugal, inclusive outreach to people on the margins of Jewish life, consciously making it easier for people to choose to be Jews.[3]

Implications for Teaching

The religious strategy outlined above has profound educational implications. It is possible, even probable, that if you are a teacher in a Reform setting, in your classroom there are students who would not be considered Jewish by the entire Jewish community. This means you need to refrain from making assumptions about the background of your students, and instead, listen to them and learn from them about the *Jewish* choices they and their parents have made. In the twelfth century, Maimonides wrote a letter to Obadiah the proselyte in response to his question about reciting the "*Avot*," the opening *tefilah* in the "*Amidah*."[4] In the opening phrase, the prayer invokes the God of our ancestors, and Obadiah's ancestors were not Jewish. He wanted to know if he could still recite the prayer. Maimonides responded by claiming that not only could Obadiah recite the "*Avot*," but also that he could do so with the awareness that while Maimonides and others who were born as Jews could trace their lineage back to Abraham and Sarah, Obadiah could trace his lineage directly to God. Advocacy for Jews who question their authenticity is embedded in Jewish tradition. As a teacher, you are responsible for making each of your students feel safe — physically, intellectually, emotionally, and spiritually. As this is true in an individual classroom, so is it true in the community as a whole.

Rounding the Learning Curve

The current big picture in Jewish education bears remarkable resemblance to a description of Jewish learning in the Babylonian Talmud (*Baba Batra* 21a) from almost two thousand years ago. Some Jewish parents were unable to teach their children Torah. So the community leaders established a school convenient for the teachers in Jerusalem. But, instead of resolving the disparity between the children whose parents taught their children Torah and those whose parents did not, the proposed solution actually aggravated the problem. The resourceful, committed parents enriched themselves and their children, while the intended students, those without parents who could teach them, did not take advantage of the school. Eventually, the leaders created schools in every district and town that were convenient for the intended learners. After trying to begin with adolescents, the local authorities decided that the schools needed to start with five and six-year-old children. The Talmudic *sugya* continues to consider issues of class size, teacher status, discipline, neighborhood schooling, and funding — all issues that reside at or near the top of the national and global agenda at the onset of the twenty-first century.[5]

---

[2]This decision, ratified at the Central Conference of American Rabbis Convention in 1983, is frequently referred to as "patrilineal descent." However, that phrase is misleading. Biology, in this case, can be through either parent, whereas Rabbinic Judaism restricts Jewish identity to the child of a Jewish mother. For further commentary, see *The Jewish Condition* edited by Aron Hirt-Manheimer (New York: UAHC Press, 1995).

[3]cf. *Divrei Giyur*, the document that articulates recom-

mended guidelines for conversion. (Adopted at the 2001 CCAR convention)

[4]Moses ben Maimon. "Letter To Obadiah the Proselyte."

[5]Education is currently (2001) near the top of the American political and social agenda. According to public opinion polls and the Congressional legislative calendar, class size, teacher training, funding, and overall educational accountability constitute vital national interests.

This context provides an historical perspective that transcends the Reform Movement, and indeed, American Judaism. Educational issues that we may see only as timely are also timeless, if not eternal. Even though we live in a culture that pursues what one bestseller entitled *The New, New Thing*, Judaism offers a counter-cultural message by insisting on the relevance of ancient questions, e.g., Am I my brother's keeper? What does God want from me? Why is this night different from all other nights?

Implications for Teaching

All Jewish schooling is supplemental. Jewish families still serve as the primary educational institution in the Jewish community. When the Judaism lived at home is dissonant with the Judaism learned in school, home wins, and consequently, too often, Judaism loses. Teachers need to set realistic goals for themselves and their students in order for both to succeed. Our work is often counter-cultural, and as with salmon swimming upstream, it often feels as though there is no time for rest unless we want to regress. Rather than harbor messianic pretensions about reaching every student at all times, seek to engage those students who are most receptive and responsive to you as a teacher. You need to succeed as a teacher, at least as much for yourself as for your students.

JEWS BY CHOICE

Jewish schools were established two thousand years ago to supplement Jewish homes, and their task has remained the same. But the homes have changed, and so have the schools. In order for us to be successful in our schools, we need to know what we are trying to supplement, and not supplant. Who are the learners in the more than 900 Reform congregations? Who are the 120,000 students in congregational schools? the 5000 children in day schools? the 10,000 in Reform Movement summer camps? The 1000+ teenagers who typically

spend a summer in Israel?[6] An increasing number of them are Reform Jews by Choice. Their parents were not reared as Reform Jews. Perhaps one of their parents was not reared as a Jew at all. Maybe one parent does not consider him or herself a Jew. Choice is the operative common denominator.

> It's a bit of a curiosity to talk about the different streams of Judaism these days. In our own community, we have people who go back and forth between different congregations, who teach in one and attend in another, and those that have been involved in one way or another in three or even four streams of Judaism in recent years. An awareness of this situation seems almost essential for the effective and sensitive teacher. I've taught for over 25 years in Reform settings, and many issues come to mind. I remember Sarah, whose family kept kosher, Bryan, whose mother was a Jew by Choice and who was more involved than any classroom parent with our congregation and ritual. It behooves us, when we design lessons and activities, to teach the tradition and also the choices that we are certainly able to make in society today. We owe it to our students and their families out of respect. I feel so strongly that we are teaching an important value of Judaism — *kavod* (respect), and we can start to do so by being tolerant of the variety of experiences, with which our students come to us.
>
> *(Michael Fixler, Syracuse, New York)*

Everyone who is a learner in this Jewish educational system is a volunteer (or a volunteer once removed!).[7] There are few, if any, Jewishly binding centripetal forces on these children. They and their families have elected to be in the minority of the American Jewish community, to affiliate and to learn as Jews. They choose consciously to identify as Jews in general, and Reform Jews in particular. As teachers, we have the honor and the responsi-

---

[6]Sam Joseph. *Portraits of Schooling* (New York: UAHC Press, 1997). Statistics regarding day schools, camps, and Israel experiences come from PARDeS (the association of Reform Day Schools) and the Union of American Hebrew Congregations Youth Division, 2001.

[7]The entire American Jewish Educational System is voluntary. A minority of American Jews affiliates with a congregation and sends their children to a religious school. Either the child

who chooses to be in the school or the child's parents (or grandparents) who decide that their child will be in the school made Jewish learning a priority. Despite recent efforts to claim the contrary (e.g., *Sh'ma* 31/582, May 2001), I am not convinced that their voluntary character distinguishes camps and Israel experiences, in contrast to congregational schools. Both mix individual and parental influence and interest.

bility to help them live with the consequences of their faithful, fateful choice.

Implications for Teaching

Dr. Michael Meyer, Professor of History at the Hebrew Union College-Jewish Institute of Religion, the seminary at which Reform Rabbis, Cantors, educators, and communal workers learn and train, claims that education involves transforming "ascribed identity into chosen identity."[8] As teachers, we provide the texts and the context that enable our students to make informed, intentional identity choices. We are engaged in a process of affirmative action, in which we are passionate advocates for Judaism in general and for Reform Judaism in particular. What distinguishes Jewish education from Judaic studies is precisely the educational goal. Learning is necessary, but not sufficient. Teachers are part of a recruiting effort to enlist membership. We want our students to choose to live as Jews, not only to learn about Judaism, to acquire distinctive Jewish memories, not only to study Jewish history.

TEACH THE STUDENT, AND THEN TEACH THE SUBJECT

When a student asks a teacher, "Why should I pray?" or, "Do I have to read the Torah?" or even, "Why do I come to this school?" the inquiry is not purely intellectual. It is existential and personal. Therefore, the teacher has an opportunity, if not an obligation, to respond on an existential and personal basis. "We need you. The Jewish community depends on you. Ultimately, you will decide whether and how to live as a Jew. But in order for you to decide, you need to learn how to pray, to experience reading Torah, to participate in the life of this school, and above all, to be open. Eventually, we want your commitment, your loyalty, and your spirit. For now, we will accept your openness, your willingness, and your trust."[9] This approach reflects

an appeal to reason and passion. It is cognitive and affective, consonant with *na'aseh v'nishma* (we will act and we will obey) – the words with which the children of Israel assented to Torah.[10]

This teaching strategy, in which habit precedes reason, is non-dogmatic, egalitarian, and consonant with the belief that Jewish identity is a matter of choice, not accident and not coercion.

Implications for Teaching

Teaching is always personal. We may be holding a textbook, but when we teach, we often become the text. Students learn about, with, and from us. As we teach, we are asking our students to rely upon us, to trust us, to walk with us in a tentative, tolerant manner in order to learn. Just as the first of the Ten Commandments asks for the acceptance of the Commander, so must we, as a preamble and prerequisite to our teaching, prove to our students that we deserve to be accepted as their teachers.[11] Our authority often rests upon our humility. The words "I don't know" are among the three most important ones we will ever say — in a classroom and everywhere else.

THE AUTHORITY OF AUTONOMY

Despite the increasing blurring and permeability of boundaries within the Jewish community, there is a discernable, meaningful Reform Movement. Even though individuals who affiliate with different movements exhibit similar, if not identical, Jewish practices, like a vector, the Reform Movement has both magnitude and direction. In general, Reform Jews are becoming more receptive to Jewish distinctiveness. The growth of Reform day schools, the increasing use of Hebrew in liturgy, the presence of *kipot* and *tallitot* in the sanctuary, and the renaissance of holiday observances such as a *Tikkun Leyl Shavuot* (A Night of Torah Study) all bear witness to this trend. These public acts of Jewish identification reflect private considerations of Jewish

---

[8]Michael Meyer. "Reflections on the Educated Jew from the Perspective of Reform Judaism," *CCAR Journal*, Spring 1999.

[9]This fictive dialogue is intended to suggest a strategy that responds to the questioner more than the question.

[10]Exodus 24:7

[11]Nehama Leibowitz. *Studies in Shemot.* (Jerusalem: Haomanim Press, 1978), 303-314. Leibowitz cites a wide spec-

trum of opinion, from Abravanel, who claims that the first of the Ten Words is not a commandment at all, to Maimonides, who argues that the "first word" constitutes the most fundamental of positive commandments. Following the lead of Maimonides, we offer a perspective on teaching that places the mutual acceptance of a teacher-student relationship as a precondition for effective teaching and learning.

identity. After having succeeded as Americans, it is now a challenge to succeed as Jews, which means being "continual rather than episodic Jews." In the Reform Movement, there is a growing awareness of the need to engage in *tikkun middot*, repairing the world inside us, in dynamic equilibrium with *tikkun olam*, repairing the world around us. Often, spirituality is contrasted with ethics, the former being characterized as personal and private, and the latter as social and public. This dichotomy is a false one. Rather, spirituality and ethics are complementary, two aspects of a Jewish life, which like a chemical equation, seek a dynamic equilibrium.[12]

> As a Reform Rabbi who grew up in the Reform movement, I am still frequently surprised by the gulf that exists between my experience and outlook and that of many of my students. Although I was not raised in a very observant home, I was raised with a strong sense of Jewish identity. In a Confirmation class, I was not that surprised when no one felt it was important to marry another Jew. I was very surprised when only one student out of ten felt it would be important to pass on Judaism to their children. Identification with Jews and Judaism can no longer be assumed; it has to be cultivated.
>
> *(Rabbi David Feder, Morgantown, West Virginia)*

Despite the complementarity of *tikkun olam* and *tikkun middot*, it is a challenge to defy the tendency to specialize and compartmentalize. For example, the Religious Action Center in Washington, D.C., in concert with the Commission on Social Action, leads the Movement-wide *tikkun olam* agenda. A different constellation consisting of the UAHC (Union of American Hebrew Congregations) Department of Religious Living and the Commissions on Synagogue Music and Religious Living and various Ethics Task Forces spearhead the Reform Movement's *tikkun middot* initiatives. At its best, the Reform Movement functions as a collaborative system, providing life-long opportunities for formal schooling and experiential learning. This system depends upon the trust among its partners and the ability of its leaders to inspire their members. The Reform Movement is

consciously non-*halachic*, accepting the axiom that the prize of autonomy, for individuals and for congregations, is worth the price.

Implications for Teaching

No two Reform congregations are identical. If you teach in more than one Reform synagogue, you may experience very different attitudes toward *kashrut*, intermarriage, Israel, Hebrew, and holidays. That diversity is not only recognized, it is encouraged as a sign of health. Pluralism is not only a value within the Jewish community as a whole; it is also a value within the Reform Movement. This approach to Jewish life leaves little, if any, room for making categorical statements such as: Judaism says____ or, All Jews____, or even All Reform Jews____. This educational strategy emphasizes tolerance and tentativeness. Rather than conceive of a teacher as an authority figure, it projects a teacher as a source of reflection, a generator of pointed questions, and a catalyst for understanding rather than an answer machine. This approach to teaching addresses subject *manner* even more than subject *matter*; the way you teach your students profoundly influences what you teach your students. How can you model tolerance when you teach?

TEACHER: A MOST INTENSIVE LEARNER

"The *talmid-chacham* . . . has an educational goal. I would go so far as to say that he embodied the most sublime educational goal for the Jewish people in the last two thousand years . . . The *talmid-chacham* fulfilled a central social function for the Jewish community. He was an authority in the domain of tradition, but one who did not evade his responsibility of applying the ancient Torah to contemporary needs."[13]

Gershom Scholem, of blessed memory, was not a Reform Jew. But he articulated a principle of Jewish learning that is as Reform as it is Jewish. The *talmid-chacham* is a worthy, if not holy ideal form that teachers of Torah pursue. Rather than being a "master teacher," a *talmid-chacham* is a "master learner," a construct supported by the Hebrew language itself. The infinitive "to teach" (*lilamed*) is the intensive form of the infinitive "to

---

[12]Jan Katzew, "Repairing the World from the Inside Out," *Reform Judaism Magazine* (Winter 1999), 38-40.

[13]Gershom Scholem, "*Shelosha Tipusim shel Yirat Shamayim*," in *Devarim B'Go*. (Tel Aviv: Am Oved, 1982), 544.

learn" (lilmode). Rather than being distinct and apart from his or her students, a "master learner" is an accessible role model for students, on a continuum of lifelong Jewish learning.

The link between Jewish learning and Jewish living has almost always been a struggle to forge. The generation of our people who were *free from* slavery was not *free to* live in the Land of Promise.[14] Separation anxiety is not limited to early learning, either for a person or a people. The dual obligations to history and community provide an ongoing Jewish educational challenge. How can we bring the past to life at the same time as we live fully in the present? The application of Torah to our current concerns is our perpetual sacred task. It is both a burden and an honor to bridge tradition and modernity. It is a very narrow bridge, one we must marshal the courage to traverse.

Implications for Teaching

Taking teaching seriously requires taking learning seriously. What are you studying? How are you applying it to your teaching, either in form or content? What are you learning about yourself as a learner that can help you be a more effective teacher? Without being solipsistic or narcissistic, use your identity as a learner to identify and empathize with your students. Consider how much time it takes you understand a key concept and apply it. Then be patient with your students, allowing them the time and space to internalize an idea and own it. Consider yourself as a student. Have you ever had an anti-educational experience? Write it down and make a promise to yourself and, when you are ready, to your students, that you will not recreate that experience for any of your students. How do you learn best? Write down your response. Be clear and concise. Understanding how you learn best will help you understand how you teach best

TEACHING FOR THE LOVE OF TORAH

Orient yourself on the bridge that leads from tradi-

tion to modernity. *Ayeka?*[15] Where are you? This was the first question God posed to a human being. It is a question we should always be prepared to address as people in general and as teachers in particular. Wherever you are on that bridge, work to widen it where it is most narrow, and strengthen it where it is most feeble. This process can foster personal and professional growth.

A new "learning" is about to be born — rather, it has been born. It is a learning in reverse order — a learning that no longer starts from the Torah and leads into life, but the other way round: from life, from a world that knows nothing of the Law, or pretends to know nothing, back to the Torah. That is the sign of the time."[16] Although Franz Rosenzweig said these words at the opening of the Lehrhaus (adult learning center) in Frankfurt, Germany, in 1917, they apply here and now. Most of the children who are learners in our schools and their parents who are also learners are more comfortable in the social hall than they are in the sanctuary or the classroom. Hebrew is a foreign language to them, not (yet) a second language. Torah is an ancient text, not (yet) a living context. We must strive to understand the lives of our students — what music they listen to, what television they watch, what language they use — and relate it to Torah. That means we have a great burden, to know Torah well enough so that we will be able to make plausible, authentic references to the lives of our students.

Abraham Joshua Heschel spoke about the overwhelming need for "text-people." He might as well be in the room with each one of us. We need to hearken to his voice and work to internalize Torah so that it will be natural for us to relate life to Torah and back again. Not only is this a prodigious assignment, it is counter-culture in our society. It asks us to prioritize communal responsibilities, not individual rights, to place commitment above fulfillment and uniqueness ahead of universality. In the Reform Movement, this is a particularly delicate, difficult process, which flouts the assimilationist tendencies of prior generations. When *Sha'ar'ei Tefillah: The Gates of Prayer,*[17] which is the *Siddur*

---

[14]This distinction is made in a classic essay by Isaiah Berlin entitled "Two Concepts of Liberty," 1958, his inaugural lecture as the Chichele Professor at Oxford University.

[15]Genesis 3:9. This is the first question in the Torah, and it is God's question through the first human being to every human being.

[16]From the inaugural lecture at the Frankfurt Lehrhaus, in *Contemporary Jewish Thought*, edited by Simon Noveck (Washington, DC: B'nai Brith Books, 1985), 223.

[17]*Gates of Prayer* (New York: Central Conference of American Rabbis, 1975), 635.

most commonly used in Reform congregations, was first published in 1975, the Havdalah service deleted the phrase that distinguishes the Jewish people from the other nations. Later editions reinstated it. Reform Jews are becoming increasingly comfortable with the distinctiveness quotient of the Jewish people. It is relatively recent that even in English the most common preposition to follow the word "discriminate" is "against"; it used to be "between." We have taken a cardinal virtue and turned it into a vice. But the original meaning did not disappear. Indeed, it is reappearing.

"According to Martin Buber, the aim of education is determined by the general trend or spirit of each age, which leaves its imprint on education and gives it its ultimate direction . . . [O]ur age is characterized by the disintegration of traditional beliefs, by lack of spiritual orientation, and the absence of a clear and common aim . . . Instead of educating for a way of life, we seem to be educating for a comfortable livelihood."[18] While there has been a resurgence, if not a renaissance, of adult Jewish learning, day schooling, camping, family education, and early childhood education, as well as a concentrated effort to innovate and improve congregational education, we face principally the same obstacle that Buber recognized. We live at a time of material wealth too often coupled with moral poverty. We must not be seduced by fad or fashion. Jewish education must maintain balance and ballast, providing an anchor to counteract moral drift.

CONCLUSION

The Reform Movement in North America originally contrasted the ethical and ritual domains of Jewish life, arguing that the ethical was enduring, whereas ritual was ephemeral.[19] However, the Reform Movement has lived up to its name by reforming

its ideology. We continue to learn that ritual behavior does not supplant ethical behavior. They are not a part of a zero sum game in which one must prosper and the other suffers. Nevertheless, this argument is much easier to articulate than to practice. Teachers of Torah share the responsibility with parents to orient the moral compass toward what is just, and kind, and humble — in a word, holy.

Implications for Teaching

New textbooks, programs, and projects abound, but they will not, by themselves, resolve the challenges we face in the current system of Jewish learning.[20] "Continuity" became "transformation" became "renaissance" became "identity and renewal." The names change, but the underlying malady lingers on. There will be no magic categorical response to the questions we have regarding Jewish education in North America. There is no substitute for a teacher building a relationship of trust with a student, inspiring a learner to live Torah. As teachers, we have the opportunity to develop subject mastery, a passion for learning, a caring for students, a love for Torah, and awe of God. Even this is not a formula for our success. There is, thank God, mystery at the heart of learning, and therefore, at the heart of teaching. Teaching is an act of faith. We believe that, in spite of ambivalence and indifference, we can inspire another student to spend her/his life *immersed* in Torah. Perhaps that is why the blessing for Torah study concludes with the words "*la'asok b'divray Torah*" (to *immerse* ourselves in the words of Torah). One by one, each of us can make a difference in the quality of Jewish life. Sometimes, we can make *all* the difference. Take the time to count your blessings as a teacher. List the names of students who have been blessings, who have reminded you that you are doing holy work.

[18]Zvi Kurzweil, "Education According To Martin Buber" in *Judaism* (Winter 1961).

[19]The Pittsburgh Platform of the CCAR, 1885, #3: "We recognize in the Mosaic legislation a system of training the Jewish people for its mission during its national life in Palestine, and today we accept as binding only its moral laws, and maintain only such ceremonies as elevate and sanctify our lives, but reject all such as are not adapted to the views and habits of modern civilization. #4: We hold that all such Mosaic and Rabbinical laws as regulate diet, priestly purity, and dress originated in ages entirely foreign to our present mental and spiritual state . . . By contrast, the 1999 Statement of Principles affirms, "We are committed to the ongoing study of the whole array of *mitzvot* and to the fulfillment of those that address us as individuals and as

a community. Some of these *mitzvot*, sacred obligations, have long been observed by Reform Jews; others, both ancient and modern, demand renewed attention as a the result of the unique context of our own times." The difference is profound, even categorical.

[20]Isa Aron, Sara Lee, and Seymour Rossel, *A Congregation of Learners* (New York: UAHC Press, 1995), and Isa Aron and Lawrence Hoffman, *Becoming a Congregation of Learners: Learning as a Key to Revitalizing Congregational Life* (Woodstock, VT: Jewish Lights Publishing, 2000). These texts outline, in theory and in reflective practice, the extensive and intensive efforts to reorient congregations around Jewish learning. They are valuable tools and records for understanding the desirability and possibility of engendering systemic change.

BIBLIOGRAPHY

Symposium on Jewish Education, *CCAR Journal,* Winter 1998.

Symposium on the Educated Jews, *CCAR Journal,* Spring 1999.

These two symposia address important and urgent questions in Jewish education. What is an educated Reform Jew? What is a coherent, compelling curriculum? What is the place of Hebrew in Jewish education? How do we set priorities for learners and teachers in Jewish schools? While these essays are grounded in theory, their aim is practical.

Aron, Isa, and Lawrence Hoffman. *Becoming a Congregation of Learners: Learning as a Key to Revitalizing Congregational Life.* Woodstock, VT: Jewish Lights Publishing, 2002.

The "Experiment in Congregational Education," spearheaded by Isa Aron, and "Synagogue 2000," led by Lawrence Hoffman, represents two important efforts to catalyze change and growth in American Jewish life. This work provides a thoughtful, reasoned analysis of the processes of organizational change in synagogue cultures.

Aron, Isa; Sara Lee; and Seymour Rossel. *A Congregation of Learners.* New York: UAHC Press, 1995.

This work offers a vision for changing congregational perspectives on education. Learning is larger than schooling, and the essays in this volume consider multiple points of entry into Jewish learning for children and adults. Some essays reflect upon experience; others offer imaginative educational scenarios.

Babylonian Talmud, *Baba Batra* 21a.

This *sugya* is remarkable in its timelessness, offering insights into the origins of the Jewish educational system, as well as its current incarnation. We have yet to develop a system that is symbiotic, bringing together the best thinking and practice in the various spheres of Jewish learning.

Bolman, Lee G., and Terrence E. Deal. *Reframing Organizations: Artistry, Choice, and Leadership.* San Francisco, CA: Jossey-Bass, 1997.

This book offers several lenses through which it is possible to gain insight into the dynamics of schooling and learning. It provides accessible, useful tools for educational leaders, professional and volunteer, to understand congregational schools as organizations in search of dynamic balance.

Evans, Robert. *The Human Side of School Change: Reform, Resistance, and the Real-Life Problems of Innovation.* 2d ed. San Francisco, CA: Jossey-Bass, 2001.

While this book does not focus on Reform Judaism in particular or Judaism in general, it addresses a universal challenge in education, i.e., mobilizing, motivating, and maintaining a team of human beings toward realizing an educational vision.

Fishman, Sylvia Barack, and Alice Goldstein. *When They Are Grown They Will Not Depart: Jewish Education and the Behavior of American Adults.* Waltham, MA: Brandeis University Cohen Center for Modern Jewish Studies, and New York: Jewish Education Service of North America, 1993.

This study provides quantitative and qualitative evidence in support of Jewish education as a powerful means of Jewish continuity and growth.

Joseph, Sam. *Portraits of Schooling.* New York: UAHC Press, 1997.

This book represents the most recent attempt to quantify the state of congregational schools in the Reform Movement. How often do schools meet? How much time do schools devote to teacher training? Who engages full-time educators? How much *tzedakah* do schools raise? What subjects do schools teach in what grades?

Reimer, Joseph. *Succeeding at Jewish Education: How One Congregation Made It Work.* Philadelphia, PA: Jewish Publication Society, 1997.

This is an ethnographic study, which resulted from more than two years of living inside a congregation and learning about its educational vision and program. The book can be a catalyst for any congregation open to scrutinizing its own educational thinking and acting.

While the qualitative analysis is more descriptive than prescriptive, there are lessons herein that all congregations could and should learn.

Wertheimer, Jack. "Jewish Education in the United States: Recent Trends and Issues." In *The American Jewish Yearbook*. New York: American Jewish Committee, 1999, pp. 2-115.

This monograph-length article provides a sober, but not necessarily somber view of Jewish education in the United States at the end of the twentieth century. The author is the leading historian in the Conservative Movement, but the scope and depth of this study extends beyond any single stream of Judaism. The article lends itself to ongoing, serious study for anyone striving to understand the development of Jewish education in the United States. The conclusions offer challenges we must face in the next generation, if not the next century, as our schools, synagogues, camps, Israel trips, and academic programs compete for limited human and financial resources.

Other Resources

The UAHC Department of Jewish Education produces print and online resources for teachers in Reform congregations. These include "Torah at the Center" for professional educators; *"V'Shinantam"* for avocational teachers; "Galilee Diary," classroom perspectives on Jewish life in Israel; "Family Shabbat Table Talk," activities related to the weekly Torah and Haftarah portions; and "The Parent Page," parent education. See www.uahc.org for further information.

CHAPTER 5

Conservative Jewish Education: Walking Purposefully toward God's Holy Mountain

Robert Abramson and Serene Victor

Conservative Jewish education has many settings: the home, the synagogue school, Solomon Schechter Day Schools, United Synagogue Youth, Camp Ramah, and Israel trips. These settings reinforce or complement one another and each requires a different skill and knowledge set.

Because 70% to 80% of Jewish children affiliated with the Conservative Movement receive their basic education in the synagogue school, we have chosen to gear this chapter primarily to those teaching in our synagogue schools, and for those thinking about teaching in them. We also hope that others — Rabbis, Ḥazzanim, educational directors, lay leadership, and parents — will use this chapter to help shape a vision for their synagogue school.

In 1988, the Conservative Movement published *Emet Ve-Emunah: Statement of Principles of Conservative Judaism*. In its last pages, it describes the ideal Conservative Jew as a "willing," "learning," and "striving" Jew, who is "a traveler walking purposefully towards 'God's holy mountain.'"[1] These characteristics — willing, learning, and striving — describe both what we seek in teachers and what we want to nurture in students and parents. We need to work toward making these characteristics the hallmark of all Conservative synagogue communities. Below is a more in-depth view of willing, learning, and striving in the Conservative context.

WILLING

Ours is a world in which Jewish commitments are no longer internalized by virtue of living within an organic Jewish community. Jewishness and a commitment to Judaism can no longer be "picked up" in the neighborhood. Jewish memories are less and less passed organically from one generation to another. Nor are our children's parents part of a generation born in America who, though not victims of the Holocaust, grew up in its shadows, feeling an inner compulsion to assure that their children would be Jewish. We live in a world in which one can fade into American culture with little or no effort. Commitment to Judaism and being Jewish must now be nurtured through a strong and deliberate partnership between home, synagogue, and other Jewish educational contexts. Our synagogues need to be communities that lovingly invite our students and families into the tradition, opening for them the richness and possibilities of Jewish life.

In these early years of this new century, our teaching must respond to the critical question, "Why should we want to be Jewish?" Schools cannot revolve only around transmitting some information about how to be Jewish and instruction in what Judaism is. We need teachers who are joyful, questioning, wondering, passionate models of being Jewish. Their goals have to go beyond merely transmitting information to engage students in the joys and meaningfulness of Jewish living. Such engagement becomes a self-evident answer to the question why be Jewish. There is a need for cognitive learning and there is also a need for teaching skills, but these elements must be coupled with affective, experiential Jewish learning. The synagogue community and its schools must give children and parents an opportunity to "try on" Jewish behaviors and probe their meaning.

The teaching of sacred deeds as *mitzvot*, commandments, is central to Conservative Judaism. It is at the very essence of being a willing Jew. Such a Jew lives a life of observance of *mitzvot* in celebrat-

---

[1]*Emet Ve-Emunah: Statement of Principles of Conservative Judaism* (New York: The Jewish Theological Seminary of America, The Rabbinical Assembly, and The United Synagogue of America, 1990), 56-57.

ing Shabbat and holidays, observing *kashrut*, and doing *gemilut chesed*. These are some of the ways the willing Jew senses and expresses *kedushah*, holiness, in relating to God, others, and the world. The willing Jew also embraces other dimensions of Jewish culture and civic life. Finding ways to engage students and parents in the possibility of such living, of becoming a "willing Jew," is the great challenge of Conservative synagogue education. This requires a combination of the cognitive and experiential, and the creation of an organic relationship between that which is learned and that which is experienced.

> I've found that while movement "labels" do say something about school and parental expectations, it's even more important to know the particular school and congregation in which you're teaching. I've taught units on *kashrut* to sixth and seventh graders at two different Conservative *shuls* located not so far apart geographically. In one, sending the kids home to look for *hechshers* (symbols indicating Rabbinic approval of a kosher item) in the family pantry brought angry parents in, accusing me of undermining family choices. In hindsight, I really was insensitive — I should have sent a letter home in advance, explaining to the parents that this was an activity demonstrating the pervasiveness of kosher products in our corner of America. In the other *shul*, a very clear commitment to traditional *halachah* carries throughout the *shul* — it's in the membership packet, the Rabbi teaches it, and the principal backs teachers up on teaching traditional observance. So, although many (or most!) of the religious school families keep "kosher-style," there were no complaints about an extended unit on *kashrut* in which kids hunted at home for kosher products and toured the *shul* kitchen to learn how *kashrut* is enforced.
>
> *(Anne Johnston, New Haven, Connecticut)*

If a teacher is going to meet the challenge, the teacher and the school community must be mindful of two principles:

> Principle #1: The school must have the courage to permit its teachers to be authentic.

Authenticity means not using "we" where there is no "we."

Teachers should not fake it by using such phrases as, "We do _____." The other side of principle #1 is that teachers not talk about Jewish life, including *mitzvot*, as if it was something alien to them. This means avoiding speaking of "customs and ceremonies," thereby relating to Jewish living as they would to the practices of a foreign culture. If they are at least in part "willing" Jews, they can look at a set of Jewish behaviors such as Shabbat, holidays, *kashrut*, and *tzedakah* as opportunities to engage in *mitzvot*, sacred obligations that bring one into relationship with God, the Jewish people, others, and the world. They can indicate an openness to "trying on" the behaviors and exploring how they might affect their lives. They can invite parents and children to come along with them. This can work if they see themselves as travelers on a path.

> Principle #2: The starting point for all good education is where the student is. We cannot engage students by pretending they are where we wish them to be. This is true about math and literature. It is certainly true about teaching Judaism.

Among other things, this means acknowledging in the classroom that students and their families are at different places in the spectrum of Jewish living, ranging from non-practice to practice. This has two dimensions: (1) being explicit about this to the students, and (2) being explicit about this to oneself when preparing lesson plans.

So what locutions can we use? Here are a few examples: "We are going to explore together." "We are going to try on/try out." "We are going to try to understand why _____." The stance of being a willing Jew, fully or partly, if presented by teachers with authenticity, can enable teachers to engage students in an exploration of Judaism that engages the mind, hands, and heart. It can enable students to use knowledge and experiences of Jewish practice to explore Judaism and make meaning. In doing so, they just might begin to get a sense of why one would want to live a Jewish life.

LEARNING

Judaism, well taught, is its own best advocate. The

content of our sacred literature — the Torah, Rabbinic oral law and narrative, and prayer — have the power to inspire, enlighten, and guide us through life. We owe our students an opportunity to experience our texts, to engage in making meaning as they study Torah. This means not just learning about Torah or reading Bible stories. Students should have the opportunity to study sections of Torah. These will probably have to be in English translation, and must be chosen judiciously. Our students are entitled to grapple with:

- the meaning of the lives of our forefathers and foremothers and God's relationship to them.

- the Exodus.

- Moshe's leadership.

- the complexities of the relationship between God and the Jewish people.

- the lives and messages of the prophets.

- the inspiration of Psalms.

Our students are entitled to probe key biblical concepts such as revelation, Covenant (*brit*), and justice (*tzedek*). They should learn how the Rabbis interpreted biblical laws, developed and applied them, and how Conservative Judaism continues this process.

Students have to learn how to read prayers in Hebrew with fluency. However, their knowledge of prayer should not end there. It should include the acquisition of a Hebrew prayer vocabulary and a growing awareness of the syntax of prayer as they develop comprehension of selected Hebrew prayers. In addition, they also need to be empowered to engage in spontaneous prayer.

Jewish learning is not confined to sacred texts. We want students: to learn about other past and present Jewish communities; to sense the joy of being part of a community; to enjoy Jewish music, art, and dance; and to experience other modes of Jewish self-expression.

Learning our sacred literature will take time if students are to be engaged in making meaning. For the synagogue school, time is all too precious. We will have to make selections organized around key concepts and themes, if there is to be sufficient time to study text in depth. We need to remember that the romance of learning precedes precision. The goal cannot be coverage. What is studied should be paradigmatic, permit interpretation, and

have the potential of being full of meaning, illuminating a student's life and pointing beyond it.

If the students are to be "learning Jews," so must their teachers and parents. The synagogue must provide its teachers opportunities for being "learning Jews." It will have to provide time, funding, and opportunity for continuing education for every member of the faculty and the school administration. It should expect everyone in the community to be learning. The synagogue also needs to encourage parents to become part of the community of "learning Jews" by providing engaging adult education in which teachers might also participate.

STRIVING

There is no such thing as a "finished" Jew. A Jew should always be striving to understand better, do more, reach a little further.

Franz Rosenzweig was a brilliant young man who grew up in Germany in a highly assimilated Jewish family and milieu (born 1886). In a spiritual crisis, he decided to convert to Christianity. His one stipulation was that he would do so as a Jew, so that year he attended Yom Kippur services before what was to be his conversion. Rosenzweig never described what happened to him during that day (October 11, 1913), but it was apparently a deep and transformative experience. He decided not to convert, but rather embraced Jewish studies. He opened himself to Jewish practice as a way to God. He founded Das Freie Juedische Lehrhaus (The Free House of Jewish Learning), an institute for adult Jewish study. A brilliant and inspirational figure, a group of young men and women gathered around him. Once, Rosenzweig was asked if he put on *tefillin*. His answer was, "Not yet." We learn from his response that the striving posture can connect with the willing posture.

The statement *Aims of the Conservative Synagogue School* reflects this posture of "not yet" when it states:

> Since growing Jewishly is a process, it includes having an attitude that the choice is not between all or nothing but between growing and not growing Jewishly, and it may mean the partial doing of some *mitzvot*. Examples of growing Jewishly in the observance of Shabbat are lighting candles, saying *"Kiddush,"* or refraining from prohibited work; in the obser-

vance of *kashrut*, they are not eating biblically prohibited foods, eating meat only in kosher restaurants, eating only dairy and *pareve* out, or keeping kosher at home.[2]

Teachers in Conservative Jewish synagogue schools need to see themselves as "not yet" Jews — echoers of Franz Rosenzweig's majestic declaration. We need teachers who have this phrase on their lips, in their souls, and in their hearts. If it is an honest answer to a teacher's relationship to Jewish observance, it will teach a Conservative value. Such teachers will model what it means to "be a traveler walking purposefully toward God's holy mountain." What a wonderful gift to share with students and their parents!

> Teaching in a Conservative school is a real challenge. I have taught in supplementary schools and currently at a Schechter day school, as well as in other settings. I much prefer being in a Conservative setting. That is where I can most be myself. Nonetheless, it is a challenge. Students (and their families) don't usually have a clear understanding of what Conservative Judaism stands for (and I think it's our obligation to teach it better), so I have a lot of explaining to do. Students know I take *halachah* (Jewish law) seriously, so they assume I am Orthodox. I am careful to define myself as an "observant" Conservative Jew, and to stress that observant is not a synonym for Orthodox.
>
> *(Cheryl Birkner Mack, Cleveland, Ohio)*

There are lots of reasons to teach. One of them is that you are a willing Jew, desirous of exploring Judaism and doing more. Another is that teaching is one of the best ways to be a learning Jew. Still another reason is that teaching can be a way of keeping oneself a striving Jew. It can stimulate and also help maintain an openness to growing in Jewish living and learning.

AN AFTERWORD AND FOREWORD

This article was conceived before, but was finished after, September 11, 2001. While the shock of that day is still very much with us and we seem indeed to be in a different place than we were before, it is too early, at least for us, to articulate a fully developed educational position for teaching in these times. This is particularly so if as many say: we have entered a new time. Dealing with the educational aftermath of 9/11 has been in the hands of teachers in the front lines as they responded to the needs and questions of students. We thank each and every teacher, who has reached inside, listened well, and responded with honesty and words of comfort. It will take time and creativity to imagine the curriculum and articulate religious implications. Presently, we have to do what Jews have always done in the face of trauma — cherish our children.

There are two ideas in *Emet Ve-Emunah* that for us come into bold relief at this time, and we would suggest that they both, now more than ever, have to become part of the path of willing, learning, and striving Jews. They are contained in the section on "Relations with Other Faiths" where it states, "Theological humility requires us to recognize that although we have but one God, God has more than one nation." At this time, as we seek for verities that have withstood the test of time, we must temper our quest with theological humility. While seeking an anchor in transcendent truths, we must go about it with humility, recognizing the image of God in the other. We will constantly need to remind ourselves "that God has more than one nation."

---

[2] *A Framework for Excellence in the Conservative Synagogue School*, Pt. II — Aims of the Conservative Synagogue School (New York: The United Synagogue of Conservative Judaism, 2001), 2.

BIBLIOGRAPHY

A Framework for Excellence for the Conservative Synagogue School. New York: The United Synagogue of Conservative Judaism, 2001. (Two Booklets)

> The United Synagogue of Conservative Judaism developed this framework to assure a quality Jewish education for the students of our synagogue schools. The goal is to prepare them for a life of Jewish learning and Jewish living. Using the *Framework*, congregations are able to define and refine their current educational program. All synagogue schools can benefit from introspection. The *Framework* provides Conservative congregations with criteria by which to examine their educational program and determine areas in which it might be enhanced. The document consists of aims, benchmarks, and a choice of models. Single copies of the two booklets are available from the USCJ Department of Education at no cost, or it can be found on USCJ's web site, www.uscj.org.

Gardner, Howard. *The Disciplined Mind*. New York: Penguin Books, 1999.

> We associate the concept of multiple intelligences with Howard Gardner. In this work Gardner shows how the system of multiple intelligences is more than a way to nourish proclivities. It is a way to nourish and encourage in the learner a deep understanding of the gifts that cultures have to offer. Read it. Think about it. Apply it.

Gillman, Neil. *Conservative Judaism: The New Century*. West Orange, NJ: Behrman House, 1990.

> This is a concise, well written history of the Conservative Movement in the United States. It will enable teachers to understand better the concerns, beliefs, and practices of Conservative Judaism.

Golinkin, David. *Halakhah for Our Time: A Conservative Approach To Jewish Law*. New York: United Synagogue of America, 1991.

> Jewish religious movements are to a great extent characterized by their approach to *halachah*, Jewish law. David Golinkin, as President of the Schechter Institute in Israel, explains the Conservative Movement's perspective on *halachah*.

Emet Ve-Emunah: Statement of Principles of Conservative Judaism. New York: The Jewish Theological Seminary of America, The Rabbinical Assembly, and The United Synagogue of America, 1988.

> Published in 1988, this is still the best understanding of the Conservative Movement. It can be a great help in answering the question, "Am I a Conservative Jew?"

CHAPTER 6

Training and Developing Reconstructionist Jewish Teachers

Jeffrey Schein and Linda Holtzman

A surprising finding of the 1997 CIJE study on the Jewish teaching profession was the paradoxical stability and migrancy of the field. Rather unexpectedly, the study found that teachers stay committed to Jewish teaching for years, even decades. They do, however, migrate from congregation to congregation in ways that are erratic and unpredictable. The changes seem random, having little to do — at least on the surface — with ideological orientation.

The practical upshot of this for *K'lal Yisrael*, the Jewish community, is that each movement must be prepared to receive teachers who are unfamiliar with the particular orientation of a given stream of Jewish life. Knocking on the door of the principal of a Reconstructionist school will be a variety of teachers, each with a different motivation for applying for a new faculty position: a friend of mine teaches here, your pay scale is a little higher than the synagogue down the street, I loved the Bar Mitzvah ceremony of a cousin at this synagogue, I hear great things about you as a principal or about your Rabbi. As the Reconstructionist Movement grows and matures, we have an increasing number of such dialogues that begin with, "I grew up in a Reconstructionist congregation," but such instances are still in a minority.

Part of our challenge then is *hachnasat morim*, welcoming our teachers into a new Jewish culture. This chapter outlines some of the key religious and educational philosophies that guide teachers' work in Reconstructionist settings.

BECOMING A MASTER TEACHER: A PLAY IN THREE ACTS

Once in the classroom it is helpful to adopt a "developmental" model of how a teacher will grow as a Jewish Reconstructionist teacher. We are particularly indebted in this regard to a short selection from *Towards a Theory of Instruction*[1] by Jerome Bruner in which Bruner distinguishes between the "enactive," "iconic," and "logical" modes of learning a new skill or discipline. Bruner asks us to think of riding a bike. There is an enactive mode of knowing how to ride when one simply gets on the bike and manages to ride. Later "images" (icons) of how to ride raise the level of awareness and perhaps the level of adaptivity in taking new bike rides. Finally, one could provide for the act of bike-riding a rational foundation of principles of physics linking the movement of human mind, arms, and legs to the gears that move the wheels of the bike.

It is helpful to think of the development of a good Jewish teacher in somewhat similar terms. The first task (Act One) is indeed enactive, ideally providing the supporting conditions that enable you as a teacher to learn from your own teaching, the failures as well as the successes. This not only includes the best of pre-service workshops, but also much opportunity for observation of, and mentoring by, master teachers (including the Rabbi, if he or she is a good teacher).

As you gain confidence, it is time to raise the stakes to the iconic challenge (Act Two) by increasing your storehouse of images of good Reconstructionist teaching. This is a perfect time to read some of the general articles in *The Reconstructionist Educator's Study Packet*,[2] available from the director in most Reconstructionist schools. Conversations with the great teachers and further observations, help build this desired vision or image of good teaching.

Act Three is characterized by reflective practice in Jewish education. A growing ability to deal with

---

[1]Bruner, Jerome, *Towards a Theory of Instruction* (Cambridge, MA: Belknap Press, 1966).

[2]Gluskin, Shai, Moti Rieber, and Jeffrey Schein. *The Reconstructionist Educator's Study Packet* (Philadelphia, PA: JRF, 2000).

complex teaching challenges marks this stage of development. Sometimes the complexity is embedded in the subject matter taught: challenging classical texts with conflicting messages about Jewish particularism and universalism, topics beyond the normal cognitive grasp of a particular age group, etc. Sometimes the complexity lies in what the student brings to the learning table: multiple religious backgrounds, apathy or alienation, or values gleaned from general American culture that are antithetical to Judaism. In both instances, your increased capacity to analyze the source of the challenges and respond in a creative way will earn you the accolade of being a reflective practitioner.

The simply "doing it"/enactive mode (Act One) of good Reconstructionist teaching is beautifully illustrated in the following excerpt of a talk (six of ten sections[3]) given by Rabbi Linda Holtzman to Jewish educators in Philadelphia (2000). The iconic mode (Act Two) is illustrated below through a resource called "Frequently Asked Questions about God, Torah and Israel," from *The Reconstructionist Educator's Study Packet*.[4] If interested in "Act Three" and the transition to a more fully rational model of reflective teaching we'd suggest taking a careful look at "Becoming a Reflective Practitioner," by Rabbis Jeffrey Eisenstat and Jeffrey Schein.[5]

ACT ONE: JUST DO IT . . . SUGGESTIONS FOR GOOD RECONSTRUCTIONIST TEACHING[6]

Following are six suggestions for good Reconstructionist teaching:

1. *Accept each child. Respect each child. Celebrate each child . . . exactly as he/she is* - The diversity of views and experiences, the diversity of families and backgrounds, the diversity of ways each person connects to Judaism, are all vital. There is no one person who adequately represents Jewish life — even Reconstructionist Jewish life. It takes many different approaches to Judaism, to God, to learning, to create a vital, interesting community.

Each child has a part in that community that is uniquely his or her own and that is uniquely valuable. When the children of one Reconstructionist congregation[7] drew pictures of God and described their drawings, each one was entirely different. There were clouds, sunlight, pastoral scenes, and old men with beards. There were airplanes, animals, and blank pages. No one was told that he/she was wrong. Each child taught every one of us something enriching in our own spiritual understanding. Our job as Reconstructionist educators is to foster the growth of each individual as fully as possible.

2. *Encourage intellectual honesty* - We need to give this gift of honesty to the children we teach. We should not lie and we need not be afraid of revealing the truth. Magic will still happen when we tell the stories of our tradition, but it should not happen at the expense of honesty. When children ask us, ''Did it really happen that way? Did the Red Sea really split? Did Adam and Eve really exist?" we can honestly say we don't know. We may not be sure that the events really happened, but we may be very sure that the stories are powerful myths that speak to our hearts and to the hearts of the children we teach. Our answer does not need to be their answer. If we respond that we are not sure, but would love to know their views, a profound dialogue can take place. Our willingness to be honest with our students can foster the deepest learning.

3. *Bring Jewish tradition into the children's lives* - One day during religious school, there was a rainstorm. After the rain ended, a glorious rainbow appeared in the sky. The entire school left their classes and went outside to look at the rainbow and to recite together the traditional blessing said upon seeing a rainbow. Everyone was moved, and I believe the children learned an important way that Jewish tradition is a real part of their lives.

Most Reconstructionist congregations are

---

[3]The full talk can be found as "Ten Things I Learned as the Education Director of JRF Congregation Mishkan Shalom" under "Education" on the Jewish Reconstructionist Federation web page, www.jrf.org.

[4]Gluskin, ibid.

[5]Jeffrey Eisenstat and Jeffrey Schein. "Teacher as Reflective Practioner" in *Tithadesh: Initiating Renewal and Reflection in*

Jewish Education (Philadelphia, PA: Jewish Reconstructionist Federation, 1991).

[6]Adapted from a keynote talk by Rabbi Linda Holtzman at the Jewish Reconstructionist Federation's November 2000 Mid-Atlantic Regional Educators' Day. Full text available at: http://www.jrf.org/edu/tenthings.html.

not *halachically* observant communities, yet as educators we can find ways that Jewish tradition can have a place in the lives of our students. We can teach Jewish ethical texts that deal with the actual problems our students have. We can tell stories that mirror their concerns. We can find ritual observance that adds a depth of spirituality to their lives.

4. *Balance content and the sharing of thoughts and feelings* - Our students need to know that they are learning. They need their minds to be stimulated by the knowledge they gain, and they need the opportunity to process the new material so that it becomes a part of them. Our curricula must reflect a balance between acquisition of content and discussion, between "right brain and left brain" activities.

Working on gaining Hebrew skills must be balanced with discussions about God. Reading the words of the Torah text must be balanced with discussions of the Torah stories. Learning the words and tunes of prayers must be balanced with conversations that delve into the meaning of the prayers. One without the other leaves everyone unsatisfied.

5. *Build a community* - Reconstructionist synagogues work very hard at creating a real sense of community among our members. Our religious schools should reflect that sense of community, as should every class within the school. Students need to be presented with real ways to care for each other and to give help to each other when needed. Students need to know that mutual respect is the base on which the school is built. Monthly meetings of the whole school can be held in order to give students a place in the community decision making process. The meetings then can become a time when congregational issues can be brought to the students and for students to bring their concerns to the community.

6. *Include families in learning* - Family education has become the centerpiece of much of Jewish education, yet it often does not seem to reach families in a significant way. In order for family education to be effective, it needs to start early and continue throughout the children's education. We also need to be realistic about who the families in our congregations are. We cannot expect

them to have greater knowledge or commitment than they have. Nor can we demand so much time that the already overcommitted members of our communities simply stop attending.

Our relationships with the families in our communities are like any relationships. They cannot be contingent upon the other partner in the relationship changing to meet our desires. Shifts may happen, but only if we first show the families we reach that we accept them as they are. Then, we can begin to teach.

I always do some research on the ideology of the movement of the school where I am teaching. I make sure that I am teaching a topic with the emphasis on the belief of the movement. If the children are old enough to understand more complex things, I might tell them what the other movements teach so that they have a perspective (and also because they may hear something different from a friend who attends another religious school), but I stress the belief of the school where I teach. When I talk about Chanukah in the Reconstructionist school in which I work, I focus on the theme of Jewish freedom, rather than on the "miracle" of the oil. I mention that there is a story that talks about the oil lasting eight days, and it's probable that there was some sort of event that happened to inspire that story, but that it's unlikely that the story really happened the way it has come to be told.

(Nancy Hersh, Chatham, New Jersey)

ACT 2: TEACHING GOD, TORAH, AND ISRAEL

Before a teacher can master and integrate enduring understandings of Judaism and education, he/she needs to "see," "hear," and "imagine" these responses. In a certain sense, we talk ourselves into new ways of thinking; thus "talking the talk" is a prerequisite for "walking the walk." What follows are responses to three questions, one each about God, Torah, and Israel. As you read them, consider the philosophical and theological ideas that Reconstructionist Judaism brings to our educational process.

God

"If all conceptions of God are allowed, what do we teach the students? That there might be a supernatural power? That kind of ambiguity would disturb me . . ."

In dealing with issues of faith and belief, there is nothing but ambiguity — certainly nothing can be proven scientifically. In any kind of talking about God, we are in the position of trying to express the inexpressible, explain the inexplicable, and help our students comprehend the incomprehensible. That this is difficult, or is usually done imperfectly, should be of no surprise to us.

Remember, first of all, that children of different ages are at different stages developmentally, and that the kind of ambiguity and abstract thinking about God that 14 or 15-year-olds might understand would be completely incomprehensible to a 4 or 5-year-old, and vice versa. So we need to deal with our students where they are.

Second, all language about God is metaphorical. If we call God Healer, or Peacemaker, or even Father, it is because these words are a metaphor for some aspect of God that we focus on at that moment. Younger children are more likely to use concrete language to represent abstract concepts, which means that it is our job to point out that no description can capture what God really is. Educating about God is on some level a gradual process of teaching what metaphor is, and how it applies to talking about God, as well as creating an environment that engages with profound and ultimate questions about our lives and our world.

When a question about God's nature comes up, understand and respect the student's opinion. Do not try to convince him of something else, but go deeper into his/her own point of view. Answering, "Yes, that's one way to view God or God's presence. What might be another view?" or, alternatively, "What makes you think of (picture) God that way?" or sometimes, "Hmm! I might not have thought of that. What does it mean to you when you say _____?" fulfills these functions of respect and deepened understanding.

Torah

"I'm a vegetarian, and I don't like all the animal sacrifice in the Torah!"

Remember that Reconstructionists say that Judaism evolves over time. That means that the way we worship today is very different from the way we worshipped 100, 500, or certainly 3,000 years ago. Way back at the beginning of Jewish history, the Jewish people worshiped by sacrificing animals. This was pretty common at the time; the Greeks and Romans also used animal sacrifice in their prayers. We can look at the parts of the Torah that deal with animal sacrifices as a history book, a description of how things were then.

When the Temple was destroyed, the Jewish people had to find a new way to worship. They stopped sacrificing animals and began to pray with words in synagogues, and to observe events like Shabbat and holidays at home. These practices have continued to this day.

Although we don't do or want to do sacrifices today, we can still look to what the sacrifices were supposed to mean. To give only one example, the Torah says that Jews were to offer sacrifices on the three festival holidays of Sukkot, Shavuot, and Pesach. We can take this to mean that these holidays are important and that they should be celebrated in special ways. We can do this today, even if we do it in a manner that is different from how it was done in biblical times, or even different from the way the Torah says we "should" do it.

Israel (The Jewish People)

"I was at my cousin's Bat Mitzvah last week and, at her synagogue, some of the prayers are different. What's that about?"

One of the most important ideas that the founder of Reconstructionism, Rabbi Mordecai Kaplan, had was that Jewish civilization evolves — that it changes in response to its times and the situation it finds itself in. One of the ways Judaism changes is in its prayers.

When a Reconstructionist is deciding how to pray, he or she looks at the prayers that we have inherited and sees how they fit the way we live and believe now. If a prayer doesn't fit what we believe, we can revise it so that it is closer to what we mean to say.

This really comes into play in the idea of Jews as the "chosen people." Reconstructionists, starting with Kaplan, have rejected the idea that there is anything necessarily superior about Judaism or Jews, compared with other peoples or religions. Unfortunately, many of our prayers were written at a time when Jews did think they were superior to other peoples. This might have been compensation for being oppressed by these other people, but in any case, for Kaplan, the idea of claiming chosenness was a moral issue. Asserting that we are chosen — and by implication superior — exacerbates ethnic conflict. So he felt that the time for such language had passed, and most Reconstructionists have followed his example.

For instance, the Reconstructionist prayer book has changed the blessing before reading the Torah from *"asher bachar banu mikol ha'amim"* (Who has chosen us from among all peoples) to *"asher kervanu la'avodato"* (Who has drawn us to Your service). In this way, we acknowledge the special nature of our relationship with God, while not putting down anyone else. Several of the prayers have been revised in this way, including the Shabbat *"Kiddush"* and the *"Alaynu."*

CONCLUSION

May you, as teacher, be stimulated and engaged on the journey from intuitive to more guided, focused Jewish teaching, within a Reconstructionist context. We encourage you, wherever you might be teaching, to examine your guiding assumptions and think about creative alternatives. From every such place of Jewish education, the road leads to the *yeshivah shel ma'alah* (the "school of schools on high"), where each of us studies and learns with Moshe, Akiba, and the other great teachers and learners of Jewish tradition.

BIBLIOGRAPHY

Alpert, Rebecca, and Jacob Staub. *Exploring Judaism.* Philadelphia, PA: JRF Press, 2000.

> This is the best and most contemporary primer of basic Reconstructionist Judaism for teachers.

Gluskin, Shai; Moti Rieber; and Jeffrey Schein. *Reconstructionist Educator's Study Guide.* Philadelphia, PA: JRF Press, 2000.

> This volume explores the practical implications of Reconstructionist thought for teachers in the Jewish religious school. Special attention is paid to concrete strategies for teachers in presenting God, Torah, and Israel.

———. *Connecting Prayer and Spirituality: A Creative Resource Guide for Teaching Kol Haneshamah.* Philadelphia, PA: JRF Press, 1996.

> This volume provides an in-depth exploration of the challenges of teaching about God, prayer, and spirituality in a Reconstructionist mode.

Holtzman, Linda. "Ten Things I Learned as the Education Director of JRF Congregation Mishkan Shalom." Elkins Park, PA: Jewish Reconstructionist Federation, 2000, http://www.jrf.org/edu/tenthings.html

> This is the text of a keynote by Rabbi Linda Holtzman to the JRF's Mid-Atlantic regional educators in November, 2000.

Schein, Jeffrey, ed. *Tithadesh: Initiating Reflection and Renewal in Jewish Education.* Philadelphia, PA: JRF Press, 1992.

> The volume contains the most in-depth examples of professional development for Jewish teachers and for training teachers as reflective practitioners.

Schein, Jeffrey, with Leah Mundell and Joe Blair. *The Reconstructionist Curriculum Resource Guide.* Philadelphia, PA: JRF Press, 1998.

> This volume provides the broadest array of examples of Reconstructionist curricular thinking applied to various topics in the Jewish curriculum.

Schein, Jeffrey, and Jacob Staub. *Creative Jewish Education.* New York: Rossel Books, 1985. (Distributed by the Reconstructionist Press)

> This volume is the most "topical" Reconstructionist educational publication, and deals with a range of issues related to formal and informal Jewish education.

CHAPTER 7

Orthodox Jewish Education

Leonard A. Matanky

In the twenty-first century, Orthodox Jewish formal education is primarily, if not exclusively, synonymous with day school education.[1] Yet, day schools, in one form or another, have been part of the Jewish communal scene since the Talmudic Sage, Joshua ben Gamla, first established Jewish "public" schools in the first century. Whether known as a *Cheder*, a *Talmud Torah*, or a *Yeshivah Ketanah*, day schools have always played a critical role in the continued growth and stability of the Jewish people.

The first American Jewish day schools appeared during Colonial times. However, the true precursors to the modern American Jewish day school did not appear until the late nineteenth century with the founding of *Yeshivat Etz Chayim* (1886) and *Yeshivat Rabbi Yitzchak Elchanan* (1897).[2] Both of these institutions were under Orthodox auspices and combined an intensive Judaic studies curriculum with a general education.

As the immigration from Europe continued, more and more day schools were established in America. The greatest growth occurred following World War II and then again during the last two decades of the twentieth century. At present, there are nearly 200,000 students attending more than 600 Jewish day schools that have an annual combined budget of close to two billion dollars.

In America today, 80% of all Jewish day schools are associated with Orthodox Judaism and nearly 80% of all Jewish day school teachers are themselves products of Orthodox day schools.[3] Therefore, it is only logical to assume that in order to understand a teacher's role within an Orthodox

Jewish day school, it is necessary first to understand Orthodox Judaism.

ORTHODOX JUDAISM

Unlike other movements within the Jewish religious world, Orthodox Jewish observance has been essentially unchanged for hundreds of years. True, the modern world presents new challenges and opportunities, yet what distinguishes Orthodox Judaism from other movements is its allegiance to a well-defined and immutable set of beliefs and actions (*mitzvot* — commandments).

One of the most famous expressions of Orthodox Jewish belief was developed by Moses Maimonides, (1135-1204), the great medieval Jewish scholar. Commonly referred to as the "Thirteen *Ani Ma'amins*" (literally, Thirteen "I Believes"), Maimonides wrote that the following principles are, "the fundamental truths of our religion and its very foundations."

1. The belief in the existence of G-d, who is perfect and is the Primary Cause of all existence

2. The belief in G-d's absolute and unparalleled unity

3. The belief in G-d's incorporeality

4. The belief in G-d's eternity

5. The imperative to worship G-d exclusively

6. The belief that G-d communicates with humanity through prophecy

---

[1] Until the late 1960s, Orthodox supplementary school education was still an option for many parents. However, by the 1970s, the vast majority of American Orthodox Jewry viewed day school education as the only valid option. This shift in perception was due to a number of factors, including: the growing "openness" of American society and the need to place limits on Orthodox youth, the decline of public school education, the growing commitment of young Orthodox Jews to Orthodox

practice and Torah study, and the successes of Orthodox day schools.

[2] These schools merged to create Yeshiva University (their Rabbinical school still bears the name of the latter Yeshiva).

[3] The Teachers Report: A Portrait of Teachers in Jewish Schools (New York: CIJE Research for Policy, 1999).

7. The belief that Moses was the greatest of all prophets

8. The belief in the divine origin of the Torah

9. The belief in the immutability of the Torah

10. The belief in divine omniscience and providence

11. The belief in divine reward and punishment

12. The belief in the future arrival of the Messiah and the messianic era

13. The belief in the future resurrection of the dead.

While *all* of these beliefs have an impact on the nature, method, and content of Jewish education, there are but a few basic Orthodox Jewish principles that have direct and identifiable educational impact:

Torah m'Sinai ("Ani Ma'amin" #6-#9)

Orthodox Jews believe that G-d gave Moses not only the entire text of the Pentateuch at Mount Sinai, but also its accompanying Oral tradition. While there is a Talmudic debate about whether Moses received the entire Torah at Sinai, or received it gradually over the ensuing 40 years in the desert, *Torah m'Sinai* (the Torah as given at Mount Sinai) is key to establishing the divinity of Jewish law.

Educational Impact:

- The divinity of the Bible leads to a reverence of the text and all of its intricacies.

- Since the text was originally written in Hebrew, knowledge of Hebrew is critical to understanding all of the nuances of this divine text.

- Studying the Bible is a means to a better understanding of G-d, Who transmitted this divine text to Moses, and the Jewish people.

Rabbinic Power

Orthodox Jews believe that its Rabbinic leadership cannot negate or modify biblical law. However, Rabbis do have the power to institute laws that safeguard the 613 basic biblical commandments, to legislate new laws to address the needs of Jewish

life, and to articulate the Bible's Oral tradition that was given by G-d at Mount Sinai.

Orthodox Jews also believe that the further a generation is historically distanced from the Revelation at Sinai, the less capable it is of understanding that unique experience. Therefore, the power of later generations of Rabbis is limited and cannot overturn decisions and enactments of earlier generations.

Educational Impact:

The words and actions of Sages who lived more than 2,000 years ago, continue to be revered, and the legal *("halachic")* texts must be studied as a basis to understanding current practice.

The Oral tradition, which first appears in written form as the Mishnah (third century) and the Talmud (sixth century) is an integral part of Jewish education.

Talmud Torah

The study of Torah is a constant, never ending obligation of every Jew, not only as a practical means to understand and fulfill Jewish religious obligations, but also as a means to grow closer to G-d. Therefore, the study of Torah, purely for its own sake *("Torah lishma")* is greatly valued and the Torah scholar is revered.

The most all-encompassing obligations of Torah study are directed toward Jewish men, and the primary responsibility to educate children rests with parents. However, parents who are unable to teach their own children may hire an "agent" (i.e., a teacher) to perform this duty on their behalf.

Educational Impact:

- While the ability to live a "Jewish life" (i.e., conform to Jewish practice) is a major goal of Jewish education, not all education must be "practically oriented." Rather, some study can be purely for the sake of study.

- Jewish education must prepare its students for lifelong study.

- Jewish study is a cross-generational activity.

- The wisdom and advice of Torah scholars is much sought after.

- Historically, the most intense Jewish education

(i.e., advanced Yeshivah education) was directed toward men.

- Jewish educators serve "in loco parentis," and Jewish schools are the vehicle to organize that education.

AMERICAN ORTHODOXY AND ITS SCHOOLS

Many Subgroups

In twenty-first century America, Orthodox Judaism cannot truly be identified as a "movement" because of its lack of organization. There is no single "Chief Rabbi" of American Orthodoxy, no single all-inclusive synagogue movement and no single body of day school administration, oversight, and governance. Rather, American Orthodoxy is splintered into many different subgroups, all of which share the same basic beliefs outlined above, but may differ about such basic issues as: the interaction with and value of general culture, the importance of post-secondary general education, and the theological meaning of the State of Israel.

Therefore, it is not surprising (especially in America where schooling is a decentralized enterprise) that Jewish day schools have been established to address the needs of nearly every possible subgroup within the spectrum of Orthodoxy. There are schools that are Zionistic and others that are anti-Zionistic; schools that use Hebrew as the language of Judaic instruction and others that teach in Yiddish; schools that are coeducational and others that are separate gender (and often, housed on separate campuses); schools that are college preparatory and others that forbid their graduates from attending college; schools that cater to Ashkenazic Jewry; and others (though a small minority) that cater to Sephardic Jewry.

Educational Impact:

- Due to the decentralized nature of Jewish day schools and the varied philosophies of the schools, it is difficult for day schools to pool their resources to create standardized curriculum and textbooks.

- Standards for academic excellence are varied, and measures of success are often ill-defined.

- Communities often find themselves with too many day schools (each with its own variation of Orthodox philosophy) for too small a population of students.

National Affiliation

Even in matters of school affiliation, there are divisions in American Orthodox day schools. The vast majority of Orthodox day schools associate with an organization called Torah Umesorah (founded in 1944 and strongly identified with right-wing *Yeshivot*), while a minority of day schools identify with one of the day school associations supported by Yeshiva University (the bastion of what is often identified as "centrist" or "modern Orthodoxy").[4] Some schools are members of both associations. However, generally, those schools that are coed, college preparatory, and strongly Zionistic will more likely associate with the Yeshiva University supported associations.

Educational Impact:

- Affiliation of schools to a centralized governing body is voluntary and, therefore, national associations yield minimal influence (both in terms of governance and curriculum) upon member schools.

Affiliation with Local Agencies

Locally, most day schools are also affiliated with a local agency (known as the central agency for Jewish education, bureau of Jewish education, or BJE). Generally, the degree to which Orthodox day schools interact with the central agency is a function of three factors: (1) the services the agency can offer to Orthodox day schools, (2) the agency personnel who have experience with and an understanding of Orthodox day schools, and (3) the amount of financial support the agency can offer the day school. Financial support of day schools (either directly from the central agency, or channeled from a local Jewish Federation through the education agency) is the strongest means to establish an affiliation between the agency and the day school. However, unless the education agency understands the needs and *halachic* parameters

---

[4]For many years, the Educators' Council of America was just such an association. However, since its demise, a number of subsequent organizations have been established, the most recent of which is the Association of Modern Orthodox Day Schools.

under which an Orthodox day school operates, there cannot be a successful relationship. For example, the central agency must understand that some matters of curriculum or methods of instruction are based on tradition and may be "non-negotiable" — no matter what current educational research may suggest. Or, since nearly all central education agencies are cross-denominational[5] and there are many Orthodox day schools that, philosophically, will not participate in cross-denominational educational programming, greater affiliation with the central agency may be altogether impossible.

Educational Impact:

- Unless central Jewish agencies are willing to hire staff that understand Orthodox day schools and are willing to work within the philosophical/*halachic* parameters of these schools, community-wide resources may be inaccessible to Orthodox day schools. However, when the agencies understand the unique nature of Orthodox day schools, there can be (and have been) significant partnerships created for the benefit of the education of Orthodox youth.

- Often, traditional functions of local central Jewish education agencies, such as Teachers' and Principals' Licensing as well as other means to encourage the professionalization of Jewish education, may not be designed for or implemented in Orthodox day schools.

The individual governance of Orthodox day schools typically follows one of two general organizational schemes. In most modern Orthodox day schools, a lay leadership "board of directors" sets school policy and the principal is charged with implementing that policy. To assist the board in this function, various subcommittees are established, among which is an "education committee." This committee is comprised of interested lay leaders (some of whom may have professional backgrounds in education), and together with the principal they review the curriculum and discuss

means of improving learning and instruction. Issues that require a *halachic* decision are generally referred by the principal to the school's *halachic* authority (typically, a communal Rabbi or *Rosh haYeshiva*), and other matters may be referred to the board for policy decisions.

In most right-wing Orthodox schools, there is a separation of power between the board of directors and the education committee (*Vaad haChinuch*). The lay leadership board of directors sets school policy in all matters, excluding education, while the *Vaad haChinuch* operates independently, often selecting its own membership, setting educational policy, and overseeing its implementation.[6] The school principal is responsible to both of these groups. In these schools, not only are *halachic* issues referred to an appropriate *halachic* authority,[7] but many other issues are referred as well. This expanded Rabbinic role is referred to as *Daas Torah*, and is based upon the belief that Rabbinic leaders possess a greater understanding in all matters than common lay leaders. Practically speaking, when invoked, the decisions of *Daas Torah* have the same import and demand the same fealty as any other *halachic* decision. As such, *Daas Torah* serves as the ultimate authority in these schools, with veto power over the board and the *Vaad haChinuch*.

JUDAIC CURRICULUM

Elitist Underpinnings

Unlike their European predecessors, American Jewish day schools are the inheritors of two traditions: the elitist curriculum of European Jewish schooling and American popular "public education."

As a result, despite the natural differences of student abilities and learning styles, the curriculum of the vast majority of Jewish day schools is geared toward advanced Yeshiva/Seminary[8] study. The Talmud, which in Europe was studied only by the most promising of young students, is taught to all boys as they reach middle school (and in some modern Orthodox schools, to all girls). All students

---

[5]The one exception is in Chicago, where there are two bureaus: one serving primarily the Reform and Conservative communities (Community Foundation for Jewish Education), and the other serving the Orthodox community (Associated Talmud Torahs of Chicago).

[6]In this structure, the *Vaad haChinuch* is often deemed a quasi-*Bet Din* (literally, ecclesiastical court) and, therefore,

according to *halachah*, its membership is limited to men.

[7]The authority may be a member (or members) of the *Vaad haChinuch* or, on major issues, a *Rosh HaYeshiva* or Torah Umesorah's Rabbinic Advisory Committee.

[8]A seminary is a common term for women's advanced Judaic programs.

are urged to continue their formal Jewish studies well beyond high school; few day schools, if any, provide options for vocational training.

Educational Impact:

- Students who are not capable of mastering the intricacies of Talmud and other advanced texts may not be offered appropriate Jewish educational options. Therefore, for some children, public school may be the only educational option.

- Students who fail to succeed in day schools may develop low self-esteem and find other inappropriate avenues for self-identity. The rise of "at-risk children" in the Orthodox community may be partially due to the elitist underpinning of day school curriculum.

The Role of the Home and the School

For boys, the study of Talmud generally takes precedence over all other Judaic instruction. For girls who traditionally were excluded from Talmud study, the Bible and its commentaries are the primary focus. Daily Jewish law is studied sporadically (driven primarily by the Jewish holiday cycle) and it is still assumed that many of the basic "daily life issues" (i.e., Shabbat, *kashrut*, and family life) will be transmitted from the home.[9] Classic biblical and Rabbinic texts are studied in their original Hebrew, and some schools (though diminishing in number[10]) still use Hebrew as the primary language of Judaic instruction (*Ivrit b'Ivrit;* Hebrew taught in Hebrew).

Educational Impact:

- For those boys who will not be continuing on to advanced *yeshiva* study, many basic issues of Jewish philosophy and law may never be studied.

- The assumption that many basic Jewish issues will be addressed mimetically (via the oral traditions of families) may no longer be true, either due to the lack of such family traditions, or through the reality of both parents working and thus unable to devote the necessary energies to transmitting values. Therefore, the role

of the school may be expanding and the validity of relying upon the home to help educate the child diminishing.

Time Spent on Judaic Studies

While the *raison d'être* of all Orthodox day schools is their Judaic curriculum, there is wide variance in the amount of time spent on Judaic studies. Typically, in the more "right-wing" schools, the Judaic curriculum commands all but a small portion of the day necessary to satisfy the various state standards for general studies. In the more "modern schools" (those that advocate for advanced general studies — e.g., college degrees) general studies may occupy up to 50% of the instructional time.

Educational Impact:

- Despite all claims to the contrary, it is impossible to achieve identical outcomes in general studies that devote 70% (or less) of time to this curriculum. How will schools determine what areas of study can be ignored without compromising that academic discipline?

- In recent years, some families (especially in the modern Orthodox community) have begun to question the ability of day schools to offer a competitive general education. When combined with the high cost of Jewish education (the average cost of a day school education is now approximately $10,000), these families have begun to consider public education a viable educational option.

- Inevitably, some students are not destined to become great Torah scholars. Can day schools prepare these students to be economically self-supportive?

FACULTY

Variation in Background and Training

Most Orthodox Jewish day schools maintain two separate faculties, one for Judaic studies and one for general studies. As a rule, the Judaic studies faculty members are also practicing members of the

---

[9]Unfortunately, with the changing dynamics of family structure, this assumption may be erroneous.

[10]While many more schools may strive for this method of instruction, there is a paucity of teachers skilled enough in conversational Hebrew to allow this to be implemented.

Orthodox community (a necessary prerequisite to guarantee consistency between the lessons taught in classes and the lifestyle of those who teach these lessons). However, sometimes in smaller communities, exceptions are made due to the lack of qualified staff, and in some schools (even in larger communities), Hebrew language teachers may also be an exception to this rule.

Most Judaic studies teachers today are, themselves, products of the day school system and, therefore, tend to be a close-knit group who share both philosophy and educational experiences. Since most day schools do not require their teachers to have completed an academic program of teacher preparation,[11] many teachers learn how to teach "on the job," relying heavily on peer input and personal memories of favorite teachers. In fact, while many schools do participate in an annual in-service day, most schools initiate increased professional standards only when required to do so by some outside governing body (i.e., a major funding organization or an accrediting agency).

Educational Impact:

- This lack of an academic prerequisite for Judaic teachers has led to two interesting phenomena: (1) a difference in the variety of instructional methods used by Judaic vs. general studies teachers, and (2) the high percentage of Judaic teachers who are members of the right-wing Orthodox Jewish community. While the dedication and enthusiasm of many Judaic studies teachers may more than compensate for their lack of formal training, the latter issue has resulted in a crisis in "modern Orthodox" schools that are largely staffed by Judaic teachers to the "right" of the school's philosophy.[12]

General Studies Teachers

Depending on the philosophy of the day school, general studies faculty members may find themselves greatly valued or simply tolerated. Often, in those day schools in which general studies is grudgingly taught, students "pick-up" on this attitude and do not take these studies seriously. However, when schools place great emphasis on general studies, Orthodox day schools often find themselves in a dilemma — the general studies teacher may be beloved, and yet may personally live a lifestyle abhorrent to *halachic* Judaism. Therefore, there are day schools which, in the absence of being able to hire only Orthodox general studies teachers, prefer to hire non-Jewish general studies teachers over non-observant Jewish general studies teachers!

Educational Impact:

- Teachers must work to understand and respect the religious philosophy of the school. Conformity to dress code, manner of speech, religiously acceptable materials, *kashrut*, and strict limits on physical contact between the genders must be respected and supported by faculty.

- No matter the philosophy of the school, respect and human dignity must be expected of the students, Teachers have a right to expect the administration of the school to reinforce the value of *derech eretz* (appropriate behavior to others) across the curriculum.

SCHOOL DAY

Long Hours

In order to address both a dual curriculum and properly prepare its students for the next level of study, students in Orthodox day schools have a long school day. From the middle school onward, boys (and in some modern Orthodox schools, girls) are required to arrive at school around 7:30 a.m. for morning prayers, and the school day continues until 4:00 or 5:00 p.m. Following school, students are expected to review their studies and complete a significant amount of homework.

Educational Impact:

- All teachers must be aware of the difficulty of participating in a dual curriculum, and must try to minimize the amount of unnecessary homework. Homework should be reserved for independent practice of skills already developed in school.

---

[11]Less than half of all Orthodox day school teachers have certification in Jewish education (*The Teachers Report*, 6).

[12]It has been suggested that this may be one of the key factors associated with the growth of "right-wing Orthodoxy" in traditionally "modern Orthodox" families.

- Often, teachers expect parents to review and/or complete those subjects the student is having difficulty learning. Because of the large size of Orthodox families and the need for both parents to work, many parents are not in the position to supervise and teach their children at night.

- Increasingly, students from larger families are being sent to school without adequate meals. Teachers should pay close attention to students who arrive to school hungry and, whenever possible, find opportunities to make sure that proper nutrition is provided.

Structure of the School Day

While Orthodox day schools typically begin the school day with prayers, not all schools immediately continue with Judaic studies. Some schools, either out of a desire to "integrate" the general and Judaic subjects or because of necessity (the lack of qualified teachers or the need to offer teachers a full-time wage), alternate subjects throughout the day between general and Judaic studies. Other schools (and nearly all right-wing boys' day schools) place all of the Judaic subjects in the morning, when the students are "freshest" and most attentive. This latter configuration of studies presents yet another challenge to general studies teachers — not only "how to teach the subject in less time," but also "how to do so when the students may be tired."

Educational Impact:

- When schools are organized into two separate and distinct curricula, teachers are often excluded from what is happening in the other part of the day. This can be true of both Judaic and general studies teachers and must be addressed by the administration.

- Often, children with academic difficulties exhibit those difficulties in both Judaic and general studies classes. Teachers must find ways to communicate about students and schools must provide opportunities for the review of the "entire child."

It is also important to note that, because the Jewish High Holy Days (Rosh HaShanah, Yom Kippur, and Sukkot) occur in the months of September and October, the beginning of the school year can include as many as 15 vacation days.[13] As a result, each year, teachers are faced with the immediate challenge of helping students to readjust to an intensive academic program, despite a month-long series of interruptions

CHALLENGES FACING ORTHODOX SCHOOLS

While many of the challenges facing Orthodox schools have already been discussed, at the beginning of the twenty-first century, there are at least three major issues that jeopardize the continued survival and success of Orthodox Jewish education: American society, finances, and personnel. Each of these is described below.

American Society

As North American society continues to accept a wider range of lifestyles, behaviors, and beliefs, Orthodox Judaism is finding itself at greater odds with general society and its morality. Whether it is television and the issues that are now acceptable to present (even during "family hour"), the Internet, advertising, or the disappearance of the "nuclear family," Orthodoxy is often forced to chose between interaction *with* society in general and isolation *from* the "evils" of that society.

This clash between societal mores and Orthodox practice has severely impacted Orthodoxy's children, contributing to the emergence of an epidemic of "children at risk." These children whom day schools have been unable to affect, *have* been affected by American culture, and, painful as it is to admit, every ill of society has crept into the Orthodox world.

For Orthodox day schools, issues such as the disintegration of families, substance abuse, sexual abuse, physical abuse, and eating disorders must now be tackled. Mental health professionals (e.g., social workers and psychologists) must now be added to school staffs, and curriculum must be modified to address these issues. The Orthodox

---

[13]Rosh HaShanah eve (1 day), Rosh HaShanah (2 days), Fast of Gedalia (1 day), Yom Kippur eve (1 day), Yom Kippur (1 day), Sukkot eve (1 day), Sukkot and Shemini Atzeret (8 days). While

some schools hold classes on the intermediate days of Sukkot (up to 4 of the 8 days), most do not, and some even give the day after Sukkot as a vacation day.

community and its schools have begun to grow fearful of general society, and the demand to separate from society is gaining strength. Therefore, it is not unusual to find Orthodox day schools that forbid Internet access, television, movies, and even newspapers. In fact, some day schools have even begun to search for alternative sources for English language literature to avoid the issues of general society.

Tragically, as schools try to insulate their students from society, there is often a concomitant increase in demand for students to conform. Minor deviations in behavior, performance, or practice, which may have once been overlooked, are now reason to remove a child from school — only exacerbating the communal problem of "children at risk."

The challenge that now confronts Orthodox educators, is not only *how* to find the balance between general society and Orthodoxy, but to determine if such a balance is even possible in the twenty-first century!

Educational Impact:

- No part of the Orthodox community is completely unaffected by American societal mores. Therefore, teachers must address issues within the classroom that may never before have been discussed. Even young children are exposed to attitudes, practices, and beliefs antithetical to Judaism.

- Teachers must refocus the curriculum to provide more opportunities for affective (vs. cognitive) education.

- With the added pressures of Orthodox Jewish families, teachers must often assume the role of a parent, providing students with a needed sense of safety, security, and love. Without such a relationship, students may not be able to develop into well-adjusted Jewish adults.

- Teachers must be taught how to identify and respond to the needs of potential "children at risk."

- Schools must carefully review their academic

and behavioral standards, finding ways to allow for greater flexibility for students to avoid excluding some children who may deviate from current expectations.

Finances

The cost of living an Orthodox Jewish lifestyle that mandates, among other obligations, day school education, is staggering.[14] With day school tuition ranging from $5,000 to $18,000 per child, and the size of Orthodox families growing, day school education is placing extraordinary financial pressures on Orthodox families.[15] As a result, some families have begun to reconsider their commitment to a day school education, opting instead to send their children to public school. Others apply to the schools for need-based scholarships.

Orthodox schools have generally adopted the policy that "no child will be denied a Jewish education because of financial need," often placing an untenable financial burden on the school. While non-Orthodox day schools can typically expect more than 90% of their budget to be raised by tuition, Orthodox day schools must raise between 30-60% of their budgets from sources other than tuition.[16]

Jewish Federations, often viewed as the "savior" of organized American Jewry, only offer about 5% of the support needed to educate children, leaving the remaining fund-raising needs to the lay leadership of the school. Since there is near perfect correlation between fund-raising needs and scholarship requests, it is also true that those schools with the greatest financial need serve a population least suited to respond to the need (i.e., to contribute funds to offset the school's deficit). As a result, many Orthodox day schools have begun to enter an era of financial crisis for which American Orthodoxy has yet to find a solution.

At present, a number of different experiments have been initiated to try to address this crisis. The National Jewish Day School Scholarship Committee has proposed the "5% solution," recruiting donors to commit 5% of their estates to Jewish education. Foundations, such as SAMIS, Avi Chai, and Gottesman Family Foundation have each

---

[14]In 1992, the American Jewish Committee estimated that the cost of full Jewish affiliation for a family of four would require an annual income of $80-125,000. Not only are many Orthodox families larger than four, but since 1992, costs have continued to spiral upward! See: J.J. Goldberg, "Jewish Sticker Shock," *Jewish Week* (February 26, 1999).

[15]These pressures (and the frustrations they cause) may also be a contributing factor to the emergence of "children at risk."

[16]Jack Wertheimer, "Talking Dollars and Sense about Jewish Education" (New York: Avi Chai Foundation, August, 2001).

experimented with programs for tuition assistance. Yet, others have proposed pressuring Jewish Federations to increase their level of support, or have begun to advocate for tuition vouchers from state governments.

The impact of this crisis is self-evident. Some schools may be forced to limit their scholarship programs, thereby relinquishing the historic commitment to day school education for all children. Other schools will continue to offer scholarships, but will be forced to slash their budgets, reducing or completely eliminating expenditures for such basic needs as curriculum development, academic support services, or even teacher salaries and benefits — thereby compromising the future success of Orthodox day schools.

Educational Impact:

* As the day school financial crisis grows, schools will be forced try to find ways to reduce their budgets, often at the expense of their academic program. Teachers may find even greater limitations on the purchase of new academic resources, increased class sizes, and fewer support services for students.

* The financial crisis will also impact on the stability of those families in lower income brackets. Such financial pressures may further exacerbate the crisis of "children at risk."

Personnel

Related to the issue of financing Jewish education is the issue of personnel recruitment and retention. Fortunately, studies have consistently found that there is a high rate of teacher retention in day schools.[17] While there are many contributing factors to this reality, one of the most important is the commitment of day school teachers to their profession — their sense of responding to a "sacred calling." Surprisingly, this commitment exists despite the fact that few of these teachers are professionally trained, adequately paid, or offered the neces-

sary support and opportunities for continued professional growth.

Nevertheless, in order to strengthen day schools and to respond to the many new complexities of day school education (including "children at risk," single parent families, and the rise in learning disabled children), it will be necessary to commit significant efforts to the professionalization of day school teachers. In-service training must be expanded, compensation increased, and benefit packages designed to reward excellence and encourage continued professional growth.

One encouraging change has occurred due to the emergence of *Kollel* study.[18] Today, the once common shortage of Orthodox day school teachers no longer exists. These men (and their wives) are naturally drawn to Jewish education and have strong Judaic backgrounds. With the appropriate support (and the necessary measure of natural talent) many of these individuals make excellent teachers.

However, *Kollel* alumni do present two new challenges to day schools, one to modern Orthodox day schools and the other to right-wing Orthodox day schools.

Most *Kollelim* (plural of *Kollel)* are adherents of right-wing Orthodoxy, and when their alumni are hired by modern Orthodox schools, a dissonance is created between their personal philosophies and the philosophy of the school. Often, students conclude that their teachers (whom they hopefully admire) represent a more valid expression of Judaism, leading them away from the philosophy of modern Orthodoxy.

On the other hand, even in right-wing Orthodox day schools, there are potential pitfalls. These are the result of the lack of professional alternatives for *Kollel* alumni and the dearth of available teaching positions. Therefore, day schools have their choice of the "best and the brightest" as future teachers. While this should portend well for the day schools, such individuals are often overqualified for the grades they may be hired to teach, and often have difficulty accepting the reality that they

---

[17]For example, see Adam Gamoran, et al, "The Teachers Report: A Portrait of Teachers in Jewish Schools" (New York: Council for Initiatives in Jewish Education, 1996).

[18]A *Kollel* is an advanced non-degree-granting institute for Judaic studies. Especially popular in the right-wing Orthodox community (which views continued Torah study as the highest form of religious expression), young married Orthodox men will

continue their studies in a *Kollel* for a number a years, before entering the work force. Typically, these *Kollel* students do not pursue secular academic degrees and, therefore, are not prepared to enter most professions. However, many day schools will hire these men (or their wives, who must contribute to the family income — because of the low stipend offered *Kollel* students) even though they lack formal training.

may remain a primary or middle school teacher for many years. This can be demoralizing and can lead to early teacher burnout.

On the administrative level, day school education is already in crisis. Too few qualified candidates are available for too many unfilled educational leadership positions. Turnover within the first five years is high (more than 50% of all educational leaders are in their positions for less than five years), and many express dissatisfaction with their positions.

Of course, much of this can be directly attributed to the complexities of twenty-first century educational leadership. The vast majority of the parent body are themselves products of day school education, and this familiarity seems to foster an unrealistic sense of the "simplicity" of the day school endeavor. High tuitions further contribute to a parent's sense of entitlement, and the demands placed on many educational leaders are unrealistic.

Therefore, despite the current financial crisis of Orthodox day school education, the forces of supply and demand have led schools to offer to educational leaders salaries double, triple, and sometimes quadruple of what was offered just a few years ago. Principals earning $150,000 to $200,000 are no longer uncommon, and while it may be long overdue, it also places additional burdens on the budgets of schools, and unfair expectations of the recipients.

New programs need to be developed to identify talented educators and offer the necessary training to enter the administrative field. Currently, The Avi Chai Foundation in partnership with Yeshiva University, Jewish Educational Leadership Institute in partnership with Loyola University of Chicago, and Torah Umesorah offer such programs. However, it is still too early to know their impact.

Educational Impact:

- As the complexities of educating twenty-first century American Orthodox children continue to grow, teachers will find even more pressure to increase their preparedness and enhance their professional credentials.

- While merit pay for teachers remains a controversial issue, as the call for professionalization grows, the likelihood of such programs increases.

- The high turnover rate of educational leaders can create a real (or perceived) sense of instability in the organization. Veteran teachers may find themselves asked to "reinvent the wheel" as each new educational leader attempts to restructure/modify the organization.

CONCLUSION

While Orthodox day schools are one of the great success stories of the twentieth century, in the twenty-first century Orthodox day school education stands at a crossroads. Today, day schools must confront the new challenges of the Jewish and general communities while continuing to provide a strong education and sense of commitment to Jewish life.

At the forefront of that challenge, as with all educational challenges, are the teachers who must work together with parents, schools, and students to create an environment that will transmit both cognitive and affective traditions of a warm and caring community.

BIBLIOGRAPHY

A Time to Act: The Report of the Commission on Jewish Education in North America. Lanham, MD: University Press of America, 1991.

> This groundbreaking report was the basis of many initiatives for Jewish education over the last decade.

"Children on the Fringe . . . and Beyond." *Jewish Observer Magazine* 32:9, November 1999.

> *Jewish Observer Magazine* is the voice of much of America's right-wing Orthodox community. This particular issue dealing with "children at risk" was the most requested issue ever published.

"Financing Jewish Education." *Agenda: Jewish Education* #14, 2001.

> JESNA, the lead agency of the United Jewish Communities, issued this survey of key financial challenges facing American Jewish education.

Gamoran, Adam, et al. *The Teachers Report: A Portrait of Teachers in Jewish Schools.* New York: Council for Initiatives in Jewish Education, Research for Policy, 1999.

> As a follow up to *A Time to Act* (see above), the Mandel Foundation supported a number of research projects to help direct future funding and training initiatives.

Goldring, Ellen B., et al. *The Leaders Report: A Portrait of Educational Leaders in Jewish Schools.* New York: Mandel Foundation, Research for Policy, 1999.

> As a follow up to *A Time to Act* (see above), the Mandel Foundation supported a number of research projects to help direct future funding and training initiatives.

Helmreich, W.B. *The World of the Yeshiva: An Intimate Portrait of Orthodox Jewry.* New York: Free Press. 1982.

> Helmreich's study of Orthodox Jewry remains one of the most important sociological and historical studies of this segment of Jewry.

Kelman, Stuart L., ed. *What We Know about Jewish Education.* Los Angeles, CA: Torah Aura Productions, 1992.

> In this collection of "research into practice" articles, Kelman succeeded in presenting many of the key issues facing Jewish educators and the supporters of Jewish education.

Kramer, Doniel Zvi. *The Day Schools and Torah Umesorah: The Seeding of Traditional Judaism in America.* New York: Yeshiva University Press, 1984.

> In this book, originally written as a doctoral dissertation, Kramer presents the history of Torah Umesorah — the largest Orthodox day school association in North America.

Schick, Marvin, and Jeremy Dauber. *The Financing of Jewish Day Schools.* New York: Avi Chai, September 1997.

> Avi Chai is one of the most creative funders of Jewish education. Part of the reason for this is the research they have conducted into the needs of American Jewish education. This study, is an important example of such research, and presents the financial challenges facing American day school education.

Schiff, Alvin I. *The Jewish Day School in America.* New York: Jewish Education Committee Press, 1966.

> Schiff's study of Jewish day schools was the pioneering history of this movement, tracing its development from colonial times to the mid-sixties.

———. *Fortifying and Restoring Jewish Behavior: The Interaction of Home and School.* New York: David J. Azrieli Graduate School, Yeshiva University, 1994.

> One in a series of studies conducted by Schiff on the impact and effectiveness of Jewish education.

Twerski, Benzion. "Orthodox Youth and Substance Abuse: Shattering the Myths." *Jewish Action Magazine* 58:2, 1998.

> Dr. Twerski, an expert in the field of drug counseling, literally "shattered the myths" in this pioneering article in the leading American Orthodox periodical.

Wertheimer, Jack. *Talking Dollars and Sense about Jewish Education.* New York: Avi Chai and The American Jewish Committee, August 2001.

> Dr. Wertheimer's study of the funding needs of education offers both cogent arguments against current practices and recommendations for the future.

CHAPTER 8

Teaching in a Jewish Community School[1]

Marc N. Kramer

The majority of Americans see themselves as products of, and committed to, what has been called "the best expression of American democracy" (Ravitch, 1992) — public schools. This linking of public education and American democracy is especially strong among American Jews (D. Z. Kramer, 1984). Yet, a large and growing number of American Jews today are actualizing their understanding of life in a democracy by enrolling their children in private Jewish all-day schools (Schiff, 1988). Whereas once Jewish day schools were exclusively under Orthodox auspices, soon Conservative and Reform day schools appeared on the American school landscape (M. Kramer, 2002). Simultaneous with the rise of the non-Orthodox, denominationally supported day schools was the appearance of communal day schools — schools independent of any denominational influence, open to all Jewish children and supported by local Jewish communities. In recent years, this notion of a communal school embracing all mainstream movements of the Jewish community has been bolstered by the American Jewish community's increased interest in pluralism.

A HISTORICAL PERSPECTIVE

In order to understand what it means to be a non-denominational Jewish school, one must first understand something about the social, political, and economic development of the American Jewish community over the past 100 years.

For the Jewish masses that arrived in the United States between 1880 and 1920, accustomed either to the *yeshivah* world or the state sponsored schools of Central Europe, enrollment into America's public schools was a collective statement of faith in their new host country. In free, public schools, they — through their children — became both English speakers and "Americanized" Jews (Cowan and Cowan, 1989). Public school represented the "bridge to the new society and the key to self-improvement" (Ehlich, 1997).

The process of Americanization rapidly transformed the immigrant Jewish community into an elemental part of the urban and suburban middle class (Dash Moore, in Sarna, 1986) where, as novelized by Philip Roth, Meyer Levin, Chaim Potok, Herman Wouk, and others (Sachar, 1990), they mitigated their bifurcated identities by "proving themselves" as good Americans. Enrolling children in public schools was an essential proof text of their acculturation. To put one's children in a Jewish all-day school was to remain steadfastly distanced from one's neighbors, friends, and even coreligionists, all of whom accepted, if not fully endorsed, public schools. The parochial school "was anti-American because it seemed to reject America's invitation to the Jew to integrate into American life and because it would impede the molding of ethnically and religiously heterogeneous masses into a homogeneous nation" (Fuchs, 1978).

JEWISH COMMUNITY DAY SCHOOLS[2]

Between the years 1940 and 1964, the number of Jewish day schools in the country increased from 35 to 306 in what Alvin I. Schiff calls the "Era of

---

[1]Sections of this chapter are excerpted with permission of the authors from Bruce S. Cooper and Marc N. Kramer, "The New Jewish Community: New Jewish Schools," *Catholic Education* (Spring, 2002); Bruce S. Cooper and Marc N. Kramer, "Jewish Schools Grow and Change," *Private School Monitor, 23,* (Spring, 2002); and Marc N. Kramer, *The Pathways for Preparation: A Study of Heads of Jewish Community Day School Affiliated with the Jewish Community Day School Network 1998-*

1999 (New York: Teachers College-Columbia University, 1999). The complete texts, as cited in the Bibliography, p. 73, are available for further reading.

[2]While this chapter offers its examples from the day school world, staff in *communal supplementary schools* and in *camps that span the Jewish denominations* will find clear ways to apply to their work in the final section of this chapter, "Thoughts on Working in a Community Setting."

Great Expansion" (Schiff, 1966). A new wave of Jewish immigrants from Eastern Europe, either fleeing the war or emerging from its ashes, "provided the impetus and clientele" (Edelman, 1982) for these new schools. In the period of time immediately following The Six Day War, American Judaism underwent a cultural and religious renaissance (Silberman, 1985). Inspired by the unlikely combination of Israel's miraculous military victories (Sachar, 1990) and the emergent Black Power movement, non-Orthodox Jews in the U.S. begin actively to reclaim their Jewishness, if not through religion, through a devotion to Jewish culture, modern Hebrew, and the arts. Jewish day schools grew in number and size to accommodate the increased number of Jews who sought for their children a kind of Jewish identity that their parents sought to subsume (Schiff, 1966).

Besides the growth and dynamics of the total Jewish day school effort, and the exponential growth of day schools of all types, a new type of school has quietly emerged that is substantively different from the traditional Jewish day school. Since the 1960s, the U.S. has witnessed a geographic dispersion of Jews (numbered at 6,061,000 in 1998) from the great metropolitan centers such as New York City, Chicago, Boston, Philadelphia, and Los Angeles, to smaller communities and ex-urban locations — from the older cities to the newer ones. Although nearly three-quarters of all Jewish day schools in the United States are currently under Orthodox auspices, only 13.8% of the American Jewish population self-identifies as Orthodox (Council of Jewish Federations, 1991). Similarly, approximately 2,100,000 Jews, representing nearly one-third of the American Jewish community, live in Jewish communities of 10,000 or fewer Jews and/or in communities that presently support only one Jewish day school. Paralleling this great migration has been the emergence of a new synthetic type of Jewish full-time education institution, called the Jewish community day school.

The independent, non-denominational Jewish community day school represents both:

- a return to a traditional mode of schooling, one in which the community establishes and supports a full-day school for all of its children with both Judaic and secular subjects taught, and,

- a movement toward a new type of Jewish school, one which is post-denominational, co-educational, egalitarian, and pluralistic.

Today, there are over 80 Jewish day schools in the United States that fall under the rubric of non-denominational Jewish community day schools (RAVSAK Databank, 2002). These schools are located in 23 states plus the District of Columbia, and are responsible for the primary, middle school, and in some cases high school education, for over 15,000 students (RAVSAK Membership Directory, 2000).

> I like being a role model of a progressive Jew for the community day school students whom I teach. I help students see that being a "religious" Jew is not solely an option for those who practice traditional Judaism, nor is it only about prayer services. Whether I am teaching Judaic Studies or General Studies classes, there are opportunities to share my own religious journey and how it affects the choices that I make daily, from reusing scrap paper to greeting each student by name.
>
> Truthfully, I had never even considered teaching in anything but a public school. I felt a strong civic and even moral duty to provide the best education that I could muster to urban, public school children. I found myself interviewing at a day school after a cross-country move to a city with a teacher surplus. What I discovered was that I had special skills to bring to the children of the Jewish community and an important mission to broaden a Judaic studies curriculum beyond the traditional "Jews should _____ and you must _____" to "Some Jews _____, because _____, while some Jews _____."
>
> *(Diane Schon Wirtschafter, Berkeley, California)*

Characteristics of Jewish Community Schools

Jewish community schools have the following characteristics that parallel changes in the American Jewish community:

- *Pluralistic* - These schools are not identified with one of the branches of Judaism (Orthodox, Conservative, or Reform), but attempt to serve Jewish children from all three groups, as well as those whose families do not subscribe to a particular view of Jewish practice. Often, these smaller towns and communities (between 2,500 and 12,000 Jews) have insufficient supporters of one movement to have a Reform, Conservative, or Orthodox school alone. Instead, in the new era, Jews of different persuasions pool their resources (and children) to create and sustain a local community day school (usually elementary). In some larger communities, Jewish community schools offer another educational alternative (e.g., the Cleveland Hebrew Schools, which complement its synagogue skills curriculum with a strong Hebrew language program) or allows a combining of synagogue resources (e.g., the Minneapolis Talmud Torah, with the majority population students from the area Conservative congregations, all of whom do not have their own in-house Hebrew school).

- *Inclusive* - Jewish community schools tend to operate under an assumption of "maximal inclusion," suggesting that all Jewish children and their families, regardless of their level of practice or commitment to Judaism, are welcomed members of the school community. This maximal inclusion is often extended to children from multicultural and multi-religious homes, children who are likely to be outside of the purview of Orthodox and Conservative schools, which require that either both parents be Jews by birth or conversion, or that, minimally, the mother be a Jew by birth or conversion.

- *Egalitarian* - Jewish community schools provide coeducational settings in which boys and girls access identical programs of study. This varies greatly from most Orthodox day schools in which some (and in many cases, all) classes are segregated by gender and where boys and girls may have divergent religious curricula. The egalitarianism of the Jewish community school is also reflected in the teaching staff, administration, and lay leadership of the school.

- *Independent* - Unlike the majority of Jewish schools in the U.S. that are affiliated with a specific denominational movement of Judaism, the community school is independent of denominational affiliation and self-identifies as "non-denominational," "pan-denominational," or "pluralistic."

- *Self-Determinant* - Jewish community schools, unlike movement-affiliated schools, determine their own policies, curricula, and governance structures. In many cases, those that are day schools turn to the local boards of education for state determined standards in secular education, although the Judaic program of studies remains the sole purview of the individual school.

- *School in lieu of synagogue affiliation* - As part of the movement toward inter-denominationalism, community day schools are independent of a particular branch of Judaism and the local synagogue. In fact, many families may enroll their children in the community Jewish day school without being active in a temple or synagogue, if members at all. This affiliation with the school may in part take the place of synagogue membership and activities; families utilize the school as a religious and cultural center, rather than joining a synagogue. Parents may, in fact, be trying to connect themselves and their families with Judaism by enrolling their children in a day school. In this way, they acknowledge that their children may soon know more about the religion, about Hebrew as both a modern conversational language and a language of prayer, and about Jewish identity than their parents. In a sense, then, the community Jewish day school throws a Jewish lifeline to Jews who had strayed from affiliation, identification, and participation in Jewish worship and life. Whereas this phenomenon is also true of the denominational schools, Jewish community day schools reach out to, and into, the largest segments of the American Jewish community: the intermarried and the unaffiliated.

- *Identified with RAVSAK* - The overwhelming majority of Jewish community day schools in North America align themselves with an organization called RAVSAK: The Jewish Community Day School Network. RAVSAK serves as a link between the growing number of non-denominational schools, providing resources, professional development, guidance, and support without proscribing policy or curriculum. Of the estimated 80 or more Jewish community day schools in North America, currently 68 schools in 27 states are associated with RAVSAK.

- *Geographically dispersed* - 160 communities in the 50 states and the District of Columbia had 2,000 or more Jews; among those cities or communities, those with around 4,000 Jews or more were likely to have a day school. Thus, a major demographic change in the U.S. is the dispersion of the Jewish community, and the spread of day schools as a consequence.

The Benefits of Jewish Community Schools

Jewish community schools are important for several reasons. First, these schools show a rising concern among contemporary American Jews to give their children a Jewish education, even if the family is not traditionally observant at home. Second, those that are day schools are scattered in virtually every community with 4,000 or more Jews, meaning that Jewish cultural and communal life is shifting — as is the population — from north and east to south and west. Third, community schools indicate a new inter-denominationalism, a willingness of Jews from various religious positions to band together around a school for the benefit of their children. Although it may be desirable to have denominationally organized schools, such an insistence could undermine the ability of smaller communities to provide the resources needed to operate a full-time school. Fourth, community schools have for an increased number of Jews replaced the synagogue as the center of Jewish life. For the majority of American Jews, who do not affiliate with a synagogue, the community school might represent entrée into the organized Jewish community.

Finally, and more interestingly perhaps, the Jewish community school is more tolerant of the internal pluralism and multiculturalism of the Jewish community, as evidenced by a general willingness to accept children who may not have, by traditional convention, been considered "Jewish." It is this striving for maximal inclusion that has helped foster so much new growth in this sector of day school education, for it not only opens the doors to otherwise excluded children, but it simultaneously opens doors to excluded families and the support they bring.

Because these schools are both independent and not affiliated with any particular denominational movement of Judaism, they function in nearly autonomous realms. In some regards, Jewish community schools are more like Jewish Federations or JCCs than they are the typical school; serving the entire Jewish community is at the heart of their mission. In the absence of a centralized denominational or Rabbinic authority, seminary, or school of education, they must find guidance and inspiration on the local level. Likewise, the schools and the local communities themselves must serve as the source of curriculum and *hashkafah* (viewpoint).

This autonomy is both a blessing and a curse for teachers. Although the implications for teaching in a Jewish community school vary from community to community, the hard work of teaching is made harder, especially for a novice teacher, when the school is driven by a vision of Jewish pluralism. Teachers need to understand fully what it means to work in their particular Jewish community school and to transmit the school's vision of Jewish life into the classroom and curriculum. This means that teachers need to decentralize their own denominational holdings and to articulate a learning environment in which no one view of Judaism is promoted — especially at the expense or degradation of another. Their classrooms must reflect the community's view of what is means to live a meaningful, knowledgeable Jewish life.

Given that teachers working in Jewish community schools must operate within the same paradigm as the schools themselves, how do they prepare and sustain themselves in these wonderful but challenging schools? I would be foolish to attempt a single, universally true response, but instead, I share with you a few thoughts.

THOUGHTS ON WORKING IN A COMMUNITY SETTING

Everyone in the School Has Something to Teach

Who is wise? One who learns from everyone. (Ben Zoma in *Avot* 4:1) Professional development is not something that happens once or twice a year at a conference or a retreat; it happens every day. Studies on how educators learn to become better teachers all indicate that most learning happens on the job. This may be true to an even greater extent in a community school, in which the vision, curriculum, and *hashkafah* vary from community to community. The version of *"Birkat HaMazon"* (blessing after the meal) that you say at home may well be different from that used in the school. Try to think of yourself not only as a community school teacher, but also as a community school learner, one who is constantly absorbing the culture from peers and students in addition to what you learn from books and formal workshops. It is essential to think carefully about what you can learn from whom. The principal can help guide your teaching, instill the school's vision, and help blend your work with that of your peers. More senior teachers can help you understand not only how to become a more skilled classroom manager, but can also share with you insights on particular units, students, families, co-workers, and even how best to work with your head of school. Of course, you will learn most from your students.

> Teaching in the community day school means that I have students who are involved in Chabad House, children from non-affiliated families, and new students from Israel with very little English all mixed into one classroom. The differing worldviews of these children enrich our school. The variety of questions that come from them is fascinating. I am convinced that if they were more homogenous, school would not be half as interesting a place in which to work and learn.
>
> (Maura Pollak, Tulsa, Oklahoma)

Find a Mentor[3]

More experienced teachers bring history, relations, and a sense of how to teach to the vision of the school. Without question, they know more about the school, curriculum, students, family, community, and principal than anyone else, and if they are, in fact, committed both to the school and the profession of teaching, they will *want* to help you know what they know and teach how they teach. Ask permission to observe them in the classroom, and make note of the "art" and "science" they bring to teaching. Listen for how they attend to issues of pluralism and how they model for students respectful Jewish discourse. Ask them for ideas to make your lessons more rich and complex. Ask them to observe you in the classroom and to give you feedback on ways to improve your work.

[3]For more about mentoring and being mentored, see Chapter 53, "Partnering with a Mentor" by Judy Aronson, pp.

As we learn in *Pirke Avot:* Get yourself a teacher, acquire for yourself a friend (Joshua ben Perachya in *Avot* 1:6).

If you are a new member of a community school faculty, you may want to ask a more seasoned teacher to walk you through the past year's calendar, recounting how the school attended to holidays, life cycle events, and community-wide celebrations. Remember, a more seasoned teacher can observe you and provide you with useful guidance in ways that your supervisor cannot — that is, without the added pressure of knowing that you are being evaluated.

Develop Your Own Style

According to legend, Rabbi Zusya of Hanipoli said to his disciples as he was dying: "In the world to come they will not ask me 'Why were you not like Moses?' They will ask me 'Why were you not Zusya?'" I share this anecdote with you now in conjunction with the advice that you not try to become the mentor-teacher you have found but, rather, be yourself. Develop your own style that draws on your best and allows you to challenge yourself in areas in which you are less skilled or experienced (in ways that do not negatively impact student learning). Teaching is, perhaps more than any other profession, a delicate balance of "art" and "science." This balance is not formulaic; how you achieve it is up to you entirely. More important, how you achieve this balance will evolve over time. One of the challenges of "being yourself" in the community school classroom is refraining from teaching the Judaism you personally practice, which may be substantively different from that of the school. The Jewish culture and curriculum of your school may draw heavily on the various denominations, perhaps echoing one movement more than others; likewise, it may focus on some non-theological aspect of Jewish life, such as Hebrew language. Ideally, what this "norm" is will be spelled out in the curriculum, discussed among faculty members, and actively promoted by the head of school. Given that we do not live in an ideal world, you may need to do some investigating as to what constitutes the school's Judaic vision and how best to impart this vision without feeling inauthentic with your students.

653-661 in this volume.

Make Room in Your Classroom for All Kinds of Jews

One of the greatest challenges of teaching in a Jewish community school is ensuring that your classroom and curriculum accurately reflect the school's vision of pluralism. This challenge is extended into the life of the classroom: Is there "room" for all kinds of Jews in your class? Do children from traditionally oriented homes and children from liberal or non-observant families feel equally at home in your class? Are certain denominational practices prized, while others are, even inadvertently, deemed "second rate"? When learning Torah, are you teaching text or denominational interpretation? In a Reform/Conservative/Orthodox day school, many of these questions would be nullified by the school's guiding, denomination principles. In such cases, families understand that regardless of personal practice, the school is teaching a particularistic way of being Jewish. But in a community school, there may be no one way for doing or believing, so what is a teacher to do?

First, in keeping Elazar ben Shamua's advice, "Let your student's honor be as dear to you as your own" (*Pirke Avot* 4:15), try to find ways to acknowledge and dignify each child's family experience. Note that I did not say "validate" each experience, nor did I suggest claiming each student's way as your own. Both would be inauthentic and, ultimately, disrespectful. Instead, consider this example: When learning the *mitzvot* associated with Purim, ask each student to explore at home what his or her parents did as children on Purim and which of these practices they continue to this day. Children who come from families deeply concerned with these *mitzvot* thus get the same acknowledgement as those for whom the customs are not followed at home, with all judgment withheld. As you come to know the children and families you serve, this becomes easier to do.

Next, when learning text, be sure to distinguish the *p'shat* from the *drash*. Let students know when they are studying the written text and when they are exploring *midrash*. Use language that distinguishes the letter of the law from how it might be interpreted or applied. For example, consider the difference between "The *halachah* is clear that all Jews must keep kosher" and "*Halachah* prohibits the mixing of meat and milk. What are some ways that this can be understood?" The second statement, in addition to being more specific, avoids embarrassment or judgment and allows for students to share both their knowledge of Jewish practice and how this practice is actualized in their homes. Keep in mind that when using inclusive, nonjudgmental language, you are also modeling tolerance and respect for your students.

Assume That Your Students Are Brilliant

A common misperception is that Jewish community schools promote a "middle of the road" approach to Jewish life, one which is palatable, if unappealing, to Jews of every stripe. Now that you teach in a community school, you will not make this error yourself. However, there is a temptation to carry the same sort of misperception into the classroom and to teach to the "middle" of the class, granting Judaic enrichment to the students from traditionally observant families and forgiving detail in the learning of students from liberal homes. This is a tremendous disservice to all of your students and could even create an unspoken (and unspeakable) classroom hierarchy of expectations. Teach instead to the highest common denominator. Give all students access to the same richness and complexity at all times, keeping in mind that your job is to teach the child and not the curriculum. "Educate a child each according to his way" (*Mishlei* 22:6).

Improve Your Hebrew

There is an old proverb that claims that learning Torah in translation is akin to kissing through a handkerchief: The action takes place, but the essence is totally lost. Jewish community schools need teachers who speak Hebrew, and by "speak Hebrew," I mean speak, read, write, and understand Hebrew to the advanced degree that would allow you to conduct your classes in Hebrew with little to no translation, should you be asked to do so. Outstanding Hebrew is a requisite skill for teaching *tefilah*, Torah, Rabbinical texts, and, of course, *lashon* (language). Without excellent Hebrew conversation and grammar skills of your own, you hinder your capacity to make excellent consumers of Hebrew and traditional text out of your students.

Be Present in the Community

In many Jewish community schools, especially in

smaller communities, tremendous emphasis is put on the *community* of the school and how the school fits into the larger Jewish community of which it is an essential part. If you are fortunate enough to teach in such a school, you may be called upon to be present at community events including B'nai Mitzvah, synagogue programs, and the like. The "plus" is that you will quickly discover just how important your presence is at these events — as a member of the community, as a *dugmah ishit* (personal role model) for your students, and as a teacher/leader. As the old saying goes, "Your presence is a present," a gift to your students and their families. The "negative" is that you will quickly discover how challenging it is to be at all of these events, especially those held in venues in which you may not be fully comfortable, such as a synagogue of a denomination different from your own. To the degree that you are able respectfully to be a part of community events, you should be. That said, you should let your head of school know your limitations so that he/she can advocate on your behalf if and when it is necessary.

Ask for Help When You Need It

Given that so many additional challenges are presented to you as a teacher in a community school, the work place learning curve can be steep and time-consuming. Much of what you may need and want to know may exist in between the lines of the written curriculum. Many of your personal practices, melodies, ritual behaviors and textural understandings may differ from those in your school. How are you supposed to know all of this? What can you do to keep yourself from burning out before you even get your fire started? Take the very advice that you would give your students: Ask for help when you need it. You, as a teacher, know the

reward of being the source of another's guidance, so allow your peers this joy with you. Remember the words of Hillel: "An ignorant person cannot be pious; the timid cannot teach" (*Pirke Avot* 2:6).

CONCLUSION

There is no setting within the Jewish community that does not require top-notch, thoughtful, reflective Jewish communal professionals. Each and everyone of these settings — camps, schools, synagogues, JCCs, Federations, family service organizations — is demanding and essential to the ongoing success of North American Jewry. Those of us fortunate enough to work in places that forego denominational boundaries face particular challenges and reap particular rewards. Ultimately, each of us must find ways to bring our whole selves to places of work, yet operate in ways that withhold our denominational stances. If and when we are successful, we contribute to *K'lal Yisrael* in ways that surely represent the best we have to offer as professionals to the Jewish community.

A Postscript

RAVSAK is the affiliating organization of non-denominational Jewish day schools across North America. Its task is to support the community day schools and the professionals who work in them. If your school is not a member of RAVSAK, ask your head of school to join. If your school is a member of RAVSAK, make use of the hundreds of resources, ideas, contacts, networks, and more, which they provide. Let RAVSAK know what they can do to support you in your pursuit for excellence in Jewish community day school education. You can reach them by e-mail at RAVSAK@aol.com.

BIBLIOGRAPHY

Cooper, Bruce S. "Jewish Schools." In *Religious Schools in America: A Selected Bibliography.* T.C. Hunt, J.C. Carper, and C.R. Kniker, eds., pp. 185-210. New York: Garland Publishing, 1986.

> This bibliography is an excellent resource on religious education in America. It is not exclusively devoted to Jewish education.

Cooper, Bruce S., and Marc N. Kramer. "The New Jewish Community: New Jewish Schools." *Catholic Education,* Spring 2002.

> This article in *Catholic Education* can also be obtained in a monograph from RAVSAK.

————. "Jewish Schools Grow and Change," *Private School Monitor* 23, Spring 2002.

> This resource is very similar to the one immediately above.

Cowan, Neil M., and Ruth Schwartz Cowan. *Our Parents' Lives: The Americanization of Eastern European* Jews. New York: Basic Books, Inc., 1989.

> This is an excellent resource for gaining a broad understanding of the Eastern European Jewish community in the United States.

Elazar, Daniel Judah. *Community and Polity: The Organizational Dynamics of American* Jewry. Philadelphia, PA: Jewish Publication Society, 1999.

> An important, academic work on the American Jewish community.

Fuchs, Jay Levi. "The Relation of Jewish Day School Education To Student Self-Concepts and Jewish Identity." Unpublished doctoral dissertation for UCLA, 1978. (Find in any university library through the ERIC System.)

> This is an excellent piece for school leaders on the impact of education on identity; a strong case for Jewish education.

Himmelfarb, Harold. "The Impact of Religious Schooling: Comparing Different Types and Amounts of Jewish Education." *Sociology of Education 50*, April 1977, pp. 114-129.

> An academic piece on how various types of education impact overall religious understanding and behavior.

Jaffee, Bernette K. *The Evolution of Jewish Religious Education in America in the 20th Century.* Doctoral Thesis for Case Western Reserve University, 1980. Ann Arbor, MI: University Microfilms International.

> An interesting look at the history of Jewish education in America. Especially good for those with limited knowledge of the subject.

Kramer, Marc N. *The Pathways for Preparation: A Study of Heads of Jewish Community Day Schools Affiliated with the Jewish Community Day School Network 1998-1999.* Unpublished Doctoral Dissertation, Teachers College-Columbia University, 1999. (Find in any university library through the ERIC System.)

> This study explores the educational paths of day school heads and the various influences on day school leadership.

Schiff, Alvin I. "Public Education and the Jewish School." *Journal of Jewish Communal Services* 6, Summer 1985, pp. 305-311.

> Read everything by Alvin Schiff! This is an interesting reflection on the relationship between the public and private sectors in education.

————. *Contemporary Jewish Education: Issachar, American Style.* Dallas, TX: Rossel Books, 1988.

> This is a classic read and a useful text for understanding contemporary issues on Jewish education.

Silver, Allen Eli. "Cultural Transmission in a Jewish Day School: An Ethnographic Case Study." Unpublished Doctoral Dissertation, University of Oregon, 1993. (Find in any university library through the ERIC System.)

> Available on microfiche, this study evidences the influence of a day school education on the transmission of knowledge and belief.

CHAPTER 9

Connections and Journeys: A New Vocabulary for Understanding American Jewish Identity[1]

Bethamie Horowitz

Our ideas about American Jewish identity are due for an update, since some of our basic ideas and assumptions reflect an earlier era of the American Jewish experience. Previous generations of American Jews knew that their Jewishness was a given, but they were striving to become American. Consider the following old joke: Chauncey Fontleroy III, formerly Shimon Fogelberg, was determined to join the elite, restricted New York Athletic Club. It took him ten years to rid himself of a Yiddish accent, to improve his manners, and to change his clothing — in short, to create a whole persona who had gone to all the right schools and who had all the right connections. Finally, the day of the interview arrived. He met with the admissions committee, and they were very impressed with him. At the end of the interview the chairman said, "I hope you won't mind, Mr. Fontleroy, but it is our policy to ask you about your religion." "Religion?" said Chauncey, "I am of the *goyish* persuasion."

This joke seems dated because Jews have managed to move from the Lower East Side to the Upper East Side in the space of a generation, and Jews today no longer feel that their Jewishness stands as an obstacle to be shed in the service of their social and economic advancement. Jews have made it in America, where they find themselves securely in the mainstream.

America itself has changed, along with the Jewish experience in America. We can see these changes most clearly by comparing the conditions that typically led to intermarriage in the 1940s and then in the 1990s. Before 1960, Jews were cut off from the American mainstream, and the phenome-

non of a Jewish "boy" finding a *shiksa* became the stereotyped image of one way to gain access to the *real* America, a path taken by only a tiny percentage of American Jews. However, by the end of the twentieth century, the barriers that had kept Jews separate from other Americans had fallen away. It had become possible to go to the college of your choice, to live in the location or work in the profession of your choice without having doors shut in your face. And you could marry the partner of your choice. Between 1970 and 1985, nearly half of the Jews marrying chose partners who were not Jewish.

What are we to make of this dramatic rise in intermarriage between 1960 and 1990? Usually, such an increase would be seen as evidence of assimilation — the rejection or shedding or diminution of Jewishness as one became "American." However, I believe that such high rates of intermarriage do not reflect a collective rush to marry out. Rather, the rates have risen because Jews are now freely interacting with people of diverse backgrounds. For most Jews living in America today, the chances of shaking hands with somebody who is not Jewish are greater than, say, in 1930, and with this increase in the quantity and quality of the interactions between Jews and other Americans, there has been a commensurate increase in the number of Jews who happen to end up with non-Jewish spouses. The sharp rise in intermarriage between 1960 and 1990 should be viewed not so much as evidence of Jewish disaffection with or rejection of their own Jewishness as reflecting the changes in Jewish social location and acceptance in America.

[1]This chapter is adapted from a 1999 lecture sponsored by JESNA about the then preliminary findings from the "Connections and Journeys" study, commissioned and largely funded by the Jewish Continuity Commission of UJA-Federation of New York, with additional support from the Avi Chai Foundation, The Chazen Family Fund, and The Lucius Littauer Foundation. The full report about the study was published by UJA-Federation in 2000, and is the basis of a book Horowitz is writing on American Jewish identity.

We can say that in the past, people intermarried by choice, whereas today they intermarry by chance. Nowadays, *Haredim* exemplify those Jews who consciously choose to limit their social interaction by segregating themselves from the rest of America, but in contrast to Jews living in America 75 years ago, they are not *forced* to make that choice. High rates of intermarriage arise from the integration (though not necessarily the assimilation) of Jews into American society.

Another significant change for American Jews is that today being Jewish in America makes one part of a rather advantaged group, and we hardly think about how much we take our being "mainstream" American for granted. Thus I myself was shocked by the insight contained in the title of a recent book, *How Jews Became White Folk*, because in my own lifetime I had not understood that in the beginning of the twentieth century, America Jews were seen as Other, as another "race." Today most American Jews are not caught between being Jewish and being American. Rather, it is more likely that a person would adopt a Jewish name or acknowledge Jewish roots than attempt to shed them (unlike Chauncey Fontleroy/Shimon Fogelberg). Chauncey could not escape his essential Jewishness despite his ability to "pass," while today a person need not even think about his/her Jewish origins it at all. A person can be Jewish by birth or by background, but unless it is part of one's psychological identity, a person's Jewish background need not be a factor in determining a person's fate.

Earlier generations of American Jews seemed caught in a dynamic of accepting or rejecting their Jewishness in order to become American, whereas today the main distinction among American Jews is between those who find Jewishness meaningful and central in their lives and those who are indifferent about it. Indifferent Jews do not actively reject their Jewishness, rather, to be more accurate, they are simply not motivated to act Jewishly.

The world has changed, yet our collective self-understanding continues to be shaped by some unspoken, tacit assumptions about Jewish identity. These became apparent to me when I was asked by UJA-Federation of New York to describe the state of American Jewish identity and I had to rely on the then most recent studies (the 1990 National Jewish Population Survey[2] and the 1991 New York Jewish Population Study[3]). Since the 1960s, socio-demographic studies of the Jewish population have formed the basis for collective stocktaking. These studies have very little to say about how people view themselves as Jews, but have a lot to say about what American Jews do. Typically, having determined that a person actually has some Jewish connection (on the basis of a person's self-reported religion, his/her parents' religion, his/her upbringing), these studies have queried respondents extensively about their particularly Jewish actions: Do you light candles on Shabbat? Do you donate money to Jewish charity? Do you fast on Yom Kippur? Do you belong to any Jewish organizations? This battery of questions — I call it *the mitzvah list* — is skewed toward conventional Jewish behaviors and practices. Yet after 30 or 40 years of this line of questioning, I wonder, is the *mitzvah* list good enough? Do we have an analytic vocabulary up to the task of providing an insightful description of contemporary American Jewish identity?

I posed this challenge in 1995 when I began formulating my research entitled "Connections and Journeys." The purpose of this study was to explore the place and meaning of being Jewish in the lives of younger, American-born Jews. Now, on the basis of this research, I propose that we revisit our underlying assumptions about Jewish identity. From the Connections and Journeys study it is apparent that there is a range of attachment to Jewish experience and meaning among American Jews that may elude the typical categories for describing American Jews.

Analytically, looking at Jewish behavior alone has been a workable strategy in differentiating the extremes: the *Jewish* Jews who practice a lot, as well as Jews who do nothing Jewish at all. For instance, a person who fasts on Ta'anit Esther, the Fast of Esther, probably performs a whole host of other practices and is pretty deeply involved in Jewish life. On the other hand, a person who doesn't fast at all, not even on Yom Kippur, may also be very involved. But what about the people who are somewhat observant — they do some stuff but not other stuff? How well do we understand them by examining only their behavior? This approach (i.e., tracking outwardly observable behavioral practice

---

[2]B. Kosmin, et al, *Highlights of the 1990 National Jewish Population Survey* (New York: The Council of Jewish Federations, 1991).

[3]Bethamie Horowitz, *The 1991 New York Jewish Population Study* (New York: UJA-Federation of Jewish Philanthropies of New York, Inc).

without tracking internal attachment to Jewishness) is easier and perhaps more clear-cut, but it can lead us to underestimate the persistence of Jewish identity. For instance, this conventional way of tracking Jewishness leads us to miss out on those people who practice very little outwardly, yet whose sense of Jewish identity is strong, as well as those people who conform outwardly, yet may not feel strongly identified or committed.

Even the best classes of students present challenges *and* frustrations. My favorite recollection comes from a Sunday morning when I felt that everything we had done was met with a barrage of negativity, especially from Becky, a bright girl, but one who was always complaining and often finding ways to "get out of the classroom."

At one point, I asked the class as a group whether they wanted to come to religious school. They said "NO!" I then asked them if, when they grew up and had children, they would have their own children come to religious school. They answered, almost as unanimously and almost as loudly, "Yes, of course!" We then proceeded to have a fascinating interchange on the issue of Jewish continuity.

I remember Becky talking about how she realized that even though she personally didn't enjoy being in school, she knew it was the only way she could really feel Jewish. It amazed me then — and still does to this day — how much the students were aware of the meaning of the concept of Jewish continuity. Yet, their hormones rage and they fight us all the way!

(Michael Fixler, Syracuse, New York)

The focus on conventional actions provides only a partial view of a person's sense of Jewishness. For instance, consider the case of Sharon: a woman in her mid-40s, raised Orthodox, who described her experience for much of her life as keeping the practices of her upbringing as if by rote. Lately she has been reevaluating what she does and why. Meaningfulness has become a criterion for her, which for her stands in contrast to doing things by rote or mindlessly. She sees herself now as making choices. For instance, she used to keep kosher until she was in a car accident and was hospitalized. Many friends came to visit, bringing food, but not kosher food. She had a moment of realizing that she had been keeping kosher just by rote, and she decided that it no longer made sense to her, because it prevented her from accepting the food and more importantly the company of her friends. At around the same time, she has joined a synagogue for the first time in her adult life. This pattern of practice — no longer keeping kosher, but joining a synagogue — looks like inconsistent behavior — one represents a decrease in Jewish practice, the other represents an increase. But from the point of view of the *meaning dimension,* Sharon's choices are very coherent. She sees herself as figuring out a Jewishness that works for her, that fits into her life.

Sharon's case argues for adding a new dimension to our understanding: In addition to tracking her Jewish *practice,* we need to look at *the internal, subjective aspect of what being Jewish means to her.* Here we are asking how meaningful or important is being Jewish in a person's life: Is it something psychologically central and meaningful, a motivating force in a person's life? Or, is it simply a fact of background?

By conceptualizing Jewishness as being expressed in two dimensions it is possible to explore the relationship between one's internal subjective connection to Jewishness and the external, outwardly observable actions that may or may not go along with that commitment. So in addition to collecting data on people's Jewish behaviors, we must gain greater insight into their internal Jewish commitments and attachments. We must come to understand the meaning of being Jewish to each individual.

Some people reveal their Jewish commitments in surprising ways. For example, I interviewed a female lieutenant in the New York City Police Department. I asked her about her Jewish practices, and she described her minimal religious involvement. Yet, she vividly described how her commander asked her, the one woman in her precinct house, to decorate the Christmas tree, even though he knew she was Jewish. She delighted in recounting their surprise the next day when they came to work and discovered that she had decked the tree with blue and white cookies shaped as menorahs and stars of David! Decorating the tree in this manner was her unconventional and combative way of asserting her own Jewish identity in that context.

With these examples in mind, in Connections

and Journeys, I decided to create the map of people's Jewishness, using two dimensions. Along the vertical axis, the person's Jewish attachment can range from low to high, while the behavioral aspects of low and high activity are plotted along the horizontal axis (see figure 1 below). Logically, people can be located in one of the four quadrants. The upper-right quadrant contains people who experience both high commitment and intense feeling and are highly active. The lower-right quadrant contains the people who feel little attachment and do little. In other words, these two quadrants contain the types of Jews we most often imagine — highly affiliated, active Jews on the one hand, and those who are highly assimilated on the other. The current analysis presents the possibility that there are people in other quadrants who feel deep connection to being Jewish and do very little (high disposition/low activity) or, in contrast, people who are outwardly conforming to Jewish practice, but without strong commitment. For instance, someone who marries into a community that is more observant than they were in the past may demonstrate high activity and low disposition. It is important to keep the distinction between the dimensions in mind in order to avoid the tendency to confuse people's subjective states with their outwardly apparent actions. This tendency is problematic for those creating Jewish programs and policies because the people who do the least are most likely to be written off. Yet, this group is likely to include many who feel positive toward their Jewishness and may therefore be open to various initiatives or programs, and eventually, to doing more things.

In addition to the centrality or importance of being Jewish in a person's life, I also examined the "content" of Jewish identity. In contrast to the older model of research, which was rather normative, in the Connections and Journeys study, I adopted a *self-anchored* approach to defining the

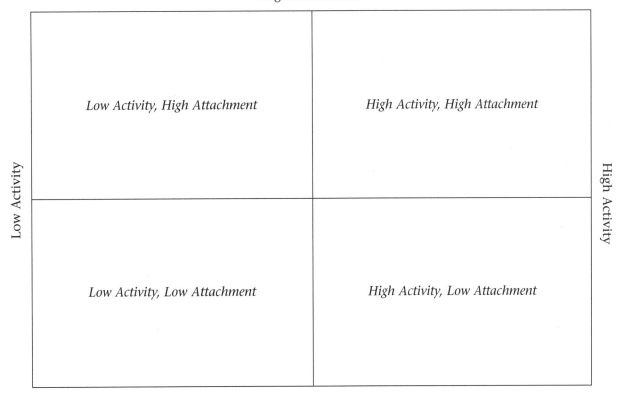

Figure 1[4]

[4]Taken from B. Horowitz, *Connections and Journeys: Assessing Critical Opportunities for Enhancing Jewish Identity* (New York: UJA-Federation of New York, 2000).

content of Jewishness. Rather than defining Jewishness according to the prescriptive norms set out by policy makers, communal leaders, Rabbis, or educators, we asked respondents to speak about themselves and to describe their Jewishness in their own terms. Rather than asking them to measure themselves against the image of "what is a good Jew?" the emphasis in this new study was, "for you, personally, what does being Jewish involve?"

The Connections and Journeys study revealed a sector of the American Jewish community with "mixed" Jewish engagement. For these people, Jewishness is not a set piece, but includes whatever ingredients they find particularly meaningful in describing the components of their Jewish identity. These may range from *halachah*, Holocaust, and *challah* to a person's Uncle Harry, spirituality, Seinfeld, and even being afraid of dogs! Imagine a salad bar containing the full array of things that people might associate with being Jewish — conventional and shared ideas, as well as novel or idiosyncratic, happy or difficult. When we think about describing a person's own sense of Jewishness, we must remember that every plate has a different set of ingredients, representing different images of what being Jewish means.

The fact that today's Jewish identity is characterized by such tremendous diversity makes research difficult. On the one hand, just because Jewish identity is not always consistent does not mean that it is not personally meaningful. On the other hand, the uniqueness of every individual is more difficult to track than the conventional person who defines Judaism according to "normative" rituals. Therefore, it is easy for researchers to lose sight of what is happening in the "non-normative" part of the Jewish community.

There are many people who discover inventive ways to act Jewishly. Daniel, a musician in his mid-40s, was raised in a minimally practicing Jewish home in Manhattan. He described his minimal religious practice — lighting Chanukah candles and perhaps a *Seder* at Passover. A very successful graduate of a top conservatory, Daniel described himself as particularly drawn to jazz. But because he was not African-American, he felt like an interloper in that world, "a fish out of water." Daniel was always drawn to the playful and improvisational nature of jazz, but when he encountered klezmer music, by accident, he said, "It felt like it was [his] and [his] grandmother's music." For him, klezmer music

became an authentic means for him to express his Jewish identity, and his klezmer gigs brought him into Jewish settings. With more contact with Jews, his Jewish involvement evolved. For years, he has not fasted on Yom Kippur, but explained that of late he had begun to feel guilty about teaching students on that day. To my mind this feeling is noteworthy because it marks a change in Daniel's feelings about his Jewishness, but this change in emotional openness had been beyond the reach of our existing means of detecting Jewish identity.

Daniel utilized his past experiences and the raw materials he inherited to formulate new meaning that would work for him in the present and future. At the time of the interview, he had begun to reevaluate and to think differently about his family experiences while growing up. He talked about childhood visits to his Uncle Louis in Brooklyn:

> When I was a little kid, we did *Seders* at a very religious uncle of my mother's, a great uncle of mine, and it was practically all in Hebrew. The *Seder* was very strict, and I think I relate more to that kind of expression of Jewishness than the synagogues on Long Island, which I considered physically ugly and spiritually bare. There was something about my great uncle doing the *Seder* in a very tense way that I connected to a lot . . . It was very authentic; he would go off on *"Chad Gadya."* He would chant the *"Dayenu,"* more than sing it. I think that was a good thing for me to see. His house was out in Brooklyn, in Grand Army Plaza, so I always felt that was where the Jews lived. Since I grew up in Manhattan, visiting Grand Army Plaza seemed like visiting a new world.

Daniel expressed that Brooklyn seemed like a "new world" to him. In his forties, Daniel related the childhood image of his Uncle Louis to the music and chanting of Judaism. As a musician, Daniel could retrieve the memory of his uncle and incorporate it in his own life through his music. So in addition to the unique constellation of elements that comprise Daniel's sense of Jewish connection — klezmer music, his Uncle Louis, among other things — it is noteworthy that Daniel's experience of his Jewishness is not static.

We do not know when or if a person's Jewish background will start to become meaningful. But it is certainly the case that for many people Jewishness is a fluid, dynamic and evolving experience. The Connections and Journeys research demonstrated the diverse ways of being Jewish; there are so many different influences and ways of being Jewish that have psychological power for people. Moreover, the research also found that Jewishness changes over time. In the past, we have taken snapshots only every ten years, at best (by conducting a National Jewish Population survey every ten years). In relying on these snapshots, we have assumed that everything remains constant. In fact, when we talked to people about their lives over time we discovered that the process is much more fluid. Identity is not a static concept; it is an interactive process.

CONCLUSION

To summarize, in what ways should our ideas about American Jewish identity be updated? First, we have learned that people's ways of identifying Jewishly are more complex than we have thought — including images, beliefs, feelings, associations, not just actions. If we limit ourselves to the conventional measures we miss a significant group of people — those for whom being Jewish is important even if they do not express their Jewishness at least through lighting candles or studying Jewish things or in other recognizably Jewish actions. We do not know what it would take to exploit this fact in order to get these people more involved, but they are typically missed in socio-demographic studies.

Second, we see that people's sense of Jewish connection emerges out of their own experiences and autobiographies. Their sense of attachment to, ambivalence about, or rejection of Jewishness comes from the experiences they have had, some more significant than others.

Third, we have learned that Jewish identification is much more fluid than we had thought. Although we may take a snapshot of where people are at a point in time, we now know that Jewish identity is dynamic and Jewishness changes in relation to other aspects in individuals' lives.

Thus, Jewish identity is complicated, diverse, and dynamic. The conventional approach used to study American Jewry has potentially skewed or predetermined the answers we have been finding. If we ask only certain kinds of questions we get only certain kinds of answers. But if we start exploring Jewish identity with a different set of questions and an openness to different ways of seeing, then we begin to develop a more complex, more nuanced way of understanding what's going on with American Jews today.

We are not talking about a cookie cutter situation here; we cannot simply manufacture Jewish identity and transmit it. It is not a thing that can be separated from the people who experience it. The fact that people are inventive nowadays raises questions about how transmittable Jewishness will be in the future. There are people who are internally committed who may move to being more outwardly committed regardless of conventional standards. Our research teaches that we cannot judge people by where they are today, and we should not write them off, because who knows where their journeys will take them.

FOR FURTHER READING

Cohen, S.M., and A. Eisen. *The Jew Within: Self, Family and Community in America.* Bloomington, IN: Indiana University Press, 2000.

Horowitz, Bethamie. "Connections and Journeys: Shifting Identities among American Jews." *Contemporary Jewry*, 1998, p. 19.

———. "Reframing the Study of Contemporary American Jewish Identity." *Contemporary Jewry*, 2002, p. 23.

CHAPTER 10

Ethics and the Jewish Teacher

Zena Sulkes

In classrooms throughout the world, Jewish students study traditional texts focusing on our obligation to complete creation and to "repair the world" (*tikkun olam*). They read of our biblical ancestors, learn of the prophets, and discuss *Pirke Avot* (Ethics of our Sages), all marked by ethical issues and exhortations. But note that the focus is on students, and *their* obligations to "do justly, love mercy, and walk humbly with Your God" (Micah 6:8). Yet, what is a Jewish *teacher's* ethical obligations to his/her students, school, community, and the Jewish community at large? This chapter concentrates on the nexus of Jewish educators and Jewish ethics, with special focus on the values of *tzedekah*, *K'lal Yisrael*, personal and business ethics, reaching out to the disabled, and *lashon hara*. All these are Jewish values that a Jewish classroom leader should exemplify. As you read on, think about how many of these values you exemplify.

TZEDEKAH: GIVING MONEY TO THE POOR

Naomi considers herself to be a great teacher and a good role model for her students. Every week, she puts a tzedekah box in front of her religious school class and reminds her students of the importance of giving their own money. She then records on a chart the children who contribute each week.

One day, after Jessica puts money in the tzedekah box, she raises her hand and asks, "Why do you tell us how important it is to give as much as we can, but I never see you put any money in the container?"

Before Reading Further - What do you imagine could be Naomi's response to Jessica? (Brainstorm 3-5 different answers, depending on whether you imagine Naomi to be a generous donator to various causes, or not.)

Texts to Think About

- There are eight degrees of *tzedakah*, each one superior to the other. The highest degree . . . is one who upholds the hand of a Jew reduced to poverty by handing a gift or a loan, or entering into a partnership, or finding work, in order to strengthen his hand, so that he will have no need to beg from other people. (Maimonides, *Mishneh Torah* 7:7, "Laws Concerning Gifts To the Poor")

- If, however, there is a needy person among you, one of your kinsmen in any of your settlements in the land that *Adonai* your God is giving you, do not harden your heart and shut your hand against your needy kinsman. Rather, you must open your hand and lend him sufficient for whatever he needs. (Deuteronomy 15:7-8)

- The world is like a revolving wheel: one who is rich today may be poor tomorrow. Let a person therefore give charity before the wheel has turned. (Rabbi Israel al-Nakawa, fourteenth-century Spain, *Menorat Hammaor* — Lamp of Illumination)

Questions to Consider - How do you, as a Jewish educator, give *tzedekah*? Do you give a portion of your earnings to the needy? Do you contribute to a synagogue, your local Federation, worthy community causes? Do your students see you drop coins in the *tzedekah* box? Children frequently respond to the manner in which a teacher models appropriate behavior. Modeling is frequently unintentional. To teach a child a new way of behaving, we must allow him/her to observe an important person performing the desired behavior. What is your ethical obligation to give? How might the teacher, Naomi, have responded in a way that shows her understanding of *tzedakah*, and her role as a model for her students?

One of the ways Jews pursue righteousness is through *tzedekah* (a word derived from the Hebrew, *tzedek*, meaning "justice" or "what is right"). In the Torah the word literally means *righteousness*, but in later years it took on the meaning of "the money we give to help others." According to the Talmud, those who give *tzedekah* get more out of it than those who receive it because the donors are given the opportunity to perform a *mitzvah*.

K'LAL YISRAEL: CONNECTION TO JEWS

Mrs. Levy's seventh grade day school class was deep into a unit on comparative religion. The course was important because this was a community day school, one that welcomed students from all of the Jewish movements. Mrs. Levy's focus was on having her students understand that Jews affiliating with different branches of Judaism were more alike than they were different. When Jon raised his hand and defined Reform Judaism as being the least strict, the easiest of all ways to be Jewish, Mrs. Levy told the class that when she was young, her grandfather told her Reform Jews didn't know anything about being Jewish.

Before Reading Further - What message does Mrs. Levy give to her students in her response to Jon? How does her story negate the message of community that her day school wishes to engender? How else might she have answered in a way that sets her as a more positive role model?

Texts to Think About

- Hillel said: What is hateful to you, do not do to your neighbor. This is the entire Torah — all the rest is commentary. Go and learn it. (*Shabbat* 31a)

- All Jews are responsible for one another. (*Shevuot*, 39a)

Questions to Consider - How do you, as a Jewish educator apply these principles in your daily life? How can you demonstrate in your classroom that what is hateful to you is not done to your neighbor? How can you make sure that your students learn to respect other Jews, no matter what their denomination or belief? In what manner can you

role model this for your students? How might Mrs. Levy have responded?

The teachings of Judaism are based on three basic rubrics: God, Torah, and Israel (the people). While each movement interprets these three principles slightly differently, this should not be as significant as our commitment to Judaism and the Jewish people. The concept of *K'lal Yisrael* teaches us that all Jews care for one another. We are supposed to behave toward others as we would want them to behave toward us; the *mitzvah* of loving one's neighbor should certainly apply to our fellow Jews.

More and more, I have come to appreciate Dr. Maurice Elias's words, "teachers are the hidden curriculum." Children learn more from what we do, than what we say. We set the tone for what is allowable in our classrooms, what is acceptable in our tradition. For many of our supplementary school students, Jewish teachers are their only connection to an adult who seriously practices Judaism. We have to live what we teach so that the *middot* (personal values) are reflected in our actions. If we want to create students who will be involved in lifelong Jewish learning, then we need to be involved in lifelong Jewish learning . . . and our students need to know that. If we don't know something, we need to admit it. I have apologized to my students for not realizing that I have hurt their feelings, for not marking tests in a timely matter, or forgetting something I promised them. My experience is that they don't then perceive me as weak, but rather respect my honesty. When I make a promise I do my best to keep it. Children remember broken promises for a long time.

(Cheryl Cash-Linietsky, Philadelphia, Pennsylvania)

BUSINESS ETHICS

Mrs. Kaplan teaches first grade in a religious school in which the educator trusts each teacher to buy consumable supplies that they need for particular class projects. Mrs. Kaplan tends to buy items she needs for her family at the same time that she buys glue, poster board, etc., for her classroom. When she must turn in the bill for reimbursement, she somehow forgets to separate her personal purchases from those for the school and turns them all in for reimbursement.

Before Reading Further - Why is what Mrs. Kaplan is doing unethical? What conversation might you have with Mrs. Kaplan about her actions?

Texts to Think About

There are several comments made by the Prophets who were concerned that in any dealings within the Jewish tradition there be a sense of fair play.

- For among my people are found wicked men:
  They lay in wait, as one sets snares:
  They set a trap, they catch men:
  As a cage is full of birds, so are their houses full of deceit:
  Therefore they've become great and rich.
  They are waxen fat, they shine — yea, they overpass the deeds of the wicked:
  They don't plead the cause, the cause of the fatherless. Yet they prosper: And the right of the needy do they not judge.
  (Jeremiah 5:26-28)

- The people of the land have used oppression and have exercised robbery and have vexed the poor and needy: yea, they have oppressed the stranger wrongfully. (Ezekiel 22:29)

- The wages of a laborer shall not remain with you until morning . . . You shall not falsify measures of length, weight, or capacity. You shall have an honest balance and honest weights. (Leviticus 19:13 and 19:35-36)

- When you sell property to your neighbor, or buy any from your neighbor, you shall not wrong one another. (Leviticus 25:14)

- You shall appoint magistrates and officials for your tribes . . . and they shall govern the people with due justice. (Deuteronomy 16:18)

- Letting spirituality and faith speak to us in our work will teach us to act on the basis of our better moral impulses and values. It will help us be more creative and socially responsible. It will also increase our enthusiasm for our work, especially when work becomes wearisome, and help us avoid burnout and stress. (Jeffrey Salkin, *Being God's Partners: How to Find the Hidden Link between Spirituality and Your Life*, p. 37)

Questions to Consider - How do these texts relate to the issue of Mrs. Kaplan's expenditures? What is the right thing for her to do? In what ways can she "let spirituality and faith speak to (her) in (her) work"? What things do you do to demonstrate that you are God's partner in the business dealings of your teaching job? What are the business ethics that inform your work? Do you take care of the administrative needs of your position? Do you take supplies or ideas from others without permission? Do you reach out to other staff and strive to meet their needs? Do you see *shalom* in your workplace? How do those in your setting work to create a moral community?

Many people may feel that considerations of business ethics have no place in our educational programs, but in truth this subject needs a forum. As employers and employees, we have an obligation to do the right thing, to choose the moral path. The concept of "doing God's work" should be an active component of each educational leader's value system and programming.

STUDENTS WITH SPECIAL NEEDS

When Mrs. Cohen arrives in August to set up her third grade day school classroom, the principal pulls her aside and informs her that a special needs child will be in the class. Mrs. Cohen's heart stops a moment, but she forces a smile as she takes the child's psychoeducational diagnosis from principal's hands. Mrs. Cohen is asked to read it and follow all the suggestions at the end of the report. When Mrs. Cohen leaves the Principal's office and goes to her classroom, she reads the report and then wonders how she might be able to get the student switched to the other third grade room.

Before Reading Further - What do you think was upsetting Mrs. Cohen? Why is her reaction part of a chapter on ethics for Jewish teachers?

Texts to Think About

- You shall not insult the deaf, or place a stumbling block before the blind. (Leviticus 19:14)

- A teacher must not become angry with students if they do not understand him/her, but must repeat his/her explanation as many times as necessary until they do understand. (Code of Jewish Law, *Yoreh Deah* 246:10)

Questions to Consider - What are our obligations as Jews for those who are not like everyone else? What are some ways a teacher can handle a special needs child in a mixed classroom in which everyone's needs are supposed to be met? What is the teachers' obligation? How can you respond in the future when your principal tells you that he/she has a special needs child for your class? What kind of help might you give your colleague Mrs. Cohen with this situation?

> I think being a Jewish teacher implies a greater responsibility. We need to be role models in every sense of the word. If our students see us in the synagogue on Shabbat, or at the grocery store or movie theater, or just walking around our neighborhood, they need to see a consistency in our actions and behavior. The values I teach through Tanach or *Tefilah* don't end when the lesson or the school day is over.
>
> *(Cheryl Birkner Mack, Cleveland, Ohio)*

Special needs advocates interpret "do not put a stumbling block before the blind" as the impetus for the American Disabilities Act: equal education for all and equal access to all buildings and programs. Yet, many of our buildings in the Jewish community are not handicap accessible! Still, what goes on in classrooms is even more important as we attempt to meet the needs of all Jewish students. More educational materials specifically designed to meet the learning styles of special needs learners are essential, and all teachers must dig deep inside themselves to find the means to become accepting of each child and his/her individual needs.

LASHON HARA: GOSSIP

Each morning, the teachers in the school gather in the teachers' lounge. Frequently, the conversation revolves around students and/or parents in a negative fashion. Today, Mrs. Greenberg says, "I hope Adam's parents make sure he had a bath and put on clean clothes. Can you imagine what that house looks like?" Mrs. Stein adds, "I don't even want to think about it! I hate to open the door to their van at carpool time because it's so dirty that stuff falls out!"

Before Reading Further - Why is this kind of conversation considered to be *lashon hara* (gossip)? In what other kinds of conversations do teachers in Jewish schools contribute to *lashon hara*?

Texts to Think About

- *Lashon hara* harms three people — the person speaking, the person listening, and the person spoken about. (*Arachin* 15b)

- My God, guard my tongue from speaking evil and my lips from speaking falsely. (The *"Amidah"*)

Questions to Consider - How do the texts respond to the situation faced by Mrs. Greenberg and Mrs. Stein? What would you tell these two teachers? Why do we as educators tend to gossip about students and/or their family? How can we stop doing so?

The Torah provides more examples of *lashon hara* (e.g., Sarah talking about Abraham's age and laughing at the thought of him fathering a child, and Joseph bringing bad reports about his brothers to their father). We must help our students to understand the differences between minor gossip and slander. As role models, educational leaders should not engage in *lashon hara*, whether in public with students nearby or in private. Jewish tradition is clear that engaging in *lashon hara* at any time or in any place is wrong.

CONCLUSION

Educational leaders, no matter what their role, should focus on helping children and adults develop good character, not just intelligence. This means modeling ethical behavior, both in public and in private. Our Jewish sources have much to say about the choices we make. This chapter has raised many issues involved in ethics for the Jewish teacher and the guidance provided by our Jewish tradition. Our students deserve strong, ethical role models, for if we do not live what we teach, our greatest lessons will not succeed.

BIBLIOGRAPHY

Artson, Bradley Shavit. *It's a Mitzvah — Step-By-Step To Jewish Living*. West Orange, NJ: Berman House, Inc., 1995.

> This book features a look at the spiritual life, an explanation of the *mitzvot* and their significance, and advice on putting them into practice.

Borowitz, Eugene B., and Frances Weinman Schwartz. *The Jewish Moral Virtues*. Philadelphia, PA: Jewish Publication Society, 1999.

> A very readable book on Jewish ethics that uses traditional texts to address modern situations.

Feinberg, Miriam P., and Rena Rotenberg. *Lively Legends — Jewish Values: An Early Childhood Teaching Guide*. Denver, CO: A.R.E. Publishing, Inc., 1993.

> Stories about Jewish values for teachers to use with young children, as well as many activities in different modalities.

Freeman, Susan. *Teaching Jewish Virtues: Sacred Sources and Arts Activities*. Denver, CO: A.R.E. Publishing, Inc., 1999.

> A wonderful teaching companion, featuring over 20 *middot* (Jewish virtues). Includes a wide variety of activities for the classroom, with special emphasis on the arts.

———. *Teaching Hot Topics: Jewish Values, Resources, and Activities*. Denver, CO: A.R.E. Publishing, Inc., 2003.

> A handbook about topics of interest to teenagers, including abortion, euthanasia, animal experimentation, consumerism, school violence, cloning, ethics of business, death penalty, the ethics of war, and sexuality. Jewish views about these issues are presented through texts, scenarios, and activities. A Student Companion is also available.

Fox, Marvin, ed. *Modern Jewish Ethics*. Columbus, OH: Ohio University Press, 1975.

> A collection of essays that addresses practical moral problems of concern to modern Jews.

Ingall, Carol K. *Transmission and Transformation: A Jewish Perspective on Moral Education*. New York: Jewish Theological Seminary of America, 1999.

> A practical guide that defines best practices in the area of character education and moral development.

Isaacs, Ronald H. *Exploring Jewish Ethics and Values*. Hoboken, NJ: KTAV Publishing House, Inc., 1991.

> This book provides Jewish teens with an opportunity to explore their own personal values in areas of ethical teaching.

Kadden, Barbara Binder, and Bruce Kadden. *Teaching Mitzvot: Concepts, Values, and Activities*. rev. ed. Denver, CO: A.R.E. Publishing, Inc., 2003.

> A practical guide to 41 *mitzvot* that includes the historical development of each, as well as great teaching ideas for a variety of age levels.

Mandel, Scott. *Wired into Teaching Jewish Virtues: An Internet Companion*. Denver, CO: A.R.E. Publishing, Inc., 2002.

> A companion book to *Teaching Jewish Virtues* by Susan Freeman, which provides online resources for each of the 22 *middot* featured in that volume. The resources can be used with any Jewish virtues curriculum.

Salkin, Jeffrey. *Being God's Partners: How to Find the Hidden Link between Spirituality and Your Work*. Woodstock, VT: Jewish Lights Publishing Co., 1994.

> An exploration of spirituality can enhance one's life and work.

Sulkes, Zena, and Al Sulkes. *Mitzvot Copy Pack™*. Denver, CO: A.R.E. Publishing, Inc., 1989.

> A collection of activity pages to be used as supplemental and enrichment materials for the teaching of *mitzvot*.

Warshofsky, Mark. *Jewish Living*. New York: UAHC Press, 2001.

> This guide for Jewish living, including *tikkun olam,* is a source book for Reform Jewish practice.

Yedwab, Paul. *Sex in the Texts*. New York: UAHC Press, 2001.

> A collection of primary texts in Hebrew and English that includes topics on ethical issues related to sex.

CHAPTER 11

Developmental Psychology

Roberta Louis Goodman

Many of the narratives in Genesis remind me of the "just so stories" of Rudyard Kipling. Kipling's fanciful collection of stories includes explanations of how things in the natural world came into being — how the leopard got its spots, how the camel got its hump, and how the rhinoceros got its skin. Some of these stories are about important events in human history, such as how the first letter was written and how the alphabet was made. The stories in Genesis give us a view of the order of the universe, a glimpse of God's plan. The tower of Babel narrative explains how it happened that the peoples of the world, who trace their lineage to common parentage, Adam and Eve, speak many languages instead of one.

The narrative of Adam, Eve, the snake, the Tree of Knowledge, and the infamous piece of fruit, is a "just so story" about human development. While clearly this episode tells us why women have great pains during childbirth and why human beings must toil the earth and work to survive, more deeply, it provides an explanation of why human beings should develop and mature. Even though *Gan Eden* has its idyllic characteristics, staying innocent or naïve is not what God had in mind for human beings. While Adam and Eve are expelled from this setting and punished for their behavior, what they did was necessary in order for human beings to grow and become God's partner in the world.

What Adam and Eve did was not unlike the behavior of elementary school aged children or adolescents. They defied the directions of an authority figure and instead took the advice of a peer. They gave in to their desires and sense of mystery. They were not convinced that taking the fruit was such a bad thing to do. They exercised free will and moral judgment, choosing to taste the forbidden fruit. They showed their humanness trying to blame someone else, not wanting to take responsibility for their actions, and attempting to hide their wrongdoing from God. By hiding, they

knew they admitted that they did something wrong and were fearful of punishment. By acting, they were testing their relationship to God. The knowledge they gained immediately after the tasting of the fruit was about their physical anatomy; they became aware of their nakedness and physiological differences as male and female. They lost their magical, mystical qualities, no longer being able to communicate directly with animals. Clearly, they were separated out from angels or other creatures in God's heavenly court; they were now earth dwellers who had to worry about food, clothing, and shelter. This type of scene gets played out over and over again today in households, schools, and even the workplace.

Gan Eden represents the loss of childhood and the movement toward adulthood physically, socially, psychologically, morally, and spiritually. This transition involves the behaviors of questioning authority, establishing a relationship to God, learning about responsibility, achieving free will, and gaining knowledge about life, including sexuality. It is a transition that often precipitates mixed emotions of sadness, joy, expectation, anticipation, possibility, and hope. Without human beings leaving *Gan Eden*, there would be no Jewish people accepting the Torah, entering into a mature covenantal relationship with God. Gan Eden is not a model of paradise to be longed for or lamented as others, including Carl Jung, the renowned psychologist, would have us think, but rather a start to a long journey of human growth and development in relationship to and partnership with God that will shape the world.

If growth and development are valued in Judaism, then what can we learn from modern developmental theorists who discuss these issues in working with our learners of all ages? Twentieth century psychology reveals a view of growth and development similar to that which the Torah teaches. For the most part, the various theories affirm the value or goodness of growth and development. These psychological theories show that people differ at various ages or stages in their lives physically, cognitively, morally, socially, and spiritually. These theories outline how people develop and provide insights on how to foster or nurture development.

This chapter presents the work of the classical developmental theorists, Piaget (cognitive), Erikson (psychosocial), Kohlberg (moral), and Fowler (faith). The chapter has four parts:

1. It addresses reasons why developmental psychology can be helpful to educators.

2. It provides a basic understanding of what a developmental theory is.

3. It describes the four theories and mentions the work of other significant developmental theories.

4. It applies the four theories to Jewish educational dilemmas or situations involving learners, curriculum, and teaching.

This chapter presents theory as it relates to the practice of Jewish education. Regardless of a person's familiarity with a particular developmental theorist mentioned above, each educator has a working idea of what human development looks like. In the workshops I do, I find that early childhood educators are often the best at describing the development of the children with whom they work. Perhaps this is because the capabilities of children at this age change so dramatically in such a short period of time. It may also be due to the fact that many early childhood programs focus on helping children grow and structure their curriculum around developmentally appropriate concepts and activities. Before you read on, take a few minutes to write a brief description of the development of a particular group of learners with whom you work. Think about your learning setting and jot down responses to these questions:

- Physical: What do they like to do? What physical needs do they have? What physical capabilities do they struggle with?

- Knowledge: What do they know? What topics, questions, or issues are of interest to them?

- Psychosocial: How do they feel about themselves? How do they interact with others?

- Moral: How do they make decisions? What life situations pose problems for them?

- Faith: How do they relate to God? What questions or struggles do they have about or with God? What questions do they have about their own lives?

Now, with your responses in mind, read on in this chapter. Consider how the comparison of similarities and differences in the development stages between you, the teacher, and your students, affects their learning.

DEVELOPMENTAL THEORIES CAN BE HELPFUL

Development implies that noticeable changes occur in a person over the life span. These changes occur in regard to intellectual abilities, physical acumen, social interactions, emotional capacity, moral decision making, relationship to God, values, and life and ultimate questions.

Developmental theories can help educators think about how their learners grow and develop cognitively, socially, morally, and spiritually when guided by the wisdom of experts. Developmental theories help identify needs, issues, ways of viewing the world, and tasks that are common among human beings. These theories help explain both similarities among people of the same stage and differences between those of the same stage. These pictures provide the broad brushstrokes, but not the individual details that make lives so interesting.

The fact that development occurs throughout the lifetime is a good argument for the value of lifelong learning. People need to confront the texts, traditions, values, and views of the Jewish people throughout their lifetime. One of my least favorite titles for an actual adult education course is: "What I Would Have Learned in Religious School If I Had Paid Attention." The point is that even if a person had paid attention as a child, that individual would have heard and learned something very different from learning the content as an adult. We hear and focus on different things as an adult, which has as much to do with our development as with the content presented.

One of the major issues in teaching learners of any age is that they are often at a developmental stage that is different from that of the teacher. We need to be careful not to impose our developmental needs and ways of being, knowing, and doing on those of our learners. The more awareness that we have of the learner's developmental stages and the similarities and differences to our own developmental stages, the better able we will be to foster the learner's growth.

Thinking about developmental issues in designing curriculum is a useful step. The concept of "spiral curriculum" fits well with this notion that people change. A spiral curriculum is designed to address similar topics or subjects in different ways at different points in one's development and education. We need to revisit concepts, our relationship to God, values, and even history throughout our lifetime. Otherwise, the adult who only learned Bible stories as a child and has not studied the text as an adult might not find the lessons learned from those Bible stories helpful, interesting, or relevant to the issues of today. We can take the same text, tradition, value, or concept, and shift its emphasis stage by stage to examine the developmental issues. For example, when looking at the text of Abraham welcoming the strangers, it might be useful for children to think about how they treat classmates whom they do not like so much. For married adults, it might be useful to apply this concept of hospitality to how we treat our in-laws or stepparents and their families.

While developmental theorists often do not explicitly suggest techniques for learning, it is possible to extrapolate approaches, strategies, and activities that are compatible with their theories. For example, Piaget emphasized the importance of experimentation and exploration for a child's growth concepts, paralleled in the educational philosophy, approaches, and theories of educators such as Dewey, and also Reggio Emilio, an early childhood program in Italy (Mooney, 2000).

Why These Four Developmental Theories?

Four developmental theories were picked for review in this book. They are Piaget's theory of Cognitive Development, Erikson's Psychosocial Development, Kohlberg's Moral Development, and Fowler's Faith Development. These theorists were picked from the wide array of theorists for several reasons:

1. All four theorists are among the most renowned. Each did groundbreaking work in his own area. Their theories have contributed to understanding a particular aspect of human development and have contributed to understanding developmental theories overall. Their work has influenced that of many others.

2. All four theorists cover the life span. Each of their theories allows the reader to see the changes that occur from stage to stage or phase to phase. They show both the beginning of life and its end. Since this book is aimed at teachers who deal with learners of all different ages, it was important to pick theorists who had something to say about the entire life span and not just a portion of it.

3. Each of their theories has important implications for Jewish educators in particular, and for religious educators in general. All have written about issues related to religious education. Beyond their own writings, they raise many important issues that a Jewish teacher should address in the philosophy and practice of Jewish education.

What Is a Developmental Theory?

Developmental theories describe people in general at different points in their lives. They emphasize the commonalities of people at a certain age, phase (period of life), or stage (step in development), and contrast these commonalities across time, people of two different ages, phases, or stages. In this way they describe how people change.

The developmental theories of the four thinkers reviewed in this chapter in detail share a number of other common characteristics.

1. Each theorist provides a developmental scheme outlining stages or phases from early ages throughout adulthood.

2. Each theorist collected empirical data to support his views, some primarily through observation and others primarily through interviews. The claims that these theorists make are based on scientific standards (even though some of their methodology is disputed).

3. Each theorist claims that his theory is universal, meaning common to people of all races, cultures, and religions.

4. Each theorist presents a structure for development, but not the specifics, the content.

There are Jews, Christians, Muslims, Buddhists, aetheists, and others who populate Fowler's Stage 4. While these people structure their faith in similar ways, the content of their faith, the actual values and stories that guide their lives are very different. The details of each person's faith and life are unique.

5. Each theorist claims that people go through the phases or stages in the same sequence. People do not skip stages or revert back to previous stages.

6. Each tries to capture and describe an aspect of human development: Piaget cognitive (knowledge or intellect) development, Erikson psychosocial development, Kohlberg moral development, and Fowler faith development. Fowler, however, in describing faith development, not only incorporates the work of the other three, but essentially outlines a theory for understanding the individual or self as a whole.

These basic characteristics are important to understanding what they are trying to accomplish.

Piaget, Kohlberg, and Fowler present stage theories that are more like one another than they are like Erikson's phase theory. These three theories share some similarities that are not characteristic of Erikson's theory: Piaget, Kohlberg, and Fowler designed stage theories.

1. Stages are not guaranteed or automatic, they are learned or acquired. Some people never reach the later stages, although most people go through all of Piaget's stages.

2. Stage and age are not the same thing, nor are they necessarily well connected. In Fowler's scheme you can have an eight-year-old Stage 2 individual and an 88-year-old Stage 2 individual.

3. Each subsequent stage is considered more adequate and integrative than the previous stage. For example, once one moves out of Piaget's sensorimotor stage, which is dominated by learning through senses and reflexes and manipulation of objects in one's environment, and into the Preoperational Stage, when one gains understanding based on one's perspections and

experiences, the new stage dominates. The previous stage disappears and diminishes as it is encompassed by the new ways of thinking, perceiving, doing, or being.

4. One stage is not better than the other. Looking at Kohlberg's theory of moral development, the world is not necessarily better off with more Stage 3 conventional moral reasoners who are guided by relationships and interpersonal expectations than with more Stage 4 conventional reasoners who have worked out a social system and rely on their conscience. Many of the stories of the Holocaust rescuers are about people who felt compelled to save people whom they knew or had some connection to rather than acting primarily out of the need to fulfill a moral law, duty, or expectation. In fact, rescuing a Jew meant violating a national law, duty, or expectation, so this orientation was problematic.

These four characteristics are typical of other stage theories.

The major problem with any developmental theory is it is assumed to be describing normal or normative behavior. As a statement of the norm, it is a statement about power. This can be problematic for the individual who is not viewed by an established system — educational, legal, religious, etc. — as not seeming to fit the norm for whatever reason. These theories describe people in the aggregate. People still need to be viewed and treated with compassion and sensitivity as individuals for all the peculiarities and differences that they bring.

THE THEORIES OF PIAGET, ERIKSON, KOHLBERG, AND FOWLER

This section contains background information on each theorist and an overview of his theory. Major critiques of each theorist are included and implications of each theorist's ideas for Jewish education are provided.

Piaget's Theory of Cognitive Development

Piaget (1896-1980) was a Swiss-born biologist who became interested in psychology and epistemology, the science of knowing. Piaget worked in the Binet laboratory in Paris named for the originator of the early intelligence quotient (IQ) examinations. He became curious as to why children of certain ages tended to make the same mistakes on the IQ tests while older children were consistently able to get the answers correct. Piaget began to inquire into children's thought processes. He wanted to understand better how children come to know what they know rather than what they know or when they know it (Mooney, 2000).

Through his experiments and observations, Piaget found that children grow in the capacity to understand relationships between objects (Riemer, 1983). At different points in their lives, children develop systems or approaches that have an internal logic to them. At a particular stage in life, their answers to problems and how they come to understand the world is consistent, even though from the perspective of an adult, it might not fully explain the situation. The classic Piagetian experiment is to take two beakers, one that is tall and thin and the other that is short and stout. Fill the tall beaker half way with water. Pour the water from the tall beaker into the short and stout one. Children at the preoperational stage will consistently say that the tall and thin beaker contains more water than the short and stout beaker. These young children are not able to understand the property of conservation that the water maintains its volume when poured from one beaker to the other even though they are different sizes and shapes. They are distracted by the size of the beakers, equating the tall beaker as being bigger and therefore holding more water, as opposed to the short beaker that they perceive to be smaller and holding less water.

Piaget believed that children were naturally curious about the world around them. This curiosity prompted their development. For Piaget, cognitive development is not solely intrinsic, genetically encoded inside each individual's brain, nor is it totally reliant on extrinsic forces imposed by the environment or taught by adults. Rather, cognitive development is a product of the construction by children of their own meaning through interactions with their environment and with others.

Through his experiments and observations, Piaget concluded that most children's thinking goes through four distinct stages. The stages are described briefly in figure 1 below (adapted from Mooney, 2000, p. 64; Crain, 1992, p. 102):

Age (Approximate)	Stage Name	Behaviors
Birth-18 Months	Sensorimotor	• Learn through physical action schemes such as senses and reflexes • Manipulate materials
18 Months-6 Years	Preoperational	• Form ideas based on their perceptions of the world • Use language to develop their thinking • Tend to focus on one variable at a time • Overgeneralize based on limited experience
6 Years-12 Years	Concrete Operational	• Form ideas based on reasoning • Limit thinking to objects and familiar events • Can think systematically, but only about concrete objects
12 Years and Older	Formal Operational	• Think abstractly • Think systematically • Think hypothetically

Figure 1

The change from one stage to another is precipitated by the acquisition of an intellectual skill. For example, the toddler's ability to look for objects not in view pushes toddlers from a stage that is based on sensing objects that are present to one in which they can internally represent an object as through language. This process is called accommodation, meaning that an idea or object leads to new ways of knowing that replaces an existing way of knowing. Assimilation refers to an experience or stimulus being absorbed into existing ways of knowing. Organization refers to the tendency to put our ideas and thoughts into coherent systems.

Piaget was interested in moral judgment. He began his studies of moral judgment by observing boys at play. Since the girls often stopped playing when a dispute over the rules arose, Piaget chose to focus only on how the boys resolved their conflicts. Piaget discerned a cognitive progression in regard to how children understand law, responsibility, and justice. He saw children as moving from a moral order of obedience imposed by adults, to a sense of morality that was autonomous and internally based. The latter stage in a child's moral development, emerging around age ten, was based on an understanding, primarily from playing games, that "rules are human devices produced by equals for the sake of cooperation" (Crain, 1992, p. 116). Unlike Freud who viewed morality as under unconscious and irrational forces, Piaget was rationally and intellectually oriented. Piaget saw cognition and affect as developing on parallel tracks in regard to moral judgment (Riemer, p. 43). Piaget's view that moral judgment was a discernible, cognitive process distinguished him from other theoreticians of the time.

Critiques of Piaget

Piaget is often criticized for his methodology. While he observed and interviewed numerous children, much of his work was based on observations of his own three children. Additionally, his moral judgment studies were based solely on males.

Piaget's theory is limited in that he described no stages beyond that generally reached in adolescence. Some of the people who work on cognitive development have since examined the ways in which cognitive development goes beyond formal operational thinking in adulthood.

Perhaps the most serious critique is that he does not account enough for children's feelings or the social world around them. One of his major critics was his contemporary, Lev Vygotsky, a Jewish Russian psychologist. Vygotsky viewed Piaget as advocating for the influence of nature, innate capacities that we are born with, over the influence of nurture — environmental factors, such as care, education, resources, and the setting in which one grows up (Crain, 1992; Mooney, 2000). Piaget was suspect of formal instruction, of teachers imposing their viewpoints rather than allowing children to make discoveries on their own. Vygotsky believed that one's culture and social setting are the primary factors affecting a person's cognitive development. Family, friends, and environment figure heavily into one's learning. For Vygotsky, education plays an important role in cultivating learning and serves to strengthen what is found in one's environment and overcome its limitations rather than waiting for cognitive growth to unfold in due course as Piaget professed.

Implications for Jewish Education

Children learn best when they can determine the meaning and significance of something rather than being told or led. Piaget's emphasis that children construct their own meaning fits well with the perspective that every learner needs to internalize the values, stories, rituals, and *mitzvot* of the Jewish people for him/herself. The Pesach *Seder* is a microcosm of this, as we are instructed to experience the Exodus as if we were there.

Piaget's emphasis on the child developing from interactions with the environment and other people translates into learning opportunities that promote exploration, experimentation, and inquiry. Playing, imitating others, and trying out new roles and ideas are all ways that children can learn. These activities serve to promote the child's intellectual curiosity, a critical component of his theory of what leads to development.

Piaget contributed to establishing the notion of making curriculum in a school developmentally appropriate. He explained the cognitive capabilities of students in different stages. While some argue that it is possible to teach anything to children of any age, Piaget outlines the ways that people of all ages are more capable of learning. If content is presented in a way not compatible with a child's cognitive capacities, regardless of how compelling the topic or project might be, the child is unlikely to learn.

ERIK ERIKSON'S THEORY OF PSYCHOSOCIAL DEVELOPMENT

Erik Erikson's own life, 1902-1994, exemplifies the struggle for identity. Erikson was the child of a Jewish woman and a non-Jewish Dane. His mother raised him primarily on her own until he was three, at which time she married a Jewish man. Erikson had trouble fitting into either Jewish or German society, where he was raised — to the Jews, he looked more like a Scandinavian non-Jew; to the Germans, he was in the minority as a Jew. After high school, Erikson both traveled and pursued studies in art, a period of his life that he later called a "moratorium." At age 25, he accepted an invitation to teach children in a new Viennese school founded by, among others, Anna Freud, the daughter of Sigmund Freud, thus beginning his formal training in psychoanalysis. In 1933, at the age of 27, when Hitler rose to power, Erikson advisedly left Europe to continue his work in psychoanalysis. He moved to the United States where he became a child analyst, furthered his studies, and taught in universities, including Harvard, despite never having received a college degree. In the 1950s, he experienced prejudice in another form. During the McCarthy era, his loyalty to co-workers and refusal to make false claims about their views, caused him to leave one university and move on to another position.

Erikson saw biology and society as serving one another. He acknowledged the interdependence of body, psyche, and cultural organization in fostering development (Erikson, 1982). He gave credence to both nature and nurture — the unfolding of the natural order and the nurturing and socialization that society contributes to the development of human beings.

Elaborating on the work of Freud, Erikson developed a theory of psychosocial development throughout the life cycle that was based on ages or time periods in one's life. In other words, for the most part, everyone passed through these phases. In some way, the phases were automatic. What was not automatic, was a successful resolution of a phase's main developmental task. Erikson presented each phase as focusing on a main developmental task, a challenge, a tension between two tendencies that are both present. Just as Judaism posits that the *yetzer tov*, the inclination to do good, and the *yetzer ra*, the inclination to do evil, necessarily exist alongside one another, so, too, Erikson postulates a similar struggle between two opposite forces that exist side by side in each phase of life. The successful resolution of each one of these developmental tasks lead to an ego strength, an emerging quality. For example, the school age child who masters the *alef bet*, helps lead prayer services, does the *mitzvah* of visiting the sick, collects food to donate to the poor, is kind to his or her classmates, beautifies the Shabbat table with decorations, and the like, gains a feeling of competence. That child successfully resolves the struggle between industry and inferiority.

Unlike the stage theorists, Erikson explained that the developmental task of previous phases can be reworked, as can the resulting psychosocial strength or quality. For example, an infant who is not consistently provided for is not necessarily scarred for life. A stable, caring, supportive grandparent, teacher, scout leader, or sports coach who helps the individual recognize his/her abilities in resolving the developmental task of industry versus inferiority with the strength of competence, can help this school age child regain a sense of trust rather than mistrust. This new sense of hope can affect the individual's perceptions of the world around him/her and also his/her own future.

While Erikson labeled the phase of adolescence as identity versus role confusion, he views identity formation as a lifelong task. Struggling with self-definition represents the shift from childhood to adulthood for Erikson. In childhood, one learns and absorbs from the world around him/her a sense of who he/she is and what he/she is supposed to be. When one enters adolescence, the responsibility for understanding who one is and what one wants to do with one's life shifts to being one's own responsibility. As adolescents gain an understanding of the future, they begin to assert their autonomy in answering the questions of "who I am" and "what I want to be" for themselves.

In Erikson's theory, as well as Jewish identity theory, identity involves a sense of self and of others, belonging to or identifying with other groups (Horowitz, 2000). For Erikson, identity is not about the self in isolation. It is also about how one defines oneself in relationship to others. Erikson writes that identity "connotes both a persistent sameness with oneself (selfsameness) and a persistent sharing of some kind of essential character with others" (Erikson, 1980, p.109). Erikson's theory fits well with the ideas that Jewish identity is about sharing views about the roles, purpose, and meaning of life with other Jews, as well as considering oneself to be a Jew. In her studies of the journeys of Jews throughout their lifetimes and their connections to Jewish life, Horowitz (2000) presents some findings about Jewish identity that resonant with Erikson's ideas. Her findings emphasize that Jewish identity is formed and expressed

through the personal or psychological interiority of feelings and attitudes about belonging to the Jewish people, as well as the sociological or communal actions, both those dictated by tradition and those that have emerged through creative expression. How Jews see themselves and relate to other Jews are important in their Jewish identity formation throughout the life span.[1]

Erikson's phases of psychosocial development are described briefly in figure 2 below (adapted from Crain, 1992; Wright, 1982, pp. 51-54):

Age	Phase Name – Developmental Task and Ego Strength Developed	Characteristics
Infancy (0-1 Year)	Trust vs. Mistrust Leads To Hope	• Regulate urges • Display confidence in caretakers and self • See world as trustworthy place • Experience mistrust
Early Childhood (2-3 Years)	Autonomy vs. Shame and Doubt Leads To Willpower	• Practice holding on and letting go of toys, hair, and limbs of others, own bodily functions • Respond to parent(s) • Learn about life through everyday rituals • Discover limits
Play Age (4-5 Years)	Initiative vs. Guilt Leads To Purpose	• Imitate others through play and making of things • Follow own curiosity • Move physically into unknown • Dream of roles might fill, tasks might accomplish • Listen to one's inner voice • Regulate own behavior • Test roles through play and real life experiences

(continued on next page)

---

[1]For more on Horowitz's assertions, see Chapter 9, "Connections and Journeys: A New Vocabulary for Understanding American Jewish Identity" by Bethamie Horowitz, pp. 74-79 in this Handbook.

Age	Phase Name – Developmental Task and Ego Strength Developed	Characteristics
School Age (6-12 Years)	Industry vs. Inferiority Leads To Competence	• Form relationships with others in neighborhood or school • Make things • Go to school
Adolescence	Identity vs. Role Confusion Leads To Fidelity	• Listen to peers and peer groups • Form ideologies • Share oneself with others • Formulate a sense of who one is and what one wants to be as an adult
Young Adulthood	Intimacy vs. Isolation Leads To Love	• Develop intimate relationships • Develop love relationships • Develop relationships with those involved in either cooperative or competitive pursuits • Come to understand oneself more fully through relationships
Middle Age	Generativity vs. Stagnation Leads To Care	• Mentor others • Share labor with others • Provide education to others • Explore a variety of interests • Continue to be productive, contributing member of society, family • Care for the next generation
Old Age	Ego Integration vs. Despair Leads To Wisdom	• Care about the whole world and all humanity • Confront one's mortality and death • Review one's life

Figure 2

Jewish Educational Implications

The social environment in which a person exists is important to his/her development. Jewish schools, synagogues, camps, and other educational institutions all provide a *context* in which these developmental tasks are worked through in a person's lifetime. Jewish learning experiences can be designed to address these developmental tasks at each phase in a person's life, thereby supporting a successful resolution of each ego strength, hope, will, love, and so forth. In young adulthood, learning can be structured in *chevruta* style, with two or three peers studying text with one another, often with the assistance of a Rabbi or educator. Through this *chevruta* experience, they can develop Erikson's ego strength of love, which has to do with creating relationships of intimacy, of getting to know another person in a deep and meaningful way. The context or setting can reinforce the importance of the emergent ego strength. Schools commonly reinforce competence, such as rewarding students with a *Siddur* upon learning the *alef bet,* but they can do it for any of Erikson's ego strengths.

These same institutions — schools, synagogues, camps, and other educational institutions — can provide *content*, which guides and informs the fulfillment of these developmental tasks. For example, the Bar or Bat Mitzvah can be a learning experience, providing a sense of roles and responsibilities, expectations and values, role models and mentors. This can occur through studying and discussing texts, performing *mitzvot*, and gaining rapport with Rabbis, educators, parents, and community members, which supports identity formation throughout adolescence.

Jewish education needs only to tap the power of Judaism as a way of life to support the psychosocial development that Erikson describes. The symbols, rituals, stories, texts, and values of a religion, a community, and a family are designed to help prepare and support the individual's growth throughout his/her lifetime. They create an environment in which meaning and purpose are experienced through celebrating, learning, and observing throughout the life cycle. We as Jewish educators have only the challenge of capturing people's attention and imagination in our learning experiences as we tap into the wisdom, mystery, and majesty of Judaism as a way of life.

KOHLBERG'S THEORY OF MORAL REASONING

Lawrence Kohlberg, an identified Jew who studied at the University of Chicago, was interested in Piaget's work. Piaget described two stages in the moral development of children. Children's moral behavior appears "conformist" when children follow the rules presented to them by authority figures. Children move from this conformist stage to an autonomous stage in which they on their own resolve dilemmas, determine the rules, and act out of an internalized sense of what is right.

Kohlberg furthered Piaget's work on moral development as a cognitive driven activity through the development of a multi-staged theory of moral development for children and adults. Kohlberg viewed all human beings, children and adults alike, as philosophers, capable of determining what is moral. Kohlberg was concerned that the prevalent moral developmental theories of his time led to moral relativism, whatever one thinks is good is good. He found problematic theories that attributed moral judgment to a product of early social learning or unconscious processes, as did Freud. He felt that moral reasoning must be connected to action, thereby connecting thought with feeling. Furthermore, these other theories were unable to explain how people resolved value conflicts, which is a central concept in moral reasoning (Riemer, 1983).

Kohlberg wanted to understand how one can educate people toward creating and sustaining a just society. He directed his efforts to apply his theory of moral judgment to educational settings and schools, as well as to refining his theory. Kohlberg recognized that the hypothetical dilemmas he created and the dilemmas that emerge in the day-to-day interactions at a school were the material for creating a learning environment in which moral judgment could be nourished and flourish. His fascination with the Israeli *kibbutz* as a social collective that supported a community predicated on justice and equality was evidenced by the amount of research that he and his students did on this topic.

Kohlberg spent much of his career as a professor of education at Harvard. He conducted his initial experiments with boys, ages ten to 16, while in graduate school at the University of Chicago. This research led to the formation of his theory on moral development. Kohlberg presented the students with a hypothetical situation that described moral dilemmas. The respondents had to indicate what they would do in the situation. Perhaps his most well-known dilemma is the Heinz Dilemma: Heinz's wife is going to die unless she receives some medication. The drug is so expensive that the only way Heinz can obtain the drug is to steal it. The question posed is: if you were Heinz, would you steal the drug? Why or why not? The responses are analyzed not so much for the content of what subjects have to say, but rather for how they go about presenting their argument justifying their choice. While Kohlberg understood that such a dilemma has its emotional, social, and practical, even economic aspects, he was concerned about the moral questions that such a dilemma posed. Moral judgment for Kohlberg involved a "weighing of claims of others (including those of society) against one's own" (Riemer, et al, 1981, p. 49). How one resolved this conflict revealed the form or stage of a person's moral judgment.

In presenting Kohlberg's stages of moral development below, it is important to remember that moral reasoning (the way we think about moral issues or dilemmas) and moral action (the way we act and respond to those issues or dilemmas) are not the same. Someone at Stage 4 is not necessarily going to "behave" more morally than someone at Stage 2. In this sense, Stage 4 is not better than Stage 2. What is interesting is that Kohlberg and others found some connection between moral reasoning and action in what they call a sub-stage phenomenon. In this sub-stage, the person not only explains what they think *ought* to happen in the moral dilemma presented, they also comment on how they would feel *personally responsible* to act. A justice ethic is mediated by a responsibility ethic, acting on what one believes to be right (Riemer, 1981, p. 112). For example, this expression of personal responsibility was more highly connected to action in studies of students who completed these dilemmas and protested the war in Vietnam (Riemer, 1981, p. 112). Helping learners consider how they would personally act might lead to a stronger connection between moral reasoning and moral action.

Kohlberg's stages of moral reasoning are described below in figure 3 (adapted from Kohlberg, 1981, pp. 409-412; Riemer, 1979, pp. 58-59; and Fowler, 1981, pp. 244-245). Most people never reach Kohlberg's two highest stages.

Earliest Age of Onset	Stage	Characteristics
2 years	Stage 1 - Preconventional: The Stage of Punishment and Obedience	• Behave out of a sense of fear of physical, not psychological punishment • Listen to authorities • Unable to distinguish the interests or perspectives of others, including authority figures, from one's own
6 years	Stage 2 - Preconventional: The Stage of Individual Instrumental Purpose and Exchange	• Behave out of a sense of fairness, equity, or reciprocity to others • Do right to serve one's own interests or needs • Regulates conflicting interests of others by exchange of services, goods, or goodwill
13 years	Stage 3 - Conventional: The Stage of Mutual Interpersonal Expectations, Relationships, and Conformity	• Act in response to the expectations of, and loyalties to, recognized others — family, peers, friends, groups • Take on the perspective of others, putting oneself in someone else's shoes • Give priority to shared feelings, agreements, and expectations over that of individual interests

(continued on next page)

Earliest Age of Onset	Stage	Characteristics
20 years	Stage 4 - Conventional: The Stage of Social System and Conscience Maintenance	• Take on the society's perspective of what is right and wrong, good and evil • Keep in place the social order, welfare of the society or group • Respond out of a sense of duty • Respond out of a sense of maintaining the system
Middle Age	Stage 5 - Postconventional and Principled: The Stage of Prior Rights and Social Contract or Utility	• Act out of a sense of justice that is prior to or higher than society's laws, e.g., a conscientious objector during a war • Criticize laws or practices of society that are unjust • Act on principles, rights, and values that would benefit all if a society were fair, even when in conflict with actual laws • Examines both the moral and legal points of view
Late Adulthood	Stage 6 - Postconventional: The Stage of Universal Ethical Principles	• Express a loyalty to all human beings • Evaluate laws and governments based on their principles • Regard all human beings as equally deserving of justice, dignity, and rights • Upholding justice, righteousness are ends, not means

Figure 3

Kohlberg spent a great deal of time doing cross-cultural studies of his theory, trying to prove its universal applicability to people of all countries, races, and religions. By proving this, and by showing the ability to nurture people's moral reasoning, he could demonstrate how moral judgment was a cognitive capacity and a process achievable by all human beings. One implication of this finding was that a just world could be formed and that education could play a critical role in forming a just world. Tragically, it was on one of his cross-cultural study trips that he contracted a disease that eventually led to his death in 1986.

Critique

The strongest, most well-known critique of Kohlberg's theory was launched by Carol Gilligan. In her book *In a Different Voice*, Gilligan presents the work that her colleagues and she did showing that women are more oriented to the views of others than are men. In fact, men tend to become more attuned to the voices of others after individuation and not before as is more typically the case of women. Gilligan disputes Kohlberg's hierarchy as it penalizes, tends to score women lower, on Kohlberg's stages of moral reasoning, when in fact their developmental paths are actually different according to her empirical studies. Kohlberg had always tried to bring women into his theory, saying that they more or less fit the same pattern of moral reasoning as the men in his initial and later studies.

Jewish Educational Implications

Kohlberg proposes a theory of moral development and theories of how to adapt moral development to an educational setting. Kohlberg recognizes the centrality of hypothetical and actual situations in which values are in conflict as a key to nurturing and shaping moral development. Furthermore, Kohlberg postulates a vision of justice through living models of a just school and a just community toward which one can aspire.

Kohlberg's theory is based on a conception of justice. His theory is useful in a Jewish context as Judaism is a religion in which ethical behavior, following the *mitzvot*, and believing in God are inextricably linked. Piety and righteousness are connected in Judaism as part of living in covenant with God. God is also viewed as essentially just in contradistinction to the gods of the Greeks, who were known for their capricious, amoral behavior.

Kohlberg's work has been adapted for use in religious schools, including Jewish schools. In 1980, A.R.E. Publishing, Inc. published a book by Earl Schwartz (now out of print) on adapting Kohlberg's work for use in Jewish schools. Schwartz has created a network of schools, Jewish and Christian day schools and public schools, in the Twin Cities that strive to create a just community within a school. He created a *va'ad din*, a court, at the Talmud Torah of St. Paul Day School to which students bring cases involving conflicts between students or even between a student and a teacher. Fifth graders spend a year studying Rabbinic texts related to situations in which students might find themselves: lying and cheating, relationships with peers and teachers, and so forth. In the sixth grade, a selected group of students serves on the *va'ad din* to make binding decisions resolving the conflicts presented. In addition, the *va'ad din* oversees what happens to lost and found items applying Rabbinic categories and concepts. In an article in *Religious Education*, Schwartz presents his view of a school's moral development (Schwartz, 2001).

Despite the seeming compatibility with Judaism, Kohlberg's theory provides insight into just part of what it means to live as a religious person, Jew or otherwise. His theory has limited application because of the understanding of justice on which his system is based and because he does not explicitly connect his conception of justice to religious ways of knowing and being. In many ways, Kohlberg is part of Western enlightenment philosophy that upholds rationality. In this philosophy, reason and rationality are a unifying force in creating a just civilization through righteous laws. Religion, including belief in God, is perceived as irrational and a divider of humanity rather than a unifier. The rise of Fowler's explicitly religious developmental theory in a post-modern society that appreciates the nonrational, emotive, social, and religious aspects of life is not a mere coincidence. From post-modernism we recognize that the enlightenment that emphasized rationality produced the Holocaust. Post-modernism seeks to give credence to other forms of knowing and being while acknowledging and incorporating rationalism as but one factor among many. Furthermore, Fowler, whose theory is described in the next section, bases his theory on religious ways of knowing and acting.

FOWLER'S FAITH DEVELOPMENT THEORY

The stage and phase theories of Piaget, Erikson, and Kohlberg, as well the theories of others, influenced the formation of Fowler's theory of Faith Development. In fact, he incorporates the work of all three theorists into his stage theory.

Kohlberg made a special contribution to Fowler's formation of Faith Development theory. Fowler was an ordained minister when he arrived at Harvard to do his doctoral studies. Kohlberg became a teacher and mentor for Fowler at Harvard. He was very helpful in suggesting ways of empirically substantiating some of Fowler's ideas that emerged from more theological and philosophical sources. As recommended by Kohlberg, Fowler formed his theory from interviews with subjects from North America, of both genders and different ages, from different religious groups as well as unaffiliated individuals, and from different socioeconomic backgrounds. These interviews were then analyzed for patterns that led to descriptions of the stages.

Faith development is a theory of human development about the whole person and what it means to be a human being. Fowler claims that our nature, our humanness, involves making meaning of our lives. This activity of faith, or faithing, incorporates the cognitive, affective, social, moral, conscious and unconscious, and all other aspects or domains of a person's development throughout one's lifetime. Just as faith binds together these components, so, too, these components can be conduits through which faith is nurtured.

"Faith or 'faithing' is the process by which a person finds and makes meaning of life's significant questions and issues, adheres to this meaning, and acts it out in his or her life" (Goodman, 1985, p. 1). Faith is common to all people. Yet, we each choose a particular path in pursing this universal phenomenon.

Faith has a narrative quality. We are continuously creating and recreating a story or stories about who we are. These stories embody our meaning making systems. They reveal to others and to ourselves our values, struggles, conflicts, and hopes. These stories guide our daily decisions, life choices, and actions.

Faith formation occurs in relation to others. These others can be individuals, such as family members, friends, classmates, work place associates, youth group workers, Rabbis, and/or educators. Or, these others can be groups, such as a synagogue, team, youth group, school, and/or *havurah*.

What Fowler calls "shared centers of value and power" mediate the relationship between the individual and others. These centers of value and power include: trust, fairness, financial gain, possessions, recognition, strength, beauty, integrity, humanism, holiness, and/or God. Fowler identifies God as one possible center of value and power. In doing so, his theory overcomes the split between rationality and passion, religion and secularism, that has characterized the modern era since the Enlightenment. According to Fowler, all people,

whether they are atheists or religious zealots, have faith. How we organize these centers of value and power, whether we assign more importance to financial gain than to fairness, or to beauty than to integrity, or to humanism than to holiness, reflects who we are and how we conduct our lives.

Faith changes over time, both in its content and structure. Faith development theory examines the structural changes in one's faith. Fowler outlines six "stages of faith" that describe people's faith. Most people get through at least Stages 1 and 2. Few reach Stages 5 and 6. Although our formal schooling may end, faith, or meaning making, is a lifelong process. The choice, perhaps the obligation, is for us as educators to intervene in people's meaning making processes. We have an important role to play in nurturing faith. By understanding how people construct their faith, we can better address their needs in this area.

It is important to remember that because faith stages describe how people structure their meaning making system, the stages reveal little if anything about the content of each stage. Their structural orientation gives them their universal quality as they encompass people of all religious groupings. We do not go through faith stages in the abstract. We each pursue a path filled with particular ideas, beliefs, experiences, practices, symbols, rituals, and customs. Catholics and Jews who are Stage 3 share a way of organizing, presenting, discussing, and thinking about their lives, irrespective of the content. In the same way, a concrete operational thinker who is Mexican-American and a concrete operational thinker who is Anglo-American think similarly about the math concepts of sets or addition.

Fowler's stages are summarized in figure 4 on the next page (based on Goodman 2002).

Age (at which it might emerge)	Stage	Characteristics
Birth	Primal or Undifferentiated Faith	• Develop sense of trust through daily rituals of nurturing • Develop first images of God based on trust of caretaker
18 months	Stage 1 - Intuitive-Projective Faith	• Use language to build relationships and control environment • Differentiate self from others • Rely on imagination and images to understand world • Imitate rituals and roles • Lured by symbols, the mysterious or magical • Respond with emotions and whole body especially in prayer • Obey out of a fear of punishment
6 years	Stage 2 - Mythical-Literal Faith	• Develop relationships with adults other than parents and peers • Learn legends, lore, symbols, and rituals of a religious group • Distinguish between fantasy and reality • View life as linear and predictable • Interpret stories literally • See symbols as one-dimensional • Explore limits of own strength and power and consequences for these actions through stories of heroes, role models, and villians • Judge actions by their fairness • Can be self-righteous, susceptible to prejudice • View God as being like a fair, caring, consistent parent or ruler

(continued on next page)

Age (at which it might emerge)	Stage	Characteristics
12 years	Stage 3 - Synthetic-Conventional Faith	• Become attuned to ways others perceive self as part of abstract thinking • Form own identity based on roles and relationships • Seek and value approval and acceptance of others • Look to non-parental role models in all aspects of life, including religion; makes them susceptible to cult leaders • Seek and grow in personal relationship to God • Describe God primarily in interpersonal terms • Seek groups to belong to; make them susceptible to gangs and cults • See meaning of texts, opinions as being self-evident; can get stuck on one viewpoint • Respond evocatively to symbols • Interpret texts, people, and events in tacit, unexamined way
20 years	Stage 4 - Individuative-Reflective Faith	• Establish one's self professionally and personally • Form own coherent view about all aspects of one's life • Assert own authority, own voice • Take responsibility for and control over commitments, lifestyle, beliefs, and attitudes • Make explicit meaning of symbols, stories, rituals • Seek rational explanations and answers
Mid-life	Stage 5 - Conjunctive Faith	• Open up to and often explore or experiment with a variety of religious experiences and expressions • Appreciate paradox, ambiguity, and inconsistencies in truth and life • Tolerate differences • Recognize the relativity of one's views, including one's religious group • Renew sense of mystery found in ritual • Focus on the transcendence of God and holiness

(continued on next page)

Age (at which it might emerge)	Stage	Characteristics
Late Adulthood	Stage 6 - Universalizing Faith	• Relinquish self, lose self-consciousness • Actualize universal truths • Universalize the bonds of social awareness • Become one with God • Embody the Divine, the sacred • God is both imminent and transcendent

Figure 4

Critique

Perhaps the most common critique of Fowler's stages is the feminist critique of Stages 3 and 4. Fowler presents Stage 3 as a more communal and relationship oriented stage, whereas Stage 4 is much more individually and independently oriented. Gilligan's feminist critique of Kohlberg (Gilligan, 1982) applies here, too. Gilligan claims that women tend to be relationship and group oriented, whereas men are more independent and individually oriented. To claim that one orientation is a lesser stage than another is to make women look morally inferior as in Kohlberg's moral development theory, and thus, extrapolating, is to relegate women's faith to a lesser form of development.

For a similar reason, Fowler is often critiqued by more traditional societies or religions, especially some of those in the Far East or Middle East that are communally rather than individually oriented. As a whole, the hierarchical nature of Fowler's theory implicitly implies that that type of society or religion is less sophisticated.

Jewish Educational Implications

The stages of faith are outlined in this chapter. Fowler claims that the role of education or of any intervention is not to move a person from one stage to the next. Rather, the task is to fill out each stage. For example, imagine the person who in Stage 1 is not introduced to any Jewish rituals or symbols until she or he is in a higher stage, and obviously older. This person who lacks an early introduction to Jewish symbols and rituals is likely to feel a void in his or her Jewish upbringing. The

introduction of ritual and symbols into a Stage 3 person's life must be done in a different way than with a Stage 1 person. A Jewish education needs to address a person at every stage of his or her faith development to bring out the richness of our heritage. Different faith issues, transitions, crises, and dangers can arise at each stage. The stages of faith help us appreciate the importance of lifelong Jewish education.

No educational or spiritual advantage is derived from having people in one stage versus another. The richer and deeper the Jewish experience at each stage, the more our lives are filled with meaning. This approach deepens, strengthens, and renews our commitment to living a Jewish life as evidenced by our actions, values, and beliefs.

APPLYING THEORY TO PRACTICE

This next section attempts to take some student and curricular or instructional issues and apply the developmental theories to see how they can aid the Jewish educator. All of the scenarios are based on real situations.

Early Childhood

Student Issue: Everyday in class, Josh and Michael, both young three-year-olds in a Jewish preschool, seem to gravitate toward one another. They end up in the housekeeping area where they never fail to get into a shoving match over "setting the table for Shabbat."

Piaget suggests that children learn by role-playing and watching models. It might be helpful to role-play this type of situation and show different ways of resolving the problem before the behavior escalates. In other words, if the two children can pretend and play out the situation themselves or watch others in a similar situation — not about setting the table, but perhaps sharing another type of toy such as blocks or bicycles — then they may learn how to resolve their own confrontation.

There are a number of ways into this issue based on Fowler: reading a book about sharing or taking turns, being kind to others, learning to resolve problems with words not fists, making peace with our brothers and sisters. The book would show what the school and Judaism value in the way of how we treat others.

Kohlberg might suggest engaging the two young children in helping resolve their own conflict. In other words, the teachers could make suggestions about what to do to avoid this problem in the future. The children could help identify which way of resolving the problem they might follow. While it might seem early to have a child in the two to five age range making up rules, what is being modeled here is helping the children internalize ways of or strategies for resolving moral conflicts. Engaging the two children in a conversation is a proactive approach that would help strengthen the child's sense of will, of wanting to interact appropriately with the other child. This approach could lead to a successful resolution of the tension between autonomy versus shame or doubt that Erikson describes for this age group.

Curricular Issue: Using an emergent curricular approach (letting the learners' interests and curiosity direct the choice of topics and activities), the birth of a new sibling for two of the children has become a major focus in this Jewish preschool classroom. The teachers want to tie the arrival of these children into units on family and Jewish life cycles.

This particular curricular issue presents many conceptual or thematic spin-offs, such as sibling rivalry, concepts of birth and death, beginnings and ends, family members, family trees, relationships among family members, caring for our family members, celebrating special moments in our lives, life cycle marker events, or naming. While Piaget points out that young children cannot think abstractly, they do think conceptually even if they do not express their thoughts or feelings by naming a concept. For example, most young children become experts early on in coveting. They just

don't articulate the concept, but they understand the behavior.

Piaget would instruct the educator to have pictures of the new siblings, concrete examples of whatever concept was being taught. For example, if it is about death and life, looking at leaves falling off of trees in the fall could be used to help convey the concept. Reading about the life cycle of a caterpillar conveys how animals' lives change. Looking at pictures of their parents when they were born, became Bar/Bat Mitzvah, got married, became parents, is another way of mapping out the life cycle. Piaget might encourage the children to play out these different times with props. Fowler would encourage the teachers to read stories or show videotapes about these different life cycle events. Sharing the rituals, symbols, blessings, and stories of these different occasions would help the children feel the connection between these special times and Jewish traditions and practices.

Both Kohlberg and Erikson would advise addressing the moral issue and dilemma of sibling rivalry, competition, or basic jealousy. It only took two weeks before our three-year-old daughter asked how long our newborn son would be staying with us. One colleague, now a minister, spoke about how he used to steal his sister's bottle and drink her milk, a pattern his parents discovered only after taking the baby to the doctor for her weigh-in. Erikson's issue of initiative versus guilt working on the ego strength of purpose is applicable here. Is the older sibling going to help care for the child, take initiative in helping the new sibling, or do nasty deeds, disobey one's parents (Kohlberg stage for this age group), and experience guilt for feeling competitive with the new child's appearance on the family scene? Acting out situations that the children can identify as good behavior toward one's new sibling or bad behavior is a possible approach. Reading stories from Jewish sources, both traditional and modern, that acknowledge the range of feelings one can have with a new sibling are helpful too. Having the children share ways that they can be kind to their sibling can lead toward the children taking initiative, developing the sense of purpose in caring for others.

Elementary School Age

Student Issue: Rachel is a new third grader in the class. The majority of the children have been together since Kindergarten. During the second month of school, Rachel was the only girl in the class not invited to a classmate's birthday party. All the girls are talking about the great birthday party they went to over the weekend, and wrote about it in their creative writing exercise. Rachel is obviously upset about this.

This situation presents a moral dilemma that has much to do with the character of the individual and her classmates. Fairness, according to Kohlberg, is a key concept in the types of moral choices that children make at this stage. Issues about fairness from the perspective of Rachel surface immediately in this scenario. Part of the problem is how to confront this issue and not embarrass Rachel or the others. Discussing stories about fairness in different social situations can help these children think through the issues.

Another part of the problem is that it seems that the classroom teacher did not address the social issue, the Jewish value of welcoming the stranger, i.e., integrating the new student into the school at the beginning of the year. Her inferiority has overcome industry for both Rachel and her classmates. The teacher, by initiating discussions about how to welcome a new student, can help build a sense of competence for the new child in a new social situation and the children who have been in the school for an extended period of time. Left to their own devices, many children will fail, as did the ones in this day school class.

Curricular Issue: The fourth grade class is studying Genesis and Exodus. The students say that they have heard and learned the Bible stories when they were in preschool and Kindergarten.

All four developmental theories support the importance of a spiral curriculum in which the students feel that they are learning something different and in a different way. These children have changed cognitively, socially, morally, and spiritually. While the biblical text remains the same, it is important to find those issues that are of concern to this age group. Based on his understanding of Erikson, Fowler would emphasize how studying heroes or role models who struggle with issues of competence, ability, success, and power, who show the extremes to which one can go either in terms of good or evil, would be of interest to these fourth graders. They are struggling with their own sense of competence, of industry versus inferiority. Looking at the characters in the Bible shows them what

they can do to be respected human beings.

Piaget might suggest that moving from the telling of Bible stories based on the original text to giving them the actual text to study acknowledges their cognitive or intellectual growth. Rather than using a collection of Bible stories, a textbook like *Being Torah* that presents a simplified, but sophisticated rendering of the biblical text, introduces the student to the skills and methods that biblical scholars use in interpreting texts. The different wording and approach found in *Being Torah* would signify to the children the change in their cognitive capabilities. They can now analyze the stories, looking for the meaning in the stories themselves. In some cases, the children can read the original text in either Hebrew or English again to show the change from their earlier studies.

> The fourth grade teacher told me that Jon was the "perfect student," a real *mench*, and that I will "love having him in the fifth grade class." Something happened, because the Jon I had was distracted by his peers and rolled his eyes when I attempted to refocus his attention. His parents were shocked when I informed them of his behavior. Was it me? His parents confronted him and discovered that their ten-year-old, like many kids in this age group, was suddenly more interested in his peers than in his work and his teacher's approval. Trust your own observations and help parents recognize developmental shifts.
>
> (Diane Schon Wirtschafter, Berkeley, California)

Adolescence

Student Issue: Four kids from the high school were in an auto accident over the weekend. The driver of the car was speeding on a road and lost control of the car. He is in a coma. The passengers in the back seat who were not wearing their seat belts were killed instantly, as was the teen in the front passenger seat, even though he was wearing a seat belt. The father of one of the passengers begged her not to get into the car as the driver had a reputation for driving too fast. He is feeling very guilty about not having insisted that she not go in the car. Both the teens and their parents are feeling miserable and unsure what to do to prevent this type of tragedy in the future.

This type of tragedy needs to be addressed in the context of a Jewish school. Multiple issues surface, such as comforting the mourners immediately, having teens recognize their mortality, the need to control new powers and take responsibility for themselves and others, responding to peer pressure versus listening to parents or utilizing their own common sense. While Kohlberg focuses on justice in his theory of moral development, situations related to character development, how human beings relate to one another, and not solely the ethics of justice, are part of moral development. At stake is more than discussing what type of justice — punishment or penitence — that the driver of the car and/or his parents, since he is a minor, should receive for this situation. Of greater consequence are the types of choices surrounding values related to a person's character that the teens need to make.

Taking this situation or related scenarios and uncovering the wisdom that Jewish texts, both traditional and modern, hold about responsibility, peer pressure, parental authority, and death would help the teens heal and learn how to respond in the future. This strategy fits with Fowler's view that the stories and texts of our people can serve as a guide in how we relate to others, the values we find most important, and the meaning and purpose we identify for our lives. Furthermore, the students and their parents need the support of Jewish professionals, Rabbis, Cantors, educators, social workers, and their community to help them through this experience. These people will, hopefully, help them feel that the rituals and customs of mourning and the views on death bring comfort.

Finally, the teens especially need to know that it is acceptable to raise questions about God and struggle. They are going to ask: Why did this happen to my friends? Why do bad things happen to good people? As Erikson reminds us, this is the phase in which identity versus identity confusion is the major developmental challenge, even though identity is an issue throughout one's life. These teens need to know that Jewish tradition allows for questioning and struggling with God, that it can provide answers about the ultimate questions that we have about life, and finally, that it is a religion that can provide comfort and hope even in the face of personal tragedy. Otherwise, the risk of their

rejecting a particular view that they held as a child about God, their questioning of the unfairness of life, can lead to the rejection of God and Judaism as a whole.

Curriculum Issue: The Confirmation (Grade 10) class is studying God, Torah, and Israel. One lesson of the God curriculum is devoted to having students identify which of four views or metaphors of God most closely represents their own view: God as watchmaker, God as Jimminy Cricket, God as coach with clipboard, God as Mother Nature (scientific laws, natural rules, and other truths).[2] Independently, several of the students come up to the instructor stating that they cannot relate to any of the four images.

This situation actually happened to me. At first, I thought it was an honest intellectual stance that their view of God was different. I realized that something else was happening only after so many of the group members came up to me to say that they could not support any of these views.

This situation evolves because of two phenomenon occurring simultaneously. One has to do with social perspective taking, and the other with identity formation. I see you seeing me. I see the you that I think you see — that is key to Fowler's Stage 3. Teens have the capability of looking at themselves through the eyes of others. It is the obsession with looking in the mirror. While at the same time that they want to appear to be individuals and develop their own unique identity as Erikson would suggest, they are very much influenced by their peers. They are concerned what their peers will say about the views and opinions that they express.

This session was preceded by a panel of well respected lay (not religious) leaders in the community who modeled sharing their own personal quest for and views of God. Even that modeling was not sufficient to support these teens who still did not have the ego strength, the certainty in their viewpoints, to subject themselves to whatever critique might come from advocating for a particular view.

A better strategy might have been to assign them to a position. Then they would be required to defend the position without having to claim it as their own. That would allow them to explore a viewpoint without having to put their personhood

---

[2]This concept was originally developed and recorded in *Shema Is for Real* by Joel Lurie Grishaver in 1973.

on the line and open themselves to comments from their friends on a subject about which they feel uncertain and vulnerable.

What would have been helpful to this group was not this four corners values clarification type of exercise, but rather looking at the theologies of different Jews. That is the approach used in the developmentally appropriate book for teens as well as adults, *Finding God: Ten Jewish Responses* (Sonsino and Syme, 2002). By looking at these different views, they could explore some ideas about God, learn how these theologians addressed life's important questions, and then select one or a combination of views that made sense to them. In this way, they could develop their own personal theology about God. In the scenario described, they were not ready in terms of their knowledge about God, to take a personal risk.

Children see things through such innocent eyes. I'll never forget when one of my three-year-old students said to me as we were preparing for a Chanukah party: "There are two kinds of people in this world — Jewish people and Christmas people!"

(Kim Lausin, Beachwood, Ohio)

Adults

Student Issue: Julie is 40 years old. She was a respected and accomplished human resource vice president for a medium-sized corporation until about three years ago. She graduated with her undergraduate degree in business nearly 20 years ago, and has not been back in school until today. In recent years, she has shifted from working full-time to taking care of her family, volunteering in the community, especially in her congregation where she has taught religious school for two years. A supplementary school graduate herself, she adores teaching in her congregation's supplementary school. She is now taking a course for credit in Jewish studies at a local Jewish institution of higher learning to help her be a better teacher and possibly to open up new career possibilities in the long term. All the students in the class are required to write a research paper on a topic of interest to them in Jewish history. Julie has not studied Jewish history since her days in religious school. She feels

that she has gaps just in the "facts" of Jewish history, the main time periods, events, and figures. To present, analyze, and critique an issue in Jewish history seems an overwhelming task. On top of these content problems, she has not written a paper of note, including for work, since graduating from college. She is very nervous about this assignment.

Julie is in the Erikson stage of generativity versus stagnation. Motivated in part by Erikson's strength of care, the normative resolution of this phase — caring for her family, her congregation, her students — the other issue here is that as an accomplished businessperson who is shifting into other avenues, she needs to feel capable and confident with these new endeavors. Her Jewish education as a child and her experiences in business have not fully prepared her for the challenges that she now faces in the classroom. Having been successful in business, she now needs to feel a sense of success in this situation to help propel her down this new life path that she has chosen to pursue. While she achieved Piaget's highest level of thinking in terms of her business life, she needs some foundational Judaic knowledge in history in order to be able to apply her hypothetical thinking skills to the problems of Jewish history. To some extent, Julie just needs to practice and refresh research and writing skills that go back to her undergraduate studies. But she also needs to acquire an internal sense of what constitutes a good research paper. In this case, feedback and support from the instructor become extremely important in building confidence as well as skills.

Curricular Issue: The course's curriculum is to present an overview of Jewish History. Rather than choosing a chronological approach, the decision was made to focus on such issues such as anti-Semitism and immigration and to look at them throughout history. The learners are having difficulty with this approach and putting events into context.

As in Julie's case, these adult learners are struggling because they lack content knowledge and a framework for understanding Jewish history. In terms of applying Piaget's theory, while most have achieved formal operational thinking, they are not well grounded enough in this particular subject area to be able to look comfortably at issues across time. Stage 4 in Fowler's theory of faith development provides some illumination here, too. In that stage, people try to develop coherent, consistent, and rational theories or systems. They would rather use a chronological framework for examining history, seeing how events unfold and relate to one another, than the more phenomenological or sociological approach to looking at an issue as it affects Jewish life throughout time. While they can think hypothetically, they are demonstrating a preference for a framework that they consider more meaningful, useful, and helpful.

Extrapolating on Kohlberg's theory, the learners are presenting a dilemma to the instructor: to follow the curricular design or to adjust to the preferences and needs of the learners. While this is not the type of dilemma that Kohlberg addresses, it shows that the conflict between two values produces the need for reviewing a situation, weighing options, and examining values in determining a course of action.

CONCLUSION

The developmental theories described in this chapter come from the world of psychology, education, and theology. They reveal numerous insights about human growth and development that have implications for teachers and for Jewish education. The knowledge presented here is designed to help make each Jewish educator more age appropriate in his/her teaching and to tap into the energy that comes from reaching a learner where he/she is in the life span. Hopefully, the chapter succeeded in making the reader more knowledgeable about and a better observer of their student's growth and development, as well as his/her own.

Utilizing the wisdom of each of these four theorists depends upon the ability of each Jewish teacher to translate the important lessons about human development into a Jewish framework. The four theorists are experts in human development, not in Jewish education. Now those immersed in teaching and living as a Jew must bring the wisdom of Jewish texts and traditions, the theories of Jewish education, their own expertise and insights, in fully maximizing the wisdom of these developmental theorists to strengthen Jewish education. Go and do!

BIBLIOGRAPHY

Dykstra, Craig, and Sharon Parks, eds. *Faith Development and Fowler*. Birmingham, AL: Religious Education Press, 1984.

> This collection of essays is perhaps the most comprehensive critique of Fowler's theory of faith development. The two editors are both prominent theologians.

Erikson, Erik. *Identity and the Life Cycle*. New York: W.W. Norton & Co., 1980.

> This work contains three essays that Erikson presented in the 1950s, including one of particular importance in outlining his views on identity formation.

———. *The Life Cycle Completed*. New York: W.W. Norton & Co., 1982.

> Erikson provides a detailed description of each phase of the life cycle.

Fowler, James W. *Stages of Faith: The Psychology of Human Development and the Quest for Meaning*. San Francisco, CA: Harper & Row Publishers, 1981.

> Fowler's seminal work in which he describes faith development theory and the stages in detail.

Fowler, James W.; Karl Ernst Nipkow; and Friedrich Schweitzer. *Stages of Faith and Religious Development*. New York: Crossroad, 1991.

> This volume is a collection of articles about faith and religious development by some of the most prominent theologians and thinkers of the time. A variety of theories, both stage theories and other approaches, are included.

Gilligan, Carol. *In a Different Voice*. Cambridge, MA: Harvard Press, 1982.

> In this work Gilligan critiques Kohlberg's moral development theory. Besides questioning a theory devised originally solely on interviews of men only, Gilligan contends that woman's moral development is based more on relationships. Therefore, she contends that Kohlberg's theory is flawed, particularly in terms of his sequencing of Stages 3 and 4. In fact, Gilligan claims that the two stages should have their orders reversed.

Goodman, Roberta Louis. "Nurturing a Relationship To God and Spiritual Growth: A Developmental Approach." In *Teaching about God and Spirituality*, Roberta Louis Goodman and Sherry Blumberg, eds. Denver, CO: A.R.E. Publishing, Inc., 2002.

> Goodman reviews Fowler's theory of Faith Development and Fritz Oser's theory of Religious Reasoning, linking their work to that of other developmentalists, specifically Piaget and Kohlberg. Descriptions of both theories and their implications for Jewish education are presented. In addition, the author outlines her own approach to nurturing faith and spirituality.

———. "Nurturing Students' Spirituality and Prayerfulness." In *Connecting Prayer and Spirituality: Kol HaNeshamah as a Creative Teaching and Learning Text*, Jeffrey L. Schein, Editor-in-Chief. Wyncote, PA: The Reconstructionist Press, 1996.

> This piece focuses is on what faith development has to say about nurturing prayer, prayerfulness, and spirituality.

———. "Faith Development." In *What We Know about Jewish Education*, Stuart Kelman, ed. Los Angeles, CA: Torah Aura Productions, 1992, pp. 129-135.

> This chapter reviews the major work and research in faith development and identifies the implications of this theory for Jewish education.

———. "Test of Faith." (Instant Lesson) Los Angeles, CA: Torah Aura Productions, 1985.

> Perhaps the first piece published that uses faith development theory in a Jewish setting, this Instant Lesson is directed at Grade 6 to adult. It challenges students to think about how they make meaning out of their lives. Activities include: trying to figure out at what stage the learner is and interpreting a story by answering significant meaning making questions.

Grishaver, Joel. *Being Torah*. Los Angeles, CA: Torah Aura Productions, 1985,

> In this textbook for Grades 2-4, the presentation of the biblical text from Genesis and Exodus models the way that scholars over the ages approach interpreting the text. The textbook is successful in guiding both teachers and students through this classic way of doing biblical interpretation. This approach helps the learner find meaning in the text.

Horowitz, Bethamie. *Connections and Journeys: Assessing Critical Opportunities for Enhancing Jewish Identity*. (A Report to the Commission on Jewish Identity & Renewal) New York: UJA-Federation of New York, 2000.

Horowitz presents her groundbreaking research and conclusions. She stresses the importance of personal, inward Jewish identity as conveyed in attitudes and feelings that reveal connections to Judaism that were not previously captured by the conventional population studies of the last several decades, which focused on actions.

Kipling, Rudyard. *Just So Stories*. New York: Penguin Books, 1902.

These classic children's stories explain how different things in the natural and physical world came about, such as how the camel got its humps, how the alphabet came into existence.

Kohlberg, Lawrence. *The Psychology of Moral Development: Volumes I and II*. San Francisco, CA: Harper & Row, Publishers, 1984.

These two volumes contain some of Kohlberg's most important thinking about his work on moral development. The epilogue is dedicated to Janusz Korsczak, whom he saw as a model of his postulated seventh stage of moral development, a stage beyond justice. This epilogue lays the foundation for seeing the multitude of ways in which Kohlberg's work was inspired by that of Korsczak.

Mooney, Carol Garhart. *Theories of Childhood: An Introduction To Dewey, Montessori, Erikson, Piaget & Vygotsky*. St. Paul, MN: Redleaf Press, 2000.

Written for the early childhood educator, this book is an easy read about these five theorists. Mooney gives examples from her work in early childhood settings to illustrate many of the main points of these theorists.

Reimer, Joseph; Diana Pritchard Paolitto; and Richard H. Hersh. *Promoting Moral Growth: From Piaget To Kohlberg*. 2d ed. New York: Longman, 1983.

The lead author, Joseph Reimer, was a student of Kohlberg's at Harvard, and today teaches at Brandeis University in the Jewish communal service program. Written as a textbook for college courses, this book provides a good overview of Kohlberg's work in moral development and its connection to Piaget's work.

Schwartz, Earl. *Moral Development: A Practical Guide for Jewish Teachers*. Denver, CO: A.R.E. Publishing, Inc., 1983.

Using Kohlberg's stages of Moral Development, Schwartz presents Jewish source material that address major moral issues. Then he presents dilemmas adapted from life for the students to resolve as a way of connecting Jewish texts and values to moral reasoning. The curriculum he presents is a basis for empowering learners to construct a school on Jewishly grounded moral principles.

———. "Three Stages of a School's Moral Development." *Religious Education* 96, Winter 2001, pp. 106-119.

Influenced by the work of Kohlberg, Schwartz applies his theory to Jewish tradition and a Jewish school setting. In this essay, Schwartz provides an accounting of a day school's moral development, and describes the moral development curriculum that he instituted.

Sonsino, Rifat, and Daniel B. Syme. *Finding God: Ten Jewish Responses*. rev. ed. New York: UAHC Press, 2002.

While there is only one God, views about God have not been monolithic. Sonsino and Syme present ten different views of God from biblical through modern times in an accessible but sophisticated way. Some of them are collective views of the Bible and Rabbis, and others are individual views of such thinkers as Philo, Maimonides, Luria, Spinoza, Buber, Steinberg, Kaplan, and Fromm. The book helps people connect to Jewish sources and perspectives on God beyond their images as young children.

Wright, Jr., J. Eugene. *Erikson: Identity and Religion*. New York: The Seabury Press, 1982.

One of Erikson's first writings was about the life of Martin Luther. Yet, too often, the religious world ignores the wisdom of Erikson, discarding this philosopher and psychologist as too humanistically, rather than religiously, oriented. Wright examines the key concepts and explores their implications of Erikson's theory for religious practitioners.

CHAPTER 12

Jewish Early Childhood Education

Maxine Segal Handelman

At Purim time, Linda's four-year-olds wrote letters to their families with pictures taken of the children in their costumes. As the children copied their addresses onto their envelopes, the teachers asked, "What town do you live in?" The children came from several local towns. The teachers got out a map and began to mark the home of each child. The class took a walk to the post office to mail their letters. Along the way, they looked at trees and bushes getting ready to sprout new leaves, saw houses with children's bikes and scooters parked in front, and enjoyed the new warm weather. When they returned to their classroom, they made a list of all the things they had seen, and then went on to talk about the other things that made a community. The children mentioned stores, doctor's offices, a synagogue, and a fire department. The teachers asked, "How could we make our community in our classroom?" and the children exploded with suggestions.

INTRODUCTION

Jewish early childhood education has existed in one form or another through the ages. Not too long ago in North America, this education largely consisted of synagogue nursery schools geared toward three and four-year-olds for a few hours a day or a week. Recently, such education has expanded well beyond nursery school. Jewish preschools and day care centers, serving infants through kindergartners and hosting parent/child classes as well have begun to emerge. Jewish early childhood programs have also begun to focus on the Jewish education of families, as well as children.

A major goal of Jewish early childhood education is to nurture in children the development of a strong, positive, warm Jewish identity and a love for Judaism. We strive to foster in children the desire and the ability to grow into Jewish adults who are proud of their heritage and happy and able to participate in Jewish life. This is not some-thing achieved in a vacuum, with children alone. Our work includes the families of the young children in our care. If the family is not involved in its own process of Jewish education and development, then the Jewish growth of the child will have no foundation on which to stand and no basis from which to continue growing once the child leaves the Jewish early childhood educational setting.

To achieve this goal — the foundation of a Jewish identity that will sustain the child, indeed the family, through an entire lifetime — the Jewish education made available to the child and family must be absolutely the best education possible. The curriculum, defined as everything that happens while the child is at school and then some, must be tailored to offer each and every child the best access to a warm, positive Jewish world. Teachers who strive to reach this goal must be able to balance, on a day-to-day basis, what they know about teaching and how children learn with what they know about their particular students. Teachers must also be able to bring to the classroom a wealth of secular and Jewish knowledge and then weave these areas together.

The same concepts that sustain us as Jews sustain the early childhood classroom. God, Torah, and Israel must inform the foundation that supports the classroom. Similarly, Shabbat and the Jewish holidays serve to provide the basic framework upon which everything else in the early childhood classroom is built. Even so, God, Torah, Israel, Shabbat, and the holidays can not be concepts separate or apart from the general curriculum. These elements must be threaded through, with secular themes peppered with Jewish concepts and vocabulary.

Judaism does not happen separately from the rest of a child's life. Children are busy learning about the entire world. It is as easy for a child to go from observing a worm slithering on the ground to wondering about God as it is for that child to pick a couple berries off of a bush and declare them to be a pair of eyes. For Jewish early childhood education to be effective, it must integrate everything in the child's world. Separating Jewish concepts and experiences from secular concepts and experiences builds the foundation of a fragmented Jewish identity. An excellent Jewish education strives to make connections between Jewish events and everyday events. The excellent Jewish early childhood classroom is a model of Jewish living, in which the atmosphere and the environment is Jewish every day.

JEWISH EVERY DAY

The children in Linda's class began creating their houses, and other buildings in the community, out of different shaped boxes. Not all the children in the class were Jewish, so rather than ask them to look for mezuzot at home, Linda took them on a mezuzah hunt through the JCC of which the school was part. Even before Linda could make the suggestion, one of the children exclaimed, "I need to make a mezuzah for my house." All the children began to discuss what materials they could use to make their mezuzah. Pretty soon, every house in the children's community had a beautiful, and different, mezuzah.

Jewish is not something we do when we go to synagogue or to grandma's house for *Seder*. Jewish is who we are all the time; it is a part of every decision we make and every activity we choose. A young child does not divide experience into compartments until he/she is taught to do so. If we compartmentalize the Jewish experience for children, if we have one circle time a week in which we sing Jewish songs and make Shabbat, but do not include anything Jewish into the rest of the circle times that week, then we do our children a disservice. This teaches children that Judaism is just another thing to do, and that is not honest. Judaism needs to flavor everything that happens with children. In other words, Judaism must inform every aspect of the curriculum.

The Unspoken Curriculum

Flavoring every aspect of the curriculum with Judaism begins with the physical set up of the classroom, the unspoken curriculum. Jewish images should be integrated with the secular images that fill the room. In classrooms for older children that

post vocabulary lists, or "Words we know," Torah should be included alongside "train," and *lulav* right next to "lollipop." Jewish holidays and Shabbat should be added to the circle time calendar. In classrooms of younger children, Jewish symbols should be visible everywhere alongside secular symbols: Jewish symbol-shaped cookie cutters mixed in with the rest of the play dough toys, Jewish party store glitter in water bottles to play with, teacher-made shaker jars with Jewish symbols sponge painted on the sides. In every classroom, Jewish books should fill the children's bookshelf along with secular books, Jewish and Israeli music should be heard in classroom throughout the week, Jewish puzzles should be available alongside of secular puzzles. Other images and materials that help integrate Judaism into the classroom every time a child or parent walks into the room include:

- signs on the door in Hebrew and/or transliteration declaring *Shalom* or *B'ruchim HaBa'im* (Welcome).

- information about and explanations for families about what their children are doing and learning Jewishly. ("On Fridays, we eat *challah* for Shabbat" "At nap time, we listen to Jewish lullabies.") Signs can be laminated and used from year to year ("We are carrying flags for Simchat Torah!").

- posters of Jewish life cycle events, Jewish holidays, Israel scenes, map of Israel, Noah's ark, Hebrew *alef bet*, number chart with Jewish pictures etc. The posters should be laminated and rotated between rooms.

- pictures of Jewish values and *mitzvot*, such as *bikur cholim* (visiting a person in the hospital), *shalom* (a child helping two other children to stop fighting), or *tikkun olam* (children recycling).

- photos of the children in the class engaged in Jewish activities (eating *challah*, looking at a *lulav*, touching the *mezuzah*), enlarged, laminated, and mounted at eye level. These pictures can also be collected into a photo album for children to look at and share with their families.

- Israeli flag.

- pictures from Jewish calendars and Jewish catalogs, cut out and mounted with Contact paper at children's eye level, or even on the floor in younger classrooms.

- Jewish calendar for the teachers to use, hung in the classroom at adult's eye level.

- children's art work, related to Jewish things happening in the room (e.g., body outlines with Hebrew and English labels, apple prints, *mitzvah* tree leaves, handmade *tzedakah* box, Bible scenes created by children).

- sponges and cookie cutters in Jewish shapes for painting.

- Hebrew newspapers for covering the tables during art projects.

- Jewish foods (plastic *challah*, *matzah*, etc.) and kosher/Jewish ethnic food boxes in the house corner.

- stuffed Torahs.

- Jewish stamps mixed in with other stamps and stamp pads.

- Jewish star pasta, Jewish stickers, and Jewish glitter shapes (obtain from a party store).

- punches for cutouts in the shape of Jewish objects.

- real Jewish objects for children to see and touch: metal *Seder* plate, *graggers*, large *dreidels*, *chanukiyah*, candlesticks, *Kiddush* cup, spice box, etc.

- Israeli scarves for dress up.

- Jewish holiday cloth napkins and tablecloths for the house corner.

- stencils of Hebrew letters and Jewish objects.

- Jewish software for schools with computers.

- Jewish games - Games like *Lotto*, matching games, and *Dominoes* are commercially available with Jewish themes and graphics. Commercially produced board games, such as *Torah Slides and Ladders* or *Magical Mitzvah Park*, may also be appropriate for your classroom.

- props for the block area to facilitate synagogue, Jewish life, and Israel play (for example, camels, stained glass blocks, Jerusalem stone blocks, people with *kipot*, castle blocks, etc.).

- blocks with Hebrew letters and Jewish pictures.

- magnetic Hebrew letters, as well as English ones.

- catalogs from Judaic stores and old New Years cards to cut up.

Laying the Foundation

Of course, a physical environment that integrates Judaism into the whole curriculum is just the first step toward establishing a classroom that is Jewish every day. We must go beyond the unspoken curriculum and examine what really makes us Jewish. It is not only Shabbat and the holidays, for being Jewish is far more than sharing in a common religion. Judaism is a culture, and for all our differences, Jews are One People – *K'lal Yisrael*. We are united in our commitments to God, Torah, and Israel (both the People and the country). We are bound by common values, language, stories, music, food, and traditions. Judaism even guides how we treat other people and our relationship with God.

All of these factors are essential in the Jewish early childhood classroom, if we seriously strive to give children a foundation for Jewish life and identity that will last their whole lives. Employing Jewish values, Jewish culture, and Jewish "ways of being" as underlying features of everything that happens in the classroom will create an environment that serves the whole Jewish child.

Jewish values, and the rituals and behaviors they lead to, serve to make us *kadosh* — distinct, special or holy. Anyone can go visit someone who is sick in the hospital. In and of itself, that is not a Jewish behavior. But when one considers that *bikur cholim*, the *mitzvah* of visiting the sick is just that, a *mitzvah* — a commandment — then visiting the sick takes on a unique significance. It's not just a nice thing to do, it's something we are *expected* to do, *commanded* to do. Visiting the sick is part of what makes us Jewish, because when we visit the sick, we model our behavior after God's behavior when God visited Abraham as he recuperated from his circumcision. Modeling our behavior after God's makes our own actions holy and, in turn, makes us holy.

Many Jewish values, *mitzvot* and *middot* (Jewish virtues) are an essential part of the fabric that makes an early childhood classroom Jewish every day. Some of these include *shalom* (peace), *tikkun olam* (repair of the world), *tza'ar ba'alay chayim* (compassion to animals), *bikur cholim* (visiting the sick), *hachnasat orchim* (hospitality), *kavod* (respect), *gemilut chasadim* (acts of loving-kindness), and *tzedakah* (charity). (For more information about these and other values, *mitzvot* and *middot*, see Handelman, 2000; and Freeman, 1999.) A teacher who familiarizes him/herself with various Jewish values can make them come alive in the classroom. When a child helps pick up garbage from the playground, a teacher can say, "Molly, you are doing the *mitzvah* of *tikkun olam*! You are helping to take care of the world God made for us." If a child is home sick from school, the teacher can present the challenge to the children at circle time, "Ari has the chicken pox. This gives us a chance to fulfill the *mitzvah* of *bikur cholim*, taking care of the sick. What can we do to make Ari feel better?" When we explicitly bring Jewish values and *mitzvot* into the classroom, our children begin to learn how to approach the world with a Jewish viewpoint. When a child understands and bases his/her behavior on Jewish values, and not just human decency, the child is building a Jewish vocabulary and a Jewish foundation that will serve the child throughout his/her whole life.

GOD, TORAH, AND ISRAEL

The community being built by Linda's class continued to grow, even though the class had largely moved on to other things. As the class began to prepare for Yom HaAtzma'ut, the children asked, "Where is Israel?" They looked on a globe, and then Linda got out a map of the Middle East and clearly marked Israel. She hung the map on the wall some distance from the map that marked each child's home and the teacher's, and connected the two maps with a string. A few days later, two of the boys asked Linda to hang an airplane they had made from a paper towel roll above the map of their community. Linda asked, "Where is the plane going?" Without hesitating, the boys answered, "To Israel!"

God, Torah, and Israel are fundamental Jewish concepts. How we interpret these concepts may vary from person to person, but they form the foundation for Jewish life in general and life in the Jewish early childhood classroom as well. You may wonder whether it is possible to run a classroom while always looking at the curriculum and thinking about God, Torah, and Israel. It is not only possible, it is essential. When these concepts form the framework from which all the rest of curriculum

emerges, then your classroom will naturally be Jewish every day. When God, Torah, and Israel are filters that color everything that takes place, the children gain a better sense of who they are, and are better prepared to go out into the world and feel pride as a Jew and competency as a human being.

> When Omer came into my kindergarten class with no English skills, I was forced to summon every scrap of Hebrew that I knew to communicate with her and to allay her fears. I would spend time after school looking up terms in my Hebrew-English dictionary so that I could give her instructions in math and reading. I arranged for the specialty teachers to come into my classroom to give instruction to the class because she felt safe in class, but cried when she had to move around the school. The class also learned to use Hebrew terms. We all were delighted when Omer began to open up to us, making jokes in a mixture of English and Hebrew. That class went on to excel as Hebrew students, perhaps because Omer made Hebrew a living, important language for us. I, too, went on to study Hebrew.
>
> *(Maura Pollak, Tulsa, Oklahoma)*

Inviting God into your classroom, sharing Torah in a meaningfully consistent way, and making Israel a daily part of your environment and routine, requires a shift in how you approach student learning. Each is a worthwhile, meaningful layer of the Jewish early childhood setting. However, do not try to add all of them at once! The task will seem too overwhelming and, as a result, no meaningful changes may occur. It may be helpful to think about which of these layers feels most natural to you right now, and start with that one. As the year progresses, or as you are reflecting on your teaching next year, you can add still another layer to the one with which you have already become comfortable.

Inviting God In

In order to let God into the classroom, teachers must be at least somewhat comfortable talking and thinking about God. This is certainly not to say that teachers must know what God is. If that were the case, very few people would consider themselves qualified to teach about God. Rabbi David Wolpe (1993) assures us that when it comes to God and making meaning of our lives, we can often give what we don't have. In fact, it is not our task as adults to transmit to children an exact copy of our faith and idea of God. Rather, it our task to use our own faith — questions, ideas, and even doubts — to help children develop their own paths. It is our responsibility to help children develop their own ideas of God in a way that is valuable and true, both to the traditions we hold and to what we know about the world.

To help children, we do need to have some sense of our own spirituality, or idea of God. Before we can really hear and deal with children's questions, we need to have asked our own questions about God, and have sought out some answers. We don't necessarily need to have *found* the answers, but we must be looking. Rabbi Daniel Gordis (1999) tells us that Jews are God-wrestlers — doubt is part of the equation. Yet Gordis warns us about sharing too many of our doubts with young children. In every aspect of life, it is our duty to assure children that they are living in a good, secure, safe world. The same guidelines apply to helping children think about God. Though we should never lie to children, it is not dishonest to help them grow up believing that God is loving, caring, and treasures every human being, including them.

Never be afraid to tell a child, "I don't know." It's okay, in fact important, for children to know that grown-ups don't have all the answers about God (or almost anything else in life). Making up an answer to a child's question could lead to mistrust and/or the necessity to unlearn later. Instead, say to a child, "I don't know. What do *you* think?" Then listen to the child's answer, and ask questions to help the child expand on his/her own ideas of God.

Our job as teachers is to allow children the space and safety to explore God. There are many strategies to help children think about how the world works. The most valuable world explorations come when children learn that each person is created *b'tzelem Elohim* — in the image of God. Being created in God's image means that every person has value, every person is deserving of respect and caring. When children know that they are created *b'tzelem Elohim*, their own self-worth is bolstered, and it is safer, and easier, to ask questions about God and the rest of their world.

There are countless ways to find evidence of God in a child's everyday world. Try watching the clouds for a few minutes, or wondering together over the miracle of a child's hands as you wash up for snack. It is possible to create opportunities to explore God, as well. Following are a few of the best ways to help children think about God; there are many others.

Shirley Newman teaches about "discovering God's secrets" (Wachs, 1998). She suggests having children collect leaves that, at first glance, seem to be exactly the same. As the children examine the leaves, they will discover that indeed, none of the leaves are identical to any other. Then, show the children a sheet of postage stamps or stack of matching postcards. Upon examination, the children will discover that these person-made things are all identical. They have just discovered one of life's secrets. When people make things using machines, the objects all come out the same. When God makes things in nature, no two are the same. The question then becomes, "Why did God do that?"

When children ask where God is, or how we know God exists if we can't see God, take a glass of water and some sugar. Let the children taste the plain water. Put the sugar in the water and stir it until all the sugar dissolves. Can the children see the sugar? Let the children taste the sugar water. Can they tell the sugar is in the water, even though they can't see it? It is just the same with God. We can find evidence of God in the world, even if we cannot see God.

The easiest, and also the hardest, way to help children explore their questions about God is to make "God-talk" a regular, normal part of the classroom. Gordis tells us that God-talk is not teaching our children anything specific. "Rather, God-talk is about making our children comfortable with the word 'God' as a part of their regular vocabulary" (1999, p. 60). If teachers refer to God in a comfortable, regular manner, then children will know it is safe for them to talk about God and explore their own understandings (e.g., Let's thank God before we eat our snack. Why do you think God made the animals talk differently than us? Did God build this table? How did God help build this table?).

Sharing Torah with the Youngest Children

The Torah is the greatest treasure of the Jewish

People. When we see the Torah, we are filled with joy. This is a very important concept, that can be taught to very young children, even infants. It is possible to foster this love and excitement in the classroom setting. Begin by exposing the children to Torah. A few stuffed Torahs, store-bought or homemade, should be permanent residents of every classroom. (These are not just for very young children; fours and fives should have stuffed Torahs, too, in addition to Torah scrolls they can unroll and "read.") These stuffed Torahs should be a special part of the classroom. Children should be encouraged to hug their Torahs, kiss their Torahs, and treat their Torahs with a little more respect than the average stuffed toy. One day care child I know always napped with the classroom stuffed Torah as his pillow.

Our regular preschool curriculum is interspersed with Hebrew vocabulary, beginning prayers, and blessings. We teach about the various Jewish holidays both culturally and traditionally, through song, story, art projects, and cooking activities. We stress a love for Shabbat from the first week of school. We try and teach the kids respect for each other, the earth, animals, and the community. Our children are proud to be Jewish.

(Kim Lausin, Beachwood, Ohio)

If a sanctuary is available, young children (infants, too) should be taken to visit the Torah scrolls. If there is no sanctuary on site, arrange to take a field trip to a nearby synagogue where children will be welcomed and where they can "meet" the Torahs. With an air of great awe and excitement, open the *Aron Kodesh* (Holy Ark). Help children touch the Torahs and marvel at their beautiful decorations. If older preschool children (four and five-year-olds) study the Torah portion every week, perhaps the younger children could join them just for the dancing and singing when they take out the Torah. Even if no one else is present, teachers can take out a Torah (with permission) and dance and sing with infants and toddlers. Teach children to give the Torah a kiss, touching the Torah and then kissing their hand. Tell the children that inside the Torah are the best Jewish stories ever. Use the Hebrew names for Torah decorations and related synagogue items, so children can learn them, too.

With the permission or help of synagogue clergy, open a Torah so two and three-year-olds can see the Hebrew writing inside. With close supervision, let children touch and hold the Torah decorations. Shake the *rimmonim* (bells) for infants so they can hear the bells. Twos and threes can hold the *yad* (pointer) and pretend to read from the Torah. Encourage the children to feel the *k'tonet* (mantle), and talk about the beautiful clothes the Torah wears. When children come on to the *bimah* (platform where the pulpit and *Aron Kodesh* are), remind them that it is a place where we respect the Torah, not a place to jump and play.

Looking, touching, and talking are just the beginning. Dancing and singing with the Torah will directly expose children to the joy that Jewish People everywhere feel about the Torah. If you have a small Torah, a homemade Torah, or even a stuffed Torah, a child or several children can hold it while everyone else sings songs such as *"Torah Torah,"* or *"Atyz Chayim Hee"* and marches behind the Torahs. You can adapt more difficult songs by replacing some of the Hebrew with English, while maintaining the meaning of the words. For example, the song *"Torah Aura"* may be transformed into: "I love the Torah, Torah Torah, it teaches me to do the things I should. Torah Aura, Torah Aura, Halleluyah!" You can follow the same model and adapt other songs, such as *"Al Shloshah D'varim"* or *"Aytz Chaim Hee."*

By familiarizing very young children with the Torah and its rituals, you pave the way for children to discover the wonders contained *inside* the Torah as they get older. When three-year-old children hear Torah stories, the stories should be specifically identified as stories that come from the Torah. These children can experiment writing a Torah as a *sofer* does, using black ink (thinned black paint) and big feathers. Spread Hebrew newspaper on the tables to show more of the written language that is inside the Torah. If children have been exposed to the joy of the Torah from the youngest age, they will be ready to study the Torah stories in a real way by the time they are four.

Sharing Torah with Four and Five-Year-Olds

The goal of sharing Torah with young children is not just to introduce children to a wonderful source of Jewish literature. The Torah is the root of many concepts and values which are essential to the development of Jewish identity. These concepts and values include:

- God created the entire world and everything in it.

- We are partners with God in caring for the earth and all living things.

- We are responsible for helping and caring for other people.

- The Torah is the story of the Jewish People.

- All Jewish people are one family.

- People can learn and grow, even if they make mistakes.

- God rested on Shabbat; therefore, we rest and celebrate Shabbat.

- The Land of Israel is the Jewish home, and our special place.

- Prayer is a way for us to talk to God, as individuals and as part of a group.

(Adapted from *First Steps in Learning Torah with Young Children* by Rivka Behar, Floreva Cohen, and Ruth Musnikow)

When sharing Torah with young children, we can integrate these concepts into their lives. Through the drama and beauty of the Torah stories, children will begin to develop their own concepts of and connection to God. Values found in Torah stories begin to take on new meaning as their relevance to the children's lives becomes apparent. When children hear the story of Jacob and Esau making up after being apart for so many years, the value of carefully maintaining their own sibling relationships comes into clearer focus. When children learn about God speaking to Abraham, to Rebecca, to Jacob, and to Moses on Mount Sinai, the possibilities of their own relationships with God begin to emerge. Torah stories link children to the vastness of the Jewish experience, and connect them to the wider Jewish community — for Torah is our story.

Israel Every Day

Israel is an essential element of any Jewish early childhood program. Israel is not just a country, not even just a Jewish country, which is a pretty amazing thing in itself. In 1903, when Theodor Herzl, the father of modern Zionism, proposed that the Jews accept the British offer of land in Uganda on which to establish the Jewish homeland, he was soundly voted down. Why? It wasn't because no one could find Uganda on a map, but because Israel has been the Jewish dream for thousands of years. In the Torah, the first thing God said to Abraham, the father of the Jewish people, was "Go forth from your native land . . . to the land that I will show you" (Genesis 12:1). God was talking about *Eretz Yisrael* — the Land of Israel. Throughout its history, the Jewish People has struggled to get to the land of Israel and stay there. A Jewish homeland just anywhere would not do. Only a Jewish homeland in *Eretz Yisrael* would suffice.

Our connection to, and love for, Israel is at the core of a Jewish identity. Our relationship with Israel connects us to other Jews all over the world. We strive to instill in young children a feeling of belonging to Israel because that particular place gives us so much: a sense of national pride, a connection to our history, a gathering place for all Jews, and a place to feel holy and close to God. While the concept of "country" is very difficult for young children, the concept of "home" is not. Israel is our Jewish home. We want children to love Israel, even if they don't understand just how far away it is.

To help children build a relationship with Israel, Israel needs to be an underlying theme not only during Tu B'Shevat and Yom HaAtzma'ut. It is important to help every child to think of Israel as his/her Jewish homeland. When a child leaves preschool, he/she should recognize the flag of Israel. Every child should know many words in Hebrew. The more Israel is personalized — with pen pals, stories of personal visits — the more concrete Israel will become.

What might we do to facilitate this? Have Hebrew and English food boxes in the house corner, Hebrew and English books on the bookshelf, and a map of Israel hanging in the class all the time. Teachers need to keep Israel constantly in mind. During a unit on winter, for example, you might say, "In Israel it almost never snows." There are many simple strategies, games, and props that will help bring Israel into your classroom. Integrating Israel will take some conscious thought and effort to become familiar with a basic Hebrew vocabulary. Many classes take an imaginary trip to Israel sometime during the year. This trip can only be meaningful if Israel is already a part of the children's every day classroom experience.

At a World Zionist Organization Early Childhood Conference in Israel in 1997, Dr. Ruth Pinkenson-Feldman discussed thematic approaches to teaching about Torah and the land of Torah (i.e., Israel). She said that the child in the Diaspora is born into an Israel of the imagination.[1] Unless (or until) children go to Israel, they can only imagine what it might be like (Zeskind, 1997). Thus, Jewish children need to be welcomed into a relationship with Israel. Through the thematic study of concepts such as the geography of Israel, seasons, lifestyles, music, dance, people, foods, and the holy sites, children can begin to construct social knowledge of our Jewish homeland. Using books, stories, pictures, and any other strategies they have at their disposal, early childhood educators need to do everything in their power to help flesh out each child's imagination of Israel so that each child understands basic concepts about the country.

SHABBAT AND HOLIDAYS

Jewish life is choreographed by the Jewish calendar. Shabbat gives us pause each week; Rosh Chodesh marks the passing of each month. And, scattered throughout the months are the Jewish holidays, each one with a story connecting us to our past, adding to the rhythm of Jewish life. Some of our holidays have a basis in Torah, such as Shabbat, Rosh Chodesh, Rosh HaShanah, Yom Kippur, Sukkot, Pesach, and Shavuot. Other holidays developed later, such as Chanukah, Purim, and Yom HaAtzma'ut. Whatever their origin, each of the holidays has something to teach us about ourselves and about who we are as a Jewish People.

The Jewish holidays are full of concrete symbols, exciting rituals, and important values. Beginning with the observances outlined in the Torah and combining those with all the foods, ceremonies, and celebrations that have been added through the generations, the Jewish holidays are designed to make Jewish life attractive and captivating for all Jews, adults and children alike.

All together, the Jewish holidays comprise a framework around which much of Jewish life revolves. In Israel, people can always be heard to say, "I'll do it after the *chagim* (holidays)." No matter what day it is, it seems there are always more *chagim* right around the corner. Still, the Jewish holidays do not define the entirety of Jewish life. God, Torah, and Israel are important parts of each holiday, yet these concepts also have great significance of their own. The same is true of Jewish values and *mitzvot*. Thus, it is important to remember that while learning about and celebrating the Jewish holidays should be an integral part of the early childhood curriculum, the holidays represent only one of many meaningful aspects of Judaism.

So, celebrate the Jewish holidays with your class. Make each holiday as rich and exciting and creative as possible. Resist the urge to water down adult observances so that the are "suitable" for children. Each holiday is already bursting with symbols, rituals, and celebrations in which children can participate. Then, always go beyond the holidays as you strive to make your classroom a Jewish place all of the time.

Shabbat

Shabbat is the holiest day of the week. From sundown Friday night, until an hour after sundown on Saturday night, Jews are blessed with a day of rest, a day of reflection and rejuvenation. The earliest mention of Shabbat is in Genesis 2, the account of creation story. In six days, God created the entire world: light, darkness, day, night, fish in the sea, animals, plants and human beings. By the seventh day, God finished the work of creating the world and rested. "And God blessed the seventh day and declared it holy, because on it God ceased from all the work of creation that God had done" (Genesis 2:3).

Most of us rush through the weekdays, packing in as much as possible into each day and night. Shabbat is our reminder to slow down, appreciate everything we have, and give back to the world instead of taking from it. Shabbat, especially Friday night, is filled with rituals to guide our experience. Friday is a busy day, getting ready for Shabbat. Shabbat is an island in time, and we want our stay there to be as pleasant as possible.

---

[1]This idea of "an Israel of the imagination" is beautifully represented in the children's book *And Shira Imagined* by Giora

Carmi, (Philadelphia, PA: Jewish Publication Society, 1988). The book is out of print, but well worth looking for.

In the classroom, Friday (or Thursday, if the children are not in school on Friday) should be a day which is different from every other day, a day which is special and distinctly given over to Shabbat preparations. Jewish or Shabbat music may be played all day, there may be special visitors or foods, and everyone might dress a bit nicer. All of this lays a foundation for the class to "make Shabbat" — to celebrate the Friday night rituals together.

Following are some tips to remember as you celebrate Shabbat with your class.

Blessings

1. *Involve the children as much as possible in saying the blessings* - Select a child to lead each blessing. Set the Shabbat objects on the table where the children are, not at a separate table.

2. *Tie meaning in to each blessing* - Encourage the children to wave their hands around the candles, even if the candles are only in front of you. With younger children, pass out the juice immediately before you say the blessing, or as you say it. Do the same with the *challah*.

3. *Make the moment as magical as possible* - Learn to sing the blessings. Tell impromptu stories as you make Shabbat. (It's magic! The candles are magically lit when we say the blessing and cover our eyes. Why do we cover the *challah*?) Sing Shabbat songs at the table. Use things the children have created (e.g., Shabbat place mats, flowers and vases, tablecloth, *kipot*, *challah* cover) during your classroom celebration. In adult/child classes, teach parents the blessing over the children, and bless the children after lighting candles. Make sure hugs and kisses are exchanged after the blessing.

A note about lighting candles:

Shabbat candles present early childhood educators with a dilemma. These candles are not birthday candles — we don't blow them out. One of our goals is to teach children this distinction. Yet, as early childhood educators, with classrooms full of active children, our number one job is to keep the children safe. It is sometimes risky to leave candles burning on a table with children nearby. One must carefully balance these two goals.

Light the candles, and move them to a safe location (a high shelf with nothing flammable nearby, a sturdy table or counter that children can't reach). Say something like, "We might not move our candles at home, but our *nayrot* (candles) are going to watch us make the rest of Shabbat from up here." Never leave burning candles unattended. When the children leave the room or move on the next activity, blow the candles out.

If there is no safe location for the candles, light the candles with the children, say or sing the blessing, then take the candles off the table, turn your back to the children and blow the candles out. If children ask why you blew the candles out, simply explain you blew the candles out to keep the children safe. Never encourage the children to blow out the candles. It gives the concrete message that we blow out Shabbat candles, even if you tell them every time, "We only blow out the candles in school."

> I did a great project with both a three-year-old and four-year-old class. After we learned the *parashah*, each child drew a picture of it. One of the teachers then wrote the child's description of his/her picture on the paper. We saved the pictures, glued them together, and attached them to paper towel rolls, so the child had a "Sefer Torah." Parents liked seeing the development of the children's drawing: for instance, in a number of cases you could tell the week that child started adding a body detail — like fingers!
>
> Once, the week we did the giving of the Torah, I told the class the *midrash* about every Jewish person standing at Mount Sinai. One little boy had me label the people he drew with his names and his friends — because they were there!
>
> *(Cheryl Cash-Linietsky, Philadelphia, Pennsylvania)*

Jewish Holidays in a Developmentally Appropriate and Emergent Curriculum

Generally, Jewish preschools have followed a time-bound curriculum, based on the framework of the Jewish calendar. In the fall we study relationships and forgiveness for Rosh HaShanah, we plant in the middle of winter for Tu B'Shevat, we bake *matzah* and tell the story of Moses in the springtime. Every Friday, we light candles, drink grape juice and eat *challah*. It is important that the rhythm of the early childhood classroom mirrors the rhythm of the cycle of the Jewish year. This study of each holiday in its turn unites the life of the classroom with the life of each family. As children study and celebrate Jewish holidays in preschool, they experience joy and gain the mastery they need to build a strong foundation of a Jewish identity.

Children learn best through play. Children play at the things that interest them the most. Acknowledging this, early childhood educators have begun to move away from pre-set themes and curriculum units toward topics and classrooms that are based on children's and teachers' interests. In a developmentally appropriate classroom, the curriculum is not directed by children or teachers alone, but rather results from interactions between teachers and children, with both providing ideas and developing them to create attractive and worthwhile themes (Cassidy, 1993). Emergent curriculum is a strategy designed to guide teachers through the process of DAP (developmentally appropriate practice), utilizing knowledge of child development, knowledge of individual children and knowledge of the families' cultural context. While it is essential that teachers formulate and strive toward long-range goals and objectives for each child and the group as a whole, emergent curriculum helps teachers balance long-range objectives with moment to moment opportunities based on child-teacher interactions and interests (Kostelnik, 1992).

Emergent curriculum is not a time-bound strategy. Topics in a developmentally appropriate classroom are studied as the interests of the teachers and children make them relevant. We study relationships and forgiveness when two children have a fight. We plant when children notice the trees beginning to bud. We bake and tell stories to support what the teachers and children bring to the classroom. We create classroom rituals based on the members of the classroom. Emergent curriculum does not proceed according to any pre-set calendar. Judaism imposes a calendar on us — a calendar based on the moon, the sun, and our rich tradition, preset by generations and unbending to the whims of young children and their teachers.

Idie Benjamin (1998) points out that too often Jewish teachers who do an incredible job making the secular aspects of their curriculum developmentally appropriate fall flat when it comes to the Jewish aspects of their curriculum. For the Jewish curriculum, many teachers revert to an overemphasis on teacher-directed lessons and art projects. While DAP does not rule out teacher-directed lessons, it does seek a balance between teacher-directed and child-directed activities.

How then does one go about a Jewish curriculum in a developmentally appropriate way? How do we balance the Jewish calendar that we are mandated to teach with the importance of making the curriculum relevant to the interests of the members of the class? The solution lies in the balance between those parts of the curriculum the teacher introduces and the parts the teacher allows the children's interests to dictate. It is developmentally appropriate for a teacher to introduce a holiday into the curriculum in its proper season, so long as he/she does not forget to address it in a developmentally appropriate manner.

Implementing Jewish developmentally appropriate curriculum requires a leap of faith. It requires the belief that children can and should be allowed to play with and absorb Judaism the way we allow them to play with and absorb other concepts in the curriculum. We want young children to grasp number concepts — to recognize numerals, master number concepts, love math. Do we sit children down and lecture them about the rubrics of addition and subtraction, make them recite their numbers one to 20 three times a day, give them precut numbers, and make sure they paste the numbers on their paper in the right order? Of course not! We give children objects to sort and classify. We count the children sitting at the table. We graph the children's favorite foods.

Judaism can be part of the life of the classroom in the same natural way as math. Children can be given the opportunity to paint with Jewish symbol shapes, wear the costumes of the biblical characters they have heard stories about, and to experiment with different Jewish candles. Many teachers fear that children won't develop the Jewish identity their parents sent them to Jewish preschool to obtain unless, for example, they impart every single bit of information about each holiday, unless the stripes on the children's Israeli flags are straight, and unless there are exactly eight branches plus a *shamash* on their *chanukiyah*.

In a developmentally appropriate Jewish classroom, there is a balance between the Jewish calendar and the everyday lives and interests of the members of the class. Teachers in such a classroom carefully consider the concepts of a Jewish holiday or topic and go with those that most closely connect to the lives of the children. Teachers in such a classroom are careful to engage children in the concept of the theme or holiday at hand with open-ended art experiences and those that result in recognizable ritual objects. Teachers in such a classroom employ strategies that will engage their students in the story and rituals of each Jewish holiday in the way that will best connect with each child. When this balance is struck, and when the Jewish areas of the curriculum are truly developmentally appropriate, then children can begin the process of building a strong, deep foundation of Jewish learning, a love for being Jewish and the foundation for a positive Jewish identity that will serve them their entire lives.

FAMILY EDUCATION

After the children in Linda's class had been working on their neighborhood for a while, it was time to move on. Rather than dismantling the children's work and sending the pieces home, Linda moved the entire neighborhood, with the maps and other documentation, displaying it in the hallway outside of the classroom. As they dropped off and picked up their children, the parents took time really to look at the neighborhood and ask their children lots of questions, learning volumes about how and what their children were learning every day.

The child is only one of the students in the early childhood classroom. The families of the children we teach are not only essential partners in the process, but also students of our classrooms and schools. Earlier it was noted that the building of a Jewish identity does not happen in a vacuum, taught by the school alone. The family must be engaged in its own process of Jewish education and development in order to provide a foundation for the child's developing Jewish identity and support for continued growth once the child leaves the Jewish early childhood setting.

Still, the parents, and indeed all the members of the child's family, are important learners in their own right. For many families, enrolling their child in a Jewish preschool begins the family's "return to Judaism." Some families may include a parent who converted to Judaism, or who is not Jewish. Many adults may have had marginal relationships with Judaism, with Bar or Bat Mitzvah marking their last period of Jewish study. Choosing a Jewish preschool over all the other secular options is a significant decision. The family is opening itself up to grapple with a tradition perhaps set aside for a long time. It is the responsibility of the early childhood program to provide parents with a quality Jewish education along with their children.

There are many strategies for teaching parents. Some of these are detailed below.

- *Make the learning visible* - Post brief descriptions of the process children went through, things children learned, and simple explanations, along with children's finished work. ("The children used apples cut in half dipped in red paint to stamp designs on the New Year's cards. This gives the children small motor practice, teaches the color red, and helps connect apples to Rosh HaShanah.") Photographs of the children working toward the displayed finished project really help bring the documentation alive.

- *Send home written materials aimed at adults* - Include explanations of holidays and holiday customs, information on ways to celebrate Shabbat, and resources of where to find more information. While the materials should be geared toward the life of a young family, it must written for an adult audience.

- *Send home children's projects with adult-level explanations* - Always enable your parents to act as their child's teacher. The projects you send home do not always need to look like what they are supposed to be. Children will learn more about *matzah* by examining and sketching a piece of *matzah* than they will by painting on corrugated cardboard. Providing parents with a bit of information about the project will enable them to be their child's teacher (For example, "We eat *matzah* for the eight days of Passover to remind us of our Exodus from Egypt. Your child examined a piece of *matzah* and drew his/her image of *matzah*. Ask your child what *matzah* tastes like to him/her.")

- *Invite parents in for Jewish moments* - Shabbat, Torah study, holidays — engage parents in the Jewish learning going on in the classroom. Whenever possible, use parents for Jewish field trips as well. For example, go on a *sukkah* hop to the homes of children in your class, and invite parents who do not build a *sukkah* at home (yet!).

- *Create theme backpacks* - families can borrow backpacks on such topics as new siblings, moving, divorce, death of a grandparent, and so on. Be sure to include Jewish resources, such as books and blessings.

I love taking my preschool Shabbat morning group on "field trips." Each trip provides not just a chance to reinforce the theme for the week, but also connections with the larger *shul* building and community. For many parents of young children, this is also their first introduction to the world beyond the children's room. When Pesach approaches, we always read *Everything's Changing, It's Pesach!* by Julie Jaslow Auerbach (Kar-Ben Publishing, 1986). Then we go outside looking for signs of spring. We peer through the fence at the garden next door, and walk down the sidewalk in front of *shul* looking for buds on the trees. We do the same trip at Rosh HaShanah, this time looking for signs of fall. At Shavuot, we make flower wreaths to wear (use the flowers with stems of flexible wire that can be easily twisted together). Then we each take a small handful of flowers (pre-cut from larger fake sprays) and go through the building looking for all the places where we learn Torah. At each place, we put flowers — on the *Aron*/Ark in the children's room and in the chapel, on the Rabbi's doorknob, on the stairs where the teenagers have their discussion group. When we walk through the building, I talk about what the big people are doing in the big *bayt knesset*/sanctuary, and we stop to peer *very quietly* through the door. I use the language of the service (Torah service, *Haftarah*, *D'var Torah*, Musaf), reinforcing the terms they hear the adults use around them, and helping them to practice some *shul* deportment (although in general ours is a very kid-friendly *shul*, with children coming and going from the sanctuary at all times).

(Anne Johnston, New Haven, Connecticut)

- *Send a Shabbat bag home with a different child each week* - The bag could include candlesticks, *Kiddush* cup, *challah* cover, candles, a small bottle of grape juice, and *challah*, along with the appropriate blessings. You might also put in a small stuffed animal as a Shabbat guest. Including a journal encourages families to reflect on their experience and read past entries to see what other families have done. This journal also helps teachers and directors to evaluate the use of the bag and the project.

- *Offer parent workshops* - A Rabbi or other community educator could be the perfect person to offer learning opportunities for your parents that combine parenting concerns with Jewish life.

- *Include Jewish learning in all family events* - Make sure that no matter what the program is, Jewish moments are integrated, even if it's just the blessing before snack.

- *Suggest Jewish activities for play groups* - Provide or suggest Jewish books, music, games, activities, and even Hebrew vocabulary, that can bring a Jewish layer to play groups in which the families in your school are involved.

When we teach our parents as well as our children, we help each family build a strong foundation of Jewish identity. This ensures that as our children move out of early childhood, their families will have the skills to help them continue growing and developing Jewishly.

NON-JEWISH TEACHERS

Many Jewish schools employ non-Jewish teachers out of necessity; not enough qualified Jewish ones apply. A non-Jewish teacher can be a real asset in a Jewish school, providing diversity on the staff by offering different viewpoints, helping other staff members consider their own opinions, and putting a new spin on old ideas. The non-Jewish teacher can also act as a connection to non-Jewish children who may be in the program.

Furthermore, a non-Jewish teacher is often an eager learner in a Jewish setting. Recognizing that he/she is now being required to teach about Judaism, this teacher ideally asks many questions and seeks out opportunities to learn more about Judaism and the Jewish holidays. These teachers sometimes possess no less Jewish knowledge than some of their Jewish counterparts. An excellent early childhood educator is someone who is constantly learning. *Pirke Avot* (Ethics of the Fathers) tells us, "Provide yourself with a teacher, and acquire a friend" (1:6).

A non-Jew can be a very good educator in a Jewish setting, with some intentional thought and study. A teacher with a weak or non-existent Jewish background should take an honest look at what he/she doesn't know, and find ways to learn more. One shouldn't aim to learn it all this week; savor the process of learning. Make it a habit. A teacher seeking more Jewish knowledge could find a friend to teach him/her the *alef bet*. He/she could join a Jewish current events discussion group or ask the school director or Rabbi to suggest a list of good Jewish books or authors, and set a reasonable reading goal. He/she could pair up with a friend and read the same Jewish book, then do lunch and discuss it. One might do something for each holiday that will help him/her to learn in action, for example, going to synagogue or getting invited to someone's home celebration. A teacher could research enough to write the classroom newsletter. One could read the Torah portion, regardless of whether he/she plans to go to synagogue to hear it read. Basic Judaism or conversion classes often welcome all learners, not just those planning to convert. Other strategies for building a stronger Jewish knowledge base include visiting a Jewish museum or Jewish exhibit, taking a Jewish cooking class, or simply searching the word "Jewish" on the Internet. A teacher would be wise to call up an observant Jewish friend and ask questions about his/her practices and to ask the families of the children in the class about the Jewish things they do in their family, and the reasons for doing them. The more a teacher knows about and feels for Judaism, emotionally and intellectually, the more easily he or she can make her classroom a place where Judaism is a natural, daily occurrence.

Once a non-Jewish teacher has begun to learn about Judaism, a director, mentor, or other teacher can be instrumental in helping him/her implement and integrate Jewish aspects into the classroom. Teaching and transmitting a culture that is not one's own is a challenging task. Besides enriching their own Jewish knowledge, non-Jewish teachers are encouraged to create a Jewish atmosphere, integrating Judaism into the classroom with Jewish music, visuals, etc. Inviting a Jewish grandmother or grandfather to volunteer regularly in the classroom can also help supplement the Jewish atmosphere in the classroom.

Always Remain Honest

While it is certainly the job of a non-Jewish teacher in a Jewish school to create a Jewish atmosphere and to teach and transmit Jewish culture and religion, a non-Jewish teacher should never lie about who he/she is. Young children are very much engaged in the process of figuring out who they are. One of the ways they do this is by comparing what they know about themselves to what they know about others.

As children come to understand that they celebrate or observe certain things, they seek to find out who around them celebrates the same thing. One standard conversation that comes from four-year-olds in almost any Jewish preschool around December goes like this: "I celebrate Chanukah. Do you?" Because of more and more intermarried families with multiple observances, a not-uncommon question is: "I only celebrate Chanukah. What do you do at your house?" Children not only ask other children these questions, they ask their teachers, too.

Non-Jewish teachers should always be honest when children ask them questions about their own practices or celebrations. It is perfectly appropriate to tell children, "No, I don't celebrate Chanukah in my home, but I like to light the candles at school." With any response a non-Jewish teacher gives, he/she must always be honest, expose children to non-Jewish people and practices in a positive way, validating the child's Jewish self and practices, and teaching respect for others. It is also important to validate Jewish ways of being and identification for Jewish children, especially since this is most likely why their parents sent them to a Jewish school in the first place.

THE JOYS OF JEWISH EARLY CHILDHOOD EDUCATION

Nowhere in the field of education can you touch the heart of a family the way you can in early childhood. At no other time do children rely on their teachers as much, cuddle or nourish their teachers as much, as in early childhood. Ilene Vogelstein notes, "Nowhere else can we instill Jewish values and a sense of Jewish identity unencumbered by years of resistance, absence, or misinformation." (Vogelstein, 2002). Toddlers who motion their hands for you to sing *"David Melech"* again and again, three-year-olds who work together to build an *Aron Kodesh* for their stuffed Torahs, four-year-olds who, after studying the Torah portion week after week ask, "Why did God talk to Moses on the mountain?" — all these are part of the day-to-day joy of Jewish early childhood education.

Young children are amazing in their ability to learn from every situation, their eagerness to explore and find out why, their vulnerability at trying to make new friends. Framed in a Jewish context, the whole experience is raised to a higher plane. In a Jewish preschool, the task is not only to set children on the road to becoming good people, but good *Jewish* people. Watching this Jewish identity begin to form and helping children take ownership of their Jewish selves is a breathtaking experience.

Jewish early childhood education is the key to our continuing community, the link to our future. It is incredible to be part of the journey.

CHALLENGES OF JEWISH EARLY CHILDHOOD EDUCATION

Finding teachers to rise to the task of early childhood Jewish education is sometimes a daunting challenge. Teachers with strengths in Judaism as well as early childhood education are even more difficult to find. By and large, the field of early childhood is a low paying field; Jewish early childhood education is no better. It takes incredible dedication to stay in a highly demanding, albeit highly rewarding, field for very little money.

Integrating Jewish and secular curriculum can be a challenge for many teachers. For too many teachers, "Jewish" only happens on Shabbat and holidays. The challenge comes in making every day feel Jewish, in establishing a classroom where Jewish books are read every day, Jewish music is as likely to be heard on a Tuesday as on a Friday, and where children don't distinguish between the Jewish parts of their lives and the secular.

It can also be a challenge to remember to teach the Jewish parts of the curriculum in the same developmentally appropriate way that the rest of the curriculum is taught. Many teachers are so concerned that the *Seder* plate the children make look like a real *Seder* plate that they forget children learn best by investigating and making their own decisions, not by assembling pieces the teacher pre-cut into a project that looks exactly like every other child's project. Early childhood teachers often feel that there is so much information that must be covered for each Jewish holiday that they forget what they know about how children really learn. A three-year-old need not know everything about Rosh HaShanah. She will study it again when she's four, and five. Slow down. Letting children learn Jewish content the same way they investigate other things will result in a stronger foundation, and a true love of learning.

CONCLUSION

May you go from strength to strength as you embark on this journey. May you discover the joy of a classroom that is grounded in Jewish values and the basics tenets of Judaism. May your children always benefit and prosper from your dedication. Amen.

TEACHING CONSIDERATIONS

- Young children learn best through active, hands-on exploration. Their environment, therefore, must be filled with real things for them to work with. Jewish objects, such as Shabbat candlesticks, *Kiddush* cups, non-breakable *Seder* plates, Israeli flags, and various kinds of "Jewish candles" (Shabbat, Havdalah, Chanukah, *Yahrzeit*) must be available for children to play with, not just on a shelf or in a cabinet for Shabbat or holiday times.

- In order to help children build the foundation of a warm, meaningful Jewish identity, Judaism must be a meaningful part of every day, integrated into the general curriculum, not something added on. Jewish books and music must be available and used throughout the week. Jewish and Hebrew vocabulary must frame each day and be woven into each curriculum unit.

- Remember the fundamental concepts that make us all Jewish. God, Torah, and Israel must be active, living elements of every day.

- More than the People have kept Shabbat, Shabbat has kept the People. Shabbat in the early childhood classroom should be a vibrant weekly celebration, filled with song, story, food, and friends.

- Jewish holidays should be prepared for and celebrated in the same excellent, developmentally appropriate way the rest of the curriculum unfolds. Children's interests should be a determining factor in the direction of the curriculum. Within the framework of the Jewish calendar, time should be used as flexibly as possible to allow children to explore fully the concepts that most interest them.

- The families of young children are our students as well. Each family is involved in its own process of Jewish education and development, which must be nurtured by the early childhood professionals. Jewish identity is formed in early childhood; the family must have a strong foundation as well in order to help the child continue growing beyond the Jewish early childhood setting

ADDITIONAL VIGNETTES FOR DISCUSSION

Passover has just ended. The next two weeks include Yom HaAtzma'ut, the Week of the Young Child, and parent conferences. In addition, the snow has finally melted and spring has arrived.

1. How can the teachers include the celebration of Israel Independence Day and the Week of the Young Child in developmentally appropriate ways, given that much of their energy is being diverted to parent conferences?

2. How can Israel be a part of the classroom the entire year, and not just now for Yom HaAtzma'ut?

3. What are some common themes that might connect Passover, Yom HaAtzma'ut, and springtime?

To help the children feel a real ownership in their classrooms, the school has decided to dedicate each door with a mezuzah hung at the children's level. In the process of teaching the children about mezuzot, one of the teachers asked her children to search their homes and count the mezuzot on their doors at home. Some of the children in the class are not Jewish, and the parents come to the director to complain, claiming that their children are now upset that they do not have a mezuzah at home.

1. How could this situation have been avoided?

2. Now that the mistake has been made, what are some steps the teacher and director can take to address the parents' concerns?

3. How can a unit on *mezuzot* be taught, with sensitivity to both Jewish and non-Jewish children who might not have a *mezuzah* at home?

BIBLIOGRAPHY

Books and Articles

Behar, Rivka; Floreva Cohen; and Ruth Musnikow. *First Steps in Learning Torah with Young Children.* New York: Board of Jewish Education of Greater New York, 1993.

> Comprehensive curriculum for learning Genesis with four to six-year-olds. A companion curriculum for Exodus was published in 1995. For more information and an order form, consult the BJE web site: www.bjeny.org/early_child-hood_education_depa.htm

Benjamin, Idie. "Doing Early Childhood Education Appropriately and Jewishly." *Jewish Education News* 19(3), 1998, 25-26.

> Benjamin defines the current trend toward developmentally appropriate practice — a stage based, child-sensitive approach to early childhood education — and shows how it may be applied to the Judaic program. She suggests ways to make the Jewish curriculum more experiential and sensory, and less concrete and factual.

Cassidy, Deborah, and Camille Lancaster. "The Grassroots Curriculum: A Dialogue Between Children and Teachers." *Young Children* 48 (6), 1993, pp. 47-51.

> Follows the development of an emerging curriculum, covering the teacher's role in the planning process and patterns of emergent curriculum.

Freeman, Susan. *Teaching Jewish Virtues: Sacred Sources and Arts Activities.* Denver, CO: A.R.E. Publishing, Inc., 1999.

> A helpful introduction to *middot* (Jewish virtues) and ways to become a *mensch*. For teachers of students in K-adult.

Gordis, Daniel. *Becoming a Jewish Parent: How to Explore Spirituality and Tradition with Your Children.* New York: Harmony Books, 1999.

> A guide for parents who want to introduce Judaism into their homes so that their children can grow up loving, understanding, and cherishing their heritage.

Kostelnik, Marjorie. "Myths Associated with Developmentally Appropriate Programs." *Young Children* 47(4), 1992, pp. 17-23.

> Debunks nine of the most widely held myths about developmentally appropriate practice.

Vogelstein, Ilene. "Jewish Early Childhood Education: The Gateway To Synagogue Renewal and Renaissance." *Jewish Education News* 23 (1), Winter 2002, pp. 37-39.

> In making the case for Jewish early childhood education as a tool for synagogue renewal, Vogelstein paints a clear picture of the need and benefits of Jewish early childhood education for all.

Wachs, Saul. "Talking To Little Children about God." *Jewish Education News* 19 (3), Fall 1998, pp. 35-36.

> We can encourage children to "do theology" — to think about God. As we do so, they are learning to make meaning of their experience through God-talk.

Wolpe, David J. *Teaching Your Children about God: A Modern Jewish Approach.* New York: Henry Holt and Company, 1993.

> A beautiful book, filled with *midrashim*, perfect for helping adults help children to discover God.

Zeskind, Margie. *Teaching Israel in the Diaspora.* Miami, FL: Central Agency for Jewish Education of Greater Miami, 1997.

> Curriculum inspired by attendance at a WZO Early Childhood Conference in Israel in 1997. A good look at early childhood education in Israel and how we can use that to teach Israel outside of the country. Available from the CAJE Curriculum Bank, 800-CAJE-ERC.

Curriculum Guides

Chubara, Yona; Feinberg, Miriam P.; and Rena Rotenberg. *Torah Talk: An Early Childhood Teaching Guide.* Denver, CO: A.R.E. Publishing, Inc., 1989.

> This book contains Bible accounts from Abraham through Moses retold for young children, each of which is followed by a huge number of creative activities in various modalities. Includes ideas for introducing the stories that are both age appropriate and true to the biblical text.

Feinberg, Miriam P., and Rena Rotenberg. *Lively Legends — Jewish Values: An Early Childhood Teaching Guide*. Denver, CO: A.R.E. Publishing, Inc., 1993.

> Ready to read stories from the Jewish tradition about Rabbis and Sages, kings and common folk, donkeys and bees, each of which is followed by creative activities in a number of modalities. Age appropriate in language and length, the stories teach important Jewish values.

Goodman, Roberta Louis, and Andye Honigman Zell. *Head Start on Holidays: Jewish Programs for Preschoolers and their Parents*. Denver, CO: A.R.E. Publishing, Inc., 1991.

> A three-year cycle of holiday programs for two to four-year-olds and their parents. These 25 programs include quality projects, patterns, and stories to take home and use when celebrating the holidays.

Handelman, Maxine Segal. *Jewish Every Day: The Complete Handbook for Early Childhood Teachers*. Denver, CO: ARE Publishing, Inc., 2000.

> A guide to help integrate into the Jewish classroom the best that the secular field has to offer. This outstanding and comprehensive book will enable every teacher to create a Jewish developmentally appropriate classroom, one in which Jewish values and themes permeate every learning experience every day. God, Torah, and Israel, the cornerstones of Judaism, are fully explored.

Machon L'Morim: B'reshit Curriculum Guides. Baltimore, MD: Center for Jewish Education, 1998.

> A professional development program for Jewish Early Childhood Educators designed to facilitate the integration of Jewish concepts and values into everyday secular themes. For more information, contact Program Director, *Machon L'Morim: B'reshit*, Center for Jewish Education, 5800 Park Heights Avenue, Baltimore, MD 21215, 410-578-6948, FAX: 410-466-1727.

Mushnikow, Ruth. *First Steps: Learning and Living for Young Jewish Children*. New York: Board of Jewish Education of Greater New York, 1980.

> A curriculum for young children three through eight that follows the Jewish calendar, with sections devoted to holidays and special events. Includes practical suggestions for integrating Jewish living with the developmental and cognitive needs of young children.

Regosin, Ina, and Naomi Towvim, eds. *Milk and Honey: Five Units Integrating Jewish and General Curricula in the Early Childhood Setting*. Boston, MA: The Early Childhood Institute, Board of Jewish Education of Greater Boston, 1990.

> Each of these five curricula units helps teachers of young children to integrate Jewish values with general curriculum areas such as music, math, science, art, language arts and dramatic play. Units include: Reading Plus — children's books with Jewish Themes and Values (Ages 3-5); Noah and the Flood (Age 3); Noah's Ark (Ages 4-5); The Mishkan — Building Community from Biblical Bases (Ages3-5); and Familiar Games the Jewish Way (Ages 3-5).

Silverberg, Sheila, and Margie Zeskind. *Webbing Out with the Jewish Holidays: Connecting the Holidays, Israel, Jewish Values and the Torah To Our Young Children*. Miami, FL: Helene and A.B. Wiener Early Childhood Department, Central Agency for Jewish Education, 1999.

> A compilation of original poems, webs, concepts, and curriculum ideas with additional selected recipes and curriculum projects taken from sources on the reference list. Wonderful examples of webs for each holiday.

Jewish Early Childhood Web Sites and List Serves

Note: We are fortunate, in today's era of the Internet, to be benefiting from resources specifically for Jewish early childhood educators. All of the following resources are relatively new. Some of the list serves are more active than others. I expect this list will be in need of corrections in six month's time. In any case, explore the web sites, join the list serves, and become part of the conversation. We have so much to learn from each other, so much to teach. Thank you to Avital Plan, Amy Weisman, Ruth Pinkenson Feldman, Ilene Vogelstein, Martha Katz, Rhonda Mlodinoff, and Betsy Rotberg and others (please forgive any omissions) who continue to work to make these resources available to all of us.

www.bjesf.org/ECEhome.html

> The BJE of San Francisco established this site in December 2000, and it is dynamic — full of Jewish early childhood ideas and information that changes monthly. To join their list serve, send an e-mail to ece@bjesf.org

www.jewishearlychildhood.com

Amy Weisman is a pre-kindergarten teacher in South Florida who, tired of the lack of Jewish EC teaching sites, decided to establish her own. It is rich with resources for every holiday, and includes reviews of teacher resources and a place for a teacher exchange.

www.groups.yahoo.com/group/JECEE

On the web site is a link to the Jewish EC Educator's Exchange list serve, or you can go to it directly.

www.jcca.org/thisnewmonth

The JCCA (Jewish Community Centers Association) web site primarily focuses on ideas for celebrating Rosh Chodesh (the New Jewish Month).

www.machonlmorim.org

This is the web site of Machon L'Morim B'reshit, the amazing program of Jewish education for early childhood teachers in Baltimore. Besides information about the program, the site provides a wonderful assessment tool for Jewishly evaluating your classrooms and school.

cajeearlychildhood-subscribe@yahoogroups.com

This is a list serve through the CAJE Early Childhood Network. You can sign up by e-mailing them.

www.groups.yahoo.com/invite/jewishreggio

One more new list serve is designed specifically for Jewish early childhood educators who are interested in or who already are implementing the Reggio approach in their school or classroom. Discussion topics focus on integrating Jewish concepts and values in a Reggio classroom. To sign on, go to the site.

www.uahc.org

This is the official web site for the Union of American Hebrew Congregations. Go to the Youth site to find a curriculum bank with lesson plans. "The Parent Page" has some great ideas, activities for parents to do with their children at home.

www.jajz-ed.org.il/child

This web sites is from the Early Childhood Division of the Department of Jewish Zionist Education, the Jewish Agency for Israel. On this site you will find information, activities, projects, and articles relating to Jewish early childhood education in Israel and around the world.

www.jesna.org

JESNA has an "ECE Toolkit," a large collection of both Jewish and secular resources for early childhood educators on the web. The Jewish Early Childhood Educators' Electronic Toolkit is designed to bring together a broad range of Judaic and general education curricular materials, activities, and resources for the professional development of early childhood educators in Jewish settings. Go to the site and click on the early childhood focus area.

www.torahtots.com

This is a very active, busy, and colorful site. They have games and activities for preschoolers. The *parashah* on parade" tells the story in a fun way and can be used as a teacher resource. The site is from an Orthodox perspective, and provides lots of valuable information.

CHAPTER 13

Creating Programs That Captivate Jewish Teens

Debbie Findling

THE SCENE[1]

The scene is familiar to most of us who work with adolescents:

A group of teens, gathered on a weekend retreat, are assembled at Shacharit morning services. The requisite prayers are squeezed in between syrupy rhyming poems about love, and ubiquitous pop songs like "You've Got a Friend." The 50 or so teens are sitting in a circle on folding chairs or lounging on the floor. Most are not paying attention. Rather, they are braiding each other's hair, giving choo-choo-train formation shoulder massages, or simply daydreaming.

Now imagine a different possibility (same weekend retreat, same 50 teens), but replace apathetic interest with dynamic engagement.

On Saturday afternoon, the teens are divided into several groups based on the various prayers of the morning service. Each group receives an educational packet describing their prayer. The materials include historic information about the derivation of the particular prayer, both traditional and alternative methods of praying, and spiritual-theological connections. The groups meet to learn about their assigned prayer and to create methods for leading it at services the following morning.

After dinner on Saturday night, 16-year-old Gabrielle introduces herself as the spokesperson for the Birchot HaShachar group. She distributes Siddurim, and cryptically asks her peers to place the Siddur by their bed before going to sleep that night. Everyone giggles, but most comply.

Early Sunday morning, the teens awake to find brightly colored construction paper signs plastered

throughout the dorm (surreptitiously hung the night before — after lights out — by the Birchot HaShachar group). The sign above 15-year-old Jaimie's cot reads, "Upon opening your eyes this morning, for what are you grateful? Read Birchot HaShachar on page 13 of your Siddur." On another floor, bleary-eyed Derrick ignores the sign above his bed and the Siddur on his nightstand. However, upon stepping into the warm steam of the shower he sees a sign posted on the shower curtain that reads, "May the Force Be with You," along with a request to read the section of Birchot HaShachar about the force of God's holiness.

As the teens make their way to the recreation hall for services, 14-year-old Sara is there to greet them on behalf of the Shema group. She hands each teen a wedding invitation announcing the marriage between the teens and God. During their assigned part of the service, the Shema group holds a makeshift tallit chupah overhead and asks the others to sign a ketubah covenant outlining God's obligations to them and their respective responsibilities toward God and each other.

Later in the service, the Amidah group explains that one of the 18 benedictions that comprise the "Amidah" is a sort of cheer in praise of God. The Amidah group then leads an Adonai Wave — complete with explanations about and chanting the various names for God.

How does a random group of teens evolve from lethargic apathy to one filled with resolute energy? Specifically, what does it take to create engaging and meaningful opportunities for Jewish teens? Although there are many possible answers to this question, I believe the answer with the most prom-

---

[1]The examples and vignettes in this chapter are an amalgamation of case studies of Jewish teen programs and classes. They are drawn, in part, from the experiences of educators of Jewish teens who were fellows in Tikea: A Fellowship for Educators of Jewish Teens in the San Francisco Bay Area, which was funded by the Richard & Rhoda Goldman Fund. Names, locations, and specifics have been changed.

ise lies in the professionals who work with teens. The question then becomes: "What do educators need to know to create enticing and engaging opportunities for teens?"

JEWISH TEENS TODAY

To answer the question of what educators need to know, it is first necessary to have an understanding of Jewish teens today.

Jewish teens are, first and foremost, teens. They share the same quirks and desires, challenges and accomplishments as their classmates and neighbors. In general, North American teens are more programmed and overburdened than teens of previous generations. They spend the majority of their waking hours inside a single institution — school — engaged in curricular and extra-curricular activities. As Charles Kedushin and his co-authors put it, "High schools constitute mini-communities with their own norms, sub-cultures, and status hierarchies."[2] Extracurricular activities confer status and popularity within the school community; therefore, unstructured activities and those unrelated to the school community are neglected.

Furthermore, "as they get older, adolescents spend more time in paid employment. More than 80% of U.S. adolescents work during their high-school years, typically 15-20 hours per week."[3] Moreover, "more than 90% of high-school seniors expect to go to college and more than 70% look forward to working in professional jobs." However, they are "unsure and anxious about how to negotiate what has become a difficult transition into adulthood. What they do know is that they must excel in the competitive school environment."[4] Teens have little extra time for activities unrelated to the real demands of school and the perceived and oftentimes real pressures of getting into a good college and competing in the professional marketplace.

Given the high demands on teens today, one might conclude that Jewish activities don't stand a chance. However, that doesn't have to be the case. In addition to being self-absorbed, rebellious, and withdrawn, teens are also altruistic. Religion can be

an avenue for teens to explore magnanimous values by providing opportunities for them to give back to the community. Judaism, in particular, emphasizes *tikkun olam* (repairing the world) as meritorious, and many *mitzvot* (commandments) obligate us toward humanitarian acts. Judaism offers a plethora of possibilities for teens to explore their benevolent spirit.

> I was amazed how teaching seventh graders turned me into a self-conscious adolescent! After a couple of girls gave me some sarcastic compliments, I found myself worrying about which clothing I would choose — would they whisper to each other about the length of my skirt or the colors in my scarf? I had to remind myself that it doesn't matter that I won't meet their fashion criteria and that, most importantly, I needed to model confidence in my personal choices, whether it be to don a *kipah* or to wear long strands of beads.
>
> (Diane Schon Wirtschafter, Berkeley, California)

Furthermore — and perhaps surprisingly — research indicates that teens today place significant value on the role of religion in their lives. In a national survey, close to 60% of high school seniors reported that religion was important to them. In another survey, more than 75% said they believed in God and had prayed at least occasionally.[5]

Although teens report that they are interested in philanthropic endeavors and religious activities, participation in Jewish life among teens continues to decline. Current research reveals that nearly 50% of 13-year-olds participate in a Jewish educational program of some type. But by age 18, fewer than 25% of these young people will be involved in any organized Jewish activity.[6] There is a clear discrepancy between what captivates the interest of teens and what the Jewish community currently offers.

Teens participate in Jewish life through the auspices of community centers, summer camps, social action and educational agencies, youth movements, synagogues, and Hebrew schools, among

[2]Charles Kedushin, et al, *Being a Jewish Teenager in America* (Waltham, MA: Cohen Center for Modern Jewish Studies, Brandeis University, 2000), 7.

[3]Ibid.

[4]Ibid.

[5]Ibd., 8.

[6]Ibid., 26.

others. While teens carry a heavy load, like most of us, they make time for activities and events that they deem worthwhile. Given the array of attractive options for teens today, Jewish teen programs must provide compelling programming if the level of disaffiliation that occurs after B'nai Mitzvah is to be reduced. One way to achieve this goal is to strengthen the educators of Jewish teens.

For pre-teens, sometimes solving interpersonal issues is more important than teaching the lesson I've planned. Or, maybe more correctly, sometimes I have to change my lesson so that they learn Jewish values by solving their crisis of the moment. I was teaching seventh and eighth graders in an isolated community. The *yid-dishkeit* in this town was tremendous — they had 100% affiliation! But that meant that the children saw the same faces, year in and year out, from the time they were preschoolers until they left for college. One Sunday morning, following an away *Shabbaton* (retreat), I walked into a class where my eight students had each burrowed into a corner (quite a feat in a small square room!), refusing to talk to the others. I made the mistake of trying to teach my planned lesson, thinking I could draw them out using non-emotional history. But at this age, anything can be made emotional, and every comment offended someone. In the end, it was clear to me that the lesson needed that day was about *sh'lom bayit* — about making peace at home. The secondary lesson that they needed was that in the Jewish community, we have professionals to whom we can turn when everything looks bleak. I walked across the hall and told the Rabbi that we needed to trade classes. I taught his lesson, and he helped the middle schoolers learn that there are Jewish ways to make peace, and that to do so is essential to the continuation of our people.

(Anne Johnston, New Haven, Connecticut)

WHO ARE EDUCATORS OF JEWISH TEENS?

Unlike other professions with well-defined demarcations and protocols, the field of Jewish teen work has no clear modus operandi. In general, Jewish teen education and programs can be divided into two categories: formal and informal. Formal education usually refers to school-based education and activities, whereas informal education encompasses camps, community centers, youth groups, and other after school programs. Unfortunately, the term "informal" is often incorrectly construed to mean trivial or superficial experiences, as opposed to casual, relaxed, yet nonetheless important learning. In response, some educators have adopted the term "non-formal" education to describe these activities. That term, however, is also predisposed to similar misunderstandings.

Complicating matters, there is an assortment of terms used to describe the professionals who work with teens. These include program provider, youth worker, teen worker, teen communal worker, teacher, and educator. Furthermore, agency titles — which reference one's role in an organization — span the gamut: worker, counselor, coordinator, supervisor, director, and manager. Moreover, when describing what they do, many teen professionals see their work in relation to the teens rather than in relation to their portfolios or organizational hierarchy. They often describe themselves as guides or mentors. In need of a more descriptive title, the teen manager at one Jewish Community Center, for example, used to refer to himself half mockingly as "the cool teen guy."

As the field of Jewish teen education evolves, the need for some shared language is imperative. Until that time, I prefer the term "educators of Jewish teens" as a catch all description of the professional and the term "teen education" to describe the field. In my opinion, whether you are the lifeguard at a Jewish resident camp or a history teacher at a Jewish day school, you are undeniably engaged in the holy work of Jewish education.

Indeed, many professionals are drawn to Jewish teen education because they possess a natural rapport with teens and a passionate desire to connect them to Judaism in new ways. Countless educators joined the field while still teens themselves — working as teaching assistants in their synagogue's religious school or as counselors-in-training at summer camp. However, many lack the education and experience necessary to provide significant Jewish learning and connections. A sort of catch-22 exists in the profession of Jewish teen education. Professionals who are attracted to working with teens and who possess that enigmatic teen chemistry are often young — generally in their 20s and early 30s. However, many lack the requisite education and experience to integrate Jewish content into their programs and to navigate successfully the nonprofit organizations under whose auspices Jewish teen programs occur.

The result is that far too many young professionals burn out quickly. Agencies frequently report yearly turnover in their teen program staff — ultimately a disservice to the teens the organization is aiming to serve. In exit interviews, these professionals report low pay, little recognition, and most importantly, a lack of training and professional development opportunities as reasons for leaving the field.

Yet, national and local experts consistently cite knowledgeable, qualified professionals as a key to creating successful Jewish teen programs. Some researchers emphatically regard the teen educator not merely as *a* key factor, but *the* key factor. A recent Brandeis University survey noted that 92% of respondents identified staff as a key to successful teen programming — the highest percentage given to any contributing factor.[7] Another study notes that the personality and experience of the teen communal worker is the most important factor in developing a strong teen program.[8]

Given the magnitude of a qualified educator in relation to a successful teen program, supporting their erudition is imperative. Specifically, then, what do educators of Jewish teens need to know in order to succeed?

WHAT EDUCATORS OF JEWISH TEENS NEED TO KNOW

In order to create enticing and engaging opportunities for teens, Jewish educators need to be knowledgeable in four overlapping areas: (1) adolescent theory, (2) organizational development, (3) pedagogy, and (4) Jewish content. Each of these areas is described below.

Adolescent Theory

Most of us have at least some vague recollection

from Introduction To Psychology courses about the pioneering Swiss psychologist and philosopher Jean Piaget.[9] For those who need a refresher, Piaget's four stages of cognitive development include sensorimotor, preoperational, concrete operational, and formal operational.

As a brief summary, the sensorimotor stage is designated roughly during the first two years of infancy. During this stage children discover relationships between their own bodies and the environment through touching, sucking, tasting, and feeling. Ages two to six — encompass the preoperational stage, wherein a child's thinking is self-centered. During the concrete operational stage, typically occurring between the ages of 7 and 12, children learn to reason logically and to organize coherent thoughts; however, abstract reasoning is challenging. The formal operational stage begins at approximately 11 to 12 years of age and continues through adulthood. This stage, of most concern to those of us who work with teens, is characterized by the ability to formulate hypotheses and systematically test them to arrive at answers to problems. Other characteristics include the ability to think abstractly, to understand mathematical structures, and to present an argument — even one contrary to fact.

This chapter is not intended to imply that educators of Jewish teens should plan theoretical mock trials debating mathematical tables. Rather, even a basic understanding of adolescent maturation cycles is helpful to those who work with teens. In general, we can glean from Piaget and the work of other child and educational psychologists that adolescence is a fraught with huge cognitive, developmental, physical, emotional, psychological, and spiritual changes. As we plan activities and programs for teens, it is imperative that we create safe spaces that are both explorative and challenging. For example, one educator of Jewish teens monitors popular culture, including movies, music, television, and the Internet, to glean ideas for teen programs. He explains, "I try to put myself in their shoes — whether it is something like the Columbine shootings or the tags that the Muslims have to wear in Afghanistan. I try to find things that directly affect their lives."

---

[7]Amy L. Sales, *Jewish Youth Databook: Research on Adolescence & Its Implications for Jewish Teen Programs* (Waltham, MA: Cohen Center for Modern Jewish Studies, Brandeis University, 1996).

[8]Gary Tobin et al, *Bay Area Teen Needs Assessment*, (New York:

JCC Association of North America and Waltham, MA: Cohen Center for Modern Jewish Studies, Brandeis University, 1995).

[9]See Chapter 11, "Developmental Psychology" by Roberta Louis Goodman, pp. 85-108 in this Handbook.

Another factor in adolescent development relates to the context of family. Recognizing that teens live in a family system is fundamental toward creating meaningful opportunities for them. It is perhaps surprising (yet reassuring) to note that research consistently negates the myth that parents and teens are inevitably at war. "Contrary to the popular image of adolescent rebellion and parental impotence, only 5-10% of families experience a significant deterioration in parent-child relations during adolescence."[10] Moreover, parents "exert a strong influence on adolescents' values, aspiration, and behaviors."[11] Parents and teens are partners in the family structure; therefore, teen programs would benefit by supporting the family dynamic.

When teaching American Jewish History to seventh and eighth graders, I often read picture books aloud. Recently our focus was Eastern European immigration to America from 1880-1920. I discovered that there are many, many excellent picture books on this topic, with wonderful illustrations. When I first read aloud to middle school students, I thought they would think it was babyish, but they loved it. Once children are past third or fourth grade, teachers rarely read to them, but they still really enjoy it.

(Cheryl Cash-Linietsky, Philadelphia, Pennsylvania)

Teen family education programs, however, are admittedly controversial. Based on the philosophy that teens need time and space away from their parents in order to explore their identity, many educators consider teen family education programs lethal. Nevertheless, to extradite teens completely from the family system is neglectful. At minimum, it is advantageous for educators to have an appreciation of the parent-teen family construct when conceiving of and planning activities for teens.

In addition to the influence of parents on teens, the teen programs themselves occur at Jewish organizations. This leads us to the second area of what teen educators need to know — organizational development.

Organizational Development

Teen programs occur within the auspices of Jewish organizations, which are complex systems with several interconnected components, including lay leadership structures, professional staff, customers or populations served. Furthermore, these organizations exist within the framework of the larger Jewish community. Grounding teen programs in an understanding and appreciation of these milieus is crucial. To navigate this complex system successfully, what do educators of Jewish teens need to know?

Understanding of the limitations, capacities, culture, norms, structures, and policies of the larger Jewish community and the organizations through which the teen programs occur are all compelling factors toward creating engaging offerings to teens. Savvy educators of Jewish teens understand that certain conditions need to be in place before success can occur, and the most skilled professional can actually help build readiness for change.

These conditions include three basic ingredients: awareness, knowledge, and commitment. Specifically, lay leaders, professionals, parents, funders, and other stakeholders must be aware of the importance of teen programs, knowledgeable about what it takes to create vibrant teen programs, and, finally, committed to providing the necessary resources and support to ensure success.[12] Networking with stakeholders and marketing dynamic teen programs are two ways educators can bolster the significance of such programming.

Moreover, the organization itself must be committed to teen programming. Even part-time educators of Jewish teens can build organizational awareness and knowledge. Where appropriate, educators can get involved in organizational decision making to ensure that the agency supports a wide range of teen activities. Furthermore, involving youth in those planning and decision making venues both empowers the teens and extends the web of stakeholders.

In Jewish nonprofit organizations, the stakeholders typically include lay committees and boards, volunteers, management level directors and supervisors, and direct service professionals (also called line workers and program staff).

---

[10]Charles Kedushin, et al., 6.

[11]Ibid., 7.

[12]See Chapter 44, "Creating a Synagogue Youth Culture" by Tami Miller, pp. 474-489 in *The Jewish Educational Leader's Handbook*, Robert E. Tornberg, ed. (Denver, CO: A.R.E. Publishing, Inc., 1998).

Educators of Jewish teens are usually direct service professionals whose name derives from the fact that unlike purely managerial or supervisory roles; they work directly with a specific population, namely teens. The function of lay committees and boards may include setting policy, fund-raising, development, and in some cases management and supervision. Far too often, the professionals who work with teens are distant from the influential lay leaders and, in turn, the lay leadership knows little about the teen professional or teen programs. Developing a good rapport with lay leaders is beneficial to the organization, the professional, and ultimately to the teens. The same is true for the supervisory relationship. Depending on the culture and norms of each organization, most educators of Jewish teens have a supervisor assigned to provide guidance and support to them. Developing a good working relationship, including regular meetings for reflection and feedback, is essential. Regular or periodic evaluation from supervisors and colleagues is also indispensable. Feedback from others can validate and affirm what one is doing well and serve to point out areas that need attention.

In addition to good relationships with lay leaders, supervisors, and colleagues, educators of Jewish teens should have at least a cursory knowledge and at best expertise in other organizational components. These include budgeting, fund-raising, grant writing, public relations, and marketing. Furthermore, many teen programs are in competition with one another for limited resources. Coordination, cooperation, and collaboration are too often absent in Jewish teen programming. One educator of Jewish teens recently commented, "It's frustrating that we can't all work together because everybody is struggling with not getting enough support — everybody is trying to hold on to what they've got."

Pedagogy

In addition to an understanding of adolescent theory and organizational development, educators of Jewish teens should indeed *be* educators. That is, they should understand pedagogy — the art of teaching. After all, our mission is to offer teens various avenues to learn about, find meaning in, and take pleasure in being Jewish.

Here, we need to go back to Introduction To Psychology and our friend, Piaget. Although not an educator and never enunciating rules about pedagogy, Piaget's work has been "revered by generations of teachers inspired by the belief that children are not merely empty vessels to be filled with knowledge (as traditional pedagogical theory had it) but active builders of knowledge."[13] Piaget likened adolescents to little scientists who are constantly creating and testing their own theories in the world. To push the metaphor, as educators of Jewish teens, it is our role to set up the lab. We provide the beakers, the slides, and the specimens, allowing the teens to look through the magnifying glass of life and Judaism to test their own hypotheses and create their own conclusions. This is not to say that we simply set up the lab and depart; rather, we can and should simultaneously guide and co-create along with them.

Jewish Content

Finally, along with an appreciation of adolescent theory, organizational development, and pedagogy, educators of Jewish teens should have a relationship with Judaism. Unlike the other three areas, Jewish content seems to be the hardest to quantify. How much Jewish content is enough? Does an educator need to be observant of *mitzvot*? Can an educator of Jewish teens question or struggle with a belief in God? I believe there are two simple answers to these seemingly complicated questions.

First, and foremost, all educators must also be learners. Educators of Jewish teens should invest in their own learning. It is hoped that the organizations in which they work will value and support professional development and learning opportunities. Judaism has a lot to say on the matter. For example, Maimonides taught that a parent must not ignore his/her own study of Torah, for just as it is a commandment to educate his/her child, so, too, is the parent commanded to educate him/[her]self (*Mishneh Torah* 1:4). We can reinterpret this teaching to apply to educators as well. Later in the same chapter, we read that every Jew is required to study Torah, whether poor or rich, healthy or ailing, young or old and feeble. Furthermore, Rabbi Menachem Mendel of Kotzk

---

[13]Seymour Papert, "Child Psychologist Jean Piaget," in *Time 100: Scientists & Thinkers — Jean Piaget*,

http:www.time.com/time/time100/scientist/profile/piaget.html, 2.

taught that if you truly wish your children to study Torah, study it yourself in their presence. They will follow your example. Otherwise, they will not themselves study Torah, but will simply instruct their children to do so.

Jewish tradition certainly values lifelong learning, but how much study is enough? Again, Jewish sources weigh in on the subject. Proverbs 24:7 teaches that a foolish student will ask, "Who can possibly learn the whole Torah . . . ?" While a wise student will say, "I will start with a beginner's book, then I will study the Five Books of Moses, and continue from there until I have mastered the whole Torah." Similarly, Isaiah 28:10 teaches that learning Torah should be precept by precept, line by line, here a little, there a little. Educators must be committed to their own learning, at the same time recognizing that learning takes time.

Second, in addition to study, I believe that educators of Jewish teens should have a meaningful relationship with Judaism. Each of us must decide for ourselves what constitutes a meaningful relationship. Teens are also struggling with creating meaningful relationships with Judaism. As we learned from Piaget, the formal operational stage may begin in late adolescence, but it continues through adulthood. Depending on the organizational culture and the particular Jewish community in which you work, talking with teens about your own joys and challenges in your relationship with Judaism may not only be appropriate, but also encouraged.

Each of the four areas of focus — adolescent theory, organizational development, pedagogy, and Jewish content — is equally essential in creating vibrant, engaging activities for teens. And as mentioned earlier, there are no clear-cut delineations between them, and overlap is a necessary condition.

CASE STUDIES

The following two case studies provide illustrative examples of the four areas of focus. The first case study, "The Night Hike," presents a case in point in which the educator effectively incorporates each of the four areas of focus. The second case study, "Playing Our Roots," illustrates a situation in which a lack of organizational support proves costly.

The Night Hike

Jake, a 27-year-old outdoor educator at a Jewish resident camp in Colorado, provides an illustrative example of utilizing key elements of each of the four areas of focus to create a more vibrant teen program at camp.

Jake spent his childhood summers at the camp, worked as a counselor-in-training, a senior counselor, and was eventually promoted to oversee the camp's teen wilderness program. Although he describes himself as Jewishly committed, he acknowledges the limitations of his Jewish education, which is based mostly in his hazy memories of Bar Mitzvah preparation and the informal Jewish education he gleaned at camp. Jake is a skilled environmentalist, particularly knowledgeable about the local flora and fauna. He holds undergraduate and graduate degrees in environmental planning, and is able to translate that knowledge into engaging outdoor adventures for teens. Jake reports, however, that his ability to incorporate Jewish content into his environmental curriculum is limited to vague understandings about tikkun olam as the Jewish value of repairing the world.

One of the highlights of the teen wilderness program is the annual solo night hike. The teens begin the hike at dusk, when the summer sun still dances through the trees. The hike continues in complete darkness (save for a few flashlights) and ends at a campfire, complete with s'mores and ghost stories.

The teens set out along a winding path, staggered one by one so they are a fair distance from the person in front of them and behind them. Reminiscent of the fairy tale about Hansel and Gretl, as the teens gingerly walk into the woods, they stumble upon strategically placed notes along the path to guide them. The first note reads, "What color is the sky?" Farther along, a note prompts the teens to listen to the sound of the birds. After the path creeps slightly uphill and the sun sinks below the horizon's crest, a note posted near a fern grove asks, "How many colors of green do you see?" The experiential reflections and trigger questions continue as the teens hike deeper into the woods: "What does dusk look like?" "Can you hear the insects?" "Close your eyes and smell the woods."

While proud of the environmental education that the hike offers, Jake yearned to find content rich avenues for incorporating Jewish education into the night hike beyond the ubiquitous tikkun olam concept. In a proactive response, Jake talked to his supervisor, who suggested he read several passages from Beresheet (Genesis). Jake also consulted with the camp Rabbi and several teens.

As a result of his study and consultations, during the following camp session, Jake moved the solo hike from a weeknight to Saturday evening. And this time, the trigger questions read: "In the Torah we read that God created light by separating the light from the darkness. As the sun sets, can you separate the light from the darkness? Squint your eyes until darkness appears." And, "Thinking about ecology, why do you think God created trees and plants before animals?" And, "In the Torah we read that God gave all the seed-bearing fruit to us to eat and the green plants to the animals to eat. Can you find and name a seed-bearing tree and a green plant?"

Finally, before concluding with the bonfire and marshmallows, Jake asked the camp Rabbi to help him lead the teens in a star-filled Havdalah service that extols the beauty and power of nightfall.

In this way, Jake used his knowledge of adolescent theory — solo night hikes appeal to teens' need for individuation and sense of adventure. He tapped into the organizational structure — accessing the wisdom and guidance of his supervisor, colleague, and teens. Through an understanding of how teens learn, he incorporated pedagogic techniques to engage them, and integrated Jewish content into his teaching methodology.

For Discussion

1. In addition to incorporating passages from Genesis, what other Jewish sources might Jake consider to deepen the Jewish content of the night hike?

2. Jake was fortunate that he had access to a network of support — his supervisor, a colleague, and teens — to help him integrate more Jewish content into the night hike. However, some educators of Jewish teens work in environments in which they don't have ready access to colleagues. What might these educators do to tap into networks of support?

3. Can you think of other creative ways that Jake could incorporate Jewish content into wilderness education? What about your work? Is there

a program or class that you offer that teens find exciting and engaging, but lacks significant Jewish content? What could you do to pump up the Jewish volume?

Playing Our Roots

Elana has been entertaining her family and friends since she was a child — composing and singing silly songs that poked loving fun at family members or corralling her sisters into performing original plays in their small kibbutz apartment. Some of the plays were so good that she even charged admission to the other kids on the kibbutz, who eagerly forked over their meager ice cream allowance to be entertained by Elana's theatrical performances on hot summer afternoons.

After serving in the Israeli army and graduating from college, Elana moved to the United States to pursue a graduate degree in theater. It wasn't long before she was discovered by the local Jewish community and recruited to teach Hebrew in the community-wide afternoon high school. The teens loved Elana's classes because she infused her Hebrew teaching with dramatic elements. On any given day, a passerby might see the teens standing on tables making animal noises as Elana called out the names of animals in Hebrew. On other days, the teens would be engrossed in reading Hebrew poetry then composing poetry of their own. Although Elana enjoyed teaching Hebrew in the high school, she wanted to incorporate more drama into her work and longed to connect her teaching to extended family that she remembered from her childhood on the kibbutz.

Elana had an idea for an intergenerational drama program for the twelfth graders in the school. She had noticed an attrition pattern whereby the incoming class of nearly a hundred ninth graders would shrink to less than half that size by the twelfth grade. Elana's dream was for the twelfth graders to learn about drama techniques and theatrical production while connecting them to their Jewish roots.

Elana had a good relationship with the school principal, whom she liked and respected. In the teacher's lounge one afternoon, Elana casually proposed her dream to the principal. The principal immediately loved the idea and enthusiastically encouraged Elana to implement it the following semester. The school principal was so committed to the program that she agreed to allocate extra money from the school budget to cover the necessary added costs involved in producing such a large-scale performance. And, once the project started, the principal often dropped by to lend needed assistance and even donated props and building materials.

Elana's program, "Playing Our Roots," attracted 35 teens — more than twice as many as anticipated. The teens interviewed elderly residents of the nearby Jewish Home about their lives and their Jewish journeys, then turned their stories into a play, which was performed on graduation night to a full house of parents, friends, and the Jewish Home residents.

"Playing Our Roots" was a resounding success at the school. Lena, a 17-year-old participant explained, "I really enjoy learning the history of my people through an artistic way and not in a formal way." Elana was thrilled, and the teens were encouraging their friends to sign up for the class the following fall. However, some time toward the beginning of the summer, the principal of the school resigned. Neither Elana nor the principal had thought to market "Playing Our Roots" outside of the teens, their families, and the Jewish Home residents. Therefore, the school committee — and most of the community – were not familiar with the program or it's meteoric success. When the new principal was hired, "Playing Our Roots" wasn't her priority because it was time-consuming and costly, and there was no one, other than the graduating high school seniors, to advocate for it.

"Playing Our Roots" was like a falling star that briefly illuminated the sky, then quickly and quietly disappeared. By the following semester, Elana was back to teaching Hebrew with only dim memories of the previous semester's brightness. She quickly grew disillusioned and bored, and eventually left the school altogether.

For Discussion

1. As mentioned earlier in this chapter, successful teen programs grow out of organizations that comprise three conditions: awareness, knowledge, and commitment. This means that lay leaders, professionals, parents, funders, and other stakeholders must be aware of the importance of teen programs, knowledgeable about what it takes to create vibrant teen programs,

and committed to providing the necessary resources and support. Although the school principal, teens, and elderly participants were aware of, knowledgeable about, and committed to "Playing Our Roots," the school committee and larger community were not. What could Elana have done to promote "Playing Our Roots" more effectively?

2. Given the added staff time and budgetary costs involved in "Playing Our Roots," what other stakeholders needed to be involved from the beginning of the program to ensure that it was considered a priority in the school (e.g. parents, funders, the local Jewish newspaper)? How might Elana have widened the web of stakeholders?

3. If you were Elana, what would you have done?

CONCLUSION

Four Strategies For Creating Programs That Captivate Jewish Teens

You don't have to be an outdoor wilderness guru to aspire to the type of engaging and innovative success that Jake achieved with the teens at camp; nor do you need to be a *macher* in the Jewish community to ensure that your program is valued by the organization and community. Successful teen programs are born out of passion, creativity and a bit of elbow grease. Start by focusing on the following four strategies that will lead to steps in the right direction.

1. *Make teens a priority in your work and at your agency* - The Bureau of the Census recently estimated that the teen population in the United States is expected to reach 31 million by the year 2006, the greatest number ever. Based on sheer numbers alone, teen programs must be considered a priority in Jewish organizations and within the local and national Jewish community. This means that teen programs ought to have sufficient budgets, educators of Jewish teens should be treated as professionals, and teens should have a voice in communal decisions that affect them. Be an advocate for teens and teen programs in your community by encouraging their participation on lay committees and boards and be an advocate for yourself as an educator of Jewish teens by setting and attaining professional standards.

2. *Teens are your best advisors* - Although Jewish teens are busier than ever before, like the rest of us, they make time for events and activities that they deem worthwhile. Ask teens what they would make time for, then plan *those* types of events.

3. *"If you build it, they will come" is a great line from a great movie, but not a great way to plan teen programs* - Rather than creating elaborate teen programs only to spend all your time finding teens to attend, go where the teens are. Jewish teens (like all teens) hang out at the mall, attend sporting events, and work part-time. Find ways to incorporate teen programming and Jewish content into those venues. Plan a Jewish treasure hunt at the local mall, raise money for *tzedakah* at a football game based on the number of goals each team scores, or create internship programs for teens to work part-time at Jewish agencies.

4. *Be innovative and take risks* - The grammatically incorrect, but inspiring Apple advertising campaign, "Think Different," doesn't just apply to computer users. Educators of Jewish teens can provide young people with a safe haven in which to explore and stimulate issues of morality, ethics, identity, and heritage and to encourage individual development in a way that may not be available to them in traditional school settings. It takes only a dose of study, a bit of creativity, and a playful heart.

BIBLIOGRAPHY

Note: The following reading list is categorized according to the four overlapping areas about which educators of Jewish teens should be knowledgeable: (1) adolescent theory, (2) organizational development, (3) pedagogy, and (4) Jewish content. It is a selection of the available literature and is not intended to be a comprehensive canon. This is particularly true in the area of Jewish content, where the body of literature is considerable. Therefore, only texts that directly or indirectly address teaching Jewish content to teens have been included. Obviously, any study in this area must be augmented by other ancient and modern Jewish sources.

Adolescent Theory

Hersch, Patricia. *A Tribe Apart*. New York: Ballantine Books, 1998.

> This book presents a portrait of adolescent culture that tells the real life stories of eight American teenagers.

Kedushin, Charles, et al. *Being a Jewish Teenager in America*. Waltham, MA: Cohen Center for Modern Jewish Studies, Brandeis University, 2000.

> This recent study provides a comprehensive analysis of the attitudes and behaviors of American Jewish teens.

Pipher, Mary. *Reviving Ophelia*. New York: Ballantine Books, 1994.

> Written by a clinical psychologist who argues that the escalating levels of sexism and violence in America stifles teenage girls' ability to succeed.

Pollack, William S. *Real Boys' Voices*. New York: Random House, 2000.

> Often compared to *Reviving Ophelia*, this book tells the stories of American teenage boys, who speak out about relationships, sex, parents, school, and more.

Riera, Michael. *Uncommon Sense for Parents with Teenagers*. Berkeley, CA: Celestial Arts, 1995.

> Written by a former high school teacher, this handbook offers a new twist on advice for parents of teenagers.

Riera, Michael. *Field Guide To the American Teenager*. Cambridge, MA: Perseus Press, 2000.

> This handbook for parents and other adults offers a glimpse into the psyche of the American teenager.

Sales, Amy L. *Jewish Youth Databook: Research on Adolescence and Its Implications for Jewish Teen Programs*. Waltham, MA: Cohen Center for Modern Jewish Studies, Brandeis University, 1996.

> This survey provides a compilation and analysis of current research and writing on Jewish adolescence and youth services.

Woocher, Jonathan, ed. "New Approaches To Teen Issues." *Agenda: Jewish Education*, Issue #13, Summer 2000.

> This issue of *Agenda* focuses on Jewish teens and on Jewish community initiatives that engage and serve the needs of adolescence.

Organizational Development

Covey, Stephen R. *The 7 Habits of Highly Successful People: Powerful Lessons in Personal Change*. New York: Simon & Schuster, 1989.

> Covey presents a holistic and integrated approach to creating organizational and personal change.

———. *Principle-Centered Leadership*. New York: Simon & Schuster, 1991.

> This companion guide to *The 7 Habits of Highly Successfully People* offers leadership techniques for dealing with organizational and professional challenges.

Gladwell, Malcolm. *The Tipping Point*. New York: Little, Brown and Co., 2000.

> This book introduces the types of personalities and reasons behind cultural, business, religious, and social phenomena.

Kelley, Tom. *The Art of Innovation: Lessons in Creativity from IDEO, America's Leading Design Firm*. New York: Doubleday, 2001.

> IDEO, the widely respected development firm behind cutting-edge products and services like the Apple mouse and the Palm Handheld, reveals the secrets of innovation.

Senge, Peter M. *The Fifth Discipline: The Art & Practice of the Learning Organization.* New York: Currency Doubleday, 1990.

> This blueprint for learning organizations includes the theory and practice behind what it takes to make an organization effective.

Senge, Peter M., et al. *The Fifth Discipline Fieldbook.* New York: Currency Doubleday, 1994.

> This follow-up guide to *The Fifth Discipline*, offers strategies and tools for building a learning organization.

Sergiovanni, Thomas J. *Moral Leadership: Getting To the Heart of School Improvement.* San Francisco, CA: Jossey-Bass, 1992.

> The author offers a new model of leadership that incorporates a moral dimension to school transformation and improvement.

Pedagogy

Brelsford, Theodore, ed. "Religious Education with Adolescents and Youth, Religious Education." *The Journal of the Religious Education Association and the Association of Professors and Researchers in Religious Education* 97, no. 1, Winter 2002.

> *Religious Education* is an academic interfaith journal. This issue focuses on religious education with adolescents and youth.

Brookfield, Stephen D. *Becoming a Critically Reflective Teacher.* San Francisco, CA: Jossey-Bass, 1995.

> Author Brookfield provides an accessible guide for faculty at any level and across disciplines to improve their teaching.

Maran, Meredith. *Class Dismissed: A Year in the Life of an American High School.* New York: St. Martin Press, 2000.

> Reveals the real-life stories of three Berkeley, California, high school seniors and delves deep into the complexities of being an American teenager.

McDonald, Joseph P. *Teaching: Making Sense of an Uncertain Craft.* New York: Teachers College Press, 1992.

> McDonald offers an insightful analysis of understanding the craft of teaching.

Meier, Deborah. *The Power of Their Ideas: Lessons for America from a Small School in Harlem.* Boston, MA: Beacon Press, 1995.

> Documenting over three decades in education, Meier presents a glimpse into the capacity of the public school system.

Sh'ma, 31/582, May 2001.

> This issue of *Sh'ma* explores the challenges of informal Jewish education.

Jewish Content

Alexander, H. A., ed. "Religious Education: Teaching, Texts, and Language." *The Journal of the Religious Education Association and the Association of Professors and Researchers in Religious Education* 92, no. 1, Winter 1997.

> This issue of *Religious Education* focuses on teaching, texts, and language.

Cohen, Steven, and Arnold Eisen. *The Jew Within.* Bloomington, IN: Indiana University Press, 2000.

> Through in-depth interviews, the authors uncover the foundations of belief and behavior among moderately affiliated American Jews.

Grishaver, Joel Lurie. *Forty Things You Can Do to Save the Jewish People.* Los Angeles, CA: Alef Design Group, 1993.

> This book offers concrete and down-to-earth ideas for parenting Jewish teens.

Freeman, Susan. *Teaching Hot Topics: Jewish Values, Resources, and Activities.* Denver, CO: A.R.E. Publishing, Inc., 2003.

> A manual for teachers that contains background material, text study, and discussions about such issues as abortion, euthanasia, harmful behaviors, animal experimentation, consumerism, school violence, cloning, ethics of business, death penalty, sexuality, and the ethics of war. A Student Companion is also available.

Tucker, JoAnne, and Susan Freeman. *Torah in Motion: Creating Dance Midrash.* Denver, CO: A.R.E. Publishing, Inc., 1990. (Available from http://www.E-Reads.com as a print on demand book or for downloading via the Internet.)

Torah in Motion is a how-to book for creating and teaching dance *midrash*.

Yedwab, Paul. *Sex in the Texts*. New York: UAHC Press, 2001.

Using original and primary texts in Hebrew and English, this collection presents controversial texts and related commentary on sexuality, love, dating, marriage, adultery, abortion, and rape.

CHAPTER 14

Teaching Jewish Adults

Diane Tickton Schuster and Lisa D. Grant

INTRODUCTION

Melissa was a 33-year-old Assistant Rabbi in her third year at a large suburban congregation. She taught a variety of adult education programs and found them to be among the most rewarding moments in her packed schedule. She led an ongoing Torah study group on Thursday evenings and taught a "Women in Midrash" class on Monday afternoons, an adult B'nai Mitzvah class on Wednesday evenings, and a range of topical programs on Sunday mornings. The Torah study class was designed for working people. It started at 6:00 p.m. with a light supper, so people could stop on their way home from work. A consistent core of about 30 participated in this class, including six married couples. Most were middle-aged "empty-nesters" who no longer had children at home. While people did not attend weekly, usually more than 20 came to each class. This was a serious group of "regulars," people who attended services often and were active Jewish learners. They spent the first 20 minutes of each class eating and socializing, and the next hour engaged in serious study of the weekly Torah portion. Melissa brought them a range of commentaries and asked probing questions about the texts. The group's textual analyses flowed comfortably and freely.

The Monday midrash class met at lunchtime and attracted mostly stay-at-home moms, or those with part-time jobs. Most of the women knew each other well and they enjoyed one another's company. Typically, their conversations began around the texts they were reading, but then frequently went on tangents into realms more immediately related to their contemporary lives. Often, the class would run over the scheduled time, but no one seemed to mind. Melissa was a full participant in the women's conversations, and did not try to bring them back to the texts until they were ready.

Melissa's adult B'nai Mitzvah class had 15 women and three men. Most of the women were in

their thirties and early forties, though there were two women in their seventies as well. Two of the men were Jews by Choice, and the third was an immigrant from the former Soviet Union who had received no formal Jewish education as a child. Half of the two-hour class focused on synagogue skills, such as reading Hebrew, chanting Torah, and learning the structure of the Shabbat morning service. Melissa would spend ten to 15 minutes of this first hour exploring the meaning of a particular prayer or the passage of Torah the group was practicing. The second hour of the class covered the Jewish calendar and life cycle events. Here, the students eagerly absorbed the information Melissa presented, but also spent time sharing their own experiences, questions, and feelings about ritual observances and practices. Melissa generally encouraged this kind of exploration in the second hour, especially as the group grew closer together over time.

After teaching for three years, Melissa thought she had a pretty good understanding of what and how adults wanted to learn. She remembered from her education class at Rabbinical school that there are three different motivations that bring adults to study. Some people — like those in her Thursday evening Torah study — are interested in Torah Lishmah, or learning for the sake of learning. Melissa found that these people were experienced learners who engaged in lively discussions and often cited commentaries or brought in midrashim independent of what Melissa introduced. In contrast, the students in her Monday afternoon midrash class seemed motivated by the social aspects of their gathering as much, if not more than, the actual learning. As with most so-called "activity learners" (Apps, 1991), conversations of these students would frequently digress from the themes of the texts they were studying. In contrast, her adult B'nai Mitzvah students had a more goal-centered orientation. They were highly motivated learners who wanted to learn to read Hebrew and become more active participants in services, as well as mark what they perceived to be an important but missing milestone in their Jewish lives.

Sunday mornings were reserved for short courses that might attract congregants who were unwilling or unable to commit to the longer ongoing classes that met during the week. This winter, Melissa decided to offer a four-part Sunday morning class, "Jewish Perspectives on Midlife." She planned to combine a mix of biblical and Rabbinic texts on aging, along with a selection of readings from a contemporary reader titled *A Heart of Wisdom: Making the Jewish Journey from Midlife through the Elder Years* by Susan Berrin, 1997. Like most of these Sunday morning classes, she expected that a mix of adult education "regulars" would come, along with some newcomers who were attracted by the topic. Sixteen women and five men came to the first class. Melissa knew about two-thirds of them from other adult study. The participants ranged in age from the mid-forties to early sixties.

At the first session, Melissa introduced the topic and her plan for the four sessions. She said the class would explore a variety of issues relating to responsibilities and changes that occur at midlife. During the introduction, she asked each person to say what brought him or her to this class. She also said she hoped everyone would find the class immediately relevant and be able to relate the texts she had selected to their own life experiences.

During the first two sessions, Melissa tried to strike a balance between making sure those with weaker backgrounds would not be lost in the material and keeping the more advanced learners engaged. She was open to people who wanted to share their experiences, but was also mindful of getting through the texts she had chosen for study. In the first week, she prepared handouts with short readings and a series of guiding questions. She then divided the class into small groups to work through the material. As she circulated among the groups, she noticed that several did not seem to stay focused on the topic for very long. The following week, the attendance dropped from 21 to 15, so she decided to keep the group together and lead a whole-group discussion.

For the third session, Melissa wanted to move away from just discussing topics to engaging the participants in a more active learning process. She decided to introduce the idea of ethical wills and get people started thinking about writing their own. Fourteen people showed up for this class. Two people who had been at the first class returned, and three who had been there the week before did not come back. Melissa opened the class by distributing three short biblical passages about the temporality of life. Using these texts, she asked the group to reflect on the difference between bequeathing a physical and a spiritual legacy. Many class members seemed to agree that leaving loved ones with a sense of one's values and teachings was more important than any material goods that might be left behind. However, two women vociferously disagreed. Gloria said, "The furniture I inherited from my mother is incredibly important to me. I honor her memory every day by using her things in my home." Phyllis added, "I agree. My son wore his grandfather's tallit at his Bar Mitzvah. and that was one of the most moving things about the ceremony." Melissa attempted to offer some words of appeasement. She said that both legacies were appropriate. She spoke of the Jewish tradition of writing an ethical will, which can serve as a counterbalance to the secular, legal equivalent that focuses more on the distribution of one's material estate. She then asked the class to read three different ethical wills from different time periods to gain a sense of the variety of themes different people chose to address.

Melissa distributed a template of questions and possible themes to help people begin to write an ethical will. She suggested the class members spend about 20 minutes privately, taking notes, jotting down reflections, or actually writing. While most of the students took pencil in hand, Phyllis and Gloria, who had protested earlier, sat stone-faced with arms clenched. Gloria muttered, "I've already taught my children what's important." Shortly after that, both women got up and left the room, about ten minutes before the class was scheduled to end.

Melissa was distraught. What had she done to provoke these women so much that they walked out of class? Had she offended them by giving priority to an ethical rather than material legacy? Had she not prepared the class well enough for the exercise she wanted them to do? Had she misjudged the readiness of the class to engage in a hands-on learning exercise?

Based on the discomfort she perceived from the week before, Melissa decided to deliver a frontal lecture for the last class, leaving time at the end for *discussion and wrap-up. Twelve people from the week before came, including Phyllis, but not Gloria. Just before class began, Mark, who had attended all the previous sessions, approached to show her some additional sources he had found as he continued to work on the ethical will he had begun the week before. Melissa was comforted by this unsolicited encounter, and thought, "Well, at least one person got something out of this class." At the end of her lecture, Phyllis came up to her and said, "That was a really good class. I wish they had all been like that."*

This case illustrates many of the challenges teachers of adult Jewish learners face. Drop-off in participation is typical in most multi-part adult learning situations. Even in the Torah study group, with its committed learners, Melissa found that attendance could be sporadic. She had expected some drop-off in this Sunday morning class for less engaged learners. However, she did not expect the dissonance that occurred in the third session. Perhaps, she had not prepared the group for what was ahead by laying out her expectations and a clear road map. Perhaps she had not provided the participants with enough opportunity to relate their own experiences to the topics. Her problems were not due to any lack of subject matter expertise. Rather, it may have been that she created a learning culture that positioned her as the dominant voice about Jewish midlife issues. Perhaps when she tried to give her students a task that required their active participation, some did not feel prepared or ready to engage.

You have to know your audience, but sometimes the adults want to do silly things, too. When I was teaching beginning Hebrew to adults, they told me they wanted to learn the same fun games their kids were learning in their Hebrew classes. I thought they would have disliked learning on the same level as their children, or thought I was treating them in too babyish a fashion, but they loved it — and learned a lot in the process!

(Amy Appelman, West Bloomfield, Michigan)

Adults participate in Jewish study for a variety of reasons. All are looking to "make meaning" out of Jewish study, but they come with different motivations, different questions, different learning styles, and different anxieties and concerns. Some may have a specific goal in mind, such as wanting to learn Hebrew or wanting to be a better Jewish role model for their children or grandchildren. Others are looking for a way to connect to a community of people with shared interests. Still others come with existential questions about their own identity or about God that they may not even be able to articulate, but which are nevertheless propelling them to study. To be effective, teachers of Jewish adults must be able to identify and address all these varying motivations, interests, and needs, so that participants feel valued and respected, and will keep coming back for more.

This chapter presents a framework for helping teachers of adult Jewish learners to understand better who their learners are, and how they can most effectively plan and organize their teaching to meet the varied, complex, and often competing, if not contradictory, needs that are bound to be present in any class of adults.

TWELVE PRINCIPLES OF EFFECTIVE ADULT JEWISH LEARNING

What are the qualities of good adult education? Knowing who the learners are is a critical part of good practice, but it is just the beginning. In *Learning to Listen, Learning to Teach* (1994), Jane Vella, who has worked in adult education for almost 50 years, identified 12 principles for effective adult learning. When we began to map out what our own research and experience told us about adult Jewish learning, we found that our list of points was virtually identical to Vella's. So we decided to apply Vella's principles to Melissa's experience and, within this framework, to review the decisions and assumptions this teacher likely made when planning to teach Jewish adults.

Principles provide an analytical framework for the design and teaching of adult learning experiences. They can serve as a template for understanding what a teacher needs to think about before, during, and after instruction. Teachers must be able artfully to organize, adapt, and represent subject matter in such a way that it is accessible, relevant, and meaningful to their students. Lee Shulman (1987) calls this skill "pedagogic content knowledge." In adult education, the essential quality of pedagogic content knowledge is dialogue. Certainly, well constructed and delivered lectures or sermons can be powerful, but generally the learning is fleeting. More enduring knowledge builds over time, through an interactive process between teacher, learner, and content. To have a lasting impact, adult educators must be able to help their learners engage in reflective dialogue that interweaves their own life experiences with the subject matter they are studying.

Vella's principles can provide a useful guide for how to create a learning environment in which this type of conversation can flourish. Each principle is an important building block for effective practice in teaching adults. Yet, each also is closely interconnected with the others. As Vella writes: "You can hardly use one without using all the others" (p. 17).

1. Needs Assessment

Adults want to learn things that help them do what they need to do, both in their personal and professional lives. Sometimes, the needs people are able to articulate are only part of the underlying motivation that leads them to an adult learning experience. This might be especially true in adult Jewish learning settings. For instance, women who study in an adult Bar Mitzvah class may first join because they want to learn to read Hebrew and/or feel more comfortable and competent in services. As they progress, however, they may find that their thirst for Jewish study grows far beyond this initial instrumental goal (Grant, 1999/2000). Vella asks, "How can we discover what the group really needs to learn, what they already know, what aspects of the course that we have designed really fit their situations?" (p. 4). This question must be asked at the beginning of any extended learning process, and also as it proceeds.

Melissa perceived that a course on Jewish perspectives at midlife would attract congregants at that stage of life because of its relevance to their current life experiences. She crafted the course based on what she assumed people at midlife would be interested in studying. At the first class, she presented her goals and provided a basic overview of each session. She also asked participants to tell her why they decided to come to the class. Adult learners want to know that the time they invest in learning will be worth their while.

This does not mean that the entire course of study need be fluid until the group convenes. However, it does suggest that teachers must be open and amenable to adapting and shifting focus depending on what motivations, questions, and concerns people bring.

Melissa took the time to ask participants what they wanted at the start of the class, but she did not discern reasons to reframe her original teaching plans. After the second class, however, she made an assessment of the learning needs and changed the class dynamic — with mixed results. She did not "check in" to get the learners' reactions. Both Vella and adult learning expert Stephen Brookfield (1991) strongly recommend that teachers solicit ongoing student feedback as courses progress, both about the content and process of learning. This kind of assessment provides teachers with important information about how the students perceive the experience and whether any adjustment to content or process should be made. When teachers adapt their teaching in response to student feedback and needs, they build trust and also promote student reflectivity about what they are learning.

2. Safety

Adult learners want to be assured that the learning experience will work for them. Typically, adults who engage in Jewish study are well educated and feel quite competent in handling most of life's challenges. However, when it comes to Jewish study, they are often novices and may feel embarrassed or inadequate about what they do not know (Schuster, 1999; Schuster, in press). Teachers in adult Jewish learning settings must create a learning climate in which people feel comfortable asking questions and expressing opinions. As we have seen above, trust is first established when teachers show that their students' questions and concerns matter. When students are encouraged to express their thoughts and offer suggestions, they are affirmed as adults who can contribute to the learning process even without subject matter expertise. Vella notes that creating a safe learning environment "does not obviate the natural challenge of learning new concepts, skills, or attitudes" (p. 6). Adult learning experiences should be intellectually engaging and challenging, but also inviting.

Did Melissa create a safe space in her Sunday

morning class? Did the drop in attendance over time signify anything more than the reality of people's busy schedules? Did she adequately prepare the students for the active learning experience of writing an ethical will? How might she have presented the exercise in a way that would not have alienated Gloria and Phyllis? Since we do not have a full transcript of the exchange that took place in class that day, we cannot really determine why and when things went awry. We can surmise, however, that the two women took offense because of Melissa's actions, statements, or expectations. Teachers create safe learning spaces by providing learners opportunities to share their views and actively engage in a learning conversation. Safety is assured when teachers remain open to and accepting of learners' opinions without passing judgment on learners' values and choices. Whether intended or not, Melissa passed judgment on Phyllis and Gloria for valuing their material inheritance over a potentially ethical one. They were either offended or discomfited by Melissa's opinion, by the activity itself, or by both. As a result, they no longer felt safe, and likely protected themselves by leaving the class.

3. Sound Relationships

Listening and responding to learners' needs and creating a safe space that provides students with opportunities to participate actively are the foundation for establishing a positive relationship between adults and their teachers. Students in adult Jewish learning settings are often awed by their teachers' knowledge, but they also want to relate to them as "real people." They want the teachers to share a bit of themselves, and to demonstrate concern for who the learners are as well.

Melissa was particularly successful in building relationships in two of her classes: her ongoing text study group and her weekly "Women in Midrash" class. She had an appreciation for the former group because of their passion for text study that she shared; she also developed strong relationships with the Monday women's group because their life experiences were close to her own. As a beginning teacher of adults, Melissa discovered the many challenges of building sound relationships with groups where there is no preexisting affinity. She hadn't been sure who would come to her "Jewish Perspectives on Midlife" class. Self-conscious about

her age and lack of adult life experience, she wondered whether she could really relate to the midlife concerns of the group. Instead she relied on textual sources to shape the course and thus focused more on content than on stimulating learner-centered conversation.

Teachers of adults must maintain a delicate balance between content and discussion. Adult learners want a content rich and intellectually challenging program. They also want to engage in meaningful conversation and share personal experiences that are relevant to the topic. The challenge, of course, is that different adults prefer different mixes of content and conversation. Melissa's Torah study group was relatively homogeneous, filled with content-centered learners who stayed on task. Her other classes seemed to lend themselves to an easy blend of content and group interaction. In the midlife class, Melissa struggled with how much time to devote to fostering intragroup relationships and how much time to the course topic. She seemed to assume that the group would be interested in what Judaism could teach them about challenges at midlife rather than getting to know one another. While she expressed her hope that the class would be able to relate their own experiences to the subject matter, she did not provide an appropriate framework to allow them to do this in a substantive way.

As Parker Palmer (1998) describes in *The Courage to Teach*, teachers like Melissa often make the mistake of focusing more on covering material than on making sure that participants have time to share and reflect on their own experiences. In Melissa's case, neither she nor the learners achieved a sense of positive interpersonal connection.

> I look forward to my adult education classes. Unlike some of the classes with teenagers, all of the adults want to be there. There always seems to be at least one adult who is discovering Judaism as a grown-up. What he or she might lack in basic background information is offset by an enthusiasm to learn and a willingness to ask whatever questions are necessary until they arrive at a satisfactory answer.
>
> *(Rabbi David Feder, Morgantown, West Virginia)*

4. Sequence and Reinforcement

Resh Lakish said: "If you see a disciple whose studies are as hard as iron for him, it is because he has not arranged his study in systematic fashion. What is his remedy? To attend the sessions of the Sages more regularly." (*Ta'anit* 7a-b)

This Rabbinic teaching shows the significance of an ordered sequence of instruction, as well as the importance of regular attendance. Vella writes that sequence "means the programming of knowledge, skills, and attitudes in an order that goes from simple to complex and from group-supported to solo efforts" (p. 9). Adults value and benefit from a sequentially structured curriculum, as shown in our recent study of students at the Florence Melton Adult Mini-School, one of the premiere programs of adult Jewish learning in North America. In our interviews with Mini-School students, we regularly heard comments such as, "Melton took things in sequence and put ideas in a fashion that was organized," or "I liked finally getting the time line of Jewish history organized in my head better than I had in the past" (Grant, Schuster, Woocher, and Cohen, forthcoming).

The ordering of material is important, but so, too, is its reinforcement. Another Rabbinic text shows how the teacher must be both patient and attentive to the student for the learning to be absorbed.

Rabbi Perida had a pupil to whom he had to repeat his lesson four hundred times before he was able to learn it. One day Rabbi Perida was invited to a religious celebration. That day, Rabbi Perida also kept repeating the lesson, but the student did not learn it. Rabbi Perida: "Why are you different today?" The student: "The moment the master was told, 'There is a religious celebration,' my attention wandered, for I kept saying to myself: The master is about to get up and leave, the master is about to get up and leave." Rabbi Perida said: "Pay attention now, and I will teach you [once] more." He repeated the lesson and the student learned it. (*Eruvin* 54b)

Melissa's midlife class serves as a cautionary tale about the importance of sequence and reinforcement. Her first class began with and focused on texts. Such an approach may be appropriate for a group like her Thursday night learners, who are comfortable with and already committed to text study. It might also work well with her adult B'nai Mitzvah students, who have a concrete goal of learning the texts of the Shabbat morning service. The people in her Sunday morning class, however, more likely were attracted because of the "real-life" topic rather than the opportunity to engage in text study. Starting with texts may have alienated and confused some of the learners, especially those who expected the class to focus more on their own midlife concerns.

Most Jewish educators are deeply committed to text study as the way into understanding and connecting with Judaism. Many adult Jewish learners, though, are strangers to the tradition of text study and must be gradually and carefully introduced to its complexities and content. As the Jewish philosopher Franz Rosenzweig (1920) observed over 80 years ago, teachers cannot assume that Torah will have immediate relevance to life; rather educators must teach from "life to Torah and then back to life again." The sequence of study must begin with affirming the learners wherever they are Jewishly. It must continue by helping adults find meaning by giving them opportunities to connect their own life experiences to the texts. Learning is reinforced when teachers make texts accessible, both in language and presentation. Learning is also reinforced when teachers listen to their students carefully and thoughtfully tailor responses to their needs.

5. Praxis — Action with Reflection

Vella writes that learning becomes praxis when it includes "not only significant action but time for reflection on that action" (p. 96). In *Preparing to Teach*, the faculty handbook for the Florence Melton Adult Mini-School, good teaching is defined as being reflective and self-evaluative: "Reflective teaching is a critical component of the ethos of the Melton Mini-School. It is a vital opportunity to learn from our practice . . . Underlying reflective teaching is a commitment to individual and colleagues' growth" (p.27). The handbook encourages Mini-School teachers to ask themselves soul-searching questions after each class session: "What was the best learning moment in class? If there was none, why not? Was there any time when you felt the students were not focused on what you were teaching? Why? Could you have done anything differently? Did the lesson reach the students at their appropriate level? Did you accomplish your purpose?"

In the same way that teachers should ask their students for feedback, they should also take the time to reflect on their own about what worked and what didn't. Melissa's decision to change the instructional approach of her last class showed reflection on practice. She realized that the sequence and structure of the course did not prepare the class for such a self-directed activity. In the first session, she tried to encourage the students to study texts on their own in small groups. Many did not seem comfortable with that approach, so she reverted to a lecture mode in the second class where she remained the principal mediator of the texts. She later wondered if the group would have been more amenable to the active learning component if the sequencing had been reversed, starting with an emphasis on the learners' lives in the first session, turning to Torah in the second and third, and the returning to "life" with the ethical will exercise in the final class. Her reflections provided her with new insights for planning future classes.

Finding time for reflection is crucial to the enhancement of teaching. This can be accomplished in a number of ways. Course evaluations are one valuable source of information. Some teachers make notes on their lesson plans following the class session to help them remember what worked well and what not so well. Others keep more extensive reflective practice journals where they record exchanges and experiences that raise questions. Still others meet with colleagues on a regular basis for support, and to share ideas and experiences. All these methods help teachers reflect on their teaching and strive continually for improvement.

6. Learners as Subjects of Their Own Learning

Though adults come to Jewish learning wanting to learn from master teachers, ultimately what they learn is up to them. Vella observes that adults "need to know, insofar as possible, that they themselves decide what occurs in the learning event" (p. 12). Malcolm Knowles (1980), one of the pioneers in adult learning theory, was the first to note that adults are largely self-directed in their learning. They choose when, where, and how they will

engage in learning. They also determine whether they are going to be active partners in the learning process (like Mark, in Melissa's class, who continued the process of writing an ethical will) or be more passive recipients of information. Though the decision is up to the individual learner, the teacher's instructional style can encourage (or inhibit) the learner's interaction with the content. As a practical guide, Vella suggests: "Don't ever do what the learner can do; don't ever decide what the learner can decide" (p. 13). Although not all learners want to engage actively with material or dialogue, Vella recommends a teaching approach in which open-ended questions call for analysis and critical thinking.

Franz Rosenzweig's reflections on adult Jewish learning from the early part of the twentieth century extend Vella's point. He wrote that people come to adult Jewish learning because they want to connect with their Judaism in some way: "People will appear who prove by the very fact of their coming to the discussion room of a school of adult Jewish education that the Jewish human being is alive in them" (Rosenzwerig, 1955, pp. 68-69). Rosenzweig counseled that the teacher's task is to cultivate and enhance that desire for connection by listening to students before planning a full course of study. He also suggested that learners need to see their teachers as both masters and learners themselves — as people who are actively engaged in seeking meaning through Jewish study. In other words, Jewish adults need to have role models who themselves are "subjects of their own learning."

7. Learning with Ideas, Feelings, and Actions

More than 50 years ago, social psychologist Kurt Lewin (1951) demonstrated that enduring learning must address a combination of ideas, feelings, and actions. Vella points out that these elements can and should be integrated in adult learning programs. Teachers can elicit feelings about ideas and concepts as they teach the content. They can also help learners to reflect on ideas and feelings as they build skills and engage in active learning. Teaching plans should incorporate all three elements. For example, Melissa's adult B'nai Mitzvah class spent a significant portion of their time on developing skills, such as reading Hebrew and chanting from the Torah. Yet, the learning went beyond an exercise in rote memorization when Melissa made sure, in each class session, to address participants' affective and cognitive needs. She accomplished this by exploring the meanings of the prayers and texts the group was studying and by inviting people to express their questions and feelings about religious observances and Jewish life in general.

Melissa was less effective in integrating all three elements into her midlife class. She felt more comfortable remaining in an intellectual realm rather than facilitating an open conversation about midlife issues of aging, loss, and coping with change. Instead, she relied primarily on the selected texts as the authoritative sources of information. While she offered opportunities for participants to share their experiences, the way she structured the class gave a clear signal that feelings were secondary to the exploration of the source material. By the time Melissa planned for more active engagement in the third session, some participants had already checked out of the experience, either by not showing up altogether, or in the extreme case of Phyllis and Gloria, by walking out when they felt the teacher's expectations were inconsistent with their own.

I remember a senior adult who always showed up for every adult education offering. She didn't remember much from one week to the next, but was enthusiastic about being there. So long as I could make each unit self-contained and not reliant on knowledge from previous sessions, she could enjoy attending and learning.

(Rabbi David Feder, Morgantown, West Virginia)

8. Immediacy: Teaching What Is Really Useful

In addition to creating a safe space for exploring ideas and feelings and for trying out new actions, another key aspect of an effective adult learning experience is ensuring that the subject matter and its presentation are immediately relevant. Adults want a well structured and sequenced program of study with ample opportunity for reinforcement. At the same time, they want and appreciate immediate results.

Immediacy relates to our first principle, which described the importance of assessing learners' needs and adapting instruction to meet them as

the course of study unfolds. Vella observes that situations in which the teacher leaves everything up to the learners are *not* effective in meeting immediate needs or producing relevant results. Instead, she proposes a structured partnership between teacher and learners that is based on a "problem-posing approach" to dialogue. This approach requires teachers to hold back their knowledge, beliefs, and opinions, until the learners have the opportunity to explore their own. It requires teachers to facilitate dialogue based on questions that invite learners to consider multiple perspectives and interpretations. It also requires teachers to enable learners to reflect on their learning by asking them how they might apply the skills or knowledge they acquired in the class to their lives as Jews. And, it requires teachers to ask for feedback about the learning process itself. Problem-posing strategies require a confident teacher and a trusting relationship between teachers and learners. In the Perspectives on Midlife class, Melissa failed to create the necessary climate for open dialogue about the learners' midlife concerns. She never got to the problem-posing processes that could help learners like Phyllis and Gloria reflect deeply on their Jewish experiences. Without this reflection and discourse, the learning process derailed and the women saw no immediate reason to stay engaged.

Another way teachers can foster immediacy in learning is to encourage "experiential" learning — in which learners move through a cycle of having concrete experiences, reflecting on those experiences, and identifying new areas for action or inquiry — which then leads to new concrete experiences (Kolb, 1984). Experiential learning helps adults engage directly with their learning and build on what they already know. Reflecting on experiences and identifying new goals prompts learners to apply what they have learned to new situations. Adult learners find this kind of synthesis of past experience and new application especially relevant.

Although Melissa attempted, via the ethical will assignment, to create an experiential learning activity, she was not able to get everyone to enter into the cycle of experience and reflection. Mark certainly found immediate relevance and created new areas of inquiry for himself, but apparently Phyllis and Gloria were not able to move from their concrete experiences to broader philosophical reflection. Melissa was unable to help these learners to find a useful connection between the content and their lives. Perhaps she could not do this because she had not asked them enough about their backgrounds or motivations for attending the course; or perhaps she started in the wrong place by urging the ethical will activity before these women had worked through their mixed feelings about what one's legacy to future generations ought to be. By concluding the course with a lecture, Melissa risked further closing off immediacy for the students, leaving them with limited insight to Jewish perspectives on their own midlife experiences.

9. Clear Roles in Communication between Learner and Teacher

> Ben Zoma taught: "Who is wise? One who learns from all persons, as it is written, 'From all my teachers have I gained understanding'" (*Psalm* 119:99). (*Avot* 4:1)

Adult learners want and need role equity between teacher and learners. They want to be respected and valued as adults. Vella points out that there can be no role equity if the learners perceive that their voices are less valid than those of their teachers, a condition for many adult learners. This can be quite tricky when the teacher has greater knowledge, skills, and comfort with the material than their learners. Helping such learners find their voice, strengthen their intellectual reasoning, and express their points of view are key tasks for teachers of adults (Belenky, et al., 1986; Schuster, 1998; Schuster, in press). Melissa did indeed have a deeper background in Jewish texts than any of the participants in that class, yet she made room for them to express their views, to explore different perspectives, and to read and make meaning out of the texts on their own and in community. Melissa functioned both as teacher and co-learner in this group. When she tried a similar approach with the "Jewish Perspectives on Midlife" class, however, it did not work. Many of the students were unfamiliar and uncomfortable with texts and felt lost, so they wandered off task. Whereas Melissa's Torah study group could grapple with text and life issues, the Sunday morning class did not have accumulated text familiarity to draw upon. What they did have was their adult life experience. However, Melissa did not structure the course to tap into these stories and experiences. The group's hesitancy was compounded by the fact that most adults come to study programs expecting a frontal lecture style of teaching; this is the format they know best. In such situations, clear communication becomes all the more essential because the teacher is asking the group to share opinions and reflect on their own experiences. Since Melissa did not cultivate strong lines of communication, she didn't know how to "read" the group or get them to self-disclose comfortably. When she thought the learners were ready to engage in active learning, she found she hadn't allowed sufficient opportunity for dialogue or trust building. As a result, communication broke down and the students did not synthesize their thoughts, opinions, and stories in a meaningful way.

10. Teamwork: How People Learn Together

> When ten persons sit together and study Torah, the *Shechinah* hovers over them, as it is written, "God is present in the divine assembly" (*Psalms* 82:1). (*Avot* 3:7)

Studying Torah is considered a religious act in Judaism. Though later in the passage quoted above it states that God is present even when one studies alone, studying in community is the preferred mode according to Jewish tradition. We are instructed to "acquire a colleague for study" (*Avot* 1:6) with whom we can enter into dialogue and debate about meanings and interpretations. As we see elsewhere, the Rabbis of the Talmud were aware that learning partners sharpen each other's intellectual and creative acuity.

> Rabbi Hama ben Hanina said: What is the meaning of the verse, "Iron sharpens iron"? This is to teach you that just as in the case of one iron sharpens the other, so also do two scholars sharpen each other's mind by *halachah*." (*Ta'anit* 7a)

The prescience of the Rabbinic Sages is reflected in much more contemporary literature that demonstrates the positive impact of learning in groups. People who study together feel less isolated, more supported, and more intellectually challenged (Boyd, 1991; Cranton, 1994; Kasl and Elias, 2000). When they feel safe and supported in their learning environment, they are more inclined to take intellectual and behavioral risks and to develop shared commitments to continued learning (Aron and Schuster, 1998; Bruffee, 1993; Senge, 1990).

In team learning, the balance of authority shifts from the teacher to the learners. Vella writes that peers "can challenge one another in ways a teacher cannot. Peers create safety for the learner who is struggling with complex concepts and skills or attitudes" (p. 20). Teachers who promote team learning generally function more in a consultative role than a directive one. They create learning experiences that allow their students to determine the structure of the learning experience, not necessarily *what* will be taught, but how. Generally, such teachers employ participatory instructional approaches rather than frontal lectures. They listen carefully to understand their students' needs. They pose opening questions, ask for students' opinions, facilitate conversations by providing guiding questions and support, and encourage dialogue across the group, not just between student and teacher.

Melissa intuitively employed this approach with her Monday "Women in Midrash" class. She determined that the class would focus broadly on women's stories. She selected the texts for study, but let the group determine the nature of the conversation and its pace. This mode of learning is best suited for what Jerold Apps (1991) calls Intuitive Learners — people who prefer learning when both feeling and thinking are combined. These learners value dialogue about the meaning of what they are studying. What appeals to this group is not well suited to everyone. Apps contrasts them with Practical Learners who generally have concrete, immediate goals and like fast paced teaching and ready application; these learners are rarely interested in class activities that rely on critical analysis or meandering discourse. Apps explains that different groups develop different norms depending on their interests, learning styles, and needs. The teacher needs to spend time determining what those interests, learning styles, and needs may be, and then cultivate a community that accommodates their differences. This is very challenging with groups that meet only a few times, but it still can be done by teachers who take the time to listen, watch, and give the learners room to describe who they are and what they hope to accomplish.

11. Engagement: Learning as an Active Process

Engagement is closely connected to the sixth principle (Learners as Subjects of Their Own Learning).

Vella writes that when learners are deeply engaged, "it is often difficult to extricate them from the delight of that learning" (p. 21). Teachers of adults often note how much they enjoy teaching classes of engaged learners. Such engagement might begin in a formal classroom, but extend beyond it as well. Adult learners are engaged when the subject matter is relevant, when the learning environment is welcoming and secure, and when they feel appropriately challenged and touched by the learning experience. Engagement is also a necessary component for critical reflection that may lead to a transformation of learners' assumptions, perspectives, and even behaviors (Mezirow, 2000). Here's an example of how one active learner's engagement, with the support of her teacher, both within and beyond a structured classroom environment, led to a profound change in the assumptions that shaped her understanding of the Divine.

Sandra was a regular participant at many of her synagogue's adult education offerings. Recently, she enrolled in a three-part Sunday morning course on prayer, taught by Ilana, the Education Director. During the second session, Sandra told the class about her ambivalence in reciting the "V'ahavta" and thereby claiming to "love God." She questioned whether she could love something she isn't sure exists. A few weeks later, Sandra came to see Ilana to tell her about attending a friend's conversion ceremony and watching her struggle to recite the "Sh'ma" correctly and precisely. Sandra said that in witnessing her friend's public declaration she suddenly felt "God's love fill up the room" and unite the community. She described this moment as one of undisputed holiness that, in the moment, reaffirmed her faith. However, she said, since the ceremony, her lingering skepticism had reappeared. Ilana suggested that Sandra embark on a focused reading program about God. In subsequent months, she met with Sandra to discuss what she had been reading. Her readings and conversations with Ilana helped Sandra realize that "finding answers" isn't the point. Rather, she reported, "It's asking the questions and reflecting on possible meanings that really matter."

12. Accountability

Vella describes this final principle as a synthesis of all the others. As such, it is the most essential. She sets lofty goals: "What was proposed to be taught must be taught; what was meant to be learned must be learned; the skills intended to be gained must be manifest in all the learners; the attitudes taught must be manifest; the knowledge conveyed must be visible in the adult learner's language and reasoning" (p. 21). Later, she writes that it is the educator's task to make learning "so accountable, the engagement so meaningful, the immediacy so useful" that education will become an essential part of people's lives (p. 169).

Melissa clearly understood how important it was to be accountable to her learners. Not surprisingly, she was more successful in situations in which her experiences, passions, and commitments were more consistent with those of her learners. For the most part, these were groups of already engaged learners (at least the ones who regularly attended). They had specific learning goals that were compatible with Melissa's. She was less effective in meeting the needs of the less engaged learners of the Sunday morning group because she did not spend sufficient time trying to understand who they were and what they wanted. Instead, she did what she was comfortable doing, teaching text, and hoped that the group would trust her enough to come along.

We have learned from the other principles that adult learners need and deserve to be heard. They need and deserve to feel safe, to have a clear sense of sequence and reinforcement of subject matter, to have a voice in determining the direction of the learning. They need to be appropriately engaged, intellectually, emotionally, and behaviorally. They want and need their learning to be relevant. They want and need to draw upon their experience in making meaning from their learning. Teachers who meet these needs and expectations are accountable. They develop strong relationships based on their personal integrity, their subject matter expertise, and their respect for their learners. It is these relationships that are at the heart of effective adult teaching and learning.

JEWISH ADULT LEARNERS: GROWING AND CHANGING

The framework we have just presented identifies many of the *adult learning* dynamics that Jewish educators should consider when they take on the challenges of teaching adults. A second framework derives from the study of *adult development* and focuses on the dynamics of growth and change during the adult years. Educators — especially those who were trained to work with children or teens and who see themselves as most comfortable working with younger populations — may need to take some time to learn about adulthood and the factors that bring adults to new learning experiences.

Interest in adult development has blossomed in the past 30 years and has shown that one of the most important realities is that adults are *highly variable* — that while there may be commonalities among certain groups, the likelihood is that, within any group, there will be wide-ranging differences. Thus, in a group of religious school parents in a congregation, there will be a dramatic spread of ages (ranging from under 30 to over 60), a wide variety of family groupings (two parents, single parents, joint custodial parents, grandparents, stepparents, etc.), a range of social and cultural backgrounds (people from different kinds of communities, geographical regions, countries, lifestyles, etc.), and diverse experiences in the realm of Jewish life and Jewish learning. Jewish adult learning settings may include singles in their twenties, widows in their eighties, *ba'alei teshuvah* of all ages, immigrants who received no Jewish education, conversion candidates, non-Jewish spouses and partners, and an array of other individuals who want to come closer to Judaism and Jewish ideas. This variability is part of who Jewish adults are today, and responding to the diversity of learners' experiences is an ongoing challenge for any Jewish professional.

Another reality of contemporary adulthood is the *normalcy of change:* during the adult years, people now expect to have changes in residence, career, marriage and family constellation, identity, and lifestyle. The average life span is now nearly 80 years. Adults see that, beyond the conventional roles of career and child rearing, they will have many years to do many things in many places. Because of the constancy of change, adults need to learn how to adapt and adjust to the stress and demands of new circumstances. They need to accommodate to the disruptions of transitions from "the familiar" to "the unfamiliar." The bright side of this reality is that life is filled with continually evolving possibilities and new opportunities. For some, however, there is a dark side that, given so many disruptions, adults cannot create (or sustain) the sense of continuity and tradition that has been the hallmark of human society throughout the generations. Jewish populations in transition — disrupted or dislocated families, elderly adults who lack family support, newly Jewish individuals who lack Jewish community, adults in shifting employment situations — have concerns that appropriately should be addressed by Jewish educators. Increasingly, professionals and lay leaders who serve the Jewish community must anticipate the learning needs of these disparate subgroups.

Over the centuries, adult transitions have been associated with changes in social status: marriage, birth of first and last child, entry into career, retirement, widowhood, and so on. Traditionally, family members and communal leaders guided and affirmed people as they worked their way through various shifts in social position. Today, however, as adults adapt to changing personal and professional circumstances, they find themselves turning to alternative sources of support and direction. According to an oft cited study for the College Board (Aslanian and Brickell, 1980), when Americans are "in transition," they tend to take on new learning projects (both formal and self-directed) in order to reinvent themselves and their lives. More significantly, throughout the adult years, they tend to see *education* as the most useful support for coping with new demands and times of change.

> It is such a different experience working with adults as opposed to children. They are usually extremely motivated, yet nervous about being in class. I try to use many of the same techniques with them as I do with children — offering positive reinforcement, lavishing praise, having much patience, and providing much repetition.
>
> *(Nancy Hersh, Chatham, New Jersey)*

Jewish adults in transition similarly look to new educational opportunities when they are adapting to new times or circumstances in their lives. In the face of loss (loss of health, of parents, of marriage partners, of children at home, of economic or national security — the list goes on and on) and of change (becoming parents, grandparents, in-laws, divorcees, new residents in communities, retirees, and so on), Jewish adults find themselves rethinking about the role Judaism and Jewish tradition plays in their lives. They wonder how Judaism can help them understand the changes they are experiencing. They think about "unfinished business" or their interrupted (or neglected or absent) Jewish education. People who for years haven't considered involving themselves in Judaism suddenly find, in response to a life change, that they want to explore their Jewish identity or heritage in a systematic way. And in response to these various transitions, Jewish adults seek Jewish education to help them.

Jewish adults feel *most* pulled to new Jewish learning experiences during middle adulthood, roughly ages 35-60. These are the years when (1) children enter Jewish education and parents find they want to be better informed themselves; (2) children prepare for their B'nai Mitzvah, and parents become interested in participating in the preparation and/or the celebration in a meaningful way; (3) intermarriage or family disruption pushes adults to realize that the transmission of Jewish values and rituals is their responsibility — and cannot be delayed; (4) illness or death of parents or peers alerts adults to their own mortality and their lack of spiritual preparation for dealing with loss and "the unknown"; (5) the reality of aging compels Jewish adults to think about the meaning of their lives, their legacy to others, and the continuity of the Jewish people. During these years, especially for working adults, the time available for Jewish adult education is at a premium.

Nonetheless, as middle-aged Jewish adults confront the realities of their lives, their desire for positive connections with Judaism and Jewish tradition grows. Moreover, if a Jewish adult has a meaningful Jewish learning experience during midlife, he or she is more likely later on — when freed from child rearing or employment — to seek to extend that Jewish education. Thus, Jewish educators need to invest in the learning of midlife learners on the assumption that these adults will return for more later in their lives.

At the same time, educators must also attend to the learning needs of an increasingly wide range of adult constituencies. In a recent seminar on Jewish adult learners, education and Rabbinical students brainstormed the many formal and informal teaching opportunities they might face in their careers; the (ever expanding) list alerts us to the complexity of learning needs in today's Jewish adult community:

Introduction to Judaism course

Jewish Community Center *Derech Torah* course

Sisterhood lunch and learn program

Hebrew class

Parashah HaShavua study group

Talmud study group

Parent portion of family education activity

Conversion class

Rosh Chodesh study group

Tikkun Layl Shavuot study sessions

Downtown early a.m. Torah study

Adult B'nai Mitzvah class

Melton Mini-School course

Wexner Heritage course

Museum or Jewish neighborhood visit

Elderhostel class

Bereavement group

Jewish book review group

Senior citizen "Ask the Educator" session

Jewish holidays and life cycle events course

Synagogue *havurah* study session

Panelists on community interfaith symposium

Confirmation parents class

Nursing home Friday afternoon discussion group

Israel trip

Shabbaton retreat

Regional synagogue *kallah*

Topical short course (Israel, *Kabbalah*, *Midrash*)

Women's spirituality retreat

Avocational teacher training program

Meditation group

Jewish Internet or distance Jewish Internet or distance learning course

This list highlights the reality that today's Jewish adults are seeking more Jewish learning opportunities and also are looking for that education in diverse places. Whereas 20 years ago the synagogue was the primary address for study in a Jewish community, today classes and workshops are held in community centers, colleges, book stores, retirement communities, museums, retreat centers, and so on. Effective teachers find themselves in demand, and quickly discover the joys and challenges of working with an increasingly motivated and informed Jewish adult learning population.

DEVELOPMENTAL TASKS OF JEWISH ADULTHOOD

Chronologically, Jewish adults are "grown up," but many do not feel genuinely mature when they find themselves in situations that involve functioning as a competent, comfortable Jew. All too often, these adults are stuck in a mode of "pediatric Judaism," in which their understanding of Jewish texts or tradition is childlike; people who grew up with minimal or no formal Jewish education find they need the equivalent of "elementary education" to take on even the most basic Jewish roles (such as making *Kiddush* or planning a *Seder*). The dissonance between feeling authoritative in other domains of life (say, at work or in community roles) and feeling unschooled in Jewish ideas or behaviors causes many adults to avoid Judaism or participation in Jewish life. Jewish educators stand in a particularly strong position to help such adults "work through" what psychologists call "developmental tasks" — learning what they need in order to function effectively in Jewish society. Seven tasks that are part of healthy psychological development overall are especially salient in the experience of Jewish adult learners. The adult learning principles we discussed earlier in this chapter relate, as well, to the needs associated with each of these tasks.

Taking initiative - It is not enough for Jewish adults merely to follow the lead of others in their quest for a meaningful Jewish life. They need to take risks toward exploring Judaism and discovering what being Jewish means to them. Taking initiative means practicing a ritual for the first time or learning the Hebrew alphabet or participating in a *tzedakah* project. It means joining with other Jews for a group activity. It can take the form of reading a book on a Jewish theme or writing to a governmental leader about Israel. Such exploration needs to be suggested, encouraged, and reinforced. Keeping in mind Vella's principle of *safety,* educators have to remember that, for many Jewish adults who are new to Jewish learning, "small steps" feel like "big steps." Just as children who are beginning learning journeys need to be rewarded for "trying," so adults need to be reassured by professionals in the Jewish community that their initial efforts make a difference. At the same time, it is important to help adults focus on what they are doing and not on what they haven't done or have yet to do. As Erik Erikson (1950) pointed out, guilt can undermine one's motivation to try. Jewish adults need to be encouraged to try.

Becoming competent - One of the hardest challenges undereducated Jewish adults grapple with is feeling Jewishly ignorant. People who don't know Hebrew avoid attending worship services where their lack of knowledge will be evident. Parents who have never prepared a Shabbat dinner feel self-conscious about their lack of basic skills. Individuals who don't know the difference between the Torah and the Haftarah don't want to be in conversations during which such understanding is assumed. For many adults, even if they attended Hebrew school and other Jewish education classes as children, the problem with feeling Jewishly illiterate looms as potentially insurmountable. Fortunately, with increasing opportunities to acquire basic Jewish education, more and more adults are discovering the joy of becoming "competent" Jews. As we pointed out in our discussion of Vella's principles of *sequence* and *immediacy,* Jewish adult learners report that what they most value is being given a "map" of Jewish knowledge that they can readily and systematically follow. They like being shown what they should learn and what resources are available for study. In classes, they like to review what's been taught so that they can feel in command of new information. While they don't like to be "tested" on their learning, they like to have opportunities to apply what they've been studying. Adults thrive on experiential learning activities that help them increase their personal sense of mastery and familiarity with content.

Finding peers - Like schoolchildren who learn about cooperation and planning by participating in soccer teams, Girl Scouts, and camp bunk activities, adults benefit from having peers with whom to share Jewish learning experiences. Peers provide

support and collaboration; they model behavior for one another and offer opportunities for practice and rehearsal. Peer groups help socialize newcomers into the "rules and roles" of a community, forgiving the initiate the awkwardness that comes with new learning. As we noted in our discussion of Vella's principles of *sound relationships* and *teamwork,* Jewish adult learners respond enthusiastically to finding others who share their interest in learning. They embrace opportunities for *chevruta* study (especially when a teacher thoughtfully pairs them with appropriate study partners and provides them with a task that they don't find too daunting or complex). They like finding peers with whom to attend services or lectures, create rituals, explore new ideas, and share Jewish holidays and life cycle events. They are drawn to book groups and family education experiences in which they can find others who have common interests. They join *havurot* that will help them to feel "less alone" in the development of their Jewish life. Jewish educators can play a crucial role in creating learning partnerships that encourage support and ongoing participation in Jewish life. Consistent with the point we made in our analysis of Vella's eighth principle (*learners as subjects of their own learning*), the educator can serve as the peer, sharing his or her expertise, while also learning from the experience of the learner. Jewish adults appreciate learning environments that are essentially democratic — in which learners and teachers all learn from one another, helping each other to stretch and grow.

> In many ways, teaching adults is more difficult for me than teaching children. Adults come with an agenda — something they want me to teach them, or a perspective they want to have represented. There is a limit to the patience of adult learners. If I don't satisfy their learning needs, they go away. It helps me if I am very clear about what I intend to do in each session, and if I open the lesson plan to their input early on.
>
> *(Sally Stefano, Worthington, Ohio)*

Developing a Jewish identity - Many contemporary Jews feel a disjunction between the "label" of being Jewish and the lives they are leading as Jews. They recognize that they need consciously and deliberately to develop their Jewish sense of self —

through learning and practice and reflection and coming together with other Jews. In 1990, educators Perry London and Barry Chazan suggested that Jewish adults (and children) could benefit from "Jewish identity education" that could systematically help them to explore Jewish values and how they live their lives as Jews. London and Chazan recommended that Jewish educators take lead roles in creating learning experiences in which Jewish adults could talk about why they were Jewish, which Jewish values have meaning for them, and what they need to better understand about Judaism. Recent studies of Jewish identity (Cohen and Eisen, 2000; Horowitz, 2000) have found that Jewish adults have an abiding sense of themselves as Jews, but their "Jewish identity" is rather fluid and changes over time. In other words, there are times in people's lives when their Jewish identity becomes especially dynamic and salient, and other times when their Jewishness holds less centrality.

The timing of Jewish identity development is idiosyncratic — different triggers will prompt different individuals at different times to embark on a purposive Jewish identity journey. Accordingly, Jewish educators have to be prepared for adults of all ages to suddenly say (by word or deed), *"Hineni"* — I am ready to deepen my Jewish commitments, to explore my Jewish values, and to put Judaism more fully into my life. In response, Jewish educators need to be available to support adults on these quests by providing opportunities for active participation in Jewish practice or communal life, time for one-on-one dialogue and personal sharing, and educational programs that address what it means to be a Jew. These responses all are part of what Vella describes as elements of the principles of *needs assessment* and *clear communication*, which optimally are ongoing in a teacher's relationship with his or her students.

Participating in community - Adulthood is the time of career and family building, both of which require individuals to cultivate mature interpersonal skills and make commitments beyond the self. Adults increasingly select their social groups and invest themselves in their preferred social milieu. During the past half century, with increased social mobility and ease in living apart from established Jewish communities, Jewish adults have made increasingly diverse choices about the extent to which they associate or affiliate with other Jews. For some Jewish adults, forming ties with the

Jewish community occurs as a comfortable and natural extension of social experiences in youth groups, summer camps, day schools, college fraternities or sororities, Israel trips, or other Jewish youth programs. For many others, however, separation from the Jewish community begins during adolescence or during college and is later reinforced by intermarriage. Some Jewish teens push away from Jewish social or organizational groups and avoid affiliation as part of their need to individuate from parental expectations. There also are some American Jews who grow up with little sense of Jewish community, either due to geographic isolation or family rejection of ties with Jewish people. Thus, during adulthood, the task of participating in a Jewish community may have little meaning or appeal, may be fraught with resentment or "baggage," may be a totally new experience, or may be an easy and socially gratifying experience.

Educators cannot assume that all Jewish adults who engage in Jewish organizational life are at ease in Jewish settings or understand the communal values traditionally associated with Jewish living. They need to help adults build ties with other Jews and create mutually supportive networks that reinforce communal interdependence. They need to educate Jewish adults about the *mitzvot* that celebrate human cooperation and giving. They need to engage people in studying texts that pertain to *tzedakah* and community obligation. And they need to model for others the benefits and blessings of community caring and sharing. In this sense, Jewish educators need to keep in mind Vella's principle of *engagement*, which emphasizes that learning extends beyond the classroom walls. By living *in community* with other Jewish adults, educators demonstrate directly their commitment to communal interdependence and support.

Making meaning - In a thoughtful discussion of why "meaning making" is a crucial dimension of adulthood, religious educator Leon McKenzie (1986) commented that all humans come into the world striving for "intelligibility and purpose," seeking a "perspective or framework for our being-in-the-world" (p. 11). Throughout our lives, we look for ways to understand our experiences and to cope with things that are confusing, frightening, or hard to accept. Religious education provides valuable structures that help people to acquire and deepen meaning in their lives. McKenzie describes the religious educator as "a facilitator who helps people gain meaning, explore and expand the meaning structures they possess, and express their meanings effectively" (pp. 10-11). In contemporary American Jewish society, many midlife (and also younger) adults actively raise questions about the meaning of Judaism in their lives. Confronted with rapid social change and a sense of vulnerability in an unpredictable world, these individuals are pulled to spiritual searching to make sense of life's changes. They want to know why they are Jewish and how Judaism can respond to the uncertainties of modern existence. They are attracted to being part of a tradition that might give some order and explanation to the upheavals around them. And they welcome the discovery of "wonder" that comes with thinking about life and God and the mysteries of the universe.

As Vella points out in her principles of *immediacy* and *learning with ideas, feelings, and actions,* educators who can help adults to grapple with meaning making in an immediate and holistic way are deeply appreciated by their students. This is particularly true of Jewish learners who look to their teachers for help in their search for meaning. Effective Jewish educators invite learners to discuss Judaism on very personal terms, to explore prayer and meditation, to link study and spirituality, or to write about their Jewish life journeys. They share with learners their own Jewish questions and non-judgmentally support them through their experiences of "God wrestling." Together, Jewish learners and their teachers explore issues of faith and accept the questioning that is at the heart of Jewish meaning making.

Growing from generation to generation - The leading theorist of human development, Erik Erikson (1950), described the developmental task of adulthood as "generativity," or the transmission of knowledge and values from one generation to the next. Erikson pointed out that adults derive their sense of well-being and purpose by passing on what they have learned to children, apprentices, employees, and others in the community who receive what they have created. The adult years are organized around one generation helping the next

to benefit from lessons learned, thus ensuring the continuity of culture and community across time. When adults fail to be generative, they and the world around them stand to become stagnant and devitalized.

Jewish generativity is enlivened by educators who can help adults to see themselves as culture bearers for their children, grandchildren, and others in the community who need to learn about Judaism and Jewish life. The more Jewish adults are helped — through learning and spiritual support — to consolidate their own sense of themselves as Jews, the more they are able to convey the meaning of Judaism to others. Consistent with Vella's principle of *action with reflection*, the more Jewish adults reflect on their Judaism and how they can pass along what they have learned, the more connected they will feel to the continuity of the Jewish people. Educators are important role models who, by example, show adults positive ways to pass along what they have learned. They help adults to translate Jewish ideas into Jewish living, thus enabling them to serve as guides to those who need their tutelage and support.

CONCLUSION: FROM THEORY TO PRACTICE

The foregoing sections provide a comprehensive introduction to key principles of adult learning and adult development that Jewish adult educators should keep in mind when seeking to reach out and meet the needs of the burgeoning Jewish adult learning population. These principles are expanded on in the sources listed in the bibliography at the end of this chapter. These sources also offer a number of insights and empirical research findings that we believe Jewish adult educators will find instructive. Figure 1 below summarizes these insights, and provides some practical suggestions for ways to implement these ideas in Jewish adult education. Implicit in the table are questions for reflection and discussion that Jewish educators should address as they strive to meet the developmental and learning needs of Jewish adults.

FROM THEORY TO PRACTICE IN TEACHING JEWISH ADULTS[1]

Insights about Adult Learners	Practical Applications for Jewish Educators
Adult life is filled with ongoing change. People tend to seek new learning when their self-esteem is threatened or their life circumstances are changing. Transitions are eased by new learning experiences. (Aslanian and Brickell, 1980; Kegan, 1994; Schlossberg, 1989)	Offer workshops on life transition themes, including transition to midlife, retirement, grandparenthood, relocation, empty nest, elder care, changes in health.
	Invite people in transition to form study groups on shared concerns.
	Engage adults in the creation of rituals associated with change and renewal.
Adult learner motivations generally include three types:	
Goal-oriented learners who use learning to gain specific objectives, such as learning a new language, learning to deal with specific family problems, learning more effective business practices.	Offer "how-to" activities that help learners become more engaged in Jewish living or observance; teach prayer book and modern Hebrew; offer workshops on intermarriage, holidays, life cycle events.
Activity-oriented learners who participate primarily for the sake of the activity itself (including the social aspects) rather than to develop a skill or learn a subject.	Feature programs that include discussion, storytelling, retreats, cooking, and other forms of community building.
Learning-oriented learners who pursue learning for its own sake, who possess a fundamental desire to know and to grow through learning. (Houle, 1961)	Arrange text study groups, book discussion groups, learners' *minyanim*.
Adult learners are more interested in application and utility than theory. They are pragmatic and place a high value on efficiency, convenience, and relevance. The first question adult learners are likely to ask is: "What is the fastest, easiest, and cheapest way for me to learn whatever I want to learn?" (Knowles, 1980)	Offer short-term as well as long-term classes.
	Assure learners that they can conveniently enter and exit learning activities without penalty.
	Schedule and locate classes to meet learners' convenience.
When adults encounter "disorienting dilemmas," they can be helped to engage in a process of self-reflection and perspective transformation. (Mezirow, 2000)	Pose questions that challenge learners to reflect on their assumptions about Judaism and their lives as Jews
Transformative learning involves: questioning old assumptions, confronting paradoxes, testing new ideas, developing critical thinking skills, and transforming perspective.	Offer support to individuals whose assumptions are being challenged. Meet with learners one-on-one to identify options and plan for ways to test new ideas.
	Help learners to reflect on their Jewish experiences in a critical or systematic way.
Engaging in reflection and discourse helps adult learners to consolidate ideas and develop wisdom. (Brookfield, 1987)	Model reflection by sharing with learners stories of your own Jewish journey.
	Encourage discussion about the tensions between old and new perspectives.

(continued on next page)

[1]Adapted from Apps, 1991; Brookfield, 1986, 1991; Bruffee, 1994; Daloz, 1999; Draves, 1984; Jackson, 1986; Knowles, 1980; Lowman, 1995; Palmer, 1998; Schuster, in press; Westmeyer, 1988.

(continued on next page)

Help learners to assess their previous experience and to evaluate learning needs.

When offering "concrete experiences," build in strategies for observation and reflection that can lead to exploration of alternative possibilities and new ways of thinking.

Help learners to move beyond the immediate activity and look for future levels of engagement.

Assist learners in their continuing movement from experience to analysis to new ideas to experience, and so on.

Help Silent knowers to:
• "unlearn" their assumptions about Judaism and Jewish learning.
• tell their Jewish story.
• meet for tutorial sessions with the Rabbi or educator.
• explore how their lives can be enriched by Jewish texts or rituals.

Help Received knowers to:
• identify gaps in their Jewish knowledge and contract for new learning.
• share their knowledge with others, especially with *chevruta*.
• articulate what Judaism or a particular Jewish issue personally means to them.

Help Subjective knowers to:
• research a Jewish tradition or belief they care deeply about.
• experiment with alternative practices.
• discuss their views and experiences with other Jews.
• create their own *midrashim*.

Help Procedural knowers to:
• locate and study commentaries.
• probe nuances of Hebrew translation.
• develop tools of exegesis (e.g., repeated words, text comparisons).
• study *midrash*.

Help Constructed knowers to:
• interpret texts.
• write *D'vray Torah* and prayers.
• teach others.

Adults bring experience to their learning and thrive in situations that honor past knowledge. Cycles of experiential learning (Kolb, 1984) enable people to move from real life experiences to reflection to consideration of new possibilities — a progression that provides immediacy, relevance, and increased personal authority.

observations & reflection   formation of abstract
                                   concepts & generalizations

concrete
experiences
                        active experimentation,
                        trying out new ideas

Learners may be described as different types of "knowers." (Belenky, et al., 1986)

Silent knowers who
• don't know they have the right to know
• don't know how to begin to acquire knowledge
• tend to be silent observers

Received knowers who
• see knowledge as coming from outside authorities
• are dependent on others when forming opinions
• prefer lecture and "facts"

Subjective knowers who
• rely on personal experience as the basis for knowledge
• have strong convictions that their knowledge is correct
• use intuition

Procedural knowers who
• recognize the value of multiple perspectives
• develop tools to analyze data
• are able to conceptualize and debate opposing views

Constructed knowers who
• develop their own knowledge base after careful analysis
• push back boundaries of their own perspectives
• create new ways of seeing old ideas
• take risks in teaching others

Adult learning styles may be categorized in three ways. (Apps, 1991)

Sequential learners who • appreciate carefully planned learning experiences in which they know exactly what is to be learned and now they should learn it • prefer to learn things in order, first this, then this. Each thing learned builds on the previous information *Practical learners* who • want fast-paced teaching that has immediate application • have little patience for "getting acquainted" teaching tools and other activities that foster a sense of community • prefer teaching approaches that use examples directly applicable to their situation • have little time for what they perceive as theoretical material unless they can see immediate application to practice *Intuitive learners* who • prefer learning when both feeling and thinking are combined • want to find meaning for themselves in what is presented • resent having a teacher tell them what they should learn/how they should learn it • like to make their own judgments about how they can apply what they are learning • appreciate getting to know other learners as people and for the knowledge fellow learners have to share	Anticipate the diverse learning styles present in any Jewish adult learning situation . . . Employ tools more concerned with facts than feelings: Lecture Print materials Interactive computer Employ tools that focus on concrete examples: Case study Group project Result demonstration Skill demonstration Simulation game Employ tools that foster in-depth understanding: Breakout group Role-playing Group project Group discussions Dyad and triad Seminar Simulation game and tools that develop multiple perspectives: Drawing Panel Guest speaker Simulated TV show and tools for providing information: Field trip Lecture Interview Print materials
Adults value teachers who • begin with the needs of the learner. • anticipate the physical needs of adults. • provide an "organizing vision" and "maps" of content and context.	Involve learners in diagnosing learning needs, formulating learning objectives, designing learning plans, and evaluating the learning experience. Adapt teaching to needs and interests of learners. Set up adult learning spaces that have appropriate furniture, good lighting and acoustics, climate control, easy access. Use materials and equipment that ensure readability/visibility. Schedule breaks every 60-75 minutes. Provide coffee; have learners confer about preferred refreshments. Announce plans verbally and in writing. Use visual aids to show linkages in material.

(continued on next page)

• help learners learn "how to learn."	Demystify access to and use of resources. Show learners how to engage in processes of inquiry and discovery. Disclose how they themselves learn and overcome obstacles to learning.
• encourage and model collaborative learning and dialogue.	Organize meaningful discussion groups. Match study partners. Collaborate with learners on projects.
• utilize multiple modes of instruction.	Incorporate lecture, discussion, demonstration, experiential activities, and other methods of instruction. Anticipate needs of visual, aural, and hands-on learners.
• are efficient.	Start and end on time; adhere to prepared schedule. Delimit discussion.
• are reflective about teaching and learning.	Critically reflect on their teaching and adapt teaching approaches as appropriate. Invite and respond to learners' feedback.
• function more as a "guide on the side" than a "sage on the stage."	Facilitate rather than dominate as the expert. Show that the teacher is also a learner.
• teach with both head and heart.	Demonstrate mastery of material and the ability to teach it with rationale and conviction. At the same time, be willing to self-disclose biases and limitations. Respond to the learner from an authentic, congruent, and caring interpersonal stance.

Figure 1

REFERENCES

Apps, Jerold. *Mastering the Teaching of Adults.* Malabar, FL: Krieger, 1994.

Aron, Isa, and Diane Tickton Schuster. "Extending the Chain of Tradition: Reflections on the Goals of Adult Text Study." *Journal of Jewish Education* 64, Winter/Spring 1998, pp. 44-56.

Aslanian, Carol, and Henry Brickell. *Americans in Transition: Life Changes as Reasons for Adult Learning.* New York: College Board, 1980.

Belenky, Mary F.; Blythe Clinchy; Nancy Goldberger; and Jill Tarule. *Women's Ways of Knowing: The Development of Self, Mind and Voice.* New York: Basic Books, 1986.

Berrin, Susan. *A Heart of Wisdom: Making the Jewish Journey from Midlife through the Elder Years.* Woodstock, VT: Jewish Lights Publishing, 1997.

Boyd, Roger. *Personal Transformation in Small Groups.* London: Routledge, 1991.

Brookfield, Stephen. *Understanding and Facilitating Adult Learning.* San Francisco, CA: Jossey-Bass, 1986.

———. *Developing Critical Thinkers.* San Francisco, CA: Jossey-Bass, 1987.

———. *The Skillful Teacher.* San Francisco, CA: Jossey-Bass, 1991.

Bruffee, Kenneth. *Collaborative Learning.* Baltimore, MD: Johns Hopkins University Press, 1993.

Cohen, Steven M., and Arnold M. Eisen. *The Jew Within.* Bloomington, IN: Indiana University Press, 2000.

Cranton, Patricia. *Understanding and Promoting Transformative Learning.* San Francisco, CA: Jossey-Bass, 1994.

Daloz, Laurent. *Mentor: Guiding the Journey of Adult Learners.* San Francisco, CA: Jossey-Bass. 1999.

Draves, William A. *How to Teach Adults.* Manhattan, KS: Learning Resources Network, 1984.

Erikson, Erik. *Childhood and Society.* New York: Norton, 1950.

Grant, Lisa D. "Adult Bar Mitzvah: An American Rite of Continuity." *Courtyard,* 1999/2000, pp. 42-171.

Grant, Lisa D.; Diane T. Schuster; Meredith Woocher; and Steven M. Cohen. *Meaning, Connection and Practice: Issues in Contemporary Adult Jewish Learning,* forthcoming.

Horowitz, Bethamie. *Connections and Journeys: Assessing Critical Opportunities for Enhancing Jewish Identity.* New York: UJA-Federation, 2000.

Houle, Cyril. *The Inquiring Mind.* Madison, WI: University of Wisconsin Press, 1961.

Jackson, Philip W. *The Practice of Teaching.* New York: Teachers College Press, 1986.

Kasl, Elizabeth, and Dean Elias. "Creating New Habits of Mind in Small Groups." In *Learning as Transformation,* edited by Jack Mezirow. San Francisco, CA: Jossey-Bass, 2000.

Kegan, Robert. *In over Our Heads.* Cambridge, MA: Harvard University Press, 1994.

Knowles, Malcolm S. *The Modern Practice of Adult Education.* New York: Cambridge, 1980.

Kolb, David. *Experiential Learning.* Englewood Cliffs, NJ: Prentice Hall, 1984.

Lewin, Kurt. *Field Theory in Social Science.* New York: HarperCollins, 1951.

London, Perry, and Barry Chazan. *Psychology and Jewish Identity Education.* New York: American Jewish Committee, 1990.

Lowman, Joseph. *Mastering the Techniques of Teaching.* 2d ed. San Francisco, CA: Jossey-Bass, 1995.

McKenzie, Leon. "The Purposes and Scope of Adult Religious Education." In *Handbook of Adult Religious Education,* edited by Nancy T. Foltz. Birmingham, AL: Religious Education Press, 1986.

Mezirow, Jack. "Learning to Think Like an Adult: Core Concepts of Transformation Theory." In *Learning as Transformation,* edited by Jack Mezirow. San Francisco, CA: Jossey-Bass, 2000.

Palmer, Parker. *The Courage to Teach.* San Francisco, CA: Jossey-Bass, 1998.

Preparing to Teach: Florence Melton Adult Mini-School Faculty Handbook. Florence Melton Adult Mini-Schools Pilot Version, 2001.

Rosenzweig, Franz. *On Jewish Learning*. Nahum Glatzer, ed. New York: Schocken, 1953.

Schlossberg, Nancy. *Overwhelmed: Coping with Life's Ups and Downs*. Lexington, MA: Lexington, 1989.

Schuster, Diane Tickton. "Telling Jewish Stories/ Listening to Jewish Lives." In *First Fruit: A Whizin Anthology of Jewish Family Education*, edited by Ron Wolfson and Adrianne Bank. Los Angeles, CA: The Whizin Institute, 1998.

———. "New Lessons for Educators of Adult Jewish Learners." *Agenda: Jewish Education* 12, Summer 1999, pp. 16-21.

———. *Jewish Lives, Jewish Learning: Adult Jewish Learning in Theory and Practice*. New York: UAHC Press, in press.

Senge, Peter. *The Fifth Discipline: The Art and Practice of the Learning Organization*. New York: Doubleday, 1990.

Shulman, Lee. "Knowledge and Teaching of the New Reform." *Harvard Educational Review* 57, 1987, pp. 1-22.

Vella, Jane. *Learning to Listen, Learning to Teach*. San Francisco, CA: Jossey-Bass, 1994.

Westmyer, Paul. *Effective Teaching in Adult and Higher Education*. Springfield, IL: Charles C. Thomas, 1988.

BIBLIOGRAPHY

Note: A vibrant and informative literature on adult development and learning has mushroomed in the past 25 years. Resources on Jewish adult education are only now beginning to appear. The following list comprises the resources we turn to most often for guidance about teaching Jewish adults.

Our Favorite Adult Development and Learning Resources

Agenda: Jewish Education, Issue #12, Summer 1999.

Entitled "Adult Jewish Learning," this issue of *Agenda* contains a historical overview of the changing field of Jewish adult education, recommendations for educators of Jewish adults, and a discussion of text study as a religious experience. Other articles provide personal testimony to the impact of adult teaching and learning on Jewish adults.

Apps, Jerold. *Mastering the Teaching of Adults.* Malabar, FL: Krieger, 1994.

Apps provides a practical guide for teachers of adults that includes guidelines for creating a good learning environment, planning lessons, delivering lectures, teaching critical thinking, and assessing quality. In each section of teaching tools, Apps lists "tips" and "things to avoid." He also gives a quick overview of learning styles and teaching styles.

Bee, Helen, and Barbara Bjorklund. *Journey of Adulthood.* 4th ed. Englewood Cliffs, NJ: Prentice-Hall, 1999.

Of all the textbooks on adult development and aging, this is the most comprehensive and reader-friendly. Bee weaves her own developmental journey into the text. This is an excellent introduction to the physical, cognitive, social, and emotional issues of aging. There is also a useful summary of Fowler's theory of faith development — unusual in a college text.

Brookfield, Stephen. *The Skillful Teacher.* San Francisco, CA: Jossey-Bass, 1991.

Brookfield's books on adult teaching and learning are first-rate. He is committed to learner-centered adult education, and consistently urges teachers to be reflective about their own experiences. Here, he describes how to use critical incidents and learning journals to understand what is occurring in the classroom. He also offers guidelines for facilitating discussions, lecturing creatively, using simulations and role-playing, and overcoming student resistance to learning.

Daloz, Laurent. *Mentor: Guiding the Journey of Adult Learners.* San Francisco, CA: Jossey-Bass. 1999.

A highly reflective practitioner, Daloz describes his experiences of mentoring adults in a non-traditional adult learning program. He summarizes theoretical material (Erikson and Levinson on adult development; Mezirow, Kegan, and Perry on adult learner transformation; Gilligan and Belenky on gender issues), and uses dynamic case material to link theory to practice. Daloz's message is that mentoring is an art that involves engendering trust, issuing challenges, providing encouragement, and offering vision.

Hayes, Elisabeth, and Danielle D. Flannery. *Women as Learners.* San Francisco, CA: Jossey-Bass, 2000.

Recent feminist scholarship has surfaced issues specific to women's learning experiences: identity and self-esteem, voice, connection, narrative, positionality, and ways of knowing. Hayes and Flannery situate these issues in a variety of adult learning contexts (formal classrooms, workplace, home, family, community), and provide a sensitive introduction to how educators can pay closer attention to helping women to grow and learn. This book is a good resource on the views of Carol Gilligan (*In a Different Voice*) and Mary Belenky, et al. (*Women's Ways of Knowing*).

Jewish Education News 22, no. 1, Winter 2001.

The special focus of this issue is "Adult Education: Making Jewish Learning Life-long." Articles describe successful Jewish adult learning programs and review key principles of adult learning that educators should incorporate into their program planning.

Kegan, Robert. *In over Our Heads: The Mental Demands of Modern Life.* Cambridge, MA: Harvard University Press, 1994.

In a changing society, adults face a range of unanticipated life demands. Kegan proposes that, to be successful as a parent, worker, learner, and community, adults must develop "fourth order thinking" in which they move beyond the socially constructed meanings of others and "self-author" their own meanings. This book is a helpful reminder to educators to think about their own meaning making and how they cope with the "mental demands of modern life."

Merriam, Sharan, and Rosemary Caffarella. *Learning in Adulthood.* 2d ed. San Francisco, CA: Jossey-Bass, 1999.

This is the "bible" of the adult learning field: a comprehensive overview of adult learning in contemporary society, adult learner characteristics, adult learning theories, and the integration of theory and practice. Although it is dense with information, the book is a gold mine and summarizes key concepts in very reader-friendly fashion.

Mezirow, Jack, and Associates. *Learning as Transformation: Critical Perspectives on a Theory in Progress.* San Francisco, CA: Jossey-Bass, 2000.

Transformative learning theory has been developing for 20 years. This book brings together summary essays by the leading thinkers in the field: Mezirow on theory basics, Robert Kegan on constructive-developmental approaches, Mary Belenky and Ann Stanton on connected knowing, Stephen Brookfield on critical thinking and ideology, and many others. Each essay is a good introduction to how meaning making and transformation occur in quality adult learning enterprises.

Schuster, Diane Tickton. *Jewish Lives, Jewish Learning: Adult Jewish Learning in Theory and Practice.* New York: UAHC Press, in press.

Using a case study approach, Schuster shows how Jewish professionals can apply adult development and learning theories to the experiences of Jewish adults who seek to find deeper meaning in their Jewish lives and learning. The book includes insights from leading Jewish adult educators, as well as numerous practical strategies for creating high quality, learner-centered adult Jewish learning environments.

Taylor, Kathleen; Catherine Marienau; and Morris Fiddler. *Developing Adult Learners: Strategies for Teachers and Trainers.* San Francisco, CA: Jossey-Bass, 2000.

Taylor, Marienau, and Fiddler are committed to "linking learning with development" and offer a practical model for how teachers can design activities that genuinely promote the intellectual growth of the learner. The first part of the book lays out the model and explains why "developmental intentions" matter. The second part is a compendium of 70 examples submitted by adult educators from diverse settings. The examples offer concrete strategies that have been used in learning situations and may be adapted by others.

Vella, Jane. *Learning to Listen, Learning to Teach.* San Francisco, CA: Jossey-Bass, 1994.

Vella's Twelve Principles for Effective Adult Learning reflect her deep understanding of who adult learners are and what they need in their learning situations. After presenting the principles, Vella describes learning situations around the world in which she tested these principles and learned the importance of starting with the learner's needs and creating meaningful dialogues. The examples make the principles come alive.

CHAPTER 15

Family Education

Jo Kay

THE JEWISH FAMILY IS IN TRANSITION

"To serve the Jewish-American family adequately today, a better fit must be re-established between the reality of the lives and needs of individual Jews and the community that seeks to enfold them."[1]

The family educator must help bridge the gap between the reality of the lives and needs of individual Jews today and the stereotypical image held by the Jewish community. This chapter will seek to define family education in the broadest sense, describe the changing American Jewish family as understood by researchers and demographers, and connect this *new* image of Jewish family to Jewish education. Teachers need to know who they are teaching before determining what to teach, and how "teacher," "student," and "content" affect one another in a dynamic interaction. A discussion of the distinctions between adult education and parent (or parallel) education, and how adult learning theories inform the work of the family educator will also be addressed. The chapter will conclude with points for all teachers to consider, regardless of the context in which they work.

Family education is a framework for planning education in a family context. Through such planning the teacher can connect the classroom to the home.

What do we mean when we refer to "family"? Family implies all those individuals to whom the learner (regardless of age) is related. They may or may not be related by blood, they may or may not live together, but they are "related," "connected," to one another in a significant way that cannot be ignored. Looking at the learner through the lens of the family impacts our perception of whom we are teaching. The learner is no longer an individual without a context, but rather a member of a family

and *the family is ultimately the "student"* we are trying to reach. Our learners, whether children or their parents engaged in family education, whether learning together or apart, or whether adults learning without a connection to a "family education" program (but rather in an "adult education" course) are all members of families. And, the families to which the learners belong today, in most cases, do not resemble the "traditional Jewish family" of the past.

"A new Jewish family is taking shape, or more aptly put, new variations on the traditional Jewish family that a mere generation ago would have seemed almost unthinkable. There are more single parents than ever struggling to raise Jewish families these days; and more dual-faith families, too, negotiating theological mine fields; adoptions are soaring in the Jewish community, creating Jewish families across cultural lines; more and more gays and lesbians are rearing Jewish children; multiracial Jewish families are also on the rise — the number of Jewish families with a nonwhite [member] may now be at 10 percent. These families are changing the face of American Jewry, and they are creating the new ties that bind."[2]

Education implies a dynamic interaction between "teacher," "learner," and "content." It is what happens when the teacher enables the learner to interact with the content in such a way as to construct meaning for himself or herself. It is what happens when what is learned is reflected upon, questioned critically, and then leads to some movement or change in attitude or behavior. Jewish Family education implies that the "content" will focus on *genuine Jewish study* or *experience* within the framework of positive family growth and

---

[1]Rela Mintz Geffen, "The Jewish Family: An Institution In Transition." *Journal of Jewish Communal Service* (Winter/Spring 1996/97): 116-121.

[2]Robert Goldblum, "A Family Gathering." *The Jewish Week* (June 3, 2000): 3.

dynamics. For some, the focus will be family. What can be learned to strengthen the functioning of the family? What can be learned from other families and how they interact with one another? What can be learned from the sharing of other parents? What does Jewish tradition have to say about parenting and related issues of concern?

For others, the focus will be Judaic knowledge. What skills can be learned to enable adults to raise their own "Jewish self-esteem"? What knowledge can be learned to enable adults to become literate and fully functioning Jews in the synagogue, at home, and in the world? What can be learned from Jewish tradition that will help adults better understand how they might face life's challenges? What does Jewish tradition have to teach adults about functioning within families?

Coping with Divorce

My name is Arlene. My ex-husband and I have joint custody of our child. Although we are both Jewish, I never really had a Jewish education. I don't know very much about the holidays since my upbringing was almost entirely secular. I moved to a community that is largely non-Jewish, because it is financially easier for us to live there. My son has made many friends in the community and although that is good, he is beginning to question his own identity as a Jew. I want to enroll him in Hebrew school and I want us to spend time together learning what it means to live a Jewish life. How can you help me?

Trying to explain to a group of children why Susie's daddy doesn't live at home anymore was one of the most trying events of my teaching career. I didn't know where to begin or how to explain it in an age appropriate way. I was just about to go into this big speech when Susie took care of it herself. "Mommy and Daddy love me and my brother very much, they just don't like each other, and so Daddy got his own house." I could not have said it any better myself.

(Kim Lausin, Beachwood, Ohio)

Divorce can be terrifying to elementary school children. Because most children know someone whose parents have split, even routine arguments between parents can be threatening to children. Before the divorce, the "family" was an identifiable unit to the child. It had a history. The child knew where he/she fit into that history. The child understood what the family valued and how to look at the world. Jewish family education can bring back the balance needed in the divorced family. It can provide concentrated, focused time together for the parent and the child. By providing support and acceptance within a Jewish setting, both the parent and the child may begin to feel *connected* again. The synagogue can become the missing extended family for which both parent and child yearn.

What are we doing as educators and Jewish professionals to serve the needs of this growing population in our synagogues and schools? How can we form "extended family units" for divorced, single parents? What might we do to offer sensitive and meaningful programs that enable our students — adults and children — to find meaning for themselves within our history and tradition?

Intermarriage

When Jim and I married, I thought we would be able to negotiate our religious differences and also strongly support the Jewish identity of our son Ryan. Yet, after Ryan was born, it was clear that our difficulties had just begun. Jim's family, who lives close by, wanted to share their Irish-Catholic religious and cultural heritage, and I was at a loss, because we live so far from my family. I need help in balancing the differences and similarities and in celebrating Jewish life. Ryan's Brit Milah was only a beginning. I want him to feel deeply connected to his Jewish heritage and to the Jewish religion. I can't do it alone.

The issue of intermarriage affects the family educator in several ways. On the congregational level, how can we become sensitized to the needs of this segment of our community? Frequently, we find the non-Jewish spouse very involved in synagogue life and completely supportive of raising the child Jewishly. However, just as often, we find intermarried families with feelings of alienation and of being "outsiders." The messages that come from the congregation, through fliers, bulletins, even membership forms, do not always speak to the needs and concerns of intermarried families. How are we welcoming them? How are we helping to support the Jewish identity of their children? How do we respond to the non-Jewish spouse/parent?

Steven M. Cohen and Arnold M. Eisen, in their book *The Jew Within: Self, Family and Community in America,* speak of the growing number of American Jews who feel that "intermarriage has no bearing on their Jewish identity." Being Jewish is personal and related to how they view themselves, and the religious identities of their spouses are also personal. What this means is not completely clear. But one thing is certain, say Cohen and Eisen: when the Jewish partner decides it is time to step into the synagogue, the Jewish professionals need to be ready to listen to what they are seeking and find a way to provide what they need. Only then will the Jewish community be able to hold onto this independent, *new* Jewish population that cares less for community and more for the individual.

Single Jews with Children

My name is Nancy and at the age of 40, when it was clear that "mister right" had not entered my life, I decided to become pregnant through artificial insemination with sperm from an anonymous donor. Now, nine years later, my son Evan is a bright and funny boy who fills my life with joy. Although I agree that it would be best for a child to be raised by two parents, marriage was not in the picture for me and I wanted to have a child. I had dreamed about becoming a mother, and my own mother was completely supportive.

Clearly, Nancy and her son Evan force us to expand our understanding of what constitutes a family. "We are in a deep demographic crisis, and if [single] Jews want to have children and raise them as Jews, we as a community have to support them."[3] Although parts of the Jewish community agree with such a decision, many do not. We need to understand the position of the institutions in which we work and find ways to respond to our families that are both helpful and sensitive. Whether parents are single because of the death of a spouse, a divorce, or a conscious choice, they are all part of our community, and they all have different needs that must be addressed if Jewish family education is to strengthen the family unit and help it grow Jewishly.

In our *shul*, we have children who are Asian and African-American, with Caucasian parents. We have African-American families and singles. We have Jews with blond, straight hair, and Jews with black, nappy hair. But all of the pictures in our Jewish books and the posters from Jewish publishers show Jewish kids who are white, and most of them have black hair. The books will change, eventually — today we can buy textbooks with girls wearing *kipot*, and there are children's books about women Rabbis. But for right now, we need to use magazines, scissors, and glue to make our own classroom posters, flash cards, worksheets, and children's *Siddurim*.

Congregational artists are a tremendous resource: When we made a new *Siddur* for our kids' *havurah* (a weekly Shabbat morning *davening*/prayer and activity group), a congregant made beautiful ink wash pictures of children in our congregation, so that even our youngest congregants would be able literally to see themselves in their *Siddur*.

(Anne Johnston, New Haven, Connecticut)

Interracial Adoptions

I will never forget the magic of the moment when I first held this beautiful infant Chinese baby girl in my arms. I sang to her, softly, a melody my own parents had sung to me when I was just a tot. It was a melody I have sung many times since in the synagogue. I knew it would comfort this beautiful stranger from a faraway land whom I held cradled in my arms. I knew it would comfort my new baby daughter. But I also knew she had to learn songs from her own Chinese heritage as well. She needed to know where she came from, and yet belong to all that I have always cherished in Jewish tradition.

This story is representative of the hundreds of Chinese baby girls who have been adopted by Jewish families throughout North America. Jewish-Chinese children will grow up with a deep knowledge of two ancient traditions that value family, study, and food. Jewish-American parents with Jewish-Chinese baby girls will walk through the

---

[3]Adeena Sussman, "Parenting: And Baby Makes Two." *Hadassah Magazine* (June/July 2000): 56-57.

doors of our synagogues and schools asking for support and assistance in building a positive Jewish identity that also respects the child's Chinese culture. (Many of the same issues apply to families with adopted children from other countries and cultures as well.) What kinds of programs will be created to welcome this new Jewish family into our communities? How can we creatively rethink what we are teaching and broaden our understanding of the *new* Jewish-American family and the challenges it faces?

I try to include some text study in each of the family or congregational programs I plan. Two segments of a recent program on "Synagogue Symbols and Ritual Objects" that seemed especially to encourage some of our more senior members to work together with our youth both included biblical text. In the first, the project invited participants to take the challenge to follow the instructions God gave regarding the design of the cover of the Ark of the Covenant. I printed out the descriptive text (Exodus 37:6-9 and Exodus 37:17-24) and provided drawing paper and materials. The second project sent participants on a Biblical Scavenger Hunt to answer a variety of questions having to do with altars, the Law, the construction and decoration of the Ark of the Covenant, the construction of the Tabernacle and its ritual objects, and the description of the priestly garments. The location of each answer was cited and had the participants leafing through the pages of the Bible, often with our senior members helping our youth understand what the numbers cited meant. Our senior members later shared with me how pleased they were to have had a chance to help our children learn.

(Carol Cohn, Orlando, Florida)

Gay and Lesbian Parents

I am Michael and my life partner is Jon. Jon and I have adopted two boys. We want our boys to grow up with a really positive sense of Jewish family. While I never liked Hebrew school, I always loved being Jewish. I learned how to read Hebrew and going to services really helps me get close to my spirituality. But, because we are different — gay men with adopted boys — we are feeling very isolated in the synagogue. We get mixed messages from the community and from our own families. We aren't thought of as a serious Jewish family and we need help in creating a Jewish home.

Gay and lesbian Jews, like heterosexual Jews, share Jewish and American values and behaviors. However, they have very specific concerns involving family, synagogue membership, and Jewish culture and theology.[4]

What mechanisms have we, educators concerned with the needs of families, put in place to identify such family issues and concerns as those described above? How closely are we listening to what these families perceive as their needs and what they actually want from the synagogue and the Jewish community? What responses are we prepared to make when these families present themselves and their concerns to our synagogues and schools?

The changing nature of the American Jewish family is seen by some as a reflection of the "collapse of family values," by others as "the weakening patterns of Jewish identification, particularly among 'alternative families,'" and by still others as a celebration of the long awaited recognition of "family diversity."[5]

Nevertheless, there are certain assumptions about Jewish family life that do find general acceptance within the greater Jewish community:

- Family has served as the primary conduit for transmitting Jewish identity from generation to generation.

- The Jewish family in North America cannot be understood outside the context of family life in North American culture.

- Strengthening family life in America requires greater societal recognition of the needs of today's changing families.

- Family as a Jewish value has been one of

---

[4]Fishman, Sylvia Barack. "Jewish Gay and Lesbian Households," in *Jewish Life and American Culture* (Albany, NY: State University of New York Press), 106-108.

[5]Steven Bayme and Gladys Rosen, eds. *The Jewish Family and Jewish Continuity.* (Hoboken, NJ: KTAV Publishing Company, 1994), xi.

the key ideals of Jewish society throughout the ages.[6]

These assumptions can only support the work of those looking at education through the lens of family. We know that we must work with the "family" when supporting and strengthening Jewish identity. We know that learners are set in a context that affects how they learn. The context of the American culture affects the culture of the Jewish family and must be taken into consideration. We acknowledge that strengthening families is a goal of Jewish family education and that to have any affect in this area requires an understanding that families are diverse and changing. And, finally, since "family" has always been a Jewish value and a key ideal held by Jewish societies throughout the ages, what better place to begin our thinking about Jewish education than from within the context of the family?

FAMILY AND COMMUNITY ASSESSMENT

As the Jewish community continues to expand and change, it is becoming more and more like an unfamiliar mosaic. Regardless of how familiar or divergent our families are, the family educator, any educator, must know them before thinking about how to help them construct meaning for themselves within the context of Jewish tradition.

Knowledge Building

Conducting intake interviews often yields much of what we need to know to begin our work. But what are the questions we should be asking? Here are some questions that will help Jewish professionals actually "see" their students and their families.

- Who are the families?

- What unique characteristics do they bring to the community?

- What talents or skills can they share with the community?

- How do they spend their leisure time?

- What do they enjoy doing as adults? as families?

- What do they want and expect from the synagogue or school?

- What are they telling us they want?

Planning and Implementation

- How well are we listening?

- What do they (the parents) reveal in the stories they tell?

- What can we learn about what they want and need?

- How can we help our teachers "see" our families and their needs?

- What do the professionals, clergy, and educators, want and expect?

- What already exists — curricula, programs, structures — that can be built upon?

- What new curricula, programs, structures, must be developed to meet the needs of the *new* Jewish community?

- How can we move toward a shared vision that sees education through the lens of the family?

- Who must be involved in developing the shared vision?

- What resources — human, financial, and material — can we draw upon?

- What steps must be taken to move forward?

- Who needs to do what?

- When shall we begin?

FAMILY EDUCATION AND PARENT PARALLEL EDUCATION

When your children ask you, "What do you mean by this rite?" you shall say, "It is the Passover sacrifice to *Adonai*, because God passed over the houses of the Israelites in Egypt when God smote the Egyptians, but saved our houses." (Exodus 12:26-27)

---

[6]Ibid.

These verses are the origin of having children ask questions at the *Seder*. It underscores the parents' responsibility to teach their children. The story of the "four sons" is a device to teach parents that *all* their children must understand the customs and traditions, regardless of their ages and capacities. We learn further, from Maimonides, in *Hilchot Torah* 1:6, that parents are obligated to begin teaching their children from they time they can speak, and that the parents are obligated to continue their own study "until the day they die." (*Hilchot Torah* 1:10)

The goal of the Passover *Seder* is to ensure Jewish continuity by having parents teach children our people's story, from slavery to freedom, and the role God played in that story. The *Seder*, with its repeated concern for the education of the entire family, becomes a paradigm for "family education."

Jewish family education occurs when parents and children, together, or in parallel settings (either apart, but at the same time, or at a different time), are involved in Jewish experiences that enable both child and adult to construct meaning, and therefore have learning as the primary objective. Although most family education experiences currently taking place in congregational schools, day schools, camps, JCCs, museums, etc., are interactive family programs, it is not the only way for families to study and learn.

If we see family education as a "framework for education," many additional creative and meaningful opportunities to help families study come to mind. What are the "teachable moments" that parents and children share each day? Bedtime, bath time, meals, shopping, car pools, a walk in the park, to name a few, are all opportunities for parents to teach their children. It is the job of the family educator to help parents identify those "moments," and then to provide them with the resources and the skills they need to construct meaning for themselves and their children, using Jewish sources and texts. Only then can they become generative by teaching what they have learned to their children.

Parents and children can study text together in *chevruta* (Jewish study technique of studying in pairs with a study partner). They can make a ritual object together after researching how, when, and why it is used, and what materials are needed.

They can cook special holiday treats, read stories, watch a movie, visit a significant Jewish site, etc., and ask questions to discover its meaning and how it is connected to their lives. These learning experiences can happen in a formal school setting, at home, on a field trip to the planetarium, to the zoo, to the theater, or any place where families can enjoy being together while discovering — uncovering — the mystery of Jewish life and tradition.

What the family educator — in fact, all Jewish professionals — must keep in mind is that there is no one way to reach the members of our families. Every avenue possible should be used to connect the home to the synagogue and the family to the school. As Jonathan S. Woocher, President of Jewish Educational Services of North America (JESNA) has said, "The more, the more."[7] We understand this to mean that synagogues and schools must constantly be looking for ways to bring the learning home. Learning happens in programs, in conversations at home, on trips, through newsletters, through formal study, etc. The *more* opportunities created for learning, the *more* possibilities exist for transformation to occur. Once we move from thinking of family education as a program, to thinking of it as a framework around which to build programs, it takes on a new focus and impetus.

Parallel learning is an alternative format for fulfilling the *mitzvah* of family study. In this format, unlike family study, parents study independent of their children. They may be in a room down the hall while the children are in class with their teacher; or they may study at a completely different time, perhaps an evening during the week. However, while designed for adults, parallel learning keeps the family in focus. An adult parallel learning Torah study class, focusing on the Book of Exodus, may take time out from text interpretation to discuss the *Seder* rituals and how to make them more "family friendly." Or, discussions about Abraham as someone who demonstrates caring for others, might also include an opportunity for adults to share how they demonstrate this *mitzvah* in the context of their own families. Regardless of the subject being studied, the family is always part of the picture and the learning is projected onto the home whenever possible. Adults may be studying on an adult level what their children are study-

---

[7]Jonathan S. Woocher, Keynote Speaker, Commission on Lifelong Learning, Union of American Hebrew Congregations, New York, February 10, 2002.

ing, or something totally different, but ultimately a connection to their children's studies is made. The goal is the transfer of learning to a family setting. The emphasis is on family values and family issues as they relate to the subject being studied.

> We can teach the parents of our students about Judaism and parenting. Frequent positive communication through notes and telephone calls is a good way to start. I promise parents on Back To School Night that I will let them know the strengths and the weaknesses of their children. I rarely have a problem with cooperation when I ask parents to help me solve a classroom dilemma that involves their child. They are my partners in education, my colleagues. I tell them that I know a lot in general about elementary age children and how they function in a group, and that they are the specialists, knowing one particular child in depth. Together we can form an unbeatable team of experts.
>
> *(Maura Pollak, Tulsa, Oklahoma)*

In the parallel learning classroom, the teacher's perception shifts from students as adults, to students as parents and as members of families. Parents are encouraged to "take the discussions home." Parallel learning enables parents to share their experiences and discussions with other parents. Parents are encouraged to learn from one another as they grow and develop personally, as parents, as adult Jewish learners, and as teachers of their children.

As teachers, we must be ever aware of these important goals of working with families. Not only are we seeking to help our parents grow Jewishly, but we are also seeking to help them become better parents to their children and better friends to one another. In many cases, successful family education classes actually turn into family *havurot* for study, for celebration, and for support.

WHAT IS ADULT EDUCATION?[8]

Adult Education, usually defined in terms of the motivating factors encouraging adults to choose to

study, generally involves a process of self-actualization. An expressed or felt need has moved the adult to seek out opportunities to learn and grow. It is usually voluntary and in response to some life transition. While this is very different in its focus and motivation from parent education, what has been learned about why adults chose to study has a great deal to teach family educators. Even when a family educator is working with whole families, the needs of the adults in those families — parents, grandparents, older siblings, other relatives, and friends — must be kept in mind.

One of the complaints often heard from professionals who are trying to run family education programs is, "Why don't they [parents] want to come?" Unless you have taken a close look at "who your families are" and "what your families enjoy doing," this is a question that is difficult to answer. Nevertheless, we have learned one lesson over the years: parents are too busy to have their time wasted. They want to be with their children. They want to enjoy the time they have together with their children. They want to know that their children are happy and learning. And, especially in parent education (adult only) sessions, they want *their needs as parents* to be addressed.

Conceptualizing how to define the education of a family greatly broadens the scope of family education. Jewish professionals, regardless of their roles, work with people who are members of families, who come from families with a history and a context that affects how they learn. And, there is considerable literature available on how adults learn. This literature informs how we work with families (adults in families) as we attempt to understand who they are and what they need.

A set of assumptions about adult learners known as "andragogy" has been most closely associated with Malcolm Knowles, noted writer in the field of adult education. These assumptions can be helpful for thinking about the adults in family programs, adults in parent programs, or adults studying in our adult education programs. They are:

- Adults are inclined toward self-directedness in most learning situations.

- Adults learn best through experiential techniques such as discussion and problem solving.

---

[8]For a fuller discussion of adult education, see Chapter 14, "Teaching Jewish Adults" by Diane Tickton Schuster and Lisa D. Grant, pp. 140-163 in this volume.

- Adults are aware of specific learning needs generated by real-life tasks or problems.

- Adults are competency-based learners and wish to apply newly acquired skills or knowledge to their immediate circumstances.[9]

How can family educators use these assumptions in the development of family and parent learning programs? Returning to the importance of "family and community assessment," it would be extremely helpful to involve parents in the design of family learning experiences. By asking, "What would you like to learn? How can the synagogue or the school help you in meeting your goals?" the educators can encourage involvement and personal investment on the part of the adults. When we listen carefully to the adults in our communities, we can often "hear" about some of the "life transitions," the issues and problems that the adults are presently experiencing and that could generate a need on the part of the adult to learn.

Diane Tickton Schuster, developmental psychologist and director of the Institute for Teaching Jewish Adults at Hebrew Union College — Jewish Institute of Religion in Los Angeles, writes that life's transitions are often an impetus for adults to seek out learning opportunities. Moving to a new place, the death of a parent or a spouse, becoming a parent, becoming part of the sandwich generation, or, the need to keep up with the Jewish education of their children are all specific learning needs generated by life's problems.[10]

> . . . My name is Harold . . . Actually, I'm here because I lost my father last spring, and since that time I have been thinking a lot about my life as a Jew. You know, I was really involved with my synagogue's youth group when I was a kid, and I was so good at Hebrew that I even thought about becoming a Rabbi. But in college I got turned off by my parents' pressure to marry a Jewish girl, and for a long time I rejected anything Jewish. Funny thing, I did marry a Jewish girl, and now that our kids are studying Hebrew, we want to learn it — really learn it — too.[11]

After listening to Harold, the family educator might choose to create an adult basic Hebrew language class (many congregations around the country have created successful parent-child beginning Hebrew programs, as well as Hebrew classes for parents), a class on the Jewish life cycle, or the educator may direct this parent to other Hebrew language learning opportunities. The responsiveness on the part of the synagogue or school to an expressed need places the school in a very positive context: the school has an understanding of this family's needs and is prepared to respond. Adults value such immediate actions and are likely to return again as they continue to seek additional avenues for personal adult Jewish growth.

The concept of "transformative learning" has been incorporated into the working definition of Jewish family education. If we agree that the word "education" refers both to the dynamic interaction among teacher, learner, and content, and to the ability of the learner to construct meaning that leads to movement or change in values, attitudes, beliefs, or behavior, then we must also agree that there can be a transformative component for the adults (parents) in certain learning situations. Not all family education is transformative, nor should it be. It depends on what goals have been established by the educator and the learner. When the focus is to learn a skill (candle blessings, how to conduct a Passover *Seder,* how to navigate the prayer book, etc.), neither the educator nor the learner is looking for transformation; rather, knowledge acquisition becomes the goal.

Educators and writers concerned with how adults learn have also addressed the concept of "transformative learning." Patricia Cranston, writing about adult learners, says that the "primary difference between education for adults and education for children is that children are 'forming' and adults are 'transforming.'" Cranston believes that in using the approach of transformative learning, "the educator goes beyond simply meeting the expressed needs of the learner, as in self-directed learning, and takes on the responsibility of questioning the learner's expectations and beliefs."[12]

---

[9]Stephen D. Brookfield, *Understanding and Facilitating Adult Learning* (San Francisco, CA: Jossey-Bass, 1999), 91.

[10]Diane Tickton Schuster, "Adult Development and Jewish Family Education," in *First Fruit: A Whizin Anthology of Jewish Family Education,* edited by Ron Wolfson and Adrianne Bank

(Los Angeles, CA: The Shirley and Arthur Whizin Institute of Jewish Family Life, 1998).

[11]Ibid., 523.

[12]Patricia Cranston, *Working with Adult Learners* (Dayton, OH: Wall and Emerson, 1992), 145.

She continues, "if we are working *only* with the learner's expressed needs, we [as educators] are not challenging the learner to question the assumption underlying the need."[13]

In questioning the way they see the world, their values and assumptions, adults are forced to think critically about their behaviors and why they act as they do. Then the work of constructing personal meaning begins. This may lead to reflection, reevaluation, and possible changes or adjustments in behavior.

> It's important to be sensitive to the fact that your students may have a parent who is not Jewish. When I ask the children to practice Hebrew reading at home, they tell me that their parents don't know Hebrew. I suggest that they read to a grandparent, or to a student who has already become a Bar Mitzvah. I also have to be careful when I ask them to question their parents on celebrations or traditions. For example, if I ask a child to interview their parents to find out a memory that they have from their childhood regarding Passover, it's possible that the child can't do this type of assignment. I try to reword the assignment in a way that makes it possible for every child to complete it. I might suggest that they ask a grandparent, or a friend, if their parents aren't able to respond to the assignment.
>
> *(Nancy Hersh, Chatham, New Jersey)*

Jewish Family education programs, in attempting to empower parents to reclaim their role as primary Jewish teachers of their children, must find ways to support these behavioral changes, regardless of how small. Providing "scaffolding,"[14] structures that enable parents to extend their reach, to accomplish a task not possible without support, while slowly becoming accustomed to new behaviors, is also the responsibility of the family educators. Just as training wheels are used when learning to ride a bicycle for the first time, so, too, must adults/parents be supported and mentored until they become confident enough to continue on their own.

As family educators or Jewish professionals concerned with education as seen through the lens of family seek to design meaningful programs, courses, interactions, and activities that challenge the parents' assumptions within a supportive environment, they (the educators) serve as guides, encouraging exploration and experimentation that is safe and responsive. Keeping in mind that each adult brings his/her own family history and experiences with Judaism and Jewish living, the educator is challenged to see and respond to the different needs and different paths necessary for learners to confront meaningfully their own assumptions, and to move forward.

TEACHING CONSIDERATIONS

- The American Jewish family is in transition. It is changing in makeup, attitudes, values, and behavior. The "traditional" Jewish family is no longer the norm. Family educators and all Jewish professionals must acknowledge the changes and be responsive to them.

- Family education is not about programs. It is a framework for thinking about education through the lens of the family.

- Family educators shift their focus from the individual as the student to the family as the student they are trying to reach.

- There is a dynamic interaction between the teacher, the learner, and the content. Each component impacts the other.

- Whether working with families, students alone, or adults alone, the teacher must know the learners. Family and community assessment is a necessity.

- Working with groups of families, or with groups of adults, requires special skills in "group dynamics." Teachers should seriously address the following questions:

  - Do I have procedures to get to know everyone? Have I planned procedures to help everyone get to know each other?

---

[13]Ibid., 146.

[14]"Scaffolding," a metaphor originated by Wood, Bruner and Ross as a complement to Lev Vygotsky's theory of zone of proximal development, has been made popular within family

education circles by Vicky Kelman in her article, "Zones and Scaffolds: Toward a Theory of Jewish Family Education," in *Jewish Family Retreats* by Vicky Kelman (New York and Los Angeles, CA: Melton/Whizin, 1992), 9-23.

- Is it *safe* for students to express their fears, concerns, needs, and ideas?

- Do students *listen* to one another? How can the teacher facilitate the use of good listening skills?

- Have I, the teacher, developed several different strategies to encourage positive interaction among students, among families, and/or among students and parents?

- Have I, the teacher, considered the *different learning styles* represented in the groups?

- Do I, the teacher, use visual, audio, written and experiential strategies to *help students construct personal meaning*?

- Are individual differences respected? Can these differences be heard in a *nonjudgmental* way?

- Are conflicts and issues recognized and discussed, while not imposing a particular point of view?

- Family educators should develop a plan that includes the articulated needs of the families and the stated goals of the program.

- Family educators will work to build upon existing structures, curricula, programs.

- Family educators will work toward involving learners (parents/adults) in developing a shared educational vision seen through the lens of the family.

- A vision for the education of all members of the family must be BIG, but it should be addressed in small steps.

- Family education is the responsibility of all the professionals in synagogue, school, camp, etc. It requires a team effort and must be approached through all existing venues in many different ways.

- By developing a shared plan of action, no one person is responsible, rather, everyone is invested in the success of the plan.

- Being responsive to the needs of all the learners, enabling learners to construct personal meaning, thinking beyond the school to the homes and communities from which our learners come, is very challenging and labor intensive work.

- Family education can be transformative. It can help parents support the Jewish identities of their children. It can affect the future of the Jewish community.

- Family education is *avodah kodesh*, holy work!

It's hard to imagine what the future of Jewish education will be. It seems like so many parents are juggling their own schedules and that of their children that Religious School seems often not to get its fair share of time and attention. I try to be sympathetic to the fact that my students are involved in so many things, and that if I ignore their other interests, I will turn them off to Judaism. I always tell them that while it's fun to play soccer (and maybe they are even good at it), it's unlikely that they will be career soccer players. However, they'll be Jewish their whole lives, so they need to spend time learning about and participating in Judaism.

(Nancy Hersh, Chatham, New Jersey)

BIBLIOGRAPHY

Changing Jewish Family

Bayme, Steven, and Gladys Rosen, eds. *The Jewish Family and Jewish Continuity*. Hoboken, NJ: KTAV Publishing Company, 1994.

A compilation of essays that assess the current situation of the Jewish American family. The authors discuss such issues as intermarriage, low birth rate, adoption, divorce, abortion, feminism, and pornography in an attempt to minimize whatever adverse affects these trends may pose for the Jewish family and Jewish life.

Cohen, Debra Nussbaum. "Shades of Gray." *The Jewish Week,* June 23, 2000, p. 10.

This article introduces the reader to the rapidly growing multiracial families that are changing the face of American Jewry. These are Jewish families in which at least one family member is not white. Whether the child is adopted, or a converted parent is black, Asian, Hispanic, or biracial, these Jewish families constitute a growing population. The question raised is, "Are they being accepted?"

Cohen, Steven M., and Arnold M. Eisen. *The Jew Within: Self, Family and Community in America*. Bloomington, IN: Indiana University Press, 2000.

Through in-depth interviews with Jews across the country, the authors seek to uncover the foundations of belief and behavior among moderately affiliated American Jews. Beautifully written, this important book raises some of the most serious questions confronting Jewish professionals today.

Fishman, Sylvia Barack. "Forming Jewish Households and Families." In *Jewish Life and American Culture*. Albany, NY: State University of New York Press, 2000.

By analyzing the fluid boundaries in the ethnic identity of Jewish and non-Jewish Americans, Fishman suggests that Jews combine aspects of American and Jewish culture and often lose sight of the greater Jewish picture to which they belong. The book combines narrative and scholarly research details.

Geffen, Rela Mintz. "The Jewish Family: An Institution in Transition." *Journal of Jewish Communal Service,* Winter/Spring 1996-97, pp. 116-121.

This article discusses the lack of fit between how the community defines family and the actual configurations and ways of life of Jewish-American families. This lack of congruence results in the exclusion of many Jews from Jewish communal life. Jewish professionals are challenged to rethink their language and their structures to be more welcoming.

Goldblum, Robert. "A Family Gathering." *The Jewish Week,* June 23, 2000, p. 3.

This article focuses on the new variations of the traditional Jewish family that only a generation ago would have seemed unthinkable. This writer suggests that whether these families will be accepted into the fold is yet to be determined.

Keysar, Ariela; Barry A. Kosmin; and Jeffrey Scheckner. *The Next Generation: Jewish Children and Adolescents*. Albany, NY: State University of New York Press, 2000.

Using the 1990 National Jewish Population Survey as its starting point, the authors examine the critical issues concerning the Jewish community in the United States. It raises questions and concerns for all Jewish professionals about the future of the Jewish community's next generation.

Linzer, Norman; Irving N. Levitz; and David J. Schnall, eds. *Crisis and Continuity: The Jewish Family in the 21st Century*. Hoboken, NJ: KTAV Publishing, Inc., 1995.

This book presents a series of papers that emerged from a seminar at the Wurzweiler School of Social Work. The writers focus on the changing values and mores facing the Jewish family and offer possible approaches to coping with the issues.

Family Life Concerns

Cardin, Nina Beth. *Tears of Sorrow, Seeds of Love: A Jewish Spiritual Companion for Infertility and Pregnancy Loss*. Woodstock, VT: Jewish Lights Publishing, 1999.

This book is meant to be a spiritual companion for people grieving infertility, pregnancy loss, or stillbirth. It offers passages drawn from

Jewish tradition as sources of consolation. It can help the family educator understand the special pain experienced by those confronting such loss.

Green, Jesse. *The Velveteen Father: An Unexpected Journey To Parenthood.* New York: Ballantine Books, 1999.

This is a beautifully sensitive memoir of a gay man becoming an adoptive father. It discusses issues of parenthood, alienation, and love associated with this unconventional Jewish family.

King, Andrea. *If I'm Jewish and You're Christian, What Are the Kids? A Parenting Guide for Interfaith Families.* New York: UAHC Press, 1993.

This book explores a series of questions confronting interfaith families as they try to determine how to help their children develop religious identities. Some questions discussed are: How will religious rituals affect a child's developing self-concept? When should a couple decide on the child's religious identity? How difficult is it for teens in an interfaith family?

Rosenberg, Shelley Kapnek. *Adoption and the Jewish Family: Contemporary Perspectives.* Philadelphia, PA: Jewish Publication Society, 1998.

Rosenberg takes an informed look at the adoption process from the Jewish perspective. Readers are prepared for the many challenges that may develop when working with adoptive families.

Seltzer, Sanford. *When There Is No Other Alternative: A Spiritual Guide for Jewish Couples Contemplating Divorce.* New York: UAHC Press, 2000.

Rabbi Seltzer examines what traditional Jewish sources have to say about divorce, as well as the issues associated with it. He offers guidance in working with families that are going through this difficult time.

Sussman, Adeena. "Parenting: And Baby Makes Two." *Hadassah Magazine*, June/July 2000, pp. 56-57.

Single motherhood, once worn as a badge of shame, is today the answer to some women's prayers. In several cases, this status has even received the community's blessing. This writer has interviewed several mothers who are single parents "by choice."

Jewish Family Education

Grishaver, Joel Lurie, with Ron Wolfson. *Jewish Parents: A Teacher's Guide.* Los Angeles, CA: Torah Aura Productions, 1997.

Beginning with questions confronting Jewish family educators, the book presents responses from experienced colleagues. Also interspersed are several stories from the field to which educators have been asked to react. The book provides much useful advice to teachers working with families.

Kelman, Vicky. *Family Room: Linking Families into a Jewish Learning Community.* Los Angeles, CA: The Shirley and Arthur Whizin Institute for Jewish Family Life, 1995.

This book comprises a two-year curriculum for small groups of families with children. Its goals are to strengthen Jewish life, to strengthen the family, and to create community for the participants.

————. "Zones and Scaffolds: Toward a Theory of Jewish Family Education." In *Jewish Family Retreats.* New York and Los Angeles, CA: Melton/Whizin, 1992.

This article, which is in an excellent manual for running Jewish family retreats, presents a theory of Jewish family education. Looking at the needs of the family in general and the Jewishness of the family in particular, the article discusses transformative educational methods.

Schein, Jeffrey, and Judith S. Schiller, eds. *Growing Together: Resources, Programs, and Experiences for Jewish Family Education.* Denver, CO: A.R.E. Publishing, Inc., 2001.

This book addresses the needs of today's Jewish family, seeking to become involved in Jewish life. It addresses changing family structures, lifestyles, and learning styles, and provides many practical programs that can be adapted in various settings.

Wolfson, Ron, and Adrianne Bank, eds. *First Fruit: A Whizin Anthology of Jewish Family Education.* Los Angeles, CA: The Shirley and Arthur Whizin Institute for Jewish Family Life, 1998.

Focused on the field of Jewish family education, this anthology brings together 36 articles that relate to the personal experiences and expertise of family educators associated with the Whizin Institute. It represents the "first fruits" of these professional educators who have worked with families and have sought to define the field.

Jewish Parenting

Danan, Julie Hilton. *The Jewish Parents' Almanac.* Northvale, NJ: Jason Aronson Inc., 1994.

A guidebook to raising Jewish children, including Judaic insights, suggestions for Shabbat and holiday observances, family projects, games, recipes, and personal stories.

Diamant, Anita, with Karen Kushner. *How to Be a Jewish Parent: A Practical Handbook for Family Life.* New York: Schocken Books, 2000.

The authors have organized this useful parenting guide into two parts: "parents as teachers" and "ages and stages." In each section, careful attention is paid to Jewish values and age appropriateness.

Fuchs-Kreimer, Nancy. *Parenting as a Spiritual Journey: Deepening Ordinary and Extraordinary Events into Sacred Occasions.* Woodstock, VT: Jewish Lights Publishing, 1996.

This book looks as the spiritually transformative possibilities experienced when raising children. Rituals, prayers, and inspiring Jewish texts are interpersed throughout.

Parent and Adult Education

Belenky, Mary Field, et al. *Women's Ways of Knowing: The Development of Self, Voice and Mind.* New York: Basic Books, Inc., 1997.

Based on in-depth interviews with 135 women, this book explores why women still feel silenced in their schools and their families. It focuses on the feelings of alienation and mistrust. Family educators must be particularly sensitive to how such feelings present themselves and how to respond to them.

Brookfield, Steven D. *Understanding and Facilitating Adult Learning.* San Francisco, CA: Jossey-Bass Publishers, 1999.

Brookfield presents an analysis of current approaches to adult learning, reviews the research on how adults learn, and identifies ways of developing creative and innovative adult education programs.

Cranston, Patricia. *Working with Adult Learners.* Dayton, OH: Wall and Emerson, 1992.

This book discusses the connection between adult learning and transformative learning. It identifies a step-by-step process necessary for transformation to occur, and speaks to the goals of good family education.

Katz, Betsy Dolgin. "Adult Education and Jewish Family Education." In *First Fruit: A Whizin Anthology of Jewish Family Education,* edited by Ron Wolfson and Adrianne Bank. Los Angeles, CA: The Shirley and Arthur Whizin Institute of Jewish Family Life, 1998.

This article discusses adult learning theories as they relate to familiy education curricula and programs. It connects the two, adults and families, on practical and theoretical levels.

Kay, Jo. "Parallel Learning and Parent Empowerment." In *First Fruit: A Whizin Anthology of Jewish Family Education,* edited by Ron Wolfson and Adrianne Bank. Los Angeles, CA: The Shirley and Arthur Whizin Institute of Jewish Family Life, 1998.

This article describes how parents are empowered to become teachers of their children through their own learning. Parents learning in adult education or parent education programs always remain parents and their learning is focused in that direction.

Schuster, Diane Tickton. "Adult Development and Jewish Family Education." In *First Fruit: A Whizin Anthology of Jewish Family Education,* edited by Ron Wolfson and Adrianne Bank. Los Angeles, CA: The Shirley and Arthur Whizin Institute of Jewish Family Life, 1998.

This article discusses developmental theories as they relate to adults. It describes what adults need in order to learn and then relates those needs to parents in family education settings.

CHAPTER 16

Special Needs Students

Ellen Fishman

This chapter focuses attention on learners in Jewish classrooms with special needs. While some of the larger cities across North America have taken the lead in providing the necessary teacher training and student opportunities, until quite recently, Jewish children with special needs have not had access to Jewish day or supplementary education. There are still many schools that are far behind in understanding the nature and needs of these individuals and providing appropriate support to the teachers who work with them. In this chapter, we will explore how best to serve the range of students in the classroom, including those with high incidence special needs.

SOME HISTORY AND THE LAW

The history of special education dates back to the passage of Public Law, 94-142, The All Handicapped Act, originally passed in 1975, and reauthorized in 1990. In 1997, it reemerged as IDEA, Individuals With Disabilities Education Act, providing the opportunity for students who differ from the norm to be educated alongside their typically developing peers. A Free Appropriate Public Education (FAPE) is among the rights to which these individuals are entitled. The legislation mandates that children with special needs receive FAPE in the "least restrictive environment" (LRE). The term "least restrictive environment" is a legal principle requiring students with disabilities to be educated as closely as possible with students without disabilities. While there is no mention of "inclusion" anywhere in the law, it did develop out of the concept of the LRE, and has become one of the hallmarks of the legislation.[1] What is most important to understand about the intent of the LRE is the notion that special education is not a place, but rather a continuum of services provided to the student.

Although parents who send their children to Jewish day school effectively waive their rights to FAPE available in the public school system, they still expect that their children will receive special education support and that proper interventions will be developed to assure their student's academic success. Families that send their children with special needs to supplementary school have similar expectations. For Jewish educators who find themselves teaching and working with these students, the challenge is to provide for the student's individual needs and the needs of every other student for whom they are responsible. While it can be a daunting task, it can also be an extraordinary opportunity! Research tells us that many regular educators receive little or no training in the area of special education. Thus, they have limited experience when planning for students with a broad range of needs. Typically, regular classroom teachers concentrate more on content and less on delivery. While this is more evident among secondary education teachers, it is not uncommon for teachers of students as young as second grade to develop a "one size fits all" approach, which meets only a small percentage of student needs. Often, the result is a frustrated teacher and a group of students unengaged in the task. Planning for students with an eye toward "access to the information" will assure greater success for all. This, then, will serve as the framework for this chapter. It is not meant to be comprehensive, but rather to provide some insights into the students enrolled in our schools. It is a stepping-stone to further exploration, and an examination of the joys and challenges of teaching all of our students.

IN THE CLASSROOM

Consider the first day of school — a classroom

[1]Mitchell L. Yell, "The Legal Basis of Inclusion," *Educational Leadership* 56 (October 1998), 70.

filled with a group of anxious children seeing old friends and new, a new teacher, new expectations, new rules, new books, and a new curriculum. In older grades, where students have more than one teacher, the expectations and rules can change many times throughout the day. It is a landscape comprised of students who are anxious and excited by the prospects of the unfolding year and spoiled and bored by the lazy days of summers. It is also an environment in which the teacher is filled with anticipation and excitement about the new group of students he/she will guide over the coming months.

Each child and, indeed, the teacher and parents have high expectations for the school year. Everyone anticipates the fresh start, the new beginning. Nevertheless, it won't take long for the students to assume their status in the classroom: most promising, most troubled, most needy, most helpful, and so on. And it won't be long either for the teacher, maybe without realizing it, to pigeonhole students into the various categories, and attach labels to some who will be destined to carry these designations for the entire academic year and beyond.

Mrs. S. has just received her class list for the academic year. In addition, the school's education director has provided her with a description of each student who has an academic, social, or medical issue about which Mrs. S. needs to be aware. There will be 21 students in her class.

Of the 21, three suffer from significant food allergies. There is one student who is diabetic. Three students are taking Ritalin[2] and/or Clonidine[3] for Attention Deficit Hyperactive Disorder; of these, there is a suspicion that two have a learning disability. One can safely assume that a number of these students who have been brought to her attention, and possibly others, too, are at risk, and will experience academic difficulty over the course of the year. Mrs. S. knows that one or two may also have significant behavior issues that will impact their ability to learn. She is also sure that there will be a few who are very able students. They will finish the assignments quickly and will be at ease with the material.

Currently, her understanding of the class composition and the information she has received from the education director is the only data Mrs. S. has to rely on as she contemplates the best way to develop and execute her lessons. Her education director has presented her with the class list, a scope and sequence for the course, and her books. The first thing she does is meet with her colleagues to plan for the year.

Throughout her training, Mrs. S. has studied a little about students with special needs. She is certain that the knowledge she possesses will be very useful to her as she begins the year. She comes to class prepared with her first lesson. Each student is instructed to read the first ten pages of the chapter in the text. She allows students about 20 minutes to accomplish this task. Mrs. S. then leads an interactive discussion. She tells those who have not been able to complete the work to do so at home. As the bell rings, Mrs. S. reminds her students that for homework they need to answer the questions found at the end of the reading.

David is one of the students in this class. He has not been diagnosed with a specific learning disability, but has had academic problems since entering school. He has a particularly hard time with reading comprehension and his writing skills are very weak. He has poor organizational skills and has difficulty remembering to bring his books, pencils, and folders to class. Nonetheless, he is a very motivated student.

Although he has made a sincere effort to complete the assignment, David is able to finish only the first page of the reading. And, although he has read it several times, he still has very little understanding of the material. As a result, he is not really engaged in the class discussion led by Mrs. S. Moreover, he feels frustrated because his classmates, who understand the material, are involved in a stimulating conversation.

Throughout the day, David has similar experiences. Each of his teachers assigns homework, most often as he and his classmates rush out the door for the next class. By day's end, he is not sure about his assignments. All he knows is that the buses are

---

[2] "Ritalin, often used in the treatment of Attention Deficit Hyperactivity Disorder (ADHD), is a psychomotor stimulant, even though its effect often seems paradoxically calming. It appears to activate the brain stem arousal system." From *Medication Fact Sheets, 2000 Edition*. Dean E. Konopasek (Anchorage, AK: Arctic Tern Publishing Co., 2000), 60.

[3] "Clonidine, frequently used in the treatment of anxiety and hypertension, is an antihypertensive medication that exerts a calming effect by reducing blood pressure, pulse rate, and central nervous system stimulation." Ibid, 10.

leaving, so he has to get his things to be ready when his bus is called.

Multiply David's issues with those of the five other special needs students in Mrs. S.'s class, and those in every other classroom in the school. The number is staggering! Some weeks into the school year, it becomes apparent that David is having difficulty in almost all of his classes. Mrs. S. asks for assistance from the special educator who is on staff at the school.

This scenario bears a striking resemblance to any classroom in any Jewish school across the country and to the diversity of the students we encounter. We would probably all agree that homogeneous classrooms do not exist. Teachers have always taught marginal, average, and very able students. What seems to be different today is our acknowledgement of, and attention, to this diversity. While not directly responsible for this new classroom composition, the Federal Law referred to at the beginning of this chapter has been the guiding force in the changing attitudes.

INCLUSION AND THE JEWISH SCHOOL

"Inclusion is an extremely controversial idea because it relates to education and social values, as well as our sense of individual worth."[4] In a Jewish environment, the moral issue is as important as the educational implications.

Since Jewish schools are not bound by the law, and receive nominal funding to support students with special needs in day and supplementary school, it follows that Jewish schools would not have the resources to serve these students as well as they can be served in the public school setting. This does not change the fact that many parents elect to send their children to Jewish day school and expect educational services for their children. Those who send their children to public school often send them to the supplementary system with the same expectations. The trends we see in the public school to provide more and more services within the regular classrooms have spilled over into the Jewish classroom. The challenge in the Jewish schools is to provide services in an atmosphere of competing demands, fewer resources, ill equipped teachers, and less time in which to accomplish the school's goals and objectives.

I am a Jewish special educator who has also been a classroom religious school teacher. So I know the frustrations of having students with special needs in a heterogenous class, and I know the frustration and isolation of students with special needs who are excluded from the regular life of the school. While there are many challenges that come with trying to integrate students with special needs into the mainstream or, conversely, to meet the special needs of students in the mainstream, I've found that one very basic issue often gets overlooked — scheduling!

I've had students who are assigned to come to resource room at a given time each school day. But instead of always missing Hebrew instruction, for example, sometimes they end up missing a part of history, or a holiday project, or other subjects, all because the classroom teacher did not take into account the resource schedule of his/her students when putting together a lesson plan. I also have students who are mainly not integrated — but who could function for short periods in a regular classroom. But I cannot schedule them in for non-Hebrew language subjects, or for the hands-on projects with which they are more successful, when the classroom teacher does not keep to a schedule.

(Anne Johnston, New Haven, Connecticut)

This, of course, is not to say that children who learn differently should be barred from enrollment. As a matter of fact, it is a moral imperative to open the doors of our schools and other community agencies to include these individuals in Jewish life. Furthermore, there are any number of ways that a school and its staff can modify the environment to meet the individual needs of their student body.

Those in the field of special education already know that "special education is good education." Those teachers who employ some of the strategies routinely used by special educators also know that with little effort, they can create the likelihood of student success.

---

[4]*Teaching & Learning*, Education Issues Series, http://www.weac.org/resource/June96/speced.htm.

A VARIETY OF DISABILITIES

Before we can consider these strategies, though, it will be helpful to examine the disabilities that are referred to as high incidence. That is, they occur often in the population. Of these, we will look at specific learning disabilities and attention deficit hyperactive disorders. While pervasive developmental disorders, including Asperger Syndrome, are not considered high incidence, there is a dramatic increase in the number of individuals diagnosed with this disorder, and thus an increase of these children in our classrooms. For that reason, we will briefly explore instructional interventions to accommodate the needs of these students.

Specific Learning Disabilities

Federal Law defines a learning disability as a "disorder in one or more of the basic psychological processes involved in understanding or in using spoken or written language, which may manifest itself in an imperfect ability to listen, think, speak, read, write, spell, or to do mathematical calculations. Specific learning disabilities characteristically affect spoken and written language, arithmetic, reasoning, and memory."[5]

The signs of these disorders can be seen in a variety of ways, including delays in listening, speaking, reading, writing, and spelling. Individuals with a learning disability often have difficulty in organizing and assimilating their thoughts. Since memory can be significantly affected, these students may have difficulty remembering instructions and holding information in their short-term memories. Individuals with specific learning disabilities may also experience difficulty in math.

Regardless of the type or manifestation, the *Encyclopedia of Special Education* suggests that "there are five reasons that educators have difficulty identifying children with specific learning disabilities. First, many teachers equate specific learning disabilities with any learning problem; second, there is no single, observable characteristic or syndrome of behaviors that can be considered typical; third, each child has his [her] own learning pattern; fourth, behavioral symptoms depend on the type of disability, its severity, the child's intact abilities

and the child's coping mechanism; and fifth, behavioral symptoms of specific learning disabilities might also arise from problems other than specific learning disabilities."[6]

Thus, it is easy to understand why a student with a learning disability would pose a considerable challenge to the untrained educator.

> We make room in our schools for more of our Jewish children if we open up our expectations of appropriate goals. I have a student who has been known to be physically violent who is now flourishing as a role model in the school — because we have designed a functional curriculum, allowing him to accomplish high profile jobs. He has a title — *Shammes* (helper) — and he sets up the sanctuary for *davening (*and puts it back in order afterward). He's allowed in the back room with the light panel, and he's allowed to touch the thermostat, both very special privileges. He also helps with snack. To accompany this, he also has a focused Hebrew learning time, and he learns about Jewish life as he learns his jobs — he learns about the late, beloved *Shammes* of the *shul*, and through his life story learns about the *Shoah* (Holocaust) and Jewish immigration, as well as about memorial boards and lights and saying "*Kaddish*." He's learning basic *kashrut* and working toward an individual field trip to the kosher market as a reward for good service to the school. And he's being prepared for roles that he can potentially take on as an adult.
>
> *(Anne Johnston, New Haven, Connecticut)*

Attention Deficit (Hyperactive) Disorder

Students "with attention deficit (hyperactive) disorder present an altogether different type of dilemma. According to the American Psychiatric Association (1994), children who are excessively active, are unable to sustain their attention, and are deficient in impulse control to a degree that is deviant for their developmental level are now given the clinical diagnosis of attention deficit

---

[5]"Education of Handicapped Children," *Federal Register* 42, no. 163 (23 August 1977).

[6]*Encyclopedia of Special Education*, vol. 2, Cecil R. Reynolds and Lester Mann, eds. (New York: John Wiley & Sons, 1987), 925.

(hyperactivity) disorder (ADHD). Their problematic behavioral characteristics are thought to arise early, often before age seven years, and to be persistent over development in many cases. Approximately 3-7% of school-age children are believed to have this disorder, with most estimates erring toward the higher end of this range.[7]

There are three main symptoms, of ADHD. These include problems with paying attention, being very active (called hyperactivity), and acting before thinking (called impulsivity).

Pervasive Developmental Disorder

Autism and Pervasive Developmental Disorder-NOS (not otherwise specified) are developmental disabilities that share many of the same characteristics. Usually evident by age three, autism and PDD-NOS are neurological disorders that affect a child's ability to communicate, understand language, play, and relate to others. In the less severe form, and among those students we encounter in the classroom, we might observe the following characteristics: difficulty in relating to people, objects, and events; difficulty with changes in routine or familiar surroundings; unusual responses to sensory information — for example, loud noises, lights, certain textures of food or fabrics, a limited range of interests, and impaired social skills. Those with advanced language skills tend to use a small range of topics and have difficulty with abstract concepts. Children with autism or PDD vary widely in abilities, intelligence, and behaviors.[8]

In terms of the successful strategies used to meet the individual needs of these students, we can draw some general conclusions that will serve all three distinct groups, and offer intervention ideas that, in general, support the wide variety of needs. As we understand more about the nature of these types of disabilities, it is critical that we also recognize that individuals will exhibit different manifestations of their disorders. We need also to recognize that the successful strategies we employ on one day may be not be successful on later attempts. Unfortunately, there is no clear-cut recipe that exists to assist us in meeting the needs of these exceptional students. It is up to us, therefore, to identify the ways in which to engage them in

the learning act using whatever innovative means there are available to us.

BUILDING STUDENT SUCCESS

What arsenal of teaching strategies is needed to ensure success for each one of the students placed in our care? All of the research indicates that learning is very complex; each individual learns at his/her own pace, in his/her own way. The research also tells us that it is not unusual for teachers to teach in the way they best learn.

> Having a special needs child in the class provides the opportunity to put Jewish values into action. This year in my Aleph class, I have a child with high functioning autism. She has been in religious school with this class all along, but this year the children began to comment and ask questions. With her parents' permission, the school director and I explained to the class on a day when we knew she would be absent what autism is and why their classmate acts so differently. We also discussed why my standards for her were different from those of other class members. We asked them to be her helpers, especially on the weekday afternoon when we had no aide for her. The students' response has been terrific. They are patient, understanding, and kind; many of them have learned exactly how to deal with Dina effectively.
>
> How we treat the differently-abled in our classrooms is the real test of our commitment to our traditions, values, and *middot*. I don't know how much this student is learning, or will learn this year, but I am certain of what she has taught her classmates.
>
> *(Cheryl Cash-Linietsky, Philadelphia, Pennsylvania)*

Thus, it isn't difficult to imagine that, among the host of issues that might contribute to the student's difficulty, there might be a mismatch between the teacher and one or even more of her students. Teachers need, then, to be flexible in their teaching and consistent and fair in their lesson goals and objectives. Too often, teachers indi-

---

[7]Russell A. Barkley, *ADHD and the Nature of Self-Control* (New York: The Guildford Press, 1997), 3.

[8]*Diagnostic Statistical Manual*, 4th ed. (Washington, DC: American Psychiatric Association, 1994), Table 1.1, 15.

cate that reduced homework assignment, different tests, and varying academic expectations are not fair. Being mindful of the concept that "*fair* does not mean *equal*"[9] will allow teachers to provide students with what they need to be successful.

Let's begin by looking at some of the easy accommodations teachers might put into practice to allow all students to access information. Later, we will examine strategies that will take more planning, and provide some suggestions to get best results when seeking assistance from other professionals in the school and beyond.

> Our school is too small to have a resource room, but we try to mainstream kids as much as possible. One of my students has Downs Syndrome, yet she is an active participant in class. Whenever possible, I e-mail texts or lesson plans for her to prepare in advance. I also make sure that she always has an opportunity to read aloud, present her work, and participate in activities. Some activities do have to be modified, but this tends to benefit the entire class. For instance, if the class is working on their own *midrashim*, everyone is given the opportunity to illustrate rather than write. This underscores the idea that Torah can be approached on many levels and in many ways.
>
> *(Dena Salmon, Montclair, New Jersey)*

Consider Mrs. S.'s classroom and take a closer look at David. Recall that David is not diagnosed with a specific learning disability, although his academic problems are becoming more pronounced as the school year unfolds. For David, and others like him, the teacher's standard classroom operating procedures put him at a disadvantage the moment he enters her room. Mrs. S. has assigned a reading passage, and led a discussion. She has rattled off the homework assignment just as the bell is ringing, while students are rushing off to their next class. She has not taken the time before class to write either the in class reading or the homework assignment on the board. In addition, she hasn't provided any advance organizers, "information,

often presented as organizational signals, that makes content more understandable by putting it within a more general framework"[10] to help provide context to the reading passage. Further, she hasn't given students time at the beginning of class to write the assignment down. Finally, she hasn't left enough time at the end of the class to review the salient points of the discussion and prompt students about the homework assignment. For David and others like him, these simple steps are critical to academic success.

This behavior, while fairly typical, is not a result of some purposeful act on her part. Rather, it is the result of lack of time and teacher pressure to fulfill a variety of responsibilities that fall to her as a teacher in the field. Unfortunately, this comes at the expense of student needs. Some changes in her approach could benefit the typically developing students, and most assuredly would assist David. Now consider how much extra time all of this might take Mrs. S. The entire activity, taken together, would require a few minutes of teaching time. Mrs. S. might consider incorporating some or all of the following techniques into her repertoire. While not exhaustive by any means, the following are proven methods to support all students.

- Write class work and assignments on the board (or photocopy assignment sheets and hand them out).

- Allow students a minute to copy down assignments.

- Provide a written daily schedule.

- Provide advance organizers to convey a context for new information.

- Allow students to review information presented to assure understanding.

The following simple adjustments in classroom organization and technique will also support David: simple adaptations in organization of the class period, reduced assignments, chunking materials into manageable related segments, and a shift in teaching techniques can alter the environment in ways that support all students, regardless of their academic and/or behavioral needs. To ameliorate problems, pay attention to things as simple as:

---

[9]In other words, what is "fair" for one child, is not necessarily what is right for another child. Fairness is making sure that everyone gets what he or she needs, individually.

[10]Marilyn Friend and William Bursuck, *Including Students with Special Needs* (Boston, MA: Allyn and Bacon, 1996), 483.

anticipating issues before they occur, providing a written schedule, cueing students of a transition from one activity to another, prompting when the schedule changes, providing a consistent routine, providing variety, and possessing the necessary negotiating skills when struggles occur between teacher and student. These can be categorized as those that require the least amount of teacher time, and, without question, serve the needs of the greatest number of students. In making these minor adjustments, teachers create an atmosphere in which the possibility exists for every child to reach his/her potential.

Creating a nurturing environment in which students feel safe to question and seek assistance from both teacher and peers is another important aspect of creating a positive classroom atmosphere. It is the responsibility of the classroom teacher to foster tolerance among students, helping each to understand that we are all created in God's image, and as such, should be accorded the utmost respect.

Today, establishing respect as normative behavior in the classroom is a real challenge for all educators. Unfortunately, bullying[11] has become a fixture in the typical classroom. It is the peripheral students, those who are the topic of this chapter, who require academic and social support, and remain the primary targets of these assaults. Teachers must reinforce this idea of respect and, indeed, demonstrate how to respect students. While we could spend a great deal of time analyzing what comprises a nurturing setting, and establishing guidelines for its creation, for our purposes, teachers should reflect on how they run their classrooms and make appropriate changes to foster a zero tolerance policy as it relates to bullying. Meaningful questions teachers might ask themselves include: Am I consistent? Do I mete out consequences fairly? What tone do I take when addressing students? Is there any hint of sarcasm in my interactions?

Behavior management is another important feature of the classroom. While long debated, it lends itself to foster student learning as it continues to be a valuable avenue for communicating with students that they are doing a good job. There are a number of management strategies to employ.

Teachers need to identify one — or a number of techniques — with which they are comfortable and utilize them to advance learning among all of their students.

The physical plant of a classroom also helps to build the classroom environment. While teachers have little control over the type of furniture they find in their classroom, they do have some ability to arrange it in ways that encourage learning. The teacher should be cognizant of the best seating arrangement. An easily distractible student, or one with an auditory difficulty, should be seated near the teacher in the front row, away from windows and doorways. Further, teachers should consider which of their students might be a distraction to others. Materials should be displayed on the walls, but not to the extent that they are a distraction. Teachers should be aware of the delicate balance between too much stimulation and too little.

Taking learning styles into account allows the teacher to consider a variety of instructional activities. This affords students the opportunity to explore and learn through modalities other than the traditional lecture and paper/pencil tasks. Countless activities exist that teach students through auditory, visual, and kinesthetic channels, thus allowing everyone some access to the material. Finally, sometimes only minor curricular accommodations are required to create an effective learning atmosphere. Examples include: underlining or circling important points for the student, providing practice questions in advance of the test, requiring students to complete only a portion of the homework, and allowing students to demonstrate mastery in a variety of ways.

Maximizing opportunities for success by employing alternative means of demonstrating knowledge will allow all students to shine. Teachers should allow students to take agreed upon breaks throughout the day to accommodate restlessness. While these suggestions may seem insignificant, taken together they will impact the entire learning environment.

Generally, the teacher can employ peer tutoring, and the use of multiple intelligences[12] to promote learning. "Effective heterogeneous cooperative learning strategies that are differentiated will also help students grow academically, socially, and

[11]For more information on bullying, see Chapter 17, "Dealing with Children at Risk" by Steven Bayar and Francine Hirschman, pp. 187-201 in this Handbook.

[12]For more information on multiple intelligences, see Chapter 27, "Multiple Intelligences" by Renee Holtz and Barbara Lapetina, pp. 323-333 in this Handbook.

emotionally."[13] Many texts are available that describe these educational approaches in depth.

> This year I have a child with severe learning issues. Sam reads English below grade level, has memory issues and other difficulties. Additionally, his parents are not that committed Jewishly; they have made that very clear. But Sam is the sweetest, kindest, most helpful child. I take every opportunity to let him know how much I value his qualities as a *mensch*.
>
> Sam, however, clearly measures himself academically against the other students and sees himself as a failure. I gave a quiz on the vocabulary words in Hebrew and Sam got 2/3 of them correct. He felt like he had failed (the majority of the class got 100s). I spoke to him and his mom, telling them how proud I was of him, and that I would not measure Sam against anyone else, due to his learning difficulties. I pointed out to him that given his issues with memory (which he clearly knows about) getting 2/3 correct was a real achievement, deserving of a lot of credit. I also offered to give him another test on just the words he got wrong, an offer he quickly took up. It's hard for children not to judge themselves in comparison to others. We need to point out the upside to them.
>
> *(Cheryl Cash-Linietsky, Philadelphia, Pennsylvania)*

Some of the current teaching strategies, especially cooperative learning,[14] do not support competitive activities. Given the nature of these exceptional students, one can imagine that competition among peers is generally counterproductive. Routinely, it is the student with academic and/or behavioral issues who ends up the loser in a competitive environment. If, on the other hand, a student is trying to improve his/her own performance, and is being reinforced by the teacher, the likelihood of success will increase appreciably.

"Modifying a curriculum to improve behavior and increase classroom performance is a strategy that is based on an extensive research literature."[15] In the case of students with more persistent problems, classroom teachers will be required to make greater changes, and give deeper thought to instruction. These changes will entail an understanding of student needs, and in-depth curricular modifications. Sometimes, these students will require a parallel curriculum, or at the very least, different readability textbooks. These modifications generally require the assistance of a special educator or someone well versed in the field to assist with the modifications.

If such becomes the case, and the teacher cannot cope with the educational and behavioral demands of the student, it makes sense to seek assistance from other professionals in the school. Before seeking advice and assistance, however, the teacher needs to assemble a student profile that pinpoints the areas of concern. This is easier said than done. Often, teachers simply say: the student doesn't pay attention. The implications of "not paying attention" are enormous and mask the issues that are at the source of the problem. It is, therefore, imperative that the teachers carefully observe and describe, in as much detail as possible, concrete examples of the behavior.

Since David has not presented any behavior problems for Mrs. S., let's take a look at Hanna, who is presenting Mrs. S., and indeed, all of her teachers, some serious inattention issues. Hanna "refuses" to stay on task. The problem is compounded because she is falling behind academically, to say nothing of the effect on others in the class. This description, however, will not assist anyone in getting at the source of the problem. Why is Hanna off task? Why is she a distraction to others in the classroom? Mrs. S. needs to describe the behavior and indicate when it is occurs. Is there a particular time of day, or a particular time of the week? With whom does it occur? In other words, Mrs. S. needs to try to determine patterns in the behavior and document what she sees. Perhaps someone other than herself (another teacher or specialist in the building, or even the school principal) can monitor Hanna's conduct, taking careful notice of the particular behavior. Or, Mrs. S. can

---

[13]Nancy Schneidewind and Ellen Davidson. "Differentiating Cooperative Learning," *Educational Leadership* 58 (September 2000), 24.

[14]For more information on cooperative learning, see Chapter 30, "Cooperative or Collaborative Learning" by Carol

K. Ingall, pp. 357-362 of this Handbook.

[15]G. Dunlap and L. Kern, *School Psychology Quarterly* 11, 297-312, 1996, cited in Nancy Mather and Sam Goldstein, *Learning Disabilities and Challenging Behaviors* (Baltimore, MD: Paul Brookes Publishing Co.), 2001.

record each time Hanna demonstrates the inattentive behavior and later summarize her findings. Other observations might include Hanna's ability to organize her work and work area, any discrepancies between oral and written abilities, obvious letter and word reversals, length of time it takes to complete work, and handwriting.

In order to discover the cause of the difficulty, Mrs. S. needs to obtain a clear picture of the behavior, gathering her information over a reasonable period of time. Only then will she be in a position to seek assistance. It does take certain skill and practice effectively to uncover the presenting issue, and it often requires help from others. In any case, this effort is critical in identifying the root causes of the problem.

Current research tells us that what often appears as an attention problem may likely have to do with a deficit in in other areas of functioning. According to Mel Levine, "problems with attention are the most common source of learning and behavioral difficulties in school age children . . . Children with attentional dysfunction clearly are highly diverse. To lump all of them together and say they have ADD or ADHD is to tell us very little about them. Not only do students vary in their precise traits and the severity of their manifestations, but they differ as well in their strengths and weaknesses in other relevant areas, such as motor skills, language ability, and memory capacity.[16]

This research underscores the vital importance of collecting the essential data that will bring the problems to light. Perhaps an adjustment in academic expectation is all that is necessary to turn the tide for Hanna. On the other hand, it is possible that more serious issues are impeding her ability to learn. Before reaching any conclusions, a team of educators should evaluate the information that has been gathered.

CONCLUSION

All of the suggested strategies in this chapter support good teaching. With the proper evaluation and intervention steps in place, even David and Hanna might well succeed in becoming more than adequate students. It is within their teacher's power to identify their academic and behavioral problems and to deliver instruction consistent with their needs. When a variety of opportunities are provided, these students, and others identified as at risk, will be able to deepen their understanding of the information they acquire and make linkages to other knowledge they have accumulated over time. Isn't this indeed what we hope for each of our students, no matter what their functioning level? It is clear that much of their success rests in their teacher's hands.

Teaching Considerations

Prior to the start of school, or as soon as possible:

- Learn as much as possible about your students by gathering pertinent information from other professionals and reviewing records.

Throughout the school year:

- Develop and maintain a positive relationship with parents. They can provide vital insights about their child.

- Establish rapport with your student(s). Ask them how they learn best.

- Provide a friendly, safe, nurturing environment that encourages student learning.

- Recognize differences among students. Provide opportunities for each to learn through his/her strengths.

- Provide opportunities for students to demonstrate mastery.

- Develop and execute lessons that allow students to access information in a variety of ways.

- Don't be afraid to ask for help. Seek assistance when student(s) don't respond to the techniques and strategies.

- Expand your arsenal of teaching methods and techniques.

---

[16]Mel Levine, *Educational Care* (Cambridge, MA: Educators Publishing Service, Inc., 1996), 13.

BIBLIOGRAPHY

Armstrong, Thomas. *ADD/ADHD Alternatives in the Classroom*. Alexandria, VA: Association for Supervision and Curriculum Development, 1999.

> This book explores a number of perspectives related to the behavior of children with ADD/ADHD. Using a holistic approach, it provides numerous strategies to support these children in school.

Friend, Marilyn, and William Bursuck. *Including Students with Special Needs*. Needham Heights, MA: Allyn & Bacon, 1996.

> This text explains the foundations for educating students with special needs, along with an explanation of special education terminology. It is a practical guide for classroom teachers that provides suggestions for programming and specific strategies to meet student needs.

Greene, Roberta M., and Elaine Heavenrich. *A Question in Search of an Answer*. New York: Union of American Hebrew Congregations, 1981.

> This practical handbook for religious and Hebrew school educators provides an overview on students who are diagnosed with specific learning disabilities. It contains case studies and a complete lesson plan based on Genesis 18:16-33.

Greene, Ross W. *The Explosive Child*. New York: HarperCollins Publishers, 2001.

> This book provides a unique approach to understanding and working with children who have extreme outbursts and are noncompliant.

Hartmann, Thom. *Attention Deficit Disorder: A Different Perception*. Grass Valley, CA: Underwood Books, 1993.

> This book provides an innovative framework for understanding ADD. The author theorizes that when the environment is properly structured, this "disorder" can be turned into a skill.

Heacox, Diane. *Differentiating Instruction in the Regular Classroom*. Minneapolis, MN: Free Spirit Publishing, 2002.

> This text provides the tools for developing a variety of tasks to meet the needs of the range of learners in classrooms. Differentiation is discussed at length, and the instructor is provided with a list of options for planning.

Konopasek, Dean E. *Medication "Fact Sheet."* Anchorage, AK: Arctic Tern Publishing Co., 2000.

> This reference guide provides a listing of facts related to medications currently in use. It is written for the non-medical professional.

Lehr, Judy Brown, and Hazel Wiggins Harris. *At-Risk, Low-Achieving Students in the Classroom*. Washington, DC: National Education Association of the United States, 1994.

> This pamphlet explores the nature of the at-risk learner and suggests ways in which to organize the environment so these students can access information.

Mather, Nancy, and Sam Goldstein. *Learning Disabilities and Challenging Behaviors*. Baltimore, MD: Paul Brookes Publishing Co., 2001.

> This guide discusses various aspects affecting learning. It provides interventions to improve both student behavior and learning.

Shore, Kenneth. *Special Kids Problem Solver*. Englewood Cliffs, NJ: Prentice Hall, 1998.

> This spiral binder is filled with ready to use interventions to help students with academic, behavior, and physical problems. It categorizes problems and provides interventions to help students. Each chapter contains a section on "how teachers can help."

Sousa, David A. *How the Special Needs Brain Works*. Thousand Oaks, CA: Corwin Press, Inc., 2001.

> This book examines how the special needs brain learns. The author explains various disorders and provides strategies to maximize success.

Wright, Peter W. D., and Pamela Darr Wright. *Wrightslaw: Special Education Law*. Hartfield, VA: Harbor House Law Press, 2002.

> This text details key sections of special education law. It highlights significant court cases and provides comprehensive information.

Yell, Mitchell. "The Legal Basis of Inclusion." *Educational Leadership*, October 1998.

> This article discusses the foundations of inclusion.

CHAPTER 17

Dealing with Children at Risk

Steven Bayar and Francine Hirschman

Many of our students live with "interesting" challenges and difficulties that are far beyond "normal" adolescent dilemmas. Many come to our schools and programs with emotional and physical baggage that, just a few years ago, would never have been imagined, including profound depression and chemical, food, sexual, or physical abuse.

It would be unreasonable for any Jewish educator to believe that he or she could remedy some, let alone all, of the ills afflicting quite a few of our students. Yet, it would be wrong for us not to try to be of help.

When it comes to dealing with a child at risk, it is natural to want to rationalize away suspicions and avoid the signs and signals. The thoughts that come most easily to mind are: "It's probably not that serious," "It's a passing phase," "Just a natural part of adolescence," "This is none of my business," "How can I be certain that what is being implied here is really happening?" "The child is just angry at parents and this is a way of getting back at them," and so forth. Yet, when the signs persist, it is time to desist from such rationalizations.

STUDENTS WITH PROBLEMS: GENERAL WARNING SIGNS

Depending on which statistics one accepts, a fourth to a half of any given group of children may have physical, emotional, or learning problems — an alarming number indeed! Is it any wonder then that the number of students, campers, and youth group members who exhibit attitudes and behaviors that are deemed disruptive or unmanageable seems on the increase?

Since our task is to educate an entire class or group, we tend to focus immediately on the negative behavior itself. Management techniques, much as in any damage control situation, would call for isolating the behavior — removing the child — so

that we can go back to the task of education. Yet, if we could but take the extra minute to be less reactive and more proactive, if we had the patience or the insight to ascertain the causal factors behind a child's negative attitudes and behaviors, we might actually be able to do more to influence that child's life than we could with all the lesson plans ever implemented. To remove the child is to make him/her more unreachable. Ironically, it is those who disturb us who could most benefit from our compassion and understanding.

If we are to impact youngsters who have problems, our first task is to identify who they are. While they may try to hide anger, frustration, and fear, it will find release in some form. Thus, in working with children, look for any of the following signs:

- Changes in behavior

- Difficulty in paying attention

- Difficulty in making eye contact

- Peer social problems

- Not working up to expected ability

- Reluctance to share information about home life

- Consistent behavior problems

- Excessive absences

- Total immersion in one activity to the exclusion of other activities, or lack of involvement in anything

- Written assignments or drawings that consistently reflect negative or dark thoughts and deeds

Youngsters exhibiting such signs are not necessarily ill or being victimized in any way; they simply bear watching closely. Remember, too, that children undergo many changes in the course of a school year. It is possible that a student might exhibit such behaviors for a short period of time because of a temporary life situation. As a general rule, a child who persists in any of the above behaviors for an extended period of time may be in need of attention and help.

Resources

Educators are usually not well versed in law, psychology, or enforcement policies. Therefore, problems that require such expertise should not be handled alone. Every person who works formally with groups of children should maintain an up-to-date resource list — a card file — in which at least the following phone numbers are listed:

1. The director in charge of your program (Education Director, Camp Director, Youth Coordinator, etc.)

2. The Rabbi, if he/she is ultimately responsible for the educational setting or organization in which you work.

3. A social worker and/or psychologist (preferably one who works with the age group that you teach; this person is usually one recommended by the director of your program)

4. A lawyer (preferably one knowledgeable in criminal law; also recommended by the director)

5. Police Department

6. Alcohol and drug abuse hot lines

7. Rape hot line

8. Social services.

Don't be surprised by entries #1 and #2. Before taking any action, *always* contact your supervisors so they may be aware of, and become a part of, the situation at hand. They usually have more expertise and experience in handling such problems and often have information about a family that teachers lack. They may be aware of steps already being taken that address the situation, and they may prefer to be the one to contact any of the others on this list. Therefore, it is especially important for a teacher, counselor, or youth group advisor *not* to make decisions or take actions without the input and support of his or her supervisors.

What follows is a partial list of problems facing students today, the signals to look for, and how to respond. This is not an all-inclusive listing so much as a general guide.

BULLYING THREATS AND AGGRESSION

There is probably no more sensitive subject than intimidation and bullying by overly aggressive students. While there is a great difference between playground or classroom bullying and the extreme of violent shootings and deaths of students, schools and youth programs were meant to be safe havens for students to learn about life, not killing fields.

The time to stop any escalation is before it starts. Often, students will feel "empowered" to bully others as they imitate what they see in the media. The teacher must set the rules for mutual respect that must be strictly enforced. In this way you take the first step by setting an example.

Watch your students. Watch their behavior as they walk in and out of class. Do they come in late and take seats away from one certain "group"? Do they leave quickly to avoid this "group"? Listen to them. What are they talking about? Who are they talking to? You will soon learn who the aggressive students are.

Don't keep the information to yourself. If you find an overly aggressive student, he or she may well be acting out in other venues. Help the administration gather information in order to identify and deal with the student.

We have learned through tragic inaction, that zero tolerance is a necessary policy when dealing with threats and aggression. No student can be allowed to belittle another. No student can be allowed to speak of destruction with impunity. There is too much at stake.

Below are two vignettes that show different facets of the issue.

Sam I

Sam is a third grader with a chip on his shoulder. His father, lately returned to religion, has placed him in religious school for the first time in his life. Sam, uprooted from his normal weekend and after school regimen of sports, retaliates by picking on two students who sit near him in class. He is always following them, muttering to them, intimidating them, though he never touches them.

All this is discovered when the school director follows up on a child who was absent for an unusual period of time. Upon investigation, the mother reports that her son chose to hide in the bathroom each of these class sessions because Sam has been "picking on him." When Sam is asked why, he responds that he does not like students who "like to be in school."

After meeting with his parents, Sam is put on probation and watched.

Sam II

Sam doesn't want to be in school. He will do just about anything to prove this. Over the years, he has pushed the system as far as it will go.

Sam is big for his 12 years. The teachers have noticed that when Sam wants something, no matter if it is an object or attention, he is willing to push students out of the way in order to get it. He always seems to pick on students at least two years younger than he, studious students who are enthusiastic about learning.

Calling in Sam's parents does not seem to help. While his mother and father are more than willing to support consequences and punishments, they use the opportunity to belittle and berate him. Because administrators come and go, and there is no consistency from year to year, Sam has been allowed to use his size to intimidate other students.

Sam's aggressive behavior, his cursing of teachers and students, and kicking went unchallenged until a parent called the Rabbi and congregational president and threatened to withdraw her child from the school because he was threatened by Sam. That night, Sam returned to school with his parents to meet with the Rabbi and principal. Though Sam at first denied the allegation, he was forced to admit his threat when confronted by three witnesses.

Sam was expelled from school and the police were called. Eventually Sam was allowed to return, but only after months of counseling.

The not so ironic conclusion to these two vignettes is that they are about the same person, Sam in third grade and Sam several years later.

What to Look For:

All information points to the fact that bullying students show their behavior in one way or another. The evidence is there, for those willing to see. The key is to "ask questions." Do not allow any suspicious behavior to go without question.

1. Does this student evince a particular arrogance toward others?

2. Does this student challenge your authority in front of others?

3. Does the student appear to be the "leader" of a pack?

4. Does the "group" engage in verbal or physical intimidation of individual students?

5. Do other students seem to avoid or fear him/her?

Resources

This is one area in which a classroom teacher or youth educator cannot function alone. Because of the danger of situations left unchecked, the program's director and Rabbi must be contacted as soon as possible. A behavior plan, with specific consequences, should be drawn up with the cooperation and involvement of the student, parent, teacher, and school administration. This then needs to be monitored, with zero tolerance for any infractions.

The threats of one student to another must be taken seriously and intervention must occur immediately. Most schools have a policy delineated for these situations in the Student and/or Teacher Handbook.

LEARNING DISABILITIES[1]

It is estimated that 10% of all students have some type of learning disability, usually manifested by a gap in expectations of performance and the actual performance. (In other words, a child who has capabilities beyond that shown by his or her actual work.) Even if that number is an overestimation, it is likely that every educator will confront at least one student with learning disabilities every year.

Children with learning disabilities tend to be bright and capable in some areas, while showing weaknesses in cognitive, verbal, and/or motor skills. A student may be unable to write down correct or legible answers, even though we know that he/she could do an excellent job explaining the same information orally or demonstrating it visu-

---

[1]For more information on learning disabilities, see Chapter 16, "Special Needs Students" by Ellen Fishman, pp. 177-186 in

this Handbook.

ally. A youngster, though obviously bright, may be unable to concentrate on an activity for an extended amount of time. To be considered as having a learning disability, a child needs to be tested.

The following case study illustrates a child with learning issues.

Rachel

The Cantor of Congregation Kol Ami usually starts working with sixth grade students in preparation for their B'nai Mitzvah. This year, she approaches the principal with a complaint about Rachel, who can't read Hebrew. How can a student get through sixth grade without knowing the alef bet?

Teachers are spoken to and records are checked. Rachel has never been a good student, but she always got by. Her attendance was spotty, but within the minimum number of school sessions. Her homework was rarely done, but she passed the courses. Rachel's behavior was within the norm. Sometimes she acted out, but most of the time she was fine.

The Cantor called Rachel's parents to tell them that their daughter would need extra tutoring to bring her up to standard. Their reply was simply, "We expected this. After all, she has learning disabilities that make it almost impossible for her to learn a second language."

Rachel had compensated for her issues with memorization and bravado for several years. That, and her ability to "blend into" to the class, allowed her to pass until the end of sixth grade.

What to Look For:

The following are signals to look for when suspecting learning disabilities:

1. A student who seems to be performing well below his or her ability

2. Significant differences in ability in different subjects, for example, the student cannot read Hebrew, yet can learn and understand complex aspects of Jewish history and Bible

3. Tremendous effort leading to tremendous frustration (i.e., a student who tries hard, yet finds little or no success)

4. A student who avoids performing by acting out in class, or by causing a distraction that will circumvent his/her being forced to perform

Resources

Every school should have a list of referral possibilities for students with suspected learning disabilities. Aside from private psychologists, the local Jewish Family Service, university, or other communal institutions may have educational testing services available. Good resources for the individual teacher or school director include special education teachers from local public and day schools, psychologists, pediatric physical therapists, and occupational therapists. When making a referral recommendation, remind the parents to keep the school in the loop by sharing reports and evaluations. Assure the parents that all such reports will be treated as confidential.

Youngsters with learning disabilities are often helped when in learning situations that pay attention to multiple intelligences[2] and learning styles, offering children a wide variety of learning avenues beyond traditional reading or paper and pencil activities.

Note: Parents in denial of their children's learning issues are prone to allow their children to attend supplementary school or camps without notifying the administration of the issues. In this way, they hope to keep their children from being "stereotyped" by the other students and teachers. These parents can place obstacles in the way of an educator trying to find the right "mix" to teach their child effectively. In such cases, the director of the program will need to determine the best way to proceed.

DRUG AND ALCOHOL ABUSE

"Jews don't drink!" How many of us grew up believing that statement to be fact? Today, we know that many Jews drink, abuse drugs, and fall prey to the same temptations and problems as the rest of the world. Worse, these behaviors may start as early as elementary school and are much more common among our high school students than teachers would like to believe.

---

[2]For more information on multiple intelligences, see Chapter 27, "Multiple Intelligences" by Renee Holtz and Barbara

Lapetina, pp. 323-333 in this Handbook.

Joel

"Our child doesn't drink or take drugs!" was the response of Joel's parents when called in by the principal when Joel appeared woozy and unfocused in the Hebrew high school. While there was no tell-tale smell, his behavior was suspicious, especially on the evening his parents were called.

In the office, with parents present, Joel denied taking anything, but admitted that he had given up on grades because he wasn't one of the "smart" kids who would compete for the Ivy League schools. Indeed, Joel was doing poorly in public school and rumors abounded that he hung out with the druggie crowd.

Before Joel was sent home with his parents that night, the principal made very clear the school's behavior expectations and its policy on drugs. Each class session following, the principal made sure to greet Joel personally and schmooze about things of importance in his life. In these short exchanges, the principal also informally evaluated Joel's physical well-being, making sure that he was in compliance with the school's policies.

What to Look For:

Students who drink or abuse drugs come from every part of the socioeconomic spectrum. They may seem tremendously exhausted and sleepy all the time, or they may always seem to be "up." They may have dramatic mood swings and be unable to concentrate or finish a task. They may be secretive and spend long amounts of time in the bathroom or alone in a classroom. Often, the first hint of such a problem may come from the student's peers. Such confidences must be carefully protected.

If you do suspect drugs or alcohol, contact your director, Rabbi, or guidance counselor/school expert on the subject (if you have such a person on staff). The classroom teacher, camp counselor, or youth advisor should not act alone on his or her suspicions. Be aware that parental denial is the almost invariable reaction to such a suspicion.

It's the Law

It is important to be aware of the following: In many localities, if you know, or have sufficient knowledge to suspect that a student is abusing alcohol and/or drugs and you do not report it, you may be held partially responsible for any actions he or she takes, or crimes committed.

Resources

JACS (Jewish Alcoholics and Chemically Dependent Persons and Significant Others) is one of the few organizations under Jewish auspices that focuses on alcohol and substance abuse. Alcoholics Anonymous has teen programs, and your local Y, Jewish Family Service, Jewish Community Center, or Federation may have educational programs for prevention and/or ongoing help for students addicted or at risk. Getting to know the Community Patrol Officer or Youth Officer in your local police precinct is, surprisingly, often a good way to get effective referral possibilities. Make sure that you know your legal responsibility to report drug problems, and know the local rulings on what action you may take with regard to searches, confiscation, etc.

> How do I integrate low-attendance students in class and help them feel a part of things? I have a reward system of dots and prizes for completion of Hebrew assignments, but how could my "seldom there" students ever earn enough for a prize? I decided to do a "lottery" of sorts. Every time any student completes a Hebrew assignment, his/her name goes in a jar. At the end of the year, I draw from the jar some names for leftover prizes. Even a low-attendance child will have a chance (albeit a smaller one) of winning a prize. Maybe they will come more often to increase their chances!
>
> (Sheila Lepkin, Denver, Colorado)

INAPPROPRIATE RELATIONSHIPS AND SEXUAL HARASSMENT

In preparation for writing this chapter, we consulted with our resources and spoke to many lay people, including our students. We asked them to list what they thought were the most pressing problems facing them as individuals and groups. While in most instances we anticipated their answers, one unforeseen response involved sexual harassment and inappropriate relationships. Many of them related anecdotal material concerning teachers of one gender becoming too familiar verbally or physically with students of the opposite sex. Several spoke about relationships between teacher and students that were questionable at best, and criminal at worst.

Beth

Beth is a good teacher. She is young, pretty, exciting, bubbly. She has changed the face of the religious school in the few months she has been working there. Children are excited to be in her classroom or her presence.

Beth is also a very physical person. She is forever touching her students and anyone to whom she talks. No matter how many times she is cautioned about her "inappropriate physical behavior," she is unable — or unwilling — to modify her actions.

Although a wonderful and effective teacher, Beth is forced to resign because she is perceived as overstepping the lines of appropriate contact with others in a school setting.

At what point does a friendly, supportive relationship cross the line? Indeed, it is often difficult for the person engaging in a behavior to be fully aware of how inappropriate it may be. For example, a young male teacher who "innocently" flirts with his female high school students may be leading a particularly vulnerable teen to interpret the flirting as an invitation to a "special" relationship. Observers on the scene can often be more objective in assessing the behavior of the teacher and warning of its potential for harm.

What constitutes sexual harassment? As this question remains subjective in the courts, we certainly do not have specific answers either. But most of us know the difference between appropriate and intentionally inappropriate behavior, between constructive and destructive language, and between that which is respectful and that which is embarrassing or provocative. Most of us know what "appropriate" means.

What to Look For:

When suspecting an inappropriate relationship or sexual harassment, the general rules to follow are:

1. If it looks questionable, question it.

2. If it appears unhealthy, it probably is.

3. Don't hesitate to confront a colleague.

4. Don't begin rumors or allow rumors to fester.

Resources

First and foremost, contact the school director and/or the Rabbi. He or she needs to know what is (or what you suspect is) happening. Whatever action is taken must come from those responsible for the institution. Do not handle the situation yourself. If we have learned anything from other religious organizations, it is that we cannot allow these situations to go unattended, or attended alone. Many schools do have a written policy for handling harassment issues; check the school handbook for guidelines and procedures.

PHYSICAL AND SEXUAL ABUSE

More than in any other area, teachers are required by law to be aware of state rules and regulations for reporting sexual and physical abuse. Most schools and programs review their state laws with staff before each school year, and record that information in the faculty/staff handbook.

Physical abuse at home is more than just an occasional spanking of a young child. Physical abuse may or may not leave marks on the student. A child who is being abused may explain away multiple bruises or injuries as being the result of various accidents. Confronting the student even with assurances that "nothing will happen to you if you tell" is not enough. Abused children, for whatever reason, will often protect the abusive parent. Health professionals should be involved in any evaluation; a teacher or educator has the same reporting responsibility as the pediatrician or family doctor.

Sexual abuse is even more devastating and harder to detect. The acting out component of this sort of abuse may be promiscuous behavior, severe timidity, or even suicidal intimations. This case study exemplifies such a situation.

Melody

A new student in the school, Melody was extremely pretty, bright, and admired by her peers. Yet, from the outset, she was always late to school, argued with teachers about class requirements, and violated most school rules. Her attire for school was inappropriate — low cut blouses, jeans with rips in the seat, and excessive makeup. Her language, especially when boys were around, was seen as provocative. When confronted by the school director about these issues, she said, "That's the way I am. If you don't like it, you'll have to change. I won't."

When her parents were called in, they threw up their hands in frustration. They could not control Melody at home either, and she was rude to them in front of the principal. It was obvious that she had no respect for any kind of authority. After this behavior continued for several months, she was asked to leave the school.

This might have been the end of the story had it not been for a concerned administrator who, even after she left the school, made a psychological referral for Melody. It was discovered in those sessions that Melody had been raped by a cousin when she was four. Her parents moved from the city and neither dealt with the incident themselves, nor got her counseling or help. Melody has no memory of that rape.

When Melody was about seven, she was bullied for over a year by another relative and the parents did not intervene. In therapy, Melody said, "You couldn't protect me. You didn't help me."

Obviously, Melody had no reason to respect authority; it had never been able to protect her. Hence, her tremendous disdain for rules and authority.

What to Look For:

If you suspect abuse of any sort, look for the following signs:

1. Inappropriate sexual behavior

2. Exaggerated fearfulness and shyness

3. A preoccupation with sexual and physical matters

4. Serious social adjustment problems and problems with authority

It's the Law

It is incumbent upon every person who works with children to know the legal aspects and the obligations concerning physical and sexual abuse because, as a general rule, the law in the United States mandates reporting evidence or even suspicions of same. While laws vary from state to state, every educator and youth worker must be aware of the following general guideline: *If you have reason to suspect that a child is being abused, unless you have*

overwhelming evidence to the contrary (and who has?), you must report the alleged offense to your local state agency.

While we might gasp at the thought of getting so directly and personally involved in these legal matters, perhaps a more compelling reason for taking appropriate actions is that, as educators, we are models for the tradition we represent. Therefore, we should be bound by the ethic we purport to inculcate in our students. So, to suspect that a child is being abused (or has an eating disorder or is suicidal) and ignore it, in effect places that life at risk, which is morally indefensible.

While this chapter has concentrated on what can happen at home within the family unit, more and more sexual abuse occurs in school settings. Unsupervised locker rooms, class trips, and even bathroom visits all provide opportunities for predatory students. It takes a moment for the perpetrator to act. It can take a lifetime to recover. Our alertness as teachers is incredibly important.

Resources

If there is behavior that may indicate abuse, you must know your legal obligations. Do not let yourself be talked out of taking action. Anyone dealing with adolescents should have the name of a good pediatrician with connections to a university affiliated hospital with adolescent facilities, psychologists and/or psychiatrists who can be called on for advice, and legal advisors who specialize in family matters.

Do not think that abuse that has ended is damage that is over. As Melody's case clearly shows, the effects of abuse clearly outlive the abuse itself.

EATING DISORDERS

Anorexia nervosa and bulimia are psychological disorders that manifest themselves as compulsive starvation, overeating, and self-induced vomiting. They are most often associated with young women and are frequently seen in Jewish adolescent females. These disorders are life threatening.

Anorexia is increasingly perceived as a disturbed adolescent's attempt to exert control over herself, when she is unable to control a chaotic or hostile environment. By starving herself the adolescent can retard the physical changes of maturity and can prevent or delay sexual development. The issue is never whether or not the girl is overweight; her self-image is so distorted that an emaciated, hospitalized teenager weighing 70 pounds can still see herself as being too fat.

Bulimia, the purging cycle, can be found independently or in conjunction with anorexia. It is not up to a youth worker, teacher, or director to make a certain diagnosis, and treatment is certainly not within the educator's purview. Indeed, a cure may not be possible by medical professionals either. However, with these diseases, standing aside altogether is tantamount to participating in a suicide.

Chavi's story is a sad one.

Chavi

In junior high school, Chavi was a plump, happy student. She started changing in many ways during her sophomore year of high school. She lost a great deal of weight (which first appeared to be a major improvement in her appearance), became withdrawn, was often late to school and to class, and was frequently absent because of illness. By the end of that year, she was pale, sickly looking, and very thin.

Chavi's teachers and principal were concerned about these changes, as were her friends. Several of them spoke to members of the faculty about the fact that Chavi spent long periods of time in the bathroom and seemed to be eating little.

The principal decided to discuss with Chavi the changes she had seen, but Chavi denied any problems. With the aid of the school psychologist, a conference was set up with Chavi's parents. The parents also denied any problems. Chavi had always been and was still a perfect daughter, a perfect student.

Chavi was also the perfect example of an anorexia/bulimic student, starving and gorging, vomiting repeatedly to make herself really "perfect." The parents made some cursory attempts at medical evaluation, but have, to this point, refused to deal with the main problem. And Chavi's behavior continues.

What to Look For:

If you see any of the following signs, an eating disorder is a possibility:

1. Students who never eat, especially when others do

2. Binge eating followed by bathroom visits

3. Student gossip about destructive eating habits

Note: Conversation among students is invaluable for detecting problems. These symptoms are most often manifest outside the classroom. Students talk a great deal about each other and almost always know when someone exhibits the symptoms of eating disorders.

Resources

There are many types of health professionals; in this case, the student needs someone who specializes in eating disorders. Many hospitals have (inpatient) eating disorder clinics. A frank conversation about suspicions between the school director, parents, and youngster is an important step to beginning a referral process.

DEPRESSION AND SUICIDE

Depression is the feeling of overwhelming sadness, worthlessness, and hopelessness that can affect anyone at times, but becomes a serious illness when it takes over a person's life. With adolescents, it is one of the surest and clearest warning symptoms of an impending suicide attempt.

Suicide has reached epidemic proportions among American teenagers. Jewish teens are at the same risk as others, so no adult who suspects/hears about a threatened suicide threat can take it lightly. Teenagers are most susceptible to attempting suicide when their lives seem hopeless or out of control (often the same motivation as in anorexia or bulimia, the eating disorders that threaten the lives of teenage girls), following the loss of someone important to them, or as a result of abuse they have suffered.

Suicide is often glorified in teen literature, movies, or music and, consequently, seems romantic and dangerous. Twice as many girls as boys attempt suicide; more boys are successful. Three quarters of those who commit suicide have threatened or attempted to commit suicide beforehand. The following is a case in point.

Gary

Gary was a young man from a seriously troubled

family. He had lost a younger brother, and there was another sick child in the family. Lost in their grief and bitterness, his parents were unaware of how little attention their oldest child was receiving.

When Gary entered high school, there were two significant things noticed: his poor academic performance and his "invisibility." He seemed to shrink against the walls, slouched, and wore his oversized coat indoors — one literally could not see the person inside. As the year wore on, Gary's constant sadness and sense of unworthiness seemed to be a cloud floating around him. He could neither perform, nor be upset about not performing. He seemed to disappear a little more each day. No teacher seemed able to reach him.

Gary's behavior and performance indicated a deep depression, and he eventually did tell the school social worker that he really had no reason to live. But even without explaining this thought, Gary's behavior was a cry for help. He felt guilty over his brother's death, guilty over the next child's illness, guilty over his parents' arguments, and even guilty about his own continuing existence. These feelings paralyzed him and pushed him to shrink and disappear, first in the sense of his physical presence, and then possibly out of life itself. This was a young man who needed serious counseling, both individually and as part of a family, and that was the recommendation that was made by the school.

What to Look For:

Not every suicidal adolescent will "wear" his depression as clearly as Gary did, but adolescents are especially at risk for both depression and suicide. There are certain behaviors and warning signs that must be taken seriously as possible indications of suicidal intent or need for immediate professional consultation. One or more of the following signs are danger signals:

1. Depression, withdrawal, mood swings

2. Changes in normal behavior and friendships

3. Giving away prized possessions

4. Writing/reading death and suicide related poetry

5. Extreme preoccupation with death

Resources

Keep handy your local suicide prevention hot line number. Make sure all of your students have it, too. The student contemplating suicide may not call, but his or her best friend may. Let your students know whom they can see or call *immediately* if they or a friend is feeling very depressed.

CULTS

It is estimated that there are over 5,000 cults in the United States today. While many are small organizations with few members and little influence, a goodly number of well organized, well funded "communities" do exist that recruit in many local areas.

Complicating the matter in recent years have been the successful attempts of several of the largest and best known cults to achieve a sort of mainstream status. The Moonies (followers of Sun Myung Moon) own one of the two daily newspapers in Washington, D.C., and offer clergy and lay leaders expense paid trips to "leadership sessions." L. Ron Hubbard's Scientology literature has found its way into school curricula. The list is very long.

Cults tend to use common symbols and idealistic language and attractive causes to lure the unsuspecting "prospect." Once enticed, the newcomer is worked on by an amazingly modern array of mind control techniques.

Youngsters most at risk are those who are lonely, troubled, and angry. They may be the very students who seek justice and are imbued with the spirit of *tikkun olam* (fixing the world). It is common for such a student to be approached to work on some social action project by an organization he/she never heard of. Once involved in a first project or a first meeting, the indoctrination begins. Jason/Sanji demonstrates such a sad situation.

Jason/Sanji

Soon after Jason's mother and stepfather moved into town, they visited the local synagogue. His mother explained to the Rabbi that she had only just come back to Judaism. Her first husband was Jewish, but anti-religion. Jason, 13 years old, had never been given a Jewish education. And, in this new city, Jason attended an exclusive private school with a schedule that did not allow him to enter seventh grade with his peer group at the synagogue. Could Jason become a Bar Mitzvah?

After much discussion, a private tutor was engaged, a system of study and service attendance was devised, and the Bar Mitzvah ceremony was tentatively set for a little after Jason's fourteenth birthday. The tutor, in monthly reports, remarked how interested Jason seemed in social action projects. Other synagogue members noticed that Jason aggressively criticized his peers for "not caring enough" about the world. Jason's mother was concerned that her son was not getting a "spiritual feeling" from his Jewish education.

After several months, the Rabbi suggested that Jason attend a Jewish summer camp to develop friendships and have a more intense religious experience. Jason replied that he already attended a religious summer camp with his father each year. The truth, as it came out, was that Jason's father and mother were cult members and had raised their son within it. When his mother left the cult and divorced his father, she took Jason with her. The terms of the divorce agreement mandated that Jason spend each summer with his father at the cult's summer encampment. At that time, he dressed as a cult member and went by another name "Sanji."

Jason believed himself still to be a member of the cult and was unsure of his Jewish identity. He did not accept his becoming a Bar Mitzvah as anything other than an accommodation to his mother.

What to Look For:

Be alert to the following signs that may signal involvement in a cult:

1. Literature of, or meeting notices for, a group that is unfamiliar; obtain a copy and take notice of what it says.

2. Discussion about a charismatic person or leader of a group; find out about him/her.

3. A student suddenly has a friend (often older by a year or two) of the opposite sex who is taking him/her to meetings; look into the nature of the meetings.

Note that while Jason was exposed to a cult by his parents, many older teens are seductively enticed to join a cult by school friends or strangers they meet on the street. Youngsters should be taught the signs of the "approaches" used by cult members and educated as to why the Jewish community feels that cults are dangerous for them to join.

Resources

There are too many cults to list here, and a wide variety of symbols and methods of operation. The local Anti-Defamation League, Community Relations Committee, or American Jewish Committee will have information about the cults operating in your area. Check the bibliography of this chapter for some specific books that will be helpful.

Meeting the needs of at-risk children and families in our school has meant rethinking our roles as teachers and as a school community. We are already accustomed to arranging meals, rides, cards, visits, and so on for families with a parent or child experiencing acute physical illness. Dealing with families at risk has led us into much more complicated arrangements. For example, we have a child whose only parent will be deployed overseas for three weeks — we found respite care and partial funding. This proved to have a terrific educational bonus, as the child will be staying with an observant Jewish family, and will be able to live some of what she has been learning in class.

(Anne Johnston, New Haven, Connecticut)

JEWS FOR JESUS AND CHRISTIAN MISSIONARIES

The gravest concern to those who are aware of the goals and methods of Jews for Jesus and Christian missionaries is that very few outsiders seem to take the threat seriously. It is often held that Jews for Jesus represent a fringe group with no clear purpose. Nothing could be further from the truth.

There is a great deal of money and clear motivation behind the attempt of Jews for Jesus to lure Jews away from their religion. There are also many more such groups than we realize. One of their main goals is to achieve recognition by the Jewish community as informed and respected teachers. Thus, their first target is Jews who are not familiar with scripture. This includes most who attended supplementary school and not a few ex-day school students as well.

There are several fundamentalist groups that train their members to "witness" to those who are not "saved." Some of these (e.g., Seventh Day Adventists) have written pamphlets detailing "how to witness to your Jewish friends." These booklets show the missionary how to reword Christian theological terms into less "loaded" expressions, what specific arguments to employ when debating religion, and what phrases to use to begin a conversation on the topic of Jesus. To the unsuspecting, these groups can and do pose a clear and present danger. Mindy could have been a victim, had her Rabbi not intervened.

Mindy

The Rabbi met Mindy, one of her Confirmation students, at the supermarket. Mindy was very distraught because in school that week, one of her friends had given her a pamphlet about a Rabbi who had converted to Christianity. The cover of the pamphlet, with the friendly face of an Orthodox man, was filled with quotes extolling his rebirth as a Christian.

Her Rabbi spent some time talking to Mindy in the store, and invited her to the office for a more in-depth conversation. There, Mindy spoke of her friend's constant pressure to consider conversion to Christianity, just as the Rabbi in the pamphlet had. After all, her friend had said, how could such a pious and observant man be wrong?

Mindy's Rabbi talked to her about the differences in belief between Judaism and Christianity, and the issues involved in being a Jew for Jesus. She also warned her of some of the recruitment tactics used by members of the group, and left Mindy with an open invitation to come back and talk, as she needed to.

Afterward, Mindy's Rabbi wrote to Jews for Jesus, the publishers of the pamphlet, for more information about this Rabbi who was also Christian. It turned out that he had been ordained in 1895! While the questions concerning his conversion still existed, the blatant lies concerning his observance, the attempt to portray him as Orthodox, and not mentioning that only one Rabbi in the last hundred years converted to Christianity did much to allay Mindy's fears and frustrations.

What to Look For:

When suspecting involvement in a Jews for Jesus or other Christian missionary group, watch out for:

1. pamphlets and other written materials brought to class.

2. questions about religion that would not otherwise come up in class.

Resources

There is a helpful organization called Jews for Judaism that works to counter the Jews for Jesus movement. (The address of their main office is P.O. Box 15059, Baltimore, MD 21208.) Write them for information and for addresses of branches in other cities. Synagogue Rabbis also serve as good resources in case of suspected involvement in either of these groups.

AIDS AND COMMUNICABLE DISEASES

In all the other categories discussed in this chapter, we have presented a case to illustrate our text. The cases available to us for AIDS and communicable diseases are too tragic and painful to portray. Numbers of teens have already become HIV-positive and will carry this plague forward, infecting the unwary.

Here again, the first rule is: yes, Jewish teenagers are at risk. Concerning AIDS, ignorance can be terminal. While many of our schools take this matter seriously and educate the student population, not all families do the same. Proper education is imperative. Abstinence is the first and best line of defense. But, realistically, teenagers now need to know about safe sex, about not using/sharing needles, and about the risks of homosexual and heterosexual sex. Religious school classrooms, youth group programs, and camp settings are all valid venues for such discussions.

Concerns about sexual behaviors and choices can and should be aired in discussions between youngsters and respected Jewish educational professionals who can bring both their moral outlook and practical advice to bear. Just as we need to inform teens about condoms and other precautions, we must also lead them to consider the moral implications of their choices.

Resources

The first resources in this instance are your school director and/or Rabbi. Will he/she support your educational efforts? If not, know where to send the students to find out what you may not be able to tell them. Locate a good speaker on AIDS and local clinics, doctors, and testing centers. Check with your community's Jewish Family Service. Know enough so as not to be shocked when kids speak to you, but know also the limits of your ability to help or to answer questions.

DEATH OF A LOVED ONE

You may assume that the death of a family member or close friend, or even a death in the family of a close friend, will create tension and behavior changes in youngsters. This is a normal part of the grieving process which takes months — even years — to restore balance to a young mind.

In many of the other situations described above, some type of aggressive action is usually recommended. In the case of grief work, giving the student time to feel the pain and hurt is perhaps the best strategy to use. Many tend to hurry along the process, becoming impatient with a child's inability to cope with a life process they themselves cannot fully comprehend. They demand responses and communication that only complicate an already trying time.

This is not to say that a child should be allowed to wallow in self-pity, nor left to feel alone in sorrow. An understanding attitude and the message that you care and are there as a support will bear fruit down the road. The case study of Phyllis is about a teenager whose father died.

Phyllis

Phyllis was 13 years old when her father died suddenly. An outstanding student and a very responsible young woman, she helped her mother with her four brothers, and continued to excel in her studies. The only visible effect of her loss was a significant weight gain.

It took a crisis three years later for her Rabbi to see what was behind the "coping" front Phyllis had adopted. She had fought with her father the night before he died, and for three years she had lived with (and stuffed herself over) the guilt she felt for "causing" his death. Once she spoke about this

problem, and realized how silly it sounded to her, she was ready to stop punishing herself by overeating, overworking, and overcompensating in every other aspect of her life, and to begin trying to rethink this critical point in her life. A recommendation for further counseling was made and brought Phyllis back to "life."

What to Look For:

Any of the following signs should be taken as danger signals:

1. Lingering depression

2. Constant weeping, or weeping for no apparent reason

3. Inability to concentrate

4. Preoccupation with death in conversations, writings, or drawings

5. A total lack of affect — no emotion about anything.

In most instances, time and emotional support from others should be enough to help the student through the grieving process. Should the grieving dynamic continue for an overextended period of time, action should be taken. Also, if the student exhibits no behavioral changes and carries on as though nothing has happened, be concerned.

Resources

The school director and/or Rabbi should be apprised of any behavior changes on the part of a grieving child. A skilled therapist is another member of the support team who may be utilized as needed. In many communities there are Jewish support groups that normally meet for six to ten sessions. Most suggest that a mourner begin with such a group no sooner than six months after a loss, as it often takes that long just for emotions and new family dynamics to sort themselves out. The Rabbi or local Jewish Family Service would know about such a group.

PARENTAL SEPARATION AND DIVORCE

We deal last with the category that is first among our concerns. Of all the possible problematic situations with which an educator can be faced, the issues surrounding the children of divorce and separation are at the same time most prevalent and most often ignored. Perhaps this is because so many of our students come from single parent homes or live with combined families (thus giving them three parents and six grandparents). Perhaps this is because many Jewish educators are also single parents who deal with the realities of the situation every day, thus acknowledging in other children the problems with which they and their children cope at home.

Whatever the reason, we must be especially vigilant in attending to the unique concerns of these students who are stretched and pulled by every adult around them.

Allen

Allen was a personable junior high school student who, while frequently involved in small acts of mischief, seemed unaffected by the anger or discipline of his teachers. His grandmother, the adult responsible for him, called frequently to check on his progress. Allen's parents did not attend parent-teacher conferences and were detached from their son.

Allen's continued acts of mischief finally aroused several faculty members to action. At the January staff meeting, all concerned admitted they did not understand the child or the family dynamics. It was determined that the school social worker would look into the matter.

Some detective work revealed the nature of Allen's world. His parents divorced shortly after he was born. His father moved across the country. His mother worked long hours and had moved near her mother for support, but no longer had any relationship with her except through Allen. Allen spent after school time with his grandmother. She supervised homework, watched out for him, gave him supper, and sent him home to his mother at night and on weekends. He spoke to his father once a week and spent summers with him. His parents were not on speaking terms.

Unraveling Allen's complex world, we understand that he had learned to negotiate his life through separate universes: his mother's, his grandmother's, and his father's. He had become adept at playing one off against the other and, sadly, he had no consistent parenting, expectations, or demands from any of these adults. His school experience was like an extension of his home life — compartmentalized, with no one person laying down consistent rules.

The principal decided to begin an aggressive approach for this young man. Allen's school would really act in loco parentis, providing a unified network of rules and expectations. During the next months, Allen's behavior and performance improved.

What to Look For:

Although Allen's case is markedly unusual and exaggerated, every divorce or separation brings fragmentation into the lives of the youngsters affected. Generally, the home situation prior to the divorce is probably less than ideal, but at least there is one home with (hopefully) one set of rules. Two (or, in this case, three) homes with different expectations and "cultures" seriously compound the confusion, guilt, and anxiety of the child of divorce. He or she can become severely confused, anxious or, like Allen, adept at maneuvering among warring parties (or engaging in antisocial behaviors such as lying, cheating, stealing, drugs, etc.). The school must be aware of and able to deal with some of the child's conflict.

The behaviors that signal problems for a child living in this situation are similar to symptoms described in categories shown above. The proper responses are also similar. Identifying the problem and working (sometimes with the parents, sometimes despite the parents) with the child present the greatest challenges.

Resources

Staying neutral, between mother and father, is important. When possible, meet with both parents simultaneously for any discussions regarding the child, including school conferences. Use the school director, Rabbi, or social worker to help you learn about a child's specific family situation and ways to work with both parents, for the good of the child. Alert parents to any distress signals provided by the child, for what parents see at home may not match the child's behavior at school or with friends.

CONCLUSION

All of the above may make you say, "Stop, I just wanted to teach Hebrew/*Chumash*/History!" or "But I just want to enjoy playing with my campers out on the ballfield!" or "It's just a youth group that meets twice a month!" But consider: a good educator or youth worker doesn't teach topics; he/she teaches children. Youngsters today seldom enter the classroom with undivided focus on the subject at hand. Their lives are "interesting, and so, beyond the curriculum, they often need our concern, support and . . . intervention. That doesn't mean you don't teach Hebrew/*Chumash*/History. It just means that you may be called upon to teach other life lessons as well. And it is those lessons that can make a decided difference to our students.

BIBLIOGRAPHY

Allen, Nancy H., and Michael L. Peck. *Suicide in Young People*. West Point, PA: American Association of Suicidology, Merch Sharp & Dohme, 1992.

> This is an excellent introductory pamphlet to the issue of suicide in young people.

Bayar, Steven, and Francine Hirschman. *Teens & Trust: Building Bridges in Jewish Education*. Los Angeles, CA: Torah Aura Productions, 1993.

> This is our book on this topic. How can it be bad?

Cohen, Susan, and Daniel Cohen. *Teenage Stress*. New York: M. Evans & Co. 1984.

> This is a must read for anyone working with teens. It is a well written, easily accessible book.

Giffin, Mary, and Carol Felsenthal. *A Cry for Help*. Garden City, NJ: Doubleday & Co., 1983.

> This well written book details the many ways people communicate their distress, and the many "hints" a teacher needs to be able to understand to help those in need.

Gordon, Sol. *When Living Hurts*. New York: UAHC Press, 1985.

> This book helps teens cope with issues of depression, suicide, and death. A good resource for teachers, as well.

Grollman, Earl A. *Suicide: Prevention, Intervention, Postvention*. rev. ed. Boston, MA: Beacon Press, 1988.

> A well written book on the topic of suicide.

Kaplan, Aryeh. *The Real Messiah: A Jewish Response To Missionaries*. New York: National Council of Synagogue Youth, 1985.

> Although this book has a clear religious agenda, it is most effective in teaching us to understand the strategies used by missionaries and how to combat them.

Klagsbrun, Francine. *Too Young to Die*. New York: Pocket Books, 1985.

> A good resource book on issues related to death.

Kubler-Ross, Elisabeth. *On Children & Death*. New York: Macmillan Publishing Co., 1983.

> Kubler-Ross is a pioneer of the Hospice movement. She writes from great experience and with great sensitivity on working with children who are terminally ill and their attitudes toward death. It is an in-depth look at these topics.

Note: For in-depth case studies on these and similar topics, refer to *Teens & Trust: Building Bridges in Jewish Education* by Steven Bayar and Francine Hirschman. The authors would like to thank Dr. Marilyn Sperling and Sara Shuter for their help with this chapter.

CHAPTER 18

Creating a Learning Environment

Rivkah Dahan and Nachama Skolnik Moskowitz

*A*dam left the staff meeting with his head swimming. He thought that offering to teach ninth grade would be a nice thing to do for his synagogue, as well as a feather in his cap professionally – the firm in which he worked encouraged its lawyers to work in the community. He was excited about teaching a course on Israel, but he didn't realize that he was expected to do things like "decorate." He was a lawyer, not an interior designer!

In so many schools, little attention is paid to the physical environment. Bulletin boards languish with a paper or two stapled to their cork surfaces. Chairs remain in the row-by-row pattern that custodians remember from their youth. The teacher's desk stands stiffly in the front, overstuffed with supplies from years past. High school students sit in classrooms used by the preschool during the week.

This chapter will help teachers like Adam focus on issues such as: room arrangement, educational displays, and organization of materials. Many of the suggestions are quick and easy to implement. Others take some time and effort. The importance of the physical environment as a complement to learning is crucial to student learning and to teacher success.

ROOM ARRANGEMENT: WHERE TO PLACE THE TABLES AND CHAIRS

Creating a physical environment that is organized, welcoming, conducive to learning and suited to the needs of both student and teacher is essential for effective instruction. The decisions teachers make about the physical arrangement of the classroom can have an impact on classroom discipline, as well as student learning.

As with a home, a classroom reflects a teacher's personality and teaching style. However, in Jewish schools, due to a dual curriculum classroom or multiple uses of the same room, setup can ultimately be a challenge. Often the classroom is shared by both the general and Judaic studies teacher or, in some cases, a synagogue may rent space from a public school. There are a number of approaches that can be taken to surmount these challenges.

Novice teachers consider room arrangements to be functional — they simply offer a place for students to sit and work. But experienced teachers understand the impact of their choice in furniture arrangement. Below is a variety of room setups with explanations of why each might be chosen for particular learning tasks.

> Our storefront congregation's essentially one-room space alternately serves as our sanctuary, meeting place, social hall, and school. Our school is set up and torn down each week, and so, easily moved furniture is a must. The wheels we put on the bottoms and handles we put on the sides of several of the cabinets that house our school's texts, games, and arts and crafts materials, make it possible for a single person to move them. These rolling cabinets then serve as dividers between the three multi-aged class groups so that, although not eliminated completely, there is a reduction for our students in both visual and auditory distractions. We also have a four-foot high, folding, canvas divider, purchased at an Army/Navy store that can also be used to help delineate class space. Our three class groups are located along three of the room's four walls. In the middle of the room are the rest of the chairs, still set up for services, and ready for us to use for whole-school *Tefilah* and music sessions.
>
> *(Carol Cohn, Orlando Florida)*

Traditional Classroom Setup

In the traditional classroom setup, the focus is at the front, on the teacher. His or her desk is "front and center," with the white board or blackboard behind. In the back there might be cabinets, cubbies, or lockers for storing books, papers, and supplies. Student desks sit in neat columns and rows, all facing the front (see figure 1). Some rooms have a long table pushed under a bulletin board that is used for teacher-student discussions, small group work, artwork, display, or a collection spot for student papers.

Some teachers like this setup for opening weeks of school while introducing rules and procedures. This is the most comfortable arrangement for a teacher who is unsure of his/her ability in classroom discipline. This setup immediately sets the tone for a learning experience with order and discipline at its core. This arrangement, however, makes it hard for teachers to walk freely among student desks. It also precludes the comfortable building of classroom community.

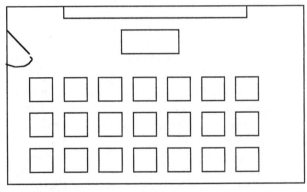

Figure 1

Pods

In a "pod" situation, students are divided into groups of three of four, with desks arranged facing one another to facilitate students working together (see figure 2). The pod setup encourages cooperative learning, allowing some students to focus on seatwork while the teacher works with students individually or in groups. In placing students in close proximity facing each other, a buzz flows through the room. The teacher's desk is often situated in the back or to the side of the room. Novice teachers may be uncomfortable with this setup, as this classroom gives the message that the teacher is a facilitator of learning, not firmly in charge of everything.

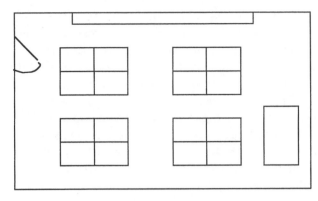

Figure 2

Quadrants

In the quadrant setup, student desks are grouped into three or four sections (see figure 3). For example, four desks might be pushed together on each side of the room, angled at a slant toward the front, and four other desks pushed together in the middle of the room. A few other student desks might be against the wall, allowing space for individual or one-on-one pairings. The teacher desk is pushed against, or is near one of the walls and is rarely sat in by the teacher during a class. This arrangement creates a number of walkways for the teacher and students to pass through freely. It encourages community, but has the disadvantage that some students have their backs to the board.

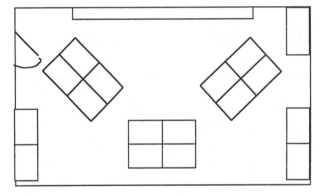

Figure 3

Big U

In a U shape, students are able to see each other, regardless of their seating placement. This setup has a row in the back (facing the front) and some rows on both sides (see figure 4). This arrangement allows for a lot of space in the center of the classroom, allowing the teacher more freedom of movement, and offering better teacher-student proximity.

Students have less opportunity to "hide in the back," though the people in the side corners of the U sometimes have trouble seeing the board. The teacher's desk may be in the center of the U, slightly over to the side, or against one of the walls.

This arrangement is best for a teacher who does not focus all his/her lessons on the board, but rather encourages lots of discussion among students. Every student is in the "front row" in this format; no one can hide behind another for mischief or sleeping. For films and videos, the seating remains basically the same, but about half the students need to move their desks around a bit to see the screen better.

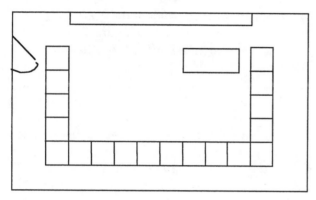

Figure 4

Large Circle

For class discussions, desks can be arranged in a large circle, with the teacher taking a student desk as an "equal" partner in the conversation (see figure 5). This allows everyone to participate. This setup is less efficient for lectures and other activities.

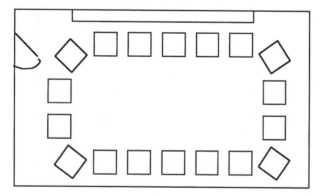

Figure 5

Seminar-Style

Much like a professional seminar, in the seminar-style setting, students and teacher sit around a large table and "discuss" (see figure 6). Sometimes the class is actually located in a board or seminar room and, at other times, this is simply an arrangement achieved by pushing all the desks together in a solid "block." The teacher has the choice of placing herself at the head of the table, or along the side, depending on the centrality of the role he/she wishes to play in the discussion. A seminar-style arrangement gives students a more grown-up feeling, important especially for adolescents.

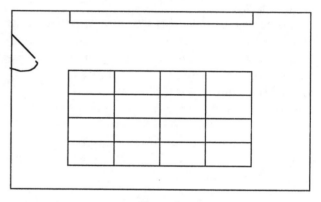

Figure 6

Right after the initial staff meeting, Adam took a walk to his classroom. He sat down at the desk and looked at the size, shape, and current arrangement in his room. He realized he needed to consider some questions about his own comfort level and classroom management style before making his final decision about how he would set up his classroom. These included the following:

- *What kind of learning-situation do I prefer: group work? discussion? lecture? What arrangement of desks makes the best sense for this preference of mine?*

- *Can every student see me? see the board?*

- *Can I see each student?*

- *Does the placement of the door or windows in the classroom make a difference?*

- *Where should my own desk be placed?*

- *Will the students have assigned places?*

- *Have I left sufficient space between student desks so that I can reach any student easily?*

- *Where will I stand?*

Adam decided to begin the school year with his ninth graders in a U-shape. He wanted to engender discussion, but he placed his desk center-front so as to send a message that he was in control of the room. Adam understood that his initial decisions were not etched stone, and that he could change the seating arrangement as he got to know the students and his own management style better.

Other Room Arrangement Considerations

Room arrangement decisions move beyond the placement of student and teacher desks in conducive locations. In deciding how to set up for the year, other issues need to be resolved:

- *Traffic flow* - Leave ample space for students and teacher to move about the room, including free and clear paths to the door in case of an emergency evacuation of the building.

- *Noisy and quiet areas* - Consider having a corner or corners of the classroom designated for things like a reading corner (with a small rug remnant and or a bean bag chair, as well as a variety of books from which children may choose), a games corner (where students can go when they have completed their work, or at recess), or a space for learning centers.[1]

- *A whole group area* - Many teachers who encourage small group work, find a spot in their room for the entire class to gather. Sometimes this is designated by an architect (a special seating area), sometimes it's a place to *shlep* chairs, and sometimes it's just a little spot on the carpet.

- *Safety* - Besides making sure that there are clear paths to the door, teachers need to make sure that computer cords are safely tucked away, that desk corners are turned in such a way that students don't get bruises on their thighs, and that any cleaning chemicals are locked safely away.

DYNAMIC DISPLAYS

Adam's next challenge was interior decorating. As a lawyer, his office manager took care of this aspect of his office, but at school Adam was on his own.

[1]See Chapter 29, "Learning Centers" by Marci Rogozen and Ronna Fox, pp. 340-350 of this Handbook.

He understood that room decorations were an important part of teaching. He looked around the room and made a mental note of the available wall space. As a Sunday school teacher, Adam was grateful that the room decorations were not his burden, alone — the room was occupied during the week by the seventh grade Hebrew class. He appreciated the brightly decorated bulletin boards, and wanted to make sure that the after school program was represented as well.

There are many different aspects of his classroom to which Adam could pay attention at this point. Displays include: bulletin boards; mobiles that hang from the ceiling; items that hang on the window, classroom door, or are tacked to the open part of the teacher desk; stand-alone displays propped on a table (much like a science fair project); and items set up on a table for students to explore. There is an unfortunate truth about schools that the older the student, the less attention teachers pay to the physical space in which they learn; this is true for high school students and even more so for adult learners. Luckily for Adam's students, he is willing at least to consider the environment in which they will reside for the year, albeit for only a few hours a week.

> When I have my room set up and it is quiet before the students come, I sit in one of the student chairs and imagine the activity of the room from the student's perspective. Where will students need to walk? How easy is the movement to and from desks? What do students see? How easy are the display materials to see? This helps me see what students see and anticipate their responses.
>
> *(Sally Stefano, Worthington, Ohio)*

A classroom should be visually appealing, not overly stimulating, and a reflection of the learning that takes place inside. On a simple level, the lights should be turned on, the temperature regulated, glare from the sun taken care of, torn items on bulletin boards removed, old no longer needed papers disposed of, and perhaps a few plants placed on the window ledge or shelves. It is relatively easy to purchase and put up bulletin board paper and a coordinated border, bringing color cohesion to the space. (Most large office supply stores have a school supply section with such paper, negating the need to staple tens of sheets of construction paper to the boards.) Teachers with very little time or artistic skill can minimally cover the boards and then staple to them some theme-appropriate posters.

While it may be the minimal aesthetic consideration, the "Jewishness" of the room must also be attended to. Students should know that they are sitting in a Jewish classroom, as differentiated from one devoted to general studies subjects. A *mezuzah* on the door welcomes students immediately into their Jewish environment. Depending on the age of the student and subjects taught, the classroom might also have a Hebrew *Alef-Bet* chart, posters of Jewish holidays and Israel,[2] a Jewish calendar (and/or a way to display student birthdays according to the Hebrew and "English" months), Jewish books or computer programs on a shelf for lending, a *tzedakah* box, and ritual objects to touch.

I share a room with a preschool class. While there are plenty of drawbacks, one great plus is that the room is partially carpeted. And so, for part of the day, my students work on the carpet, sometimes stretched out on their bellies, but working. I especially use the carpet during the week. It is very difficult for my students to sit still for religious school after five or six hours in secular school. Also, when reading or discussing feelings, it's a lot cozier on the carpet.

(Cheryl Cash-Linietsky, Philadelphia, Pennsylvania)

In today's ever mobile, cost effective society, not all Jewish education goes on in classrooms that belong to the Jewish community. Some classes are held in public schools and some in office buildings. These create "display challenges" for the teachers involved. Similar issues abound when two very different classes (e.g., the weekday preschool class for four-year-olds and a ninth grade evening class) share space. One solution is to ignore the issue and

do nothing to change the environment. But another is to think of creative ways to bring in temporary displays, perhaps on (science fair-type) display boards, or a piece of fabric that is rolled out over a bulletin board for a few hours and then packed away again. Some teachers share space, with a "half-for-me and a half-for-you" attitude. If such is your situation, read the rest of this chapter with an eye to creative ways of dealing with it.

Students are required to sit in their classroom for many hours a day. What goes up on the walls, doors, and even ceilings, will ultimately be imprinted on their memories. Use your displays to introduce a unit, spark your students' curiosity, or extend learning. Not surprisingly, there are some ways to categorize displays that help teachers consider what they might wish to place in their rooms.

Student Displays

Displays of student work show off and reward students for creative activities such as art projects, writing samples, and photographs of classroom life (the latter are often labeled with information about the specific activity). At the beginning of the year, such boards help introduce students to each other. Parents especially enjoy viewing student displays as these showcase their children's activities and "open the door" to the classroom. Students appreciate seeing their "name up in lights," leading to greater self-esteem.

Consider these caption titles (and hints) for student displays:

- My House - For a "get to know me" bulletin board that spotlights primary grade children and lasts all year, create a page-sized template of a house, photocopy it, and distribute one to every child. During the first week, have students decorate their houses to represent themselves and their own homes, perhaps with photos and/or drawings. Ask them to write or dictate one sentence about themselves to add to the house. As the year progresses, use the houses as an anchor point for displaying children's work, adding their writing and drawings, and watching the houses grow!

---

[2]A special word about Israel-related displays, even if Israel is not the "subject-of-the-year": With the continued issues in Israel, and the decrease in visits by our students and their families, it is imperative that teachers find ways to bring Israel to the hearts of their students. Attention to visuals of Israel in the classroom (posters, a display of postcards, photo albums, a photo of Israel screen saver) is one easy way to accomplish this.

- _____ in a Nutshell - Ask students to summarize a specific piece of learning (e.g., the weekly Torah portion, a prayer, a personality in Jewish history) using bullet points or an illustration of key ideas. Post these on a bulletin board with pictures of nutshells as the border.

- Take a "Step" in the Right Direction - Use a sneaker border and post student work in the center.

- Follow the Road to Jewish Learning with __(name of class)__ - Draw a path and place student work on "picket signs" scattered along the way.

- Leap into Learning - Place a frog on a lily pad in the center of the board and other lily pads scattered around. Student work (or photos of a class project) is placed on the pads.

- We're all Part of One Whole" - Cut an oak tag (poster board) apart and distribute a piece to each student. They glue on a photograph and some key words and interests.

Interactive Displays

Interactive displays contain hands-on materials that can be manipulated by the students and provide an exceptional way to maintain attention. Whether tacked on a bulletin board, classroom door, or front of the teacher's desk, these displays should be placed at a level that is accessible to students. Examples include:

- Question of the Week - Cover a bulletin board with blank butcher paper. At the top, write a thought provoking question. Let the students write their thoughts on the paper (as well as read what others have written) in their free time, such as before class begins or after an assignment is done. The question may be related to a particular unit, a springboard to something new, or a review of something learned earlier.

Some possible questions include the following:

- What is your favorite holiday, and why?

- What makes a good friend?

- What do you already know about (upcoming lesson topic)?

- What do you want to know about (upcoming lesson topic)?

- If you could meet any historical figure, whom would you want to meet and what would you ask them?

This board may also be done with a factual question. Include some slips of paper with Internet addresses that have answers. Students take these slips and use either a school or home computer to find the answers. Responses can be posted by students on file cards.

- Jews around the World - Cut out a number of house shapes from colored construction paper and create window openings and doors. Find photographs of different Jewish observances (online or in books or magazines that are okay to cut up) and place them under the house shapes in such a way that the observance shows through the window or door. On each house, or perhaps on a "mailbox" outside, record some reference sources (web sites, books, and page numbers, etc.) for the students that explain about the holiday, country, or ritual. As students learn about the photograph, have them record the information on a file card and staple it under the house.

- What's Kosher? - Cut a variety of food pictures from magazines, or find them in a computer clip art program. Paste one item each on the front of a folder turned so that the fold is at the top and the opening at the bottom. Inside the folder write whether or not the food is kosher, along with an explanation. Staple these to a bulletin or display board and encourage students to consider each item and then check for the correct answers.

Teaching Displays

Teaching displays reinforce specifically information learned in class. They may be as simple as placing in the room such items as a map, Hebrew verb chart, blessing posters, photographs, or a Jewish quote that focuses the unit. These may be bought (e.g., a poster of Jerusalem's key religious sites), teacher-made (e.g., a poster that illustrates the shape of the moon on each day of the Hebrew month), or student-made (e.g., student illustrations of prayer vocabulary dangled from the ceiling).

	What	When	Who	Where	Why	How
Shabbat candle						
Havdallah candle						
Yartzeit candle						
Chanukkah candle						
Ner Tamid (eternal light in synagogue)						

Figure 7

Some teacher displays specifically grow out of a class lesson. These can include:

- pieces of chart paper on which the teacher records student brainstorming or key ideas.

- a chart with items down the side, and related questions across the top (see figure 7). For example, a picture of different Jewish candles can be placed down the left of a chart, with the words "what, when, who, where, why, how" across the top columns.

As students learn about the candles and their rituals the teacher records information in the squares. (This kind of a chart not only displays information, but can be categorized as an interactive display if student groups each filled in the squares and then posted them to share with the class.)

Creating a Display

Planning a display step-by-step makes the process less overwhelming. Using the format we call SCE-MEES offers a structure, especially helpful to novices. This stands for Subject, Caption, Etch-a-Sketch, Materials, Execute, Evaluate, Store. Each of these is explained below.

Subject: Consider the *subject matter* that the display will teach/reinforce. Make a list of the main points that pertain to that unit.

Tips:

- Themes that last year-round are real time-savers.

- Certain items can last year-round, as well. These include *alef bet* charts, months of the year display, calendar, "feelings" charts, class rules, and other general knowledge to keep in front of students.

- Save one display strictly for information: memos, menus, emergency procedures, etc.

A canvas shoe bag makes a good mail center. It can hang on the back of a door, if wall space is at a premium. Pin a name badge on each pocket. Gently roll corrected work and other individual work into the pockets.

(Diane Schon Wirtschafter, Berkeley, California)

Caption: Think of a catchy slogan that will be an attention grabber. (This step is skipped in the case of dangling mobiles.)

Tips:

- Magazine and newspaper ads will give clues to catchy titles, as will books. (If this is not an area of expertise, ask a friend to help.)

- Captions can be printed out on a computer,

or put together using purchased letters (available at a teacher supply or large office store), cut by hand, or punched out using something like an Ellison Machine (available in some schools or community teacher resource centers; for information, see the Bibliography).

Etch-a-Sketch: Draw a rough sketch of the display.

Tips:

- Make sure the diagram is to scale, so proportions can be anticipated.

Materials: Gather the materials needed. Be creative in the use of textures, if possible and do not go "wild" with a lot of clashing colors.

Tips:

- For large areas, try backgrounds from sheets, fabric remnants, plastic tablecloths, fadeless paper (available at teacher or office supply stores), or gift wrap.

- Textures and three-dimensional effects help make a display stand out. Consider using actual objects (e.g., real branches to make the top of a *sukkah*) or helping normally flat items "puff" (e.g., create a large circular map ("globe") of the world and stuff the underpart with crumpled newspapers, bubble wrap, or tissue paper).

- Mobiles should be light enough not to pull down the ceiling! Find out from the custodian or school director permissible ways to hang displays from the ceiling. (Drop ceilings offer a way to attach an opened paper clip to the metal bars that hold up the ceiling panels.) Items that could be used to "anchor" a mobile include:

  - wire hanger
  - paper plate
  - fishing net
  - strainer/colander (cooking utensils, food pictures, plastic food, food boxes, etc., can hang from them with their Hebrew terms attached)
  - small laundry basket (hang pictures of clothing from it, labeled with Hebrew terms)

- breadbasket (hang Hebrew names of fruits and/or blessings)

- hang small toy vehicles from something for a transportation unit

- cake/pizza wheels (available from a baking supply store)

- crown (hang symbols and characters from the Purim story)

- basketball hoop

- umbrella

- Clotheslines are great for hanging time lines, schedules, and a variety of pictures. Hang these either against a wall or, if across the room, up high enough so that they are not a safety hazard for students.

- Use yarn, fabric, pipe cleaners, and other objects to add spice to your display.

Try to keep the easels and sand/water tables near the sink. Your art projects and play dough activities will be walked all over the carpet, so setting up a table off the carpet and on a hard surface is also suggested. Don't put your block corner near the reading corner; it becomes too noisy for your budding readers to concentrate. Change your dramatic play corner often. I hate seeing the same dolls, cookware, and plastic food in April that has been there since September. Be creative . . . think like a pre-schooler!

(Kim Lausin, Beachwood, Ohio)

Execute: Some people prefer to do messy work in a school workroom or teacher center. Others do not mind spreading out at home on the kitchen table or in front of the television.

Tips:

- Use your home computer's font and color capacity to type labels and find interesting clip art.

- Not artistic? Ask your school for help transferring a picture to a transparency (easy to do on the photocopier, or simply traced) and then use an overhead projector to project the image onto poster board, bulletin board paper, or a piece of fabric (attached to a wall, bulletin board, or a glass surface, such as a large window panel). Move the projector closer to or farther away from the material to vary the size of the image. Trace the image that is projected onto the material for posting on your display.

- Use rubber cement or glue stick to back paper to paper. A glue gun can be used to attach items to covered bulletin boards that might normally defy attachment: small tree branches for Tu B'Shevat, empty boxes of food for a display on *kashrut* or a blessing-match interactive activity, old markers for a back to school theme, etc.

- For interactive activities, consider these "stick-to" items: Velcro, magnetic tape, looseleaf rings, and library pockets.

- Find out what is permissible to use to attach things to the door, wall, or ceiling. Blue sticky tack (available in hardware, office, and teacher stores) works well and usually does not pull off paint from the surface to which it sticks.

- Photos, pictures, and designs can be blown up to poster size at a photocopy specialty store.

Evaluate: While the display is up, consider whether the learning goals were accomplished through this particular design. Make notes for future use.

Store: After a lot of hard work, it is nice to find ways to store materials so they may be used another year.

Tips:

- Consider reusing boxes in which poster or display boards arrive.

- Tape two poster boards together along three sides to store oversize flat items.

- Purchase plastic or cardboard containers at an office supply or home renovation store (Walmart, Target, The Container Store, etc.).

- Place bulletin board cutouts and letters in a large manila envelope with a picture mounted on the outside. File the envelopes by subject area or month in a filing cabinet

or large box. (Manila envelopes can be laminated to hold letters and small bulletin board pieces. Attach a photo or sketch of the bulletin board to the envelope before laminating it to remember exactly how the display was created.)

- Attach a press-on pocket to the largest piece of the bulletin board stored in a box. Use this to store the letters and smaller pieces.

- Use a clear dress bag to store bulletin boards. You can see what is inside and get to it easily.

For starters, Adam decided to put fadeless bulletin board paper and colorful borders on each of the two bulletin boards to give the room a neat look. He stapled to one of them some posters provided by his school director that related to the curriculum, and used his home computer to print out a large caption. He wanted to feature student thinking on the other board, so for now he posted the title, "What do we know?" The first week of school, he planned to staple onto that board the sheet of chart paper used to record what students knew about the topic they would be studying with him. Adam knew that as a new teacher, there was much to focus on and, without formal training, he had lots of preparation for his class lessons. But his room now looked welcoming. Later, once he'd gotten to know his students and the curriculum better, he'd have time to decide how better to utilize his two bulletin boards.

ORGANIZATION OF MATERIALS IN THE CLASSROOM

A wonderful term from Physics is "entropy," which refers to the world moving to a state of chaos. One of the key jobs of a teacher is to minimize chaos in a classroom, for with order, learning proceeds much easier. Sometimes, such organization comes from thinking through the streamlining of certain procedures. For example, a great way to take attendance is to use a pocket chart display (either store-bought or teacher-made) that contains cards with each student's name and/or photograph on them. When children arrive in class, they turn their cards over, allowing the teacher to see the one or two names still in their original faceup position. The materials each have a spot, fulfill an organizational function of the class, and streamline the taking of attendance.

Other ways to organize materials in classrooms include:

- Purchase a shoe bag and hang it over a door. Use it either for small supplies or as a "mailbox" for each student.

- Use plastic see-through stackable boxes to store supplies.

- If students work at tables together, consider creating table supply baskets that contain all that the group needs so they don't need to jump up to find markers, scissors, pencils, etc.

- Place an extra table in the classroom for learning centers, small group work, or a small display area.

- Cover the bottom of a large shoebox with Jewish-themed gift wrap, and then cover the entire box bottom with Contact paper. Use as an "in-box" for student work.

- If students are cramped for personal storage space (i.e., they work at long tables together or do not have a storage area in their desk), consider having a talented set of parents create a storage pocket for placement over the back of each student chair.[3] Books, notebooks, and other items can be placed inside.

Adam wasn't quite sure what organizational issues he would have in his classroom. He noticed that one cabinet in his room was filled with supplies, including little baskets with pencils, crayons, markers, and scissors. He made a mental note to use them, rather than ask his students to remember pencils from home every week.

---

[3]There are companies that make these. One manufacturer is "Seat Sack, Inc., www.seatsackinc.com.

CONCLUSION

The content, aesthetics, and organization of classroom environments impact on student learning. It behooves teachers to be planful about the space in which they and students think, challenge each other, and learn about Judaism. Also, the care and attention teachers pay to their classrooms give subtle clues to their students about the importance of the learning that goes on there. The ideas in this chapter range from easy (take down droopy, torn sheets on an existing display) to complex (creating a coherent bulletin board display). Each teacher will need to determine what is within his or her time, talent, and energy abilities to execute. But it is important to do.

PEEKING INTO CLASSROOMS

Vignette 1

Mrs. Katz was beginning her tenth year of teaching at the local Orthodox day school. Her parallel teacher for general studies, Mrs. Goldberg, was a novice teacher. The two shared a classroom. Mrs. Katz was a very traditional teacher and wanted the seats arranged in rows with students seated alphabetically. Mrs. Goldberg, who did not yet know the students, did not want inadvertently to put the quiet children in the front and the active children in the back. And so she arranged the students' desks in a semi-circle. She felt that this setup would allow her to use the first few weeks of school to get to know the children better, have everyone in the "front row," and have less opportunity for misbehavior.

- How might students be affected by the constant shifting of desk space?

- What issues do you anticipate between the two teachers?

- What advice do you have for Mrs. Goldberg? for Mrs. Katz?

- How do you think they might best "live" together in the same room?

Vignette 2

Risa Gelbfish was a veteran teacher looking to put some new life into her classroom. She had just completed a course on cooperative learning and was anxious to incorporate her newfound skill into her classroom. She arranged the desks in groups of four to facilitate students working together. She moved her desk to the corner of the room where it was no longer the focal point of the classroom. Each table now had its own caddy of supplies so student groups could work independently. There was also a small mailbox-like storage display that housed the student/group folders.

- In what ways do you think that Risa's arrangements will complement her decision to try cooperative learning?

- What issues might she anticipate?

Vignette 3

Josh Kahn was hired in the middle of the school year to take over for Mr. Shapiro, the fourth grade teacher who had taken a leave of absence. It was right before Purim and there was plenty to teach. Josh was taken aback by the room — he strongly believed that a classroom should be warm, inviting, and conducive to group work. Yet, it was set in traditional rows with the teacher's desk at the front.

- How might Josh's decisions about the room impact on the students' transition from their previous teacher to him?

- What do you recommend he do first?

Vignette 4

In one week's time, The Hannah Senesh Day School would be hosting an open house for parents. The purpose of this meeting was to give the parents and teachers an opportunity to meet and for the teachers to give an overview of their curricular goals for the year. In preparation, the principal asked teachers to prepare their classroom displays to reflect the student's work. Danielle Cohen, the kindergarten teacher, had already filled her bulletin boards, but not with student work.

- What options are open to Danielle for display of early childhood work?

- What advice would you give Danielle about the kinds of displays she might consider for her room in general?

"When are we going to have Hebrew?" "When do we get recess?" To answer these and other similar questions, I simply gesture to the board where I always post the day's schedule. This helps students learn time management skills and fosters independence. Transitions are smoother and anxiety is reduced.

The white board reads: "*Boker Tov.* Greet everyone by name. Hand in your Hebrew homework. Take out your Tanach and begin reading page 38." Every day my students know to look at the *La'asot Achshav*, the "Do Now," listed in the front of the room. Students get into gear at a reasonable pace, while I am free to greet students and meet the individual needs of a few students. The day begins calmly and efficiently.

(Diane Schon Wirtschafter, Berkeley, California)

Vignette 5

For years, Mrs. Fink taught the first grade Judaic Studies curriculum in a room that she shared with the General Studies teacher, Mrs. Hirsch. Their colleagues joked about who would bring a larger bag of new materials to school for each day's lesson. Their room was cluttered with art supplies, tables, boxes, class pets, and everything but the kitchen sink. At the start of each school year, they faced the same dilemma — how would they divide up the display, storage, and center space in their already crowded classroom.

- What arguments might convince these two teachers to change their vision of a classroom?

- How might the teachers best negotiate this situation, knowing that both are pack rats?

- What storage solutions might help these two teachers?

Vignette 6

The teachers all had a "caught in the headlights" look in their eyes as their principal explained that due to a building project in the synagogue, mid-week classes would be held at a local public middle school. Visions of chalkboards that said, "Do not erase," of bulletin boards that reflected the latest science experiment, and no in-class storage space, had at first shocked the teachers. But the principal said that they had use of a large storage closet in the hall, and that the synagogue board gave approval for expenditures of supplies that might make their lives a little easier (such as display boards, carts, shoebags to put over the door, etc).

- What issues might the religious school teachers anticipate in relation to room environment or displays?

- How might these issues be solved creatively?

Vignette 7

Ben Rosen really enjoyed teaching Talmudic studies to his sixth graders. This year's students were having difficulty understanding the challenging texts. His principal had been after him to put up some displays in his classroom, reflecting the various tractates that lent themselves quite well to illustrations. The problem was that Ben had two left hands, and even stick figures were beyond his artistic ability.

- How might Ben use a computer to solve some of his display issues?

- How might students help create learning displays?

BIBLIOGRAPHY

Bemer, Lynn, and Marcia Harmon. *The Big Collection of Teacher Tips: Book 1*. Greensboro, NC: The Education Center, 1988.

> Over 1,000 ideas first featured in *The Mailbox* magazine. Includes activities, bulletin board ideas, and management tips for seasons and holidays throughout the year.

Bruce, Lori, et al. *The Big Collection of Teacher Tips: Book 2*. Greensboro, NC: The Education Center, 1992.

> Over 1,300 ideas first featured in *The Mailbox* magazine. The ideas, spanning the curriculum, were written by teachers for teachers. Some topics include: organization of the classroom, seasonal holiday ideas, recycling, and a special section on student teachers and substitutes.

Clayton, Marlynn K., with Mary Beth Forton. *Classroom Spaces That Work* (Strategies for Teachers Series, 3). Greenfield, MA: Northeast Foundation for Children, 2001.

> This very practical book is filled with ideas for arranging furniture, organizing materials, eliminating clutter, taking care of students with special needs, and keeping the classroom clean and healthy.

Hierstein, Judy. *Interactive Bulletin Boards*. Columbus, OH: Frank Schaffer Publications, Inc., 1993.

> Simple yet striking bulletin boards utilizing inexpensive and found materials, including source suggestions. Projects are designed to enlist middle to upper grade students in the creative process.

Michel, Margaret, et. al. *The Best of Mailbox Bulletin Boards Preschool/Kindergarten*. Greensboro, NC: The Education Center, 1996.

> The best ideas from *The Mailbox* magazine for this age group for creative bulletin boards — 112 pages of eye-catching displays included for every month. Ideas presented are for easy-to-create teacher and student-made displays. Monthly themes with patterns included.

Moskowitz, Nachama Skolnik. *Original Bulletin Boards on Jewish Themes*. Denver, CO: A.R.E. Publishing, Inc., 1986.

> This innovative book, appropriate for teachers of all grades, contains complete instructions for over 60 basic bulletin board formats and over 250 bulletin board ideas. Special features include: descriptions and drawings of each bulletin board, additional variations and an index by subject matter. (While this book is out of print, it is available in many libraries and resource centers.)

Schmidt, Janie, et al. *Big Book of Bulletin Boards - Intermediate*. Grand Rapids, MI: Instructional Fair, Inc., 1995.

> These pages provide interactive bulletin board ideas covering a range of topics and curriculum areas. The book includes directions, variations, and explanations of objectives.

Catalogues of Helpful Materials

Ellison
http://www.Ellison.com

> This company has a special die-cut machine that stamps out letters (including Hebrew) and shapes in a variety of sizes. While expensive, it makes bulletin board creation a snap!

Teaching Resource Center

http://www.trcabc.com

> Pocket charts, storage containers, magnetic and white boards, big book storage ideas -- this company has lots of ideas for organizing the classroom.

Building a Classroom Community through Thoughtful Classroom Management

Marilyn A. Gootman

All Israel are responsible for one another. With what may the responsibility be compared? With a ship in which one compartment has split apart. Of something like this, it is not said, "A compartment in the ship has split apart." What people say is, "The entire ship — the whole thing — split apart."

(Seder Eliyahu Rabbah)

Judaism is a community-based religion. We are commanded to pray together, celebrate together, study together, and to take care of each other. Respecting and preserving community is a fundamental precept, the basis of our survival. Accordingly, it is vital that we instill the value of community in our students.

But isn't this particularly challenging for American Jewish educators? After all, aren't our children surrounded by the message that individual effort, competition, and self-reliance will lead them to achieving the American dream? Just think of how many of them have been entranced by the "survivor" television shows, the ultimate expression of looking out for #1. Of course, community support and public service have always been a part of American culture, and even more so after September 11, 2001, but nevertheless the individual reigns supreme.

How can we meet this challenge? By transforming our classrooms into living Jewish communities. Teaching our students "about" Jewish communal concepts just won't work. As Rabbi Simeon Ben Gamliel says, "Not learning but doing is the chief thing." In our classrooms our children can practice the skills they need to become responsible members of the Jewish community. As an added bonus, our students will enjoy their learning more, they will be better behaved, and teaching will be more pleasant for us.

Now let's take a look at some of the compo-

nents essential to creating thriving Jewish communities in our classrooms: a caring teacher, structure, communication, and responsibility.

A CARING TEACHER

When Jared's mother died, his teacher Mrs. Cohen came to the house before the funeral to sit with Jared and returned during the week of shivah. With Mrs. Cohen's guidance, Jared's classmates showed up every evening for the minyan. The class planned a meal and brought it to the family.

In any community, the leader, i.e., the teacher, sets the tone and is the key to a successful dynamic. In relating to each and every student, conveying that we care about them as people, as learners, and as Jews can have a powerful impact on their future commitment to Judaism. Today, 40 years later, Jared recalls how moved he was by his teacher's compassion and credits her with his decision to become a Rabbi.

We don't usually think of it this way, but we teach many at-risk children — they are at risk of losing their Judaism. There is a considerable body of research about at-risk children that suggests that having a warm, caring relationship with a teacher can help those students become resilient, to adapt successfully despite risk. This is particularly the case during stressful life events like Jared's loss of his mother. The way we teachers, as community leaders, relate to our students can have a lifelong impact on their commitment to Judaism. There are many ways that we can convey a Jewish message of caring — a visit to a child or family member who is sick, preparing a meal for a family in crisis, sending *mishloach manot* baskets to our students. A smile, a question about how they are doing, sharing a newspaper clipping you think they might enjoy, chatting after services, paying a condolence call —

while each of these takes just a moment, the effect can last for years.

Was there someone who inspired you to become a Jewish educator? Was there someone who sparked your commitment to Judaism? Which of their attributes touched a chord in you?

Here are some responses others gave to these questions: Believed in me, never gave up on me, patience, nonjudgmental, had high standards, loved Judaism, cared about me as a person and my life outside school (e.g., visited me when my mother died, brought dinner to us when my baby sister was born, phoned me when I had pneumonia), made me feel special, had confidence in me even though I wasn't doing well.

We are fortunate that Judaism gives us guidelines for caring — *bikur cholim* (visiting the sick), *hachnasat orchim* (welcoming guests), *mazon* (feeding the hungry), *gemilut chasadim* (bestowing loving-kindness), *menachem avel* (comforting the bereaved), among others. Try to think of how you can reach out and plant a Jewish seed in the hearts of each and every one of your students, particularly the most vulnerable ones.

STRUCTURE

Ms. Levy was proud of her creativity and flexibility. She wanted to make Hebrew school fun for her students. She didn't want her students to be bogged down with rigid rules — let them just enjoy learning, she felt. Yet, an uneasy tension permeated the air. Books and papers were scattered around the room, bits of scrap paper randomly dotted the floor, students' desks were in disarray. Some students were working intently while others were chatting or bickering. The chaos seemed to be putting students on edge.

The Talmud tells us that Joshua was deeply concerned with Israel's well-being, so he provided roads and highways for them.[1] Our classroom communities also need roads and highways for everyone's well-being. When we map space and time for our students, we facilitate cooperative living, and thereby take a major step in avoiding discipline problems. Ms. Levy mistakenly thought that structure stifles creativity. Just the opposite is the case —

kids have a hard time getting anything accomplished if they are surrounded by chaos.

Space

Establishing specific locations and containers for homework, class assignments, pencils, and tools, such as scissors, rulers, and dictionaries, makes it convenient and possible for students to work. Clear labels help them locate supplies and make it more likely that things will be returned to their proper location, as Ms. Levy soon realized. Without some sort of organization and stability in the classroom, students will not have the time and space to be creative.

Where we place items is just as important as how we place them. Keep in mind traffic flow. Can your students get to supplies without disturbing others? Is there a homework basket by the door waiting to be filled as students enter the classroom?

And let's not forget interpersonal chemistry. Do your seating arrangements take into consideration interpersonal chemistry that is either too good (leading to chatting and fooling around) or too bad (leading to fighting or bullying)?[2]

Time/Routines

Routines provide security and confidence. Routines help communities function smoothly. When students know what is expected of them and when, they can concentrate their efforts on their work rather than on trying to figure out what they should be doing.

It is up to us to determine the routines that will enhance community living. We need to consider our preferences, the classroom setup, and the particular students. The following are some routines or procedures we can clarify for our students as we also instill important Jewish values:

- *Seder Hayom* (order of the day): What to do upon arrival in class, where homework is listed, where to hand in homework, what to do when a pencil breaks, where papers should be turned in, where book bags and other supplies should be placed, what to do when they have a question, bathroom breaks, quiet signal, dismissal.

---

[1] *Eruvin* 22b

[2] For further information, see Chapter 18, "Creating a

Learning Environment" by Rivkah Dahan and Nachama Skolnik Moskowitz, pp. 202-214 in this Handbook.

- *Tefillot* (prayers): When and where prayers are said. Who leads the prayers and what kind of participation is expected.

- *Tzedakah* (money for the poor): Collection procedure

- *Mazon* (food for the hungry): Where to place contributions

- *Bikur cholim* (visiting the sick): What to do when someone is absent

- *Bal tashchit* (do not destroy): Where to place recycling items

- *Hachnasat orchim* (hospitality): What to do when a guest enters the room or a new student arrives

Because routines vary from teacher to teacher and class to class, they must be clearly spelled out for students right from the start. And we need to remind students periodically about these procedures. Some teachers prepare a handout that describes procedures to help new students adjust when they join the class, as well as to remind students who may need a refresher.

Time/Schedules

Our Rabbis were very wise when they said, *"Aseh toratcha keva"* (Fix a time for your study of Torah).[3] Schedules provide assurance that we will accomplish what we intend. They have a calming effect on the community because students know what to expect. Writing the schedule on the board can be helpful.

Keep in mind that time has a different meaning for children. Children live in the present. They do not have experience with deadlines or the adult notion that time is limited. We hurry them, yet they persist in taking their time. When possible, it is helpful to allow students a little more time than we think they will need to clean up their supplies or prepare to move to the next subject.

I personally found this challenging when I taught in a synagogue school because our time was so limited. Every minute seemed so precious. I hated to waste the time on what I thought of as minutia. But I soon realized that I got less accomplished when I rushed my students through transitions — there was more tension, more confusion,

and more mess in the room. I discovered that an extra few minutes spent on transitions had a tremendous payoff in terms of student attention and focus on the next lesson.

Ms. Levy's overly loose policy may have been a reaction to her own teachers whom she felt stifled her creativity. Yes, routines and schedules are important, but *"yesh gevul,"* there is a limit. Routines and schedules don't have to be etched in stone. We do not want our students to become rigid, inflexible people, nor should we model rigid behaviors. Such people don't function well in communities. It helps when we are flexible in our routines and schedules, revising them for exceptional situations, explaining when and why we are changing them. It also helps to explain why we generally do not change them.

If it has been raining and you see a rainbow, by all means stop the lesson and say the *brachah* for a rainbow. If there is a death of someone in the community whom students know, by all means take time out from the regular lesson to talk with the students. These are examples of teachable moments that should take precedence over the regular schedule. But these are exceptions, not daily occurrences.

> There are two rules in my classroom: (1) everyone is respected, and (2) everyone is free to make mistakes without fear of ridicule. I am strict. I am consistent. I try to be fair. I freely admit my own mistakes to my classes. I try to reward behavior that I want in my classroom by verbal praise, sending home written notes, and giving positive comments to parents in person or on the phone. I ignore inappropriate behavior when I can. I cut it off with a warning and then action when necessary. If I need help with misbehavior, I draw on the reservoir of good will created by my good comments and ask parents to help me solve the problem. My students know they can count on this sequence of events. As a result, my classroom problems are minimal.
>
> (Maura Pollak, Tulsa, Oklahoma)

Rules

Kids need limits to help them feel safe and secure

---

[3] *Pirke Avot* 1:15

and to help them adjust to the needs of others and the community. Limits teach them how to behave like *mentschen* (good, decent human beings).

Rabbi Nathan warns us: "Once the wall of a vineyard collapses, the vineyard is as good as destroyed."[4] If our rules and limits collapse when the slightest pressure is placed upon them, our classroom community can fall apart.

So how can we decide with confidence what limits and rules to set down? How could we help Ms. Levy set limits without stifling her students' creativity?

First, try to categorize the rules as follows:

- Rules that protect mental health (e.g., name calling, teasing, bullying not allowed)

- Rules that protect physical safety (e.g., place books in desks so people won't trip on them)

- Rules that protect property (e.g., return supplies to the proper location)

- Rules that encourage cooperative living (e.g., one person talks at a time, avoid distracting others)

- Rules that uphold religious practices (e.g., bring only kosher foods to class)

Now, here's how you can figure out how to set these limits and rules.

Clear:

If we want kids to obey us, then we have to be very clear about what we expect. "Be neat" can be interpreted in many different ways. "Place your book bags on the hooks" states very clearly what is expected.

Appropriate:

It's important to remember to adjust our rules and limits to students' ages and stages of development. Some rules that are necessary in kindergarten may be ridiculous in high school, and vice versa.

Necessary:

Limit classroom rules to those necessary to assure behavior that makes learning possible and safe for all. Keep in mind the *midrash* that warns us: Do

not make a fence that is more important than what is fenced in.[5] Yet, Rabbi Yose reminds us that we need a strong fence: Better a fence of ten handbreadths that stands firm than one of a hundred handbreadths that is sure to fall down.[6]

One very successful approach for establishing rules is to engage students in the process of creating them during a class meeting. Such meetings are discussed in the following section.

Richard was a third grader who dearly loved to tease Ana. I had talked to him about it a few times, but Richard did not stop teasing her. "It's so much fun to hear her scream," he explained. Instead of talking to Richard again, I taped an index card to my desk and wrote his name on top of it. I wanted to count how many times a day the teasing was occurring. Richard noticed the card within an hour of my taping it down. "What's that for?" he asked. "I'm just trying an experiment." I answered. That day, no teasing took place. The next day, Richard checked the card. "There's nothing on it," he said, "and I didn't tease Ana yesterday. You're keeping track of my teasing!" I grinned. There was no more teasing. The change in behavior came about because I changed my behavior from scolding Richard to charting his actions.

(Maura Pollak, Tulsa, Oklahoma)

COMMUNICATION

"What two events do we celebrate on Shavuot?" asks Mr. Cohen. "Okay, Ilana, you've raised your hand, what's the answer?"

"The giving of the Torah and the harvesting of the firstfruits."

"Great! Now who knows how much time there is between Pesach and Shavuot? I see Chaim's hand. Chaim, what's the answer?"

" Six weeks."

"Good try, but no. Does someone else know?"

And the lesson goes on with Mr. Cohen standing in front of the class, his students arrayed before him in four rows, some raising their hands, some

---

[4]*Avot de Rabbi Nathan* 24

[5]*Genesis Rabbah* 9:13

[6]*Avot de Rabbi Nathan* 1

daydreaming, and some whispering and passing notes to each other.

How can students learn to function in a community if the only chance they have to interact with each other is when they're off task and fooling around? Let's explore how we can design classroom communities that give students the opportunity to communicate and cooperate with each other.

"*Boker Tov*, Marnina. How'd your recital go? Good morning, Eli. Did you have a chance to read your poem to your parents? *Boker Tov*, Rachel." The message each morning is, I know who you are and I care about you. I expect reciprocity and won't allow a student to talk to me about anything until he/she has greeted me. "Show me how today went for you — from one finger for lousy to five fingers for excellent. Within seconds, I survey the students gathered in a circle at our class meeting. "I'll choose three people to say how they ranked today and why." "I put up a fist, because I hate this school," asserted Nathan. "Wow, that's a strong statement. I'm sorry you feel that way! Can you name a few things we can do to improve the situation for you?" Nathan didn't want to talk any further, but he knew that he was heard and that we were there for him as a class community.

What better way to come together as a community than with the singing of "*Mah Tovu*" and "*Elohai Nishmah*." Both affirm the goodness — one in community and the other in our souls. We cannot be too explicit in letting children know that these prayers need to inform the way we interact in our classroom and school community.

(Diane Schon Wirtschafter, Berkeley, California)

Grouping

Certainly, teaching the whole group is appropriate at times. But it's also vital to the classroom community to find opportunities to regroup students so that they interact directly with each other. Although cooperative learning, in which students work in small groups, is a fairly recent educational trend, Judaism has been espousing a similar approach for centuries.

"As one piece of iron sharpens another, so do two students sharpen each other when they study."[7] Our Rabbis designed the concept of *chevruta*, study with a partner, because they knew that both partners would grow from such an experience, intellectually and interpersonally. Why not incorporate this Jewish way of learning into our classrooms? Keep in mind that groups can be composed of anywhere from two to five or six students.

There is an art to designing successful classroom groupings. Here are some guidelines:

1. Start small. Don't suddenly switch to groups for every subject. Try it with one subject and then move on.

2. Structure some groups with students who are at the same ability level (homogeneous) and others with students at differing levels (heterogeneous). Different kinds of challenges work well with each of these compositions.

    Homogeneous grouping works well for drill and practice and learning new challenging material. Practicing Hebrew lends itself well to this kind of grouping.

    Heterogeneous grouping works well with open-ended activities, discussions, tasks that require divergent thinking, projects with many possible answers, current events, and brainstorming. Designing a *gemilut chasadim* project would lend itself well to heterogeneous grouping.

    Sometimes, it is appropriate to let students choose their own groups (as long as we can assure that no one feels left out). Other times, we can assign students to groups. In the latter case, keep in mind interpersonal chemistry, abilities, and student interests.

3. Before trying group learning, teach students the necessary interpersonal skills, how to behave with *derech eretz* (proper, decent behavior) in the group. Help them practice by modeling the behaviors and engaging them in role-play. Here are some of the skills necessary for success in groups:

    • Talking in quiet voices

    • Listening with both eyes and ears

---

[7]*Ta'anit* 7a

- Disagreeing constructively

- Resolving conflicts when they arise (problem solving)

- Providing others with positive feedback

- Moving into groups efficiently

4. Students can help brainstorm a list of *derech eretz* guidelines to help the group function smoothly. Many of these overlap with our general classroom rules and can be developed in a class meeting as described in the next section. This is a good time to discuss the Jewish concepts of *kavod* (respect) and *bushah* (embarrassment) and to stress that Judaism emphasizes not embarrassing anyone in public. As the Talmud states, "Shaming a fellow person in public is like shedding blood."[8]

    Here are some suggested *derech eretz* guidelines:

- Use quiet voices.

- No put-downs.

- Hands and feet should be kept to oneself.

- Everyone participates.

- One person speaks at a time and the others look at that person.

- Share materials.

- Help each other.

- Don't interrupt.

5. Give very clear instructions before breaking into groups.

- Tell students how much time they have for the activity.

- Remind them about the guidelines.

- Be very specific about what you expect to be accomplished.

- It may be helpful to assign each person a specific task (e.g. scribe, discussion leader, etc.). Explain that when the Children of Israel were building the *Mishkan* (tabernacle) in the wilderness, each person was assigned a specific task according to his talents.

Knesset — Class Meeting

It was a small class, only eight children. But discipline problems abounded. The teacher was at wit's end, about to quit. Teachers are hard to come by everywhere, but especially in small congregations in small cities like Athens, Georgia, where I live. The education director panicked and called me in. The students and I gathered in a circle and I asked them, "Tell me what's going on. What seems to be the problem?"

Anna said Lisa keeps whispering to her. Alex taps on his desk, annoying his neighbor. Andy hums to himself. Rachel complains that she can't concentrate . . . After discussing how people felt about the situation (it became clear that everyone was feeling frustrated) and asking for strategies for controlling behavior (such as tapping on one's arm instead of the desk), I asked them if they could come up with some rules for the classroom. This is what they came up with: "We can do whatever we have to to learn as long as it doesn't interfere with the learning of someone else." And it worked — end of problem.

Success didn't come just from setting a brilliant rule — it came because all the students were involved in the discussion. They listened to the feelings and frustrations of their peers, everyone had a voice, and everyone felt that he/she had a part in the final decision.

Sitting in a circle, facing each other, all at the same level (chairs on floor), teacher and students can share ideas, solve problems, and plan together. We can explain to our students that we are establishing this *knesset* because we treasure their ideas and because their participation in decision making is important for the successful functioning of our classroom. Next, we can teach them the mechanics needed to conduct a successful *knesset*. Two suggestions follow:

- *Circle formation* - The circle formation facilitates good communication because everyone can see everyone else and no one has a preferential seating position. Convening a circle can be awkward and clumsy, depending on the room's regular seating arrangement. Why not ask our students to plan the most efficient and comfortable way to arrange the circle? Once the class chooses the arrangement they think will

---

[8]*Baba Metziyah* 58b

work best and that will take the least time to set up and break down, they can practice setting it up.

- *Communication guidelines* – Ask students to all talk at once. This can be an effective entry into a discussion about guidelines that would be helpful in order to assure that everyone is heard. What happened when we all talked at once? How did it make you feel? Were you able to get your point across? After this discussion, students can design procedures for successful communication. As they discuss the guidelines, we can interject concepts such as *derech eretz* (manners), *kavod/bushah* (respect/embarrassment), and *rachamim* (compassion.)

In addition to solving class problems, a *knesset* is ideal for making class decisions, such as delineating appropriate rules and procedures, planning a field trip or class party, figuring out how to arrange the classroom, or choosing a *gemilut chasadim*, *mazon*, or *tzedakah* project.

What about competition?

"When were the Jews expelled from Spain?"

"1494."

"No, Sarah please sit down. Brad, in what year were the Jews expelled from Spain?'" "1492."

"Okay, Brad, you stay standing."

The students were playing *Around the World*. If you get the question right, you stand. If you're wrong, you sit down, and the next person gets a chance. At the end of the game, the last student standing gets a reward.

Teachers often take situations like these for granted. After all, don't our students seem to love competitive games like these? But at what price? What toll does competition take on our classroom community?

With competition, one person's success requires another's failure.[9] Yes, children who have a chance of winning may like it, but what about those others who never win? What happens to the Jewish values of *kavod* (respect), *rachamim* (compassion), and *sh'lom bayit* (peace in the home)?

Doesn't competition enhance performance? Not usually. Research has proven that competition often diminishes performance, particularly when it comes to creativity, while cooperation and collaboration promote higher achievement.

---

[9]For an interesting, thorough discussion of competition, see the book *No Contest: The Case Against Competition* by Alfie Kohn

But don't our students love games, and don't games help to keep kids interested? Non-competitive games abound that can help us vary the pace of our classes and keep our students involved without compromising the community.

I have a cardboard chart that sits on the chalk tray and leans against the chalkboard. On it is a vertical list with examples of five *menschlich* behaviors, such as mercy (*rachamim*). I have five clothespins fastened to the top of the chart. As I see the students exhibit the behaviors listed, I move a clothespin and attach it to the side where the behavior is listed. If all the clothespins are moved (and none moved back), then everyone in the class gets a small candy. With this procedure, the behavior of a few can effect the entire community. I find that students watch out for each other more this way.

(Sheila Lepkin, Denver, Colorado)

RESPONSIBILITY

Required Helpfulness

Almost weekly, Sarah's mother interrupts class to give her her forgotten snack, book, or money for tzedakah. When Joey neglects to complete his homework, his mother usually writes a note explaining that he was too tired or busy to do it and requesting that he be excused. When Chaim wrote on the school desks and was asked to clean them after school, his mother protested.

Many of our students have few if any responsibilities at home. They are pampered and protected by their parents. While their parents mean well, they may not realize that responsibility builds character. Community responsibility is only possible when individuals are taught responsibility. How can we teach responsibility to all our students, including those who may never have had many demands placed upon them? We are fortunate that our Rabbis have not only taught that all Israel are responsible for one another and that responsibility builds community, but they have also provided us with the tools of responsibility.

(New York: Houghton-Mifflin, 1992).

Let's explore how the following Hebrew words/concepts can become part of everyday classroom community language, living, and learning:

Bal Tashchit/Be Not Destructive

Talmudic law prohibits the willful destruction of natural resources, or any kind of vandalism, even if the act is committed by the owners of the property themselves.[10]

This concept can help us explain to students the need to protect school property as well as to avoid wastefulness of resources. Having recycling containers in the classroom fits in with *bal tashchit*, as does teaching students how to be respectful of school property.

Bikur Cholim/Visiting the Sick

Visiting the sick is a *mitzvah*. The purpose of such a visit is to lighten the suffering of the sick person through pleasant conversation, tasty food, and sensitive care.

The class can design a *bikur cholim* plan for reaching out to sick classmates — by e-mail, phone, a visit. They can design a system for informing absent students about classwork. Perhaps the group might also like to design cards and/or poems, or bake, etc., not only for sick classmates, but also for those in the wider community who are sick. Some students may wish to volunteer to assist the sick. Students can plan together with the Rabbi or educational director.

Dignity to the Elderly

We are advised to treat the elderly with respect. The Torah instructs us to rise before an elderly person.

Visiting nursing homes, sending holiday treats to the elderly and shut-ins, and collecting oral histories are among the ways students can reach out to the elderly.

Gemilut Chasadim: Bestowing Loving-kindness To Others

Gemilut chasadim can involve either money or one's personal service, and can be done for both the rich and for the poor.[11]

There are all sorts of ways students can bestow acts of loving-kindness on others. Some class meetings begin with students telling about a kindness someone (usually a classmate) has bestowed upon them and how it made them feel. Some classes have a *gemilut chasadim* chart instead of a duty or helper chart. Helping someone with a difficult task, teaching a friend a new skill, sweeping the floor, putting away books are all appropriate categories for this chart.

Hachnasat Orchim/Hospitality

Hospitality has been an important Jewish value ever since Abraham welcomed the strangers who came to visit him.[12]

Inviting guests to the classroom on special occasions provides an opportunity to teach students how to welcome guests (greeting them personally, offering them a seat, assuring that they are comfortable). It is also beneficial to discuss with students the proper behavior when an unexpected guest stops by the classroom (perhaps a parent or the principal).

Sharing/Taking Charge/Acting Now

Hillel says, "If I am not for myself, who will be for me? If I am only for myself, what am I? If not now, when?" (*Pirke Avot* 1:14)

This is a wonderful quotation to explore with students and to use in context as the opportunity arises. It relates not just to sharing, but also to taking charge and acting now. You might say, "It's okay to speak up for your rights. After all, if you are not for yourself, who will be." Or, "Let's share the materials. Keep in mind, If I am only for myself, what am I?" Or, "Let's write letters right away in support of Israel. After all, if not now, when?"

Love Your Neighbor as Yourself

The statement "Love your neighbor as yourself" from Leviticus 19:18 can be the basis for a class discussion on rules and acceptable behavior that is respectful of the feelings and needs of others.

---

[10]*Mishneh Torah, Hilchot M'lachim* 6:10

[11]*Sukkah* 49b.

[12]Genesis 18:1-8.

Reciting this passage when a problem arises (e.g., when one student laughs at another's mistake) can serve as a reminder.

> At the beginning of the school year, I take photographs of all my students, two to a picture to save money. I use my computer to scan all the pictures onto one sheet of paper, and keep it in my notebook as an aid in memorizing their names. The originals go on a chart labeled "Know Your Classmates," which is on my classroom wall. Next year I may give each student a black and white copy of my picture sheet for their folders.
>
> (Sheila Lepkin, Denver, Colorado)

Mazon/Providing Food for the Hungry

Place a container in the classroom for cans and other food items or donate food or money from a class party to teach students to think of the needs of others.

Sh'lom Bayit/Peace in the Home

When discussing our rules, we can examine what behaviors are necessary to achieve *sh'lom bayit* — one person talks at a time, no name calling or put-downs, using kind words, etc. When problems arise we can refer to the need for *sh'lom bayit*: "For the sake of *sh'lom bayit*, let's try to work out our differences today." Some classes designate a *"sukkat shalom"* area where students can resolve their conflicts.

Tikkun Olam: Repairing the World

The class can select a *tikkun olam* project to work on together, for example, repairing library books, beautifying the school grounds, or selecting a particular social action project. A wonderful resource is *The Kid's Guide To Social Action* by Barbara Lewis.

Tzedakah (Charity)

The root of the word *"tzedakah"* means justice. Giving money to the poor is the just, right thing to do and is an obligation for us all. Judaism teaches that even the poor are expected to give *tzedakah* to others.

Allowing students to select the organizations that will receive their *tzedakah* contributions makes the act of giving more meaningful. Many children just receive the money from their parents. Perhaps the class could undertake a fund-raiser, the proceeds of which could go to an organization the students select.

These are but a few suggestions for teaching students responsibility. Take a few minutes and think how you can incorporate these concepts into you classroom community.

Assuming Personal Responsibility for Misbehavior:

Here's a familiar scenario:

"It's not my fault! She should have been more careful where she walked and she wouldn't have tripped on my foot."
"But your foot was in the aisle."
"Where else can I keep it? I'm too tall for these desks."
"Go over and apologize to her."
"I'm sorry you tripped on my foot."

Will an apology stop this from happening again? Unlikely. In *Hilchot Teshuvah*, Maimonides explains that we know someone has repented when he/she has the opportunity to commit the same offense, but doesn't because he/she feels penitent and not because he/she is afraid or lacks the courage to do so. The key is to help our students figure out how they can resist the temptation to do the same thing again — to teach them to replace inappropriate behavior with appropriate behavior.

And how do we accomplish this? Maimonides gives us the guidelines. First, in his *Laws of Character*, he reminds us, "One who rebukes another person, whether because for a wrong committed between the two of them or between the other and God, should give the rebuke privately. They should speak to them patiently and gently."[13] This means that we should have a private conversation with the student. Of course, we can't conduct this conversation in the middle of class, but it's important to find some time (before or after class,

---

[13]Maimonides, *Laws of Character* 6:7

during break time, even if it means making alternative transportation arrangements) if we want long-term solutions to behavior problems that sap our time and energy.

I have adapted Maimonides's approach to repentance into an English version: the 3 R's of repentance (or the three R's of responsibility), which can provide the format for our discussion with students who misbehave.

The first R is Recognition. Before a behavior can be changed, a child must first recognize that it is problematic. Sometimes children will be aware on their own that they have erred. At other times, we may have to help them realize that a problem exists ("I noticed you tripped Sarah." "No, I didn't, I was just stretching my foot.")

Even if students deny their transgression at first, if we stay calm and nonjudgmental and hear them out, they will usually admit it. Once we have reached this point, then we can go on to the next step.

The second R is Remorse. Having remorse means regretting what we have done. Having remorse means having a conscience. Only if we feel remorse about what we have done will we be willing to change.

There are two facets to remorse: (1) understanding the negative impact of our actions on ourselves (people will not want to go near you, people will keep away from you), and (2) understanding the negative impact of our actions on others (Sarah could fall and get hurt).

We can help our students come to these conclusions themselves by guiding the discussion. In talking to Ben about taking Glenn's eraser, it would be helpful to ask: "How do you think Glenn might feel when he can't find his eraser?" "How do you think Glenn might feel about you when he realizes you took his eraser?" Again, it is important that we stay calm, nonjudgmental, and matter-of-fact so that the child sees us as an ally and not an adversary. This means no lectures, no guilt trips, no harangues — tempting though they may be. If our students are made to feel helplessly bad about themselves, or if they feel threatened, or if they think we think they are a bad person, they will be less likely to change.

It is certainly tempting to avoid this step, which can be uncomfortable and time-consuming. But our students and the whole classroom community really lose out if we make excuses not to bother ("He really didn't mean it," "It wasn't so bad," "I haven't got the time," "It's just a stage"). Kids will be responsible only if we teach them how to be. We save a lot of time and pain by putting our efforts into these discussions at an early stage.

The final R is Resolve, helping students resolve to change the inappropriate behavior. As with the previous two steps, the ideas should come from the child with our guidance. "The next time the situation arises, I will cross my legs so I won't be tempted to trip someone."

A few months ago, I was sitting with a parent of a former student, Laura, at services. I noticed that Laura wasn't sitting with us, but instead was with another girl, Chelsea, and her parents. I said how glad I was that they were still friends, as I remembered that they had first met in my class two years before. The parent told me that their friendship had grown and become quite strong, and that each family often invites the other girl to go along with them now on vacations. We never know when this kind of relationship can develop, but we must recognize that every opportunity that we give students to work together and get to know each other can lead to such a blossoming.

(Michael Fixler, Syracuse, New York)

First, we can brainstorm solutions together with the student: Here are some ways I can help myself not trip someone who walks by me — cross my legs, tape up my legs, sit somewhere away from everyone. Then, we can help them evaluate these solutions to see which one will work best. "I don't want to be isolated from everyone. The teacher won't let me tape my legs. I think crossing my legs will help."

Students may need some help with this process. We can throw in some ideas of our own and help them evaluate each suggestion. By involving them in the process and not making the decision ourselves, we make it likely that true *teshuvah* will occur and that the next time, when in that situation, the student will chose an alternative way to behave.

Let's not expect miracles. Our students may need reminders, they may regress at times, but with our encouragement, they can indeed change.

CONCLUSION

We are fortunate to be educators in Jewish schools. As *Am HaSefer* (People of the Book), we have a strong tradition of respecting learning. As *Am Yisrael* (People of Israel), we have a strong tradition of respecting community. Thus, our Jewish values provide the keys for optimal living and learning in the classroom and beyond.

> I've become much more aware this year of "presence" as a quality in a teacher. Teachers with presence are self-confident and it shows in their actions in the classroom. They wait for the class to quiet down before speaking. They are the focus of the class. They use their voices in a variety of ways to capture interest. Frequently they build relationships with the students as individuals, which encourages cooperation. They seem to be comfortable with themselves as humans, as teachers, as role models. They are consistent in discipline and in praise.
>
> Teachers without presence are usually inconsistent and slow to react decisively when students disrupt class. They try to talk over the noise in class, often shouting. They are clearly uncomfortable.
>
> I think it is possible to change. Work toward consistency in expectations and discipline. View your students as individuals; get to know their strengths and weaknesses. Respect yourself. You have knowledge to impart and you should be willing to wait for the class to be quiet enough so that everyone can learn.
>
> (Maura Pollak, Tulsa, Oklahoma)

TEACHING CONSIDERATIONS

- One goal of Jewish education is to instill the value of community in students.

- A peaceful, cohesive community enhances all classroom learning.

- A caring teacher sets the tone and is the key to a successful dynamic in the classroom community.

- By organizing space and time for our students, we facilitate cooperative classroom living.

- Rules help children adjust to the needs of others and the community.

- Varying the grouping of students helps them learn to cooperate and collaborate with others.

- Class meetings enhance classroom communication and build community.

- Jewish values provide the tools for teaching students responsibility.

- In order to achieve *sh'lom bayit* in the classroom community, students must be guided to assume responsibility for their own behavior.

VIGNETTES

Greg

Greg is really annoying his teachers and his classmates. He blurts out answers without being called on, hums to himself, and always seems to be bickering with someone. Because his parents are powerful and wealthy members of the congregation, his teacher is afraid to say anything to him.

- How could Greg's teacher engage in a 3 R's discussion to help him change his behavior?

- What might be some other ways to help Greg become more responsible?

Jack

Jack's parents went through a bitter divorce five months ago, and he is still having a hard time concentrating on schoolwork. He turns in assignments late and seems to be inattentive in class.

- How could his teacher bring the classroom community into action to help Jack?

- What can the teacher do to help Jack through these tough times?

Noisy Kids

The students in Kitah Bet are so loud when they go to the assembly hall that they disturb all the other classes. The other teachers are complaining to the Kitah Bet teacher. She has punished the children, even keeping them from the assembly, but nothing seems to work.

- How could the teacher use a class meeting to remedy this problem?

BIBLIOGRAPHY

Beane, Allan L. *The Bully-Free Classroom: Over 100 Tips and Strategies for Teachers K-8*. Minneapolis, MN: Free Spirit Publishing, 1999.

Excellent strategies for the prevention of bullying and intervention, which you can start using immediately. Easy to understand and simple to implement.

Blueprints for a Collaborative Classroom. Oakland, CA: Developmental Studies Center, 1999.

More than 250 concrete activity suggestions for fitting collaboration seamlessly into classroom life. Ideas for making partner and group work easy and natural.

Gootman, Marilyn. *The Caring Teacher's Guide To Discipline*. Thousand Oaks, CA: Corwin Press, 2000.

Practical, realistic approach to classroom discipline — a comprehensive guide to teaching students to do the right thing. The focus is on helping teachers acquire the skills they need to help students practice self-control, solve problems, use good judgment, and correct their own misbehavior.

Kohn, Alfie. *No Contest*: *The Case Against Competition*. New York: Houghton Mifflin, 1992.

A thorough exploration of competition in our schools and the problems arising from competition. A thought provoking book for teachers.

Lewis, Barbara, *The Kids' Guide To Service Projects: Over 500 Ideas for Young People Who Want to Make a Difference*. Minneapolis, MN: Free Spirit Publishing, 1995.

Marvelous, practical suggestions for *tikkun olam*. Includes simple projects as well as large-scale commitments for a variety of topics.

Lewis, Barbara, *The Kids' Guide To Social Action*. Minneapolis, MN: Free Spirit Publishing, 1998.

Excellent, practical suggestions for *tikkun olam*. Step-by-step instructions show how to write letters, conduct interviews, make speeches, take surveys, raise funds, get media coverage, and more.

Ways We Want Our Class to Be. Oakland, CA: Developmental Studies Center, 1996.

Ideas for organizing successful class meetings distilled from the Child Development Project (CDP). The CDP is a comprehensive school change effort to help elementary schools become inclusive communities and stimulating, supportive places to learn.

CHAPTER 20

Advancing through Retreating

Judith S. Schiller

What makes a retreat such a unique, high impact experience? Many educators, Rabbis, youth advisors, Jewish communal professionals, and participants often reflect on the effect of taking a group away for a weekend of learning, community, and fun with Judaism. They often report on how the group becomes closer and experiences "aha" moments in their learning. Some participants may experience Shabbat in an authentic and creative way for the first time. For others, the retreat is an initial time away from home. For a family, it becomes a special opportunity to spend quality Jewish time together, and deepen their involvement in Jewish life. A congregational group finds renewed strength and connection to each other, and energy to contribute to their synagogue community. Here is a sampling of actual feedback from participants and staff:

- The retreat encouraged the practice of Shabbat as a natural extension of our lives.

- This retreat program offered an important opportunity for students actually to live the Judaic life and values we teach.

- A strong sense of community was maintained throughout Shabbat.

- Students gained a deeper understanding of their strengths and weaknesses and their willingness to take responsibility for their actions.

- We like the outdoor setting. It gives everyone a chance to be in nature and connect to the outdoors.

- The retreat experience enabled the students really to understand that Judaism has a lot to say about *bal tashchit* — taking care of the environment.

The "magic" of these experiences is the result of thoughtful planning, staffing, and preparation.

In particular, staff is critical to the success of the retreat. While this chapter cannot address all the facets of retreat planning and implementation, it provides an overview and key points that are relevant to teachers who may be asked to staff or coordinate a retreat.

This chapter is divided into two sections. The first part provides an overview of retreats in general. In the second part, the multi-faceted role of a teacher staffing a retreat is addressed, encompassing what to anticipate, how to prepare, and keys to working with different age groups, families, and intergenerational groups.

WHAT IS A RETREAT?

Simply put, a retreat experience provides an opportunity for "living the learning." It often takes place over Shabbat. Retreat participants engage in learning within a highly experiential framework of Jewish time, space, text, and community. Anyone who has had a positive Jewish summer camp or youth group experience understands firsthand how a group of individuals can become a community, connected to and through Jewish life and values. When skills and knowledge are experienced within real Jewish time and context, they have deeper meaning.

Imagine a group of fifth graders sitting together in a camp dining hall on a Friday evening, sharing in Shabbat celebration, reciting the *brachot* (blessings) and sharing a festive meal. They sing with *ruach* (spirit), socialize, and learn more about each other. After dinner they sing/pray *"Birkat HaMazon,"* the blessing after the meal. Prior to the retreat, these blessings were taught in the classroom, providing the opportunity to feel comfortable utilizing them in the context of real Jewish time and community.

Another example: a group of tenth grade students explores the notion of *Brit* (Covenant), and the challenge that *B'nai Yisrael* (the Children of

Israel) faced in becoming a community with freedom and responsibility. They engage in trust, cooperation, and problem solving activities (led by a skilled facilitator), during which issues of communication, leadership, and respect emerge within the group. As they debrief the experience, the students gain insight into their functioning, both as individuals and as a whole. Their exercise is then "processed" on a metaphorical level, as the challenge of *B'nai Yisrael* wandering in the wilderness is mirrored in their own struggle to work together. The Jewish concept of *Brit* and the Jewish value of personal obligation to each other, comes alive.

Ideally, a well constructed retreat program addresses the whole person, nourishing the intellectual, emotional, physical, and spiritual dimensions of each participant. While some of the activities and learning experiences at a retreat could possibly be done within the classroom, the use of extended time, space, and context serve to create a learning journey, enabling participants to make powerful connections and work collaboratively as a community. Ideally, a retreat is more that the sum of its parts, with participants coming away with both new understanding of a topic and an association of fun and friendship with learning and Judaism.

Retreats vary structurally in many ways, including:

- the size of the group (large — 70 to 100+, medium — 30 to 50, and small — 10 to 20).

- age(s) of participants (upper elementary, middle school, and high school students, families with young children, and intergenerational groups spanning eight months to 80 years old).

- length of time.

- type of setting.

A retreat can be scheduled as a one-day event, a Shabbat overnight, or three or more day programs (such as a family camp or youth *kallah*). Sites vary, depending on the size and needs of the groups, and the type of accommodations available. Camps, nature education centers, hotels, conference centers, and state parks may be among the options.

(Some communities may be fortunate to have their own Jewish retreat site.) A retreat program could be based at the school or synagogue and, if so, the setting would be used in a way different from during normal school time. (Sites will be discussed later in this chapter.) The combination of all these factors presents opportunities and challenges in the use of space, program design, staffing, accommodations, and logistics.

For example, a large retreat requires sufficient space for the group to convene for meals, prayer, large and small group programs, staffing at a reasonable ratio to participants (generally, one staff for every eight to ten participants. Younger participant groups require more staff and often assistance from *madrichim*.[1] High school groups require less staff.) Retreats also have an energy and personality of their own. Some groups can be easy to manage and cooperative from the start, while others offer behavioral challenges.

A retreat program can be developed by an educational team from a school, based on the institution's goals and tied to curriculum. Other times, it may be a packaged program offered by a professional group or facility. It can also be a combination of both, in which the resources from a facility (e.g., education staff, nature experts) are utilized in the retreat program. A retreat has the most impact educationally when the program revolves around a central theme and a "Big Idea" that weaves the different parts of the program together. Ideally, the program engages a variety of modalities and learning styles, incorporating dramatic arts, moral dilemmas, role-plays, games, group challenge, cooperative activities, outdoor nature experiences, and creative arts, with the strong emphasis on the experiential and group process. Importantly, a retreat should be a time that feels relaxed and fun for the participants.

Community Building

Many educators look to retreats to build community in their groups. Community building is particularly challenging in supplementary schools and congregations that often draw membership from different communities and school systems within a greater metropolitan area. Indeed, a retreat experi-

---

[1]Literally translated as "counselors," in a retreat setting this often refers to junior staff members who are typically aides in the religious school.

ence can further the development of a group. However, to be fully effective, it must be part of a larger vision of a school and classroom community, with specific approaches and understanding of the process of building community. Community building takes work. It is predicated on trust, risk taking, and open communications. It is a process that needs constant attention.[2]

Building community is foundational to the whole experience of creating a sacred space for Jews to learn, pray, socialize, eat, sing, play together, and care about each other. Evidence of a group bonding on a deeper level or even being aware that they are part of a whole and have some level of responsibility within it, is reflected in their interactions, listening skills, communication, how they sit together, help each other, and participate in problem solving. Here are some reflections of retreat participants relating to their group experience:

- Being a Jew is hard, but if we work together, we can do it. We need teamwork. (Fifth grader)

- I learned about caring, being nice, and having fun with other Jews. (Fifth grader)

- I would have liked to stay more than one day and night. I had a great time. (Fourth grader)

BEING A RETREAT STAFF MEMBER

The role and responsibilities as a member of a retreat staff is both multifaceted and varied. Often, roles are defined in relation to the type of group and its needs. However, there are basic functions and expectations of staff that apply universally. They include ensuring safety, enthusiasm and warmth, flexibility, comfort in working in an informal context, role modeling positive Jewish identity, willingness to learn about Judaism, preparation, working as part of a team. Each of these is described in brief below.

- *Ensuring safety* - Retreat staff is responsible for ensuring the physical and emotional safety of the group. Physical safety is fairly obvious — no horseplay, jumping off bunk beds, playing with matches, hiking alone in the woods, etc.

Emotional safety means the participants feel that they are operating in an atmosphere of comfort, trust, and respect. The group needs to have ground rules from the beginning that (preferably) the participants have had a hand in defining. Staff must pay attention to the participants' interactions throughout the time of the retreat, from the bus ride and arrival time to the concluding program. Watching for how group members interact, overtly and subtly, often requires "big antennae." It is helpful for the staff to have some check-in time to compare notes on their observations of the group.

- *Enthusiasm and warmth* - Staff sets the tone in the way that they interact with the participants. They need to be upbeat and inviting, with an attitude that says "Glad you are all here." Enthusiastic and prepared staff help facilitate the smooth flow of all areas of the retreats.

- *Flexibility* - No matter how well planned, a retreat program is subject to change for any number of reasons: weather, group dynamics, programs taking more time, late arrival, etc. Therefore, staff needs to be able to improvise and go with the flow. A sense of humor is an essential survival skill, especially in a situation with potentially unpredictable and surprising moments.

- *Comfort working in an informal context* - By definition, a retreat is informal. The atmosphere is more relaxed than school. The social dimension is heightened, as students interact on many more levels, sharing living, eating, and sleeping space. For some teachers, the transition from the formal to the informal setting requires some conscious thought about the difference in role, or wearing two hats, that of both the teacher and the *madrich(ah)*. For example, a teacher may need to decide what he/she wants to be called — by first name, rather than Mr. or Ms. or possibly by a nickname.

- *Role modeling positive Jewish identity* - The retreat staff is most influential on the behaviors of participants as a role model. Fostering a sense of *menschlichkeit* begins with staff acting as *men-*

---

[2]Laurie S. Frank, *The Caring Classroom* (Madison, WI: Goal Consulting, 2001), 11.

schen, encompassing interactions with the group, participating in ritual and prayer, joining in singing, taking on roles in the service, focusing on the participants, and reflecting a connection to and joy in Jewish life and values. (A word about informal attire: avoid wearing T-shirts with potentially provocative statements. "Save the Whales" is okay, but "Co-ed Naked Sunbathing" or problematic language is not. Be especially thoughtful regarding how you appear on family retreats, as you will be under the scrutiny of parents.)

- *Willingness to learn about Judaism* - Retreat staff members may have a variety of backgrounds in Judaism, with different levels of knowledge and experience. Preparing for a retreat creates an opportunity to learn more within a community of educators. Be open to exploring texts, asking questions and hopefully, enjoying the process of enriching your own Jewish learning and growth. Importantly, be sure you are familiar with the ritual practices, *halachic* (legal) parameters, and *minhagim* (customs) that are part of the group's culture.

- *Preparation* - In some cases, teachers may be expected to develop their own lesson plans for the retreat program. This might be done collaboratively in a group, or independently. Sometimes, the retreat coordinator will develop programs and materials for the staff to implement. Be sure to review materials provided in advance so that you understand the educational goals and focus of the retreat. If little information is provided, ask the retreat director or coordinator for the theme and topics, and try to do some of your own research.

- *Working as part of a team* - Teamwork and cooperation are critical components of any retreat process. Everyone needs to be "on the same page," which supports all the facets of retreat implementation. In addition, this implicitly models teamwork, sending a message to the participants about cooperation.

Chain of command and protocols must be followed. Staff should be briefed on the checklist of "what to do when: a child is ill, problematic behavior occurs, medication is needed, bedtime is too wild, etc. The retreat leader may need to be consulted when certain issues arise, and should definitely be kept informed of any problems. Staff should have opportunities to debrief together during the retreat, often to deal with adjustments to the schedule, groupings, logistics, and program setups.

Roles and Responsibilities of Staff

The roles and responsibilities of staff include the following: assisting with travel, arrival, settling in; mealtimes; facilitating programs; supervision of bedtime and wake-up time; *Tefilah*; logistics; monitoring and helping during free time; working with families; community building; follow-up after the retreat. Each of these is described in brief below.

- *Arrival and settling in* - With younger age participants (Grades 3-6), arrival time can be a bit noisy, especially with a large group. Staff should be stationed in different parts of the living areas, assisting students in getting settled. The students may have a lot of energy and excitement, along with some anxiety about being away from home and embarking on a new experience. Many of them will ask questions (similar to questions in the classroom setting): What are we doing now? What do we do next? Can I be in the same group as Sarah? Can I sit where I want at dinner time?" Staff should be prepared to orient the students.

  It is helpful to post the bunk arrangements (prepared in advance) and the schedule. Check with the retreat director on questions that arise about changing bunk assignments. If arrival time is late Friday afternoon, the time may be rushed as everyone prepares for Shabbat. You will need to help students with their luggage and help them mobilize for the next activity. If dinner is not being served first, it's important to have healthy snacks available.

  For middle school groups, staff should be watching for the "coolness factor" (who's cool, who isn't) and the participants' level of maturity, which can vary a great deal between boys and girls. If there appears to be a "cool clique" that is excluding others, look for opportunities to help the group get acquainted. A mixer activity should begin right away, helping diffuse cliques. Wall charts with general questions, e.g., favorite ice cream, sport, music, etc., on which participants fill in information about themselves can be a non-threatening way to begin to know who is in the group, and discover similarities and differences; staff should be part of the activity.

High school students are more mature and can take more responsibility. They need less assistance with shlepping and settling. Provide them with a schedule and instructions. For example, "Please get yourself settled in the next 20 minutes, change clothes for Shabbat, and be back here by 5:30 for our opening program." Sometimes high schoolers can help with setting up the retreat, a great way to involve the group in preparing and welcoming Shabbat and taking ownership of their space.

• *Mealtimes* - For Friday night, it is often helpful to have assigned seating with a staff member at each table. This helps to diffuse the discomfort of participants who are not connected to other people in the group, and encourages mixing and getting acquainted. Table tents with names of participants can facilitate the seating process. An alternative is to have each staff member invite participants to his/her table. However, for some retreats, there may not be a seating plan, so staff needs to pay close attention to how the group is clustering and sorting itself; they may have to get involved in the process by limiting the number of people at a table and negotiating the seating so that there isn't a table of "outsiders" and another overcrowded with a "clique." Seating at other meal times can happen more organically, as the group becomes better acquainted. While the initial meal may require some structure later, the participants need to feel that the staff trusts them to choose their own seats. This allows for a modicum of individual choice, so the retreat does not feel overly structured and confining.

As a staff member, you should be a "host" *and* a member of the group seated at the table, engaging in informal conversation. If sharing does not occur naturally, you can ask an icebreaker question: What movies have you seen recently? What's the best day of the week for you, and why?

• *Facilitator of programs* - Facilitation is the art of empowering the participants to "own" their

learning and construct their own meaning. The learning then unfolds as a process of discovery, inquiry, cooperation, sharing, problem solving, teamwork, and reflection. The facilitator's role is to guide the participants in their journey, and support the bonding of the group. A few examples:

1. During an icebreaker activity, staff should be involved as both participants and facilitators, mixing with the group while modeling positive social interaction. As a participant, you should be comfortable sharing a bit about yourself. In the facilitator role, you watch for and nurture opportunities for the participants to get acquainted and feel comfortable.

2. Text exploration - Text exploration requires the facilitator to ask questions about the text studied, rather than explain what it means. Questions[3] need to be sequenced, beginning with those that are concrete, factual, and assess basic comprehension (e.g., What happened in this story? What did Moses see? Where did B'nai Israel travel to? What do we know about this character from the text?) They need to become more analytical and interpretative (e.g., What do you think Abraham was thinking at this moment? Why did B'nai Israel react in this way? What *mitzvah* relates to this situation, and why? Can you think of an example from your own experience that relates to this situation?).

The group process should be one of "circling around an idea," inviting different perspectives and reactions, and encouraging sharing and dialogue among the group members. For older students, the tension of conflicting points of views can generate a great deal of energy and insight among group members, as long as it is handled with openness and respectful communication skills. It can sometimes be helpful for the facilitator to play "devil's advocate" offering a divergent view or a dilemma. The goal is for the group to become a community of inquiry, strengthened through work-

---

[3]For further information on asking questions, see Chapter 44, "Teacher May I . . . and Other Classroom Questions" by

Janice P. Alper and Shayna Friedman, pp. 529-541 of this Handbook.

ing together with respect and cooperation. The facilitator must be very alert as to *how* things are said, as well as what is said.

Children's literature is an excellent source for teaching ethics and values to younger and even upper elementary students, and can be used as a text for dramatic play or story theatre. (A big container of costumes and props can add to the fun and creativity.) Stories about friendship, respect for parents and grandparents, taking care of the earth, which are not necessarily Jewish in content, often provide issues that connect to Jewish texts and values. Sometimes connections are made through a critique of a story. For example, *The Giving Tree* by Shel Silverstein is viewed by many educators (myself included) as problematic in that it tells a story of a tree that gives and gives and a boy who throughout his life takes and takes. When this familiar story was read to a group of first to third graders as part of a family retreat on Judaism and the environment, they were asked to figure out what was wrong in the story. The students were able to identify that this boy never said thank-you to the tree. Their observation led to a discussion of what it means to be thankful, show appreciation, and the *mitzvah* of *bal tashchit* (care for the environment). The older students, fourth, fifth, and sixth graders, studied Jewish texts relating to Judaism and the environment and interpreted the same story as a "Rabbinic panel," explaining how the story would be viewed through a Rabbinic lens.

3. Cooperative games and group challenge activities are often part of a retreat program. These can consist of icebreakers, trust building, problem solving, ground initiatives, low and possibly high ropes elements. Essential aspects of these programs are safety (physical and emotional) and proper sequencing of challenges (moving from lower to higher levels of challenge as the groups demonstrates its ability to work together). The group should have ground rules for behavior, preferably in the form of a group contract or *Brit* developed together, in advance. The staff's role in this type of program (often run by skilled professionals in the field, although not exclusively) is sometimes to participate along with the group members, other times to observe, and always to help ensure group safety. Even if you are not directly involved in the program, you should not separate from the group's experience by standing on the sidelines.

It is important to allow the participants to recognize the issues they are confronting. When a group is stuck and not effectively problem solving, staff needs to resist the urge to direct or offer a solution. A more effective intervention is to call a "time out," and invite the group to sit and process what is going on. You may have an opportunity to offer feedback to the group with a statement like: "Something I observed was . . . ," or "It seemed from where I was watching that there were communication gaps."[4]

The key to the effectiveness of challenge programs is in the reflection and debriefing of the activity. How well did the group work together? How was the communication? A simple and effective guide to debriefing is to ask the group first "what happened?," then "so what?" (what did we learn?) and finally "now what?" (how can we use this learning for: our next challenge . . . being a team . . . committee . . . class, etc?). Importantly, you want to help the group make Jewish connections to the activity, e.g., how does this experience relate to the text we read: "All Israel are responsible for each other," or "If I am not for myself who will be for me; If I am only for myself what am I?"

As a facilitator, you want to look for the teachable moments. Listen to participant responses and see where connections can be made from one program to the next, or how one insight opens up new meaning to an earlier discussion. The facilitator threads and weaves the learning, making the

---

[4]Refer to the Bibliography at the end of the chapter for sources on experiential/adventure-based learning.

implicit explicit. In addition, there may be materials that the facilitator chooses to enhance learning — a poem, song, quote, or reading. As the learning community develops, be aware of positive interpersonal behaviors and label them with a Jewish value or concept. Identify the actions that contribute to the well-being of the community. (You may need to find a way to communicate this subtly, or through a "back door" to avoid sounding preachy and "too teachy.") Or, ask the group for feedback on how they are doing as a community.

- *Bedtime supervision* - Staff needs to be prepared for some chaos and resistance from the participants around getting to bed. For younger students (third to sixth grade) supervision is critical at this time; often ground rules need to be reinforced (no jumping off bunk beds, no food in the room, no horseplay, etc.). Bedtime rituals and structure can help, for example, giving the bunk mates 15 minutes to have play time before washing up, P.J.s, and quiet time. A bedtime story or music can help a group wind down. Saying the *"Shema"* at bedtime can have a calming, quieting effect, as well as reinforce the sense of Jewish time and behaviors. However, don't be surprised if after bedtime rituals and being tucked in, there are rumblings from the group. Staff needs to stay calm and work to quiet the participants. For some groups, there needs to be a heroic staff member who can stay up late, monitoring the behavior of students who are having trouble getting to sleep.[5] Sometimes a child may be sick or may have some issues at bedtime that require tending to. Getting a group to be quiet at bedtime can be one of the biggest challenges for staff, especially when they themselves may be in need of rest. It requires patience and planning strategies in advance.

  There needs to be some flexibility in regard to curfew and *Lilah Tov* (good night) for teens. They may need time to unwind later in the evening. Staff needs to be able to monitor the late night activity, and set a reasonable lights out time (between midnight and one at the latest). If the students stay up all night, they will

be too exhausted in the morning to participate in the program.

- *Wake-up time* - Very often with younger groups, some students may wake up early, before the others. A staff member should be designated to supervise the early risers, so that they do not cause disruption to the rest of the group. They can be taken to the non-sleeping area of the dorm for quiet play, assist with breakfast setup, or perhaps go on an early morning hike, led by a staff member.

- *Tefilah* - Staff must model participation in prayer, as a way of transmitting expectations to students. If Hebrew or prayer skills are lacking, staff members should still participate as well as they can, demonstrating that they are interested in learning with the students. At the same time, staff needs to pay attention to the group, intervening quietly if and when behavior issues arise.

  During *Tefilah*, it is possible that some staff members may wish to organize materials for the next program. However, this sends a mixed message to the participants. It is preferable to wait for a break or take time to set up before the worship experience.

- *Logistics* - There are always logistical tasks that require tending to. Room setups, food management, supervising *toranut* (chores) by the students, and organizing supplies are all part of the process.

- *Free time* - *Hafsakah* (break time) in a retreat needs some light structure and clear guidelines for participants. Staff needs to monitor campers, checking in to be sure that they are safe and involved in appropriate activities. If there is an extended *hafsaka*h after lunch, there should be options, including quiet and active games (this can be an optimal time for a *Frisbee* game outdoors), hiking the trails with a staff member supervising, and "downtime" in the bunk. Participants must be given firm boundaries on where they can and cannot be. Energy levels among the staff may lag, especially if some were occupied the night before with bedtime challenges. Staff should regroup and deter-

---

[5]Participants who are disruptive to those who *want* to sleep, may need a separate room or space, as well as a review of expec-

tations. Or, students wishing to sleep may need a quiet space away from the noisy group.

mine who is able and willing to take on which roles. Also, having some *madrichim* can be particularly helpful during *hafsakah*, allowing some older staff to have a breather and set up for the next program.

- *Working with families* - When a group of educators was asked for the *"mah nishtanah"* (the differences) between working with families rather than with youth, they said they felt sometimes uncomfortable or even intimidated under the parental gaze. They expressed both relief at not having to deal with bedtime, and the polar concern that parents are quick to forget to take charge of their children, sometimes assuming staff is on duty round the clock. Working with families is different in many ways. The staff role is not limited to facilitation of children's programs, but encompasses welcoming a whole family to a special Jewish experience. First and foremost, parents want to feel confident and comfortable with you as their child's teacher/ *madrich(ah)*.

- *Community building* - It is incumbent on the retreat staff to seize opportunities to nurture the growth of community. These could include interactions during meal times, playing during free time, empowering participants to resolve conflicts with some coaching, modeling positive communication, and giving constructive feedback. Staffing a retreat is a special opportunity for teachers to become better acquainted with their students. This relationship building process can hopefully impact classroom dynamics after the retreat.

    Keep in mind that building community takes time and is done in small steps. Groups vary a great deal in motivation, personalities, connectedness, skill, emotional needs, culture, and behavior. This year's sixth grade class could be very different from last year's or the next year's class. Therefore, keep expectations realistic, and reasonable.

- *Follow-up after the retreat* - A key question for educators is how to capture the retreat experience back in the classroom and extend and reinforce its impact and meaning to the participants afterward. A bulletin board with photos, art, and projects done by the participants serves as a visual reminder of the experience. Make excerpts from evaluation forms into a poster

with the heading, "Here's what we said about our retreat." Post texts or quotes that were used on the retreat in the classroom and refer to them in subsequent lessons. Some of the approaches to learning that were part of the retreat can be integrated into the classroom. For example, a cooperative game or group challenge could be incorporated into a lesson plan.

I have taught several summers at the National Havurah Institute, a week-long residential retreat with a full day program for the children (separate from the adult learning). I love getting to know a new place intimately, and discovering its possibilities for teaching. I love to use the outdoors for exploring new dimensions in *davening*.

One year, in my fifth/sixth/seventh graders' group, we talked our way through the weekday *Shacharit* — what do each of the *tefilot* (prayers) say to us, how do they make us feel, and what do they make us think about? We each made a marker that symbolized a *brachah* — I still have the crown with little bells for the *"Amidah"* in my living room. Then, as a group, we went outside and walked around our part of the campus, asking which environment, which landscape, which vista seemed to direct our thoughts in the direction of each part of the service. We hung our markers, and were blessed with a week without rain! We sometimes *davened* with our markers, and sometimes tried entirely new environments — like *davening* on the dock in the still of the morning. We shared our project with the adult community, and asked them to respect our markers, and to share in our explorations. It was my group, on the edge of leaving the children's program, that took a tentative step toward making their own contribution to the community that year.

(Anne Johnston, New Haven, Connecticut)

BEING PREPARED

In the best of scenarios, a retreat process begins with the staff getting acquainted and investing in the program. Optimally, the staff meets at least one time to review the program, logistics, staff roles, and participants. (For an example of a well planned, well thought out retreat, see the Appendix on p. 237.)

If the retreat program is developed internally within the school, the staff may be involved in the planning, possibly requiring additional meetings. Classroom teachers can contribute richly to program planning because of firsthand knowledge about students, their learning styles, and their engagement in the curriculum. The retreat staff needs to be familiar with the schedule and content of the program and, in some cases, may be asked to develop lesson plans on a specific topic or text.

If the program is being handled by the staff of a retreat facility, the learning goals, materials, and philosophy of the retreat site should be provided well enough in advance that the staff can review and plan for teacher input. An educator can gather additional materials to complement the experience.

However, not all retreat processes are handled in a planned, systematic way. A teacher could find her/himself thrust into the role of retreat staff with little background information or organized preparation. While this is not a recommended approach, nonetheless it can and does happen. Hopefully, the points outlined in this chapter will provide an overview of what to expect. In addition, staffing any retreat requires thinking on your feet and being resourceful.

Greg spent most of his time in the classroom trying to figure out how many different ways he could disrupt the class and in general succeeded brilliantly. I was dreading what havoc he might wreak at the seventh grade retreat. I was absolutely amazed at how differently he behaved in a different environment. The informal setting allowed him to be much more comfortable and much better able to cooperate and participate.

The more important change was in my attitude toward Greg. Before the retreat, I was beginning to resent his presence in the classroom. Once I was able to see that he was more than just a surly adolescent, my attitude toward him changed and I was able to make some changes in the classroom as well, such as more work done in dyads and triads, greater use of drama and skits, and more use of games.

(Rabbi David Feder, Morgantown, West Virginia)

CONCLUSION

The components of a retreat process can be likened to separate strands of a *challah* that individually have their special textures and qualities, but braided together have a full flavor and aroma. Each part needs attention, and complements the whole.

The comments below are from educators who participated in retreats. They reflect the all-encompassing aspect that the experience potentially offers:

- An effective retreat is . . . one in which the participants come out feeling enriched, physically, emotionally, and intellectually. This should be accomplished by achieving particular activity goals and by creating an atmosphere that allows dialogue, exploration, investigation. An effective retreat is one in which people come out feeling that not only were they able to gain, but to contribute to the experience.

- An effective retreat is . . . one in which individual people become a community; one in which the participants thirst for more information; one that allows you to explore an environment you normally wouldn't be privy to; one that allows you to explore your relationship with the Most High; one in which you are exposed to mentors and role models; one in which you come home exhausted, but spiritually charged.

- A retreat is an experience made up of many components. It is a union, a set of activities, a series of learning experiences, and a united community. Often retreats are simulations of life experiences. Retreats are also blocks of time that are held together by common goals and bonds. They are solidified by relationships and communication. A retreat is also a unique experience because of the elements of time and space. Retreats tend to take on "personalities" of their own. An effective retreat will revolve around a single theme, but also expand out into many levels and meanings (like a spiral twisting upward and outward at the same time and never ending). Retreats can be measured or assessed by the meanings that are made by all the participants.

CONSIDERATIONS FOR STAFFING RETREATS

1. Participants first - The needs of the participants are the primary concern.

2. Teamwork - Work as part of a retreat staff team, in consultation with the retreat leader.

3. Be part of the community that you are fostering and have fun getting to know the participants.

4. Be flexible and ready to shift gears.

5. Be prepared, do your homework, and find out what you need to know to be effective with the group.

THINK ABOUT THE FOLLOWING:

• The theme of a retreat is Holiness. Find some resources on the subject and brainstorm ways to approach the subject for different ages.

• A group of students wakes up earlier than the rest of the group and starts to get disruptive. How might you handle the situation?

• During cooperative games, a fifth grader is frustrated and angry at another student and begins to act out inappropriately. How do you handle him? How do you handle the group?

• At dinnertime, some of the people seated at your table are talking to each other, but a few are not part of the conversation. What could you do to engage the whole group at your table?

• A group of high school students wants to stay up late, while others wish to get to bed. How could you handle this situation?

Note: With deep appreciation, I want to acknowledge Leslie Brenner, my dear friend, mentor, and retreat guru, for all the training, guidance, support, and wisdom she has shared with me, which inform this chapter in many ways. In addition, the title of this chapter and the educator reflections in the summary are from a course that she taught.

APPENDIX
SAMPLE SHABBATON SCHEDULE
CONGREGATION BRIT EMETH - 5TH/6TH GRADE SHABBATON

TIME/ACTIVITY		THEME & DESCRIPTION
FRIDAY		
2:00	Advance team sets up site.	
4:00	Students meet at synagogue.	Check-in; car pools coordinated.
4:15	Depart for site.	Car pools leave synagogue; one car remains for stragglers.
5:00	Arrive and settle in.	Room assignments. Put away things. Snack. Change into Shabbat outfit. Name tags.
5:20	Program Introduction - *Dining Room* Orientation from site host.	Kick-off to a great retreat. Introduce staff and Review *"Brit"* - *Rabbi, Miriam, Judy*
5:40	Candle lighting - *Dining Room*; Kabbalat Shabbat MPR (Multi-Purpose Room)	Candle lighting; sing a *niggun* as we travel to Multi-Purpose Room (MPR) for Kabbalat Shabbat service.
6:30	Shabbat Dinner - *Dining Room*	Shabbat dinner rituals - *brachot*, *"Kiddush,"* hand washing, *"Motzi," "Birkat HaMazon," zemirot.* Celebrating a special time in our week, for rest and giving thanks. (Assigned seating on table tents. Staff member at each table with students.)
7:30	**Program I - Mixer – CONNECTING TO ISRAEL** *MPR & Dining Room*	**THEME: CONNECTING TO ISRAEL** Warm-ups and Mixer activities - MPR *Meraglim L'aretz* - scouting activity - *White Pines Building.* Scavenger hunt with clues, done in teams. Debrief with each group giving report in skit form of what they found on their Israel scouting mission.
8:45	Change into warm clothes for outdoor activity.	
9:00-9:45	Night Hike/outdoor activity, stargazing.	Divide into 2 groups with retreat staff and site staff.
9:45-10:15	Oneg Shabbat - *Dining Room*	
10:15	Bedtime Prep	Wash-up, P.J.s, Bedtime Stories in sleeping rooms; *"Shema"* before sleep.
11:00	*Lilah Tov* - In bunks Lights out	

(continued on next page)

TIME/ACTIVITY	THEME & DESCRIPTION
SHABBAT	
8:00 *Boker Tov*	
8:30-9:00 Breakfast - *Dining Room*	Cold cereals, pastry, juice, milk, hot chocolate
9:00-10:15 Tefilah and Torah Service - *MPR*	Students to lead parts of service. Incorporate student writing into service. *D'var Torah* on *Terumah*.
10:15 *"Kiddush"*	
10:30 -12:00 **Program 2 - NESIYA L'YISRAEL** - *MPR*	**THEME: NESIYA L'YISRAEL through Time and Texts - FOCUS: What Israel has meant to the Jewish People at different times** - Five learning stations, each from a different period of time in Israel's history.
12:00-1:00 Lunch - *Dining Room - (Toranut group helps with setup)*	
1:00-2:30 **Program 3 - ISRAELI ARMY** *Dining Room and Outdoors*	**THEME: BUIDING COMMUNITY IN THE ISRAELI ARMY** Army Initiatives with Moshe
2:30-4:00 *Hafsakah*	Options of indoor and outdoor games and activities, loosely structured and supervised; downtime in bunks
4:00-5:15 **Program 4 - NESIYA L'YISRAEL - A journey to different places in Israel** *MPR*	**THEME: NESIYA L'YISRAEL - A journey to different places in Israel.** Stations with activities related to specific places in modern Israel. Spice sack for Havdalah prepared by each student at Jerusalem station.
5:15-6:15 *Seudah Shlishit*; Sing Down *Dining Room*	Israeli cafe with hummus, pita, felafel, etc. Ice cream sundae bar for dessert. (DAIRY UTENSILS ONLY)
6:30-7:00 Havdalah; Closing Activity Evaluations Pack up Car pools arrive	Closing activity - Israel is _____. Evaluations
7:15 Car pools coordinated and depart	
7:45 Return to synagogue	

BIBLIOGRAPHY

Biers-Ariel, Matt; Deborah Newbrun; and Michal Smart Fox. *Spirit in Nature —Teaching Judaism and Ecology on the Trail.* Springfield, NJ: Behrman House, 2000.

This invaluable resource offers ways "to turn an ordinary walk in the woods into a journey of the spirit." The activities have the potential of creating "Aha" moments, linking Jewish texts, prayers, and blessings with nature experiences. Easy to use and well organized and formatted, each activity provides ages, hiker's goals, timing, materials, procedure, and questions for discussion. Each chapter focuses on a different aspect of outdoor experience, with topics such as Opening Our Eyes To Miracles, Trees: The Torah of Life, Making Makom: Places in Nature, and more.

Cain, Jim and Jolliff. *Teamwork and Teamplay — A Guide To Cooperative, Challenge and Adventure Activities That Build Confidence, Cooperation, Teamwork, Creativity, Trust, Decision Making, Conflict Resolution, Resource Management, Communications, Effective Feedback and Problem Solving Skills.* Dubuque, IA: Kendall/Hunt Publishing Company, 1998.

A most comprehensive resource with a very easy to use format, this book contains all the elements for creating challenge and adventure programs. Hundreds of resources for challenge games, event planning tips, get acquainted activities, processing and debriefing ideas, games of all kinds, and detailed instructions for designing equipment are included.This book is highly regarded by professionals in the experiential education field.

Elkins, Dov Peretz. *Jewish Guided Imagery.* Princeton, NJ: Princeton Academic Press, 1996.

An explanation of guided imagery as a dynamic way to "hook" the learner into a subject and create deeper, more personalized levels of understanding. The exercises can be used in a wide variety of formal and informal educational settings and occasions. Elkins provides insight into the goals and purposes of guided imagery, along with guidelines, preparation techniques and "how to's" of setting the atmosphere for experiences of high impact. Included are nearly 20 guided imagery scripts for the Bible, Rabbinical literature, Jewish history, prayer, Shabbat, and much more.

Escapades! Las Vegas, NV: Talicor, Inc., 1996, Item #6600.

Escapades! Consists of an index box full of activities that require minimal preparation. It is divided into sections, including Cooperative Group Games, Cooperative Challenges, Partner Games, Sound & Movement, and Thrills & Skills. Each section is subdivided according to varying energy levels. One side of each card outlines and describes the specific activity, and the other side illustrates the activity in picture format. There are hundreds of activities and games that can be used in classrooms, on retreats, at educational programs and events, and that can be facilitated indoors and outdoors. The activities are adaptable for all age groups.

Foster-Harrison, Elisabeth S. *More Energizers and Icebreakers: For All Ages and Stages: Book II.* Minneapolis, MN: Educational Media Corporation, 1994.

All of the activities in this book were developed to enhance the learning environment in a class or group. Easy to use, well designed with illustrations, set up to be photocopied.

Frank, Laurie S. *The Caring Classroom: Using Adventure to Create Community in the Classroom and Beyond.* Madison, WI: GOAL Consulting, 2001.

A process-oriented approach that gives students a chance to learn and practice the life skills of collaboration and conflict resolution. It describes a developmental sequence and offers activities that can be used, and processed, at each step of the sequence. It is a guide for teachers that is packed full of activities, tips and information that help facilitate the growth of a classroom as a community. (Available through Project Adventure, www.pa.org)

Grishaver, Joel Lurie. *You Be the Judge — A Collection of Ethical Cases and Jewish Answers.* Los Angeles, CA: Torah Aura Productions, 2000.

A collection of 52 real or realistic ethical problems that are submitted to the test of Jewish Law. Great resource for role-plays, and *Bet Din*, appropriate for youth and families, Grade 4-adults.

Kelman, Vicky. *Jewish Family Retreats — A Handbook*. New York and Los Angeles, CA: The Melton Research Center of the Jewish Theological Seminary of America and the Whizin Institute for Jewish Family Life, 1993.

A thorough overview of Jewish family education with particular focus on family camp/retreat. The book strikes a balance between the theoretical and practical, with sections titled: A Theory of Jewish Family Education, Why Do a Retreat?, Practical Arrangements, Programs, Staffing, Lesson Plans, and Resources.

Musikant, Ellen, and Sue Grass. *Judaism through Children's Books: A Resource for Teachers and Parents*. Denver, CO: A.R.E. Publishing, Inc., 2001.

A guide to children's books on a spectrum of Jewish topics: Bible, ethics, folklore, history, holidays, Holocaust, and life cycle. Featured books in each category identify the appropriate age range and contain summaries, main ideas, discussion starters, and activities. Recommended for supplementary and day school teachers, group workers, librarians, and parents of children PK-12.

Orlick, Terry. *The Cooperative Sports and Games Book — Challenge without Competition*. New York: Pantheon Books, 1978.

Terry Orlick has created and collected over 100 games based on cooperation, not competition, for people of every size, shape, age, and ability, from preschool to senior citizens. User-friendly, this book is organized by age groups and contains photos, descriptions, and instructions. This rich resource offers lots of group building, non-competitive physical activities that foster cooperation and group problem solving and that nurture acceptance and sharing.

Rohnke, Karl. *Silver Bullets*. Dubuque, IA: Kendall/Hunt Publishing, 1984.

———. *Cowstails and Cobras II*. Dubuque, IA: Kendall/Hunt Publishing, 1989.

These two books are resourceful guides for group building programs that include adventure leadership, icebreakers, initiatives, and trust building. They unpack the essential concepts of sequencing, debriefing, and closure. While not everyone needs to be an expert in the application of these activities, it is important for educators to understand the basic concepts and potential opportunities, in order to plan effective Jewish educational experiences that utilize these strategies.

Rohnke, Karl, and Steve Butler. *Quicksilver Adventure Games, Initiative Problems, Trust Activities and a Guide To Effective Leadership*. Dubuque, IA: Kendall/Hunt Publishing, 1995.

In the tradition of *Cowstails* and *Cobras II* and *Silver Bullets*, this book contains over 150 new games, initiatives, icebreakers, variations on old standards, trust, closures, and more. In addition to the activities, there is a leadership section, in which the authors impart many of the secrets they use when leading and designing programs.

Rohnke, Karl, and Jim Grout. *Back Pocket Adventure*. New York: Simon and Schuster Custom Publishing, 1998.

This is a collection of activities that do not require any props or equipment whatsoever. Some of these are new activities, and others are adaptations of older activities revamped to be done without adventure paraphernalia.

CHAPTER 21

Beyond the Classroom — Reaching and Teaching in the Home

Enid C. Lader

*A*aron Marcus enjoyed teaching seventh graders. They were enthusiastic and energetic, but seemed so overwhelmed by their upcoming B'nai Mitzvah that engaging them in classwork — and getting them to do any homework — seemed impossible.

Sharon Milder has taught in a day school for over 20 years. She has received a note from the parents of one of her students requesting a conference. Their child views homework as "home wars." They need to talk.

Tova Cohen looked at her calendar, looked at her lesson plans, and looked again at her calendar. The fall holidays managed to land on almost every Sunday. She had hoped to teach the story of Noach to her first grade class, and had wanted the students to perform a puppet show of the story for the kindergarteners. When would she have time to introduce the story, make the puppets, and rehearse with her students two Sundays after Simchat Torah?

The preceding vignettes pose some interesting questions for consideration:

- How can teachers reinforce concepts taught in weekly classes, knowing that homework will probably not be done?

- How can teachers reconcile a very full curriculum with not having enough time to teach it all?

- How can teachers help parents whose children come home not remembering what to do for homework?

- How can one build bridges between school, home, and back again?

The focus of education is often set within the four walls of the classroom. Yet, with strong partnerships between teachers and parents, the walls of the classroom can expand to living rooms, kitchen tables, and even family cars. This chapter offers rationale and strategies for how the home in general, and parents in particular, can be our partners in this endeavor we call Jewish education.

This chapter will focus on developing home support for learning, and on developing strategies for engaging parents as our partners and as learners themselves. Interactive Family Homework will be introduced as a way of expanding the walls of the classroom and engaging families in Jewish conversations, along with ways that teachers can communicate with parents, enlisting them as ready partners in their child's education.

HOME-SCHOOL PARTNERSHIPS: THE WORK OF JOYCE EPSTEIN

Joyce Epstein is the director of Partnership-2000 Schools, a project affiliated with Johns Hopkins University.[1] She has studied various ways of developing partnerships between the home, school, and community that can "improve school programs and school climate, provide family services and support, increase parents' skills and leadership, connect families with others in the school and in the community, and help teachers with their work."[2] This is accomplished through involving

---

[1] Partnership-2000 Schools is under the auspices of the Center on School, Family, and Community Partnerships and the Center for Research on Education of Students Placed at Risk (CRESPAR) at Johns Hopkins University.

[2] Joyce L. Epstein. "School/Family/Community Partnerships: Caring for the Children We Share," in *Phi Delta Kappan* (May 1995):701.

each of the partners — home, school, and community — in various ways. Epstein details six types of involvement in her work. This chapter builds upon Type 4: Learning at Home.[3]

> Every Rosh Chodesh, teachers have to write a newsletter to parents about what we had done in the past month and what was coming up next. The parents really appreciated these communication, which provided a way to start a dialogue between parents and children about religious school.
>
> Secular school supply stores have cute postcards for teachers to send to students. At the beginning of the year, I have the students address two cards to themselves. I write a note on a card when a child does something special or makes a big improvement. Parents love these cards because their children don't always share information about school with them. My students love getting mail, especially postcards that praise them!
>
> (Cheryl Cash-Linietsky, Philadelphia, Pennsylvania)

Partnerships with our students' families can be built by "by providing information and ideas to them about how to help students at home with homework and other curriculum-related activities . . . "[4] There are a number of ways this can be accomplished. Teachers can:

- share with families policies regarding homework.

- provide information on improving student skills.

- offer home-based activities that require students to interact and discuss with family members what they are studying in class.

- create calendars that are sent home with family activities or "car talk questions" to reinforce topics learned in class.

- develop summer learning packets or activities.[5]

Just think of the possibilities!

CLEAR HOMEWORK INFORMATION: HELPING PARENTS HELP THEIR CHILDREN

Sharon Milder met with Rivka's parents and found out that there was a good reason that homework had turned into "home wars." Rivka did not understand what to do and, therefore, could not complete the assignment. Her parents felt very inadequate with Hebrew, and felt frustrated in not being able to help her. Ms. Milder thought about what she could do to help both Rivka and her parents.

What kinds of things can teachers do to help make homework assignments understood — by both the students *and* their parents? Is the homework assignment given quickly at the end of class — or is it posted in a special location so the students know where to find it and write it down? Do students have time to ask questions about the assignment? Do students ever have the opportunity, after being given the specific concepts and/or skills the teacher would like them to develop, to create their own assignment? If the students do have questions, where can they go for help? Is there a "homework hotline" number to call or an web site to access? Are there resource people who can be contacted if questions arise? Do students have "homework buddies" — classmates they can call on for assistance? (These buddies can change as various kinds of knowledge and skills are developed.) And, how can parents help?

A class update sent home to parents can help them keep track of how the curriculum is moving along. If a special project is coming up that includes specific supplies, objects from home, or interviews with family members, a special "heads up" sent to parents before the project is set to begin will be greatly appreciated.

The Internet is a useful tool for parents when reinforcing their children's learning; it also serves as a tremendous resource for gathering information. There are Hebrew curricula that are complemented by textbook-based web sites where students and parents can go to check homework. Teachers can develop, or enlist parents in the creation of

---

[3]Epstein's Framework of Six Types of Involvement includes: Type 1, Parenting; Type 2, Communicating; Type 3, Volunteering; Type 4, Learning at Home; Type 5, Decision Making; and Type 6, Collaborating with Community.

[4]Joyce L. Epstein, "School/Family/Community Partnerships: Caring for the Children We Share," *Phi Delta Kappan* (May 1995):704.

[5]These are examples of Sample Practices suggested by Dr. Epstein. Our challenge is to think of these in the context of our own teaching situations. How much can I do? What is my relationship with the families? What are the policies of my school? Can I just do this, or do I need to discuss this with my principal/supervisor?

class bulletin boards on the Internet to post questions and encourage discussions. As parents gain comfort in and with their child's curriculum, it is quite possible that they themselves will be intrigued and challenged to explore topics and look to further their own education.

As can be seen, keeping the lines of communication open between the school and the home, and providing for support can be ideal ways of engaging parents in the partnership of educating their children.

SKILL IMPROVEMENT: BRINGING PARENTS ON AS PARTNERS

Sharon turned to Rivka's parents and offered them some options that would help them begin to be able to help Rivka with her homework. She asked them if they would be interested in the "Hebrew on One Foot"[6] program being offered in their community. She also shared with them various resources for learning Hebrew on their own. Sharon offered to take some time to transliterate specific Skill Builder sheets she had developed for her students. This transliteration (for parents' eyes only) would enable Rivka's parents to help her review in a practical way.

If teachers want to provide parents with information on improving their children's skills, it has to be offered in a way that is thoughtful and considerate of the parents' own skills and abilities. Adults, as well as children, need to feel comfortable — and not anxious — in learning situations. By providing user-friendly materials and support, teachers can bring parents on as partners in a non-threatening way.

INTERACTIVE FAMILY HOMEWORK: OPPORTUNITIES FOR JEWISH CONVERSATIONS

Within the framework of Epstein's Type 4 Involvement — Learning at Home — is the concept of Interactive Family Homework. The Interactive Homework model provides opportunities for students to share, in a meaningful way, what they have learned in their classes, as well as to develop those concepts and ideas with their parents. This "expanded learning process" extends the walls of the classroom into the students' homes, helping parents make connections with their children, the curriculum, and the school. Of course, in religious schools and day schools, they are also making Jewish connections.[7] Interactive Family Homework provides opportunities for families to talk about the curriculum because the assignments *are* part of the curriculum!

As developed by Epstein, there are five components to Interactive Family Homework: (1) a short letter of explanation to the family, (2) introduction of elements or concepts, (3) the "development" section, (4) the family survey, and (5) home-to-school communication.

Below (figure 1) is a sample piece of interactive homework for a fifth grade class that has been studying the concept of *Shalom* (peace). It begins with a letter of explanation:

Name _____ Date _____

Dear Family,

   In our class we have been learning about the Jewish concepts of *"Sh'lom Bayit"* (peace in the home), and *Rodef Shalom* (pursuing peace). For this assignment, we will be creating a "prescription for peace." Our family should discuss the questions, and develop a prescription that we can try out. This assignment is due (in one week) on _____ .

Sincerely,

_____
(Student's signature)

Figure 1

[6]"Hebrew on One Foot" is a Hebrew literacy program founded and created by Rabbi Noah Golinkin. It is offered in a number of communities around the country. This program is designed to give adults the basics in learning to read Hebrew in one day.

[7]See also *Growing Together*, a collection of Family Education programming, edited by Jeffrey Schein and Judith S. Schiller, (Denver, CO: A.R.E. Publishing, Inc., 2001) for more homework samples.

Here are some Jewish texts we have studied about peace:

- "Seek peace and pursue it." (Psalm 34:15.)

- "The Torah does not obligate us to pursue the commandments, but if they come your way, you are commanded to perform the duties connected with them. In the case of peace, however, 'seek peace' wherever you happen to be, and 'pursue it' if it is elsewhere." (*Numbers Rabbah*, 19:27)

- *Rodef Shalom* - The Hebrew term for "Pursuer of Peace"

- *Sh'lom Bayit* - The Hebrew term for "Peace in the Home," referring to the value of harmony and mutual respect in the home

Figure 2

Key ingredients include a short explanation of the basic concept, the assignment, and the expectations: family involvement and when the assignment is due. The student is asked to sign the letter as a way of making sure that the student understands what is expected and can further explain it to his parents.

In figure 2 above, comes the introduction of elements or concepts.

At this point, the students can share with their parents, and perhaps other family members, a review of the material studied in class. The student, in fact, becomes the "teacher" as he or she shares this information. It also helps update the parents on the curriculum. This serves as the preparation for the extension of the lesson, or development section (see figure 3 below).

This assignment asks the family to consider how their home could become more peaceful. The development section involves family members in meaningful conversation (based on Jewish texts), and culminates with a finished product. The assignment begins with the student, in his/her home with the family, on a specific topic. The Family Survey (see figure 4 on the next page) allows the conversation to expand beyond the scope of the assignment to other areas.

The Family Survey extends the conversation and the lesson. It is important to consider how the results of the survey, and the central assignment, will be used. Are they a bridge to the next class? Do they introduce a new theme? Will they be used to prepare for a family education program? Can they provide a bridge between the Judaic and General Studies curriculum? There are many possibilities.

Before the homework is returned, the student's parents fill out the feedback section, the Home-to-School Communication (see figure 5 on the next page).

For this assignment you will need: pen/pencil and paper.

1. As a family, using the first two Jewish texts on your list, discuss what it means to "seek peace." What does it mean to "pursue peace"? Write down the main points of your discussion.

2. If your home is to exemplify a peaceful home, a home that reflects *"sh'lom bayit,"* how can this be accomplished? Make a list of your suggestions. Prioritize the actions on your list and write them out as if you were writing a prescription. Have all the members of your family sign the prescription.

3. Post your prescription so that all can see (perhaps on the refrigerator). Try your prescription out for a week. Come together again as a family and discuss how your home reflects *"Sh'lom Bayit."* Be prepared to share your experience with the class.

Figure 3

FAMILY SURVEY

Interview family members and write down their responses.

1. The Hebrew word *"shalom"* (peace) also means "wholeness." In what ways do you think these two words are related?

Figure 4

This feedback form provides an opportunity for you as a teacher to hear from the parents. It keeps the communication going in *both* directions, from the school to the home and from the home to the school.

> To consider: How could Tova Cohen utilize Interactive Homework as a bridge between the two weeks she has to prepare her class for a Noach puppet show?

LEARNING "ON THE WAY": CLASS CALENDARS AND "CAR TALK"

Aaron Marcus thought hard about the "homework" situation. Did the students really know what was expected of them? Did the parents know this as well? "Perhaps," he thought, "assumptions have been made that are not quite accurate." What if the homework invited the students to have conversations with their parents about topics studied in class? What if the assignment was then incorporated into the following class session? Even if parent and child talked about the assignment in the car on the way to class, it would be a "Jewish conversation."

How many of our families have opportunities to discuss "things Jewish"? their feelings about Israel? their thoughts about the Torah portions? And how can these conversations connect with the subject matter of the classroom?

Class calendars can provide students and their families with both an idea of what is going on in class, as well as starting points for Jewish conversations. For example, if Aaron's seventh graders (and their parents) received calendars that included information about the class, count-downs indicating when special homework assignments are due, and/or topical questions based on the content of the class, then all could see how the class and its assignments are connected. Figure 6 on the next page is an example of a calendar page for one week. In this case, the Shabbat school class is preparing to study *Bereshit* (Genesis).

As Aaron prepares to teach his Shabbat class,

HOME-TO-SCHOOL COMMUNICATION

Dear Parent: Your comments about your child's work in this activity are important. Please write yes or no beside each statement and feel free to add any additional comments.

_____ My child understood the activity and was able to discuss it.

_____ This activity helped me understand what my child is learning in class.

_____ I/We felt that the amount of time (one week) suggested for the activity was appropriate/realistic.

Other comments:

____

____

____

____

Parent's Signature: ______________________________ Date: ______________

Figure 5

chances are that some of the students have thought about and talked about some of the questions and are ready to be active participants in learning more about *Bereshit*.

With a packet of questions that reflects concepts and ideas from the curriculum, the family car becomes another opportunity for Jewish conversations.

Of course, it is very important that parents have a clear understanding of what "all this" is for, why they are doing it, and how it will help them and their child. Again, one cannot underestimate the importance of communication. Letters or phone calls at the beginning of the year that offer a positive outlook and a clear explanation of the goals for the class and expectations of students *and parents* can be first steps to fostering a good relationship and partnership with families.

> To consider: How would you design a packet for use with your students? Would you give out the whole packet at once, inviting families (or carpool groups) to turn to a specific question on a given date . . . or would you provide one question card at a time?

OCTOBER — Tishri/Cheshvan						
Sunday	Monday	Tuesday	Wednesday	Thursday	Friday	Saturday
1 *Simchat Torah*	2 Think about beginnings . . . Are they easy or difficult for you? Give an example.	3 Translations can be a challenge. What is the difference between "In the beginning God created . . ."[8]	4 . . . and "In the beginning of God's creating . . ."[9]	5 Two Creation stories??? Check this out: Gen. 1:1-23 & make a sketch of the different sections.	6 Now check this one out: Gen. 2:4-25 & make a sketch of these different sections. Do they match up??	7 Bring your sketches to class. *Parashat Bereshit*

Figure 6

---

[8]Translation from *The Living Torah* by Rabbi Aryeh Kaplan (Brooklyn, NY: Moznaim Publishing Corporation, 1981).

[9]Translation from *The Stone Edition — TANACH*, edited by Rabbi Nosson Scherman (Brooklyn, NY: Mesorah Publications Ltd., 1996).

SUMMER LEARNING PACKETS: EDUCATION BEYOND JUNE

The weekly calendars for Aaron's class were a great success. He has thoughts about creating some calendars for the summer with the questions and activities more spread out.

Sharon would love for her students to keep up their Hebrew skills over the summer. She thought about her Skill Building sheets. What if she added some summer artwork, created a few new pages, and sent them out to her students in July and August?

Tova received her class list of the fall's first graders. She wanted to introduce herself and her curriculum in a fun way. She decided to create a booklist for her students, inviting them to go on a summer Scavenger Hunt in the public and synagogue libraries to find and read as many books as they could. Some books are on a higher reading level and provide parents an opportunity to read to their children.

The final bell rings. The students scamper out of their classrooms for the final assembly. Three months of vacation! Yes, but wait. How about a few reminders during the summer to keep up those skills that have been learned over the year? How about continuing to build on the partnership developed with parents? Basically, the challenge is to help our families continue to "think Jewish" and have Jewish conversations all year long. Many families are with us all the way, and many are just looking for a little direction.

FORGING STRONGER LINKS

This chapter has focused on expanding the walls of the classroom into the homes of our students and, in the process, creating stronger partnerships with their parents. Ideally, parents should feel comfortable in their partnership role, and should have the resources they need — or at least the knowledge of where to find them — at their fingertips. School and synagogue libraries are "first stop" resource stations for many parents. Providing parents with a list of resources specific to the curriculum at the beginning of the year can be very helpful. The

Internet has become another invaluable resource for parents and teachers alike. In the case of smaller congregations and schools, the Internet . . . greatly enhances resource possibilities.[10] Typing "Jewish family," "Jewish holidays," or "Hebrew language" into any search engine automatically connects families with a wide variety of resource possibilities. Teachers can utilize parents' computer skills in assisting them in developing a selection of sites appropriate for specific classes.[11]

> I once had a class web site for my students and family. I filled it with bells and whistles, such as songs and graphics. However, I found that not all my families had the computer hardware and software to access all the goodies on my site. Now I send out a monthly e-mail called "Sheila's Schmooze, the Fourth Grade News." The main categories are: In Class this Month, Hebrew, Parashah Picks (story from Aish.com), Jew Crew Schmooze (birthdays and special events, snack list), Joke of the Month, and See the Sites (my favorite web sites as Internet links). Links to the Temple and Youth Group web sites are always listed. I invite parents to give me other e-mail addresses to add to the distribution list (e.g., grandparents). Students without e-mail (1/5 of the class) are given a paper copy in class, and it is always posted on my classroom door.
>
> *(Sheila Lepkin, Denver, Colorado)*

Communicating with parents often takes the form of flyers, bulletins, and class letters. E-mail is yet another way to "get the message home," receive homework, and open the door to parents communicating with the teacher. Meetings with parents provide yet another opportunity to develop important relationships that lead to stronger partnerships. One-on-one, or with a group, these provide special opportunities for parents to get to know the teacher, the school, and the curriculum better. Inviting parents to assist in planning special programs, developing some of the specific projects discussed in this chapter, building on their expertise, and expanding it within the Jewish framework

---

[10]For more information on technology, see Chapter 22, "Jewish Learning in the Digital World" by Caren N. Levine, pp. 250-268 in this Handbook.

[11]See *Wired into Judaism: The Internet and Jewish Education* by Scott Mandel (Denver, CO: A.R.E. Publishing, Inc., 2000).

offers the chance to enhance and develop Jewish skills and knowledge.

One year, I taught an overview of Jewish history and used the book *Mystery of the Coins* by Chaya Burstein (UAHC Press). After giving a bit of a tease about chapters in class one morning, I assigned chapters to be read at home. I posed questions in a written assignment and encouraged families to write in the margins of the books, if they were so inclined. I remember Barry came in one week and told how he and his dad had had a big argument/discussion on whether the character should have joined the Karaites or not, considering the circumstances, as presented in the book. We had an interesting discussion about traditions and time periods, all launched from this read-aloud experience that took place in the home.

I do recognize that some families did not do the reading. It never works for everyone, and we must accept that when we try to work with the home; we are dealing with an even more diverse population there than we are in the classroom. The underlying principle here has to be that if we don't make an effort to extend what we do beyond the classroom, we are missing out on something important.

(*Michael Fixler, Syracuse, New York*)

CONCLUSION

In the process of forging stronger links with families, teachers will find that this special relationship is invaluable. Teachers and parents alike can become partners in the process of *"v'shinantam l'vanecha,"* teaching their children diligently, both *"b'vaytechah . . . u'va'derech,"* in their home and on their way.

TEACHING CONSIDERATIONS

- Parents can be valuable partners with teachers in the Jewish education of their children.

- Communication between the school and the home, and the home and the school, plays an important role in helping parents feel connected to their children's educational programming. This can be accomplished through printed materials, phone calls, face-to-face meetings, and the Internet.

- Adults, as well as children, need to feel comfortable, and not anxious, in learning situations. By providing user-friendly materials and support, teachers can bring parents on as partners in a non-threatening way.

- The Interactive Family Homework model provides opportunities for students to share, in a meaningful way, what they have learned in their classes, as well as to develop these concepts and ideas with their parents.

- Models of learning that extend beyond the walls of the classroom provide families with opportunities to have "Jewish" conversations.

BIBLIOGRAPHY

Epstein, Joyce L., et al. *Partnership 2000 Schools Manual: Improving School-Family-Community Connections*, Baltimore, MD: Johns Hopkins University Center on School, Family, and Community Partnerships, 1997.

This manual is designed to be user-friendly. It provides the reader with background information on the importance of creating school-home-community partnerships, and then offers all the material one might need to develop the concept and staff. It includes presentation summaries, planning forms, etc. Although geared to the secular school and curriculum, these materials can be adapted to the Jewish studies curriculum.

Schein, Jeffrey, and Judith S. Schiller, eds. *Growing Together: Resources, Programs, and Experiences for Jewish Family Education.* Denver, CO: A.R.E. Publishing, Inc., 2000.

Note specifically Part IX: "Family, School, and Community Partnerships," Chapters 38 and 39, which focus specifically on adapting the Joyce Epstein model for your school (by Meryl Wassner), and interactive homework in a Jewish context (by Enid C. Lader).

Swap, Susan McAllister. *Enhancing Parent Involvement in Schools: A Manual for Parents and Teachers.* New York: Teachers College Press, 1987.

The author lays out the barriers to parent involvement in the school, and then proceeds to break them down by suggesting the importance of: positive contacts, productive conferencing, finding out what parents want, and involving parents in solving problems and making decisions. Appendixes include activities for Parent/Teacher discussion groups, case materials for communication exercises, and media resources.

CHAPTER 22

Jewish Learning in the Digital World

Caren N. Levine

The technological revolution does not replace the gifted teacher, but it does represent an extraordinary resource for the teacher. It offers new ways to interact with a broader world, opening doors to exciting new visual, textual, and intellectual discoveries and engaging students with Jewish history. It is our generation's challenge for the next century.

(Eli Evans, *Telecommunications and World Jewish Renewal*)

INTRODUCTION

The purpose of this chapter is to provide educators and educational stakeholders with an overview of how the Internet and software can be integrated into Jewish learning settings. The chapter is also meant to help educators become familiar with a variety of resources for Jewish education, develop technology-enhanced materials, and understand how to make good educational choices.

The chapter includes:

- a brief overview of software and the Internet as educational resources and their potential to enhance and transform learning in Jewish education.

- an orientation to resources for the Jewish learning environment.

- models for curriculum integration and design for education settings and beyond.

Throughout history, Jewish educational settings have employed the various technologies available to them to support learning, whether through oral transmission, parchment scrolls, books, chalkboards, filmstrips, audiotapes, videos, software, or telecommunications. The development of new, digitized technologies, such as computer software and the Internet, provide Jewish educators and learners with unprecedented abilities to create, access, and disseminate resources. Used to their potential, these technologies can facilitate engagement in Jewish lifelong learning and community participation in new and meaningful ways.

E-LEARNING AND JEWISH EDUCATION

Vignette 1

Sara is a new teacher. She just completed her degree in education and is eager to challenge her students and impart her love of learning. She is an avid user of the Internet for personal use. Sara likes to surf, buy music and books online, and once in a while participate in an online auction. She also likes to download audio files of music, play interactive card games against competitors around the world, and stay in touch with news from Israel by scanning its major newspapers in English and, when she is feeling ambitious, in Hebrew. She even found her teaching job through an online service. While in graduate school, Sara scoured the Internet for resources such as bibliographies, academic papers, and educational reports to include in her course work research. Sara has some sense that software and the Internet can be used in her professional life as an educator, but she isn't quite sure where to begin or how to think in a productive way about the tacit technology-related knowledge she holds.

Noah is an accomplished teacher who has been refining his craft over the past seven years. At home, his children spend time nearly every evening on the Internet. A relative Internet novice, he marvels at how easily and fearlessly they surf the Web and chat online with their friends. Although he is skeptical of claims that technology is "the latest and greatest" answer to education, he understands that, like any good resource, it can be a powerful and motivating tool for learning. He also recognizes that there is a strong role for teachers to play in developing meaningful learning experiences sup-

ported by technology, and that students and educators alike need to develop literacy skills that will enable them to become critical connoisseurs of multimedia resources. Noah is curious and wants to incorporate new technologies into his work, but he isn't sure where to begin or how to adapt it into his already considerable teaching repertoire.

Jewish learning occurs in many contexts — at home, in synagogues, classrooms, summer camps, retreat settings, in families, youth groups, senior centers, and other social and cultural venues such as JCCs and museums. Jewish learning can also occur in cyberspace, facilitated through the use of computers, whether through online communications or software-created environments. Learning with computer-based (digital) resources is commonly referred to as e-learning, and includes the use of software, CD-ROMS, DVDs, PDAs, as well as the Internet. The National Staff Development Council (NSDC) describes e-learning as that which:

> includes learning experiences enabled or enhanced by technological resources that support the development, exchange, and application of knowledge, skills, attitudes, aspirations, or behaviors for the purpose of improving teaching and increasing student achievement. (National Staff Development Council, p. 7)[1]

As educational theorists such as Seymour Papert point out, there is a subtle shift in the way the educational community views the use of technology. Practitioners are beginning to think of technologies less as "teacher technologies," or resources for teaching, and more holistically as tools for learning.

What does this mean for the learner and his/her educational partner, the teacher? The Internet and software can be used as creative tools with which to develop learning supports or as a medium in which to express one's ideas in a publishable, multimedia format. They can be used as a way to reach out to possible constituents and provide infrastructures to support learning communities. When applied appropriately, e-learning can be an asset to Jewish learning by:

- scaffolding and customizing individual learning experiences.

- creating enriched learning by tapping into different learning modalities and multiple intelligences.

- providing adaptive strategies and techniques to overcome barriers to learning (i.e., special keyboards, touch screens, voice recognition software).

- engaging students in complex projects.

- providing access to resources, ideas, and professional development for educators that broaden the learning experience beyond the local community.

The use of digital media, of course, is only as good as its relevance to educational vision and its related learning goals and objectives: how it meets the needs of the learners, accessibility, and, implementation by skilled educators. As an educational tool, the Internet and software provide a number of resources that educators can use to help individualize Jewish learning. The multimedia attributes of some of these media — including text, graphics, sound, and "drag and drop" manipulatives like those demonstrated on Zigzagworld's Hebrew for Me (www.zigzagworld.com)[2] — can accommodate different learning styles by providing supports for multi-modal learning.

Software and the Internet can be used for traditional learning exercises, such as remediation through interactive tutorials and drill and practice. They can also be used to support different types of inquiry-based and constructivist learning:[3] educators can employ these tools to design and access resources; students can use them to create projects and develop electronic portfolios that reflect their ability to transform information into learning.

For teachers, the Internet is also a means for accessing resources for educators' own professional development, including web sites, online workshops, and more formal courses that address subject matter content, teaching skills, and administrative tools. Discussion boards and e-mail can be

---

[1]*E-learning for Educators: Implementing the Standards for Staff Development.* (Oxford, OH: National Staff Development Council, 2001).

[2]Note: Web sites cited in this chapter portray only a sampling of such resources and are not meant to represent a comprehensive listing. Every attempt has been made to provide accurate information as of publication; however, web sites and web addresses often change over the course of time.

[3]For more information on constructivist philosophy, see Chapter 28, "Empowering the Learner: A Look at Constructivism" by Nachama Skolnik Moskowitz, pp. 334-339 in this Handbook.

used to develop collegiality by providing emotional supports and intellectual sustenance. The digital world is a new educational medium in which to work, learn, and play.

> When I teach *Parashat HaShavua* (the Torah portion of the week) on the Internet, I miss the more immediate response and energy elicited by learning in the classroom. I also miss the differences and shadings that can be conveyed by tone of voice. On the other hand, the Internet allows both teacher and student the opportunity to be more thorough and develop more detailed questions and answers.
>
> *(Rabbi David Feder, Morgantown, West Virginia)*

TOOLS FOR LEARNING — TOOLS FOR TEACHING

The Internet

The Internet is conventionally described as a network of interconnected computer systems. These systems provide tools and services that allow users to publish and retrieve information. The information can be represented in many different multimedia formats, for example, sound, pictures, text, and movies. In the area of education, the Internet can be considered one big global online clearinghouse for communications, research, and publishing. The availability and exchange of ideas and information can potentially open new venues to enrich people's lives. However, with this explosion of information sharing and online interaction comes the responsibility of critically evaluating resources for appropriateness and reliability, a topic that is addressed later in this chapter.

There are many ways in which to categorize the types of online resources from an educational framework. For example, some Internet resources relate to content knowledge, while others focus on developing particular skill sets. Still others include curricular resources such as interactive projects and activities.

Below is a sampling of types of resources that can be of particular use to Jewish educators:

- *Content Knowledge*

  Subject matter by topic

  Reference materials, primary sources, archives

  Museums, libraries, databases, online resource centers, online exhibits

  Schools, organizations, religious movements, academic institutions

  News services

- *Skills*

  Pedagogy and androgogy

  Learning styles

  Learning the Internet

- *Tools*

  Search engines

  Discussion lists and discussion boards

  Templates for designing materials, including worksheets

  Online school administration and classroom management tools

  Multimedia resources (i.e., audio, video, images, timelines)

- *Curriculum, Projects, and Activities:*

  Lesson plans, curriculum units

  Puzzles, games

  Online learning for students

  Online learning for professional development of educators

LOCATING AND IDENTIFYING RESOURCES

Finding resources online is a first step, followed by evaluating appropriateness (more on that later). There are two basic ways of finding Internet resources of potential value online — search engines, such as Google (www.google.com), and subject directories, like Maven (www.maven.co.il). Search engines are particularly useful for general searches based on key words or concepts. These automated programs will seek out matches to the query and pull up links to web sites that contain those terms. Another way to conduct a search is to use a subject directory, which organizes topics compiled by the proprietor of the directory in a way that makes it easy to browse, like a library card catalog.

Search Engines

A search engine is a computer software program that searches web pages throughout the Internet and catalogs its findings based on a user's request. With the plethora of different types of search engines, there are now available online tutorials, such as the Spider's Apprentice (www.monash.com/spidap.html), to evaluate various search engines and compare their distinctive features. Meta-search engines, such as Dogpile (www.dogpile.com) act as front-ends to other search engines so that a user can search multiple engines with one query.

Let's say a teacher is looking for material on Jewish food for a curricular unit on Jewish cuisine around the world. How would this educator conduct an effective search? Here are a few tips:

- Always follow directions according to each search engine's syntax.

- Basic searches are generally based on keywords; for example, entering the words *matzah* and *ball* will call up all documents that contain both of those words.

- Literal phrases can be searched by placing quotation marks around them

  - "matzah ball"
    This search will result in web pages that contain the phrase *matzah ball* (i.e., the word *matzah* immediately followed by the word *ball*.)

- Searches can be refined through the use of Boolean operators, *and* (also represented as a plus sign), or, *not* (also represented as a minus sign). Some examples are:

  - matzah AND ball (+matzah +ball)
    In this search, results will include web pages in which all of the indicated terms (words) in the phrase appear; that is, *matzah* and *ball* will appear somewhere in the document, but may not bear any relationship to each other (i.e., a recipe for *matzah ball*; however, the following may also come up: Sammy ate *matzah* while Leora played *ball*;)

- matzah OR ball
  In this search, results will include web pages with at least one of the terms in the phrase; that is, pages will come up with either the word *matzah* or the word *ball*.

- matzah NOT ball (+matzah –ball)
  In this search, results will include web pages that include the first term, but not the second term; that is, the results will only include pages with the word *matzah* but not the word *ball*.

Try searches using these phrases and note the differences in the results. Also try out meta-search engines that conduct multiple searches, for example, www.dogpile.com. Note that each search engine may return a different list of web pages that match the criteria. This is because when each search engine scans the web pages on the Internet, they may catalog this information differently from one another.

There are many free web search engines available on the Internet. Some of the more popular engines are www.google.com, www.yahoo.com, www.altavista.com, and www.dogpile.com. Each of these sites explains how the specific engine performs its search, and provides guidance for the most efficient way to structure a query for fast and accurate results. The success of finding an appropriate match is highly dependent on the specific query issued. In general, using common words, such as *and, it, from, but, so,* etc., will cause the search engine to answer with many pages (though some search engines ignore popular words to help refine the search more quickly). Using specific words, such as *recipes, Jewish,* etc., will help to refine results.

Jewish Web Directories

Web directories are self-contained indexes that organize web sites by subject, much like the Yellow Pages in a phone directory, or a library card catalog, through which the user can browse. There are several directories devoted to resources of Jewish content. A few examples:

- *Jacob Richman's Hot Sites — Jewish*
  www.jr.co.il/hotsites.jewish.htm

- *JewishNet: Global Jewish Information Network*
  www.jewishnet.net

- *Maven*
  www.maven.co.il
- *Shamash*
  http://shamash.org
- *Zipple*
  www.zipple.com

Print resources include *The Jewish Guide To the Internet* by Diane Romm, which is accompanied by a web site: www.jewishinternetguide.com.

Software

There are different ways to think of software. Some software programs are created as tools that let users create their own materials, keep track of records, or facilitate organization of ideas and projects, such as *Inspiration*, a graphical organizer. Hebrew word processors, presentation tools such as *PowerPoint*, spreadsheets, and databases fall into this category. Other tools include reference materials, such as dictionaries; encyclopedias; Judaic libraries, including the Bible, Talmud, and prayer books; clip art; and, text databases such as the *Encyclopaedia Judaica* and the *Bar Ilan Responsa*. Other software might focus primarily on learning activities. These include drill and practice software for learning Hebrew, a simulated tour of the Temple in Jerusalem, games such as *Who Stole Hanukkah*, and extensive multimedia learning environments such as *Survivors: Testimonies of the Holocaust*, which includes interactive maps and video clips of survivors' accounts of their experiences, and Gesher's *Bible Multimedia Adventure Series*. The *Heritage: Civilization and the Jews* DVD-ROM is an example of an environment that uses a blended approach that takes advantage of the Internet to disseminate new material, post teachers guides, and share lesson plans.

The categories below suggest types of software programs that serve as tools and learning activities:

- *Tools*

    Desktop publishing

    Graphics

    Presentation tools

    Organizational tools

    Research and reference tools

    Spreadsheets and databases

    Word processors

- *Learning Activities*

    Drill and practice

    Instructional games

    Problem solving software

    Simulations

    Tutorials

DEVELOPING TECHNOLOGY-ENHANCED CURRICULA AND ACTIVITIES

Designing learning that takes advantage of digital media is a nascent field of curriculum development. Integrating the Internet and software into a lesson can be viewed as a continuum — at the most basic end of the spectrum, an educator can choose to direct learners to specific online resources just as he or she would do with print resources; at the other end of the spectrum, the lesson plan can be delivered, conducted, and assessed entirely online using the Internet and/or software. As both technology and digital learning evolve, there will be many new and exciting ways to incorporate them into Jewish education. Regardless of the medium, however, there are certain basic principles of good curricular design based on learning theory that should be considered, many of which are discussed elsewhere in this book.

As with other curriculum design, educators ask:

- What is the rationale for including this resource/activity/program?

- How is it linked to the overall curriculum?

- How does it support the learning objectives?

- Does it reflect applicable education standards, where they exist?

- How can achievement be assessed?

There are several popular frameworks for designing educational activities that incorporate digital technologies. Tom March, Bernie Dodge, and Judi Harris are three educators who have been instrumental in thinking about different types of online learning modules and activities. Although these resources and activities are presented in the context of K-12 formal education, they can be adapted for other educational settings and populations, and are relevant frameworks for using more traditional, "offline" resources as well. A major focus of their work is the use of communication, collaboration, research, and presentation to transform information into knowledge and learning through interpretation and application. The material that follows is summarized and adapted from publications by March, Dodge, and Harris and is cited in the Bibliography at the end of this chapter.

Models of Curricular Activities

Tom March developed a taxonomy of goal-based learning activities that uses the Internet. These formats tend to build on each other and the same resources can be used for different projects and adapted for different Jewish learning settings. This taxonomy represents a range of activities, from resource collection, which is a basic way of organizing simple, web-based activities, to the more sophisticated type of activities associated with WebQuests. Readers are encouraged to read March and Dodge for more detailed information. A few brief examples are provided below.

Hotlists

Hotlists help learners quickly identify resources that will be helpful for completing projects or are tailored to individual interests. They serve as predefined, topic-centered "bookmarks" or "favorites" lists. Creating hotlists is one way to begin to enhance already developed lesson plans with online resources. Hotlists generally include content sites, but can also take the form of multimedia scrapbooks that include media resources to enhance student projects, such as maps, time lines, photographs, sound bites, video clips, Jewish clip art, etc.[4] Teachers can also assign students to create their own hotlists in preparation for research projects. Fully developed hotlists are more than just listings of web sites. They are a collection of sites or resources on a topic that were selected for their usefulness and grouped into an organizational framework that is helpful to the user. For example, a hotlist about Israel might include links under the following categories: "Economy," "Geography," "History," "Religion," etc.

A good hotlist includes the following components: Hotlist Title; Introduction (goals of the hotlist; the student's tasks, etc); and, Annotated Links. When developing a hotlist, think about how to organize the links to guide the user more effectively.

Knowledge Hunts

Knowledge hunts, also referred to as treasure hunts, are analogous to online scavenger hunts. Learners are asked to collect information based on a series of questions by investigating pre-defined web sites. The hunts provide students with contexts for acquiring and synthesizing resources to investigate a topic.

A well-designed hunt includes: the Title of the hunt; an Introduction with goals and instructions, Questions to be answered by the students, Annotated Links to resources which provide answers, and a Big Question designed to help students piece together the information and synthesize it in a meaningful way. A general formula is to direct students to one web site per question. These differ from hotlists, which provide multiple sources of information, in that hunts focus on important areas within a topic.

WebQuests

WebQuests are inquiry-based activities that involve a central question and related tasks that cultivate higher order thinking. WebQuests are often designed as group activities that promote collaborative research and decision making. They are particularly useful for uncovering and analyzing complex ideas. Although many projects consider themselves as WebQuests because they follow a particular format, a truly robust WebQuest takes into account transformational learning; that is, upon successful completion of the project, the learner has not only developed an expertise in the area of study, but is able to put this expertise to use in new ways.

Bernie Dodge developed the WebQuest format with Tom March, and he maintains the WebQuest site: (http://edweb.sdsu.edu/webquest/webquest. html), which includes many examples of well-crafted activities, step-by-step instructions, and

---

[4]Note: As with print and other materials, educators should make sure that these resources are cleared for copying before assigning them. Appropriate citations should be included with other references (i.e., bibliographies).

evaluation rubrics. Dodge also suggests pedagogic techniques to help scaffold student learning by providing the resources for:

- reception - resources with which students may not be already familiar, such as tips on conducting interviews and online dictionaries.

- transformation - assistance on meaning making processes such as comparisons, pattern discernment, decision making.

- production - providing templates, writing guides, and other tools for creating original materials.

No matter which format is chosen, the essentials of good lesson planning are key to successful learning experiences. Each activity should begin with an introduction that includes the goals of the activity, some background to help the learner frame the activity, such as the "big idea" behind it as well as clear directions, annotated resources and links (the annotations help guide the user and highlight the content of the selected web sites and their usefulness), and criteria for successful completion.

One example is represented by Maury Greenberg's *Virtual Field Trips WebQuest* (www.jecc.org), which was created to help teachers learn the basics about creating virtual field trips. While reviewing this WebQuest, think about how the content was developed. Note how the material is structured, with clear directions and authentic tasks. Consider how this WebQuest takes advantage of techniques such as simulation, and how it presents the skills and knowledge tools needed successfully to complete the activities.

A good WebQuest includes: a Title, an Introduction with goals and instructions, the Process needed to accomplish the task and Roles that need to be addressed, Annotated Resources related to the task, Guiding questions to support the process, Evaluation rubrics, and a Conclusion that summarizes the learning activities.

Activity Structures for Online Projects

Another way to think about online curriculum is in terms of activities. Judi Harris identified a framework with which to categorize Internet-enhanced educational activities that actively engage students. This framework, which she refers to as "activity structures," serves as an instructional design tool for teachers to build educational environments. Harris identified three genres of online activity:

- interpersonal exchange

- information collection and analysis

- problem solving

These projects can be used to frame online activities for Jewish learning and engagement in a variety of settings.

Interpersonal Exchange - individuals or groups talk electronically, using e-mail, web conferences, videoconferencing, etc. Some examples:

Keypals - Student-student or group-group electronic exchanges, often between schools in different communities, or between different grades within a school

Global classrooms - Classrooms in different locations study a common topic over a specific period of time, either short-term or over one or more semesters

Electronic appearances - Accessing guests who have expertise on a particular topic; generally a "limited engagement"

Telementoring - mentoring at a distance; matching students with access to experts in a particular subject area who will support and encourage mentees as they proceed on projects

Question and Answer Activities - Opportunities to "ask an expert" specific questions related to understanding a particular topic

Impersonations - Participants exchange views based on a particular character's perspective

Interpersonal exchanges can include e-mail exchanges and videoconferencing between schools in Israel and the Diaspora to share experiences about growing up Jewish; another example might be a veteran teacher who provides online support to a more novice educator in another school.

Information Collection and Analysis - collecting, compiling, and comparing information. Some examples:

Information Exchanges - Classes collect, share, and analyze data.

Database Creation - Classes build on data collection by organizing information into a common database.

Electronic Publishing - Creating and posting online magazines, newspapers, exhibits, etc.

Telefieldtrips - These may include sharing online travel experiences interactively online, or a virtual expedition, in which students take part in field trips conducted by scientists, educators, or other types of adventurers. A variation on the theme is the "virtual tour," in which an online field trip is designed by the teacher or learner, and which may include the use of webcams, photographs, video, etc.

Pooled Data Analysis - Data is compiled at multiple sites and combined for analysis to reveal patterns.

Information collection and analysis in a Jewish setting could include a project in which different schools around the world trace their Jewish roots, share this information, map it out, and analyze it within the context of recent Jewish history.

Problem Solving - online collaborations or competitions using frameworks for problem-based learning. Some examples:

Information Searches - Students are provided with clues and resources to use in response to guided questions.

Peer Feedback Activities - Participants offer feedback and critiques of peer work, including writing assignments and position papers.

Parallel Problem Solving - Students in various locations are given similar problems to solve and discuss their problem solving methodology.

Sequential Creation - Participants create a piece of text or visual image together, as each adds to it in turn.

Telepresent Problem Solving - Computer-mediated meeting to report back on similar activities based on real-world issues undertaken at various locations.

Simulations - Sustained projects that engage participants in simulated events or model making.

Social Action Projects - Participants develop an understanding of real-world issues and take action toward resolution.

Problem solving activities can include online *tzedakah* projects that students research and devise strategies to address. Another idea is an intergenerational "campfire" story, in which participants of all ages take turns developing part of a story and pass it on to others to continue.

Vignette 2

Sara reviewed some of her lesson plans and realized that she could enrich them by directing her students to online resources. She created a hotlist of sites about Israel. The students worked in groups based on specific themes relating to the study of Israel. Sara found that she was able to move around and assist each group as they discussed the resources and determined how best to use the information they uncovered. She realized that, with guidance, her students were not just surfing randomly online, but were actively manipulating and transforming material into learning. Later, she revisited her hotlist and selected resources that would be beneficial to her WebQuest that compared election procedures in Israel with those in the United States.

Noah always wished his students could interact with other Jewish children throughout the world to foster a personal sense of K'lal Yisrael (connections with other Jews). Noah wanted them to understand that Jews live all over the globe and share a varied and rich history, and that Jews are responsible for each other's welfare. He was happy to discover that e-mail and the World Wide Web could support rich student exchanges through educational Internet twinning projects between Israeli and Diaspora schools, such as those sponsored by Partnership 2000 and the Department for Jewish Zionist Education's Pedagogic Center. Students were able to practice their written Hebrew using word processors, and their spoken Hebrew through videoconferences, facilitating individual relationships among young Jews the world over. Noah implemented twinning projects with his day school class, as well as with the congregational high school class he teaches on Sundays. One result was a joint social action project with the Israelis in which students recorded oral histories of elderly family members.

Jewish E-Learning in Action

How are Jewish educators incorporating digital media for learning? Here are just a few examples:

Congregational School/Lesson Planning/Jewish Holidays

Lauren Resnikoff developed curriculum units for students attending congregational schools as part of her own learning under a Master's program sponsored by the Board of Jewish Education of Greater New York (the Technology Collaborative). Her materials on teaching Jewish holidays were designed to meet state standards and to incorporate ISTE (International Society for Technology in Education) standards for technology literacy. She used software to design and post the curriculum on the Internet. Students are expected to use the Internet as a content resource and multimedia software to demonstrate their understanding of the material. These units and others can be found at the web site of the Board of Jewish Education of Greater New York (www.bjeny.org).

Day School/Student Projects/Jewish History and Culture

Sol Novick, an educator at the Solomon Schechter Day School of Essex and Union, New Jersey, works with his students to develop technologically-enhanced learning through courses and projects. Sol has developed Teacher and Student Booklets and other materials on topics such as "Studying Bamidbar: A Multi-Resource Approach," "Holidays and Events on the Jewish Calendar," "One People: A Multi-Media Jewish History Project," "Realizing the Dream: The History of Zionism through its Heroes." The materials include models for integrating technology into research and final projects. In addition, Sol disseminates annotated lists of web sites for Jewish education. Information about these resources at: www.ssdsofessexandunion.org/courses.html

Day School/Learning Tools and Student Projects/Jewish Text Study

RabLab, developed by Jeff Spitzer, is a Rabbinic text project that was first piloted at the Solomon Schechter Day School of Greater Boston. It is a curricular initiative that takes advantage of traditional text learning, digital databases of Rabbinic literature, and web publishing skills. Students learn text study skills as well as computer skills that help them master *Torah Sheh'b'al Peh* (the Oral Torah). Students learn in small groups and are challenged to engage in the inquiry-based process by creating Talmudic-style responses to the text and publishing them on the Online Beit Midrash constructed for this purpose. The original RabLab page can be found at: www.ssdsboston.org/main.htm.

Adult Learning/Student Design/Jewish Values in Secular Studies

ACEiT (Association of Collaborating Educators for Instructional Technology) is an example of how a face-to-face Master's class sponsored by the Board of Jewish Education of Greater New York (www.bje.org), in partnership with the New York Institute of Technology, transformed itself into an online academy as part of its learning experience. Modeling a constructivist approach, participants developed their own self-paced online course in their individual subject areas as part of the larger educational environment.

Online Lifelong Learning/Small Group-Large Group-Individual/Jewish Text Study

Gemara Berura is a computer program meant to help students develop skills for analyzing Gemara text. The program focuses on helping the learner map out and decode the text using graphical cues to understand the context. Support materials include databases, biographies of the Sages, reference tools, and an Aramaic-Hebrew Dictionary. The software is supplemented by a web site with lesson plans and teacher guides (www.gemaraberura.com).

TorahQuests are activities meant to engage students of all ages in creating Torah commentary using a variety of media. Although TorahQuests can be constructed "off-line," the TorahQuest web page offers a number of interactive, online Torah study activities (www.jrf/torahquest).

These types of online learning initiatives provide schools and other educational settings with the ability to expand course offerings for its core population, including their teachers, and to accommodate gifted and talented populations and other students with special needs.

Vignette 3

Through their school's online discussion list, Noah and Sara discover their common interest in using technology in their work. They complement each other's skills and become mentors to one another: Sara helps Noah become more adept at using the Internet and software applications, while Noah shares tips about teaching and classroom management. Together they develop lesson plans to use with their students. Sara is also a youth group leader. She uses e-mail to stay in touch with the teens during the week, and she checks the web site of the national office for suggested activities. She recently enrolled in an online professional development course for new teachers. With Sara's assistance — and that of a few of his students — Noah creates a class web site on which he and his students post weekly assignments, publish an online magazine with a class in Israel, present student projects for peer review, and highlight specific web sites that supplement in-class work and help parents make connections between their children's lives in school and at home. Sara and Noah's classes worked together with schools in Israel to develop a multimedia PowerPoint presentation, "A Day in the Life of Israeli and North American Kids" that was shown at a school. The presentation included photographs, audio messages and music, video segments, and text. Each participant received his/her own copy on CD-ROM.

THE "ONE COMPUTER-NO COMPUTER" EDUCATIONAL SETTING

Many times an educator would like to use Internet and software resources, but does not have easy access in the classroom or learning setting. Teachers and students may have better access from home or the library, and so printed copies of online materials might be distributed or homework assigned. When asking students to use computers at home, teachers need to be cognizant that not all students are "wired" and should make alternative arrangements. A school might invest in one or more "floating" laptops or palmtops (handheld computers like Psion or AlphaSmart) that can be circulated to classrooms as needed or given to individual students and educators for extracurricular work. In settings in which there is access to at least one computer, teachers can use it as a learning sta-

tion for individual or small group work. The computer can also be connected to a large screen video monitor using a video display device for class presentations and group work. There are a number of web sites that offer suggestions for classes with one computer, many of which are mentioned in Kathy Schrock's article, "The One-Computer Classroom: A Review of the Internet Literature (http://kathyschrock.net)."

A growing number of students and teachers use personal digital assistants (PDAs, like the Palm Handhelds) to keep track of important personal information. PDAs, often referred to as handheld computers, are also being used in educational settings for data collection and information sharing. Collaborative worksheets, such as those developed for general education at the Center for Highly Interactive Computing in Education at the University of Michigan (www.handheld.hice-dev.org) can be developed and "beamed" from teacher-to-student, student-to-teacher, and student-student. PDA resources for Jewish education such as Hebrew software, traditional Jewish texts, Hebrew calendars, blessings, Israeli newspapers, and dictionaries can be downloaded from the Pilotyid site (www.pilotyid.com). In addition, educational services, such as Scholastic Wireless (www.scholastic.com), are increasingly making resources available for users to download news, activities, and other information onto their PDAs.

E-LEARNING AND PROFESSIONAL DEVELOPMENT

The Internet offers a wealth of resources for professional growth and a variety of educational professional development opportunities through electronic discussion lists, web sites (including online resource centers), and online courses or workshops.

Just as there are online activity sites for students, there are sites, discussion lists, and online courses for educators. Some of these initiatives are sponsored by educational departments of the religious movements, others are offered by universities or educational agencies, and still others are under independent auspices.

RESOURCE CENTERS

Online resource centers are specific types of web

sites designed to provide access to resources and tools for teachers and students, such as lesson plans and teacher-made materials for Hebrew and Judaic learning. They may also offer online templates to help teachers design technology-enriched learning in the form of projects, worksheets, puzzles, and sustained student activities such as WebQuests. The following are examples of online resource centers for Jewish educators:

- CAJE, the Coalition for the Advancement of Jewish Education (www.caje.org)

- e-Chinuch.org: Pinchas Hochberger Creative Learning Pavilion (www. e-chinuch.org)

- The Jewish Education Center of Cleveland (www.jecc.org)

- JESNA's Jewish Educator's Electronic Toolkit and Sosland Online Resource Centers (www.jesna.org)

- The Lookstein Virtual Resource Center for Jewish Education (www.lookstein.org)

- The Pedagogic Center of the Jewish Agency for Israel, Department of Jewish Zionist Education (www.jajz-ed.org.il/index1.html)

ONLINE LEARNING

Many Jewish institutions of higher learning in North America and Israel offer online courses for educators, some leading to Master's degrees or professional development credits. Other courses, which may be under independent auspices, may be more informal in nature, and are geared toward *torah lishmah*, learning for its own sake.

Online learning encompasses a range of experiences. They include, by are not limited to:

- Informal e-mails of resources or more structured lessons that are sent from the faculty to the learner, such as *Divray Torah* from a scholar or suggested activities from central agencies for Jewish education.

- Self-paced, online tutorials, such as Maury Greenberg's online tutorial for creating virtual field trips (www.jecc.org) and Nancy Messinger's professional development tutorial for her educators on the use of the

video *The Prince of Egypt* as contemporary *midrash* (www.acaje.org).

- Interactive videoconferences and web-based courses that focus on building communities of actively engaged learners who participate in online discussions and activities, such as the Jewish Agency Contact Center (www.jacontact.org) and JSkyway (www.jskyway.com).

Other professional development or learning opportunities take advantage of "blended learning," offering multiple means of learning settings, including face-to-face seminars combined with online components.

> I am still learning how to integrate the computer into my teaching, but I did use one computer resource recently in an eighth grade class when we were reviewing Samuel I. I found a web site with artwork from the Bible, and downloaded four pieces of art showing David. I photocopied the pictures and asked students to locate where in the texts the action depicted in the picture occurred and then to assess the accuracy of the artist's representation. We then discussed their conclusions. It was an efficient way to review much of David's life (the pictures I found showed David as a shepherd boy, Samuel coming to anoint David, David singing to Saul, and a battle scene. Students identified anachronisms such as clothing and architecture, but also focused on the details (or lack of them) in the text.
>
> *(Cheryl Birkner Mack, Cleveland, Ohio)*

STRENGTHENING HOME-SCHOOL-COMMUNITY CONNECTIONS

The Internet can be used to bring the outside world in, as described above, and, conversely, to extend the "brick and mortar" boundaries of classrooms, synagogues, camps, retreat centers, youth groups, religious movements, and other religious and cultural organizations that play roles in Jewish life. Schools, for example, use class web sites to engage parents further by posting assignments and electronic portfolios of student work online, and by providing families with pointers and links to assist with homework. Camps and retreat sites create online photo albums to highlight activities and share events. School, camp, and youth group trips to Israel use the Internet to document their experiences and as a way to report back to peers and parents and to supplement face-to-face encounters with newfound friends.

Homework Helpers

Educational organizations can tap into the Internet to develop "homework helpers" for learners and their parents. A homework helper for students might include hotlists of Jewish-related sites to assist research projects in their general education courses (i.e., Jewish immigration and genealogy sites) or resources to learn more about a particular subject area for those who want to explore an area in greater depth and pursue additional independent study. Homework helpers can also be chosen to review and reinforce classroom exercises; NewSlate (www.newslate.com), for example, is an online tool that generates individualized quizzes to practice Hebrew and Yiddish comprehension.

Online "handouts" with annotated links are also helpful for supporting extracurricular family activities and for providing parents with resources to assist their children's education. For example, a handout posted online about upcoming holidays might include detailed information about home rituals and links to holiday sites for further, self-guided learning. Lauren Resnikoff extended the physical boundaries of her congregational school by compiling companion links and family activities to accompany in-class curriculum (www. tbdcommack.org). The Jewish Family Resources web site compiled by Rabbi Amy Scheinerman (http://scheinerman.net/judaism) represents another way of approaching this type of resource. The site, designed to help congregants become more familiar with Jewish rituals and texts includes a virtual tour of the synagogue, an introduction to Jewish holy books and rituals, and links to Jewish stories that parents can read to their children.

Online Hebrew tutorials, such as those collected on About.com or offered by some Jewish publishers to complement to their Hebrew programs, can provide an introduction or refresher course for parents and children who need assistance with the language. Sites like "A Page from the Babylonian Talmud" (www.ucalgary.ca/~

elsegal/TalmudPage.html) guide novices and veterans through basic understandings of traditional Jewish texts. These resources can be used and distributed to learners who do not have regular access to the Internet.

Other types of online homework helpers include educational sites that feature reference materials, subject-specific links, and study tips and sites that contain question and answer formats in which the user submits a question and receives responses from staff or other users. Some general education sites provide online tutors and tutorials, often for a fee.

Connecting Communities

As discussed above, telecommunications can be used to bring together different groups of people, such as Israeli and Diaspora Jews, for cultural exchanges and community building. It can also be used to deliver more formal courses, such as the online series developed for North American high school students by WebYeshiva and the Lookstein Center in Israel, which provides access to Israeli scholars and resources.

The Internet can also facilitate connections beyond the school or local environment through social action projects. Resources can be found online for developing social action projects, and the Internet can be used to foster these types of projects. For example, iEARN, the International Education and Resource Network (www.iearn.org), enables students to engage in meaningful educational projects with local and international peers. iEARN's Holocaust/Genocide Project is one model developed for learners to read, research, discuss history and current events, and take action to make the world a better place. In addition to online curricular resources and collaborations, participants have taken part in study trips to Poland and Israel.

Connecting Communities

The Internet can be employed as a means of communicating with the stakeholder community and providing information and feedback for decision makers, like PTO members. Specialized online resource centers, like those found on the JESNA site (www.jesna.org) are designed with educational stakeholders in mind, and provide resources on issues such as congregational education, day schools, Jewish educational research, Jewish special needs, media and technology, and youth initiatives for professionals and lay leaders. PEJE, the Partnership for Excellence in Jewish Education (www.peje.org), disseminates resources and publications of interest to day schools through its web site.

MAKING GOOD CHOICES

As with any resource, considerations regarding the use of the Internet or software for learning should be made in context of its overall impact and how it fits into desired learning goals and objectives. There is value in including resources and activities that are fun, motivating, or that fill social and affective purposes. Educators and learners should not feel obligated to use an entire site or software program; rather, they should pick and choose those segments appropriate for their purposes. Guiding questions include, but are not limited to:

- Does the material reinforce or enhance the curriculum's learning goals?

- Does it facilitate learning that students or educators could do before, but better?

- Does it enable students or educators to do something unique that they can't do by another means?

- Does it engage and/or support learning? Does it support a variety of learning styles?

- Does it detract from learning?

- What is the best use of this resource? Is it best used as a resource for research, a project site, with information and activities, or a supplement that can be adapted for education?

Integrating the Internet and software goes hand in hand with critical evaluation to assess reliable and appropriate materials. Criteria for evaluating web sites and software are somewhat similar to reviewing other media such as print material and videos. Media literacy is an essential tool for educators and learners alike. The nature of the Internet in particular, in which anyone can publish anything, rather than being centralized through specific publishers or producers, makes it more of a challenge to test reliability of content. Consider the following:

- *Authorship or sponsorship* - Who is the author? Is the publisher a reliable source of information? Under whose auspices is the material, and are they a legitimate/appropriate source of information?

- *Content* - What is the purpose of the web site or software, and does the content meet these goals? What is the quality of the information? Are there particular biases in the content? Does the site conform to issues of copyright? If a web site, is it regularly updated and are the links maintained? Is this material an appropriate resource for the activity or curriculum?

- *Presentation* - Is the material easy to navigate technologically and also in terms of content continuity? Does it take useful advantage of design features, such as graphics, audio, etc.? Does it exhibit sufficient levels of interactivity for the type of resource it is?

- *Technology* - Are there technical difficulties associated with the site or software? Does it work with all web browsers or computers? Does it require special software or a specific computer platform?

DEVELOPING TECHNOMENSCHEN

The term *technomenschen* has been used to describe people who use technology in a way that is ethically responsible. Ethical issues related to the use of the Internet and technology in the educational setting need to be addressed by educators, especially in the context of Jewish values. In school settings, this generally takes the form of a contract called an Acceptable Use Policy. These AUPs (also known as Responsible Use Policies) are reviewed and signed by students, faculty, and families, when applicable.

A typical AUP for Jewish settings might address: Jewish values and ethics, school/agency values, online conduct (also know as "netiquette"), copyright concerns, game playing policies, and security issues. Individual class AUPs that incorporate Jewish values might be developed by students in conjunction with a unit on Jewish ethics that incorporate Jewish values.

KEEPING PERSPECTIVE: STAYING GROUNDED IN CYBERSPACE

Integrating educational technology into one's skill set takes time. As it is with acquiring any new skill, there is a big learning curve involved, complicated by the occasional quirkiness of technology. There will be moments of great frustration and, more often than not, moments of great achievement.

As educators become more familiar and comfortable with using these media, they often pass through a continuum of beliefs and practice regarding their ability to reflect on and integrate technology into their work. The stages, identified by the ACOT (Apple Classrooms of Tomorrow) project are summarized here, along with examples:[5]

Entry - Teachers are uncomfortable using technology and don't see how it can be used in the curriculum; they tend to rely on others for technology-related projects and support.

A teacher in a congregational school might at first be overwhelmed by demands of time and lack of computer skills. He/she is planning a lesson on Israel and, unfamiliar with the Internet, asks a colleague to help locate and print out maps of Israeli cities from the Internet that she can have enlarged and use as posters around the classroom.

Adoption - Teachers use Internet applications that they find useful and some software, mostly as productivity tools such as word processing.

The teacher learns to use a Hebrew-English word processor to develop bilingual worksheets and vocabulary lists instead of typing the English and writing the Hebrew entries by hand.

Adaptation - Teachers begin to use computer resources with their students in a way that supports the curriculum by giving them traditional tasks that make use of technology.

Students are taught research skills, including resource evaluation and analysis to use for an assignment on Israel. Instead of traditional paper reports, students develop PowerPoint slide shows about Israel's history and deliver detailed presentations to the class.

Appropriation - Teachers begin to think about and implement ways of using technology as a new tool to achieve overall curricular objectives.

When planning a curricular unit on Israel, the teacher integrates historical time lines, interactive maps, photographs from Israeli archives, audio clips of Israeli songs, and webcameras that provide real-time video of Israeli locations, including the Kotel. All of these resources become part of his/her repertory as he/she designs the curricular unit.

Innovations - Teaching practice is transformed as teachers experiment and integrate technology in a transparent and seamless way; the technology becomes another resource to foster learning.[5]

The teacher creates a companion web site for the class that supports their Israel studies. The web site is used to post weekly assignments and links to other resources for those students who wish to learn more. Background materials and home-based activities are collected and posted for intergenerational family education projects in the home. Students post portfolios of their best work to share with classmates. The class uses the discussion area on the web site for online conversations with peers in Israel to compare lifestyles and what being Jewish means to them. A joint student newsletter published on the web highlights differences and similarities in holiday observances.

An additional challenge to integrating multimedia into the educational setting is the fact that students may be more adept at using software and the Internet than are their teachers. As described above, learning to use these digital resources is a gradual process, although there will always be the "innovators" and "early adaptors" — teachers who jump right in. Even the most novice teacher can develop skills in order to become a critical connoisseur of educational technology, to determine more effectively what is useful, and to become familiar with basic issues of media literacy. As with any new resource or innovation, teachers will better integrate these resources into their work as they sharpen their technical skills and gain increased confidence in curricular design using multimedia.

Educators who are interested in using the Internet and software in their work — as a means of intensifying their own learning and as a way to embellish and support student learning — might be guided by the following questions:

- Will this use of the Internet [and software] enable students [educators] to do something that they COULDN'T do before?

[5]Adapted from Debra Rein, *What Is Effective Integration of Technology and Does It Make a Difference?* Paper presented at the International Conference on Learning with Technology, 2000. (Available from www.l2l.org/iclt/2000)

- Will this use of the Internet [and software] enable students [educators] to do something that they COULD do before, but better?[6]

CONCLUSION

There is a tendency when adapting new technologies to employ them to do traditional tasks in a more efficient manner. At some point, however, there may be a technological evolution in which the tools become mechanisms for transformation. That is, resources and opportunities made possible through the distinct features of the Internet and software can spark the imaginations of educational stakeholders to "think different" — to borrow a phrase from Apple Computer — about teaching and learning by prompting them to reconceptualize the meaning of "Jewish education" and learning Jewishly. In other words, what does it mean to learn Jewishly and to "do Jewish" in the fifty-eighth/twenty-first century?

The digital world provides a means to make powerful connections between home, school, and the work place; between "formal" and "informal" educational environments; between Judaic and secular studies. The interplay of formal and informal education, the blending of online and face-to-face activities, the availability of unprecedented access to resources and expertise, and the ability of the educational community to create meaningful and flexible learning experiences through the use of these tools hold the promise of revolutionizing life-long Jewish learning.

This chapter serves as a brief introduction to a complex topic. Readers are encouraged to learn more. A Bibliography with suggested resources is provided below.

TEACHING CONSIDERATIONS

A Few Helpful Hints for Getting Started

- There are a number of good web sites that can serve as a "launch pad" for locating resources. The JESNA site (www.jesna.org), for example, includes a database of Judaic software, categorized and annotated links to other sites of interest for Jewish educational settings, and original materials for educators and lay leaders to facilitate the integration of media and technology. The Associated Talmud Torahs site also contains a listing of software and reviews (www.att.org).

- Educators and administrators looking for telecollaborators in Jewish education can turn to e-mail discussion lists, such as the Lookstein Center's lookjed list (www.lookstein.org) and Inter-Jed (http://shamash.org). Partners can also be found through CAJE networks, central agencies for Jewish education, JCCs, camp associations, student associations, national organizations, or other educational institutions that promote electronic learning, such as the Pedagogic Centre and Partnership 2000 communities, which specialize in twinning projects with Israelis.

- Let students use the Internet and software to produce projects. Instead of a traditional report, an assignment might take the form of designing a web page that reflects certain criteria; if students don't have web skills or access to online templates, they can storyboard and map out the content or design it in a word processor, save it as a web page, and submit the completed assignment on a disk.

- Online museums and exhibits are rich environments that can help contextualize ideas and objects important to Jewish cultural and spiritual life. The Jewish Museum web site (www.jewishmuseum.org), for example, provides historic, cultural, and artistic interpretations of its collection online.

- Online newspapers can be used to compare news from local sources with Israeli newspapers in English or Hebrew. Hebrew language radio broadcasts can be downloaded as well.

- Create "favorites" lists for the learning setting or classroom and categorize them according to subject areas that align with curriculum or topics that are studied: Israel, family and Jewish living, early childhood,

---

[6]Judi Harris, "Wetware: Why Use Activity Structures?" *Learning and Leading with Technology* 25:4 (December/January 1997-1998):13-17. Bracketed words added by the author.

genealogy, history and culture, kids, Jewish text and commentaries, Hebrew, holidays, Jews around the world, ecology, stories, etc. Share these lists with colleagues.

- Tap into secular resources such as About. com, in addition to Judaic resources. For example, genealogy projects can take advantage of government records, such as the immigration material found at the Ellis Island American Family Immigration History Center site (www.ellisislandrecords. org), as well as JewishGen (www. jewishgen.org), an international resource for Jewish genealogy worldwide.

- A good way to find out more about how to use technology for Jewish education is to have a better understanding of the target audience. Interview students and learn how they use the Internet and software in their studies. Take a look at the other institutions in their lives — camps, youth groups, publics schools, work place, senior center (if they are older students), other classes — and see how software and the Internet is used, if at all. Ask students how much time they spend online each day. For what purposes do they use the Internet — for chatting with friends, downloading music, locating resources for homework. How do they decide the relevance and accuracy of online resources? What types of software hold the most appeal, and why? Remember that the perceived facility with the technology of some users does not mean they are equipped to discern information critically or use it in a transformational way.

- Find out from colleagues if and how they use technology in their work and leisure time. Do they have favorite sites or software? Are they interested in incorporating it into their work, but aren't sure how? Form a study group together to share curricular ideas or start an e-mail teacher discussion list.

- What training, facilities, and equipment do educators in the learning setting need to integrate digital media into the curriculum? How does it fit into the organization's vision of education? What are next steps?

- Investigate new initiatives, such as the ORT/JECC Partnership for Technology in Education (Cleveland) and the Jewish Technology Collaborative, sponsored by the BJE of Grater New York, in which cadres of teachers are trained to infuse technology into the curriculum. These "lead teachers" then serve as mentors to fellow educators. Participate in face-to-face or online professional development opportunities, such as workshops and conferences.

- Start small and build on successes; experimenting with any new innovation takes time and a sense of adventure. Play with existing curriculum and experiment, perhaps beginning with hotlists to complement lesson plans. When comfortable, start developing new curriculum that takes further advantage of different software and internet resources. Note any change in teaching and learning activities. Always have a low-tech "Plan B" and expect the unexpected, especially when technology is involved. For example, have printouts of online materials available to hand out in case the Internet is down, or make sure that equivalent, off-line resources are readily accessible.

- Be aware that commercial Internet service providers often offer customers templates and space to create web pages. A few of these services offer free e-mail accounts, the ability to create free e-mail discussion lists, and online learning templates.

- Educational web sites, such as Kathy Schrock's Guide for Educators (http://school.discovery.com/schrockguide) and www.4teachers.org feature worksheet and quiz templates for teachers to create materials. NewSlate (www.newslate.com) is a multilingual (Hebrew, Yiddish, English, and more), customizable quiz generator.

- And finally — take risks and experiment!

BIBLIOGRAPHY

Note: In addition to the books and web sites listed below, be sure to check resources available from local central agencies for Jewish education and other educational organizations.

Note also that web sites and web addresses do change over the course of time.

Barrett, Helen. *Electronic Portfolios = Multimedia Development + Portfolio Development: The Electronic Portfolio Development Process.* (Available from electronicportfolios.com)

> Resources for using technology toward assessment, with a focus on developing electronic portfolios.

Becker, Henry J. *Internet Use by Teachers: Conditions of Professional Use and Teacher-Directed Student Use.* (Teaching, Learning, and Computing: 1998 National Survey Report 1.) Irvine, CA: Center for Research on Information Technology and Organizations, The University of California, Irvine, and The University of Minnesota, 1999. (Available from www.crito.uci.edu/TLC)

> Results and implications from a national survey of teachers' use of computer technology, their pedagogies, and their school context.

Brunner, Cornelia, and William Tally. *The New Media Literacy Handbook: An Educator's Guide to Bringing New Media into the Classroom.* New York: Anchor Books, 1999.

> An introduction to media literacy and curricular integration, with a focus on history and social studies, arts education, language arts, and science.

Curtis, Michael, et al. *Palm Handheld Computers — A complete Resource for Classroom Teachers.* Eugene, OR: ISTE, 2003.

> Rationale, sample lessons, templates, and tips for using handheld computers in the classroom. Includes companion CD-Rom with Palm OS Freeware programs.

Dockterman, David A. *Great Teaching in the One Computer Classroom.* Watertown, MA: Tom Snyder Productions, 1998.

> Provides a rationale and suggestions for using computers in the classroom, with an emphasis on successful ways of incorporating even one computer into the setting.

Dodge, Bernie. "FOCUS: Five Rules for Writing a Great WebQuest." *Leading and Learning with Technology* 28:8 (May 2001). (Available from www.iste.org)

> Recommendations for creating educationally productive and challenging WebQuests.

E-Learning for Educators: Implementing the Standards for Staff Development. Oxford, OH: National Staff Development Council, 2001. (Available from www.nsdc.org)

> Publication for staff development leaders that describes different models of e-learning for the professional development of teachers.

Evans, Eli. *Telecommunications and World Jewish Renewal.* Keynote address presented at the Conference on Media and Technology in Jewish Education for Developers and Educators, "Shaping the 58th Century with 21st Century Technology," 1997. (Available online from www. jesna.org)

> A vision of Jewish education and the telecommunications revolution.

Harris, Judi. *Design Tools for the Internet-Supported Classroom.* Alexandria, VA: ASCD, 1998.

——. "Wetware: Why Use Activity Structures?" *Learning and Leading with Technology*, 25:4 (December / January 1997-1998):13-17. (Available to ISTE members from www.iste.org)

——. *Virtual Architecture: Designing and Directing Curriculum-Based Telecollaboration.* Eugene, OR: International Society for Technology in Education, 1998. (Supporting materials available online at http://ccwf.cc.utexas.edu/~jbharris/Virtual-Architecture)

——. "Virtual Vantage Points: Using Webcams for Teleresearch." *Learning and Leading with Technology*, March 2001. (Available from www.iste.org)

> These four entries by Judi Harris are resources for designing inquiry-based educational activities and projects using the Internet.

Gordon, David T., ed. *The Digital Classroom: How Technology Is Changing the Way We Teach and Learn.* Cambridge, MA: Harvard University Letter, 2000.

> A compilation of articles and essays addressing the challenges of educational technology for the classroom.

Greenberg, Maury. *Web Page Evaluation Form*. Cleveland, OH: Jewish Education Center of Cleveland. (Available from www.jecc.org/edres/medtech/wwwevalform.pdf)

———. *Software Evaluation Form*. (Available from www.jecc.org/edres/medtech/softevalform.pdf)

———. *Virtual Field Trips: An Online WebQuest for Educators*. (Available from www.jecc.org/edres/medtech/vft/home.htm)

Online resources created for Jewish educators to facilitate the integration of software and the Internet into their practice.

Isaacs, Leora, and Caren Levine. *Technology Planning 101*. New York: JESNA, Jewish Education Service of North America, 1999. (Available from www.jesna.org)

A planning guide for integrating technology into educational settings.

Isaacs, Leora; Caren Levine; and Rebecca Goldwater. *Preliminary Survey of Distance Learning in Jewish Education*. New York: Jewish Education Service of North America, 2002. (Available from www.jesna.org)

A study of different models of e-learning for Jewish education, with an emphasis on programs for the professional development of Jewish educators.

"Technology and Jewish Education." *Jewish Education News* 23:2, Summer 2002.

This issue of JEN includes articles on integrating technology, teacher training and professional development, the school setting, and special projects in Jewish education.

ISTE, International Society for Technology in Education (www.iste.org).

Leading organization for educational technology professionals, ISTE also works to develop national educational technology standards for students, teachers, and administrators.

The Jossey-Bass Reader on Technology and Learning. San Francisco, CA: Jossey-Bass, 2000.

A collection of articles, reports, and essays by leading experts on educational technology and its impact on learning.

Kathy Schrock's Guide for Educators. (Available from http://school.discovery.com/schrockguide/index.html)

A categorized list of sites useful for enhancing curriculum and professional growth. It is updated often to include recommended sites for teaching and learning.

Kathy Schrock's Homepage. (Available from http://kathyschrock.net)

Additional resources collected by the educator, including "The One-Computer Classroom: A Review of the Internet Literature" and "The ABC's of Web Site Evaluation."

Kent, Todd W., and Robert F. McNergney. *Will Technology Really Change Education? From Blackboard To Web*. Thousand Oaks, CA: Corwin Press, 1999.

An overview of the history of technology integration into schools and lessons learned.

Mandel, Scott. *Wired into Judaism: The Internet and Jewish Education*. Denver, CO: A.R.E. Publishing, Inc., 2000.

Resources for integrating the Internet into Jewish educational settings.

———. *Wired into Teaching Jewish Holidays*. Denver, CO: A.R.E. Publishing, Inc., 2003.

———. *Wired into Teaching Jewish Virtues: An Internet Companion*. Denver, CO: A.R.E. Publishing, Inc., 2002.

———. *Wired into Teaching Torah: An Internet Companion*. Denver, CO: A.R.E. Publishing, Inc., 2001.

These three volumes are especially designed for teachers without Internet access at school, but who are online at home. Each parallels a book in the A.R.E. Teaching Series, and provides dozens of web sites related to specific subject areas. Step-by-step methodology helps Internet novices, as well as those with experience.

March, Tom. *Working the Web for Education: Theory and Practice on Integrating the Web for Learning*. (Available from www.ozline.com/learning/theory.html)

———. *The Six Web-and-Flow Activity Formats — Working the Web for Education: Activity Formats*. (Available from www.web-and-flow.com)

———. *Working the Web for Education*. (Available from www.ozline.com/learning/theory.html)

———. *Thinking Thru Linking.* (Available from www.ozline.com/learning/thinking.html)

———. *The Six Web-and-Flow Activity Formats.* (Available from www.web-and-flow.com/help/formats.html)

———. *Ten Stages of Working the Web for Education.* (Available from www.infotoday.com/MMSchools/may99/march.htm)

> In these entries, Tom March provides resources for designing inquiry-based educational activities and projects using the Internet.

Matanky, Leonard A. "What We Know About . . . Computers in Jewish Education." In *What We Know About Jewish Education: A Handbook of Today's Research for Tomorrow's Jewish Education*, edited by Stuart L. Kelman. Los Angeles, CA: Torah Aura Productions, 1992.

> An overview of Jewish education and educational technology, research, and implications for Jewish settings.

McKenzie, Jamie. "The New Lesson Plan." *From Now On* 9, no. 8, April 2000. (Available from www.fno.org/apr2000/newplan.html)

> Essay on how the Web can be used for creating content-rich curriculum.

Media Media

> An electronic newsletter published by JESNA for those who use technology and media in Jewish education (www.jesna.org).

Milken Family Foundation (www.mff.org/edtech)

> Research and resources for educational professionals and lay leaders.

Papert, Seymour. *Technology in Schools: To Support the System or Render it Obsolete?* (Available from www.mff.org/edtech)

> Article on new ways to envision education in the digital age.

Rein, Debra. *What Is Effective Integration of Technology and Does It Make a Difference?* Paper presented at the International Conference on Learning with Technology, 2000. (Available from www.l2l.org/iclt/2000)

> Lessons learned on the integration of technologies and related professional development.

Romm, Diane. *The Jewish Guide To the Internet.* 3d ed. Northvale, NJ: Jason Aronson Inc., 2003.

> A guide to the Internet that includes resources for Jewish education. The companion web site is found at www.jewishinternetguide.com.

Schneider, Roxanne. "Homework Helpers To the Rescue." *Technology and Learning*, October 2001. (Available from www.techlearning.com)

> Overview of different models of homework helpers that are currently available.

Shaping the 58th Century with 21st Century Technology: Proceedings from the Conference on Media and Technology in Jewish Education for Developers and Educators, 1997. (Available from www.jesna.org)

> Papers and presentations on educational technology and its implications for Jewish education.

Sink or Swim: Internet Search Tools & Techniques (www.sci.ouc.bc.ca/libr/connect96/search.htm)

> Overview of search engines, subject directories, and practical tips for using them.

Schrumm, Lynne. *Online Professional Development — Suggestions for Success.* (Available from ww.att.com/learningnetwork/virtualacademy/success.html)

> Article that discusses a range of models of online learning and how individual learning styles can be matched to appropriate learning environments.

Tapscott, Donald. *Growing Up Digital: The Rise of the Net Generation.* (1998). New York: McGraw-Hill, 1998.

———. *The Net Generation and the School.* (Available from www.mff.org/edtech)

> Essays on the media habits of young people, and how these characteristics can impact learning styles.

Summer Camping: Teaching in Your Pajamas

Gerard W. Kaye

"Just how Jewish is this camp anyway?" is a regular question that parents ask camp directors when they want to be sure that their child will have a "fun" time during the summer and not wind up at summer-school-in-the-woods. Most of the time, the answer that they are given is something like, "Well, camp has lots of recreational activities and we do have occasional fun discussions about Jewish themes." That's usually a lot more palatable to some parents than explaining that there are worship services, Hebrew learning sessions, Jewish content presentations, and, of course, "fun discussions" as well. But both are really true. Camp is a place where Jewish life can be fun, and the excitement of the out-of-doors can allow counselors to talk about the values of Judaism.

Jewish camping has emerged as a popular and recognized tool for Jewish education in the past decade. Over the years, kids returned from Jewish camp knowing previously unknown prayers, singing Hebrew songs (the meaning of which they don't usually know), and able to make Havdalah — a ceremony that most liberal Jewish families rarely incorporate into their weekly ritual.

The influence and importance of the camp experience is recognized by a number of relatively new mainstream organizations, including The Foundation for Jewish Camping, The North American Alliance for Informal Education, and Jewish Federations across the country. Major Jewish research facilities are studying camping in order to discover the "big secret" of why it works so well.

Staff members of Jewish camps understand the influence and importance of camping experiences for a child's social and identity formation; camp obviously offers a world in which Jewish life and learning can be integrated. Soccer is played every day, drama rehearsals are led by the same people sitting at the lunch table, and Hebrew is the language of announcements, activities, and names of buildings. The essential circumstance that camp offers is a unified community in which the members are mutually supportive and behavior is comparative within a peer cohort. At camp, there is no need for mom or dad to tell a child what to do and when to do it. Therefore, the norms of the community become the norms of the individual.

"THE NORM" OF CAMP AS A LEARNING COMMUNITY

Weekly and daily worship services are an assumed activity in which everyone participates. The same is largely true in all of the learning at camp, for just as worship is part of the regular schedule at camp, so it is likewise true of the educational program. Regularly scheduled Jewish learning sessions are part of each youngster's activities and are assumed to be the norm by the camper, by the staff, and (to a greater or lesser degree) by the parents as well. In simplest terms, when each part of the day reinforces the rest, then the importance of Jewish identity becomes apparent. Art activities that focus on a Jewish learning theme make the interpretation of a Jewish lesson clearer.

The importance of peer reinforcement cannot be too strongly emphasized. Coming to synagogue with one's parents after a rushed dinner (dressed in clothes of which mom approves) at the same time that friends are at the movies, doesn't make prayer wonderfully attractive. At camp, everyone participates in *Tefilah* (worship) — not only the children, but all of the adults as well. The truth is that we have an easier job of getting youngsters, or for that matter anyone of any age, to appreciate and "buy into" the worship experience. Worshipers can wear blue jeans (or on Shabbat pick clothes from the suitcase of the kid in the next bunk), and might just get to touch forearms with the girl or boy standing nearby during the *"Amidah."*

Give me a group of junior high or high school teens, services written and timed into the camp schedule, a couple of bad guitars, photocopied and dog-eared versions of the *"Barchu," "Shema," "Amidah," "Alaynu"* and *"Kaddish,"* interspersed with two poems by Rod McKuen and a couple of Joni Mitchell songs, a rousing chorus of "Miriam's Song," and I will show you real spirituality!

THE EDUCATIONAL PROGRAM

The whole business of learning in camp comes down to a simple reality: education can fit anywhere during the camp day. The hardest part of camp is a mirror image, and can feel quite overwhelming — that we have full days and immense space available for education. Most of us aren't accustomed to working this way. We usually have a slice of time to implement whatever it is we are trying to do; our enemies are the Palm Pilot and wristwatch. Camp directors always want to make things fit so that they don't aggravate the folks in the kitchen too much. Great programs take this into account, making mealtime part of an activity so that everybody wins.

Most camps have regularly scheduled learning times during the day or the week, whether with a focus on Jewish content, Hebrew, worship, or even song. (Most of the songs we sing either come from biblical or other Jewish texts, and the Hebrew words provide a chance to teach a little more Hebrew.)

Selection of Curriculum

What to teach is a crucial decision in camp planning. Religious schools and day schools start with a curriculum designed to span the years that the students are enrolled (for example, every year between kindergarten and twelfth grade). Camping is very different, given the fact that children don't necessarily attend every summer. Even campers who are regulars often don't remember a lesson taught 11 months earlier. Even when they do remember, their developmental stage has changed, along with their public and Jewish education.

Camp curricula frequently include topics that are relatively universal. Israel is a popular theme because of our desire to connect campers to the Jewish homeland, and there are often a number of

Israeli counselors in camp, providing human resources for a currently difficult to teach subject. Torah narratives and Jewish values are also the focus of learning in camps across the country.

Informal education in a camp setting does not mean that there is no curriculum or lesson plans. Quite the opposite — learning is intentional and deliberate. In fact, in many camps, the goal is to integrate Jewish learning into as many activities of the day as possible. Therefore, themes can be part of the arts activities, the evening program, worship, and Hebrew class, as well as recreational times.

The best themes are those that the available staff can make come alive. Even though it might be interesting to develop a program in camp about the Talmudic explanation of charitable giving, the staff may not be up to the challenge. On the other hand, taking advantage of the gifts and talents of specific individuals can yield significant results.

Just because we have three or four full-time weeks with children does not mean we can teach everything in the *Encyclopaedia Judaica*. Actually, narrow casting is much more effective than broad casting. Emphasizing three or four key issues in a theme is much more effective than trying to convey the entire breadth of Jewish knowledge. Messages need to be clear and direct and the counselor needs to understand the content and values they are passing along. If the counselor doesn't get it, the campers surely won't. Know what you want to say, and say it concisely.

Teachable Moments

Don't overlook any moment of the day as a teachable moment. Mealtimes are great for conversation and discussion with the campers at your table.[1] If your camp begins meals with *"HaMotzi"* (the blessing before eating) and ends with *"Birkat HaMazon"* (the blessing after the meal), discuss the content of those blessings and the obvious Hebrew words your campers might know. When you and your campers go down to the waterfront or the pool for the first time in the session, the waterfront director can teach them one of Judaism's mandates to parents — you must teach your children a craft and teach them how to swim.

---

[1]When you sit at the table, always sit in the middle not at an end . . . that way you can see and talk with all of the kids. And slouch. They are shorter than you and want to be talking to your face.

One prayer in the morning service lists values, among which is the importance of visiting the sick. Camp nurses, however, generally prefer that campers don't visit their friends in the Health Center so as not to spread whatever variation of camp crud is going around. However, passing out paper and pencil (either during the service or just after) for campers to write a get well note to their bunkmates reinforces the impact of this prayer.

Even though Genesis is far from the summer weekly Torah portion, reviewing the responsibilities that God gave to Adam in overseeing the earth is a great way to open a conversation about environment. Don't forget nighttime as well. Your Camp Director may not be enthusiastic about keeping the campers up late to see the rotation of the night sky, but the majesty of creation is rarely better felt.[2]

Informal Education Techniques in a Camp Setting

It has been over 25 years since Dr. William Cutter brought Confluent Education to the Jewish educational world from the sphere of general education. Confluent Education is the "bringing together" of the cognitive (thinking/intellectual exercises) with the affective (the emotional). When we tap into students' (or in this case, campers') feelings (via guided fantasies, values clarification activities, or bibliodrama during which they put themselves in the shoes of a character), we also affect the intellectual realm. We have worked hard in the world of Jewish education to create good feelings and a sense of spirituality. Yet, we sometimes forget the real need to substantiate good feelings with good knowledge. This is at the heart of confluent learning.

When religious schools are successful, they are able to convey both a substantial knowledge base, as well the feeling of being engaged with the subject matter. The advantage that camp provides is the ability to merge the two into the third level of confluence — psychomotor response — or doing something. In plain words, having been taught a lesson and then feeling the application or importance of it can then change behavior. Action can follow learning so that the sense of accomplishment is more complete.

Many camps exemplify this with the *tallit*. Most youngsters received a *tallit* at their Bar or Bat Mitzvah. In liberal synagogues, a parent or grandparent often presents it; the youngster wears it for the ceremony, and the *tallit* may then emerge for special occasions. However, at camp, counselors can help each camper to make a *tallit*. Campers learn how to tie the knots as the meaning of *tzitzit* is explained. They can decorate the fabric with tie dye or intricately sewn patterns, and then regularly wear their *tallit* at camp services before taking it home. Thus, the teens tie their own feelings to the knots and fringes.

But the learning isn't over! You can bring campers to the ropes course where they will learn how important it is to belay their friends on the other end of the rope. This makes the point that the *tzitzit* — the knots and fringes on the *tallit* — can play the same anchoring role between the Jew and God. The ropes course is where campers also learn the mandate of *Kol Yisrael Arayvim Zeh BaZeh* — all Jews are responsible one for another.

So you see that Jewish learning goes on all day . . . and we haven't even talked about soccer yet.

ROLES OF THE COUNSELOR

Counselors in camp (usually in their late teens or early twenties, recently graduated from high school or are in college), are as much the client of the camp as is the camper. It is the counselor's role to be both teacher and student. Camps frequently create a learning process that reflects this need. When the process works well, the learning begins before camp as counselors become part of the process for selecting what will be taught and how. Throughout the summer, counselors are discussion leaders, skit performers, individual tutors, and curriculum designers. The counselor is older sibling, first nurse, play leader and playmate, guide and teacher — always a friend, but never a buddy.

Counselor as Role Model

One cannot say too much about the notion of role modeling. While this point is usually made in staff orientation, it would be wonderful if a staff trainer videotaped each counselor individually during the day. Seeing a video of your eyes rolling in disgust, your head nodding asleep during a program, and

---

[2] A nightwalk program is described in further detail in Chapter 13, "Creating Programs That Captivate Teens" by

Debbie Findling, pp. 127-139 in this Handbook.

the silliness of you, a six-foot tall counselor talking to the air over the head of a four-foot tall camper, makes a much bigger impact than just about anything that could be said.

Although my title may be "musical director" of a Jewish theater camp that caters to children ages five through 13, I wear many hats in serving the needs of these young campers. I am coach, teacher, counselor, and friend. Sixteen years of teaching preschool has taught me that what is really important when preparing children for a camp theatrical experience is not dwelling on that final performance, but rather working on building self-esteem, self-confidence, and the responsibility of being a team player. If I have to review one song or one dance 50 times to give one child the chance to say, "Wow, I can do this," then I feel that the time was well spent.

I have only two rules at camp: you must try your hardest, and you must never laugh at another child who is trying his/her hardest. When children are able to follow these simple rules, their final performance is always a smash hit.

(Kim Lausin, Beachwood, Ohio)

Counselor as Educator

Find out the thematic focus of your unit as soon as possible. Don't assume that you really don't know anything about it — you probably have gained some background along the way in your own Jewish education. Thirty minutes with a book (or the Internet) will not make you an expert, but will offer you some beginning background that will serve you well.

Many Jewish camps have educational specialists who prepare materials for you before camp and who can help you during the summer as well. In fact, there may even be staff at camp whose job it is to be the program organizers for special Jewish learning pieces. If such individuals call upon you for help, ask them to spend a little time with you in advance of the event.

Counselor as Discussion Leader

Most learning events at camp focus around a presentation and are followed by activity or discussion groups. Remember that learning events don't have to be limited to a single time during the day. They can come in on the waterfront by ski boat or show up in fortune cookies at dinner. Here are a few more ideas that you might use:

- Slip a note into each camper's pillowcase with a question or a quote.

- Set up a question box in the dining hall into which kids can drop answers (put pencil and paper next to it!).

- Put together a marching band and make a big announcement on the ball field.

- Develop a treasure hunt that leads campers to the next theme.

- Use a political convention motif to set off the discussions.

- If there are horses at camp, some major figure (you dressed up) should come riding in.

- Ask Israeli staff to show you how to make a "fire sign" to announce a project.

- Interview historical characters on your camp radio or TV station.

Remember, you are limited only by your imagination (and your camp director's worries about the budget). If you are charged up by the idea, your kids will be, too.

You will likely be called upon to lead the discussions. When that happens, you will no doubt be given a series of questions designed to help campers think further about the topic. If you are not given this guidance, sit with a fellow staff member (other counselor, Rabbi, unit head, educator) to brainstorm leading questions in advance. Questions that contribute to a flowing discussion might include:

- Does this sound like something you have ever seen, heard, felt?

- Who do you know who has this kind of idea?

- Do you agree with Lisa/David?

- Do your parents ever say things like this to you?

- Is this something that only Jewish people think about?

- Are there people who say this is really right/wrong?

In many camps, discussions are held on the grass under a tree. If your group is a consistent one, always meet at the same tree so that campers don't hunt around for the group — and you don't either. Second, sit in a circle and ask all of the kids to sit up without leaning against each other. Don't bother trying to get them not to pull the grass — this is a battle you can't possibly win. The first and second time you meet with the group (when you are still a little hazy with names), ask one of the campers whose name you know to move next to you. This will establish for the rest of the group that you are familiar with some of the kids. However, when you call on a camper, ask for his/her name until you learn it.

Now here's a key to your success as a discussion leader: don't be afraid of silence. When you ask a question, wait until someone answers it. You can rephrase the question if you think that it wasn't well framed, but do not provide the answer yourself just because the campers aren't popping up with it instantly. Some won't know the answer, and others won't talk because they don't want to appear as if they are know-it-alls. It takes time to think of thoughtful answers to thoughtful questions; thinking time is important to a good discussion.

Be sure to listen to the words and ideas that the kids present. As often as not, their thoughts will flesh out Jewish ideas in ways that the author of the learning activity might not have considered. Campers' perspectives, albeit totally different from the expected focus, are often unusual and insightful. Help campers to be right, rather than jumping on the bandwagon of "my opinion is the best." Find a way to interpret an idea so that it can nourish the premise, even when it seems to contradict it. This is a counselor's role throughout the day.

Finally, do not always call on the campers who have their hand up all the time. It is okay to call on those who don't volunteer to speak; some are more shy than others and are pleased to be asked an opinion. Be careful of calling on your "favorites" all the time. Look to the child who no one else knows how to respond to as your personal contact. Find an opening to have a private chat with those kids who just don't seem to be part of the group, helping them to discover the questions that are burning to be asked. The Passover *Haggadah* tells us that there is a child who doesn't know how to ask, and we are mandated to open their mouth. Such kids come to summer camp, too.

When should you end a discussion? Not necessarily when the clock strikes the appointed hour, and certainly not when every question has been answered completely. Rather, end the discussion group when there are still lots of campers waving their hands, and yet most of the information has been unfolded. That way, campers will want to come back for more. Sometimes they get to come back tomorrow, and sometimes not for years until you bump into them in the Los Angeles Farmers' Market or in Times Square.

Counselor as "Continuing Educator"

Are formal educational programs and discussion groups the only learning time during the day? Certainly not. Every part of the camp lends itself to the notion that it is a laboratory for Jewish identity and understanding. A quick look in a prayer book will show campers that Jews have *brachot* for all kinds of occasions in daily life, from rainbows to tough crossings on the canoe trip. You don't need to be a Rabbi to find them; just skim the table of contents and turn to the right page in most *Siddurim* (prayer books).

Counselor as Learner

About this time, you may be frustrated, thinking that you just don't know this much "Jewish stuff." Yet, you surely do know some of it, or have opinions on it. Hopefully, your camp supports your Jewish growth before the summer, when they send preparatory materials, and at staff orientation. Some camps also look to create opportunities for staff to learn at other times during the summer, for example, sessions during which a few staff join together at a meal for "Food for Thought." Sometimes, there are separate hours during the day for Judaica, as well as counseling techniques. The camp library often has books and displays set aside for counselors to select stories for lights-out programs or to learn more about the session theme itself. One camp has dedicated a day of its orientation week to a mini-conference; local Jewish educators teach a variety of mini-courses that tie into the summer program and are topics of interest to staff.

Rabbis, educators, program directors, and worship coordinators seem like obvious folks to help.

There are lots of others, though, who can assist in teaching your campers as well. Consider the sports director, waterfront director, and horseback riding staff who can be co-opted into your goals. For example, these specialists can be helpful in setting up situations that teach campers alternative ways of understanding that "All Israel is responsible one for another." Share a quote from Talmud with the wrangler, showing that Jewish law requires that we must treat animals kindly *(tza'ar ba'alay chayim)*.

Finally, when you absolutely don't know the answer to a question that campers ask about Judaism (or anything else), remember the old staff maxim: "I don't know either — let's go find out together."

Counselor as Tone Setter

And now a word about energy — yours! Everybody who works in camping lives by the first and most essential maxim: enthusiasm radiates enthusiasm! If you are hoping that campers will feel energized and involved in what goes on throughout the day, they must see their counselor leading the way. A depressive counselor who is always complaining about the program, the unit head, the director, and the kids will surely be the head of a bunk of campers who do the same (except they will also complain about their counselor and be homesick to boot!). Starting with *Tefilah*, staff needs to set a tone of involvement with clearly apparent singing, reading, and attentive focus on the *Siddur*. From here, the ball field is easy. Cheering for your campers, telling an animated story at the campfire, and leading the way when a volunteer cabin is needed, makes kids feel like they should each win the Best Camper Award.

JEWISH VALUES IN A CAMP SETTING

Camp is a perfect place for Jewish values to focus the community's actions. Setting up a "direction pole" for personal Jewish values in the center of camp reminds everyone of those unique Jewish issues. (Direction pole? You know — those poles with cute little arrows that point the way to different cities with miles on them.)

Language among campers and staff alike is a real opportunity in camp. On Yom Kippur, the traditional prayer book has 44 lines that begin *"al chet"* (For the sin which we have sinned). Eleven of these lines (fully one quarter of the ways that we can really mess up) have to do with language. In most camps that I have ever been in, at least ten of these pop up every few hours. You can ignore them, join in, rebuke the campers or take advantage of the opportunity. Rabbi Joseph Telushkin, in his short book *Words That Hurt, Words That Heal*, reminds us of the Talmudic teaching that whoever shames a person in public, it is as if they shed their blood. You can teach this to your bunk when one youngster becomes the butt of embarrassment.

While the entire spectrum of Jewish values could certainly be taught at camp, some values lend themselves more naturally to camp life than others. The following is an incomplete, but beginning list:

- *Bayn adam l'chavero* - relationships between people (what do we do with the camper we aren't crazy about)

- *Bayn adam l'Makom* - relationships between people and God

- *Bal tashchit* - the mandate against destruction of nature (the environmental issue including food fights at lunch)

- *Bikur cholim* - visiting the sick (remember the note to kids in the infirmary)

- *Hachnasat orchim* - providing hospitality to strangers (welcoming visitors to camp)

- *Kashrut* - watching what and how much you eat

- *Klal Yisrael* - concern for Jews everywhere (even those who go to other camps)

- *Ma'asim tovim* - the practice of general decent acts

- *Mazon* - providing food for people

- *Rodef shalom* - pursuit of peaceful relations (great for cabin disagreements)

- *Shmirat haguf* - respect for one's own body as well as others (not just physical)

- *Talmud Torah* - Jewish learning in all its forms

- *Tikkun olam* - repairing the world (starting with the trash on the camp's grounds)

- *Tza'ar ba'alay chayim* - compassion for animals

- *Tzedakah* - providing for the needs of all, Jewish and non-Jewish

There are many more such values, and it really depends on your creativity as to how you can translate them to your campers. Sometimes it can be done through a poster in the cabin after voting on the values that campers and staff prize most highly, and sometimes it can be done by using an appropriate word in the midst of a *vikuach* (conflict). Most of all, success in teaching values of any kind depends on a decision by the entire camp community that it counts at least as much as soccer skills.

And the whole business of tattooing and piercing? See *Randy's Navel Piercing* for a good resource.

JEWISH RELIGIOUS ISSUES IN CAMP

Do you think that it would have messed up some "vast eternal plan" if Chanukah was in the middle of the summer and Tishah B'Av was commemorated at another time? Couldn't we have a wonderful upbeat celebration rather than the sad commemorations of the most troubling events in Jewish history? On the other hand, if not for summer camp, most Jews would never really know about the ninth day of the month of Av on the Hebrew calendar.

Camp religious practice is frequently confusing, even in those camps that are sponsored by a specific synagogue movement such as United Synagogue of Conservative Judaism's Ramah camps, the Reform Movement's camps, and B'nai Akiva's Moshava camps. This is largely due to the fact that campers, staff, and faculty come from different communities, each with different customs.

For those who are knowledgeable enough and open enough to listen to new ideas, this is really exciting and interesting. But for a ten-year-old, it can just feel "wrong" because the practice is not what he/she has been taught. Telling a child that he/she is wrong is to deny his/her parents, Rabbi, friends, and, ultimately, the child him/herself. Certainly we don't want to do that. Opening a camper to other ideas doesn't repudiate him/her, but adds to knowledge and experiences.

On the other hand, not every idea that somebody presents is automatically correct. Camps frequently mistake novelty for creativity, especially in Jewish practice, and so we might construct an Ark

facing west rather than east just to try something new. We rise on tiptoe or bow in the service for prayers that "speak to us," creating a worship experience that more resembles Pilates than *Tefilah*. Camp is a place where creativity is essential. This is true in the realm of the arts, in sports, and also in Jewish practice. But no one would think that it's okay to swat a soccer ball with a baseball bat or to hoist a sail upside down and expect the boat to move. Why do some take similar uninformed liberties with Judaism?

An ancient Jewish maxim instructs us to find ourselves a teacher. This is particularly useful in camp where Jewish learning is frequently on the fly. Hillel directors are great at 45-second Jewish lessons in the university corridor. Counselors need to be able to do that, too.

When you don't quite "get it," ask the question yourself. Better, of course, is to create an intentional community in which many of these ideas have been thought out in advance of the summer. You don't have to depend on the "Jewish specialist" in camp to learn a few practical notions that interest and concern you. Go to the list of Jewish values above and type them into the search engine on the Internet, and do some serious reading. Only in relatively modern times did "Rabbi" become a job title. Before that, Rabbis taught Judaism on Shabbat and led services, while the rest of the week they were carpenters and cobblers.

CONCLUSION

Chances are that your camp has wonderful facilities including (perhaps) a high ropes course, a great waterfront with sailboats, sports facilities that could rival those of many high schools, meeting spaces of all kinds, arts facilities, and more. The single most important spot in camp is none of these. Cut the horses loose, let the sailboats go downstream, take down the ropes (both high and low), and leave just a log — that's right, just a simple log on the ground. A log that has a camper on one side and a caring and devoted counselor on the other, with nothing in between. After all, this is the powerful relationship that camp fosters. When a counselor and camper go to brush their teeth at bedtime and the child looks up and asks, "You know that stuff we were talking about today about God, do you believe it?" this is the teachable moment. This is when you teach in your pajamas.

BIBLIOGRAPHY

Barish, Shirley. *The Big Book of Great Teaching Ideas: For Jewish Schools, Youth Groups, Camps and Retreats.* New York: UAHC Press, 1998.

> Organized by age group and content area (Bible, holidays, etc.), this book has a plethora of ideas that enrich any Jewish teaching situation.

Cogan, Lainie Blum, and Judy Weiss. *Teaching Haftarah: Background, Insights, and Strategies for Understanding the Prophets.* Denver, CO: A.R.E. Publishing, Inc., 2002.

> In this comprehensive teacher manual, a concise summary of each Haftarah is followed by Rabbinic interpretations, literary and historical analyses, exploration of the connection between the Haftarah and its Sedra (or holiday), as well as creative discussion questions and exercises that enable students to relate personally to the text.

Elkins, Dov Peretz. *Jewish Guided Imagery: A How-To Book for Rabbis, Educators, and Group Leaders.* Princeton, NJ: Growth Associates, 1996.

> A classic that applies humanistic psychological principles and practices to Jewish themes. While some of the activities may be a bit dated, the book's goal is useful for today's situations.

Freeman, Susan. *Teaching Hot Topics: Jewish Values, Resources, and Activities.* Denver, CO: A.R.E. Publishing, Inc., 2003.

> A valuable resource for teachers of teenagers on complex issues, such as abortion, euthanasia, animal experimentation, consumerism, school violence, cloning, ethics of business, death penalty, sexuality, and the ethics of war. Each chapter features an overview, scenarios, text study passages from both Jewish and secular sources, and numerous activities based on a wide variety of pedagogic methods. An accompanying Student Companion is also available.

———. *Teaching Jewish Virtues: Sacred Sources and Arts Activities.* Denver, CO: A.R.E. Publishing, Inc., 1999.

> This resource for teachers features background material, extensive texts, and imaginative arts activities for 22 key *middot* (virtues). See also *Wired into Teaching Jewish Virtues: An Internet Companion* by Scott Mandel (A.R.E., 2002).

Goodman, Robert. *Teaching Jewish Holidays: History, Values, and Activities.* rev. ed. Denver, CO: A.R.E. Publishing, Inc., 1997.

> In addition to a complete historic overview of each holiday and extensive lists of holiday vocabulary with definitions, this teacher manual contains dozens of creative individual and group strategies for every grade level, as well as all-school and family activities. See also *Wired into Teaching Jewish Holidays: An Internet Companion* by Scott Mandel (A.R.E., 2003).

Goodman, Roberta Louis, and Sherry H. Blumberg. *Teaching about God and Spirituality: A Resource for Jewish Settings.* Denver, CO: A.R.E. Publishing, Inc., 2002.

> This source book aims to encourage and guide educators in their own learning and teaching about God and spirituality. Fifty-two chapters written by over 40 experts are divided into four sections: theology, education, teacher education lessons, and learner lessons for all ages, including family education.

Kadden, Barbara Binder, and Bruce Kadden. *Teaching Jewish Life Cycle: Traditions and Activities.* Denver, CO: A.R.E. Publishing, Inc., 1997.

> This book for teachers features background information on every stage of life, insights from Jewish tradition, and hundreds of creative activities for all ages.

———. *Teaching Mitzvot: Concepts, Values, and Activities.* rev. ed. Denver, CO: A.R.E. Publishing, Inc., 2003.

> Each of the 41 chapters in this teacher manual features a different *mitzvah*. An overview, text study, and activities for every age group round out this exceptional resource.

———. *Teaching Tefilah: Insights and Activities on Prayer.* Denver, CO: A.R.E. Publishing, Inc., 1994.

> This teacher handbook on prayer offers chapters on each section of the worship service. Each begins with an overview and text study and is followed by provocative and creative activities, including Hebrew enrichment and ideas for families.

Loeb, Sorel Goldberg, and Barbara Binder Kadden. *Teaching Torah: A Treasury of Insights and Activities.* rev. ed. Denver, CO: A.R.E. Publishing, Inc., 1997.

This classic manual for teachers provides a synopsis of each of the 54 weekly Torah portions, insights by commentators of yesterday and today, and over 1,000 strategies that analyze, extend, and personalize the text. See also *Wired into Teaching Torah: An Internet Companion* by Scott Mandel (A.R.E., 2001).

Reisman, Bernard, and Joel Reisman. *The New Jewish Experiential Book.* 2d ed. Hoboken, NJ: KTAV Publishing House, 2002.

This is the return of a classic! A new edition of what was the "bible" of many involved in the informal Jewish educational world.

Rosenak, Michael. *Tree of Life, Tree of Knowledge: Conversations with the Torah.* New York: Perseus Books Group, 2001.

A sweet treasure of a book that uses Torah study to address philosophical issues of Jewish education.

CHAPTER 24

Curriculum Planning: A Model for Understanding

Nachama Skolnik Moskowitz

*A*nne sat at her kitchen table, a large mug of coffee by her side. Today, she thought about her class of second semester fifth graders and their upcoming unit on Pesach. For years, she taught this class pretty much the same way. She had them make a "Ten Plagues Kit" to use at their own Sedarim at home. They visited the "matzah factory" to see how matzah was made, they did a play for the lower grades on Elijah visiting different homes during Pesach, and corresponded with a class their age in Israel to see how they celebrated the holiday. Students (and their parents) loved this particular unit — it was fun and engaging. But Anne was dissatisfied, and she wasn't quite sure why.

Many teachers plan their units pretty much the same way as Anne — they think about what worked in previous years, perhaps checking textbooks or teacher guides for ideas, or even going online and asking if "anyone has any great ideas" for the particular subject. But unit planning, and preparation for a specific class, should be more thoughtful and coherent. Anne's particular unit, while fun, has several problems, including that it is disjointed, lacks a "big idea" about the holiday, and has no depth for students in fifth grade. This chapter offers a format for planning that helps create developmentally appropriate, interesting, and engaging learning for students, no matter whether they are four-year-olds, 14-year-olds, or adults.

STEP 1: THE BIG PICTURE

Many teachers, because of time pressures, take a one-day-at-a-time stance to lesson planning. While they might have a sense of what they want to teach ("I'm in the Henrietta Szold unit," or "We're getting ready to cover the value of *derech eretz* — appropriate behavior"), they often feel that planning a specific unit up front, in detail, will take too much time. And so, each lesson is planned separately: ("I think I'll show the movie of the Torah scribe working, and then I'll give students a quill to try it themselves."). While this may seem time-efficient, it really is not. Moreover, groundwork that might need to be laid in the second lesson for what the teacher decides to do during the fourth can become a moot point.

Unit planning, rather than lesson planning, is an important beginning point to assure learning success. When a full unit is planned in advance:

- More time may be spent up front, but less is spent on a lesson-by-lesson basis. Teachers later flesh out specifics, but the broad brush strokes and the hard work of learning design will already have been accomplished.

- Learning has the potential to be coherent — with lessons building logically upon each other, and learning tied together. Anne, our Pesach teacher, has a smorgasbord of activities, with no flow from one to the other. One can only imagine what important ideas students remember about Pesach a month after her unit is concluded.

- A teacher can avoid the wistful sigh, "I wish I had done X when starting this unit, but I didn't realize I'd needed to lay that groundwork." A planned unit helps anticipate those issues.

- Supplies can be ordered well in advance of any administrative deadlines.

Anne knew that she needed to begin in a different way. She prided herself on the strong Jewish background she gained in college 20 years ago, and rarely did any new research in advance of lesson planning. This time, however, she decided to read the chapter on Passover in the holiday book her school director bought the staff last year as a "thank-you" for their commitment. She roped her husband into joining her in study ("two heads are better than one," she told him). They spent a couple of hours reading and talking, making sure they both understood the information. Anne was surprised by how superficial her knowledge of Pesach had been — basically, the facts of the story and the ritual observances gleaned from years of family Sedarim.

I write my lesson plans twice, first in pencil, then in pen. The first time through, I write down everything that I think I need to accomplish in the coming week. Then I look over what I have written and ask myself some questions. How many of the senses have I involved in a week's plans? Have I offered any opportunities for academically weak students to use their strengths? Do the students get a chance to move around?

Usually, at this point, I have to make some changes. I am still covering the same ground academically, but now I turn to my reference library for different ways to teach those lessons. I also look back over the past month's plans at this time. Have I used music, drama, food, or games in the past 30 days? If the answer is no to any of these areas, then it is time again to incorporate them into this coming week's work. Now I can write my plans in ink.

(Maura Pollak, Tulsa, Oklahoma)

There are many ways to describe the lack of depth that occurs in Jewish (and general) educational settings. "A mile wide and an inch deep" describes a curriculum that:

- has no depth of meaning.

- offers a lot of often disparate information ("here are the 20 facts I'm going to test you on when the Pesach unit is done").

- includes "cute" projects that take an inordinate amount of time when weighed against the importance of what is learned (Anne's

ten plagues kit is one example, as it doesn't build understanding of key ideas of Pesach).

An "iceberg curriculum" is similar, in that teachers often focus on the tips of the icebergs, ignoring the important depth of information below the surface (see figure 1).

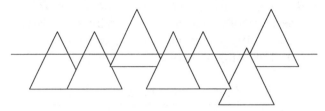

Figure 1

Anne's flitting from project to project, each not connected to the other, is a great example of a teacher jumping from tip to tip of icebergs. She taught "about" the Ten Plagues, how *matzah* is made, Elijah's significance, and how Pesach is celebrated in Israel. However, she missed a lot of depth of meaning that lay below the surface.

Note in the iceberg diagram, how the blocks of ice touch and meld into each other under the water, pointing to the possible integration of content and concepts. To gain the benefit of the icebergs, learners must go deep to uncover concepts and information lying below the surface. But that means that the teacher must also "go deep" in his or her preparation.

In her reading about Pesach, Anne was especially taken by one statement, "Why is it that so many Jews were active in the civil rights movement of the 1960s, though their own Jewish education was so minimal? Could it be that they had sat year after year at their Seder and heard the impassioned plea to "let my people go"? Could it be that these Jews took seriously the injunction, "in every generation, each person must see him or herself as if he/she personally left Egypt"?

Stirred by this idea, Anne remembered a workshop she had attended the year before on a model of planning called "Understanding by Design."[1] In this model, the beginning point is the development of an "enduring understanding," a big idea that organizes learning. Anne decided to try to develop an enduring understanding for her Pesach unit.

[1]Grant Wiggins and Jay McTighe, *Understanding by Design* (Alexandria, VA: Association for Supervision and Curriculum Development, 1998).

Understanding by Design began sweeping the country at the end of the 1990s. Starting with what is called "enduring understandings," this model is unique in its "backwards design process." Rather than setting a goal for learning, then creating learning activities, and finally deciding on the assessment process, UbD (as it is affectionately called) moves from the enduring understanding to the assessment (what the authors call "evidence of understanding"), and only then to the development of learning activities (see figure 2).

The Backwards Design Process[2]

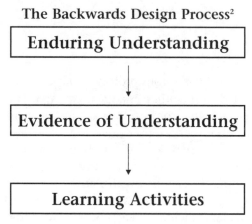

Figure 2

While it sounds rather simple, the power of good UbD units comes from attention to the backward process and to developing each stage completely before moving on to the next. A good enduring understanding (to be explained, below) can take two or more hours of study and conversation to develop. The evidence of understanding, often a performance assessment, provides a clear learning goal that students need to be able to complete successfully to demonstrate their attainment of the enduring understanding. Finally, the learning activities help prepare students for the evidence of understanding stage.

The Beginning: Enduring Understandings

Traditional curriculum development begins with the articulation of goals or objectives. An *Under-*

standing by Design unit has a different starting place, that of an enduring understanding (EU) . . . or a really big idea that frames learning. Because of the largeness of the EU, students will dig into one aspect of the big idea during their course of study. Over time, with multiple exposures at different ages and stages, students come to grasp the many facets of the enduring understanding.

Assume that the full circle (figure 3 below) represents the following enduring understanding:

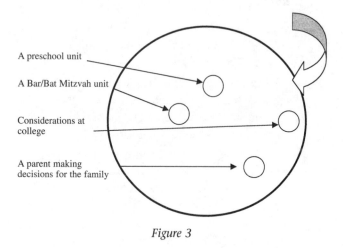

Figure 3

Attention to the ideas behind ritual observance strengthens the chain of Jewish tradition and leads to a deeper connection with *K'lal Yisrael* (the connections among the Jewish people).[3]

This is an *enduring, big idea that has lasting value beyond the classroom.*[4] A person can approach one aspect of it as a preschooler, another aspect when considering the significance of her Bat Mitzvah, another as she wonders how to observe Rosh HaShanah while at college, and yet another as a parent weighing issues of home holiday observance with his toddler. This is the meaning of lasting value.

An enduring understanding is also the *big idea or core process at the heart of a discipline.* "Discipline" here refers to the areas of study (e.g., science, math, philosophy, theology). As a core process or big idea, an EU is not a set of facts, but rather something that a professional grapples with in his her area of expertise. The following are enduring

---

[2]Note that this is the design, or curriculum development process. It is not the process by which students learn. When a UbD unit is taught, the starting point for students is in the learning activities, culminating in the assessment (evidence of understanding). They may be introduced to the enduring understanding at any point along the way.

[3]All enduring understandings listed in this chapter were used in curriculum developed by the Jewish Education Center of Cleveland, and are reprinted with permission.

[4]The italicized definitions of enduring understandings are taken from *Understanding by Design* (1998, 1999), with the exception of the last two, which have been added by this author.

understandings that are at the heart of a discipline; in parentheses, after each, are the names of people who might still study and consider their implications, professionally:

- Religions shape behaviors, beliefs, and values. (Clergy)

- The Jewish people is a like a reed: alone it can be easily broken, but as a group together stands strong. (A Jewish Federation leader)

- The Judaism experienced *b'shivt'cha b'vaytecha* (when sitting in your house) transmits Jewish values, beliefs, and memories. (A Jewish family educator)

- Conflicting claims of inheritance create emotionally charged tensions that are difficult to resolve. (A Middle East politician or peace mediator)

Enduring understandings are *abstract, counterintuitive, and often misunderstood ideas*. They are not facts, nor are they statements of objectives or goals. The following are not enduring understandings:

- *Sh'lom bayit* (peace in the home) is an important goal to work toward.

- The Torah is important to the Jewish people.

- Students will understand why study is important in Jewish tradition.

- Jacob prayed to God in different ways.

Enduring understandings are sophisticated statements that offer a lot of room for study and consideration.

EUs are *potentially engaging*, drawing students into discussions and arguments. Look at the bulleted list of enduring understandings at the top of this column, and note how each statement has the potential to engage students. Then, look at the list immediately above, and note how these "clunk" — they are not sophisticated ideas and therefore do not have the power to draw students into conversation with our tradition.

Anne kept in mind the characteristics of enduring understandings as she considered the big ideas of Pesach she wished her students to learn. She and

her husband (who hung in with her on this discussion) talked a lot about Pesach and its central ideas. They considered the impact of Pesach in the lives of Jews throughout history, and the way it served as a master story for the actions taken to help those in need. For example, the Soviet Jewry movement in the 1960s and 70s was shaped by the values learned by Jews, who sat each year at their Seder and read the words of the Haggadah.

After a couple of hours of conversation (including some jumping up to grab their family Haggadah to check references), Anne decided on the following as her focus for her fifth grade unit: Collective Jewish memory has shaped the Jewish obligation to cherish and promote "freedom throughout the land" (Leviticus 25:10).[5]

While this was a bit bigger than Pesach itself, Anne felt that the statement could actually focus much more than just a holiday unit. Anne spent some time checking this statement against the list of characteristics of an enduring understanding. She realized that Jews who serve in political office, those who work for Jewish social justice organizations (e.g., the Religious Action Center — www.rac.org), individuals who compile new editions of the Haggadah, and historians all struggle with this idea. Anne decided that using this as the big idea, represented by a large circle (as in figure 3 above), she would focus her Pesach unit with three essential questions:

- Why is freedom so central a value to Jews throughout history and across the globe?

- How has seeing ourselves as personally having been part of the Exodus from Egypt motivated the actions of Jews throughout history?

- How does the celebration of Jewish holidays, remind us of our obligation to "proclaim freedom throughout the land"?

Carving Out the Unit

While enduring understandings give a focus to a unit in very broad terms, teachers need to delineate the specifics of a unit. The essential questions above (as developed by Anne) take one cut into the big ideas, but they are still quite broad. Anne's

---

[5]This enduring understanding was developed by the Jewish Education Center of Cleveland's Curriculum Department, with educational leaders of Park Synagogue (Cleveland, Ohio) for use

in a fifth grade curriculum. This, and most examples for "Anne," are taken from that unit.

questions could be used to focus a unit on Chanukah or even Yom HaAtzma'ut (Israel Independence Day).

To help focus even farther, Anne needs to think about what she wants her students to *know* and be able to *do* by unit's end. In many ways, these look like objectives, but they are only one small part of the unit's focus. Anne, therefore, writes down what she wants her students to know and be able to do:

Know:

- What Jewish texts say about freedom, especially the Torah (as it describes the Exodus), and the *Haggadah.*

- The obligation of all Jews to "proclaim freedom throughout the land."

- How Pesach reminds us of the Jewish emphasis on freedom.

- Points in our history when Jews remembered that they had been slaves in the land of Egypt . . . and acted accordingly in a modern situation.

Be able to do:

- Explain the centrality of freedom in Jewish life.

- Read fluently prayers and songs from the *Haggadah* that complement the value of freedom.

- Discuss events beyond the Exodus through the lens of our people's eternal struggle for freedom.

Anne knows that there are parts of the Seder that her school director requires fifth graders to read or chant fluently; she adds them to her lists, but makes a note to ask that some of the requirements get shifted to other grade levels in future years. This clears the way for her to focus on the parts of the Haggadah that truly complement her big idea.

STEP 2: EVIDENCE OF UNDERSTANDING

When most teachers plan curriculum, they decide how to assess students *after* they decide on the learning activities. In an *Understanding by Design* unit, this is the second step of the process, creating strong coherence between the enduring understanding and the actual learning activities. The evidence of understanding refers especially to a final assessment (often an authentic or performance assessment) that pulls together student learning. But this evidence can also be collected along the way of a unit, with checks for understanding or specific facts that a teacher requires of her students.

Final Assessments

Here are a few assessment examples developed for specific enduring understandings. Note how they check a student's grasp of the big ideas.

Enduring understanding:

- Conflicting claims of inheritance create emotionally charged tensions that are difficult to resolve.

Evidence of understanding:

- Students "ghostwrite" a speech for a person opening "The Children of Abraham Café" in Jerusalem, a place where Jews and Arabs are welcome. The speech must show understanding of the historical claims of the two peoples to the land, and also be welcoming in tone. (High School)

Enduring understanding:

- Liturgical music shapes and is shaped by faith and culture.

Evidence of understanding:

- Students create a service with attention to their choices of liturgical music. They write a program for worshipers that describes the influence of the specific selections on Judaism and worship, as well as ways Jewish culture influenced music. (Middle/High School)

Enduring understanding:

- Pesach encourages us to relive the past, connects us to Jews worldwide in the present, and helps us teach Jewish values to our children.

Evidence of understanding:

- Students interview a neighbor or family friend who was not at the student's *Seder* this year. They compare their own *Seder* with that of the person they interviewed. The class charts/graphs comparisons (what is the same and what is different) and together decide why it is important for Jews to have a *Seder* each year. (Primary)

Enduring understanding:

*   Jewish families stand witness to Jewish history, transmitting memories through ritual, realia, and stories.

Evidence of understanding:

*   Students create a museum exhibit of moments in Jewish history that their own family witnessed and passed along to future generations. (Middle School)

Anne realizes that creating an assessment takes her beyond current experience. To help figure out what to do for this particular unit, she turns to the Understanding by Design Handbook (1999) for a step-by-step process the authors call GRASPS[6] for the acronym that describes the steps.

Goal - Anne decides that she wants her students to demonstrate how collective Jewish memory has shaped the Jewish obligation to cherish and promote "freedom throughout the land."

Role - Many years ago, Anne saw Judy Chicago's Dinner Party, place settings representing famous people. Today, she notes that various cities have had theme-based outdoor art exhibits (e.g., Cleveland, in honor of the Rock and Roll Hall of Fame, provided guitars to various artists to decorate . . . and then positioned these around the city). With this in mind, Anne decides to put the students in the role of arts collective members.

Audience - The audience for Anne's students will be those coming to the art exhibit.

Situation - This will be the exhibit.

Product - Anne's fifth graders will need to pick a Jew active on behalf of the freedom of others, who lived anytime beyond the Exodus from Egypt, and create a pillow for this person to lean on during the Seder. The pillow must reflect how this person promoted "freedom throughout the land."

Standard - For this assessment, Anne decides to create a Performance Assessment Task List. This is a chart (see figure 4 below) that tells students what they need to include in their work to have completed the assessment successfully.

	Possible Points	What I think I earned	What the teacher says I earned
I picked a Jewish person who wanted freedom for others.	20		
I have a summary sheet of this person's life, and explain clearly when this person fought for freedom.	30		
My pillow shows what "cause" this person stood up for.	20		
My pillow includes *Seder* themes.	10		
My pillow was created with care; it is obvious that I put effort into this project.	10		
I include a bibliography of where I found this information.	10		
Total Points	100		

Figure 4

---

[6]For more information on GRASPS, see pp. 144-159 of *Understanding by Design Handbook* (Alexandria, VA: Association of Supervision and Curriculum Development, 1999).

Developing an assessment can be difficult. Wiggins and McTighe use the GRASPS system to offer a step-by-step way to create an interesting assessment. Sometimes it takes moving through all the steps to see the final product. At other times, once the role and audience are developed, the rest just fall into place.

Creating an evaluation tool (such as the Performance Assessment Task List) offers a relatively fair way of seeing if students truly grasped the enduring understanding. In Anne's case, she included the elements of her EU that she wanted to assess in the statements to which students responded. For older students, the EU can be written specifically into the grid, asking them if they showed their understanding.

Note, though, the difference between a Performance Assessment Task List and a "rubric." The latter is more detailed, offering specific behaviors needed to earn a specific grade. In the case of Anne's project, a rubric might state that to receive an A, the student must have demonstrated a clear understanding of the connection between the way our memory of the Exodus has shaped the obligation of Jews to promote freedom throughout the land. The research on the person must include at least three different bibliographic sources, and the paper must clearly state the stance of this person toward the right of people to be free. The pillow must be neatly designed and show evidence that the student took care in the execution of the project.

Needless to say, such a statement is written beyond the comprehension capabilities of a typical fifth grader. Anne's decision to write a Performance Assessment Task List was in part a result of the frustration she felt her students would have if they had to deal with a written rubric.

On-the-Way Assessments

While Anne initially focuses on the final assessment project, she also knows that there are smaller steps along the way she wishes to assess during her unit. She wants to know if students understand the idea of "collective Jewish memory" in relation to Pesach — what does it mean that each of us should feel as if we, personally, left Egypt? So, she decides that one of the assessments she will do early in the unit is a writing sample, asking students to talk

about their lives in Egypt — what they did, how they felt about leaving, etc. After that, she would do a learning activity in which students begin to match up current situations to "their lives" back in Egypt (e.g., if they were tired working as slaves all day long in an unfair situation, who might *today* be tired from working in an unfair work situation?).

Some teachers include on-the-way quizzes of information to be learned (e.g., the rules of *kashrut*, important historical dates, specific places on maps, or applications of Jewish values to real-life situations). Homework can also be given and graded. They key, however, in a UbD unit, is that each assessment checks on important information and understandings that build to a student's grasp of the enduring understanding. If the assessment is superfluous, then it doesn't belong in this particular unit.

> My lesson planning extends from macro to micro. For my Saturday school class, I lay out the year on four pieces of notebook paper. Holidays, Torah portions, student birthdays, focus units that take multiple weeks, and special activities/events are listed for each session. Then each week gets its own sheet of paper. Each activity is planned to take about 20 minutes, and I always schedule one more activity than I need or may get to. This schedule is posted on the blackboard for the kids to see. Then one more sheet, my "to do" list: the materials I have to prepare and have ready for each activity. Finally there are sticky notes slapped on the Saturday sheet that serve as an anecdotal record. Notes such as, "Hannah likes to work with Shelby" and "Next time explain this more before the kids try it" go here.
>
> *(Sheila Lepkin, Denver, Colorado)*

STEP 3: LEARNING ACTIVITIES

The final step in a UbD *planning* process[7] is the development of the learning activities. These wait until the very end, for they need to prepare students in a variety of ways to handle the evidence of understanding assessment.

---

[7]This chapter will suggest additional steps in the process of developing a viable classroom lesson. However, the UbD model has only three steps in total.

When Anne looked at the learning activities she used before for her Pesach unit, she was dismayed. Not one of these helped prepare students for the assessment — not one helped them learn the concepts that were so crucial to considering a famous Jew's impact on the freedom of others (which was the focus of the pillow making project). And so, Anne had to start from scratch.

Simplistic as it seems, I try to ensure that each lesson has a goal that can be stated in a single sentence, and then plan an activity that will accomplish that goal. Since my classes are only 45 minutes long, I need to break subjects into fairly small bites. For instance, when we started a unit on Exodus, I introduced Rav Huna's *midrash* on four reasons why the Jews were redeemed from Egypt, one of which was that the slaves kept their Hebrew names.

To make this idea feel immediate to the students, I had the following goal: "Using name books and family histories, students will learn how their own Hebrew names preserve and reflect their Jewish heritage." It took two class periods for the students to complete their research and make their presentations, but by the end of the lesson, they did achieve the goal that I had planned.

(Dena Salmon, Montclair, New Jersey)

One of the hardest things for teachers working to create a coherent unit of study is making sure that the learning activities prepare students for the assessment, which in turn tells whether or not they "got" the enduring understanding. This demands "letting go" of past teaching ideas that might have been interesting, fun, or even challenging. The power of a UbD unit is in its coherence.

What does it mean, then, when students spend hours working on:

- honey dishes, with bees perched on the side, for Rosh HaShanah?

- creating mosaic rainbows when studying the Noah story?

- the creation of a Western Wall out of paper bags stuffed with newspapers?

It is important to think about our goals for student learning, and find ways to accomplish them. In the cases above, instead of learning about bees and honey, we can focus on forgiveness; instead of gluing colored paper onto large arches, we can learn about responsibility and promises; instead of stuffing newspapers into paper bags, we can learn about the power of a site over a people. In each of the new lessons, we can still be hands-on and creative — we just need to find the connections to the learning we really want for students.

Anne spends some time thinking about the learning activities she wants to include in this Pesach unit. She asks her school director to brainstorm with her a bit, and she hauls out some teacher guides and other resources to see what ideas might spark her planning. By the time she is done, her unit includes:

- *showing the segment of the film "Prince of Egypt" when Moses goes to Goshen and seems to be aware for the first time that the Children of Israel are slaves. Students work in small groups to discuss questions Anne gives them about slavery and freedom, as seen in the video.*

- *reading from the Book of Exodus about the life of the Hebrews under Egyptian slavery, and doing a "dance midrash" with a parent.*

- *a symbol creation activity, in which students pretend they are a committee of Israelites creating symbols of their slavery to pass along to future generations so that others remember what it was like to be without freedom.*

- *a four-station activity that focuses on the four names of the holiday.*

- *checking in the Haggadah for references to freedom (students are given stickies and asked to mark the places in the Haggadah that refer to freedom). Anne structures this in a way that the Haggadah doesn't become overwhelming — students roll dice to see what page to look on.*

- *reading the quote from David Ben-Gurion on the Jewish memory of the Exodus, and comparing it to the American/English memories of the Pilgrims' arrival in America. Students study pictures of Jews celebrating Pesach over time and around the world. Why do we have such memories? How have we built such memories over time? What memories do I (the student) have about Pesach and its message?*

- *looking at the statement, "Let all who are hungry, come and eat," and developing a campaign to raise food and money for the local food bank.*

- *interviewing adults (family members and friends) to see what memories they have of Pesach, and what messages they think it gives us.*

- *learning/activity centers on people in our history who stood up for the freedom of others.*

Anne discovered with her husband that "two heads are better than one" when it came to brainstorming the enduring understanding; the same holds true for thinking about the learning activities. If you don't have a large repertoire of activities up your sleeve, spend time with someone who does. Think also about activity formats that worked for one unit, and can be transferred to this one. Interviews and learning centers, for example, are formats that can be used in a variety of settings.

STEP 4: LESSON PREPARATION

A teacher who moves through the UbD planning steps that Anne took will end up with a coherent, challenging, and interesting unit of study. But more needs to happen before a class is actually taught.

Calendaring

Decisions need to be made regarding how long a specific unit will take and in what order each of the lessons will happen. It is helpful to plot each unit out on a calendar, not only looking to see how many weeks are available overall, but how many sessions will be devoted to each activity. Planning this on an actual calendar is helpful, as holidays, special school-wide events, etc., need to be taken into account. Figure 5 on the next page allows an entire year of Sundays to be seen at glance, making chunking of units a bit easier.

I always work out a schedule for myself for the year, and decide what my goals are. I study the curriculum guide, if there is one, and try to develop a timetable that will help me to accomplish my goals and complete the curriculum. I may not always adhere to the schedule that I originally devise for myself, but having it does help me to keep on track. If there is no curriculum, I do some research on my own, and find materials that I think will be appropriate for the subject that I am teaching. I also find it helpful to ask the teacher who previously taught that class for guidance and suggestions as to what worked, and what didn't, especially when I'm teaching something for the first time.

(Nancy Hersh, Chatham, New Jersey)

Resources

Years ago, Jewish education was "resource poor." There were few materials available to teachers either to enrich personal background (especially at 11 p.m. on a Saturday night, at home, while planning for the next day's lesson), or more important, in the hands-on resources that enrich student learning (e.g., flash cards, contemporary Jewish graphics, bulletin board supplies, access to texts). While the field has a long way to go, the proliferation of Jewish computer software and Internet resources offers teachers materials that were not available in the past.

No one would dispute that locating resources and creating hands-on learning materials takes time. However, it is important to remember that our students are used to the niceties of educational supplies in their general studies classrooms. Unless such materials are also offered in their Jewish subjects, Jewish education is relegated to second class status. Taking the time to do personal research, create activity packets and instruction sheets on the computer, and finding the resources needed to illustrate learning,[8] is crucial to solid student understandings.

---

[8]This author vividly remembers going into a classroom in the midst of a history lesson. The teacher, who hadn't thought to bring a map, was gesturing in front of a blank chalkboard and saying, "From here in France, to here in Russia . . . " It was unclear how students, who didn't have a clear picture of Europe in their heads, assimilated that piece of the lesson.

September					
October					
November					
December					
January					
February					
March					
April					
May					
June					

Figure 5

(Reprinted with permission from *The Jewish Educational Leader's Handbook*, edited by Robert E. Tornberg. © A.R.E. Publishing, Inc., 1998.)

> I don't truly develop my curriculum for the year until I get a chance to meet the children. What works with one group of kids doesn't necessarily work with another. One year, I had 16 students with 11 boys and five girls. Another year I had a class of ten with eight girls and two boys. I have a skeleton curriculum of what I'd like to get accomplished in the course of the year. But I don't fill it in until mid-September.
>
> *(Kim Lausin, Beachwood, Ohio)*

Lesson Structure

Each lesson can be unique, according to the needs of the particular focus. However, each lesson must also have a purpose, as well as a discernable structure. The following steps offer one such format for teachers to follow:

Step A: Set Induction

The technical term "set induction" refers to the opening of a lesson in a way that gets students ready for the key learning. This can be done in a variety of ways, including:

- a quote written on the board that students discuss.

- a picture, photograph, or video clip that students examine for a purpose determined by the teacher.

- a teacher demonstration.

- a short activity or structured discussion between pairs of students, or small groups.

- a personal question related to the lesson's focus that students answer privately, putting the sheet away until the end of the session.

It is important that this initial part of the lesson sets the groundwork for the learning to come. A wise person once said, "Tell them what you are going to teach, teach it, then tell them what you taught." This stage of a lesson matches the first part of that quote.

Step B: Idea Development

While there are many ways to describe this step, it is really the "formal part of the lesson." So many chapters in this Handbook describe wonderful ways to engage students in learning that they seem redundant here. The key, however, is to find learning activities that prepare students with the skills, knowledge, and understandings to approach the final assessment in a thoughtful way. This part of the lesson takes the most time, and requires teacher attention to:

- flow and coherence - What sequence of activities, "telling," and questioning best develop the ideas behind this lesson?

- questions that guide learning - What high level questions might advance student thinking and learning?

- groupings - How can students be grouped for optimal learning? Which students are working well together? Which students should be separated? Can this class handle multiple groupings (pairs, foursomes, etc.) during the course of one session?

- engagement in learning - Do students understand the task before them? Are they on task? Are they working well with each other?

- learning styles - Is there enough variety in the lesson to accommodate students with different learning styles?

- issues of misunderstandings - What verbal and nonverbal clues do students give of their grasp of the material? Are they responding correctly, whether in writing, orally, or via an art form?

- smooth transitions - How will students be introduced to "next steps" in the day's activities? How can confusion be minimized?

- pacing - How much time do students need for each activity segment? Are there some students who need different tasks or reminders of timing, because of personal learning styles? Will time run out before the class has a chance to finish an activity?

- material use (and abuse) - How can classroom learning materials be best distributed in a way that minimizes chaos? What materials need to be collected before students find "creative" ways to use them (e.g., turning worksheets into paper airplanes)? How can student work be stored so that parents can see evidence of student learning at a later time in the unit?

- bridging - How can this learning bridge to other lessons? to the home? to students' synagogue(s), school(s), or communities?

- assessment - How can student learning be assessed throughout the lesson? What kind of personal notes made by the teacher would help him/her remember comments and questions by students? How can an assessment of student learning in this session shape the planning of future lessons?

Key, however, to success of a unit based on *Understanding by Design* is the teacher's attention to the enduring understanding, with consistent "threading" of it throughout the day's lesson. Students need to be reminded *how* specific learning activities relate to the big idea so they more easily grasp the connections the teacher is working to create throughout the unit.

It is important to note that in a UbD unit, most of this middle section class time will be spent on the development of concepts. However, toward the end of a unit, the focus will shift to the assessment activity.

Step C: Conclusion

So many classes end with the ring of a bell and the teacher's cheerful, "See you next time!" Yet, at the end of the day students need to be reminded of what they were taught. Brain research teaches that a review of information immediately after it is taught helps cement learning. This can be done in a variety of ways:

- The teacher can quickly summarize the key points of the day's lesson.

- The teacher can quickly whip around the room and ask each student to offer one piece of information learned that day.

- Each student can fill out an end-of-day feedback form that includes the open ended sentence, "Today I learned _____."

- Each student, provided with three file cards, can be asked to write on each one thing learned that day. Working in groups

of three to four, students share their cards to see what others learned and to correct together any misinformation.

- The teacher can stand at the door, asking each exiting student to share one piece of learning (and give a handshake).

Step D: Evaluation

Just as individual lessons often conclude with a wave out the door, so, too, units often end with the teacher's quick focus on the next task at hand. To learn and grow as a teacher, it is important to step back and evaluate successes and failures. Here are some ways to do this:

- *Reflect on student work* - Too often, student work is used simply to provide a grade for the report card, rather than serve as a window onto issues of teacher effectiveness. In studying student responses, it is important to consider what they really did learn, as well as areas of continued confusion. Not only is the question, "How might I have *taught* this better" critical, but it is also important to think about ways *now* of going back to clear up fuzzy issues in students' minds. Student work, viewed over time, also helps show growth (or lack thereof) in individual students. Remediation may be a key need of certain students.

- *Consider other directions the unit might have* taken - Experienced teachers know that what works for one class of students might not necessarily work for another. After a unit has ended, it is interesting to consider which other learning paths might have been followed. Notes placed in files will help shape the next teaching of the particular course.

- *Make note of new resources discovered along the* way - In the course of a unit, colleagues and education directors will often say, "Look what I found that meshes with what you are teaching!" Collecting these new materials creates an enriched starting point for a future teaching of the unit.

Anne found that the first time through her unit planning and teaching, things did not go as smoothly as she would have liked. There were questions students asked that she could not answer. She found, however, over time that it became easier to respond, "I don't know, but let's figure out together where we might find that answer." It took more effort than she originally thought to shift from unit planning into the specific lessons she wanted to orchestrate. But she was also pleased with the interest of her students in the activities accomplished. A lively discussion grew out of the "Prince of Egypt" film segment, and some very quiet students excelled in analyzing the photographs of Pesach observed in various communities. The dance midrash worked well, quite to her surprise, but she gives a lot of credit for that success to the congregant who was a dancer in a "past life," and came to help her with that particular session. The students did very credible final projects. She discovered by accident that by asking for an oral and a written commentary, different students shone in each of the reporting forms; some did better orally, and some did better with writing.

Anne thought back to her previous years' lessons, filled with fun, exciting Jewish activities. But in retrospect, she realized that this year's unit was just as engaging, and that it offered students stimulating Jewish ideas to ponder. She was hooked on teaching in a way that promoted understanding, and excited about the possibilities this provided —

not only to her professional growth, but to the Jewish growth of her students.

CONCLUSION

Lesson planning is hard work. Unit planning, with a focus on developing a Jewish enduring understanding is even harder. But the results are worth the effort. Students who move beyond the facts of Jewish life to the bigger ideas have a wealth of learning to draw on in a multitude of situations. And that really is what Jewish education is all about.

TEACHING CONSIDERATIONS

- Initially, plan globally — for a unit, not a particular lesson.

- Keep focused on the big ideas of Judaism.

- Study, for without personally developed deep understandings of Judaism, teachers will find themselves skipping along on the peaks of icebergs, rather than getting under the surface into the depths of our tradition.

- Work with others in the planning process; two heads are better than one . . . but three are really ideal.

BIBLIOGRAPHY

Wiggins, Grant and Jay McTighe. *Understanding by Design*. Alexandria, VA: Association for Supervision and Curriculum Development, 1998.

A book (1998), handbook (1999), and video series (1999, 2000) that demonstrate a curriculum development process that leads to understandings of the big ideas in life. For more information on UbD, click on the Resource button on the UbD Exchange web site, www.ubdexchange.org.

Wiske, Martha Stone, ed. *Teaching for Understanding: Linking Research with Practice*. San Francisco, CA: Jossey-Bass, 1998.

This book describes the Harvard University, Project Zero's Teaching for Understanding (TfU) project. It offers the philosophy and research principles of TfU, opening a window into curriculum development using this process.

Applying 4Mat[1] To Jewish Curriculum and Instruction

Cynthia Dolgin, Bernice McCarthy, and Marcey Wagner

Vignette 1: Marcia, the Seasoned Teacher

Marcia was taking a shower. Her hair was soaped, but her mind was at Hebrew School. A seasoned religious school teacher, she had ten years experience, and a reputation for succeeding with even the most difficult, "spirited" classes.

Marcia has been teaching a unit on Passover to her fourth graders over the past several years. It seemed to go over well, but now she was having second thoughts. Did her students really connect with Passover? Were any of them actually moved to change any aspect of their behavior and become more Pesach observant? Did they make any personal meaning out of her lessons? What changes could she make to her lessons so that the classroom experience could be truly transformative in the lives of her students? She needed to reinvigorate her teaching, so that her students' learning would be more about "really knowing" and not just about fact and skills. She knows that her students can successfully recite the "Four Questions" and give a stellar performance at the school model Seder. But how could she help them make meaning of their newly acquired knowledge and skills so that these impacted on students' identity as Jews?

Vignette 2: Peter, the Novice Teacher

Peter was so excited! It was Tuesday. He'd be teaching that afternoon, and he couldn't wait to see his classroom full of fifth graders. Peter loves Judaism and gets great satisfaction passing on that love and his knowledge to his students. Peter is also a lawyer with a busy, successful practice. At 50, he is a past president of his synagogue, and — since the death of his mother — a regular at the morning minyan. For the past few years, he has been toying with the idea of giving something back to the community by teaching Hebrew school. This past August, he was approached by a principal of a synagogue nearby asking him to teach the Tuesday class. He thought about it, realized that this position would not conflict with being an NFL season ticket holder, and he jumped at the opportunity.

Driving to class, he thought about his students. Relying on a nice textbook, Peter's Bible lessons had been going fairly well, and he usually succeeded in keeping the rambunctious kids under control. He got through the first three chapters of the book, and felt confident enough at this point to try a "creative" suggestion from the teacher's guide, selecting a recommended activity that sounded like fun. Last Tuesday, he found in the principal's office a book of Bible skits, photocopied one skit, and gave it a try. The class was noisy, but the students seemed to have a great time. Most students that is. Adam spent the class period sulking. When called upon and gently pressured to take a part, Adam looked like he was about to throw up. Peter didn't seem to be reaching Adam, who reminded him so much of his own eldest son. How could an activity be so engaging for most of the class and so repugnant for one child? No matter what Peter has tried so far, reaching Adam continues to elude him. The more "fun" the activity, the more Adam retreats. As the light turns green, Peter wonders what to do.

---

[1]Much of the material contained in this chapter is adapted from Bernice McCarthy, *About Teaching: 4MAT in the Classroom* (Wauconda, IL: About Learning Inc., 2000). While About Learning Inc. has graciously granted permission to use portions of their published materials, they look with strong disfavor on those who would copy and use their materials without proper arrangements and without regard for international copyright law.

INTRODUCTION

4MAT is a meta-model for instructional design, exemplifying a natural cycle of learning, and illustrating profound insights into the learning act itself. 4MAT was created by Bernice McCarthy, and has recently been gaining attention for its applicability to the field of Jewish education. As the creators and writers of Project Etgar, a new middle school curriculum for Conservative congregational schools, Dolgin and Wagner have been utilizing 4MAT for the past few years as our preferred model for developing curriculum and instruction. We were introduced to 4MAT by Dr. Steven M. Brown, Director of the Melton Research Center and Dean of the Davidson School of Education at the Jewish Theological Seminary of America, who has incorporated it into teaching curriculum development to students in education classes at the seminary. Out of our sincere love of Jewish teaching and learning, and our conviction that 4MAT has deep and broad implications for Jewish curriculum and instruction, we invited Dr. McCarthy to co-author this chapter, introducing readers to 4MAT and the Natural Cycle of Learning. With permission from About Learning Incorporated, much of the content of this chapter was adapted from the book *About Teaching: 4MAT in the Classroom* (McCarthy, 2000). We fleshed out its applicability to the field of Jewish Education.

We have personally found that the nature and conditions of Jewish education — whether in religious schools or in day schools — makes it difficult to achieve a balance between meaning making, knowledge and skills acquisition, and creative application of new learnings. In religious schools, spotty attendance and irregular schedules with numerous interruptions make it difficult to think in terms of learning units — ongoing, connective learning, that spans several days and weeks. As teachers, we often felt that circumstances turned us into "masters of the one-shot," where every class began with a grabber, ended with a grand finale, and hopefully included some *tachlis*[2] in the middle. Some of our classroom encounters had been heavy on experience, but light on conceptual learning or skill acquisition. Others aimed to drill the skills at the expense of the opportunity for making personal meaning. Rarely, though, had we attained a true balance between:

- eliciting and connecting to prior knowledge *and* teaching new content.

- practicing skills *and* helping students make personal meaning.

- creativity *and* rigor.

- process *and* product.

- being tellers *and* being facilitators of student learning.

These past few years, we have achieved greater balance in our teaching by using 4MAT to structure the lessons we teach into coherent curricular units. Within a 4MAT unit, learning occurs in a natural cycle of connecting, examining, imagining, defining, trying, extending, refining, and integrating, utilizing a wide variety of modalities. Because it honors the whole learner, provides a framework to achieve the elusive balance of educational goals, and makes room in the classroom for all kinds of learning preferences, 4MAT has uniquely salient implications for religious and spiritual education, and ethnic cultural reclamation. This may explain why 4MAT has been adopted and adapted for many types of educational systems with concerns similar to ours. Native American tribal schools, Hawaiian language immersion schools, day schools of other faiths, and after school religious education have all gravitated to 4MAT as a vehicle for curriculum development, teacher preparation, and ongoing professional development.

McCarthy's model builds upon the work of Kurt Lewin and David Kolb, and the social constructivist tradition of Vygotsky and Dewey — a belief in active engagement in learning. According to the model, human beings come to meaning by:

- experiencing their inner lives, prior knowledge, and personal life experiences.

- perceiving the external world.

- learning about and conceptualizing that world.

- mastering concepts and skills.

- acting on those conceptualizations.

- adapting and integrating those conceptualizations to their inner lives so that the

---

[2]In this case, loosely translated as "deep content."

learner comes to "own" his or her new knowledge, skills, impressions, and beliefs.

McCarthy's 12 principals of learning that form the foundation of the 4MAT system are:

1. Learning is fundamentally social.

2. People need to learn about what matters to them.

3. Learning needs a supportive environment.

4. Learning is conceptual in nature and creates visual images.

5. Learning is functional.

6. Learning by doing is more powerful than memorizing, and coaching is the key.

7. Learning needs to promote a mindset that endures beyond the teaching.

8. Self-directed learning is the core.

9. Cracking the whip stifles learning.

10. Failure to learn is often the fault of the system.

11. Sometimes the best learning is unlearning.

12. Real learning leaves us changed.

As you read, you may be saying to yourself, "Gee, I already *do this*, and I've never even heard of 4MAT." What 4MAT does is take healthy, intuitive concepts of teaching and learning that have long been the hallmark of excellent education, and structure them in an accessible way. For the novice teacher, 4MAT provides the framework for launching a career in Jewish education that centers instruction on the learner. For the experienced teacher, 4MAT helps organize practices and methodology into coherent units that maximize learner potential and meets learners where they are, with the guiding principle that learners develop and come to speak in their own voice. For the truly expert teacher, 4MAT validates and concretizes salient educational beliefs and practices.

4MAT fits neatly with the Jewish belief that every person is wholly unique and created *B'tzelem Elohim*, in the divine image of God (Genesis 1:27). 4MAT is compatible with Gardner's cognitive theory of the multiple intelligences[3], which has greatly broadened our understanding of the various domains involved in problem solving and product making. However, it might be worthwhile to consider implementing 4MAT in conjunction with the implementation of the multiple intelligences (MIs), because 4MAT reaches beyond the cognitive into the religious, by honoring the spiritual, emotional, and affective domains.

HONORING LEARNER DIVERSITY AND THE NATURAL CYCLE OF LEARNING

At its core, 4MAT honors learner diversity and the natural cycle of learning. Each of these is explained below.

Learner Diversity

Learners are legitimately different in the ways they perceive and process information in formal and informal ways. Every learner is wholly unique. No two people are exactly alike. In a one-on-one tutorial, the instructor can tailor the curriculum and pedagogy to match the specific needs of the sole learner. However, in the classroom, teachers must work to meet the diverse needs of all the unique learners within the group. 4MAT enables the teacher to identify and adapt instruction to four profiles of learner preferences, helping him/her to keep instruction varied, and appealing to a variety of proclivities through multiple modalities in order to allow every learner his or her moment to shine and other moments to stretch:

- *Imaginative Learners*, who seek personal meaning, and prefer to learn by sensing/feeling and reflecting. (Type 1)

- *Analytic Learners*, who seek to understand the facts and conceptual knowledge, prefer to learn by thinking and reflecting. (Type 2)

- *Common Sense Learners*, who are pragmatic problem-solvers and hands-on learners, prefer to learn by thinking and doing. (Type 3)

- *Dynamic Learners*, who seek to integrate experience and apply it in new and often creative ways, prefer to learn by sensing/feeling and doing. (Type 4)

---

[3]For more information on multiple intelligences, see Chapter 27, "Multiple Intelligences" by Renee Holtz and Barbara Lapetina, pp. 000-000 in this Handbook.

McCarthy's four learner types builds upon the work of earlier theorists, e.g., Carl Jung's four psychological types (Feelers, Thinkers, Sensors, and Intuitors) and David Kolb's four learning skills (Valuing, Thinking, Decision Making, and Acting).

Interestingly, Jewish wisdom literature preceded all of these researchers at classifying people into four types. In *Pirke Avot* 5:12-17, we see people categorized into four character traits, four temperaments, four types of students, four types of *tzedakah* givers, and so on. Within each of the ancient Rabbinic foursomes, however, the Sages find one negative "type" either "a scoundrel," one who is "wicked," or "one who has bad fortune." For example:

> There are four types of students:
>
> - One who is quick to understand, but quick to forget — his gain is canceled out by his loss.
>
> - One who understands with difficulty, but forgets with difficulty — his loss is canceled by his gain.
>
> - One who is quick to understand and forgets with difficulty — this is a wise person.
>
> - One who understands with difficulty and is quick to forget — this one has bad fortune.
>
> (*Pirke Avot* 5:14)

In a more metaphoric description, the Rabbis explain:

> There are four types among those who study with the Sages: the sponge, the funnel, the strainer, the sifter.
>
> - The sponge — absorbs everything.
>
> - The funnel — in one end and out the other.
>
> - The strainer — passes the wine, retains the dregs.
>
> - The sifter — removes the chaff, retains the groats.
>
> (*Pirke Avot* 5:17)

In both of these *mishnayot*,[4] Analytic or Type 2 learners fare the best, and earn Rabbinic praise. So, too, in general education today, schools focus on

Type 2 learners. Most schools do not honor and reach out to other types of learners, even though the majority of people are not Type 2 learners.

The Natural Cycle

4MAT's Natural Learning Cycle is composed of four quadrants, each of which engages learners in both verbal and nonverbal ways. At the heart of each natural learning cycle is a core concept that focuses the cycle of learning. Following the Natural Cycle is a way of designing instruction that begins with personal meaning (Quadrant One), moves to concepts (Quadrant Two), to usefulness (Quadrant Three), and finally to adaptation (Quadrant Four). Within each of the four quadrants in the cycle, both left-mode and right-mode processing skills are integrated into instruction.

- *Quadrant One: Experiencing* - The learning cycle begins with *connecting* to experience, with personal meaning and relevance, with our perceptions of what happens to us and how we feel about those experiences. We come to understand what we see and act on our conclusions by *examining*, reflecting upon, and analyzing experience. We begin in Quadrant One by wondering, "Why do I need to know this?" and "What do I already know about this?"

- *Quadrant Two: Conceptualizing* - With our interest raised, we move to Quadrant Two. Our perceptions lead to individualized images that we then form into cognitive and visual conceptualizations. We ask, "What more do I need to know?" and "What do the experts have to say about this?" We *imagine* or "picture" the concept and are then *informed* by the experts, learning new concepts, facts, and skills.

- *Quadrant Three: Applying* - Once we have learned the facts associated with the core concepts, we proceed to Quadrant Three where we try, practice, manipulate, and tinker with our new learning, gaining skill and confidence in our new skills. In Quadrant Three, we answer the questions, "How does this work?" and "How do I use this?" by *trying out* the content, and then *extending* our new skills to more complex experiences.

---

[4]*Mishnayot* - plural form of *mishnah*, a small section of text found in the Rabbinic text called Mishnah. (Calling something a *mishnah* is like referring to the small section of text in the Bible called a "verse.")

- *Quadrant Four: Creating/Adapting* - Once we have gained dexterity with new knowledge and skills, we can incorporate them into who we are, by moving to Quadrant Four and *refining* application of what we have learned in ways that are personally relevant and useful. We *integrate* our new learning into our lives, and we share and celebrate what we have learned. In Quadrant Four, we answer the question, "What if?" This leads to more complex understanding, greater readiness for the next experience, and ongoing growth. This is the cycle of deep and life changing learning.

Looking back to the two examples from *Pirke Avot*, one imagines that the author is referring to formal study — a Sage instructing students — in order to transmit knowledge and skills. We envision instruction focused on Quadrant Two — learning concepts and skills, most suitable for Type 2 learners. We also imagine that studying with the Sages also involves a good deal of Quadrant Three learning — trying out and practicing the concepts and skills, perhaps in *chevruta*, the traditional Jewish methodology of peer-coach and pair learning. It seems that this kind of learning with the Sages focuses on verbal, analytical, and logical skills — left-mode skills — and not on intuition, visuo-spatial, nonverbal learning. If our assumptions are correct, then it is understandable that not all learners being instructed by the Sages will be considered successful.

Historically, schools validate the way a Type 2 learns, and emphasize Quadrant Two teaching and learning modes, despite the fact that about 70% of learners are *not* Type 2s. (Good for the 2s. Not so good for the rest of us.) Unlike the foursomes found in *Pirke Avot*, 4MAT's four learner types are all positive, valued, and honored. Learning episodes put emphasis on meaning making and creativity/integration, as well as on conceptualizing and application. We believe that this cycle — if implemented by teachers of Jewish studies — can reach learners down to their core and can vastly improve the quality of instruction in Jewish classrooms by elegantly connecting the transmission of the Jewish tradition with its transformative powers.

MORE ABOUT THE FOUR KINDS OF LEARNING STYLES

During McCarthy's public school teaching career, her affinity for students whom other teachers had given up on, her ability to help them accept their strengths and learn to capitalize on them while developing a healthy respect for the uniqueness of others, led to the development of 4MAT.

Facing the truth that every learner is wholly unique can be overwhelming for classroom teachers who must make learning accessible to all. By rotating instructional methodology to appeal to each of the four diverse learning styles, teaching becomes more manageable. Each learner has an opportunity to thrive in his or her most comfortable place, and also to stretch in ways that come less naturally. Differences in learning styles should be acknowledged and celebrated, not seen as deficits.

Teaching around the cycle and reaching out to the different learning styles means that teachers themselves are stretching beyond their naturally comfortable place. Teachers also have their preferred learning style and teaching style as well, though few of us ever stop to think about what these might be. The LTM[5] (Learner Type Measure) developed by Dr. McCarthy is an easy self-assessment instrument that helps people identify and learn about their *own* learner type and learning preferences. Teachers who encounter, learn about, and think deeply about their own learner type are in a better position to understand, honor, and plan for the diversity of learners in their classroom.

Whereas each individual teacher and learner feels most comfortable in one quadrant of the cycle, fairly comfortable in other parts, and downright uncomfortable with certain modes of teaching and learning, all the steps of the cycle are critical for authentic learning to occur. Teachers who teach through the natural cycle spend part of the time out of their comfort zone, but at the same time will reach a broader spectrum of learners. It takes practice, but it is possible and worthwhile for teachers to broaden their repertoire. Following is a description of the learner types:

---

[5] Administering the LTM instrument should be an early step in 4MAT professional development for teachers. It is available online at www.aboutlearning.com.

- *Type 1 Imaginative Learners* perceive concretely and process reflectively. They seek meaning and clarity. They integrate experience with the self. They learn by listening, sharing ideas, and personalizing information. They are insightful and work for harmony. They create supportive cultures and are great mentors. They thrive on taking the time to develop good ideas, and like to brainstorm with others. They are caring individuals whose favorite question is "Why?"

  - *Type 1 Imaginative Teachers* are interested in facilitating individual growth, helping people become more self-aware, see knowledge as enhancing personal insights, and like discussions and group work.

- *Type 2 Analytic Learners* perceive information abstractly and process it reflectively. They seek goal attainment and personal effectiveness. They are eager learners who think through ideas. They excel in traditional learning environments because the lecture and reading modes suit them. They are excellent at details and sequential thinking. They tackle problems with rationality and logic. They seek to understand the facts and their favorite question is "What?"

  - *Type 2 Analytic Teachers* are interested in transmitting knowledge. They try to be as accurate and knowledgeable as possible, believe curricula should further understanding of significant information, and encourage outstanding students.

- *Type 3 Common Sense Learners* perceive information abstractly and process it actively. They seek utility and results. They are pragmatic and hands-on. If it works, they use it. They cut right to the heart of things. They thrive on plans and time lines. They tackle problems by acting (often not consulting with others). They seek to encourage practical applications and their favorite question is "How does this work?"

  - *Type 3 Common Sense Teachers* are interested in productivity and competence. They try to give learners the skills they will need in life. They see knowledge as enabling learners to be capable of making their own way.

- *Type 4 Dynamic Learners* perceive information concretely and process it actively. They seek to influence others. They learn by trial and error. They believe in self-discovery. They are flexible and adaptable. They are risk takers, and often reach conclusions in the absence of logical justification. They tackle problems by intuiting possibilities. They enrich reality: they add their own ideas to what is. They seek to integrate experience in new and often creative ways. Their favorite question is "What if?"

  - *Type 4 Dynamic Teachers* are interested in enabling learner self-discovery. They try to help people act on their visions. They see knowledge as necessary for improving larger society, and like variety in instructional methods.

All four learner types are equally valuable and should be given their moment to shine.

All teachers have also been learners, but our learner preference does not necessarily correspond with the way we teach. Most people who teach are more influenced by the way they were taught than by learning about teaching or even by their own learning preferences. We tend to adopt teaching methods that are most familiar to us, not necessarily the ones that best suit us, or that best suit our learners.

MORE ABOUT THE NATURAL CYCLE

The cycle is a combination of two intersecting continua, the first, how we *perceive*, how we take in and experience the world, and the second, how we *process*, how we act upon what we take in. The natural learning cycle is the act of making meaning, the rhythm between how we perceive and how we process. Learning is the realization of something new and our response to that newness. In happens in a unique way for each of us.

Perception (תְּפִיסָה)

We perceive newness first without senses, in direct experience. Then we move to the task of describing it, abstracting it, conceptualizing it (see figure 1 on the next page).

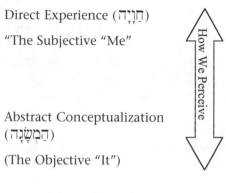

Direct Experience (חֲוָיָה)

"The Subjective "Me"

Abstract Conceptualization
(הַמְשָׂגָה)

(The Objective "It")

Figure 1

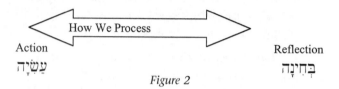

Figure 2

Some people like to linger in the experience, stay in the subjective, while others like to move on quickly to the abstract, to the objective, and want to know what the experts have to say.

In general, secular education asks us to move to abstraction too quickly, before we have had a chance to feel what this new thing is about. While early childhood education thrives on experiential learning, as children get older, they are expected to learn more passively, listening or reading, and absorbing without the benefit of direct, personal experience. In religious education, we fare somewhat better in experiential learning, in part because we are not bound to externally imposed standards and in part because we understand that religious instruction is very much about personal experience of the Divine. We care very much about creating experiences that will reach deep into the souls of our learners and connect them to God, Torah, and *Klal Yisrael*. Very often, however, particularly in part-time congregational education, we linger in the experience and then move on to the next experience without engaging in the rigor of abstracting, conceptualizing, and mastering skills. Think of all those marvelous set inductions, followed by the creation of beautiful and creative artifacts, but which lack cohesive connection to the *tachlis* — learning and mastery of texts and skills. Jewish educators tend to divorce the mastery of knowledge (like *halachah*, ritual, and observances) and skills (like learning to read Hebrew and to *daven*) from the more imaginative and creative aspects of Jewish life (like discussion about our feelings/reactions and engaging in the arts).

Process (עִיבּוּד)

The movement along the perceiving dimension,

from Direct Experience to Abstract Conceptualization, is propelled by the associated Processing dimension. We process our perceptions by reflecting on them. This leads us to abstract those experiences, to create concepts about them, to generalize them. The other end of the processing continuum is action (see figure 2 below).

Schooling tends toward the reflective and shies away from the active. Many general educators, as well as Jewish educators, feel most comfortable when learning is quiet and still, when children are sitting and listening, or reflecting and thinking. They become tense when learning is noisy and active. For these teachers, active learning feels too chaotic and they fear "losing control." But learners who learn best while actively engaged in hands-on doing, tinkering, manipulating, and experimenting are left frustrated and disengaged in a classroom whose teacher demands stillness and quiet.

Process in the Jewish Tradition

Balancing "Learning about Mitzvot" and "Doing Mitzvot"

At the heart of Jewish education is the interconnectedness and tension between transmission and transformation — to transmit the tradition and to have it be transformed and transforming in the hands, minds, and hearts of each person who is touched by Torah. Our desire is to perpetuate Jewish living and practice *MiDor L'Dor* (from generation to generation), and for Jewish living and practice to be meaningful and relevant for each person and for each generation. Personal connection, understanding of concepts, mastery of skills, and practice imbued with personal meaning makes for the kind of balanced cycle of learning and doing that can keep Judaism fresh and constantly relevant. The question is, how do we create learning episodes so that our students stay balanced between subjective, personal experience and the collective canon of the Jewish tradition? Can we create lessons and units that balance *learning about* and *reflecting upon* the *halachah* (law) of *mitzvot* (commandments), for example, and the actual performance of the commandments? By designing curriculum that is true to 4MAT's natural learning cycle, Jewish educators have the scaffolding in place to keep the learning in balance.

Are reflection and action always equally balanced? Some of the Sages seem to indicate the supremacy of action over study. Rabbi Hanina ben Dosa teaches that: "When a person's good deeds exceed his wisdom, his wisdom will be enduring. But when a person's wisdom exceeds his good deeds, his wisdom is not enduring" (*Pirke Avot* 3:12). Just as John Dewey believed and taught in the early twentieth century, Hanina ben Dosa seems to have believed many centuries ago that learning by doing what one has learned is much more enduring than just passively learning the facts and skills without putting them to practice.

Ben Bag-Bag, on the other hand, seems to favor reflection and says nothing about action when he teaches, "Study it and review it: You will find everything in it. Scrutinize it, grow old and gray in it, do not depart from it. There is no better portion in life than this" (*Pirke Avot* 5:24). In fact, for thousands of years, whenever action in the Diaspora has been difficult or impossible, reflection has sustained us as a people and a religion.

In the following teaching from *Pirke Avot* 5:16, we see an equal reward in action and in reflection, a strong preference for a balanced combination of *both* action and reflection, and distain for those who neither act nor reflect:

> There are four types among those who attend the House of Study:
>
> - One who attends, but does not practice the *mitzvot* — he receives a reward for his attendance.
>
> - One who practices the *mitzvot*, but does not attend regularly — he receives a reward for his performance.
>
> - One who attends and practices the *mitzvot* — this is a saintly person.
>
> - One who neither attends nor practices the *mitzvot* — this is a scoundrel.

Our efforts in Jewish education, at the very least, seek to avoid the perpetuation of scoundrels, and in the ideal, seek to evoke a personal commitment to both action and reflection. Classroom instruction is only one small piece of the overall learning experience of our students, and not all factors are subject to the control of the classroom teacher. Nevertheless, the closer we come to honoring the natural learning cycle within our teaching episodes, by honoring experience, study, practice, and personally meaningful action, the better our chances that Jewish learning and living will be sustained and enriched.

4MAT: HOW PERCEPTION AND PROCESS INTERSECT

In conceptualizing putting perception and process together, think of a clock (see figure 3 on the next page). Learning starts with ME, in the sensory place at 12 o'clock, where we directly experience, and moves toward reflective observation at 3 o'clock. Then we assimilate the experience and abstract it into a concept. We stand back and examine, we name It. The 6 o'clock place is the "It" place, where things are objects to be examined and understood.

Then we try things out, finding out what personal meaning we can make of this experience, this thing, transforming abstract concepts into actions via active experimentation (9 o'clock).

Once again, we return to 12 o'clock, to a new direct experience, bringing with us our prior knowledge and newly acquired skills, expanded mental images, and previous experiences. Each of us who has experienced the cycle together has integrated meaning, concept, and action, each in our own way, and is ready to act on our unique conceptualizations by trying them out in the real world.

For each person, the point of intersection between perception and process is wholly unique. Some linger longer in the subjective, abstract experience while others want to quickly move to the objective, concrete concepts. Some like to watch for a while, figure things out and then take action, while others like to jump right in.

BRAIN-MIND LEARNING

In order to understand something about the uniqueness each person brings to the learning act and to design classroom instruction that honors that diversity, it helps to understand and then infuse both left-mode and right-mode methods into classroom teaching and learning. For our pur-

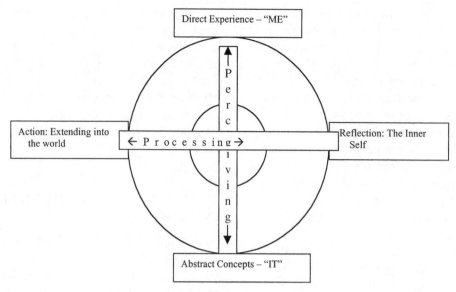

Figure 3

poses, we do not need to understand precisely *where* in the brain different learning functions are located, whether in the left hemisphere or in the right. We recognize that brain research and the application of brain research to education is in its infancy. We see the relationship between right and left-mode characteristics as relative, not absolute. The point is that learning is richer, deeper, and has the power to fuel both transmission and transformation when both left-mode and right-mode teaching strategies are applied in the classroom, when the whole brain is engaged.

For left-mode tasks, ask students to sequence, to name, to remember names, to relate verbally, to break down into parts, to follow procedures that lead in similar directions, and to repeat what they have been told. For right-mode tasks, ask students to synthesize, to hunch, to intuit, to tinker and play with ideas, to visualize in pictures, to polish and refine skills.[6]

Learning traditionally puts the emphasis on left-mode strategies, such as reading, listening, and sequencing. Emotion, memory, intuitive insights, imagination, spiritual openness, social interaction, spatial manipulation, doing, and being in the moment are all expressions of right-mode strategies. Some kinds of learning involve both left and right-mode. In music, both modes are integral parts.

Neuroscience has illuminated the duality between the left-mode and right-mode dimensions, between

- thinking (left) and being (right)

- cognition (left) and intuition (right)

- objectivity (left) and subjectivity (right)

- symbolism (left) and patterning (right)

- sequence (left) and simultaneity (right)

- linear (left) and round (right)

- language (left) and space (right)

Education is constantly attempting to apply the newest understandings from neuroscience, but the right-mode remains elusive — not easy to describe in words. It is very important, but hard to assess. It is difficult to communicate the understanding of the right-mode, simply because of the ineffable qualities of insight and intuition. Nevertheless, the right-mode is the heart of religious experience, and so it needs to be well integrated and honored at the heart of religious education. We need to be aware not only that our students have different strengths when it comes to right and left-mode processing, but also the kinds of tasks we ask of them, in order to create real thinkers for our world and for *K'lal Yisrael*. Learning episodes that help to

---

[6]Chapters 3 and 4 of *About Teaching* offer rich explanations on Brain-Mind Learning that are accessible and reader-friendly.

Student Learning Strategy Preferences	
Those who favor the Left-mode	**Those who favor the Right-mode**
• Prefer verbal instructions	• Prefer demonstrated instructions
• Like controlled, systematic experiments	• Like open-ended experiments
• Prefer problem solving with logic	• Prefer problem solving by hunching
• Find differences	• Find similarities
• Like structured climates	• Like fluid and spontaneous climates
• Prefer established information	• Prefer elusive, ambiguous info
• Rely heavily on the verbal	• Rely on the nonverbal
• Like discrete information recall	• Like narratives
• Control feelings	• Are free with feelings
• Are intrigued by theory	• Need experiences
• Excel in propositional language	• Excel in poetic, metaphoric language
• Draw on previously accumulated information	• Draw on unbounded qualitative patterns, clustering around images

Figure 4

develop the processing abilities of both the left-mode and the right-mode will improve individuals' internal and interpersonal lives. Figure 4 on the next page describes the characteristics of left-mode and right-mode learners.

Richard Restak has said that "uniting the activities of the two hemispheres is the highest and most elaborate activity of the brain."[7] Any experiences that help to develop the processing abilities of both hemispheres, of the verbal with the nonverbal, will have longer-term efficacy and impact on the person, and improve individuals' internal and interpersonal lives.[8]

THE COMPLETE 4MAT CYCLE

4MAT puts together a system of curriculum and instructional design that accounts for individual learning differences and maximizes whole brain-compatible learning.

"We sense and feel, we experience, then we watch, we reflect, then we think, we develop theories, we conceptualize, then we try out our theories, we experiment. Finally, we apply what we have learned to the next similar experience. We get smarter, we apply experience to experience."[9]

Within each of the four quadrants, both right-mode and left-mode pedagogy is utilized, for a total of at least eight steps in the learning cycle,[10] as represented by the cycle in figure 5 above.

Quadrant One – כַּוָּנָה

We begin where the students are. The purpose of Quadrant One is to create meaning, to answer the question, "Why?" The right-mode is sensory, it comes from feeling. It synthesizes things, puts them together. The first step begins in the right-mode, in the subjective experience, and then reflects on that experience, in the left mode.

---

[7]Richard Restak, *The Modular Brain* (New York: Simon and Schuster, 1994).

[8]For a more thorough delineation between the left-mode and right-mode, see Chapters 3 and 4 of *About Teaching* (McCarthy, 2000).

[9]Bernice McCarthy, *The 4MAT System* (Barrington, IL, Excel, Inc., 1987).

[10]For a full discussion about assessing around the 4MAT Cycle, see Chapter 6 in *About Teaching*.

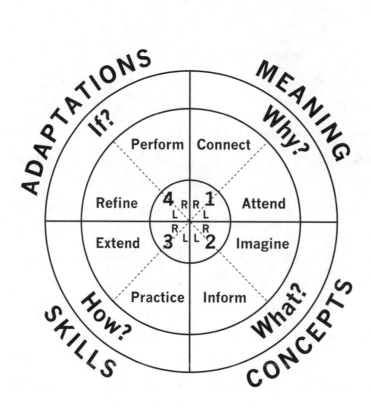

Figure 5

Step 1: Connect – הַקֶּשֶׁר הַהֲדָדִי

Establish a relationship between your learners and the content, connecting it to their lives, not telling them how it connects, but having something actually happen in the classroom that will bring them to make the connection themselves. The "connect" is personal and subjective, piquing students' interest and curiosity. It is a right-mode activity. The experience created must be based on the essence of the *concept*, not on the discreet facts that make up the *content*. Every learner must be able to be and feel successful at participating in the connection. For example, asking students to brainstorm and share the different ways they acknowledge special occasions is a good Quadrant One connect question. However, asking children to share all the ways their families acknowledge Shabbat is not a good connect question if not all families in your group observe Shabbat. It is the kind of question that would immediately shut down learning for some members of the class. The connect activity can be: participating in an event, hearing a story,

or seeing a judiciously selected film clip that leads them to the content to be learned in Step 4. The experience needs to touch their hearts.

Step 2: Attend – בְּחִינַת הַהִתְנַסּוּת

Have your students examine what just happened in the first step. Have them attend to their own experience and to the perceptions of their fellow students: how it went, what really happened. Allow students to reflect on the experience together, discussing, sharing, seeing similar patterns. After the created experience, have your students examine the event by stepping out of the experience, applying the left-mode's analyzing skill — standing aside the better to understand.

As learners step outside the experience to discuss it, they will help each other understand the value of the material, the relationships, the discrepancies, and the inherent possibilities. Figure 7 on the next page shows the skills in Quadrant One and the modalities that can foster their development.

QUADRANT ONE

Skills:	*Try:*
Self-knowledge	Journals
Searching for meaning	Stream of consciousness mind-maps
Making connections	Nonverbal representations of connections, such as art, film, etc.
Relating to individuals	Discussions of idea possibilities
Generating ideas	Essays that explore personal reactions
Owning one's message	Trusting insights
	Contributing to the group
	Listening
	Paraphrasing
	Expressing support
	Describing feelings
	Finding patterns

Figure 7

Quadrant Two – דֵּעוֹת

The purpose of Quadrant Two is to inform and enlarge the learner's understanding of the content, to answer the question, "What?"

Bring the right-mode to bear on the concept under study before delivering the expert knowledge through the left-mode.

Step 3: Image – הַדְמָיָה

Your students need to imagine, to picture the concept as they understand and have experienced it, before you take them to the experts.

Right-mode activities such as analogies, metaphors, visuals (collage, clay, paper tearing, color, sketching) that capture the conceptual essence — as it is presently known to your students — will bring them to the expert content not as "strangers in a strange land," but as persons who can say, "I already know something about this."

Step 4: Inform – לִימוּד

Students are now ready for the left-mode step of Quadrant Two, receiving and examining the expert knowledge. Inform them of the content they need to understand, give them the expert knowledge. Whereas Step 1 is very much a subjective experience, in Step 4 the learner takes a more objective stance. The teacher or the text (or other form of media) is presenting commonly accepted, objective "truths."

This is the telling and receiving time for your students. This is where a fine, organized, well delivered lecture belongs — illuminating texts, guest speakers, films, information from Internet resources, information gathered from interviewing parents, grandparents, and so on. If you do this well, you prepare your students to receove the learning from you and from the experts, and begin to take ownership of it for themselves. (See figure 8 below for Quadrant Two skills and the modalities that foster their development.

Skills:	Try:
Acquiring pertinent information Relating to ideas Understanding theory and structure Thinking reflectively Being objective Classifying Patterning	Self-testing for conceptual, theoretical and structural understandings Conceptualizing the essence of content Imaging the concept and its connections (collage, sculpt, sketch, pantomime, story) Spatial tests (nonverbal depictions of ideas and relationships) Oral exams/articulating a concept Metaphoric expressions of content Informal student/teacher dialogues Essays Critiques Research reports A good lecture Seeing relationships Explaining

Figure 8

Quadrant Three – יְכוֹלוֹת

The purpose of Quadrant Three is to practice, to become skilled, to move toward mastery, to answer the question, "How?" First, bring the left-mode to bear to develop skills for enacting the concept under study, so that it will be possible to extend the concepts and skills back into personal meaning through the right-mode.

Step 5: Practice – תִּירְגּוּל

Your students must practice the learning as the experts do it. It is not yet time for innovation or adaptation. This is the time for tinkering, manipulating, and sometimes drilling.

Students need to learn by practicing. They need to become sufficiently skilled before they can innovate. Think of a musician who practices first, then interprets. Practicing Hebrew reading and mastery of the skills to *daven* a prayer become so much more meaningful once the essence of the prayer has been experienced and its content fleshed out in previous steps.

Our experience has been that it makes the most sense to build a unit of *Tefilah* (prayer) study that incorporates the mastery of several prayers connected by a common concept. For example, in a unit on *Bikur Cholim* (visiting the sick), it makes sense to study several prayers that relate to the concept of "healing," such as *"Mi Shebayrach," "Birkat HaGomel,"* and the *"Refa'enu"* blessing from the weekday *"Amidah."* In order for students to learn about and master a large amount of content and prayer skills, the teacher would "warp" the 4MAT wheel. Warping entails multiple iterations of "Step 4 - Inform" and "Step 5 - Practice," repeating the Inform step and Practice step for each additional prayer included. During each iteration, more information from the liturgists is added (Inform), and then students practice these new prayers to gain skill mastery and understanding (Practice). After mastering the technical skills of several liturgical segments, movement through the wheel continues.

QUADRANT THREE

Skills:	*Try:*
Direct communication	Tinkering
Relating to objects	Exploring
Problem solving	Inquiring (questioning the expertise of experts)
Computing	Experimenting
Decision making	Making things work
Formulation	Taking things apart
Analysis to action	Problem solving by defining, strategizing, evaluating, refining
Strategy selection	Interpreting
Perspectives taken	Finding applicability to real life
Discovering elegant solutions	Finding usability
	Bringing insights to bear

Figure 9

 Step 6: Extend – יִישֹּׁום וְהַרְחָבָה

This is where innovation begins and *the student's own voice starts to take over*. Students know enough, have enough skills to tinker, to see how it works for them, to play with the content, the skills, the materials, the ideas, the wholes and the parts, the details, the data and the big picture, to make something of this learning for themselves — to be interpretive.

The right-mode's ability to see possibilities, patterns, wholeness, roundness is a major asset here. There is not set path, just the processing. Now the various centers in the classroom become very busy. There is no set-in-stone algorithm, just hunches and nuances. There is no sequence; insights arrive as the doing comes together. When this happens in a classroom, it is really something to see. Students and the teacher are engaged in major quality time. Figure 9 above shows the skills and modalities that pertain to Quadrant Three.

Quadrant Four – הִסְתַּגְּלוּת

The purpose of Quadrant Four is to adapt, to create, to integrate the learning so it can be used by the students in their future. It answers the question, "What If?"

 Step 7: Refine – עִידוּן וְשִׁיפּוּר

Again, stay with the left-mode. In the previous step, the students started to extend the learning into their lives. They need to evaluate that extension in the cool light of left-mode analysis. Some students can critique their own work and that of their classmates (students are often the best evaluators of their own work) by engaging in peer-edits, and self assessment, comparing one's own work to a previously agreed upon rubric. After having begun the process of extension, this step is a chance to improve a rough draft and make corrections before a product is finished. In Jewish education, too often we shy away from being rigorous; we are generally uncomfortable about pushing students to give us their best. We praise mediocre work because we're grateful for anything students will produce for us. But our experiences applying 4MAT in Jewish schools is that religious school students are willing to give more of themselves than many of us think, when we are specific in our expectations and in our critiques. The teacher suggests, helps with resources, offers. Have students analyze, improve, refine their work.

Step 8: Perform – הַגְשָׁמָה

Lastly, have students perform. Look for originality (while expecting "correctness" in those aspects of the learning that involve mastery of a set formula), relevance, new questions, connections to larger ideas, skills that are immediately useful, values confirmed or questioned anew.

Here the students display their understanding, how relevant the content is to them, its connection to larger ideas, how it fits into their world. Values are confirmed or challenged, and knowledge assumes new form. The students are now the true center of the action, the context of the student now embodies the text of the experts. Their accomplishments are celebrated and, in whatever venue is possible, publicly acknowledged.

Figure 10 below shows the skills in Quadrant Four and the modalities that foster their development.

Real learning moves from the personal, perceived connections of Quadrant One, to the conceptual knowing of Quadrant Two, to the practice and tinkering of Quadrant Three, and then to the creative integration of Quadrant Four. Our knowledge must be used and it must operate in our lives. Being unique, each of us uses and integrates learning in our own inimitable, incomparable way.

What we learn is transformed inside of us. It is in the transformation that real understanding happens. And it can only happen when we complete the cycle. *All real learning leaves us changed.*

PUTTING TOGETHER A 4MAT UNIT

Not all steps need to be of equal length. Sometimes it makes sense to repeat steps (for example, to layer the teaching of several chunks of content and skills within one conceptual unit), but it rarely makes sense to skip steps. The pressure of time makes it tempting to abandon the cycle. A unit can consist of one or more completed cycles, each focused on a specific core concept or "big idea." For example, a substantial Project Etgar[11] learning unit on *kashrut* consists of three connected learning cycles:

- The first is on the concept of *Na'aseh V'nishma*, (we will do and then we will understand).

- The second on the development of positive character traits.

- The third on the Jewish dietary laws in practice.

As a second example, we would not write a 4MAT unit on "Jewish history" per se. We would, however, mind-map — or create a web of — the content of a period of Jewish history and look for an emergent concept or concepts that distinguishes

QUADRANT FOUR

Skills:	Try:
Creative integration of things learned	Recognizing and acting on serendipitous occurrences (unexpected discoveries)
Relating to groups	Creating publications or other original works
Reality checks	Merging new material with yourself
Ability to synthesize	Performing
Ability to use synergy (associating two or more elements in a new way)	Finding alternative/additional uses for learning
Ability to self-evaluate	Expressing learned material
Social action	Portfolios (both professional and academic)
Creative expression	

Figure 10

[11]Project Etgar is the New Middle School curriculum under development for the Conservative movement, based on 4MAT and authored by Dolgin and Wagner.

that period, and then create a 4MAT unit around that concept. So, for example, an integrated unit may emerge that focuses on the concept of *Kol Yisrael Arayvim Zeh BaZeh* (all Jews are responsible for one another). Through the 4MAT unit, the learners would connect to, learn about, master, and apply the idea that every Jew is responsible for every other Jew. Using both left-mode and right-mode activities — in many cases corresponding to the multiple intelligences — learners would come to understand how the concept of *K'lal Yisrael* has shaped Jewish history, *halachah* (law), literature, and liturgy. Learners would then decide how to adapt their learning on behalf of their fellow Jews, in their own community, in Israel, and throughout the world, in a personally meaningful way.

Suggested Order for Constructing a 4MAT Unit

The order in which one ultimately teaches a 4MAT unit flows through the Natural Learning Cycle as described in the previous section. However, we recommend following a different order to plan and construct a 4MAT unit.

1. **Content** — First, answer the question "what are you teaching?" and determine the *content* you are expected to teach when you get to "Step 4 - Inform." If you are relying on a textbook, then read and reread it to begin seeing what "big ideas" emerge in the content. We find that, in any case, it is almost always impossible to cover everything contained in a textbook. Furthermore, it is usually deadly to plow through a textbook in a linear fashion. We recommend using 4MAT to help proactively select the content that is interconnected and that can be presented in a way that makes sense and can fully engage your students in a meaningful way.

2. **Mind-Map the Content** - The next step is still focused on Step 4 — Inform. Your task is to mind-map — or create a web of — your content. What concepts arise, and how can the content be clustered into related concepts? What ideas do you want your students to know? We find yellow sticky notes to be invaluable for mind-mapping the content. Write a word or two on a note about each

area of content you think needs to be covered (which is always more than is possible to cover). Then rearrange the notes in clusters of content that seem to share a common concept. You are likely to end up with one, two, or several "main clusters" and then a few "stand alone" content pieces that are conceptually unrelated to any others.

3. **and** **and** **Results** - Now it is time to determine what results you expect of your learners. What will all learners be expected to know? What can be mastered by some, but not all, students? How will you know that they know it? In other words, what forms — both verbal and nonverbal — will the final product take? In this stage of the unit planning process, you are beginning to flesh out the form and forum for steps 6, 7, and 8, the extend, refine, and perform steps.

4. **Mind-Map the Skills** - The next step is still focused on Step 5 — Practice. Your task is to mind-map — or create a web of — skills to be acquired. What skills need to be taught? What do you want students to be able "to do?" How will you provide a variety of practice options that will work for your diverse learners? Will you need to pair students with practice partners? provide tapes? budget time for skills practice?

5. **Mind-Map Activities** - What are all the possible activities that can be used to teach this unit? What makes sense in terms of the content, in terms of time and space constraints, and in terms of multiple modalities that appeal to different learner preferences? Remember that covering less content that involves deep and meaningful learning will tend to be more transformative than rushing to cover lots of discrete facts.

6. **and** Begin to fill in the wheel, particularly the inform and practice steps.

7. **and** **Create the Connection** - What experiential activity will connect the content to the lives of your learners *now*? Once you are sure

of your core concept, the content and skills that relate to that concept, plan the Quadrant One activities, connect and reflect.

8. **Application** - What activities will engage the learner to create unique applications? In other words, how will you help students move from practicing new skills and concepts to incorporating them into their lives? Since the students' own voices begin to take charge of the learning in this, the extend step, what choices and options for venues might you suggest? What resources (art supplies, reference books, field trips, and so on) do you need to provide or arrange for, in order for your students to be successful at applying their new learnings?

9. **and Celebrate** - How can the learners edit, refine, present, and celebrate their accomplishments? At this stage, you are looking once again and refining your plans for the Quadrant Four refine and perform steps.

10. **Bridge to the Essense** - The last, and for many people, the hardest step is to find the perfect right-mode activity that will create a mental image for your students that bridges the core concept of the unit to the content you will be teaching and students will be learning. What activity will enable the learner to bridge from personal meaning to new learnings they will be exposed to in this unit? For example, if your unit is a study of anti-Semitism and your core concept is "Jew as Other," you may want the "Image" exercise to be an examination of pictures of how Jews have been characterized in European art. Depending on the *content* you will be teaching and the *concept* that unifies the unit, bridging to the essence can take many nonverbal forms, such as collage making, drawing, sculpting, pantomime, seeing a movie clip that helps students visualize the concept, listening to a story told by the teacher or through a recording, and so on. If you are showing unflattering pictures of Jews from church frescoes and political cartoons, the purpose is to create a mental image, not to teach the content. You may want to come back to the pictures later and

explain them, but not during the image step.

11. Reassemble your unit, get the supplies you need in order, and enjoy the fruits of your labor!

CONCLUSION

This chapter has introduced the reader to 4MAT, a model for the development of curriculum and instruction that is centered on the learner, that honors all kinds of learners, and that is particularly well suited to religious education. Dolgin and Wagner have been experiencing, learning, practicing, and implementing McCarthy's model to applications in Jewish education over the course of several years, and have gotten better at it over time. It has not been easy to change old habits, and it continues to be tempting to teach the way we like to be taught, instead of teaching so that everyone's learning modalities are accessed. We are still uncomfortable when we lead our learners through steps with activities that are out of our own comfort zone, but are deeply moved when the eyes of a learner we would otherwise have missed come alive while engaged in learning that is embedded in *his/her* comfort zone. We are sure that our teaching is profoundly better and that we are successfully reaching more of our students since we began to use 4MAT to structure our curriculum and instruction.

Our mastery of this model came slowly, through ongoing professional development at various levels of 4MAT training, plenty of practice, and other people to be engaged with along the journey. We are both Type 1 "Imaginative Learners," and prefer to construct 4MAT units collaboratively. Being Type 1s often makes our work move slowly, and we get as much help as possible by collaborating with the 2s, 3s, and 4s in our professional world, to push us along and enhance our work. For us, two heads have proven to be better than one, and a team approach has made it even more effective. We learned from Dr. Steven M. Brown, who learned from others, that human beings learn best in cooperation with other human beings by actively processing information that they find personally meaningful. This principle not only applies to children in classrooms, but also to their teachers, whose own learning about teaching and curriculum planning and decision making should be ongoing and collaborative with colleagues and master educators.

In schools where there is more than one class on the grade level, teachers may find natural partners for curriculum planning. For those who teach alone, it is invaluable to find and team up with another, so you can help each other brainstorm and sketch a unit outline. Your principal can also serve as a planning partner, if he or she becomes familiar with 4MAT. Co-planning of teaching units makes for meaningful and valuable professional development opportunities.

As we learn from Joshua ben Perahyah:

עֲשֵׂה לְךָ רַב, וּקְנֵה לְךָ חָבֵר,
וֶהֱוֵי דָן אֶת־כָּל־הָאָדָם לְכַף זְכוּת.

Select a master-teacher for yourself;
Acquire a colleague for study;
When you assess people,
tip the balance in their favor.

(*Pirke Avot* 1:6)

For those to whom the 4MAT model speaks, you may be interested in attending 4MAT training in your area, or in bringing a 4MAT instructor to your school, agency, or community. Reading an article or attending a few sessions will not in and of itself change your teaching practice. Practice time, trial and error, reflection, peer coaching, adapting, and refining are all necessary if your goal is to transform your teaching and reach all of your learners.

Vignette 3: Denise, the Teacher of All Learners

Child care difficulties caused Denise to abandon her high-power corporate job and to become a full-time stay-at-home mom. Denise really enjoyed the first few months at home with her two boys. She didn't even mind driving the Hebrew School carpool. She toyed with the idea of a part-time job, but nothing seemed interesting enough to disrupt her now peaceful home life. That is, until a very astute Educational Director, Shirley Applestein, approached Denise when she was dropping off the Sunday morning carpool. "Denise, do you have a minute to come into my office? There's something I want to discuss with you." "Uh oh," thought Denise, "which one of my boys has gotten into trouble?"

"Sure," Denise replied, somewhat sheepishly. She pulled into a parking spot and the two women disappeared into Shirley's office.

The topic of discussion totally surprised Denise. It wasn't about one of her boys, but about her! Shirley wanted to recruit Denise to become a religious school teacher. "But I have zero teaching experience!" exclaimed Denise, as she broke into a sweat. "Oh, nonsense," said Shirley, "you have a strong Judaic background, you're great with kids, and I know you've been looking for something meaningful to do part-time. What could be more meaningful that educating Jewish youth?" Denise was beginning to soften. "Besides," continued Shirley, "we just lost a Dalet teacher, and I really need you!"

Denise was stunned, but tempted. Shirley was such a wonderful principal and Denise had a great deal of respect for her. If Shirley said she would help Denise and coach her, Denise knew she meant it. "Okay, I'll give it a try," Denise said hesitantly. And with a great big hug from Shirley, Denise became a religious school teacher.

Shirley did her best to mentor Denise, but with such a large school to run, it was difficult to find spare time to meet alone with her new teacher. Denise had a pile of beautiful textbooks and teacher's guides to work with and was doing pretty well for a novice teacher, but still wished she had a better grasp on her students' abilities, and a better way of structuring her lessons.

Then 4MAT entered Denise's life. Her synagogue's school had been accepted as a Project Etgar test site, and the new curriculum was based on core concepts of Jewish life, using 4MAT as the framework for structuring the curricular units. Denise and Shirley attended a training session given by the directors and writers of Project Etgar, which included a basic introduction to the theory and application of 4MAT. Denise was enthralled. Here was the user-friendly approach to religious school lesson planning that she was looking for. Understanding the four learner types helped her better understand the variety of strengths and proclivities of her students, as well as the challenges they faced in her class. It even helped her better understand her own boys' learning styles. The 4MAT Natural Learning Cycle made sense to Denise, though admittedly, some of the suggested activities seemed unnecessary or too time-consuming. The eight steps gave Denise a concrete framework on which to plan her lessons.

A few months later, Denise and Shirley attended another 4MAT workshop, and took the plunge. Denise agreed to help Shirley work on restructuring the Hebrew High School curriculum. Denise already had good instincts, a love of children, and a love of Judaism, but 4MAT helped her reach out to all kinds of learners, and become a successful, fulfilled teacher, who feels that she is truly doing something meaningful.

BIBLIOGRAPHY

Dewey, John. "How We Think: A Restatement of the Relation of Reflective Thinking To the Educative Process." In *John Dewey: The Later Works, 1925-1953*. J.A. Boydston, ed. Carbondale, IL: Southern Illinois University Press, 1986. (Original work published in 1933)

> Dewey's belief that knowledge is constructed by individuals and not dispensed as a commodity from "the outside in" significantly impacts on our understanding of the relationship between teachers and their students and students and their learning.

Foote, Chandra J.; Paul J. Vermette; and Catherine F. Battaglia. *Constructivist Strategies: Meeting Standards and Engaging Adolescent Minds*. Larchmont, NY: Eye on Education, 2001.

> This book may be of interest for teachers who are interested in exploring and applying hands-on, constructivist teaching and learning at the high school level.

McCarthy, Bernice. *About Learning*. Wauconda, IL: About Learning Inc., 1996.

> This book is about the learning process, offering an explanation of how learning works. Written as poetry and brimming with quotes from great thinkers. The Appendix includes examples of five 4MAT instructional units for primary, middle, and high school, community college, and law school.

———. *About Teaching: 4MAT in the Classroom*. Wauconda, IL: About Learning Inc., 2000.

> *About Teaching* is the base upon which this chapter stands. It explains in detail how to teach around the 4MAT cycle, and includes key chapters on assessment (you may have noticed that assessment is not addressed in this chapter), brain research, and lesson writing guidelines. It will assist teachers who are learning to use and implement the 4MAT System to develop curriculum and enhance instruction.

National Research Council. *How People Learn: Brain, Mind, Experience, and School*. Washington DC: National Academy Press, 2000.

> This substantial volume appraises the scientific knowledge base on human learning and its application to education. The objective is to ascertain what is required for learners to reach deep understanding, to determine what leads to effective teaching, and to evaluate the conditions that lead to supportive environments for teaching and learning.

Silver, Harvey F.; Richard W. Strong; and Matthew J. Perini. *So Each May Learn: Integrating Learning Styles and Multiple Intelligences*. Alexandria, VA: Association for Supervision and Curriculum Development, 2000.

> Easy reading and interactive exercises to facilitate teachers' success in addressing both multiple intelligences and multiple learning styles in curriculum, teaching, and learning.

www.aboutlearning.com

> From this web site, you can sign up to receive a free, weekly e-mail called "The Week in Learning," which contains ideas and tips for teaching and learning through the natural learning cycle.

CHAPTER 26

Studying Curriculum Materials: A Strategy for Improving Teaching

Gail Zaiman Dorph

Curriculum materials are used by teachers on a daily basis; they are the "stuff" of lessons and units, activities, and worksheets. This chapter will suggest ways of helping teachers investigate curriculum materials as a vehicle for increasing their subject matter knowledge and improving the quality of teaching and learning in their classrooms.

Lee Shulman has explained curricular knowledge in the following ways: "The curriculum and its associated materials are the *materia medica* of pedagogy, the pharmacopeia from which the teacher draws those tools of teaching that present or exemplify particular content and remediate or evaluate the adequacy of student accomplishments."[1] Curricular knowledge defined in this way is analogous to a kind of knowledge that doctors have. For example, given a patient's profile and history, doctors are aware of the pluses and minuses of various medications. They have strategies for trying out medications and combinations of medications, taking in knowledge from the patient's subjective reports, as well as from objective tests to measure the effectiveness of the treatment plan. This kind of knowledge has several components:

- A familiarity with the range of available instruments

- Analytic tools used to decide among alternatives based on a range of considerations, including context

- Strategies for monitoring and assessing effects so that modifications can be made

In order to drive home the importance of this kind of knowledge, Shulman asks: "Would we trust a physician who did not really understand the alternative ways of dealing with categories of infectious disease, but who knew only one way?"[2]

Extending the metaphor from medicine to education suggests that in order to use materials well, teachers (as well as principals and other educators) need to know at least the following:

- There are *alternatives*; that is, there are curricular choices to be made among various materials designed to teach the same subject matter to students of the same age, learning in similar settings.

- Teachers need *analytic tools* to help them study these materials in principled ways, thinking about which materials can be best used for what purposes.

- Teachers need *strategies* to help them learn how to monitor and assess the ways in which teaching and learning are proceeding as they use the materials.

The medical model does not go far enough, however. While it is true that educators need diagnostic and evaluative strategies, they also need to think pedagogically about ideas and materials to be able to choose and design paths for students to explore and learn those ideas and materials. Close study of curriculum materials can lead to more profound understanding of the subject matter, as well as to an understanding of ideas that enable teachers to use, revise, and tailor the materials to their own students. Although learning to study curricular materials does not sound complicated, stories that teachers and principals tell about how they use them suggest that structural and conceptual work needs to be done to move us from where we are now to where we ought to be.

---

[1] Lee Shulman, "Those Who Understand: Knowledge Growth in Teaching," *Educational Researcher* 15 (32), 1986, 10.

[2] Ibid.

The following three stories describe two different challenges we need to address in order to change the ways in which teachers and principals think about using curriculum materials. Each story is based on a conversation or experience in which I was involved.

THREE STORIES

Story 1: Curriculum Materials Are Not Recipes

I observed a class in which a teacher was using new materials designed to help teachers and students become "close readers" of Torah. The materials included questions, and urged teachers to ask questions in order to help children learn to read a biblical text and make sense of its meaning. The teacher used the questions suggested in the materials. When children did not respond with answers that were "the same" as those provided in the sample lessons as possible answers, the teacher supplied the suggested answer as the "correct" answer.

On that day, the teacher was asking students to compare the place of man at the end of Chapter 1 of Genesis versus the place of man at the end of Chapter 3 of Genesis. Her questions included:

- When does man appear in the Creation narrative?

- What is his place in the story?

- When does he appear in the Eden story?

- Do you think that there is any difference in the place of man in each story?[3]

When students did not understand the line of questioning, rather than asking them to go back to the text and read the verses from chapter 1 and then the verses from chapters 2 and 3, she supplied answers that she found in the materials:

In the Creation story, man appears almost at the end of the story.

He is the last creature to be created, he is the ruler of the earth, with him the creation is completed.

In the Eden story, man appears at the beginning of the story.

In the first chapter, man is treated as a part of the whole creation. In the second and third chap-

ters, man is the center; he is the important subject of the story.[4]

By using these materials in this way, the teacher actually subverted the goals of the materials. Instead of helping her students learn to read carefully and use investigative strategies for making meaning, she actually taught them a set of facts (i.e., "correct" answers) using the questions provided in the curriculum materials as a vehicle.

This story points to one particular understanding or misunderstanding of curriculum materials: that they are designed to be used as recipe books. They provide technical instructions written by experts, designed to be followed more or less exactly as written in order to be "fail-safe." In this case, the curriculum developers encouraged this misunderstanding by providing answers to each question as a guideline and by presenting the materials in "recipe" fashion.

While it is true that curriculum documents are written to be used, they are not meant to be recipes. Recipes assume that if the same ingredients are used in the same measure, and cooked or baked for the same amount of time, the results will be predictable. We know that although you may be teaching the same subject to the same age children in the same setting, and even have the same goals, each instance of teaching is actually different. The students are different, the community is different, the teacher is different, and interactions between students and students, as well as between teacher and students, are different. Materials must be adapted for each new set of conditions. Few teachers or principals act on that challenge sufficiently.

Story 2, Version 1: Curriculum Materials Are Not the Subject Matter

In interviews that I conducted with novice teachers, I asked a young Hebrew School teacher, "How do you prepare to teach?" "What do you mean?" she asked. I reframed my question, "How are you going to get ready to teach this afternoon?" She answered, "I'm going to read the textbook and when I get to class I'm going to have a discussion with the kids about what it says."

This story highlights a significant problem: confusing the curriculum materials or textbook

---

[3]Leonard Gardner, *Genesis: The Teacher's Guide, Experimental Edition* (New York: Melton Research Center, 1996), 17.

[4]Ibid.

with the subject areas they are designed to teach. In this particular case, this novice teacher was *teaching* the textbook, not Torah or Jewish Values or Holidays. Because she was such a novice, her case represents an extreme version of this problem. Lacking even the simplest form of pedagogical thinking, she had no idea that she needed to create a lesson plan. She was not certain if the textbook she was using came with a teacher's guide. It had never occurred to her to ask. Nor had she ever asked herself: what do I want children to learn from what we will do together this afternoon? And what is my role in making that happen?

Story 2, Version 2: Curriculum Materials Are Not the Subject Matter

I was talking with a school principal about the ways in which teachers in her school were using curriculum materials to teach Torah. She talked glowingly of reinforcement exercises that teachers had created to make the materials come alive. I asked: "What role does reading the text of Torah play in teachers' preparation?" She replied, "I don't think they ever read the Torah itself." I asked, "Have you suggested that to them?" "Not really," she replied. "Why?" In exasperation, she said, "Gail, I'm surprised that you are asking this question. No parent has ever called to say, 'Why did the teacher not prepare by at least reading the original text,' but they often call to say, 'Why is class so boring?' These teachers are focusing on making class interesting!"

While this approach represents a more appropriate and sophisticated stance than that of treating materials as recipes, and while it represents a deeper understanding of the role of the teacher, it is another version of mistaking the materials for the subject matter. The starting point of this teacher's pedagogic work was to embellish the materials in order to make them appropriate and interesting for her class. She did not think about the text itself or about the appropriateness of these materials for her school or her class.

A Torah story summarized, retold, or edited by a curriculum developer is not the same as the account of the narrative found in the Torah. The curriculum developer's story represents choices that the curriculum developer and/or publisher have made about what they want children to learn. Consequently, it is often choices made by curricu-

lum developers, not teachers or the principal, which shape the opportunities learners have for understanding not only the "basic facts" of a subject, but in a larger sense, what it means "to know" a subject.

THE PROBLEM

These three stories suggest that many teachers have only a minimal understanding of what they are supposed to do with the curriculum documents they have. The teachers described in the stories above did not understand that they needed to study, understand, and evaluate the materials in their hands in order to use them in the service of teaching. No matter how materials are presented, no matter how good they are, they require teacher work to transform them from words and suggestions on a page into learning opportunities for children in their classrooms.

Thinking about the work that curriculum transformation entails on the part of teachers will require a change in stance toward curriculum materials. Teachers must learn to see "curriculum" neither as a given nor as an ideal, but as a *possibility* that needs their active review and reshaping. Teachers will need to understand that curriculum materials are not neutral tools. They embody various assumptions both about what is worthwhile learning and how learning ought to take place. Teachers must learn to analyze materials in order to understand the assumptions upon which they are based, and then actively work with and on the materials in order to transform them in the service of teaching a given group of students.

We can improve the quality of teaching and learning in our schools by creating opportunities for teachers to come together regularly to study and analyze the curricular materials they are using or asked to use. Such opportunities would help teachers develop curricular knowledge and would support both teacher and student learning. Instead of providing easy answers to the question, "what should I teach tomorrow?" materials would become texts for study and opportunities for teachers to work together to deepen their content knowledge and sharpen their approach to teaching this content. It would require them to confront the "original," the true subject matter and their own understanding of it. Unpacking materials in this way and then learning to think about them pedagogically will help teachers know more and become "smarter" about choosing and designing learning opportunities for their students.

PURPOSES OF CURRICULUM STUDY GROUPS

In *Knowing and Teaching Elementary Mathematics*,[5] Liping Ma describes how teachers in China meet on a regular basis to study curricular materials. It is instructive for us to think about what she learned from visiting these teacher study groups and interviewing teachers who participated in them. For these teachers, participation in such study groups provided a window for better understanding of mathematical ideas. It enabled them to use, revise, and tailor the materials to their own students in more productive ways. Interestingly, these teachers claimed that such study was instrumental in helping them develop what they called PUFM, "Profound Understanding of Fundamental Mathematics." Given that one of the challenges facing us in Jewish education is creating a knowledgeable group of teachers and students, the idea that studying the materials that we use in teaching can help us learn more about PUJS, the Profound Understanding of Jewish Subjects, is very appealing.

As one reads Ma's description, it is easy to picture the process that she is describing. Imagine what it would be like to be involved in such a process with your colleagues.

> They study it constantly throughout the school year when they teach it. First of all, they work for an understanding of "what it is." They study how it interprets and illustrates the ideas . . . , why the authors structured the book in a certain way, what the connections among the contents are . . . At a more detailed level, they study how each unit of the textbook is organized, how the content was presented by the authors, and why. They study what examples are in a unit, why these examples were selected, and why the examples were presented in a certain order. They review the exercises in each section of a unit, the purpose for each exercise section, and so on. Indeed, they conduct a very careful and critical investigation of the textbook.

Although teachers usually find the authors' ideas ingenious and inspiring, they also sometimes find parts of the textbook that from their perspective are unsatisfactory, or inadequate illustrations of ideas in the framework.[6]

What is clear from reading this description is the seriousness with which these teachers approach this task. Their study groups resemble in some ways good adult Torah study groups. In both, the written word is studied carefully; it is unpacked and analyzed. In the curriculum study groups described by Ma, there is one difference. Not only does this close study of curriculum materials lead to more profound understanding of the subject matter, it also leads to a kind of understanding of ideas that enable teachers to use, revise, and tailor the materials to their own students. Both of these outcomes seem critical in improving teaching in Jewish settings as well. Curriculum study groups would help us reach both these goals. Let us examine each of these processes — unpacking and adapting — in more depth.

UNPACKING CURRICULUM MATERIALS FOR GREATER UNDERSTANDING

The backbone of this strategy lies in determining what a given set of materials is about, what its stated purposes are, and what teachers and students must do together in order to reach its goals. It is critical in using this approach to understand that curriculum materials represent choices that curriculum developers make as they construct their materials. These choices center on what Joseph Schwab has called the four commonplaces of education: teacher, subject matter, learner, and context.[7]

Studying two sets of materials allows us to compare the way each deals with the same issues and will give some sense of what can be learned from unpacking and comparing materials in the service of the first purpose above, selecting appropriate materials). In the excerpts from curricula on the Tower of Babel that follow, some of the choices that two curriculum developers made can be seen. I will focus particularly on subject matter in this

---

[5]Liping Ma, *Knowing and Teaching Elementary Mathematics* (Mahwah, NJ: Lawrence Erlbaum Associates, 1999).

[6]Ibid., 131, 132.

[7]Joseph Schwab, "The Practical: Translation into Curriculum," *School Review* 81, 1973, 501-522.

example in order to indicate *how* teachers studying together might develop more PUJS (Profound Understanding of Jewish Subjects) and thus improve their capacity to teach. After the example, I will suggest a template that can be helpful in unpacking a curriculum from the vantage point of any one of the commonplaces.

An Example

The account of the Tower of Babel (Genesis 11:1-9) is commonly taught to children between the ages of eight and ten. Since the text of the Bible is difficult, even in translation, most curriculum developers prepare simplified versions of the story in addition to developing questions for teachers and worksheets and activities for children. In retelling the story, curriculum developers are already *interpreting* the original subject matter. To understand fully the choices made by the developers requires teachers to read the text of Genesis before they teach the story.

Comparing and contrasting two sets of materials (in the following examples) allows teachers to understand that different materials:

- tell the biblical story differently.

- posit different goals for Torah study.

- provide students with different opportunities to learn both "the facts" of the text and "the norms" by which it is studied.

The Tower of Babel opens with a decision by humanity to build a city and a tower with its top in the heavens. The two different sets of materials represent the people's decision, their motivation, and God's decision to intervene in different ways. In order to understand clearly the choices that the developers are making, take the time to read the text of Genesis 11:1-9 before reading further:

Textbook #1[8]

They decided to build a mighty city and a tower of brick. "We will make the tower so tall it will touch the clouds in the sky," they said. "People will then remember us and praise our name. People will want to live in our city forever . . ."

God saw the bricks becoming a city and a tower. God watched as the hearts of the people became as hard as bricks. The people of the earth stopped loving one another. They forgot how to love God, . . .

Textbook #2[9]

(3) People said to their neighbors: "Okay, let us make bricks and burn them hard . . . "

(4) Then they said: "Okay, let us build a city and a tower with its top in the sky. Let us make a name for ourselves, to keep us from being scattered over the face of all the earth."

(5) The Lord came down to see the city and the tower that Adam's children were building.

(6) The Lord said: "Now, they are one people with one language. This is only the beginning of what they will do. From now on, they will be able to do whatever they feel like doing."

(7) Okay, let us go down and babble their language so that people will not understand their neighbors' language.

In Textbook #1 the builders' motivation is clear (people will remember us and praise our name), as is the reason for God's intervention (people stopped loving each other; people stopped loving God). In Textbook #2, people want to make a name for themselves; God decides to prevent them, as otherwise "they will be able to do whatever they feel like doing." The actual biblical narrative is closer to the version of the story in the second textbook. Although people's intentions are mentioned in both, the moral overtones are not clear in the second. The biblical text and the version of it in this textbook are opaque. A reader is left to puzzle over the meaning of the narrative. What did the people do wrong? What is so bad about building this tower? Why does God decide to punish the people?

In trying to "unpack" these two sets of materials, teachers need to ask two different kinds of questions:

---

[8]Seymour Rossel, *A Child's Bible* (West Orange, NJ: Behrman House, 1988), 41.

[9]Joel Lurie Grishaver, *Being Torah* (Los Angeles, CA: Torah Aura Publications, 1986), 57.

1. What is the curriculum developer's perspective on the subject matter?

2. What will students learn about the Torah and about studying the Torah if these materials are used well?

Examining more than one set of materials designed for use in comparable settings makes it easier to discern that choices have been made in how curricula "represent" subject matter.

From the excerpts above, we can infer that the curriculum developers of Textbook #1 are concerned that students learn that the Torah contains moral values because they chose to make explicit the moral they wished to teach. We might infer that the curriculum developers of Textbook #2 want to create a text that is close to the one in the Torah, while leaving the interpretation of the text open to the learners.

The Teacher's Guides

These inferences are borne out when we examine portions of the teacher's guide to each of the textbooks. In Textbook #1, there is a section entitled: "What does it mean?" In this section of the materials, the developer summarizes lessons that students should learn from their reading:

> The builders on the tower looked down and saw everything below getting smaller and smaller. It made them feel stronger and more important than the people below. They began to think that they were as mighty as God.

> You do not have to be on top of a tall tower to look down on other people. You can just say or think that a person is someone to "look down on," someone less important than you.

> But really, God makes each of us special, so every person is important. Every person has something special to offer the world. "Looking down" on people is always a mistake. It's like "making war with God."[10]

The underlying assumption that the Bible communicates religious and moral values and that its narratives are to be understood as helping the reader learn how to act in the world are explicit. This is an approach to the teaching of Torah that is

familiar in the context of religious education.

This is not the approach of Textbook #2, which adopts what might be termed a literary critical method for studying and teaching the Bible. This method aims at opening up the complexity and ambiguities of the biblical narrative. Its pedagogic approach asks readers to "read the text closely" in order to uncover its multiple meanings. In these materials the biblical stories are recounted in words that closely conform to the Hebrew text. Just as the biblical text omits attributions of personal motivation and intention, so, too, does this textbook. Thus students are often left puzzling over the message of a given story. In this lesson, children learn that the Bible is a book with multiple messages for them to discover.

The differences in these textbooks extend to the assignments and questions in the materials and teacher's guides. Textbook #1 tells us what the people did wrong; in Textbook #2, the students are asked, "What did they (the people in the story) do wrong?" Children learn that this question has multiple answers through three different ways: (1) The question is asked and they themselves generate possible responses. (2) After the story, there is a page in the textbook called "Commentary."[11] Such a page follows each narrative. This page has photographs of four children, each of whom has presumably grappled with the same question, and their responses to the question being posed. (3) The teacher's guide brings additional texts from the Jewish tradition that contain Rabbinic responses to the same question. Studying these two sets of materials raises many questions for teachers, particularly: What are our purposes for teaching Bible? What do we want the children who are eight years old in our school to be learning? How will we help children reach these goals, no matter which textbook we use?

This example vividly illustrates that curriculum developers have a point of view about subject matter. This is not only true in a subject area such as Bible, in which developers are creating the story line itself. Examples abound in other disciplines as well. For example, history can be studied from a political or social perspective; history books can be organized chronologically or thematically; and primary sources can be made accessible to students or not. Each of the decisions made by the curriculum

---

[10]Rossel, 43

[11]Grishaver, 58.

developer represents history in a different way and, therefore, creates different opportunities for students to learn some things and not others.

A TEMPLATE FOR UNPACKING CURRICULAR MATERIALS

Exploring the stance of curriculum materials toward each of the four commonplaces (outlined by Schwab, p. 314) can be used as an opening for a curriculum study group's investigations. The former example demonstrated what teachers might learn if they focused on unpacking materials from the standpoint of subject matter. Questions can also be developed that promote the study of each of the commonplaces. An example of a "generic"[12] set of questions that can be adapted/developed for a variety of subject matters follows:

About the Subject Matter:

1. What are the goals of these materials? Or, what goals seem to be implicit in the design of these materials?

2. What are the main concepts that this curriculum is trying to teach?

3. What is the basis for the organization and sequence of the content?

4. What disciplinary lenses shape the curriculum? What other lenses could be used?

5. What orientations to the subject matter inform these materials?

6. What modes of inquiry are presented or implied in the materials?

7. What is the role of primary sources (texts) in developing the concepts?

About Teacher and Teaching:

1. What roles for teachers are anticipated in the materials (e.g., are teachers to be sources of knowledge, guides for independent learning, other)?

2. What assumptions does the curriculum make about the personal knowledge and attitudes that the teacher brings to the content?

3. Do the materials state specific teaching strategies? Are teaching alternatives offered?

4. Do the materials disclose to the teachers the developers' choices and reasoning?

5. What does "good teaching" using these materials look like?

About Learners and Learning:

1. What image of learning is implied by the materials (e.g., active inquiry, the acquisition of specific knowledge/habits/skills, others)?

2. How do the materials take into account the different motivational needs of learners (e.g., the need to excel, the need for social interaction, curiosity)?

3. Does the curriculum treat learners as individuals or as members of a uniform group?

4. How could the materials be adapted to varied populations of learners?

5. If students learn the ideas/concepts/skills "well," what will they actually learn?

About Context:

1. Do the materials reflect an ideological or denominational stance? If so, what is it?

2. What is the fit between the materials and the family background of students and the local community?

3. Do the materials mention the impact of the subject on society?

4. What is the fit between the materials and your classroom situation (e.g., time, resources)?

5. How would you adapt the materials to fit your context?

Developing questions such as these and using them to unpack and study curriculum materials can be a first step for teachers' groups when dis-

---

[12]Many of these questions were developed by Miriam Ben-Peretz, Gail Dorph, and Sharon Feiman-Nemser for a seminar of teacher educators who were part of the Mandel Foundation's Teacher Educator Institute.

cussing curriculum. These explorations have the potential to lead to deepening understanding not only of the subject material, but also of the role of the teacher and the developers' ideas about what it takes to learn something.

ADAPTING MATERIALS FOR INDIVIDUAL CLASSROOMS

In her book *The Teacher-Curriculum Encounter,*[13] Miriam Ben-Peretz suggests that teachers are freed from the "tyranny of textbooks" when they understand that curriculum materials themselves are interpretations. Knowing more about what is "behind" the materials they are using allows teachers to engage their students in more sophisticated and far-reaching ways. The questions teachers investigate and the knowledge they gain will make an impact on their choices as they plan what to teach. Thus, their planning will become more sophisticated and comprehensive, and their capacity to enact the curriculum will be expanded.

In her work, Ben-Peretz suggests that curriculum materials not be viewed as static suggestions of the ideal but rather as expressions " . . . of educational potential, of intended, as well as unintended, curricular uses which may be disclosed through deliberate interpretation efforts."[14] The idea that a teacher's use of materials may go beyond the intention of a curriculum developer, emphasizes the notion that in the enactment of curriculum, teachers themselves actively become partners in its development.

When teachers spend time investigating curriculum, they can develop an understanding of how the material impacts on the subject matter, its explicit goals, what the materials contain and what they omit, the projected role of the teacher, and what children are expected to learn. Such knowledge can be a building block toward teachers actively and intentionally uncovering multiple uses for curriculum in their setting and can prepare them for the role of curriculum developer (suggested by Ben Peretz). By studying materials together, teachers become aware of their role in adding to, adapting, and modifying the materials at hand.

> . . . the notion of curriculum potential is dependent on the interaction between teachers and materials. Materials offer starting points, and teachers use their curricular insights, their pedagogical knowledge, and their professional imagination to develop their own curricular ideas on the basis of existing materials . . . The spectrum of ideas about potential uses of curriculum materials that teachers may generate is dependent on their knowledge of subject matter, their past teaching experiences, their feeling for and understanding of classroom reality, their interpretative skills, and their openness to new ideas.[15]

Adapting Curriculum — Developing Curriculum Potential: What's the Big Idea?

The following example of teachers studying curriculum materials takes place in the context of an afternoon school setting.[16] A consultant works with three teachers who are about to begin teaching a unit about Shabbat. They begin by stating their understandings of the goals of the written curriculum. Barbara, one of the teachers, explains: "These are the objectives of this unit. This is what I want kids to come away with. They need to know all three prayers and they need to realize that everyone celebrates Shabbat differently."[17] The group tries to understand how the objectives of the unit could, on the one hand, be so specific (all three prayers) and, on the other hand, so open-ended (everyone celebrates Shabbat differently). As they talk, they realize that they are ambivalent about how to present Shabbat to the children in their classes. They have some ideas about "traditional" ways to celebrate, as well as an understanding of the reality of their community, a community in which traditional observances are not the norm. On the one hand, they want children to understand that the day is "special" and, on the other hand, they don't want to teach them some version of "correct practice" that they may not have seen

---

[13]Miriam Ben-Peretz, *The Teacher-Curriculum Encounter: Freeing Teachers from the Tyranny of Texts* (Albany, NY: SUNY Press, 1990).

[14]Ibid., 45.

[15]Ibid., 53

[16]Ibid., 463.

[17]Erich Fromm, *The Forgotten Language: An Introduction To the Understanding of Dreams, Fairy Tales, and Myths* (New York: Grove Press, 1951).

and that parents may resent. The only idea that the materials contain is the notion that Shabbat is special. But when they try to fill in what makes the day special, it is hard to distinguish between the concept "week-end" and the concept "Shabbat."

The consultant suggests a conceptual framework that she feels offers a Jewishly authentic and substantive way of thinking about Shabbat and that she believes will be meaningful to the team members and consonant with the school community. Fromm's *The Forgotten Language*[18] develops the concepts of work and rest in the following way:

> "'Work' is any interference by man, be it constructive or destructive, with the physical world. 'Rest' is a state of peace between man and nature."[19]

These ideas about work and rest still present a challenge because decisions must still be made about how Shabbat is to be celebrated. However, it is an idea that teachers feel they can work with because it explains the restrictions of Shabbat in a way that might be more understandable and relevant to the members of this community.

Now that they have a conceptual framework on which to build, the teachers turn back to the curriculum and discuss ways in which they can use this new big idea both to frame the unit and adapt the learning activities suggested by the curriculum developers. Just because they have figured out an idea that helps them make sense of Shabbat does not mean that they have figured out what and how to teach their students. They now need to address the questions:

1. What exactly do we hope these young children will learn?

2. How will we help them learn those things?

3. How will we need to add/modify the materials that we are using to reach these goals?

These questions are different from those that were addressed in the unpacking investigation above. Although one can unpack curriculum materials from the perspective of any one of the commonplaces (preferably from the perspective of all four) the work of adaptation cannot stop there.

Teaching happens in the interaction between and among teacher, students, content, and settings. Thus the questions that need to be asked require not only analysis, but imagination.

Teachers must navigate among: (1) their own knowledge, beliefs, and ideas of learners, content, and setting; (2) the real students who sit before them (and those students' abilities and capacities as well as their prior beliefs, knowledge, understandings); (3) the subject matter, its complexities and the ways in which they are represented in specific curriculum materials; and (4) the unique features of the setting and community in which they teach. It may be helpful to visualize this dynamic with teacher, learner, and content as points of a triangle, each one linked to the other two, and set inside a larger circle indicating the setting, as in figure 1 below:

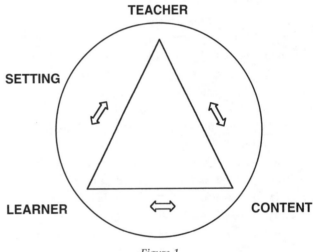

Figure 1

The arrows represent the dynamic interaction between and among the various corners of the triangle. Groups of teachers figuring out issues of curricular adaptation must have this dynamic in mind as they work.

During the process of curricular adaptation, the teachers in this school decided to look for a story that would capture the idea of the specialness of Shabbat and chose the classic story "The Sabbath Taste."[20] The story develops the idea that intention and effort are the ingredients that make Shabbat

---

[18]Ibid., 244.

[19]Sadie Rose Weilerstein, *What the Moon Brought* (Philadelphia, PA: Jewish Publication Society, 1942), 55-62.

[20]To learn more about Brenda and her seminar, see: Gail Z. Dorph, Susan Stodolsky, and Renee S. Wohl, "Growing as a Teacher Educator: Learning New Professional Development Practices, *Journal of Jewish Education*, 2002.

and the foods that we eat on it different from those that we enjoy during the rest of the week. In addition to finding the story, they created a set of questions to help children understand the ideas that are developed in the story. They brainstormed possible answers that children might give and tried to imagine the pitfalls they might encounter. In essence, they were working on giving "some meat" to the concept of "special."

> We have a Partnership 2000 *shaliach* (emissary) in our religious school, who comes from a *kibbutz*. He is a very visible presence, and so it was important that he spend time with the children in my resource class who are not mainstreamed. In looking for background material to use with my students, I found myself forced to refine my goals for teaching this mini-unit on Israel/*kibbutz* several times. I began by looking at other curricula with an eye toward reading level. I asked myself if my students could read and comprehend this material in English. In so doing, I began questioning why a particular textbook or unit was designed the way it was. What were the goals of the authors, and were they appropriate goals for my students? What goals did *I* have beyond not having the students feel left out of the general excitement over the emissary? In the end, I created worksheets to use with an adult video on the *kibbutz*. This process helped me to identify my key goal of having students gain a visual sense of Israel, as well as a visual context in which to place the emissary's stories of *kibbutz* life.
>
> *(Anne Johnston, New Haven, Connecticut)*

VALUE-ADDED: BONUSES ACCRUING FROM THE WORK OF CURRICULUM STUDY GROUPS

There is more to curricular knowledge than the development of subject matter expertise and the ability to adapt materials for use in a given classroom. Curriculum study groups may take on at least two other critically important tasks:

- Setting goals and choosing materials that "teach toward those goals"; this would include studying alternative materials for a given topic or subject within a grade.

- Aligning a school's curriculum (making sure that the goals and approach to teaching and learning proposed in materials chosen for one year match up with and build on goals chosen in other years) in order to create a more coherent educational experience for learners.

Such work could be instrumental in informing curricular choice and selection and could lead to productive discussions about goals for the students with regard to a particular subject area across the grades.

An additional gain of curriculum study groups comes under the heading of adult learning. This important secondary gain can be demonstrated from the case of Brenda,[21] a principal of a Reform religious school with 450 students in a medium-size Jewish community. She has been conducting voluntary monthly study groups for her faculty for the last four years. This group began as a series of teachers meeting to align the school's holiday curriculum. Teachers came together to examine the materials they were using to teach holidays over the course of the five years of religious school. They wanted to know what ideas and practices they were actually teaching and to understand how a child's ideas about these holidays would grow and deepen over the years.

As their work together developed, teachers realized that they needed to learn more about the holidays and to get in touch with their own beliefs and commitments. Brenda organized a series of meetings devoted to studying the holidays, including study of appropriate primary texts,

> in order to connect it to our lives today, and also to figure out how to teach this . . . to create different curricular objectives and activities for each holiday and . . . by the end of the year, a holiday curriculum . . . that was developmental throughout the grade levels.[22]

They developed a strategy that included monthly meetings with the whole faculty during

---

[21]Ibid., 7.

[22]J.W. Little, "Teachers' Professional Development in a

Climate of Educational Reform," *Educational Evaluation and Policy Analysis* 15, 1993, 129-151.

which they studied the holiday, and also grade level groups during which there was careful study of the curriculum materials in use. In advance of each of these holidays, they would work through their ideas about what would be important to teach that year and why. They brainstormed activities that would add "meat" to the ideas embedded in the curriculum and decided what they would skip, either because they felt it did not add to their current sense of what it was important for children to learn or because they realized there would not be enough time to do everything.

Over the course of the years, not only did they deepen their personal knowledge of holidays (the focus on adult learning of Jewish content was becoming stronger), they also developed some common language for talking about teaching and learning and developed more trusting attitudes toward each other. Last, but not least, they improved the curriculum for their students!

There is one final rationale for creating ongoing curriculum study groups in your own educational settings. Educational research (Little, 1993[23]; Little and McLaughlin, 1993[24]) has shown that significant teacher learning and development occur over long periods of time. Thus effective professional development programs must be sustained and coherent, providing enough time for teacher reflection and growth. Ongoing curriculum study groups can provide one such opportunity for teacher learning. Because working on curriculum means working both on the content of teaching and on its enactment, it is a powerful strategy for working on improving both teaching and learning.

CONCLUSION: HOW TO BEGIN

Simply put, the way to begin would be to follow the advice of *Pirke Avot*, (Ethics of the Fathers): *"K'neh lecha chaver"* — find a study buddy, another teacher who wants to investigate what students in their classes are learning, and just begin. Reread your materials and ask yourselves: If we use these materials well, what would students be learning? Is this what we want them to learn?

The insights you gain from this first inspection can be the springboard to constituting a small or large study group in your institution to continue studying curriculum materials in a systematic way. Your process may include using or adapting the questions found in the template suggested above or devising your own questions. Your path may lead you to adapt the curriculum you have in hand or to study other materials in order to develop a more eclectic approach to your students and to the subject matter.

---

[23]Little, J.W., "Teachers' Professional Development in a Climate of Educational Reform," *Educational Evaluation and Policy Analysis* 15, 1993, 129-151.

[24]J.W. Little and M.W. McLaughlin, *Teachers' Work: Individuals, Colleagues, and Contexts* (New York: Teachers College Press, 1993).

BIBLIOGRAPHY

Ball, Deborah, and David Cohen. "Reform by the Book: What Is — or Might Be — the Role of Curriculum Materials in Teacher Learning and Instructional Reform?" *Educational Researcher* 25 (9), 1996.

Ball and Cohen develop our thinking about ways in which curriculum materials can be an agent for the improvement of instruction.

Ben Peretz, Miriam. *The Teacher-Curriculum Encounter: Freeing Teachers from the Tyranny of Texts.* Albany, NY: State University of New York, 1990.

Ben Peretz teaches us how to treat curriculum materials as the "embodiments of potential," that is, as dynamic documents that teachers must interpret and develop. Her book encourages teachers to "read" curriculum imaginatively and develop its potential, building on what curriculum developers create, but not being confined to their ideas and suggestions.

Blythe, Tina. *The Teaching for Understanding Guide.* San Francisco, CA: Jossey-Bass, 1998.

The *Teaching for Understanding Guide* offers teachers guidance in applying the four critical components of the "teaching for understanding" framework developed by Project Zero and the Harvard Graduate School of Education. The approach itself is described in *Teaching for Understanding: Linking Research with Practice.*

Ma, Liping. *Knowing and Teaching Elementary Mathematics: Teachers' Understanding of Fundamental Mathematics in China and the United States.* Mahwah, NJ: Lawrence Erlbaum Associates, 1999.

This book describes the nature and development of "profound understanding of fundamental mathematics." Although based on practices developed in the teaching of mathematics found in Chinese schools, the ideas and strategies that she describes have important implications for anyone interested in the development of profound understanding of Jewish subject matter areas.

Shulman, Lee. "Those Who Understand: Knowledge Growth in Teaching." *Educational Researcher* 15 (32), 1986.

In this article Shulman introduces a framework for thinking about what teachers need to know and understand in order to teach. One such framework is curricular knowledge.

Wiggins, Grant, and Jay McTighe. *Understanding by Design.* Alexandria, VA: Association for Supervision and Curriculum Design, 1998.

Understanding by Design and its accompanying handbook were developed to help educators design units and courses of study that focus on the development of students' understanding. It offers criteria not only for selecting "big ideas," but also for thinking more carefully and deeply about assessment, promoting methods that allow teachers to determine the degree of student understanding. (For more on Understanding by Design, see Chapter 24, "Curriculum Planning: A Model for Understanding" by Nachama Skolnik Moskowitz, pp. 278-291 in this Handbook.)

CHAPTER 27

Multiple Intelligences

Renee Frank Holtz and Barbara Lapetina

*A*t back-to-school night, the parents of your students all inform you that their children are "very smart." You are a new teacher at the local day school and you certainly don't wish to question the parents of your 24 geniuses, but it is clear to you — after only one week of school — that while all of your students may be smart, they seem to be smart in different ways. Some seem to like to draw (doodling all over their book covers), while others are clearly gifted in physical activity. One student brought his saxophone to school and played beautifully, while another brought you the gift of a poem she wrote.

So, you do what many teachers do on back-to-school night — you nod and tell all of the parents that, yes, you recognize that their children are very smart. In the meantime, though, you decide that you need to discover how your students are intelligent and how these intelligences can play out both in and out of the classroom.

Ahad HaAm said, "Learning, learning, learning: that is the secret of Jewish survival." However, children learn in such different ways that it often seems as if the *path* to learning is the specific secret to our longevity. One possible foray down that path is through an examination of the multiple intelligences that students exhibit. Howard Gardner viewed intelligence as "the capacity to solve problems or to fashion products that are valued in one or more cultural setting" (Gardner and Hatch, 1989, pp. 4-10). He suggested that we each have varying strengths in combinations with intelligence (Gardner, 1993).

Gardner initially formulated a list of seven intelligences that he called verbal/linguistic, musical/rhythmic, logical/mathematical, visual/spacial, bodily/kinesthetic, interpersonal, and intrapersonal. One added later is naturalistic. Robert Sternberg (1997) did similar research. He suggested that we have differing strengths in an amalgamation of intelligence. He referred to schoolhouse

intelligence as a preference for learning in the linear ways often typical of classrooms, contextual intelligence as a preference for seeing how and why things work in the world, and problem solving intelligence as a preference for making new connections and innovations (pp. 107-108). Tomlinson (2001, p. 62) noted that, "Indications are that when students approach learning in ways that address their intelligence preferences, results are quite positive."

Gardner's theory of multiple intelligences has met with a strong, positive response from many educators. It has been embraced by a range of educational theorists and, significantly, applied by teachers and policy makers to the problems of schooling. The first two intelligences are ones that have been typically valued in schools. The next three are usually associated with the arts, and the final two are what Gardner called personal intelligences (Gardner 1991, p. 12). At the time of this writing, Gardener was considering two additional intelligences: existentialist and spiritualist. Gardner claimed that the seven intelligences rarely operate independently. They are used at the same time and tend to complement each other as people develop skills or solve problems (p. 81). A number of schools in North America have looked to structure curricula according to the intelligences, and to design classrooms and even whole schools to reflect the understandings that Howard Gardner develops. Project Spectrum from Tufts University and Project Zero from Harvard are two such curricula that encompass entire schools.

An offshoot of Project Zero is Project SUMIT (Schools Using Multiple Intelligences Theory). Mindy L. Kornhaber, a researcher involved with Project SUMIT, has identified a number of reasons why teachers and policy makers in North America have responded positively to Howard Gardner's presentation of multiple intelligences. One suggested reason is that the theory validates educators' everyday experience: students think and learn in many different ways. Gardner's theory also provides educators with a conceptual framework for organizing and reflecting on curriculum assessment and pedagogical practices.

In turn, this reflection has led many educators to develop new approaches that might better meet the needs of the range of learners in their classrooms. However, the question arises: if it is hard to teach one intelligence, how can educators teach if there are seven? Gardner responds to this question by making the point that seven kinds of intelligence would allow seven ways to teach, rather than one. Powerful constraints that exist in the mind can be mobilized to introduce a particular concept (or whole system of thinking) in a way that children are most likely to learn it and least likely to distort it.

Each of Gardner's seven intelligences is described below.

VERBAL/LINGUISTIC (WORD SMART)

"Pleasant words are like a honeycomb, sweetness to the soul, and health to the body." (Proverbs 16:24)

Your sixth graders are responsible for this month's school newsletter. Articles have been submitted by other classes, but your students have to work on the layout. You really want to make the project a collaborative effort, but you have found that your students do really well with independent projects or activities that involve verbal skills. In order to help reach those students who have strengths in these areas, you decide to rework the project so that you can help students emphasize their verbal/linguistic skills.

Linguistic intelligence allows individuals to communicate and make sense of the world through language. Students who enjoy playing with rhymes, who like puns and jokes, who can tell a good story, who acquire other languages easily, all exhibit linguistic intelligence (Blythe, White, & Gardner, 1995, p. 5).

You divide your students into groups of four. You assign each group an article and ask members to come up with a word game or puzzle that reinforces the theme of the article. You also ask each group to develop a short word bank of Hebrew words that are translations of some of the article's key words. After each group has finished their assignment, you move on to layout.

To try in the classroom:

- Formal presentations
- Study of poetry
- Word games
- Journals

MUSICAL/RHYTHMIC (MUSIC SMART)

"Sing unto the Lord a new song." (Psalms 96:1)

Mr. N. is dreading the upcoming review session for his midyear evaluations. He believes that his students dislike reading Hebrew and thinks that his approach to the subject is less than interesting — both for him and for his class. He usually spends about 15 minutes a day having the whole class involved in choral reading. Then he has students work independently or in pairs on their word banks, and complete the pages in their textbook. Now that his students are studying their Hebrew tenses, he finds that things have become even more tedious. His lessons are not reaching enough of his students, and he would like to make them more exciting.

Musical intelligence involves skill in the performance, composition, and appreciation of musical patterns. It allows people to create, communicate, and understand meanings made out of sound. Students who are attracted to the singing of birds outside the classroom window or who can tap out intricate rhythms with a pencil exhibit musical intelligence (Blythe, et al., 1995 p. 6).

Mr. N. reads about the musical/rhythmic intelligence. He really isn't sure which of his students might enjoy or have strengths in these areas, but decides that emphasizing these activities might be a good idea. He divides his students into small groups and assigns each one of these grammatical forms (1) future tense of the verb A-H-V, (2) past tense of the verb Sh-M-R. He asks each group to create a song or "jingle" that articulates or emphasizes the prefixes and suffixes that go with these conjugations.

To try try in the classroom:

- Use music to create moods.
- Write lyrics to music.
- Use choral reading and musical instruments.

LOGICAL/MATHEMATICAL (REASONING/ NUMBER SMART)

> "Logic supplemented by the social sciences . . . becomes the instrument of advances." (Cordozo, *Growth of the Law*)

Josh has been the youth group advisor at the nearby synagogue for three years. He takes his job very seriously. The highlight of the year is the annual tzedakah (justice/charity) teacher-student basketball game. However, the game attracts mostly those students who are interested in "getting physical." He has always invited all other students to come and cheer on their classmates, but few attend. He decides to ask his kids what else they might like to do, in hopes of reaching out to students who might be excited to participate in other ways.

Logical/mathematical intelligence consists of the capacity to analyze problems logically, carry out mathematical operations, and investigate issues scientifically. It enables individuals to use abstract relationships. Students who enjoy baseball statistics, who love to analyze the components of a problem (either personal or school-related) before systematically testing solutions, exhibit logical/mathematical intelligence (Blythe, et al., 1995, p. 12).

> *Josh's youth groupers agree that there are a lot of kids who would like to participate, but who don't feel comfortable playing basketball. The group decides to sell tickets to the game and to sell food at the game. A group of 20 youth groupers forms a committee. They create tickets on the computer, make lists of food to buy and prices to be charged. Josh is thrilled; there are now many more teens involved in the program!*

To try in the classroom:

- Use list making.
- Find patterns and categories.
- Use logic puzzles, calculations, scientific methods, and graphs.

VISUAL/SPATIAL (PICTURE SMART)

> "True vision requires far more than the eye. It takes the whole person." (Guggenheimer, *Creative Vision*)

Sandra is so excited to be starting her first year of teaching at the day school downtown. She will teach four sections of history and two of economics. She wants to make sure that her classroom is a stimulating place for her students. She knows that many of her lessons emphasize verbal/linguistic intelligences and wants to expand the repertoire she is offering to her students. In addition, she is worried that the study of ancient Israel might be something that her class considers dull. She is looking for ways to liven up the activities she plans.

Visual/spatial intelligence makes it possible for people to use visual or spatial information, to transform this information, and to recreate visual images from memory. The students who turn first to graphs, charts, and pictures in their textbooks, who like to web ideas prior to writing a paper and who intricately doodle in their notebooks, show evidence of spatial intelligence. (Blythe, et al., 1995, p. 8)

> *Sandra decides to have her students create a topographical map of ancient Israel, focusing on the journey of Abraham. She provides them with clay, poster paper, and markers. They have to work together and create a visual representation of ancient Israel.*

To try in the classroom:

- Color combinations
- Layouts
- Mapping
- Graphic organizers
- Newspapers
- Bulletin boards
- Posters

BODILY/KINESTHETIC (BODY SMART)

> "Blessed are You, Eternal our God, Source of the Universe, who has made our bodies with wisdom, combining veins, arteries,

and vital organs into a finely balanced network." (Morning worship service, from *Brachot* 60b)

Tzipporah has been studying Prophets with her fifth graders. She has been discussing the Book of Judges as a cycle — time and again the Israelites sin and break their Covenant with God, Who then brings an oppressor. The Israelites cry out, and ultimately God hears them. God brings a judge, often someone unknown, to save them. In actuality, it is God who really saves the people. At peace, the judge dies. Then Israel sins and breaks the Covenant and the cycle starts all over again.

In the past few years, she has discussed this cycle and asked her students to complete the exercise in figure 1 below.

This year, Tzipporah wants to add another dimension to the discussion. She has observed that while many of the students seem to assimilate the information the class is discussing, some are still uncertain how the cycle operates.

Bodily/kinesthetic intelligence entails the potential of using one's whole body or parts of the body to create products or to solve problems. The student who can accurately toss a crumpled piece of paper into a wastepaper basket located across the room displays this intelligence. Students who love physical education class and school dances, who prefer to do class projects by making models instead of writing reports, display bodily/kinesthetic intelligence. (Blythe, et al., 1995, p. 7)

Tzipporah consults with some colleagues and decides that a bodily/kinesthetic activity would help cement the information she is trying to impart. She gives students a worksheet with the various parts of the cycle written on it and asks them to use their "muscular imagination" to act out the cycle physically. The results are bodily/kinesthetic and are an excellent active learning activity.

To try in the classroom:

- Active learning programs

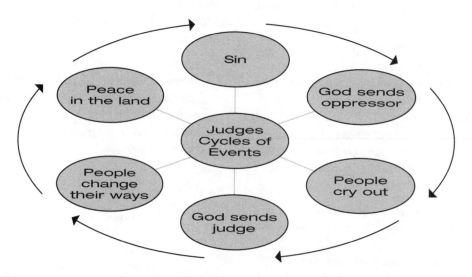

What does it mean to sin? How might an individual's sins be different from the sins that the Israelites committed? Describe below at least four sins that an individual might do and four that a nation might commit.

Individual		**Nation**

Figure 1

- Emphasize awareness of body to task

- Puzzles

- Physical exercise

- Field trips

INTERPERSONAL (PEOPLE SMART)

"Wherever you go, you will find friends." (Ladino saying)

Adam is an amazing Kitah Gimel teacher and Tefilah leader. He uses many "traditional" methods, and primarily teaches in a lecture format. Yet, he is dynamic and charismatic; most of his students find his classes motivating and say that they learn a lot. Still, Adam understands that he is not reaching all of his students. He asks the Staff Developer to observe his class. She notes that while the pedagogic style that he has created encourages his students to interact with their teacher, it does not seem to give students the opportunity to interact with one another. She suggests trying to include some methods that would foster the use of interpersonal intelligences.

Interpersonal intelligence entails the capacity to understand oneself, to appreciate one's feelings, fears, and motivations. Students who thrive on small group work, who notice and react to the moods of their friends and classmates, and who are able tactfully to persuade their teacher of the need for extra time to complete an assignment display this intelligence. (Blythe, et al., 1995, p. 9)

Adam decides to approach his teaching of Tefilah from with a perspective different from his usual frontal style. He pairs up the students and asks them to discuss the meaning of several Tefilot prior to their "drills and skills" practice. Each pair is responsible for joining with another group that has discussed the same Tefilah. The pairs compare their thoughts. The larger groups will then present their conclusions to the class. In this way, the student-driven lesson will assist those with strengths in the interpersonal intelligences to participate fully in the lesson.

To try in the classroom:

- Learning stations

- Cooperative learning activities

- Mentoring

- Peer tutoring

INTRAPERSONAL (SELF SMART)

"It is depth of understanding, nobility of thought, that constitutes the crown of the righteous." (Commentary by Figo on Brachot)

Unlike the study of Tefilah described above, the study of Talmud is usually a collaborative effort called chevruta, which is performed with a partner. It can be difficult to conceive of how to make what is usually a task that capitalizes on interpersonal intelligences, one that can make good use of the reflective nature of intrapersonal intelligences. Nonetheless, when Miriam was preparing to teach her tenth year of Talmud at the nearby day school, she had decided that she needed to find a way to include those students whose strengths lay in the intrapersonal areas.

Intrapersonal intelligence helps individuals distinguish among their own feelings and to build mental models of themselves. This is the most difficult intelligence to assess, but it is often evidenced by how well students use their other intelligences — how well they capitalize on their strengths and are aware of their weaknesses, and how thoughtful they are about the decisions and choices they make (Blythe, et al., 1995, p. 9).

Miriam decides that she wants to include reflective activities that accompany the normative chevruta work. She asks students to keep individual journals describing their Talmudic studies — the frustrations they encounter in trying to decipher the text and the feelings they have when they believe they have successfully interpreted a passage. These journals are intended as a log of their private thoughts and are meant to reflect how students feel about their Talmudic studies when they go home every evening.

To try in the classroom:

- Journals

- Reflective activities

- Offer choices of activities

NATURALIST (NATURE SMART)

"The power of nature is the power of God."
(Spinoza, *Theologico-Political Treatise*)

It seemed to Daniel that his lessons on Hebrew language made use of many of the intelligences displayed by his students. Certainly they had emphasis on the verbal, but he had excluded the naturalist intelligences. Utilizing an appreciation of nature and the environment seemed to him like the farthest thing from modern Hebrew, but he wanted to find a way to include those students who had strengths in this area.

Naturalistic intelligence allows people to distinguish among, classify, and use features of the environment. Students who are interested in botany, geology, and archaeology display this intelligence. The student who can name and describe the features of every make of car also possesses this intelligence (Blythe, et al., 1995, p. 10).

Daniel decided to start with some basic brachot that related to nature. He had his students examine what Rambam (Maimonides) wrote about the rules for saying the brachot over aromas. He reviewed with his students the brachot that are said upon seeing lightning, an ocean, or wonderful trees or fields. Then, he had students make flashcards of some vocabulary words that related to types of flowers, trees, and other things a person might see when they go on a nature hike. Finally, he sent his students outside once a week for ten weeks and asked them to report back (in Hebrew) on what they saw and experienced.

To try in the classroom:

- Make use of animals.
- Nature
- Weather
- Museums
- Being outdoors

Figure 2 on the next page explains each intelligence and shows how one might capitalize on it in the classroom. It also lists some individuals who exhibited these intelligences.

Six years ago, I rejected the idea of multiple intelligences. My students have changed my mind. There are children who are gifted musically, who effortlessly learn a new language, who play with ideas in math the way other children play with Legos, who struggle in reading but can read a social situation flawlessly. Since I have begun to appreciate the diverse strengths of my students, I have changed the way I teach. I vary my approach to topics so as to incorporate the skills of the specific group. A high energy group responds well to creating puppet shows that portray the stories from Genesis. A logical, argumentative class likes to discuss the cases in *You Be the Judge* (Torah Aura Productions). A quiet class that is unresponsive to discussion of ideas may come alive when working in small groups to create a mural.

I also plan assignments that allow individual students to show off their stronger points. Shira struggles in reading, and feels discouraged when she notices how quickly everyone else in class can finish a workbook task. But Shira has great social skills. I choose her to model introductory conversations for the class before we all go off to visit senior citizens at our Jewish retirement center. For 20 minutes, Shira is queen of the class. She won't forget that experience.

(Maura Pollak, Tulsa, Oklahoma)

LESSONS THAT COMBINE INTELLIGENCES

Sample lessons and strategies that employ Gardner's multiple intelligences may be found below following figure 2. Be aware that you will not use every intelligence in every lesson. A realistic goal would be to make certain that you do use every intelligence over a period of time.

Hebrew Reading

Sarah teaches Kitah Gimel (third grade). She is responsible for helping her students acquire a general knowledge of Hebrew phonics. She thinks she does a pretty comprehensive job: students create

Intelligence	What This Means When Your Students Utilize These Intelligences	How You Might Capitalize on This in the Classroom (Campbell, 1994)	Some Famous Jews Associated with These Intelligences (Nicholson-Nelson, 1998)
Verbal/ Linguistic	Hears sounds of language, reading, labeling, and listening.	Use formal presentations, study poetry, actors, word games, humor, idioms, dictionaries, journals, and word lists.	Billy Crystal, Gilda Radner, Judy Blume, Jerry Seinfeld, Robert Klein, Bette Midler, A. B. Yehoshua, Ari Fleischer, Isaac Bashevis Singer, Leon Uris, Howard Cosell
Musical/ Rhythmic	Hears music and rhythm, sound, and vibration.	Use music to create moods, demonstrate situations. Write lyrics to music, try different rhythms, change the environment. Use choral reading and instruments.	Art Garfunkel, Paul Simon, Barbra Streisand, Irving Berlin, Leonard Bernstein, Aaron Copland, George Gershwin, Jan Peerce, Itzhak Perlman, Phish
Logical/ Mathematical	Seeks patterns, logic, and may be analytical.	Use list making, finding patterns and categories, sequencing, logic puzzles, calculations, scientific methods, and graphs.	Albert Einstein, Jonas Salk, Rube Goldberg, Alan Greenspan, Judith Resnick
Visual/ Spatial	Thinks in pictures and images, shapes, patterns, textures, and colors. Knows where objects are in relation to other things.	Employ color combinations, pictures, descriptions, layouts, mapping, graphic organizers, use of color. May work well with newspapers, bulletin boards, posters, and other visual arts.	Marc Chagall, Agam, Calvin Klein, Mel Brooks, Steven Spielberg, Marty Feldman, Peter Max
Bodily/ Kinesthetic	Can easily make use of body language, enjoys activity and sensory processing situations.	Employ active learning programs, emphasize awareness of body to task. Use puzzles, physical exercise, and field trips.	Marx Brothers, Jerry Lewis, Marcel Marceau, Sandy Koufax, Hank Greenburg, Harry Houdini, Michael Andron (Tora Dojo Dynamo), Penninah Schram, Jeff Halpern, (Bill) Goldberg, Kerri Strug, Shari Lewis
Interpersonal	Uses verbal and nonverbal communication, works cooperatively, sensitive to needs of others.	Make use of learning stations, cooperative learning activities, team activities, mentoring, and tutoring.	Henry Kissinger, Joseph Lieberman, Elie Wiesel, Shimon Peres, Yitzhak Rabin, Ruth Bader Ginsburg, Ann Landers
Intrapersonal	Can concentrate easily in the midst of activities, may be introspective and aware of the feelings of others.	Use journals, reflective activities, higher level thinking skills, and choice of activities.	Sigmund Freud, Hannah Senesh
Naturalist	Appreciates nature and the environment.	Make use of animals, nature, flora, fauna, weather, museums, and being outdoors.	Daniel Ziskin (founder of the environmental group Jews of the Earth, Boulder, Colorado), Martin Buber

Figure 2

their own letter and word banks, and they practice choral reading. Most of the work is done as a whole group. However, she now recognizes that all of these activities help students with strong *verbal/linguistic* skills develop. She wants to add additional activities that will broaden the number of intelligences being used in students' study.

MI Options

- Students can also work individually, listening to tape recordings (*musical/rhythmic*).

- They can also work in pairs, using the computer software that reinforces their textbook work (*interpersonal*).

- Students can take the new vocabulary words and make the back bulletin board into a word wall, grouping the words together into categories, designing the display, and then mounting the words onto the board (*visual/spatial and logical/mathematical*).

Torah

David usually teaches his Torah class of sixth graders by having them take our their *Chumashim* (books of Torah) and dictionaries and begin to translate the text. Finally, students discuss what they have read. At a faculty meeting, David asks colleagues for input into strategies for including students whose strengths lie in intelligences other than *verbal/linguistic*.

MI Options

- David can add the reading of several verses of the text in Hebrew so students hear the cadence and rhythm of the language in its original (*musical/rhythmic*).

- Working in groups, students can create a large map of biblical Israel and surrounding countries as a classroom mural. Then, as they continue their study of Torah, they may map out the geography of the central characters (*interpersonal and visual/spatial*).

- Students can dramatize some of the appropriate portions, as well as some of their interpretations (*kinesthetic*).

- Students can create a small-scale model of the ark Noah built, based on the instructions given to Noah in Torah (*visual/spatial and logical/math*).

- Students can write in their journals about how they would have responded to some of God's tests of our ancestors (*intrapersonal*).

Holidays

You are about to embark on the annual teaching of Chanukah. You must prepare your students for their annual visit to the nearby children's hospital where they will deliver gifts and play *Dreidel* with the patients. You want to be sure to have activities that include as many of the intelligences as possible.

MI Options

- Students can explain to the patients the history of Chanukah, including the Maccabees, *chanukiyah*, *dreidel*, and exchange of gifts (*verbal/linguistic*).

- Students can figure out how many pieces of *gelt* each class member should receive (*logical/mathematical*).

- Students can take turns spinning the *dreidel* (*bodily/kinesthetic*).

- Students can create a poster that lists all of the rules of the *Dreidel* game (*visual/spatial*).

- Students can play the game, helping one another read the Hebrew letters and understand the rules of the game (*interpersonal*).

- Students can create a journal that relates their family's customs and traditions about Chanukah, which they will share with the patients (*intrapersonal*).

- Students can sing Chanukah songs (*musical/rhythmic*).

- Using materials found in nature, students can make gifts for the patients (*naturalist*).

CONCLUSION

The ways in which Howard Gardner's theory of multiple intelligences have been translated into policy and practice is varied. Gardner did not initially spell out the implications of his theory for educators in any detail. Subsequently, he has looked more closely at what the theory might mean for schooling practice (e.g., in *The Unschooled Mind, Intelligence Reframed,* and *The Disciplined Mind*). Teachers need to attend to all intelligences, not just the first two, which have traditionally been their concern.

As Kornhaber (2001, p. 276) has noted, this involves educators opting "for depth over breadth." Understanding entails taking knowledge gained in one setting and using it in another. "Students must have extended opportunities to work on a topic" (p. 276). Gardner's interest in deep understanding, performance, exploration, and creativity are not easily accommodated within an orientation of a detailed curriculum. An MI setting can be undone if the curriculum is too rigid or if there is but a single form of assessment (Gardner 1991, p. 147).

The delineation of multiple intelligences has helped a significant number of educators to question their work and to encourage them to look beyond the narrow confines of the dominant discourses of skills, curriculum, and testing. For example, Mindy Kornhaber and her colleagues at Project SUMIT have examined the performance of a number of schools, concluding that there have been significant gains in SAT scores, parental participation, and discipline with the schools themselves attributing this to MI theory. To the extent that multiple intelligences theory has helped educators reflect on their practice, and given them a basis for broadening their focus and attending to what might assist people to live their lives well, then it must be judged a useful addition.

TEACHING CONSIDERATIONS

- Very few lessons should contain approaches directed toward all of the various multiple intelligences.

- The important thing is to try to vary the modalities and appeal to different intelligences as often as you can.

- The seven intelligences rarely operate independently of one another, so students can "tap into" several of their intelligences at one time.

- As teachers, we often prepare lessons that are directed toward our own intelligence preference. It may be helpful to analyze our strengths in order to make certain that other intelligences are included in our lessons.

BIBLIOGRAPHY

Armstrong, Thomas. *Multiple Intelligences in the Classroom*. 2d ed. Alexandria, VA: Association for Supervision and Curriculum Development, 2000.

This book presents a practical introduction to the theory of multiple intelligences for individuals new to the model.

Blythe, Tina; Noel White; and Howard Gardner. *Teaching Practical Intelligence: What Research Tells Us*. West Lafayette, IL: Kappa Delta Pi, 1995.

A brief pamphlet describing what students need to know in order to succeed in school. This is a part of the Project Zero research.

Brualdi, A, C. *Multiple Intelligences: Gardner's Theory*. ERIC Digest, http://www.ed.gov/databases/ERIC_Digests/ed410226.html, 1996.

This digest discusses the origins of Howard Gardner's theory of multiple intelligences, his definition of intelligence, the incorporation of the theory of multiple intelligences into the classroom, and its role in alternative assessment practices.

Campbell, Bruce. *The Multiple Intelligences Handbook*. Standwood, WA: Campbell & Associates, 1994.

This book gives an excellent user-friendly approach to multiple intelligences and contains many valuable lesson plans.

Campbell, Linda; Bruce Campbell; and Dee Dickinson. *Teaching and Learning through Multiple Intelligences*. Needham Heights, MA: Allyn & Bacon, 1999.

A wonderfully organized book on the instructional applications of multiple intelligence theory.

Gardner, Howard. *The Unschooled Mind*. New York: Basic Books, 1991.

A valuable book for teachers and parents who want to know how children think and how schools should apply multiple intelligences to the classroom.

———. *Intelligence Reframed*. New York: Basic Books, 1999.

A compendium of theory by the psychologist who created the idea and structure of multiple intelligences.

———. *The Disciplined Mind: Beyond Facts and Standardized Tests, the K-12 Education That Every Child Deserves*. New York: Simon and Schuster, 1999.

Merging cognitive science with educational agenda, this book shows how ill suited our minds and natural patterns of learning are to current educational practices.

Gardner, Howard, and Thomas Hatch. "Multiple Intelligences Go To School: Educational Implications of the Theory of Multiple Intelligences." *CTE Technical Report Issue No. 4 EDC Center for Children and Technology* [online, 1990]. Available at www.edc.org/CCT/ccthomereports/tr4.html.

This essay sketches the background and major claims of a new approach to the conceptualization and assessment of human intelligence.

Nicholson-Nelson, Kristen. *Developing Students' Multiple Intelligences*. New York: Scholastic, 1998.

This book is an excellent composite of teaching strategies for Grades K-8 using the framework of multiple intelligences.

Project SUMIT. *SUMIT Compass Points. Practices*, 2000.

The Project on Schools Using Multiple Intelligences Theory (SUMIT) is a three-year national investigation of schools using Howard Gardner's theory of multiple intelligences. It seeks to identify, document, and promote effective implementations of MI.

Scherer, Marge. "The Understanding Pathway: A Conversation with Howard Gardner." *Educational Leadership* 57, (3) 12-17, 1999.

Howard Gardner reflects on how students who learn in many different ways might grapple with their deepest questions about life.

Sternberg, Robert. J. *Thinking Styles*. Cambridge, England: Cambridge University Press, 1997.

Using a variety of examples, this book presents a theory of thinking styles that aims to explain why aptitude tests, school grades, and classroom performance often fail to identify real ability.

Tomlinson, Carol Ann. *How to Differentiate Instruction in Mixed-Ability Classrooms.* 2d ed. Alexandria, VA: Association for Supervision and Curriculum Development, 2001.

This book provides guidance for teachers who are interested in creating learning environments that address the diversity typical of mixed ability classrooms.

Williams, Wendy M., ed., with Noel White and Tina Blythe. *Practical Intelligence for School.* Boston, MA: Addison-Wesley, 1996.

This handbook provides lessons for developing practical intelligence for schools as students carry out common school tasks.

CHAPTER 28

Empowering the Learner: A Look at Constructivism[1]

Nachama Skolnik Moskowitz

Let's look into two fifth grade classrooms:

In the first class, Mr. Schwartz is teaching a lesson on Israel's geography. He wants students to be able to identify Israel's major cities and land/water forms. He spends the first ten minutes of his lesson pointing out some of Israel's key geographical features on a large wall map. Then, students are brought two at a time to the map to touch quickly whatever city or land/water form their teacher calls out. After every student has had a chance to participate in this reinforcement game, Mr. Schwartz shows a 15-minute, upbeat Israel travel video. Finally, in the last eight minutes of the class, students work in groups of three on a geography sheet, unscrambling the names of Israel's cities and geographical areas.

In the second fifth grade classroom, Ms. Gratz also is teaching Israel's geography. She has decided that she wants her students to be able to distinguish the geographical differences between (1) northern Israel (she focuses on Haifa, but includes the Galilee), (2) the central area of Jerusalem, including the Judean Desert, and (3) the southern Negev and Eilat. She gives each group of six students a geographical map and 20-25 postcards of their region. The postcards show not only the physical features of that area of the country, but also people "interacting" with the environment (recreational activities, the types of buildings in the area, etc.). Youngsters are set up in cooperative learning groups and asked to use clues from the postcards to locate their area of Israel on the map and then fill in the chart (figure 1):

What we notice about nature	What we notice about buildings and other things people added to nature	What we notice people doing or what people could do in this area of the country

Figure 1

[1]A version of this chapter originally appeared in *Jewish Education News* as "Bringing Authentic Learning Experiences into the Classroom," (vol. 17, no. 1, Winter 1996). It is reprinted here, slightly adapted, with permission of the Coalition for the Advancement of Jewish Education (CAJE).

Each issue of *Jewish Education News,* which is published three times a year, is devoted to a different topic of relevance to Jewish educators and all those interested in Jewish education. Selections from current and previous issues of JEN can be found on the CAJE website, www.caje.org.

As the class works, Ms. Gratz circulates throughout the room. She asks questions to help students notice details in the pictures that they overlook. She tells one group that declares itself finished in five minutes that they missed a lot of information. She has them study other information in their pictures and the descriptions on the back of the postcards (Ms. Gratz eventually gives this particular group the specific instructions to find 12-15 things for each column).

Ms. Gratz praises students for finding clues to information she would have missed in a particular picture. She asks "Why did you come to that conclusion?" when youngsters seem to have faulty information on their chart. Most of the time, as her students retrace their logic, they find where they went wrong. But, Ms. Gratz makes a couple of notes about some things she will need to correct when the group gets back together to share information. She enjoys listening to her students discuss among themselves — they ask each other good questions such as, "Why do you think . . . ?" and "Did you notice. . . ?"

There's a comfortable working "buzz" in the room as the students work in their groups for most of the class period. Ms. Gratz then brings the class together for the last 15 minutes so that they can share their conclusions with each other. She asks each group to locate its region on the map and discuss some of the more interesting information they learned. During this interchange, Ms. Gratz helps groups clearly present their findings, sometimes by asking them questions that help them identify the important "facts."

COMPARING THESE CLASSROOMS

Both Mr. Schwartz and Ms. Gratz teach the geography of Israel to fifth graders. Chances are that lessons like the one Mr. Schwartz planned take place nationwide in many upper elementary Jewish classrooms. He expects his students to know the facts about the map of Israel, and spends an hour finding ways to pour that information into his students' heads. Even though his lesson is lively, his students are relatively passive participants — his foundational question, "What are the major cities and land/water forms of Israel?" is not compelling to students. They don't gain a deeper understanding of Israel's geography when they memorize places on a map and connect them with video images.

Indeed, in this lesson, Mr. Schwartz takes on the role of a traditional teacher in a traditional classroom. He sees his students as blank slates needing to be filled with information. Today, he expects his students to spit back their knowledge in a word scramble worksheet. Next week, perhaps he'll ask for it in a multiple choice test. His curriculum is fact driven and, because of that, is rather dreary.

My *Midrash* teacher (Marc Bregman) in Jerusalem once said, "This is your class not mine." Those words have stayed with me and given me a new perspective in teaching. I think we need to give students more of a hand in developing their education. Yes, a teacher can create the curriculum, teach the course, and facilitate the learning experience, but the class does not belong to the teacher. We need to allow the students to feel as if the educational enterprise is theirs to shape and mold — and not the teacher's to dictate.

(Amy Appelman, West Bloomfield, Michigan)

When his students sing the "we're bored refrain," their parents and Mr. Schwartz are surprised, for they see him as having an upbeat classroom. What they don't understand, however, is that Mr. Schwartz has not sparked his youngsters in any meaningful way. His foundational questions don't have depth, and for that reason his lesson, and certainly his students, never take off.

Ms. Gratz, on the other hand, develops a lesson that challenges her students to the core. She begins her planning by asking herself how she could help students internalize information on Israel's geography. She realizes that memorizing city names and locations are pretty low level tasks. So, she decides to up the stakes by having students analyze pictures (the postcards) and, through their discoveries, draw conclusions about Israel's physical and human geography. Her foundational question, though never spoken aloud to the students, forms the basis of her highly complex lesson.

Ms. Gratz is a teacher who uses the theories of constructivist education to guide her teaching. In constructivist classrooms, students are active participants in the learning process as they reshape and internalize information by "constructing" knowledge. Constructivist education, "place(s) in students' hands the exhilarating power to follow trails of interest, to make connections, to reformulate ideas, and to reach unique conclusions."[2] In constructivist classrooms, students often work with primary sources (Ms. Gratz's youngsters used a geographical map and picture postcards). They collaborate to gain a deep understanding of the material studied. They are encouraged to ask questions of the material and of each other.

The teacher's role is quite different in a constructivist classroom from that in a traditional class.

> If you believe that knowledge has to be constructed by each individual knower . . . teaching becomes a very different proposition from the traditional notion where the knowledge is in the head of the teacher and the teacher has to find ways of conveying it or transferring it to the student . . . What you present is never something that you expect the student to adopt as it is, but what you present is something that you think will make it possible for the student to find his or her own way of constructing.[3]

Constructivist teachers emphasize broad concepts (the geographical differences in Israel) instead of specific skills (naming all the major cities in Israel); however, students often learn the subskills anyway because they need them to solve the problem presented. Constructivist teachers empower students to respond to each other's questions and draw their own conclusions. They do a tremendous amount of pre-class preparation framing the questions that will drive the lesson, and finding the primary sources or hands-on materials that will enrich student understanding. They engender student collaboration and conversation, often in formal cooperative learning groups. And, most of all, these teachers listen and ask probing questions.

Constructivist teachers look to create conversations — among students, and between students and the teacher. They consider how to get students to classify, to analyze, and predict. Because their questions are of a higher level, these teachers make good use of "wait time," allowing students ample opportunity to process answers before expecting a response. They engage students in the deeper and more important questions of Jewish study.

I believe children construct their own learning so as to make sense of their world. I see this over and over again in my classroom. So often, the children become the teachers and I the student. For example, one little girl asked me if she could have the big box that was out in the hall waiting to be thrown out. When I brought it into the room, she asked for brown paint. Soon, half the class was busy painting. Another child asked me to cut open one side, in a "round kind of way." Still another brought over the pillows from the reading center and stuck them inside the box. Then, without any prompting from me, they started crawling around the floor. I asked what they were doing and the first little girl told me that they were looking for food to eat before their hearts stopped.

It took me awhile, but I finally realized what was going on. We had read a book about a bear who was preparing for winter before his long hibernation. Words weren't enough for them to understand the process. They needed to experience it.

(Kim Lausin, Beachwood, Ohio)

AUTHENTIC LEARNING EXPERIENCES: A CONSTRUCTIVIST SUBSET

Some teachers who subscribe to constructivist learning theory, work to create authentic learning experiences for their students. These are tasks that integrate academic content with complex thinking and communication skills. These experiences also have an "authentic" application in the world, i.e., the students are given a real task with a real audience.

Authentic learning experiences have compelling applications for Jewish education. As in Mr. Schwartz's class, our students are too often asked to learn isolated information that has no direct application or interest. Imagine, though, a group of high school students asked to research an itinerary to propose to the Rabbi and educator for a family trip to Israel. Students would have to research the sites, decide what would be of intergenerational

---

[2]Jacqueline Grennon Brooks and Martin G. Brooks, *The Case for Constructivist Classrooms* (Alexandria, VA: Association for Supervision and Curriculum Development, 1993), 22.

[3]von Glaserfeld, quoted in "Experience, Problem Solving, and Discourse as Central Aspects of Constructivism," *Arithmetic Teacher* (December 1990), 34.

interest, plan a route, and make a formal proposal to the synagogue staff. They might have to interview families that have visited Israel and speak to the congregation's travel agent to find out what parameters need to be considered. They would be part of the renegotiations with the travel agent if the plan was not feasible from a time or budgetary standpoint. Would these students learn the geography and city names of Israel? You bet! They'd learn a whole lot more as well.

What other authentic learning experiences might educators develop? We can ask students to:

- write a monthly column for the synagogue newsletter that gives families help in celebrating Jewish holidays at home. (They would need to research the holidays, survey families to discover what kind of information would be helpful, and spend time learning what activities are appropriate for what age.)

- design a logo for the Federation Youth Campaign. (Students would need to learn about the Federation and its mission. They might meet with a graphic artist and learn about the power of logos.)

- develop a book list for Kindergarten teachers to use to complement their holiday teacher, based on specific criteria.

- create and lead a "Tot Shabbat."

- develop an art exhibit for the local JCC. Develop the criteria for inviting artists based on the mission statement of the JCC (and/or its art department), choose exhibitors, and help the JCC staff carry out the plans.

- research and brainstorm ideas to use at college for "Ten Minute Judaism." (This concept came via a Cleveland Family Educator, Laurie Bar-Ness, who tells college students that no matter how busy they are or how far away from home, they can find ten minutes on the day of a Jewish holiday to celebrate it. The challenge is to figure out a Ten Minute Sukkot, a Ten Minute Chanukah, etc.)

- develop a statement on the ethics of computer usage for their day school, including the Jewish aspects of the issue.

- write background statements for the congregation's ritual committee on a topic the group needs to discuss. Research both sides of the issue, present the arguments to the committee, and participate in the ensuing debate.

Imagine the energy generated by students involved in developing solutions to the projects mentioned above! They have a real problem and a real audience. Consider the research questions they need to generate to come to the heart of their issue.

Consider, too, the role of the teacher in: setting the problem; facilitating the use of print, computer, and human resources; and shepherding the students along paths of inquiry. This is very different from what has traditionally been expected of teachers. It is, indeed, challenging to teach within the framework of constructivist theory. It is also very easy to teach the way we were taught — pouring in the information and "covering" the material. It may also be intimidating to give up the locus of control, for in constructivist classrooms, the students help direct the flow of the learning.

Teachers who use a constructivist approach, or who develop authentic learning experiences, must themselves learn a tremendous amount about the subject matter. Ms. Gratz had to know that geography is more than maps; it also includes people and their environments. She had to understand the differences between Israel's geographical areas and their effect on how people live in each region. She then had to develop an activity that would help her students process this information through their own eyes.

Time, subject matter coverage, and resources are three issues with which constructivist teachers wrestle.

Time

It takes a lot of time to prepare a lesson in which the locus of control is in the students' hands. It also takes a lot of time for students to think, discuss, and draw their own conclusions. When teachers take this into account, issues of curricular coverage come to the fore.

Coverage

As teachers take students into greater depth, they find that they cannot "cover" everything they think should be in the course outline. Decisions need to be made as to what is important, and what is not. These are often broad curricular decisions that need to be made in conjunction with the school's director, for a change in one aspect of the educational system greatly impinges on the other areas of student study.

Resources

Teachers cannot rely on a textbook to provide them with the rich information they need to develop constructivist lessons. Ms. Gratz asked some friends to gather "tons" of postcards when they visited Israel; she then saved them for a future use. Another teacher may need help locating the Rabbinic sources that respond to the problem before her class. Another may want to locate eight different "how to" holiday guides to help her students plan their Ten Minute Judaism guide. Our school directors need to be resource *mavens* (experts) to help support the needs of teachers working with constructivist educational models.

Indeed, the element that helps guarantee the success of a teacher implementing constructivist theory is *support*: support of a school director who allows the teacher to take risks . . . and sometimes fail, and support of other teachers who bounce ideas off each other, who celebrate successes and rethink areas of difficulty.

CONCLUSION

So, is the time and energy worth it? Yes, unequivocally! Think about the energy level of Ms. Gratz's class as they probed the information on their postcards. Think about Hebrew students who examine a list of words to figure out their commonalities, and thus discover for themselves the principle of Hebrew *shorashim* (roots). Think about a group of students who undertake a study of *chanukiyot* to compare their characteristics with information they find in Rabbinic sources before working with an artist to design a personal *chanukiyah*. Think about students who use a concordance, traditional commentaries, and a computer modem to pursue a question that popped up during a Torah study session.

Teachers and their students become exhilarated when challenged by lessons designed with constructivist theory. To ask, to answer . . . this is so much more enriching than "listen to me and then fill in the blanks on your worksheet."

TEACHING CONSIDERATIONS:

- Constructivist teachers shift their role from the "sage on the stage" to "the guide on the side." Their task is to facilitate learning, not direct it.

- Constructivist classrooms empower students to pursue paths of learning. However, this does not mean that there is no attention to curriculum, for, as seen in the opening vignette, Ms. Gratz was very planful about her teaching outcomes.

- In constructivist classrooms, students work with primary sources as much as possible.

- Teachers must often retool schedules so that optimum time is available to constructivist explorations, must plan on going into more depth instead of breadth, and must seriously consider which resources would best help students in their paths of inquiry.

BIBLIOGRAPHY

Association for Supervision and Curriculum Development (ASCD), 1703 N. Beauregard Street, Alexandria, VA 22311, (800) 933-2723, www.ascd.org.

> ASCD has quite a number of resources on constructivism. Go to the web site and do a search for "constructivism." Up will pop items for sale from the organization (e.g., books and videos), as well as articles from the web site. Also, click on the "Tutorials" in the home page and scroll to the bottom of the page. Click on "Constructivism" for definitions, articles, and video clips.

Brooks, Jacqueline Grennon, and Martin G. Brooks. *The Case for Constructivist Classrooms*. Alexandria, VA: Association for Supervision and Curriculum Development, 1993.

> This is a short, easy to read book that explains constructivism. It's considered a practitioner's "bible" for this philosophy.

Marlowe, Bruce A. *Creating and Sustaining the Constructivist Classroom*. Thousand Oaks, CA: Corwin Press, 1998.

> This is a great overview of constructivism that includes case studies and checklists to help guide teachers in implementing this philosophy in their teaching.

Martin Ryder Web Site, University of Colorado at Denver, School of Education. http://carbon.cudenver.edu/~mryder/itc_data/constructivism.html

> Martin Ryder has created an incredible compilation of web sites with an emphasis on constructivism, which is well organized and very comprehensive.

"The Constructivist Classroom." (Issue Theme) *Educational Leadership* 57, no. 3, November 1999.

> This journal focuses on constructivism, with a variety of articles by different authors.

Torp, Linda, and Sara Sage. *Problems as Possibilities: Problem-based Learning for K-12 Education*. Alexandria, VA: Association for Supervision and Curriculum Development, 1998.

> Problem-based learning (PBL) is one instructional model that supports constructivist philosophy. This particular book walks teachers through the process of creating and facilitating a problem.

CHAPTER 29

Learning Centers

Marci Rogozen and Ronna Fox

*M**r. Fine makes a quick stop in Mrs. Gold's classroom on his way to a meeting. This is not the quietest class in the school; a steady hum is heard from the room. Yet, Mr. Fine is pleased by what he sees. Children are busy working in stations throughout the room, some individually, some in small groups. Mrs. Gold is calling students to her desk one at a time to review their progress and set new short-term goals. How has Mrs. Gold managed to keep all these children engaged in such diverse activities? Why has she chosen to conduct her class in this manner?*

Mrs. Gold discovered that using learning centers allows her to be more flexible in meeting student needs in her classroom. What is a learning center? For our purposes, learning centers are considered to be "any learning, reinforcement, or interest activity in which a student can direct his own learning."[1] Learning centers can be used in any classroom, in any subject matter, and with any grade. We are most accustomed to seeing them used in early childhood classrooms, but they are also successfully used throughout the grade levels. Even adults can benefit from using learning centers.

THE BENEFITS OF LEARNING CENTERS

Learning Centers afford teachers the opportunity to plan appropriate instruction for individual students, each of whom has personal strengths, weakness, and interests. Imagine how much learning could take place if each student was challenged at his/her own academic level, and could advance at a personally appropriate pace. In a classroom with learning centers, students work independently (or in small groups) on predetermined center-based tasks. With class members working on structured assignments, the teacher has the time and ability to monitor progress and help individual students set new goals, whether in the areas of reinforcement, enrichment, or new learning.

Learning Centers also allow teachers to meet with various ability groups without sacrificing the learning of other students. While students with similar needs meet with the teacher, others are involved in centers around the room.

While planning an upcoming unit on introducing her students to Hebrew script, Mrs. Gold reflects on each student's learning style. Many of them learn visually, and will benefit from seeing how the letters are produced. Some learn best from information experienced kinesthetically. For them, a combination of tracing the letters in the air and following raised letters on cards will lead to producing them on paper. Others gain the most through verbal cues. All of the children will benefit from some exposure to a variety of approaches.

Research has identified multiple types of intelligence,[2] and a variety of learning styles. Student success is higher when information is received in a manner complementary to personal learning preference. In their book *So Each May Learn*, Silver, Strong, and Perini write:

. . . what works for one person might not for another because of individual's different intelligence profiles. By allowing students to process information according to the intelligence they use best, you provide a scaffolding for students, helping them gain mastery over essential content.[3]

---

[1]Louise F. Waynant and Robert M. Wilson, *Learning Centers . . . A Guide for Effective Use* (Minneapolis, MN: Judy/Instructor, 1974), 1.

[2]For more information on multiple intelligences, see Chapter 27, "Multiple Intelligences" by Renee Frank Holtz and

Barbara Lapetina, pp. 323-333 in this Handbook.

[3]Harvey F. Silver, Richard W. Strong, and Matthew J. Perini, *So Each May Learn* (Alexandria, VA: Association for Supervision and Curriculum Development, 2000), 17.

Learning Centers give teachers a structure within which to present content in different ways, thereby increasing learning.

Another benefit of using learning centers is the ability to offer students some choices in the material to be learned, the *way* it will be learned, as well as the means of assessment. Students who have choices feel greater ownership of the learning process and are generally more motivated. Students also take on increasing levels of responsibility as they master new skills, and are thus more likely to succeed in future endeavors.

> When I utilized learning centers in my seventh grade classroom, the students really got into it. Each station taught about a different aspect of *tefillin*, and students had to complete a worksheet at each one. The only drawbacks to the stations were that they were time-consuming to plan. and at the end I had a lot of worksheets to grade. However, with this group, it was worth it. The students enjoyed having independence and freedom to move around during class.
>
> *(Amy Appelman, West Bloomfield, Michigan)*

PLANNING LEARNING CENTERS

Learning Centers can be categorized in different ways. It is important to examine these variations before proceeding so that the centers created help to meet specific goals.

Process-based vs. Content-based Learning Centers

A process-based learning center is defined by the process by which students interact with subject matter in the center (e.g., Listening Center, Art Center, Computer Center). Process-based learning centers are often seen in early childhood classrooms, but can be appropriate for any age. The advantage of these centers is that they are created for long-term use, often becoming permanent fixtures in a classroom.

One process-based learning center can be used for a variety of subjects. For example, the Computer Center may be a place for designing an art project, learning Torah trope, or composing a Hebrew story. A Listening Center could provide an opportunity to listen to a story, learn a new prayer, or hear an Israeli news broadcast. The activities found in the center change regularly, but the process of learning remains constant.

A content-based learning center is defined by the subject matter to be covered there. Examples may include a center for learning about a specific holiday, Israeli history, Talmud, or *kashrut*. These centers might be set up only while teaching a specific unit, or may have interchangeable activities that would be available over an extended period of time.

Single Center/Multiple Centers

For the teacher using centers for the first time, it may be easier to start with a single center. Once comfortable creating and managing one, a teacher may expand the number of centers in use at any given time.

Some teachers set up a single enrichment center with activities available for students who complete their work early. Some use multiple centers to teach aspects of a unit. For example, in the weeks leading up to Passover, one center might contain activities related to the *Haggadah*, another to cooking, and yet another to the biblical text. The number of centers needed would depend upon specified curricular goals and the teacher's personal preference as to how much of the material is teacher directed, and how much is to be the responsibility of the students.

Learning Center Activities

Having determined the types of learning centers to be used, it is time to consider the activities in which the students will engage. As with all other learning activities, it is appropriate to begin by considering curricular goals on which all the activities in a learning center will focus. While it may be tempting to add activities that simply seem like fun, learning centers actually teach the class. It is therefore important to show the same level of focus here that would normally be given to classroom lessons. The learning center format will, however, allow creativity in terms of how to move through these goals. With this opportunity to think more flexibly, new ideas will arise, allowing for varied learning activities and increased student interest. Figure 1 on the next page contains an extensive list of verbs that may spark new ideas.

Identify	select	investigate	label
predict	design	categorize	define
observe	analyze	explain	separate
recall	suggest reasons	convince	locate
survey	evaluate	classify	choose
draw	write	match	collect
list advantages of	make a model	distinguish	describe
act out	summarize	give examples	compile a list
solve	visit	answer	plan
list	sequence	translate	read

Figure 1

For example, if the students are learning about various *brachot* (blessings), consider any of the following activities suggested by different verb choices:

- Compile a list of foods for each *brachah*.

- Categorize these foods according to their *brachot*.

- Match the following foods to their *brachot*.

- Design a wall chart to be used as a guide in deciding what *brachah* is appropriate for various foods.

- Solve the mystery of what Joshua ate for lunch using the following clues.

- Write an essay on the impact of saying *brachot* on character development.

- Give examples of foods for which the *brachot* are commonly misused and explain the appropriate use of its *brachah*.

- Compile a list of daily opportunities to say *brachot*.

In the brainstorming process, there may arise more than one activity to match the stated goals, providing an opportunity to consider various needs of different students. Is there a student who should reinforce her knowledge through the written word? another who could best express himself through verbal presentation? a third who would benefit from physically manipulating objects?

Allow for these choices in the learning center. As long as each activity leads the students to classroom goals, it is reasonable to provide options. For younger children, for those who find choice difficult, or those just learning to use centers, it may be preferable to assign specific projects to each child. Another approach is to create some assignments that are mandatory, leaving one or two items to choice.

When I first learned about and began using learning centers, I was amazed at all the things that teachers thought a learning center should look like. In early childhood settings, I saw work spaces, fully equipped with furniture and materials. In classrooms, I saw beautiful displays and color-coded file folders on walls and tables. I saw plain cardboard boxes, and scraps of paper stapled to the walls. I didn't know which style was mine and which was necessary to success. I finally discovered that I could use any and all styles (except color-coded file folders — I draw the line at that much effort for externals), and I learned that the success of a learning center depended on the time I took to conceive it, and teach it. If kids knew what was there and how to use it, and the content was engaging, the center would be a success. The best ones have always been the ones with cool stuff that I was excited about giving the kids an opportunity to explore.

(Sally Stefano, Worthington, Ohio)

In planning centers, it is important to consider how many children can realistically use each center at a time.

- Centers may be set up so that the students work directly at the center. This is desirable when there are special materials and equipment that must be used. In this case, it is helpful to decide how many students can easily work in that space without distraction. Fewer students may need to be assigned to center work at a given time, or more centers might need to be provided.

- If the materials being used are easily transported, the design of the activities may allow them to be picked up from a central place and used either at the student's desk or another part of the room.

Be sure to provide enough materials so that everyone expected to be doing center work is able to do so.

I've seen many wonderful things that can happen because of learning centers. I never feel that I can do learning centers all the time, every week, but know that the benefits derived from them make it worth the time spent setting them up and teaching with them at least a few times a year.

I normally have about four students in a group. In January one year, I had four groups of four students. It started at a game center where a teen aide led them in playing a Hebrew concentration game. After ten minutes, they moved to an art activity that was self-directed (though I had explained it before we started). After that they came to my center, where we had an exercise in reading Hebrew. Finally, I had the group listen to a story about planting trees in Israel for Tu B'Shevat read by a seventh grader who was given the reward of doing this for my class.

Clearly, there are many reasons for doing learning centers, and I find that the students almost always leave the class with a positive feeling from engaging in them.

(Michael Fixler, Syracuse, New York)

Another consideration when planning activities is the amount of time it will take students to complete each. This, of course, relates to the class schedule. Is there enough time for long-term activities? Will the students be able to return to their assignments in the next day or two so as not to lose momentum? Are the students adept at working on a project over time? Are there some students for whom assignments must be completed in one class period? The more the assigned activities reflect the realistic needs and abilities of the class, the higher the likelihood of success.

CREATING THE CLASSROOM ENVIRONMENT

A floor plan allows smooth flow from center to center and ease of material use. Begin with a sketch of the classroom drawn to scale, then add the permanent features, such as windows, bulletin boards, electrical outlets, doors, and sinks. Does one center area require access to an electrical outlet? Does another need to be close to a sink? Is there something going on outside a window that may be distracting? Will one center need to be in an especially quiet environment? Perhaps one center should be near a bulletin board so that its content can be part of the center's activity.

Once general areas have been assigned, consider the types of furniture needed at each center. In some instances, a round table for small group discussion is helpful. In other centers, quiet individual work space may be important. Carrels or table top dividers work well. Be sure to place quiet centers away from those that produce a lot of noise. Sometimes creating a barrier with file cabinets or shelving muffles some noise; carpets and wall hangings work as well. Are bookshelves needed to store resources and materials? Does one center require open floor space for student seating? Many classrooms also need reserved area for full group instruction. All this should be included in the layout.

Managing the Materials

Materials management is an important part of using learning centers. It is well worth the time to establish a system, allowing for easy access to materials. Students could have a small supply box containing frequently used basic supplies such as pencils, crayons, glue, etc., that could be carried from center to center. Another option is to leave all materials in a particular center that requires those supplies. This approach takes more maintenance on the teacher's part, but assures that students have everything they need. The age of your students may be a factor in making this decision.

There are many ways to store materials for centers. Many storage containers can be found around the house. Students may be able to bring some from home. Be sure to label these containers clearly (for younger children, include a picture). Boxes, baskets, files, carts, shelves, and cans may be helpful. If you have multiple centers running, it may be necessary to have duplicate materials in some centers. Borrowing supplies from one center to another in the middle of a project can be frustrating to students.

Instructions

In planning her Hebrew language center, Mrs. Gold has paid close attention to the instructions given to the students. While there will be some opportunity to give oral instructions, she knows that it is important that the students have something to refer back to. Each activity is clearly labeled with the steps needed to complete the assignment, as well as where to put the assignment when it is completed. In the past, Mrs. Gold has needed to create illustrations for her pre-readers, but this particular class handles written instruction well. Mrs. Gold always has someone proof read the instructions to ensure that they are clear.

The very nature of learning centers assumes that the students will be doing work without a teacher present. Therefore, it is vital that there be clear instructions available for every activity. Waynant and Wilson[4] recommend making sure all instructions are legible. Use a computer to print them out. Make sure the terms you use are familiar to students. Where helpful, have examples of what a project looks like at various stages of completion. Provide a picture or audiotaped instructions for those who need them. Be sure students know whom they can ask for assistance when the teacher is not available. Finally, always do a dry run with a small group of students to see if changes are needed.

Scheduling

As each school year begins, Mrs. Gold plans how she will use learning centers in her classroom. Once she knows the types of centers she will use, and what her classroom environment will look like, she considers how to create a class schedule that maximizes the effectiveness of these centers. She considers whether all students will be working in centers at the same time, or if groups will rotate. How much of her curriculum will be presented through the centers and how much will be presented by the teacher? Are the centers primarily used for enrichment, or is basic curricular material presented there? All of these issues influence the type of schedule that will work well in Mrs. Gold's classroom.

One can learn a lot about a classroom simply by looking at the daily schedule. Waynant and Wilson present a variety of scheduling approaches[5] each of which reflects a different teaching approach.

In Schedule I (see figure 2 on the next page), the teacher has chosen to have groups working either directly with her, or independently. Students working independently can use the centers once their work is complete. This type of scheduling is ideal when using centers to provide enrichment for those students who tend to finish their work quickly. It may not allow all students an opportunity to work in the learning centers.

Schedule II (see figure 3 on the next page), illustrates a different approach to using learning centers. In this example, the entire class uses the learning centers at the same time. The teacher may use center time for special enrichment projects, reinforcement activities, and individual conferencing.

Schedule III (see figure 4 on the next page), indicates that this teacher has chosen to do most of her teaching through the learning centers. This takes a great deal of planning, but can be an exciting approach. Note that the teacher does meet with groups and individuals, as needed. These meeting times are vital if the teacher is to manage this setup well.

---

[4]Waynant and Wilson, op. cit., 23.

[5]Ibid., 31-35.

Schedule I

Group	Time			
	9:30-10:00	10:00-10:30	10:30-11:00	11:00-11:30
A	**Teacher Directed Activity**	**Non-Center Activities** / Learning Centers when finished	**Non-Center Activities** / Learning Centers when finished	**Teacher Directed Activity**
B	**Non-Center Activities** / Learning Centers when finished	**Teacher Directed Activity**	**Non-Center Activities** / Learning Centers when finished	**Teacher Directed Activity**
C	**Non-Center Activities** / Learning Centers when finished	**Non-Center Activities** / Learning Centers when finished	**Teacher Directed Activity**	**Teacher Directed Activity**

Figure 2

Schedule II

Group	Time				
	9:30-10:00	10:00-10:30	10:30-11:00	11:00-11:30	11:30-12:00
A	**Teacher Directed Activity**	**Non-Center Activities**	**Non-Center Activities**	**Teacher Directed Activity**	C E N T E R S
B	**Non-Center Activities**	**Teacher Directed Activity**	**Non-Center Activities**	**Teacher Directed Activity**	
C	**Non-Center Activities**	**Non-Center Activities**	**Teacher Directed Activity**	**Teacher Directed Activity**	

Figure 3

Schedule III

9:30-11:00	1:00-12:30	1:30-3:00
Language Arts Centers	**Math Centers**	**Science and Social Studies Centers**

Conferences, large group and small group teacher directed activities scheduled as needed.

Figure 4

Schedule IV

Group	\multicolumn{5}{c}{Time}	
	9:30-10:00	10:00-10:30	10:30-11:00	11:00-11:30	11:30-12:00	
A	**Teacher Directed Activity**	**Non-Center Activities**	Centers	**Teacher Directed Activity**	**Non-Center Activities**	C O N F E R E N C E S
B	Centers	**Teacher Directed Activity**	**Non-Center Activities**	**Teacher Directed Activity**	Centers	
C	**Non-Center Activities**	Centers	**Teacher Directed Activity**	**Teacher Directed Activity**	Centers	

Figure 5

Schedule IV (see figure 5 above), is a very commonly used structure. Students divide their time between working with the teacher, working independently, and working in learning centers. Other time is spent in whole group instruction. Groups may have additional time in learning centers or independent work, allowing time for the teacher to meet with individual students.

Schedule V (see figure 6 below), shows another variation. The majority of learning takes place in learning centers, but each group meets regularly with the teacher.

Clearly, there are endless variations. It is up to you to create a schedule that will be most comfortable for you and that will meet your needs.

Schedule V

Group	\multicolumn{4}{c}{Time}	
	9:30-10:00	10:00-10:30	10:30-11:00	11:00-11:30	
A	**Teacher Directed Activity**	Centers	Centers	Centers	C O N F E R E N C E S
B	Centers	**Teacher Directed Activity**	Centers	Centers	
C	Centers	Centers	**Teacher Directed Activity**	Centers	

Figure 6

Record Keeping

In order for learning centers to be effective teaching tools, clear records must be kept. The teacher decides what assignments are appropriate for each student, monitors progress, and then evaluates the progress the students have made. The process continues in a circular manner (see figure 7 below). Once an evaluation is complete, new assignments are provided that review, reinforce, or build upon previous knowledge.

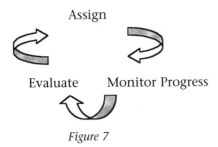

Assign

Evaluate   Monitor Progress

Figure 7

There are a variety of ways to assign work to the students. Many teachers find that it is convenient to assign work while meeting with each group. However, when a class is rotating through different work stations, some must begin assignments prior to a daily meeting with the teacher. Therefore, a mechanism is needed to help students keep track of their assignments between meetings. This is commonly done through the use of contracts, essentially a written form listing work to be completed (see figure 8 on the next page). Students refer to their contracts to organize their time and their assignments, keeping a record of what has been completed and what to work on next. Many teachers make the contract a part of a center's folder that students return to a central location at the end of center time. This allows the teacher to access the folders for monitoring and evaluation. The folder can also be used for the teacher to communicate back to the student through written notes and instructions.

DEALING WITH SPECIAL ISSUES

A Shortage of Space

Many teachers are discouraged from using learning centers due to a shortage of space when classrooms are small or shared with other teachers. With a bit of planning, however, these obstacles can be overcome.

In a smaller room, be sure to maximize the use of available space. Use clotheslines or hooks to display work, and reference items can hang from the classroom ceiling. Consider using a bulletin board as a learning center by making it an interactive area. Check to see if there are available spaces for work outside the classroom, for if center activities can be picked up and taken to the library or hallway, space may not be an issue at all.

There are many ways to create centers in a shared classroom as well. Centers that are created in folding display units are easily put away at the end of class time. Lightweight luggage carts make it easier to move small boxed activities from the car to the classroom. Don't forget your allies in administration. There may be an available closet nearby that could be yours for the asking.

> I have used learning centers while teaching Hebrew. Many of my activities were as simple as file folders with library pockets glued to the inside to hold index cards, file folders with "trail games" on them, file folders with task sheets. Folders are literally a flexible learning center. And the advantage of using them is that individual students can proceed through a learning center at their own pace.
>
> *(Karen Elson, Columbus, Ohio)*

A Shortage of Funds

Learning centers need not be a great expense. While it is possible to create elaborate centers with everything printed in color, a simpler approach can be used. Instead of purchasing colorful display boards, cut appliance boxes to size. Mounting instructions onto colored construction paper enlivens a display at a minimal cost. Storage containers, magazines, and other materials may be brought from home. Sometimes, however, an initial investment saves money over time. Any pieces that you intend to use from year to year and that receive a lot of handling are worth protecting. If a laminator is available, make use of it. Otherwise consider clear Contact paper. This one step may save you from having to recreate materials in future years.

Name _____

Activity #1	☑
Activity #2	☐
Activity #3	☑
Activity #4	☐

This is a very simple contract that allows the student to keep track of the work that has been completed — assuming all of the students are working on the same assignments. A similar table could be made with varied assignments written in for different students.

Name _____

Color in the flame for each activity you complete.

1 2 3 4 5 6 7 8

This is similar to the contract above, allowing student choice. It uses thematic graphics to maximize interest.

Name _____

Assignment	Teacher Comments	Student Comments	Date Completed
Create a skit using our vocabulary words	Please work as a group with Shimon and Ari. Let me know as you complete the script.	Shimon has been absent. We will return to this assignment later in the week.	
Rewrite the dialog on page 16 in the feminine form	Pay close attention to adjectives as well!		3/14
Design a postcard illustrating the mitzvot of Purim.			

This is a more involved format. The teacher determines the specific assignments for each student. Space is made available for teacher/student communication.

Figure 8

A Shortage of Time

There is no doubt that developing centers is time-consuming, especially the creation of learning activities. Any shortcuts that allow you to streamline the rest of the project are usually welcome. There are often resources available nearby.

The first to consider is a local teacher center. Some Jewish communities fund centers with professional staff available to assist in materials creation. These centers, gold mines of information and inspiration, often have equipment that can save an enormous amount of time. Computers, laminators, and die cut machines are only a few of these time savers.

If the Jewish community doesn't have a teacher center, look for centers available through your school district, county, or local colleges. Many allow visitors to use them for a small fee. General teachers stores can also provide a source of pre-made materials at a reasonable price. English text on secular materials may be covered and replaced with Hebrew, and items that have interesting shapes (apples, lightbulbs, globes) can be used in a Jewish setting with just a little bit of creativity.

Another source of assistance is the parents of your students. Every class seems to have a parent or two who enjoys creating displays. Others may be willing to lend a hand with cutting and other chores. Don't forget to check with the school director for any policies regarding parent involvement.

CONCLUSION

As the school year comes to a close, Mrs. Gold thinks back on it. It has been a busy year, full of satisfaction. Students have mastered the curriculum, each in his/her own way. It has been a positive experience for everyone. Next year she will meet a new group of students. While most of her material will be useful in helping them achieve their goals, she knows that some adjustments will be made for their unique needs. A new year and a new challenge, but one she can anticipate with excitement and confidence.

TEACHING CONSIDERATIONS

- Learning centers give teachers the opportunity to individualize instruction so that each student's needs are specifically met.

- To be effective, learning centers must be planned with attention to clear teaching goals.

- The flexibility of learning centers allows them to be utilized in any teaching environment.

- Organizational systems, such as contracts and work folders, assist the teacher in the ongoing management of learning centers.

BIBLIOGRAPHY

Holliman, Linda. *The Complete Guide To Classroom Centers: Hundreds of Ideas That Really Work*. Cypress, CA: Creative Teaching Press, Inc., 1996.

This book is for both novices and longtime users of learning centers. It can be used as a guide, as a reference in taking the next step in using centers, as well as a source for many new ideas to enhance your learning centers.

Ingraham, Phoebe Bell. *Creating and Managing Learning Centers: A Thematic Approach*. Peterborough, NH: Crystal Springs Books, 1997.

This book includes information on creating learning centers that are tied to the curriculum, ways to help students use learning centers, and types of learning centers (cognitive development, creative development, literacy development, physical and social/emotional development centers).

Marriott, Donna. *What Are the Other Kids Doing? . . . while you teach small groups*. Cypress, CA: Creative Teaching Press, Inc., 1997.

This book includes 30 independent literacy center activities, assessment tools, and management techniques to enable students to be responsible and accountable for their work giving the teacher time to work, with small groups.

Opitz, Michael F. *Learning Centers: Getting Them Started, Keeping Them Going*. New York: Scholastic Professional Books, 1994.

A step-by-step guide to incorporating learning centers into classroom instruction, including floor plans, sample schedules, activities, and more.

Rice, Dona. *How to Manage Learning Centers in the Classroom*. Westminster, CA: Teacher Created Materials, Inc., 1996.

This book is created to enable teachers to help each student realize his/her potential for learning. It shows how learning centers can enhance your teaching and your students' learning.

Silver, Harvey F. *So Each May Learn: Integrating Learning Styles and Multiple Intelligences*. Alexandria, VA: Association for Supervision and Curriculum Development, 2000.

A readable text that includes research-based principles that support integrated learning, information on understanding multiple intelligences and learning styles, and templates for designing integrated lessons based on curriculum.

CHAPTER 30

Cooperative or Collaborative Learning

Carol K. Ingall

INTRODUCTION

Michelle has been teaching fifth grade Chumash in a Jewish day school for two years. This year her class is a large one, with 20 students, five more than customary. Michelle, like most teachers, teaches the way she was taught. She presents new vocabulary to the group, gives an overview of the material to be mastered, then asks the class to read and translate. At the end of class, the students work individually on worksheets she has prepared. The system had worked well for her in the past. This year, however, some students are staring at the ceiling or at the clock. Some finish the worksheet in five minutes and proceed to disturb their neighbors; others tearfully ask for additional time. Michelle is both bored by the routine and troubled by the growing number of discipline problems it has evoked. Over coffee in the teachers' lounge, Ariella, the fourth grade teacher, has shared her impressions of the group she taught last year. The operative adjective is "diverse." She confirms what Michelle has intuited during the first week: the students differ markedly in their facility with Hebrew, in their analytical and verbal skills, and in their interests outside the classroom. Ariella advises Michelle to experiment with some cooperative learning techniques.

Cooperative learning is more than the latest fad to sweep secular education. It is a truly Jewish way of teaching our children. Cooperative learning builds group skills at the same time as it stresses individual accountability. In addition to acquiring these important social skills, children in cooperative classrooms learn as much, or more, than in traditional classrooms.

Although cooperative learning has been around since the days of Colonel Francis Parker in the 1890s, it has captured the public imagination since the early 1980s. Its advocates see cooperative learning as an antidote to the rampant "me-firstism" of the Yuppie Era, a form of moral education that creates a firsthand experience with democracy. The Attleboro, Massachusetts public schools are so convinced of the efficacy of cooperative learning, they have mandated its application for 20 percent of each teacher's instructional time.

Detractors see cooperative learning as yet another fad. They raise concerns for the gifted child, the loner who is uncomfortable in group situations, the suitability of all subjects to cooperative learning techniques, the necessity of retraining teachers in the technique, and the potential of sacrificing skills to content. Should the group rewards in cooperative learning be extrinsic ones, such as bonus points or prizes, or should they be intrinsic? Is cooperative learning a set of techniques or a philosophy of living?

This chapter will address these questions by reviewing the current literature in the field. It will also provide readers with *tachlis* — examples of how cooperative learning can be applied to the curriculum of the Jewish school.

WHAT IS COOPERATIVE LEARNING?

Let's begin with a definition of cooperative learning. You have been teaching using groups for years. Students in Jewish history work on group reports; you divide your Hebrew language students into slow and bright groups. This is cooperative learning, right? Wrong.

One of the hallmarks of cooperative learning is positive interdependence. Positive interdependence means the creation of a "we" instead of a "me" atmosphere. Such an atmosphere can be created by establishing mutual goals. An example of a mutual goal is that all students must learn a given amount of material (e.g., ten vocabulary words from *Parashat Toledot*) and they must see to it that all members of the group have mastered the material.

A second example of the creation of positive interdependence is the introduction of joint rewards. For example, if each person scores above

70% on a quiz based on the vocabulary in *Toledot*, each member of the group will receive five bonus points.

A third method of effecting positive interdependence is for the teacher to limit materials and information. By sharing resources, students have to depend on each other. The students working on a biography of Herzl would turn in *one* report. Each member of the group might have been assigned a specific role: one to research Herzl's life and work before his "conversion" to Zionism, a second to study the impact of the Dreyfus Affair on the young journalist, a third to deal with Herzl's efforts in setting up the Zionist Congress. Students might be assigned one copy of a text to interpret, forcing them to sit "eye-to-eye and knee-to-knee."

A fourth method of fostering positive interdependence is to assign roles to students in the group. Thus in the *Toledot* vocabulary example, one student might be responsible for teaching the English translation of the words, a second for teaching the Hebrew spelling, and a third for conducting the practice drills and checking the completed work.

Another characteristic of cooperative learning is individual accountability. There are no "hitchhikers" in cooperative learning groups. Not only does each student have an integral role, but each student must also show mastery over the entire body of material. Our Herzl project would not be completed by the students working on their discrete assignments, binding them together, and turning in their project. In addition, each student would be responsible for sharing his/her area of expertise with the other members of the group. To assure individual accountability, the teacher might give each group member individual exams, or the teacher might randomly select one member of the group to summarize for the entire group. (Of course, the group would be given time to prepare for this method of evaluation.)

Still another characteristic of cooperative learning is building social skills. Cooperative learning groups may be somewhat noisy. They should be. There is a lot of face-to-face interaction going on. Students are summarizing for each other, quizzing one another, explaining material to each other. Sounds familiar? This aspect of cooperative learning is old fashioned *chevruta* learning. In *yeshivot*, *chevruta* (or learning with a partner) is the norm. For hundreds of years, Jews have been explicating

their texts with study partners. The exchange of divergent views, the "ownership" of a text gained through teaching it to another, and the bonus of camaraderie are easily transplanted from the *bayt midrash* to the secular, religious, and day school.

Cooperative learning differs from *chevruta* in that the teacher has a responsibility for teaching the social skills needed for collaboration. Cooperative learning practitioners must address the questions of teaching how to develop leadership, how to make effective decisions, and how to resolve conflicts.

The remaining characteristic of cooperative learning is group processing. Students must have the opportunity and know-how to assess how well they and their groups are functioning. This aspect, although critical to the cooperative learning experience, is most often lacking. The groups can process their effectiveness individually through self-assessment forms turned in to the teacher immediately after the experience or through student journals. The group can evaluate itself. One member can serve as evaluator, giving his/her report as to how many times each member participated, whether or not members added their remarks onto those of previous speakers, or noting "put-ups" instead of "put-downs." A further method of group processing is to have the teacher circulate with a checklist while the groups are working. She can then report on her findings to the class. Still another method is to review the group processing with the entire class. The teacher would pose the question, "How are we doing?" and facilitate a class-wide assessment.

A warning: this group processing is one of the most valuable aspects of cooperative learning, one which is usually sacrificed in the interests of time. Bypass it at your own peril. You lose the community building that is so valuable, particularly in Jewish schools, and you run the risk of having your cooperative learning experience become routine group work.

By now you should have the idea. Cooperative learning moves the locus of authority from the teacher to the students. Practitioners call this "student as worker; teacher as coach." The teacher is no longer the showman or actress, but the facilitator. The heavy duty work is done before class: creating the groups, assigning the roles, structuring the materials to provide positive interdependence, deciding how to ensure individual accountability, determining which social skills would be taught as well as how to encourage and assess them and, finally, building group processing into your lessons. Needless to say, you have to determine what aspects of your curriculum are suitable to cooperative learning. Don't overdo it; it is but one arrow in your quiver of strategies. Lecture has its place, as do individualized activities and healthy competition.

> The secret to cooperative learning is to give each member of the cooperative group a stake in the outcome. I will often give two responses to work done in a cooperative group. One is on the final product — everyone has a stake in the outcome of that. The other is individual. I try to let each student reflect on how the group functioned and his/her contribution to the work of the group. I encourage the students to keep track of each other. If I am using cooperative learning groups for a longer assignment, I suggest they call each other to make sure each member of the group has completed his or her part.
>
> *(Sally Stefano, Worthington, Ohio)*

A REVIEW OF THE CURRENT LITERATURE

Among the original gurus of cooperative learning were David Johnson and Roger Johnson. They popularized the concept through workshops given for the Association for Supervision and Curriculum Development, by their contributions to the literature, and through their Minnesota center. They helped create the vocabulary that characterizes cooperative learning, such as positive interdependence, individual accountability, shared leadership, emphasis on task, and maintenance[1] — all of which describe learning "eye-to-eye and knee-to-knee." Their bias was a social one: cooperative learning was good for what ailed democracy. Social skills could not be assumed by the teacher; they had to be taught.

Robert Slavin of Johns Hopkins University came to cooperative learning from a different per-spective. Originally interested in mainstreaming learning disabled students, his concern was achievement rather than community building. He writes: "Once thought of primarily as social methods directed at social goals, certain forms of cooperative learning are considerably more effective than traditional methods in increasing basic achievement outcomes, including performance on standardized tests of math, reading, and language."[2] Unlike the Johnsons, who advocate cooperative learning for both the three R's and interpretive realms, Slavin concentrates on the three R's. Like most of the advocates of cooperative learning, Slavin insists on heterogeneity in grouping. He is opposed to ability or homogeneous grouping for pragmatic reasons: it doesn't work, even though teachers seem to feel that it does. "It is surprising to see how unequivocally the research evidence refutes the assertion that ability-grouped class assignment can increase student achievement in elementary schools."[3]

Alfie Kohn has challenged Slavin's assumptions and techniques. Like the Johnsons, Kohn is more concerned with a philosophy of living rather than a set of techniques. Kohn criticizes Slavin for his team-centered learning modalities, all of which use group rewards, or as Kohn would say, grade grubbing. He feels that using group rewards has a hidden cost: a diminution of creativity. Trophy-chasing is unnecessary; the process is itself the prize.[4]

A recent newcomer to the debate is John Myers. Writing in *Cooperative Learning*, Myers raises a semantic question. He asks us to differentiate between cooperative learning a la Slavin and collaborative learning a la Kohn/Johnsons. The former is concerned with techniques, product, and transmission, the latter with a *Weltanschauung*, process and transformation. Preferring the British nomenclature of collaborative learning to differentiate the transformational from the transmissional, Myers is an advocate of collaborative learning. He says: "I contend that the dispute is not about research, but more about the morality of what should happen in schools."[5]

[1]David W. Johnson, et al, *Circles of Learning: Cooperation in the Classroom* (Arlington, VA: Association for Supervision and Curriculum Development, 1984), 10.

[2]Robert E. Slavin, "Cooperative Learning and the Cooperative School," *Educational Leadership* (November 1987), 7.

[3]Robert E. Slavin, "Ability Grouping and Student Achievement in Elementary Schools: A Best Evidence Synthesis," *Review of Educational Research* (Fall 1987), 307.

[4]Alfie Kohn, "Group Grade Grubbing versus Cooperative Learning," *Educational Leadership* (February 1991), 83-87.

[5]John Myers, "Cooperative or Collaborative Learning? Towards a Constructive Controversy," *Cooperative Learning* (July 1991), 19.

APPLICATIONS TO JEWISH SCHOOLS

If you wish to apply cooperative or collaborative learning techniques to your classroom, reflect on the following questions:[6]

1. What do I want my students to know and be able to do? How will I know? What will I measure? Is there a balance between social skills and content skills?

2. Is this task appropriate for cooperative or collaborative learning? Have I built in positive interdependence and individual accountability?

3. Have I clearly defined the criteria for success for the students and for myself?

4. Have I built in time for group processing?

Start modestly. Your groups should consist of no more than three or four students. Watch for a heterogeneous mix; consider ability, cliques, neighborhoods, and gender — then mix them accordingly. Spend about 20 minutes on the first project.

If you want to practice before committing yourself to a long-term experience, you might want to try Think-Pair-Share. Ask a question that requires a thoughtful opinion, not one for which there is a right or wrong answer. For example, "Why has Chanukah, a minor Jewish holiday, become so important in the United States?" Give students a minute or so to ponder, then ask them to jot down their thoughts. (They may decide it's the American love of the underdog, the similarity of the American Revolution to the Hasmonean Rebellion, or just the proximity of Christmas.) Then give students a few minutes to share their ideas with a partner and come up with an answer each pair agrees to. The teacher can then call on the pairs to share their conclusions with the entire class. Think-Pair-Share guarantees reflection and participation. You can graft processing onto this technique by asking students what new insight they gained through working with a partner or how they resolved conflict in their dyads. Think-Pair-Share can be used in any part of the curriculum that requires interpretation: *Chumash*, Hebrew literature, *mitzvot* or values, Jewish history, or current events.

Another task that builds consensus is to have students analyze a Jewish text using the following questions:

1. What does the text say?

2. What does the text mean?

3. What does the text mean to me?

4. What word or phrase is central to the understanding of the text? Why?

"Jigsaw" is a technique developed by Elliot Aronson. The Herzl project described earlier in this chapter is an example of adapting "Jigsaw" to the study of Jewish history. In "Jigsaw," students are assigned to four to six member teams to work on academic material that has been broken down into sections. For example, Sukkot might be broken down into the laws of building a *sukkah, ushpizin*, biblical references to Sukkot, *brachot*, traditional Ashkenazic and Sephardic foods eaten on the holiday. Each team member is assigned one of the five areas in which to gain expertise. If there are 25 students in the class, there would be five teams, each having a *sukkah, ushpizin*, Bible, *brachot*, and foods expert. Team members studied their materials individually, then met in "expert groups" to discuss and master their sections (all five *sukkah* experts, the five *ushpizin* experts, etc.). Then all the experts returned to their team to teach their teammates their expertise so that all the material is covered. The teacher could then evaluate each team on their mastery of all the Sukkot material.

Hebrew language teachers may want to experiment with some of Robert Slavin's methods. STAD (Student Teams-Achievement Divisions) works well with subjects for which there are well-defined teaching objectives with single right answers. In STAD, students are put into heterogeneous four-member groups. The teacher presents a lesson frontally, then students work within their teams to make sure that everyone has mastered the material. Each student individually takes a quiz during which they may not help each other.

The teacher compares quiz scores to students' past averages. Then he/she awards points based on the degree to which students can meet or exceed their own past performances. Students receive team scores based on their individual improvement. Teams that improve receive certificates or rewards.

By basing team success on individual improvement, students are encouraged to help each other prepare for the quizzes. STAD makes it easy for a

---

[6]Thanks to Amy Gerstein for her help in formulating these questions.

weaker student to succeed, since that student is competing with himself/herself, not with brighter teammates. The downside of STAD are the objections that Alfie Kohn has raised.

Hebrew language teachers might want to experiment with the writing of a group poem.[7] The following exercise uses groups of four students to create a group poem using a procedure developed by Kenneth Koch in *Wishes, Lies and Dreams.* Following is an outline of this procedure:

1. Assign students to groups of four.

2. Assign roles as follows:
   Director: gets materials and keeps track of time.
   Facilitator: makes sure everyone's ideas are expressed and listened to.
   Recorder: makes a clear, legible copy of the final version of the poem.
   Reporter: reads the poem aloud to the class.

3. Have the director distribute 12 index cards (three per team member) and four felt tip pens, one color for each team member.

4. Show an overhead acetate with sentence starters for use in creating the group poem. Explain any unfamiliar words.

5. Ask the students to take a piece of scrap paper and fill in the blanks as best they can, making full sentences. Allow them five to seven minutes to complete the assignment. (You can use vocabulary words from your reading series.)

6. Ask students to select their two best lines and write them, one per card, on their two index cards.

7. Explain the roles of the director, facilitator, recorder, and reporter.

8. Go over the instructions for the composition of the group poem:

   a. Each person reads his/her two cards aloud to the group, translating if necessary.

   b. The group gives feedback after each person shares (words they liked, correcting spelling or grammar).

   c. After all have shared, the team must pick at least one card from each person, decide on

the order of the lines to create a good group poem, and finally, determine a one or two word title for the poem.

The group must agree to use at least one card from each person, to modify the lines only with the consent of the author, to agree on the final product, and to sign the poem with their names. This should take about 15 minutes.

After each of the recorders copies the poem onto newsprint, the poems should be displayed and then read by the reporters. Any member of the group might be called on for explication. Group processing:

1. Ask the students to reflect on the following questions:

   a. How is writing a poem in a group different from writing a poem alone?

   b. How did I feel about my contribution to the group?

   c. How do I feel about my role within the group?

   d. Were everyone's ideas encouraged and listened to?

   e. What could we do better next time?

2. Give the students time to answer the above questions in their groups (four to five minutes).

Whatever models you choose to implement, be sure to keep the groups heterogeneous, and change them every four to five weeks. (Students will work with anyone if they know it won't be forever. During the course of the four or five weeks, they may even learn to respect, if not like, "everyone" very much.) Be sure to encourage group autonomy. Make it a rule: no group can call on the teacher until each person in the group has been asked to answer the question or solve the problem. If you find that certain students tend to dominate a group, give each member of the group five poker chips. In order to speak, a member has to ante up a chip. When all five are played, the team member forfeits the right to speak. For a group to complete its tasks, each of the members must play its chips. This system curtails the blabbermouths and encourages the *bayashanim* (shy ones).

---

[7]This exercise is adapted from "Writing a Group Poem: A Cooperative Learning Lesson in Language Arts" in *Cooperative*

Learning 11, no. 4 (July 1991).

Don't forget the encouragement of social skills and group processing. For two examples of evaluation instruments, see Appendix A and Appendix B of this chapter. Please Listen To Me (Appendix A) is for students; the Classroom Observation Chart (Appendix B) is for teachers.

Due to differences in attendance and skills, each of my fourth grade students is in a different place in his/her Hebrew instruction. The series *Z'man Likro* (A.R.E. Publishing, Inc.) lends itself easily to an individualized approach, with each student having his/her own folder and workbook and working at his/her own pace. However, I believe, as do the authors of *Z'man Likro*, that it is also important for the children to work together in pairs and groups. I try to avoid the "blue bird-red bird" groups by having flexible grouping. One day, a student may be assigned someone who is working on the same lesson; another day, he/she may be playing a letter game with someone more or less advanced. I mix them up and keep them guessing!

(*Sheila Lepkin, Denver, Colorado*)

CONCLUSION

Michelle, the caring and pragmatic teacher we met at the beginning of this chapter, knew it was time for a change. Her conversation with Ariella and a handbook on cooperative learning that she picked up at the neighborhood bookstore steeled her resolve. When the class met the following Monday, Michelle asked the students to close their Chumashim and notebooks. She explained that she was going to change the format of the class.

The students were to be divided into heterogeneous groups of four, with diverse responsibilities. They would actively teach each other, rather than listening passively to her. Each group would include a librarian, who would pick up everything needed for the lesson: the Hebrew dictionaries, supplies, and worksheets. Each group would have its own coach to prepare its members for the quizzes, which would be assigned daily. A third member would be the facilitator who would keep track of the time, make sure that everyone was contributing to the discussion, and take responsibility for the completion of the group project. The fourth member of the
team would be the editor, who would present, in final form, the group project to which all of the members of the group would contribute.

The groups would change every three weeks, as would the responsibilities. The students would receive both individual grades, based on the daily quizzes, and a group grade based on the group project, which would be presented at the conclusion of the parashah. That project might draw upon the many talents in the group: Shoshana's musical ability, Yoram's artistic gifts, or David's facility with the computer. In addition, Michelle would factor in points for social skills, such as how well students listened to one another or dealt with disagreements within the group, or helped a group member who seemed to be floundering.

After listening to Michelle's introduction, Noam asked, "If we'll be teaching one another, what will you be doing, Ms. Davis?" Michelle explained that she would meet with each group during the class, making sure that students were on task, and answering questions that no one in the group could answer. She would also engage in a daily stroll around the classroom, using her walk to get a sense of how the groups were functioning.

In addition to sharing her plans with her students, Michelle sent a letter home to parents, informing them of the new format of the class. In it she stressed her belief that cooperation would promote higher achievement, develop social skills, place responsibility for learning on the learner, and create a forum for the many talents in the group.

Barraged with questions, Michelle recognized some of the pitfalls enumerated in the teacher's handbook she had read over the weekend. She quickly understood that she would have to be attentive to the following issues:

- How could Michelle create an inventory of student talents, their preferred learning styles, their capacities for tension and empathy?

- What happens if students don't like the groups to which they are assigned?

- What if members don't fulfill their responsibilities? Would one student be saddled with the burden of carrying a group of freeloaders?

- What about the student who prefers to work alone?

- How do students negotiate disagreements: dismissively? by refusing to speak up?

- How would she balance teacher-provided structure with student autonomy?

- How would she balance the academic and the social needs of preteens?

For further discussion: Imagine the following conversations:

- What might Michelle say to Max, who comes to her after class to confide that he thinks that Rachel is too bossy and that he wants to change his group?

- What might Michelle say to Mrs. Stone whose daughter Jessica is a fine student who feels put upon having to coach weaker ones?

- What might Michelle say to her colleague, Betsy Cohen, who questions the ethics of giving students a group grade?

As a Jewish educator, I am convinced that collaborative learning, or the Kohn/Johnsons school of cooperative learning, has a great deal to offer Jewish schools. Jews live in community. Public prayer is mandated three times daily. A *minyan* (ten people) is required. We pray using collective language. Our Yom Kippur liturgy intones, "*We* have sinned; *we* have transgressed." Our goal is not individual salvation, but the creation of a holy people. Surely the use of individualization and competition is discordant in a Jewish school; the medium is the message — and collaborative learning is a much more appropriate message.

Sarah S. Shapiro and Ruth Ravid studied cooperative learning in Jewish schools. Modifying Slavin's Student Team Achievement Divisions (STAD), they assessed the success of the approach in raising student achievement in Hebrew language and Bible. They also noted a change in attitude toward Jewish education on the part of the students, and a change in attitude toward teaching on the part of the teacher.[8]

As important as the Shapiro-Ravid study is in making a case for cooperative learning in the Jewish school, a more important case can be made. As Jewish life becomes increasingly more fragmented, as secularization and modernity erode the foundations of the Jewish home, the Jewish school is increasingly called upon to recreate the Jewish community. Collaborative learning can foster that community.

Collaborative learning reinforces an essential teaching of Rabbinic Judaism: "All Jews are responsible for one another." That responsibility is what Ronald Tyrrell noted in his research on cooperative learning. He quotes a teacher who says: "My students worked much better together. There seems to be much more acceptance of each other. They are dealing with what differences there are in a more harmonious way. I hear far fewer put-downs and they are much more encouraging of each other."[9] What this teacher hears is the sounds of a caring community — the ideal of Judaism.

As educators, we have to concern ourselves with community as well as content, method as well as message. Elliot Eisner reminds us that school reform begins with the culture of the school. "How we organize the 'envelope' within teaching and how curricular activities occur also matters. That is, how schools are structured, the kind of values that pervade them, the ways in which roles are defined and assessments are made are a part of the living context in which both teachers and students must function."[10]

In a recent ASCD *Update*, Eisner commented on the purpose of schooling. "I don't think that the major aim of school is to help kids do well in school . . . *Schools exist for the kind of life that kids are able to lead outside of schools.*"[11] Using Eisner's definition, collaborative education offers the educator an invaluable resource for the teaching of social responsibility. It is equally as invaluable a resource for Jewish schools.

Collaborative or cooperative learning reminds me of the famous *midrash* about the *lulav* and *etrog*. The injunction comes from Leviticus 23:40: "Take . . . a cluster of the four species . . . " The Rabbis commented on what this phrase meant. The citron, they said, has fragrance and edible fruit. So the Jewish people has members who study and also do good deeds. The palm has an edible fruit and no

---

[8]Sara S. Shapiro and Ruth Ravid, "Student Team Learning in Jewish Schools," *Jewish Education* (Spring 1989), 12ff.

[9]Ronald Tyrrell, "What Teachers Say about Cooperative Learning," *Middle School Journal* (January 1990), 17.

[10]Elliot W. Eisner, "What Really Counts in Schools," *Educational Leadership* (February 1991).

[11]Elliot W. Eisner, "What's the Purpose of School?" ASCD *Update* (December 1990), 4.

fragrance. So the Jewish people has in its midst members who study God's word, but do no good deeds. The myrtle has a fragrance, but no edible fruit. So among the Jewish people are those who do good deeds, but do not study. The willow has neither fruit nor fragrance, like those Jews who neither study nor do good deeds. But God says that in order to make it impossible for the Jewish people to be destroyed, each is bound to the other. Each needs the other. (Adapted from *Pesikta Rabbati* 51:2.) This is the message of collaborative education — that it is imperative for us to create communities that value their members for their contributions and their differences, a message that is Jewish to its very core.

I would like to use cooperative learning more in the classroom. I often use "Jigsaw" when I want to cover a lot of material in a short time. This year, for the first time, I had my sixth graders learn different *Rashis* from the Book of Genesis in groups and then teach them to their home groups. If I had taught each Rashi to the entire group it would have taken much longer, and I'm not sure the students would have understood them so well.

(Cheryl Birkner Mack, Cleveland, Ohio)

APPENDIX A

Please Listen To Me

1. How well did I listen to others in my group?

1   2   3   4   5   6

I wasn't listening   Sometimes I listed   I listen
at all   to others   very carefully

I let others know I was listening by _____.

I could have been a better listener by _____.

2. How well did others in my group listen to me?

1   2   3   4   5   6

I wasn't listened   Sometimes I was   My ideas were
to at all   listened to   carefully listened to

Someone made me feel listened to by _____.

Someone made me feel I wasn't listened to because they _____.

3. Next time I listen to others I will _____.

APPENDIX B
Classroom Observation Chart

NAMES OF STUDENTS IN GROUP: DATE:

MOVE IN ORDERLY FASHION

STAY ON TASK

HANDS TO SELF

STAY WITH GROUP

Group Cooperative Learning Grade:

Grade Justification:

BIBLIOGRAPHY

Chinn, C.A.; A.M. O'Donnell; and T.S. Jinks. "The Structure of Discourse in Collaborative Learning." *Journal of Experimental Education* 69, no. 1, Fall 2000, pp. 77-97.

> Chinn, et al. examined the types of discourse structures emerging during peer learning and the ways in which these structures were related to learning for 105 fifth graders working in groups of four to learn about writing conclusions. They characterize the discourse structure as a network of arguments and counterarguments, with argument quality positively related to students' ability to write their own conclusions. The research could be used to make a case for the similarity between the goals of cooperative learning and *chevruta* learning.

Cohen, Elizabeth G. *Designing Groupwork: Strategies for the Heterogeneous Classroom.* 2d ed. New York: Teachers College Press, 1994.

> Features strategies for group work, a perspective on group dynamics, and examples of creative team building.

Dishon, Dee, and Pat Wilson O'Leary. A *Guidebook for Cooperative Learning: A Technique for Creating More Effective Schools.* 3d ed. Holmes Beach, FL: Learning Publications, Inc., 1998.

> A clear, step-by-step guide to implementing the Johnsons' model of cooperative learning.

Dyson, B., and S. Grineski. "Using Cooperative Learning Structures in Physical Education." *Journal of Physical Education, Recreation & Dance* 72, no. 2, February 2001, pp. 28-31.

> Research has determined that cooperative learning has positive effects in physical education. This article presents five important components of cooperative learning to help physical educators maximize learning (team formation, positive interdependence, individual accountability, positive social interaction, and group processing). It describes five cooperative learning structures: think-share-perform, pairs-check-perform, jigsaw perform, co-op play, and learning teams. The article offers yet another application of cooperative learning and confirms its applicability to any subject domain.

Johnson, David W.; Roger T. Johnson; and Edythe Johnson Holubec. *The New Circles of Learning: Cooperation in the Classroom and School.* Alexandria, VA: Association for Supervision and Curriculum Development, 1994.

> This book, authored by the pioneers of cooperative learning, includes an overview of cooperative learning and research, essential components of cooperative learning, as well as chapters on formal and informal cooperative learning, teaching students cooperative skills, and the cooperative school.

Kagan, Laurie; Miguel Kagan; and Spencer Kagan. *Cooperative Learning Structures for Teambuilding.* San Clemente, CA: Kagan Cooperative Learning, 1997.

> Includes step-by-step instructions, hints, variations, and over 100 teambuilding activities and ready to use blackline masters for each of 14 teambuilding structures.

Kagan, Spencer. *Cooperative Learning.* San Clemente, CA: Kagan Cooperative Learning, 1997.

> Includes how to form groups (randomly, homogeneously, heterogeneously), activities for establishing group rapport, how to assign effective and well defined roles to each group member, teaching social skills, ensuring equal participation and positive interdependence, and how to assess work.

Knabb, M.T. "Discovering Teamwork: A Novel Cooperative Learning Activity to Encourage Group Interdependence." *American Biology Teacher* 62, no. 3, March 2000, pp. 211-13.

> Knabb resents a new cooperative group learning strategy that encourages students to work together so that they learn the importance of sharing and synthesizing information during biology activities. This approach is equally adaptable to Jewish studies.

McElherne, Linda Nason. *Jump Starters: Quick Classroom Activities That Develop Self-Esteem, Creativity, and Cooperation.* Minneapolis, MN: Free Spirit Publishing, 1999.

> The easy to follow activities in this book are fun and meaningful, and encourage children to understand and appreciate themselves and others.

Schniedewind, Nancy, and Ellen Davidson. "Differentiating Cooperative Learning." *Educational Leadership* 58, no. 1, September 2000, pp. 24-27.

Effective heterogeneous cooperative learning helps students grow academically, socially, and emotionally. Within heterogeneous groups, teachers can differentiate tasks by complexity and quantity, use high achieving students' ideas, enhance individualized work, plan challenging peer tutoring assignments, add enrichment options, vary criteria for success, and promote social learning.

Sharan, Shlomo, ed. *Handbook of Cooperative Learning Methods.* Westport, CT: Praeger Publishers, 1999.

This broad perspective on cooperative learning methods is divided into three sections — methods, application, and implementation.

Sharan, Yael, and Shlomo Sharan. *Expanding Cooperative Learning through Group Investigation.* New York: Teachers College Press, 1992.

This comprehensive work explains the philosophy, foundations, and current practice of group investigation. The authors provide suggestions for ways of developing the necessary discussion and cooperative planning skills, as well as detailed examples of projects for elementary and upper grades.

Shaw, Vanston. *Community Building in the Classroom.* San Clemente, CA: Kagan Cooperative Learning, 1992.

Shaw's ideas on building community in the classroom help teachers pick and choose what will work for their class, whatever the grade.

Slavin, Robert E. *Cooperative Learning: Theory, Research, and Practice.* 2d ed. Needham Heights, MA: Allyn & Bacon, Inc., 1994.

A readable and concise guide on the subject that includes up-to-date ways to increase the effectiveness of cooperative methods for achievement, intergroup relations, positive mainstreaming, outcomes, self-esteem, and more.

Web Sites

www.clcrc.com - Cooperative Learning Center at the University of Minnesota

Contains essays on developments in cooperative learning pioneered by the Center, as well as newsletters, a Q & A section, and more.

www.cooperativelearning.com - The web site for Kagan Publishing and Professional Development

Features training, products, a magazine, articles, and discussion on cooperative learning.

www.iasce.net - Web site of the International Association for the Study of Cooperative Education

Contains newsletters, resources, and announcements of conferences and training pertaining to cooperative learning.

CHAPTER 31

Teaching about God and Spirituality[1]

Sherry H. Blumberg

*B*rian had been dreading this moment from the day he started teaching in his congregational religious school. He had felt he could handle anything — discipline issues, lesson planning, bulletin boards, a classroom visitor, angry parents. But all along, he was filled with anxiety about the day a student would ask a question about God. And today was that day. Brian looked at the student who cocked her head inquisitively to the right. Then, he simply sat down at his desk. What in the world, he wondered, would he answer?

Many people — Jews included — need and very much want to talk about God. Faced with a highly complex and seemingly relativistic world, most people are — at one level or another — looking for something of enduring value, importance, and sanctity that will give their lives a sense of direction and meaning. They need to explore their understanding of and their relationship to that which is sacred. To meet this legitimate and real need, Jewish educators need to teach about God. Fortunately, our tradition has an abundant and diverse supply of resources for this exploration.

What Jewish sources can we use to help these seekers answer their questions about existence and purpose of life itself? What curricular approaches will enable students to find hope in the midst of sorrow and tragedy? What values inspired our traditions? Why have the Jewish people always been optimistic and involved in this world? What are the ways Jewish educators can help students learn about the mystery of life, and the Source of life itself?

When I and many others like me think about our lives and reflect on what has given us the courage and stamina to live in this world, we arrive at one answer: our faith in God has given us a Jewish affirmation of life. It is that faith — that *emunah* — a sense of trust and truth — that gives us hope, courage, values, and the link to all other persons in time, especially to other Jews. Our faith sanctifies our lives and raises our lives above the profane, while still allowing us to accept and respond to the responsibilities of living.

For myself, the faith that sustains and nourishes me comes from my Jewish education, as well as my life experience. For people like me, our faith adds depth to the rational and intellectual content of our Jewish studies. Yet, that faith is neither blind nor unquestioning. Doubting, questioning, and dialoguing are integral parts of a Jewish study of and encounter with God. From Abraham's time to the present, we have engaged in dialogue and argument among ourselves and with God. Torah study, prayer, and our daily actions inspire the dialogue, which is at once both a statement of faith and a sign of a relationship. But, just as any relationship that has not been challenged does not know its own strength, the strength and quality of a relationship with God can be assessed only when challenged. For this reason, it is important to speak about God in a trusting and nurturing environment, one in which we can safely raise our doubts, explore our questions, and pursue our quest. This is why I believe that the Jewish school must be a place where children can go for answers and guidance while testing or affirming their faith.

In this chapter I answer the fundamental educational question of how best to structure this dialogue for students within a school's curriculum, depending upon the goals of the school and the ages of the students.

---

[1]This chapter is reprinted with permission from *Teaching about God and Spirituality: A Resource for Jewish Settings*, edited by Roberta Louis Goodman and Sherry H. Blumberg (Denver, CO: A.R.E. Publishing, Inc., 2002).

DESIGNING A CURRICULAR APPROACH TO TEACHING ABOUT GOD

Key Elements

Turning Jewish schools into places where God is encountered and discussed requires well thought-out curricular approaches. How best to approach teaching about God in our Jewish schools evokes many questions: (1) What conception or idea of God should we present? Is there an authentic Jewish God concept? (2) What if the teacher is unsure about his or her own conception or feelings about God? Can an atheist or agnostic Jew teach about God? (3) When do we begin to teach about God? What concepts or ideas are appropriate for each age? (4) Are some teaching techniques better suited than others for teaching about God? (5) With the vast amount of material available, where, as teacher and educator, do I begin, and where end?

These questions translate into five key elements in designing a curricular approach to teaching about God: (1) philosophy and goals, (2) the teacher, (3) age appropriateness of the curriculum, (4) teaching techniques, and (5) the materials. Below, I answer the questions associated with each key element.

Philosophy and Goals

What conception or idea of God should we present? Is there an authentic Jewish God concept? Normative Judaism has no doctrinal statement about the definition and conception of God. Rather, it concentrates on the relationship between God and human beings. God is One, but there are multiple understandings of what that one God is. Therefore, a variety of Jewish God concepts, ideas, and experiences should be provided to learners so they can latch onto that perspective that most strongly resonates with them. As Fritz Rothschild puts it: "Teaching about God in Jewish education must draw on the variety of formulations and approaches which have emerged in the history of Israel's religion."[2] On the other hand, this multiplicity of authentic expressions about God does not mean that everything is acceptable. Some parameters are needed in defining a Jewish God concept in order to maintain a collective understanding, a connection to the Jewish people. (For a further discussion of these parameters, see Eugene Borowitz's discussion in *A Layman's Introduction To Religious Existentialism*.)

The Teacher

What if the teacher is unsure of his or her own conception or feelings about God? Can an atheist or agnostic Jew teach about God? A person who is going to teach about God needs to have examined his or her own belief, and tested it in the light of Jewish criteria, namely, metaphors, concepts, and views of God found in texts or expressed by Jews throughout the ages. For example, a person questioning why bad things happen to good people could examine, among other things, views on the concept of free will, the Book of Job (the classic biblical text on theodicy), or the responses of Holocaust survivors to that horrifying experience.

Perhaps thinking about the agnostic or the atheist teacher raises the deeper question of whether or not a doubter or a non-believer, can or should teach about God. The best teacher to teach about God is one who has a deep religious faith, and yet doubts, questions, and struggles with his/her understanding of God. This person exemplifies the Jewish seeker, one who is actively engaged in a relationship with God. Therefore, I would rather choose the agnostic teacher who can honestly search with the students than the confirmed atheist, or even a person with a conception of God that doesn't allow for any disagreement or flexibility.

Age Appropriateness of the Curriculum

When do we begin to teach about God? What concepts or ideas are appropriate for each age? In my view, we should begin to teach about God as soon as a child begins asking questions about God. From then on, such teaching should continue throughout one's formal religious education. Hopefully, the curiosity that sparked that first question about God will continue for a lifetime. Some studies, such as one printed in *Compass* magazine,[3] identify the questions about God that most concern each age group from kindergarten through high school. Responding to questions and concerns that students themselves raise is one way of assuring that the curriculum is age appropriate.

---

[2]Rothschild, Fritz A., "The Concept of God in Jewish Education," *Conservative Judaism* 24:2-20 (Winter 1970), 6.

[3]Bernard Zlotowitz, "Teaching God To Kindergarten and First Grade," *Compass* 38 (March 1976), 1.

Teaching Techniques

What teaching techniques are best to use in teaching about God? In a certain way, teaching about God is like teaching about any other subject. The choice of technique should be guided by what will reach the students. However, teaching about God does present its own challenges in choosing a technique. The authors of *Teaching Basic Jewish Values*, Azriel Eisenberg and Abraham Siegel, warn not to discourage inquiry and not to confuse doubt with disregard for religion. While questioning and doubt challenge tradition, they do not necessarily lead to its breakdown.[4] To me, this means that any teaching technique that is honest, of interest to the students, and provides for open-minded, open-ended discussion, and takes the learner from the "known to the unknown" will work.[5]

Connecting technique to goals and purpose is particularly critical in making teaching about God relevant and effective in Jewish schools. Fritz A. Rothschild (1970) pointed out that for several reasons there is often opposition to the study of theology in Jewish schools no matter what technique you use. The Orthodox usually seek to avoid intellectual ferment and doubt, while the Conservative and Reform are afraid of a limitation of freedom and of the idea that there is one correct belief. Culturalists and secularists, on the other hand, find God study old fashioned and not applicable altogether.

Materials

With all the materials now available, which to begin with, and where do I go from there? Perhaps the best answer on what to use in beginning teaching about God is start with any text, Bible, *Midrash*, *Siddur*, or Hasidic tale. Begin with any question, concept, or idea that seems appropriate for the age group. As for what comes next, the more one seeks, reads, or learns about God, the more there is to know and experience. Magazine articles, newspaper reports, history books, nature accounts, scientific discoveries, medical reports — all of these are fertile ground for God-talk. A mix of current and classic Jewish texts can also be extremely effective.

CURRICULAR APPROACHES TO TEACHING ABOUT GOD

Thus far, we have focused on the five elements that are part of any curricular approach to teaching about God. Below you will find a typology of common curricular approaches to teaching about God. One must plan and carefully consider how "God" will be a part of the religious school curriculum. I agree with Rothschild that any discussion of God that comes about appropriately in the classroom can and should be integrated into the curriculum, and that the teacher needs to capture and respond to those special moments that present themselves as appropriate for teaching about God. Still, "God" needs purposefully and explicitly to be included as part of the formal, planned curriculum.

In presenting this typology it is important to note that this is not about teaching techniques used to present content, but rather about the conceptual framework that undergirds how we teach about God, and the philosophical underpinnings that shape the content.

None of the five curricular approaches outlined here is generally used exclusively, nor are any of these approaches entirely discrete entities. For ease of discussion, I have divided them as follows: Theologians' Approach, Emotional Approach, Conceptual Approach, Historical Approach, and Integrated Approach.

The purpose of this section is to enable the educator or teacher to make an intelligent choice of curricular approach that is consistent with the goals and philosophy of his or her school. Each of these approaches has its strengths and weaknesses. Each is a legitimate method of approaching the content. Each will be examined with regard to its philosophy and goals, arrangement of content materials, the materials available, and age level appropriateness.

Theologians' Approach

One of the most likely approaches to teaching the idea of God is through the writings of those individuals who attempt to explain the concept or experi-

---

[4] Azriel Eisenberg and Abraham Siegel, *Teaching Basic Jewish Values, A Teacher's Guide To the Confirmation Reader* (New York: Behrman House, 1954).

[5] Robert B. Nordberg, "Ideas of God in Children," *Religious Education* 66 (September/October 1971), 376-379.

ence of God, namely the theologians. The strength of this approach and its underlying philosophy is that committed thinkers, those who live by their philosophies, struggle with exploring and articulating their ideas about and relationship to God. Their theologies reflect both their insights as scholars and their experiences as human beings. In an approach such as this, the lives of the theologians are intertwined with their thinking about God.

The use of text materials from theologians such as Philo, Saadia, Maimonides, Martin Buber, Abraham Joshua Heschel, Mordecai Kaplan, Eugene Borowitz, Milton Steinberg, Eliezer Berkovits, Robert Gordis, Judith Plaskow, and others, make the ideas vibrant, since these materials are not just impersonal abstractions, but are part of the lived experiences and convictions of these thinkers as Jews.

One of the problems in using this approach is that the learner must confront several concepts at a time. While this is an excellent approach for the older adolescent learner who can compare and contrast and see a total *gestalt* of a person's thoughts, such materials might be confusing for the younger student.

There is overlap between this approach and the Historical Approach if the theologians are considered in chronological order. Many of these theologians have created a chronology of theological ideas in their attempts to explain and develop Jewish theology for and in their age. This theological chronology serves to connect them to those who came before them, while positioning them to address the issues of their time. Placing the theologians in their historical context is important, as often they are responding to the problems of their generation or era. Overlap also exists with the conceptual and emotional content areas, but the initial structuring in this first approach is around the theologians themselves, their writings and thoughts about God.

The materials available for use in teaching through this approach are *Living as Partners with God* by Gila Gevirtz (1997) for elementary students, and *Finding God: Ten Jewish Responses* by Rifat Sonsino and Daniel B. Syme for teens and adults.

Emotional Approach

Perhaps the most difficult of the approaches to explain or define is the Emotional Approach. Here, the human emotions that move us to experience God, such as awe, wonder, fear, love, reverence, humility, curiosity, and even anger, are the focus. Source materials are collected around these emotions. The philosophical underpinnings of such an approach stem from the affective elements of the curriculum (faith, hope, etc.) and the desire to make these the primary entry points into an exploration of God. The experience of God becomes magnified in importance beyond mere theological reasoning or explanations.

Why is the "experience of God" important? Eisenberg and Siegel state, "the experience of God must precede attempts at defining [God] and not vice versa."[6] Experience precedes knowledge in their estimation. Similarly, Rabbi Zlotowitz advocates for the primacy of focusing on experiencing God because of its connection to belief, conviction, and commitment:

> Children need to relate to God so that God becomes a meaningful experience in their lives. Religious belief is not an intelligence test, but an emotional experience that affects our lives and gives meaning to our existence.[7]

Fritz A. Rothschild's work describes what is involved in experiencing God. He presents five fundamental experiences that are basic to a religion's understanding of God: change, dependence, order, value, and imperfection.[8] David Cedarbaum goes further in identifying levels of experiencing God. Each one of these levels helps lead to a more mature concept. The levels of experiencing God are: beauty of nature, beauty of people, forward movement of humankind, law and order in the universe, and an understanding of the moral law.[9]

I believe that any approach to God would be incomplete without an attempt to share, relate, and explain the experience of God. The Emotional Approach is one that overlaps with each of the other approaches in some ways, but it is possibly the best approach to use as one begins teaching children

---

[6]Eisenberg and Siegel, op. cit.

[7]Zlotowitz, op. cit., 1.

[8]Rothschild, op. cit., 6.

[9]David Cedarbaum, "Developing God Concepts with Children," in *What Is the Answer?: A Guide for Teachers and Parents To Difficult Questions*, edited by Stuart A. Gertman (New York: Union of American Hebrew Congregations, 1971), 9-15.

about God. Young children in particular often have an instinctual knowledge of these emotions.

Materials for this approach include *Hello, Hello, Are You There, God?* By Molly Cone (1999) for early childhood; *The Book of Miracles* by Lawrence Kushner (1987) for elementary age students; *Judaism and Spiritual Ethics* by Niles E. Goldstein and Steve Mason (1996) for teens; and *God Whispers: Stories of the Soul, Lessons of the Heart* by Karyn Kedar for adults. The Book of Job is also an especially good resource, and, of course, the Psalms are a rich resource that should not be overlooked.

Conceptual Approach

The Conceptual Approach is the most commonly used approach for teaching children about God. It deals with concepts and ideas about God and theology, which stem from basic questions about God and our relationship to God. Ideas such as Covenant, omnipotence, omnipresence, omniscience, qualities of God, monotheism, naturalism, pantheism, revelation, and redemption are just a few of the concepts that one can study. Questions such as what is evil, why do we pray, does God answer prayer, how can we know God, and the like are the outgrowths of exploring these concepts.

The underlying philosophy of this approach is that through ideas and through questions, we confront the concept of God. Materials are arranged around a specific idea and questions that relate to it. This method of organization is used in many modern texts. Source materials from many different religions may be brought in, since the questions are often similar in many religions. Some ideas, unique to Judaism, such as chosenness, will require Jewish materials.

The Conceptual Approach is effective for every age, as long as the materials selected are age appropriate in terms of activities and level of abstraction. There are ways of simplifying concepts, but a better method would be to let wording and questions for each concept fit the age. For example, adolescent learners and adults can grapple with the concepts of mysticism and gnosticism, while even the youngest preschool learners can understand the idea of creation. It is through the use of the conceptual approach that the conflicts between science and religion, secularism and religiosity, and many other intellectual controversies can be raised and discussed.

Materials for this approach are plentiful. Some suggestions are: *Because Nothing Looks Like God* by Lawrence and Karen Kushner (2001) for early childhood students; *How Do You Spell God?* by Marc Gellman and Thomas Hartman (1995), *Partners with God* by Gila Gevirtz (1996), *and Let's Discover God* by Marlene Thompson (1998) for elementary age students; *God: The Eternal Challenge* by Sherry Bissell [Blumberg] with Raymond A. Zwerin and Audrey Friedman Marcus (1980), and *The Invisible Chariot* by Deborah Kerdeman and Lawrence Kushner (1986) for teens and adults; and *What Do Jews Believe?* by David Ariel (1995), *Sacred Fragments* by Neil Gillman (1990), and *Innerspace* by Aryeh Kaplan (1990) for adults.

Historical Approach

The easiest approach to define in the study of God is the Historical Approach. In this approach, ideas about God are traced chronologically from the primitive to Abraham through the present day. "History is the laboratory of Jewish theology," asserts Rabbi Eugene Borowitz.[10] The Historical Approach is well suited for schools that present Judaism as an evolving religion or that focus on the presence of God in history.

The arrangement of source materials is done chronologically. Concepts come up when they are confronted in history. The Historical Approach provides an emphasis on cognition. Note that this approach is ineffective with younger students whose sense of history is not yet developed. This approach is best used starting in middle grades and continuing through adulthood.

Tools for the Historical Approach are not plentiful. Some of the books previously mentioned as focusing on Jewish theologians present their views in chronological order. Both *Living as Partners with God* by Gila Gevirtz (1997) for elementary students, and *Finding God: Ten Jewish Responses* by Rifat Sonsino and Daniel B. Syme (2002) for teens, are organized chronologically. Chapter 1, "The Changing Perceptions of God" in the book *Teaching about God and Spirituality: A Resource for Jewish Settings*, and the book *Four Centuries of Jewish Women's Spirituality* by Ellen M. Umansky and

---

[10]Quoted in a Personal Interview with Eugene Borowitz, Summer 1975.

Diane Ashton (1992) for adults also reflect an Historical Approach. Additionally, teachers can pull materials from the Bible, Talmud, *Midrash, Siddur,* Medieval thinkers, and modern philosophers without too much difficulty.

Integrated Approach

As previously stated, I believe that the best way to teach about God is by integrating the questions, experiences, and emotions connected with God throughout the whole curriculum, whether the topic of study is Prayer, Bible, History, Life Cycle, or Hebrew. The philosophical underpinning of the Integrated Approach is that "all authentic religious ideas relate to the idea of God."[11]

What is the specific definition of an Integrated Approach to God in the curriculum? How do we relate God to the other subjects and materials? In this approach, God is talked about and explored in every class of the school. For example, God should be discussed in relation to God's role in the Bible, beginning with Bible tales and continuing with each new course in Bible. God should also be discussed relative to the *Siddur,* the textbook of Jewish theology and prayer, with such questions as: What do we mean when we say *"Baruch Atah Adonai Elohaynu . . . "*? What is *Adonai* or *Elohim*? In a course on Ethics or *halachah,* God may become the standard, the judge to whom we are answerable, the righteous one who is our model as in *"Da Lifnay Mi Atah Omed"* (Know before whom you stand). God is tied into history because of the traditional belief that God is present not just at creation, but throughout history. A connection between just about any topic and God can be made.

The topic, God, and the child are all integrated. The questions and challenges about life in all realms — physical, social, emotional, and spiritual — which the child confronts at each step of his/her development become part of this curricular integration. In order for the Integrated Approach to be used in the school, a commitment to developing the relationship between God and the child, in addition to teaching knowledge about God, must be a top priority.

David Cedarbaum, in his article about developing God concepts with children, states: "A cardinal principle is that we must relate God to the experience of the child at each step of his[her] development as we encourage him[her] to think about the great mysteries of the universe."[12] To go one step further, we must be conscious not only of each step of the child's development, but also of each kind of subject matter. In this way, "God" does not become a subject of discomfort, but rather becomes an important part of our living as a human being and as a Jew.

The following resources are available for the Integrated Approach: *How Does God Make Things Happen* (2001) and *What Does God Look Like?* (2001), both by Lawrence and Karen Kushner, for early childhood students; *When a Jew Prays* by Seymour Rossel (1973) and *God's Top Ten* by Roberta Louis Goodman (1992) for elementary age students; *When I Stood at Sinai* by Joel Lurie Grishaver (1992) and *Test of Faith* by Roberta Louis Goodman (1985) for teens. That the Integrated Approach is popular for adults can be seen in the abundance of available resources, including *The Busy Soul: Ten-minute Spiritual Workouts Drawn from Jewish Tradition* by Terry Bookman (1999), *Soul Judaism* by Wayne Dosick (1999), *The Extraordinary Nature of Ordinary Things* by Steven Z. Leder (1999), and *Jewish Paths toward Healing and Wholeness* by Kerry M. Olitzky (2000). In addition, the Integrated Approach will or can at other times include all of the other approaches, so that all of the materials relevant to teaching about God become usable here, too. This broad, all-encompassing approach to teaching about God requires planning, a little imagination, and a deep concern for the development of children's relationship with God.

CONCLUSION

This chapter has provided a brief overview of several curricular approaches to teaching children and adults about God. The educator may follow a single approach or use a mix of approaches. The key is selecting an approach that matches the school's philosophy and goals. Whatever curricular approach is selected, the paramount concern is the need for Jewish schools to enable learning about God to occur explicitly and with intent and careful planning.

---

[11]Nordberg, op. cit., 378.

[12]Cedarbaum, op. cit., 10.

TEACHING CONSIDERATIONS:

- It is important for teachers to spend some time thinking about the place of God in his or her life, and his or her classroom.

- It is okay to be an agnostic teacher who is willing to search seriously for God with the students.

- Different ages of students demand different approaches to the conversation about God.

- Jewish educators must choose a curricular approach that is consistent with the goals and philosophy of his or her educational setting.

BIBLIOGRAPHY

For Adults

Ariel, David. *What Do Jews Believe? The Spiritual Foundations of Judaism*. New York: Schocken Books, 1995.

> Chapters in this book address key theological concepts and questions about God, human destiny, good and evil, chosen people, meaning of Torah, *mitzvot*, prayer, Messiah, and why be Jewish.

Artson, Bradley Shavit, et al. *I Have Some Questions about God*. Los Angeles, CA: Torah Aura Productions, 2002.

> This book features 12 questions about God from children in Grades 3-4 and responses from Rabbis Bradley Shavit Artson, Ed Feinstein, Elyse Frishman, Joshua Hammerman, Jeffrey Salkin, and Sybil Sheridan. Some examples of questions are: How do we know there really is a God? Does God know what I am thinking or what I will do? Does God really make miracles? Does God punish people? The book was created to help teachers and parents feel comfortable talking with children about God.

Bookman, Terry. *The Busy Soul: Ten-Minute Spiritual Workouts Drawn from Jewish Tradition*. Woodstock, VT: Jewish Lights Publishing, 1999.

> This guide presents easy to do spiritual exercises that focus on holiday themes. For example, Purim includes themes of risk taking, *mazal* (luck), and self-esteem and self-reliance.

Borowitz, Eugene. *A Layman's Introduction To Religious Existentialism*. Philadelphia, PA: Westminster Press, 1965.

> Borowitz examines existentialism — the philosophical movement begun by Camus and Sartre — and places it in a religious context for Jews. His discussion of the limits of a Jewish God concept is still among the clearest delineations of these boundaries that I have found.

Dosick, Wayne D. *Soul Judaism: Dancing with God into a New Era*. Woodstock, VT: Jewish Lights Publishing, 1999.

> In this do-it-yourself approach to spiritual living, Rabbi Dosick provides exercises and suggestions for enriching daily life that draw upon Jewish meditation, mysticism, and *Kabbalah*. He provides several practical approaches for deepening personal relationships with God, including praying and meditating, performing rituals and following observances, and utilizing the arts — song, stories, and dance.

Gillman, Neil. *Sacred Fragments: Recovering Theology for the Modern Jew*. Philadelphia, PA: Jewish Publication Society, 1990.

> Each chapter of Gillman's book addresses a critical issue in Jewish theology today. Some examples are: revelation, knowing God, proving God's existence, encountering God, why God allows suffering. Gillman uses classic and modern texts and his own views as he responds to these essential theological questions.

Goldstein, Niles E., and Steven S. Mason. *Judaism and Spiritual Ethics*. New York: UAHC Press, 1996.

> In an attempt to identify spiritual ethics of Jewish conduct, behaviors that reflect our devotion to God, the authors present an exploration of the thirteenth century text, *Sefer Ma'alot Hamidot* (Book of Virtues and Values).

Kaplan, Aryeh. *Innerspace: Introduction To Kabbalah, Meditation and Prophecy*. Jerusalem, Israel: Moznaim Publishing Corp., 1990.

> This source provides a thorough and accessible description of the soul and *sephirot* in mysticism.

Kedar, Karyn D. *God Whispers: Stories of the Soul, Lessons of the Heart*. Woodstock, VT: Jewish Lights Publishing, 1999.

> Through interviews and stories about ordinary people and her own life experiences, Rabbi Kedar shows that the joy and pain in our lives have purpose and meaning. Some of the themes she deals with include: the divine in each of us, hope, patience, acts of loving-kindness, forgiveness, learning from death, surrender, and balance.

Kushner, Harold S. *When Bad Things Happen To Good People*. New York: Schocken Books, 2001.

> Explores the problem of evil and suffering from a Reconstructionist point of view. Kushner presents, from his own personal experience, the struggles with classic theological positions, and proposes that suffering and illness are not

caused by God, but are, rather, just a part of life. Appropriate for high school students and adults.

Nordberg, Robert B. "Developing the Idea of God in Children." *Religious Education* 66, September/October 1971, pp. 376-379

Describes key elements in approaching the teaching of God in a religious educational setting.

Olitzky, Kerry M. *Jewish Paths toward Healing and Wholeness: A Personal Guide to Dealing with Suffering*. Woodstock, VT: Jewish Lights Publishing, 2000.

Rabbi Olitzky provides a Jewish framework for understanding healing and suffering. The healing rituals, psalms, and prayers that are featured can be used to precipitate or enrich the dialogue with God.

Rothschild, Fritz A. "The Concept of God in Jewish Education." *Conservative Judaism* 24, Winter 1970, pp. 2-20.

In this article, the author identifies problems in teaching about God. He argues that in formulating an educational approach in modern times, we need to examine and consider the diverse ways in which Jews have viewed God throughout the ages.

Umansky, Ellen M., and Diane Ashton. *Four Centuries of Jewish Women's Spirituality: A Sourcebook*. Boston, MA: Beacon Press, 1992.

This volume is a collection of writings by over 100 women that reflects their Jewish, religious self-identity. The material draws on a wide range of sources, including letters, sermons, essays, Responsa, *midrashim*, diaries, poetry, ethical wills, and speeches. These sources help capture and reclaim Jewish spirituality from a woman's perspective.

Zlotowitz, Bernard M. "Teaching God To Kindergarten and First Grade." *Compass* 38, March 1976, pp. 1-3.

This article provides practical wisdom on how to approach teaching God to young children in Kindergarten and Grade 1.

For Students

Artson, Bradley Shavit, et al. *I Have Some Questions about God*. Los Angeles, CA: Torah Aura Productions, 2003.

Six leading Rabbis tell stories to answer 12 important questions. Three answers are provided for each question. Exercises follow that enable students to reflect and share, and look at their own experiences of God. The book is designed to help teachers and parents talk with their children about the difficult issues of understanding God. For Grades 3-4.

Bissell [Blumberg], Sherry, with Audrey Friedman Marcus and Raymond A. Zwerin. *God: The Eternal Challenge*. Denver, CO: A.R.E. Publishing, Inc., 1980.

A mini-course for Grades 7 up that considers frequently asked questions about God, including: Where do you live, God? How shall I speak to you? Why do you need me, God? Each question is followed by a combination of activities, Jewish sources, and responses that address each question. The relationship between God and each individual is discussed, and different ways that God can be part of our lives are presented.

Cone, Molly. *Hello, Hello, Are You There, God?* New York: UAHC Press, 1999.

This collection for Grades K-3 incorporates the stories about God found in the series *Hear, O Israel: The Shema Story Books*. These original stories convey concepts such as learning, belonging, and love of God. The Teacher's Guide contains background materials, activities for the classroom and the family, objectives, and questions for discussion.

Gellman, Marc, and Thomas Hartman. *How Do You Spell God? Answers To the Big Questions from around the World*. New York: William Morrow and Co., 1995.

Each chapter of this book begins with a universal question, such as theodicy (why do bad things happen to good people?). Answers to these questions are explored from different religious traditions. A teacher guide is available.

Gevirtz, Gila. *Living as Partners with God*. West Orange, NJ: Behrman House, 1997.

A second volume that builds on *Partners with God* by the same author (see immediately below), this book focuses on helping students formulate an understanding of community and the Jewish people's Covenantal relationship with God. Concepts are presented by focusing on role models — important Jewish figures from ancient to modern times — who have fulfilled the Covenant by living as partners with God. Their insights and actions give glimpses into ways that we can live as partners with God in today's world. A Teacher's Edition is available.

———. *Partners with God.* West Orange, NJ: Behrman House, 1996.

Gevirtz addresses children's profound questions about God by introducing a Jewish vocabulary for thinking and talking about God. The book fosters a personal search for God. The Teacher's Edition includes commentary on the concepts presented in the textbook, as well as strategies that accommodate different learning styles.

Goodman, Roberta Louis. *God's Top Ten.* Los Angeles, CA: Torah Aura Productions, 1992.

Based on narrative theology, which focuses on the use of stories to convey an understanding of God, this book presents a story from classical or modern sources to help students explore and explain the meaning of each of the Ten Commandments. Interspersed questions raise significant issues about life. A Teacher's Guide is available.

———. "Test of Faith: An Instant Lesson on Faith Development." Los Angeles, CA: Torah Aura Productions, 1985.

This Instant Lesson for teens and adults is perhaps the first piece published that uses faith development theory in a Jewish setting. It challenges students to think about how they make meaning out of their lives. Activities include: trying to figure out at what stage the learner is at and interpreting a story by answering significant meaning making questions.

Grishaver, Joel, et al. *When I Stood at Mt. Sinai.* Los Angeles, CA: Torah Aura Productions, 1992.

Written with a class of sixth graders, this volume invites students to tell their own stories about revelation and what it means to receive the Torah at Mount Sinai. The material can be used with sixth graders through adults.

Kerdeman, Deborah, and Lawrence Kushner. *The Invisible Chariot: An Introduction To Kabbalah and Jewish Spirituality.* Denver, CO: A.R.E. Publishing, Inc., 1986.

This workbook on Jewish mysticism for Grades 9-adult strives to connect mysticism and spirituality to the students' lives. It presents major ideas and concepts about *Kabbalah* in an accessible, but rich way. Learners explore and reflect on their place in the universe, the roles they can play in repairing the world, and how their lives can be connected with God. A Leader Guide is available.

Kushner, Lawrence. *The Book of Miracles: A Young Person's Guide To Jewish Spirituality.* New York: UAHC Press, 1997.

Midrash, storytelling, and evocative illustrations are used to impart the connections between God and Torah and every element of creation. Best suited to junior high school students.

Kushner, Lawrence and Karen. *Because Nothing Looks Like God.* Woodstock, VT: Jewish Lights Publishing, 2001.

Real-life examples help children and parents explore possible responses to the questions people have about God. Stories revolve around fear and hope, happiness and sadness, and other spiritual matters. Appropriate for all ages, but especially younger students.

———. *How Does God Make Things Happen?* Woodstock, VT: SkyLight Paths Publishing, 2001.

The story line in this book gives concrete examples of how God daily gives us ways to change the world for the better. Geared to babies and preschoolers.

———. *What Does God Look Like?* Woodstock, VT: SkyLight Paths Publishing, 2001.

Filled with colorful illustrations and real-life examples form a child's everyday world, this book draws parallels from what is all around us in our daily lives to God's being omnipresent — everywhere. This awareness creates a sensitivity to that which makes our lives holy and special. Geared to babies and preschoolers.

Leder, Steven Z. *The Extraordinary Nature of Ordinary Things.* West Orange, NJ: Behrman House, 1999.

In a poetic, fluid style, the author presents the connections between the ordinary events of our lives to God and spirituality. Crunching on *matzah,* pulling weeds in the heat of the summer, and even a roller coaster ride, become extraordinary events when viewed from a Jewish perspective. Leder's essays are enriched by texts from *Midrash*, Talmudic excerpts, and passages from Torah. Geared to high school students and adults.

Rossel, Seymour. *When a Jew Prays*. New York: Behrman House, 1973.

Texts and stories help illumine the art of praying and the meaning of the prayers. Geared to upper elementary students.

Sonsino, Rifat, and Daniel B. Syme. *Finding God: Ten Jewish Responses*. 2d ed. New York: UAHC Press, 2002.

While there is only one God, views about God have not been monolithic. Rabbis Sonsino and Syme present ten different views of God from biblical through modern times in an accessible, yet sophisticated way. Some of these are collec-tive views of the Bible and the Rabbis; others are the individual views of such philosophers as Philo, Maimonides, Luria, Spinoza, Buber, Steinberg, Kaplan, and Fromm. The book helps people connect to Jewish sources and perspec-tives on God that are more complex than their own childhood views of God. Geared to high school students and adults.

Thompson, Marlene. *Let's Discover God*. West Orange, NJ: Behrman House, 1998.

Basic concepts about God are presented in eight four-page booklets for Kindergarten through Grade 2. These include: our Covenant with God, why we perform *mitzvot*, how we can act in God's image. Poems, photographs, activities, discussion questions, prayers, and blessing enrich the series. A Teacher's Edition is available.

CHAPTER 32

Teaching Texts

Betsy Dolgin Katz

Judy Wiler is planning two lessons to teach her sixth graders about Jerusalem. The textbook she uses looks at the geographical location of the city, goes into its history, and then describes some of the attractions of the modern city. Judy wants more than that. She wants to get into the heart and soul of the city that is the center of Jewish life and thought. She thinks of what has helped shape her deep ties to the city. Walking over to her bookshelf, she takes down a book entitled Poems of Jerusalem by Yehuda Amichai.

INTRODUCTION

Since we stood at the foot of Mount Sinai, Jewish text has been at the center of Jewish life. In Deuteronomy 31:10-12, Moses gives instructions to the elders of Israel telling them:

> Every seventh year, the year set for remission at the Feast of Booths, when all Israel comes to appear before *Adonai* your God in the place which God will choose, you shall read this Teaching aloud in the presence of all Israel. Gather the people — men, women, children, and the strangers in your communities — that they may hear and so learn to revere the Teaching. Their children, too, who have not had the experience, shall hear and learn to revere *Adonai* your God . . .

It is not accidental that Mohammed, founder of Islam, in epitomizing who we were and what was important to us, called Jews "The People of the Book."

We are experiencing an exciting moment in Jewish learning today as more and more Jews are turning to the study of Jewish texts. Since the 1980s, Jews have been going "back to the sources" (this became the title of a well-known, oft used

book written by Barry Holtz in 1984). The return to text captivated our adult population. In addition to *yeshivot*, Jewish colleges and universities and Judaic Studies Departments at universities, the two-year Florence Melton Adult Mini-School, Wexner Heritage Program for Leadership, and Meah[1] continue to draw increasing numbers of lay students from the liberal Jewish community. More congregations are hiring adult Jewish education professionals and systematically planning offerings for adult learning. The Internet is rife with online courses. There are distance learning experiences through satellite and interactive video, many based on text. Book vendors online join the providers of audiotapes and fax subscriptions in making newly translated texts accessible. Never in history has it been easier to bring Jewish literature into our homes.

Enthusiasm is catching. Parents who become committed and excited about Jewish study want their offspring to have the same opportunity to learn from original materials. A shift from children learning *about* texts to learning the texts themselves is taking place. Once children can read, there are texts appropriate for them. After all, our young predecessors entered *cheder* (school in Eastern Europe for very young children) at the age of three and mastered Mishnah by 12. The formula presented first in *Pirke Avot* 5:24 reads:

> He used to say: At five years old one is fit for the study of Scripture, at ten years for the Mishnah, at 13 for fulfilling the commandments, at 15 for the Talmud . . .

It's time to bring our children back to the sources! Texts contain the stories that subtly shape who we are. They convey values, attitudes, concepts, and a way of seeing and understanding the world. Our texts are the embodiment of the shared memories of generations, the keen observations of contemporaries, the dreams of all of us. As Jews,

---

[1]For additional information on these adult learning initiatives visit their web sites: Florence Melton Adult Mini-School:

fmams.org.il; Meah: hebrewcollege.edu; Wexner Heritage Program for Leadership: wexnerheritage.org.

these are our birthright, a heritage waiting to be claimed.

WHAT IS A JEWISH TEXT?

For our purposes in this chapter, "text" is defined in its broadest sense as a primary source written by, about, and/or for Jews. The first of these documents is Tanach, which is made up of Torah, Prophets, and Writings. Mishnah (a compilation of oral laws), and the Gemarah (commentary on the Mishnah), collectively the work of Rabbis between 200 B.C.E. and 500 C.E., is referred to as Talmud. *Midrash*, along with Talmud, makes up the earliest Rabbinic literature. Also included as text are Rabbinic writings from the Middle Ages until today. Great commentators on Torah and Talmud such as Rashi (Rabbi Shlomo ben Isaac), Rambam (Rabbi Moshe ben Maimon/Maimonides), Ramban (Rabbi Moshe ben Nachman/Nachmanides), the mystics of Spain and Safed, and the codifiers of Jewish law, especially Joseph Karo, take us into the sixteenth century. Texts written by our scholars served to keep Judaism alive and responsive to the changing world in each generation. The writing of commentaries continues today. Jewish texts in the form of questions and Rabbinic answers called *Responsa* — explanations, elaborations, and adaptations of Jewish law that respond to and affect changing Jewish life — have been a part of our tradition since the first millennium C.E.[2]

Through the ages, Jews have written prayers and created rituals that are part of the rhythms of Jewish life. Shabbat and daily prayers, holiday prayers, prayers and commentaries that accompany life cycle events are also part of our heritage of texts. In addition, there are poetry, short stories, drama, biographical tales, and novels that make up a large section of our library of Jewish texts. Most of the information in this chapter can be applied or adapted to the teaching of any of these varied Jewish texts.

GETTING READY TO TEACH TEXTS

Study of Jewish Texts

A teacher of texts should be a student of texts. It is true, however, that someone can teach a lesson based on a text without having studied the text itself. Secondary texts (textbooks that paraphrase or summarize texts) can always be used, but they represent:

- a lost opportunity for a teacher to learn and grow.

- a lost opportunity to experience the depth and beauty of a key document that has shaped Jewish life.

- a lost opportunity to discover the secret in the power of the original text, something not present in a pale image.

Teaching without reading the original text is like teaching someone about gardening after having examined only artificial plants.

By taking the time to find and read the original text and its commentaries, a teacher is opening up the possibility for inspiration, and for spiritual as well as intellectual growth. Someone who loves text is a different teacher from someone who has never experienced it. The awe and reverence for text permeates a classroom; children can detect and be inspired by it. There is an enthusiasm born out of confidence that comes with knowledge of the original. Someone once said that when we pray, we talk to God, and when we study, God talks to us. For some, God's voice can be heard in the sounds and images of the text. Even if for you God's voice is not always clear, other voices echoing across thousands of years bespeak it through the text. Many of those who are inspired to write texts today, the prayers, the poetry and prose, are a product of studying the texts that came before.

A colleague once remarked that he can feel competent and confident teaching when he is communicating only 70% of what he knows. Even though one may be teaching a first, fifth, or eleventh grader, a teacher should know a great deal more than what he/she is actually teaching. The practice of reading the textbook ahead of the students and then packaging and conveying the information to them just won't do.

My Beliefs about Texts and Text Study

In any class we teach, we must be aware of our per-

---

[2]For more information on the nature of Jewish texts, see Barry Holtz, *Back To the Sources* (New York: Simon and Schuster, 1985).

sonal reactions to what we are teaching. Much of what we teach is a reflection of our inner beliefs about the subject and, in this case, our beliefs about texts themselves. Everyone is biased in one way or another. Our personal history, our assumptions of what is right and what is true influence how we see and present texts.

What is your perspective on the holiness of texts? Do you believe that some of the texts, Torah, Prophets, Writings, the Talmud are sacred? Does knowing that *Mikra*, the word that refers to Bible, comes from the same root as the verb "to call, to summon," cause the text make a claim on us? Is the text sacred?

Are all sacred texts holy because they come from God? Or are there other forces at play that can make a text sacred? Are some sacred texts endowed with holiness by human history? Can a text written in the twentieth century have qualities of holiness?

The way you answer these questions will reveal one dimension of your orientation to text teaching. Consider the following questions. The answers, consciously or unconsciously, influence how you teach text.[3]

- Is the text to be taught as the text itself — separate from purpose or context? Do you believe that a text, its structure, its phrases, its words should be thoroughly analyzed and understood?

- Is the text to be understood in the context of the biography of its author, its geographical source, its moment in history?

- Is the text a means toward an end, a tool for teaching a particular idea or philosophy, a prism for understanding an event or a person? Is a text a way to understand the Jewish way of looking at the world, to learn God's will or to be exposed to a specific scholar's way of understanding God?

- Conversely, can the text be interpreted and understood through the prism of a particular perspective such as Freudian psychology, mysticism, or Marxism?

- Can the text be a springboard, an entry point into one's mind and soul? Does it provide information that helps you make decisions about your life? Is it a way to find personal meaning in the world?

When I teach a class about the Jewish views on what happens after we die, I like first to present biblical and Rabbinic texts. Afterward, I have the students read Jewish folktales. It is gratifying when they recognize threads of the text material they have studied elsewhere woven into the folktales. They then identify changes and innovations contained with the tale. The unit concludes with them writing their own tale and wrestling with their view on what happens after we die.

(Rabbi David Feder, Morgantown, West Virginia)

GOOD PLANNING IS THE PREREQUISITE TO GOOD TEACHING

The Purposes/Goals of Text Study

Taking your general orientation into consideration, when you begin to plan a lesson that involves text study, the initial task is to determine the goals of the particular lesson. The goals can include:

1. exploring a particular content: the text itself, a story, a law, a belief, a custom.

2. learning Hebrew vocabulary, key phrases.

3. teaching students how to study Jewish texts.

4. providing an opportunity to enjoy the study of text and to gain satisfaction from the process.

5. forming a learning community, a group that shares knowledge, language, and their own rituals for Jewish text study.

Learning How to Study a Text

In many Jewish classrooms, the process of learning becomes an end in itself. Learning to study in

---

[3]Much of our work in the area at the Florence Melton Adult Mini-School has been informed by the research of Pamela L. Grossman, University of Washington, Seattle, in articles such as "Learning to Teach without Teacher Education, *Teacher College Record* 91, no. 2 (Winter, 1989). Her work and its application in

Jewish Education is discussed by Barry Holtz, "Reading and Teaching: Goals, Aspirations and the Teaching of Jewish Texts," in *Abiding Challenges, Studies in Memory of Mordechai Bar-Lev* (Ramat Gan, Israel: Freund Publishing House and Bar Ilan University, 1999).

Jewish ways is part of being an educated Jew. As students accumulate experience in text study, they will be learning skills that will enable them to become lifelong learners.

With apologies to Benjamin Bloom[4] consider the following Taxonomy of Text Study, otherwise known as Textonomy.[5] Although as in Bloom, the tasks are roughly organized from the least demanding to the most demanding, they do not have to be mastered in order.

Florence Melton Adult Mini-School's Textonomy

Locate and read text.

Retell the content.

Restate content in one's own terms.

Answer factual questions based on the content.

Be able to define key words and phrases.

Interpret the text from one's own perspective.

Know facts about the context that are relevant to understanding the text.

Answer and ask analytical questions.

Interpret the meaning of literary elements.

Be familiar with a variety of commentaries from classical and contemporary sources.

Understand implications of the text for Judaism, Jews, and oneself.

Draw connections to other conceptually related texts.

Create counter-texts, *midrash* on both *halachic* and *aggadic* texts.

Learning to study in Jewish ways also includes the use of traditional study strategies like *chevruta*, studying with a partner or in a small group. Not an automatically acquired skill, students participate in *chevruta* most effectively and enjoy it when guided slowly into the process. We will look at this more closely in the teaching strategy section of this chapter.

---

[4]A fuller discussion of questioning and Bloom's taxonomy appears in Chapter 44, "Teacher, May I . . . and Other Classroom Questions" by Janice P. Alper and Shayna Friedman, pp. 529-541 in this Handbook.

[5]This phrase was coined by staff of the Florence Melton Adult Mini-School as the framework for analyzing the skills involved in mastering Jewish texts.

Selecting Texts to Teach

When deciding what texts to teach children, there are some simple considerations to keep in mind. It is obvious that the text should accomplish the goal(s) you have set. An important decision to make, taking into consideration goals, the age and interest of students, is what genre of text is best. Many texts can accomplish the same goal, so the question becomes whether to select a narrative or a legal text, a prayer or a story, a poem, or an historical document. A good example of a choice made according to the nature of the students and the goals of the class is described by Joel Lurie Grishaver in *Being Torah*.[6] His model for choosing texts for your classes is:

- The text should be of high interest and "edutainment" value.

- It should arouse curiosity because it contains a compelling question, a problem to be solved, an itch that needs to be scratched.

- It should be aesthetically appealing, easy to reach. With younger students, pictures and graphics will not only make it attractive, but support key ideas you want to teach.

- The text must be intellectually appropriate for a student.[7] The subject matter must be compatible with a student's background and learning ability. There should be no difficult words or phrases that would create frustration and distractions. Knowledge of Piaget's conclusions about when learners are capable of grasping abstract ideas is relevant here.[8]

- Another theoretician whose work can shape our choice of texts would be James Fowler. A child's stage of faith development[9] can shape his/her perception and understanding of texts. Again, we avoid texts whose meaning is beyond the understanding of a child.

---

[6]Joel Lurie Grishaver, "Of Mishna and Mishegas," *Jewish Education News* (Summer, 1993), 30-31.

[7]A fuller discussion of child development appears in Chapter 11, "Developmental Psychology" by Roberta Louis Goodman, pp. 85-108 in this Handbook.

[8]Ibid.

[9]Ibid.

Some recent textbooks have built lessons on text study. Use the above criteria before accepting a publisher's choice of text. It is important to note that there are texts that can be used with any age group, from young children to adults. The goals for the use of the text would vary as would the questions or strategies used to achieve the goal. The following example will serve as our entry point into a discussion of teaching strategies.

A TEXT FOR ALL AGES

It was reported about Hillel that every day he used to work and earn one tropaik, half of which he would give to the guard at the House of Learning, the other half he spent for food for himself and for his family. One day, he found nothing to earn, and the guard at the House of Learning would not permit him to enter. He climbed up and sat upon the window to hear the words of the living God from the mouth of Shemayah and Abtalion. They say that day was the eve of the Sabbath in the winter solstice, and snow fell down upon Hillel from heaven. When the dawn rose, Shemayah said to Abtalion: "Brother Abtalion, every day this house is light and today it is dark; is it perhaps a cloudy day?" They looked up and saw the figure of a man in the window. They went up and found Hillel covered by three cubits of snow. They removed him, bathed and anointed him, and placed him opposite the fire, and they said: This man deserves that the Sabbath be profaned on his behalf. (*Yoma* 35b)

Goals and Strategies — Eight-year-olds

Goal: To learn how important study is for everyone.

Strategy: A. Read the story together from a revised version, eliminating some problematic words and phrases, but maintaining the integrity of the text.

Discussion Questions:

- How does Hillel try to solve the problems?

- How does he finally get to the House of Learning?

- Have you ever heard of anyone else for whom learning was very important?

- Have you ever wanted to learn something and been stopped by something outside of your control? What did you do?

- Why do you think learning was so important to Hillel?

Strategy B: Tell another (age appropriate) story about someone for whom learning was very important, for example Akiva, Abraham Lincoln, Harriet Beecher Stow, or Rebecca Gratz. Use similar questions as in Strategy A to develop a comparison.

Strategy C: Ask students to interview a parent or grandparent to find out how learning was important to him/her. What did he/she do to be able to learn? How does this compare to what Hillel did?

Goals and Strategies — Twelve-year-olds

Goal: To learn of the extent to which Torah study is valued and what can be compromised in order to pursue study.

Strategy: *Chevruta* — study in small groups of two or three

Chevruta Questions:

1. If you were to act out this text, how could you divide it into sections or scenes? What would be the title of each scene? (For younger children, the teacher could divide the story and ask the students to provide the titles.)

2. Discuss the following quotation from *Pirke Avot*: "Where there is no food, there is no Torah. Where there is no Torah, there is no food" (3:17). What in the text would illustrate this saying?

3. How do we know that Hillel was determined to study?

4. How was the Sabbath profaned?

Questions for the Whole Class

1. The whole story takes place because Hillel could not get into the House of Learning. What is the significance of having a guard at the door?

2. What are all the things that Hillel had to overcome, to do, or to ignore in order to study?

3. How did the other Rabbis treat Hillel? What does that show about how they felt about what he did?

4. Mohammed, the founder of Islam, called the Jews the "People of the Book." Why "the Book"? What does this say about the importance of study in Jewish history?

5. From what you know about our history, what had to be overcome at times in order to be able to study?

STRATEGIES FOR TEACHING TEXTS

In selecting strategies for teaching text, all that is said about teaching any subject holds true.

- The strategy should be appropriate for the topic. There is no straight lecture that would be acceptable in the context of text study.

- The strategy should be efficient. It should not take up more time than the idea it is teaching is worth. This includes the preparation time of the teacher as well as class time.

- Interactive strategies that create a direct relationship between the student and the subject matter, and a relationship among students studying the same material promote more involvement and more learning.

- The strategy should be one that the teacher and the students all enjoy.

- The strategy must take into consideration the limits of the classroom, unless, of course, it is a strategy that extends outside the classroom (field trip, use of technology, family involvement, homework).

Above and beyond these givens, there are methods that work particularly well when directed toward text study. Although the catalog of strategies for text teaching is an extensive one, we will look at just four of the most important categories: teacher guided discussion, small group/*chevruta* study, literary tools, and experiential activities.

> When preparing for Pesach, I usually have the Confirmation class read Chapter 10 of *Mishnah Pesachim*. I explain to them that the *Haggadah* developed over time, and that the oldest source for it (other than the Torah itself) is this chapter from the *Mishnah*. Because they are very familiar with the *Haggadah*, they are able to see how Jewish practice has changed and evolved from the time of the *Mishnah* until our own day. Once they've studied the *Mishnah*, I then ask them what they would omit and what they would add to the contemporary *Haggadah*.
>
> *(Rabbi David Feder, Morgantown, West Virginia)*

Teacher Guided Discussion

Discussion is a most effective means for sharing information or seeking answers to a problem. It is also useful from the perspective of the teacher for assessing learning and spotting learning or social problems in the class. Robert Gilstrap and William Martin report in *Current Strategies of Teachers* that:

> Teachers who generally use student ideas for some periods of discussion and those who build on student ideas are teachers whose students often have and continue to have (1) higher-than-average achievement on tests of information, (2) positive attitudes toward school, teachers, and subject matter under study, (3) lower levels of anxiety, and (4) more positive self-concepts.[10]

For our purpose of text study, teacher-led discussion allows a teacher to focus on specific aspects of the text and to engage the students in critical thinking. Students learn to listen, to organize their thoughts, and to ask good questions. They can test out original ideas in a safe environment. A skilled discussion leader can see to it that as many students as possible are involved in the learning. The pooling of information can result in insights that can't be achieved when working alone. If there are misunderstandings that surface, they can be corrected within the discussion.

---

[10]Robert L. Gilstrap and William R. Martin, *Current Strategies for Teachers* (Santa Monica, CA: Goodyear Publishing Company, n.d.), 15.

With all these positive qualities in mind, it must be pointed out that leading discussions is more challenging for teachers than giving lectures. A teacher does not have the same control over the content when he/she opens the floor for discussion. He/she has to know more — additional knowledge based on anticipated questions and problems. There is no guarantee that the discussion will go in the direction the teacher desires or even if the goals of the class will be achieved.

Demands on the teacher are not only in regard to subject matter. Leading a good discussion requires diverse skills and a repertoire of good questions.

Starting the Discussion

Having an effective way to introduce a discussion about a text can make the difference between success or failure. It is important to find an effective way to get students to focus on the issues in the text after reading it together. In *Discussion as a Way of Teaching*, Brookfield and Preskill[11] recommend strategies that fit well in our setting:

Start with a sentence completion activity:

What struck me as we read the text was _____.

The question I would most like to ask about this text is _____.

What I like or dislike most in this text is _____.

State and ask for responses to a contentious statement:

Hillel did a very stupid thing. Studying Torah is not something for which you risk your life. He should have gone home to his family.

Introduce quotations that affirm or challenge the text:

There is no food without Torah. There is no Torah without food.

One is permitted to break the Sabbath in order to save a life.

You are permitted to give up your life only to keep you from idolatry, murder, and adultery.

Ask students to recall a memorable experience related to the text:

Young student: Can you think of something more important to you than having enough food?

Can you recall a time that you wanted to do something so badly you were willing to take a risk in order to do it?

Keeping a Discussion Going

Keeping a discussion going and guiding the students to clearer and deeper thinking about a text requires a variety of skills. If one's goal is to open a discussion, it is important to ask "open" questions rather then "closed" questions. A closed question is one that has one right answer. It is particularly limiting when the answer is either "yes" or "no." Open questions encourage interpretation, commentary, more creative thinking. There may be a correct answer and wrong ones, but the question should allow for deeper thinking and personal expression. The difference between open and closed questions is implied in the work of Benjamin Bloom in his taxonomy of educational objectives. He shows how the depth of content learning that takes place in the classroom depends upon the category of questions asked. Begin with the simplest questions (Who? What? When? Where?) and move to questions that check for comprehension (e.g., ask a student to repeat a story or retell the story in his/her own words), then ask questions that require the student to respond using more advanced mental operations (e.g., analysis, synthesis, and evaluation). One caution: be ready to ask the same question more than once. Students of all ages need time to think, yet teachers often try to avoid silence.

Questioning skills do not end with Benjamin Bloom. There are questions that pertain to the nature of the discussion itself as opposed to the content. These are questions that push students to provide evidence and clarification and reactions to others. The following examples are based on Brookfield and Preskill.[12]

[11]Stephen D. Brookfield and Stephen Preskill, *Discussion as a Way of Teaching* (San Francisco, CA: Jossey Bass, 1999), 64-126.

[12]Ibid., 87-91.

Questions that ask for more evidence:

- How do you know that from the text?

- Where is that in the text?

- What does the text say to support your statement?

- Can you quote part of the text to support your illustration?

Questions that ask for clarification:

- Can you put it another way?

- What do you mean by that?

- Can you give me an illustration?

Questions creating connections:

- How is this related to what we said earlier?

- How does this fit with what Stacy said?

- What have you added to our understanding of the text?

- Does this disagree with what Haim said?

Summary of a Discussion

Finally, in a good discussion, ask questions that allow for a summary of what has been covered or a synthesis of some of the ideas. Some suggested questions are:

- What are the two most important things that you have learned from this text?

- What questions still remain unanswered?

- What do you now understand as a result of our discussion?

- What key word or short phrase captures the essence of our discussion?

Small Group Work/Chevruta

Many of the qualities for effective questioning are applicable in peer-led small group discussions. In Jewish tradition this is referred to as *chevruta*, from the Hebrew word for friend or companion. Again, we turn to *Pirke Avot*, in which it is written, "Acquire for yourself a companion." The Hebrew word used for "acquire" is the same word that is used for "buy" or "purchase." One has to find a

companion who is equal in worth to what you have to offer. Both parties give and receive. They are compared to two pieces of flint which, when they work well together, create sparks, and sharpen each other.

Although it may be possible simply to give students questions to explore in small groups, teachers can build up to effective work in *chevruta* by gradually increasing the independence of groups. Here are suggested steps to follow in *chevruta* learning:

Step 1. In a teacher-led discussion, ask a question and then direct students to discuss it with a partner before returning to a whole class discussion with their responses.

Step 2. As a lead-in to a class discussion, instruct students to read the text aloud in *chevruta* and answer one question before joining in a class discussion that will build on their answers. Reading a text aloud with another person is not something to which students are accustomed. Unless told specifically to do so, they will frequently read it quietly to themselves. Elements of a text that would otherwise go unnoticed sometimes surface when a text is read aloud. It is a different kind of experience that demands that the reader verbalize every word and hear the sounds of the text. It helps students learn to listen to each other.

Step 3. After introducing a text to a class, distribute a series of written questions that will guide a more extended *chevruta* discussion. Having students study in *chevruta* makes more demands on a teacher, not fewer. Ideally, the teacher should prepare a "roadmap" for students containing not only the questions, but also vocabulary, important dates, maps, related passages, and even illustrations. During the 20-30 minutes of *chevruta*, the teacher should circulate from one group to another listening, observing, sometimes asking a question, or commenting on a good discussion taking place. The class discussion following the *chevruta* period should build on what was discussed in small groups and not just review the past discussions.

Understanding the Nature of Oral Law: The Truth of Interpretation

The following is an example of a written guide for a class using *chevruta* as a learning strategy.

The Text: *Menachot* 29b

Rav Judah said in the name of Rav. When

Moses ascended on high, he found the Holy one, praised be He, engaged in adding crowns to the letters of the Torah. Moses said: "Lord of the universe! Does the Torah lack anything that these additions are necessary?"

God answered: "After many generations, a man by the name of Akiva ben Joseph will arise, and he will expound heaps and heaps of laws (*halachot*) based upon each mark."

Moses said, "Permit me to see him."

God replied, "Turn around."

Moses went and sat down in the back of the class behind eight rows of Rabbi Akiva's students and listened to the discussions on the Torah. He was ill at ease, for he was unable to understand their arguments. However, during a discussion of a certain subject when the students asked the teacher, "How do you know that to be so?" Rabbi Akiva replied, "It is a law given to Moses at Sinai." He (Moses) was comforted.

Vocabulary

Akivah ben Joseph

crowns

written Torah

oral Torah

halachot

Chevruta Questions

1. What question is raised for Moses when God adds crowns to the Torah passage?

2. When Moses visits Akiva's class, what emotions might he have experienced?

3. How does the story answer Moses' question?

Class Discussion

Why is there a need for interpretation, a need for Oral Torah?

What is the status given to Oral Torah in this passage? in our lives?

Literary Tools

Besides being our way to teach ideas, practices, history, and ethics of Judaism, many Jewish texts are also examples of great literature. As such, one of the best ways to understand their purposes and their message is to use literary techniques for analyzing them. Looking closely at words, motifs, and narrative structures has been a portal into understanding Jewish text used by many prominent scholars.

Language and Words

The smallest key to unlocking the meaning of texts are words. For example, what words are repeated in a text? The appearance of specific words or synonyms of the word calls attention to an idea. Their presence is a sign of what is emphasized in the understanding of a text. In the following selection of several of the "*Shevah Brachot*," the seven blessings of a wedding, notice what words are repeated over and over again. From these, what are the primary messages of the text?

May the barren land rejoice and be glad, when its children are gathered back to it in joy. Blessed are You, O God, Who makes Zion rejoice in her children.

May You grant great joy to these dearly beloved, just as You granted joy to the work of Your hand long ago in the Garden of Eden. Blessed are You, O God, Who grants joy to the bridegroom and bride.

Blessed are You, *Adonai* our God, Ruler of the Universe, Who created happiness and joy, bridegroom and bride, rejoicing and song, delight and cheer, love and harmony, peace and fellowship. Soon, *Adonai* Our God, may there be heard in the cities of Judah and in the streets of Jerusalem, the sound of gladness, the sound of joy, the sound of the bridegroom, the sound of the bride. Blessed are You, O God, Who grants joy to the bridegroom with the bride.

Another perspective is added when you recognize words or phrases from your knowledge of other texts. What reference to another text is made in the blessing above? What meaning does it add to the prayer?

What words stand out because they don't seem to belong? In this text filled with joy and gladness, why is there mention of a "barren land"? By asking students to single out that phrase and asking why it is there, the teacher will have the opportunity to teach about the theme of remembering sorrow in times of joy and link the blessing to the breaking of the glass at the end of the wedding.

For older students, one can examine what is contained in the Hebrew words that might be missed in an English translation. In this case, looking at the different words for creation, *yatzar* and *bara*, open the discussion to the complexity of human life, God's relationship to human beings and how marriage enables us to fulfill the potential for which we were created.

Structure of Narratives

In understanding the text we study, we can also look at the larger structures making up the texts. How can the text be subdivided, and what is the relationship of the parts? In studying the text about Hillel, students were asked to look at the story as a play and to divide it into scenes.

Scene I - Introduction: Not everyone can study.

Scene II - Hillel finds a way to learn.

Scene III - Hillel is rescued and honored.

The parts can be seen as related in terms of the flow of the story, but there are other themes that can be seen in the relationship of the parts. For example, what do the three sections say about rules and laws. Are they always good? Can they ever be broken?

Figurative Language: Metaphor, Simile, and Other Comparisons

In the blessings we looked at above, the bride and groom being blessed are linked to the original couple in the Garden of Eden. "May you grant joy to these dearly beloved as you granted joy to the work of your hand long ago in the Garden of Eden." In making this comparison, many qualities relative to the relationship of God to Adam and Eve and their

creation are implied to be among the qualities of the present bride and groom. The meaning of the text is deepened by what can be called "harmonics." When the string of a violin is played, other strings vibrate adding subtle sound and color. So, too, when comparisons with parallel stories are used, the meaning expands and takes on new dimensions.

A second form of comparison is found in the use of metaphors. In an article in The Melton Research Center Journal, Alvin Kaunfer applies the technique of synectics to Jewish learning.[13] Synectics is the use of comparisons to elucidate and amplify ideas and situations. It encourages metaphoric thinking that enhances creativity. In Judy Wiler's opening vignette on planning her lesson about Jerusalem, we see her looking through Yehuda Amichai's poetry and finding one metaphor after another describing the city. She can read some of these to her students, comment on them, and ask them what they can learn about Jerusalem through these comparisons. At the end of the two lessons, Judy can ask the students to write their own descriptions using this kind of language or to write their own poem using a metaphor. The kinds of metaphors Amichai includes:[14]

- The city plays hide-and-seek among her names: Yerushalayim, Al-Quds, Salem, Jeru, Yeru.

- Jerusalem is short and crouched among its hills unlike New York, for example.

- Jerusalem stone is the only stone that can feel pain.

- I and Jerusalem are like a blind man and a cripple. She sees for me
  Out to the Dead Sea, to the End of Days.
  And I hoist her up on my shoulders
  And walk blind in my darkness underneath

- Jerusalem is a port city on the shore of eternity.
  The Temple Mount is a huge ship, a magnificent luxury liner.

- Jerusalem is a cradle city rocking me.

---

[13]Alvin Kaunfer, "Synectics," *Melton Research Center Journal* 11 (1980), 3.

[14]All quotations are from Yehuda Amichai, *Songs of Jerusalem* (Tel Aviv, Israel: Schocken, Ltd., 1987).

Character, Point of View

In selecting from the wide variety of literary strategies available, one of the most fruitful approaches to text involves character analysis. Some characters are very simple, flat individuals. The guard in the Hillel text is an example of this. He has only one purpose in the text. Other characters move a narrative forward by what they say and do. They become our teachers who raise questions just by who they are and what they do. Hillel is a complex, thinking, acting individual. We learn from the decisions he makes, from his actions, how other characters interact with him. Howard Deitcher, in an unpublished paper presented at the Florence Melton Adult Mini-School Institute of the Hebrew University in Jerusalem, points out that one can also learn from a character's emotions, inner dialogue, physical gestures, speech, physical appearance, and how God interacts with the character.

After gathering as much information as possible about a character, a student can be asked to fill in some of the blanks in the texts, which is his/her creation of *midrash* (traditionally, non-legal commentaries that make up part of Jewish Oral Law). What would be Hillel's inner thoughts standing outside of the House of Learning when the guard had just turned him away? We are not told what went through his mind before he decided to climb up on the roof. One could also ask what conversation took place between Hillel and Abtalion and Shemaya at the end of the text's narrative.

Experiential Activities for Studying Texts

When teaching children text, experiential activities can build on the ways students learn best. The activities can reinforce and practice things that have been learned. Almost everything we have discussed up to now has related to the written word, to the verbally-oriented activities of discussing, writing, imagining. Experiential activities build on the "multiple intelligences"[15] of children and provide an opportunity for students to demonstrate their learning in various ways. They most frequently are used to apply ideas learned in the study of texts. Some examples of experiential activities that relate to the texts in this chapter follow:

Drama and Storytelling

Dramatize the story of Hillel and the House of Study.

Midrashic drama - In the story of Moses visiting Akiva's class, present a discussion between Moses and Akiva that takes place after the class.

Storytelling - Tell the story of Moses visiting Akiva's class, from Akiva's point of view.

Art and Photography

Make a mobile of images that represent Jerusalem.

Do a photo collage of wedding pictures showing joy.

In relation to the Moses and Akiva story, learn and demonstrate the kind of calligraphy used in Torah scrolls.

Music

Learn the song "*Amar Rabbi Akiba.*"

Learn to play (or sing) wedding music, including "*Od Yishama.*"

Learn to sing and study the lyrics of the song "Jerusalem of Gold."

Creative Writing

Write a poem about Jerusalem.

Write a news article about Hillel at the House of Learning.

Write an interview of Moses.

Values Activities

Discuss: What would you do if . . . (you were in Hillel's place)?

Write down and discuss with a partner the most important message in a text you have studied.

Discuss: Who would you most like to be in the story of Moses in Akiva's class? Moses? Akiva? God? a student?

---

[15]Howard Gardner, *The Disciplined Mind: What All Students Should Understand* (New York: Simon & Schuster, 1999). Also, see

Chapter 27, "Multiple Intelligences" by Renee Holtz and Barbara Lapetina, pp. 323-333 in this Handbook.

Four Corners Activity: Students are asked to go to the corner of the room that most closely expresses their opinion about Jerusalem.

1. The spiritual center of Jewish life

2. The city representing the history of the Jewish people

3. The source of pride and Jewish identity

4. The home of every Jew

Research

Conduct an opinion survey among classmates as to whether Hillel did the right thing by going on the roof of the House of Learning.

Interview students who have been at weddings to find out what they considered to be the most joyous part of the wedding.

Find other texts that contain the same idea as the Moses and Akiva text teaching the importance of interpretation.

CONCLUSION

To be a successful teacher of texts, here is what it takes:

1. Know the subject matter — study the texts carefully yourself.

2. Know yourself — know your beliefs about the texts and the purpose for the study of the text.

3. Develop a repertoire of teaching strategies.

4. Know your students and what is appropriate for them (consider their prior experience with texts and what is developmentally, intellectually, and spiritually appropriate).

5. Enjoy your teaching and see it as doing vital work for the Jewish people.

Professor Yehuda Schwartz at Hebrew University convinced me of the beauty and the importance of learning Mishnah. One of the advantages of teaching Mishnah in Israel is the lack of a language barrier. For students whose first language is not Hebrew, there is much in the Mishnah that needs to be explained. I have the students make their own glossary to keep in a notebook. We list Aramaic-Hebrew equivalents, common terms, and abbreviations. They can use these for all assignments including quizzes and tests except vocabulary quizzes.

I teach at least one *perek* (chapter) at a time, pairing students up in *chevrutot*. I give them a guide sheet and ask them to read through it with their partner. They list difficult words, main ideas, *tannaim* who appear, *machlakot*, and questions or problems they find. Sometimes we review much or all of the *perek* together; sometimes I teach only selected *mishnayot* (subsections; "verses"). When my seventh graders learned the fourth *perek* of *Brachot* last year, I asked each *chevruta* to pick one mishnah they would like to teach to the class. One pair taught their mishnah, gave a quiz, and rewarded scores of 80+ with a scoop of ice cream, and scores of 100 with two scoops. Another pair ordered a cake from a kosher bakery, and asked them to write the mishnah in icing. So we "ate" the mishnah. I taught the tenth *perek* of *Pesachim* to the same group. This time I assigned a mishnah to each pair. I brought in several *Haggadot*, including the Polychrome *Haggadah* that color codes the text according to its period of origin. I ask the students to identify where (if anywhere) their mishnah appeared in the *Haggadah*, what changes or additions were made in its appearance, and to prepare a graphic representation of their mishnah and its relationship to the *Haggadah*. Indeed, I have learned much from my students. (*Avot* 4:1)

(*Cheryl Birkner Mack, Cleveland, Ohio*)

TEACHING CONSIDERATIONS

Vignettes — Questions for Discussion

Although she does not consider herself to be a text teacher, Kindergarten teacher Stacy Levin does teach text. Each year for the past three years, she has taught an entire lesson on the Ten Commandments. Using the story book Who Knows Ten by Molly Cohen as the basis, Stacy designs good discussions, play activities, and arts and crafts projects based on the Ten Commandments. Has she ever read the Ten Commandments in full from the Book of Exodus? No.

- Should Stacy study the Ten Commandments and some commentaries?

- What do you think has kept her from doing it up until now?

- What would she gain by studying it?

Jeff Stern teaches his seventh graders the story of Moses speaking to God and then visiting Akiva's class. One of his students challenges him, "This story cannot be true. You can never prove that Moses talked to God and that he came back after dying. Why are you teaching us about things that can't have happened?"

- How should Jeff respond?

- What do you teach about the truth of texts?

- Would this story influence you to teach a different text next time? Which might you choose?

BIBLIOGRAPHY

An Introduction To Shared Inquiry. Chicago, IL: Great Books Foundation,1992.

> The official description of the Shared Inquiry Method utilized in all Great Books settings, which emphasizes the role of the facilitator in understanding the meaning of texts.

Amichai, Yehuda. *Songs of Jerusalem*. New York: Schocken, 1987.

> An anthology of poetry unified by the theme of Jerusalem.

Bloom, Benjamin. *Taxonomy of Educational Objectives: Cognitive Domain*. New York: David McKay, 1956.

> A classic guide to teachers and curriculum writers on creating educational goals for the classroom and for planning the questions to be asked on a particular subject.

Brookfield, Stephen D., and Stephen Preskill. *Discussion as a Way of Teaching*. San Francisco, CA: Jossey-Bass, 1999.

> A description of the tools and techniques for stimulating good classroom discussions with an emphasis on democratic education.

Deitcher, Howard. *Teaching Literary Tools for Studying a Biblical Text*. Unpublished paper, 1999.

> The application of the insights from general literature to the study of all classical texts.

Gilstrap, Robert L., and William Martin. *Current Strategies for Teachers*. Santa Monica, CA: Goodyear Publishing, 1975.

> A clear organized description of major strategies used in our classrooms.

Grishaver, Joel Lurie. *Being Torah*. Los Angeles, CA: Torah Aura, 1985.

> This book for teachers provides a model for effective text study that can be used with children of all ages in a wide variety of settings.

Holtz, Barry, ed. *Back To the Sources: Reading the Classic Jewish Texts*. New York: Simon and Schuster, 1984.

> A compilation of essays by contemporary scholars on the nature of the major Jewish texts, as well as an excellent introduction on the importance of text study.

Neusner, Jacob. *Learn Talmud*. West Orange, NJ: Behrman House, 1979.

> A good textbook for junior high and high school students that presents a model approach to the study of Talmudic text.

"Teaching Text: Opening the Gates To Life-long Learning." *Jewish Education News* 14, no. 3, Summer 1993.

> A valuable collection of essays on the hows, whys, and whats of text study.

CHAPTER 33

Teaching Torah

Joel Lurie Grishaver

INTRODUCTION

The basic premise of this chapter is simple — the Torah is an environment. Once you have spent time with the Torah, once you have let its texts stew in your mind and cook in your gut, Torah gives you a good idea of how it wants to be taught. The many ways of teaching text are for the most part interchangeable and adaptable to any content base. I am going to describe the nature of the biblical text and the kind of teaching it invites.

BACKGROUND

The Torah contains the oldest written prose in the world. Before there was Torah, stories were told through poetry. All of western fiction has its roots in the original ways the Jewish people developed and told their most important stories. Shemaryahu Talmon, an important Israeli Bible scholar, has suggested that biblical narrative, the Torah's storytelling style, was created as a unique and original art form to express a unique Israelite belief in the one God.

> The ancient Hebrew writers purposefully nurtured and developed prose narration to take the place of the epic (poetic) genre which, by its content, was intimately bound up with the world of paganism . . . In the process of total rejection of the polytheistic religions and their ritual expressions in the cult, epic songs and also the epic genre were purged from the repertoire of Hebrew authors.[1]

When we study Torah stories from the text, we are reconnecting ourselves to an important western literary tradition, but more importantly, perhaps, we are actually touching the art form created to express the revolutionary idea of the One God.

---

[1] *The Old Testament as Inspiration in Culture: International Academic Symposium — Prague, September 1995*, edited by Jàn Heller, Shemaryahu Talmon, Hana Hlavackova, and Martin

PART 1: TEACHING TORAH IS ABOUT FILLING IN FEELINGS

When you read Torah (or any biblical narrative) you quickly notice that it is primarily made up of only two kinds of statements. You have statements of action.

> And every beast, every creeping thing, and every bird, everything that moves on the group, went forth by families out of the ark. (Genesis 8:19)

And you have dialogue, the actual things that people say:

> And God blessed Noah and his sons, and said to them, "Be fruitful and multiply, and fill the earth." (Genesis 9:1)

When the text wants to display emotion, it is usually described as a physical reaction:

> So Cain burned (was angry) and his face fell. (Genesis 4:5)

And when Torah wants us to know how a person feels, it is done as a monologue, a public presentation of an internal monologue.

> And when the Eternal smelled the pleasing odor, the Eternal said in the Divine heart, "I will never again curse the ground because of people, for the imagination of people's heart is evil from youth; also I will never again destroy every living creature as I have done." (Genesis 8:21)

There is just about no description of any detail in the Torah. We don't get any more than the context and the series of actions. Torah doesn't actually tell us how people feel, any more than the things we could observe in their face and body language if we were there.

Prudky (executive editor), published by Mlyn, Trebenice 2001 for the Center for Biblical Studies of the Academy of Sciences of the Czech Republic and Charles University in Prague.

From the vantage of being teachers of Torah, the limitation of the Torah text to external observable behaviors gives us two challenges that become two advantages. First, like radio (rather than film) we get to imagine the biblical characters and the settings. We don't know who is short and who is tall. We don't know who has what color hair. We don't know what color people wore, etc. That validates the text being interpreted via imagination. But, secondly, and more important for teachers of a spiritual-ethical tradition, this narrative style forces us into "empathy" as a major learning process.

Let's look at an example:

Cain said something to his brother Abel. When they were in the field, Cain rose up upon his brother Abel and killed him. (Genesis 4:8)

We do not know a lot about this situation. We can imagine that Cain is angry, but we don't know the degree or the direction of that anger. We have no notion of what Abel is feeling. We have no sense of his reaction. We do not know how many conversations Cain and Abel had before that incident in the field. We do not know if the anger grew or began to subside. We only know that something was said (and we don't know what) and then Cain killed Abel. One aspect of Torah study, therefore, consists of painting in the emotional tones. There are lots of ways of doing this. Here are a few.

Asking - It is possible to ask directly: What do you think Cain was feeling? What do you think Abel was feeling? How long do you think this went on? Did Adam and Eve try to do anything about this? Etc. The questions can also move to, "What do you think will happen next?" We move from our feeling of empathy to our prediction and anticipation of the character's reactions. Both *I Can Learn Torah* and *A Child's Garden of Torah* (Torah Aura Productions) work on this model.

Bibliodrama - This is a process of acting out situations by inventing the missing dialogue. It would include staging a conversation between Cain and Abel after the sacrifices were accepted and rejected. It might include a conversation between Adam and Eve about their children. Also, it could have Cain's response to God about "being careful" because "sin crouches at the door." Staging each of those missing conversations and expanding the

dialogue, is a way to work on the skill of perceiving feelings and projecting reactions. To learn more about Biblodrama you can read *Scripture Windows* by Peter Pitzele (Torah Aura Productions).

Midrash[2] - *Midrash* is a body of literature created by the Rabbis. Think of the Bible as an album of family snapshots. When you look at that album with your parents, they can often tell you stories behind and between each picture. Sometimes they tell you the context, the setting of each photo. Sometimes they tell you more about the person in the photo. And, sometimes they tell you the story of the picture itself. Often, the *midrash* supplies extra dialogue for a biblical scene, revealing more of the feelings and motivation of each character. The two easiest places to find good *midrashim* are Louis Ginzberg, *The Legends of the Jews* (Jewish Publication Society), and *The Midrash Says* (Benei Ya'akov Publications). *The Rabbi's Bible* (Behrman House) and *Torah Toons 1* (Torah Aura Productions) use *midrash* in a teaching frame.

Writing original midrash - Once students have a sense of how *midrash* reads, then writing rather than acting out *midrash* is a wonderful process. This makes Torah study a creative writing experience. One only needs ask students to create "a complete scene" behind a biblical story.

Torn paper midrash - This is just one of many artistic techniques that can allow you to focus on feelings. The process is simple and the results usually stunning. Give students paper and glue and no scissors and ask them to "tear" their version of the story and then explain it. The process of tearing takes the emphasis off making a perfect image, and allows students to concentrate on interpretations. Jo Milgrom's *Handmade Midrash* (Jewish Publication Society) describes this process.

Comic books - This is a perfect vehicle. In comic books there are three kinds of writing on a panel. One is the narrator in a box. Another is the dialog in a speech bubble. And, the third are the cloud-like thinking bubbles. By cartooning specific biblical scenes, students can include the dialogue and the thinking behind the dialogue.

Common to each of these interpretive processes is a focus on the feelings of each of the biblical characters. What is clear in this process is that people use their own experience to flesh out the story. Sometimes the work is biographical,

---

[2]For more information on teaching *midrash*, see Chapter 34, "Teaching Midrash and Rashi" by Joel Lurie Grishaver, pp. 403- 412 in this Handbook.

sometimes autobiographical. The Torah clearly invites this kind of study because it asks us to make sense of an apparently incomplete story, teaching us wisdom in our process of reconstruction.

PART 2: HOLES

One of the best kid's books I have read in a long time is called *Holes* by Louis Sachar. It is the story of a 12-year-old sent to a work camp for being caught with stolen sneakers. At this camp there is a warden who makes the boys dig a hole in the desert every single day. We learn that she is hunting for something. The bottom line, however, is that what she wants is indeed found, but not in one of the holes. It is found rather by the connections and the stories that are evoked. The Torah is a book of holes — holes we are required to fill in order to make sense.

Let's work with one example. This is the end of Genesis 11.

26 When Terah had lived 70 years, he became the father of Abram, Nahor, and Haran.

27 Now these are the descendants of Terah. Terah was the father of Abram, Nahor, and Haran; and Haran was the father of Lot.

28 Haran died before his father Terah in the land of his birth, in Ur of the Chaldeans.

29 And Abram and Nahor took wives; the name of Abram's wife was Sarai, and the name of Nahor's wife, Milcah, the daughter of Haran the father of Milcah and Iscah.

30 Now Sarai was barren; she had no child.

31 Terah took Abram his son and Lot the son of Haran, his grandson, and Sarai his daughter-in-law, his son Abram's wife, and they went forth together from Ur of the Chaldeans to go into the land of Canaan; but when they came to Haran, they settled there.

32 The days of Terah were two hundred and five years; and Terah died in Haran.

We would normally skip over this passage. It seems to have no story. It seems to be just a boring list of names. But, it is at the foundation of some of the most important "oral" Torah we know. It triggers the most famous *midrash* of all times. Here is how we get there.

Imagine that the Abraham family had a photo album. It would have a series of photos with these captions:

1. Terah with his sons, Abram, Nahor, and Haran

2. Haran and his son Lot, just before Haran died.

3. Abram and Sarai and Nahor and Milcah.

4. Milcah and her children and Sarai (who had no children)

5. The Family before we left Ur.

6. Terah before he died in Haran

Anyone looking at the photo album would ask questions like these:

a. How did Haran die?

b. Why did the family leave Ur and go to Haran?

c. What was it like for Sarai to be childless?

d. How did Terah die?

If we had been looking at the album with an older family member, a grandparent or parent, he or she would reach back into the family memory, the family oral tradition, and tell us what she or he remembered or knew about these people.

Consider the Bible, with its holes, to be the family photo album. In the same manner, know that the *midrash* represents the "oral tradition," the remembered back stories of what happened behind, around, and between the photos.

The famous story of Abram smashing the idols is one such hole "filling." It is part of a longer story that explains that Abram and family were kicked out of Ur because Abram told people that Nimrod, the king, was not a god. The "background stories" that are the memories from in between the photos are called *midrash*.[3] In this chapter, I talk about how one teaches the holes.

---

[3]Ibid. That chapter includes insights on how one teaches these larger memories (*midrash*) of the story.

1. *As problems:* One can simply ask, "How do you think Haran died?" "Why do you think that Abram's family moved twice, first to Haran and then to Canaan? The process of solving these problems can involve using "facts," much like a detective gathers clues. These clues can come from other places in the biblical text, or they can come from geography or anthropology or lots of places. But the process of study here can be to use the information we have to fill in holes — project the information we don't have. Filling holes can also be a creative process, using our imagination to complete the story. Such books as *The Rabbis' Bible* by Solomon Simon and Morrison Bial (Behrman House), *A Torah Commentary for Our Times* by Harvey J. Fields (UAHC Press), and *Torah Toons 1 and 2* by Joel Lurie Grishaver (Torah Aura Productions) work on this principle. The best way to find these "holes" (in the first place) is often to work backward, using a commentary such as Rashi[4] to isolate the problem and then create the activity.

2. *As Artistic Opportunities:* It is possible to use all of our basic tools of expression to work on "filling the hole." Here is an opportunity for theater or creative writing, for dance or song writing, or any art form. Students are given a chance to work alone or in groups to create their own completion of a biblical text. When they engage in this creative act, they are paralleling the world of Rashi and of *midrash.* All this is an act of "creating one's own *midrash.*" After engaging in this process (or even before) one can study traditional responses, reading collected *midrashim* or Rashi's commentary.

3. *As a Choice:* Very often the *midrash* gives us more than one way to fill the same hole. It is very possible (and not very hard) to find two or three different answers to the same question. A good way of studying is to work backward. Start by reading collections of *midrash* such as *Legends of the Jews, The Book of Legends, The Midrash Says,* or even *Midrash Rabbah.* Pick a section that has a

"Davar Acher" (Another Interpretation). This expression denotes that more that one *midrashic* tradition already exists.

Divide the class into groups, and give each group a different *midrash*-solution to each group and have them act, draw, dance, sing, argue, etc., the point of view suggested. For example, in *Being Torah* (Torah Aura Productions) we work with the story of the Tower of Babel. We ask the traditional question, "Why did God feel the need to stop the tower's construction (when heaven is not really the top of the sky anyway)? We share three solutions: (a) Because people were trying to fight a war with God and conquer God (taking away God's authority), (b) Because people were trying to "be" gods (and take away God's authority), and (c) Because people were so obsessed about building the tower that they forgot to take care of each other. They cared more about the tower than they did the people who worked on it. These three different answers can easily be the source for three parallel groups that make a skit or a dance or a mural explaining and exploring their "solution." These can also be the basis of a debate, challenging each group to find "proof" in the Bible for their point of view. (Note that most activities done by groups can also be done by individual students.)

"Teaching the holes" is an old idea. It is the core of much Rabbinic work. In the *Zohar* it is said that the Torah is made up of "black fire written on white fire." The idea is simple, the negative space, the space between the letters, teaches us just as much as the letters themselves.

PART 3: OUR LIVES AS TORAH, TORAH AS OUR LIVES

The Insight

We start with a story:

Rabbi Shneur Zalman, the Rav of Northern White Russia (died 1813), was put in jail in Petersburg, because the *Mitnagdim* (those Jews who were against the Hasidim) had denounced his principles and his way of living to the government. He was awaiting trial when the chief of the gendarmes entered his cell. The majestic and quiet face of the Rav, who was so deep in

---

[4]Rashi is also discussed in Chapter 34 of this Handbook.

meditation that he did not at first notice his visitor, suggested to the chief that the man he had before him was a thoughtful person. He began to converse with his prisoner and brought up a number of questions that had occurred to him in reading the Bible. Finally he asked: "Why did God, the All-Knowing, have to ask Adam, 'Where are you?'

"Do you believe," answered the Rav, "that the Bible is eternal and that every era, every generation, and every person is included in it?"

"I believe this," said the jailer.

"Well then," said the Zaddik, "in every era, God calls to every person, 'Where are you in your world? So many years and days of those allotted to you have passed, and how far have you gotten in your world?' God is speaking to you, 'You have lived 46 years. How far along are you?'"

When the chief of the gendarmes heard his age mentioned he pulled himself together, laid his hand on the Rav's shoulder, and cried "Bravo!" But his heart trembled.

But let us examine the story more closely. The chief inquires about a passage from the biblical story of Adam's sin. The Rabbi's answer means, in effect: You yourself are Adam, you are the man who God asks: 'Where are you?'"[5]

In this section, we are going to visit a special kind of personalization of the Torah. There is a basic idea that flows through the reading of many biblical commentaries that the stories in the Torah are not just "history," and not just a Jewish "mythology," but actually represent archetypal moments in human experience. That is why the Maharal wrote that "the Torah is written in eternity, not in history."

The Torah tells the story of the enslavement of the Jewish people in Egypt. It goes into a great deal of detail. Basing itself on one word in that long account, the Mishnah clarifies that experience by saying, "Every person is required to see him/herself as if he/she personally went out from Egypt." The text of the *Haggadah* then personalizes that idea further by saying, "Not our ancestors alone, but us did the Holy One redeem from Egypt." Many of the Hasidic teachers, rooting themselves in the *Zohar*, push this idea even further, teaching, "Each

of us has our own Egypt. Our 'Egypt' is the thing in our life that keeps us enslaved and out of which we need to be liberated."

The tradition follows the same progression with the experience at Mount Sinai. We learn first that the Jewish people were at Sinai, then that we were at Sinai, and finally that each of us has our own Sinai experience.

When Hasidim, extending the thinking of both Talmud and *Zohar*, thinking, try to explain good Jewish teaching, they use the Maggid of Mezrich as their paradigm. His students explain his teaching by saying, "He got each one of us to tell him our own story of what it was like to leave Egypt and what it was like to stand at Sinai."

Nachmanides, the Ramban, makes a comment on the parts of Genesis in which Abraham camps here and there, digging this and that well. This is the kind of biblical detail that most of us tend to skip. The Rambam, however explains, *"Ma'aseh Avot siman l'vanim,"*[6] our ancestors' stories are signs of what will happen to their children. That is the kind of Torah learning we will explore here, using the Torah's stories as a direct parallel to our own lives.

The Practical Application

The direct approach - Long ago, I studied confluent education with Dr. William Cutter. During that process, he and a number of other educators developed a Confluent guide to Passover. I have no idea where you might find a copy of that unpublished document, but, among the activities therein was a "process" of getting students to tell the story of the Exodus in the first person. They answered such questions as, "What job did you have to do? Did you believe Moses? What was the worst part of being a slave? What were the plagues like?" It was a classroom exercise in shared fantasy that could be drawn, danced, written, acted out, or just told. Torah Aura Productions later turned that process into *My Exodus*, a video originally made for the Jewish Television Network. Its teacher's guide has good details on how to run such sessions. Later, in teaching a seventh grade class, I created the book *When I Stood at Mount Sinai* (Torah Aura Productions), which echoes this process for the revelation at Sinai.

---

[5]Martin Buber, *The Way of Man: According To the Teaching of the Hasidism* (New York: Citadel Press, 1996), 5-100.

[6]Nachmanides on Genesis 12:6.

The personal match - This is actually very simple, once you get the hang of it. It is the asking of either one of two questions. Sarah is old and barren. The lack of a child causes her much pain on many levels. God tells here that she is going to have a child. Sarah's response is a laugh and a statement of doubt. One way of studying this is trying to investigate the nature of Sarah's laugh. We would do that by asking, "Why did Sarah laugh?" or "What kind of laugh did Sarah have?" Another way of approaching this question would be, "When have you laughed the way that Sarah did?" Likewise, you can ask, "When have your feelings been tested the way Sarah's were? How did you respond?" Once again, the secret is in the question. The mode of expression could be any one of dozens of ways. It could be Sarah as a guest on a talk show, exploring her feelings with other guests who share their experiences. It could be any art form. It could be a "Quantum Leap" experience where you step into Sarah's shoes while she steps in yours. Once you have the question, the activity follows.

From my life to the Bible - This one is harder, but it is also fun. Often when people tell their own story, it is actually a Bible story. Here is a perfect example — a family story that I collected in a workshop.

I grew up downtown during the Depression. We had a big house and every day we served a big lunch. Some days it was just potatoes and sweet potatoes, but it was a big lunch. The whole family gathered, and often beggars would come to the back door and get their share, too. Later we learned that somewhere on the front of the house, hobos had put a mark indicating this house as a place that would feed them. I have taken that time into my life — and always seen my house as that kind of place.

This is clearly the story of Abraham and Sarah who spent much of their life offering hospitality to others.

The way of using this second insight is to invite students to tell family stories and then match them to the biblical text. This may sound a little risky, but it is not really that hard. Yes, you do need to know some biblical stories. Yes, you do have to be comfortable recognizing patterns, but it is really not that difficult. Practice a little with friends and you will see.

Working in these personal ways with the biblical text is a powerful way of developing connection. It gives you the chance to turn to your students and say, "This is your story."

An Example

This *D'var Torah* written in 1999 by Andrew Gomez for his Bar Mitzvah, is a perfect example of this process. (I wish I could take credit for his insights. I did part of the studying with him, but the real breakthrough in connection came when he studied with his Rabbi, Mordecai Finley.)

The Torah says that the Tower was made of brick. Once the Tower got high enough, there was a certain point where the bricks became more important than the people working on it. According to the *midrash*, if a man with a brick started to fall, they would try to get the brick first, and then maybe the man. The building was becoming more important than each worker.

Not too long ago, a magic trick called "Metamorphosis" was explained to me. In order to perform the trick, I needed a curtain, a large box, and some rope. I realized I had everything except for this large box or crate. When my Dad said that we could build the crate, I got very psyched and every ten seconds I was saying, "Can I build the crate now?" "Can I build my crate now?" I was supposed to be writing my *Drash* at this time. But instead of working on the *Drash*, I insisted on working on this crate. I was so far behind on my *Drash* work that I wouldn't have it ready for the Rabbi on time. Then it hit me, "Get your priorities together!" So thinking about the crate ceased, and I frantically prepared this *Drash* for the Rabbi. The crate was my Tower. I put so much time into it that it blinded me from my other priorities. I think everyone has a project that blinds them from either priorities with friends, family, or community. My crate kept me from doing what needed doing. It became more important than my *Drash* . . . In this portion, I started out wondering why God is being so punitive, and wound up understanding things from a different view. That's the interesting part of Torah study. I hope this *Drash* gives you a new perspective on the Tower of Babel story, and that it encourages further discussions.

One of the dangers in teaching familiar texts is that students — and even teachers! — come to feel that certain stories are so well ingrained that there is nothing new to see in them. We took a new look at the story of *Matan Torah* (the giving of the Torah) one year, bringing it to life by using our natural surroundings. Our *shul* is located next to a large ridge, which is city park at the bottom and state park at the top. On foot, the walk from our *shul* to the top of the ridge takes about one hour. Rather than act out *Matan Torah* in the classroom, we took our students — and our text — outside. We gathered at the foot of the ridge and read about *B'nai Yisrael* (the Children of Israel) stopping at the boundary God set around the mountain. Then we talked about how it felt to look up at the mountain looming above us — how it would feel to know it was forbidden, and how Moshe might have felt, knowing he was going up alone.

We walked halfway up to where we could first touch the rock face. We sat near the rock face, and read about Moshe beginning his ascent. We could not see the top of the ridge from where we were, and we talked about his walking into the fireworks around Mount Sinai. At that point, I took the youngest children back down the mountain. They took small pieces of the red rock ridge with them, and we talked about using them to remember the story in a few weeks at Shavuot. On our way down, we talked about the ecology of the ridge, and compared the things we saw growing and the different ecosystems we were seeing to the landscape of Israel/Sinai in the time of the Torah. The older kids went up to the top of the ridge with the able-bodied teachers, and sat at the top to read *Matan Torah*, and to talk about Moshe's direct encounter with God. After that, we reinforced the lessons of literally going up after that whenever we talked about having an *aliyah* to the Torah.

(Anne Johnston, New Haven, Connecticut)

PART 4: TEACHING TORAH IS MAKING CONNECTIONS

Torah was never engineered to be read for the first time. Its writing style demands an active reader, one who is always manipulating and processing the text. Here are just a few examples:

- The Hebrew word for Noah's ark, *teva*, shows up again as the name for the basket in which Moses is floated down the Nile. The Torah also makes a point of sharing the detail that both vessels were coated with the same tar.

  When you see the connection, you get to answer the question, "How was Moses' basket like Noah's ark?"

- The Ten Commandments appear twice in the Torah, once in Exodus and once in Deuteronomy. When you compare their texts, they are just about the same. The one big exception is in the *Shabbat* commandment. In Exodus, the command is to "Remember" Shabbat and the justification is "because God rested on the seventh day." In Deuteronomy, the command is to "Keep/Guard" *Shabbat* and the justification is "because you were slaves in the land of Egypt."

  When you compare the two sets of commandments, two questions immediately emerge: The first set of questions is: Why do we need both to "remember" and "keep" Shabbat? (What is the difference?) Second: How do the creation of the world and the Exodus from Egypt connect to a day of rest? How do we live each story?

- After Adam and Eve are kicked out of the Garden of Eden, God puts a set of heavenly creatures called *"Keruvim"* (cherubs, not angels) as the guards at the Garden entrance. When God gives directions to build the Ark of the Covenant, they include sculptures of winged creatures, *Keruvim* — the same word.

  When you notice the connection, you are immediately prompted to ask: What is the connection between the Holy Ark (where the Torah is kept) and the entrance to the Garden of Eden?

- If you read the language of the setting up of the Tabernacle carefully (in Hebrew) you will notice that it directly echoes the language used at the end of the first week of creation. The Torah is clueing us that our building of the Tabernacle is connected to God's creating the world.

Again, once we notice the connection, the question is clear: What is God-like in the act of building and establishing the holy space where God and people meet?

Don't panic - You might be reading this and saying, "I didn't know any of the things he is referencing." Don't worry. I was a successful Torah teacher long before I knew any of this. To help you get started, let me first explain where these kinds of connections can be found, and then let's look at a number of classroom activities that use the "comparison" mode. These activities will work even if you don't have the Hebrew background to compare the words the Torah is using, and even if you don't read the commentaries that center in this kind of study.

> The kids loved hearing the stories with visuals and I would leave the set on the flannel board for free play. The kids would chose to go over and retell the story to their friends.
>
> *(Cheryl Cash-Linietsky, Philadelphia, Pennsylvania)*

Finding the Echoes and Repetitions in the Torah

The Rabbis believed that nothing in the Torah is an accident. Every paragraph, every sentence, and every word has a specific meaning to convey. One of the keys to unlocking the Torah's real meaning is repetition. The *midrash* and all of the literature that descends from it affirms that nothing is repeated without a purpose. Every repetition is there either to make a connection or to establish a contrast.

Here are two examples of different kinds of connections that teach different kinds of lessons.

- When Abraham is leaving for what he believes will be the sacrifice of Isaac, the Torah tells us that *"he saddled his donkey"* (Genesis 22:3). It seems funny that a rich man would do this kind of menial labor. Later, when Pharaoh changes his mind and chases after the families of Israel in order to return them to slavery, the Torah tells us that *"he harnessed his chariot"* (Exodus 14:6). In each case it would be possible to assume

that these men in power actually had these common actions done for them, but the commentators see a conjunction — a common obsession that was being manifested in both men taking personal responsibility for their journeys. The noticing of both actions leads to the question: How were these men the same — and how were they different at these similar moments?

This kind of "repetition" invites "compare and contrast" as its learning style.

- God gives Adam a blessing, "Be fruitful, multiply, fill the earth, *and master it*" (Genesis 1:28). When God repeats the blessing for Noah and family after the flood it comes out, "Be fruitful, multiply, and fill the earth" (Genesis 9:7). The last phrase, *"and master it,"* has been removed. The obvious question is: What has changed that led God to change the instruction? In the *midrash*, the answer emerges from a focus on (a) the previous failure of humankind and (b) the presence of a new element, the Covenant.

In this case, the *repetition* always demands that we first find what has changed and then explain the difference.

Much of classical Torah commentary centers on interpreting not only the words in a given story, but in finding their relationship to other words used in other stories. The first place to go to find such connections is in the commentaries. Know that most Torah scholars do not discover these connections on their own, rather they are like someone walking through the forest, following a trail that has been blazed and marked by other scholars. Let's look at an example.

A Sample Unpacking

At the beginning of the book of Exodus, Moses, who has grown up in Pharaoh's household, kills an Egyptian taskmaster to protect a "Hebrew man." Exodus 2:15 tells us: "Pharaoh heard about this matter and wanted to kill Moses." Two questions immediately emerge: How would a minor event like this reach Pharaoh's ear and, why would Pharaoh care if a son of his household killed a minor official? Egypt was not America! Look at what Rashi says about this:

Pharaoh Heard: Dathan and Abiram informed against him.

This probably makes no sense — yet! It takes some unpacking. First you need to look up Dathan and Abiram. If you do (and I used the *Anchor Bible Dictionary*), you will find that Dathan and Abiram were two priests who sided with Korach in his rebellion against Moses much later in the Torah. Korach was a guy who manipulated people for his own power. So there is a connection. Here, someone must have told Pharaoh about what Moses did and made it sound dangerous. Later, a crew of priests tries to manipulate the entire people so as to oust Moses. The *midrash* takes the bad guys from there and moves them into the mysterious bad guy slot here. (This is why the Torah can never be understood when reading it for the first time.)

A teacher has a wonderful lesson to exploit if he/she can find the pieces. Let's start at the end and move back to the beginning. The class is asked: What leads a person to become a traitor — to do things that they know are wrong and will hurt other people? This leads to the final question: When are you a traitor? What leads you to do things you know are wrong — and not act as your best possible self?

The actual lesson ends with skits that represent Dathan and Abiram visiting their therapists and talking about their actions.

So let's go back to *The Beginning* so as to get to this point.

- The teacher needs to teach something about Moses becoming the leader of the Jewish people.

- He/she opens up the Torah and decides that the moment when he stops being an Egyptian and starts defending Jews is the interesting moment.

- He/she takes out a commentary because you can't do the next part out of your own head — *Rashi's Commentary*, a collection of *midrashim* like *The Midrash Says . . .* , the notes in either the *ArtScroll* or *Plaut* versions of the Torah, etc. Many other resources would also do nicely.

- The teacher finds a comment that is interesting. In fact, the focus of the lesson may change through study. We started out interested in Moses becoming a leader and

wound up teaching about becoming a traitor. Torah works like that.

- Having found a comment by Rashi that is cryptic (not knowing who Dathan and Abiram were), the teacher goes to the next step. He/she looks them up and finds that they are the archetypal traitors in Jewish history. He/she learns that their own "needs" (greed and the desire for power) lead them to manipulate situation after situation in ways that hurt Israel and benefit them. In this way the lesson emerges just by checking into sources that annotate the biblical text.

I teach Torah as our mythic, historical, and cultural heritage. For example, we read our creation stories in Genesis 1 and 2 and compare them to creation stories from around the world. The students find many points of similarity as well as some differences. We study Mosaic law and compare it to the Code of Hammurabi, and contrast how slavery is depicted in Egyptian culture and the Israelite culture.

I encourage students to question the text. I want them to feel connected to a long line of Jews who spent their lives trying to learn and understand its complexities.

(Dena Salmon, Montclair, New Jersey)

Some Activities

Here is a collection of activities that any teacher can develop and do (even if not a Torah scholar). Each of these activities builds on the idea of comparing and contrasting different parts of the Torah.

- The Torah tells us that Isaac and Ishmael came together to bury Abraham. Imagine the conversation between their walking sticks. How were their lives similar? How were they different? (The idea of looking at stories through objects comes from *Scripture Windows* by Peter Pitzele.)

- Adam and Eve were kicked out the Garden. Jacob and Family had to go down to Egypt when there was a famine. Israel was carried away to Babylon when the Temple was destroyed. How were all of these exiles the same? What hopes, what fears, what feelings did these groups share? Think art or drama or writing. Write a diary entry for each group, etc.

- What does it mean to be a Jewish parent? Design a series of picture frames, one made by each of the Patriarchs and Matriarchs. How would each student make it personal? Or, have each parent create a scrapbook of his/her children's big life moments. How are the moments similar and different?

- Have Eve talk to Sarah and Tziporah (Moses' wife) about the problem with men. And then have the two of them move on to talk about the power of forgiveness.

- God revealed laws to Noah after the flood and laws to Moses and Israel at Mount Sinai. Do a mural of these two moments of law giving (revelation).

- There are two different stories of when Moses hit the rock. They are found at Numbers 13 and Deuteronomy 1. Have a debate about which one is correct. Spend time looking at how they are the same and how they are different.

The secret to this last kind of teaching is to be asking constantly: How is this biblical moment like other biblical moments? This will lead to asking: How are they both like moments in my own life? The big lesson that can emerge is the insight that studying Torah is about making connections, first between the Torah we are studying and other places in the Torah, then between the Torah and the pages of our lives.

PART 5: LEARNING TORAH IS ABSORBING SYMBOLS

Now we will work with a really simple idea. One important part of learning Torah is the process of playing with and absorbing individual images and symbols. Let's take a very simple, wonderful example. In Genesis 28, we have the story of Jacob's dream with a ladder that goes from earth to heaven. It is one thing to study the text of this story by investigating its biblical and *midrashic* context, it is another thing to pluck the image out of the story and examine it on its own.

Here are some examples:

- The *midrash* is filled with stories of ladders that take people from earth to heaven. One example grows out of a passage in the Talmud in which Moses goes up to heaven to battle with the angels to receive the Torah.

- Several different sources compare the *Siddur* (prayer book) to Jacob's ladder. It is a way we climb from earth to heaven.

- The poet Denise Levertov used the image of climbing Jacob's ladder as a metaphor for the process of art by writing a poem.

The Jacob's Ladder

The stairway is not
a thing of gleaming strands
a radiant evanescence
for angels' feet that only glance in their tread, and need not
touch the stone.

It is of stone.
A rosy stone that takes
a glowing tone of softness
only because behind it the sky is a doubtful, a doubting
night gray.

A stairway of sharp
angles, solidly built.
One sees that the angels must spring
down from one step to the next, giving a little
lift of the wings:

and a man climbing
must scrape his knees, and bring
the grip of his hands into play. The cut stone
consoles his groping feet. Wings brush past him.
The poem ascends.

(By Denise Levertov, from POEMS 1960-1967, copyright © by Denise Levertov. Reprinted by permission of New Directions Publishing Corp.)

What we learn from this poem is that many biblical metaphors/images have lives of their own that transcend the texts in which they are found. Some other clear examples are the Garden of Eden, the tree of life, Noah's ark, the Tower of Babel, the coat of many colors, basket in the bull rushes, and the burning bush. The process of mastering these strong biblical images, of playing with them, of finding connection with them, is another way of bringing Torah into our daily life.

Let's look at some practical examples of how to do this.

Synetics - Synetics is a brainstorming process. Dr. Gail Dorph, in particular, uses synetics as a Torah teaching tool — and it can be very powerful. For example, ask: How is studying Torah like climbing a ladder from earth to heaven? The same kind of adaptation can be made for most biblical metaphors.

Tell the story through objects - *Scripture Windows* contains an exercise in which biblical stories are told through objects. For example: When Moses got to the burning bush, he was told to take off his sandals because he was standing on holy ground. Imagine having your students tell the story of the burning bush from the sandals' point of view. Imagine the conversation between Moses' sandals and other famous biblical sandals. After this word play you could make sandal collages.

Personalizing the image - What else is like eating from the tree of knowledge of good and evil? Cut images and words out of magazines to tell the story of a time when you felt as if you were eating new knowledge, and the knowledge changed you forever.

Create the symbol - Design your own coat of many colors!

Literature and art search - How many different arks can you find? Collect all of the stories you can with the image of Noah's ark. Educator Debi Rowe used to have a poster in her house of a blimp loaded with oodles of animals. Some times you can compare the way different artists drew the ark, sometimes you can find stories that use the ark as a different kind of image.

Usually we try to understand the Bible in its own context. When we study symbols, we take the image out of the story and give it a life of its own.

---

[7]Wolf, Alan, *Moral Freedom: The Search for Virtue in a World of Choice* (New York: W.W. Norton & Company, 2001).

PART 6: TEACHING OUR STUDENTS HOW TO ARGUE

Why Argue?

We live in an age when arguing has fallen out of favor. We live in an age of moral freedom. Alan Wolfe, in his book, *Moral Freedom*, writes:

> The nineteenth century witnessed the triumph of economic freedom . . . The twentieth century was the century of political freedom . . . The twenty-first century will be the century of moral freedom . . . In an age of moral freedom, moral authority has to justify its claims to special insight . . . We interviewed many individuals who were reluctant to accept something as right or true just because authority or tradition has proclaimed them right and true, and were determined to play a role in creating the morality by which they will be guided. "I've started to think of God more as a love than as a father," one person said. If his comment is representative, the authority so many Americans crave does not stop with awe at the threshold of the Judeo-Christian tradition.[7]

This citation means that most of the time, when we ask our students most questions about meaning, we get back a perfectly deconstructed answer — it is a matter of opinion. And, when life is reduced to a matter of opinions, nothing is worth arguing about because it is all a question of . . . is there enough salt in this gravy?

One of the goals of Torah study is to teach two diverse lessons. One, that there is a way that God wants us to see things. God has taught us truth via the Torah. And, two, our job is to struggle to find that truth. The struggle, the argument, and the search purifies Torah and gets it to shine.

That is why Jewish tradition is really big on teaching us how to argue. In the Torah we learn the story of Korach, one of Moses' relatives, who confronts Moses and tries to take over the leadership of the Jewish people. The argument ends in a lot of violence and with a number of deaths. The *midrash* expands this story, clarifying what was wrong with the way that Korach argued. By the time we get to *Pirke Avot*, the matter is clarified and reduced to a basic principle:

There are two kinds of arguments. Every argument that is in the name of heaven will create something permanent; but those that are not in the name of heaven will create nothing. Which arguments are in the name of heaven? Those that are like the discussions between Hillel and Shammai. And which arguments are not in the name of heaven? Those that are like the controversy of Korach and his gang (5:17).

The deep notion here is that one of our Torah obligations is to teach our students how to argue.

Argument Is at the Core of the Torah

After the conflict with Korach was over, God told Moses, "No one should ever act like Korach" (Numbers 17:5). No one was quite sure what was actually being forbidden; different Rabbis have different ideas about this:

- Rabbi Joseph D. Epstein thought that it taught, "It is bad to start an argument but worse to continue it."[8]

- Rabbi Reuven Margolies taught that it means, "One is never allowed to hate."[9]

- Rabbi Zalman Nehemiah Goldberg taught that it means, "Never be the one who starts an argument — especially if you can not help worrying about being right. And especially if first saying, 'I'm sorry' will prevent it." He adds, "It doesn't matter who really did the wrong thing to begin with."[10]

In these three responses, we have an "argument" over what's bad about arguments. Taking all of the pieces, we have a great lesson:

1. Study the story of Korach in the Torah (Numbers 16). Have your class figure out what Korach did wrong. My friend, David Parker, still believes that Korach was right.

2. Study some of the *midrashim* on Korach — see the changes in the "expanded story." Either *Legends of the Jews* or *The Midrash Says* would be good places to find these "extra" stories.

3. Read the piece from *Pirke Avot* found above. Collect opinions about the ways that we should not be like Korach.

4. Read the collection of three commentators who all have different opinions of how not to be like Korach.

5. Point out that we have had a "Hillel and Shammai" type of argument over the argument of Korach.

6. End with: "*Pirke Avot* teaches, 'Every argument that is in the name of heaven will create something permanent.' What permanent things have we created today?"

The Argument Centered Classroom

Here are five things you can do to create a culture in your classroom that supports constructive arguing:

1. Develop and post a class list of Rules for Arguing. This should include such things as Be Polite, Disagree with Ideas, Not People.

2. Ask questions about texts/stories that invite opinions. These are the kinds of Torah questions that are really worthwhile.

3. Write the name and the theory of each person's opinion on the board. Review them. Maybe even have students keep a notebook of both their theory and someone else's theory each time. *The Being Torah Student Commentary* (Torah Aura Productions) is designed for doing just that.

4. Study arguments. Divide your class regularly into sides and support the notion that there are big arguments that are an important part of Judaism. The best place to find these arguments is either in the *Torah-Toons* books, especially the *Torah-Toons II* book, or in the series by Nehama Leibowitz — *Studies in the Book of Genesis, Exodus*, etc.

Honor arguments. Regularly praise students for arguing well and teaching us more Torah through their struggle and opinions.

[8]*Mitzvot ha-Shalom* 122-24.

[9]*Magoliyot HaYom* to *Sanhedrin* 110a, 6.

[10]*Moriah*, vols. 169/170, 62-72.

CONCLUSION

Bringing Torah into the classroom is at the core of Jewish education. The methodology for teaching it need not be difficult, even for the teacher who knows little Hebrew and has never mastered the text. Begin by looking for feelings. Then look for "holes" in the verses, and have students create *midrash* by filling them in. Always encourage the personalization of the Torah – each of us is Adam and Eve and Abraham and Sarah and Moses, etc. Each of us walks in their shoes and hears the questions asked by God of them in our ears.

The text often uses the same words in different contexts or repeats phrases, adding or deleting words in the repetition. In explicating reasons for such connections and nuances come fresh insights.

Torah symbols can take on a life of their own in modern expressions. Used metaphorically, they can enrich our means of expression and, conversely, can return us to the biblical text when encountered in modern usage.

Finally, studying Torah is about arguing viewpoints. It does not posit relativistic values, but rather insists that we probe it over and over again to find God's truths. Torah looked at in this way can become a never ending source of study and fascination for our students.

BIBLIOGRAPHY

Books That Model the Above Methods

Golub, Jane Ellen; Joel Lurie Grishaver; and Alan Brahm Rowe. *Being Torah.* Los Angeles, CA: Torah Aura Productions, 1985. (Grades 3-5)

A tool for involving third to fifth graders in the process of Torah study. Students learn to close-read texts and find hidden clues, surprising connections, and secret patterns, then suggest their own interpretations.

Grishaver, Joel Lurie. *Being Torah Student Commentary.* Los Angeles, CA: Torah Aura Productions, 1987. (Grades 3-5)

Includes exercises and activities for *Being Torah.*

———. *Gan: A Child's Garden of Torah.* Los Angeles, CA: Torah Aura Productions, 1996. (Grades PK-1)

Child-friendly versions of 25 classic stories from the Torah from creation to the death of Moses.

———. *Torah Toons 1: The Book.* Los Angeles, CA: Torah Aura Productions, 1997. (Grades 4-Adult)

Using the inquiry method, this textbook creates a Rabbinic study environment. Students read a summary of a *Parashah* (36 are included), then focus on specific verses involving a character's behavior, answer questions derived from those verses, and explore *midrashim* that address the same questions.

———. *Torah Toons 2: The Book.* 2d ed. Los Angeles, CA: Torah Aura Productions, 1983. (Grades 6-Adult)

Torah Toons 2 expands into the realm of the commentators and asks questions about language and ethics. Students become partners in the process of Rabbinic Torah study.

———. *When I Stood at Mount Sinai.* (Instant Lesson) Los Angeles, CA: Torah Aura Productions, 1997. (Grades 6-Adult)

A participatory exploration of *midrashim* about the giving of the Torah written by a class of 12-year-olds. Invites students to tell their own stories of what it was like to receive the Torah at Mount Sinai.

Wise, Ira, and Joel Lurie Grishaver. *I Can Learn Torah, Volumes 1 & 2.* Los Angeles, CA: Torah Aura Productions, 1992. (Grades K-2)

An innovative bible study program that involves parents as partners in the learning process.

Videos That Model the Above Methods

———. *My Exodus.* Los Angeles, CA: Torah Aura Productions, 1984. (All ages)

Six students give personal accounts of their experiences in leaving Egypt.

———. *Torah Toons 1: The Video.* Los Angeles, CA: Torah Aura Productions, 1997. (Grades 4-Adult)

Each of the 36 five-minute segments deals with the enactment of one *Parashah*, and ends with a focused question about one aspect of the material.

Books for Research

Bialik, Hayim Nahman, and Yehoshua Hana Ravnitzky. *The Book of Legends: Sefer Ha-Aggadah: Legends from the Talmud and Midrash.* William G. Braude, trans. New York: Schocken Books, 1992.

The first complete English translation of the Hebrew classic *Sefer Ha-Aggadah*, the non-legal portions of the Talmud and *Midrash*, features hundreds of texts arranged thematically. *Aggadah* includes the genres of biblical exegesis, stories about biblical characters, the lives of the Talmudic era Sages and their contemporary history, parables, proverbs, and folklore.

Fields, Harvey J. *A Torah Commentary for Our Times.* 3 vols. New York: UAHC Press, 1998. (Grades 7-9)

Includes a summary of each weekly reading and in-depth examination of a few important themes using ancient, medieval, and modern commentaries, including that of the author. Although geared to Grades 7-9, these books are ideal for beginning Torah students of all ages and scholars seeking new angles on the text.

Freedman, H., and Maurice Simon, eds. *Midrash Rabbah*. London: The Soncino Press, 1999.

This definitive English rendering of *Midrash Rabbah* contains homiletic, ethical, and moral interpretations of the Scriptures, as expounded by the Rabbis during the Talmudic and medieval times. Includes the complete *Midrash* on the Five Books of the Torah, as well as on the Five *Megillot*.

Ginzberg, Louis. *The Legends of the Jews*. Philadelphia, PA: Jewish Publication Society, 2003.

This classic, recently reissued, is an indispensable reference on the body of literature known as *Midrash*. A comprehensive compilation of stories connected to the Hebrew Bible.

Herczeg, Yisrael, ed. *Saperstein Edition Rashi: The Torah with Rashi's Commentary Translated, Annotated and Elucidated*. Brooklyn, NY: Mesorah Publications, Ltd., 1995.

A multi-volume version of the Torah. The Torah text is included, along with Rashi commentary written in Rashi script. The volume, however, expands this by including a phrase by phrase translation of Rashi – English interspersed with the Hebrew in traditional block letters. Notes and explanations by the editor fill the bottom third of the page.

Leibowitz, Nehama. *Studies in Bereshit (Genesis): In the Context of Ancient and Modern Jewish Bible Commentary*. New York: World Zionist Organization, 1974.

Teaching Torah in a deep way, this book contains analytical portions from many of the commentators in English, but with lots of contextual references and examples in Hebrew. An insightful commentary on each *sedra* in Genesis. There are similar studies in separate volumes for each of the other books of the Torah.

Simon, Solomon, and Morrison Bial *The Rabbis' Bible: Volume 1: The Torah*. Springfield, NJ: Behrman House, 1995. (Grades 5-9)

This version of the Pentateuch bridges the gap between Bible stories and scholarly exegesis. A sampling of all five books of the Torah is illuminated by traditional commentary, which is keyed to the text and appears directly beneath it on every page. Students explore biblical texts alongside *midrashic* interpretations.

Weissman, Moshe. *The Midrash Says: The Book of Berashis* (and other books in this series). Brooklyn, NY: Benei Ya'akov Publications, 1980.

A collection of *midrashim* in five volumes, each matching one book of the Torah and organized by the weekly Torah portions.

Books on Methodolgy

Pitzele, Peter A. *Scripture Windows*. William G. Braude, trans. Los Angeles, CA: Alef Design Group, 1997.

Peter Pitzele is the creator of bibliodrama, a process of stepping inside the biblical text and creating *midrash* through improvisation. This book is a how-to manual on that process.

Milgrom, Jo. *Handmade Midrash*. Philadelphia, PA: Jewish Publication Society, 1992.

Milgrom uses an innovative and interdisciplinary approach, connecting biblical study to personal growth and expression. Art and related literature are used to stimulate participants' thoughts and emotions, which are then expressed through different visual media. This process is then followed by discussion and processing of participants' work.

CHAPTER 34

Teaching Midrash and Rashi

Joel Lurie Grishaver

I am proud say that I prefer teaching Torah in a *midrashic* context to teaching just the biblical text.

In this chapter we will look at: ways of finding *midrashim*;[1] ways of making sense of *midrashim*, finding their key "lesson," and then studying them from various sources; and, finally, a number of *midrash*-oriented activities that can become part of your classroom repertoire.

> I teach Torah, *midrash*, and *mitzvot* — subjects that have no beginning or end. As a teacher, I am a perpetual student. I study the Torah portion every week and read commentaries on the Internet and in traditional sources. I often find things that amaze and intrigue me, and I try to share this enthusiasm with my students.
>
> *(Dena Salmon, Montclair, New Jersey)*

WHAT IS MIDRASH?

Midrash is a literature that was created around the same time as the Talmud (160 B.C.E.-500 C.E.), only it has continued on in various forms. It is a collection of stories and meanings about the biblical text. Often *midrashim* fill in holes in the biblical text. They tell what happened *before* a story, to make its events more clear. They tell what happened *after* a story is finished, often giving it a kinder or better ending. They sometimes focus on small moments or small details in the Bible and in a kind of "close up" give us a greater sense of meaning.

WHERE CAN ONE FIND MIDRASHIM?

There is no one book or collection that contains all the *midrashim*. *Midrash* is a diverse literature that is collected and recollected in lots of books. If you go into most good Jewish libraries, you will find an English collection that is labeled *"The Midrash."* This is actually the Soncino English translation of the collection known as *Midrash Rabbah*. This is a central collection, but it is not the only one. Such books as *Sifra*, *Sifre*, *Pirke de Rebbe Eliezer*, *Midrash ha-Gadol*, among many, contain more *midrash* in its primary form. Some *midrashim* are even to be found in the text of the Talmud.

In 1908, Hayyim Nahman Bialik and Yeshua Hana Ravnitzky, published a book called *Sefer ha-Aggadah*. The work was a collection of "greatest hits" of *midrash* and *aggadot* (non-biblically-centered legends, found in the Talmud and *midrash*). In 1992, William Braude (with some help from Everett Fox) published an English translation called *The Book of Legends*. The collection of Torah material in it is somewhat limited, but the total book is amazingly extensive. Both the Soncino *Midrash* and the *Book of Legends* are available in CD-Rom in English. A complete collection of all *midrashim* are available in Hebrew on the CD library collected by Bar Ilan University.

One of the things that makes *midrash* hard to work with are the forms in which it is originally found. Usually, *midrashic* stories are fragments found in the middle of something else. Often they involve Hebrew word plays and other technical forms of biblical interpretation. There exist a number of "meta-collections" of *midrash* that gather together the larger stories from multiple sources and strip away many of the technical language issues. Two of these collections are easily accessible. The first is a six volume academic offering from the early 1900s, *The Legends of the Jews* by Louis Ginzberg (translated by Henrietta Szold). A one volume condensation of the Ginzberg series, called

---

[1]The word *midrash* is singular, and *midrashim* is plural. "Midrashic" is an Englishized adjective form of the word.

Legends of the Bible, is also available on CD-Rom. The second comes out of the Orthodox world and uses Ashkenazic English spellings (*Shabbas*), and *"Frum"* language (*ha-Shem*). It is a series called *"The Midrash Says . . . "*

Two books that try to teach the *midrashic* process by showing it in conjunction to the biblical text are *The Rabbis' Bible* (Behrman House) and *Torah Toons 1* (Torah Aura Productions). A number of storybooks present *midrash* in a stand-alone form. My favorite is *The Family Book of Midrash: 52 Jewish Stories from the Sages* by Barbara Diamond Goldin (Jason Aronson Inc.).

Finally, Rashi and most other biblical commentators make extensive use of *midrash*. But, they usually use *"midrashic* sound bites," very condensed forms of larger *midrashim*.

WORKING WITH MIDRASH

In order to use a *midrash*, we need to remember a few things:

Every midrash starts with a question. Each *midrash* tries to solve a problem in the biblical text. *Midrash* assumes that God wrote the Torah. Thus, there should be no mistakes, there should be no contradictions, and no holes in the Torah. The first part of studying a piece of *midrash* is to find its question. These questions are not always stated.

Every midrash has both an answer and a message. Learning to tell the difference is a big deal. A solution fixes the problem in the biblical text. It tells us that the "question" we had, has an answer. We learn that there is no mistake, no contradiction, no hole. The answer conserves the biblical text. The message teaches us a generalizable lesson. It is in the message we learn a piece of Torah that is life changing.

Midrash is "real" Torah. While it is not *p'shat* (the literal meaning of the written text), it is "authentic" Torah. It is oral Torah, a telling of what the Jewish people have long remembered and long believed that the written Torah means. *Midrash* is not an absolute literature; it is comfortable presenting many meanings and many solutions. It is not just "one person's opinion." *Midrash* comes either as part of God's revelation, or the deep collective wisdom of the Jewish people. The one you chose depends on your theology. The point is that *midrash* is worth teaching as an end in itself, and not just a means to an end.

My Vav class (sixth grade), spends a year learning how to be close readers of Torah by studying the art of *midrash*. Over time, the students learn how *midrash* deals with questions and problems arising in the text, fills in gaps when details are missing, and connects or explains how to adapt ancient laws to the post-Temple world.

During this weighty undertaking, I like to show rather than tell, and I interject a bit of fun whenever possible. For instance, we might start off with a modern *midrash* such as "Kindergarten," by James E. Gunn. (This is an account of God as a kindergartener, working on a not quite successful planetary creation project.) As the students read the *midrash* aloud, they spontaneously figure out that Gunn is providing a thought provoking commentary on *Bereshit* (Genesis).

(Dena Salmon, Montclair, New Jersey)

An Example of a Midrashic Story

Moses was a shepherd in the wilderness, caring for his father-in-law Yitro's sheep. One day, one little kid ran away. Moses followed the kid for quite some time until it came to a shaded pool of water and started to drink. Moses came up to kid and said, "I am sorry. I should have known you were thirsty. It was my fault you had to run away." He then picked up the kid, placed it on his shoulders and carried it back to the flock. God then said to him, "Because you had mercy leading a flock of sheep, I know that you will have mercy when you lead My people, Israel."

The lesson of this story is fairly simple: good leaders understand and react to the needs of the people they lead. In this sense, we learn that the leader serves the people and not vice versa.

Here is the origin this story, with the problem and the solution. Note that portions in italics are the actual biblical text. The narrative starts in Exodus 3:1:

Moses was grazing the sheep of Jethro, his father-in-law, the priest of Midian; he guided the sheep far into the wilderness, and he arrived at the Mountain of God, near Horeb.

The Problem: Why did the future leader of the Jewish people have to do something as mundane as being a shepherd?

The Answer: Leading sheep is a good way of learning to lead people. (Or leading sheep was a good test of the ability to lead people.)

Notice, the question and the answer are distinct from the meaning. The answer solves the problem in the biblical text saying, "God had Moses work with sheep to learn how to work with people." The lesson, however, is generalizable, "Good leaders sense the needs of their flocks."

Here is the way this actually appears in the *midrash, Exodus Rabbah* 2:3. The following text is from the Soncino CD-Rom. The annotations in italics are mine.

Now Moses was keeping the flock.

This is the verse we are studying. It only states part of the verse, because we only need part of the verse for our problem.

It is written: But the Lord is in His holy Temple (Habbakuk II, 20).[2]

The is the "Proem Verse." Many of the midrashim *we have are transcriptions of sermons that include the stories that we know as "midrash." These sermons tie together a verse from elsewhere in the Bible with the verse we are studying. The sermon will connect the verse from Exodus with this verse from Habbakuk.*

R. Samuel b. Nahman said: Before the Temple was destroyed, the Divine Presence dwelt therein, for it says: The Lord is in His holy Temple (Psalm XI, 4); but when the Temple was destroyed, the Divine Presence removed itself to heaven, as it is said: The Lord hath established His throne in the heavens (ib. CIII, 19).

Now we get our basic sermon theme, sometimes God feels close to us, other times God seems remote. The nearness of God may have to do with our behavior.

R. Eleazar says: The Shechinah (*the part of God that can be close — our neighbor*) did not depart from the Temple, for it is said: And Mine eyes and My heart shall be there perpetually (II Chronicles, VII, 16).

Now we add, even when God seems far away, there is still a connection.

What follows is a bunch of proofs that even though we think that God has abandoned the Temple Mount and Jerusalem, that is not actually the case. We are still waiting for the connection to Moses.

(A.) So it also says: With my voice I call unto the Lord, and He answereth me out of His holy mountain, Selah (Ps. III, 5); for although it was laid waste, it still retained its holiness. See what Cyrus said: He is the God who is in Jerusalem (Ezra I, 3), *implying that though Jerusalem is laid waste, God had not departed from there.*

(B.) R. Aha said: The Divine Presence will never depart from the Western Wall, as it is said: Behold, He standeth behind our wall (Song of Songs II, 9), and also: His eyes behold, His eyelids try, the children of men (Psalm XI, 4).

(C.) R. Jannai said: 'Although His Presence is in heaven, yet, His eyes behold, His eyelids try, the children of men.' God was here like a King who had an orchard, wherein he built a tall tower and commanded that workmen should be engaged to do his work there. The King said that the one who was proficient in his work would receive full reward, but one who was indolent in his work would be handed over to the Government. This King is the King of kings, and the orchard is the world in which God has placed Israel to keep the Torah; He also stipulated with them that he who keeps the Torah has the entry to Paradise, but he who does not keep it is faced with Gehinnom (*Jewish Hell*).

Here comes the transition. It will follow. God does not abandon us. God never leaves the Temple, because God is always judging our actions. God never completely disappears, rather God waits for our "good behavior."

Thus with God; though He seems to have removed His Presence from the Temple, yet 'His eyes behold, His eyelids try the children of men.' And whom does He try? The righteous, as it says: The Lord trieth the righteous (ib. 5).

---

[2]Items written in parentheses refer to biblical chapters and verses. This particular one is Habbakuk, Chapter two, verse 20. Note that chapter numbers are written in Roman numeral form. In other citings, the Soncino editor uses "ib." to mean, "same

book as the one quoted above). The text quoted from the Soncino has been left as provided on the CD, including grammatical or editing mistakes.

What follows is an example of God judging people by their actions. The example is King David. Moses' story will follow. What both of these men have in common is that first they were shepherds and then they were major Jewish leaders.

DAVID EXAMPLE: **By what does He try him? By tending flocks. He tried David through sheep and found him to be a good shepherd, as it is said: He chose David also His servant and took him from the sheepfolds. (ib. LXXVII, 70). Why 'from the sheepfolds,' when the word is the same as and the rain . . . was restrained? (Gen. VIII, 2). Because he used to stop the bigger sheep from going out before the smaller ones, and bring smaller ones out first, so that they should graze upon the tender grass, and afterwards he allowed the old sheep to feed from the ordinary grass, and lastly, he brought forth the young, lusty sheep to eat the tougher grass. Whereupon God said: 'He who knows how to look after sheep, bestowing upon each the care it deserves, shall come and tend my people,' as it says, 'From following the ewes that give suck, He brought him to be shepherd over Jacob His people' (Psalm LXXVIII, 71).**

OUR MOSES STORY: **Also Moses was tested by God through sheep. Our Rabbis said that when Moses our teacher, peace be upon him, was tending the flock of Jethro in the wilderness, a little kid escaped from him. He ran after it until it reached a shady place. When it reached the shady place, there appeared to view a pool of water and the kid stopped to drink. When Moses approached it, he said: 'I did not know that you ran away because of thirst; you must be weary.' So he placed the kid on his shoulder and walked away. Thereupon God said: 'Because thou hast mercy in leading the flock of a mortal, thou wilt assuredly tend My flock Israel.'**

(Hence Now) **MOSES WAS KEEPING THE FLOCK.**

In other words, "Why was Moses tending sheep?" So that God could judge him. What does that have to do with our starting verse? Simply this: "Even when God seems remote, our actions matter." Even in the wilderness, when we seem all alone, God is there.

If you picked up Rashi's commentary you would not find this story at all. Instead you would find one culled from the next piece of *Exodus Rabbah*.

FAR INTO THE WINDERNESS:

He went into the wilderness in order to keep far from theft, so that his sheep would not graze in the fields of others.

The Rashi can be unpacked in the same manner.
The Question: Why did Moses lead sheep way into the wilderness (as far as Sinai)?
The Answer: To make sure that he was not grazing on land owned by anyone.
The Lesson: Righteous people work hard to make sure what they are doing is honest. Even small thefts are not allowed.

Practical Applications

Here are ten creative ways of teaching the *midrash* (and not the biblical text). None of these assume that you work with the full text. They do assume that you either told the story of the "good shepherd" or the "honest shepherd" to your class.

1. Have your class of sheep write or tell original stories of Moses as a shepherd.

2. Write, tell, draw, or act out stories of other famous Jewish leaders as shepherds.

3. Write a story about the job that Miriam did that either trained her (or let God see her) as a good Jewish leader.

4. Write a guide to being a good shepherd. Have it include things that should be done by both shepherds of people and shepherds of sheep.

5. Make a mural about the way that God is our shepherd — and how we should shepherd like God.

6. Work out ways of being careful not to steal (the way that Moses was careful).

7. Create a dance of Moses and the sheep. You could also write "The Ballad of Moses and the Kid."

8. Make up a modern version of this story. What job would God pick for Moses today?

9. Brainstorm other lessons every leader should learn.

10. Learn about other biblical characters that were shepherds. See if you can either find or make up a story of what they learned or demonstrated as shepherds.

TEACHING RASHI

Rashi is a hurdle for Torah teachers to leap. Once you feel that you can open up "The Rashi" and follow his teaching and use it to guide yours, you have been transported out of the universe of "naked" Torah (Torah is "just" what I think it means) into the universe of Rabbinic understandings.

In this portion of our discussion, we are going to: attempt to put Rashi's work in context, give some basic tools for unpacking and understanding "a Rashi," and look at a few creative ways of teaching with Rashi.

Who Is Rashi?

Rashi is *Rabbi Sh*lomo *Yi*tzchaki, a French biblical and Talmudic commentator, who lived in Troyes between 1040 and 1105. He is considered the prime Jewish commentator, and most serious text study follows his guidelines. As you can see from the italicized letters in the first sentence, "Rashi" is really a combination of the first letters of his full name.

Rashi received his early Talmudic training in his native Troyes, France, before traveling to Mainz and Worms (Germany). He returned to Troyes at the age of twenty-five, having become one of the leading Talmudists of his day. Rashi refused to take a Rabbinic position. He taught and wrote while earning his livelihood as a wine merchant.

He spent most of his life on his Talmud commentary, but his Torah commentary is equally important. Both are considered to be the authoritative guides to studying those respective texts, and each are printed along with virtually every edition of the *Chumash* (Torah) and the *Germara* (Talmud).

Rashi was also involved in *halachic* discourse and carried on a vast correspondence. His decisions are key foundations used by most legal authorities. Although he always quotes the opinions of his masters with the utmost respect, Rashi does not hesitate to disagree with their views and render his independent ruling. Rashi struggled to be lenient in his decisions, especially where monetary loss, albeit minor, was at stake. He argued with authorities who chose to be strict whenever the law was unclear.

Many statements regarding ethical behavior are found in Rashi's responsa. He stresses that the actions of a Jew should reflect high moral standards. He is constantly concerned for the weak and the oppressed and has a great respect for family life. He lauds peace as the loftiest goal, for it brings harmony and bliss to all.

Rashi's final years were scarred by the suffering of the Jews in the First Crusade (1096). It was the "Holocaust" of his time.

What is "A Rashi"?

Rashi and his students (many of whom become the *Tosefot* — another group of commentators) used to study the Torah and the Talmud verse by verse. They took notes on their classes and these notes were edited and redacted into commentaries. These notes go verse by verse, problem by problem, through the text. Part of the issue with studying Rashi is unpacking the shorthand and code used to write these notes. This is similar to what happens whenever you borrow someone else's classroom notes.

Each single comment made by Rashi is called in *Torah Lushon* (Jewish Slang) "a Rashi." One secret to understand Rashi's teaching is that while he solves the problems in the Torah one small clause or word at a time, often when you pull back and read all of the comments he has on a story, you get to see a larger picture of the way he dealt with the whole passage or story.

Rashi's commentary consists of a number of different kinds of "explanations." Sometimes he tells us what words mean, by giving us biblical verses that use the same word. Sometimes he does this by translating a word into "Old French." This makes Rashi one of the best sources for the evolution of the French language. Rashi also works like a web page creating "hyperlinks" to places in the Talmud and the *midrash* that explain or use the biblical passage. More than giving his own opinion about what things mean, Rashi sifts through all of the answers available in earlier Rabbinic sources, picks the one or two answers he prefers, and restates them in a very few words. By studying Rashi, one gets a guided tour through not only the biblical text, but the key locations in Rabbinic literature as well.

Rashi marks the trail. When you climb a mountain there are two choices, you can climb on your own, or you can follow a trail staked by previous explorers. It is exciting to climb on your own, but much easier to follow a path already explored. When you do a well-known climb, the metal pitons are already hammered into the rock at the places you will need to attach a rope. Often the handholds are marked. And, there are indications of the paths that have not worked. Studying the Torah with Rashi is like following one of these trails. Rashi marks the difficult places and lets you agree or disagree with his solution — but what he has done for you is mark the problems.

What is "Difficult" to Rashi?

The key question in studying Rashi is always, "what's bothering" him or "what's difficult" to Rashi? That is because Rashi studies problems and does not just state opinions or insights because, more often than not, Rashi does not state the problem he is answering; he just gives the answer. That makes the first part of studying Rashi a game of *Jeopardy*. To understand Rashi's questions, you need to know something about the way Rashi sees the Bible.

Torah as a Zipped File

If you want to understand the Torah the way the Rashi did, you need to start with one basic idea: God taught Moses two kinds of Torah, the Written Torah and the Oral Torah.

- The Written Torah is not only the Torah (the Five Books of Moses), but also includes the rest of the Bible, the Prophets and the Writings.

- The Oral Torah includes the Talmud, the *Midrash*, later codes, and commentaries, right up to the latest pieces of Jewish wisdom that are now being written.

But here is the catch. Do not think of Oral Torah as commentary on the Torah. Do not think of it as additions and transformations. None of that is the way the Rabbis (and Rashi) understood Oral Torah. Rather, think of it as a slow unfolding of the wisdom embedded in the Torah.

Think of a zipped or a compressed computer file. That metaphor will help. God has Moses up on Mount Sinai for 40 days and 40 nights, in that time God has to teach Moses enough Torah to last

until the messiah comes — until the messianic era is realized. It takes nine months to write a Torah scroll. Moses has to (according to the *midrash*) write down the entire Torah plus master a complex secondary literature in a little under six weeks. God's secret weapon is the nature of the Oral Torah. It is like a time release capsule, set to release as needed.

Here is the way it works. If I want to shorten the word "running" to the least number of key-strokes, I can compress or "zip" it. I can use "search and replace." I tell the computer to substitute a capital G for every use of "ing." The word "running" is now "runnG." A capital letter at the end of a word is never a usual usage. Likewise, I can tell the computer to make every double letter a single capital. "running" is now "ruNG." If I give the computer an English dictionary, I can remove the vowel "u" because "ranning," "renning," "rinning," and "ronning" are not words. An underlined "r" will indicate a missing vowel. Therefore I can compress "running into "rNG." To turn "rNG" back into running I just run my search and replace program in reverse. To make sense of the "short version," I need to know the rules for decompressing. You know the experience of sitting and watching your computer do just that with much bigger and more complicated rules. This happens every time the blue line creeps across your screen showing you the percentage of the process that has been completed.

The Rabbis believed that the Written Torah is the zipped/compressed version of the Oral Torah. All of the Jewish Law that the Jewish people would need, all of the interpretations of the text, all of the meanings that would come into play, were there, ready to be unfolded from the text. So, Moses learned on Mount Sinai two things: the text of the Written Torah and the rules for expanding it into the Oral Torah. One of the assumptions in this process is that we often find answers in the Torah, and are able to make sense of them just when we need them. Often, our perception of the problem allows an answer we already had, but didn't quite perceive, to come into focus. That is the way God revealed enough Torah to last us until the final redemption.

You need not accept this vision of the Torah, many important theologians and teachers reject it, but you will need to be able to look through its lens because all of Rabbinic Judaism starts with it as a given. (This explanation was created by your author for the Synagogue 2000 material and is used with their approval.)

Rashi's Five Problems

When you start by understanding that the Torah is a "compressed" file, everything that looks like an error is actually the clue to a kind of "decompression" that needs to take place. This is the secret to understanding Rashi. Basically, Rashi's commentary is built around finding five types of problems.

1. *Grammar and Meaning* - These are straightforward problems. What does this word mean? How can a plural noun follow a singular verb? How do we punctuate this sentence, etc. Sometimes Rashi's solution is direct, for example, telling us that *"abrek"* means bow down. Sometimes, a single word clue opens up the chance to teach a *midrash*.

2. *Next To* - Sometimes the Torah feels like Moses dropped the pile of pages he had written down and Joshua sewed them together in the wrong order. Things go next to each other in weird ways. Topics sometimes jump like the editing of a rock video. Rashi assumes that the order is the order that God wants and that we have something to learn from every unusual connection the order makes. Things are placed next to each other as an indication of a larger insight.

3. *Extra Language* - Because the Torah is divinely written, it should be perfectly expressed. This means that none of the following could be motivated by either stylistic concerns or carelessness: the repetition of a phrase or incident, or a series of descriptors (phrases or words) when a single could have been used. Phrases or clauses that don't seem to add to our understanding (writing for writing's sake) must indeed add to our understanding.

4. *Contradictions* - Conflicting details of multiple accounts cannot represent contradictions; they must somehow be complementary. Established or anticipated patterns of description must have a reason for changing (theme and variation).

5. *Behavior* - Why do characters act the way they do? Biblical heroes are supposed to be role models. If their behavior appears unethical or un-Jewish, then it is either explainable as a permissible exception or, in actuality, is not the

behavorial gap we perceived. If Abraham and Miriam's actions need to be "Torahdik," then how much the more so does God's behavior? God's behavior is sometimes even harder to understand.

If you want a great understanding of this pattern you can look in one of two places. The book, *Learning Torah*, which I authored (UAHC Press) spends a great deal of time developing these patterns and perceptions. Also, a series of Feldheim Books by Avigdor Bonchek, called *What's Bothering Rashi?* (Four of the five volumes are out of print, but are often found in libraries). These books carefully break open the process.

A Sample Rashi

I am particularly partial to the *ArtScroll, Saperstein Edition, Rashi*. I think it makes the easiest read for non-Hebrew comprehenders and absolute best choice for people with some Hebrew, but not enough to study the straight text that way. This passage comes from there.

We will be looking for three things: the question, the answer, and the message. The "answer" answers the question, the message is a piece of wisdom for us to live by.

> TORAH (Genesis 3.2): The woman said to the serpent, "Of the fruit of any tree we may eat. (3) Of the fruit of the tree, which is in the center of the garden, God has said, "You shall not eat it and you shall not touch it, lest you die."

> RASHI: AND YOU SHALL NOT TOUCH IT. She added the commandment therefore she came to detraction. (i.e. she detracted from God's words, she violated the prohibition). This is (the idea) of that which says: "Do not add to God's words" (Proverbs 30:6). (*Bereshit Rabbah* 19.3)

So let's unpack this Rashi.

AND YOU SHALL NOT TOUCH IT. This part of the phrase that Rashi quotes is the location of "the difficulty."

The difficulty in this case is "A CONTRADICTION." In order to know that, we need to look back. In Genesis 2:15, God tells Adam not to eat from the tree in the middle of the garden. God actually says nothing about "not touching" the fruit.

3. The obvious question would be, Why did Eve change God's words to Adam? But that is not the question that Rashi asks. His answer guides us to realize that he is asking: What happened when Eve changed God's words?

4. Rashi tells us two things: Eve's undoing, her fall from Eden, happens because she adds to God's words and, Rashi reminds us that God (in Proverbs) has warned us not only not to delete or change God's words, but not to add to them, either.

5. This Rashi is a condensed piece of a full *midrash* (*Bereshit Rabbah* 19:3). In the larger *midrash* (and in the next section of the Rashi), we realize that the Serpent gets Eve to touch the fruit and she does not die. Once she had touched it and lived, she tries eating it. The lesson being, had she not "invented" part of God's message, she would not have broken any of it.

6. That gets us the three parts of studying most Rashis:

    a. The Question: What happens when Eve changes God's message?

    b. The Answer: The "additions" Eve made, give the snake the opening to trick her.

    c. The Message: We need to be careful about "playing God" and "speaking for God." Adding our own opinions to the Torah can be dangerous.

This single example of how a Rashi works may well not help you feel comfortable with Rashi, but it should give you a good idea of how to get started. Both of the books recommended above will help you get inside of a lot more examples.

Teaching with Rashi

Let's examine three different options for teaching this particular Rashi:

1. Explaining Eve. The *midrash* that Rashi is quoting makes it clear that Eve changed God's words. It does not explain how this happens. Using any or all art media you can explore this question. You could write a ballad or a ballet on why Eve got God's rule wrong. You could do a mural or a cartoon about how the snake used this change, etc.

2. You could find other examples in history where people have "added" to God's word and things went wrong. (You could even make these up.)

3. You could explore the difference between "adding" and "interpreting" and figure out ways of making sure that you are learning Torah and not creating Torah.

This assumes that you, the teacher, are studying with Rashi as part of your preparation, but you are not actually teaching Rashi in your class.

1. *Use Rashi to find good midrashim.* Learn how to read Rashi's answers to find great *midrashim* to teach. Then use all of the teaching strategies found in the "teaching *midrash*" section, above.

2. *Use Rashi to find good problems.* Present your class with the problem in the story that Rashi uses as the target for his answer. Give them a chance to invent their own answer. The answers could be skits or creative writing pieces. They could be poems or paintings. They could be done by individuals, by groups, or even all-class projects. The point here is that the class involves not "learning" Rashi's answer, but using Rashi's starting point. This is the process that is at the heart of the *Torah Toons* series (Torah Aura Productions). After the creative experience you may or may not choose to share Rashi's actual answer.

3. *Use Rashi to scout an area to let your students play detective.* Find a good problem in a verse then invite them to discover, "What's wrong with this verse?" Once they have unpacked the problem, you can then teach or not teach Rashi's answer, and/or you can then invite their own creation of a solution (see above).

Considerations for Teaching Rashi

1. Sometimes just opening the book and studying the Rashi can be great.

2. You can invite groups to unpack the Rashi, finding *problem, solution,* and *message,* before you begin to discuss it.

3. You can invite the class to become the *Tosefot.* These were Rashi's sons-in-law, grandchildren, and students. They both edited and "second guessed" Rashi. Invite them to rewrite the

Rashi into a more comprehensible form and then add their own comments about where they think he is right and where they thing he is wrong.

4. You can then develop all of the creative lessons you want — following suggestions from the first two options. You can work with Rashi's *midrash*. You can work with the message and go "creative" about the big idea he teaches. In this way, as with the "Eve changing God's word" example, Rashi is only the access point to your real lesson.

BIBLIOGRAPHY

Books That Model the Above Methods

Grishaver, Joel Lurie. *Learning Torah: A Self-Guided Journey through the Layers of Jewish Learning.* New York: UAHC Press, 1983. (Grades 7-9)

Ten modules, each of which analyzes the Torah in a different manner. Students will learn the meaning of Torah and how to read, translate, and understand it.

———. *Torah Toons 1: The Book.* Los Angeles, CA: Torah Aura Productions, 1997. (Grades 4-Adult)

Using the inquiry method, this textbook recreates an authentic Rabbinic study environment. Students read a summary of a *Parashah* (36 are included), then focus on specific verses involving a character's behavior, answer questions derived from those verses, and explore *midrashim* that address the same questions.

———. *Torah Toons 2: The Book.* 2d ed. Los Angeles, CA: Torah Aura Productions, 1983. (Grades 6-Adult)

Torah Toons 2 expands into the realm of the commentators and asks questions about language and ethics. Students become partners in the process of Rabbinic Torah study.

Books for Research

Bialik, Hayim Nahman, and Yehoshua Hana Ravnitzky. *The Book of Legends: Sefer Ha-Aggadah: Legends from the Talmud and Midrash.* William G. Braude, trans. New York: Schocken Books, 1992.

The first complete English translation of the Hebrew classic *Sefer Ha-Aggadah*, the non-legal portions of the Talmud and *Midrash*, features hundreds of texts arranged thematically. *Aggadah* includes the genres of biblical exegesis, stories about biblical characters, the lives of the Talmudic era Sages and their contemporary history, parables, proverbs, and folklore.

Bonchek, Avigdor. *What's Bothering Rashi?* 5 vols. New York: Feldheim Publishers, 1997)

A valuable aid in comprehending the analytical logic that lies behind Rashi's brilliant interpretation of Torah.

Ginzberg, Louis. *The Legends of the Jews.* Philadelphia, PA: Jewish Publication Society, 2003.

This classic, recently reissued, is an indispensable reference on the body of literature known as *Midrash*. A comprehensive compilation of stories connected to the Hebrew Bible.

Goldin, Barbara Diamond. *The Family Book of Midrash: 52 Jewish Stories from the Sages.* Northvale, NJ: Jason Aronson Inc., 1998.

This award-winning book is a collection of *midrashim* retold to appeal to readers young and old.

Simon, Solomon, and Morrison Bial. *The Rabbis' Bible: Volume 1: The Torah.* Springfield, NJ: Behrman House, 1995. (Grades 5-9)

This version of the Pentateuch bridges the gap between Bible stories and scholarly exegesis. A sampling of all five books of the Torah is illuminated by traditional commentary, which is keyed to the text and appears directly beneath it on every page. Students explore biblical texts alongside *midrashic* interpretations.

Freedman, H., and Maurice Simon, eds. *Midrash Rabbah.* London: The Soncino Press, 1999.

This definitive English rendering of *Midrash Rabbah* contains homiletic, ethical, and moral interpretations of the Scriptures, as expounded by the Rabbis during the Talmudic and medieval times. Includes the complete *Midrash* on the Five Books of the Torah, as well as on the Five *Megillot*.

Herczeg, Yisrael, ed. *Saperstein Edition Rashi: The Torah with Rashi's Commentary Translated, Annotated and Elucidated.* Brooklyn, NY: Mesorah Publications, Ltd., 1995.

A multi-volume version of the Torah. The Torah text is included, along with Rashi commentary written in Rashi script. The volume, however, expands this by including a phrase by phrase translation of Rashi — English interspersed with the Hebrew in traditional block letters. Notes and explanations by the editor fill the bottom third of the page.

Weissman, Moshe. *"The Midrash Says."* Brooklyn, NY: Benei Ya'akov Publications, 1980.

A collection of *midrashim* in five volumes, each matching one book of the Torah and organized by the weekly Torah portions.

CHAPTER 35

Teaching about Prayer

Rachel Raviv

The wind is blowing. In the stillness, one hears only the rustle of the leaves. Particles of dust hang in the rays of sun that filter through the tree branches. A bird chirps merrily in the background. A group of 15 students huddles together — outside — behind the school's chapel, praying. They have no Siddurim in their hands, only journals and sketchpads; nothing is said aloud. They are experiencing nature, God's works. They have in mind the following guiding questions, presented to them before they left the classroom:

- *What do you see/notice?*

- *How do you feel?*

- *What amazes (surprises, or disappoints) you?*

- *What would you say to God about this moment or about nature in general?*

- *What might you ask God about nature, if you had the opportunity?*

When they return to their classroom, their teacher asks them about their experience, structuring their conversation to discuss each of the questions listed above. At the end of the conversation, she has them write brief poems or create original artwork on the ideas of awe and thanksgiving.

Throughout the semester, as the class studies a prayer that connects to these subjects, students review and revise their reflections tied to the traditional prayers ("Yotzer Or," "Or Chadash," etc.) so they can see the development of the prayers and connect to the authors' mood and motive, experienced hundreds of years earlier. As appropriate, students learn the traditional choreography (davening) of each prayer and spend time strengthening their decoding skills.

At some point, the teacher supplements the students' personal Siddurim with these poetic and artistic reflections, inserted in appropriate places, to act as kavanot.[1]

---

[1]A *kavanah* is a poetic prayer "from the heart," but structured within a prayer experience. The plural of *kavanah* is *kavanot.*

> I think that when schools have organized services, it is essential that teachers participate in the *Tefilah.* I don't know how we can expect our students to take *Tefilah* seriously if they see that once you are an adult you don't have to do it. They may get that message from parents or friends, but certainly shouldn't get that message from Jewish teachers.
>
> *(Cheryl Birkner Mack. Cleveland, Ohio)*

FOUR ESSENTIAL ELEMENTS TO TEACHING PRAYER

Teaching prayer involves more than merely making sure students pronounce the words correctly. An effective teacher of prayer must balance four competing elements:

1. Supervising the development of proficient prayer mechanics including pronunciation, rhythm, and choreography

2. Finding opportunities to help students express their "organic" emotion — connecting these to those experienced by the writers of prayers many generations earlier (building empathy and understanding), while weaving together the new and the old through discussion and exploration

3. Opening the conversation to big questions about such things as God, loss, thanksgiving, faith, blessings, and existence

4. Facilitating a spiritual environment, by promoting spontaneous, prayerful moments

In the opening vignette, the teacher considered all four elements. She created an opportunity for students to feel connected to God (not just through the outdoor meditative exercise, but through a semester long process of building spirituality and introspection.) She helped her students put their emotions into words and gave them the chance to express their original prayers to God.

The teacher bridged the space between her students and the writers of the canonical prayers. In the classroom, she allowed students to theologize and to come to terms with their understanding of nature, the Creator, and humankind. Yet, she did not ignore the importance of preparing students to pray in the community with others; she reviewed the prayer mechanics, making sure their pronunciation and movement was correct.

In essence, she enabled students to become engaged and thoughtful pray-ers. Had she neglected any of the four elements listed above, the students would have been ill prepared for a meaningful *Tefilah* (prayer) experience. Ignoring any element creates an imbalance; yet, leaning too far in the direction of any of the individual elements also skews the outcome unfavorably. The next section outlines ways to facilitate each of those elements necessary to teach prayer, including the following:

- developing prayer mechanics

- building understanding and empathy for traditional prayers

- opening theological conversations

- creating a spiritual environment

Some of the techniques suggested in this chapter will feel natural; others may feel foreign or uncomfortable at first. But it is important to include aspects of each of the four elements into classroom practice so as to include all learners and to connect to the varied purposes of prayers.

For this reason, teachers must discover their own starting points when teaching *Tefilah*. For some, beginning with prayer mechanics works best. These teachers can then layer on top of that learning, strands of meaning, meditation, and connection.

Others may decide to focus on meaning first. Structuring class around prayer themes (for example, concentrating on those dealing with "light" or those that are prayers of thanksgiving) might then be the starting point. These teachers might next layer the words and choreography onto the meaning building activities and meditation exercises.

Teachers must balance their own comfort level with the varied methodologies with the needs of their students. While it may feel inauthentic to try some of the meditative techniques, these might provide a breakthrough for some students in the classroom, awakening them to praying. Alternatively, relying heavily on prayer mechanics may seem cumbersome and tedious; yet, for some students, the ability to pray with a congregation in Poland during a summer trip may connect them to the community of Jews in ways not otherwise possible. Similarly, high school students might be searching for meaning and community that they don't know exists within their own religious heritage.

Developing Prayer Mechanics

In many schools, the emphasis of prayer education is on mechanics; this is in part due to the reality that parents are concerned that their children are able to lead their B'nai Mitzvah ceremonies fluently. It is also due to the feeling that only when one is able to read the words on the page can real *kavanah* emerge. Most would also suggest the importance of making students feel comfortable reading the words of the *Siddur* and participating in congregational prayer. For these reasons, teaching prayer mechanics often feels like the natural place to start.

To achieve these aims, students must be able to do the following:

- Decode Hebrew

- Join in the *nusach* (prayer melody)

- Navigate the *Siddur*

- Follow the choreography of the service

Though each teaching venue usually defines the method of instruction for mechanics, some strategies are suggested below. These include the use of reading games, audiotapes, student-led prayer experiences, and decoding tricks.

Games and Hebrew Proficiency

Perhaps the most daunting piece of teaching *Tefilah* is the inclusion of a foreign language. Yet, the ability to read Hebrew is an important part of being able to pray. Drilling for proficiency in reading can be tedious and overwhelming. For this reason, many reading games have been developed to lighten this process. This is not to say that games should be overemphasized; there is intrinsic value to spirituality and focusing too closely on making classes "fun" minimizes this value. Yet, games are a nice way of making Hebrew reading more enjoyable.[2]

Audiotapes

The use of audiotapes in the classroom is another valuable tool for teaching mechanics. Teachers can record one *Tefilah* at a time onto a tape (or burn a CD) for students to take home with them. Students can then listen at their leisure (or while riding in the car), chant along with the tape, and eventually record their own version of the prayer for the teacher to review. For aural and oral learners, this is an especially effective technique. Again, this should not be overemphasized as learning by rote and repetition deserves cautions. Yet, this method, in conjunction with meaning making and meditative activities, reaches learners of differing learning styles.[3]

Student-Led Prayer Experiences

Allowing students to lead prayer services for themselves, for their parents, and for the congregation-at-large, is also important. Not only does it give them motivation to achieve (and the added incentive of a real deadline), it reinforces their learning and lets them feel good about the process. It also makes the learning come to life and prepares them for congregational praying in a way that classroom learning cannot. These experiences can be in varied settings: in junior congregation, in classroom prayer services at people's home, in a family program at the synagogue (for example, Havdalah), or in the "big" service.

Decoding and Making Sense of the Words

There are stories of students in synagogue classrooms across the country, working to earn a "best time" for the quickest repetition of the *"Amidah"* (the central set of prayers in a service; these are said standing), as if the ultimate achievement in prayer was speed. Such proficiency may be a starting point, to enable students to take the prayer beyond the words on the page, but it must not be the ultimate goal.

Once students learn how to decode, a common goal is to help them make sense of the words on the *Siddur* pages. This includes focusing on common suffixes and prefixes and relevant repeating words. For example, one might want to teach students to recognize the word *"Melech"* (king) each time they see it in the *Siddur*. Students could draw a crown around the word or highlight it in "royal" purple. Or students could locate and highlight the suffix *"cha"* ("You") every time it appears, focusing on the "whom" of some of the word meanings in the *Siddur*.

Understand and Empathize: Individual and Community

Cantor Kaplan has recently noticed that services with his junior congregation are marked by low energy. The students follow along, sing when appropriate, and generally go through the motions, but do not seem engaged in what they are saying.

He knows their Tefilah teacher has them explore the meaning of the prayers. In her class, they are active participants and engaged in thoughtful conversations. The Cantor is interested in connecting what engages students in the classroom with what happens at junior congregation. He wants them to become aware that Jews have uttered these same words for thousands of years. He wants to show the students their link in the chain of tradition. But he does not know how to bridge what they are learning in class with what happens in his service.

Bringing meaning to the *Tefilot*, not just while in the classroom, but while involved in the actual act of communal prayer, should be a major concern in prayer education. It is essential for students to transfer this knowledge to their synagogue practice so that they can properly "enter" the *Tefilot*. When they do, they can say the words with real *kavanah*, or intent. The following are several techniques designed to demystify the words of prayer and open them up for students:

---

[2]For more information on games, see Chapter 51, "Enriching Instruction with Games" by Susan Arias Weinman, pp. 000-000 in this Handbook. For more information on decoding, see Chapter 42, "Teaching Hebrew Reading" by Dina

Maiben, pp. 495-515 in this Handbook.

[3]For more information on multiple intelligences, see Chapter 27, "Multiple Intelligences" by Renee Holtz and Barbara Lapetina, pp. 323-333 in this Handbook.

- *Midrashim*, or prayer origin stories

- Guided questions

- *Chatimot* ("praying signatures")

- Spontaneous prayer opportunities

These suggestions, which are described in more detail below, can be used both in the classroom and during services. Yet, they are most effective when used in both venues. To bridge the classroom learning with real-life application successfully, there must be cooperation between those who teach prayer and those who lead services for the students. Where this cooperation exists, the service leader can reinforce what happens in the classroom and the classroom teacher can become aware of how students progress during prayer experiences.

Before I teach the children to read a prayer, I always give them some sort of concrete concept that they can use to relate to the prayer. For example, when I teach the *"Avot,"* I begin by telling my class about my own family, and I share with them that I recently found out that my great-grandfather, who died many years before I was born, was actually a *melamed* (teacher) in a *shtetl*. I then proceed to tell the children how things are passed down from generation to generation, and sometimes we don't even realize that we carry things from our ancestors. I explain that I didn't know my great-grandfather, yet we share a profession, and somehow that must have been passed down to me through my grandparents and parents. This usually precipitates a discussion on families, and how we are connected to our past. This is a good way for the children to understand their connection to history, and I conclude that their Jewish fathers and mothers have passed on something to them, too — the Jewish religion.

(Nancy Hersh, Chatham, New Jersey)

Midrashim, or Prayer Origin Stories

Storytelling is a powerful way to connect students to the meaning behind prayers. Many *Tefilot* have *midrashim* that tell their origin. For example, the Jews escape the oppression of Egypt and reach the Sea of Reeds. Trapped at the edge of the sea — with the Egyptians close behind — they are filled with despair. God splits the Sea, and Moses leads them through. On the banks of the other side, they sing praises to God: "Who is like You?" These words of the *"Mi Chamocha,"* which is sung daily in worship services, retell that story. Exploring the *midrash* helps to build better understanding of the words of the prayer, and also connects the students emotionally to the words they are saying. Students can pray with emotion; when they are frightened or when they feel "redeemed," they are familiar with words that express similar feelings and that are a part of a long-standing Jewish tradition.

Guided Questions

Another method is the use of guided questions. Before beginning (to study) a prayer, the teacher asks a focused question or poses a statement such as, "Think of a time when you were scared." Once the conversation is opened, she (or the Cantor, during services) then weaves those ideas and feelings back into the prayer being studied (or uttered).

For example, as young students discuss being fearful in the dark at night, some might say that they feel better when they see the dim glow of the night-light or when they hold teddy bear close. In class, they write brief *kavanot* about being afraid and feeling brave. The teacher then connects those feelings and actions to a particular prayer, such as the *"Hashkivaynu"* (the prayer said in the evening service between the *"Shema"* and Its Blessings and the *"Amidah"*) or *"Shema al ha'mitah"* (the *"Shema"* said at bedtime). The class delves into why those prayers were written, uncovers who wrote them, and explores its view on the author's mood in writing it. Later, during services, after communicating with the teacher, the Cantor can remind students about their *kavanot*, or have volunteers share them, before chanting the prayer.

The teacher could also have students explore the meaning of prayers and then ask them to bring in a contemporary example on this theme. Suggest students explore poems, song lyrics, newspaper articles, and the like. Use these to trigger discussion. For example, the class could explore the prayer *"Modeh Ani,"* which expresses thanks for allowing us a new day. Students are encouraged to find examples of giving thanks in today's world. Again, these examples are woven into the service to bring additional meaning to the words and to connect the pray-ers to the prayers in new ways.

> I often have children illustrate a prayer, or at least the concepts of the prayer. One lesson that I did that was very successful was that when I was teaching the *"V'ahavta"* prayer, I focused on teaching about Judaism from generation to generation. I asked the class to think about what they would teach about the Jewish religion to someone who knew nothing about Judaism, and we came up with a list. We then made up a poster and titled it *"L'dor Vador"* (from generation to generation), and each child contributed to the list. We hung that poster in the classroom, and throughout the school year we added things to the list as they came up in our discussions. It helped the children to understand that there is more to our religion than just lighting candles on Shabbat, or eating *matzah* on Passover.
>
> (Nancy Hersh. Chatham, New Jersey)

Chatimot

Many prayers include *brachot* (literally translated as "blessings;" these always begin, *"Baruch Atah . . . "*). Some prayers have *brachot* both at their beginning and at their end. Especially in the *"Amidah,"* each ending *brachah* targets the particular meaning of the prayer. By looking at that ending *brachah* (called the *chatimah*, or seal), one gets to the essence of the prayer.

The teacher can focus the class on the words of the *chatimah*, momentarily forgoing the rest of the *brachah*. This helps students understand what they are saying. An excellent teaching technique is to have students make up a beginning part of a prayer that goes with a particular *chatimah*. In the end, the prayer that they make up can become a *kavanah* to be read before the actual *Tefilah* they are studying.

Spontaneous Prayer Opportunities

Similar to the above is the technique of spontaneous prayer during a service. In approaching a prayer to be chanted, the Cantor asks the students to reflect on the meaning of the prayer; in essence, they will be "writing" their own reflection, on the spot.

One set of appropriate blessings for this technique is *"Birchot HaShachar"* (the morning blessings). Once students know the rhythm of the *brachah* (blessing) formula, the Cantor can have them say the first part, *"Baruch Atah . . . HaOlam,"* and then pause. Each student is given the opportunity to share one thing for which he/she is thankful. After each pause, the Cantor calls out the name of a student who then must finish the *brachah* (for example, "for letting me play with my new dog"). The rest of the students repeat that ending in the same melody as the *brachah*. They then say the formula again and the next student finishes it.

Another prayer for which this technique is often used is *"Oseh Shalom."* The Cantor first establishes what it means to be an *"oseh shalom"* (a doer of peace), then asks students to share ways they have brought more peace into the world. The discussion ends with singing the *Tefilah*.

These various methods, used in the class and during services, connect students to what they are saying. In this way, the prayers are no longer empty and mysterious. They actually communicate to God ideas and emotions with which the students have struggled and interacted.

Opening Theological Conversations

After Confirmation class last week, Eliana confided a problem to Rabbi Green. Though she likes participating in the youth group and does not even really mind coming to religious school, she is not sure that she "feels" Jewish. She went to church with one of her friends, and felt very moved by the service. She has never felt that way at synagogue. No, she doesn't identify with Jesus, but she doubts her connection to the Jewish world.

Avi is in the same grade as Eliana. He is a very active student. He marches at Israel rallies, but usually on the pro-Palestinian side. At school, he hangs out with students of all different nationalities and prides himself on his liberal views. Recently, Avi has become interested in Buddhist teachings. Though a serious and committed student, Avi constantly challenges the Rabbi's views in class.

The Rabbi is at a loss. He is unsure how to deal with both Eliana and Ari. He needs help discovering a way to bridge their evolving notions of God and faith with the traditions and rituals of Judaism. He senses that Judaism feels inauthentic and empty for them when it should be rich and meaningful.

It is essential for a teacher to show students the meaning inherent in Judaism. Without demystifying the rituals, students will feel disconnected and may reject those traditions. They will look for meaning elsewhere. One symptom of this is the disconnect felt during services and with traditional prayers, especially with those said in Hebrew, a foreign and therefore distant language.

A powerful method for handling this, to demystify the words and intent behind the prayers, and to show the innate spirituality of Judaism, is through a question box. Allow students to write down their Jewish questions as they arise during *Tefilah* class. (This also helps deflect interesting questions that are off-task.) This is really important because too often students get the message that asking such questions is distracting from the lesson at hand and inappropriate when — actually — it is exactly what they are supposed to be doing in a Jewish school.

Spend some time each week answering the questions put in the box. A few tips:

- Don't be afraid to say, "I don't know the answer to this." Follow that comment with a suggestion to consult each other, the Rabbi, or other sources. Saying, "There is no right answer to this question" often opens up the conversation and allows room for philosophizing that might not otherwise happen. In the same way, asking, "What do you think?" is a great technique to help students think about big issues.

- Don't be afraid to let students answer each other. Pondering and debating these issues is very healthy. Let students answer each other, but reserve the right to structure the conversation to stay true to Jewish belief (God has no shape or form, there is only one God, etc.).

- Don't be so sure that there is only one answer to each question. In Judaism, on almost every topic, there are conflicting opinions.

As students stumble upon documented beliefs, connect them to particular prayers (for example, *"Yigdal"* and the 13 principles of faith, or the

"Shema" and the notion of one God). This is one step in the demystification process. It connects students' ideas of faith with those that are already present in the canon of Jewish prayers and beliefs.

Dr. Sol Wachs suggests great activities along these lines. For example, present students with a list of the various names of God as these appear in the prayers being studied. As a class, explore what those names mean and imply. Allow students the opportunity to try out various notions of God, and explain that Judaism not only allows for those varied beliefs, but encourages them. Prayer then becomes a clarifier of beliefs and helps students come to terms with their own beliefs in relation to Jewish ones.

Creating a Spiritual Environment

Morah Siegel looks around her room. On the walls are American flags, charcoal sketches of the western frontier, and handwritten haikus on freedom. Most of the space in her classroom is dominated by the work of the secular third grade that meets there daily. She finds it difficult to get her seventh graders into a "prayerful" mood in that same space on Monday afternoons. Seated at desks, in even rows, Siddurim open in front of them, the students sit at attention (or worse, slump in apathy), and they are definitely not in a stance of meditation. Morah Siegel is at a loss for how to change the aura of her classroom.

Creating a meditative experience in a prayer service or in the classroom is perhaps the most complex element in teaching *Tefilah*. For many, it might be the most intimidating piece, or even feel silly or inauthentic. But prayer should be a multisensory, multilevel experience; it should connect the pray-er to God, to the Jewish community both past and present, and to his/her own thoughts. To achieve these connections, some pray-ers must reach an almost meditative state. Reaching this state is not a skill that comes naturally to many; it is too often overlooked and, it is easily dismissed as too new-age or as non-Jewish. Yet, Jewish tradition not only embraces this meditative state, it provides techniques to achieve it properly.

Thinking back to prayer services may conjure up memories of Shabbat Shacharit services that seemed to go on "forever," the Rabbi seemingly plodding through the pages, just to "cover" the material, to complete every page. These are not the services to introduce to our children. Rather, students should encounter meaningful, spiritual experiences during which time flies, not drags.

Just as adult prayers set their prayer mood with appropriate prayer adornments (*Tefillin* and/or *tallitot*), children need similar rituals to help set the space and time for prayer. Traditional Judaism offers specific techniques to help set the stage. These include:

- the *niggun* (wordless melody).

- the *kavanah* (poetic prayer of intent).

- *P'sukay d'Zimrah* (the warm-up service that leads into the morning prayers).

Try opening the service with a wordless melody that repeats (such as those sung by Shlomo Carlebach). Keep it going until the energy in the room has built. Without saying a word, head right into the first prayer. The *niggun* should help a person to get lost in the moment. The melody carries participants along with it.

Similarly, the *kavanah* helps get the congregation in the mood for prayer. It not only adds meaning to the words being said, but, if chosen correctly, sets the spiritual tone for the experience. Choose a rhythmic poem to read as a *kavanah*. Try one that is awe inspiring, one that opens the mind to the words of the prayer and to the works of God.

P'sukay d'Zimrah is the opening section of the morning service. It is comprised of hymns that are intended to warm us up for the praying experience. This is an excellent opportunity to shape the way services will proceed.

In creating a spiritual environment, modeling is very important. Students can sense when their teachers are uncomfortable and will replicate that discomfort. For this reason, teachers should find their own spirituality when praying with their students. This might mean such things as fully following the choreography of the prayers (bowing when appropriate), *shuckeling* and swaying in prayer, or closing their eyes during concentrating moments.

Knowing all of this, what steps does Morah Siegel have to take before she can transform her classroom (the students and setting)? Creating the right environment is essential. Students have to be prepared properly for a powerful prayer experience. Without the proper preparation, the activity described in the opening vignette would have fallen flat; students have to learn how to "get lost" in the moment.

So, how can Morah Siegel ready her students for meaningful prayer? She might try playing with the following dynamics (setting, lighting, seating and placement, sound and voice timber, meditation, word repetition, inspirational quotes and texts, music and rhythm, guided imagery, and storytelling) to set the stage for spiritual encounters in her classroom. These activities serve as a warm-up to other prayer activity, and each is described briefly below.

Setting

Try varying the setting of prayer. Visit a park, the chapel, the sanctuary, the sea (river, or lake), a library, or a home.

Lighting

Try varying the degree of lighting from bright to dim. Ask students to reflect on how the lighting affects their mood.

- Are there moments when it's easier to get lost in the words and ideas of the prayer? How does the light affect this?

- Does a dim light help reduce feelings of self-consciousness?

- Are there times when bright lights are most appropriate?

Seating and Placement

Try letting students find their own space throughout the room. Ask them to sit on the floor, move the desks, or sit in a circle. See how the different placements affect their mood. Have the males and females sit distant from each other. How does that influence their praying? Discuss why traditional communities use a *mechitzah*. Ask how students feel about this practice.

Sound and Voice Timber

Try varying the sound of your voices as the group utters various prayers (such as *"Oseh Shalom"* or the opening lines of *"Mah Tovu"*). Start as a whisper; then build to a shout; then work back down to a whisper. Try it the other way around. Try speaking breathlessly or with wonder.

Meditation

Give students a chance to be introspective and to search within themselves for meaning. Give them a topic to explore or let their minds wander. Be sure that there is an atmosphere of trust and seriousness; it's very difficult to get "lost" when one fears being ridiculed. To achieve this atmosphere, teachers might try using some of the other dynamics mentioned above in addition to the meditation: dim the lights, play mellow music in the background, ask students to close their eyes. Give them ample time to develop their thoughts. Let them reflect and share with each other (if they choose to) what occurred during the activity (if they choose to).

Word Repetition

Try using a phrase as a mantra. There are examples of this already built into the traditional prayer service; start with those (the first line of the *"Shema,"* *"Elohai Neshamah,"* or *"Adonai S'fatai,"* the meditation said before beginning the *"Amidah"*). There are many melodies for these phrases. Ask the Cantor or Rabbi to suggest a tune or try it without any melody. Once the students are familiar with the words to be said, have them repeat the sentence over and over again, almost as a chant. Try focusing on just one word. Then, let students choose their own word and have them all say it at the same time. Have them take turns. Discuss which words they chose and how the repetition made them feel. Talk about how all of the voices sounded when they merged. Remind the students to try saying their "words" again during services. Have them chant their words at different speeds, in rounds, or in varied phrase lengths.

Inspirational Quotes and Texts

Sometimes students need a starting point. Try hanging up signs with inspiration quotes throughout the room, such as, "Know before whom you stand." Give students a "thought of the day" to ponder. Let them discuss their reactions. Allow them to experiment with spiritual thoughts.

Sometimes we get so caught up in the work of teaching the routine *Tefilot*, we lose sight of how *davening* (the experience of praying) can be connected with our immediate everyday lives — or can connect us with the lives of Jews around the world. I was in charge of leading *davening* for our small religious school the year the Iranian Jews were arrested on trumped up spying charges. Some of our students had heard about this in current events classes in their secular schools. We were all frustrated at our lack of ability to do anything, since the Iranian expatriate Jewish community was initially asking people not to protest, for fear of endangering delicate behind the scenes negotiations. So I took this opportunity to teach our students about prayer as a way of expressing our fears.

Each school day, we began *Tefilah* (the worship service) by asking volunteers to read the names and ages of the arrested Jews. We then followed this reading by singing a psalm. I explained that this is a tradition of our people in times of crisis. The psalms I taught them, however, were not the traditional psalms read in such times. Because these were children, I wanted them to find hope in the psalms they were singing. So we talked about how we were singing for these Jews who could not sing with joy right now, in the hopes that they soon would be singing again with their families. And the psalms and melodies we learned were those common for *Hallel* (a part of the worship service) at our *shul* — so that along the way, the students picked up an unexpected synagogue skill.

(Anne Johnston, New Haven, Connecticut)

Music and Rhythm

Melodies and movement have a long tradition in Jewish prayer services. Add various musical pieces to your service. Bring in CDs or sheet music from such artists as Debbie Friedman, Craig Taubman, and the group Yom Hadash. Experiment with poetry, original and not. Bring in instruments and let the students accompany the prayers.

Many people are not comfortable with movement or dance within a service. However, some students may be kinesthetic learners who require movement to connect to the *Tefilot*. Sign language is a great compromise for these students. Try using sign language along with music in a service (three popular choices are the *"Shema," "V'ahavta,"* and *"Oseh Shalom"*). This technique is especially important for early elementary school students who need movement to break up the more sedentary parts of the service.

For older students, introduce them to the custom of *shuckeling* (rhythmically swaying back and forth while praying). Ask if students have seen that done before. Talk about how it looks and feels. Ask them to try it while praying. Does it change anything? Is it comfortable? See if students can come up with why this is part of traditional praying.

Guided Imagery

In guided imagery, students close their eyes and listen to a story in which they imagine themselves taking part. This can be used in conjunction with storytelling or with the *midrashic* origins of prayer.

Once the teacher (or prayer leader) establishes the imagery to be used (such as the Jews crossing the Sea of Reeds or Moses approaching the people before he dies), students explore their own emotions and ideas connected to the event. These events tie to prayers (the *"Mi Chamocha"* and the *"Shema"*) and help students focus on the meaning and origins of the words being said.

Storytelling

Whatever the age of the students, storytelling is a fantastic way to set the tone for a calm, centered service. The chosen story can center on the weekly *parashah*, an upcoming holiday, or a value of interest. The storytelling can, if desired, be followed by a discussion.

The storybooks by Sandy Eisenberg Sasso (such as *In God's Name*) and other such picture books for children are very appropriate for this.

When the mood is set (using any one or any combination of the preceding dynamics), let students linger in their "meditative" state. Allow space for those who may not reach this state to sit quietly. This is not something that can be forced. For the others, let them focus on the spirituality of the experience. After some time, begin to discuss what took place. (This can be done through the use of a journal in which students record their reactions to these experiments. Sharing their responses with each other opens the conversation as to what aids in our spirituality. Have students reflect on what they learned about their own prayer comfort and needs.)

Discuss what helped students to enter the experience. How did they feel? How can they reconstruct these feelings within traditional prayer settings? (Are there cues to be posted in the sanctuary, readings to be read, or melodies to include?) Pass the suggestion on to the Rabbi. Perhaps they can be included in the congregational service or mentioned in the school (or synagogue) newsletter.

CONCLUSION

Prayer is more than the words on the *Siddur* page. It is about communicating one's thoughts and feelings. It is about connecting to God, to the Jewish people, and to one's self. It is both difficult and vital to give students the tools to pray effectively: the ability to read the words, the knowledge of what they mean, the skills to affect a meditative stance, and the motivation to begin the process in the first place. The ideas and suggestions put forth in this chapter represent a starting point.

TEACHING CONSIDERATIONS

- In teaching prayer, be sure to balance the four essential elements: mechanics, emotional connection, theology and personal meaning, and spirituality.

- In terms of mechanics, focus on transmitting the skills to decode Hebrew, follow along through the *Siddur*, chant traditional *nusach*, and follow the movement of the service. These skills can be achieved through the use of games, tapes, student-led prayer experiences, and decoding tricks.

- As for personal connection, teachers have the following approaches at their disposal: *midrashim* and prayer origin stories, guided questions, *chatimot* exercises, and spontaneous prayer opportunities.

- In teaching theology and Jewish belief concepts, teachers should focus on dealing with students' specific questions and doubts. This can be handled through a question box, open discussion, or as needed. These conversations should be woven back through the prayers and traditional Jewish belief.

- Finally, when attempting to create a spiritual environment, teachers should experiment with various elements in the environment, having students reflect on the comfort and spiritual states elicited. The elements with which to experiment include: the setting, lighting, seating and placement, sound and voice timber, meditation, word repetition, inspirational quotes and texts, music and rhythm, guided imagery, and storytelling.

If students are reached on all of these levels, they will no doubt be connected and moved by their prayer experiences.

BIBLIOGRAPHY

Brody, David, and Dena Thaler. *A Teacher's Guide To Ani Tefilati*. New York: UAHC Press, 1997.

Included in this guide are lesson plans organized around prayer themes. This is a great source for meaning making activities.

Cohen, E.J. *Yad B'Yad (Hand in Hand)*. Contact CAJE for more information on this video.

This video provides straightforward demonstration of hand signing. Included are specific signs for *"Kiddush," "Motzi,"* candle blessings, *"Shema,"* and *"Oseh Shalom."*

Elkins, Dov Peretz. *Jewish Guided Imagery: A How-To Book for Rabbis, Educators & Group Leaders*. Princeton, NJ: Growth Associates, 1996.

This book presents a clear introduction to guided imagery, as well as dozens of examples of exercises on a variety of topics, including Bible, Rabbinic literature, Jewish history, and holidays.

Fields, Harvey. *B'chol L'vavcha*. New York: UAHC Press, 2001.

This book contains great material to use as inspiration while leading a junior congregational service or in the classroom. It contains numerous *midrashim* on the origins of prayers and texts for use in study.

Hoffman, Jeff, and Andrea Cohen-Keiner. *Karov L'chol Korav: For All Who Call: A Manual for Enhancing the Teaching of Prayer*. New York: Melton Research Center for Jewish Education, 2000.

An innovative text with a wide variety of activities related to meditation and spirituality.

Isaacs, Ronald H. *Lively Student Prayer Services: A Handbook of Teaching Strategies*. Hoboken, NJ: KTAV Publishing House, 1995.

This book has great focusing questions and activities for use in services or in the classroom.

———. *Siddur Lev Chadash: For Shabbat and Festivals*. KTAV Publishing House, 1999.

This *Siddur* offers *kavanot*, brief explanations, and meaning making ideas for selected words and phrases from *Tefilot* of Shabbat and Festivals.

Kadden, Bruce, and Barbara Binder Kadden. *Teaching Tefilah: Insights and Activities on Prayer*. Denver, CO: A.R.E. Publishing, Inc., 1994.

This is a thick text, rich with stories and suggestions to shed light on the meaning of specific prayers.

Moskowitz, Nachama Skolnik. *A Teacher's Guide to A Bridge To Prayer*. New York: UAHC Press, 1989.

Interesting suggestions for decoding techniques. Meaning making activities and prayer enrichment ideas are also provided.

Schein, Jeffrey L., ed. *Connecting Prayer and Spirituality: Kol Haneshamah as a Creative Teaching and Learning Text*. Wyncote, PA: The Reconstructionist Press, 1996.

This text offers a plethora of activities to explore the meaning of the *Tefilot*, the order of the service, and our connection to God. It also provides some pedagogic and theological underpinnings for those activities, geared especially to Reconstructionist educators.

Silberman, Shoshana. *Siddur Shema Yisrael: A Siddur for Sabbath and Festivals and Sourcebook for Students and Families*. New York: The United Synagogue of Conservative Judaism Commission on Jewish Education, 1996.

A useful source for junior congregation, for leaders and participants, this *Siddur* includes fantastic artwork and a poetry connection to specific prayers.

Zana, Hillary, and Dina Maiben. *Z'man L'Tefilah: The Time for Prayer Program*: Teacher Guide. Denver, CO: A.R.E. Publishing, Inc., 1998.

A great overview on teaching Hebrew decoding skills, plus hands-on activities and resources are offered in this guide.

CHAPTER 36

Teaching Jewish History

Julia C. Phillips and Lauren B. Granite

Rachel and her friends were sitting on their bunks talking and writing letters after dinner, waiting to go to evening program. All of a sudden the cabin door was thrown open, and one of Rachel's counselors ran in. All the campers in her cabin were told to hurry — there was very little time left for them to make their way out of Ethiopia. Their guide was coming soon and they had to be ready. They would be going on a long journey and they could take only the few things they could carry. Rachel excitedly got down from her bunk. Should she take her stuffed rabbit or her toothbrush? Which would be more important on this mysterious trip? She decided she couldn't leave the stuffed rabbit behind; it was the only thing she had to remind her of home. Then there was a quiet knock on the door of the cabin. A counselor dressed in a robe came in and began to argue with Rachel and her cabin mates about the price of leading their group to Addis Ababa. Finally, they came to an agreement and Rachel's group sneaked out of the cabin into the growing twilight.

THE IMPORTANCE OF TEACHING JEWISH HISTORY

Judaism is a historical religion. Each year, we relive our history through the holiday cycle as participants. It is not just our forefathers and foremothers who lived through these events, but also each and every one of us today. We follow Moses out of Egypt, celebrate with Miriam the crossing of the Reed Sea, stand in awe at the base of Mount Sinai, build and dwell in booths, and celebrate the rededication of the Temple after its desecration by the Greeks. So aware are we of the significance of history in Jewish ritual life that two major Jewish events of the twentieth century — the Holocaust and the birth of the State of Israel — were added to the Jewish religious calendar. Judaism is historical because it is not only about an individual relationship with God, but also about being a people. When we speak of our people, we do not mean only those Jews living today, but also those Jews who came before us and those who will come after us. Each convert becomes the son or daughter of Abraham and Sarah, thus joining our family tree that connects them with the history of our people.

Yet, we do ourselves a disservice when we learn only the "history" of the Bible and do not continue with our historical knowledge of the rest of our family. To understand ourselves fully as Jews requires a knowledge of our history from creation to the present day. Teaching history to our children adds a layer to their ritual lives. It helps them better understand where they came from and where they are going — developing a stronger Jewish identity along the way. When taught well, Jewish history allows each individual to form an emotional connection to the past and thus a stronger connection to Judaism. Learning about the struggles, choices, convictions, inventions, and artistic creations of the Jews who came before us can help our children travel the roads of their own Jewish lives in a more effective way. The big questions of history are the same questions we deal with today and will continue to deal with tomorrow. In learning from the past, we can better choose how to answer those questions for ourselves in the future.

Given that Jewish history is central to Jewish identity, we consider it vitally important for Jewish educational institutions to make studying the Jewish past an ongoing part of the curriculum. In this chapter, we strive to provide Jewish history teachers with theoretical ideas as well as practical suggestions about presenting the Jewish past to those living in the Jewish present. Teachers will find not only resources, such as examples of activities to be used in the classroom, but also a discussion about how people create histories of the past. We believe that successful teaching happens when the teacher is clear not only about the facts or events he/she is presenting, but also about his/her own ideas about those facts and events. Thus, borrowing from educator David Kobrin,[1] we have included at the end of each segment reflection questions to aid in your thinking about the perspective you bring, consciously or unconsciously, to the issues raised in that section. We hope you reflect on these issues as you read the chapter, but they may be most beneficial after you have taught a class or unit. Applying these questions to a specific experience will probably shed more light on how you approach the material than thinking about them in general terms.

Reflection Questions:

- Why have you chosen to teach Jewish history, rather than Hebrew, Torah, Rabbinics, or prayer?

- What do you find to be the most important reason for studying history?

- What do you want to convey to your students about why history is important?

WHAT DO WE MEAN BY "JEWISH HISTORY"?

The term "Jewish history" may seem self-evident, but the meaning varies depending on the community in which it is discussed. Your working definition of Jewish history — that is, the underlying assumptions in your teaching about what constitutes historical truth about the Jewish past — is usually influenced by your personal view and the philosophy of the institution in which you are teaching. Quality teaching requires personal reflection on the perspective a teacher passes on to his or her students. Therefore, this section examines two common perspectives on Jewish history, the sacred and the academic. This issue is particularly sensitive for those teaching the biblical and Rabbinic periods.

Sacred History

Sacred history is the traditional, Jewish religious interpretation of historical events. It is the story Jews have always told themselves about the past through their sacred texts (the Tanach, Talmud,

and other religious writings), as well as oral traditions passed down over the centuries. Observant Jews have understood their history as true because the sacred texts are authoritative for them as Jews. From a religious perspective, archaeological evidence is not needed to prove that miracles happened, or that a Patriarch actually existed. Instead, the central relevant part of history from a sacred perspective is the relationship between God and the Jews, and how that relationship played out over the centuries. This perspective on Jewish history has shaped both the experience of Jews and the Jewish response to historical events.

Academic History

The academic approach to history is not concerned with religious truths, but rather historical accuracy as defined by the discipline of historical criticism (the application of scientific methods to the study of the past). The historian relies on a range of materials to determine historical truth: religious texts (analyzed as historical, not sacred, literature), ritual objects, archeological ruins, artifacts, and documents of all types written by Jews and non-Jews of the time period under study (e.g., contracts, diaries, inscriptions). Historical records are not taken at face value; they are authoritative only insofar as they can be authenticated through scientific methods of analysis. In addition, the academic historian does not accept God as a legitimate actor in human history. A variety of factors might explain a historical event, but God is not one of them.

Both sacred history and academic history contain truths that we need for self-reflection as a people and as individuals. The sacred history of the Jews has shaped the Jewish experience and kept Judaism and Jews alive for over five thousand years. But, if we teach Jewish history only from a sacred perspective, we deprive our students of the skills to analyze Jewish life in the past and in the present. Conversely, teaching only the academic approach takes away a core purpose of Jewish education: to pass on Jewish thought and traditions. While a critical historical analysis of the political, economic, and social realities of the Jewish past is indispensable for understanding contemporary Jewish life, we lose our essence as a people if we do not teach our children the sacred perspective as well.

---

[1] David Kobrin, *Beyond the Textbook: Teaching History Using Documents and Primary Sources* (Portsmouth, NH: Heinemann, 1996).

Reflection Questions:

- How much of your understanding of Jewish history incorporates "sacred history"? How much includes the academic approach?

- What part does God play in your understanding of Jewish history? How does that affect how you teach Jewish history?

- In what Jewish environment are you teaching? How does that influence your approach to God and Tanach?

DEVELOPMENTAL ISSUES IN TEACHING JEWISH HISTORY

The study of history requires that the student learn not just a specific subject matter, but also certain skills and ways of thinking. A student historian[2] needs to be able to: differentiate between the past and present; put things in chronological order; formulate questions to direct their investigations; conduct interviews; interpret data from written and visual sources such as pictures, graphs, and actual objects; develop hypotheses; organize data into historical narratives; and suggest alternative courses of action. So the question arises, at what age are students able to learn history and develop historical skills? The National Standards for History, guidelines for secular schools published by the National Center for History in the Schools, indicates that children as young as five or six can begin to understand history and develop some of these historical skills.[3] As with any kind of learning, history needs to be approached at the child's developmental level. While it is beyond the scope of this chapter to provide an in-depth discussion of child development, we will address briefly the issue of how history and historical skills can be taught at different ages, particularly to younger children.

Between the ages of five and seven, young children are still fairly egocentric. They see things mainly from their point of view and are focused primarily on their own experience. The family is very important to them, and they have active imaginations. They are not ready for abstract thinking, and ideas need to be presented in very concrete ways. However, this does not mean that young children cannot think historically, given the right environment. According to the National History Standards, teachers in Grades K-2 should give their students opportunities to learn to differentiate between broad categories of time such as "long ago," "yesterday," and "tomorrow"; to develop questions to guide their own interests; and to begin to understand the feelings of historical characters.[4] The family, myths, legends, and historical stories can become the focus of developing historical skills at this age because of where the child is developmentally. Activities at this age that could help encourage Jewish historical thinking skills might focus on Bible stories. For example, first or second graders might spend time learning stories about Abraham, Isaac, Jacob, Sarah, Rebekah, Rachel, and Leah. While learning these stories, the teacher might have the students focus on how the characters in the stories felt. The students might also come up with questions they have about the story to which the teacher can help them find the answers. Another activity might include having the students draw pictures showing scenes from the stories they have learned and putting the pictures in chronological order. This would help reinforce the concept of chronology in that the stories are about generations of one family to which we are also related.

From the age of eight through ten, children's thinking becomes less egocentric. Now they can see issues from different perspectives. While abstract thought is still difficult, given concrete situations, children at this age can come up with alternative solutions. For this reason, in Grades 3-4 students, are ready to think about areas beyond themselves and the family, and the focus of historical study can move to the local community and state where the children live. Stories are still a good resource but now the teacher may want to shift to biographies and fictional historical accounts. According

---

[2]Ibid. We borrow the term "student historian" from Kobrin, whose use of it reflects his pedagogical approach to teaching history: that students truly learn history by doing history, by becoming historians themselves. This means they generate their own questions, do their own research, and create historical narratives based on primary sources. Such an in-depth approach to history is rarely possible in Jewish educational settings, but striving toward this level of involvement in the process of creating

history should still be a goal.

[3]"Developing Standards in History for Students in Grades K-4." *National Standards for History Grades K-4: Expanding Children's World in Time and Space* (19 Oct. 2001), 2, http://w3.iac.net./~pfilio/stand.txt.

[4]Ibid, 7.

to the National History Standards, teachers in Grades 3-4 should give their students the opportunities to learn to construct and interpret time lines, empathize with characters from the past, compare different historical sources, and develop alternative ways to resolve a dilemma.[5] A Jewish history unit for this age group might focus on the local Jewish community. As part of this unit, students could conduct oral histories of local residents and design a museum exhibit after their research is done.

Beginning around the age of 11, some children start to think abstractly and deal with such conceptual principles as liberty, justice, and love. As children enter the adolescent years, they are concerned about their own future and their place in the world. Therefore, the teaching of history in upper grades continues to follow the developmental abilities of the child by moving further out into the world and dealing with some of the more abstract issues of Jewish history, such as morality, faith, and justice. Students in this age group can use primary sources to develop historical narratives of their own, taking positions on issues of the past.[6] Jewish history activities for this age group might include putting on trial historical characters, such as Moses or King David, or analyzing historical documents related to American Jewish history.

Reflection Questions:

- How does your understanding of a child's intellectual, moral, and faith development[7] influence how you teach your students?

- What ages are you teaching? Based on the above descriptions, how might you incorporate historical thinking into your lessons?

TEACHING JEWISH HISTORY

Once we recognize that history can be understood from a very young age, two questions arise: What elements in the study of Jewish history are the most important to convey? And, how do students learn most effectively? The two issues are linked because *what* you choose to teach in any given topic (which facts, issues, and ideas you will present) shapes *how* you choose to teach the material (the assignments, readings, activities you include). Our approach to these questions is grounded in the concept that history as a discipline revolves around "big ideas,"[8] underlying issues that give meaning to the facts of the past (people, dates, events), and that the most effective learning happens when students are actively pursuing the answers to the questions of history. In short, we consider the most effective learning to occur within a multilayered approach that organizes units of study around big ideas and allows students to encounter the evidence of history directly.

Based on this model, there are three elements to consider when teaching any unit of Jewish history:

1. What are the big ideas of the period of history in question?

2. What historical evidence is available for the students to engage with directly?

3. What activities enrich the encounter with historical sources and allow students actively to create their own responses and analyses?

This section will examine each of these unit elements, showing how they work together and complement each other. We begin with a vignette.

While Mrs. Adler has taught at the Temple Shalom religious school in California for three years, this is the first year she is teaching American Jewish history to fifth graders. Over the summer, she reviewed the textbook, which primarily examines the experience of Jewish immigrants on the east coast. Mrs. Adler knows that many of her students have family living back east, but otherwise it is a distant place to most of them. So, an American Jewish history unit concentrating on the Northeast probably will not capture the imagination of her California students.

Therefore, Mrs. Adler chooses specifically to focus on the experience of American Jews in the west during the late nineteenth and early twentieth centuries. The textbook discusses this topic in only two paragraphs, so she sets aside the book and searches the synagogue library and the Internet for

---

[5]Ibid.

[6]Ibid.

[7]For more information on moral and faith development, see Chapter 11, "Developmental Psychology" by Roberta Louis

Goodman, pp. 85-108 in this Handbook.

[8]Grant Wiggins and Jay McTighe, *Understanding by Design* (Alexandria, VA: Association for Supervision and Curriculum Development, 1998).

other possible sources. As she researches, Mrs. Adler realizes that there are many ways she could approach her topic. She could focus on the dates and places of famous events or the biographies of famous Jews such as Levi Strauss. But the more research that Mrs. Adler does, the more she realizes that many of the dilemmas Jews faced a century ago are related to those her students currently experience, and are almost exactly the same as those they will one day encounter. Some of these include whether or not to move, whether or not to marry a Jewish spouse, where to find a Jewish spouse, and how to practice Judaism in communities in which there are very few Jews. And so Mrs. Adler selects the core concept of "choices," and creates the following "big idea" statement: The choices made by the Jewish men and women who moved west, and many others like them, would change their lives and the lives of those who came after them. Each lesson in her unit will contribute to the unpacking of this statement. By the end of the unit, her students will be able to defend or critique this big idea.[9]

Mrs. Adler begins the unit by asking, "How many of you have ever moved to a new city?" The class works together to make a list of reasons why people might decide to move elsewhere. When possible, she highlights issues that will be relevant in the historical material. In the next few classes, Mrs. Adler introduces primary sources — reproductions of advertisements and articles out of period newspapers, letters written by Jews in the west to their families in the overcrowded cities back east — as a way of examining why American Jews chose to move west. The students read these materials and analyze them using questions Mrs. Adler provides. They make a list of why Jews chose to move out west. As background, they watch a video about this topic and read a short piece Mrs. Adler found in a collection of essays.

After the presentation of the background material and the analysis of the primary sources, a process that has taken several weeks, Mrs. Adler returns to the very first activity in the unit. She asks the class to compare their own lists of reasons for moving with the historical reasons for why Jews actually did move. She poses several questions: What are the similarities and differences between

the two lists? What different historical realities influenced each group's decision to move? Which of the reasons for moving on the two lists were influenced by the participants being Jewish? Which of the reasons were influenced by the fact that the Jews were American? Mrs. Adler concluded this unit with a discussion of what defines "Jewish" and "American" values, asking her students to reflect on to what extent they separate the two in their lives.

ELEMENT #1: THE BIG IDEAS

In the above vignette, Mrs. Adler's topic is Jews in the American west in the nineteenth and twentieth centuries. Within that topic, she chooses one core concept, an axis around which to organize the important names, dates, and events of that period. By highlighting the theme of the choices Jews made in their journey out west, she is able to raise several levels of questions for her students. Some of the questions relate to their current lives (e.g., what dilemmas do they presently face?). Some relate to questions they will encounter later in life (e.g., should they marry a Jew?). Some relate to the material itself (e.g., why did Jews move west?). These questions allow students to explore the topic on a variety of levels.

"Big ideas" are sophisticated ideas that lie at the heart of any academic discipline; they are the perennial ideas that make the discipline intriguing. Facts alone do not generate discussion; big ideas do. For example, a traditional approach to teaching Mrs. Adler's unit might (1) follow the textbook, which barely covers the experience of the Jewish move west; (2) leave the textbook, but focus on the time line of the Jewish move to the west, including how they managed the move, what life was like for Jews when they arrived and even how little the history of the Jews of the west is understood today — all of the "hard data." Mrs. Adler, however, chose a big idea as the organizing principle of the unit, a statement to be explored on many levels. Her big idea was: The choices made by the Jewish men and women who moved west, and many others like them, would change their lives and the lives of those who came after them. To "unpack" this statement, to truly understand it, Mrs. Adler's students

---

[9]For more on "big ideas" and Understanding by Design, see Chapter 24, "Curriculum Planning: A Model for Understanding"

by Nachama Skolnik Moskowitz, pp. 278-291 in this Handbook.

will have to explore: (1) What dilemmas did the Jews of that period face, and why? (2) What choices did they make in the face of those dilemmas? (3) Why did they make those particular choices? (4) How did these choices affect the lives of the people in the time period? (5) How did these choices affect future generations? (6) Do Mrs. Adler's students feel the effects of these choices in their lives today? Through this complex series of questions — questions that involve facts as well as meaning — big ideas connect students to the past by giving them the opportunity to explore issues that are also relevant for them in the present.

A big idea is usually expressed in the form of a statement, as in the previous paragraph. One way to develop a big idea for your unit might be to start with a core concept, a theme in Jewish history, and expand it to a big idea, a thesis. Some of the core concepts found in Jewish history include, but are not limited to, Covenant, building Jewish community, assimilation/adaptation, exile/Diaspora, personal responsibility and social justice, anti-Semitism,[10] pluralism within the Jewish community, and personal choices. Start with a core concept and, in the process of course preparation, play around with it to create a statement that encourages several levels of discussion: about the details of the period, about the dilemmas Jews faced, and about changes in Jewish social, economic, political, or religious life that occurred as a result of the events. Consider, too, whatever parallels might exist between the Jews of the time period under discussion and the Jews in the classroom.

Concepts such as those listed above appear repetitively throughout the course of Jewish history, which means most of them are very relevant to today's North American Jewish youth. Basing your unit on a big idea shifts the attention from memorizing dates, names, and other facts, and instead emphasizes the dilemmas, struggles, and experiences of the Jewish people. History comes alive for students through an exploration of these experiences because they can relate to them.

When studying American Jewish history, I want the students to learn also about the history of the local Jewish community. For those who have parents who grew up in the community, I have them ask the parents questions about religious school, services, Bar and Bat Mitzvah, Confirmation, and similar topics. The culmination of the history unit is interviewing a senior member of the congregation. The students spend a full session preparing for the interview by thinking of questions and also by being sensitized to working with seniors. The interviews are videotaped and then placed in the synagogue library as an oral history project contributed by the religious school.

(Rabbi David Feder, Morgantown, West Virginia)

ELEMENT #2: AVAILABLE HISTORICAL EVIDENCE

Teaching through big ideas enables students to see the big picture, but that larger perspective can be vague and sometimes confusing if students are not offered the opportunity to explore those ideas in a specific context. Thus, while big ideas serve as organizing principles of any given period of Jewish history, primary sources provide the details — the who, what, where, when, why — that make those concepts come to life. Without big ideas, history can all too easily be reduced to a list of names, dates, and facts. Without primary sources, big ideas are ephemeral and sometimes difficult to understand.

What falls under the category of "primary source"? A primary source is any object or written document from the time period under study — historical evidence that students can experience directly. Secondary sources are scholarly works that interpret primary sources.[11] Some of the primary sources that you might use in a lesson include: artifacts, diaries, contracts, sacred texts, paintings, sculpture, audio and videotapes (of an historical

---

[10]Anti-Semitism sometimes emerges as the main theme in teaching Jewish history — intentionally or unintentionally. Indeed, particularly when teaching the medieval or modern periods it is hard not to spend precious class time jumping from one anti-Semitic outrage to another. When overused, the theme of anti-Semitism can be counterproductive. We recommend try-

ing to ensure that your curriculum or unit on Jewish history emphasizes the rich and diverse past we have as Jews, spending time on anti-Semitism in small doses.

[11]Monica Edinger, *Seeking History: Teaching with Primary Sources in Grades 4-6* (Portsmouth, NH: Heinemann, 2000), 25.

event), to name just a few. Some of the secondary sources you might use are textbooks, articles, scholarly writings about the period of history you are teaching, and documentaries.

The ways in which primary sources are used in the classroom depends, of course, on the age of the students. For younger students, primary sources might include pictures, artifacts, and artwork, while older children, teens, and adults are able also to read and analyze historical documents.[12] No matter what primary sources are chosen for the lesson, there are several important steps to follow when using them. A good general rule to follow is that a primary source is only as good as its setup and analysis. That is to say, by itself a primary source teaches very little. With the proper presentation, both before and after actually encountering the primary source itself, an object or document can change the way students think of history. Below are some general guidelines to follow when using primary sources.

1. *Provide context for the primary source* - Young children, teenagers, and adults always need a context in which to place the primary source they are about to encounter. Some background considerations might include: Where did you get the object? Who is the author of the document — not just a name, but what role did he/she play in history and why are we reading this piece? Clear introductions give students the tools they need to analyze the object or document on their own.

2. *Work in small groups* - While the teacher-student ratio dictates to what extent small group work is possible with younger children, with older students we highly recommend working in pairs with a primary source, whenever possible. This allows each student to "wrestle" with the problems presented through objects or documents, actively engaging in understanding history. The teacher facilitates group work by checking in with each group, answering questions, and ensuring that students are on the right track.

3. *Provide basic questions* - Students usually do not know what to look for when presented with a primary source. Guideline questions serve two purposes: they help the students get as much as possible out of the document or artifact and they train students how to read a primary source. Clearly, younger children will need the guidance of the teacher. But older children and adults also need prompting. With objects or documents, the goal of the basic questions is to ensure that each student understands the fundamentals of the primary source. Here are some basic questions to be answered:

Objects as Primary Sources:

- What is the object?

- What is the object used for?

Documents as Primary Sources:

- Who wrote the document? When was it written? For whom was it written?

- Are there any words in the document you don't understand? (Look them up.)

- What are the main points of the document? (It is crucial that every student in the class is clear about the basic meaning of the document — even a story — before proceeding to any analysis of it.)

4. *Provide Analysis Questions* - "Students don't learn from experiences upon which they don't reflect."[13] Encountering a primary source will have only a temporary impact unless the students reflect on its meaning in a larger context. Thus, after every student in the class is clear about the basic meaning of the primary source, a critical part of the educational process is for them to analyze the object or document. The questions guiding them in their analysis will, of course, be determined by the big idea you choose and the reasons you selected the primary source in the first place. Here are a few analysis questions to consider:

---

[12]This section emphasizes the structure of the primary source activity as a way to help students analyze objects and documents. Students with learning disabilities will need further assistance, particularly with documents that might contain difficult language. Reading the text out loud, providing a vocabulary list, and continuous reinforcement of the context in which the text is being read might be helpful.

[13]"Better Endings for Classes and Courses," *ClassWise* (May/June 1997).

Objects as Primary Sources:

- What can the object tell us about the life of the person that used it? What can it tell about the times in which it was used?

- How can the above information help us understand the big idea of this unit? (Phrase this question in terms understandable to the students.)

Documents as Primary Sources:

- Why was the document written? (Is the author trying to solve a problem? Is the author trying to present a viewpoint on an important issue?)

- Is the author a reliable source on the issue at hand? How can you find out?

- Are there any contradictions in the document? If so, why do you think they are there?

- In what way(s) does this document shed light on the larger issues being discussed in this unit?

5. *Post-analysis* - In the best of circumstances, students often have a hard time recalling what they encountered in a previous class. So, in order to maximize the learning from a primary source, be very aware of the time and end a few minutes early in order to wrap up the day's work (yes, even if they are going to continue with the document or object the very next day). Whether a brief verbal summary that ties together what the students have learned so far, or an activity in which students themselves pull together the various elements of the lesson, every examination of a primary source should include some sort of concluding reflective exercise.

If you have not used primary sources before, you may be surprised at how much time it takes to elucidate the basic meanings of the texts (depending on their difficulty). This may be due to several factors: (1) Students are not used to engaging actively with the material — they are usually told what is important to know; (2) If reading primary sources from earlier periods of history, the language of the texts is sometimes difficult and the ideas may be quite foreign; (3) Part of the process of using primary sources includes teaching students

how to think like historians — this does not come naturally. For all of these reasons, successful use of primary sources always includes appropriate setup and concluding discussions or activities.

Reflection Questions:

- How does your definition of history influence *how* you teach history (methods, materials, resources)?

- Which concepts do you think are most important in the study of Jewish history, and why?

- In what ways have historical artifacts and documents in museums or historical sites helped you connect to the past? How would you recreate that connection in the classroom?

ELEMENT #3: ACTIVITIES THAT ENRICH THE ENCOUNTER WITH HISTORICAL SOURCES AND ALLOW STUDENTS TO CREATE THEIR OWN RESPONSES AND ANALYSES

Small groups of sixth graders moved around the exhibit on the Jews of Yemen. Each student had a clipboard and pencil and was writing down answers to questions on a worksheet as they looked at display cases and read labels. Mr. Rothman moved among the groups, answering questions and helping the students with unfamiliar vocabulary. The students were trying to determine what their own lives might be like if they had lived in Yemen rather than twenty-first century America. What would be the same? What would be different? How would they have learned about Judaism? Where would they have prayed? What would that structure look like? These were just a few of the questions the students had come up with before the trip. They already knew that they would be using the answers to these questions that they found at the exhibit, plus information from their textbook back in the classroom, to write two to three journal entries for a Yemenite Jew of their own age. They would also compare this Jewish community with Jewish communities in other parts of the world that they had already studied.

In science classes, students do lab work that recreates actual scientific methods. They learn by doing and become scientists themselves in the process. Thanks to new and exciting theories about how students learn and retain information, teachers in many disciplines, including history, are increasingly incorporating into their lessons activities that engage students on the experiential level and allow them to enter into the same processes used by professionals in the field. As with lab work, experiential activities teach nothing in and of themselves. To be effective — more than a fun time — they need to be part of a very structured unit or lesson plan and clearly tied to big ideas. Activities as learning tools allow students to build their own knowledge from the experience, but only when they are properly guided. When well constructed, activities tap into student creativity, helping them retain their learning longer. Given the opportunity to be actively engaged in the learning process, students find added relevance and meaning in the Jewish past. Below are a few suggested activities.

Field Trips

Purpose of this activity: To take the learning out of the classroom, to utilize local resources for the teaching of Jewish history, to provide links between students and local Jewish history.

Goal of this activity: At the conclusion of a field trip activity, students should be able to (1) describe and discuss the site or objects they visited, (2) connect information about the site or objects studied in light of the historical background studied in class, (3) produce a reflection piece about their experience.

Depending on your community, there may be museums, historic synagogues, Jewish cemeteries, or other local sites that might add to a unit on American (Canadian) or local Jewish history. These sites offer opportunities for students to use historical objects (headstones, buildings, ritual objects, etc.) to learn about history and/or experience in the same way that historians use historical materials to teach about the past. Wherever you are taking your students, it is important to spend time introducing the trip before you go and following up on the trip when you return to class so that your students get the most out of the trip. Field trips are appropriate for all ages. Follow-up projects will differ depending on the age of the students. Some of these are described briefly below.

Some Preparations before the Trip

- Create in-class lessons that will help the students put what they will see on the field trip in a larger context.

- Provide information about what the students will see, especially anything you think will be of special interest to them. Some museums will supply slides, catalogs, or written material that you can use with your class before your visit.

- Give the students things to look for or questions to think about while they are on a trip. This can be done through a student activity sheet that students work on during the trip.

Some Wrap-Up Ideas for the Classroom

Here are some suggestions for processing the field trip when you return to the classroom.

- Ask students to share highlights from the trip, verbally or in writing. These might form the basis for writing thank-you notes to anyone who helped during the visit.

- Discuss the questions students were supposed to think about during the visit, or go over information collected on their student activity sheets.

- Develop a project that uses information from the trip.

Creating Your Own Museum

Purpose of this activity: To engage students in the research, construction, and presentation of history.

Goal of this activity: To provide students with the opportunity to: (1) research a time, person, or event in Jewish history; (2) make decisions regarding how history is understood through its presentation; (3) use their creativity to tell a story.

One of the many things that historians do is to use objects, documents, and art to tell a story. Student historians can also develop museum exhibits in their classroom or for the whole school. Give the class a topic to research that will become the basis for the exhibit. After some general reading on the subject has been done, possibly from the textbook, have the class generate ideas for different aspects of the topic to be covered in its exhibit. Break the class into small groups, with each assigned the task of researching a particular aspect of the main topic. Groups might use the Internet, books in the library, primary documents that have been prepared by the teacher, and/or objects that they have at home or can be found in the synagogue. After a certain amount of research has been done, each group should choose items to put in their part of the exhibit. As a class, you might want to discuss the order of the exhibit, legends, etc. Exhibits can range from the traditional poster board displays or tri-fold science project boards to costumed student presentations to interactive web sites created by the students.

Exhibits are appropriate for students in third grade and up. The younger the children, the more direction and structure will be needed. With younger grades the teacher may want to have packets of materials available for the children to use in their research. Older children can develop their own research questions and determine where best to find the information.

As part of a unit on "The Holocaust: Resistance and Rescuers," our sixth, seventh, and eighth grade students wrote their own skit about life within the walls of Warsaw Ghetto. This was to focus on some of the forms of resistance, both passive and active, that took place in those circumstances. Prior to putting on their skit, which was replete with homemade sets and costumes, they created an "underground newspaper," by writing "articles" and notes on paper torn from grocery bags. These "newspapers" were secretly passed throughout our school, with many of our students adding their own names or messages to them. Our school snack was "stolen" from the "enemy" and secretly distributed, quietly blessed, and hurriedly eaten or hidden away for later. Many lessons were learned from this unit. Among them was that our fellow Jews did not all give up hope or go without fighting "like sheep to the slaughter," but that there were those who fought, if not with weapons, then with their wits, or through their determination to remain human in a place where humanity was forgotten.

(Carol Cohn, Orlando, Florida)

Reenactments

Purpose of this activity: To provide students with experiential learning about an event or time in Jewish history.

Goal of this activity: For students to understand the emotions, struggles, and dilemmas of Jews during a particular moment in Jewish history.

One way to illustrate a big idea or core concept is for students to relive part of the experience. This experience can either become the basis for discussion, further study or the culmination of what the students have been studying. Reenactments are often used in camp settings (see the scenario described at the beginning of the chapter). However, they also can be done in a classroom setting. For example, Julia remembers how every year for Shavuot she and the students in the religious school became a group of wandering Jews following Moses to Mount Sinai. One of the teachers in costume played Moses, leading the students to Mount Sinai (the Rabbi's house a quarter of a mile from the synagogue). Once there, Moses climbed Mount Sinai (the back porch), while students built a golden calf (in the back yard, below). To this day, it is one of her most vivid religious school memories.

Reenactments often take a lot of planning on the teacher's part and may require additional people to carry out in the classroom. The main idea is for the children to experience something akin to the actual historical event. It could be following Moses to Mount Sinai, arriving at Ellis Island, or being a pioneer on an early Israeli *kibbutz*. It is hard to generalize about how to plan such activities because they vary so much according to the time and place you are trying to recreate, but here are some things to consider when planning your reenactment:

1. *Before you begin* - determine whether the reenactment will be used as the introduction to a new unit or the conclusion. If used as an introduction, think about what activities will be used to lead away from the reenactment into further study. If used as a conclusion, consider what information students will need to already have to get the most out of the reenactment. Either way, it is important to remember that a reenactment works best if it is not left to stand on its own and relates to the core concept or big idea you are teaching.

2. *Research the event* - Before deciding what to reenact, read books, check web sites, and review videotapes to find out as much about what happened as possible. Take special note of challenges or conflicts involved in the situation. Incorporating these will make your reenactment more interesting and can give rise to follow-up discussion and study.

3. *Plan the activities* - Once familiar with the information surrounding the event or time period, decide which aspects to recreate. These decisions should be based on how the experience can further support the core concept or big idea being taught, as well as taking into consideration issues of time, space, and personnel.

4. *Develop materials and find props* - Some of the activities will require worksheets or props to be used by the students or by the facilitators.

5. *Find people to portray historical characters or be group leaders* - One advantage to doing reenactments in camp is that there are usually lots of counselors around to take on different roles. In a school setting, you may need to call upon adult volunteers or parents. Since your volunteers may not be familiar with the events being reenacted, it is important to provide them with background information ahead of time.

6. *Conclusion* - While reenactments are likely to be memorable events simply because they are a change from the ordinary school or camp routine, what the students learn from them also depends on what happens when the reenactment is over. Have the students reflect on the reenactment and come up with questions that the experience raised for them. Have them think about things about which they would like to know more. Then, brainstorm ideas of where they could find answers to their questions. This can lead to further study during the rest of the unit. In the reenactment described at the beginning of the chapter, the campers might have wanted to

know more about what happened to Ethiopian Jews when they arrived in Israel. To answer this question, a speaker could be brought in to talk to the campers, or the campers might have written letters to Ethiopian Jews in Israel, or watched a video.

Object Reading or "You Are the Detective"[14]

Purpose of this activity: To engage students in the process of analyzing objects and pictures to create an understanding of the past.

Goal of this activity: Children should leave this activity understanding: (1) that people make assumptions based on what they see, (2) how to use objects and pictures to put together a story of the past, (3) history is constructed by people.

As with the other activities, this one works best when part of a larger unit, particularly as an introduction or conclusion. Be sure you set up the activity by providing students with the background information they will need to make appropriate analyses. Invite a guest — perhaps an older member of the community, a well respected local Jewish leader, or a famous Jewish person connected to the school — and ask him or her to bring a bag or box of objects and pictures that represent important parts of their lives. The students should not be told very much about the guest. Instead, they are to examine the contents of the bag or box — either in small groups or as a group, guided by the teacher. The immediate goal is for the students to ascertain what they can about the person who brought in the objects.

By choosing objects that are not obvious to the children, the teacher and guest deliberately challenge the students to question their assumptions. For instance, if the guest brings in a picture of herself with some children, students might reasonably assume the guest has children and it is they who are in the picture. However, if the picture actually shows the guest with her nieces and nephews, or the children of a close friend, students learn to question their assumptions about what they see. Either through discussion or some other activity, the class comes to conclusions about who the guest is (likes, dislikes, religion, marital status, sense of

---

[14]Lauren Granite received this idea in a personal telephone communication with Leslie Mirchin, formerly of the Jewish Women's Archive, in February, 2000.

humor — whatever is indicated by the objects). Next, get the children to reflect on what they can and cannot learn about a person through a random collection of objects. Ask them to draw or list what they would want to put in a bag so someone could learn about them. (What objects might convey the most information, if there was no one to explain them? What pictures would tell a story that is essential to who they are in the world and what is important to them?) Alternatively, bring in a large picture or painting of an event or moment in Jewish history and have students analyze what they can learn from this picture. Particularly if you have already studied a period of history that the picture reflects, this will reinforce the analytical skills of the initial part of the activity. The long-term success of this activity depends on the conclusion you set up for the students. A concluding exercise that allows students directly to discuss or analyze their experience of constructing history can be combined with a creative concluding exercise. Creative ideas might include writing a diary entry of the people seen in the photograph or painting or, for older students, creating a skit based on what they learned from the painting or picture.

Trials

Purpose of this activity: To engage students actively in investigating and understanding a particular historical figure and/or event in history.

Goal of this activity: At the end of this activity, students should: (1) understand the moral issues involved in the event under investigation, (2) have developed the skills involved in building an argument, (3) understand the historical context relevant to the event or person under question.

Putting a historical figure on trial for his or her actions engages students in learning about a particular event, person, and/or period of history. Trials are probably most useful for students in the sixth grade or older. Examples of historical figures to put on trial would be: Moses (for killing the Egyptian), King David (for stealing Bathsheba from Uriah and having Uriah killed), Josephus (as a traitor to the Jews). The students often get carried away with the dramatics, but creating a structure for the preparation ensures there is solid educational value to this activity. There are many ways in which you might organize the preparation for the trial. Below is one example used by Lauren Granite with a sixth grade supplementary school class studying the stories of King David.

1. *Learning the material* - A successful trial is grounded in a thorough understanding of the facts, so the first step is for students to read texts, watch a video, or otherwise learn the material. Consider having the students read the stories or primary sources in small groups, followed by questions that will get them thinking about the key issues of the trial. Follow their independent learning with a class discussion to make certain that every student is clear about the main issues and facts.

2. *Building a prosecution and defense* - Divide the class into two groups, assigning one to be the prosecution and the other the defense. Each group must decide how to build their case and, in the process, what witnesses they want to bring to the stand. (Supervise this process to ensure that there is not more than one student playing each character.) The students must not only think through how to argue their side of the case, but also determine what witnesses they need to support their argument. For greater creativity, allow them to include characters that might not clearly be part of the story as told in the sources. For example, when Lauren's class put King David on trial for adultery with Bathsheba and the death of Uriah, her husband, one student wanted to play Michal, David's first wife, who is not at all mentioned in the Bible in the context of the David and Bathsheba story. The student beautifully reflected on the life of Michal in her testimony, providing the defense with an important character reference for King David.

3. *Preliminary questions* - An optional element, preliminary questions help in trial preparation by allowing everyone to hear what each witness will say at the trial. Both prosecution and defense ask the same number of questions, and the witnesses must be warned that they cannot change their testimony between the preliminary questioning and the trial. Each side should then have more time to tighten their arguments.

4. *The trial* - Invite people from outside of the class to be the jury. The teacher or some other authority figure can be the judge to ensure the

trial keeps moving and that order prevails. Encouraging appropriate costumes for all students lends excitement to the activity.

5. *Wrap-up* - Ask students to write some sort of reflection statement in the character of the person they portrayed (prosecutor, defense lawyer, character in the story), or work in small groups to answer a few analytic questions about the trial. Whatever activity you create, the students must reflect on the larger issues and themes that emerged in the course of the trial.

Oral Histories

Purpose of this activity: To engage students actively in the process of investigating history.

Goal of this activity: At the end of this activity, students should: (1) understand the broader historical context of the life of the person they interviewed, (2) have improved their ability to ask pertinent questions of a source, (3) have a clearer understanding of his or her own family's history (if the student interviewed a relative).

Within the context of Jewish education, oral histories are usually interviews of older people conducted by students as a way of learning about the immigrant or Holocaust experiences of the older generations. Also, oral histories are often used as a way for a student to understand his or her family's history and Jewish heritage. We want to emphasize the importance of placing them in a larger historical context. While conducting an oral history may be in and of itself an enriching experience for the child, the educational impact is greatly increased if the student is encouraged to make connections between what he/she learned in the interview and the broader themes of the historical period under question. It is not enough for Rivka to interview her grandmother who emigrated from Czechoslovakia to the United States at the beginning of the twentieth century. We must teach Rivka that her grandmother's experience was part of a larger trend that took place at that time and why. Rivka must learn to ask questions about why her grandmother settled in Ohio instead of New York and, perhaps, to hear the story of someone who went to New York at the same time.

Reflection Questions:

- What are some of the most memorable learning experiences you have had? What made them memorable?

- What do you know about your students' interests outside the classroom? How can you use those in your lessons?

- When your students leave your classroom on any given day, what do you want them to have learned from the lesson?

RESOURCES FOR TEACHING JEWISH HISTORY

The suggestions in this chapter about how to teach Jewish history would be incomplete without at least a few suggestions as to where to find material to implement them. The local library and the Internet are probably the first stops for research; between these two you should be able to find anything from time lines and maps to online exhibits and the latest textbooks. For videos, local video stores, university libraries, central agencies for Jewish education, Jewish Community Centers, and synagogue libraries often have both documentary videos or DVDs (e.g., *Heritage: Civilization and the Jews*) and popular historical fiction (e.g., *Exodus*). Five to 15 minute segments can be shown to illustrate a particular period or issue. Computer software in the field of Jewish history is limited at the writing of this chapter — the only CD-ROM that provides an in-depth, historical critical look at Jewish history is the *Encyclopaedia Judaica*, and that is quite difficult reading, especially for children and teenagers.[15]

Depending on where you live, you may or may not have access to two important resources: a central agency for Jewish education and a local historical society. The former often have libraries, video collections, and curricula that are very helpful in putting together a class, a unit, or an entire year's curriculum; local historical societies are wonderful resources for documents or artifacts related to the history of the local Jewish community. If you live in an area with no central agency for Jewish education, a trip to the one in the city closest to you would be worthwhile.

---

[15]To check on any new software that might be available, we recommend two web sites that specialize in Judaic computer

programs: www.davka.com and www.jewishsoftware.com.

I think we need to keep in mind that especially for students in Grade 5 and up, we not only need to teach Jewish identity, but also to give our students a safe place for processing their evolving Jewish identities. My sixth grade class was studying the Holocaust. We were looking at early anti-Semitic propaganda and violence when one of the students spoke up about harassment at school. I stopped the class — made up of students from affluent suburbs — and asked if anyone else had experienced this. Quite a number of the students spoke up, and I decided to end my prepared lesson right there. I gave them time to talk about their experiences. I asked the class to help with possible solutions, and I used this opportunity to introduce them to some of the organizations in the Jewish community that are active in anti-prejudice work. I referred the most upset student to the Rabbi immediately, and I arranged for the Rabbi to come to the next class to talk about his work in the schools and communities on reducing prejudice. The Rabbi and I sent a letter home to the parents explaining what had happened that day, and letting them know that the Rabbi was available for further consultation. When we did return later to that day's lesson, I like to think that we did so in an atmosphere of security that made it easier for the students to examine the graphic historical material.

(Anne Johnston, New Haven, Connecticut)

CONCLUSION

In Jewish educational settings, teaching Jewish history is about teaching students to reflect on Jewish identity. The Jewish past is relevant to the Jewish present because in each period we find core concepts and big ideas that are still pertinent today. Questions about God, communal life, ethnic iden- tity, ethical choices, religious rituals, and spiritual ideas have been part of the Jewish landscape since the time of Abraham and Sarah. By "taking" students to periods of the Jewish past with primary sources, you enable them to reflect on the Jewish present and the dilemmas they face today. As you take the time to create lessons that actively engage students in the learning process, you open the door for them to continue asking critical and meaningful questions throughout their lives.

TEACHING CONSIDERATIONS

- History should not be about memorizing facts. Think of ways to make the people and experiences of the past real to your students.

- Take the time to delve into one period of history, even it means you eliminate other material.

- Use concepts that your students can relate to as jumping-off points for teaching about the past, and provide big ideas for them to explore and debate.

- Move from where your students are out into the wider world, bringing them with you as you go.

- A strong setup and conclusion are necessary for any activity to have an educational impact. Students must always reflect on what they have learned.

- When possible, allow students to debate or recreate historical dilemmas in the classroom.

- Use artifacts or primary sources to understand the topic at hand, allowing students to create the historical narrative themselves, rather than relying on a textbook.

- Utilize local resources for your lessons.

BIBLIOGRAPHY

General Reference Texts for Studying Jewish History

Ben-Sasson, H.H., ed. *A History of the Jewish People*. Cambridge, MA: Harvard University Press, 1985.

> This very detailed overview of the entire sweep of Jewish history is an excellent reference for teachers interested in understanding the context of a particular event or period of Jewish history. However, it is probably too dense for students.

Gilbert, Martin. *The Atlas of Jewish History*. New York: William Morrow and Co., Inc., 1992.

> A collection of maps depicting different periods and events in Jewish history, this small book is a terrific visual addition to any Judaica collection.

Gribetz, Judah; Edward L. Greenstein; and Regina Stein. *The Timetables of Jewish History: A Chronology of the Most Important People and Events in Jewish History*. New York: Touchstone, 1993.

> This text is a straightforward chronology of the entire span of Jewish history consisting entirely of timetables laid out side-by-side: general history, Jewish historical experiences, and culture based on location (e.g., Jews in North America).

Mansoor, Menahem. *Jewish History and Thought: An Introduction*. Jersey City, NJ: KTAV Publishing House, 1991.

> This very useful, easy reference for Jewish history teachers outlines the major events, historical periods, and lives of important figures in Jewish history. It is quite helpful for a quick overview or brushup on the major elements of the Jewish past.

Sachar, Howard M. *The Course of Modern Jewish History*. New York: Vintage Books. 1990.

> This is a very readable secondary source about modern Jewish history, perhaps best used in conjunction with primary sources.

Seltzer, Robert M. *Jewish People, Jewish Thought: The Jewish Experience in History*. New York: Macmillan Publishing Co., Inc., 1980.

Seltzer's excellent survey of Jewish history from the Bible to modernity not only focuses on the historical development of the Jewish experience, but also spends quite a bit of time on theological and philosophical developments in Jewish thought.

Primary Source Text Books

Marcus, Jacob Rader. *The Jew in the American World: A Source Book*. Detroit, MI: Wayne State University Press, 1996.

> A very thorough primary source book for American Jewish history, covering religious, political, and social documents regarding Jews in America from the Colonial period to the late twentieth century.

———. *The Jew in the Medieval World: A Source Book: 315-1791*. rev. ed. Cincinnati, OH: Hebrew Union College Press, 2000.

> An excellent collection of translated primary sources from the medieval period. Each source has a small introduction written by Marcus.

Mendes-Flohr, Paul, and Jehuda Reinharz, eds. *The Jew in the Modern World: A Documentary History*. New York: Oxford University Press, 1995.

> This large collection of primary sources covers the experiences of Jews in the modern world. Well organized, with an introduction to each section and notes for every document.

Schiffman, Lawrence H. *Texts and Traditions: A Source Reader for the Study of Second Temple and Rabbinic Judaism*. Hoboken, NJ: KTAV Publishing House, Inc., 1998.

> An extensive collection of primary sources from the Second Temple period and early Rabbinic Judaism, this book is designed to be a companion to Schiffman's text of the same period, *From Text To Tradition: A History of Second Temple and Rabbinic Judaism*.

Museums, Historical Societies and Archives

The American Jewish Historical Society
2 Thornton Road
Waltham, MA 02453
781-891-8110

and

15 West 16th Street
New York, NY 10011
212-294-6160
www.ajhs.org

Their web page provides links to other Jewish historical societies across the country that may be able to provide teachers with information about regional and local Jewish history.

Goldring/Woldenberg Institute of
Southern Jewish Life
PO Box 16528
Jackson, MS 39236
www.msje.org
601-362-6357

A basic informational web site for the Museum of the Southern Experience, the Goldring/ Woldenberg Institute of Southern Jewish life site provides information about the museum, its satellite locations, and its traveling exhibits. Materials may also be purchased from their online store.

The Jacob Rader Marcus Center of the American Jewish Archives
3101 Clifton Avenue
Cincinnati, OH 45220
www.huc.edu.aja
513-221-1875

The archive and its web page may be helpful in general background. The organization also houses the records of many Jewish organizations and might be helpful in locating information about the history of specific Jewish institutions in your community.

The Jewish Women's Archive
68 Harvard St.
Brookline, MA 02445
www.jwa.org
617-232-2258

The Jewish Women's Archive (JWA) researches, creates archives for and educates about the history of Jewish women in North America. This web site offers a Virtual Archive, Exhibits, and a Resources link which includes activities and lessons about the history of Jewish women created by educators around the country. Both as an organization and a web site, the JWA is an excellent resource for anyone interested in teaching Jewish women's history.

The Library of Congress
101 Independence Ave., S.E.
Washington, D.C. 20540
www.loc.gov
202-707-5000

While not a specifically Jewish web site, the Library of Congress site can provide access to Jewish primary sources in their collection and other collections. Written documents, illustrations, personal papers, and posters can be accessed. In some cases, reproductions or microfilm can be ordered. The site also offers the "America's Library" for kids and an online version of many of the library's exhibits.

National Archives and Research Administration
700 Pennsylvania Ave., N.W.
Washington, D.C. 20408
www.nara.gov
800-234-8861

NARA is not as user-friendly as some sites. The materials here are of limited use in the Jewish history classroom, but the examples of teacher materials can be used as models for Jewish history teaching. The most useful part of this site is the "Digital Classroom," where teachers can learn about using primary sources and access lesson materials to use in their classroom. These American history lessons include background material, original documents, and teaching activities.

CHAPTER 37

Engaging with Israel

Sally Klein-Katz and Paul Liptz

INTRODUCTION

*I*n a Jewish school in Philadelphia, 70 second grade pupils were given the following assignment: "When you go home from school today, you will find out that your family received free tickets for a three-week trip to Israel. How would you plan your family's itinerary?" The children worked out the whole program based on their life experiences: listening to family speaking about Israel, older siblings' Israel visits, pictures on the walls of the school, visits to Israel by a few of them, and loads of imagination. The teachers were speechless with tears in their eyes as they realized Israel was truly a part of the consciousness of these young students.

Israel is part of the lexicon of *Am Yisrael*, the Jewish People. However, it is complicated to study and teach a country, a holy landscape, an ancient narrative, and a modern society complete with language, symbols, politics, daily news, heroes, and ordinary people. If we approach Israel in the classroom as a course in sociology or social studies, we miss its *neshamah*, its soul. If we assume a connection between our students and Israel — the Land, people, and modern state — then we could be in for a disappointing surprise. So how shall we proceed when trying to establish meaningful connections between an individual and the Jewish homeland?

GLOBAL JEWISH MALL

Many Jewish educators speak of the "Jewish bookshelf" as a metaphor for the requisite Jewish knowledge base. A more apt metaphor in this age of consumerism is that of a shopping mall. It highlights the differences between cognitively teaching about and affectively engaging with. It points to freedom of choice and exploration of individual interests. Interacting with Israel is richly diverse and potent:

- if the ultimate goal is to cultivate excitement, passion, and commitment in our students as Jews throughout their lives.

- if we are looking to facilitate the students' connecting their past, present, and future with *Am Yisrael*.

- if we are looking to cultivate Jewish identification with people, place, and time.

All malls have an open-door policy; just step toward the mat and the door opens automatically — welcoming you in no matter what is on your shopping list. Like the mall, step toward the mat in Israel, and the door will automatically open for all Jews. So in learning about Israel, the first commitment required is an intention to enter. A mall is set up to entice us to buy items not on our list, even those we may not have known existed when entering. In Jewish life, the options are endless, and exposure to their richness can entice further examination. Each product, by law, must be labeled with its place of origin or list of ingredients. By analogy, Israel is in part the place of origin or ingredient list for almost every Jewish "product" that exists. Advertisements invite us to experiment with new products. Israel is one of the greatest contexts for Jewish experimentation and exploration of diverse Jewish values.

Why the metaphor? Because it is accessible and understandable; it demonstrates the integral nature of Israel in the Jewish experience; it invites an informal and interactive notion of engaging with Israel, not as "subject matter for education," but as a real place with real people and a distinctively Jewish rhythm and time. Israel's landscape, language, calendar, symbols, narratives, heroes, and people, all connect with primal Jewish experiences. Israel connects historical perspective with contemporary context. *Medinat Yisrael* (the State of Israel) is Jewish public space, open to all Jews who wish to enter (just step on the doormat and the doors will open). It is the one country where the interests of

Am Yisrael (the People of Israel) is a permanent top priority and the major cultural context is Jewish in all of its diversity. So no matter which "store you may shop in," there are rich and diverse Jewish connections there to be seen. Because Israel is a modern society in the making, it is the responsibility of all Jews to address her beauty and her imperfections with as much information and caring as members of a family would have for one another. This can be very inviting and exciting for Jews who are looking for ways to make a difference in this world. The adventure goes on in *Medinat Yisrael*; the task of modern nation building is not finished. The State is a dynamic, living civilization with many exciting challenges yet to be addressed. Israel is not only a piece of our past, it is very much integral to our entire personal Jewish journey.

There is no adequate substitute for visiting Israel, meeting its people, and hiking its landscape. But when one does not visit, the challenge is how best to engage the learner in a process of "exploring Israel." Rather than "teaching about" the Land and her people, how do we connect the learners to something bigger than themselves? We suggest an integrated approach to interacting with *Moledet Am Yisrael* (the Homeland of the Jewish People), by which Israel becomes part of the deepening of one's Jewish self.

So let's examine now what this means by exploring some of the stops (some of the teaching aspects) in our "global Jewish mall" — our Israel. Each of these stops will be described in detail below.

1. Israel as Jewish Landscape
   Mall stop: Jewish Landscaping and Ecology

2. Israel's Jewish Language: Hebrew
   Mall stop: Community Room

3. Israel's Jewish Calendar and Rhythm
   Mall stop: Jewish Lifestyle and Appointment Books

4. Israel's Jewish Symbols and Space
   Mall stop: Jewish Homes and Furnishings

5. Israel's Jewish Narratives and Heroes
   Mall stop: Jewish Book Shop and Movie Theater

6. Israel's Jewish Family/Community
   Mall stop: Jewish Cultural Center, Gift Shop, and Food Court

7. Israel Travel and Experience
   Mall stop: Jewish Travel Agency

Although I talk about Israel in Judaic studies and my students are exposed to Israeli teachers and students from Israel, I'm not sure that my classes have much feeling for or knowledge about the country. Last year, my first graders corresponded with a second grade class in Degania, Israel. They began to be aware of Israel in the news. They had some questions about life in Israel. They were thrilled to receive nuts and dried fruits at Purim from their pen pals.

This year, all of the classes are corresponding with children in Degania. The older students are required to use their Hebrew skills to write a portion of each letter in Hebrew. They enjoy translating from Hebrew to English for the younger children. We've marked Degania on the map of Israel and have requested information about their home from the Israeli pen pals. The Hebrew teachers are working with the fifth graders, who will travel to Degania after graduation, teaching them some of the vocabulary and phrases that they will need for the trip. We try to remind them periodically why they are practicing ordering food, social graces, and counting money. I can't evaluate yet how successful this approach will be, but many students seem to be excited about and involved in the process.

(Maura Pollak, Tulsa, Oklahoma)

ISRAEL AS JEWISH LANDSCAPE

Mall stop: Jewish Landscaping and Ecology

Desert is the natural setting for much of our collective story. It is not just a place; it is where the physical and the spiritual coincide. *Am Yisrael* was formed in the desert. It is the place, the natural landscape, where one actually needs *kehilah*, a community. It is part of the beauty and the challenge of Israel. Thus, this mall stop broadly includes items (issues) such as: Survival, Ecology, Community under Adverse Conditions, Contrasts, Covenant, Relationships between People and Place, Rich Natural Diversity in such a small country, and so much more.

Practical Suggestions

As background, one can use excerpts from the Tanach or books such as *Walking the Bible: A Journey by Land through the Five Books of Moses* by Bruce Feiler as a "walking in the footsteps of . . ." approach. Or, consider *As a Driven Leaf* by Milton Steinberg as a way to bring the Talmud and its issues to life. *The Illustrated Atlas of Jerusalem* by Dan Bahat with Chaim T. Rubenstein (translated into English) provides excellent maps, charts, drawings, and photographs of Jerusalem throughout the ages. Also, you can refer to your local Jewish media center for some wonderful videos, such as the *Genesis Media Project*, which offers the Book of Genesis filmed as closely to the text as possible, with the actual Judean desert as its backdrop. Web sites can be helpful while providing some beautiful photographs to enrich the visuals for all of the units; just do a search under "Israel — photographs." Additional web sites may be found in the Bibliography for this chapter. Through these texts and web sites, one can explore the connection between people, place, and time, highlighting the impact of landscape on the Jewish experience. Teaching ideas can be found in the "steps" below.

Step 1: Connection between Am Yisrael and Eretz Yisrael

Place a variety of photographs or artists' drawings of *Eretz Yisrael* around the room that focus on nature (posters, books open to particular pages, postcards, people's photographs, etc.). If possible, play some "desert music," or have someone set the mood by softly playing a recorder or a wind instrument as background sounds as the students enter the room. On the board have the following instructions written out: "*B'ruchim HaBaim le'Eretz Yisrael!* Welcome to the Land of Israel! As you quietly wander/wonder through the Land, choose one of the pictures that most catches your eye. Sit near that picture and silently explore what drew you to it."

Once everyone is seated, invite students to share what drew them to their particular picture. At this point, either you (or a guest) should stand before the class (having quickly draped a white sheet around your body and over one shoulder and holding a tall stick in one hand and a book of the Torah in the other) and introduce yourself in a dramatic voice. "I am Moshe Rabbaynu, who led you out of Egypt and through the wilderness for 40

years. I have attempted faithfully to teach you God's word; and now, just before you cross into the Land that God has promised our people, I must review what God expects of you! And so I continue . . ." Read Deuteronomy 11:8-25 in a dramatic fashion, reading at least the first line in Hebrew. Give pairs of students a *Siddur* with the second and third paragraphs of the "*Shema*" blessings marked, and a copy of Deuteronomy 11:8-25. Have the students compare the text you just read with the paragraphs of the "*Shema*" blessings. Then ask the students to read aloud the various references to *Eretz Yisrael* commenting on what they are learning about *Eretz Yisrael*. For class discussion: "What do we learn from this Torah and *Siddur* text about the connection between *Am Yisrael* (the Jewish People) and *Eretz Yisrael* (the Land of Israel)?" As a close, have the students again review the pictures around the room, identifying which they would choose to take with them in their memory as the "landscape/background" for the next time they recite the "*Shema*" and its blessings, or the next time they see a *mezuzah*.

Step 2: Connection between Am Yisrael and Eretz Yisrael

Take the class out to a natural place with which they are unfamiliar. Upon arrival, have someone dressed up like the week before and say: "I am Yehoshua Bin Nun (also known as Joshua), Moshe's faithful servant. Now that Moshe has died, it is up to me to lead this people into the Promised Land. We are about to enter *Eretz Yisrael*, fulfilling God's promise to us. But this is a Land that we should investigate first. I need spies to check out the Land . . . and so, I assign all of you to be those spies. You are to explore silently the area that I assign to you, and then report back to the people upon your return. Each of you is to take a bag of supplies that I have prepared. Carefully read the instructions enclosed and be faithful to our people!" Assign each person a different physical area close by. The written instructions may read:

1. Close your eyes for one minute and collect impressions through your senses of hearing and smelling.

2. Collect in this bag as many impressions and artifacts from your area. You may also choose to use the paper, pencils, colored

markers, or pastels creatively to help in your reporting back to the people.

3. Prepare to share with our people, *Am Yisrael*, something particularly significant from your exploration.

The initial sharing is a quiet display of the physical elements they found and collected in their bags (their drawings, written words, or artifacts). The second level of sharing is in the role of spies, giving a brief verbal description of their area, focusing on "something particularly significant." The third part is a discussion, including questions such as:

1. How did it feel to be off on your own exploring a new place?

2. Do you feel some kind of attachment to your section, as opposed to others' sections? If so, how would you describe that attachment?

3. If we could bring others to your place, how would we want to prepare them?

4. In some way, as a group do we feel some kind of connection to this place that is different from what we may have felt when we first arrived? If so, what does that mean to us — to feel a connection with a new place that we have experienced together?

5. How do we think the Children of Israel might have felt at the moment of the end of 40 years of wandering just before they were going into *Eretz Yisrael* for their first time?

6. When you think about the ancient connection between *Am Yisrael* and *Eretz Yisrael* from the time of Avraham approximately 4,000 years ago and Moshe approximately 3,300 years ago, what are your thoughts or feelings? What mental pictures do you have?

7. The modern State of Israel, established in 1948, represents a return of *Am Yisrael* to *Eretz Yisrael*. How would we as a group describe to someone who knows nothing about what we have studied this special connection between *Am Yisrael* and *Eretz Yisrael*?

> I find it hard to make Israel come alive using just the textbook. When I have had Israelis or Americans who frequently visit relatives in Israel come in and speak to the class, then Israel really does come alive. The personal stories of everyday life, of school and shopping and holidays with family, the things that they can relate to their own lives — these are what makes Israel meaningful to them.
>
> *(Rabbi David Feder, Morgantown, West Virginia)*

ISRAEL'S JEWISH LANGUAGE: HEBREW

Mall stop: Community Room

Hebrew is a living language through which Jews dream, play, love, and experience life. It allows for the metaphors of the past to enrich our present with meaning. It is the expression of our integrated selves: ancient-modern, texts-jokes, playful-serious, delightful-difficult, meaningful-superficial, commanded-commanding, and prayer-poetry. Through interaction with Israel, Hebrew comes alive. Hebrew takes on new meaning while providing a reason to take on the challenge to learn a different *alef bet* and language. Integrating Hebrew with Israel brings the language to life. For example, the *shoresh* (Hebrew root), עלה (going up), connects Jews everywhere with Israel. The root is used for a variety of words including *aliyah laTorah* (being called up to the Torah) and *aliyah l'Eretz Yisrael* (going "up" to live in Israel), as well as *oleh/olah* (someone who "moves up" to Israel).

Practical Suggestions

Display Hebrew in every possible way in order to create an ambiance in which Hebrew is normal: posters from Israel on the walls, on every sign in the building, pictures with Hebrew words taken from the Internet, etc. Use Hebrew words and phrases at every assembly and as part of every class. Encourage students and teachers to use their Hebrew names (understanding their origins).

Establish a *Va'ad HaLashon*, a Hebrew language committee, with the responsibility to choose 100 Hebrew words that all Jews in the community should learn, know, and use. All of those learning Hebrew in the community should be part of this project, making suggestions (including the reason they propose that word or *shoresh*). The *Va'ad HaLashon* should be made up of individuals of varying ages, backgrounds, and familiarity with Hebrew, including leaders of the community. There should be a specific amount of time designated for this project, concluding with a Celebration of *Ivrit*. This celebration should involve all students of Hebrew of all ages (including elderly Jews who may have studied Hebrew in their youth in other countries). Everyone can contribute something to this celebration using the words that were chosen (making the invitations, creating posters, performing short plays, writing songs to sing and teach, baking Hebrew *alef bet* cookies, making puzzles, games, and T-shirts that use the selected words). Invite others from outside your specific community to the celebration, adding to its importance. Then, work toward ensuring that everyone learns and uses the chosen words (including the local Jewish press). A next step could be to report this celebration of the 100 words to others (even worldwide over the Internet), expanding the list of words as other suggestions come to *Va'ad HaLashon* and are accepted. Each year a new *Va'ad HaLashon* should be established to keep the project alive.

Some examples of *shorashim* to serve as the basis of words could be:

עלה (going up)

שער (gate)

ברך (blessing)

שלם (peace, wholeness)

כנס (come together, enter)

למד (learning, teaching)

ראש (head, beginning)

אחר (other, responsibility)

ISRAEL'S JEWISH CALENDAR AND RHYTHM

Mall Stop: Jewish Lifestyle and Appointment Books

Israel is the birthplace of our calendar. It is the one place where the Land and the climate support celebration of all the Jewish holidays and *mitzvot* to the fullest. In Israel, the blossoming of almond trees really does herald in *Tu B'Shevat*. Shabbat is a day with a different rhythm for everyone, secular and religious alike, with a whole week building up to it. In Israel, "Jewish" is more than just religion, it is also a way of life — a lifestyle — an all-encompassing, rich experience. Israel connects the holidays with Torah and with God.

Practical Suggestions

Base your life and that of your class on a Hebrew/Jewish calendar. See it as a way of giving meaning to your personal rhythm and that of your class. Doing so is a way of venerating time by focusing on formative moments within the Jewish calendar and rhythm. It creates an atmosphere within a place, and enables us to experience time in a different way. It is a way to connect your people (students) with our People (*Am Yisrael*). As personal examples, both of the authors have deep connections with the 1967 Six Day War. Paul arrived on *aliyah* one day before its onset, and Sally participated in a moving mass rally at the JCC in Allentown, Pennsylvania. For both, the intersection between this *Am Yisrael* event and their personal lives deepened their journeys into Jewish peoplehood and connections with Israel.

Display various local Jewish newspapers (both Hebrew and English) or bulletins with the Hebrew dates listed. Have the students locate the Hebrew dates and then find them on the large class calendar, noting also the times listed for Shabbat and holiday candle lighting, etc.

Help everyone in the class find out their Hebrew birth date. Post these "important dates" on a large Hebrew calendar and have the students put them into their own personal Hebrew date books. (You can request that the local Jewish bookstore or Internet store import Israeli students' calendar/assignment books, which are all based on the Hebrew and Julian calendars and are in Hebrew). Inquire if anyone may have another significant Hebrew date for her/his family, such as the passing of a grandparent, and have them add this occasion to the group's calendar. Some discussion questions:

1. Is your Hebrew birth date close to a Jewish holiday? If so, how has this impacted your birthday celebrations, if at all (e.g., *matzah* meal birthday cakes)?

2. How does it feel to have two birth dates?

3. What might it mean that, as Jews, we have our own calendar?

Now analyze Hebrew calendars from the past three years as they relate to the Julian (secular) calendar. Write out the secular dates of various Jewish holidays for a three-year span. The question will no doubt be asked: "Why does the Hebrew calendar change so much from year to year?" If it doesn't come up, then you can encourage the question by asking students what they observe. To answer this question, have the class do some research into the functioning of the Hebrew calendar. You can divide student's into small work teams with different foci, directing them to sources that also include photographs or illustrations:

1. How was/is Rosh Chodesh (first day of the new month) determined?

2. Why is there a solar adjustment to the lunar calendar/cycle?

3. What are the connections between the Hebrew calendar and *Eretz Yisrael?*

4. Which holidays are on a specific date because the season of the year is significant to their celebration, and which for other reasons? Why?

After collecting their responses, have each group prepare to teach the others, including visual aids. Encourage active discussion and questioning by the group, including the collection of additional questions for further research. Once you are satisfied that the group understands the basics of the calendar, move on to the larger questions:

1. What are the possible implications for a people (*Am Yisrael*) to have their own ancient calendar that they maintain to this day?

2. Is there a kind of calendar rhythm that separates us from our surroundings at times (such as the *mitzvah* to sit in a *sukkah* when it may be snowing or raining where they live)? How does this feel?

3. Even though Jews live all over the world, our calendar connects us with a specific place, *Eretz Yisrael*. Analyze the reasons for this. Ponder the implications.

4. How do you think it would feel if almost everyone around you was celebrating the Jewish holidays in her/his own way like it is in Israel (where even the school calendar is based on the Hebrew calendar)? (Use the Israeli school children's calendar/assignment books for this question, noting the national school holidays.)

In conclusion, establish this connection between people, place, and time: *Am Yisrael, Eretz Yisrael*, and the Hebrew calendar. During the remainder of the year, be sure to celebrate/commemorate as a group the dates the students have marked in their Hebrew calendars. Follow the rhythm of the Hebrew calendar through the eyes of the Israeli school children and the Israeli national school calendar. You can change the posters in the room to match the current season in Israel.

ISRAEL'S JEWISH SYMBOLS AND SPACE

Mall Stop: Jewish Homes and Furnishings

Symbols have the power to communicate ideas, elicit emotions, and make deep connections. The value of visual and tangible symbols cannot be overstated. One only needs to observe the use of the symbol of the American flag following September 11, 2001, to understand the power inherent in a symbol. The flag of Israel also has the potential to elicit powerful connections. It was based on the design of the *tallit*, the Jewish prayer shawl, because that is one of the most recognizable symbols of the Jewish people. In the center of the flag is another well-known Jewish symbol, the *Magen David* ("Shield or Star David). Combining these two powerful Jewish symbols, *tallit* and *Magen David*, brings together the forces of tradition and history. In another example, the long-standing tradition of breaking the glass at the end of Jewish wedding ceremonies while reciting Psalm 137:5-6 ("If I forget you, O Jerusalem . . . "), symbolizes *Am Yisrael*'s deep, ongoing connection with Jerusalem, while focusing on the destruction of the Temple (another ancient symbol). Although different people do apply their own interpretations, Jewish symbols help to connect us as a people to each other, to our tradition, and to the Land and State of Israel.

Practical Suggestions

Assign students to bring something from home that symbolizes Israel for them — something they received as a gift from Israel, something made in Israel, or something they associate with Israel. They should write on a little card their description of how they associate this item with Israel. Ask each student to bring both the item and the card to class hidden in a bag so no one can see it. In addition, be sure to have a small flag of Israel to add to the symbols.

Meanwhile, on the walls of the room, hang posters with various symbols of Israel (posters of the Israeli flag, the Seal/Emblem of Israel, the *Kotel* (The Western Wall), the *Knesset*, etc. (see the Bibliography for web sites where one can order such posters), and arrange the chairs in a circle or have the students sit on the floor. Prepare blindfolds for everyone in the class. As the students enter, have them place their bags on a table. Select approximately five items from the bags for the first part of the program, still keeping them concealed, and making sure that a flag is among them. When you are ready to begin, have the students sit in the circle and cover their eyes with the blindfolds. One by one, pass an item around the circle. No one should say what he/she thinks it is until everyone has had the opportunity to hold it. Replace the item into the concealing bag and have students lower their blindfolds and guess what the item is. Once they agree on the identity of the item, show it to them and put it in the center of the circle. Repeat this for up to five times in total.

Next, ask the class:

- How it was that you were able to determine blindfolded what you were holding?

- In addition to feeling its shape, did you need to know something more in order to guess what it was?

- If we pulled a stranger into our class from the street, would they have been able to make a good guess with their eyes blindfolded for all five items as well as you did (including the Israeli flag)?

Then open all the bags and have the students make a display of the items and cards they brought from home. Have them "tour" the museum. In closing the program, review the different kinds of symbols displayed and categorize them (religious, national, commercial, connected with the Land, the people, Hebrew language, etc.). Comment on the similarities and diversity of the items students brought. Point out the power of symbols as expressing who we are, and representing our connections with each other and with Israel.

> My classes were upset and confused about Israel's actions in Jenin. I did an Internet search and brought in many articles written by various people: American reporters, Europeans, Arabs, and Israelis. I also shared an e-mail from an Israeli friend whose son was involved in the actual battle. We discussed how the media reflects different political viewpoints and how to tell where the information comes from.
>
> *(Dena Salmon, Montclair, New Jersey)*

ISRAEL'S JEWISH NARRATIVES AND HEROES

Mall stop: Jewish Book Shop and Movie Theater

The narrative of *Am Yisrael* and *Eretz Yisrael* with its challenges and promises begins with the Tanach and continues throughout classical and modern Jewish literature, in which the heroes and heroines are usually remarkably human. Through the articulation of our personal narratives we express what is meaningful in our lives. The challenge of Jewish education is to facilitate the intersection of our students' personal narratives with the national narrative of our people — building connections and enhancing meaning and Jewish identity. For some students, the greater the distance of historical periods, the more difficult it is for them to connect and integrate it into their own story. Hence, the life stories of the normal citizens of modern Israel can provide diverse, accessible models of contemporary heroes. This is all the more essential in an age in which so many youth mistakenly identify superstars as their heroes, even when there is little about those superstars' lives students would truly value if pressed to determine "What is a hero?"

Practical Suggestions

Part One: Introduction To Heroes – Write on the board the Hebrew *shoresh*, גבר. Begin by looking at the Hebrew words formed by that *shoresh*: *gever* (man), *g'veret* (woman), *gibor* (hero), *g'vurah* (heroism). Note that the same root in Hebrew can mean an ordinary person and also a hero.

Have each student prepare a list of the attributes of someone they admire. Emphasize that this could be someone they know personally, not necessarily a famous person, and that it can be a composite of various people. Have the students volunteer to share the attributes while someone writes them on the board. Look for similarities and differences. Have the students explain why they chose the attributes they did, what that attribute means to them personally, and what values it represents.

Either show a 15-minute video or read excerpts from the book about Alex Singer, a young Jewish American who, at the age of 25 in 1987, fell defending Israel. His story is told through his letters, journals, and drawings in the book *Alex: Building a Life*. All of these materials, along with an educator's guide, are available through the web site: www.alexsinger.org/index.html.

Supply each person with a large piece of art paper or poster board and a variety of materials (colored markers, pastels, magazines, bits of cloth, and colored papers for collage, glue, paints). Ask them to express their personal concept of a hero using these materials. Invite the poets among them to include poetry in their creation. To allow creative juices to flow, give students adequate time and space (background music is always good to encourage the quiet that some people need). Allow a minimum of 45 minutes for the creative part. Just before finishing the individual work, distribute a blank sheet of writing paper and have students write out again the attributes of a hero, without looking at their previous list. At the end, have the students display their creation while everyone walks around looking. Then have each one sit in front of his/her own creation and verbally share their hero.

Part Two: Personal Narratives, Past and Present – This kind of assignment requires much support from the teacher in order for it to be effective. Give each student in the class an e-mail address of someone in Israel with whom they can correspond. It is best if it is someone they know, such as friends or family in Israel. However, it is also effective if it is with someone unknown, as long as there has been some kind of introduction and they have a common language in which to correspond. It doesn't matter if it is an older person or a peer.

Begin by helping your students write personal introductions of themselves: their family, hobbies, favorite music, and the context within which they are doing this (e.g., "As a class, we are collecting people's stories about themselves. It is important to us to know what your life in Israel is like these days. We also want to share with you what our lives are like here . . . "). In the second e-mail, have your students share what they consider to be important attributes for a hero, and ask that the Israeli respond with what they consider to be important or who their personal hero is. As the e-mail responses arrive, have the students print them out and bring them to class. Make a chart on the wall that includes the original list of attributes that the class created, and add the Israelis' contributions in a separate column.

As a conclusion, either individually or as a class, write a contemporary *midrash* of what it takes to be a hero in our times. Have them include their own responses and those of their Israeli pen pal. It could be interesting to have students prepare personal hero portfolios that including their artwork (it may need to be photographed in order to be preserved), their developed list of attributes, their e-mail correspondence with their Israeli partner, related newspaper or magazine articles, photographs, and the *midrash*. These could be displayed for others to see.

Beyond the context of this assignment, it is also appropriate to discuss how your students may wish to reach out to Israelis in other ways. Especially in times when people do not feel safe visiting Israel, many overseas connections have been further developed between Jews outside of Israel and Israelis. This has been done by telephone calls, sending pizzas to Israeli soldiers at their posts, purchasing Israeli products in local stores and over the Internet from Israeli stores, sending *tzedakah*, and many other wonderful and generous ways. To locate these options, do a web search under the following topics: Israel Shopping or Israel Gifts.

ISRAEL'S JEWISH FAMILY/COMMUNITY

Mall Stop: Jewish Cultural Center, Gift Shop, and Food Court

Medinat Yisrael gives depth to what sometimes becomes cliché: *"Am Yisrael Chai"* (the People of Israel lives). As an ancient people having lived among many different cultures in varied lands, *Am Yisrael* (the Jewish People) has developed into a richly diverse, living and dynamic Jewish collective. This extensive diversity is most notably present in Israel, the place of *kibbutz galuyot* (the ingathering of the exiles) where the cultural interchange is inspiring and alive, not just relegated to a folklore museum. Daily interactions of the people in Israel are part of the national collective discussion. In Israel, living and learning diverse Jewish cultural customs is unavoidable, whether through interactions with neighbors, schoolmates, coworkers, or within each extended family. Visiting a bereaved family requires knowledge of their specific customs within the Jewish *halachic* legal system. Israel is the place where Jewish cultural pluralism is thriving. This is significant for Jewish educators, as it provides an opportunity to extend the perspective of Jewish family to include an authentically richly diverse concept of *Am Yisrael* and *kehilah* that is inherently pluralistic. Music and dance are two avenues through which you can connect your students with this diversity.

Practical Suggestions

Rhythm and music connect with something deep within us, having the power to bring us to move and dance. Post pictures or photos around the room of Jewish people in diverse dress and with differing physical features. Also, post a map of the world on the wall. Prepare and play a selection of Jewish music from diverse cultural contexts, i.e., music that Jews play, sing, and use in ceremonies and celebrations. (Your Cantor or music specialist can help you locate these.) Give each selection a Hebrew letter for reference without identifying its source. As you play each, have the students close their eyes and imagine people moving to these rhythms. Following each example, ask students to describe what they had imagined:

1. Who were the people in your mental picture (Men, women, children, families)?

2. What were the people wearing? (Suggest that students are welcome to point to various pictures you have displayed.) What were they doing? Was it part of an event?

3. What was the setting of your mental picture?

4. What feelings did you associate with the music?

5. Would you have thought this music to be Jewish if you heard it on the radio?

Identify the source for each musical selection, making the connection with the appropriate photograph or picture, and then have the group find the location on the world map, placing a pin in the spot. Focus your concluding discussion on the extensive diversity of the Jewish people and how representatives of each are concentrated in Israel. Place a pin on Israel on a world map. Ask the students to add pins on the map locating where their family originated. Then ask them to connect all those countries to Israel by tying colored yarn from those pins to Israel (note that people from there also make up Israeli society).

In your follow-up discussion, discuss the universal feeling that those who are different from us are strange. We may associate their customs with travel to exotic countries or past historical times. Make the point that contemporary Israelis come from over 100 different countries and cultural backgrounds. They have brought their traditional foods, music, dances, dress, gender roles, customs and symbols with them. This impacts how they celebrate the holidays and life cycle events, as well as how they pray. (Make the point that customs are neither right nor wrong even though some people attach elevated importance to them, as if they are equivalent to Jewish law.)

1. Have you ever attended a Pesach *Seder* where there were customs different from those of your family? Did this interest you? disturb you? Explain.

2. How might it impact your Jewish life if you were surrounded by cultural diversity as in Israel (for example, there would be different foods, diverse recipes for *charoset*, different tunes for songs at the Pesach *Seder* etc.)?

3. In what ways is it like an "intermarriage" when a Jew with Hungarian roots marries a Jew from Yemen? What might the implications/complications be?

4. In what ways do you think this taking on local culture and customs has helped to keep *Am Yisrael* alive? In what ways might it complicate being a people?

In Israel, this dynamic and living interchange of diverse Jewish cultures has enriched the society.

> As teachers, we need to be careful about the assumptions we make about the Israel politics of our parents — and our colleagues. I spent a year in Jerusalem during the current intifada. I'm an ardent Zionist and leftist. And I've found myself feeling very uncomfortable at professional meetings, listening to both presenters and colleagues talking about parents who are critical of Israeli government policy as ignorant, out of touch, and undermining the Jewish community and their children's education. I never quite know how to say, "Wait a minute — you could be talking about me!" (or at least my politics). And if a teacher feels that way, how much more so might a parent feel estranged by a school in which he/she hears those views expressed.
>
> *(Anne Johnston. New Haven, Connecticut)*

Another suggestion is to select some Israeli songs known to most of the students and consider diverse musical renditions on their meanings. Begin by focusing on the literal meaning of the actual words. Next allow for free association of the students as they look for meaning through their own interpretations. Then share the background of the song (who wrote the words/or what is the source, who composed the most popular tune, when it was composed, if there is a connection with some national or personal event, etc.). Ask the question: Does the meaning of songs become transformed at different times and in different places?

Still another suggestion is to focus on Israeli folk dancing, which connects people, movement, music, and meaning. It is significant as nonverbal communication. Bring in a professional Israeli folk dancing teacher who knows the history and background of each dance and the significance of the song/tune it brings to life.

And, finally, don't overlook poetic language to create meaning and connections. Yehuda Amichai's poetry is powerful, and it was he who helped create modern Israeli poetry. Amichai wrote from a deeply personal perspective, which was integrally part of the collective experience. By studying a selection of his poetry, one can learn much about contemporary Israel's soul. In order to learn more about

Yehuda Amichai, read a selection of his poems, and order his books (including English translation). Web sites for Amichai's poetry are listed in the Bibliography.

There are also various Israeli music web sites. Search under "Israeli music." These, too, are listed in the Bibliography.

Beth Hatefutsoth's "Visual Documentation Center" documents Jewish life and creativity in the Diaspora. It is one of the most important centers in the world, and offers a comprehensive collection of Jewish photo documentation of life outside of Israel. You can access this on the Internet at: www.bh.org.il/Documentation/index.asp.

Also, posters and movies, as well as books, are available through the Beth Hatefutsoth electronic store at: www.bh.org.il/shop.asp.

ISRAEL TRAVEL AND EXPERIENCE

Mall Stop: Jewish Travel Agency

Perhaps the most effective introduction to this mall stop are four quotations from research on 104 studies of Israel trips: "Does the Teen Israel Experience Make a Difference?" by Barry Chazan with Arianna Koransky (New York: Israel Experience Inc., 1997).

> An Israel Experience enables young people to have a positive Jewish experience at a time in their lives when they are shaping the patterns of their subsequent adult Jewish identity and involvement.

> An Israel Experience is a unique kind of Jewish education that contributes to the formation of positive Jewish attitudes and behaviors through experiential rather than frontal learning.

> Young people who have participated in Israel Experiences regard their summer in Israel as one of the most positive Jewish moments and memories in their lives.

> There is a link between adult Jewish identity and participation in a teen Israel Experience.

Although less extensively researched, it has been established that Jewish adult travel to Israel has an impact on Jewish identity, as well as Jewish family educational Israel trips impacting the family as a whole. (See *The Ma Nishtana of Family Education Israel Trips*, edited by Sally Klein-Katz and

Roberta Bell-Kligler, available from Melitz through their web site, www.melitz.org.il.)

Practical Suggestions

As teachers, you have great influence on your students' connections to Israel, both spiritual and physical. If you have been to Israel, talk about your experiences. Encourage older students to share their experiences on teen or family trips to Israel. Sprinkle into your conversation phrases that assume students will visit at some point in their lives (e.g., "when you visit Israel . . . "). Encourage students and their families to consider a specific trip to Israel, perhaps one sponsored by your community or affiliate youth group. If yours is a community that sponsors a savings program for Israel trips, remind the parents of your students of the benefits of saving money each year toward a future trip.

CONCLUSION

As you may imagine, it has been a challenge to write this chapter during a difficult and painful time in Israel. However, it is precisely at such moments that we need to focus on the integral relationship of *Am Yisrael*, *Eretz Yisrael*, and *Medinat Yisrael*. Within our preparations, we were assisted through our conversations with colleagues whom we thank, noting that the contents of this chapter do not necessarily reflect their approaches: Professor Barry Chazan, Johnny Ariel, Rabbi Alan Kay, and Jo Kay.

TEACHING CONSIDERATIONS

- The goal is to establish meaningful connections with the collective Jewish homeland; linking personal past, present, and future with that of *Am Yisrael*.

- Israel is one of the greatest contexts for Jewish experimentation and exploration of diverse Jewish values. Make the most of this.

- Consider an informal and interactive

notion of engaging with Israel, not as "subject matter for education," but as a real place with real people and a distinctively Jewish rhythm and time.

- Affective education is most effective in facilitating the learners' exploration of what Israel means for their lives while forming a relationship.

- Adventure is part of Israel; developing an understanding of the continuing pioneering opportunities is to be part of all educational programs connected with Israel.

- Cultivating collective Jewish responsibility in relation to Israel facilitates enables one to engage in a dynamic, ongoing partnership.

- Hebrew is a living link that enriches connections with *Am Yisrael*, *Eretz Yisrael*, and *Medinat Yisrael*.

The prospect of teaching about Israel is both exciting and daunting. It's obvious that it would be best to take students there rather than try to teach about Israel from afar. At a CAJE conference one year, I met Sari from Ra'anana. She taught third grade as I did, and we decided to start a pen pal program with our classes. There were obstacles: her class met six days a week, they knew little English, we wanted to use e-mail (and there were problems with that on a number of levels). Yet, the experience of the students writing back and forth was so fantastic. The excitement each time they received letters was palpable for anyone who came into our classroom. I heard that it was the same for the Israelis. There was much incidental learning about similarities and differences in our lifestyles. Connection to Israel became so much greater than it would have been if we had just stuck "Israel" into our curriculum and studied the maps and time lines and watched videos.

(Michael Fixler, Syracuse, New York)

BIBLIOGRAPHY

For Teachers

Arian, Alan, and Michael Shamir, eds. *The Elections in Israel 1999*. Albany, NY: State University of New York Press, 2002.

> The editors have analyzed the elections results over an extended period of time. The series is a vital source for understanding the intricacies of the election process.

Hazony, Yoram. *The Jewish State: The Struggle for Israel's Soul*. New York: Basic Books, 2001.

> An attempt by the Israeli right to analyze the role of the intellectual left. This book has initiated an important internal debate, and challenges the dominating historical schools of thought.

Hertzberg, Arthur. *The Zionist Idea*. New York: Atheneum, 1972.

> This book includes the central ideas of the main Zionist thinkers. Hertzberg gives a short introduction on each person and then includes fascinating primary sources.

Liebman, Charles S., and Eliyahu Katz, eds. *The Jewishness of Israelis: Responses To the Guttman Report*. Albany, NY: State University of New York Press, 1997.

> An important book about the ongoing debate of how to interpret Jewishness. These two writers have played a vital role in this discussion.

Ofer, Dalia. "The Strength of Rememberance: Commemorating the Holocaust during the First Decade of Israel." *Jewish Social Studies* 6, no. 2, Winter 2000, 24-55.

> The question of the role of the Holocaust in Israeli society remains a topic of great interest. Dalia Ofer has written several works on this theme.

Sachar, Howard. *A History of Israel*. New York: Alfred Knopf, 1996.

> This is an outstanding overview of events in Israel from the end of the nineteenth century. Sachar's approach is essentially centrist, and he manages to include the perspectives of the main players in the developing historical drama.

Shalev, Meir. *The Blue Mountain*. Hillel Halkin, trans. Edinburgh, England: Canongate Books, 2002.

> An example of one of the many painful exposures of Zionist past by an Israeli intellectual. Shalev, Amos Oz, and a host of other Israeli writers have written on the unfulfilled hopes and dreams of the developing state.

Zerubavel, Yael. *Recovered Roots: Collective Memory and the Making of Israeli National Tradition*. Chicago, IL: University of Chicago Press, 1997.

> This book initiated an important discussion on collective memory and resulted in a widespread debate in Israel.

For Students

Abraham. New Media Bible, Part 2. Genesis Media Project, 1976.

> In this video, which is based on meticulous research and consultation with Bible scholars (including Harry Orlinsky and Nahum Sarna) and archaeologists, the narration remains faithful to the text, and the action illustrates the daily life of biblical personalities. The film stars Israeli actor, Topel, as Abraham, and is a good way to introduce Torah narrative using the visual backdrop of Israel.

Alexander, Sue. *Behold the Trees*. New York: Scholastic Books, 2001.

> Israel's history, from ancient times to present, is told in this beautifully illustrated tale of the Land and its trees. A 2001 Association of Jewish Libraries Notable Book. For Grades 3-6.

Bahat, Dan, and Shlomo Ketko, trans. *The Illustrated Atlas of Jerusalem*. Jerusalem: Carta, 1996.

> This book has been translated into English and it provides wonderful maps, charts, drawings, and photographs of Jerusalem through the ages.

Burstein, Chaya. *A Kid's Catalog of Israel*, Philadelphia, PA: Jewish Publication Society, 1998.

> A compendium of information and activities for upper elementary and middle school students.

Da Costa, Deborah. *Snow in Jerusalem*. New York: Albert Whitman & Co., 2001.

> A Jewish boy and an Arab boy become friends on a rare snowy day in Jerusalem, as they each help a stray cat.

Feiler, Bruce. *Walking the Bible: A Journey by Land through the Five Books of Moses*. New York: HarperCollins Publishers, 2001.

> Bruce Feiler has written a real and up-to-date "walking in the footsteps of . . . " book, a personal and spiritual exploration.

Singer, Alex. *Alex: Building a Life: The Story of a Young Jewish American Who Fell Defending Israel*. Jerusalem: Gefen Publishing House, 1997.

> This book and 15-minute video are rich in background information about Alex Singer who fell in battle at the age of 25 in 1987. The story is told through the use of Alex's letters, journals, and drawings. (There is also a web site, www.alexsinger.org/index.html.)

Steinberg, Milton. *As a Driven Leaf*. New York: Behrman House, Inc., 1939.

> This is a classic that brings the issues and daily activities of common folk and religious leaders during the Talmudic period to life.

Family Education on Israel Trips

Klein-Katz, Sally, and Roberta Bell-Kligler. *The Ma Nishtana of Family Education Israel Trips*. Jerusalem: Melitz and Project Oren, 2000, available from Melitz at their web site: www.melitz.org.il.

Web Sites for Visual Aids, Information, and Educational Ideas

- Israel Information Center, Jerusalem
  www.cidi.nl/html/info/facts/fhist1.html

- The Department for Jewish Zionist Education, The Pedagogic Center
  www.jajz-ed.org.il/100/concepts

- Israeli Ministry of Foreign Affairs: Israel Information Center Catalogue of Publications
  www.israel.org/mfa/go.asp?MFAH010w0

- Neot Kedumim Biblical Landscape Reserve
  www.neot-kedumim.org.il

- The Hebrew University of Jerusalem, The Pedagogic Resource Centre and Library for Jewish Education
  http://sites.huji.ac.il/melton/library.html

- The Israeli Posters Center
  www.israeliposters.co.il

- Biblical Archaeology Society
  www.bib-arch.org/bswbHmSitemap.html

- In Israel: Israel in 3D
  www.inisrael.com/3disrael

- Israeli Posters: Harvard University Library
  www.clir.org/pubs/reports/mcclung/inv/047.html

- Beth Hatefutsoth's "Visual Documentation Center"
  www.bh.org.il/Documentation/index.asp
  www.bh.org.il/shop.asp

Web Sites for Poetry

- Alex Singer: Building a Life.
  www.alexsinger.org/index.html

- Yehuda Amichai's poetry
  www.ithl.org.il/amichai/index.html
  www.jajz-ed.org.il/50/people/amichai.html

Web Sites for Music

- Feher Jewish Music Center, Beth Hatefutsoth
  www.bh.org.il/Music/index.asp

- Israeli Music Online
  www.sabra.net/theisraelhour/index.html

- Israeli Scent — Israeli Music
  www.israeliscent.com/IsraelStore
  IsraelMusic/e-music-israelisongs-01.htm

Web Sites for Israeli Tourism

- Israel Ministry of Tourism
  www.infotour.co.il

- Infotour — Israeli Tourism and Recreation
  www.infotour.co.il

CHAPTER 38

Teaching Mitzvot, Values, and Middot

Steven Bayar

INTRODUCTION

What are *mitzvot*, values, and *middot*? For the purposes of this chapter, *mitzvot* are defined as commandments, the laws and rules outlined in the Torah. Values are general categories and standards of behavior that can be deduced by studying the *mitzvot* we follow. *Middot* are the attitudes and actions we are encouraged/required to assume by the values to which we adhere. Thus, one cannot teach *mitzvot* without also instructing on the values derived from them. At the same time, teaching *mitzvot* and values without *middot* render the exercise without reinforcement.

TEACHING MITZVOT, VALUES, AND MIDDOT[1]

In many religious school classes across the country, the first act of a teacher after taking attendance is to pass around a *tzedakah* box. The reason most teachers would give for doing this is that the first value we teach is to help others in need.

But take a step back. Look at the first five minutes of class with a dispassionate eye and analyze the actions of taking out the *tzedakah* box, passing it around the class and having the students place money in it. What was *actually* taught? In stripping away "our" preconceptions of *tzedakah*, one finds that the only thing that has been taught by passing around the box is to impart to the students that when a person enter the classroom, he or she is supposed to put money into a box. This is an unreinforced rote action, even if the *mitzvah* of *tzedakah* is explained several times during the year. If there are no activities to reinforce the *mitzvah*, and the value, and the *middah* associated with the commandment of giving *tzedakah*, there is no point to the donation. While many teachers engage the students in discussions and empower

the class to decide where to donate money, too often the money disappears without the student knowing why Jews are commanded to give, and specifically where the year's collection has gone.

Jewish education is a challenge. Teaching values, *mitzvot*, and *middot* can be especially difficult in the supplementary school setting. Given our time and budget constraints, it sometimes seems as though we are asked to teach our students and families all there is to know about Judaism while we are standing on one foot. However, we have at our fingertips the ability to do much more — if we use our resources wisely.

The fact is that our schools and classrooms have become artificial environments. Students in our classrooms know that the values there are often different from the ones they live with at home. They know that the values they are being taught are not always shared by their parents and families, and that therefore the students are not necessarily bound by what they learn.

While many view this dynamic as adding to the challenge, it can also be an incredible gift, and is perhaps our greatest asset in this area. Yes, we may have only a small classroom under our control, but, given the proper curriculum and strategies, we can make that classroom into an important source for values for our students.

The key rests in our ability to have our students incorporate our lessons into their daily lives. To this end, our first goal must be to develop curricula that will not only teach *mitzvot*, values, and *middot*, but will allow us to "bridge" those values from the classroom into the home and into the lives of the families of those we teach. For instance, a lesson about respecting the elderly is incorporated or internalized when the student in his or her own time outside of school visits a nursing home or prepares a care package for an elderly shut-in. When

---

[1] This chapter is based in part on work I have done for and with Danny Siegel and Rabbi Elliot Kleinman. Not only have

they been my teachers, they have also been my role models.

the lesson is acted upon by the student (and the student's family), using time otherwise allotted for other activities, the lesson has gone beyond the classroom.

Given the priorities of our schools, Hebrew, prayer, holidays, and ritual observance always seem to take precedence over everything else. The practicality of our curricula, the teaching of discernable skills that can be used immediately, are seen as more vital given the time constraints we face. However, there are excellent curriculum pieces on *mitzvot*, values, and *middot* available (see the Bibliography at the end of this chapter), many of which integrate holidays and observance and behaviors, allowing all elements to be taught together.

> I'll never forget the day Caitlyn solemnly approached me before the start of class. She usually had a bounce in her step and a bright smile, but that day, she was subdued. She gently held a styrofoam container up for my inspection as she gingerly lifted the lid. Her mother explained that Caitlyn had found this butterfly alive with a damaged wing. She had tried to nurse it back to health, but it had not survived. Caitlyn had recently learned about *mitzvot* in my classroom and had, therefore, decided to name the butterfly Mitzvah, since, as she explained, that's what she had done in trying to save the butterfly's life. Caitlyn asked if she could share her butterfly with the class that day. I agreed, and as we sat in a circle on the floor, the other third graders and I had a very special lesson in how to care for others and a very mature conversation about death. The students were so interested in Caitlyn's story and so careful with Mitzvah, the butterfly. It amazed me how this frail, little creature became such a powerful lesson in a Jewish classroom.
>
> *(Amy Appelman, West Bloomfield, Michigan)*

How to Proceed

All the values, *mitzvot,* and *middot* originate from

texts in our tradition.[2] Therefore, students must first learn the value. Teach the text! Don't paraphrase it or use a synopsis. Use the actual words as they appear. Don't even clean up the grammar. Make the text a character in the lesson. Let it have an identity separate from you or the class. Let the class interact with the text.

It is said that Judaism is a religious tradition that encompasses a dialogue between the generations. That dialogue can never begin unless there is something to respond to. By teaching the text:

- Students have something concrete they can take away from the classroom.

- A teacher does not teach his or her own personal interpretation of the tradition. Rather, the students see the text and how the teacher interprets it, but have the space and freedom to "make the text their own," interpreting it uniquely and personally.

- The values, *mitzvot,* and *middot* in the lesson are given an authority greater than that of the teacher. The students have the opportunity to see the lesson as part of a tradition, not something to learn because the teacher says to do so.

- The tradition becomes interactive.

- A vehicle is provided to export the value out of the classroom.

Following are two examples that demonstrate the above method. The first focuses on *Rodef Shalom* (pursuing peace) and *Bikkur Cholim* (visiting the sick). The second provides a teaching example using *Lehadayr P'nai Zakayn* (Respect for Old People).[3]

The Text: Rodef Shalom and Bikkur Cholim

Rabbi Broka Choz'a was frequently to be found in the marketplace of Bay Lefet.

Elijah was often there with him. Rabbi Broka asked Elijah, "Is there anyone in the market who deserves to receive the rewards of the Next World?"

In the meantime, two people came by and

---

[2]See Chapter 32, "Teaching Texts" by Betsy Dolgin Katz, pp. 374-387 in this Handbook.

[3]These texts and questions are taken with permission of the author from the Ziv/Giraffe curriculum published with a grant by the Righteous Persons Foundation, Millburn, NJ, and distributed by the Ziv Foundation and the Mitzvah Clown Handbook, 2002.

Elijah said to him, "These will receive the rewards of the Next World."

Rabbi Broka asked them, "What do you do?"

They replied, "We are jokers, making sad people laugh. Also, when we see two people arguing, we work hard to make peace between them." (*Ta'anit* 22a)

Allow the text to guide the discussion. Elicit from the students what they think the text means. Use questions such as the following:

- What values does the text tell us are important? (Bringing happiness to others and making peace between those angry at each other.)

- What is special about the characters of the story? (Two non-descript characters getting into heaven at the same level as a great Rabbi, simply because they bring happiness to others.)

- The jokers were men of action, and the Rabbi was a man of study. What does the tradition think about the combination of knowledge and action? (Both are important.)

Introduce the Value

- Why does the text tell us it is important to pay attention to helping others? (To make people who are sad feel better — this comes right from the text.)

- What do *mitzvot* command/teach us about making sad persons feel better? (*Rodef shalom* — pursue peace, and *bikkur cholim* — visit the sick.)

Model the Mitzvah

There is an excellent film entitled *Patch Adams* (1998, 115 minutes, rated PG-13) about a doctor's attempt to bring joy to the patients for whom he cares. It is based upon a true story about a real-life doctor. From the start of the film, watch the clip from 0:25:00-0:31:00 (or if you object to mild profanity, 0:27:30-0:31:00). Use a section of the video as a "trigger" for discussion about the values/*mitzvot* of *rodef shalom* and *bikkur cholim*.

In addition, the Ziv/Giraffe curriculum includes profiles of *mitzvah* heroes. In it you will find a page on Mike and Sue Turk (Sweetpea and Buttercup), a couple who spend a significant part of their lives training people of all ages to be *mitzvah* clowns.

Reinforce the Values, Mitzvot, and Middot through an Activity

How about dressing as clowns and visiting the sick? In this case, the activity is used not only to reinforce the *mitzvot,* values, and *middot,* but to export these concepts outside the classroom into homes. Danny Siegel (see the Bibliography) or the local hospital can tell you where to find a pastoral clowning program in your area.

Schedule a session on Mitzvah Clowning for the entire school/congregation, welcoming the participation and involvement of families. This activity extends beyond a one-time commitment, providing access to the value, *mitzvah,* and *middot* surrounding *bikkur cholim.* In this way the *mitzvot,* values, and *middot* become important not only for those who participate, but also for the entire congregation/school.

There are many activities on a smaller scale. Check out any of Danny Siegel's books to find a multitude of *mitzvah* heroes involved in projects designed to "bring smiles to the faces of those in pain." There are programs to develop hospitality kits for people in chemotherapy, children in hospitals, and many others. The key is to involve the students and family outside the classroom.

> At the beginning of the school year, I tell my students that one of my top priorities is having respect for each other, and that I will always try to show them respect, and that I want the same in return from them. I teach them the *middah* of *derech eretz,* and explain that I expect everyone to behave properly toward their classmates, and toward their teacher.
>
> (Nancy Hersh, Chatham, New Jersey)

The Text: Lehadayr P'nai Zakayn (Respecting Old People)

For this *mitzvah,* we can use a variety of texts:

It is natural for old people to be despised by the general population when they can no longer function as they once did, but sit idle, and have no purpose.

The commandment, "Honor your father and your mother" was given specifically for this situation. (Gur Aryeh Halevi)

When we were young we were told to act like adults. Now that we are old, we are treated like infants. (*Bava Kamma* 92b)

One man may feed his father fattened chickens and inherit Gehenna (hell), and another may put his father to work treading a mill, and inherit the Garden of Eden (heaven). How is it possible for a man to feed his father fattened chickens and still inherit Gehenna?

There was a man who used to feed his father fattened chickens. Once his father asked him, "My son, where did you get these?" He answered, "Old man, old man, shut up and eat just as the dogs shut up when they eat." Such a man feeds his father fattened chickens, but inherits Gehenna. How is it possible for a man to put his father to work in a mill and still inherit the Garden of Eden?

There was a man who worked in a mill. The king ordered that millers be brought to him. Said the man to his father, "Father, you stay here and work in the mill in my place, and I will go to work for the king. For if some insults come to the workers, I prefer they fall on me and not on you. Should blows come, let them beat me and not you." Such a man puts his father to work in a mill, yet inherits the Garden of Eden. (*Jerusalem Talmud, Kiddushin* 1:7)

As before, let the text guide the students:

- What are the texts teaching us?

- Who is writing the texts?

- Are the sentiments expressed in the texts valid?

Introduce the Value

- What does it mean to respect old people?

- How do you show respect?

- How do you know when people respect you?

- How much do you know about old people?

- How do you feel about old people?

- Why do you think the Torah includes a *mitzvah* about old people?

Before moving on to the activity, show the opening five minutes of the movie *Cocoon* (1985, 117 minutes, rated PG-13) to reinforce the value and the text. In this film, the various aspects of a senior center (independent living, assisted living, and nursing care) are portrayed. The viewer sees how the seniors' expectations and lives center around little things, such as having an unmelted cupcake for snack or remembering the name of a friend.

Shlock Rock (a popular Jewish band) calls *middot* "Torah manners" in one song. Talking about *middot* can be one way, however, to bring Torah into conflict resolution. I teach in a resource room. Sometimes our students come to the brink of (or engage in) physical violence. We separate everybody and then we sit down to process what happened, and how it could have been handled differently, or even prevented. That's all standard practice, and we model our process on the practice in their special education classes in secular school. But what I add is *middot* — giving Jewish (Hebrew) names to the character traits we want to work on, such as patience and forgiveness. We also use our discussion of *middot* to talk about God — how we are all created *b'tzelem Elohim* (in the image of God), and how we can come closer to God by working on those *middot* God has shown us. We further reinforce the lessons by referring again to *middot* when teaching Torah (especially *Parashat HaShavua* (the portion of the week), a focus at our school, pointing out when Torah personalities are exhibiting positive *middot*.

(Anne Johnston, New Haven, Connecticut)

Model the Mitzvah

While most classes have visited a nursing home, consider preparing for such a visit in a way that reinforces the *mitzvot,* values, and *middot* of respecting the elderly. Invite a senior to class who will tell the students "the way it really is." Have the visitor discuss his or her concerns about growing old, of being able to care for him/herself. Sensitize the class to the issues in a way that will make a difference.

In preparation for the actual trip, have students prepare a series of interactive activities to be done *with* the residents, rather than *for* them. Make sure that during their preparations, students focus on the central *mitzvah* of respecting the elderly. For example, everyone knows that *Bingo* is a staple of nursing homes. However, a better game is *Poker*, as it demands interaction with the players, forcing a person to think and focus on the game.

> I explain the *mitzvah* of *bikkur cholim* (visiting the sick) and assign each student a *bikkur cholim* buddy. I try to pair people who are not buddies, so they have a chance to get to know each other. I also will change the pairings two or three times a year.
>
> The buddy who was in class on a given day has to call the child who was absent, find out if everything was okay, and tell him or her what was missed. The child who received the call has to tell me that their buddy phoned. This has also helped make connections between parents. I have done this successfully both in day school and supplementary school.
>
> (Cheryl Cash-Linietsky, Philadelphia, Pennsylvania)

Reinforce the Mitzvot, Values, and Middot through an Activity

While at the nursing home, help students keep focused on the values, *mitzvot,* and *middot* related to their visit. Afterward, debrief the activity, asking students to discuss their impressions. Would they go to a nursing again? How might they perform the *mitzvah* of *lehadayr p'nai zakayn* again?

Teaching Values through Other Texts in the Curriculum

The previous two examples were easy to teach because each text referred to a specific *mitzvah*. In fact, the only reason for teaching such texts is to introduce the *mitzvah*/value. This is not a problem if the curriculum calls for teaching these specific values and *mitzvot*. However, there is not enough time in most curricula for a separate course on

mitzvot — as other subjects often take precedence. So, now consider a text in which the values are not of primary educational concern. (Note: The following example is the account of Abraham and Sarah from the book of Genesis.[4] Current textbooks often paraphrase this text, telling the story instead. But the story is not the point of the text. The text is! One cannot interpret a story in the same way that one can interpret the text itself. In teaching *mitzvot*, values, and *middot*, it is important to use the actual text, for our tradition is set up in such a way that no text is devoid of values

The Text: Genesis 18:1-15

Adonai appeared to him by the terebinths of Mamre. He [Abraham] was sitting at the entrance of the tent as the day grew hot. Looking up, he saw three men standing near him. As soon as he saw them, he ran from the entrance of the tent to greet them and, bowing to the ground, he said, "My lords, if it please you, do not go on past your servant. Let a little water be brought. Bathe your feet and recline under the tree. Let me fetch a morsel of bread that you may refresh yourselves. Then go on, seeing that you have come your servant's way."

They replied, "Do as you have said."

Abraham hastened into the tent to Sarah and said, "Quick, three seahs of choice flour. Knead and make cakes!" Then Abraham ran to the herd, took a calf, tender and choice, and gave it to a servant boy, who hastened to prepare it. He took curds and milk and the calf that had been prepared and set these before them. He waited on them under the tree as they ate.

They said to him, "Where is your wife Sarah?" He replied, "There, in the tent."

The one said, "I will return to you next year, and your wife Sarah shall have a son!" Sarah was listening at the entrance of the tent, which was behind him.

Now, Abraham and Sarah were old, advanced in years. Sarah had stopped having periods of women. Sarah laughed to herself, saying, "Now that I am withered, am I to have enjoyment — with my husband so old?"

---

[4]This text and questions are used with permission of the author and publisher from the curriculum "To the Land That I Will Show You: The Story of Avraham" (Millburn, NJ: Ikkar Publishing).

Then the Lord said to Abraham, "Why did Sarah laugh, saying 'Shall I in truth bear a child, old as I am?'" Is anything too wondrous for *Adonai*? I will return to you at the same season next year, and Sarah shall have a son."

Sarah lied, saying, "I did not laugh," for she was frightened.

He replied, "You did laugh."

Again, let the text guide the discussion. However, look at every action, every nuance in order to glean as much as possible from it.

- What human interactions take place in the text?

- How does Abraham treat the visitors?

- What *mitzvah* does Abraham model for us? (hospitality — *hachnasat orchim*)

- Why does Sarah laugh?

- Why does God criticize Sarah?

- What is the difference between what Sarah says and what God reports is said to Abraham? (Sarah says that both she and Abraham are too old. God tells Abraham that Sarah only spoke of herself?)

- Why does God lie?

- What *mitzvah* does God model for us? (*sh'lom bayit* — peace in the home).

Finding values in our texts is dependent upon our ability to resist compartmentalizing our subjects. Torah not only means teaching the stories of our Patriarchs and Matriarchs, it can mean learning the values/*mitzvot* that our tradition imparts through the texts. In this way we give new life to the texts we teach.

Many of the texts we might teach in our schools can serve as models for *mitzvot* and values.

CONCLUSION

It is time-consuming and difficult to teach *mitzvot*, values, and *middot*. However, when teachers devote the necessary time and resources, they can have a profound impact on their students.

> To make the *mitzvot* more topical, I always keep my eye out for pertinent stories in the newspaper. When studying atonement, for instance, we've learned about a Chinese company that deliver apologies for a fee. We also read op-ed pieces on forgiveness after September 11th, discussed Bishop Desmond Tutu's approach to the Truth and Reconciliation Committee in South Africa, and debated Timothy McVeigh's refusal to apologize and its implications in his trial.
>
> *(Dena Salmon, Montclair, New Jersey)*

TEACHING CONSIDERATIONS

- To be effective in teaching *mitzvot*, values, and *middot*, a teacher must be able to export the topics out of the classroom.

- Students will come from a variety of backgrounds and lifestyles. In some instances, what you are teaching may come into conflict with these lifestyles.

- Communication with the home is essential.

- Most parents become supportive when they are made aware of what is coming.

- Make sure your principal/Rabbi knows what you are doing. Parents may share concerns with them rather than with you. Also, if a family is likely to be uncomfortable with what you are teaching (e.g., a grandmother has recently been placed in a nursing home, or there are difficult relationships with grandparents), your supervisor may be privy to that information.

- Make sure that the specific interpretation of the *mitzvot*, values, and *middot* you are teaching is in sync with the school's philosophy. If it is not, the strategies may backfire, causing a difficult situation.

- While there are existing curricula for teaching *mitzvot*, values, and *middot*, consider creating your own. The Bibliography at the end of this chapter suggests several books that feature texts on a variety of topics. Once you have determined the topic you wish to teach, find the appropriate texts and then develop an activity or two to support it.

BIBLIOGRAPHY

Bayar, Steven, and Fran Hirschman. *Teens & Trust: Building Bridges in Jewish Education.* Los Angeles, CA: Torah Aura Productions, 1985.

> This is an excellent tool for strategies and games in introducing *mitzvot*, values, and *middot*.

Bayar, Steven. *Pirkei Avot: Ethics of Our Ancestors.* Millburn, NJ: Ikkar Publishing, 1995.

> This text-based *Pirke Avot* curriculum explains 12 texts from "Ethics of the Fathers" and relates each to a secular film clip in order to teach values.

———. *Avot D'Rabbi Natan: The Ethics of Rabbi Natan.* Millburn, NJ: Ikkar Publishing, 1999.

> Also text-based, this curriculum is more tied to Jewish philosophy than to ethics.

———. *Ziv/Giraffe Program: A Curriculum for Tikun Olam.* Milburn, NJ: Ziv Tzedakah Fund, 1998.

> This text-based, full-year curriculum teaches about the philosophical basis for *tikkun olam* (repairing the world). It explains how different *mitzvot* and holidays can be utilized to achieve *tikkun olam*. This chapter is an encapsulation of the work done on the Ziv Curriculum. (See www.ziv.org/ziv_curriculum.html.)

———. *The Giraffe Heroes Program.* Evanston, IL: The Giraffe Project, 1997.

> Although this is a secular curriculum, it can be readily adapted to the Jewish classroom. (See www.giraffe.org.)

Borowitz, Eugene, and Frances Weinman Schwartz. *The Jewish Moral Virtues.* Philadelphia, PA: Jewish Publication Society, 1999.

> The authors base their work on the thirteenth century book *Sefer Maalot Hamiddot* (The Book of Choicest Virtues) by Yehiel ben Yekutiel, the first systematic, comprehensive, and analytic treatment of the virtues Judaism esteems. Using Yehiel's 24 categories, the authors effectively rewrite the book for contemporary Jews. (See Ingall, below, for a leader's guide to this book.)

Freeman, Susan. *Teaching Jewish Virtues: Sacred Sources and Arts Activities.* Denver, CO: A.R.E. Publishing, Inc., 1999.

> Highlights 25 *middot* (virtues) through background material, extensive text study, and hundreds of imaginative arts activities.

Gopin, Marc, et al. *Jewish Civics: A Tikun Olam/ World Repair Manual.* New York: Coalition for Alternatives in Jewish Education and Washington Institute for Jewish Leadership, 1994.

> This curriculum explores the ways we can improve and repair our world through civics. It serves as a good model for current issues in the Jewish community. A must for any high school educational program.

Gribetz, Beverly. *Issues in Halakhah: Jewish Values Curriculum for the Jewish School in the Diaspora.* Jerusalem: Melton Center for Jewish Education in the Diaspora, Hebrew University, 1982.

> For those interested in teaching texts in depth, this curriculum supplies the necessary material.

Grishaver, Joel Lurie. *40 Things You Can Do to Save the Jewish People.* Los Angeles, CA: Alef Design Group, 1993.

> Each of the 40 activities featured in this book can be readily exported outside the classroom.

Grishaver, Joel Lurie, with Beth Huppin. *Tzedakah, Gemilut Chasadim and Ahavah: A Manual for World Repair.* Denver, CO: ARE Publishing, Inc., 1983.

> A beautifully designed, interactive workbook that introduces these values to students in Grades 4-6.

Ingall, Carol K. *A Leader's Guide To the Study of the Jewish Moral Virtues.* Philadelphia, PA, Jewish Publication Society, 2000.

> Advises study groups on how best to present the material in *The Jewish Moral Virtues* by Eugene Borowitz and Frances Weinman Schwartz (see entry above).

Kadden, Barbara Binder, and Bruce Kadden. *Teaching Mitzvot: Concepts, Values, and Activities.* rev. ed. Denver, CO: ARE Publishing, Inc., 2003.

> An overview of 41 different *mitzvot*, followed by activities for classroom. A user-friendly and complete resource.

Klagsbrun, Francine. *Voices of Wisdom: Jewish Ideals and Ethics for Everyday Living*. New York: Jonathan David, 1986.

Features a very large number of quotes from Jewish sources, many of which can be readily applied to *mitzvot*, values, and *middot*.

Moskowitz, Nachama Skolnik. *A Bridge To Our Tradition: Pirkei Avot*. New York: UAHC Press, 2001. (Teacher Guide, 2002)

A middle school book on *Pirke Avot* that empowers students to think actively about the values of this ancient text in their own lives.

Reisman, Bernard, and Joel Reisman. *The Jewish Experiential Book*. rev. ed. Hoboken, NJ: KTAV Publishing House, 2002.

This book is the standard for Jewish values exercises.

Siegel, Danny. *13 Things Kids Don't Know about Tzedakah*. New York: United Synagogue Youth, 1989.

———. *Practical Mitzvah Suggestions*. rev. ed. New York: United Synagogue Youth, 2000.

Danny Siegel's pamphlets deliver exactly what their titles promise. They are succinct and to the point, and thus an excellent jumping-off point to any lesson.

———. *Good People*. Pittsboro, NC: Town House Press, 1995.

———. *Gym Shoes and Irises* — Book Two. Pittsboro, NC: Town House Press, 1987.

———. *Heroes and Miracle Workers*. Pittsboro, NC: Town House Press, 1997.

———. *Mitzvahs*. Pittsboro, NC: Town House Press, 1992.

———. *Munbaz II and Other Mitzvah Heroes*. Pittsboro, NC: Town House Press, 1988.

———. *Where Heaven & Earth Touch*, Pittsboro, NC: Town House Press, 1988.

These six books are a must for anyone teaching values. They are a treasure trove of texts, strategies, models, and philosophy.

Summers, Barbara Fortgang. *Community and Responsibility in Jewish Tradition: A Study and Action Program*. New York: United Synagogue of America, 1978.

This curriculum, a standard in the field, explores different texts as they relate to the Jewish values of community and responsibility.

Newman, Louis, *The Talmudic Anthology: Tales and Teachings of the Rabbis*. Springfield, NJ: Behrman House, 1996.

Answers to vital questions based on the great Jewish writings of the last 3500 years. Includes stories from the Bible and Talmud and the insights of Jewish commentators.

Telushkin, Joseph. *The Book of Jewish Values: A Day-by-Day Guide To Ethical Living*. New York: Bell Tower, 2000.

The author has combed the Bible, the Talmud, and the whole spectrum of Judaism's sacred writings for the manual on how to lead a decent, kind, and honest life in a morally complicated world.

———. *Jewish Wisdom: Ethical, Spiritual, and Historical Lessons from the Great Works and Thinkers*. New York: William Morrow & Company, 1994.

A collection of hundreds of quotations from the jewish religious and secular canon from the Talmud to Isaac Bashevis Singer and Amos Oz. Organized by theme and accompanied by the author's clear and insightful comments.

CHAPTER 39

Teaching Life Cycle

Bruce Kadden

Teaching the Jewish life cycle would be a new experience for Sam Steinberg. For many years he had taught Bible stories to fifth graders, and a fourth grade tzedakah unit. However, last spring, his principal asked him to teach the sixth grade life cycle class during the upcoming school year. He was confident that he could bring the rituals to life for his students, for example, by inviting a mohel to speak about Brit Milah (circumcision) and by holding a model Jewish wedding ceremony. Most of the students were already excited about their upcoming B'nai Mitzvah ceremonies, so that would be an easy topic to teach.

On the other hand, Sam was somewhat apprehensive about the many sensitive issues related to the life cycle that impacted the families of his students. Jennifer's parents had recently divorced. How would she handle that lesson, he wondered? And Adam's father had passed away a year and a half ago. Would he be able to deal with the unit on death and dying? Were any of the students adopted, he asked himself, as he pondered that topic? The more he thought about it, the more worried he became as he sat down to begin planning the course.

Many teachers of Jewish life cycle view the challenge with a mixture of enthusiasm and apprehension. The life cycle rituals are among the most meaningful in Judaism. Most of our students and their families have participated in many such observances. However, many aspects of the life cycle need to be taught with a special sensitivity to the students and their lives.

When I first began teaching religious school, I was preparing a unit about the death of Moses. In Rabbinical school, we had just studied the long and powerful *midrash* about Moses' death, and I decided to use it to compose a dramatic reading for the students. One of the other teachers of the same grade level wanted her class to join us. Shortly after

I began my presentation, the other teacher suddenly got up, appeared to be emotionally shaken, left the room, and did not return.

Afterward, I learned that this woman's son, a young adult close to my age, had recently been diagnosed with a brain tumor. Fortunately, she was a wonderfully sensitive woman, and we were able to develop a close positive relationship. But that experience taught me how sensitive we as teachers need to be, especially when dealing with material related to death, dying, and other emotional issues.

Furthermore, ethical issues pertaining to the life cycle (such as artificial insemination, surrogate motherhood, and euthanasia) offer particular challenges. We not only need to be aware of our students' sensitivities to such topics, but of our own as well. Many congregations ask members to participate in High Holy Day services. One year my congregation's Ritual Committee asked a woman to read the Haftarah for the first day of Rosh HaShanah about the birth of Samuel. Hannah, Samuel's mother, was barren many years before giving birth. After looking at the reading, she declined the honor. Like Hannah, she also had been barren for many years, but her prayers had not been answered and she had never had children. She recognized that reading that story from the *bimah* would have been too difficult for her. Would this woman have been able to teach about issues pertaining to childbirth?

Those who teach the Jewish life cycle need to be sensitive to their own feelings with regard to certain topics. Would a teacher whose friend recently took her own life be able effectively to teach about suicide? If a teacher has been trying to get pregnant for many years, would she be able to present the subjects of infertility or adoption? Many people are uncomfortable speaking about death, dying, or other sensitive issues. A teacher of Jewish life cycle must be able to evaluate his or her comfort level with each of the sensitive issues of the course. Being able to share one's feelings and concerns with the educator or Rabbi in charge of the school is vital if one is to develop and teach this topic.

If you are unfamiliar with life cycle rituals or issues, it is important to find good resources. A number of useful books are listed in the Bibliography at the end of this chapter. If you have not attended a particular life cycle ceremony, it would be helpful to do so. Speak with the Rabbi of your congregation to determine an appropriate occasion to attend. For each life cycle event you are teaching, identify at least one primary source that answers questions you or your students might have.

Sam had been to a few Jewish weddings and many B'nai Mitzvah observances, but had been to only one funeral, his uncle's, and never attended a Brit Milah. He spoke with his Rabbi and asked to be informed about opportunities to become more familiar with the rituals. After he attended a funeral, he spoke with the Rabbi to make sure that he understood each of the traditions and the meanings behind them. He was glad that he had established a good relationship with the Rabbi, and knew that he would call on her often during the year.

- What Jewish life cycle ceremonies have you attended? Which do you feel comfortable teaching? Which do you need to learn more about?

- Do you have a Rabbi or other knowledgeable person who can answer your questions about the Jewish life cycle?

DEFINING THE TOPIC

Not so long ago, the Jewish life cycle was a well defined topic. The Mishnah, a collection of Jewish teachings compiled in the second century, contains this passage describing the life cycle:

Rabbi Judah ben Tema used to say: At five years old [one should begin to study] Scripture. At ten years old [one should begin to study] Mishnah. At 13 years old [one should begin to observe] *mitzvot*. At 15 years old [one begins to study] Talmud. At 18 year old [one should] marry. At 20 years old [one should] pursue a livelihood. At 30 years old [one is ready] for strength. At 40 years old [one is ready] for understanding. At 50 years old [one is ready] to give advice. At 60 years old [one is ready] for

old age. At 70 years old [one reaches] fullness of age. At 80 years old [one reaches] strong old age. At 90 years old [one becomes] bent. At one hundred years old it is as if one has died and left the world. (*Pirke Avot* 5:24)

While we might object to certain conclusions of Rabbi Judah, we can appreciate his attempt to define the life cycle precisely. Until recently, such a course would include units on Brit Milah and Naming; Bar and Bat Mitzvah, Confirmation (in communities in which it is observed), Marriage, and Death and Dying. A few other topics, such as adoption, divorce, or conversion might also be considered. As our world has changed, so has our need to expand our understanding of the Jewish life cycle. In recent years, Jews have created rituals to mark virtually every moment of the life cycle, as well as new rituals to celebrate traditional life cycle events.

In addition, a plethora of ethical issues has arisen with regard to certain life cycle events, particularly birth and death. New technology has greatly impacted the life cycle as well. All of these matters need to be taken into account when developing a life cycle course.

In some schools, the parameters of such a course may be determined by the curriculum, a document specifying which life cycle events to teach, as well as approaches to teaching them. On the other hand, you might be told to teach the Jewish life cycle with little or no guidance.

Where do you begin? Below is an outline of the major stages of the Jewish life cycle and some of the issues that might be considered at each stage.

Childbirth

The Mitzvah of Procreation

According to Jewish tradition, in order the fulfill the commandment in Genesis to "be fruitful and multiply," one should have at least two children, at least one of whom is male. Today, some Jews are very cognizant of population concerns or do not feel it is an obligation to have children. On the other hand, other Jews, aware of the devastating loss of population during the Holocaust as well as concerns about assimilation and intermarriage, might consider having more than two children. These polar issues (procreation and population) also influence the Jewish attitude toward birth control.

Pregnancy

Judaism has a variety of rituals, both traditional and contemporary, for a pregnant woman and her partner. There are also contemporary Jewish rituals to deal with the tragedies of miscarriage and stillbirth. The challenge of infertility, which faces many women, has led to the development of Jewish positions on the issues of abortion, artificial insemination, *in vitro* fertilization, and surrogate motherhood.

Adoption

Judaism encourages couples to consider adoption when they are not able to conceive or bear children. There are rituals to welcome adopted children into the family.

Brit Milah and Naming

The birth of a child is celebrated in the Jewish community with *Brit Milah* (Covenant of Circumcision) for a boy and *Brit Bat* (Covenant of the Daughter) — the naming, or another ritual for a girl. Traditionally, Jewish firstborn males are redeemed from their priestly responsibilities with the ceremony of *Pidyon HaBen;* some have developed a *Pidyon HaBat* ceremony for a girl.

Childhood and Adolescence

Jewish Education

The role of Jewish education is crucial for passing on Judaism to the next generation. Jewish parents face a choice between sending their children to Jewish day schools or to supplementary schools. The beginning of Jewish education is often celebrated with the ceremony of Consecration. Jews celebrate their coming of age with the ceremonies of Bar/Bat Mitzvah. In addition, many synagogues also offer Confirmation, usually observed at the end of tenth grade.

Issues of Adolescence

In an effort to enhance the meaning of important rites of passage of the teen years, Jewish rituals have recently been developed for menstruation/ puberty, getting a driver's license, graduating from high school, and leaving home for college, military, or work.

Many of my students have never attended the life cycle events we are studying. Even if they have, they were not necessarily watching for the things that I wanted to stress.

I find that using a video of the event in conjunction with an outline of the ceremony is very effective. Videos of *Brit Milah* (ritual circumcision) ceremonies are available. Often a local *mohel* (the person who does the circumcision) will have a tape that is shown to perspective parents. Check out your local Jewish newspaper for a list of *mohelim* or ask your Rabbi. Many *mohelim* are willing to speak to the children about what they do. Try to find a video of a *Simchat Bat* (the ceremony to welcome a baby girl).

Since my wedding was Orthodox, and I teach life cycle in Conservative synagogues, I have used wedding videos from my friends and my educational director. We see segments from each and then stop, compare, and contrast. My middle school students are intrigued by the differences and the reasons for the differences

This year, my students paid a visit to the Rabbi, because he is an expert on Jewish divorce and actually writes *Gittin* (divorce documents). He demonstrated the process of giving a *Get*.

Besides a visit to the funeral home, invite someone from the local *Chevra Kadishah* (the burial society) to speak to the class. It takes the mystery out of the entire process. My students have been impressed with the sensitivity and dignity Jewish tradition provides to the dead. I have always discussed the importance of the *shomer* (a person who watches over a body until burial). September 11th added a new aspect to that. *The New York Times* and other publications had articles about the students from Stern College who volunteered to serve as *shomerot* for the remains of the 9/11 victims on *Shabbat* and holidays, while the bodies were waiting to be identified. The reasons the students gave and how it affected them, stirred my students deeply and touched their their souls.

(Cheryl Cash-Linietsky, Philadelphia, Pennsylvania)

Adulthood

Marriage

The Jewish wedding includes a variety of rituals and traditions. Among the more controversial issues in Jewish life are intermarriage and ceremonies for same-gender couples. Not all Jewish adults choose to marry; some remain single and some live with a significant other, without marriage; these choices have important implications for the Jewish community.

Divorce

When marriage ends in divorce, according to *halachah* (Jewish law), the man gives his wife a *get*, a written release. The issue of the *agunah*, "chained" wives who are not able to remarry because they have not received a *get* from their husbands, is a difficulty worthy of discussion.

Parenting

Parents are responsible for raising and educating their children to be *menschen* (good people) and to enjoy the richness that Judaism offers. Parenting issues are many, including: What does it mean to be a Jewish parent? How do parents handle the tension between providing their children with a religious education, and the plethora of activities in today's secular society? How do interfaith couples raise their children?

Aging

As the Baby Boomers age, the issue of growing older will have special ramifications for the population at large. Judaism demands that we treat the elderly with respect. Questions to consider for this topic include: What are the challenges that adults face as they age? What are the responsibilities of being a Jewish grandparent? What contemporary ceremonies has Judaism developed to recognize the significance of becoming a "senior citizen" and retiring?

Conversion

In recent years, especially, Judaism has tried to welcome those who have wanted to become Jewish. There is a difference in the requirements of conversion between the Reform, Conservative, and Orthodox, as well as acceptance of conversions by other movements. Jews by Choice are welcomed warmly into the community, yet also face issues because of their new entry into Judaism.

Death and Dying

Illness and Visiting the Sick

It is a *mitzvah* to visit the sick. How does this *mitzvah* apply to specific circumstances? What is the obligation of the community toward those who are physically and mentally ill? Treatment of the terminally ill can be quite controversial, especially issues such as physician-assisted suicide and euthanasia.

Preparing for Death

Creating an ethical will is a time-honored Jewish tradition; these letters provide heirs with instructions on living an ethical/moral life. In addition, much attention has been focused recently on the importance of creating a living will or a "Durable Power of Attorney" for health care; this raises issues of respect for the elderly.

Suicide

Suicide is one of the great tragedies of life. While Judaism opposes suicide, it tries to be sensitive and supportive of surviving family members. Education for signs of suicidal thoughts is important for both teens and adults.

Preparation of the Body for Burial

Judaism insists the body be treated with dignity following death. It is not to be left alone from the moment of death to burial, which is traditionally scheduled soon after. Cremation is forbidden by Jewish law and autopsy is only permitted by *halachah* under exceptional circumstances. However, donating organs is permitted. Preparation of the body includes *taharah* (the ritual washing) and dressing the body in a shroud.

Funeral

The Jewish funeral service includes certain Psalms, "*Ayl Malay Rachamim*" (a chanted prayer), the "Mourner's *Kaddish*," and a eulogy. In addition, the rituals of *k'riah* (tearing the garment) and shoveling dirt in the grave are important ways for mourners to begin working through their own pain at the death of a loved one.

Mourning Rituals

Judaism has developed a number of mourning rituals that are observed following the death of a loved one. These begin with customs at the Jewish cemetery, move to rituals marked at the *shivah* (first week of mourning) in the home, and proceed through the first year after death. What are the appropriate rituals to observe when visiting a Jewish cemetery? a home in the week following a funeral and afterward?

> For the unit on life cycle, I've used two teddy bears, "Dov" and "Dova," who experience the entire cycle from *B'rit Milah* (ritual circumcision) and *B'rit Bat* (bringing a baby girl into the covenant) through B'nai Mitzvah, wedding, and the funeral for one of their grandparents. In a small Jewish community with few opportunities to experience most of these events firsthand, the bears helped to make these events come alive.
>
> (Rabbi David Feder, Morgantown, West Virginia)

CREATING A CURRICULUM

In many ways, the Jewish life cycle is a curriculum lived. As an infant, most Jewish children have a *Brit Milah* or a *Brit Bat* or other naming ceremony. The child then celebrates becoming a Bar Mitzvah or a Bat Mitzvah at age 13, and oftentimes Confirmation at the end of tenth grade. As an adult, the person usually marries, and becomes familiar with Jewish rituals of death and mourning when burying a parent or other loved one. Is it therefore really necessary that we teach our students about the life cycle?

Whereas it was once taken for granted that all Jews would experience Jewish life cycle rituals, that is no longer the case. For many Jews, these rituals are optional. And yet, those who observe them invariably find that they are deeply moved by these rites of passage. For many Jews, the experiences of holiness and transcendence most often occur at a life cycle celebration. As Rabbi Jeffrey Salkin has written, "At their best, when the poetry works and the magic does its stuff, life cycle cele-

brations keep Jews connected to the Jewish people, to God, and to Torah."[1]

While we cannot expect our students to have the same powerful experiences learning about the life cycle as they might by actually participating in them, we can impress upon them the potential of these rituals to sanctify and transform their lives. Our ultimate aim should be for our students to recognize the importance and meaning of life cycle rituals so that they draw meaning in celebrating these rituals at the appropriate times in their lives. Furthermore, in introducing Judaism's understanding of the ethical issues pertaining to the life cycle, we want our students to be able to call upon Jewish sources and authorities when faced with important choices, and also to recognize the value of these resources in helping them make informed decisions.

With so much from which to choose, how does one decide what to teach? In addition to the above factors, you will want to take into account the following factors.

Age of Students

Life cycle is sometimes taught as young as third grade or as part of a high school program, although it can be taught to younger children and to adults. The age of the students is crucial in designing the curriculum. For younger students, you will probably want to focus on the basic life cycle rituals and practices. For older students, you may want to include newer rituals that are pertinent to their age (such as getting a driver's license for 15 or 16-year-olds). With a class of teenagers or adults, you may wish to explore some of the ethical issues that relate to the life cycle.

Time

The amount of time you have to teach the course will significantly affect its content. Obviously, a mini-course comprised of six lessons that are 90 minutes in length, will be different from a year-long, hour per week class.

Class Size

The number of students may also dictate the type of

---

[1] Barbara Binder Kadden and Bruce Kadden, *Teaching Jewish Life Cycle* (Denver, CO: A.R.E. Publishing, Inc., 1997), ix.

activities that you use in the class. A small, intimate group may be ideal for class discussions, whereas with a group of 20 students this may be more difficult. Small group work, cooperative learning, and *chevruta* (work in pairs) all break the class into smaller groups that make learning participatory.

Goals

The most important factor in determining the objectives and activities of your class will be the goals you wish to accomplish. If goals are not set out in your curriculum, you will need to create them. Here are some suggestions:

- Students will recognize the importance and meaning of life cycle rituals and eagerly anticipate celebrating/observing them at the appropriate times in their lives.

- Students will access a variety of resources (print, video, Internet, etc.) on life cycle issues, thus enabling them to locate information at a time of need.

- When faced with important choices with regard to the life cycle, students will understand the value of consulting Jewish sources and authorities to help make their decisions.

- Students will identify and explain the following life cycle ceremonies: *Brit Milah, Brit Bat*, Bar Mitzvah, Bat Mitzvah, Confirmation, Marriage, Divorce, Death and Mourning.

- Students will explain the importance of life cycle rituals to living a Jewish life.

- Students will create a life cycle ritual.

- Students will discuss the Jewish attitude toward: abortion, artificial insemination, living wills, autopsy, divorce, intermarriage, etc.

Philosophy of the School

The approach to teaching life cycle will be very different depending on the Judaic philosophy of your school. You should speak with the educator or principal of the school and/or the Rabbi to be sure you understand the philosophy and what may and may not be taught. In an Orthodox or traditional school, a life cycle class will no doubt emphasize traditional rituals and traditional understandings of those rituals. Such topics as intermarriage or cremation may be off limits or may need to be presented in a specified manner, emphasizing Jewish opposition to such practices. Not all schools may want the issues of same-gender marriage or suicide to be taught. If you are teaching about ethical matters pertaining to the life cycle, you will want to be aware of the position of the movement your school represents or, if you teach in a community school, the variety of positions of the movements representing the students in your school.

> *Sam thought a lot about his overall goals for the class. "What do I want to have these students remember about the Jewish life cycle ten or 15 years from now?" he thought. He looked at the list of topics and began to create his curriculum. He knew that in the limited time he had with the students each week he could not cover all of the topics. He also realized that while it was important that the students learn the background and meaning of the rituals, he also wanted them to experience the feelings that go along with the rituals and to struggle with some of the ethical questions that pertain to the life cycle. Although his students were only sixth graders, he knew that they were aware of such topics as abortion and adoption, intermarriage, and suicide.*

Consider the following:

- What do you want your students to remember about the Jewish life cycle ten or 15 years from now?

- What topics do you want to cover during the course?

- Do you want to focus on the rituals or do you also want to consider ethical issues?

STRATEGIES FOR TEACHING LIFE CYCLE

The Jewish life cycle presents a unique opportunity to thread lessons together throughout the course. You might, for example, create a family (using dolls or puppets) and follow "their journey" through the life cycle. Alternatively, students might be assigned the roles of family members for each lesson.

Other ways to tie the lessons together include:

- keeping a journal of one's life cycle experiences.

- creating a mural depicting the variety of life cycle events.

- making a video of the Jewish life cycle.

- creating a scrapbook of life cycle celebrations.

- finding opportunities for students to attend or participate in life cycle rituals in the congregation or community, such as a *Brit Milah*, naming ceremony, or funeral, or *shivah minyan*.

On Tuesday, January 28, 2003, I had had a discussion with my *Aleph* students about the Space Shuttle Columbia and the first Israeli astronaut, Ilan Ramon. We spoke about his being a child of survivors, the things he chose to bring into space, and the role he played as a representative of the Jewish people, observing many *mitzvot* in space. Then, to everyone's horror, on Saturday, the first of February, the shuttle Columbia broke apart upon reentry to earth and all the astronauts perished.

On Sunday morning, February 2, as I drove to school, I knew that I had to address the loss of the shuttle and the astronauts. One of students greeted me with the comment, "If we hadn't had that discussion about Ilan Ramon, I wouldn't have been so upset." Another commented on how the Torah scroll had survived the Nazis, only to be destroyed this way. We spoke about what Jews do when someone dies. Since we couldn't pay a *shivah* call, we wrote a letter as a class to Mrs. Ramon and to Prime Minister Sharon. Each child signed his/her name in Hebrew and English. We also decided to use our *tzedekah* money to plant a tree in Colonel Ramon's memory. The Rabbi also came in to talk to the children about the loss and to answer their questions.

(Cheryl Cash-Linietsky, Philadelphia, Pennsylvania)

WHERE TO BEGIN

While it seems logical to begin the teaching of life cycle with rituals pertaining to birth and continue through death, other approaches are possible. For example, you might begin with a couple getting married, and then follow their journey as they bear children, raise them, face the death of a parent, etc. Alternatively, the class might focus on an older couple who flash back to various points in their lives (birth of children, marriage, B'nai Mitzvah of children, etc.).

CONCLUSION

Teaching the Jewish life cycle can be an exciting, stimulating experience for both teacher and students. It touches on some of the most intimate and personal parts of our life, moments of life and death, moments of joy and sadness. By introducing students to the rituals and ethical issues of the life cycle, we begin preparing them to live a life enriched by Jewish values and traditions. While students will not be able to absorb all of the details about the life cycle, we can offer them resources for a lifetime and help kindle a spark in them that will be lit over and over again as they grow and experience the cycle of Jewish life.

TEACHING CONSIDERATIONS

- Identify or create goals and objectives for the course.

- Define the topics that you will be covering.

- Clarify the philosophy of the school as it pertains to the topics you will cover.

- Determine the time frame you have to cover the material.

- Consider the age and maturity of the students.

- Take into account class size, physical space and other logistical information.

ADDITIONAL VIGNETTES

Death and Mourning

You are preparing a lesson on Jewish customs pertaining to death and mourning. You remember that Joseph's grandfather recently passed away. Since that time Joseph has seemed more withdrawn in class.

- How does the death of Joseph's grandfather affect how you will design your lesson?

- Will you speak to Joseph before you teach this lesson?

- Will you speak to his parents? What if it was Joseph's mother or father who had passed away?

Marriage

You are teaching a mini-course on Jewish marriage to high school students in a communal school. The principal has clearly stated that you must convey the message to your students that Jews should marry other Jews. Yet you know that many of the parents of your students are interfaith couples.

- How do you, in a sensitive manner, present to your students the message of marrying other Jews?

- Would it be a good idea to speak with the principal about presenting this topic in a different fashion?

BIBLIOGRAPHY

Books

Adelman, Penina V., and Beth K. Haber. *Miriam's Well: Rituals for Jewish Women around the Year*. 10th anniv. ed. New York: Biblio Press, 1996.

A collection of creative women's rituals for life cycle and other celebrations.

Aqua, Risa Towbin, and Hal Aqua. *The Life Cycle Journey: A Workbook for Jewish Students*. Denver, CO: A.R.E. Publishing, Inc., 2000.

A description of the Jewish life cycle for Grades 4-6 with many engaging activities. Leader Guide is also available.

Cardin, Nina Beth. *The Tapestry of Jewish Time: A Spiritual Guide To Holidays and Life Cycle Events*. West Orange, NJ: Behrman House, 2000.

Includes detailed explanations of rituals and historical background, as well as contemporary innovations for observing life cycle events.

Diamant, Anita. *Choosing a Jewish Life: A Handbook for the New Jewish Convert*. New York: Schocken Books, 1997.

Although written for one who has converted to Judaism, this book contains much useful information for teaching about conversion.

————. *The New Jewish Baby Book: Names, Ceremonies & Customs, A Guide for Today's Families*. Woodstock, VT: Jewish Lights Publishing, 1994.

An excellent resource for rituals pertaining to birth and naming.

————. *The New Jewish Wedding*. rev. ed. New York: Simon and Schuster, 2001.

A guide to Jewish wedding rituals and traditions.

Friedland, Ronnie, and Edmund Case, eds. *The Guide To Jewish Interfaith Family Life*. Woodstock, VT: Jewish Lights Publishing, 2001.

A collection of articles from both Jewish professionals and intermarried individuals concerning Jewish life cycle observances.

Geffen, Rela M., ed. *Celebration & Renewal: Rites of Passage in Judaism*. Philadelphia, PA: Jewish Publication Society, 1993.

Essays by a number of scholars about the Jewish life cycle, including birth, parenting, Bar/Bat Mitzvah, conversion, marriage, divorce, illness, aging, and death and mourning. Contains an excellent glossary of terms relating to the life cycle.

Grishaver, Joel Lurie. *The Life Cycle Workbook*. Denver, CO: A.R.E. Publishing Inc., 1983.

A cartoon workbook for teaching the life cycle to intermediate grades.

Isaacs, Ronald. H. *Rites of Passage: A Guide To the Jewish Life Cycle*. Hoboken, NJ: KTAV Publishing House, Inc., 1992.

Offers a concise explanation of rituals and traditions associated with the Jewish life cycle. Also contains examples of some ceremonies for life cycle celebration.

Isaacs, Ronald. H., and Kerry M. Olitzky. *Sacred Moments: Tales from the Jewish Life Cycle*. Northvale, NJ: Jason Aronson Inc., 1995.

A variety of stories and traditional texts that relate to the life cycle.

Kadden, Barbara Binder, and Bruce Kadden. *Teaching Jewish Life Cycle: Traditions and Activities*. Denver, CO: A.R.E. Publishing, Inc., 1997.

A treasure trove of information and activities for teaching every aspect of the Jewish life cycle to all age groups. Each chapter contains an overview of the topic, sources from Jewish tradition, and more than 50 activities categorized by age group. Also contains activities for adult classes, family programs, and all-school programs.

Klein, Isaac. *A Guide To Jewish Religious Practice*. New York: The Jewish Theological Seminary of America, 1979.

A comprehensive guide to Jewish practice from the perspective of Conservative Judaism.

Kolatch, Alfred J. *The Jewish Book of Why*. Middle Village, NY: Jonathan David Publishers, Inc., 1981.

An excellent resource for when students ask why we do things the way we do.

————. *The Second Jewish Book of Why*. Middle Village, NY: Jonathan David Publishers, Inc., 1985.

A continuation of the first book in this series.

Kula, Irwin, and Vanessa L. Ochs. *The Book of Jewish Sacred Practices: CLAL's Guide To Everyday and Holiday Rituals and Blessings.* Woodstock, VT: Jewish Lights Publishing, 2001.

> Traditional and contemporary ways to mark important moments in one's life.

Lamm, Maurice. *The Jewish Way in Death and Mourning.* Middle Village, NY: Jonathan David Publishers, Inc., 2000.

> Traditional perspective of rituals and issues pertaining to death and mourning.

———. *The Jewish Way in Love and Marriage.* San Francisco, CA: Harper & Row, 1991.

> Traditional perspective of rituals and issues pertaining to marriage.

Musleah, Rahel. *Journey of a Lifetime: The Jewish Life Cycle Book.* West Orange, NJ: Behrman House, 1997.

> Designed for grades four to five, this book has both text and activities pertaining to the life cycle. A Teacher's Guide and family education material are also available.

Olitzky, Kerry M. *The Life Cycle Workbook Leader Guide.* Denver, CO: A.R.E. Publishing, Inc., 1983.

> This Leader Guide for *The Life Cycle Workbook* by Joel Lurie Grishaver contains ideas for activities that can be used in connection with the workbook or independently.

Orenstein, Debra, ed. *Lifecycles: Jewish Women on Life Passages and Personal Milestones,* vol. 1. Woodstock, VT: Jewish Lights Publishing, 1994.

> Essays and rituals pertaining to the life cycle from birth to death, with particular emphasis on the life cycle of women.

Schulweis, Harold M. *Finding Each Other in Judaism: Meditations on the Rites of Passage from Birth To Immortality.* New York: UAHC Press, 2001.

> A variety of meditations for the life cycle written by one of the preeminent Conservative Rabbis of our age.

Shekel, Michal. *The Jewish Lifecycle Book.* Hoboken, NJ: KTAV Publishing House, Inc., 1989.

> A textbook on Jewish life cycle rituals. A teacher's guide is available.

———. *Skill Text for The Jewish Lifecycle Book.* Hoboken, NJ: KTAV Publishing House, Inc., 1989.

> Student activity book for *The Jewish Lifecycle Book.*

Weber, Vicki L., ed. *The Rhythm of Jewish Time: An Introduction To Holidays and Life Cycle Events.* West Orange, NJ: Behrman House, Inc., 1998.

> Explains the meaning of the customs central to Jewish life cycle events.

———. *Tradition! Celebration and Ritual in Jewish Life.* West Orange, NJ: Behrman House, Inc., 2000.

> Full-color visual reference book that includes a section on the rituals of the Jewish life cycle.

Media

The Journey
Ergo Media Inc.
35-minute video

> An American Jew visiting Russia in 1939 encounters a Russian Jewish youth and realizes that it is up to him to prepare the youngster for his Bar Mitzvah.

The Eighth Day
Ergo Media Inc.
25 minutes

> In the days of the Maccabees, a couple must decide whether to circumcise their son in defiance of the Greek edict.

The Corridor
Ergo Media Inc.
25 minutes

> The meaning of death and afterlife for Jews is explored in this drama about two Americans who are involved in a car accident in Israel.

The Discovery
Ergo Media Inc.
60 minutes

> A film about the struggles of a 12-year-old boy as he prepares for his Bar Mitzvah.

Seal upon Thy Heart
Ergo Media Inc.
30 minutes

> A young Jewish couple plans and celebrates their traditional Jewish wedding with the guidance of their family and Rabbi.

When Love Meets Tradition
Direct Cinema Ltd.
28 minutes

A number of couples discuss the challenges of intermarriage.

Number Our Days
Direct Cinema Ltd.
29 minutes

Based on the book by Barbara Myerhoff, this award winning video looks at the elderly Jewish community of Venice California.

Web Sites

www.milah.net
A Parent's Guide To Brit Milah (Ritual Circumcision)

An overview of the laws and customs surrounding the mitzvah of *Brit Milah* (ritual circumcision)

http://shamash.org/reform/uahc/congs/ot/ot005/
bmnews7.html#MODEL
About Milah or Circumcision

A parent-oriented brochure about *Brit Milah* (ritual circumcision), prepared through the *Berit Mila Newsletter* — A publication of the National Organization of American Mohelim/ot (affiliated with the Reform Movement)

www.ahavat-israel.com/torat/lifecycle.html
Ahavat Torat Israel — Jewish Life Cycle

Birth and Circumcision, Bar Mitzvah and Bat Mitzvah, Marriage and Divorce, Death and Mourning.

www.Kaddish.org
Dealing with Death

Articles on the meaning of death for Jews, the relevance of Jewish rituals at this time, how to handle the subject of death in the family, and reviews of books dealing with the topic.

www.Jewish-funerals.org
Jewish Funerals Burial and Mourning

Official web site of the Jewish Funeral Practices Committee of Greater Washington, a 23-year-old federation of synagogues providing education and assistance.

www.scheinerman.net/judaism/life-cycle
Rabbi Scheinerman's Home Page

Information on the Jewish life cycle.

http://MyJewishLearning.com
Hebrew College

A personal gateway to Jewish exploration, guided learning, other life events.

CHAPTER 40

Teaching Jewish Holidays

Nachama Skolnik Moskowitz

Michael Schiller finished his first day of teaching religious school, feeling great about the students and his introductory lesson on holidays. After arriving home, he turned off his phone and spent hours with great excitement preparing his lessons for the next three weeks. During that time, he got a message from a parent. Wondering if the mom was calling to say that little Susie had a great beginning to religious school, Michael called back.

"Mrs. Schwartz? This is Michael Schiller, Susie's religious school teacher. I'm returning your call from earlier in the day. May I help you with something?" Mrs. Schwartz proceeded to tell Michael that Susie was totally bored in class this morning and did not want to return next week. "After all," her mom reported, "Susie said that she learned all about holidays each of the years she has been in religious school!"[1]

One would think that the teaching of Jewish holidays would be an easy task for a Jewish teacher. Resource books abound with background information, art projects, stories, and games. Yet, for a myriad of reasons, students like Susie complain. It is true, that when family home observance does not match what is being taught in school, students feel dissonance; holiday lessons can seem unimportant. Some teachers place the "blame," therefore, on the family. However, educators have great power to engage students in learning and meaningful ritual observance. This chapter provides direction to making this possible.

THE ISSUES

There are a number of reasons that students like Susie feel as if holidays are "overdone" from year to year:

- *The nature of the Jewish calendar* - Quite obviously, the holidays return each year! There is little that a teacher can do about this, other than embrace the calendar's cycle as an opportunity to engage students once again in the beauty, wonder, and connectedness of Jewish life!

- *The sense of obligation many teachers have for teaching holidays* - It is interesting that teachers who have not been given any contractual obligation for teaching Jewish holidays often feel that it is in their domain to spend some time teaching each holiday. In some schools, this is fine, but in others, it creates the obvious issues of overlap and repetition. That is not inherently bad, but with all the potential topics and themes for Jewish education, it's a shame to be teaching something that the school director has delegated to someone else.

- *The repetition of information from year to year* - In some schools, teachers are simply told, "Teach the holidays as they come." And so, there is no clear understanding of the focus for each grade level, creating a repetition of information and sometimes of learning activities.

- *The concern of teachers that students don't know anything about this holiday* - Conscientious teachers often spend the first part of a new unit checking to see what students remember from previous years. This is good! But many times students have a hard time "dusting off" old knowledge that is now out of context from an earlier year's work. By the time students are warmed up to what they remember, many teachers launch into a comprehensive overview of key dates, people, and rituals . . . not get-

---

[1]Thanks to Bill Bronstein for this vignette.

ting to the "new" lessons they might have taught otherwise.

- *The mindless nature of many learning activities* - Word finds, mazes, and fill-in-the-blank worksheets focus on the lowest levels of information and facts. They don't engage students in the bigger, more exciting concepts that form the foundation of Jewish thought.

- *The making "again" of certain holiday ritual objects* - How many parents have sighed as their children bring home yet another *Seder* plate from religious school?

While some of these issues are not in the teacher's hands (e.g., the return of holidays year after year, or the director's inattention to a spiral curriculum), there are a number of steps a teacher may take to mediate the issues faced by Susie and her classmates.

STEP 1: A CONVERSATION WITH THE DIRECTOR

It is important to gain some basic understanding of decisions a school has made in regard to the teaching of Jewish holidays. A first-step conversation with the education director or department head offers an opportunity for clarity and direction. Questions to consider asking include:

- What is the school's philosophy in regard to Jewish holidays? (This is not a question that gets at the "how-to" answers, but rather opens the door to a discussion of the educational institution's religious beliefs and practices.)

- What expectations are there for how I approach the teaching of holidays?

- What are the general practices of families who send their children to this school?

- Am I expected to teach Jewish holidays as part of my curriculum? If it's not part of my teaching assignment, but I wish to do so, *may* I teach the holidays?

- What was the holiday curriculum last year for these students? What will it be next year?

- What curricular guidance is there for me? a set of objectives? a list of the key concepts? a full curriculum?

- Is there a textbook? a teacher guide?

- What can I take home (books, web site addresses, videos) that will help me prepare for the specific holiday lessons I am to teach?

- What art projects have students done in earlier years? Are there any special projects or activities "reserved" for specific grade levels?

- Are there any grade-specific or all-school holiday programs?

- What information about the holidays is generally sent home to parents? How responsive are they?

- Does the educational institution have family education programs for various holidays? If so, what are my responsibilities as a teacher?

STEP 2: THINKING ABOUT THE CURRICULUM

In the summer before school begins, teachers walk out of their school director's office grasping curriculum guides, textbooks, and resource books. It is important to consider the guidance each offers for lessons about the Jewish holidays, as well as the issues presented by each.

Curriculum Guides

Some schools provide teachers with a curriculum guide, whether school-created, or something bought from a publisher. Often these move through a thoughtful spiral from grade to grade. They are helpful because they minimize overlap through the grade levels and often have specific activities for each age group.

Teachers may find the following materials either in their school resource centers, or order them online:

- *A Curriculum for a Jewish Religious School (Grades K-10)* by Audrey Friedman Marcus with Diane Samet - This is a comprehensive spiral curriculum, Kindergarten through

Grade 10, with a focus on six core areas, one of which is the holidays. The catalog description says, Holidays are stressed in Kindergarten and Grade 1, and are discussed and celebrated briefly in each grade thereafter as they occur. In each grade from K-8, there is a focus holiday or two on which more time is spent. Additionally, in each grade, different aspects of the holidays are stressed (e.g., holidays celebrated at home, holidays celebrated in synagogue, *brachot* (blessings) associated with holidays, etc.). These features are designed to avoid repetition of the same material in every grade.

To order this curriculum, contact A.R.E Publishing, Inc.[2]

- *Melton Holiday, Mitzvot and Prayer Curriculum* - Though no longer in print, many (if not most) school and central Jewish agency resource centers still have copies of the well respected Melton Holiday Curriculum, written by Gail Dorph and Vicky Kelman. Designed for four grade levels, this comprehensive lesson-by-lesson guide integrates the teaching of holidays with that of *mitzvot* and Hebrew prayers. Teacher background and resource sheets are also included.

- *Jewish Education Center of Cleveland (JECC), Project Curriculum Renewal's Thematic Holiday Curriculum (Grades 3-5)* - This curriculum offers a very different approach to the organization of holiday teaching. Each grade focuses on a theme:[3] third grade is about Cycles, fourth on Responsibilities, and fifth on Freedom. The holidays are then divided among the grades, so that four are studied in depth over multiple sessions each year. For example, in fifth grade, stu-

dents focus on the freedom-related holidays: Chanukah, Pesach, Lag Ba'Omer, and Yom HaAtzma'ut. The other holidays are usually "covered" in one lesson. This curriculum is available from the JECC.[4]

- *First Steps: Learning and Living for Young Jewish Children* by Ruth Musnikow - The Bureau of Jewish Education of New York many years ago published a wonderful curriculum guide for young children, ages three to eight. It offers an integrated approach to holiday education, combining developmentally appropriate learning (cooking, art, science, language) with the teaching of Jewish holidays. This curriculum guide is available from the BJE of New York.[5]

Other curriculum materials do exist for the teaching of Jewish holidays. These listed, however, offer distinct approaches to the organization of the curriculum.[6]

> Reflection has allowed me to see how negligent I was to assume that because my students were Jewish, they had experienced the basics of Jewish ritual. I realize now that in many instances we cannot assume that ritual behavior is reinforced in the home.
>
> *(Amy Appelman, West Bloomfield, Michigan)*

Textbooks

In many schools, teachers are given an age appropriate textbook (with teacher guide, if available[7]) and told, "teach!" The obvious advantages are that teacher preparation is focused (read Chapter X before the students do), information is structured, activities are often provided, and overlap between grade levels is minimal. However, textbooks can

---

[2]To order, go to www.arepublish.com/curriculum.html or call 800-346-7779.

[3]This curriculum was developed using *Understanding by Design*. Each grade level is organized around a formal "enduring understanding." For more information on Understanding by Design, see Chapter 24, "Curriculum Planning: A Model for Understanding" is by Nachama Skolnik Moskowitz, pp. 278-291 in this Handbook.

[4]For contact information, go to www.jecc.org.

[5]To order, go to www.bjeny.org/BookStore.asp.

[6]For thoughts on studying the approaches of different curriculum and textbooks, see Chapter 26, "Studying Curriculum Materials: A Strategy for Improving Teaching" by Gail Zaiman Dorph, pp. 311-322 in this Handbook.

[7]Be sure to ask if there is a teacher guide for the textbook you have been given, and/or check on the publisher's web site. Many directors either forget that a book has a corresponding guide, or they don't remember to give teachers the guide because it is situated in a space away from the textbook storage area.

lend themselves to a reading round-robin style of teaching ("Joe, you read the next section"), which is not very stimulating.

Prior to bringing textbooks into the classroom, teachers must still consider the lesson's focus (whether objectives or "big idea"), the initial way they will engage students, age appropriate and meaningful activities, as well as ways of bridging learning to the home.[8]

Resource Books

For beginning teachers, general reference and resource books[9] can be the most confusing materials from which to work. They offer a lot of information about each holiday and/or provide a multitude of activities from which to choose. Unless teachers in a specific school formally "lay claim" to certain teaching ideas, it is possible that students will do the same or similar activities in consecutive years.

To use these books successfully, it is important to choose a conceptual framework from which to teach each holiday and then to match learning activities with each lesson's focus. It is also important to evaluate the value of each activity for the students. Some activities are conceptually on a lower level than others and while they may be "fun," they won't engage students and/or promote deep learning.[10]

Teacher-Developed

Many teachers do create their own holiday lessons. The best are well thought-out and based on the "big ideas" of Judaism, rather than an off the cuff "discussion" followed by an art project. In this Handbook, "Part V: Curriculum Considerations" offers some formats to help shape quality lessons.

STEP 3: THINKING ABOUT HOLIDAY TEACHING ISSUES

As with any teaching topic, holidays offer their own challenges. It is important to give thought to them in advance.

Beyond the Details

Holidays are much more than a listing of facts and ritual observances. They open the door to Jewish life, offering insight into Jewish theology, history, and values. A study of holidays (as well, certainly, as their celebration) helps Jews understand the key ideas of Jewish life. The choices teachers make in their classrooms either introduce students to big understandings, or get them mired in the minutia.

Bridging Home

School is an artificial setting where learning takes place out of the context of Jewish practice. Our holidays are traditionally observed in the home and/or in the synagogue, and so bridging learning to those places must be part of the teaching plan. This can happen in a number of ways:

- Create ritual objects that may be used in the home. Send these home with appropriate instructions and blessings. (See caveat under "Ritual Objects" on the next page.) Some schools create home packages like "Shabbat in a Box" — complete with candles, a small bottle of grape juice, a small *challah*, instructions, etc.

- Send home a sheet with background information on the holiday, along with celebration ideas and family discussion questions.

- Provide families links to holiday web sites.

- Create Holiday Packs that go home to students on a rotating basis. These might include resource books, story books, music tapes or CDs, a holiday video, and a journal for recording what families found interesting or had questions about.

- Prior to a holiday establish a hotline — a phone number that families can call with holiday preparation questions.

- Help make matches between families for holiday dinners or celebrations.

- Bring to the classroom information about

---

[8]For a wonderful guide on the use of textbooks see, "Making Textbooks Work for You" by Dr. Carol K. Ingall, available at www.behrmanhouse.com/cat/free/maktext/index.shtml.

[9]See the Bibliography at the end of this chapter for a listing of such books.

[10]For a discussion of the issues in teaching disparate facts and the use of low-level activities, see Chapter 1, "Beyond Apples and Honey: The Editor's Soapbox" by Nachama Skolnik Moskowitz, pp. 1-12 in this Handbook.

family holiday celebrations "after the fact" (i.e., after the holiday has come and gone). Build upon this sharing between students. Are there new questions raised that need exploration?

Ritual Objects

As noted several times in this chapter, one "overdone" aspect of holiday teaching is the creation of Jewish ritual objects. It is true that often the only ritual objects owned by families on the "fringe" of Jewish life, are the ritual items sent home from religious school. But there is no reason for children to bring home each year of preschool a Pesach *Seder* plate made of cupcake cups stuck onto an aluminum foil covered pizza wheel! Such low quality materials put a low value on Jewish rituals.

It is much more appropriate for teachers to negotiate among themselves, with the help of the school director, as to which age group will create a quality-made ritual object for various holidays, and plan budget expenditures accordingly.

Worksheets and Other Teaching "Stuff"

Worksheets and resource sheets abound for the teaching of holidays. Some of these are part of student textbooks, and others are found in teacher resource books or "student fun books" on the general market. However, if teachers are to take seriously "teaching for the big ideas," then the value of these sheets needs to be weighed against the final goals. There are lots of ways to engage students in the importance of Jewish holidays. Before choosing a particular sheet, consider whether it helps attain the learning goals determined in the beginning stages of unit or lesson development.

Moreover, it is important to realize that the *kedushah* (holiness) of holidays is best realized through hands-on experiences and thoughtful conversations, not a fill-in-the-blank exercise.

Hebrew

Teachers should think through the place of Hebrew in their holiday curriculum. In some schools, the person who teaches Hebrew is not the person who teaches the holidays. Yet, Hebrew blessings and songs are a natural part of holiday curriculum. Coordination between such teachers, including the use of non-transliterated material for students who can decode, is important.

Integration

While holidays are often taught in a lesson unto themselves, they provide rich opportunities for integration. For example, there are some wonderful videos and children's books on holidays celebrated at important points in American and world history. A unit on *K'lal Yisrael* (the unity of the Jewish people) can include holiday celebrations by Jews in different cultures.[11]

Modeling

There are a number of ways to open students to the joy of celebrating Jewish holidays, but the most authentic way is to involve them! This may include:

- talking about your own observances of a holiday.

- inviting a guest to class to talk about his or her observances.

- asking students to share what their families did on a particular holiday (in some settings, the structuring of this sharing is important so that those whose families have minimal (or no) observances, do not feel left out or Jewishly inadequate.

- inviting students to special holiday events hosted by the school or synagogue.

- inviting students to your home or apartment to set up for a holiday, or enjoy a snack or meal together.

Age Group Challenges

Early Childhood

One of the key learning goals for our youngest children is the building of holiday memories through a variety of sensory inputs. This means the teacher must think seriously about holiday *sights*

---

[11]The JECC web site has a number of "Holiday Helpers," a listing of resources for the teaching of selected holidays:

www.jecc.org/edres/medtech/abv.htm.

(lit candles, set tables), *sounds* (blessings, songs, special noises . . . like a *shofar*), *smells* (food, Havdalah spices), *tastes* (all the yummy — and not so yummy — things we eat), and *kinesthetic experiences* (shaking a *lulav*, spinning a *dreidel*).

It is also important that teachers consider the big Jewish ideas that could inform their lesson planning. For example, four-year-olds can understand that the Maccabees stood up for what they felt was right (i.e., the value of "courage"). We are proud of them for their actions and therefore "publicize the miracles of this holiday," which in Hebrew is known as the *mitzvah* called *pirsum ha-nes*. If these two ideas are the focus of learning, then a teacher might choose to:

- read Chanukah stories telling of the courage of the Maccabees.

- place costumes for the Maccabees in the dramatic play center.

- offer pictures of The Temple in Jerusalem to those playing in the block area.

- develop art activities that families can post on their windows to "publicize the miracle."

- find songs that focus on the courage of the Maccabees.

- share different *chanukiyot* during group time, helping students see their function (as well as beauty) in publicizing the story of Chanukah.

- place *chanukiyot* on low shelves or tables for students to explore, fill with candles, or sketch.

- introduce the *dreidel* as a diversion used by the Maccabees when they did not want their enemies to know they were courageous enough to study Judaism.

These foci may also mean reevaluating projects with a long history in the class or school, but that do not bring children to the "big ideas" that have been delineated. (For example, no longer making non-functional *chanukiyot* out of empty spools of thread, burning different kinds of oil to see which produces a brighter flame, or playing pin the *shamash* on the *chanukiyah*.)

It is also important to remember that young children cannot celebrate holidays on their own, but are dependent on their families. This means that more important than the education of the young child, is the education of his or her parents in a "safe and non-threatening" way. The ideas in "Bridging Home" (see p. 475 above) provide some thoughts on helping this happen.

> Sometimes the secular calendar presents us with opportunities to break out of the box in how we think about holidays. Our *shul* has a *tikkun leil Shavuot*, a late night (though not all night) of study on the first night of Shavuot. While we have had a family education presentation for parents and children for a number of years now, we took that a step further the year that the first night of Shavuot coincided with a three-day weekend. We had a Shavuot sleepover!
>
> Parents and children were invited to attend the family education program the first hour of the study session, and then elementary-age children were invited to stay the night. We planned activities, such as playing *Jewpardy*, and had discussions on Shavuot themes, for every half-hour time slot up until midnight. But by 10 p.m., the parents had had it, so we moved up sundaes to midnight and had everybody in their sleeping bags by 12:30 or so. The *halachic* issues of a sleepover on a holiday are interesting — we had to find places where we could turn the lights out before candlelighting, but where there would be enough ambient light for kids who were afraid of the dark! Three years later, the kids still remember this night fondly — and they will always connect Shavuot with studying late into the night, getting ready to receive the Torah.
>
> *(Anne Johnston, New Haven, Connecticut)*

Elementary

It is in this age group that most holiday teaching occurs — both in Judaic and in Hebrew classes. The issues of overlap and repetition are, therefore, of greatest concern for teachers of elementary aged students.

Children are also pretty literal at the elementary school level, and will often run home to parents saying, "My teacher said we should . . . " It is therefore important to understand that teacher comments about celebrations can become problematic when weighed against the potentially inadequate or angry feelings they can create for parents. Teachers need to be careful about what and how they say what "must be celebrated," checking especially for the school's stance on such messages to children (and ultimately to parents).

Secondary

One of the key reasons to study Jewish holidays in adolescence is to help teens make the transition from an environment in which "doing Jewish" is planned for them, to one in which they will have to take responsibility for holiday observance. This *might* include a review of the holidays and their *mitzvot*, but even more does it mean pointing students to the wide variety of resources (books, web sites, stores, people, organizations, etc.) available to them when they are on their own.

Adult

Adults do not like to feel inadequate. It is therefore important to remember that classes and celebrations must be welcoming to those who are new at "doing Jewishly." As with teens, adults need resources they can use on their own. Adults also need permission to make mistakes when celebrating holidays for the first time on their own — understanding that it is not a disaster if a holiday observance may not have unfolded quite as planned or expected.

STEP 4: CALENDARING THE YEAR

Finally, one of the important planning tools for teachers is the school calendar. It is helpful at the beginning of each year to note when each of the holidays occur and when special school events are scheduled. Then, it is important to note on the calendar when the lessons on a particular holiday will begin and end. Most teachers schedule their lessons in the time that is building up to the holiday, but do not consider what might occur in their classrooms *after* the holiday, once students have had a chance to observe it in the synagogue or at home. After a holiday, the celebration is still fresh in students' minds, offering an opportunity for reflection in a different light.

I love to take the teens into the kitchen, especially when discussing holiday celebrations and different Jewish communities. For Pesach, when we do the "International House of Charoset," not only do they get the opportunity to get out of the classroom and into the kitchen, they also expand their understanding of both the variety and commonality of Jewish expressions. All Jewish communities make *charoset*, but not everyone uses apples, nuts, cinnamon, and wine. (We use that as a metaphor and talk about both fitting in and being yourself.) The teens also get to distribute the *charoset* to the rest of the school, giving them the chance to do something for others and also to have a sense of pride about their accomplishment

(Rabbi David Feder, Morgantown, West Virginia)

CONCLUSION

Jewish holidays provide hands-on opportunities for learning about our history, for thinking about theology, and for connecting with Jews worldwide. It is crucial that teachers upon whom the responsibility of teaching Jewish holidays falls consider the often unspoken of issues inherent in this area of Jewish study. The celebrations and the observances open the door to Jewish life — an important opportunity that should be exploited thoughtfully.

TEACHING CONSIDERATIONS

- Emphasize the experience of celebrating or observing holidays, instead of depending on worksheets or "cute" but non-focused art activities.

- Align holiday learning activities with big ideas or goals.

- Remember that parents and families need to be partners with teachers in Jewish holiday education.

- Coordination among teachers, and through the grades, eliminates overlap and repetition.

BIBLIOGRAPHY

Books

Abramowitz, Yosef I., and Susan Silverman. *Jewish Family & Life: Traditions, Holidays, and Values for Today's Parents and Children.* New York: Golden Books Publishing, Co., 1998.

> Designed for parents, this book offers background and family-based activities for holiday observances. The authors take into account the issues of Jewish family life, within the larger non-Jewish landscape.

Adler, David. *The Kids' Catalog of Jewish Holidays.* Philadelphia, PA: Jewish Publication Society, 1996.

> Fun and inviting, this book is written for kids with information on the holidays, along with crafts, songs, recipes, and activities.

Barish, Shirley. *The Big Book of Great Teaching Ideas: For Jewish Schools, Youth Groups, Camps, and Retreats.* New York: UAHC Press, 1998.

> Divided by age level, this resource is filled with creative ideas for teaching Jewish holidays.

Goodman, Robert. *Teaching Jewish Holidays: History, Values, and Activities.* Denver, CO: A.R.E. Publishing, Inc., 1997.

> The "bible" of Jewish teachers of every age level and in every setting. Offers background information, as well as a myriad of teaching ideas and resources for every Jewish holiday.

Handelman, Maxine Segal. *Jewish Every Day: The Complete Handbook for Early Childhood Teachers.* Denver, CO: A.R.E. Publishing, Inc., 2000.

> Geared for early childhood educators, this book has developmentally appropriate ideas, background, and activities for young children. A wonderful addition is the inclusion of songs for preschoolers.

Mandel, Scott. *Wired into Teaching Jewish Holidays.* Denver, CO: A.R.E. Publishing, Inc., 2003.

> Points teachers to online resources that complement A.R.E.'s *Teaching Jewish Holidays* manual for teachers.

Strassfeld, Michael. *The Jewish Holidays: A Guide & Commentary.* New York: HarperCollins, 1985.

> An oldie, but a goodie! This book provides great background on the holidays, offering a starting point for teacher lesson preparation.

Web Sites

www.babaganewz.com
BabagaNewz

> This monthly magazine encourages fourth through seventh graders to explore Jewish values from novel, thought provoking perspectives. Holidays are integrated into other topics and are compellingly discussed. (Note: This is a web site, but it is most especially a full color, "hard copy," slick magazine. It may be ordered as a classroom subscription.)

www.bjeny.org/102.asp?dept=Educational%20Resources
Bureau of Jewish Education of New York: Education Resource Center

> Offers links to a variety of holiday curricular resources produced by the BJE of New York. Also check out their BJE Store.

www.bkesf/prg/ECEhome.html
Early Childhood Webpage: Bureau of Jewish Education of San Francisco, Marin, the Peninsula and Sonoma Counties

> A wonderful site with holiday information for early childhood educators. See also their Battat Educational Resource Center webpage.

www.jecc.org/edres/medtech/abv.htm
Jewish Education Center of Cleveland (JECC)
Holiday Helpers

> These downloadable sheets offer listings of student books and age appropriate videos on a variety of holidays.

www.jewfaq.org/holiday0.htm
Judaism 101: Jewish Holidays

> An overview of the Jewish holidays, written in an easy to follow format.

http://myjewishlearning.com
MyJewishLearning.com

The home page includes a link to a comprehensive section on Jewish holidays, offering basic information ("Primer") to more complex ("Analysis and Interpretation.")

http://scheinerman.net/judaism/holidays.html
Rabbi Amy Scheinerman's Home Page

In this wonderful resource for teachers and families, Rabbi Scheinerman offers both background and how-to information written in a welcoming manner.

http://uahc.org/educate/parent
The Jewish Parent Page: UAHC

This web site was designed to educate parents about Jewish holidays and rituals.

CHAPTER 41

Integrating Social Justice into Jewish Curriculum

Sharon Morton

*A*nna Shapiro was getting very frustrated. Today's topic was Jewish immigration to North America at the turn of the twentieth century. She thought she had planned an engaging lesson, but looking at her sixth graders, she knew otherwise. They were not responding to the questions she was asking so as to check their understanding of the material.

Anna enlisted the help of Mrs. Bernstein, the principal. Mrs. Bernstein asked the students, "What is happening here?" The youngsters offered a variety of reasons for not keeping their focus, including issues at home, issues with friends, general stress, and "boredom." Putting the textbook aside, the principal said, "Wow, you have really big things on your minds. But now think about Ms. Shapiro's lesson. Why do you think you are studying immigration this year?"

The students connected to the question, offering a variety of answers. "Because it is important . . . Because it is like learning about our family . . . Because I learned about my grandmother today, who came from Romania . . . Because it gives us a chance to realize how lucky we are today . . . Because I need to begin to be responsible as I become Bar Mitzvah . . . Because it reminds us that we come from a long line of strong and courageous people, and we can be like that, too." And then, one of the students asked, "But what can we do for new immigrants so we understand their problems?"

Anna's mouth dropped open. She glanced at Mrs. Bernstein who then winked at her and left the room. Anna knew that she had a lot of work to do as she rethought her lesson planning, but also knew that "out of the mouth of babes" had come a way to hook her students into learning.

THE PURPOSE OF RELIGIOUS STUDIES

The purpose of religious studies is to guide a person toward knowledge, wisdom, and a sense of values. Our Jewish classrooms should help students to develop a connection with the wider community, to acquire faith in themselves and the world and a better understanding of their purpose in life. Yet, quite often, teachers get hung up on the "content" of our curriculum and the need to cover a lot of information. Jewish study is not just an intellectual exercise; it should impact the heart and soul.

It is this author's opinion that social justice, and the action that naturally follows, must be interwoven with every aspect of the curriculum in order to accomplish the purposes of religious studies. Jewish immigration serves as the example upon which this chapter is built, but every curriculum can be developed similarly. No matter what our teaching assignments, it is important to ask how "Mitzvah Day" projects, school *tzedakah* collections, or field trips connect with our curricular goals. We need to ascertain ways to integrate these acts of *chesed* (goodness) into the curriculum of every grade level. Similarly, family days and field trips can be connected to social justice/action.

OUR RESPONSIBILITY IN THE WORLD

Three areas intertwine when we consider our responsibility to others in the world:

- *Chesed* (kindness to others) - thinking, speaking, and actions toward others

- Social action (projects) - the doing

- Social justice (larger societal changes) - the transforming

Each of these areas will be discussed below.

Chesed

Chesed begins on a small level, and moves into larger spheres of influence. The ways students and teachers address one another in the classroom community, the ways they help one another, the ways they integrate a new student are of great significance as our children learn. Therefore, talking about and acting on classroom kindness fits into *every* curriculum.

Chesed is also practiced through the kindness the students show to speakers who come to class, to the projects they choose to do, how they meet people in the community, and how they present themselves in the larger community as ambassadors of *chesed*.

Chesed can also be taught as children hear stories of individuals via their curriculum and learn to understand and empathize with those characters.

Social Action Projects

There are limitless opportunities for students to do on behalf of others. Some of these possibilities are listed below:

- *The bold program* captures the imagination, such as buying an ambulance for Israel or building a house with Habitat for Humanity.

- *The simple program* doesn't take a lot of time, such as packing sandwiches for the poor or spearheading an old clothing drive.

- *The program that begins because of a commitment* and then grows and takes on a life of its own, such as a visit to a nursing home to hear immigrant stories that continues because of a growing friendship between a student and a resident.

- *The program that comes about because of a sense of outrage,* such as the response of a 12-year-old who saw pictures of children working for $1 a day and, reminded of the sweat shops in America, put a large program in action to help end such child labor.

- *The program developed by a group of people who see the "big picture,"* such as the child who learned that children with cancer suffer hair loss and sometimes self-esteem problems, and decided to make beautiful hats for them with real hair coming out the bottom.

- *The program that is repeated and sustained* by organizations for their communities, such as a group of families who decides to rescue a family from Argentina or Cambodia, and then provides them with housing, jobs, child care, etc.

- *The program that is fun, challenging, and significant, and is spearheaded by one visionary,* such as that done by a Bat Mitzvah student who concluded her Bat Mitzvah celebration by having everyone build a park together in a neighborhood of poor immigrants.

- *The program that is incidental to other programs,* such as asking people gathering for school or worship services to sign a postcard, or donate $5.00 to pay for a bus ride for a child so she could pick strawberries for her own poor family.

- *The program that is evident every time one enters your building,* as the space notifies us daily of our potential to make the world a better place through signs, collection boxes, and action.

Sample Social Action Projects

Here are further examples of social action projects that are appropriate for Jewish students in religious schools and day schools:

Tzedakah collections for a particular cause

Speakers on social action topics

Surveys on disability or the environment

Lessons on socially responsible investing

Mitzvah Days

Trips to Washington to visit Congress to lobby on behalf of social action projects

Social action newsletters

Motivational stories or videos leading to action

Discussions on ultimate regard for one another

Field trips

Special social action days in school

Applications for grants to do projects

Mitzvah Fairs

Interfaith programs

Trips to the State Capitol

Trips to Israel

Environmental Fairs

Collection bins for various kinds of donations

"Mitzvah Crib" for donations of baby items

Drives to collect items such as books, eyeglasses, wigs, prostheses, school supplies, blankets, baby toys, cribs, can tops, sports equipment, stuffed animals, video tapes, toiletries, pennies for a Holocaust Memorial, food, medical supplies, scarves, mittens, hats, etc.

Social Justice

Social justice is transformative change, advocating for issues that go beyond a specific person who needs food or shelter. It is "surgery" for a problem, instead of a bandage. The institution and the teacher must be aware of social justice issues that are coming up in Congress and choose those that will fit into the curriculum as causes for which to advocate. A helpful web site is that of the Religious Action Center of the Reform Movement (www.rac.org).

Social justice activities in the area of immigration would include such issues as petitioning Congress to provide better health care and housing for immigrants; advocating for changes in school systems to be sure that English as a second language is provided; the action required to build a community center for immigrants to learn culture, language, and ideas of our community; the opportunity to work in concert with a community organization to find jobs for new immigrants. These are changes in the "system" as opposed to changes that we can make for one person or one family.

THINKING DIFFERENTLY ABOUT CURRICULUM

Ms. Shapiro has a lot to think about before her students return for their next lesson. She begins to plan future lessons, with attention to social justice and the actions students can do related to issues of immigration. Ms. Shapiro had assumed that since her textbook treated each historical period in chronological sequence, she had to follow that pattern. But, now that she takes a fresh look at her curriculum, she realizes that she can group similar immigrations to North America into one unit and begin asking some broad questions to aid her planning:

- *Why is the study of immigration potentially important to sixth graders?*

- *What benefit is there from the study of this topic?*

- *How will this topic relate to the students' personal lives outside of the congregation, to their involvement in the community, and even to their understanding of world events?*

- *Will students live a better life because they studied immigration? In what ways?*

- *How might understanding their own family's immigration and hardships connect the student with their own past, and help them to shape their own destiny?*

- *How will knowing about the hardships of historical immigrations make the student more empathetic and compassionate toward new immigrants?*

- *What does the student need to do in order to concretize those feelings?*

- *What specific Jewish values and mitzvot underpin the immigrant experience?*

- *Can this course of study help when a new student from another neighborhood moves into the community?*

When teaching and learning take place only in class with no impact beyond, the intellectual and emotional growth of the student is limited. The curriculum, and in this case, the social action component, must move well beyond the classroom. As figure 1 on the next page illustrates, a curriculum with an emphasis on social action should affect all layers of a student's life:

As Anna builds her curriculum, she realizes she wants to have social action components that touch her classroom, the students' families, as well as the broader community. She begins listing some questions about school, family, and community to help her get started. Each of these is described briefly below.

The School

The school and synagogue setting offer students a chance to delve into history that is close and personal. Anna starts making note of some questions: What is its history? Who were the founders?

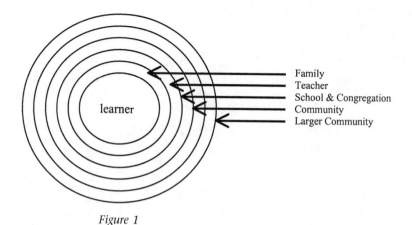

Figure 1

Where did they come from? Can they be interviewed? Why was building a congregation and community important to them? What is the purpose of the school? What are the social justice "causes" that are important to the school and the community? What are the underlying values of the school; the congregation?

Family

Where did the students' families come from? Why did they come to North America? Are there any families with relatives who are thinking about immigrating to another country? Could the class perform acts of chesed for those relatives? After studying issues related to past immigrations, what actions can we be more open to taking as a class? Might we write letters promoting equal opportunity housing? Might we get involved in projects of the ACLU or the Jewish Council on Urban Affairs?

Community

Anna thinks a bit about the issues facing immigrants in her city. She wonders about having the class work in a shelter. Are there some people in that shelter who can't find work because of a language barrier? Are there some who had no family close by to support and nourish them as they grew up? She also considers the possibility of using a small plot of the synagogue's property to plant crops that can be harvested in the fall to feed the poor. With a primary election coming up in a

month, Anna wonders if a voter registration drive would dovetail nicely into their study of immigration and the importance of the right to vote. Were there ways to help new families resettle in their community, leading into a discussion about the relationship of settlement and immigrants? Is there a time to discuss immigrants who work as grossly underpaid sharecroppers? Could letters be written to Congresspeople to discuss rights of immigrants?

Anna creates a chart (figure 2 on the next page) to help her think beyond the four walls of her classroom.

MORE RESEARCH

While lots of ideas may flow in the early part of social justice curriculum design, other questions help focus the unit plan. The excitement of the many possibilities for projects can pull a teacher off track. The actions must be connected in some way to the curriculum. Keep the following questions in mind during the planning process:

1. Is there a motivating activity, a personal story, or any *core* story that gets the students involved, invested, motivated? A compelling story of one person often encourages a student to act quickly.

2. How can classmates work together to accomplish a project?[1]

3. Will *lashon hatov* (good words) and *chesed* be a part of these strategies?

---

[1]See Chapter 30, "Cooperative or Collaborative Learning" by Carol K. Ingall, pp. 351-362 in this Handbook.

Learner	Family	Teacher	School & Congregation	Community
Help students understand concept of looking back and moving forward. Learn stories of immigrant heroes. Write stories of how each child can be a hero in the future to affect a small change in the world.	Family tour of Jewish Chicago to meet Russian immigrants, as well as to see the sites of Jewish interest What is the act of kindness that students must do as they meet people? What can they do afterward? Interest them in "Adopt a Family" program of the JCC.	The teacher must be a model of *chesed*, social action projects initiator, and a passionate social action activist.	Do students practice *derech eretz* (appropriate behavior)? Is there such a thing as the "Just School" with a code of ethics?	*Chesed* - develop programs to teach English or Jewish literacy to immigrants Become involved in community actions Talk about the organizations that immigrants set up, i.e., burial society, the free loan society.

Figure 2

4. Are there appropriate Judaic texts to study to help students understand that our tradition teaches us how we are supposed to act?[2]

5. Have the needs and interests of the students been discussed to see how their own ideas can be integrated into the program?

6. What is the value behind each potential project? What are the ramifications of the project? What project can be done at a later date with their friends, family, and community? What can we extrapolate from one activity that will help each person become involved and do more in the future?

7. How will students see the big picture? How can they have a share in selecting the projects that have been chosen?

8. Can you find a hero in the unit? Our children need to find and identify with real heroes, persons who teach us good values. (For Anna, an immigrant who learned English, studied, and became a doctor could be such a hero. An older person who has sacrificed his professional life in Russia so that his children and grandchildren could live a free life in America is certainly a hero.)

9. How can the framing of the project ensure that the students understand that the hands-on work is based on Jewish ideals and teaching? (This is vital — we must help our students know that *our* social action work is "Jewish.")

10. How can parents understand that our purpose is to give children and understanding of the need for altruistic behavior? Our role should not be merely to amass facts, but to create understanding, appreciation, and purpose based on the wisdom of our teachings.

WEBBING THE IDEAS

Anna knew that she needed to organize her many ideas on paper. Therefore, she began to create a web of her unit. She wanted to include not only concepts, but social action project ideas that would complement the topic of study.

---

[2]See Chapter 32, "Teaching Texts" by Betsy Dolgin Katz, pp. 374-387 in this Handbook.

Approaching a Jewish theme using a web is a way to uncover a vast range of concepts related to any given theme. To produce a web, put the main topic word in the center of the page and then let the ideas fly (with the children's help). Webbing enables teachers and children to see the wider context of everything that is happening, and the connections to many parts of the curriculum. If the social action theme is an outgrowth of the web, it is clearly integrated with the other work that you do, and the children can better understand its relevance to the topic.

Webbing is most easily done with one or two other people. In a group, more ideas are generated and the life experiences of each participant help to enrich the results. Anna's web is shown in figure 3 on the next page. All of the social action activities relating to the curriculum areas are in boxes. (Note that this web was made during the efforts to free Jews from the Soviet Union.)

CURRICULUM INTEGRATION

It is easy to get caught in teaching one subject without paying attention to the richness of our heritage and the multiple modalities of learning.

Anna Shapiro was teaching American Jewish history, and so she began by staying boxed into one discipline. She soon realized that she couldn't ignore other aspects of Jewish life (e.g., prayer, holidays, values, theology, Torah, etc.) and that her unit would be greatly enriched by branching out beyond history. For instance:

- *Since the Torah service includes a prayer for one's country, she thought her class might go to a nursing home to lead the residents in prayer and learn their "stories" at the same time.*

- *Since Israel is constantly faced with the absorption issues of new immigrants, Anna realized that this opened up an avenue into Israel studies.*

- *On holidays and Shabbat, Anna realized that her class could donate to new Jews much needed ritual items.*

- *Theology comes into play, too, in a discussion of B'tzelem Elohim, that we are all created in the image of God. Sometimes new immigrants are not treated in this manner. What, then, is our responsibility to them?*

- *Anna's head was swimming by now, but she created one more planning chart (see figure 4 on page 488) to help her see the possibilities for integration of other subject areas into in her unit on immigration.*

While she still had a lot to do to organize her curriculum, Anna Shapiro happily shared with her principal her new direction. Drawing students into their Jewish learning through social action was exciting to them both, and would make a difference in the life of these 15 sixth graders, as well as those whose lives they would touch.

Her principal cautioned Anna on one thing — the possibility of doing so much that students lose the focus of the lessons. In the end, Anna's curricular responsibility was to teach immigration within a historical context. Anna had now to look at her web and chart and determine which activities most clearly would help her students "get" the big ideas surrounding Jewish immigration. She also had to consider consistent and frequent ways to weave the big ideas and Jewish context throughout the various projects, so that students would come away from her class gaining Jewish learning, not just having fun.[3]

THE JEWISH CONTEXT

Our tradition is rich in teachings that help us understand our responsibilities to others. Clearly, posting them on the board or mentioning them once is not enough. These teachings must be discussed on an age appropriate level and woven into every conversation that touches on similar themes and concerns. The classroom walls should feature these teachings. They should be discussed in transition moments in class so as to remind students continually of their importance and their relationship to the curriculum.

---

[3]See Chapter 1, "Beyond Apples and Honey: The Editor's Soapbox" by Nachama Skolnik Moskowitz, pp. 1-12 in this Handbook.

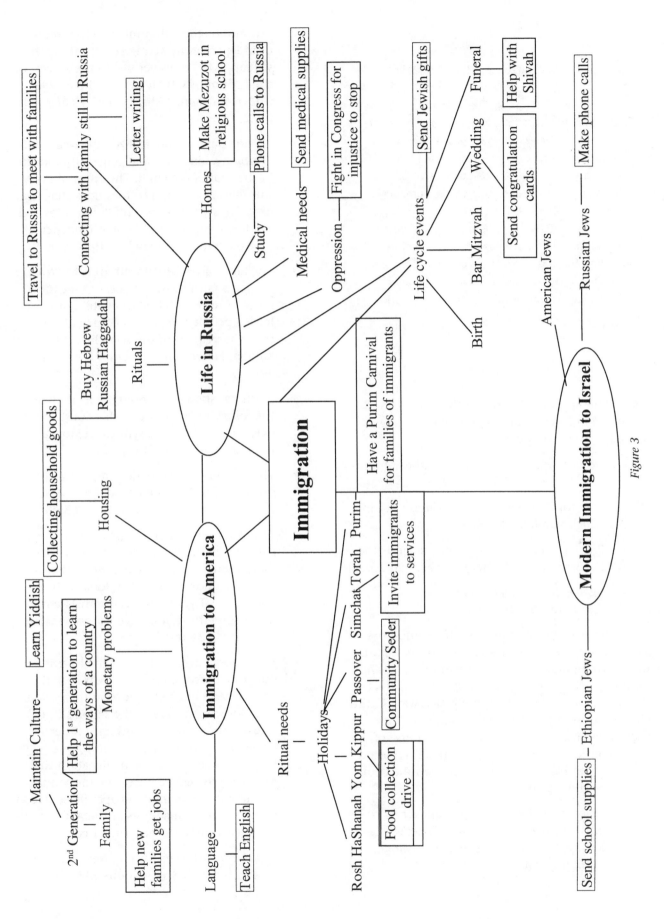

Figure 3

> One year, when I taught a course on *tikkun olam*, our local Jewish newspaper started running a series about local people and programs helped by the Jewish Federation. The students were touched and moved to take action as a result of these articles. We did a few *tzedakah* drives for the specific people or organizations we read about, but there was one person with whom the students were intrigued. This young woman was living on Disability due to HIV/AIDS. The students didn't just want to help her, they wanted to meet her. So we arranged for her to come and speak to the class about the reality of living with HIV. This really personalized for my students how they could make a difference in the world.
>
> *(Cheryl Cash-Linietsky, Philadelphia, Pennsylvania)*

Texts

Short statements catch a student's attention and can be quoted verbatim in appropriate settings. Some key texts are these:

- Do not separate yourself from the community. (*Pirke Avot* 2:5)

- Pray for the welfare of the community in which you live. (Jeremiah)

- Proclaim liberty throughout the land, and to the inhabitants thereof. (Leviticus 25:10)

- Justice, Justice shall you pursue. (Deuteronomy 16:20)

Other passages offer further information or food for thought. Those passages below emphasize that learning must be for the intention of adding purpose to this world. Each quotation suggests that we must look at curriculum in a global way. As the children learn a quote from our tradition, they should discuss its connection to their course of study, consider ways to concretize (take action on) the quote, and anticipate the impact on the community of the action.

- Learning is the raising of character by the broadening of vision and the deepening of feeling. (M. Sulzberger. *Menorah Journal*, 1916, ii, p. 58)

- The aim of education must be the training of independently acting and thinking individuals, who, however, see in the service of the community their highest life problem. (Albert Einstein, 1936, *Out of My Later Years*, p. 32)

- No one has yet fully realized the wealth of sympathy, kindness, and generosity hidden in the soul of the child. The effort of every true educator should be to unlock that treasure — to stimulate the child's impulses and call forth the best and noblest tendencies. (E. Goldman, *Living My Life*, 1931, p. 409)

- The aim (of Jewish education) is to develop a sincere faith in the holiness of life, and a sense of responsibility for enabling the Jewish people to make its contribution to the achievement of the good life. (Mordecai Kaplan, *Future of the American Jew*, 1948, p. 44)

- A scholar should not reside in a city where the following are not found: a court of justice, a charity fund, a synagogue, (or) a teacher. (*Sanhedrin* 17b)

- The person in poverty does more for the householder than the householder does for the one in need. (*Leviticus Rabbah* 34:8)

- Busy yourself as much as possible with the study of divine things, not to know them merely, but to do them and when you close the book, look around you, look within you, to see if your hand can translate into deeds something you have learned. (Moses of Everux, 1240)

- We, who are responsible for the learning of our students for a ten to 16-year period, must extend our sights beyond the period that our students are in the schools or colleges. Until we do this and until it becomes a part of our curriculum planning, we will neglect those objectives of education that related to the entire life of the individual. (Benjamin S. Bloom, in a paper presented at a General Session address at the ASCD 1978 Annual Conference, San Francisco)

- Be kind to strangers for you were a stranger in the land of Egypt. (Exodus 23:9)

Core Curriculum	Prayer	Israel & World Affairs	Holidays & Shabbat
"Justice, Justice shall you pursue." (Deut.16:20) Study Leviticus 19 (Holiness Code) to understand our role in society. Social Justice: Fight for legislation that will assist the poor immigrant — Family Leave Act, Universal Health Care, etc. The importance of one – speakers bring important core stories. Read *In My Words* by Irene Opdyke (Holocaust story). Let students know how the Jewish community helped her when she immigrated to America.	*Avot v'Emahot* – We can learn much from the goodness of our ancestors. *Sim Shalom* – people came to America for peace and for religious liberty. *Prayer for our Country* – Asks God to bless our country and its leaders (in the Torah service). Pray for Israel – imagine immigrants landing in Israel for the first time. How does this prayer speak to them?	Study the Ethiopian airlift to Israel. Send school supplies to Israeli schools. Study quotations on Statue of Liberty and the Liberty Bell. (Discuss how students can concretize quotes.) Invite in a Russian or Ethiopian Jew who has immigrated to your community.	Passover – "For you were strangers in the land of Egypt" Shabbat - *Kiddush* reminds us of creation and leaving the land of Egypt All holidays – Collect ritual items for new Jewish immigrants to your community or to Israel.

God	Hebrew Values	Music	Art
B'tzelem Elohim – we are created in the image of God to help one another. *Shechinah* – the nurturing quality of God is important to new immigrants as they leave their friends and family.	*Pikuach Nefesh* – to save a person's life *Yedidut* – friendship *Chasday Olam* – the Righteous of the World *Tikkun Olam* – repairing the world	*Aylu Dvarim Sheh-ayn Lahem Shiur* – These are our obligations without measure (lists various obligations we have as Jews to each other). "Light one Candle" by Peter, Paul, and Mary speaks of Jewish continuity. Sharing our music with the Jews who have immigrated to Israel, or another country.	Make a large banner of people who came to North America, with some focus on the organizations that helped (e.g., Hebrew Immigrant Aid Society, The American Jewish Joint Distribution Committee). Create bumper stickers or pins that focus on a Jewish text of social justice.

Figure 4

Note: See the Bibliography on p. 492 for books with similar quotations.

Values

There are many terms related to social action having to do with how we behave, what we do, and how we think. Use the key words below in everyday conversations with students: "I see you behaved with *derech eretz* today," "Today we are going to begin a very special *tikkun olam* advocacy effort," "Do you see how Abraham Joshua Heschel's statement is an example of altruism?"

- Altruism - Love of humanity that compels us to do righteous acts

- *B'tzelem Elohim* - In the image of God. The expression tells us to behave in a godly way.

- Character Building - self appreciation, self worth, self-respect, self-knowledge, self-awareness

- *Chesed* - Loving-kindness

- *Derech Eretz* - Wholesome behavior

- *Gemilut Chasadim* - Acts of love and care we do for each other

- *Ger* - Stranger (there are a series of laws governing how to treat the stranger in your midst)

- *Kavod Nashim* - A Rabbinic value to encourage the dignity and honor of women

- *Kodesh* - Unique, set apart

- *Lashon HaRa* - Slander, tale bearing or any use of words that serves to ruin relations in a community

- *Middot* - Virtues or values; principles we consider to be of central importance that influence how we act, what we do, what we stand for

- *Mitzvot* - Acts required of us because of the *Brit* (Covenant) between Israel and God; commandments

- *Pikuach Nefesh* - Life must be saved. This is more important than any other commandment.

- *Shalom* - Peace, wholeness

- *Sh'lom Bayit* - Peace in the home

- Social Action - In the broadest sense "social action" is how we act, feel, behave, and interact with others

- Social Justice - Represents the actions we take that can change an unjust, imperfect world into a better one. It is legislative, serious actions to affect change

- *Tikkun Olam* - To fix the world; a general term used to concretize our social action work

- Tolerance - Respect, understanding, and appreciation for those different from ourselves

- *Tzedakah* - Support the poor and less fortunate; doing the right thing; giving money to needy people

- Values - Those principles that are coherent in our nature and compel us to act immediately

Besides using these words and concepts regularly in your classroom, hang pictures of each on the classroom walls. Ask students what your course of study has to do with these words. Focus on these terms as appropriate during prayer services. As you discuss heroes' stories or immigrant stories, ask which quality the hero represented. Why were they important? How does each child in the class show these qualities in his/her own life? Develop cooperative and interactive strategies that challenge the students to think through social and political issues in the community and that help them to learn and practice communal responsibility.

EVALUATION OF SOCIAL ACTION IN YOUR CURRICULUM

Evaluation of social action work is difficult at best. It is easy to evaluate the success of a particular project or to count the hours that a student worked to complete a project. But it is impossible to assess whether or not the work has affected the student's thinking, values, or future life. Following are a few thoughts on how a teacher might ascertain as to whether the concept of social action has been internalized by the students.

- Spend the last five minutes of class asking, "Based on what you learned today, what will you do this week to make yourself, your home, or your community a bit better?"

- Use flash cards containing a text. Do a "whip" around the room. What social action tasks might this text suggest?

- Post Jewish quotes around the room. At the end of a session, have students stand under a quote of their choice, tell the class why they chose that quote, and how it relates to the topic of the day.

- At the end of the session, have students thank one another for an act of *chesed* that was performed during the day and/or for an act of *chesed* that was performed within the curricular study.

CONCLUSION

A Jewish educational setting is very different from that of a secular school. There students attend and then leave to go to another place. One of our goals is to "keep them in" — to have them return to us as adults with a greater understanding, appreciation, and excitement about what our tradition has to offer. Therefore, social action must be an integral part of every curriculum, involving the family and the larger community as well.

While the task may be daunting, our tradition tells us we must keep trying, as it is said: "It is not incumbent upon you to complete the task, but neither are you free to desist from it" (*Pirke Avot* 2:21).

TEACHING CONSIDERATIONS

- Think of social action globally in terms of *chesed*, *derech eretz*, social justice.

- Believe that every course of study, along with all ancillary subjects, must include a *clear* social action component.

- Believe that looking at your teaching in this way is exciting, and that *chesed*, social action, and social justice fit *every* curriculum at *every* grade level.

- Keep in mind children's needs, interests, and problems, with the hope that they can feel better about themselves and their role in society.

The most effective teacher of social justice I ever saw was our Cantor Emeritus. This aged, gentle man agreed to take on a high energy group of seventh graders who had completed their course of study for Bar and Bat Mitzvah but needed to attend one more year of midweek Hebrew. My oldest son was in this class.

As they met for the first time, the Cantor asked his students what they wanted to study. "Social justice," they answered, "we want to do something with our lives. Why can't we go places and see how we can help repair the world?" So they did, with the help of two parents with vans. They toured a day center for the homeless and were put to work cleaning the facility. They went to the city pound and handled the dogs there. They collected food for the local food pantry and delivered it. They cleaned up a creek. Week after week, they visited places, asked questions, and worked. At the end of the year, they were given an assignment. Make something that expresses what you have learned this year. Some wrote papers. Two girls wrote a play about searching for Jewish identity in middle school. One child created a sculpture with writings from the Holocaust on it.

In the course on one year, the Cantor met with these adolescents for 60 hours. Most of them went on to become fantastic Sunday school aides, youth group participants, and volunteers. "Who has been your most influential teacher?" my 22-year-old son is often asked. The answer never changes: the Cantor.

(Maura Pollak, Tulsa, Oklahoma)

BIBLIOGRAPHY

For the Teacher

Beane, Allan L. *The Bully Free Classroom — Over 100 Tips and Strategies for Teachers K-8*. Minneapolis, MN: Free Spirit Publishing, 1999.

Offers effective strategies and activities to stop bullying before it starts.

Feinberg, Miriam P., and Rena Rotenberg. *Lively Legends — Jewish Values: An Early Childhood Teaching Guide*. Denver, CO: A.R.E. Publishing, Inc., 1993.

Stories and activities that focus values for an early childhood setting.

Freeman, Susan. *Teaching Jewish Virtues: Sacred Sources and Arts Activities*. Denver, CO: A.R.E. Publishing, Inc, 1999.

Introduces Jewish virtues (*middot*) using arts, drama, movement, and music.

Gold-Vukson, Marji. *Tzedakah Copy Pak™*. Denver, CO: A.R.E. Publishing, Inc., 1997.

Twenty-nine ready-to-photocopy activity sheets for Grades 3-6 that help children discover the true meaning of *tzedakah,* the teachings of Maimonides, the pleasures and responsibilities associated with *tzedakah*, and more.

Grishaver, Joel Lurie, and Beth Huppin. *Tzedakah, Gemilut Chasadim and Ahavah*. Denver, CO: A.R.E. Publishing, Inc., 1983.

This workbook for Grades 6-12 features ancient and modern texts, along with practical action projects to help people in need and a chance to find and interview individuals who act out *mitzvot*. Students record feelings and experiences in a log. Background and additional activities are contained in the comprehensive Leader Guide.

Halper, Sharon. *To Learn Is to Do: A Tikkum Olam Roadmap*. New York: UAHC Press, 2000.

Study of *tikkun olam* (repairing the world) via *mitzvot*, Torah, and Torah commentary.

Kadden, Barbara Binder, and Bruce Kadden. *Teaching Mitzvot: Concepts, Values, and Activities*. rev. ed. Denver, CO: A.R.E. Publishing Inc., 2003.

An exceptional guide to learning and teaching about *mitzvot*. The revised edition contains five additional *mitzvot* and updated bibliographies.

Kolatch, Alfred J. *Great Jewish Quotations*. Middle Village, NY: Jonathan David Publishers, Inc., 1996.

A wide assortment of quotations from various sources in various ages.

Luvmour, Sambhava, and Josette Luvmour. *Everyone Wins*. Philadelphia, PA: New Society Publishers, 1990.

Over 150 games that build self-esteem, resolve conflict, and encourage communication.

Miller, Frye, and Myers Walls. *Young Peacemakers Project Book II*. Elgin, IL: Brethren Press, 1990.

Youth handbook with a focus on peace and human rights education.

Siegel, Danny. *Gym Shoe and Irises,* Book Two. Pittsboro, NC: Town House Press, 1987.

Shows how to personalize *tzedakah* and make it a part of one's life.

Starting Small — Teaching Tolerance in Preschool and the Early Grades: Complete Text and Video Package for Teachers. Montgomery, AL: Teaching Tolerance Project of the Southern Poverty Law Center, 1997.

This book describes a primary grade classroom in a multiracial school and how the teacher promotes esteem, tolerance, and understanding of self and others.

Strom, Margot Stern. *Facing History and Ourselves — Holocaust and Human Behavior*. Brookline, MA: Facing History and Ourselves National Foundation, Inc., 1994.

A resource book devoted to teaching about the dangers of indifference and the values of civility.

Taking the MTV Challenge — Media and Torah Values. Teaneck, NJ: Union for Traditional Judaism, 1997.

Teaches children to view images in the media thoughtfully and critically while arming them with moral values found in the Tanach.

To Till and to Tend: A Guide To Jewish Environmental Study and Action. New York: Coalition on the Environment and Jewish Life, 1995.

Promotes environmental education as it relates to Jewish life.

Vorspan, Albert, and David Saperstein. *Jewish Dimensions of Social Justice: Tough Moral Choices of Our Time*. New York: UAHC Press, 1998.

Explores Jewish perspectives in areas of social justice that American Jews deal with today.

Books for Children

Abraham, Michelle Shapiro. *Repairing My World*. New York: UAHC Press, 2001.

A "worktext" that focuses on applying Jewish values to one's own life, family life and the community.

———. *The Be a Mensch Campaign*. New York: UAHC Press, 2001.

A student "worktext" for Grades 3-4 that introduces Jewish ethical terms.

Cohn, Janice. *Christmas Menorahs: How a Town Fought Hate*. Morton Grove, IL: Albert Whitman & Co., 1995.

True story based on an actual anti-Semitic incident in Billings, Montana.

Lewis, Barbara A. *What Do You Stand For? A Kid's Guide to Building Character*. Minneapolis, MN: Free Spirit Publishing Inc., 1998.

Helps children build good character traits by teaching them leadership skills, kindness, and other positive behaviors.

Rael, Elsa Okon. *What Zeesie Saw on Delancey Street*. New York: Simon & Schuster, 1996.

A young Jewish girl learns about generosity, courage, and community in New York City during the early 1900s.

Rosen, Sybil. *Speed of Light*. New York: Atheneum, 1999.

A young Jewish girl living in the 1950s experiences prejudice and fights back.

Seuss, Dr. *The Butter Battle Book*. New York: Random House, 1984.

A cautionary cold war story that teaches the dangers of prejudice.

Web Sites

www.AJWS.org
The American Jewish World Service

This organization helps to alleviate hunger, poverty, and disease world-wide, breathing Jewish ethics and values into service to others.

www.dosomething.org
Do Something

This organization helps youth get involved in a variety of projects in their own community.

www.helping.org
The Network for Good

At this e-philanthropy site, individuals can donate, volunteer, and speak out on the issues they care about. The organization's goal is to connect people to charities via the Internet.

www.idealist.org
Action without Borders

Members of this organization "work to find practical solutions to social and environmental problems, in a spirit of generosity and mutual respect."

www.JDC.org
The American Joint Jewish Distribution Committee

"The Joint" sponsors programs of relief, rescue, and reconstruction, as the overseas service arm of the American Jewish community.

www.JFJustice.org
The Jewish Fund for Justice

This organization assists community-based groups support programs that "promote self-sufficiency and sustainable solutions to problems." See the curriculum on this website, as well.

www.just-tzedakah.org
Just Tzedakah

Provides tools and encouragement to increase the level and effectiveness of *tzedakah* among American Jews. Besides helping donors make choices, the site includes great information on the tradition of Jewish giving.

www.rac.org
The Religious Action Center

This organization educates and mobilizes the American Jewish community on legislative and social concerns, and serves as the advocate of the Reform Movement in Washington, D.C.

www.servenet.org
SERVEnet

> A program of Youth Service America (YSA) that helps match volunteers with service projects in their area, via a zip code and interest match.

www.socialaction.com

> Sponsored by Jewish Family and Life (JFL), *Social Action* is an online magazine dedicated to pursuing justice, building community, and repairing the world.

www.workingforchange.com
Working for Change

> Working for Change is sponsored by Working Assets, and offers a forum for web surfers to "speak out on urgent issues, read informative news and columns, go shopping, make a donation, or volunteer their time."

www.ziv.org
Ziv

> This is the site of Danny Siegel's *tzedakah* organization, and offers the annual report of Ziv's far-reaching *tzedakah* contributions, as well as information about an excellent curriculum guide.

CHAPTER 42

Teaching Hebrew Reading

Dina Maiben

*M*elissa's parents were worried about her ability to master Hebrew reading. She had always found English reading difficult, and was even classified in public school for problems with visual perception. Even though her parents could help her with Hebrew, they were concerned about the added burden that Hebrew studies might place on a fourth grader for whom school work was such a struggle. Equally great was their concern that additional difficulties with academic work might have a negative effect on her self-esteem.

By contrast, Craig was a fairly typical Hebrew student. He had done well in both the reading readiness program and the primer. However, when he started the prayer curriculum, he began to experience serious difficulties. A contributing factor in this situation was the fact that no one could help him with his Hebrew studies at home. Craig was the child of an interfaith marriage. His father was not Jewish, and his mother had attended Hebrew school only for a couple of years, so she had never learned Hebrew. Craig's teacher referred him for tutorial assistance. On the form, she indicated that he was uncertain about a number of vowels, and was making mistakes with visually similar letters, like vav and resh. The tutor administered a test of basic reading skills. Craig was asked to read two, three, and four-syllable words using every letter and vowel combination in Hebrew. Since Craig was able to read these combinations with 90% accuracy, the tutor sent him back to class, noting on the referral that he did not have any difficulty with vowels or visually similar letters. Two weeks later, Craig's teacher referred him for tutorial again, indicating that he was still experiencing the same problems. Although Craig passed another reading test with flying colors, he was still unable to read the prayer texts with accuracy. For example, while reciting the וְאָהַבְתָּ, he read בְּדֶרֶךְ as בָּרוּךְ.

Rachel had always been an excellent Hebrew student. She mastered new oral vocabulary with ease, and could carry on complete conversations in Hebrew. For the first couple of years, she breezed through the course, although her reading was a little slow and deliberate. However, by the middle of her third year, she began to have so much difficulty with reading that she began to dislike Hebrew studies altogether.

Any successful program of instruction must negotiate between the complexities of the subject matter and the special characteristics of the learner. This negotiation is done in part by the teaching method and instructional materials. To a far greater extent, however, the task of mediation falls on the teacher's shoulders. The teacher who fully understands both the intricacies of the subject and the nature of the students in a given class is far better prepared to stand at the side of a learner who is struggling to master the material.

The most important subject matter considerations for reading instruction center on the linguistic qualities of the language being taught and the idiosyncrasies of its script. These considerations go far beyond the specific skills focus of most reading programs, for although a number of visual, auditory, and phonological skills are involved in reading, different languages and scripts require the reader to apply these skills in vastly different ways. Hebrew reading instruction should be based on a thorough analysis of these features, employing the structures and sequences that have been shown to minimize potential learning difficulties, and promoting those reading strategies that best enable the beginning reader to apply the basic skills to the unique demands of a Hebrew text. In the Diaspora, Hebrew reading instruction is complicated by three other factors. These are: (1) the extent to which decoding is part of an overall program of Hebrew language instruction, (2) a few Hebrew phonemes that are not present in the students' native language, and (3) the needs and norms of the school and its community. The most important consideration in this last category is the community's standard pronunciation of a few Hebrew phonemes, which may or may not conform to the teacher's pronunciation or that promoted by a given reading program.

On the other side of the equation, developing Hebrew readers brings a number of additional variables to the table. These include age, previous experience with the subject matter, general knowledge, and a wide range of personal qualities, such as interest, motivation, and their tolerance for frustration. The nature of the students' families and the communities in which they live can also affect their ultimate success in learning to read Hebrew. Such factors as the amount of support that students receive for their studies at home and the ability of parents to provide assistance as well as support are very powerful influences that must be addressed.

Because success in Hebrew reading instruction depends on the ways that the teacher and program materials can negotiate between all of these complex variables, a better understanding of each should enable teachers to plan more effectively, diagnose learning problems more accurately, and remediate them more efficiently. It is with these pragmatic goals in mind that this chapter will explore the major issues and present those approaches to teaching Hebrew reading that have been shown to be most effective. In the process, we will examine the specific issues that were causing Melissa, Craig, and Rachel so much difficulty.

READING, DECODING, AND RECITATION

At the outset, it is crucial to begin with a definition of some terms. If you ask most Hebrew teachers to describe the primary goal of their curriculum, they answer with the phrase "Hebrew reading." This term, however, is often a misnomer. Reading is the process of translating visual symbols into meaningful language. This is the kind of reading that you are doing right now. The eyes move across the page, transforming the print into words and ideas. By definition, this is a language skill that requires a command of both vocabulary and grammar. While this is often the ultimate goal in a day school setting, it is a far cry from the "reading" done in a typical Hebrew school class. In most supplemental settings, "Hebrew reading" is generally limited to decoding and recitation. While reading requires a knowledge of language, decoding is translating

printed symbols into the sounds they represent, then blending those sounds back together. Recitation is the act of orally presenting a well-prepared text. While decoding is often slow and deliberate, recitation requires fluency in both word blending and phraseology. Recitation is the goal of all prayer programs, as students must be able to recite specific prayer texts in order to lead and participate in congregational worship services. The differences between reading, decoding, and recitation lead to the central question in Hebrew education — namely, the precise roles that these three different skills will play within the overall framework of the curriculum. The answer to this question will vary from school to school, based on each individual institution's priorities for different types of Hebrew programming. Dori (1992) cites three such types of programming: Hebrew for ritual, developing Hebrew literacy, and experiencing communicative Hebrew, noting that each type of program necessarily cultivates different skills. For example, if the Hebrew curriculum focuses on language, and the desired outcome is students who will understand what they read in Hebrew, the reading component will naturally concentrate first on the development of decoding and then on reading comprehension skills. On the other hand, if the curricular focus is on prayer recitation and the acquisition of synagogue skills, the reading component should naturally emphasize decoding and recitation skills, such as fluent phrasing. If the curricular focus includes elements of both, the reading program must incorporate all of these skills in its mix, stressing each skill commensurate with the weight of its curricular objective. Here again, there will be great variation from school to school, and in settings that provide a dual Hebrew track, there will be variation within the school as a whole. In the case of the schools attended by Melissa and Craig, the curricular focus of the Hebrew program was on decoding skills and prayer recitation. Rachel, a day school student, was in a Hebrew program with a focus on communicative Hebrew and developing Hebrew literacy.

Because decoding is central to both types of Hebrew curricula, it is a logical place to begin the exploration of Hebrew reading issues. Fortunately, there is a vast body of research related to general reading instruction and to Hebrew phonics in particular, and it is highly valuable to review classroom practices in its light. This research, however, is not without problems of its own. First of all, reading is a highly complex process. The complexity of English reading has led to a great deal of disagreement among researchers about the best approaches to its instruction, and there are no signs that this controversy will be resolved any time soon. This debate often informs Hebrew reading instruction because secular education has a profound impact on Jewish education. It determines how students are prepared for the work they do in Jewish classrooms and it exerts a powerful influence on the development of the methods and materials that are used in Jewish educational settings. It can also shape students' expectations of Jewish education. Because students have already learned how to read in one language, they frequently expect that Hebrew reading will work in precisely the same way, an assumption that can lead to significant difficulties for some students.

An equally significant problem with the research lies in the fact that it has been conducted with students who are learning to read their native languages. It is difficult to draw any conclusions about either the kind of Hebrew decoding taught in so many supplementary schools or the second language reading programs of Diaspora day schools based on investigations of methods that are designed to teach students to read a language that they already know. For this reason, the suggestions presented here should not be viewed as ultimate answers, but should serve as a stimulus for new thinking about the extraordinary challenges of teaching Hebrew reading.

READING, LANGUAGE, AND SCRIPT

The first cross-national investigation of reading was conducted by William S. Gray (1956). He identified a great number of similarities in mature readers of a wide range of languages. For example, eye movements during reading follow a universal pattern of quick sideways motions known as saccadic movements, which alternate with short pauses known as fixations. Occasionally, the eyes backtrack along the line of print, fixate, and then move forward again. These are known as regressions. It is only during fixations that the reader can actually see the print, and regressions are usually a means of verifying or correcting what one has already seen.

Although Gray concluded that the process of reading is essentially the same in all languages, he did note that mature readers of both Hebrew and Arabic make longer fixations and more frequent regressions than readers of European languages. Subsequent cross-national investigations of reading (Downing, 1973; Kavanaugh and Venezky, 1981; Harris and Hatano, 1999) have given further support to the notion that both the linguistic and orthographic features of a language can greatly influence the way that beginning readers encode and retrieve its printed words. A number of researchers have pointed to the nature of how Semitic languages build words and the idiosyncrasies of their scripts as likely explanations for the need to look longer and verify more frequently. Hebrew reading teachers must therefore not rely on the strategies that their students have acquired for decoding English, and must be aware of the unique qualities of the Hebrew language and its system of writing in order to provide students with those strategies that are most appropriate for Hebrew reading.

Considerations of the Hebrew Language and Its Script

The central linguistic aspect that can influence how beginning readers learn Hebrew is in the area of word building. Hebrew, like Arabic, derives much of its vocabulary from roots of three consonants which are inflected with prefixes, suffixes, infixes, or changes in the vowel patterns to create a wide variety of words. While such a system lends a mathematical elegance to the language, it can also create difficulties in reading. Because words tend to be of a similar length, and slight alterations create significant variations in meaning, readers must pay close attention to minute visual cues in order to identify individual words correctly. This issue will be addressed more fully in the section below entitled "Overall Visual Qualities of the Script." In addition to linguistic considerations, five general aspects of a writing system can influence the way that mature readers process its written symbols, and should be taken into consideration when teaching beginners. These are: the type of script, the directionality it employs, the number of different symbols that the learner must master, the regularity of the sound-symbol correspondences, and the overall visual qualities of the script.

Type of Script

Alphabetic writing, in which each symbol or combination of symbols represents a sound, differs from both logographic and syllabic systems, in which individual symbols represent words or syllables respectively. For example, dyslexia is extremely rare in Japan, where both a syllabic and logographic system are used, and in Taiwan, where the script is wholly logographic (Tzeng and Hung, 1981). It is possible that both logographs and syllables map more directly onto speech than does an alphabetic system from which the reader must be able to deduce the sound-symbol correspondence rules from the regularities of the written word.

The absence of vowel letters in Hebrew has sparked some debate about whether it originally constituted a syllabic or an alphabetic system. Gelb (1963) claimed that West Semitic writing, including Old Hebrew, was originally syllabic in nature. Other scholars disagree, noting that Modern Hebrew is adequately served by consonant representations alone because the vowels play only a minor, inflectionary role. Although Gelb's views have become fairly popular, they suffer from one serious flaw, namely that 22 symbols is not adequate to form a syllabic orthography, especially when the language has between four and eight distinctive vowels. Rather, it seems obvious that Semitic languages did not need to mark vowels because Semitic roots are characterized by their consonant patterns, and the vowels simply differentiate grammatical forms. A reader with a command of the language could easily deduce the appropriate vowels from context alone, just as fluent speakers of Modern Hebrew can today. Especially in light of the vocalization system that has been in use for more than a millennium, we should consider Hebrew to be an alphabetic language in which consonants play a more significant role.

Directionality

Directionality is the second script feature that can have an affect on the way that beginning readers learn. Some languages, such as Chinese, are written from top to bottom. Those that use Latin script, including English, French, and German, are written from left to right. Vocalized Hebrew, while written from right to left, actually requires a more sophisticated pattern of eye movements than English. In written English, the letters are all printed on a single line, allowing the reader to move his or her eyes in a straight, linear progression from left to

right. By contrast, vocalized Hebrew has meaningful elements that are printed above and below the line of consonants, including most of the vowels and one diacritical mark. A Hebrew reader must not only scan from right to left, but in an up and down manner as well.

Number of Symbols

The third feature that varies from one writing system to another is the number of different symbols that the reader must master in order to read. In this area, alphabetic scripts have a marked advantage over both logographic and syllabic systems, as alphabets always contain a significantly smaller number of symbols. It takes the average learner many years to memorize the thousands of individual logographs found in Chinese writing, while mastering the 26 letters of the English alphabet can be accomplished in a matter of hours. Hebrew has 22 basic consonants — five of which have final forms — nine vowel signs, and a handful of diphthong clusters that represent additional phonemes. Between four and seven consonants are altered by diacritical marks, depending on the pronunciation used by a given community. The phonetic values assigned to certain vowels also vary from place to place, determining the exact number of symbols that mark unique pronunciations. Because the variation in this area depends more on the nature of the community than on any inherent qualities of the script itself, it will be discussed further in the section below entitled "Hebrew Decoding: Planning for Success."

Regularity of the Sound-Symbol Correspondences

When comparing logographic, syllabic and alphabetic systems, the total number of individual symbols that the learner must memorize can be a significant factor in learning to read. When examining an alphabetic script, however, the far more pertinent question is how effectively those symbols map onto the sounds of the spoken language. As mentioned above, both logographic and syllabic systems appear to map more directly onto speech than any alphabetic system. For this reason, logographs and syllables demand far less linguistic awareness on the part of the reader than alphabetic writing (Liberman, et al., 1981). In the same way, different alphabetic systems make different demands of the reader. Some written languages, such as Finnish, are almost wholly phonetic. Their shallow orthographies comprise perfect one-to-one correspondences between graphemes and the phonemes that they represent. Deep orthographies, like English, require the reader to possess a far greater degree of linguistic awareness, as the grapheme-phoneme correspondences are highly inconsistent. Learning to decode in an inconsistent system can be a very frustrating task, as the novice reader must acquire a seemingly infinite amount of information. While the differences between deep and shallow orthographies are mainly quantitative, they can be qualitative as well. In consistent systems, the knowledge that the reader must acquire is often far less complex than that required for reading in an inconsistent system. Logic dictates that these quantitative and qualitative differences should make a consistent system much easier for the beginning reader. Comparative studies of reading in different countries (Downing, 1973; Kavanaugh and Venezky, 1981) support this notion, documenting a lower incidence of reading disabilities in countries where the system of writing is consistent. For example, Kyöstiö (1981) reports that only 15% of the second grade pupils in Finland suffer from any reading disabilities, and only one university in that country has a department devoted to training special education teachers. The picture of literacy in America is quite different, with reports of increasing reading failures, and estimates that one third of all elementary school students in the United States have difficulty learning to read (Lefevre, 1964).

Hebrew employs a fairly shallow orthography, although not as shallow as Finnish. In written Hebrew, almost every grapheme represents a single phoneme, and most phonemes can be represented by only one grapheme. However, there are a number of exceptions. Lenchner and Dori (1983b) divide these exceptions into four classifications. The first of these contains sets of different letter symbols that mark the same sound. Included in this category are those letters that have regular and final forms (ץ/צ, ן/נ, ם/מ, etc.), and a variety of unrelated [letters that originally represented different sounds, but whose pronunciations have converged over the course of time (ת/ט, ש/ס, ק/כ, כ/ח, ב/ו, and [ה]/ע/א).

In the same way, there are four sets of different vowel signs that receive very similar pronunciations (◌ֶ/◌ֵ/◌ֵי/◌ֶי, ◌ַ/◌ֲ/◌ָ/◌ֳ, ◌ִ/◌ִי, ◌ֹ/◌ֻו, ◌ֻ/◌ֹ/◌ָ). Some of these sets contain vowel signs that are visually similar, such as *patach* and *chataf-patach* (◌ַ/◌ֲ), and those that bear no visual resemblance to each other, such as *shuruk* and *kubutz* (◌ֻ/◌ֻו). The third category of potentially confusing symbols contains those letters that can represent more than one sound. This classification has a number of subcategories. First, there are the בגד״כפת letters, six letters that originally took different pronunciations depending on their placement within a syllable. Only Yemenite pronunciation retains all six dual forms. Ashkenazic pronunciation retains four dual forms (ב, כ, פ, and ת), while the Sephardic pronunciation has retained only three duals whose pronunciations are altered depending on the presence or absence of a dagesh (ב, כ, and פ). More confusing are the letters ה, ו, and י. At times, these letters represent the consonant sounds [h], [v] and [y], respectively. At other times, they occur as markers for elongated vowels (e.g., *kamatz*, *chirik* and *cholam*). Finally, the ש can represent [sh] or [s], depending on the placement of the dot above it. Closely related to the third classification, the fourth consists of individual vowels that can take different pronunciations. In Sephardic Hebrew, the *kamatz gadol* represents the phoneme [a], a sound that is essentially identical to the *patach*. However, the visually identical *kamatz katan* represents the phoneme [o], quite similar to the *cholam*. Similarly, the *sh'va* can either represent an indefinite vowel, or the lack of a vowel entirely, depending on where it falls within a syllable. Finally, a *patach* followed by a non-voweled י represents the phoneme [ay], like the sound of the English word "eye."

Overall Visual Qualities of the Script

The fifth, and clearly most complicated factor that can influence the process of learning to read, is the overall visual quality of the writing system being studied. In discussing this factor, it is necessary to examine three general areas: word shapes, letter resemblance, and the presence of unchanging word forms, as well as any special problems that arise specifically from Hebrew script.

Some instructional methods stress the importance of using ascending and descending letters to assist in word recognition. These are letters that extend above or below the line of print, such as t, h, k, g, p and q. Because these letters often occur at predictable points or in regular combinations within English words, they may assist the reader by providing a shortcut to processing a complete visual image. This technique is especially useful for recognizing whole words rather than phonetic decoding. Words that do not contain ascenders or descenders are considered to lack distinctive features, and are often avoided in the early stages of instruction.

Some scripts, however, have very few ascending and descending letters. Hebrew, for instance, has only one ascender, ל, and only one descender that occurs in every position within a word, ק. The other four descenders are all final letter forms. As a result, Hebrew words lack distinctive shape, and vary mostly in terms of length. Even this distinction is tenuous, as Hebrew's heavy reliance on its root word system for word building produces a majority of words that are three to six letters long. Because most Hebrew words lack distinctive features, the most beneficial reading approach will emphasize phonetic decoding of single letters and vowels, not attending to word shape. Another important aspect of any script's visual quality is how closely individual symbols resemble one another. This is related to the question of how much effort the learner will need to make in order to tell them apart. English, for example, has a few pairs of visually similar letters, most notably b/d and p/q. Hebrew, on the other hand, is filled with sets of printed symbols that are visually similar, although it has none of the mirror-type letters of the English example. Visually similar Hebrew symbols fall into three categories: those that are identical except for one small element, those that are virtually identical when rotated, and those that share only an overall shape.

The first category is by far the largest, and one that can cause significant problems for the beginning reader. It consists of letters that are identical except for one tiny feature: ב/כ, כ/פ, ג/נ, ד/ר, ה/ח, ח/ת, ו/ז, ר/ו, י/ו, ו/ן, ך/ן, ף/ך, ס/ם, ץ/ן, etc. In addition to some thirty pairs of these visually similar letters, the are also a few pairs of vowels in the category: ▪/▪, and ▪/▪.

The second category consists of letters that are similar when rotated, such as ה/כ, ב/ת or ש/פ, as well as the vowels ▪ and ▪. Although this is a much smaller category, and one less prone to cause problems for most readers, confusion here can indi-

cate a serious perceptual problem in the area of directionality or spatial orientation.

The third category is the most frustrating for many teachers, who are often surprised by students who confuse letters that are clearly quite distinctive. The letters in this category do not share a majority of common features like those in the two previous categories. Rather, they resemble each other in overall shape or orientation. The most common of these pairs are ם/ס and ע/צ. Students who confuse these pairs are not fully processing each visual image, but are attempting to use minimal visual clues to identify the letter. This strategy is quite similar to that of using overall word shapes mentioned above, and it is inadequate for the task of Hebrew decoding.

The sheer number of visually confusing items in Hebrew script as well as the variation of ways in which they can be similar, creates subtle differences in the interplay of the reading skills when applied to Hebrew rather than English reading. For example, the research on English reading points to phonological awareness (the ability to extrapolate sounds from syllables and syllables from words) as an early predictor of reading success (Liberman, et al., 1981). Although phonological awareness also plays a significant role in Hebrew decoding, it has been shown to be far less important than visual skills as a predictor of Hebrew reading success (Share and Levin, 1999). This finding lends support to the notion that Hebrew places a greater demand on the reader's visual processing system than is necessary for English reading.

The third general aspect of a writing system's visual quality is the preponderance of unchanging word forms. English is filled with words with shapes that remain constant, and has even more that change in highly predictable ways based on their grammatical function. Because English relies so heavily on word order to convey grammatical role, the reader is able to predict which form a word is likely to take with relative ease. This is one of the key redundancies in English orthography that can assist the reader in processing large amounts of linguistic information without the need for fully processed visual images.

Unlike English, Hebrew is an inflected language. Different words are derived from common root clusters, and this process accounts for the greatest amount of Hebrew vocabulary. As a result of creating words in this manner, slight alternations in the vowels, and the addition of affixes can produce dozens of different words, while the most salient part of the visual image, the root consonants, remains the same. The difference is both quantitative and qualitative. Not only can individual Hebrew roots produce many forms, including several words of the same grammatical type, but the visual cues that enable the reader to distinguish between them are often quite subtle. As a result, students who do not focus on the entire visual image may confuse words that are derived from the same root, especially if one form is particularly familiar. For example, it is not uncommon for novice readers to substitute the word "בָּרוּךְ" for any word derived from the root ".ב.ר.ך", and are even more prone to do so if the word occurs at the beginning of a sentence or if it contains an affix that is visually similar to the one found in the more common version, (e.g. בְּרִיךְ). In addition to the five general categories of script features that can cause difficulties for the reader, any system of writing can require specific processing strategies, and can present a number of problems that are uniquely its own. For example, Hebrew not only requires the reader to process fully every visual image, but appears to demand complete grapheme-to-phoneme translations as well. Navon and Shimron (1981) asked adult native Hebrew speakers to identify words by their letters only. They found that naming was equally fast for unvocalized words, those that were correctly vocalized and those that contained incorrect vowels that preserved the phonemic value of the word. However, word identification was significantly slower when words were incorrectly vocalized and the vowel signs did not preserve the sound of the word. A follow-up study (Shimron and Navon, 1982) compared the use of grapheme-to-phoneme translations in children and adults, and found that neither group was able to resist such translations while both groups benefited from the redundant phonemic information provided by the vowels. The only significant difference between the two groups was that the children were more sensitive to minor alterations in the graphemes even when the phonemic value of the word was preserved, suggesting that children were less able to disregard the vowels even when they were asked to do so.

Finally, a system of writing may be afflicted with a number of unique problems. In Hebrew, for instance, the vowels are much smaller than the consonants, and are generally tucked away below or above the line of print. Not surprisingly, vowels have been implicated as a primary contributor to reading failures in Israel. For example, Feitelson (1981) reports that vowel errors were more common than any other single type, accounting for 38% of all errors, in a reading aloud task given to Israeli children at the end of first grade.

> I often assign children to master the Hebrew reading of a prayer. I give them a certain amount of time to learn the prayer, and then have them individually and privately read it for me. This has the advantage of not boring the rest of the class, and it gives me a chance to evaluate the student without the pressure of having to explain to the other students why I accept different standards from different children. I will pass a child on a prayer if I think it is the best that they can do, and continued practice won't improve their reading. But if I think a student is capable of doing better, I will have a higher level of expectation for that student. It is often hard to explain that to the children, and they don't see it as being fair.
>
> *(Nancy Hersh, Chatham, New Jersey)*

HEBREW DECODING: PLANNING FOR SUCCESS

Because Melissa has a history of difficulties with English reading, the way that her Hebrew primer deals with the unique features of Hebrew script will go a long way in determining her ultimate success or failure at learning to decode Hebrew, as well as the ultimate ease or frustration that accompany her experience. First, like all beginning Hebrew readers, Melissa must be taught to attend to and fully process every visual cue. This strategy should be emphasized from the outset, and she should be told explicitly that the way one reads Hebrew is absolutely different from the way one reads any European language. Second, because Hebrew has so many letters that look so similar, everything possible must be done to reduce the likelihood that she will confuse them. Finally, her phonics program must pay special attention to the vowels, employing drill patterns that will best foster mastery of these troublesome symbols.

Israeli researcher Dina Feitelson has long

pointed to the pivotal role that instructional sequences play in the introduction of individual letters and vowels. In her research with Israeli school children, three different sequences were examined for introducing "look alike" letters. With some groups, the letters were introduced concurrently, or at the same time. In other groups, the letters were introduced sequentially with confusing items presented one right after the other and, finally, in some groups these items were introduced sequentially with confusing letters separated by strings of neutral symbols. While logic may dictate that concurrent introduction should be the most effective approach, as it would allow the teacher to draw specific comparisons and contrasts between similar items, classroom experimentation revealed a different finding. In every case, both concurrent and sequential introduction where two confusing items were presented one right after the other actually led to an increase in confusion, while the students who were given ample time with one item before the second was introduced were far more capable of making the fine distinctions necessary. Here the research emphatically suggests that learners must fully master one member of the pair before being able to attend to the subtle differences presented by the other.

Comparable experiments were conducted with the introduction of different symbols that represent similar sounds (such as וֹ, ס and שׂ, or ב and כּ), as well as those that represent identical sounds, (such as ח, ה and כ, or ◘ and ◘). In the case of similar sounding letters, sequential introduction with strings of neutral sounds separating each item was found to decrease the likelihood of confusion, while both other approaches led to greater confusion. By contrast, concurrent introduction was found to be the most advantageous approach for different symbols that make identical sounds. In this case, both kinds of sequential instruction led some students to remember one symbol, but not the other. Nevertheless, because Hebrew makes such great demands of the reader's visual system, it is of particular importance that visually similar letters are not introduced together or one after the other, because once this confusion sets in it can plague the reader literally for years. And if this is true for Israeli learners who live in a fully Hebrew environment, it is an even greater concern for students in the Diaspora whose exposure to Hebrew is often a very part-time enterprise. While this find-

ing is important for all beginning Hebrew readers, it is crucial for a student like Melissa, who does not possess strong visual processing skills.

Consideration must also be given to the manner in which vowels are presented and drilled. Here again, some vowel pairs are visually similar (such as ◘ and ◘); there are sets of different symbols that make the same sound (such as ◘, ◘ and ◘); and some make similar sounds (such as ◘ and ◘). Whenever possible, these should be introduced through the same kinds of sequences employed for letters, with concurrent instruction for different vowels that represent the same sound, and sequential introduction with strings of neutral symbols separating those that either look or sound similar.

Feitelson (1981) also reports that the drill patterns influence successful mastery of the vowels, and that the most effective approach lies in structuring reading drills around single vowels rather than consonants. As students acquire a vowel it should then be drilled with all of the consonants that they have already learned (e.g. בַּ, שַׁ, תַּ, גַּ, דַּ, etc.), instead of the more common pattern of drilling single consonants with different vowels (e.g., בֹּ, בְּ, בּוּ, בַּ, etc.).

In the Diaspora, Hebrew reading instruction is complicated by three other factors. These are a few Hebrew phonemes that are not present in the students' native language, the needs and norms of the school and its community (exemplified by the community's standard pronunciation of a few Hebrew phonemes), and the extent to which decoding is part of an overall program of Hebrew language instruction.

There are two phonemes that consistently present problems for native English speakers. The first is the [ḥ] of the ח and כ. This phoneme can be difficult for beginning readers because there is no exact equivalent in the English language. As a result, learners tend to substitute what they perceive to be the closest approximate sound, usually a [h] or [k], depending on the phoneme's placement within the word. The other phoneme that can present difficulties for the beginning reader is the [z] of צ. Although this phoneme is found in English, it occurs in the initial position in only one English word, tsetse fly, a term that is unlikely to be familiar to beginning readers. When the צ occurs at the beginning of a word, native English speakers often pronounce it as [s] or [z]. However, this phoneme does commonly occur in the middle or at the end of English words, including pizza, hats, Betsy, and lets, so most English speakers can differentiate it and eventually learn to pronounce it more readily than the [h]. There is some debate about the cause of this problem. Some researchers (Baratz, 1970; Labov and Cohen, 1973) contend that difficulties of this nature are the result of problems in auditory perception and discrimination. Others, most notably Bryen (1976), insist that this is simply a problem of production, not processing. Experience suggests that it is sometimes a simple matter of production, but that it can be the result of more serious auditory processing problems at other times.

As a first step to helping students develop proper pronunciation, it is essential that teachers consistently model the correct pronunciation of these problematic phonemes. Thus, חַלָּה should never be called "Hallah," and צְדָקָה should never be referred to as "Sedakah." This should be stressed with teachers at all levels, especially those who teach the youngest children in the school, as young children can be particularly adept at mimicking the teacher's pronunciation.

When a student makes one of these common confusions during letter identification activities or reading, the teacher should provide immediate feedback, and ask the student to reread the word. If the problem persists, it is necessary to test the student in order to determine if the problem is one of auditory perception or of production. In a simple test of auditory discrimination, the teacher reads pairs of words to the student, who is asked to determine if the words are the same or different. Some pairs are identical; others are identical except for the target phoneme (e.g., bass/bass, hits/hiss, less/lets, bass/bats, lets/lets, etc). A student who can complete this task accurately does not have a problem with auditory discrimination, but may not understand how to produce the correct phoneme. In this case, the teacher can describe how the sound is produced, modeling it in an exaggerated manner, and can allow the student to feel his or her throat if this is helpful in learning how the sound is produced.

Remediating problems in auditory discrimination can be more difficult. However, several different activities can be used to assist students in developing this skill. First, the same kind of activities that can be used to test auditory discrimination can be used to raise students' awareness of the dif-

ferences between sounds. The teacher can read pairs of words and ask students to identify which are the same and which are different, or can use rhyming and non-rhyming words. As a general rule, students are first exposed to similar phonemes that occur in the initial position of the words, as it is easier for students to perform auditory processing tasks with initial sounds (Liberman, et al., 1981). Next, students are asked to distinguish between similar phonemes in the final positions. As students master each of these types, they can be asked to generate examples of their own, a task that demonstrates considerable mastery of auditory discrimination. The teacher can ask, "What word begins with the same sound as חֶסֶד?" or "What word rhymes with קֵץ?" Once students can identify the target sound in both positions in isolation, the teacher can make the activity more difficult again by presenting words that utilize the target phoneme in either of these two positions. Only after students can readily identify the target phoneme in both the initial and final positions are they presented with words in which the target phoneme is embedded within the word. A second special concern that complicates Hebrew decoding instruction in the Diaspora centers on the community's norms, especially where Hebrew pronunciation is concerned. There is a great deal of variation in the way that Hebrew is pronounced within the Diaspora. Aside from the major differences between the Ashkenazic and Sephardic dialects, there are subtle differences in the ways that different congregations pronounce a number of vowels, some opting for an Israeli pronunciation, some using a more pure Sephardic pronunciation, and others borrowing vowel pronunciations from Ashkenazic Hebrew. It is desirable for each school to adopt a uniform pronunciation, so that students can expect their teachers' standards to be consistent as they progress from one grade to the next. For practical purposes, the pronunciation used by the Rabbi and Cantor should set the standard promoted in every classroom. Using such a "Bimah Standard" will help to reduce the likelihood of confusion.

A final consideration is the relationship between phonetic reading and language. This is a crucial consideration if the curriculum in the years following the primer contains a Hebrew language track, but it is important even in settings that place an emphasis only on prayer recitation. While there is no evidence that the acquisition of language skills detracts from a student's ability to master phonics, there is considerable evidence to indicate that learning some language can actually enhance a learner's decoding skills. Frank Vellutino and his colleagues found that learning Hebrew as a language actually improved scores on a test of visual memory, an important finding considering how crucial visual skills are to successful Hebrew decoding (Vellutino et al, 1973; 1975). Similarly, Lenchner and Dori (1983b) emphasize that oral Hebrew vocabulary instruction is particularly helpful for students who are weak in visual processing as it enables them to bring their stronger auditory skills to the task of decoding. Here again, the research strongly suggests that students benefit greatly from phonics programs that teach reading within a language framework. Minimally, a language framework would dictate that reading drills be restricted to the use of actual Hebrew words once students have mastered enough phonemes to produce ample words. Even before that point, the individual syllables and clusters should be composed of combinations that actually exist in Hebrew given the limited number of phonemes that have been introduced. This is important because these drills predispose the learner to attend to key syllabic patterns. It is both ineffective and inefficient to introduce students to combinations that they will never encounter again.

Ideally, a language framework would provide an introduction to a limited amount of authentic Hebrew vocabulary. These "key words" might be derived from the general vocabulary of Jewish life, and might include holiday terms, greetings, ritual items, and so on. Not only do such terms give students a feel for Hebrew as an authentic spoken language, but also provide them with a means of checking a symbol they may not recognize immediately against a known entity. Clearly, a complex relationship exists between learning to decode and the idiosyncrasies of a language and its script. Since this relationship produces serious consequences for the classroom, Israeli researchers have compared the efficacy of various instructional patterns for dealing with a number of Hebrew script and language features that have been linked to reading failure. A series of systematic classroom experiments revealed a set of specific instructional sequences and approaches that reduced the likelihood of confusion and enabled most learners to master the necessary decoding skills more efficiently. Because

these factors are directly related to Hebrew orthography, the strategies found most effective in Israel should also be effective for teaching Hebrew decoding in the Diaspora, especially when the additional concerns of learning to read Hebrew in the Diaspora have been addressed. By using a primer that separates both auditorily and visually similar letters, that uses concurrent introduction for different symbols that represent the same sound, that provides reading drills that center on the vowels, and that help her apply her stronger auditory skills to the task, Melissa will be able successfully to master Hebrew decoding despite the obstacles that she may face. Nevertheless, it may take her additional time to complete the program, and she must be allowed to progress at her own pace with as much support as her parents and teachers can provide. Additionally, because she has specific problems with visual processing, her teachers may wish to incorporate the following strategies:

- If Melissa continues to confuse visually similar letters, she should be given activities that employ auditory, tactile, and kinesthetic modalities with visual processing. These include tracing letters in sand, touching wood, plastic, rubber or foam letter manipulatives, and using the body to create letter shapes (Lenchner and Dori, 1983a; 1983b). She can also cut letter shapes out of sugar cookie dough, bake the cookies, and eat them as a reward for mastering the grapheme-phoneme correspondences. Similarly, Hebrew *alef bet* candy molds are available on the market, and Melissa can be allowed to make and eat chocolate letters when she can identify them correctly. These last two activities also reinforce the traditional Jewish belief that learning is sweet.

- Melissa should be exposed to as much oral Hebrew language as possible, and should be given the opportunity to decode words that she will then be able to read. This will provide her with the ability to check a phonetic item she might not recall with a known lexical entity.

- To help Melissa master Hebrew's unique directional progression, her teacher can provide her with a number of tracing activities. Using sheets of single syllables and gradually more complex words, she would be asked to trace the progression from consonants to vowels in each example using a colored pencil or marker. The teacher should model this procedure, instructing Melissa to begin on the far right and progress from right to left, and top to bottom. Once Melissa has mastered the basic concept, the teacher can suggest that she use her index fingers to trace the syllabic configurations of words that she reads aloud, eventually weaning her of this technique as her eye movements become more natural and automatic.

- Because phonemic accessing plays such a critical role in Hebrew word identification, even for mature readers, the proper phonemic encoding of graphemes should be stressed with Melissa from the earliest stages of instruction. Here, the evidence from research in a number of different writing systems suggests that in early decoding experiences the amount of information presented in each lesson should be as small as possible so that the learner is able to focus completely on the task. Initial exposures to the letter and vowel symbols should restrict the total number of items. For example, Downing (1973) suggests that concurrent introduction of both upper and lower case English letters can create unnecessary confusion for the learner. For this reason, the amount of information about each item should be strictly limited. Because the sound-symbol relationship is of primary importance, all information that does not reinforce this association can be excluded from the introduction (Feitelson, 1965; 1976).

- A number of strategies have been suggested to assist students in learning to associate consonant symbols with their phonemes. Feitelson (1976) describes three approaches. First, each consonant was introduced in association with a concrete and easily illustrated word that began with it. While the use of key words to illustrate consonants is still the most commonly used approach today, and one that has the added advantage of introducing students to Hebrew vocabulary, it has one distinct disadvan-

tage. The association of a letter with a key word can be so strong that some students have difficulty abstracting a letter's sound when they subsequently have to apply it to a new word. Although this can be true in any situation, it is most likely to cause problems when the letter occurs in the middle or at the end of a new word. In the second strategy, each consonant was introduced in combination with a vowel. While this plan worked quite well during the first stage of instruction when only one vowel was required, the same difficulties with abstraction arose as the students progressed to the more advanced stages where they had to cope with additional vowels. In the final program, each consonant sound was introduced through a story in which the sound played an important part and was repeated several times. After the story, the students were shown a letter poster that illustrated the story and the target sound. Beneath the picture was the new letter. These posters were then displayed in the classroom so that students could refer to them as necessary. Additional reinforcement was given in the form of songs that reminded students of the key sound as well as certain elements of the original story. Feitelson reported that this method proved most effective for students who had certain learning disabilities as well as those who were culturally disadvantaged.

- Finally, because Hebrew syllables are highly regular, Hebrew lends itself quite well to a synthetic approach to phonetic decoding. In the traditional approach to decoding, the reader must abstract single sounds from their printed representations, then recombine them to form syllables and whole words. This approach is analytical, and it requires a degree of linguistic awareness that many students lack. In the synthetic approach to Hebrew decoding, students are taught to focus on individual syllables, drilling them as units, rather than first learning to break them down into their smallest grapheme-phoneme correspondences. Once students master the sound-symbol relationships of the consonants and vowels, they are given lists of consonant-vowel and consonant-vowel-consonant syllables in which one element (such as the initial consonant) changes in each example. As students gain fluency and confidence, the final consonant in each C-V-C cluster is changed, and then the vowel. The teacher reads a few items to model the process of blending the sounds together. Students then drill the lists, and formulate a set of general rules about the pronunciation of each type of syllable. By combining deductive analysis with synthetic drill, students should become more aware of both the ways that consonants and vowels are blended together to form the natural sounds of speech, and the manner in which the orthography expresses these relationships. This heightened awareness should help to reduce the amount of overly mechanical reading that is so often a by-product of the traditional phonics method. Feitelson (1967) reports that such a scheme for Hebrew decoding was developed in Israel. After only 12 weeks of instruction, the students were able to move directly to an unabridged version of the Bible.

FROM DECODING TO RECITATION

While any of the items discussed above can be a source of significant problems for beginning Hebrew readers, Craig's difficulties were more complex. Initially they appeared to stem from two specific areas, the confusion of visually similar letters, and problems with the vowels. However, subsequent investigation by the tutor revealed that Craig had no significant difficulty identifying vowels or distinguishing between visually similar letters. His problems only appeared when he attempted to recite the prayers in Hebrew. The most revealing error was his substitution of בָּרוּךְ for בְּדֶרֶךְ when he recited the וְאָהַבְתָּ. Clearly, Craig was attending to the first and last letter of the word, and attempting to deduce what was in between. This is a classic English reading strategy, and one that Craig mistakenly believed could be applied to Hebrew reading as well. As noted above, this reading strategy is wholly inappropriate for Hebrew decoding because Hebrew requires even mature readers to provide full visual processing of every item. It also requires readers to make complete grapheme-to-phoneme

translations. Further, while this kind of global reading strategy may be appropriate for silent reading, it is not a good strategy for recitation because oral reading requires the reader to process every word more carefully to ensure correct pronunciation.

In his essay, "From Sumer to Leipzig to Bethesda," Richard L. Venezky points out that silent reading is a fairly recent innovation: " . . . it is clear that even among the most scholarly and literate, silent reading was exceedingly rare up to perhaps as late as the time of Chaucer. Even in complete privacy one read to himself with the full participation of the tongue, glottis, and the other elements of the articulatory system and therefore considerably more slowly than the better adults in silent reading today." He goes on to conclude that, "Oral reading, because of both its slower pace and its attention to complete articulation of each word is probably not as demanding of higher cognitive processes as rapid, silent reading. In rapid, silent reading, visual processing which tends to be relatively slow, is traded off for greater syntactic/semantic processing which tends to be relatively fast" (Venezky, 1981: 5-6).

Because Craig had mastered silent English reading, he expected Hebrew to behave in the same way. It was, therefore, a simple matter to remind him that the experience of Hebrew reading will not be the same as English reading. Further, since Craig is not experiencing trouble with individual letters or vowels, he can begin directly with whole word blending. The multi-sensory approach to word reading that was developed by Beth Slingerland has proven useful for many students in learning to blend Hebrew words with fluency. It provides an excellent way to introduce individual words from a passage, especially those that are difficult, and gives students specific practice with them before moving on to phrasing. The first step builds an auditory-visual-kinesthetic association. The teacher points to the first of eight to ten words and pronounces it aloud. The class repeats. Individual students should be called on to repeat the word individually. Continue in this manner until each word has been introduced. The second step strengthens the auditory-visual-kinesthetic association and leads to greater recall. The teacher calls an individual student up and names one word from the list. Using a pointer, the child indicates the word and repeats it. The rest of the class repeats the word, unless an incorrect word has been indicated. By the group's silence, the student should know immediately that he or she has made a mistake, and should attempt to self-correct the error. Any student who repeats an incorrect word is either unsure of the word or is not paying attention. Repeat this procedure until each student has had a few turns, and the class as a whole is able to repeat the words correctly.

If the students learned the meanings of these words, a third step allows them to associate individual words with their concepts. The teacher provides a definition or translation for one of the words. For example, if the word list contains מִצְוָה and יִשְׂרָאֵל, the teacher might say, "Find the word that . . ."

   . . . describes an action the Torah tells us to do (מִצְוָה)

   . . . names the Jewish homeland (יִשְׂרָאֵל).

The fourth step is a test of mastery. One at a time, individual students should be called up to read the entire list or at least several words at a time. The child points to each word, reads it, and the class repeats if it is read correctly. During this step, the teacher has some flexibility. If it seems that the class has mastered the material, begin with the weakest students. If they can complete the step successfully, move to the next step. If it seems that the class is still unsure, begin with the strongest readers, as this allows slower students to hear and see additional models.

Once students have mastered individual words, they can begin to practice reading the phrases that make up a prayer text. Just as students need to blend individual phonemes into syllables and syllables into whole words, they must be able to blend words into complete phrases in order to avoid the choppy, robotic reading that so often characterizes their efforts. Here Slingerland's multi-sensory approach to phrase reading can prove effective.

Use a chart that has four to eight complete Hebrew phrases written in large letters, one phrase per line. The first step creates an auditory-visual-kinesthetic association. Students hear the phrase while looking at it, creating an auditory-visual link. They then say it while looking at it and drawing an arc through the air with their arms. It is almost impossible to read in a choppy manner when moving the arm in a smooth motion.

The teacher holds the length of the pointer under the first phrase and reads it in a rhythmic, conversational manner (not word by word), while sweeping the arm through the air in an arc from right to left. The class repeats this procedure exactly. The direction of this arc is significant, as it reinforces the directionality of Hebrew reading. The teacher should note any child who has difficulty with the direction and provide immediate remediation. Repeat this procedure several times with the class as a whole, then ask individual students to perform individually, with the class repeating after them. As students master this kind gross motor activity, move from posters to individual sheets, and ask students to make the arc on the page with their fingers when reading.

Once Craig has been exposed to some of the more difficult individual words in a passage, has drilled them and practiced reading them in full phrases, he can begin working on learning to recite the full passage in earnest. To assist Craig further with proper phraseology, his teacher should use a text that introduces the prayer one phrase per line. This provides a visual cue to proper phrasing. And because mastery of recitation requires a great deal of repetitious drill, Craig's teacher should add singing, games, choral and antiphonal reading, and other activities to keep the materials interesting and enhance the students' enjoyment of this work. While building from fluent word blending to full phraseology will provide Craig with both the proper exposure and drill structure necessary for the mastery of Hebrew recitation skills, he brings an additional difficulty to the table, although one that is far from unusual in Jewish schools at this point in history: neither of Craig's parents can help him with his Hebrew homework. Three phenomena, the gender gap in Jewish education, the growing divorce rate in American Jewish families, and the increasing rates of interfaith marriage, have exacerbated this problem in recent years.

One of the most recent profound trends in Jewish education has been the dramatic increase in equal educational opportunities for girls. In her review of the changing role of women in Jewish education, Monson (1992) cites two sets of past enrollment statistics for American Jewish schools. In the mid-1950s, boys and girls were enrolled in fairly equal numbers in Sunday schools, but boys outnumbered girls by a ratio of two to one in day schools and three to one in afternoon supplementary schools. Even as late as 1970, the gender gap had not closed to a very great extent, as girls were as likely as boys to receive a primary Jewish education. However, by the age of ten boys were far more likely to attend Jewish schools. Similar studies from the 1980s and early 1990s reveal that this gender gap has been closed for all intents and purposes, as girls are now as likely to receive a Jewish education as boys (Tobin, 1992). While this bodes well for the future, the fact that this is such a recent development suggests that in many families with children currently enrolled in Jewish schools, the mother may not have received any Jewish education beyond the second or third grade, and will likely not have learned even basic Hebrew phonics.

Compounding this condition are two other trends within American Jewish families. The first of these is the increasing rate of divorce, a reflection of the general change in the American nuclear family. In some communities, children from single-parent households headed by women make up a significant percentage of the school population. In addition to the kinds of financial and emotional stresses that these families may be experiencing, many of these mothers did not receive a Hebrew education themselves, and will therefore be unable to assist their children with Hebrew homework. The second trend is the increasing rate of intermarriage, which presents a unique set of challenges for Jewish educators as a whole and Hebrew teachers in particular. The 1990 Jewish Population Survey sent shock waves through the Jewish community with its reports of a 50% rate of intermarriage, and the finding that nearly one-third of all Jewish families were interfaith (Kosmin, 1992). Where Hebrew education is concerned, students in single-parent homes and those from interfaith families are unlikely to have anyone at home who can assist them with their Hebrew studies. This situation is a great source of frustration for students, parents, and teachers alike.

In addressing this issue, it is helpful to examine a similar situation that arose in Israel during the 1950s. Feitelson (1973; 1981) details the reading instructional techniques that were employed in the European Diaspora and those that were developed in pre-state Israel. As part of their overall rejection of all things connected to life in Europe's ghettos, the early pioneers rejected the traditional approach to Hebrew reading instruction and adopted the reading instructional methods that had been developed by the early educational reformers in England and America for teaching English reading. Despite the fact that these methods were wholly unsuitable for

teaching Hebrew, there were no widespread reports of reading failure. The mass immigration of Jews from Arab lands in the early 1950s brought this happy situation to an abrupt end. Within its first three years of statehood, the population of Israel doubled. In some parts of the country the majority of school entrants came from Middle Eastern or North African backgrounds, and their families often had scant traditions of learning, especially for women. Suddenly, reading failure rates skyrocketed to 50%. Many schools blamed this rate on the poor conditions in which the immigrant children lived and the lack of motivation on the part of the parents, many of whom were illiterate themselves. However, an independent study implicated the teaching method as the primary cause of the failure. Faced with a serious threat to the entire structure of the curriculum, the Ministry of Education set up teams to investigate the situation and develop teaching materials that would resolve it.

These teams based their work on two set of considerations, the specifics of the subject matter and the nature of the students for whom the materials were intended. Of greatest significance was the determination that when the children's parents had little or no education, or when the education they had was in a language different from the one used in school, the materials and sequences would have to cover all possible contingencies, because the teacher could never rely on the parents to provide auxiliary instruction. In fact, interviews revealed that the old methods had appeared successful only because the students had received a great deal of sophisticated parental assistance at home (Feitelson, 1981). These findings reveal two important, and often overlooked truths. First, children often struggle to learn when their parents are unable to provide auxiliary instruction at home. No matter how academically gifted a child may be, if he or she develops a problem, it will likely be a greater struggle simply because there is no additional help available at home. Second, parents are used to helping their children with school work and are often very uncomfortable when they are unable to provide the expected assistance. No parent wants to feel diminished in the eyes of his/her children, and may tacitly send the message that Hebrew work is not really important since even the parents lack these skills.

Several options are suggested to assist Craig's parents in helping him to master prayer recitation.

First, they should be encouraged to bring Craig to services on a regular basis. Nothing replaces congregational participation in prayer recitation as both a motivating factor and an ideal way to practice.

Craig will certainly benefit from service attendance as this will give him wonderful opportunities to practice what he is learning in the most real of settings. It will also provide his parents with some exposure to what Craig is studying, and it will certainly send a profoundly positive message about the importance of his Jewish education. Second, the teacher can provide Craig's parents with transliterations of each prayer text that Craig is learning. Although this is not an ideal situation, it will enable them to follow along with him as he practices at home. They can also be provided with a tape to help them learn the prayers.

Ideally, the school can provide special instruction for parents who do not read Hebrew, to assist them in becoming literate enough to assist their children. Programs like the day-long Hebrew reading marathons have been used successfully in many communities to assist parents in brushing up on their skills or acquiring them for the first time. Other schools offer a series of family education opportunities, including parallel Hebrew classes. In this model, parents meet to study Hebrew at the same time their children are in class, use the same books, and stay just slightly ahead of their child's class. By studying the same lesson in advance, they are able to provide any necessary assistance for their children when it is most needed.

At first Craig's problems in Hebrew appeared to be related to visual processing and mislearned vowels. Realizing that his difficulties arose from applying an inappropriate reading strategy, his teacher was able to remediate the problem just by explaining how and why Hebrew requires a different approach. Craig was then given specific practice with difficult individual words, direct instruction in fluent phrasing, a wide variety of practice drills and activities, and strategies for working at home. Additionally, by understanding and planning for his special family circumstances, his school was able to better serve the needs of a growing segment of the community. Here are a few important considerations for teaching prayer recitation:

- Begin the study of each new prayer by giving students specific practice with its most important and difficult words.

- By using phrases from each new prayer for phraseology instruction and review, the speed of mastering the recitation of each prayer should be greatly accelerated.

- Introduce full texts of each prayer through versions that present the text one phrase per line.

- Use choral and antiphonal reading, singing, and a variety of reading games to maintain the students' interest in the work.

RACHEL'S MAGIC LOOM

As a day school student, Rachel's program stressed communicative and literary Hebrew. She was expected to speak Hebrew in class, and read Hebrew texts with comprehension. Rivers and Nahir (1989) describe six stages of reading development within the context of a communicative Hebrew course. The first three stages are characterized by the dependence on the students' acquisition of oral language. In the first stage, students are introduced to the writing system. They focus on mastering the sound-symbol correspondences and acquire as much oral Hebrew language as possible. During this stage, students learn to read only those words that they learned orally, and the written material is presented in precisely the same manner and context as it was orally. Once students have mastered basic phonics and simple Hebrew sentence structures, they enter the second stage of reading which features the recombination of familiar material. Here, the items that students have learned orally are presented in new contexts, allowing students to learn new ways of using familiar words when they speak. At this stage, reading provides students with new strategies for oral communication. For a while, students may alternate between these two stages. In the third stage, they begin to acquire reading techniques, such as a sensitivity to writing style, as well as more complex sentence structures. While most of the vocabulary used in reading passages is already known to the students through oral work, some new lexical items are presented as long as their meaning can be deduced from illustrations, context, or through the use of cognates.

Stages four through six foster students' growing independence with reading, and are characterized by the fact that the written material relies less and less on previous oral and aural exposure. In stage four, students practice their reading skills with an increasingly wide range of materials, and engage in two types of reading. Some reading materials are used to further the students' understanding of grammar and continued acquisition of vocabulary. At the same time, students are encouraged to begin reading on their own for pleasure as well as for information. In stage five, students use their skills for expanded purposes, and read some literary passages in their original form. At this point, reading becomes a technique for learning rather than an end in itself, as students learn to scan for information, extract ideas, and pay close attention to literary style. By stage six, reading should be a fully autonomous activity, and each student should be able to use a variety of written materials for fully independent study.

Even in the earliest stages of study, Rachel excelled at the oral language work, but struggled with reading. As she progressed from stage two to stage three, and especially from stage three to stage four, reading comprehension became progressively more difficult for her. Part of Rachel's problem may lie in the fact that she is being asked to read an increasing number of words that she has not learned orally and whose meaning she must deduce from context or other clues. Her success with oral language suggests that Rachel possesses exceptional auditory processing skills, but may be less adept at visual processing. To evaluate her strengths and weaknesses, her teacher can ask her to read a passage and comprehension questions aloud, answering the questions orally. If she can complete this task with relative ease, the teacher can adapt her reading program to help her make use of her stronger auditory skills.

For example, while most intermediate and advanced students can read a new passage silently during their initial exposure to it, and many benefit from the opportunity to practice the passage before reading it aloud to others, Rachel is just the opposite. Despite the fact that oral reading is necessarily slower, Rachel will benefit from hearing the words read aloud, as this is the most direct way for her to access linguistic comprehension. As a result, her teacher can continue to utilize stage two learning techniques with Rachel (i.e., providing oral presentation of new vocabulary and grammatical structures before she is given the printed matter), even as the material increases in difficulty. Rachel should be encouraged to read aloud, gradually

reducing the volume at which she reads until she can simply hear the words "in her mind's ear." Developing Hebrew readers bring a wide range of personal qualities to the task of learning. These include interest, motivation, and their tolerance for frustration. Rachel's interest level and her personal motivation have always been quite high. However, as she has struggled with the materials, she has reached the limit of her tolerance for frustration. Rachel's teacher needs to find strategies that will help her succeed in order to increase both her motivation and her tolerance for frustration.

Of all the individual learner variables that have been studied in relation to second language learning, motivation has been found to be both the most important and the one most open to the influence of the teacher (Savignon, 1976; Gardner, 1980). For example, initial success with language learning has been shown to significantly increase the student's motivation to learn, which in turn leads to greater subsequent success (MacNamara, 1973; Burstall, 1975). In other words, when it comes to second learning learning, nothing succeeds like success. By finding ways to help Rachel experience more success in reading, her teacher will greatly decrease her level of frustration while increasing her motivation to learn. The following considerations may prove helpful to teachers who work in settings that stress communicative and literary Hebrew:

- The reading stages described by Rivers and Nahir do not represent six levels of study, nor are they time-oriented sequences. Rather, they should be seen as a developmental process. As such, there is likely to be a great deal of overlap, and students may pass back and forth between different stages at any point. Moreover, some students will instinctively begin to make use of higher-level strategies before being taught to use them, while other students will continue to make use of earlier strategies for a very long time. It is neither essential to pigeonhole any student into a particular phase nor to force them to move from one stage to another. What is essential is making sure that each student learns to read as fully and easily as possible.

- The reading materials used for communicative Hebrew courses should provide real information and should not simply provide a means of introducing or drilling grammatical items. These contrived reading passages create such a distortion of the language and its uses that it can actually inhibit the opportunities for authentic language learning (Gremmo, Holec, and Rily, 1978). From the outset, reading materials should be directed toward the normal uses of reading. These include gathering information about a topic of interest; learning how to play a game or complete a task; as a means of finding out what other people think, believe, or feel; or for personal pleasure.

- The more that teachers know about their students, the better able they are to assist them with the materials. By understanding Rachel's strengths and weaknesses, her teacher was able to design an approach to Hebrew reading that would allow Rachel's strengths to compensate for her deficits.

- All good teachers know that demonstrating excitement and enthusiasm for their subject is an excellent way to stimulate their students' interest. Rachel's teachers can model enthusiasm for Hebrew in a number of ways. First, they can share interesting facts about the history of the language or how Hebrew words are developed. The Bibliography that follows contains a section entitled "Background Information on the Hebrew Language." It lists resources on the history of the Hebrew language and interesting stories about its words and their development.

> Using cut-up pipe cleaners, glue, and note cards, I had the students create fuzzy, 3-D *alef bet* consonants and vowels. Then I blindfolded students to see if they could "feel and say" the right letters and sounds.
>
> *(Sheila Lepkin, Denver, Colorado)*

CONCLUSION

In his 1979 article in the *Modern Language Journal*, Dr. Moshe Nahir reviewed the Hebrew language programs published in North America for both the elementary and collegiate levels. Nahir concluded that although the major trends in second language instruction were echoed in these programs, the reflection of these trends "has been slow and partial, with the field of Hebrew ever trailing one stage behind the theoretical and methodological mainstream (Nahir, 1979: 424)." Unfortunately, Nahir's comments are as valid today as they were a quarter of a century ago, and apply as much to the teaching of Hebrew phonics as they do to Hebrew language instruction. Despite decades of research into the acquisition of Hebrew reading in particular, most Hebrew decoding programs lag far more than one stage behind our knowledge about the process. This gap between knowledge and practice poses serious consequences, as the very nature of Jewish education, with its universal time pressures, creates the need for instructional methods and sequences that are both effective for long-term result and efficient in terms of available class time. It is only by employing such methods and materials that we can ever hope to be successful in providing whatever kind of Hebrew education we attempt to impart. The simple truth remains that we can no longer afford to ignore the research and lag one step or more behind. Only by applying the findings from the field to our classroom work can we begin to make every form of Hebrew reading a truly rich and rewarding experience for our students.

BIBLIOGRAPHY

Baratz, Joan C. "Beginning Readers for Speakers of Divergent Dialects." In *Reading Goals for the Disadvantaged.* J. Allen Figurel, ed. Newark, DE: International Reading Association, 1970, pp. 77-83.

Explores the role of auditory discrimination in learning to read.

Bryen, Diane N. "Speech-Sound Discrimination Ability on Linguistically Unbiased Tests." *Exceptional Children* 42, January 1976, pp. 195-201.

Discusses the role of culture bias and auditory discrimination.

Burstall, Clare. "Factors Affecting Foreign-Language Learning: A Consideration of Research Findings." *Language, Teaching and Linguistics Abstracts* 9, 1975, pp. 5-125.

Examines the role of many factors in second language learning.

Dori, Rivka. "What We Know about . . . Hebrew Language Instruction." In *What We Know about Jewish Education: A Handbook of Today's Research for Tomorrow's Jewish Education.* Stuart L. Kelman, ed. Los Angeles, CA: Torah Aura Productions, 1992, pp. 261-269.

This essay has informed most of the recent discussion of Hebrew language instruction.

Downing, John. *Comparative Reading.* New York: Macmillan, 1973.

An early and influential cross-national comparison of reading instruction.

Feitelson, Dina. "Structuring the Teaching of Reading According to Major Features of the Language and Its Script." *Elementary English* 42, 1965, pp. 8780-877.

———. "The Relationship between Systems of Writing and the Teaching of Reading." In *Reading Instruction: An International Forum.* M.D. Jenkinson, ed. Newark, DE: International Reading Association, 1967, pp. 191-199.

———. "Israel." In *Comparative Reading.* John Downing, ed. New York: Macmilan, 1973, pp. 426-439.

———. "Sequence and Structure in a System with Consistent Sound-Symbol Correspondence." In *New Horizons in Reading.* John E. Merrit, ed.

Newark, DE: International Reading Association, 1976, pp. 269-277.

———. Relating Instructional Strategies To Language Idiosyncrasies in Hebrew." In *Reading, Orthography and Dyslexia.* James F. Kavanaugh and Richard L. Venezky, eds. Baltimore, MD: University Park Press, 1981, pp. 25-34.

These five studies summarize Feitelson's landmark research on Hebrew reading instruction in Israel, and how Hebrew requires a unique application of reading skills.

Gardner, Robert C. "On the Validity of Affective Variables in Second Language Acquisition: Conceptual, Contextual and Statistical Considerations." *Language and Learning*, no. 30, 1980, pp. 255-270.

A look at a number of learner variables in second language acquisition.

Gelb, Ignace J. *A Study of Writing.* rev. ed. Chicago, IL: University of Chicago Press, 1963.

An early exploration of different types of orthographies.

Gray, William S. *The Teaching of Reading and Writing: An International Survey.* Paris: UNESCO, 1956.

The first cross-national examination of reading.

Gremmo, Marie-José; Henri Holec; and Philip Riley. "Taking the Initiative: Some Pedagogical Applications of Discourse Analysis." Nancy, France: Mélanges Pedagogiques, University of Nancy, Centre de Recherches et d'Application Pedagogiques en Langues, 1978.

Examines practical classroom applications of the communication patterns that typically develop in foreign language classrooms.

Harris, Margaret, and Giyoo Hatono, eds. *Learning to Read and Write: A Cross-Linguistic Perspective.* Cambridge, England: Cambridge University Press, 1999.

A recent cross-national exploration of how reading is taught and learned.

Kavanaugh, James F., and Richard L. Venezky. *Reading Orthography and Dyslexia.* Baltimore, MD: University Park Press, 1981.

A cross-national examination of the issues in reading and specific language disabilities.

Kosmin, Barry A. "The Permeable Boundaries of Being Jewish in America." *Moment* 17, no. 4, August 1992, pp. 30-33.

A synopsis of the finding of the 1990 National Jewish Population Survey.

Kyöstiö, O.K. "Is Learning to Read Easy in a Language in Which Grapheme-Phoneme Correspondences Are Regular?" In *Reading, Orthography and Dyslexia*. James F. Kavanaugh and Richard L. Venezky, eds. Baltimore, MD: University Park Press, 1981, pp. 35-49.

Explores the teaching of reading in Finland.

Labov, William, and Paul Cohen. "Some Suggestions for Teaching Standard English To Speakers of Non-standard and Urban Dialects." In *Language, Society and Education: A Profile of Black English*. Johanna S. DeStefano, ed. Worthington, OH: Charles S. Jones, 1973, pp. 218-237.

Explores how dialects influence auditory perception and reading acquisition.

Lefevre, Carl A. *Linguistics and the Teaching of Reading*. New York: McGraw-Hill, 1964.

An early indictment of reading failure in American public schools.

Lenchner, Orna, and Rivka Dori. "Why Jonathan Can't Read: Part I." *Compass* 6, no. 2, 1983, pp. 3-4.

———. "Why Jonathan Can't Read: Part II." *Compass* 6, no. 3, 1983, pp. 6-8.

An examination of how Hebrew instructional sequences can foster success or hamper the endeavors of students with specific learning disabilities.

Liberman, Isabelle; Alvin M. Liberman; Ignatius Mattingly; and Donald Shankweiler. "Orthography and the Beginning Reader." In *Reading, Orthography and Dyslexia*. James F. Kavanaugh and Richard L. Venezky, eds. Baltimore, MD: University Park Press, 1981, pp. 35-49.

A thorough examination of phonological awareness and its importance in learning to read.

MacNamara, John. "Nurseries, Streets and Classrooms: Some Comparisons and Deductions." *Modern Language Journal* 57, 1973, pp. 250-254.

Examines several variables in classroom and naturalistic language acquisition.

Monson, Rela G. "What We Know about . . . Women and Jewish Education." In *What We Know about Jewish Education: A Handbook of Today's Research for Tomorrow's Jewish Education*. Stuart L. Kelman, ed. Los Angeles, CA: Torah Aura Productions, 1992, pp. 43-50.

Examines the changing role of women in American Jewish education.

Nahir, Moshe. "Teaching Hebrew as a Second Language: The State of the Art." *Modern Language Journal* 63, no. 8, 1979, pp. 423-429.

Summarizes Nahir's examination of the elementary and collegiate Hebrew language curricula developed in North America.

Navon, David, and Joseph Shimron. "Does Word Naming Involve Grapheme-To-Phoneme Translation? Evidence from Hebrew." *Journal of Verbal Learning and Verbal Behavior* 20, 1981, pp. 97-109.

Examines grapheme-to-phoneme translation in adult Hebrew Reading.

Rivers, Wilga M., and Moshe Nahir. *Teaching Hebrew: A Practical Guide*. Tel Aviv: University Publishing Projects, Ltd., 1989.

Creates a complete framework for teaching communicative Hebrew through an adaptation of River's earlier work.

Savignon, Sandra J. "On the Other Side of the Desk: A Look at Teacher Attitudes and Motivation in Second Language Learning." *Canadian Modern Language Review* 76, no. 32, 1976.

A look at the role of motivation in second language learning.

Share, David, and Iris Levin. "Learning to Read and Write in Hebrew." In *Learning to Read and Write: A Cross-Linguistic Perspective*. Margaret Harris and Giyoo Hatano, eds. Cambridge, England: Cambridge University Press, 1999, pp. 89-111.

A recent review of research related to reading instruction in Israel and how Hebrew requires a unique application of general reading skills.

Shimron, Joseph, and David Navon. "The Dependence on Graphemes and Their Translation To Phonemes in Reading: A Developmental Perspective." *Reading Research Quarterly* 17, no. 2, 1982, pp. 210-228.

In this follow-up to their earlier study, the authors examine grapheme-to-phoneme translation in the Hebrew reading of both adults and children.

Slingerland, Beth H. *A Multi-Senroy Approach To Language Arts for Specific Language Disability Children: A Guide for Primary Teachers.* Cambridge, MA: Educator's Publishing Service, 1975.

Presents a full program of instruction for teaching English reading, including oral reading, through multiple modalities. Although designed for students who have specific language disabilities, the approach presented can be readily applied to classroom that promote Hebrew decoding and recitation.

Tobin, Gary A. "What We Know about . . . Demography." In *What We Know about Jewish Education: A Handbook of Today's Research for Tomorrow's Jewish Education.* Stuart L. Kelman, ed. Los Angeles, CA: Torah Aura Productions, 1992, pp. 71-80.

A look at the demographic research on the American Jewish community, and the changed in educational patterns that have occurred over the past several decades.

Tzeng, Ovid, and Daisy Hung. "Reading in a Non-alphabetic Writing System." In *Reading, Orthography and Dyslexia.* James F. Kavanaugh and Richard L. Venezky, eds. Baltimore, MD: University Park Press, 1981, pp. 211-216.

Examines the differences in learning to read in logographic and syllabic systems.

Vellutino, Frank R.; Robert M. Pruzek; Joseph A. Steger; and Uriel Meshoulam. "Immediate Visual Recall in Poor and Normal Readers as a Function of Orthographic-Linguistic Familiarity." *Cortex* 9, 1973, pp. 370-386.

Examines the role of language in tasks that require visual recall. This study used Hebrew as the target language.

Vellutino, Frank R.; Joseph A. Steger; Mitchell Kaman; and Louis DeSetto. "Visual Form Perception in Deficient and Normal Readers as a Function of Age and Orthographic-Linguistic Familiarity." *Cortex* 11, 1975, pp. 22-30.

A follow-up of the 1973 study conducted by Vellutino and his colleagues, this time including groups of younger children. Hebrew was again used as the target language.

Venezky, Richard L. "Overview: From Sumer To Leipzig To Bethesda." In *Reading, Orthography and Dyslexia.* James F. Kavanaugh and Richard L. Venezky, eds. Baltimore, MD: University Park Press, 1981, pp. 1-11.

Presents an introduction to the major issues explored in the book as a whole, as well as a look at the history of reading and its instruction.

Resources for Teaching Reading

Note: The following entries provide teachers with resources on the issues related to reading instruction, as well as games and activities that develop the specific reading and language skills discussed in this chapter.

Harris, Albert J., and Edward R. Sipay. *How to Teach Reading: A Competency-Based Program.* New York: Longman Inc., 1979.

This volume explores all the major issues related to reading and its instruction, from reading readiness to fostering a literary interest. This exceptional resource provides theoretical models, summaries of research, and practical classroom techniques.

Kaye, Peggy. *Games for Reading: Playful Ways to Help Your Child Read.* New York: Pantheon Books, 1984.

These English language reading games and activities can easily be adapted for use in teaching Hebrew reading.

Zana, Hillary. "Games and Other Learning Activities for the Hebrew Class." In *The New Jewish Teachers Handbook.* Audrey Friedman Marcus and Raymond A. Zwerin, eds. Denver, CO: A.R.E. Publishing, Inc., 1994, pp. 240-254.

The games presented here by a master teacher were designed specifically for the various skills necessary for Hebrew decoding, recitation, and reading.

Background on Hebrew Language

Note: The following entries offer teachers background information on the Hebrew language and its alphabet. These sources are meant to provide enrichment material for personal growth as much as for classroom use.

Chomsky, Willima. *Hebrew: The Eternal Language.* 8th ed. Philadelphia, PA: The Jewish Publication Society, 1957.

A classic study of the Hebrew language and its importance for the Jewish people.

Fine, Marilyn Z. "Classical Text and Modern Hebrew: Making the Two Worlds One." *Jewish Education News* 18, no. 3, 1997, p. 32.

A concise approach to integrating Modern Hebrew vocabulary with that of classical texts.

Horowitz, Edward. *How the Hebrew Language Grew.* Hoboken, NJ: KTAV Publishing House, Inc., 1988.

One of the earliest explorations of the development of Hebrew, including an overview of its grammatical systems and an explanation of its root word system.

Lowin, Joseph. *Hebrewspeak: An Insider's Guide to the Way Jews Think.* Northvale, NJ: Jason Aronson Inc., 1995.

This title is concerned with the marvelous workings of the Hebrew root letter system. The 105 chapters were originally published as columns on the Hebrew language in *Hadassah Magazine.*

Nahir, Moshe, ed. *Hebrew Teaching and Applied Linguistics.* Washington, DC: University Press of America, 1981.

This collection of essays presents various aspects of Hebrew instruction, including reading.

Sáenz-Badillos, Angel. *A History of the Hebrew Language.* Translated by John Elwolde. Cambridge, England: Cambridge University Press, 1993.

In this very scholarly work, Sáenz-Badillos traces the origins of Semitic languages through the rebirth of modern Hebrew in Israel. An excellent, though difficult source.

Steinberg, Samuel. "Hebrew: The Hallmark of an Educated Jew." *Jewish Education News* 18, no. 3, 1997, pp. 10-11. (Originally published in *The Pedagogic Reporter*, January 1983).

An exceptional think piece on the value of Hebrew education. Must reading for anyone who cares about this topic.

CHAPTER 43

Teaching Hebrew Language

Bunnie R. Piltch

I had an experience with Hebrew during a routine crew team practice this fall. Crew, being one of the preppiest, waspiest sports this side of Equestrian, isn't exactly where you'd expect to connect with a fellow Yid, but I lucked out. For those of you who don't know much about crew, the boat I row in has eight people, all facing away from the direction the boat is moving in. There's another person, though, who sits facing everyone else, steering and watching where we're going. This person, called the coxswain, is also responsible for cheering on the rowers and counting off the strokes. Most coxswains simply shout, "One! Stroke! Two! Stroke! Three! Stroke!" as we pull our oars through the water. Our coxswain that day, Eric, had a better idea. Imagine my surprise when, during the hardest part of the course, he started shouting, "Ahat! Stroke! Shtyem! Stroke! Shalosh! Stroke!" I remember immediately starting to pull a lot harder. I felt the boat start to move faster too, so there must have been others in the boat feeling elated at our mutual connection to a foreign culture.

To someone new enough at the college experience to still get homesick occasionally, this really made me feel good. Someone counting in Hebrew not only brought back all my feelings associated with Judaism, especially the family time spent together. Of course, it also made me think of my old Hebrew school teacher. She would always count in Hebrew to see how many had shown up for class on any given Sunday and to measure the right amount of hot cocoa mix at our afternoon Bar Mitzvah lessons. When Eric coxed that day, it made me feel like this was a place I could be happy and be myself.

(Ethan Kramer, 2002[1])

HEBREW: THE JEWISH LINK

As a Hebrew language educator, one of the most difficult questions for me has always been: why do we teach Hebrew? I never know how to answer that question because for me it is too simple, yet, at the same time, too complex a question. In the first place, why would anyone involved in Hebrew/Jewish education ask such a question? Of course, we all know that Hebrew is the language of our Torah: the origin of our theology; the legacy of our history, our ancestry, our heritage. In the second place, Hebrew is the language of Israel, our Jewish homeland. Quite frankly, I am tempted to answer this "why" question with the regular response — "Because!" But this response belies our understanding of the *interconnectedness* of Hebrew language to our Jewish heritage and community.

Moreover, it seems to me that there are also individual reasons for teaching Hebrew that go beyond the scope of our Jewish legacy. For me, teaching Hebrew originates from a love of the language that I discovered very early in my life, when I first was exposed to formal Hebrew reading instruction in *alef* class. I have carried this love of Hebrew throughout my supplementary school, day school, and university Hebrew classroom experiences. During my visits to Israel, I feel as if I "morph" into a language sponge — soaking up as much language knowledge as I possibly can during the immersion. Hence, based on my own collective experiences, it seems reasonable to believe that if I, as a Hebrew educator, have multiple understandings of why I teach Hebrew, so must others.

Furthermore, when we ask ourselves why we teach Hebrew, it is important to recognize that our students also bring multiple experiences and con-

---

[1] Ethan Kramer was a student in my Elementary Modern Hebrew I class at Lehigh University. This passage was excerpted from a class assignment to write an autobiographic essay reflecting on past and present Hebrew experiences.

nections to the study of Hebrew that may be similar to our own, as illustrated in the opening excerpt by my student, Ethan Kramer. In that passage, Ethan makes an exciting discovery that there were other Jews on his crew team. He immediately feels at home and comfortable with the knowledge that he is not alone. Ethan's discovery is accomplished when he hears the Hebrew numbers, and recalls happy memories of his former teacher counting students in her classroom, afternoons of Bar Mitzvah lessons, and hot cocoa. Hebrew was a trigger for Ethan that gave him a sense of belonging by connecting him to his Jewish identity and his past. From Ethan's perspective, Hebrew is not simply a foreign language one might study for a global purpose. Rather, Hebrew is the link to a *shared* "(foreign) culture," his religion, and his family. For Ethan, Hebrew is his heritage language.

Hence, when we address the question of why we teach Hebrew, it is important to consider that our teaching is informed not only by our own beliefs and motivations, but also by those of our students. Likewise, it is important to acknowledge the range of meanings Hebrew carries for both teachers and students as a heritage language. In a study of student motivation for learning Hebrew, Grace Feuerverger identified three "differential definitions of Jewish ethnic group membership . . . *religious* (as an expression of religious identity), *ethnocultural* (as a symbol of ingroup distinctiveness; as a sense of membership to the Jewish People), and *survivalist-nationalist* (as an identification with the contemporary state of Israel and Israeli-Jewish society)."[2] All in all, these three definitions aptly represent our discussion of why we, teachers and students, believe it is important to teach and learn Hebrew. In this chapter we will focus on two of these three definitions, *religious* and *survivalist-nationalist*, as a framework for understanding the importance of teaching Hebrew.

Suggested Exploration Questions for Teachers and Students

- What explanations can you offer for why you believe it is important to teach/learn Hebrew?

- What Hebrew contact experiences in your life have been significant (positive and/or negative) for you?

- Do you believe that factors such as time in your life, place, or other participants in the Hebrew experience you recall, had an influence on your experience?

- What are your feelings regarding the experience? Are these feelings related to your actions, the actions of others, or both?

- In what way/ways does the experience influence your past and present life as a Hebrew teacher/student?[3]

THE HEBREW CONUNDRUM: TEXT OR TONGUE

Probably, the largest and most active debate among Hebrew educators is centered on curricular goals: namely, classical Hebrew for Torah, *Siddur* (prayer book), etc., versus modern Hebrew for verbal and written communication. Some language programs emphasize one over the other and some strive for balance. Interestingly, many programs convey a somewhat confusing emphasis by labeling their class subjects in the following manner: Bible, Prayer, and Hebrew Language. In fact, Hebrew language instruction is regularly involved in all three of these subjects. Yet, since Hebrew is recognized by name only for a single course dedicated to conversation, what does that imply for the aspects of Hebrew language that are required for the study of text? Are we aware that we may be conveying messages of unequal importance regarding one type of Hebrew language study over another?

The *Religious* Program

I remember a phone call from a day school parent and board member, asking for my opinion of why, after several years of attending elementary day

---

[2]Grace Feuerverger, p. 330, in "Jewish-Canadian Ethnic Identity and Non-Native Language Learning: A Social-Psychological Study," *Journal of Multilingual and Multicultural Development* 10:4 (1989): 327-57.

[3]These questions are summarized from the class assignment referenced in Footnote 1. For more in-depth information on reflective teaching practices, see Chapter 2, "Exploring Teachers' Beliefs" in Jack C. Richards and Charles Lockhart, *Reflective Teaching in Second Language Classrooms* (Cambridge, U.K. and New York: Cambridge University Press, 1994), 29-51.

school, students were very weak in their verbal proficiency in Hebrew. Ultimately, this parent felt that this was a serious shortcoming, if not a failure, of the day school educational program with respect to curricular directions and faculty expertise. This parent believed that the school emphasized instruction of *sifrei kodesh* (sacred texts) by employing mostly Rabbis for teaching text, overlooking the need for teachers trained in language instruction.

However, key to understanding this parent's concern is understanding that this day school was primarily an Orthodox school centered on a *religious* instructional program. Since religious instructional programs tend to emphasize predominantly the study of *sifrei kodesh* and *Siddur* as fundamentals, from a language perspective, religious programs are focused on instruction of language in the form of written text. Pedagogically speaking, the skills involved in learning text discourse are concerned with developing language literacy. Accomplishing literacy requires language educators to employ the appropriate methodologies that are related to written text, such as: vocabulary acquisition, grammatical forms, reading and writing for meaning and understanding, and translation.

The *Survivalist-Nationalist* Program

One of the more common reasons students in my college Hebrew classes give for choosing Hebrew as their elective course, is based on a prior or planned visit to Israel, and/or wanting to be able to understand and converse in Hebrew with an Israeli family relation. Indeed, Hebrew language instruction is as integral to studying religious texts as it is to communicative interaction and identification with the State of Israel, albeit in differing ways.

The transformation of the role of Hebrew as *lashon hakodesh* (the sacred language) to an everyday spoken language is explained well by Spolsky and Shohamy: "First place in Israeli language policy inescapably goes to *Hebrew* [italics in original], the language whose revitalization was a central tenet of Zionist ideology, and which has become the hallmark of Israeli identity and unity . . . Hebrew is the national language, the first official language, and the language of the majority, the language in which all citizens must be encouraged and assisted to achieve functional orality and liter-

acy."[4] Simply put, the Hebrew language is inextricably linked to nationhood and peoplehood: i.e., Israel the country and Israel the Jewish homeland.

Moreover, while Hebrew language was transformed to serve the Jewish people in their homeland, Hebrew language also signifies the link of Jews living outside of Israel to their homeland. Thus, the survivalist-nationalist identification with Israel, the Jewish homeland, connects and motivates educators and students to communicative Hebrew language instruction. Pedagogically speaking, unlike the religious program that necessitates the acquisition of specific language skills appropriate for text discourse, accomplishing verbal proficiency in Hebrew involves methodologies that offer opportunities for communicative language interaction: two different language foci that involve diverse teaching and learning processes.

Finally, in order for educators to understand how Hebrew language should be taught, one needs to have an understanding of why, or in other words, what the importance of Hebrew language is to the particular instructional program and its participants. Additionally, in order to avoid misunderstandings about the success of Hebrew language instruction, it is important to explore and consider what meaning Hebrew language carries for the program's participants: namely, teachers, students, and even parents. In the case of the day school parent who was disappointed with the students' lack of communicative proficiency in Hebrew after years of studying the language, it appears that the parent had mismatched performance expectations of the students based on a misunderstanding of instructional motivations and goals — survivalist-nationalist versus religious and the specialized kind of language learning that is distinctive to each.

Listed below are some questions that I include in an initial survey of my Hebrew students to understand their motivations for studying Hebrew. The questions posed in each of the categories (language background, related interests, and beliefs about language learning), are designed to discover respondents' individual beliefs and experiences that are attributable to the identities delineated and discussed above: religious and survivalist-naturalist. These questions may also be adapted to explore teachers' backgrounds, for the purpose of a better understanding of their own attitudes toward

---

[4]Bernard Spolsky and Elana Shohamy, *The Languages of Israel: Policy, Ideology and Practice* (Great Britain: Multilingual Matters Ltd., 1999), 265-266.

instruction that contribute to their individual teaching styles and methods.[5]

Another possibility for a background survey of this type would be to adapt these questions for parents, thereby expanding the educational program to include parents as "stakeholders" in the learning partnership. In this way, one might improve educational communication between parent and school, as well as avoid potential misunderstandings similar to the one cited above involving the day school parent and her disappointment with the school's Hebrew program.

Suggested Student Survey Questions

- Language Background

  1. Number of years of Hebrew study (approximate)

  2. Type of instruction (e.g., day school, supplementary, camp . . .)

  3. Days/Hours per week (approximate)

  4. Have you spent time in Israel? When and for how long?

  5. Is anyone in your home Israeli or a speaker of Hebrew? Who?

  6. What other foreign languages have you studied? How long?

- Related Interests

  1. Have you had, or do you plan to take Jewish studies courses? If yes, which one(s)?

  2. Have you had, or do you plan to take any other foreign languages? If yes, which one(s)?

- Beliefs about Language Learning

  1. Describe briefly or list your *strengths* in language learning.

  2. Describe briefly or list your *weaknesses* in language learning.

  3. Describe your reason(s) for selecting Hebrew for foreign language study.

HOW WE TEACH HEBREW

My class is really slow. We went over the tefilah (prayer) twice in class, we went over the new vocabulary, and I gave a vocabulary quiz for reinforcement. I handed out (comprehension) questions for homework and we went over the questions in class. I don't understand. When I included the tefilah on the exam, many students had a lot of trouble and couldn't answer all the questions. When I went over the exam in class, many didn't seem to recall having studied the tefilah. I don't know what else I can do.

Teaching Text

This "lament" typifies the single most challenge teachers encounter: how to engage the students in successful learning. Insofar as teaching Hebrew literature is concerned, teachers face an additional challenge of how to present varying levels of text language to students. To be more specific, religious literature such as *Siddur*, as one example, is a distinct genre of literature that is comprised of vocabulary and language forms that are very sophisticated and advanced for most students of Hebrew. This linguistic gap is compounded by a cultural gap between our students in today's world, and the historical period in which classical religious literature (*Siddur*, Torah, etc.) was composed. Therefore, it is crucial for teachers to find a way of bridging both a linguistic and cultural gap encountered by our students with the text.

Basically, teaching *Siddur* text involves two aims: (1) to familiarize the students with how the language skills they have been exposed to can be applied to understanding the meaning of the *tefilah*, and (2) to involve the student in interacting with the text in order to develop a personal relationship with *Siddur* literature.

These two aims are applicable to any genre of text selection, for the reason that our fundamental goal of how to teach Hebrew text is to engage the student in learning to appreciate the integral relationship between language, literature, and the reader/audience. Next is an outline of teaching objectives for engaging students in text learning, which incorporates these aims into a lesson model for teaching text. Since *Siddur* literature is often

[5]For more information, see Chapter 3, "Focus on the Learner" in Jack C. Richards and Charles Lockhart, *Reflective*

Teaching in Second Language Classrooms (Cambridge, U.K. and New York: Cambridge University Press, 1994), 52-77.

poetic, this model is informed by current educational research in teaching reading and poetry.

Stage 1: Pre-reading (Warm-up)

Goals:

1. To remind the student about the stylistic appeal of poetry

2. To elicit curiosity and expectation about the language and meaning of the *tefilah*

The first stage of the lesson should introduce the student to the *tefilah* from two perspectives: form and content. This introduction is accomplished by activating the student's existing world knowledge.

Sample Questions/Activities

Goal I

1. Do you recall a favorite song, nursery rhyme, fairy tale, etc. from your childhood?

2. What was special about it? Were there particular (stylistic) features about it that you enjoyed?

3. Compare your list with a friend's. Did you list some of the same features?

Goal II

1. Class discussion: Select a key word or title word from the text already familiar to the students, e.g., *shalom*

2. What does the word *shalom* suggest to us about the meaning of the *tefilah*?

Transition To Stage 2

1. We're now going to read the *tefilah* together. Keep in mind for later discussion, whether the title fits the theme of the *tefilah* as we predicted, or not.

Stage 2: While-reading (Reading the text)

Goals:

1. To help students read the Hebrew *tefilah* text as a lyrical poem

2. To enable students to understand the literal meaning of the poem

The second stage of the lesson focuses on the mechanical aspects of reading and understanding the literal meaning of the poem. Correspondingly, the activities offer opportunities for reading skill practice and development, as well as language building for understanding and meaning.

Sample Questions/Activities

Goal I

1. Many of us know this *tefilah*. You may join in singing it with me, or you may listen if you prefer.

2. Now I'm going to read this *tefilah* as a poem. Listen the first time through, and then we will read it together a second time. Then, students are directed to read the text in pairs.

Goal II

1. Written Word-Find activity: Can you find the meaning of the words listed below in the puzzle? (Students may look up the words in the English translation of the text. The translation of the text provides a contextually related way for the students to gather the definitions of unfamiliar vocabulary. Note: In order for the translation to be useful to the students, it has to be very literal. Or, if preferred, a glossary of new vocabulary may be supplied by the teacher.)

Stage 3: Post-reading (After reading)

Goals:

1. To help students recognize some of the prominent stylistic features of the *tefilah*

2. To help students connect the use of the language with understanding the meaning of the poem

The third stage of the lesson comprises activities that engage the student in analysis and interpretation of the poem. After reading the poem for surface understanding, the student is ready to explore how the stylistic features of the *tefilah* contribute to the meaning. The process of understanding the meaning of the *tefilah* engages the student in reviewing the text vocabulary as well as using the vocabulary to communicate a comprehensive understanding of the text. This process of review and selection of vocabulary focuses the student on the textual cohesion of the *tefilah*. Hence, the student is engaged in integrating language skills with interpreting the literature.

Goal I

1. Select a salient stylistic feature of the text (e.g., alliteration, rhyme, etc.) and ask students to classify and list them. For example: Fill in the table below listing all the words having the *mem* sound in the left column, and all the words without the *mem* sound in the right column.

2. Many prayers are about God. Now go over the words you have listed above. Work with a partner and discuss the following:

    a. Who or what are the words in the left column referring to? in the right column?

    b. Are the words on the left referring to the same thing as the words on the right, or are they referring to something different?

    c. Why do you think the poet/author chose these words for this *tefilah*?

3. Which words are: Repeated in each verse? sound almost alike? Do they mean something similar?

Goal II

1. Think about the *tefilah* and note the words that suggest where the title originated from. Can you find an alternative word or phrase that would make a suitable title for this *tefilah*? (Be prepared to defend your choice of title during our class discussion!)

Stage 4: Extension (Follow-up)

Goal:

1. To provide additional creative opportunities for interpreting the *tefilah*

The fourth stage of this unit may take place over a longer period of time, such as a couple of class sessions or a series of segments of class sessions, in order to allow students ample time cooperatively to expand and produce culminating projects that can be shared with or performed for others. These tasks are designed to engage the students in interacting with the poem from a more self-directed than teacher-directed perspective, and thus, support the aim of developing a personal relationship with the meaning of the *tefilah* through interpretation.

Ask students to choose one of the following activities (working independently, with a partner, or in small groups):

1. Try becoming a poet/author yourself. By changing the first word of the verse, you can create a verse of your own. How many verses can you compose as your own? You may use your *Siddur* if you need ideas for words. (To be completed in Hebrew.)

2. Turn this *tefilah* into a pop or rap song. (Hebrew or English)

3. Imagine that a group of archaeologists made an amazing discovery recently. An ancient jar containing a fragment was unearthed in a cave. This fragment revealed a slightly different version of the *tefilah* from the one we know today. In this newly discovered version, the word "X" is replaced with the word "Y". Now, pretend you are a history professor, and write a report of this discovery explaining which version you believe to be the more accurate one.

4. Imagine that you are a TV journalist and you have invited the author of this text to interview on your talk show. Write a Q & A script of the interview between you and the poet. (In this activity, the teacher may supply some initial questions to guide the student. For example: "I noticed that the word '*shalom*' is repeated often. Did you have a specific reason for doing this?")

Stage 5: Reflection

Goal:

1. To help the student relate his/her learning to the overall aims of this unit

The fifth and final stage of this model lesson on teaching text offers closure for the student. This activity helps students to form an awareness of a connection between learning and feeling. When students are able to synthesize and internalize their learning experience, they have realized a personal relationship with the text.

1. Now that you have completed all of the activities in this unit and understand more about the meaning of this *tefilah*, has your feeling about it changed?

2. Do you have mixed feelings? Complete one or both sentences: "Yes, I _____" "No, I _____"

3. Share your feelings with at least two other people in the class. Are their feelings similar to yours?

In brief, the model lesson presented above offers a diverse range of activities that in totality help us to have a better understanding of the complexities of teaching Hebrew text.[6] In response to the teacher's "lament" that her class was "slow," I would suggest that she try to reflect on her teaching of *tefilah* in view of the aims and goals upon which the above activities are based. The most common and, therefore, probably the most crucial aspect throughout the entire lesson, is that the student is personally engaged in interacting with the text at every stage of the lesson. When we lament that our students are not learning, we need to consider that we may have failed to convey to our students the importance of connecting to Hebrew by not engaging them in the learning process. In the next section, we will expand the premise of engaging the student in the learning process as we examine the teaching of Hebrew grammar.

Teaching Grammar

Another component of the background survey I obtain from my Hebrew students (referenced earlier in this chapter) deals with what students believe are their strengths and weaknesses in language learning. Not surprisingly, the most common answer students give for weakness in language learning is grammar: by far, considered the most daunting aspect of language learning. Sadly, for many, the task of learning grammar evokes so much angst that it is perceived to be virtually synonymous with learning a language in general. As a consequence, many students are discouraged from studying a language at all. Similarly, teachers often find teaching grammar the most difficult aspect of language instruction. Perhaps this is why grammar is one of the areas of language acquisition in which a great deal of research has been, and continues to be conducted. Nevertheless, given that Hebrew carries so much meaning for us as our heritage language, it behooves us as educators to extract for ourselves some understanding of teaching grammar that we can apply to our teaching of Hebrew.

Personally, I am fascinated with discovering how Hebrew functions in comparison with English, my "native" language, and French, my third language. Conveying my fascination with Hebrew grammar to my students, is thus, a very significant motivation for my teaching. Given this interest in grammar, for me the most impressive aspect of grammar research that has influenced my teaching is referred to as "consciousness-raising." Rod Ellis defines "consciousness-raising" (CR) as that which "refers to attempts to make learners aware of the existence of specific linguistic features."[7] In the preceding section in which I discussed teaching text, a number of the activities involved engaging the student in becoming aware of specific features of the style and meaning of the text. Likewise, in this section, an example of a grammar CR task will be presented to illustrate the role of CR in directing the learner's attention to a specific grammatical feature.

Overview of a CR Task

One of the most difficult grammatical features of Hebrew grammar is learning the function of the word "*et.*" Since *et* is unique to Hebrew and entirely unfamiliar to English speakers, it is especially problematic for teachers and students. Therefore, the goal of this CR task is to introduce the learners to the usage of the Hebrew word *et.* Essentially, the word *et* has no definitional mean-

---

[6]The material presented in this section was developed from the following resources: C. Brumfit and R. Carter, Eds., *Literature and Language Teaching* (Oxford, U.K. and New York: Oxford University Press, 1986); M. Celce-Murcia, ed., *Teaching English as a Second of Foreign Language* (Boston, MA: Newbury House,

1991); and J. Collie and S. Slater, *Literature in the Language Classroom: A Resource Book of Ideas and Activities* (Cambridge, U.K. and New York: Cambridge University Press, 1987).

[7]Rod Ellis, *Second Language Acquisition* (Oxford, U.K. and New York: Oxford University Press, 1997).

ing; its only purpose is to serve as a marker that precedes the direct object.

In a CR task there are four basic principles that are involved:

1. *Isolation* of specific features for focused attention

2. *Provision* of data to illustrate the target feature

3. *Utilization* of intellectual effort to understand the target feature

4. *No Production* - There is no requirement for the students to produce/use the target feature. This is the critical difference between a grammar drill and a CR task![8]

This task is comprised of four activities. The first activity involves the students in listening to a tape recording of a short story embedded with sentences using the word *et*. In addition to the recorded story, the students may be given an accompanying picture that illustrates the content of the story in order to facilitate comprehension of the story. This activity represents the presentation phase of the grammatical feature in which the teacher provides the data to illustrate the feature for focused attention.

Script of Listening Activity

(Translated to English)

The teacher is sitting in the classroom.

The students are sitting in the classroom.

The teacher sees *(et)* the students.

The students see *(et)* the teacher.

The teacher says, "Hello. Good morning!"

The students say, "Hello Teacher!"

Danny asks, "Where is Talya? I don't see *(et)* Talya."

The teacher says, "I don't see *(et)* Talya either."

Ron says, "I see *(et)* Talya. Talya is sitting under the table reading a book."

David says, "She is reading *(et)* Noga's book!"

[8]Author's lecture notes from a course given by Professor Rod Ellis, Temple University, 1997.

Talya says, "Yes. I am reading a book. But, I am not reading *(et)* Noga's book, I am reading *(et)* my own book."

Following this introduction to *et*, the second activity in this CR task is referred to as a "grammaticality judgment" activity. A grammaticality judgment requires the student to differentiate between what is grammatically correct and incorrect. This type of activity typically involves correct and incorrect examples of the target grammatical feature, and requires the student to indicate which is correct and incorrect. Since the form is still fairly new, the student is permitted the option of listening to the tape recording as often as deemed necessary in order to complete the activity. After the students have completed the activity, they may consult with others in the class to check their answers; thus, creating an opportunity for feedback and additional interaction that is focused on the learning of the target feature.

GRAMMATICALITY JUDGMENT ACTIVITY

(Translated to English)

Check Yes or No.

	Y	N	
1.	__	__	The teacher is sitting in the classroom.
2.	__	__	The teacher is sitting *(et)* in the classroom.
3.	__	__	The students are sitting in the classroom.
4.	__	__	The students are sitting *(et)* in the classroom.
5.	__	__	The teacher sees the students.
6.	__	__	The teacher sees *(et)* the students.
7.	__	__	The students see the teacher.
8.	__	__	The students see *(et)* the teacher.
9.	__	__	I don't see Talya.
10.	__	__	I don't see *(et)* Talya.
11.	__	__	I see *(et)* Talya.
12.	__	__	I see Talya.

13. __ __ She is reading *(et)* a book.

14. __ __ She is reading *(et)* Noga's book.

15. __ __ I am not reading *(et)* a book.

16. __ __ I am not reading **(et)** Noga's book.

At this point, the teacher asks the students to attempt to explain what the target grammatical feature *et* is. While the students are making a conscious effort to infer a grammatical rule from the data they have been working with, they are demonstrating a complete focus on the grammatical form itself. This activity, which centers on rule formation, presents a learning opportunity for the class to come together as a whole group to discuss, refine, and arrive at a consensus of agreement on the most accurate rule description. It is important to note that even in this activity, students are not being asked to use/produce the target feature, merely to recognize and describe it. This de-emphasis on production in a CR task serves to minimize the student's tension by allowing the student to focus all energy and attention on the recognition of the new form.

The fourth and final activity in this CR task is referred to as a "jigsaw" activity. In a jigsaw activity students interact to exchange and share information with each other to reinforce the learning. Specifically, this activity asks the students to draw a composite picture that depicts the information supplied by the teacher. Each pair of learners is given two different parts of the story with the word *et* embedded. As one student reads her script, the other student must illustrate what is being read, and both students are required to contribute in order to complete the illustration.

Jigsaw Activity

(Translated to English)

Part A

The teacher is sitting in the classroom.

The teacher sees *(et)* Talya.

The teacher says, "Hello Talya."

The teacher sees *(et)* Dan.

The teacher says, "Hello Dan."

Part B

The students are sitting in the class.

Talya is reading a book.

Dan is reading a book, too.

Ron sees *(et)* the teacher.

Ron says, "Talya is reading *(et)* Dan's book and Dan is reading *(et)* Talya's book."

In sum, the first three activities in this grammar CR task focused on introducing the target grammatical feature to the learner aurally through listening presentations, and visually through written and pictorial presentations. These presentations of the data involved the learner in becoming aware of the new form, as well as intellectually interacting with the new form by interpreting and describing its function. Furthermore, the activities were designed to involve the students in small groups and in the class group as a whole, thus creating a number of opportunities for a range of communicative interactions during the task. The aspect of communicative interaction that is integral to the design of these CR grammar activities is what I find most exciting, because it occurs "naturally" as the students execute the assignments. Moreover, often times grammar lessons tend to be very "teacher fronted" kinds of lessons, and this CR task moves students into a more interactive and communicative setting for learning. In more advanced Hebrew language classrooms, we could expect to hear the students discussing the target feature entirely in Hebrew as they complete the activities! In the next section we will examine Hebrew language communication more closely.

All in all, the activities in this CR grammar task can be adapted to teaching other aspects of Hebrew, such as text as we discussed earlier. When I teach any class, I always ask myself what methods I can use to raise the students' consciousness to help them grasp new material, and I always find that when I can engage them accordingly, it makes for a more interesting and successful class all the way around![9]

---

[9]For more information see: S. Fotos and R. Ellis, "Communicating about Grammar: A Task-Based Approach." *TESOL Quarterly* 25:4 (1991): 91-113; S. Fotos, "Integrating Grammar Instruction and Communicative Language Use through Grammar Consciousness-Raising Tasks." *TESOL Quarterly* 28:1 (1994): 323-351.

CREATING A COMMUNICATIVE ENVIRONMENT

Conversational Hebrew

What does it mean to teach a class in "conversational" Hebrew? Many students and adults enroll in a conversational Hebrew class to prepare for an upcoming trip to Israel. Inevitably, in this type of class student abilities range from those who are looking to expand their knowledge of vocabulary and expressions to those who are looking to "brush up" on their oral language skills, to those who are beginners interested in learning some basic, introductory expressions that will help them to handle daily necessities, such as shopping and finding the restrooms.

However, regardless of the range of students' backgrounds in the class, a "conversational" Hebrew class is ultimately *content* centered on topics and language use common to life in Israel. This distinction between "conversational" and "content" is an important one for our understanding of how we teach Hebrew. That is to say that when we teach vocabulary and expressions that are characteristic of certain settings, in reality, we are teaching conversational content, or topics, as opposed to how to be conversational in the sense of conversant, or communicative.

Likewise, I would argue that, in effect, conversational Hebrew classes tend to create artificial environments that do not achieve what they set out to do. Teachers bring "artifacts" into the classroom with which to teach the vocabulary and, conversely, pretending to be in Israel. In actual fact, these environments are contrived, and the communication among the students is often artificial and not for the purpose of negotiating meaning, as it would be in "natural" conversation.

Another type of conversational Hebrew class is one centered on discussions, for example, of current event topics selected from the media. This type of conversational class seems more "natural" in focus, as the students participating in the discussion are purposefully engaged in expressing their own viewpoints with each other. The limitation of this type of class is that only students who have achieved a certain level of oral language proficiency can participate satisfactorily in class discussions. For beginning students, participating in a discussion produces a level of anxiety and frustration as students do not have sufficient language to understand and respond. Students also may feel "infantilized" as their language abilities are too limited and constraining, and thus, students are unable to express themselves in the way that they see themselves as individuals.[10]

Teacher Knowledge

On balance, teaching conversational Hebrew per se is narrow in scope, especially from the objective standpoint of wanting our students to be able to communicate in Hebrew at varying levels in any number of settings. Hence, a more relevant goal for teaching Hebrew conversation might be to create communicative learning opportunities and environments that are integrated into the extant subjects of the Hebrew curricula. In order to do so, we need to recognize a number of critical factors that have an impact on communication in the classroom. For one, teaching Hebrew communication would require teachers to possess not only academic knowledge of the subject they are teaching, but also the ability to develop materials, plan activities, and converse in Hebrew "comfortably" so that they are " . . . able to surround learners with language, an essential component of an effective language learning environment."[11]

Second, creating a communicative environment requires teachers to have an understanding of the types of behaviors and interactions between teacher and student and among the students themselves, which may be encountered in the communicative language learning process. There is a vast amount of literature on communicative teaching, but I would like briefly to discuss two of them that I find particularly interesting and helpful in the learning process: affect and language play.

Student Anxieties

As I alluded to earlier in this section, affect plays a significant role in the language classroom with respect to communication. Specifically, language anxieties have been shown to have detrimental effects on language performance. Rebecca Oxford explains that while certain physical behaviors

[10]Guy Spielmann and Mary L Radnofsky, "Learning Language under Tension: New Directions from a Qualitative Study." *Modern Language Journal* 85 (2001): 259-78.

[11]Helena Curtain and Carol Ann Pesola Dahlberg, "Planning for Success: Common Pitfalls in the Planning of Early Language Programs." *ERIC Digest* ED 447 726 (December 2000): 2pp.

point to the existence of language anxieties such as: tardiness, fidgeting, complaining about headaches, "clowning," etc.; other behaviors such as solitariness and "conversational withdrawal" are less obvious. Oxford offers a number of ways teachers can facilitate the reduction of anxiety in the language classroom, some of which are: encourage risk-taking and permit students to make errors without correction;[12] explain class goals, assignments, and tests clearly; minimize competition; and, give rewards that reinforce self-esteem and support language use.[13]

Language Play

On the other hand, in contrast to language anxieties, language play is an aspect of communication in the classroom that reflects the learner's "online"[14] language skill development. Researchers Maggie Broner and Elaine Tarone examined two forms of language play in the classroom, *ludic language play* and *rehearsal in private speech.*[15] The former, *ludic language play* refers to "pretend" or "fun" play in which the learner makes fun of the sound or form of the target language, or fabricates language to mix new forms of language together with existing language in ways that do not exist in either language. Ludic language play is a phenomenon that allows the learner to practice and grow accustomed to new language in unconventional and non-threatening ways, since the language the learner is producing is entirely under her individual control, and not for the purpose of negotiating meaning. Additionally, ludic language play is a form of language input created by teachers and adults. (Dr. Seuss stories come to mind as a wonderful example of a kind of ludic language play.) In short, ludic language play provides a source of amusement for the learner during the process of learning the language.

Further, the language play classified as *rehearsal in private speech,* refers to what is commonly known as the phenomenon of "talking to oneself." Basically, in private speech the learner practices new language that the learner has not fully mastered. As Broner and Tarone point out, while ludic language play is for fun, rehearsal in private speech is serious language production.[16] In sum, I would argue that it is important for us to understand the significance of both kinds of language play as potential strategies for the student in developing communicative language skills; and thus, one should not try to restrict language play in the classroom by insisting on a policy that permits Hebrew speaking exclusively.

Suggested Exploration Questions for Teachers and Students

- How does your school's curriculum/instructional program list Hebrew and other Judaic Studies course offerings?

- Is Hebrew language integrated into your classes or is it taught separately?

- Have you observed student behaviors in your class that suggest affect, such as, language anxieties and language play?

CONCLUSION

In the final analysis, when we consider why and how we teach Hebrew, we realize again and again that Hebrew is an inseparable component of the subjects we teach. Hebrew is inseparable from our literature — historical and liturgical. Hebrew is interwoven into our identity as Jews. Metaphorically, teaching Hebrew is synonymous with living Hebrew. Hebrew is our legacy: our heritage language that links us to our people, our culture, and

---

[12]Although, it should be noted that a great deal of research in language acquisition on this subject identifies and supports specific types of feedback and correction that are potentially helpful to the learner in certain settings. For a more in-depth review of the literature, see: Howard Nicholas, Patsy M. Lightbown, and Nina Spada, "Recasts as Feedback To Language Learners." *Language Learning* 51:4 (December 2001): 719-58.

[13]Rebecca L. Oxford, "Anxiety and the Language Learner: New Insights," in *Affect in Language Learning,* edited by Jane Arnold (Cambridge, U.K. and New York: Cambridge University Press, 1999), 58-67.

[14]"Online" is used here in the figurative sense to mean cognizant and on-the-spot language production.

[15]The term "private speech" or "inner speech" originates from the psychologist, Lev Vygotsky. Related research on this topic can be found in: James P. Lantolf and Gabriela Appel, eds. *Vygotskian Approaches To Second Language Research* (Norwood, NJ: Ablex Publishing Corporation, 1994).

[16]Maggie A. Broner and Elaine E. Tarone, "Is it Fun? Language Play in a Fifth Grade Spanish Immersion Classroom." *Modern Language Journal* 85 (2001): 363-79.

our ancestral homeland. The most beautiful thing a teacher could ever hear is what I heard from Ethan that day when I read his essay, " . . . I had an experience with Hebrew . . . "

TEACHING CONSIDERATIONS FOR HEBREW

- Learning Hebrew is *not* like learning any other foreign language; Hebrew connects students to their Jewish heritage.

- Expand your teaching of Hebrew to include exploring your personal beliefs about why you teach Hebrew.

- Expand your teaching of Hebrew to include exploring your students' beliefs about why they want to learn Hebrew.

- Find ways to utilize students' existing knowledge of Hebrew to engage them in learning new material.

- Allow students ample opportunities to receive and practice language before they are expected to produce and use the language for grading/evaluation purposes.

- Plan creative opportunities for the students to use their new knowledge of Hebrew.

- Opportunities for purposeful oral communication can be built into classroom learning.

- Be sensitive to the affective climate of the language classroom to minimize learner anxiety.

- There is no single way to teach/learn Hebrew. Our teaching must be fluid, diverse, and all-embracing.

BIBLIOGRAPHY

Arnold, Jane, ed. *Affect in Language Learning*. Cambridge, U.K. and New York: Cambridge University Press, 1999.

> This book comprises 18 chapters on a range of topics that are concerned with improving language teaching through a greater awareness of the role affect plays.

Bialystok, Ellen, and Kenji Hakuta. *In Other Words: The Science and Psychology of Second-Language Acquisition*. New York: Basic Books, 1994.

> A very well written and interesting book on second language acquisition by two renowned researchers in the field. This book is not exclusively for teachers, but for anyone interested in how languages are learned.

Collie, Joanne, and Stephen Slater. *Literature in the Language Classroom: A Resource Book of Ideas and Activities*. Cambridge, U.K. and New York: Cambridge University Press, 1987.

> This resource book demonstrates the role of teaching literature in language learning. It offers a variety of ideas and techniques for integrating literature work with language teaching.

Ellis, Rod. *Second Language Acquisition*. Oxford, U.K. and New York: Oxford University Press, 1997.

> This brief survey book from the Oxford Introductions To Language Studies series, outlines the research and development of the field of second language acquisition. It explains the key concepts and terminology associated with this field of study.

Kramsch, Claire. *Language and Culture*. Oxford, U.K. and New York: Oxford University Press, 1998.

> This brief survey book from the Oxford Introductions To Language Studies series, illuminates the relationship between language and culture. It explains the key concepts and terminology associated with this field of study.

Lee, James F. *Tasks and Communicating in Language Classrooms*. New York: The McGraw-Hill Companies, 2000.

> An important, practical teaching resource for understanding and facilitating communicative language teaching. One of its key points is how to reformulate traditional language texts into interactive communicative tasks.

Lightbown, Patsy M., and Nina Spada. *How Languages Are Learned*. Oxford, U.K.: Oxford University Press, 1993.

> A highly recognized and readable overview of first and second language acquisition, this book considers the implications of language acquisition for language teaching.

Richards, Jack C., and Charles Lockhart. *Reflective Teaching in Second Language Classrooms*. Cambridge, U.K. and New York: Cambridge University Press, 1994.

> This book presents an introspective approach to teaching and learning that has probably been one of the most informative and influential in my teaching experience to date.

Spolsky, Bernard, and Elana Shohamy, *The Languages of Israel: Policy, Ideology and Practice*. Great Britain: Multilingual Matters Ltd., 1999.

> This book primarily explores the educational policies and ideologies of languages taught and spoken in Israel. It offers interesting insight into the role of Hebrew for the Jews and Israel from ancient times to the present.

Ur, Penny. *A Course in Language Teaching: Practice and Theory*. Cambridge, U.K. and New York: Cambridge University Press, 1996.

> A complete introduction to teaching languages for use in both pre-service or in-service settings, this manual contains a wealth of teaching modules for teachers new to foreign language teaching. The book also presents a good and useful overview of theory and classroom techniques for experienced teachers.

CHAPTER 44

Teacher, May I . . . and Other Classroom Questions

Janice P. Alper and Shayna Friedman

Asking questions is deeply rooted in Jewish tradition. One such example, familiar both from the Torah[1] and our worship[2] is the prayer, *"Mi Chamocha"* (Who is like You?) in which we rhetorically ask about and reaffirm God's greatness.

The Talmud is rife with questions that occurred to the Rabbis as they studied biblical texts. In fact, the very first verse of *Brachot*, and, therefore, of the Talmud, opens with a question, "From what time may one recite the *'Shema'* in the evening?"

Traditional Jewish study, based on asking and answering questions about texts, demonstrates the importance of questions to develop critical thinking skills. Adin Steinsaltz notes that the Talmud allows us to go from passive to active learning. He states that in order to understand a text fully, a student raises questions and attempts to find solutions to them.[3] This style of thinking is a process that leads one to lifelong investigation and understanding of core Jewish ideas and concepts.

Asking questions about Jewish practice and text continues to this day. Through the centuries, when Jews had questions about a particular practice or relationship, they would ask their Rabbis. If the local Rabbi did not have an answer, he would forward the query to a Rabbi in another town who might then write a response. Thus Judaism has a whole body of legalistic Jewish literature, with the bearing of *halachah* (law) known as *She'aylot u'Teshuvot – Responsa*, or questions and answers.

Today, responses to queries may be found on the Internet or in current Jewish periodicals. The technological age has raised a series of questions on issues that the Rabbis of yesteryear could never have imagined, such as end-stage life care and organ donations, the *kashrut* of artificial ingredients in foods, surrogate parenting, and issues surrounding copyright of materials on the Internet. In providing the answers to the questions of modern life, the authorities (generally Rabbinic scholars held in high esteem in the larger Jewish community) use the same methods we see in the Talmud — reliance on a series of instances or cases that give credence to their answers. No answer is given in a vacuum.

This chapter provides teachers with the tools to develop questions that stimulate critical thinking skills and that allow students to develop a lifelong relationship with Jewish learning. As teachers of children in Jewish school settings, the questions we ask offer students an opportunity to exercise their minds and process information that will have a long lasting effect on their lives. Judaism is, after all, a window into a lifestyle, a culture and religion that guides our behaviors. Asking basic questions that require brief, often one or two-word responses, does not allow our students to delve deeper into the richness of our Jewish heritage. Our questions to students and their questions of us and of our tradition should ultimately reflect Judaism's centuries old questioning paradigm.

BLOOM'S TAXONOMY OF QUESTIONS

In the late 1950s, Benjamin Bloom at the University of Chicago developed a Taxonomy of Educational Objectives.[4] His work has had a seminal influence on educational practice over the last 40 years, especially on the ways teachers asked ques-

---

[1] Exodus 16:11

[2] In the section called *"Shema* and Its Blessings."

[3] Adin Steinsaltz, "Guidelines for Talmudic Study," *The Talmud, the Steinsaltz Edition, A Reference Guide* (New York:

Random House, 1989), pp. 79-80.

[4] Benjamin Bloom, *The Taxonomy of Educational Objectives* (New York: Longmans, Green), 1956.

tions.[5] Bloom noted six domains in which students may apply cognition or learning: knowledge, comprehension, application, analysis, synthesis, and evaluation.

Bloom's Taxonomy serves as a guide when structuring lessons, offering options for question development, from low level (e.g., knowledge, interpretation) to higher levels that demand critical thinking (e.g., analysis, synthesis). What follows is a listing of the six domains outlined by Bloom, with key defining words and sample questions in a Jewish context.

Knowledge

The key defining words for the domain of knowledge are:

Remembering

Memorizing

Recognizing

Recalling

Identifying

Responses to questions on the knowledge level of the taxonomy reflect a student's ability to absorb information on a factual level and provide it to the teacher when prompted.

Examples:

- Who can tell me the name of the holiday we are celebrating this week?

- Look at the Hebrew words on the page in your book. Which words do we use when we say a blessing? Which words tell us about Shabbat?

- How many days did it take God to create the world? What was created on each day?

Comprehension

The key defining words for the domain of comprehension are:

Interpreting

Translating from one medium to another

Describing in one's own words

Organizing and selecting facts and ideas

Retelling

Responses to comprehension questions indicate that the students are able to apply what they have learned on a factual basis by restating or reorganizing the materials.

Examples:

- What happened when Moses went to Pharaoh to ask him to free the Jewish slaves?

- Interpret in movement (dance) the words of the "*Shema* — Hear O Israel, *Adonai* is our God, *Adonai* is One."

- Read the chapter in your book that talks about the uprising of the Warsaw Ghetto in 1943. Create an outline of the order of the events.

- When you pray or say a blessing, how do you imagine the presence of God?

Application

The key defining words for the domain of application are:

Problem solving

Applying information to produce some result

Use of facts, rules and principles

How is _____ an example of _____?

What is the relationship between "X" and "Y"?

Why is _____ significant/important?

Questions at this level help the students to find relationships to other things they have learned.

Examples:

- Billy noticed that one of our classmates has been out of school for more than a week

---

[5]While others have developed schemata for thinking about questions, these seem to fall into the same general areas that Bloom presented in his seminal work in 1956. For example, The Teaching and Learning Center of the University of Nebraska-Lincoln, provides six domains or question types: Probing Questions, Factual Questions, Divergent Questions, Higher Order Questions, Affective Questions, and Structuring Questions (see www.unl.edu/teaching/teachquestions/html).

and called him to find out why. How is this an example of an act of *chesed* (kindness)?

- How is the story of Purim related to other Jewish holidays, such as Passover and Chanukah?

- How would you design a *chanukiyah* that follows the laws in the *Shulchan Aruch*?

- (After studying a unit on Jewish laws of mourning) - What can we do as a class to respond to a bombing in Israel?

Analysis

The key defining words for the domain of analysis are:

Subdividing something to show how it is put together

Finding the underlying structure of a communication

Identifying motives

Separation of a whole into component parts

What are the parts or features of _____?

Classify _____ according to _____.

Outline/diagram _____.

How does _____ compare/contrast with _____?

What evidence can you list for _____?

Questions for analysis allow students to begin to examine information for tacit understanding — what is *not* being said.

Examples:

- In the story of the *Akedah* (the binding of Isaac), God tests Abraham. What do you think are God's motives for the test? Why do you think Abraham is motivated to obey God so willingly?

- What comparisons can you make between the stories of the Maccabees (Chanukah) and the plight of the Jews in Shushan (Purim)? What is similar? What is different?

- Read "*Hatikvah*" (Israel's national anthem) in English and Hebrew. What message is

being communicated to the Jewish People? to the world?

- Compare the Shabbat "*Amidah*" with the weekday "*Amidah*." What is similar? What is different?

- In your own words, what do you think are the most important or main ideas about the story of Jacob and Esau?

Synthesis

The key defining words for the domain of synthesis are:

Creating a unique, original product that may be in verbal form or a physical object

Combining ideas to form a new whole

What would you predict/infer from _____?

What ideas can you add to _____?

How would you create/design a new _____?

What might happen if you combined _____?

What solutions would you suggest for _____?

Synthesis questions open the door to original thinking and creativity. They encourage the students to explore, and in some cases imagine, alternative solutions to a situation.

Examples:

- Review the blessings before and after reading the *Haftarah*. What messages do they convey? Are there any other messages you would want to add? Write an original blessing that you would find appropriate after reading the *Haftarah*.

- Look over the various objects that are representative of Jewish practice, such as a *mezuzah*, a *chanukiyah*, a *Magen David*, etc. Create a new symbol or design that you think could represent the Jewish people today.

- Examine the missions of various organizations that support the food bank in your community. What are some of the ways they act to help people? What might happen if several organizations got together to fight world hunger instead of each one working separately?

- If you were to write a new four questions for the *Haggadah*, what would they be?

Evaluation

The key defining words/phrases for the domain of evaluation are:

Making value decisions about issues

Resolving controversies or differences of opinion

Development of opinions, judgments, or decisions

Do you agree that _____?

What do you think about _____?

What is the most important _____?

Place the following in order of priority _____.

How would you decide about _____?

What criteria would you use to assess _____?

At the evaluation level, students begin to make decisions based on the materials studied.

Examples:

- If you were Jacob, what do you think you would do if you were asked to fool your brother? How would you make your decision?

- You are going to soccer practice in your family car when you see a mother with a small baby in a fancy stroller come up to you and ask for money. What do you think about this situation? How would you go about deciding to help her or not help her? Justify your answers using the texts we studied about *tzedakah*.

- What is your opinion about the movement to allow a moment of silence in public schools? Offer supporting data.

- For the past year, you have put your babysitting money aside for a special trip

you want to take. However, your parents insist that you give a small portion ($50) to a charity of your choice and they tell you that they will match the amount. First, do you agree with your parents' condition? Second, how would you go about determining how to distribute the money? What criteria would you use?

Bear in mind that all of Benjamin Bloom's domains or levels may be used for students of all ages. Some of the wisest and most thoughtful answers are from young children who are not burdened with other opinions or a need to please. These are frequently insightful, candid responses to higher level questions posed in developmentally appropriate language. However, know that when preparing lessons and writing questions you do not have to have all levels of the taxonomy represented, but you should know which levels you are including.

Lessons in Jewish school settings are often replete with questions that are often used to determine if the information or the focus of the lesson has been absorbed or "learned" by the students. Without knowing it, teachers often test themselves to see if they have been effective in the class. Yet, once teachers are introduced to Bloom's Taxonomy, they are more thoughtful about their questions and begin to see how these can be used not only to measure a student's understanding of a subject, but to push them to higher levels of thinking.

Good questions are hard to come by. Sometimes I approach the process from the other side. What am I looking for in an answer? My class lights up when I say, "Now this question may have several correct answers. Let's see how many we can figure out." Suddenly everyone's hand is up. The risk just went out of giving an answer.

My fifth graders groan when I ask a question and refuse to hear the answer until tomorrow. Some of them, I hope, go home and talk about the question at dinner. The delaying tactic gives the students who like to ponder their ideas before speaking a chance to have an answer ready as well.

(Maura Pollak, Tulsa, Oklahoma)

THE IMPACT OF BLOOM'S TAXONOMY ON JEWISH CLASSROOMS

As you read the following vignettes describing three Jewish classrooms, try to determine the levels of questions the teachers are asking. Put yourself in their shoes and see what you might do if you were the teacher.

Vignette 1: A Bible Story in a First Grade Religious School Class

Sunday mornings in Sheri's first grade classroom are full of excitement and energy. She plans a variety of activities that meet both her teaching objectives and the needs of her students. On this particular day, she is teaching the story of Jacob and Esau. Sheri asks the children a number of questions that she believes helps students better connect to the story, such as:

- *What do you think it must be like to have a twin?*

- *Did you ever feel jealous of someone?*

A number of other classroom activities follow to reinforce the content of the story. As her students eagerly line up for carpool, Sheri asks each a question about something she covered in class today: Joshua, what kind of stew did Jacob use to tempt Esau? Hannah, who were Isaac and Rebekah's two sons? Jonathan, who was older, Jacob or Esau? After sharing their answers, the students each receive a piece of candy and are dismissed.

Before you read on, try to determine the level of questions Sheri asks her students. Do the questions elicit higher level thinking skills? help the students gain enduring understanding that will last them a lifetime? help them develop critical thinking skills?

Now write down three or four questions you might ask to measure what the children are learning and understanding.

Vignette 2: The Confirmation Class Dilemma

Rabbi Mandelbaum wants her Confirmation class to learn how to make life decisions, based on their ability to access Jewish texts. Each week, she presents the class with a different contemporary issue along with relevant Jewish texts. Tonight, the Rabbi asks her class to consider the issue of respect. She has given her students a scenario in which a

teenager, who believes he has been unfairly grounded, decides to go out with friends against his parents' wishes. Along with this scenario, the Rabbi asks her students to read Rabbinic commentaries on the fifth commandment. After giving them time to read silently, Rabbi Mandelbaum opens the floor for discussion. "Well," she begins, "what should our friend have done?"

"No way should he have stayed home. His parents were unreasonable, and he shouldn't have to suffer for it!" answers one student.

"Yeah, but by going out, he just dug himself into a deeper hole," replies another.

"I would just refuse to speak to my parents the whole time I was grounded, even if they asked me a question," decides a third.

"Maybe his parents are always giving him mean punishments. Shouldn't he take the opportunity to show them they're wrong?" asks a fourth.

"Yeah, what if the punishments they give him are cruel and unusual?" adds another.

While the discussion is lively, and the students are engaged, Rabbi Mandelbaum drives home feeling unsure of whether her students were really affected by their exposure to the texts.

Before reading on, determine for yourself how you might have presented this material. Are there questions you could have asked that would help the students see a synergy or dissonance with the texts based on their opinions? How could the lesson move from a diatribe about being treated unfairly by parents, to understanding that we sometimes have to examine our own opinions and ideas in light of more universal and "Jewish" ideas that underscore a parent's concern for one's well-being? In other words, what kinds of questions could Rabbi Mandelbaum have developed to help her students move to a higher order of thinking while integrating the texts?

Take a few moments to write down questions that would have helped the students and Rabbi Mandelbaum see the relationship between Jewish texts and the dilemma. In a situation like this, the order of questions may need to proceed from the knowledge level through evaluation. Try to develop one question for each level.

Vignette 3: The Torah Service — A Sixth Grade Class

Mr. Schwartz, an Israeli who teaches Hebrew in a

four-hour-a-week program, has been working with his class on the Shabbat morning service. His class meets for 2¹/₂ hours on Sunday morning and 1¹/₂ hours during the week. The first thing the students do after attendance and all the administrative work, is to practice reading from their Siddurim. Since the focus is on the Shabbat morning service, the students have been spending the last few weeks learning the Torah Service. Mr. Schwartz has set up the class so that the students work in small teams on their decoding skills and then he tests their mechanical reading in these groups.

Today, Mr. Schwartz takes them to the sanctuary, sits them in the front row, and says, "Now we are going to talk about the Torah service. In many ways, the Torah service reminds us of the great moment described in the Torah when the law from God was brought down from Mount Sinai to the Jewish people. I want you to watch me act out for you what happens in our Torah service, and you think about how it is like the bringing down of the Torah from Mount Sinai."

Mr. Schwartz then goes up to the Ark, signals the class to rise, takes the Torah out, brings it down to the class to touch/kiss with their Siddurim, then takes it back up to a reading stand. He lays the Torah down and calls up someone to say the blessings before he reads it. Stopping there, Mr. Schwartz asks the class to draw some comparisons between the moment at Sinai, and what we do each time we read the Torah.

After a lively discussion with the class on the comparisons, Mr. Schwartz moves on, "After we complete the reading of the Torah, there are other things that take place in the service before we put the Torah back in the Ark. Look in your Siddurim and find the prayers we recite while the Torah is still out of the a Ark. Why do you think we say these blessings and prayers at this time?"

Before returning to class, Mr. Schwartz asks these other questions that are part of his lesson plan:

- When it is time to put the Torah back in the Ark, what do we do in this congregation?

- Is this a powerful and meaningful act at this moment? Is there something that we might say or do at this moment to add to the drama or majesty of the occasion?

- How will this moment feel to you at the service of your becoming a Bar/Bat Mitzvah?

Stop and think about Mr. Schwartz's questions. Again, consider what questions, if any, you might ask about this segment of the liturgy. What levels of the taxonomy are reflected in his questions and your questions — where are the points of synergy and dissonance?

When it came time to assess what my students had learned during a semester, I decided I would let them ask the questions. I put the names of people, places, and things we had studied (and I thought were important for them to remember) on strips of paper. I folded these up, threw them into a hat, and each student got to pick one. Each student then had to write a question that would correspond with the "answer" on his or her strip of paper. They could use their books and whatever resources they had. When everyone had finished, I wrote each student's question on an overhead projector and the rest of the class tried to guess the answer to each one.

(Amy Appelman, West Bloomfield, Michigan)

An Analysis of the Teaching Scenes

In the first scene, Sheri uses questions as a tool for her own self-evaluation. She wants to make sure that her students learned *something* in her class, and their answers serve as a great comfort to her that she is doing her job.

But is Sheri really succeeding as a Jewish educator? Certainly, her students will be able to answer basic Jewish literacy questions, and this is an important part of identifying with the Jewish people. However, Jews also need to be critical thinkers. We are a people who delves deeply into our tradition, studying it both as a guide for living and for its own sake. It is not enough to possess factual knowledge about Bible stories and Hebrew letters. A Jew needs to learn what these things tell him about how to live, and that the act of studying sacred text is a lifelong process.

While first graders are young, they are capable of more than memorization. Yet, Sheri's questioning style does not encourage them to do more than that. She remains consistently on the lowest level of Bloom's taxonomy, and she is not alone in this. According to an article by Dennis Palmer Wolf in *Academic Connections*, "There are many classrooms in which teachers rarely pose questions above the 'read-it-and-repeat-it' level. Questions that demand inferential reasoning, much less hypothesis formation or the creative transfer of information to new situations, simply do not occur with any frequency."[6]

Jerome Bruner writes, in his benchmark work, *The Process of Education*, " . . . any subject can be taught effectively in some intellectually honest form to any child at any stage of development." He goes on to say, "The task of teaching a subject to a child at any particular age is one of representing the structure of that subject in terms of the child's way of viewing things. The task can be thought of as one of translation."[7]

Both Wolf and Bruner write about the situation in secular schools. While the goals of secular learning may be different from those of Jewish learning, the need to move students beyond the knowledge level is crucial in both, and it is as important an endeavor for first graders as it is for adult learners. Sheri is probably underestimating the ability of her first graders to think critically about the information she feeds them, and therefore she fails to let them interact with the Torah and the Hebrew language. Furthermore, she rewards them for their answers, sending the message that remembering this information is a necessity for immediate material gain.

Compare Sheri's questions to those of Mr. Schwartz. The questions he poses almost follow a hierarchy from basic knowledge to some analysis and synthesis. He first describes the parallels to the events at Sinai, then reminds students of the order of the Torah service by acting it out for them, and then asks them to make comparisons. Finally, he asks the students to put themselves into the picture to consider their own thoughts and feelings. Unfortunately, he makes some jumps in his questions, not allowing a smooth transition from one thought to another.

Now think about Rabbi Mandelbaum's class. She asks only one question that happens to prompt a lively discussion, including some critical thinking by the students. However, because there is no integration of the text with the question, the students fail to see the relationship between the two. Perhaps, had Rabbi Mandelbaum been aware of Bruner's work of teaching a subject on a develop-

mentally appropriate level, she might have been prepared with a series of questions that would have engendered lively discussion, but would also have helped the students to gain an enduring understanding of the value that the Jewish text presented as an anchor for their lives.

In all three vignettes, it is appropriate that the teachers reviewed basic information: Sheri to review the facts, Rabbi Mandelbaum to have a quick synopsis of the Fifth Commandment, and Mr. Schwartz the order of the Torah Service. But where might they go from there?

Keeping Bruner in mind, Sheri could have asked her first graders: Why is Esau upset with Jacob? How did Isaac feel when he found out he gave the family blessing to the wrong son? If you were starving, what would you give up for a delicious smelling meal? How would you have felt if you were Esau? Does this story remind you of any other stories we've learned about from the Bible? Why do you think the Torah includes this story? When faced with analysis, synthesis, and evaluation questions such as these, Sheri's students learn that the Torah is more than a big scroll full of names, places, and events. They begin to see it as a guide, full of lessons that are always relevant. They learn that it contains a lifetime supply of issues for contemplation. As they get older, their answers to Sheri's questions will certainly change, but more important than their answers is their interaction with the sacred text as an ongoing Jewish activity. By asking better questions, Sheri can engage her students in the *mitzvah* of Torah study rather than merely exposing them to random Torah facts.

Similarly, Rabbi Mandelbaum could have created a level of discussion about the dilemma by asking students first to understand what the fifth commandment says — i.e., what does it mean to honor your father and mother? Are there times you might not honor them? If so, what situations would prompt this? There are Rabbinic answers to this dilemma. Rabbi Mandelbaum could have prompted the students use the Jewish sources as proof texts for their decisions, maybe even writing them as cases with responses.

While Mr. Schwartz has a hierarchy of questions, there are a number of them that are missing from the incident we have seen. The questions he

---

[6] "The Art of Questioning," *Academic Connections*, Winter 1987; republished by the Institute for Inquiry (www.exploratorium.edu).

[7] Jerome Bruner, *The Process of Education* (Cambridge, MA: Harvard University Press, 1977), 33.

asked about the order of the service and possible student feelings as a Bar/Bat Mitzvah, have no relevance to the big idea he was developing in the beginning of the lesson about the dramatic comparison with Sinai. His concluding questions should have helped students delve into the idea of acting out important Jewish ideas within our liturgy (service).

> I include a list of questions in my lesson plans whenever I want to have a discussion.
>
> Rather than speaking to the class all the time, I like to give students the chance to speak about their thoughts and opinions. I stress to the students that I may not agree with their remarks, and they may choose to disagree with my feelings, but we accept that we are all entitled to our own thoughts. Usually, there is much discussion, and I rarely get a chance to ask all the questions that I have on my list, but it's always better to be more prepared.
>
> I ask questions that can be answered by everyone, and while many of the questions require definite answers, I like to have questions that don't have right or wrong answers, but make the children think about the question. If I get an answer that isn't what I was looking for, I always give the child positive feedback because I don't want him or her to hesitate to answer questions in the future. Typically, I might say, "Gee, that's an interesting thought . . . not quite what I was looking for, but I like that answer."
>
> (Nancy Hersh, Chatham, New Jersey)

A TEACHER'S ROLE AS FACILITATOR OF QUESTIONS

How can we, as teachers in Jewish settings, learn to ask questions that will be challenging to our students and help them develop the critical thinking skills that will lead to deeper understanding of Judaism? What is it that we need to know and what is it that we can do?

The Passover *Seder* is often seen as the a paradigm for asking questions and stimulating answers. Noam Zion and David Dishon in their *Leader's Guide To the Family Participation Hagaddah, A Different Night*, devote a whole section on questions.[8] We are reminded that in order for questions to stimulate thinking there are a number of elements to consider. For one thing, questions should be in words that a child understands. Once a child understands the words, he/she can begin to seek the answers.

The ritual of the *Seder* is a stimulus for numerous questions merely by the activities associated with it — washing hands without saying a blessing, breaking *matzah* and hiding a piece of it, dipping and eating unusual foods, opening a door for a mysterious guest. In the course of one's life, experiencing a *Seder* at different stages engenders questions of all kinds. We can all probably relate to this from our own life journeys. At first there is the wonder of it all — *kashering* a home, preparing the foods, having guests . . . always asking why. As we progress in life, our questions take on different nuances and we ask more about how this could happen, what lessons are there for me, what will I take away from the *Seder* this year and bring back next year?

Rabbi Leo Baeck said:

> It is an age old saying: Ask a Jewish a question, and the Jew answers with a question. Every answer given arouses new questions. The progress of knowledge is matched by an increase in the hidden and mysterious.[9]

At the *Seder*, the leader may begin by asking the questions, but it is the participants around the table who may respond with additional questions. So, too, in a classroom. A teacher may prepare a lesson with a series of questions designed to help the students gain understandings about particular subjects. However, it is the students' questions that often stimulate further discussion and help engender higher level critical thinking skills that lead to enduring understandings.

As teachers, it is important to listen to stu-

---

[8]Noam Zion and David Dishon, "The Four Questions in Depth," in *The Leader's Guide To the Family Participation Hagaddah, A Different Night* (Jerusalem: Shalom Hartman Institute, 1997), Chapter 6.

[9]Leo Baeck, in a series of lectures he gave at Hebrew Union

College, Cincinnati, Ohio, and published as follows: "The Interrelations of Judaism, Science, Philosophy and Ethics, the Dr. Samuel Schulman Lectures," December 13-15, 1949. "Judaism, the Jew and the State of Israel, The Dr. Nathan Krass Lectures," New York, March 27-29, 1950.

dents' questions. These provide insight into absorption by the students and their processing of the content, and they serve as a barometer on how you are doing as a teacher. Keep an ear open for their questions. Do students want clarification, are they relating to other areas covered in class, are they moving in a direction other than the one intended? If students are going off track, is the issue in the way you thought about the material? Did you phrase your questions in language they understand?

> I like to start off my *Mishnah* classes by teaching *Avot* 2:6 (A shy person cannot learn), and I encourage students to be good learners by asking good questions. I also relate the story from the *Haggadah*, *A Different Night*, about the Jewish Nobel prizewinning scientist who was asked to what he attributed his success. He credited his mother who never asked him what he learned in school, but instead greeted him at the door with "Nu Izzy, did you ask a good question today?"
>
> *(Cheryl Birkner Mack, Cleveland, Ohio)*

QUESTIONING TRICKS OF THE TRADE

Question Types

The Teaching and Learning Center of the University of Nebraska at Lincoln offers an interesting piece of information: "Research on the questions teachers ask shows that about 60 percent require only recall of facts, 20 percent require students to think, and 20 percent are procedural in nature."[10] This points to the importance of thinking about the various types of questions that Bloom's Taxonomy pushes us to consider. It is key that teachers plan their lessons with specific thought to the higher levels of thinking on the upper end of the taxonomy.

Lesson Evaluation

What questions did the students ask? Were they relevant to the topic? Did they lead you away from where you were planning to go? Should you follow the students' lead because it indicates there are missing elements to their knowledge base or are there pressing concerns relating to the issue?

Wait Time

Don't just ask a question and expect immediate answers. Give the contemplative student time to formulate an answer; encourage the first student who raises a hand to think more about it. Waiting for three seconds after you ask a question (one/one thousand, two/one thousand, three/one thousand) is usually enough time for someone in the class to offer a response.

Ways to Encourage All Students to Think

Some students know that if they sit quietly, one of their classmates will answer the question posed. There are a number of ways to encourage all students to consider the answer to a question, before calling on one person in the class or having an overall discussion:

- Do not call on anyone, until at least half the class has its hands up.

- Ask each student to take a few moments to write the answer down on a sheet of paper or a white (erasable) board. Walk through the class, checking and commenting to individuals about their answers before discussing as a class.

- Have students discuss the answer to a question in pairs for a few minutes, before opening class discussion.

Encouraging Questions

Pause after explaining a topic and ask if there are questions. Acknowledge body language and facial expression: "Some of you seem puzzled, What don't you understand?" or "Do you need me to go over this again?" Sometimes it is helpful to have one student answer another's questions: "This is what I think you are asking," or "Did you mean to say _____?"

---

[10]See www.unl.edu/teaching/teachquestions/html.

Student Directed Questions

Help students learn to ask questions by partnering them with others or in small groups. Give them something to read or, for younger children, provide a picture to look at. Have them write or dictate one or two questions about the "text." When students pose questions of each other, give them the opportunity to answer them as well.

Avoid Yes/No Questions

One of the best ways to guarantee a failed discussion is to ask yes/no questions. Once students have answered the question, the task is complete. Consider the difference in discussion with the yes/no questions, and those rephrased:

- If you keep kosher, does this mean you cannot eat milk and meat together?

  - Rephrased: What are the rules of observing *kashrut*?

- Was Noah the person who built the ark?

  - Rephrased: Why does the Torah say that Noah was chosen to build the ark?

- Do we say the "*Shehecheyanu*" each night of Chanukah?

  - Rephrased: Why do we recited "*Shehecheyanu*" only on the first night of Chanukah?

Inappropriate Questions

What about students who ask a question that does not fit with the current lesson? When this happens, it is the teacher's job to acknowledge that the student has a legitimate question, but that it is not relevant to the present discussion. Some teachers write such questions on the board and review them all before class is over. Together, the teacher and class determine if the questions should be dealt with at a future time.

THINKING ABOUT ANSWERS

Thus far we have focused on asking questions. The teacher has a responsibility to answer questions as well. Keep in mind the following:

- Repeat the question and paraphrase it. This will ensure that everyone hears the questions and lets the questioner know you understand the question. It is also a good idea to have students paraphrase your questions or ask them in their own words.

- Answer a question directly, especially if students are asking for more information or clarification. Check your response by asking the questioner, "Does that answer your question?" or, "Was that what you were asking?"

- Admit it when you do not know an answer. You may let students know you will investigate, or ask them to investigate the answer and come back with it at the next class.

- Validate each student's questions. Avoid embarrassing students who ask questions that may not be relevant or appropriate at the time.

CONCLUSION

This chapter has focused on why and how to ask questions. Bloom's Taxonomy of Educational Objectives served as the basis for organizing and developing questions in a Jewish classroom. Our challenge as Jewish educators is to plan lessons that include a variety of questions to help students gain understanding of Jewish values, tradition, culture, religion, and peoplehood.

Now, what questions will you ask your class?

BIBLIOGRAPHY

Anderson, Lorin W., and David Kratwohl, eds. *A Taxonomy for Learning, Teaching, and Assessing: A Revision of Bloom's Taxonomy of Educational Objectives*. New York: Longmans, 2001.

This revision of the earlier work published in 1994 evaluates the taxonomy within the context of a specific topic in contemporary educational study. Comparison is made between the historical period in which the original taxonomy was developed and the present educational environment. There is a discussion about the future of education in the United States and the world at large. It is designed specifically to help teachers understand and implement standards-based curricula.

Anderson, Lorin W., and Lauren A. Sosniak, eds. *Bloom's Taxonomy: A Forty-Year Retrospective*. Chicago, IL: NSSE, 1994. (Distributed by the University of Chicago Press)

This book contains a series of essays reflecting on the development and use of the taxonomy. There are discussions about the impact of the taxonomy on testing and evaluation, curriculum, teaching, and teacher education. There are also documents from educational scholars reflecting on the taxonomy in other countries, among them continental Europe, the Mediterranean, the Middle East, and the Republic of Korea.

Bateman, W. L. *Open To Question*. San Francisco, CA: Jossey-Bass, 1990.

The author organizes this easily read text around three central questions: (1) Why teach by inquiry? (2) How can you teach by inquiry? and (3) How can you start? Based upon the author's experiences teaching at both the K-12 and college levels, this book stimulates readers to engage in both self-reflection and instructional skill building.

Bean, John C. *Engaging Ideas: The Professor's Guide to Integrating Writing, Critical Thinking, and Active Learning in the Classroom*. San Francisco, CA: Jossey-Bass, 1996.

A practical guide integrating critical thinking skills and writing skills in the classroom. This book offers ways of designing interest provoking writing and critical thinking activities. It is a good resource for faculty looking for ways of improving student writing and thinking skills. Four sections explore: understanding connections between thinking and writing; designing problem-based assignments; coaching students as learners, thinkers, and writers; and reading commenting on, and grading student writing.

Bloom, Benjamin. *The Taxonomy of Educational Objectives*. New York: Longmans, Green, 1956.

This seminal work provides teachers with a layout of a variety of different types of questions a teacher may ask students. In the book, Bloom applies research from cognitive, affective, and psychomotor theories to support his work. This work provides a useful structure in which to categorize questions for discussion or tests.

Bonwell, Charles C., and James A. Eison. *Active Learning: Creating Excitement in the Classroom*. Hoboken, NJ: John Wiley & Sons, 1991.

This book defines active learning and offers many suggestions for making classes more interactive and engaging. Chapter subjects include the modified lecture, questioning and discussion, and strategies to promote active learning.

Bruner, Jerome. *The Process of Education*. Cambridge, MA: Harvard University Press, 1977.

This book views children as active problem solvers who are ready to explore difficult subjects. It features four main ideas: the role of structure in learning and how it may be made central in teaching, thus building on what has been learned before; readiness for learning underpinning the idea of a spiral curriculum in which one revisits basic ideas repeatedly as a child goes through his/her education; intuitive and analytical thinking to enable one to judge valid and invalid conclusions based on prior knowledge; motives for learning whereby one learns best if one is truly interested in the material presented.

Dantonio, Marylou. *How Can We Create Thinkers? Questioning Strategies That Work for Teachers*. Buffalo, NY: National Education Service, 1990.

Research indicates that teachers spend 80% of their instructional time asking questions. But are they asking the type of questions that will engender thinking among students? This publication demonstrates how to ask questions that prompt students to focus, expand, and support their answers. Proper use of questioning techniques presented in this document will help increase students' ability to think creatively, comprehend better, and retain information. It also includes specific and practical steps for developing a successful questioning skills training program.

Davis, Barbara Gross. *Tools for Teaching*. San Francisco, CA: Jossey-Bass, 1993.

This book is a rich compendium of classroom tested strategies and suggestions designed to improve teaching practice. There are 49 teaching tools organized into 12 sections that cover both traditional tasks and newer, broader concerns. Each tool includes a brief introduction, a set of general strategies, and concise descriptions of practical ideas culled from distinguished teachers, and from the literature on teaching and learning. It has a very useful format that complements its content.

Hyman, Ronald T. *Strategic Questioning*. Englewood Cliffs, NJ: Prentice-Hall, 1979.

This concise text is designed to help teachers become more effective and strategic questioners. It contrasts several different types of questions instructors might use, describes five general strategies for asking questions, identifies 15 specific questioning strategies, and offers a manual illustrating 25 sample questioning dialogues.

Marzano, Robert J. *Dimensions of Thinking: A Framework for Curriculum and Instruction*. Washington, DC: Association for Supervision and Curriculum Design, 1988.

Originally conceived as a book for use in designing staff development programs for teachers as a basis for curriculum planning, this work is beneficial to students as well. The monograph draws from a number of models designed to help students develop higher order thinking skills. The authors present several ways of framing curricular content to allow for students questions and responses that allow them to grow and develop. A precursor to some

of the work that comes later (see Wiggins and McTighe), it is deeply rooted in the taxonomy-like framework first presented by Bloom, to show how one can move through the curriculum allowing the development of thinking to pervade all of schooling.

Saphier, Jon, and Robert Gower. *The Skillful Teacher, Building Your Teaching Skills*. Carlisle, MA: Research for Better Teaching, 1987.

This handbook for both beginning and seasoned teachers uses questions throughout the text to illustrate how to become a better teacher. The whole volume serves as a model for how to use questions in a classroom and provide reflection and action for the teacher. Specific chapters help teachers to frame questions for use in lessons and in the classroom: "Clarity" (Chapter 7) "Principles of Learning" (Chapter 8), "Learning Experiences" (Chapter 13), and "Objectives" (Chapter 15).

Steinsaltz, Adin. "Guidelines for Talmudic Study." In *The Talmud, The Steinsaltz Edition: A Reference Guide*. New York: Random House, 1989.

In this chapter of *The Talmud, The Steinsaltz Edition*, Rabbi Steinsaltz reminds us of the way Talmud is developed. While preserving the sanctity of the text, the reader can see that many different viewpoints are expressed in the content presented. This chapter helps the reader understand that we often have questions that cannot be articulated, and we sometimes have to go back to basics to determine what our questions may be.

Wiggins, Grant, and Jay McTighe. *Understanding by Design*. Alexandria, VA: Association for Supervision and Curriculum Development, 1998.

This book helps educators to determine what are the most important concepts and ideas to get across to students. The premise is that there are a series of "essential" questions we can ask on almost any topic that will help students gain deeper understanding of content and knowledge. The structure of the book allows educators to move step-by-step through course content to identify areas that will lead to enduring understandings — learning for life. Developed for educators in all settings, it is particularly meaningful in Jewish educational environments, encouraging teachers to examine what they teach year to year in subjects that are often repeated.[11]

Wilen, William W., ed. *Questioning Skills for Teachers*. 3d ed. Washington, DC: National Education Association, 1991. (ED 332 983)

This edited collection of nine papers offers educational practitioners and researchers a review of relevant research on questioning techniques and an examination of the characteristics, purposes, and values of different kinds of questions. It also includes a look at how silence or wait time after asking questions and receiving responses from students can be strategically used to produce significant educational outcomes. Finally, there is an exploration of the characteristics, principles, types and phases of class discussions, and a research-based look at ways to improve teachers' questions and questioning.

Wolf, Dennis Palmer. "The Art of Questioning." *Academic Connections*, Winter 1987, pp.1-7. (Republished by the Institute for Inquiry, www.exploratorium.edu)

This article was adapted from a talk delivered to more than one hundred high school and college teachers. It focuses on the issue of questioning in the classroom in order to improve everyday teaching practice, and includes questions raised by teachers in order to improve their delivery of content material.

Zion, Noam, and David Dishon. "The Four Questions in Depth." In *The Leader's Guide To the Family Participation Haggadah: A Different Night*. Jerusalem: Shalom Hartman Institute, 1977.

In this chapter, the authors discuss different ways to stimulate questions. They cite the Rambam as setting the example for asking different kinds of questions at different times in the *Seder*. There are also tips on how to ask the questions and when. Finally the authors provide a list of "Quotations to Encourage a Questioning Mind" (p. 29) from various Jewish sources.

Web Sites

Note: The Internet can provide a wealth of information about questions. Here are three of the sources we used in preparing this chapter.

www.depts.washington.edu/cidrweb/CIDRbooks.html
Center for Instructional Development at the University of Washington, Seattle

This site provides an annotated bibliography on questions and other subjects. While focusing mostly on faculty in higher education, there are a number of items relevant to teachers in all classrooms and in Jewish school settings as well.

www.eric.ed.gov
ERIC Education Resource Information Center

The ERIC resource refers teachers to articles, practical strategies, bibliographies, and the like.

www.oir.uiu.edu
Office of Instructional Resources, University of Illinois at Urbana-Champaign

This site yielded information on the kinds of questions one may ask using Bloom's taxonomy. It describes the taxonomy and then goes through the process of rank ordering the questions asked, giving suggestions of key words and phrases.

---

[11]For more on *Understanding by Design*, see Chapter 24, "Curriculum Planning: A Model for Understanding" by Nachama Skolnik Moskowitz, pp. 278-291 in this Handbook.

CHAPTER 45

Active Learning

Melissa Bailin Bernstein

This chapter is based on the premise that students who are active learners, rather than passive recipients of information, not only gain deep understandings, but enjoy their educational experiences more. As Jewish educators, we should want no less for our students. As you read the following vignettes, consider which teacher has developed a classroom in which students are active learners.

Vignette 1

In Mrs. Katz's Tanach class, students are seated in rows, while Mrs. Katz sits at the front of the room at her desk, facing the students. Avi reads the story of Noah out loud, Jennifer and Aaron listen attentively, while Shira passes a note to Sara, David daydreams, Alex plays with his PDA, and Jenny is staring out the window.

After Avi has finished reading, Mrs. Katz asks the question, "So what happened in the story?" Students stare back at Mrs. Katz with blank looks — and even surprise — because the task has changed from reading to questioning.

Vignette 2

In Mr. Simon's Tefilah class, students are divided into groups of three. Each group is reading a different section of the translation of the "Shema and Its Blessings" and taking notes on what they read, preparing to teach their section to another group.

Desks are arranged in groups of three, with the teacher milling between tables. There is a loud mumble in the room as students discuss and interpret the prayer. The students are engaged; each one is assigned a job within their small groups: leader, reader, or recorder.

HOW DOES ACTIVE LEARNING LOOK?

If you chose the second vignette, then you picked the classroom in which students are actively learning. They are on task and engaged. To see how Mr. Simon accomplished this (and how Mrs. Katz's teaching differs), we will explore five main indicators of an active learning classroom, each with specific examples: focus, noise level, student behavior, community, and understanding gained.

Focus

The first indicator of an active learning situation is the focus of a classroom. In the first vignette above, Mrs. Katz is the focus of the lesson. She is the director, manager, and the giver of information, while the students are directed, managed, and passive recipients. Mrs. Katz called on the students to read, and they did. Much of the conversation was teacher-to-student. A classroom that is teacher-focused will answer the question, "What is the teacher teaching?"

In an active classroom, the focus is on the student and the student's learning. The teacher is the facilitator and creator of the activity, while the students are the directors and managers of their own learning and work. This was clearly seen in the second vignette as the students were leading the discussion and preparing to teach to their peers. In Mr. Simon's classroom, one could ask the question, "What are the students learning?"

Noise Level

Imagine walking into Mrs. Katz's class. What do you hear? Probably a pattern resembling the following: Mrs. Katz's voice, then a student's voice, then Mrs. Katz, followed by another student. The only outside noise is that of students fumbling through their bags, finishing snacks, or having off-task conversations. Now, imagine the sounds heard in Mr. Simon's class. Most likely, the classroom is buzzing with several students' voices, pages of books turning, and maybe Mr. Simon's voice.

The noise level in a classroom is the second indicator of an active classroom. In a traditional class, there is order, and the teacher is the director of all conversation. This was seen as Mrs. Katz asked a question of the class, expecting one student to answer, thus creating a teacher-to-student dialogue. In Mrs. Katz's class there is very little student initiated conversation and almost no student-to-student conversation.

In an active classroom, the goal is to create a three-tiered conversation, student-to-student, student-to-teacher and teacher-to-student (see figure 1).

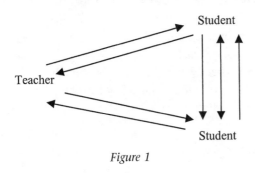

Figure 1

In an active lesson, students speak to each other, share information, and teach one another. The teacher may facilitate the lesson, but the students are actively involved.

Student Behavior

The third indicator of an active learning situation is the students and their behavior. So often, in religious school classrooms, we see disengaged students, who are inattentive or misbehaving. As seen in the above examples, the more traditional classroom made it possible for students to disengage from the lesson. Mrs. Katz created a lesson that drew in only one or two students at a time. If an individual was not the student reading, there was nothing to keep him/her involved in the lesson. In Mr. Simon's class, all the students had a job and were responsible for a task. In an active lesson, each student participates. Whether working individually or in a group, each student has a task with an expected outcome. Students become involved in

the learning and are responsible for the learning process.

> I use materials requiring groups of children to work together. For example, in our study of "Bible People," I lay on the table cards containing the name of one biblical person or individual facts about them. Working together, students first place the names in chronological order and then identify which facts go with each person. Expected to be able to explain why the cards "fit" in each place, students engage in much animated discussion that, in and of itself, provides review of the information. A variation of this has each student receiving a card containing either a name or a fact, with instructions to "find your partner."
>
> *(Carol Cohn, Orlando, Florida)*

Community

Again, imagine yourself in Mrs. Katz and Mr. Simon's classroom. Consider the room arrangement. Are the desks in rows or clusters? Does the arrangement invite conversation, or are students' backs to each other? Where is the teacher's desk? Where is the teacher? Does the teacher sit among the students or is he/she standing in front of the class in "lecture position"? Are the students talking to each other? Are they respectful of each other?

For many of our students, the social aspect of religious school is their incentive to attend class. Students need friends and peers whom they want to see each week, and they need time to be able to socialize. Thus, the fourth indicator of active learning is community. Community in this instance is defined as a classroom in which the students talk to each other and respect each other. No one is put down for his/her thoughts and everyone is included in the activities, including the teacher.

Understanding Gained

The final indicator of an active learning classroom is that students are gaining deep knowledge from the lesson. There is a difference in the level of understanding between a classroom in which the teacher simply pours information into the students and a classroom in which students have an opportunity to gather the information on their own, then discuss, process, and somehow transform it.

In Mr. Simon's class, the students studied the prayers, gaining a deeper understanding of their meaning. They could then take the information and put it into their own words and teach it.

Active learning techniques create a medium for the teacher to assess continually the depth and amount of understanding throughout the activity. When comparing the two vignettes above, Mrs. Katz had no method of assessing her students. She may have gained some knowledge from those few who did get a chance to answer her questions, but for the most part, the students were simply reading words on the page. No thought was required for this activity! In Mr. Simon's class, he could not only assess understanding from the final product of each group, but he could also assess the understanding at any given time, simply by listening in to a group's conversation.

ACTIVE LEARNING TECHNIQUES

When creating an active lesson it is important to keep in mind how the brain learns. According to Eric Jensen (*Brain-based Learning*, p. 48), "learning is best when focused, then diffused, focused, then diffused." Focused can be defined as the time that students are receiving information. Diffused is defined as the activity that asks students to process or transform the information received. For example, in Mrs. Katz's class, the students were constantly focused on the reading. She could have "diffused" the information by stopping the class, and asking them to "Think, Pair, Share" (see the definition of Think, Pair, Share," below). Jensen states, "constant focused-learning becomes increasingly wasted time." He suggests that a good rule of thumb for timing of a focused activity is the age of the learner, plus two minutes. The maximum focus time should not exceed 20-25 minutes.

Thus, creating an active lesson takes a lot of retraining and rethinking. Like any new habit, practice, patience, and time are essential. While creating a completely active lesson is the goal, the reality of a Jewish classroom may not allow for this. Because of time constraints and other issues inherent in Jewish teaching, it is not suggested

(nor is it possible in most Jewish classrooms) to "do away with" frontal teaching completely. There are many instances and lessons during which frontal teaching is necessary. However, in implementing some basic techniques, a lesson can be converted from teacher-focused to learner-focused, thus achieving deep knowledge.

The following activities are ways to diffuse your students' thinking and to get them active. These techniques can be used one at a time as a way to vary a more traditional lesson (e.g., a lecture). Or, many can be combined to enhance engagement or to further deepen student understanding and, of course, used for a whole lesson.

> I give each student a card with the name of a prayer used in *Tefilah*, the name of a Jewish holiday, etc. The students arrange themselves in the correct order of the prayers, the holidays, etc., order according to their cards. Should there not be enough cards for the entire group, it is the responsibility of the rest of the students to determine if the sequence is correct, and to fix it if it is not.
>
> (Carol Cohn, Orlando, Florida)

Think-Pair-Share

This simple three-part technique, originally developed by Frank Lyman,[1] can be a staple to any classroom plan. In the first step, the teacher poses a question to students and the students formulate an answer individually. Once students compose an answer (or complete a worksheet, or whatever the task may be), they pair off and share and compare their answers. Each person is either a speaker or listener, fostering respect and listening skills, as well as encouraging socialization. This technique also enables students to deepen their knowledge by putting their thoughts into words and then teaching their partner.

During a "frontal" lesson, this technique allows students an opportunity to share and process new information. In the case of Mrs. Katz's class above, she could periodically ask students to "think-pair-share" the main ideas of the story, keeping them

---

[1]Frank Lyman. "The Responsive Classroom Discussion," in *Mainstreaming Digest*, A.S. Anderson, ed. (College Park, MD: University of Maryland College of Education, 1981).

more focused on the learning as it unfolds, rather than waiting until the end.

Divide and Conquer

Another excellent way to break up a reading class is to divide and conquer. In the example above, Mr. Simon's class demonstrated this activity. Divide the reading, possibly giving each group a different book, article, or even section of the chapter. After each group has read the material, they discuss it and prepare to teach it to others. This can be done in groups, or in pairs. In a pair, each student reads a section and then teaches the material to his/her partner.

One year, I had a class of students who just could not grasp that the *erev* Shabbat service (or any service for that matter) was more than a random collection of prayers. It wasn't until I brought in a box of Legos and asked them to build the *erev* Shabbat service that they could visualize that the service did have a structure.

(*Rabbi David Feder, Morgantown, West Virginia*)

Voting

Voting can be as simple as the teacher stopping the lesson to take a poll of what students are thinking. "Raise your hands if you think we should light the *chanukiyah* right to left. Raise your hands if you think we should light it left to right." Voting doesn't always mean raising hands. Alternatively, it could mean write votes on a dry erase board or paper and holding it up for everyone to see. Voting can also involve movement. For example, "If you agree with what Queen Vashti did, go to the windows, if you disagree, move to the blackboard." Voting is a quick and simple technique that encourages students to think, form an opinion, and then share with others. It gives students an opportunity to have a say (especially if the vote determines an outcome, as in the question, "Who is ready for a break?"), as well as instills confidence in students to share opinions and thoughts in an informal, non-threatening manner.

After voting, a further step may be taken to deepen knowledge and understanding of material, by asking students to "think-pair-share" (see above)

with each other to discuss their views. In the above example, one student who voted to light the *chanukiyah* from right to left may pair with someone who voted to light from left to right. The students can try to persuade each other to change their view, or simply share why they chose that particular answer. Through doing this, knowledge is deepened as students discuss and "teach" their understandings.

Go around the Room

In the middle of a lecture, lesson, or even a large group discussion, the teacher or facilitator could stop the lesson and then ask each student to say something, while also giving a pass option. It can be a comment, opinion, an answer to a question, etc. The focus of "Go around the Room" is to encourage everyone to say something. This technique gives the teacher or facilitator an opportunity to assess student understanding and engagement. If all the students opt to "pass," the teacher may need to change the direction of the lesson to encourage more participation. If all the students give responses that are on task and show understanding, the teacher knows to continue.

Do the students need to stretch? A nice variance on this activity is to ask the students to stand up. Each student shares a thought; however, if someone said their thought, they either need to think of another idea, or sit down. In this activity, everyone has a chance to say something and nothing is repeated.

Another next level can be added to the "Go around the Room" technique by asking students to pair (see "Think, Pair, Share," above) to discuss their answers before offering them to the larger group. This step allows students to "check" their work with someone else and gives them an opportunity to organize their thoughts out loud.

Writing

Writing (or drawing for younger students) is a great way to get students active. The teacher can stop a lesson, ask a question, and have students write their answers. Students either hold their work up for the teacher to see, or share it with a friend. This can be done with short answer questions, paragraphs, thoughts, or even Hebrew letters (e.g., the teacher may ask students to draw the letter *bet*, or the letter that makes the "B" sound).

Another writing technique is sentence reflection. Students are given open-ended questions and an opportunity to answer. Some examples of sentence reflections are: Three things I learned today: _____, I am wondering _____, I was surprised by _____, I don't understand _____, I would like to know more about _____. Students can discuss their answers in small groups, or this activity can simply be for the teacher's assessment. This type of writing allows for self-reflection and self-evaluation, and provides an opportunity for students to make meaning of new information.

An advantage to having students write is that it allows the teacher to do a quick assessment of student understanding and engagement. As students write, the teacher has a moment to walk around the room and give individual attention to some.

Make writing "different" with dry erase boards, which are a treasure for younger students (and some older ones, too!) and work like a charm to help students be more positive about writing. Most students like to write on the board, and having an individual one allows them to feel as if they are always at the board. Dry erase boards can be bought in a school supply store. Or, teachers can make the boards at school by laminating a sheet of card stock or poster board. To complement the set, purchase dry erase or wet erase markers at an office supply store. (Most teachers prefer wet erase markers over dry erase markers, as there is less ink smudging.)

Be creative with your dry erase boards. Don't limit yourself to traditional smaller boards. No white board in the room? (A white board is the opposite of a blackboard, which uses chalk; a whiteboard uses colored markers.) Create a white board by laminating a large sheet of chart paper. This is great for color coding directions or student work.

By using other forms of dry erase boards, teachers can create a permanent "dry erase chart." A text study dry erase board has questions printed on it to help guide students through a text study. Questions should be general, for example: "If you could, what questions would you ask the author (or one of the characters in the text)? What do you think the author of this text (or speaker or God) wanted us to know or think about? What is the "big idea" of this text? What is this text teaching? For each text study, students reuse the board.

Ask Your Friend

When a student has a question, recommend that he/she "ask a friend." This nurtures a sense of community among students and encourages them to have conversations with each other, rather than relying on the teacher. "Ask Your Friend" allows one student to be the "teacher," enabling him or her to process the newly learned information and thereby deepen knowledge.

> When I am a student, I learn best when I can take an active approach to learning. I don't get much from sitting passively in lectures. As a teacher, I strive to get students actively involved with the text the way I like to be involved myself. My goal is to give them the tools they need to teach each other and teach me.
>
> *(Dena Salmon, Montclair, New Jersey)*

Graphic Organizers

A graphic organizer is an instructional tool to help students organize their thoughts. A popular and easy organizer is a chart that students fill in as they acquire information. For example, rather than simply watching a video and looking for evidence of characters performing *mitzvot*, students might be asked to fill in a chart, listing the scenes that correspond to specific values (see figure 2).

Describe movie scene ↓	What *mitzvot* are depicted in the scene? ↓

Figure 2

Another chart is the KWHL chart, created originally by Donna Ogle (1986). It allows students to call to mind earlier learning and gives them space to record new information as the unit progresses. At the top of the chart, the headers read

- What do we already *know* about the subject?

- *What* do we need to know?

- *How* can we find the information?

- What did we *learn*?

Note: A KWHL chart would make a great permanent dry erase board.

Charts don't have to be in the form of squares. Be creative! For example, the outline of a body helps students organize their thoughts about Israel, with each body part prompting for something related to its function. For example: in the *head* of the chart students can write information (facts) they know about Israel; in the *feet* they can describe the path of a trip; in the *hands*, what they can do to help; and, in the *heart*, their hopes and prayers for the country.

A Venn Diagram is comprised of two (or more) intersecting circles. It helps students examine similarities, differences, or even categorize elements. For example, students can show the behaviors that honor parents in one side of the diagram and behaviors that do not show honor to parents in the other circle. A comparison of two Jewish personalities can be done, for example, by placing the characteristics of Moses in one circle and the characteristics of Abraham in the other. Qualities of both can be placed in the intersecting area.

Folded paper can be a quick, easy, and interesting graphic organizer. Simply ask students to fold the paper into as many sections as needed to organize their thoughts. For example, ask them to fold the paper into three sections, like a brochure. Then on each section ask them to write one main point of the story. At the end of the task, they will have a brochure about the story.

Fun with Stickies

Everyone enjoys colorful office supplies, including students. Invest in a few packages of stickies (more commonly known as Post-It notes). File cards also serve the purpose. Give students three stickies and ask them to write one fact they remember about the story of Chanukah on each. Divide the students into small groups and have them share their stickies. Can they put the stickies in order to tell the whole story?

Stickies can also be used as an active form of assessment or review. Give each student three stickies and request that they write one piece of information learned in the lesson on each. Then, divide students into small groups in which they can share their answers. Using this technique, students share what they learned and hear other facts they might not have remembered. A further step can be taken to increase understanding by asking students to

categorize the stickies by time period, holiday, etc., depending on the lesson.

Stickies can also be used as conversation starters for text study. Instruct students to read a piece of text. Then, give each student two stickies. On one, they should write the meaning of the text and, on the other, write how they can incorporate the text into their work or life, depending on the lesson.

Group Work

Many of the active learning techniques mentioned above include group work. Group work offers a myriad of benefits for a class and fulfills all five indicators of active learning.

- Group work is student-focused, placing students in charge of their own learning.

- Community is created because students work as a team to complete tasks.

- More students have active involvements, lessening behavior problems.

- Conversations are fostered among students, raising the noise level in the room and serving as an opportunity for students to socialize.

- Understanding is deepened as the groups work together, accomplish learning tasks, and process information in different ways.

Often, teachers shy away from group work because of the misconception that student conversations will pull them off task. Yes, students do socialize, but as noted earlier, there are benefits to this. To minimize extraneous conversations while channeling the students' efforts into more productive work, do the following:

- *Give clear directions with clear expectations from the group*. Often, because of time restrictions, teachers tend to skip this important part of the lesson. Rather than verbally giving directions (which always needed to be repeated several times), write them on the chalkboard, on a chart pack, or even have them on a worksheet with discussion questions. If you recall in the second vignette, the students were given the task of having to learn their prayer well enough to be able to teach it to the rest of the class. Rather than busying themselves with social talk, they gathered information, interpreted it, and discussed how they would teach it.

- *Create jobs for each group member* so that everyone has a task. In the vignette featuring Mr. Simon, students were assigned tasks. It may help to give students a sheet of paper or card with their jobs written down, so that each time group work is done, students are handed their job assignment. Or, they can pick blindly, as in choosing a card from the deck. Some jobs may include reporter, secretary, researcher, or leader.[2]

INTEGRATING ACTIVE LEARNING INTO A LESSON PLAN

Now that active learning has been defined and explained, it is time to implement the techniques into a lesson. Begin by taking an already created lesson plan and thinking about the five indicators discussed in the beginning of this chapter. Ask yourself the following questions.

When I examine my lesson plan:

1. What is the focus? What I am teaching or what are the students learning?

2. Is there room in my lesson plan for students to talk to each other?

3. Who will be engaged by this lesson? Will each student have a chance to play a role in the lesson?

4. Have I created an atmosphere in which students respect each other?

5. How is knowledge deepened by the activities planned? How will I know what students understand?

To see how this works, turn Mrs. Katz's lesson in vignette 1 into an active lesson. First, consider the lesson she taught in light of the five indicators (see figure 3).

When Looking at Mrs. Katz's Lesson:	
What is the focus? What is Mrs. Katz teaching and what are the students learning?	Mrs. Katz is the focus of the lesson. She is directing the students to read the story of Noah. The students are reading the story of Noah.
Is there room in Mrs. Katz's lesson plan for students to talk each other?	There is no opportunity for students to talk to each other in this lesson.
Who will be engaged by this lesson? Will each student have a chance to play a role in the lesson?	One student at a time will be engaged. Maybe others will pay attention while the one student is reading.
Has Mrs. Katz created an atmosphere in which students respect each other?	Students are not respecting each other. As Avi is reading, Shira and Sara are passing notes, David is daydreaming, Alex is playing with his PDA, and Jenny is staring out the window. They are not respecting the reader. Only Jennifer and Aaron are paying attention.
How is knowledge deepened by the activities planned? How will Mrs. Katz know what students understand?	Students will be exposed to the story of Noah, but no knowledge is deepened. Mrs. Katz has learned that the students understand very little when she sees their blank looks after her question, "So what happened in the story?"

Figure 3

---

[2]For more information about Cooperative Learning, see Chapter 30, "Cooperative or Collaborative Learning" by Carol K. Ingall, pp. 351-362 in this Handbook.

Based on the answers to the five questions, this lesson is clearly not active.

Using the active learning techniques described earlier in this chapter, a revised active lesson plan would look like this (figure 4).

Name: Mrs. Katz   Date: Sunday, December 3   Class: Tanach (Bible)

Topic: The story of Noah

Goal: Students will read the story to determine God's message

Lesson Plan:

Task 1: Text Study of Genesis

Divide students into pairs to complete the text study sheet. Give each group a "text study dry erase board" and wet erase marker. Assign one partner to be the reader, the other to be the recorder.

> **TEXT STUDY SHEET**
>
> THINKING ABOUT THE TEXT
>
> Use the following guide to help you read Genesis 6.
>
> 1. Read the text.
>
> 2. Are there any words you don't understand? (Be sure to find the definition for these.)
>
> 3. If you could, what questions would you ask the author or one of the characters in the text? (Be sure to spend some time answering your questions as a group.)
>
> 4. What do you think God wanted us to know or think about?
>
> 5. If you were Noah, would you do as God commanded? Why or why not?

Task 2: Sharing and comparing the information using "Think, Pair, Share"

Join each pair with another, making a group of 4. Have students share and compare their answers for questions 4 and 5.

Figure 4

I have learned the importance of speed, energy, and flexibility. Flexibility is obvious: jumping into a classroom at the last minute requires that you have resources at your fingertips, always having something in the back of your mind. Energy is also obvious: if you enter a room and begin with high energy, students will follow and will be grateful. Speed is a little more elusive. I have seen teachers spend what seems like an eternity on a page of reading or finding the meaning of one Hebrew word. Teachers don't always feel the slowness of the lesson. But high energy leads to a faster paced lesson. Whether "the material is covered" or not, students will feel that they have learned something because they did not perceive their time to be wasted.

(Karen Elson, Columbus, Ohio)

Now that the lesson is "re-done," let's ask the five questions again (as in figure 5 below).

What is the focus? What is Mrs. Katz's teaching or what are the students learning?	The students will explore Genesis 6, by using the "text study" dry erase board.
Is there room in Mrs. Katz's lesson plan for students to talk each other?	Students will have an opportunity to work in pairs and in a group of four.
Who will be engaged by this lesson? Will each student have a chance to play a role in the lesson?	All students will be engaged. While working in pairs, one student is the reader, while the other is the recorder. Then they must share their work with another pair.
Has Mrs. Katz created an atmosphere in which students respect each other?	Students must respect their partner, value their opinions, and come to an agreement. Then each pair must share their work with another pair.
How is knowledge deepened by the activities planned? How will Mrs. Katz know what students understand?Has Mrs. Katz created an atmosphere in which students respect each other?	Students are studying the text closely and are asked to synthesize the information by answering, "What do you think God wanted us to know or think about?" and "If you were Noah, would you do as God commanded? Why or why not?" Mrs. Katz will know what the students understand by what they are writing, as well as from hearing their conversations as she is milling around the room.

Figure 5

CONCLUSION

A frequent comment made about incorporating active learning into Jewish schools is, "It seems like it will take so much time to make a lesson plan for an active class." Like doing anything new, it will take a little longer initially because it requires a new way of thinking. One must consider not only the material, but also how it will be learned by the students. The more you practice, the easier it will become. While several techniques have been suggested, many more exist, or are waiting to be created . . . so get active!

TEACHING CONSIDERATIONS

- The first indicator of active learning is that the teacher is not the focus, rather it is the students who are in "control" of their learning during the actual lesson. This takes structure and planning by the teacher.

- Don't be concerned if you feel your room is too noisy. This is actually a good thing! As long as the students have roles and tasks, that means that your room is active.

- As stated earlier in the chapter, not all lessons need to be completely active; however, be considerate of your students' learning and always keep in mind Jensen's formula: "Learning is best when focused, then diffused, focused, then diffused."

BIBLIOGRAPHY

"Graphic Organizers." NCREL North Central Region Education Laboratory 20 2 2003, www.ncrel.org/sdrs/area/issues/students/learning/1r1grorg.htm.

This web site gives several examples of various graphic organizers.

Harmin, Merrill. *Inspiring Active Learning: A Handbook for Teachers*. Alexandria, VA: Association for Supervision and Curriculum Development, 1994.

This handbook offers a wonderful definition of active learning, as well as a myriad of techniques to motivate and engage students.

Jensen, Eric. *Brain-based Learning*. Del Mar, CA: Turning Point Publishing, 1996.

Based on research on how the brain learns, Jensen offers ways to promote better learning, including classroom environment, varying learning styles, thinking strategies, motivating students, and more.

Lyman, Frank. "The Responsive Classroom Discussion." In A.S. Anderson, ed. *Mainstreaming Digest*. College Park, MD: University of Maryland College of Education, 1981. See www.wcer.wisc.edu/nise/CL1/CL/doingcl/thinkps.htm.

A description of "Think, Pair, Share" can be found at this web site.

Silberman, Mel. *Active Learning: 101 Strategies to Teach Any Subject*. Boston, MA: Allyn and Bacon, 1996.

Active Learning offers many techniques for teachers including: ways to set up a classroom to encourage team building and promote discussion among the students, activities to help partners work together, strategies to make a lecture more active, and methods of getting all students involved with learning at once.

Silver, Harvey F.; Richard W. Strong; and Matthew J. Perini. *Tools for Promoting Active, In-Depth Learning*. Trenton, NJ: The Thoughtful Education Press, 2001.

This book offers several active learning "tools" and graphic organizers that encourage "in-depth" learning.

Starin, Carol Oseran. *Let Me Count the Ways: Practical Innovations for Jewish Teachers*. Los Angeles, CA: Torah Aura Productions, 2000.

Planning lessons, school-to-home communication, holiday celebrations, classroom management, and effective teaching tools are among the many topics covered in this book.

CHAPTER 46

Enriching Instruction with Art

Eileen Ettinger

Adonai spoke to Moses, saying: See, I have singled out by name Bezalel . . . I have endowed him with a divine spirit of skill, ability, and knowledge in any kind of craft . . . and in all manner of workmanship. (Exodus 31:1-3)

Bezalel was given the task of building the Tabernacle. Thus was born the partnership between the divine Creator and the human creator. We are partners with God in creation. All of us are endowed with the divine creative spirit.

Working with our hands connects us with the creative spark that God gives us. By providing hands-on art activities we, as teachers of Judaica can help students make a connection with their inner selves, with God, and with Judaism.

Our tradition is text based. Therefore, much of our teaching in the Jewish classroom is based upon text. We study Torah, Midrash, and Talmud and look for meanings. We scrutinize our prayers to make them more meaningful to us. We read Jewish literature and explore its messages. Our challenge as teachers is to make the texts come alive. It is my premise that, through using hands-on art activities, our students make connections between the texts and their inner selves, their minds and souls, to become partners with God in creation. In pedagogical terms, the hands-on art process makes a connection between the cognitive and affective, or the intellectual and emotional aspects of learning to produce personal, meaningful learning.

Furthermore, the process of creating meaning visually releases words through which to interpret texts verbally and in writing. Mordecai Kaplan said, "Art possesses the magic whereby it is able to express the seemingly ineffable and to communicate what is ordinarily regarded as incommunicable."[1]

ART AND PROCESS

In her book, *Footprints and New Worlds*,[2] art educator Temina Gezari tells a story about a five-year-old boy named Bobby. He sat next to her with a brush, paint, and paper, and proceeded to paint a broad brush stroke across the top of the paper. "This is the sky," he said. He painted a broad stroke across the bottom of the paper and said, "This is the earth." He continued to paint a tree with branches, leaves, grass, a rose under the tree, the shining sun, a cloud in the sky, and rain coming down from the clouds. He painted a bigger rose and said that the rain made the rose grow. He painted and talked more until he said, "And now the moon is rising," and painted the moon. He thought for a few minutes and said, "It's getting dark. Night is coming." He took the brush and with big strokes he covered the entire paper with black paint. He put his picture down and went on to something else.

Bobby was not interested in the finished product. It was the process that counted. He needed to express something and he did so. The paintbrush was a vehicle of expression. Once he was finished with the joy of creation, he was done.

Young children's inner selves are open. They pick up a brush, tap into their feelings and experiences, and paint them. We all possess the creative divine spirit within us. Unfortunately, as we mature, we do not look at artwork as a vehicle of expression. All too often, emphasis is placed upon the finished product. We want it to be perfect, or better than that of the person next to us. As a result, we often try too hard to make it good and thereby lose the joy of the experience. Some of us shy away from the art activity all together. Yet, it is the process that counts. We need to invite the students in with non-threatening art projects that help them connect with their creative spirits.

---

[1]Mordecai Kaplan, *The Future of the American Jew* (New York: Macmillan, 1948), 357.

[2]Temina Gezari, *Footprints and New Worlds: Experiences in Art with Child and Adult* (New York: Jewish Education Committee Press, 1964), 10-13.

It is in the process that the sparks fly and learning occurs. That doesn't mean we should not hang the students' art work all over the walls. The finished product is a bonus, and we should certainly acknowledge the "beautiful things" they create.

ART AND SELF-ESTEEM

In her kindergarten class, Suzy was taught the significance of the customs of Shabbat and *Hiddur Mitzvah*, elevating the *mitzvah* by using beautiful ceremonial objects. Through the process of making a *challah* cover, she explored and expressed her personal connection with Shabbat. But we cannot forget the importance of the connection with tradition and esteem building that occurred for Suzy when the *challah* cover was placed on her Shabbat table at home.

We need to emphasize the process and we need to encourage the students to do their best, but it is important also to honor what they produce. It may not be beautiful in our eyes, but it is a reflection of their inner selves and that makes it lovely and meaningful.

> During my students' seventh grade Shabbat service, I could tell that they really saw the importance of it. This being their Bar and Bat Mitzvah year, they each had made a *tallit* with the guidance of the school's art teacher. They each wore the new *tallit* that had been made in class, and they were so proud. We put on the *tallitot* for the first time as a class at the beginning of the service, a moment that many said was the most meaningful part of the service for them.
>
> (Amy Appelman, West Bloomfield, Michigan)

GOALS OF USING ART IN THE JEWISH CLASSROOM

For the purposes of this chapter, I define art as the "hands-on creative process."

The goals of using art in the Jewish classroom are for the students to:

1. use the hands-on creative process to connect the text with their inner feelings, thereby finding personal meaning.

2. use the hands-on creative process to find verbal and written words to explain the texts in a personal way.

3. study Jewish ceremonial art and develop aesthetic appreciation.

4. study and create Jewish ceremonial objects and develop aesthetic appreciation and a connection with our heritage.

5. use the hands-on creative process to connect a sense of joy and satisfaction with Jewish learning.

THE FORMAT OF THIS CHAPTER

Art Projects

In this chapter I present a variety of art projects to use in the classroom, along with suggested Judaic lessons. I have chosen projects that are non-threatening to the art novice and materials that are inexpensive and easily accessible. The general procedures for doing the projects are presented first and are followed by specific lesson suggestions.

Keep in mind that the projects and lessons are interchangeable and that you can combine two or three techniques in one project. For example, you can include micrography and stenciling in a collage.

Share and Write

At the end of each lesson, I include the reminder, "Share and Write." After the students create their visual image, ask them to share their visual interpretations with the whole class, in pairs or small groups. When sharing is done, the students write their interpretations, completing their connection to the text. If they are too young to write, they may dictate to someone. When displaying the art projects, hang them with their written interpretations.

ART PROJECT: MICROGRAPHY

Background Information

Micrography is a Jewish art form of miniature Hebrew writing done in the shapes of objects, animals, buildings, and geometric designs. Micrography began with the writing of the Masorah in ninth century Israel. The scribes of the Masorah studied the Bible and established exactly how it should be written and read. The words of the Bible are very sacred and the scribes could not put their comments on the original scroll. The notes of the Masorah were written in separate manuscripts. As the scribes commented on the Bible, many of them formed their writings into interesting designs of objects, animals, buildings, and geometric shapes. Their creative inscriptions developed into the art of micrography.

This art form was passed on from generation to generation and from country to country throughout Europe and into North America. Today it can be found in *ketubot* (wedding contracts), prayer books, *Mizrachim*, sukkah decorations, Purim *Megillot,* and in fine art. See figure 1 for an example of micrography.

Figure 1

Preparation

Place construction paper, pencils, and lined white paper in front of each student as you begin the lesson.

Materials

- Pencils
- Lined paper
- Large pieces of construction paper
- Thin felt markers

Procedure

- Introduce the lesson by explaining what micrography is.
- Show students an example.
- Emphasize that this is a Jewish art form.
- Tell students that they will have a chance to do micrography themselves.

Directions

Say to the students:

- Close your eyes. What pictures come to mind when you think about the text (use the appropriate word, i.e., prayer, story, etc.) and the questions?
- Keep the pictures in your mind and make simple line drawing of them, lightly, with pencil, on the construction paper.
- Make a list of words, with pencil on the lined paper, that you think of when you look at the drawing and think of the text. They can be single words, sentences, or poetry.
- Write the words, with felt markers on the pencil drawing. Cover all the lines. You can repeat the words if necessary.
- Write in any language, any script. You can combine languages. If you repeat words, you will create a pattern. You can experiment with color patterns created by the markers.
- When you are finished writing the words erase the penciled lines.
- Share.
- Write.

Micrography Sample Lesson 1: Where Do You Find God?
(Grades 3-Adult)

Procedure

- Introduce the art form of micrography and show an example.

- Read the story, "The Princess Who Wanted to See God" from *Who Knows Ten*,[3] by Molly Cone.

Directions

- Continue with the following questions and directions:
    - What happened to the princess at the end of the story?
    - Where did the princess find God?
    - Where do you find God?
    - Sit quietly for a minute. Close your eyes and think about where you find God.
    - Ask students to open their eyes and then continue with the general micrography directions, above.

Micrography Sample Lesson 2: Shabbat Brachot (Grades 2-4)

Micrography is an excellent medium for interpreting and personalizing prayers. For example, when beginning Hebrew students finally master writing the whole Hebrew alphabet, a good way to celebrate is to do *brachot* micrography in Hebrew. One example of this is a *Shabbat Brachah Sign*. This is a multi-lesson project with one *brachah* per lesson, but all done on one sheet of paper. Below is the *brachah* lesson for the candles. Follow through with the wine and *challah* and add them to the paper. (See figure 2.)

Figure 2

[3]Molly Cone, *Who Knows Ten* (New York: UAHC, 1965), 14-20.

Procedure

- Practice saying the Shabbat *brachah* over the candles with the class.
- Say the translation together and discuss what it means.

Directions

Say to the students:

- Pretend that it is Friday night and you are getting ready to light the Shabbat candles with the *brachah*. (Light candles and say the *brachah*.)
- Look at the burning candles and think about how you feel when Shabbat candles are lit.
- Make a simple line drawing, in pencil, of Shabbat candle sticks and candles.
- Write the *brachah* over the candles, in Hebrew, over the lines that you drew, using felt pens. If you need to, write the *brachah* over and over until you cover all the lines.
- Erase the pencil lines. (Details of the art lesson are below.)
- Share how you feel when the Shabbat candles are lit on Friday night.
- Write a few sentences about how you feel.

Micrography Sample Lesson 3: Rainbow Brachah

Micrography may be done over images of any other *brachah*. For example, teach the *brachah* over a rainbow. Discuss how students feel when they see a rainbow. Have them do a drawing of a rainbow and micrography over the image.

ART PROJECT: WIMPELS

Background Information

A *wimpel* is a fabric binder that is wrapped around the Torah. The art of creating personalized *wimpels* began in Germany in the sixteenth century. A *wimpel* was made from the cloth used to wrap a baby boy after his circumcision. It was cut into strips and sewn from end to end. The mother or a scribe painted or sewed the boy's Hebrew name, birthday, and father's name, and the saying: "May he grow in Torah, the marriage canopy, and the doing of good deeds." Images found on the *wimpels* were illustrations of the saying, folk designs, animals, and whimsical letters. *Wimpels* were not made for girls.

When the boy was weaned, he was brought to the synagogue and his family presented the *wimpel* to the synagogue. It was stored until his Bar Mitzvah when his *wimpel* was wrapped around the Torah that he was to read. It was wrapped again on his *Aufruf* when he was called to Torah on the Shabbat before his wedding.

The Skirball Museum in Los Angeles has a large collection of *wimpels*[4] obtained before World War II. In North America, the custom of making wimpels is still alive — parents continue to make them for their baby boys (and girls).

Figure 3

MAKING WIMPELS USING STENCILING
(Grades PK-Adult)

Background Information

Stenciling is easy and has endless possibilities. It is good to start a picture off with stencils and then add free-hand designs and pictures. It works with all ages. Preschoolers use large, simple stencils. Adults may want to create their own stencils. Commercially prepared Jewish stencils of Jewish and holiday symbols and Hebrew letters are available. Be sure to explore the variety of secular stencils, too, such as flowers, animals, English letters, shapes, etc. (see Bibliography). Stenciling may be done on paper or on fabric. See figure 3 in the next column and figure 4 on the next page for examples of wimpels made by stenciling.

Preparation

- Cover tables with newspaper.
- If stenciling on fabric, put cardboard under the cloth because the fabric paint seeps through.

Materials

- Pre-cut stencils, commercially made: Hebrew and English letters, numbers, Jewish symbols, flowers, animals, etc.
- Homemade stencils - designs can be traced on oak tag or stencil paper and cut out with an X-acto knife (done by teacher or adult students).

Paper Stenciling

- Paper
- Thick and thin felt markers
- Crayons
- Poster paint applied with brushes or sponge pieces.
- Glitter
- Glue

Fabric Stenciling

- Fabric (100% cotton or muslin)
- Fabric markers
- Fabric paint
- Glitter

---

[4]www.skirball.org/Visions/index2a.html, "Life Cycle," *Visions and Values: Jewish Life from Antiquity To America*. (Click on the life cycle icon, then scroll down to the *wimpel*.)

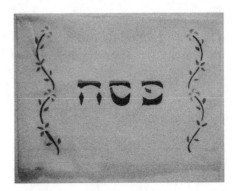

Figure 4

- Glue
- Brushes
- Pieces of sponge
- Pieces of cardboard to put under fabric as you work

Directions

Say to the students:

- Place stencil on paper or fabric.
- While holding down the stencil, fill it in with markers, crayons, or paint. (For young students, hold down stencils as they fill them in.)
- When using special materials:
  - If using glitter, fill the stencil with glue, pick up the stencil, scatter glitter on glue, shake excess glitter off, and let dry.
  - If using a paintbrush, dip brush into paint and lightly dab brush all over inside of stencil.
  - If using a sponge, dab it into paint and tap the sponge all over the inside of stencil. Use paint sparingly on sponge to create an interesting texture (in contrast to the smooth texture made by brushes or markers).
- Special instructions for different ages:
  - Primary grades: Use water-based paint on paper with large stencils and large brushes and sponge pieces.
  - Intermediate grades through adults: Use permanent fabric markers and fabric paint on fabric with any size stencils
- Overlap stencil impressions to create interesting designs. Make sure the first stencil design is dry before you put something on top or around it. This prevents smudging.
- After designs are created with stencils, add other freehand images with markers or paint.

Group Stencil Project: Directions

- Try out designs on paper.
- Decide and mark where designs will be placed.
- Copy paper designs onto fabric.
- Have only two or three students at a time working on the large piece.
- Variation: Students put their designs on individual pieces of fabric and these are then sewn on the large piece.

Program Ideas

- Camp banners, family days, intergenerational programs, projects

Project Ideas

- Stenciling on Paper: *Ketubot*, holiday cards, illustrated *Siddur*, *Haggadot*, posters
- Stenciling on Fabric: *Tallitot*, *kipot*, *challah* covers, *matzah* covers, Passover pillow covers, wall hangings, *Shalach Manot* bags, T-shirts, banners

Wimpel Sample Lesson 1: Bar/Bat Mitzvah Family Wimpel
(Grade 7)

We all know that the experience of becoming a Bar/Bat Mitzvah is as significant for a student's parents as it is for the student. The months leading up to the "big day" are extremely busy, stressful, and emotional. All too often party preparations overshadow the significance of the life cycle event.

Many religious schools have pre-Bar/Bat Mitzvah family day programs, sometimes monthly events spanning the whole year.

I suggest that families create a family *wimpel* to wrap around the Torah on the day the youngster becomes Bar/Bat Mitzvah. This is a multi-session project. The parents and the child study the meaning of the child's Torah portion. They are given a set of questions that help them make personal connections to the story. They then interpret it together and use stencils and brushes to paint their interpretations on a *wimpel*.

This shared creative activity accomplishes many things. The family replenishes their spirits by spending quality time together away from the pre-party stress; together they make a lasting connection to the Torah portion and thus to Torah; the Bar/Bat Mitzvah experience becomes a deep, Jewish family experience that can create a stronger bond to each other and to Judaism. See general stenciling directions below.

Wimpel Sample Lesson 2: Confirmation Class Memories
(Grade 10)

I used stenciling with a Confirmation class to create a *wimpel* to wrap around the Torah when they were confirmed. It was a symbolic summary of their years of Jewish education. We did it on a piece of muslin that was approximately 14″ x 90″.

Tenth grade students are reluctant to pick up a brush and start painting. I gave them stencils of many Jewish symbols as a jumping off point. On and around the stencils they added details by hand. I made *Chumashim* (books of the Torah) available, and they included stories that had significant value to them. One student did a stark rendition of Mount Sinai from which sparks of light emanated. I encouraged them to be creative and overlap the stencils and images and include Hebrew and English words. They planned their designs and made them on paper. Then decided which design should go where on the *wimpel*.

This was a long process that took place over months, using part of class time each week. When the *wimpel* was finished, a member of the congregation put trimming around to finish it off. After the completion of the project, discussions ensued about shared experiences in religious school. These were recorded on paper. Some of the students had

been together since kindergarten. The project gave them the opportunity, as a group, to reminisce, which brought them closer together in their last months of formal religious school. During their Confirmation service, the students presented their *wimpel*, shared their written memories, and wrapped the *wimpel* around the Torah.

Wimpel Sample Lesson 3: Confirmation Class — The Story of Ruth
(Grade 10)

The class reads the story of Ruth and creates a visual interpretation of the story on a *wimpel*. They start with stencils and add freehand drawings. They write a joint interpretation to be presented at the Confirmation service.

ART PROJECT: PAPER MIDRASH
(Grades 3-Adult)

Background Information

Dr. Jo Milgrom, a scholar and artist, created the process of Paper Midrash. This is a hands-on method of interpreting text. Students express their visual interpretations with torn pieces of paper. This leads to verbal written interpretation. Dr. Milgrom has given workshops all over the country and has inspired many Jewish educators to use this technique. See figure 5 below for an example of a paper *midrash*.

Figure 5

Materials

- Large pieces of construction paper for backing, one large piece for each student

- Small pieces of construction paper for tearing, assorted colors

- Glue or glue sticks

Directions

Say to the students:

- You will create a visual interpretation of the biblical passage.

- Tear, only tear, small pieces of paper and glue them on to the large piece to tell the story that we just read.

- Include all the characters, God, and you.[5]

- Questions that might help you create your visual interpretation (make these specific to your passage).

    - Why do you think the people did what they did?

    - How did the people feel about each other?

    - How do you feel about them?

    - What role did God play in all of it?

- Share your pictures by telling who is in the picture, how they feel about each other, how you feel about them, and what happened.

- Write.

Lessons Ideas

- Any text interpretation

Paper Midrash Sample Lesson 1: Adam and Eve
(Grades 7-Adult)

Give students copies of Genesis 3:1-7. Review what took place in the Garden of Eden prior to these verses. Then read the verses together.

Directions

Say to the students:

- You will now have an opportunity to make *midrash*. *Midrash*, meaning "search out," is a collection of writings done between 100 and 900 C.E. In the actual Bible text, very little is said about peoples' motives, feelings, or reactions. The Rabbis, in writing their interpretations, filled in the blanks of the text, so to speak. Any time you interpret a biblical story, you are making *midrash*. You will have a chance to do that today. First, you will interpret Torah with your hands by creating a visual interpretation of the biblical passage.

- Your task is to tell the story by tearing, only tearing, pieces of construction paper, then gluing them on the large piece. Include all the characters of the story: Adam, Eve, Serpent, God, and you.

- Here are some questions that will help you interpret the story:

    - Why do you think the serpent tempted Eve to eat of the tree?

    - Why did Eve eat of the tree?

    - How did Adam feel when he learned of what Eve did?

    - What role did God play in all of it?

    - How do the characters relate to each other?

    - How do you feel about the characters?

- Share.

- Write.

ART PROJECT: COLLAGE
(All ages)

Background Information

Collage is a catchall term for art that contains a collection of anything. Collecting the materials to use can be one exciting aspect of the collage project. Look outdoors, in your garage, among tools, at broken toys, broken dishes, old jewelry, old clothes for interesting fabric, etc. Ask students for ideas for materials. A collage is a design made up of an

---

[5]I include "you" because I am trying to have the student relate personally to the story. I add God so that the student will think about the role God plays in biblical narratives and, therefore, in people's lives. It is fascinating to see children and adults resist at first, but then come out with wonderful interpretations.

assortment of materials overlapping each other, with words, paint, markers, etc., all pasted on a backing. It challenges the artist to use his/her imagination.

Preparation

- Cover tables.
- Place long strips of butcher paper on tables for collage backings.

Materials

- Long strips of butcher paper
- Scissors
- Glue
- Construction paper
- Throw away materials, such as: egg cartons, paper rolls, fabric, buttons, beads, rice, Styrofoam, wallpaper, old holiday cards, old magazines
- Glitter
- Sequins
- Tissue paper
- Cellophane
- Pipe cleaners
- Magazine and newspaper photos
- Sand
- Crayons and or markers
- Paint and brushes
- Fabric, wallpaper, wrapping paper scraps
- Noodles
- Old beads and pieces of jewelry
- Place long strips of paper on tables for collage backings.

Procedure

- Have groups of 3 to 5 working on different part of the paper.

Directions

Say to the students:

- Using scissors and glue, make a design with the collage materials to interpret the text.
- You can add words, letters, magazine letters and photos, glitter, paint.
- It is effective if you overlap the materials and cover the whole paper.
- Share.
- Write.

Lesson Ideas

- Text interpretation, map of Israel, *kibbutz* life, scenes of times and places in historical and contemporary life, i.e., *shtetl* scene, sanctuary scene.

Project Ideas

Use collage materials to:

- enhance other art projects.
- decorate hand made ceremonial objects.

Collage Sample Lesson 1: Taking Care of the Trees (Grades 3-Adult)

This lesson can be done as part of Tu B'Shevat observance or *Shomray Adamah* (taking care of the earth). It can be a whole school or camp program, camp weekend, or family day. It can be done in a park or a camp setting. The lesson is best done outside where students can walk around and collect materials that relate to trees (i.e., branches, leaves, bark, seeds, pine cones, acorns). If the lesson is done indoors, provide the nature materials for the class, in addition to the regular collage materials.

Procedure

- After students have collected the tree materials have them sit in a circle, share what they collected, and talk about what trees mean to them.

- Break class up into groups of two or three (or family groups, if applicable).

- Give out the following quotations, assigning one quote to each group. If you are working with a lot of students, some groups will get the same quote, providing an opportunity to compare how each group interprets the same text.

  God said, "Let the earth sprout vegetation — plants and trees of every kind."

  And it was so. And God saw that it was good. There was evening and there was morning, a third day. (Genesis 1:11-13)

  God said, "See I give you every seed-bearing plant upon all the earth, and every tree that has seed-bearing fruit; they shall be yours for food . . . " And it was so. And God saw all that had been made and found it very good. (Genesis 1:29-31)

  When you pick the fruit of your trees for food, you shall not pick the fruit all the way to the edges of your field. You should leave some for the poor and the stranger. (Leviticus 19:9-10)

  All trees speak with one another. All trees speak with people. All trees were created to be friends with people. (*Genesis Rabbah* 13.2)

  The world is a tree and the people are its fruit. (Solomon ibn Gabriel)

  Deuteronomy 20:19 states that one is not to cut down food trees even when engaged in warfare. *Midrash* goes on to say that one who smashes household goods, tears clothes, demolishes a building, stops up a spring, or destroys food on purpose violates the command — "you must not destroy."

Directions

Say to the students:

- Each group will receive a quotation from a Jewish source.

- Read the quote among yourselves and discuss what it means to you.

- Discuss how you would describe it visually, with your hands.

- You are going to make a group collage to describe your quote using the materials you collected. You may also use the collage materials on the tables.

- This is a group effort. Therefore, you need to discuss and decide as a group what you want to say and how you will use the materials to make your collage.

- Everyone contributes to the discussion and to making the collage.

- Now create your collage.

Collage Sample Lesson 2: Holiday Collage Mural
(Grades K-Adult)

In preparation for a holiday study, have the students make a collage, "Our [name of holiday] Story." This can be a class project or for family day or grandparents' day.

Invite visitors to bring in a special ceremonial object, song, story, or food to share with the class. Ask everyone share what they brought and tell what the item is used for, where it came from, memories associated with it. Display all the objects on a table and then review the ceremonial objects, prayers, songs, activities, and meals of the holiday.

Prepare a display of all the objects that were shared.

Procedure

- Divide the class into groups of 3 to 5.

Directions

Say to the students:

- Each group is going to make a holiday collage that describes the holiday.

- Think about what was shared today.

- Talk with your group about what you want to put in the collage and what materials you want to use.

- You can also use words, prayers, songs, recipes.

- When you are finished, each of you write a few sentences about how you feel about the holiday. (Primary grade students may dictate to adults.)

ART PROJECT: PAINTING

Background Information

Before beginning the curricular task at hand, give students a piece of paper, a brush, and some paint. Give them the chance to swish the paint around, experiment with colors, and play. This will awaken in them the pleasure of working with paint.

Preparations

- Cover tables with plastic covering.

- Put paint into wide containers so that it is easily accessible.

- Give each student a container of water in which to clean brushes when changing colors.

Materials

- Plastic tarp or plastic table cloths to cover tables

- Tempera paint in assorted colors

- Large brushes

- Large pieces of newsprint

- Cups to hold the paint

- Cups of water

- Paper towels

- Aprons (parents' old shirts are good)

- Sponges for clean-up

Procedure

- Show students how to dip brushes into paint and paint on the paper.

- Go over basic rules of painting, such as: paint only on the paper, clean brushes before changing colors. (Primary grade students may have some difficulty with this.)

- Explain how to clean brushes — dip brush in water, swish around, wipe off on paper towel. Do this a couple of times.

- Have students play and experiment with painting before they start the real project, i.e., mixing colors to make new colors, experimenting with lines, textures, shapes.

- Make the paintings.

- Share.

- Write.

- Save time for cleanup.

Lesson Ideas

- Text Interpretation

Project Ideas

- Incorporate painting into any of the other art projects.

Painting Sample Lesson 1: Becoming a Torah
(Grades PK-2)

One Sunday afternoon, as religious school was ending, the preschool teacher showed me a painting that one of her four-year-old students had done of a Torah scroll. The Torah was hugging the *aytz chayim* (the wooden pole/handle of the Torah) with streams of brightly colored light swirling around. The following activity was done before the students painted a Torah.

The teacher had taken the preschoolers into the sanctuary to see and touch the Torah scroll and to learn the names of the parts of the scroll. Back in the classroom, they talked about what they saw. She told them to become Torahs. They stood up and stretched their arms straight up high over their heads like the *aytz chayim*, then whirled around as Torahs. When they were finished whirling, they painted Torahs, with the *aytz chayim* reaching up to heaven and down to the earth.

Painting Sample Lesson 2: The Seven Days of Creation
(Grades 3-Adult)

Painting can be intimidating in and of itself. However, painting the seven days of creation is less threatening because we don't really know how these things looked. All we need to do is use abstract lines, shapes, textures, and different colors to show how we think it looked. There are many beautifully illustrated books for all grade levels that depict the seven days of creation. Find one for your class, at the appropriate grade level, and use it in the lesson.

Materials

- *Chumashim*

- Printed copies of Genesis 1:1-2:3.

- Grade level appropriate illustrated book depicting the seven days of creation

- Painting materials

Procedure

- Read the biblical account of creation.

- Read a storybook rendition of the creation.

Discussion and Directions

Say to the students:

- What do you think is the difference between the two stories?

- The Bible doesn't tell us how things looked. We need to use our imagination to show visually what happened, which is what the storybook did. When we do this, we engage in a form of *midrash*. (Explain what *midrash* is using the explanation on p. 559.) You will have the opportunity to use your imagination to create *midrash* as you paint the seven days of creation.

  - Use color, line, texture, and shapes to paint what you imagine happened.

  - Give out printed copies of the verses for reference as the students work. (You do not want students to get paint on the *Chumashim*.)

  - This may need to be a multi-session lesson, depending upon the grade level and time constraints.

ART PROJECT: MOSAICS

A classical mosaic is a design made with small chips of glass, stone, or ceramic that are set in plaster or cement. Mosaic art goes back as far as Mesopotamia, and was developed into a high art form by the Greeks and Romans. It was used extensively in early Christian art. Excavations have uncovered many Byzantine era mosaic floors all over Europe, the Middle East, and in Israel. A series of floor mosaics, possibly done by Jewish artists, were found in the Bet Alpha Synagogue in Israel that date from the sixth century.[6] They contain the representation of the sacrifice of Isaac, signs of the Zodiac, and objects from the Tabernacle.

Mosaics Sample Lesson: Scenes of Jerusalem (Grades 8-10)

I worked with eighth to tenth graders on mosaic scenes of Jerusalem. We studied the history and architecture of Jerusalem. In the library we researched books of photographs of the stone buildings in Jerusalem. I showed slides of stone buildings and structures and projected them on a wall. Each student picked a scene, placed a large poster board on the image on the wall, and traced the outlines of the buildings.

They took the silhouettes and filled them in with tile chips of varied stone-like colors to create mosaics. (Home improvement stores have such tiles, which can be smashed with a hammer.) The students put the chips of the tiles on their drawings and made mosaics. When the mosaics were finished, we hung them up along with their writings about the buildings.

Mosaics Sample Lesson 2: Scenes of Jerusalem (Grades 4-7)

The same mosaic project can be done with intermediate grades. Use greeting cards or photos with scenes of the stone buildings of Jerusalem. Cut out the silhouettes of the buildings and paste them on boards. Fill in the buildings with small tile chips.

---

[6]"Bet Alpha Synagogue," *The Universal Jewish Encyclopedia*, vol. 3, 249-250.

Materials

- Heavy cardboard for backing

- Tile chips, produced by hitting tiles with a hammer

- Tile sources: Leftover tiles from building projects, discontinued tiles from stores

- Student-made clay chips from oven baked polymer clay, which are baked in a regular oven. (A suggested brand of polymer clay is Sculpy. It can be found in any art supply store.)

- Ceramic glue

Directions for Making Clay Chips

- Roll out slabs of polymer clay with a rolling pin.

- Cut slabs into small square and triangle chips.

- Bake in oven according to directions on package.

ART PROJECT: MASKS

Background Information

How many times have you walked through religious school and been delighted by Purim masks hanging on the walls? Seeing the faces of Esther, Mordecai, King Ahasuerus, and Haman reminds us of the playful fun that is in store when Purim arrives. It is traditional for students to make masks of the Purim characters. However, you can take advantage of the mask making excitement that Purim generates and create masks with other themes.

Three different projects are suggested, depending upon the grade level. The first of these is a suggested all-school mask project for Purim. You can make such masks at any time during the school year. It is important to note that these masks are not made to be put on the face. The main thing is the process of making them. The students make the masks in order to connect with heroic people and their acts.

Masks Sample Lesson 1: Heroes in Jewish History
(All-School Project)

Studying about heroes provides students the opportunity to be inspired by and emulate heroic acts. Ori Z. Soltes said, "Heroes are that link between human and Divine which offers an idealized model of what we all would strive for were we big enough to do so."[7] When students create masks, they actualize that link.

Jewish history is filled with heroes from Abraham to Hillel, and even non-Jews who helped us such as Raoul Wallenberg. For ideas for heroes, consult *Jewish Heroes, Jewish Values*, a book about contemporary heroes by Barry Schwartz.[8] Two other good sources are *Jewish Education News*[9] and *Professional Jewish Educator*.[10]

Preparation

- When doing a whole school hero mask project, plan to display the masks for Purim, start the project about two months before the holiday. This will provide enough time to finish a couple of weeks before Purim so that the masks may be displayed for a while before the holiday.

- Before the students make their masks, they will need to explore the characteristics of a hero, chose their hero, and research that person.

Directions

Say to the students:

- You are going to make a mask of a hero, a historical figure you admire.

- Put things on the mask that identify who the person is, i.e., a ladder on Jacob's face, one of her poems of the face of Hannah Senesh, or E=MC^2 for Albert Einstein.

---

[7] Ori Z. Soltes. "What Defines a Jewish Hero?" *Jewish Education News* 15:2 (Spring 1994): 10-13

[8] Barry Schwartz, *Jewish Heroes, Jewish Values* (West Orange, NJ: Behrman House, Inc., 1996).

[9] *Jewish Education News* 15:2 (Spring 1994). May be ordered online from www.caje.org.

[10] Coalition for Jewish Learning, "Who Is a Hero?" *Professional Jewish Educator* XIX (January 2001): 2-10. The complete text is online at www.cjlmilwaukee.org.

- Create an expression on the face that shows how you would feel if you were that person.

Remember that it is the process that counts. The finished products may not portray exactly what you would expect to see. The important part is the process in which the students make personal connections with the heroes.

Project: Stocking Wire Hanger Masks
(Grades PK-2)

See figure 6 for an example of a stocking wire hangar mask.

Figure 6

Materials

- Knee high stockings or panty hose cut at the knees
- Wire hangers
- Scissors
- Glue
- Yarn
- Collage materials (see above)

Directions

Say to the students:

- Bend the body of the hanger to form an oval.

- Pull a knee-high stocking over the oval and tie it with yarn right above the handle.

Show students how to glue collage pieces on the stocking to make a face, use yarn to make hair, and other collage materials for decoration. (For younger students, you may need to make the facial features for them.)

Project: Two-Faced Masks
(Grades 3-7)

A good way to show the hero's face and the student's reaction is to make two faces. This is a flat mask with two cardboard profile cut-outs placed on a flat piece of cardboard. See figure 7 for an example of a two-faced mask.

Figure 7

Materials

- Prints of Piccasso's paintings of faces
- Pencils
- White paper
- Cardboard or poster board
- Construction paper
- Heavy scissors
- Strong glue
- Paint
- Brushes
- Collage materials
- Thin felt markers

Directions

Say to the students:

- You will need three pieces of cardboard: two pieces for faces, one piece for the backing of the faces.

- Cut out two profile faces from cardboard — one of your hero and one of you.

- Paint the faces or cover them with construction paper.

- The facial features — eyes, nose, mouth, etc., can be made any way you want, going in any direction, much like a Picasso painting of faces. (Show Picasso prints.)

- On the hero's face, put something that would identify who the person is.

- On your face, create an expression that shows how you would feel if you were that person.

- On the backing, write what the hero did and how you would feel about it if you were the person.

- When you put the faces on the backing leave enough space in the middle to put what you wrote about the hero.

Project: Papier Mâché Masks
(Grades 8-10)

See figure 8 for an example of a papier mâché mask.

Figure 8

Preparation

- Prepare wallpaper paste, according to directions.

- Blow up balloons.

Materials

- Wallpaper paste prepared according to directions

- Newspapers torn into strips

- Large balloons

- Tempera paint

- Large and small brushes

- Collage materials

Procedure

First Session:

- Blow up a balloon and hold it down on the table with the tied-off knot on top.

- Dip newspaper strips into wallpaper paste.

- Cover half of the orb of the balloon with the strips, creating the oval shape of a face.

- Put on two layers of strips.

- Allow to dry, usually a few days.

Second Session:

- Using paint and collage materials, create the hero's face, following the directions for the two-faced mask lesson.

- Share.

- Write.

Lesson Ideas

- Stocking wire hanger masks can be used in acting out characters in a story.

- Two-face masks can become two, three, or multiple face masks for use in interpreting Torah. Each face would be another character in the story.

MAKING CEREMONIAL ART

Ceremonial objects play a significant role in the lives of the Jewish people. Torah says, "This is my God, and whom I will glorify" (Exodus 25:2). The Rabbis interpreted this to say, "Adorn thyself before God in the performance of the commandments. Make before God a beautiful *sukkah*, a beautiful *lulav*, a beautiful *shofar*, beautiful *tzitzit*, and a beautiful *Sefer Torah* . . . and bind it up with beautiful wrappings" (*Shabbat* 133b). We adhere to this decree by creating beautiful ritual objects and using them to elevate the *mitzvot*.

Through the study of ceremonial objects, we learn Jewish history, rituals and ceremonies, *mitzvot*, aesthetic appreciation, the importance of memory, and the appreciation of our culture. Create a series of lessons on appreciation and understanding of ceremonial objects and the roles they play in Jewish celebrations. Use the art projects in the chapter and explore other art media to make ceremonial objects with your students.

> When I was teaching about Jewish history at the time of the Romans to sixth graders, we designed a model of Jerusalem (like the one at the Holyland Hotel in Israel). Steven, a big kid who struggled all year with the conceptual discussions and Hebrew prayer, had a ball just designing and laying out the streets, buildings, and lives of people from this time. Using research and readings, the class was able to have fun and learn. There was also a great deal of surprise on the students' part that we even got involved in this kind of project, for they know that teachers of the upper grades generally spend less time and energy using a creative hands-on approach.
>
> *(Michael Fixler, Syracuse, New York)*

TIPS FOR THE TEACHER

- Do the project yourself first. It is very important that you are comfortable and familiar with the process.

- Show students a finished product so they have an idea of how it might look. Put it away before they start the project so that they do not think they have to copy it.

- Use exciting and unusual materials.

- At the beginning of the school year, write a letter home to parents requesting odds and ends and throwaway items that they have at home such as buttons, yarn, old holiday cards, old beads or jewelry, fabric, and wallpaper samples, etc.

- Circulate around the room while students are working to give them encouragement and help when necessary.

- Show individual students' work to the rest of the class as they are working. It gives encouragement to the student whose work you are showing and gives ideas to the other students.

- Do group projects. Group work provides a variety of viewpoints, fosters listening, socialization, cooperation, and compromise, and builds community.

- Keep a stack of newspaper available to cover all work space.

- Provide cover up clothes, such as old shirts for students. Parents don't like it when their children come home with stained clothes.

- Display all the student work wherever you can. This builds self esteem, teaches others, and creates an aesthetic environment that lifts the spirit.

CONCLUSION

There is great value in using art in the Jewish classroom. After doing some of the art projects in this chapter, I hope you will be motivated to create similar projects for other parts of your curriculum. Art projects will surely produce meaningful learning and joyous experiences. Look for the divine sparks.

BIBLIOGRAPHY

Reference Material

Campbell, Anne. "Reaching Others through the Arts." *Art Education* 32:5, September 1979, pp. 24-25.

> Proposition to use art to facilitate learning.

Korn, Irene. *The Celebration of Judaism in Art.* New York: Smithmark Publishers, 1996.

> A collection of folk art, fine art, ceremonial art, including micrography and *wimpels* with brief descriptions of holidays and customs associated with the works of art.

Milgrom, Jo. "Hand-Made Midrash." *The Melton Journal,* Winter 1984, pp. 6-18.

> Description of one of Jo Milgrom's experiments with paper *midrash.*

Outwater, Myra Yellin, *Judaica.* Atgen, PA: Schiffer Publishing Ltd., 1999.

> Presentation of Jewish ceremonial objects, their uses and connection to Jewish history and culture. With color photographs.

Sosin, Doris. "The Wimpel: A Jewish Folk Art Expression." *The Paper Pomegranate* VII, no. 3, Winter, 1983.

> History and detailed description of the art of wimpel making.

Jewish Craft Books

Adler, David A. *The Kids Catalog of Jewish Holidays.* Philadelphia, PA: Jewish Publication Society, 1996.

> Comprehensive compilation of Jewish holiday history, crafts, recipes, stories, songs. Good book to recommend to parents. (Ages 10-13)

Brinn, Ruth Esrig. *Bible Story Crafts for Little Hands.* Minneapolis, MN: Kar-Ben Publishing, 2000.

> Stories presented with crafts that include puppets, costumes, and musical instruments. (Ages 4-8)

———. *Jewish Holiday Crafts for Little Hands.* Minneapolis, MN: Kar-Ben Publishing, 1993.

> Contains craft projects for and information about Jewish holidays. (Ages 4-8)

Kops, Simon. *Fast, Clean and Cheap.* Los Angeles, CA: Torah Aura Productions, 1989.

> Large and varied collection of craft projects for the Jewish classroom. (All ages)

Reyder, Rimma. *Jewish Ceremonial Designs.* Owings Mills, MD: Stemmer House Publishers, 1987.

> A collection of drawings of Jewish ceremonial objects. Good source of Jewish images and designs to be applied in creating ceremonial objects. (Ages 13-adult)

Ross, Kathy, and Melinda Levine. *The Jewish Holiday Craft Book.* Brookfield, CT: Millbrook Press Trade, 1997.

> A variety of interesting crafts for the Jewish holidays. (Ages 3-10)

Secular Craft Books

Day, JoAnne. *The Complete Book of Stencil Crafts.* New York: Dover Publications, Inc., 1974.

> Comprehensive book of instructions for making stencils and how to use them. Variety of applications and stencil patterns. (Ages 10-adult)

Jackson, Paul. *The Art and Craft of Paper Sculpture.* Radnor, PA: Chilton Book Co., 1996.

> A comprehensive survey of paper craft with techniques, materials, and instructions. Good source for paper sculpture, mask making, framing works, and more. (Ages 10-adult)

Kafka, Francis, J. *Batik, Tye Dying, Stenciling, Silk Screen, Block Printing: The Hand Decoration of Fabrics.* New York: Dover Publications, Inc.,1974.

> Clear guide with well illustrated instructions. (Ages 10-adult)

Kohl, MaryAnn. *Preschool Art — It Is the Process That Counts.* Beltsville, MD. Gryphon House, 1994.

> Theory and practice in preschool art. Art lessons with clear directions and good illustrations. (Ages 3-6)

Solga, Kim. *Make Scupltures!* Cincinnati, OH: McGraw Hill Ryerson, 1992.

> Collection of easy to make sculpture projects in all media from homemade clay to stone sculpture. Good mask projects. Clear directions and excellent illustrations. Many of the projects can easily be adapted to the Jewish classroom. (Ages 5-11)

Thomas, John E., and Danita Pagel. *The Ultimate Book of Kid Concoctions*. Strongsville, OH: The Kid Concoctions Co., 1998.

A complete guide to recipes for all sorts of paints, clays, doughs, and solutions. (Ages 4-8)

Wigg, Philip R, and Jean Hasselschwert. *Handbook of Arts and Crafts*, 10th ed. New York: McGraw-Hill Higher Education, 2001.

A high quality, comprehensive book written by teachers. Covers basic concept of art instruction, background and use of all materials, and thorough presentation of a variety of lessons in many media. (Ages 5-12)

Wiseman, Ann. *Making Things — The Handbook of Creative Discovery*. Boston, MA: Little Brown & Co., 1973.

A comprehensive collection of interesting craft ideas. Many can be adapted to the Jewish classroom. Very reader friendly for those not trained in art. This is a basic book that every classroom teacher should have. (Ages 5-12)

SOURCES FOR CRAFT MATERIAL

CRAYOLA
30 Centre Square
Easton, PA 18042-7744
610-515-8000
www.crayola.com

Excellent resource for craft materials and art lesson ideas.

KTAV
930 Newark Avenue
Jersey City, NJ 07306
201-963-9524
http://ktav.com

Hebrew alphabet stencils and craft materials.

S & S WORLDWIDE
P.O.B. 513
Colchester, CT 06415
800 243-9232
http://snswide.com

Offers a wide variety of craft materials for teaching, reinforcing, and observing the Jewish holidays and *mitzvot*.

INTERNET RESOURCES

CAJE Curriculum Bank
www.caje.org

Good source for lesson ideas.

Israel Museum, Jerusalem
www.bh.org.il

Presentation of programs and resources the museum offers on art, history, etc.

Jewish Museum, New York
www.JewishMuseum.org

Resource for Jewish art and Jewish education.

Jewishnet
www.jewishnet.net

Connection to Jewish lists and academic sites.

Shamash
www.virtual.co.il.

Major Jewish web site for everything Jewish, including educational sources.

Skirball Museum, Los Angeles
www.skirball.org

Resource for Jewish art and Jewish art education.

CHAPTER 47

Enriching Instruction with Drama

Gabrielle Kaplan-Mayer

INTRODUCTION

Another Sunday morning assembly. Half an hour for parents, children, and teachers to start the day with prayer, songs, morning announcements, and a little Torah study. Lately, the assemblies had all felt the same . . . kids zoning out, parents flustered and looking at their watches, teachers making last minute lesson plan decisions. Where was the kavanah, the intention about making this learning time meaningful? Sharon, the school director and assembly leader, shrugged. Time to try something new. "How do I engage restless four-year-olds, cynical seventh graders, and parents from all different backgrounds?" she wondered. She thought about a workshop she had taken recently about using drama in the classroom. She didn't have much experience in theater (except for having the lead in her high school play), but she was willing to try anything to make these people wake up and get engaged in Jewish learning. She could adapt some of the workshop ideas for the morning assembly. Would it work? What have I got to lose, she thought, why not take the risk?

The next week, the students led the morning prayers as usual. Then Sharon shortened the school announcements, and then it was time for Torah study. She explained that Torah study would be a little bit different this week. The group was midway through the Book of Exodus. Rather than go on with the next Parashat HaShavua, they were going to review the stories they had learned so far. But not with discussion, not with question and answers. She had people count off by ten and form ten groups of eight people each. In a paper bag, she had put small pieces of paper with a short synopsis of what happened in each Parashah, such as, "The Hebrew slaves finally make it to the Sea of Reeds. As the Egyptian soldiers were coming behind them, God parts the Sea for them and they are able to cross. Miriam leads the women singing and dancing." Each group drew one slip of paper out of the

bag. "Okay, everybody, here are your instructions," Sharon said. "You have ten minutes to figure out a way to act out your scenario. Everyone in the group should be involved. You can use movement, voices, singing, dancing — anything you want. It doesn't have to be Broadway. Have fun."

The social hall filled with a buzz of energy, excitement, laughter. Sharon moved from group to group, seeing if anyone had questions or was feeling stuck. "Wait, wait," kids would say, "We're not ready to show you yet." Even the youngest ones gave their input, and the shy parents took roles as a tree or rock, finding a way to be involved without having to be the skit's focus. In ten minutes, the groups had bonded and collaborated. They connected their creative energies and brought a Torah moment to life.

Sharon called them back together. "Everyone take a seat. Welcome to Exodus Theater. This morning, just sit back, relax, and let your imagination guide you through the people and places in the Book of Exodus."

Each skit was unique. People moved their bodies in waves as the Sea. Children jumped up and down as frogs. Moses, in various groups, was played by a kindergarten girl, a middle-aged father, and a boy with autism who had never participated in an assembly before. Stealing the show was one kid's Bubbe, who happened to be visiting that week. She played God in the Burning Bush scene. "Oy, vey es mir, Moses, would you listen to me already?" she pleaded.

Sharon looked at her watch. Whoops! Assembly ran five minutes over. She thanked everyone for experimenting with her, and for all of their engagement with the Torah stories. She wished everyone a great morning in classroom. No one moved too quickly. "Do we have to go to class?" asked one student. "This was really fun, let's do more."

We'll try it again, thought Sharon. There must be other ways, too, other frameworks that allow students to work so collaboratively. There must be other ways to use drama to engage our families in Jewish learning, to bring our texts to life. Sharon was committed to finding them, creating them, bringing them to her community.

WHY DRAMA?

My own professional training is in theater and creative writing, as well as in Jewish education, and over the last ten years I have been working on ways to integrate drama into Jewish learning. I believe that all Jewish educators, like Sharon, regardless of their background in theater, can simply and easily use drama as an educational modality. With a little guidance and a willingness to play, Jewish educators can greatly enrich their schools, youth groups, camps, and communities with this form of creative expression.

Often, in my teacher workshops, I hear a list of concerns, and sometimes objections, too. These include, "It takes too much time to do a play," "The kids get too silly and don't learn anything," and "I can't find a play about the subject matter I need to teach." These concerns and others are valid, but there are solutions to these worries. Using drama successfully takes some forethought, guidance, and planning on the teacher's part. In this chapter, I will outline some subject areas, techniques, and situations in which a little drama training can go a long way. I will demonstrate that the positives of using drama far outweigh any anxieties that may arise from trying out something new.

MULTIPLE INTELLIGENCES: WHAT ALL DRAMATISTS KNOW

Howard Gardner's pluralistic theory of multiple intelligences[1] has revolutionized the way we think about reaching our students. The "old school" model of frontal teaching — a lecture format with little room for creative engagement — clearly misses those students whose intelligence is measured outside the linguistic mode. In Jewish education, thinking in terms of multiple intelligences offers a wealth of creative opportunities. Yet, using

this theory can also feel a bit daunting when planning actual lessons. With two hours a week to teach Hebrew, Bible, Holidays, History, Ritual, and Ethics — and using all of the seven (no, now it's nine) intelligences, it's a challenge!

Have no fear, teachers. Drama is here. Long before Gardner's theory, drama teachers knew that doing plays engaged students creatively and intellectually in a wide variety of ways. Let's take a walk through a drama experience prototype.

Pesach is coming. There will be an all-school family program. The principal has asked every teacher to come up with a short presentation about some aspect of Pesach. What to do? How about a play? You talk to the students about what part of Pesach they would like to focus on. Suggestions include: Elijah, Passover in the concentration camps (you've just read an article about it), different kinds of charoset, and the Four Questions. Okay. Where to find a play touching on any of this?

Why not have the students write the play? This will engage the kids with linguistic intelligence. Meanwhile, those with the logical-mathematical intelligence can start designing and building a set. Their friends with spatial intelligence can decorate the set and start making costumes. Musical intelligence? Please, they'll be rapping and dancing before the script is even finished. The kinesthetic Intelligence kids will shine as actors. Those who have a flair for interpersonal intelligence make excellent assistant directors, stage managers, or publicity people. You can engage the sense of intrapersonal intelligence after the play, by giving all the students time to journal and reflect on their experience.

But how much time does this process take? It absolutely depends on how much time you can allow. You can do a "quickie" process, taking a bit more time than Sharon's impromptu exercise, or you can build the play making into a special project that spans a few weeks. If you want to be very elaborate, see if parents will support scheduling an extra rehearsal or two after or outside of class. But, realistically, most of us don't have that luxury of time. What follows is an outline for creating a short, original play in two classes.

---

[1]For more information on this theory, see Chapter 27, "Multiple Intelligences" by Renee Holtz and Barbara Lapetina, pp. 323-333 in this volume.

CREATING A CLASS PLAY: BREAKING IT DOWN

Setting Guidelines

Before starting any creative project, talk with students about your expectations for behavior. Emphasize that in collaborations, students really want to use their listening skills; and make sure that everyone in the group is able to contribute his/her ideas. More often than not, you won't have problems with behavior issues because students will be engaged and enjoying the social component of the drama experience. However, as a teacher, no one knows your class better than you; use your judgment. If you have a particularly unruly group, let them know ahead of time that working on a play isn't "goof-off" time, and that if they can't handle themselves with *derech eretz* (appropriate behavior), you have alternate, very boring assignments lined up for them.

Outlining the Play

(Time: 10-15 minutes)

As a class, talk through the structure of the play. In the above example, the class wants to focus on the meaning of Pesach, touching on Elijah, maybe the Holocaust, and include elements of the *Seder* like *charoset* and the Four Questions. To start, brainstorm about a topic, story, period in history, value, or issue until you come to a general theme on which everyone can agree. Then, brainstorm together about the following dramatic elements:

Characters: Who are the characters in the play/skit? What are their goals/needs? How will they achieve them?

Setting: Where does your play take place? Does the setting change within the play? What would happen if we put the characters in an unusual setting?

Action: What *happens* in the play? How do the characters change? What do they learn that they didn't know at the beginning of the play? What obstacles do they face?

Let's say that a class decides that the main character is Elijah and that he visits a family at their *Seder* (we'll need kids, parents, grandparents, etc.). The youngest child is supposed to sing the Four Questions and is nervous. One of the grandparents is a Holocaust survivor. She tells about what it was like not being able to have a Passover *Seder*. The play is set at the family's *Seder* in the grandparents' home. The main action is that the youngest child is afraid to sing the Four Questions, but Elijah comes early to encourage her to do it. Only the little girl can see/talk to Elijah. He convinces her that she will sing beautifully. The girl is able to sing the questions, and everyone is proud.

Writing the Play

(Time: 30-45 minutes)

Now, everyone is on the same page and ready to get started. Depending on the size of the class, you may want to select a small group to be the writers. If you have a very small class, everyone may work together. Here are a few techniques to take the initial idea and transform it into a play.

Two Person Scene Writing (Great for Grades 4 and up)

Assign each student a character (say, Elijah or the Young Girl). Use one piece of paper. One person writes an opening line and then passes it to the other person. Without talking, he/she responds by writing another line. Continue in this back and forth fashion until a scene is written. For example, first student writes:

Elijah: Hello, Sarah. Don't be afraid, I'm the Prophet, Elijah.

(He then passes the paper to student number two. She reads it and writes the second line.)

Sarah: I thought you would come to the *Seder* later, when we open the door for you.

(She gives the paper back to "Elijah." He reads it and writes.)

Elijah: I was in the neighborhood, thought I'd drop in. So what's up?"

(They continue writing and in a few minutes, *voila*! You have a scene.)

Group Improv (K-3 with guidance. Grades 4 and up very easily)

Assign each "writer" a character. If doing the *Seder* scene, give each person a family member's identity. Ask him or her to sit at the table. Outline a few "beats" for them to improvise with. For example:

1. Everyone comes to the *Seder* table, greets each other, and sits down.

2. Grandpa begins the *Seder*.

3. Sarah is really nervous and tries to make excuses about singing the Four Questions.

4. Elijah comes and talks to Sarah. No one notices her getting up from the table and talking with him.

5. Sarah returns and sings the Four Questions beautifully. Everyone is happy.

6. Grandma tells the family about how when she was girl in the concentration camps, she couldn't celebrate Pesach. She explains how happy she is to be together with the family.

7. Time for dinner — everyone eats!

As "director," give the improvisers the directive and then let them play for a few minutes. You can assign one student as scribe to take notes or you can use a tape recorder and later transcribe and edit the scenes.

Designing the Play and Adding the Details

(Time: 30-45 minutes)

Remember the multiple intelligences? While engaging the acting/writing group, other participants can work on painting sets, assembling costumes, etc. How can all of this be going on simultaneously? This is a great time to use *madrichim* (teen assistants) or parent volunteers. I have always found parents more than willing to help out with a class play. In fact, I have been surprised by the wonderful skills and talents of the parents — some have tremendous background in the arts! Send out an information form or e-mail at the beginning of the year, asking parents to list any special skills or hobbies and any background or experience in the arts. They will be flattered to be called and asked to come help out with scene painting, etc.

Special Touches

The following are a few inexpensive, easy ways to add those special touches to your play.

Costumes

Every teacher should have a class costume box full of scarves, shawls, hats, sticks, beards, etc. A ten dollar investment can acquire a very large traveling costume trunk. Go through closets and ask friends and family to donate any out-of-style or just-don't-fit-anymore garments. Kids will take a polyester dress from the 1970s and transform it into the perfect gown for Queen Esther! Visit a novelty shop (or your local drug store right after Halloween) and pick out a few special items, such as funny noses or glasses.

As the writing crew is developing a play, let the costumers pick out and put together outfits for each character. By analyzing what Elijah might wear, they are learning about the essence of the character.

Set Building

In most schools, plays are staged in the classroom or maybe the social hall. At a teacher's disposal are a few chairs or folding tables to arrange and use as a set. Just add a few cardboard boxes, and with the right actors, miracles occur! Let students attach the boxes to make doorways, arches, pyramids, whatever you need. In this case, it might be a door from which Elijah enters and exits.

Scene Painting

Ah, the joys of butcher paper, some markers, or even paint and a little tape! Put the visual artist types together, and they'll create Bubbe and Zayde's living room, complete with bookshelves and *tzotchkes*. Tape the decorated butcher paper to your blackboard and let the imagination do the rest!

The Song and Dance Number

Don't forget those kinesthetic kids! While you've got your basic script cooking, why not add a little musical number, just for kicks? What if Elijah sang a number with a backup chorus about his travels on Pesach? Where else in this little play might a song go? Give the musical kids a chance to work together and put together a song or two.

Putting It All Together

(Time: 30-45 minutes)

If you can afford the time, do a dress rehearsal with the entire cast. If not, do a quick read-through. Invite your guests to come take a seat, and then . . . lights, camera, action. You've got a show.

OTHER USES FOR DRAMA

Working together to create an original play is just one way to use drama in the Jewish classroom or camp setting. There are hundreds of ways to incorporate drama activities into regular lesson plans. Adding a drama activity can increase student participation and encourage cooperative learning. Drama can reinforce history, Torah, *tefilah*, values, holidays — absolutely anything that's in the curriculum. Drama can work just as well in the early childhood classroom as in a Hebrew High School situation.

The following are a range of activities for different developmental ages.

Early Childhood

Holiday Pantomimes

Pick any holiday and ask students to show a "movement" associated with the holiday. For example, some Shabbat movements might include setting the table, baking *challah*, lighting candles, pouring juice, etc. Have the class try each movement together. Then put on some music related to the holiday and invite students to do the holiday movements in rhythm with the music. Students can play with repetition, try new movements, work together and alone, etc.

Torah Statues

Read a Torah story. Talk about the different characters in the story. Ask students to find a way to "physicalize" each character. How would Moses walk as he climbs up Mount Sinai? How did Queen Esther look when she was chosen to be queen? Let the students walk around the room, trying the different characters in the story. Call "freeze" and invite the students to look around at the statues. Ask students which character they are.

Kindergarten-Grade 3

Soundscape

In sharing a Torah or other story, stop at appropriate moments and ask students to create the sounds they imagine. They can use their bodies, voices, and instruments (if you like). For example:

- In teaching creation, ask students to make the sounds for each separate day of creation.

- In telling Noah's ark, have students to make the flood sounds, animal sounds, etc.

- When telling any "traveling" tale (such as one about Abraham and Sarah), have students make the clip-clop noise of the camels.

Also, pause and ask students what characters might be saying to each other that is not written in the story. For example, what did the Hebrew slaves say to each other as they were leaving Egypt?

Make Puppets and Prepare Puppet Show

Share a Torah or holiday story with students and allow them to create their favorite character using paper bags, socks, etc. The teacher can tell the story while puppets act it out. For older students (Grades 2-3) give them time to "re-create" the story on their own in small groups and allow them to practice a more formal puppet show.

Grades 4-7

Writing Monologues

Read a short bit of Torah text out loud. Ask students to write down questions as they hear the text. Write all of the questions on the board (but don't discuss). Ask students to pick a character from the text (can include inanimate characters or animals, such as Moshe's stick, the ram from the *Akedah* — binding of Isaac, etc.). Now do the "circling exercise" in which students write character's name in the middle of a piece of paper. Around it, they make circles containing answers to the following questions:

- What does the character look like? What is his/her emotional state?

- Does he/she have a best friend? In whom does he/she confide?

- What does the character want? What does he/she fear?

- Does he/she have any pastimes (hobbies)? What things does he/she like to do? hate to do?

Next, ask the students to write a short monologue, answering one of the questions from the discussion, but writing from the character's perspective. If students are stuck, have them start with a sentence like one of these: "I want _____." "I fear _____." "I need _____." Time the students (five minutes is sufficient to begin with). Ask students to share their work. Have them exchange monologues and work on performing each other's monologues.

Using Games

The following games can be used with teaching history, Bible, etc.

- *The Object Game* - Assign students a biblical or historical character. Hand them an everyday object (stapler, chalk, tape, etc.). Ask them to explain how they use that object in their life. The object can become anything — a stapler might be a tool the Israelites used in Egypt when making bricks, etc.

- *The Pantomime Game* - Write cards that tell an action for part of a story you have read (for example, Joseph's brothers sell him to a caravan for money). Divide students into pairs or small groups and have them practice pantomiming the action. The other students watch each pantomime and guess what the action is.

- *Who Am I?* - Students take on the identity of a character from the weekly Torah portion, a famous person in history, a literary character, etc. Other students ask yes and no questions until they figure out the character's identity. For example: Are you married? Do you live in Egypt? Do you have children?

Grades 7 and Up

History Party

This activity can focus on characters from one historical period or from different times. If doing the party as an introduction to a unit, assign each student a character and then provide time for research about the person's life. For the party itself, students should "meet and greet" as many guests as possible and share at least three facts about themselves. They can begin by saying, "Hello, I'm Moses Maimonides and I lived _____." You can stop guests periodically and ask them to share a bit about the person they're speaking to. Provide drinks and snacks to make the atmosphere festive!

Television Format

Let's face it, our kids *know* TV. Why not use it to our advantage? Choose among television's many formats and find a creative way to explore history, ethics, current events, or Bible. Ideas include:

> *Live and Late Breaking!* - Students play reporters covering major events: the ten plagues, the first World Zionist Conference, etc.

> *Talk Show* - Explore a topical issue in a talk show format with students playing out experts from various angles of the issue.

> *Commercials* - Students can create commercials for "products" used in historical periods. Take everyday objects (staplers, coffee mugs, telephones, etc.) and explain what they were used for back then.

DON'T FORGET TZEDAKAH PROJECTS

Nothing delights people in a senior citizen's home like watching a group of young people perform a play. For many elderly Jewish people, visits from school groups are their only contact with young people. When you create a class play, perform a short skit, or put together an original show by using the drama activities above, you can extend the *mitzvah* of learning by bringing your students to a nursing home to perform. This experience can also help the students, who have not all experienced this type of setting before. The play will "break the ice" and will allow students and residents to mingle more easily afterward.

USING THEATER IN THE COMMUNITY

Many of our communities are fortunate to have a professional Jewish theater in our midst, or to have professional theaters that, from time to time, perform plays of Jewish interest. A wonderful way to introduce students to the rich world of Jewish theater is by taking them to such a play of Jewish interest. In most instances, the play's director will be happy to talk with you about the play's subject matter, and you can determine how it might connect to your curriculum. For example, in the last two years, I have taken students to see a production of Chaim Potok's classic, *The Chosen*. This powerful play touches on many different themes found within a typical religious school's curriculum: Zionism, the Holocaust, different denominations/traditions within Judaism, Jews in sports, etc. When taking a group of students to see a play, I ask them questions ahead of time so that they will look for or pay attention to specific things. For example, for *The Chosen* production, I asked students: How does the play portray people in a Hasidic context studying Talmud? How does this form of study differ from that of Reuven and his father who are modern Orthodox Jews?

Planting a seed in the students' minds ahead of time enables them to focus on something relevant to the curriculum, while also taking in the play as a whole entity. As a follow-up, have a discussion in class. If desired, use the play to inspire other activities, such as having the students recreate some of the scenes or write their own skits about one of the play's themes. It is also helpful to contact the theater ahead of time to see if they have prepared a special teacher's guide for the play or to arrange a talk-back session with the director and cast following the show.

To find a Jewish theatre close to your community, contact the Association of Jewish Theaters at their web site, www.wjt.ca/ajt.htm.

TEACHER AS CHARACTER

One last suggestion: Whether you are an early childhood teacher, a camp director, a parent volunteer, or any other leader in a Jewish context, please consider the idea of "taking on a character." What better way to introduce students to a historical, literary or biblical figure than to allow them to meet and ask that figure some questions? Sure, it will take a little guts on your part, and perhaps some research, but the results will make any initial cringing worth it!

Where to begin? Think about what costume or prop would help you "feel" like the character. What prop could introduce Eve? Well, why not an apple? How about Noah? Maybe a raincoat or an umbrella. Joseph — that's too easy! Think about some of the characters who aren't given much description and allow your imagination to open up the possibilities of their character. You can also tell a story from a made-up character's perspective. For example, tell the Purim story through the eyes of a maid in King Ahashuverus's palace. Just put on a little apron, grab a feather duster, and go!

It works really well to have a teen assistant or parent volunteer give a big introduction while a teacher steps out of the room to put on the costume, take a deep breath, and get "into character." Think about how the character would walk, talk, and stand. As the character, tell the students a bit about yourself and about your story, and then allow them to ask questions.

This activity can be adapted to any situation. One of my co-teachers and I used to begin every day of our second grade class as the letter in the *alef bet* that we would be studying that day. For example, for *gimel*, I ran into the classroom with cheerleader pom-poms and a big "*gimel*" taped to my sweatshirt. "Gimme a *gimel*!" I cheered, and then called out words that started with *gimel* that I made into little cheers. The kids got the "g" sound before we formally started class and remembered some of the *gimel* words that we learned later in our lesson. Silly, yes — but worth it for the learning!

HEBREW THROUGH DRAMA

Many of the above activities and suggestions can be adapted for learning and reenforcing Hebrew. Students could write simple skits in Hebrew or could role-play using vocabulary words. For example, suppose a class is learning words associated with the home or family. Assign each student to play a member of the family and ask them to act out a simple conversation, perhaps about making dinner or planning a family outing. Translate a short play into Hebrew for the students to perform or have them act out a Hebrew poem or song. Be creative and have fun!

CONCLUSION

Sharon, the school director in the opening vignette, was really thrilled with her experiment in using drama at the opening assembly. During the week following her experiment, she thought about ways that drama could help some of the "challenge areas" in her school.

How do you think Sharon could use drama to:

1. help improve the morale of both teachers and students with a rather unruly group of seventh graders whose curriculum includes American Jewish History, Hebrew, Jewish Values, and current events? Teachers had tried a wide variety of techniques, including films, discussions, and field trips. Still, the group had never really come together as a community, and many students dropped out after their B'nai Mitzvah. Sharon desperately needed a way to energize both teachers and students. How could drama help this situation?

2. make prayer more meaningful for students in Grades 3-6? Sharon has observed that while her teaching staff is excellent at seeing that students are able to sing or recite *tefilot*, she often wonders how comfortable they are discussing the meanings of the prayers with her students. Sharon cringes at hearing the students always going through the prayers by rote, without having an opportunity to connect to the prayer's meaning. What methods might she suggest for teachers to use creative drama techniques to explore *tefilot*?

3. create exciting, interactive family education programs? Looking at her calendar, she has a Shabbat family education program for kindergarten and first grade scheduled and another family education program for Grades 4 and 5 about *tzedakah*. Sharon wants to put all of the parents at ease; some are much more Jewishly knowledgable than others. How could she use drama games, skits, or other such activities to connect all of the families?

By now, you are surely convinced that Jewish teachers can greatly increase the excitement, joy, and learning in their classrooms through the use of creative drama. Drama reaches students according to their natural intelligences and offers an opportunity for true collaboration and community building. Drama reenforces learning and sparks the imagination so that students can step in and explore Jewish subjects from the inside out. Depending on the time a teacher gives drama, it can be used as a simple opener or can become a greater class project, full of extended learning. Perhaps most important of all is the result you will see when students are creatively engaged: a happy classroom, full of productive students.

Unused corners can make for marvelous spaces for creative dramatization. We moved our *Tefilah* (worship service) into the forest one Yom HaShoah with partisans by turning off the lights. Each class had learned about the partisans in class. On Sunday morning, we crept together down to the back basement hallway, which connects the two wings of our *shul*, and which can be completely darkened. We had asked beforehand about anyone who was afraid of the dark, and those who were went with teachers and went last, once there was some light in the hallway (from the end door being opened by the first groups out). Everybody was asked to imagine that they were partisans in the forest, and that they must move as silently as possible. Feeling their way along the cold concrete blocks of the hallway, the students moved from one end to the other, then crept on tip-toe into an unheated classroom without chairs. Surrounded by trees left over from Tu B'Shevat, they sat on the floor and each class led the silent version of each prayer that they had prepared (during *davening* workshops the previous week). Everyone left quietly, and went back to class to debrief. It was a powerful experience, which we shared with parents in a letter home. And it took up little more time than a regular *davening*.

(Anne Johnston, New Haven, Connecticut)

TEACHING CONSIDERATIONS

- What do you need to use drama successfully in your classroom? Follow this simple checklist and you will be sure to succeed.

- Examine your curriculum and find themes or subjects that would lend themselves to drama.

- Set guidelines and expectations for class behavior.

- Send out a form to parents, asking them to list background or interest in the arts.

- Clear an area of the room or arrange to use the social hall so that you have sufficient room for drama activities.

- Look in your Jewish newspaper or the arts and entertainment section of your local paper and see if there are any Jewish plays in production.

- Collect used or oversized clothing, hats, jewelry, etc., to use for costumes, and cardboard boxes to use for set building.

- Talk with your school director and find out if there are any school assemblies coming up, for which a drama performance would be appropriate.

- Browse the A.R.E. Publishing Catalog and select books of Jewish plays for use in your classroom.

- Select a character that your students will be studying and plan out your costume/props for that character's "visit" to class.

- Talk to other teachers on your staff and find out how they might like to collaborate with you on a theater project.

BIBLIOGRAPHY

Books about Drama in the Classroom

Albert, Eleanor. *Jewish Story Theater.* Los Angeles, CA: Torah Aura Productions, 1989.

This book provides simple instructions and examples for turning textbook stories into story theater-style plays.

Citron, Samuel J. *Dramatics for Creative Teaching.* New York: United Synagogue of America, 1961.

Citron's classic anthology gives examples, play samples, and ideas for using drama in the Jewish classroom.

Lepkin, Biela. *Creative Drama in the Hebrew School.* Haifa, Israel: Pinath-Hasefer, 1978.

This wonderful book, written by a creative Jewish theater teacher, supplies drama exercises for subjects including Hebrew, holidays, and Bible.

Pitzele, Peter A. *Scripture Windows: Toward a Practice of Bibliodrama.* Los Angeles, CA: Torah Aura, 1998.

Pitzele is the founder of the "Bibliodrama" movement and his book offers insight into this very specific practice of bringing biblical characters to life.

Books of Jewish Plays

Allen, Richard J. *Parashah Plays.* Denver, CO: A.R.E. Publishing, Inc., 2000.

A play (often humorous) for every single *parashah*!

Beiner, Stan J. *Class Acts.* Denver, CO: A.R.E. Publishing, Inc., 1992.

Thirty plays, for ages preschool through high school, and ranging in subject from Torah to contemporary issues.

_____. *Bible Scenes: Joshua To Solomon.* Denver, CO: A.R.E. Publishing, Inc. 1988.

Short plays inspired by the books of Joshua, Judges, Samuel, and Kings.

_____. *Sedra Scenes: Skits for Every Torah Portion.* Denver, CO: A.R.E. Publishing, Inc., 1982.

The first book of plays based on every Torah portion, now a classic.

Kaplan, Gabrielle Suzanne. *Extraordinary Jews: Staging Their Lives.* Denver, CO: A.R.E. Publishing, Inc., 2001.

This book of plays by the author of this chapter is appropriate for teenagers. The plays focus on the lives of eight Jews who have made a difference through *tikkun olam* — healing the world: Hannah Senesh, Bella Abzug, Ida Kaminska, Emma Goldman, Leonard Bernstein, Rabbi Abraham Joshua Heshel, Aaron Lansky, and Yitzhak Rabin.

_____. *The Magic Tanach and Other Short Plays.* Denver, CO: A.R.E. Publishing, Inc., 1999.

Twenty-four imaginative plays for elementary to high school, students that focus on sacred texts, wisdom stories, Jewish values, and holidays.

Patera, Meridith Shaw. *Kings and Things: 20 Jewish Plays for Kids 8 To 18.* Denver, CO: A.R.E. Publishing, Inc., 1996.

This book contains plays for elementary to high school students on such topics as major holidays, Bible stories, Israel, Holocaust, folktales, and Jewish values. Each can be produced with minimal costumes and props or as Readers Theater.

———. *Skits and Shpiels: 14 Plays for Grades 4 To 9.* Denver, CO: A.R.E. Publishing, Inc., 2002.

This set of 14 fun, original scripts, each about 15 to 30 minutes in length, is ready to photocopy for actors. Production notes and a CD-ROM are also included. Topics include: holidays, Bible, Jewish folktales, *midrash*, Talmud, *tzedakah*, and Israel.

Shakow, Zara, ed. *Curtain Time!* New York: Jonathan David Publishers. 1985.

More skits, plays, and drama ideas with Jewish themes.

CHAPTER 48

Enriching Instruction with Music[1]

Julie Jaslow Auerbach

When a replacement for an ailing Kindergarten through third grade music teacher was needed, my child's preschool teacher recalled that I played guitar and loved to sing. The preschool teacher recommended me, and a new world opened up.

Many a Jewish music teacher has come into the profession through the love of Jewish music and an eagerness to share a passion and a love for singing and a desire to encourage others to lift their voices, too. Music is in our blood. It is as ancient as the "Mi Chamocha," the song our people sang at the shores of the Reed Sea while Miriam led the women in dance (Exodus 15:1-21), the Psalms of King David, and the Torah trope we chant each week. *Piyyutim* (religious poems) fill our *Siddur*. Melodies that were sung in the *shtetls* have been combined with jazz to become the Klezmer music we know today. Classical compositions, Broadway theatre and Hollywood films, Cantorial, liturgical, Israeli folk, dance, popular, and rock — you name it, it's a part of our Jewish musical heritage!

Jews have sung throughout the generations when praying, when reading Torah or Haftarah, to teach each other, to express feelings, to tell a story, or to preserve a memory. With words from liturgy, the Torah, poets, and our own hearts, there is a magnificent abundance of Jewish music today!

As I prepared for my first class with the kindergarten children, I tried to recall the songs that appealed to me. Since it was September, I would begin at the beginning, of course, with Rosh HaShanah songs. As that first year went by, encouraged by the Education Director, Judy Lichtig, we began to organize our musical curriculum to create cohesion between the religious school classroom and the music classroom. Picking up on the themes

presented by the Union of American Hebrew Congregations in 1982 in their experimental edition of "To See the World with Jewish Eyes," which stressed integrating the holidays, we came up with lists of songs that would guide us through the years to follow. It was then, with Judy's encouragement, that I began to write songs.

When instinct told me that I needed to start with a song that would let students know that a music session was to begin, I slipped into the synagogue's ready culture and led off services with "Bim Bam," even though it was Sunday and not Saturday morning. At the suggestion of the Rabbi of the congregation, I wrote a song I called "Boker Tov" and presented it to him as a birthday gift.

While a lot of music exists already, some may be in a music teacher's head waiting to be created. How we integrate the known and obvious songs with the less well-known or obscure song may make all the difference to a challenging setting or class of students. There are broad aspects of Jewish music to cover in the teaching of Jewish music as a subject; several will be considered in this chapter. But there are also ways that Jewish music can enhance the curriculum or teaching of Jewish subjects. That, too, will be discussed in the pages that follow.

INTEGRATING MUSIC WITH CURRICULUM

Prayer

A group of third and fourth graders are assembled in the sanctuary for music. Each has a copy of the lyrics to the song "So Many Questions" by Doug Cotler.[2]

The teacher says, " I am going to sing a song through for you. You have the words, so please fol-

---

[1]This chapter is dedicated to the memory of Alice Epstein Weinstein, who graced the Cleveland Jewish community, and later the American educational community, and who, with her

vast knowledge of Jewish music, lovingly supported and enabled friends and colleagues.

[2]On his CD, *Listen*, and in *The Doug Cotler Songbook*.

low along. After I finish singing the song, we are going to talk about it."

After modeling the song, the teacher then asks the students, "Have any of you ever thought of any of the same questions that are included in this song?" Immediately, many hands go up. A lively discussion ensues about God, the world, and our place in it.

Since the song ends with the words of the "Barchu," the teacher teaches the students to sing the song, thus, moving the group into Tefilah.

Prayer is a difficult subject to teach, for one must get both the keva (meaning) and the kavanah (intent). A songwriter like Doug Cotler makes the job a little easier with songs that include both the prayer lyrics and his own personal interpretation of the prayer. It gives children an opportunity to explore a prayer in a safe way.

We are fortunate today, as so many songwriters have written songs with lyrical explanations. Rabbi Joe Black's "Nikavim Nikavim"[3] describes both feelings and intentions for "Asher Yatzar," the prayer from the Shacharit (morning) worship service that speaks to the healthy functioning of our bodies. Debbie Friedman's "Mi Shebeirach"[4] also provides such opportunities in its elaboration on the theme of healing.

Long-standing prayer melodies — the traditional nusach — echo the fervor and flavor of yesterday's minyanim and continue to resonate in the present. Who can deny the connection made when singing the Torah trope for "Az Yashir Moshe" (Exodus 15) when students realize just how many generations have come and gone since then. Nor can we overlook the kind of spiritual power latent in "Dayenu" that we sing each year at our Pesach Sedarim.

In the Conservative settings in which I work, it is customary to chant the appropriate nusach for the prayers. Nonetheless, I have recently begun experimenting with some of the more popular melodic tunes that now exist. The chanted "Barchu" has thus been supplanted with a melody by Ben Siegel, and the Debbie Friedman "V'ahavta" has also been introduced.[5] I have discovered that alternating the melodies helps students learn the words. My first and second graders were having dif-

ficulty with the "Barchu" until I introduced the catchier melody. Similarly, they readily learned the words of the "V'ahavta" because of the compelling nature of that melody. Later on, at the weekly Shabbat service, they can learn the traditional melodies. Just as there are different kinds of learners who need different kinds of curricular stimulants, so, too, are there different kinds of melodies that appeal to different personalities in a classroom.

In a class conducted for adults, two prominent Cantors spoke about Jewish music. They talked about their individual career paths, their own early interests in Jewish music, as well as the history of hazzanut (Cantorial music), and the role of the Cantor in history and today.

A Cantor's knowledge and repertoire is not limited to the pulpit. Cantorial music tells a Jewish historical story through individual melodies as well as in liturgical pieces. Each Cantor is a musical person, who has a strong insight into music beyond what is sung on the bimah.

At a CAJE workshop at the University of Massachusetts entitled the "Shema through the Life Cycle," educator Ben Zion Kogen beautifully sang through several versions of the "Shema," asking the attendees if they could place each melody. Some were easy, some a bit harder. After a few guesses, all answers were revealed.

Doug Cotler told a story in that same workshop about a man who came to Cantor Cotler (Doug's father) to complain that he had not sung the traditional "Mi Chamocha." Cantor Cotler sang a very "cantorial" sounding melody and asked the man if that was the one he wanted. Happily, the man replied, "Yes, yes, that's it!" to which Cantor Cotler responded, "I just made it up."

One Friday night, the Rabbi with whom I work asked me to sing the traditional "V'shamru." Which one was it? It was the one the congregation usually sings each week. Traditional is often in the ear and mind of the beholder.

Prayer melodies not only vary from generation to generation, but from part of the service to part of the service — and from service to service! Culturally, there are the Ashkenazic melodies from

---

[3] On his CD and audiotape, *Leave a Little Bit Undone*.

[4] On her CD, audiotape, and in the accompanying Songbook, *And You Shall Be a Blessing*.

[5] Both of these melodies can be found in *Manginot*, edited by Stephen Richards (New York: Transcontinental Music Publications, 1992).

Europe with which most Americans are familiar. Yet, of late, we also sing the distinctive, highly rhythmic Sephardic melodies from Mediterranean and Arabic countries in which Jews have lived. And then there is the whole proliferation of Hasidic Song Festival melodies, like Uzi Hitman's *"Adon Olam"*[6] or Tzvika Pik's *"Shema."*[7] Finally, we have what has been called American *nusach*, the folk/pop/rock music that American Jewish musicians have been creating over the last several decades.

Thus, even in the traditional setting, the melody for the *"Shema"* could be sung using several melodies through the course of a week, in addition to what we refer to as the "traditional" one. With each melody we teach, we enrich the child's repertoire and add another layer to the child's understanding of the prayer itself and also of the context in which the song is sung or the origin of its composer.

Hebrew Language

I walked into my son's day school Kindergarten classroom many years ago and watched Judaics teacher Anne Sportas talk about the weather. Immediately, my mind connected to the ever present weather chart I had seen in preschool classrooms. I saw a "window of opportunity" within a Hebrew song for language and sound development. When Anne finished, I asked her if she could use a weather song. She said yes, and I wrote "Mah Mezeg Ha'avir" (What Is the Weather?), available on my audiotape Seasoned with Song.

The acquisition of Hebrew language is an important part of a Jewish child's education. However, developing the ability to hear and duplicate the sounds is not an easy task when you consider that most of the average Jewish child's life is *not* spent in an environment in which he/she hears the language. In your classroom, play CDs, tapes, and recordings of Israeli songs and music. Acquire some of the many available Israeli children's recorded songs from a Jewish library or a Jewish bookstore. Browse through Israeli children's songbooks. Every Hebrew word heard by a child affects the Hebrew sounds that will later be duplicated by that youngster.

Here are some tips regarding Hebrew:

- Begin playing Israeli music as early as possible for the language, the tempo, and the melodies.

- Enunciate the Hebrew words clearly when teaching a song, and be sure to provide the meaning, preferably through action or pictures.

- Students must also learn by doing. So, introduce the words and concepts and then have them echo the words back and forth to you.

- Phrases are important. Gather the words into appropriate phrases and repeat them.

- Watch for syntax. Too often a composer will "tweak" a word to have it fit a melody.

- Use popular Israeli songs that have simple repetition patterns. These represent a great way to teach language.

- Find words in the *Siddur* and use them with a song to connect to the language of Hebrew prayer.

- Ask the students to find or isolate words they know and then introduce the newer words in the song.

- Identify a movement to associate with a Hebrew word or introduce Hebrew sign language. (There are several books that contain the symbols. These include *Signs in Judaism* by Adele Kronick Shuart, and *Celebrating Judaism in the Home: A Manual for Deaf Families* by Rabbi Miriam Baitch.)

- Rewrite well-known English songs to include or use Hebrew words or phrases. (For example, the "Hokey Pokey" can be done using words for Hebrew body parts.)

- Visual learners will need to see those words. Make song sheets, or use an overhead projector with any book in which the words may appear.

---

[6]On his CD, *Uzi Hitman Sings.*

[7]This song can be found in any collection of Hasidic Song Festival recordings.

MUSIC AS A CURRICULUM ENHANCER

The Song as Text

I was once asked to teach some Purim songs to a group of third through fifth graders. I chose a selection of songs, some modern, some folk, traditional, English, and Hebrew. One song, "A Wicked, Wicked Man," had been the most popular Purim song of my youth, so I included it with all the verses.

Have you ever really looked at all the verses of "A Wicked, Wicked Man"? In this post 9/11 world, they are really scary. All of a sudden I had found myself teaching a song to children with frightening lyrics! What to do?

The students and I completed the song and then I asked them to take a good look at the lyrics. "Anyone see anything troubling here?" I asked. Hands went up and a wonderful discussion about lyrics and contexts and history took place.

We sometimes take the lyrics of songs for granted. Perhaps we have sung the song so often that we don't think about the words, or we become too absorbed in the melody. However, it is important not to overlook them.

Sixth graders are studying the tallit. The lyrics of Craig Taubman's "V'havienu"[8] are in front of them. "Collect into one, the memory . . ." Students are asked to comment on what Craig is saying in his song. "How do we collect the memories when we pull our tzitzit together?" the teacher asks. And "Who are in the memories?"

First graders are learning about the Jewish life cycle. A CD player is playing Julie Auerbach's "The Jewish Life Cycle Song"[9] as they enter the room. The song describes life cycle events from birth through Consecration, B'nai Mitzvah, and marriage, with the whole cycle starting over again with a new birth.

In a fifth grade Jewish history class, students read through the lyrics to Auerbach's "Once We Were Nomads." They try to identify the period during which each of the occupations written about occurs. When were Jews farmers and shepherds? When were we artisans? teachers? lawyers? peddlers? They find out more about the people in the song such as Ben-Gurion or Maimonides. The song lists in a historical context many people and many occupations.

Music is not for music teachers alone, but for classroom teachers as well. We read in the Talmud (*Eruvin* 54b) how Moses was taught the lesson by God. He in turn taught it to Aaron, then to Aaron's sons, then to the Elders, and then to the people of Israel. Then Moses left, and Aaron took up the teaching of the lesson, first to his sons, then to the Elders, and then to the people of Israel. He left, and his sons taught the lesson, first to the Elders and then to the people. Lastly, the Elders taught the lesson to the people of Israel. Everyone heard the lesson four times. "From the aforementioned procedure, Rabbi Eliezer inferred: It is a person's duty to repeat a lesson to his pupil four times, a practice that may be deduced by an argument *a fortiori*: if Aaron who learned from Moses, and Moses who learned [directly] from the Almighty, had to have their lesson repeated four times, all the more so by far an ordinary pupil who learns from an ordinary teacher." Thus we moderns can infer (and this is borne out in Gardiner's theory of multiple intelligences)[10] that it is not enough to teach a lesson in one modality, but one must use four. Music should be one of these because of its objectivity, its accessibility, and because of the enjoyment it provides.

Consider for Jewish history: Doug Cotler's "Standing on the Shoulders" (on the recording, *Listen*), or Safam's "World of Our Fathers" (on the recording, *Sons of Safam*).

Consider for life cycles: "*Shema B'ni*" by Cotler and Taubman (on Cotler's recording, *Whispers in the Wind* and Taubman's recording, *Journey*).

Consider for biblical stories: "Miriam's Song" by Debbie Friedman for the Exodus story (on the recording, *And You Shall Be a Blessing* and in the accompanying songbook), Sam Glaser's "Across the River" for Abraham (on his recording, *Kol Bamidbar* and in the accompanying songbook), and for Joseph (of course!) songs from "Joseph and the Amazing Technicolor Dream Coat."

Consider for the history of Israel: "*V'ulai*," "*Ufaratza*," and "*Shir Lashalom*." The lyrics are wonderful discussion triggers. The songs can be found in any good collection of Israeli folk music or in one of the many collections of Israeli songs published by Tara Publications.

Consider for a Jewish values discussion: "*Justice Justice*" by Doug Cotler (on his recording, *Everyone's*

---

[8]From his recording, *Heaven and Earth.*

[9]On her recording, *Seasoned with Song.*

[10]For more on multiple intelligences, see Chapter 27, "Multiple Intelligences" by Renee Holtz and Barbara Lapentina, pp. 323-333 in this Handbook.

Invited); "I Count" by Sam Glaser (on his recording, *Kol Bamidbar*); "Chazak, Chazak" by Julie Silver (on her recording, *Strength To Strength*); "The Empty Chair" by Jeff Klepper (on his recording, *In This Place*); or *"Kadosh"* by Doug Cotler (on his recording, *A Rose in December*).

More songs for specific topics can be found by checking Internet sites and those listed at the end of this chapter; for example, Zemerl's: *www. princeton.edu/zemerl*.

Movement and Dance[11]

It's almost the end of the afternoon. Judaics teacher Yehudit Sharaby, whose classroom is set up with tables in a U-shape, has moved her third grade students into the open section of the U to teach an Israeli dance. Because it is close to Tu B'Shevat, she is teaching "Tzadik Katamar Yifrach." Being a sensitive teacher, she will often put on a CD with an Israeli dance just to give the restless kids a break. Yehudit is a master at bringing in movement to enhance her lessons whether by using musical instruments or through an Israeli dance.

In the second grade classroom down the hall, Nurit Barnard has brought in many instruments, each of which relates to one mentioned in Psalm 150. The children are going to use the instruments to accompany a familiar melody and then learn a new one.

Meanwhile, across town, another teacher is preparing to continue a lesson on Israel in advance of Yom HaAtzma'ut. Last week she taught "Achshav" to her first graders, and she is thinking about bringing in some Israeli flags to use with the song as props this week. She will eventually teach them the simple partner dance that matches the tune.

In each of these cases, the teacher is planning more than just the song, but an activity to accompany the song, or the use of Jewish music as a transitional tool. We are, after all, in Jewish schools. In each case, the teacher has recognized that children need to move. This is especially true for those who come to an afternoon religious school. Would some Israeli dancing at the beginning of the class help settle students more quickly? Would having to create a movement for a phrase of a song help the child think a little more about the content of the

song? You can start your own movement experiences using one of the many CDs and tapes available (see the Tara Publications Internet site for ideas — www.info@jewishmusic.com) with lively Israeli dances, both classical and new.

> One year, I taught *gimmel* level Hebrew to Rachel. I remember how much she struggled to gain the fluency and flow that is expected at that level. I also remember attending her Bat Mitzvah and hearing her chant beautifully. I talked to her parents afterward and they told me how quickly she caught on when she was able to lend a musical component to the recitation of Hebrew sounds. How often do we discover the wisdom of our Rabbis! After that, I tried to include a song, a rhythm, a musical interlude in my lessons.
>
> *(Michael Fixler, Syracuse, New York)*

TECHNIQUES

Ages and Stages

It was just before Purim. I walked into the pre-school classroom with my guitar and a big red straw bag filled with Purim props. I sat down on the floor with the children in a circle and began to sing a "Hello" song. Then I began the lesson. "What do you like about Purim?" I sang, revising the song "What Do You Like about Shabbat?" by "Miss Jackie" (on her recording, Sing Yeladim). As each child answered, I pulled the item he/she mentioned from my bag. Pretty soon we had all the Purim props on the floor in front of us.

It was again just before Purim. We were concluding a Middle School program on Purim. I passed out words to Jeff Klepper's "You Can Change the World" (from the Kol B'Seder recording, Growin') and taught the chorus. When we finished the song, I asked the students, "Tell me something about this song. What is the composer's message?" A lively discussion on what it means to change the world, connections to tikkun olam (fixing the world), and references to "Lo Alecha Hamlacha Ligmor" (It is not our job to complete the task, but neither is it ours to desist from it — Pirke Avot 2:21) unfolded. How can one person change the

---

[11]For a fuller discussion on movement, see Chapter 49, "Enriching Instruction with Dance and Movement" by Ofra

Backenroth, pp. 592-607 in this Handbook.

world? Can our choices affect outcomes in the world? Did Esther's choices change the world? Did Mordecai's?

In each of these cases, a song was used to introduce Purim — with concrete objects for the little ones and more heady ideas for the older ones. In each case, the song was the trigger for a kind of discussion. For younger children, a discussion focuses on objects — what do we need in order to celebrate the holiday of Purim? What are the days of the week? Preschool children need the tangible. They need easy words. Using visuals helps them to understand concepts more readily. Older children need to wrestle with ideas. They need songs with words that have meaning and songs that have catchy popular sounding melodies.

Songs for younger children can be extended through props, movement, and dance. But don't underestimate these activities for older students, too. While some teens are reticent about Israeli dancing, many are not. They dance at camp, they dance on youth group Israel trips. Perhaps the right association helps.

All age groups need relevance to the subject they are studying, to their lives, to the person each student is. To bring in a popular song and change the words is fun for an adolescent, but not appropriate for a preschooler. Piggyback songs (songs pairing new words with the melodies of already existing songs, e.g., "Where is Thumbkin?" which is to the tune of *"Freres Jacques"* — and there are many variations on that melody!) are popular in preschool, but would be deadly with a teen.

The musical key in which you place a song also makes a difference to different age groups. Preschoolers through third grade prefer the key of D major or E minor; they have a narrow vocal range. Older students have a broader vocal range, but for many of them their voices have lowered, and so D is too high. I've found that for them the keys of C major and D minor tend to work better. But don't expect them to reach high notes. You'll need to remind them to take a deep breath as you approach such a note.

Beyond the Song: Beginnings and Endings

Songs can help to build community. Consider the *"Mah Tovu"* we sing at the beginning of Shacharit. The song functions to gather those present into one group to begin to pray together. For several

years, I conducted a Tot Shabbat service that I began each week with *"Mah Tovu."* I brought with me a puppet of Abraham and talked about the tents in which he lived. I pointed out that while we no longer live in tents, our earliest ancestors did. Now we come together in modern day tents or synagogues. A *"Hineh Mah Tov"* can serve the same function since the words talk about how good it is to be together. Fran Avni's "Togetherness" ("How Happy We Are/*Hineh Mah Tov*") on her recording, *Mostly Matzah,* can provide a good guessing game — students hear the English words and are asked for the Hebrew equivalents.

It is the day of Purim. Middle school students in a day school have spent the afternoon studying in small groups the first seven chapters of the Megillah, focusing on the choices that the characters make throughout the story. When they come together to share their discoveries, the discussion will be followed by Jeff Klepper's "You Can Change the World" (on Kol B'Seder's recording, Growin', and "Or Zarua" (on their recording, Shalom Rav).

As you plan your lessons, whether they include music for music's sake or as a curriculum enhancer, keep in mind the ability of a song to gather people together. Remember, too, that while a song can be a trigger for a unit or lesson, it can also provide a good way to conclude the material.

Beyond the Song: Focusing and Shifting

Ulpan teacher Yehudit Sharaby was ready to move her adults on to another topic in their Hebrew class, but she knew that they had been focused long enough on grammar and needed a modality shift. Yehudit took out a CD and passed out the words to "BaShanah Haba'ah." She turned on the CD player and asked her students to listen to the song and identify the words that looked like they were in the future. Students were then poised to move on to an analytical lesson on the future tense.

In the worship service, we mark transitions with the *"Kaddish."* At the end of *P'sukay D'Zimra,* after the Torah service, and before *"Alaynu"* there is a *"Kaddish."* But in the classroom we don't often think to use music as a transition. It provides a natural way to shift gears that tells the student politely but firmly that we are moving on to something else. Preschool teachers are used to using songs to mark transitions. However, why sing "Clean-up time in the Nursery" in a Jewish preschool classroom when a *niggun* (song without words) could also do? Words and melody and mode set the tone of a classroom and speak volumes about who we are and what is important for us to learn. In the same way, songs can enable students to pause and refocus in order to get ready for what is about to come.

Motivational Tips for Teaching

One day I had to teach Chanukah songs to a large group of third through fifth graders. The kids were not in the mood to sing. I had prepared song sheets with songs that I thought they would like, but the group was not responding. I had to think fast.

Most teachers, at one time or another, have probably considered bribery. There are, however, other ways to motivate a group to sing:

- Create a competition between groups to see who sings the loudest. This can be boys versus girls, one grade versus another, one row of students versus another, etc.

- Vary the dynamics or speed.

- Sing part of the song, leaving out some of the words, which the students fill in, or sing the words incorrectly.

- Have students go on a scavenger hunt for themes, words, or a story line.

- Watch the students to see where they are and what they are doing. Then build on that. For example, while working with some teens in preparation for Purim, I noticed one student singing *"Rash Rash Rash"* as I was playing the introduction to *"Chag Purim."* Picking up on that, I put him and another boy in charge of a rhythmic ostinato bass that we ran throughout the song using those words and his idea.

- Shift to a song the students like and then come back to the new one.

- Add a movement piece to correspond to the lyrics.

I have found music to be a very useful tool when studying prayer. After studying the meaning of *"Mi Chamocha,"* I usually play seven or eight different melodies for this passage, asking students which one best captures the spirit of the prayer. The students then have to list every secular song they can think of on the theme of redemption and see how well its melody demonstrates the same theme.

(Rabbi David Feder, Morgantown, West Virginia)

SAMPLE LESSON PLANS

Advice for the Music Teacher

Regardless of the age group or curricular goal, each lesson should have a thematic center, be it holidays, Hebrew language, *Tefilah*, Israel, values, history, etc. Decide on the main point you want to get across through the songs you intend to teach. Select an opening and closing song (which can be the same from session to session), a familiar song to make everyone comfortable and a new song as a challenge. For older students, this format is less rigid, as one could spend an entire music class period on one song, discussing the lyrics, learning it, singing it, and then playing with it through song extenders (movement, dance, props, drama, etc.).

Teaching Considerations for a Music Lesson

1. Select core songs that are crucial to your curriculum or to the topic for the day.

2. Select songs you like to sing, want to share. It is easier to teach a song you really like than one you don't.

3. Select songs the kids can play with. Children like to become part of the song and to take control of it. Music class is also more fun when the children are involved and not just sung to.

4. Integrate, adapt, vary, and add to the songs. Never do a song just once and in one way. Learning will not necessarily happen the first time a song is sung, but often the third or fourth time through.

Following are some sample lesson plans for Pesach broken out by age group. In each lesson below, I encourage you to think about a story line or a contextual patter that you use between songs and as connectives to curriculum. Music teachers can be prone to a "sing, sing, sing" syndrome, without giving the children explanations before or between each song. In such a case you are losing the "teachable moment" when a reiterated theme can be a more effective learning modality for some children. Examples are given following each suggested song. In some cases, the songs presented represent a clear thematic connection; in others, they are reflective of a need for variety in type of song on the same Pesach theme.

Preschool

As mentioned above, every music class should have an opening song and a closing song. This structure is especially crucial for preschool. To the extent that they are consistent each time, these songs then act as signals or cues for the transition taking place.

Lap chants are good vehicles to use during each class with younger children. Involving a simple tapping of the hands on the knees and some kind of rhyme, they enable the child to connect with body and beat to words. In the example below, the "Dayenu Lap Chant" is an introduction to the song "Dayenu": "1-2-3-4, here we go out the door; 1-2-3-4, we won't be in Egypt any more!"

Theme/Goal: Beginning Preparation for Pesach Seder

Here are some suggestions for incorporating music as you prepare children for their *Sedarim*:

- Hello song - choose one that you like. It can be "*Heyveynu*" by David Feingold (on the recording, *NFTY at 50*) or one of the many simple versions of "*Hineh Mah Tov*" (in *The New Jewish Children's Songbook* by Tara Publications).

- "Lap Chant Dayenu" (see above and the book *Jewish Every Day*) - Begin by instructing the children to tap their knees with their hands. Ask them if they can hear the Israelites marching out of Egypt. Then begin singing.

- Four Questions - Introduce an adapted version or the first two questions by pointing out that there are so many different things we see and do at our *Seder* that we have a special way to ask questions about them. (I have taught the first line of the "*Mah Nishtana*" in Hebrew and then the second line as "Oh why is this night so different tonight? Why do we eat only *matzah* tonight? Oh why, oh tell me why, oh why, oh tell me why.")

- "Make Charoset Chop Chop Chop" - To introduce it say: On our *Seder* table we find many interesting foods. One is *charoset*. It reminds us of the mortar that the Israelite slaves used for their bricks. Here's the recipe for *charoset*.

- "Bake a Matzah" - Introduce the song by saying: Now let's make some *matzah*!

- "If You're Happy and You Know It" - Use this song to review all of the things done during the music session. Say: We've had such fun today. Let's try to recall what we have done and learned.

Note: Props are excellent for the early grades — preschool though second grade. Consider using a big basket or shopping bag with all the items needed to celebrate a holiday as you introduce it.

Grades K-2

Theme/Goal: Aspects of Slavery and Freedom in the Seder

The following ideas relate to slavery and freedom in the *Seder*:

- "*Heyveynu*" by David Feingold (on the recording, *NFTY at 50*), or "*Modeh Ani*" (depending upon your setting).

- "Lap chant Dayenu" - No introduction is necessary for this age group. In this way the song serves as an introduction to the class.

- Four Questions - Say: We have many questions to ask at our *Seder*. Jews have been asking these questions for many generations through this song.

- "*Avadim Hayinu*" (traditional) - Introduce with: The *Seder* reminds us that we were slaves, but now we are free. I'll sing a line and you sing it back to me. (Note: *"Avadim Hayinu"* can be done very effectively in this manner as an echo song.)

- *"Building Cities"* (in *The New Jewish Songbook*) - Say: Follow me with this as we remember how hard the Israelite slaves worked. Make sure to use dramatic motions, including mopping your sweaty brow!

- *"Hineh Mah Tov"* or *"Oseh Shalom."*

Grades 3-5

Theme/Goal: Pesach Seder

Here are some songs to use when studying about the *Seder*:

- *"Heyveynu"* or *"Modeh Ani"* - see above

- *"Kadaysh Urchatz"* - The word *"Seder"* means order. Here is the order of the *Seder* in song.

- Four Questions - see above

- *"Avadim Hayinu"* - see above

- *"Dayenu"* - Say: At last the slaves are free!

- *"Hineh Mah Tov"* or *"Oseh Shalom."*

Grades 6 and Up

Theme/Goal: Freedom through the Generations

On the theme of freedom through the generations, I suggest the following:

- *"Bechol Dor Vador"* - Introduce this by saying: Freedom has been a Pesach theme throughout the generations. The words of *"Bechol Dor Vador"* give us a glimpse into how the Rabbis understood this theme as it appears in the *Hagaddah*.

- *"Make Those Waters Part"* by Doug Mishkin (on the recording, *Woody's Children*) - Say: Song-writer and social activist Doug Mishkin's song reflects certain themes in recent history. Can you find them as we sing through the song?

- *"Go Down Moses"* (folk song) - Say: Let's learn a traditional folk song that is related to the *Seder* and freedom. Black slaves used to sing this song many years ago in the United States. Why do you think it had meaning for them?

- *"World of Our Fathers"* (on the recording, *Songs of Safam*) - Say: The theme of freedom also can be seen in the stories of our own families, in the stories you might hear from your great-grandparents or grandparents.

- *"Standing on the Shoulders"* by *Doug Cotler* (on his recording, *Listen* and in the *Doug Cotler Songbook*) - Say: For many of us, Doug Cotler's words remind us that we stand on the shoulders of all of those relatives who have come before us.

Kabbalat Shabbat

Here are some suggestions for a 20-minute *Kabbalat Shabbat* service for Grades 7 and 8 in a day school setting.

As students enter, play *"Or Zarua"* from Doug Mishkin's recording, *Woody's Children* (words and music are available on *NFTY at 50)*. When students are settled, and as the song finishes, hand out song sheets with the words to *"Make Those Waters Part"* by Doug Mishkin and *"Anu Beta Yisrael"* by Jack Schechtman Gabriel (on his recording, *Rock Yourself To Glory)*.

1. Tell students that they will be listening to several songs that have to do with Pesach. Tell them to follow along with the words as the songs are being played.

2. Give some background on the composers/ singers and the attitudes/values they may show through their songs. For instance, Doug Mishkin is an attorney who has been very involved in social action. Jack Gabriel is a Rabbi in Colorado.

3. Play Mishkin's *"Make Those Waters Part"* first.

4. Ask students to comment in general about the song. What did they notice in the song? What is the composer singing about?

5. Ask students to reflect further on each of the "exoduses" Mishkin sings about.

6. What does Mishkin mean when he says, "Make those waters part"? About whom is he talking?

7. Recall other "exoduses" with students, specifically Operation Magic Carpet and Operation Moses, which brought Ethiopian Jews to Israel. Urge the students to think about words in the *Hagaddah* that speak to the exoduses of every generation (*Bechol Dor Vador*).

8. Play Jack Schechtman Gabriel's "*Anu Beta Yisrael*" next. (This is about the exodus from Ethiopia by the Beta Yisrael Jews.)

9. Solicit comments on this song as well.

10. Remind the students about the *Hagaddah*. Divide them into small groups for a brief brainstorming to uncover the many other exoduses that have taken place, as well as the current situation in Israel. Conclude by asking the students "What is freedom?"

11. As the session concludes, discuss the role and responsibility of each student in the room to act as a Nachshon "to make the waters part." Remind the students about Elijah and our continual hope for peace and freedom for all.

12. If time allows, students can be led through the motions that accompany "Pharaoh, Pharaoh" by Mah Tovu. (The song is available on the single CD of the same name.)

CONCLUSION

There is music for every subject and every teaching situation — for happy, holiday times (e.g., the familiar and fun songs we sing at the *Seder)*, and even for the dark times of war (e.g., the song "*Kol HaOlam Kulo,*" which my daughter Marissa used as a meditation during the Iraqi War of 2003). This chapter has provided just a few suggestions and tips for using music to enrich and enhance your curriculum. I hope you will feel free to use these ideas and to expand on them, always remembering that "Sweet are the songs of Israel" (II Samuel 23:1).

TEACHING CONSIDERATIONS

- Choose a song wisely to be sure that it fits with the lesson and/or topic you are trying to teach. Is it age appropriate? Can the words be easily grasped?

- Review words in advance to make sure that you are comfortable in presenting the song.

- Check activities. Is there a smooth transition between activities? Are they appropriate in tempo and timing for the group and your lesson plan? Are there any supplies you will need?

- Integrate, adapt, vary, and add to the songs, either through discussion or summary activity.

ADDITIONAL VIGNETTES

You are teaching Pesach music for Grades 3-5 on a Sunday morning. You and the Cantor have been told the songs the school director would like you to sing. As you go through her list, however, you realize that the song sheets you used last week are not present and that each child has a different Hagadah. In addition, as you begin to teach "Avadim Hayinu," the weekday Hebrew supervisor informs you that she has been teaching it another way. Sound familiar?

- What is a music teacher to do? Which problem do you address first: the lack of the song sheet or the different version of the song?

- Do you teach the weekday version in order for there to be consistency?

- Do you piece together what you can, using the different *Hagaddot,* and turn this into a lesson involving the *Hagadah* as a text?

The Middle School students in the day school are a rowdy bunch, but Kabbalat Shabbat has to happen each week at 11:45 a.m. before lunch. You have about 15 minutes to present something relevant to Shabbat/the parashah/an upcoming holiday/a value. You want to use a song or two.

- Where will you look for an appropriate song?

- What techniques do you anticipate using to focus the group on the music you wish to teach?

- Is there another staff member who can give you some ideas?

BIBLIOGRAPHY

Note: For an extensive list of recorded and published music, see *Jewish Every Day* by Max Segal Handelman, ARE, 2000.

Jewish Sign Language Resources for Movement

Baitch, Miriam. *Celebrating Judaism in the Home: A Manual for Deaf Families*. Tarzana, CA: Temple Beth Shalom of the Deaf, 1996, o.p.

Shuart, Adele Kronick. *Signs in Judaism*. New York: Bloch Publishing Co. Inc., 1986.

Note: There are also three videos available to help teach Jewish sign language: "Yad B'Yad" and "Yad B'Yad Sheini," both available through E.J. Cohen at EJ2323@aol.com, and "Singing and Signing Hebrew Blessings and Songs," available from Judy Caplan Ginsburgh at judy@jewishentertainment.net.

Publishers and Distributors of Jewish Music

A.R.E. Publishing, Inc.
700 N. Colorado Blvd. #356
Denver, CO 80206
www.arepublish.com

Tara Publications
P.O. Box 707
Owings Mills, MD 21117
www.jewishmusic.com

Transcontinental Music Publications
633 Third Ave., 6th Floor
New York, NY 10017
www.eTranscon.com

Sounds Write Productions, Inc.
P.O. Box 601084
San Diego, CA 92160
www.soundswrite.com

Jewish Book Stores and Libraries

Each Jewish community generally has a Jewish bookstore or at least a Judaica shop in a local synagogue. Synagogue libraries, day school libraries, college libraries, and public libraries are all good sources for Jewish music. Don't forget the Cantor's library in the synagogue.

Radio Stations and Programs

In many communities there may be local Jewish radio and television programs, usually once a week. Check your community's Jewish newspaper and cable TV guide for listings.

The Internet

The Israel Music Institute (IMI)
www.aquanet.co.il/vip/imi

> This is a publicly owned, nonprofit music publishing house run by the Israel Ministry of Education and Culture. IMI holds the copyright to some 1700 works by more than 160 Israeli composers. The IMI catalogue contains orchestra, chamber, and choral works. The IMI also serves as the Israel Music Information Centre. The web site features catalogs, including forthcoming publications, and a gallery that provides brief biographical sketches of composers and a listing of their compositions.

House of Musical Traditions
Recordings Department and CD Archives
www.hmtrad.com/records/rec.html

> Contains a listing of Klezmer and Yiddish, liturgical, Israeli, Ladino, and other Jewish recordings. Some listings have selected audio tracks.

www.israelhour.com/links.html

> Israeli music artist sites, news and links. Lyrics and sounds of Eurovision contest entries and winners from Israel.

www.israel-mfa.gov.il/mfa/go.asp?MFAH00tx0

> Fifty Years of Song - The Israeli Ministry of Foreign Affairs offers a lyrics database for 25 famous Israeli songs with English and Hebrew lyrics as well as the musical score (as a graphics file) for each song. If the URL doesn't work, go to www.israel-mfa.gov.il/mfa. Use the GO box for "Israel at 50" and go to the "50 Years of Hebrew Song" link.

Tara Publications
www.jewishmusic.com

> An extensive selection of music both recorded and published and the ability to browse.

Jewish Music Megasites
www.jmwc.org/jmwc_webres.html

> Gives subject listings of resources; helpful for research.

The Jewish Midi Library
http://members.aol.com/israelmidi/index.html

> Listen to melodies of many Jewish songs from Israeli to folk to movies and plays.

Jewish Music WebCenter
www.jmwc.org

> The purpose of this site is to provide a forum for gathering and presenting information on academic, organizational, and personal activities in Jewish music today. Information is provided to encourage and support the enjoyment, study, creation, and knowledge of Jewish music.

Maven Music
www.maven.co.il/subjects/idx196.htm.

> Maven is a megasite that lists various Internet sources around the world. The music page contains an extensive alphabetic listing of Internet sites concerned with Jewish music. There are some annotations. Sites are ungraded.

Radio Hazak: Israel Music on the Web
www.radiohazak.com

> Information on artists, news, reviews, and a message board about Israeli pop music.

Sabranet
www.sabranet.com

> This site purports to be a complete guide to Israeli related Internet sites. The main page connects to links on Israeli music files with excerpts from popular Israeli music in Real Audio file format.

Shulmusic
http://shulmusic.org

> This web site is devoted to music of the synagogue and all Jewish liturgical music. The aim of the site is to become a global resource for

Jewish liturgical music. Musical scores for various holidays and events are provided online.

Jewish Music Research Centre
http://shum.cc.huji.ac.il/~jmrc/jmrc.htm

> The Jewish Music Research Centre of the Jewish National and University Library of Hebrew University on Givat Ram contains the National Sound Archives and several large special collections of Jewish music. Among these are the A.Z. Idelsohn Archives, the recordings collection of Robert Lachmann, and recordings of music from Jews around the world.

Sounds Write Publishing
www.soundswrite.com/swjewish.html

> This site has links to artists and is ready to answer your Jewish music questions.

Hava Nashira
http://uahc.org/hanashir

> A Jewish song leader's page offering articles and announcements for youth group and lay song leaders. Information for leaders of youth group singing and other events. Includes a useful list of publishers, songbooks, and recordings, as well as tips on song leading.

Zamir
www.zamir.org.

> Choral music, links to publishers, songs about Jerusalem, bibliography of music pertaining to Holocaust, Sephardic music, music for Chanukah, etc.

Zemerl The Interactive Database of Jewish Song
www.princeton.edu/zemerl

> Provides lyrics, information, and sounds of Jewish songs in Yiddish, Hebrew, and Ladino. The songs in the database are available by general thematic categories. The information includes title, composer, lyricist, and language. Sometimes a short commentary is included about a song. The web site invites inquiries about new songs and features articles and recommended readings.

CHAPTER 49

Enriching Instruction with Dance and Movement

Ofra Arieli Backenroth

INTRODUCTION

*W*hile different Tanach classes at Schechter have always looked at the Bible in different ways, and while it is not uncommon to find a Tanach class meditating after completing a section of the Bible or reading the text, it is very rare to find a room full of teenagers dancing through the events that formulated and shaped the Jewish religion. Yet, in the Bayt Knesset, on February 10, a piece of the text was being performed through modern dance. Dance is one way to bring life to the pages Schechterites have been studying for many years. (Kaminsky,[1] 1999)

In spite of the latest research into learning modes that claims that students learn concepts at a deeper level of understanding and empathy when their bodies — all their senses and emotions — are engaged, it is a rare occurrence that dance is introduced as part of content learning activity. But in Solomon Schechter High School of West Orange, the initiative of bringing the arts into the classroom was greatly appreciated. The choreographer JoAnne Tucker and the dance ensemble Avodah were invited to the school to help teachers and students integrate dance into the Jewish studies curriculum. "Normally I hate dance," said Danielle Friedman, 15, "but this was really creative." The choreographer explained that dance is spiritual worship and a form of liturgy through which she is able to reinforce Jewish identity and facilitate cognitive and affective understanding of Jewish texts.

Dance has existed since the beginning of humankind. Before verbal or written communication existed, people used movement to communicate. This medium was instrumental in comprehending and making meaning of their world, as well as influencing the universe. Moving rhythmically is innate to human beings and is an intrinsic form of self-expression. Dance communicates in a kinesthetic form. Its vocabulary is steps, movements, and patterns. There are moments in life that are ineffable, and can be expressed solely through arts, music, and dance. Isadora Duncan, the pioneer of modern dance once remarked, "If I could tell what it is, I would not have to dance it." Dance is able to express these moments and to reflect the essence of Jewish learning. Since dance is not a linear process and may include more than one participant at a time, it can present divergent points of view and multiple layers of meaning simultaneously. Addi-tionally, since dance has been a form of cultural expression for many years, dance history is an excellent source of learning about multiculturalism and the styles of different ethnic groups. Being a group project it also reflects the cooperative *chevruta* (studying with a partner) style of learning.

The goal of this chapter is to familiarize the teacher with creative dance as a part of content learning and to introduce the possibilities of learning text with dance and through dance. Accordingly, questions that are raised by the text are going to be answered through creative dance and choreography. As they learn through dance, I hope that the students achieve mastery of both the cognitive and the affective layers of the text, reinforce the knowledge of the content matter in an experiential way, and establish a connection with the emotional content of the lesson. Using dance as a form of learning helps the teacher target the students who are learning best through a kinesthetic approach, engage the students who can never sit still during class time, and reach the very quiet ones who seem not to be touched by letters and words.

---

[1] Blair Kaminsky, "A Biblical Experience: Leaps, Turns and Flailing Arms." *The Flame* (March 24, 1999), 1.

I will first introduce general principles of creative dance and movement improvisation, which are at the core of any movement activity. (I will not include any discussion about Israeli and folk dancing, since they are dealt with in many other books and seminars.) I will explore several examples of lesson plans that are connected to biblical narrative, liturgy, and curricular units of Hebrew language and poetry. These units can be used in a variety of educational settings, such as day schools, synagogue schools, informal education, camps, and adult education. All the units can be adjusted and modified according to the cognitive level of the students and their stages of motor development.

Why should we teach dance in conjunction with content learning?

I was always shy. I never participated in class discussion. During recess time, I read books. But one day I went with my friend to dance class. She had Polio, and it affected her arm. The doctor told her that she should exercise her arm to build up the remaining muscles. I loved the class. It was the best thing that ever happened to me. Suddenly I could speak. Not with words, but with movements. As time went by, I became the dance expert in school. I choreographed the dances for all the holidays and end of the year celebrations. (Tali, a student)

Susan Langer says that "what is expressed in a dance is an idea . . . of the way feelings, emotions, and all other subjective experiences come and go — their rise and growth, their intricate synthesis that gives our inner life unity and personal identity."[2]

Dance is an exuberant and compelling form of physical communication and expression. Composed of patterned sequences of nonverbal body movements that are purposeful and intentionally rhythmic, dance has always been part of human culture and rituals that celebrate significant life passages. Through dance, students learn to appreciate different cultures, examine religious and secular beliefs, and express statements about social and political issues.

Integrating dance into content learning provides the student with the ability to solve problems through choreography and express meaning in a creative way. While dancing and moving, the students' bodies are the medium of expression. As a result, learning is authentic and in context. Since dance is experiential, authentic, and personal, what is learned becomes an integral part of the educational experience and is less likely to be forgotten. Dance can make learning relevant to students' lives and connect to their personal experiences. The art of dance engages the passive learners and transforms them into passionate actors. It enables students to connect with the text through their bodies. It forces the learner to think about the meaning of the narrative, the emotions and the feelings that the story evokes.

Creative dance offers an alternative avenue to interpretation of material and a new way of exhibiting understanding and acquisition of new knowledge for many students, especially those who learn well in a bodily-kinesthetic mode. Howard Gardner[3] argues that teachers should provide pathways for success for students and should look for ways to identify and build a curriculum that encourages students' use of their strengths and multiple intelligences. Eric Jensen[4] claims that the kinesthetic arts contribute to improved cognitive skills, improved learning, creativity, self-esteem and self-concept. It helps to reduce stress, increase energy, and make learning fun.

The creative process is not a one-time event, but a continuous journey. The actual doing and practicing of improvisation are just as important as the final product. Just like any other skill, creative dance can be learned and needs to be done regularly and practiced. The exploration of the ideas that initiate the movements, and the process of putting the movements together into a phrase are the practice of being creative. The students learn that creativity is not an "awakening" to a grand idea, but a result of hard work, thoughtful and purposeful practice, and trial and error (Howard Gruber and Doris Wallace[5]). Therefore, creative dance is a

---

[2]Susan Langer, *Problems of Art* (New York: Charles Scribner's Sons, 1957), 9.

[3]Howard Gardner, *Frames of Mind: The Theory of Multiple Intelligences* (New York: Basic Books, 1983). For more information on this theory, see Chapter 27, "Multiple Intelligences" by Renee Frank Holtz and Barbara Lapetina, pp. 323-333 in this Handbook.

[4]Eric Jensen, *Art with the Brain in Mind* (Alexandria, VA: Association for Supervision and Curriculum Development, 2001).

[5]Howard Gruber and Doris Wallace, *Creative People at Work* (New York: Oxford University Press, 1989).

process that requires mastery not only of the content, but also knowledge of the elements of dance.

Creativity needs fostering and nurturing. The teacher's belief that everyone can create new and exciting dances based on innovative and interesting ideas is a crucial aspect of the creative process. He or she needs to support the students by showing interest in what they create, responding positively, providing reinforcement, and giving them opportunities to discuss their creations. The teacher needs to recognize the individuality and uniqueness of each student and point it out. In addition, teachers should help students articulate the reasons for the choice of movements and how they combine them together in a dance phrase. They should also reinforce the creation of new movements and interpretations by giving ample time for thought and concentration on the composition. This encourages students to come up with meaningful expressions.

Teaching dance may be done in two ways:

1. The teacher choreographs a sequence of steps, and later on takes the phrase apart, isolates each movement, and teaches the movements one by one before reassembling them into a dance. In this case, the teacher models and the students follow.

2. The teacher introduces a problem to be solved through a movement. Here, students experiment with movements by matching the movements to an idea. The students, rather than the teacher, are the choreographers, and they create their own sequence in response to a stimulus.

Since this chapter focuses on teaching through dance, I concentrate mainly on the second way. However, learning the language of dance necessitates a clear, direct, and unambiguous experience in movements. Only after students learn and practice the basic dance "vocabulary" can they create new independent expressions with the movements they have learned and practiced. Gradually, the teachers add to that vocabulary.

This chapter describes only one set of outcomes of dance solutions that might come up during a class. In a classroom situation, the teacher might anticipate a variety of dance solutions that exemplify a variety of points of view held by the participants.

ELEMENTS OF DANCE

Dance takes the body through space, in a certain way or shape, using a certain amount of effort or force, and at a certain speed or tempo. Gradually introduce new elements into your practice. There is no need to introduce all elements in each session, and some will be explored naturally. During the dance, the student conveys an idea through movement instead of words. The students need to put movement together in a certain order and with a certain quality. It may include any of the elements described below: body, space, force, and time.

Body

The body includes all the body parts — head, torso, limbs, joints, muscles, and bones.

- There may be whole body actions or stillness.

- Different body parts may lead the movement.

- The body can move from place to place (locomotion movements): walk, run, jump, skip, leap, slide, etc.

- Body parts can move in isolation (e.g., feet may be motionless, but the rest of the body moves).

Space

Movements can be performed in various ways:

- Different directions (front, backward; side, above, below)

- Different levels (high, low, medium)

- Different pathways (straight, angular, curved, circular)

- Varying relationships (around, near, far, inside, outside, above, under)

- Different focus (eye contact, distant gazes)

- Various groupings (solos, partnering, groups)

- Different dancer connections (leading, following, mirroring, copying, responding)

Force

Movements differ from each other in their dynamic and qualities.

- Movements can be smooth/light, forceful/heavy, etc.

- Movements can be long and flow from one to another, or be short and abrupt, angular, or curved, etc.

- Movements can be direct or indirect, firm or soft.

- Movements may reflect surfaces (hot, cold, sticky, smooth, rough).

- Movements may reflect moods (dancing happily, sadly, excitedly, etc.).

Time

Time is another quality of movement that varies.

- A movement is performed at a certain speed: slow or fast or anything in between with a certain tempo.

- Movement has duration: long or short, interrupted or continuous, accented or even.

- Dances can be performed seriatim (one after the other) or in unison.

Movement Suggestions

For the novice teacher and students, opposites are easier to conceptualize and practice. Slow/fast, smooth/angular, high/low should be explored before subtle nuances are introduced.

Use pedestrian movements; these should be at the core of the dance. Everyday activities like work, brushing teeth, sports, locomotion, etc., are a way to connect students' lives to the dance activity.

Once teachers are aware of the possibilities of movements, they can gradually introduce different ideas and expand the movement vocabulary of the students. As a result, students master the dance "language" to use when they create their dances and participate in dance performances.

Creative dance sessions should not have musical accompaniment initially, since the music tends to influence the style, dynamics, and tempo of the movement the students choose. Hence, it is better first to explore the questions and then find the movements solution. After the selection and combination of movement is accomplished, the teacher can ask students to choose music to accompany the dance.

Some Movement Ice Breakers

Following is a variety of ice breakers to use prior to movement activities:

Introductions - Have the class stand or sit in a circle and ask students to introduce themselves one by one with one gesture that describes the way other people perceive them. In the second round of introductions, have students make a gesture that describes the way they think about themselves. Ask students to find a partner and together explore the discrepancies between the gestures. They can come up with some ideas and suggestions about why there are differences between the way we see ourselves and the way others see us.

Body awareness - This serves as a physical warm-up and as a way to break the ice for further movement activities. Ask students to imagine that there is a little ping-pong ball moving each of their joints while going through each of the steps. Start the movement session sitting down to alleviate anxiety.

- Scan the body with your movements. Start with the head, move each part of your body in isolation all the way down until you reach the toes. Gradually introduce different dance elements into the process (e.g., shake, push, wave, etc.).

- Ask students to:

  - circle the head, move it from side to side, bring the ears close to the shoulders.

  - move the head from side to side and look at the people who stand next to them.

  - circle the shoulders forward and backward.

  - lift the shoulders up and drop them down.

  - stretch the arms to all directions wiggle the elbows, and wiggle the shoulders.

  - bend the torso down, and lift it up.

  - round the back and arch it.

- tap the feet on the floor, move the feet as far as possible away from the chair, then move the feet close to the chair.

- move a pretend ball from the top of the head to the toes in continuous motion.

As someone who has taught both early childhood education and special education, I've come to love using movement when teaching or reinforcing the *alef bet*. We do *alef bet* yoga! Today there are books to teach you positions, but I have found that my students like the challenge of trying to come up with their own interpretation of the letters. As each student or pair demonstrates (pairs work much better for some of the letters, such as *hey*, *chet*, *kuf*, and other letters with more than one leg), I ask the rest of the class to coach them (a kinder version of critique) to make their letter as accurate as possible. In this way, both the students in position and those watching at that moment have an active role.

It's best to warn your students — or at least their parents — in advance, so that the girls will come in pants or tights. It's also much more comfortable on carpeting than on cold tile! Students with physical or visual conceptual disabilities can be included by giving them letters with shapes easier to visualize or create, such as *samech* or *mem sofit*.

(Anne Johnston, New Haven, Connecticut)

TEACHING VALUES: TRUSTWORTHINESS — EMUNAH[6]

Creative Dance Session

- How does movement express trust?

- How would one's movements demonstrate trust or mistrust?

- How would you explore the concept of *emunah* with movement? (Introducing the problems to students generates many solutions.)

- Explore the concept of trust in movement: What happens in a free fall? Think about falling from the security of perfect balance, falling on a roller-coaster, falling in love.

- What happens in all of those? We lose balance, control, we let go, we trust someone/ something will hold us back, support us, or prevent us from falling.

Essential question:

- What are the different manifestations of trustworthiness that God shows to God's creatures?

Leading (opening) questions:

- How is God depicted in the prayer book? in the Bible? (As a loving parent, teacher, maker of peace, etc.)

- What does it mean to have faith in God? to trust God? (The Hebrew word for trust is *emunah*.)

Procedure:

Ask students to stand still. The first thing they discover is that the body's natural movement is a letting go, similar to a fall. When one stands perfectly still and does not try to control the movement, one loses balance and self-control, and tends to fall.

1. Ask students to stand still and keep their arms close to the torso. Then they should let go of any control of the body, and let it fall. The students catch themselves in the very last moment.

   - Ask students to share how it feels to lose control.

   - Ask students to explore different directions — forward, backward, and sideways.

   - Ask students to find the point at which the body is suspended, supporting itself in a non-balanced way.

   - Ask students to choreograph a movement phrase in three parts of fall, suspension, and rebound.

---

[6]This lesson plan is based on one by Carol K. Ingall, in *A Leader's Guide To the Study of the Jewish Moral Virtues* (Philadelphia, PA: The Jewish Publication Society, 2000).

2. Ask students to find a partner and find movements that cannot be executed unless one supports the other (standing on one foot for a long time, standing facing the partner with toes touching, holding hands and pulling away from each other so that students create a V form with their bodies. There are many more ways — let the students explore.)

   • Ask students to take turns in falling out of balance, relying on the partner to catch them in time.

   • Ask students to consider the question of how the supporter needs to prepare for the catch? What is more difficult to do, let go or catch? Why?

3. Ask students to try different directions (sideways, front, backward), different speeds (slow fast), different qualities (sudden, planned, etc.).

   • Discuss in pairs the differences in free fall unassisted and free fall supported and assisted by a partner. What does it teach you about the concept of trust?

   • Ask students to share the findings with the group.

   • An option: Let students rehearse a short combination of the two types of falls, and create a dance of *emunah*, of trust.

   • Perform the dance.

Debrief:

   • What do students notice about the differences in trust and distrust during free fall? What made them trust their partner?

   • When people are in a vulnerable situation, do they tend to exhibit trust? Why? How?

   • How can one represent in dance trusting relationships between a loving parent and a child, a teacher and a student, a bird watching its chicks?

TEACHING BIBLICAL STORIES: JACOB'S DILEMMA (Genesis 27)

Note: All units are based on the MaTok curriculum.[7]

Rebekah takes the lead in laying plans for tricking Isaac into giving the *brachah* to Jacob instead of to Esau. Jacob hesitates and asks, "Yes, but what if . . . ?" In the end, however, he is convinced to follow Rebekah's lead. The reason for the deceit is the value of the *brachah*, which is high. Such accounts invite students to make moral judgments. It is important that students not see Rebekah and Jacob in absolute terms, but rather see them as complex characters. Rebekah is prepared to go to great lengths so that Jacob acquires the *brachah*. Basing their thinking upon the actions and words of Rebekah and Jacob, the students explore the motivations and possible consequences of Jacob's potential reasons for taking various courses of action.

Creative Dance Session

Essential question:

What is the value of Isaac's *brachah* — the *brachah* for the firstborn?

Leading questions:

   • What are Rebekah and Jacob willing to do in order to get the *brachah*?

   • How did Rebekah convince Jacob to acquire the *brachah*?

Movement questions:

   • How would you convey leadership in dance?

   • How would you convey forcing someone to do what you intend them to do?

   • How would you demonstrate deceit?

A possible solution:

   • Ask students to explore two different kinds of relationship through movement. The first one is following the other person's

---

[7]D. Miller, ed. *Matok* (New York: Melton, 2001).

rhythmic movement. The second one is finding one's own rhythmical pattern and trying to keep it going. A discussion about the experience follows the exercise.

- Ask the group to stand in a circle so they can see each. One of the participants leads the class in a "follow me" game of rhythmical movements like stamping with feet on the floor, using small wood blocks, or clapping hands. Variations can be achieved by moving around, using one foot, clapping in different directions, at at different levels, and using varying dynamics.

- Ask students to pair up and continue with the same routine while you make suggestions to vary the movements by using contrasting quality of movements. For example: high/low, fast/slow, inward/outward, etc.

- Ask students to form small groups and explore one rhythmic pattern of movement. The movement and rhythm should be easy to follow. The aim is to convince another group to join them in the same pattern and rhythm.

- Ask two groups at a time to perform their patterns.

- While they perform, ask the rest of the students to notice whether they were able to maintain their own pattern or eventually followed the other group's pattern?

- Ask students how difficult it was to keep one's own group identity and not follow the other.

Debrief:

- Relate the exercise to the *brachah* lesson.

- Ask students to reflect on the methods the group used to overcome the other group.

- Ask students to think about the body language Rebekah used to talk Jacob into taking the *brachah*. Are they similar? In what way are they different?

- Finish the session by creating a duet dance *Midrash* (commentary/explanation) of the conversation between Rebekah and Jacob.

TEACHING BIBLICAL STORIES: JACOB'S WRESTLING (Genesis 32)

Jacob's struggle with the unnamed man at night changes him physically, emotionally, and spiritually. This struggle signals the personal growth that is necessary before he can resolve his "unfinished business" with Esau and meet the challenges of the next stage of his life — being the leader of Israel. In the wake of the mysterious wrestling scene, Jacob is left with a limp that is perhaps evidence of the emotional scars of the struggle. A spiritual change is also suggested when Jacob receives both a blessing and a new name ("for you have striven with beings divine and human, and you have prevailed") (Genesis 32:29). The change of name signifies a change in personality as well as destiny. The struggle was not only for victory, but also about withstanding and enduring. Jacob now claims to have met God face-to-face. The encounter with God equips him emotionally and spiritually to face Esau.

Creative Dance Session

Essential question:

- What happened to Jacob during that night?

Leading questions:

- With whom did he fight (with another human being, with an angel, with God, with himself)?

- What happened to him during the fight?

- Why was his name changed?

Movement questions:

- How does the battle with the unknown influence the choice of movements?

- What will be the choice of movements for an internal struggle?

Procedure:

- Ask students to have an argument without words using no voice, only facial expressions and arm movements.

- Ask students gradually to add body parts to the argument.

- Ask students to pair up and conduct a no-touch physical battle. (Be firm about the limits of this battle.)

- Lead a discussion with students about Jacob and the fight with the unknown figure.

- Ask students to chose one of the above options and create a dance *midrash*. (Remind the students that following the fight they are limping. What does the limp mean?)

- Ask students what they learned about themselves as a result of the fight?

Debrief:

The observers can answer the following questions:

- Does Jacob look different from the other figure? How? Who is bigger, stronger — Jacob or the other? Why? What are their facial expressions and body positions like?

- Does one figure seem to be winning? Who? How can you tell?

- Does the activity look like a fight or something else?

TEACHING BIBLICAL STORIES: JOSEPH
(Genesis 37)

The ideas of "descent" and "ascent" are important themes of Joseph's life. His life paves the way for and symbolizes the Israelites' descent to Egypt and their eventual redemption. The story unfolds on two levels. On one level, the characters' own actions have implications. For example, Jacob sends Joseph from Hebron to Dothan to look after his brothers. At the same time, events are interpreted as divinely predestined. Some traditional commentators see the man who directs Joseph to his brothers (verses 15-17) as a divine messenger. Even if the stranger is not a divine messenger, is it only coincidence that he happens to be at the crossroads just when Joseph needs directions to his brothers?

According to Everett Fox, the paradox of fate and free will or destiny and choice is a central tension in the biblical relationship between human

beings and God.[8] There is a dramatic reversal of fortune in the Joseph narrative; while the brothers sell Joseph into slavery to be rid of the dreamer, ultimately Joseph's dreams come true and the slave becomes master. This reversal not only makes for gripping drama, but also underscores divine determinism.

Creative Dance Session

Essential question:

- Were the events in the story of Joseph predestined, or were they caused by the participants?

Leading question:

- What is the role of God in the events?

Movement question:

- What is the difference between a spontaneous movement and a dictated movement, in practice and in performance?

Procedure:

The dance unit will focus on the tension between free will and destiny.

- Ask students to pair up, then take roles as a puppeteer and a puppet.

- Ask each puppeteer to find four gestures that can be performed smoothly and accurately and teach them to the puppet.

- Practice the movements a few times with the puppeteer holding "the strings" and leading the puppet.

- Ask students to add short locomotion movements between each of the gestures so that you travel across space.

- Ask students to practice the pattern.

- Discuss how it feels to be a puppet, worked by strings.

- Ask students to repeat the same phrase, but without the restrictions of being moved by a puppeteer.

[8]Everett Fox, *The Five Books of Moses: A New Translation with Introductions, Commentary, and Notes* (New York: Schocken, 1995).

- Ask students to discuss how this changed the movement's style. Were they compelled to change some of the movements? Why or why not?

- Ask students to connect the idea of the puppet to Joseph's change of fortune. Was it predestined?

- Ask students to choreograph a dance pretending to be Joseph rising from slavery to be a ruler. Ask them to choose between divine intervention and personal achievement.

- Ask students to perform for your class.

Debrief:

- Discuss the differences in the movements and how the dance activity impacts the understanding of the biblical narrative and the implication of divine determinism.

- How does the difference between a spontaneous movement and a dictated movement impact students' feeling toward human responsibility in the biblical events?

TEACHING BIBLICAL STORIES: MOSES
(Exodus 2)

Exodus 2:11-17 relates the first actions of Moses and gives us insight into his character. Three different situations arise in which he acts on behalf of a person being mistreated. The students look at the similarities and differences of these three events in order to learn about Moses. Through these comparisons, students become aware of his leadership qualities.

The discussion refers to Exodus 2:10, which tells how Moses grew up as the son of Pharaoh's daughter. It seems that Moses grew up among Egyptians as if he were Egyptian. However, in the very next verses we read about Moses's strong identification with the Hebrews. His unique upbringing contributes to his great understanding of the Egyptian culture while maintaining his identity as a Hebrew.

Creative Dance Session

Note: These chapters are rich with many movement ideas and scenes that can be acted. I will con-

centrate only on Moses's character as indicated in the three incidents of helping the weak.

Essential question:

- Who is Moses?

Leading question:

- What do we learn about Moses's character from the three stories?

Movement questions:

- Considering the fact that the Egyptians were the masters and the Hebrews were slaves, how would you represent the two in movements?

- How would art assist us in making the distinctions in learning about the way people move?

Procedure:

- Ask students to discuss why and how Moses's upbringing as an Egyptian is advantageous when dealing with Pharaoh.

- Ask students to explore the cultural and social/class differences and how these differences are visible in the movements they select. (To help students, have them look at Egyptian art and determine how it depicts people and their motions.)

- After students explore the two different types of movements, bring up the issue of Moses's identity as an Egyptian and later on as a Hebrew. How does movement convey the idea of a changing identity?

- An additional activity: Create a dance about being welcomed or not welcomed by a community. Ask students how being different from their neighbors influences the way they act and move.

- Facilitate a discussion on Moses's character and the instances in which he risked his life to help the weak. Have students combine information from various "scenes" to extrapolate a portrait of Moses and his characteristics (e.g., courageous, fearless, strong, fearful, Egyptian, coward, running away, secretive, helping the weak, etc.).

- Ask students to make a list of the qualities of Moses that make him the right leader for the Hebrews.

- Ask students to chose three characteristics and explore them in movements, creating a scene of Moses in action.

Debrief:

- In a discussion following the dance, ask students why they chose a particular scene.

- What did the dance contribute to their understanding of Moses's actions?

TEACHING A PRAYER

Prayers are read from a *Siddur*. Dancing a prayer is a Hasidic practice that favors the idea of serving God with joy and happiness following the biblical verse, "You shall love the Lord your God with all your heart and all your soul and with all your might" (Deuteronomy 6:5). This inspired the Hasidim to imbue their worship with full-bodied song and dance.[9]

The morning service opens with the verse: "Praised are You, *Adonai*, our God, Sovereign of the universe, who creates light as well as darkness, who has endowed life with the ceaseless urge for harmony; You are the creator of all things." The prayer starts the continuum of God as the creator of light and darkness and continues to the universal theme of creating the universe. It concludes with the idea that the Torah is the ultimate light. The prayer reminds us about the story of creation and that God is the creator of light and darkness.

Creative Dance Session

- Ask students to compile a list of contrasting words such as light and darkness (e.g., Happiness/Sadness, Beauty/Ugliness, Wholesomeness/Fragmentation, Harmony/Dissonance, Beginning/End).

- Ask students to pair up. Each pair chooses one pair of contrasts for which to brain-

storm many adjectives that relate to one of the contrasts. (In a proficient class this can be done in Hebrew.)

- Each pair then chooses three contrasting pairs of adjectives. (Example: Harmony/Dissonance: Smooth/Rough, Curved/Angular, Pleasant/Screechy.)

- Ask students in pairs to explore through movement one grouping from the list of contrasts (e.g., Happiness/Sadness, Beauty/Ugliness, Wholesomeness/Fragmentation Harmony/Dissonance, Beginning/End).

- Ask students to explore the rest of the contrasts in the same manner.

- The students by now have a variety of motions representing different feelings.

  - Ask students to choose one motion from each set of adjectives, put them together into a dance phrase, and practice.

  - Ask students to perform the phrase for the whole class.

Debrief:

Facilitate a discussion about the meaning to the dancers and the rest of the group of the phrase, "You shall love the Lord your God with all your heart and all your soul and with all your might" (Deuteronomy 6:5). How does the movement connect the dancer to the idea that the Torah is the ultimate light and that the prayer reminds us about the story of creation.

TEACHING THE "SHEMA"

"Hear, O Israel, *Adonai* is our God, *Adonai* is one. Praised be God's sovereignty forever and ever."

Creative Dance Session

Essential question:

- What does each word mean in the context of the prayer?

---

[9]Fred Berk, *The Chasidic Dance* (New York: Union of American Hebrew Congregations, 1975).

Leading questions:

- What are the key words in this phrase?

Movement questions:

- How would you express the above key words in movement?

Procedure:

- Find a gesture or short movement phrase and practice it few times.

- Ask students to form a "dance machine" (students repeat their movement phrases simultaneously. When the motions are performed together, they create the complete "*Shema.*")

- Assign to each student one word of the "*Shema*" to be explored in movement.

- After each one has a movement that expresses the assigned word, the students reassemble the phrase. They may perform their movements one after another in the same order as in the "*Shema*" phrase. They may improvise by repeating each other's movement so the first one does all the movement and the last one has only his/her movements to add to the phrase.

- As students gain experience in improvising, they will be able to come up with countless ways of improvising on the theme.

Debrief:

- Explore with students how the activity of dealing with each word of the "*Shema*" enhanced their understanding of it.

- Discuss how dancing a prayer in a group transforms their concept of God as one.

TEACHING STORIES: BROTHERS: A HEBREW LEGEND

Long ago, in the Land of Israel, two brothers grew up together on their father's farm. They helped their father work the land. When the father grew old, he divided his land equally between the brothers. He told his sons to be friends, and always to help one another.

The sons always obeyed their father's wishes. One year, when there was little rain and the wheat harvest was poor, the brothers worried about each other. The brother who had a wife and family thought, "My brother is all alone. I have sons to take care of me when I am old. I will take some of my wheat to him." The brother who lived alone thought, "My brother has a wife and three children while I have only myself to feed. I will bring him some of my wheat."

Secretly, at night, each carried wheat to his brother. One night, as they were doing so, the brothers met and discovered the other's compassion. We are taught that the holy Temple in Jerusalem was built on the spot where the two brothers met.

The students study the narrative of why *Bayt HaMikdash* (the Temple) was built where it was, and explore the value of brotherly love, responsibility to one's family and one's neighbors. The values this story teaches are embedded in the fabric of Judaism: *gemilut chasadim* (doing deeds of loving-kindness), *hidur p'nay zakayn* (caring for the elderly), and *kavod av v'aym* (honoring one's parents).

Creative Dance Session

Essential question:

- What does the legend tells us about trust and loyalty?

Leading questions:

- When are we worthy of others' trust?

Movement questions:

- Which movements utilize trust (e.g., suspension or leaning on each other, jumping into one's arms, balancing on one foot in a toe shoe for a long time)?

Procedure:

- Discuss with students possible relationships and feelings among siblings — jealousy, competition, love, etc.

- Divide the classroom into different zones of movements (e. g., label areas/zones with statements such as love vs. hate, goodness vs. malice, war vs. peace). Ask students to move freely among the zones, and change the movement style according to the zone.

- Ask students to discuss how it felt to be in the various zones. What did they like or dislike about the zones? Where did it feel the most comfortable?

Debrief:

- Facilitate a discussion of the story, and ask students how they can expand on the narrative after doing the zone exercise.

- After doing trust and loyalty movements, why do they think the holy Temple was built on the spot where the two brothers met?

TEACHING HEBREW: "THE BIRD'S NEST" BY BIALIK

Unlike the previous examples, teaching Hebrew with movement should be direct and accurate, and include only unambiguous examples of matching language with movements. If the text calls for a jump, make sure that it is a jump and not a hop. (Later on, when you teach about animals and you want them to hop like rabbits, you may introduce hopping as a variation.) If you are uncertain about a movement, it is better not to do it, so as not to confuse the students.

In his book *Total Physical Response*, James J. Asher[10] explores the possibilities of teaching a language with the assistance of movement.

Goal:

Note: The poem *"A Bird Nest"* by Hayyim N. Bialik[11] tells about a bird in a nest that is very quiet so as not to waken the baby bird.

- Teaching new vocabulary in the context of a story or a poem

Creative Dance Session

Props:

A hoop may serve as a nest.

Activity before teaching the poem in Hebrew:

- Identify all the action verbs.

- Teach students the following verbs through movements and mime: to sit, to fly, to look for, to catch, to return, to eat, and to be quiet.

Procedure:

- Practice the action verbs in isolation in a game form.

  - Contrast to fly/to sit

  - To look for/to find

- After the class is proficient in the action verbs, create unambiguous movement phrases and link them to the spoken Hebrew language.

- Practice the phrases with the students.

- To keep students' interest, do not show the storybook or the poem at this stage.

- After students are able to follow the phrases without the teacher's modeling, show some pictures to extend the word bank — e.g., egg, a baby bird.

- Make new phrases and ask students to move. (Make sure the sequence always has a beginning, middle, and an end.)

- You are now ready to read the whole sequence, show the pictures.

- Ask students to make a new dance using the movements they learned.

- Ask students to tell the story in Hebrew.

TEACHING HEBREW: "THE ELEPHANT'S SWING" BY OWEN AND BRUNER

As students become more proficient in the language, you can gradually ask them to move in different ways (e.g., slowly, fast), then introduce the matching vocabulary in Hebrew.

---

[10]James J. Asher, *Learning Another Language through Actions* (Los Gatos, CA: Sky Oaks Productions, 1981).

[11]Hayyim N. Bialik, *"Ken Lazipor,"* in *Chagiga Shel Shinim*, edited by M. Regev (Tel Aviv, Israel: Am Oved, 1980).

The story "The Elephant's Swing" by Miriam Owen and Esther Bruner[12] is about a little elephant that wants to have a swing just like children have.

Procedure:

- Ask students to practice the action verbs: to walk, to sit, to move, and to swing.

- Ask students to practice the concepts of up and down, forward and backward, side to side.

- Add the emotions of sadness and happiness, and ask students to explore those in a dance form.

- Always have students practice the verbs alone, and gradually introduce the spatial concepts to the movement phrase. Example: Dan and David swing up, Gila and Rachel swing down, the children walk forward, and the children walk backward.

- After students are proficient in the above words, the story can be read by the teacher and danced by the students. With older students who have a richer vocabulary, you can go into more complex issues of emotions and abstract situations.

Each of these stages presents multiple opportunities for introducing new vocabulary words to the learner. The teacher can review and practice words already known, while physically acting out the meaning of the words.

TEACHING A RITUAL

Many times, students object to rituals, saying that they see no use for them and don't understand the meaning or see the connection to their life. As a preparation for teaching a religious ritual, teachers may introduce a technical dance challenge. An example might be a pirouette, or doing strength exercises like lifting weights in order to be able to move more freely and fluidly later. Max Kadushin says that in our tradition rituals are performed before there is a complete understanding of why and what are the reasons for them.[13] Preparing for a

dance performance involves extensive practicing movements that initially seem to be out of context and are unclear in terms of their contribution to the dance performance. These are done simply because they need to be practiced in order to be able to further develop the movement once the dancer is experienced. Working on the technical aspects of dance might also shed light on the practice of religion.

CONCLUSION

In case you feel intimidated or overwhelmed by the idea of using movement and creative improvisation as a teaching tool, remember that students like to move and are happy to supply all the physicality needed for a successful lesson. Your job is to find the appropriate themes, to help students come up with questions, and to allow the students to be creative. The idea is not to have the students imitate your movements, but to discover their own kinetic language. If you are not comfortable with what might seem like uncontrolled energy, set up a system of freedom and restraints that supplies a secure structure for everyone. In my classroom, when I bang once on my drum, everyone freezes. It is effective to establish certain routines, like warm-up and closings. Always start simple and build up; the students, too, feel better knowing that the teacher is in control.

You might find that representing academic concepts in physical ways makes the learning more accessible and memorable for children, and fosters creative and dynamic energy in the classroom. Besides learning specific content from these kinesthetic activities, children exposed to creative movement as a language for learning become more aware of their own natural resources. They expand their concepts of creativity and of how they can use their own bodies. They learn through their own creations. The combination of discipline and imagination is an invaluable foundation for creative thinking. Encouraging children to work both alone and with others, to give and to take, to evaluate and to edit, to feel and to think, is empowering to them, and ultimately, therefore, to their teachers.

---

[12]Miriam Owen and Esther Bruner, eds., *The Elephant's Swing* (Jerusalem: The Melton Center for Jewish Education, 2000), experimental issue.

[13]Max Kadushin, *Worship and Ethics: A Study in Rabbinic Judaism* (New York: Bloch Publishing Co., 1963).

TEACHING CONSIDERATIONS

Dancing, I feel free, weightless and limitless. I feel I can fly. (Arielle, a student)

- Freedom as well as discipline is the essence of a creative dance.

- The time dedicated to dance expression should have clear goals and structure.

- Limits and constraints of behavior should be clear and unambiguous.

- Ask students to move the furniture so they can move freely and safely.

- Students and teacher should respect each other's personal space.

- Teach students the terms and names of movements.

- Teach students to observe and articulate what they observed.

- Observe students, and describe positively your observations.

- Give students time to reflect on their dance creations.

Guidelines for Teaching Content Matter through Dance

- Identify a narrative or a situation that provides possibilities for movements.

- State the key concept.

- What are the essential question and the sub-questions?

- Identify the questions students will answer with the choreographic process.

- Explore the possible movements that can be used to answer the question.

- Clearly define the requirements in terms of content learning and also the dance elements to be explored.

- Make sure time was allocated for the process of creating a dance.

- Allocate time for reflection upon the dance activity and the connection to the content matter.

Putting It Together Check List for the Teacher

1. Keep it simple.

2. Be concrete — what exactly do you want to accomplish?

3. Be specific — elbows not arms.

4. Use technical terms.

5. Encourage creativity.

6. Point out different ways of solving the same problem.

7. Repeat activities — students like to do what they know and improve on it.

8. Introduce new material within a familiar context.

9. Vary dance activities — groups, pairs, singles.

10. Use students' ideas as well as your own.

BIBLIOGRAPHY

Ackerman, Karen. *Song and Dance Man.* New York: Alfred A. Knopf, 1988.

Grandpa demonstrates for his visiting grandchildren some of the songs, dances, and jokes he performed when he was a vaudeville entertainer.

Garfunkel, Trudy. *On Wings of Joy: The Story of Ballet from the 16th Century To Today.* E-Reads, 2002.

An engaging history of dance that introduces readers to the major choreographers, performers, and composers who influenced the development of ballet.

———. *Letter To the World: The Life and Dances of Martha Graham.* New York: Little, Brown, and Co., 1995.

The life story of the choreographer and modern dancer Martha Graham for young readers.

Gelsanliter, Wendy, and Frank Christian. *Dancin' in the Kitchen.* New York: The Putnam & Grosset Group, 1998.

A story book for children in rhymes about a family dancing in the kitchen. Illustrated.

Lewis-Ferguson, Julinda. *Alvin Ailey, Jr.: A Life in Dance.* New York: Walker & Co., 1994.

The life story of the dancer and choreographer Alvin Ailey for young readers.

Satterfield, Barbara. *The Story Dance.* Minneapolis, MN: Fairview Press, 1997.

A young girl enjoys looking at the family treasures with her grandmother and hearing about the adventures of a great-aunt who danced the Flamenco in Spain.

For the Teacher

Armstrong, Thomas. *Multiple Intelligences in the Classroom.* 2d ed. Alexandria, VA: Association for Supervision and Curriculum Development, 2000.

Armstrong describes how educators can bring Howard Gardner's theory of multiple intelligences into the classroom every day.

Dewey, John. *Art as Experience.* New York: Perigee Books, 1980.

Dewey discusses art from different points of view: the artist and the observer, the substance of art and what it expresses, the criticism of art and the observer's reflections, the different philosophies of art, and the way art reflects culture and civilization.

Fraser, Diane L. *Playdancing: Discovering and Developing Creativity in Young Children.* Hightstown, NJ: Princeton Book Company, 1991.

Games and stories that help to discover and develop creativity in young children.

Gardner, Howard. *Frames of Mind: The Theory of Multiple Intelligences.* 10th ed. New York: Basic Books, 1983.

Gardner challenges the notion that intelligence is a single general capacity possessed by every individual to a greater or lesser extent. He posits the existence of a number of intelligences that provide a unique profile to each person.

Humphrey, James Harry. *Child Development and Learning through Dance.* New York: AMS Press, 1987.

Humphrey discusses dance education, how to teach dance in elementary school, and child perceptual-motor development, among other issues.

Jensen, Eric. *Arts with the Brain in Mind.* Alexandria, VA: Association for Supervision and Curriculum Development, 2001.

Jensen is a strong advocate for the arts. In this book he offers suggestions for the integration of movement in the curriculum.

Joyce, Mary. *First Steps in Teaching Creative Dance To Children.* 3d ed. Mountain View, CA: Mayfield, 1994.

The author explores elements of dance and how to introduce these to children. With photographs.

Mann, Kate. "Moving Metaphors for God: Enriching Spirituality through Movement." In *Teaching about God and Spirituality: A Resource for Jewish Settings.* Roberta Louis Goodman and Sherry H. Blumberg, eds. Denver, CO: A.R.E. Publishing, Inc., 2002.

The focus of this chapter is on using movement to nurture spirituality. Three examples of movement activities are offered, each including the prayer connection, vocabulary, a teacher script, and questions for discussion.

Minton, Sandra Cerny. *Choreography: A Basic Approach Using Improvisation.* 2d ed. Champaign, IL: Human Kinetics, 1997.

The author addresses three of the dance standards — understanding choreographic principles, creating and communicating meaning, and using critical and creative thinking skills.

Tucker, JoAnne. *Creative Movement for a Song: Activities for Young Children.* Denver, CO: A.R.E. Publishing, Inc., 1993.

This book features 30 movement activities for lively songs by Kol B'Seder, Fran Avni, Julie Auerbach, and Steve Reuben. There is also an overview of using movement in the early childhood classroom, as well as an outline of Jewish concepts and dance concepts for each musical selection.

Tucker, JoAnne, and Susan Freeman. *Torah in Motion: Creating Dance Movement.* Denver, CO: A.R.E. Publishing, Inc. 1990. (Available from www.E-Reads.com as a print on demand book for downloading via the Internet)

This book provides creative movement activities for each week's Torah portion.

CHAPTER 50

Enriching Instruction with Stories and Storytelling

Meryl Wassner

INTRODUCTION

The ancient art of storytelling has been, since earliest times, integral to civilization as a means of transmitting values, history, and dreams. Some stories are best read — their language is rich, poetic, unique and to be savored. Other stories beg to be told with all the *ruach* (spirit), body language, and emotions possible. In either case, stories are meant to be passed on from generation to generation in families, in places of worship, in political circles, while mentoring in the workplace, and in our schools.

We have not made the most of all that storytelling and stories can bring to the teaching and learning experiences of participants in synagogue, day school, camp, JCC, retreat, and adult educational settings. This chapter, therefore, will guide you through some of the issues to consider when thinking about adding stories to a full range of materials and teaching formats. The following questions are addressed by the author:

- How does a story enrich a lesson?

- When are good opportunities in the lesson to weave in a story and how does one do it?

- How does one select the best story for the content/objectives of a lesson?

- How capable and receptive are students to responding to stories and storytelling, and why?

- Why are teachers reluctant to utilize this rich medium and wealth of information to build on their lessons (programs)?

- Considering both the subject matter and the ages of our students, what are some of the special challenges we face in teaching? How can incorporating stories meet the challenge?

To help teachers add stories to their teaching, examples of both materials and teaching strategies are included here to assist teachers, program coordinators, Rabbis, Cantors — in fact, anyone who teaches our Jewish values and history to a group.

Stories are a two way street. I love to tell stories, and so do my students. My lessons were not as complete when I insisted that I tell all the stories and that my students do all the listening. I was angry when John said, "You sure do a lot of talking." It took quite a while for the sense of his criticism to sink in.

I began to observe the teaching style of our school's social studies teacher. Every year, she did a project that required stories from the children. One year, they told about family members who had immigrated to the United States. Another, year they made time lines of their lives. Last year, they interviewed senior citizens about their childhood memories. Each project was bound into a book and copies were given to each participant. What a great way to teach the value of stories!

As a result of my observations, I now ask for more stories from my students. I ask them to retell the biblical stories that I teach in Judaic studies. I ask for holiday stories. Sometimes I proclaim their stories "*midrashim*," which fills them with pride. I've learned that I love to hear stories as much as I love to tell them.

(Maura Pollak, Tulsa, Oklahoma)

HOW/WHEN TO USE A STORY IN THE LESSON

Stories can be used to open a lesson, inviting students in, to end a lesson, leaving a lasting impression, or they can be inserted into the body of a lesson to provide another style of teaching after, perhaps, some introductory frontal instruction. A story itself can *be* the lesson, giving students an opportunity to interpret and extract Jewish values or messages from its events, language, and tone.

The teacher must determine which technique will be more effective — asking the students to read the story for themselves, or having the teacher *tell* a story that illustrates the point in the lesson to be made, expanded upon, or challenged. With preschoolers, it is obvious that a story will be told. But with classes of older students, good readers can be asked to read a tale silently or aloud in pairs. Through a sheet of questions to guide discussion in small groups, students can be prompted to think about the meaning of the story by themselves, rather than having the teacher become the transmitter.

> For K-3 students, a story with associated actions is very appealing and increases their attention. Bible stories are more fun when the children are assigned an action/motion to do each time they hear a character named. Hear "Moses" and stroke your imaginary beard, Miriam pretends to shake a tamborine, Pharaoh pounds his fist in his hand. I let the students offer suggestions.
>
> *(Sheila Lepkin, Denver, Colorado)*

SELECTING THE CORRECT STORY

Once the instructor has made the decision to incorporate a story (through reading or storytelling), has determined at what point to weave it into the lesson, and has narrowed down the focus of the lesson, he/she is faced with a decision: which story to use. We are blessed today with extensive congregational libraries and the enormous resources of the Internet. We, therefore, have literally hundreds of stories to chose from to cap off a lesson, or teach a *mitzvah*, or lead us back to another time in our history. But even when the theme is clear, the selection process can be overwhelming. So how does the teacher choose the perfect story for the lesson? Here is a true story that may answer this.

At the age of 38, I found myself returning to college to complete my Bachelor's degree. I was very excited

and terrified at the same time. Would I have the right stuff to go back and finish this important personal and professional goal? I had loved literature when I had been in college two decades earlier. So I decided to register at Spertus Institute of Jewish Studies in Chicago for the spring semester, hoping to find a literature course. I scanned the selection, and lo and behold, there it was: "Medieval Jewish Literature." I was about to embark on a long-standing love affair with our culture and values, embodied in the vast collection of Jewish folklore, taught by one of the finest folklorists, writers, and editors of our time, Howard Schwartz.

Professor Schwartz was the visiting professor at Spertus that term, on loan from the University of Missouri. He often would set the tone of the class by opening with a story. His stories were an enchanting introduction to the rich material he was teaching. I was taken by his relaxed, yet animated delivery. There was tenderness in the words and ultimately the message. Often, a good deal of humor was also packaged in. I loved the class, looking forward each day not only to discussions of the materials we had read, but to Professor Schwartz guiding us back through time with such eloquence and verve.

One year, I was asked to lead off a High Holy Day service at my synagogue with a story. I was not nervous about getting up in front of the congregation, but for the life of me I could not decide upon which story to tell. A few weeks before Rosh HaShanah, I attended an all day seminar on storytelling by Professor Schwartz, who was visiting the Chicago area. I approached him with my dilemma.

Professor Schwartz listened very carefully, as is his usual manner, and he answered my question with a question or two of his own: "Meryl, have you found any story in the recent past that you find yourself returning to again and again? Think about it. What story really speaks to you?"

His questions took me by surprise. I thought he would simply offer a few recommendations and I would be on my way, grateful for his suggestions. What story did I find myself going back to again and again? He waited very patiently, silently, as I thought. I replied to him that I had always enjoyed the Zalman Schachter-Shalomi story entitled "The Midwife of Souls."

He asked me what about it kept bringing me back to it. I responded that it had touched me deeply each time I read it. Much to my surprise, I felt a swelling of emotion in me, and I know I had tears in my eyes. He then just smiled at me and said: "Then you know the story you must tell. "The Midwife of Souls" is your story, Meryl . . . and you must tell it."

I will never forget that exchange. I cannot tell you how many times I have told the "Midwife of Souls" story — in my classes, giving storytelling workshops, doing storytelling programs in congregations. As I maintain eye contact with my audience or students, I consistently notice a palpable energy in the room. People are moved. It becomes an authentic experience for them and me. Connections are made.

There may be 20 stories written on a specific theme that you might chose. Select those that draw you in. Reread them, feel the language, the message. Tell them aloud to yourself and then find a gentle listener. One story will stand out. If it resonates for you, you have found the right story for your lesson.

HOW THE STORY ENRICHES THE LESSON

From a pedagogical standpoint, stories offer a change from the teacher "teaching" values or ideas in his/her own words. They give a different "voice" to the lesson, for even if the teacher tells the story, he/she becomes the transmitter, not the originator of the ideas.

A story can also add information, expanding the lesson in a style that adds texture and color to the content. It allows the students to use their imaginations, offering images they may not have seen, and evoking places in their minds and spirits that they may not have experienced before.

When telling a story, the teacher may use language that expands student vocabulary. Because many favorite, colorful stories come from different lands, students are exposed to cultural diversity. When hearing the story of Chusham, the sweet little boy from Iraq,[1] the children enter a world with open markets, alive with activity, commerce and distinctive social mores.

As storytelling is incorporated into the curriculum of older children, they can be encouraged to become the storytellers themselves, developing

their own language skills, elocution, creativity, and confidence. When researching the stories, they expand their knowledge of literature from many time periods and countries.

Stories offer the potential for a special kind of magic to happen in the classroom, a level of intimacy and sharing that cannot be matched by a more traditional method of instruction.

> My students learned about Holocaust rescuers through the personal story of one of our members, who told how he came to be a Holocaust survivor. This was so much more meaningful than the reading of such a story would have been! Another time, a different member asked to talk to our students about his experiences as a Jew in the Pacific arena during World War II — how important it was to him to have been given a miniature *Siddur* to carry with him, and how he celebrated Chanukah and Pesach while overseas. Both stories were interesting to the children and generated good questions and lively discussion.
>
> *(Carol Cohn, Orlando, Florida)*

OUR STUDENTS AS CONSUMERS

When we teach, we must always consider if the material we select will accomplish the goals we set out to achieve. Our goal might be the acquisition of a new skill, the integration of new information on a topic, an esthetic experience that touches student souls and subsequently facilitates their self-expression in some medium. We must try to anticipate how students will receive the material, asking ourselves what enables them really to take it in, to work with it on some internal level, and then to utilize it in the future. It is important not to underestimate students' capacity to interpret, then integrate materials. We must also not look at stories and storytelling as some "childish" form of communication; they offer great depth.

Children are the best readers of genuine literature . . . Folklore plays a most important role in children's literature. The tragedy of modern adult literature is that it has completely divorced itself from folklore . . . Without folklore and deep roots

---

[1] "Chusham and the Wind," in *The Diamond Tree* (New York: HarperCollins Publishers, 1991).

in a specific soil, literature must decline and wither away. Luckily children's literature is even now more rooted in folklore than the literature for adults.[2]

Children are consumers who expect authenticity. They want what is true, and paradoxically that truth can come in the form of magic or mysticism. Isaac Bashevis Singer comments on the child's psyche and why he writes about a realm beyond everyday realism:

> Because children like clarity and logic, you may wonder how I can write about the supernatural, which by its very definition, is not clear and not logical. Logic and "realism," as a literary method, are two different things. One can be a very illogical realist and a highly logical mystic. Children are by nature inclined to mysticism. They believe in God, in the Devil, in good spirits and bad spirits and in all kinds of magic. Yet, they require true consistency in these stories. There is often great logic in religion and there is little logic in materialism. Those who maintain that the world created itself are often people without any respect for reason.[3]

> During Jewish Book Month, I always have my Confirmation class read stories to the students in the younger grades. To prepare them, I find a story to tell to the high school students. They would never admit that they still enjoy having someone read to them or tell them a story, but I can tell by the expressions on their faces that they still do. The younger students light up when they see the older students walk into their classroom to spend time with them reading a favorite story, and the older students enjoy the adulation and responsibility.
>
> (Rabbi David Feder, Morgantown, West Virginia)

STORYTELLING WITHOUT FEAR

Once one is convinced of the legitimacy of stories and of our students' receptivity, there is just one more obstacle to face: that is, getting over personal self-consciousness about telling stories to students.

For some, it is the performance anxiety; for others, there is the concern of telling the story in a way that will be true to the author's intention. Perhaps the teacher doesn't know the students that well yet, and is concerned about being critiqued (especially by older students). When serving as the education director at various congregational schools, I have conducted workshops on storytelling to help my faculty become comfortable with the idea of weaving stories into their curriculum. Below is the exercise in which my teachers participate.

Introduction: I begin by sharing a story that I am comfortable telling and that touches me in some way (either my heart or my funny bone). This "safe" introduction, opens teachers up to the idea of telling stories.

I divide the faculty into three groups. To personalize the experience, I ask them to find a partner within their assigned group, someone with whom they don't generally have an opportunity to work.

I distribute sheets that help the teachers reflect on growing up experiences. Each sheet contains questions related to one particular generation (see Appendixes A, B, and C). The questions or phrases are meant to trigger memories to be shared orally with a partner.

After the pairs have shared their "stories," the groups reconvene. I ask individuals to retell the story they heard, and I make certain that we touch on the contents outlined in each of the Appendixes. I then ask them how it felt to be telling the fragments from their past. To the listeners, I ask what it felt like to be hearing these stories.

This has been a favorite exercise for, without exception, it engenders peals of laughter, pregnant silence, and even tears of gratitude from the participants. It bonds teachers together in a very intimate way that facilitates their staying in touch throughout the balance of the year. It creates community among the faculty, builds their confidence in being able to share personal stories with their classes, and reduces their inhibitions regarding incorporating more storytelling in their classrooms

Fifteen minutes of each subsequent teacher's meeting includes an opening or closing, with one of the faculty telling a story. This provides good practice and good modeling. By the end of the

---

[2]Introduction to Isaac Bashevis Singer's *The Power of Light* (New York: Farrar, Straus & Giroux, 1990).

[3]Ibid.

year, a wide selection of stories has been shared, which I keep on file for the faculty to access during subsequent calendar years.

SPECIAL TEACHING CHALLENGES

Teaching Torah To Middle School Students

The answer to how to make Torah relevant to middle school students takes many forms. For this age group, I would suggest introducing *midrashim* (stories that fill in the blanks of the Torah narrative) as one answer. The filling in the blanks, the creative extensions, the questioning nature of *midrash* are perfect for interpretation and discussion among 11 to 13-year-olds. With some skilled facilitation by the instructor, there is a wide variety of answers to questions, all of which can be "correct." This encourages active participation in class discussions, as well as a curiosity and appreciation for the original verses of Torah. The Lillian S. Freehof series, *Bible Legends*, is particularly well suited for this age student, both male and female. I have used it often with sixth graders, resulting in lively discussions.

> I have developed a set of "Magic Stories." These are well-known children's books for which I have created flannel pieces, magnetic pieces, small stuffed characters — anything possible to enhance the story. I use my flannel apron or mitten, magnetic chalkboard, or my hide and seek apron to draw the children's attention to the story. My hide and seek apron is one I made that has six pockets on the front and six on the back. The children are delighted every time I pull another character or prop out of one of the pockets. It really helps keep them focused on the story.
>
> (Kim Lausin, Beachwood, Ohio)

Working with Teens

Books have been written on how to get and keep teenagers' attention in the later years of their formal Jewish education. "Stories," which can help accomplish this, come in many shapes and forms. The autobiographical vignettes that are a part of ethical will accounts are intimate, real life stories. The writers share what they felt were the highlights of their lives, and express gratitude to those important to them. They often make references to the Jewish values that sustained them throughout their lives and the legacy they hope to pass on to those who follow them.

Family Education

Families have rich stories to share from previous generations. Frequently, it takes some prompting to get the generations to share these family treasures. Families are very busy, going in so many directions, with both parents working in the majority of households. A synagogue program offers a perfect forum for this intimate, intergenerational sharing. We need to impress upon families the necessity, the richness, and the joy of sharing experiences from holidays and times past. This sharing creates connections between the generations and the values that have pervaded the Jewish experience.

One year, I developed a family program for a *Shabbaton*. The overarching theme was: "Holiday Traditions in Time Past and Present: From Eastern Europe To Naperville" (a town west of Chicago). We had some activities during which entire families were in the same room, for example, immediately after a brief Shabbat morning service. I officially opened the weekend with a story entitled "Every Name Has a Story," a precious tale about a little boy's experience of being prepared for his first day of school. In a story rich in imagery and nostalgia, he is told about the time when his *"Tateh"* was going off to school. The young children in the room had just begun school (this was around the High Holy Days) and the parents had just experienced this bittersweet life passage with their offspring. The day had many short, parallel programs for children and their parents, and culminated in one last intergenerational activity, just before Havdalah.

During the *Shabbaton*, I used the questions in the Appendixes (the same ones that focused the faculty workshop described earlier in this chapter). I introduced the exercise (much as I did with my teachers in workshops) with the proviso that all questions can be answered, even if the adults came to Judaism later in life. (Cherished family traditions from other religions were also shared, with attention to the characteristics that made them rich, family bonding experiences. Participants were asked how the characteristics — not the specific tradition — could enhance Jewish practice as well.) I gave each family unit the opportunity to choose the sheet they wanted to complete. The guidelines were that the adults were to ask the questions of one another and the children were to listen to each parent's responses. The children who ranged in ages from four to 12-years-old, were permitted to ask brief, clarifying questions.

After the families rejoined as one group, I then asked the children to tell me something they learned for the first time about their parent's experiences growing up, or to share what their family now does together during the holidays. There were smiles, giggles, and sweet tears all around. The children and the parents referred to this experience throughout the entire school year. Many parents subsequently told me that they devote time every week, at least once, either at bedtime or on Shabbat, or during that down time in the car when driving from place to place, to share some remembrance with their children. Simply put, there is no bad time to do that!

Adult Learners

Many Jewish communities conduct adult learning institutes. A multi-week course on Jewish folklore, designed for Jewish adults, can introduce learners to a number of tales, storytelling techniques, great storytellers, and provide an opportunity to write an ending to an existing folktale.

Below is a brief outline of some of the potential components of a class for adults:

- Definition of a folktale

- Distinguishing features of Jewish folklore (compared to tales from other cultures)

- The traditional four levels of Jewish text interpretation

- **P**shat (the simple understanding of a text)

- **R**emez ("hints" or implied meanings in a text)

- **D**rash (explanation or application of the text)

- **S**od ("secret" — the mystical interpretation)

- Rabbi Nachman of Bratslav and the Baal Shem Tov, and their influence on modern folklorists

- Commonly found motifs in Jewish folklore

- Reading, comparing, and contrasting folktales

- Interpretive endings by students to a previously written story

Variations on this multi-week course can be designed to suit teenage learners; a survey course for a Jewish high school can be a fine addition to a curriculum that includes Jewish literature and values. It can also be adapted for a fourth or fifth grade family education program with parents and their children. The creation by each family member of an ending to an existing story can foster an appreciation for one another's creativity and self-expression. The Nachman of Bratslav story entitled "The Treasure,"[4] which teaches us to value our families above all else, is a fine choice for the family education format.

CONCLUSION

Educators can utilize stories and storytelling in their classrooms and programming in Jewish settings without reservation. The value is immeasurable and the students, be they children or adults, will respond favorably to this enrichment of the materials presented. Stories can be woven into any part of a lesson or unit of study.

There is no shortage of materials to incorporate into our lessons. It is important to take time to select the stories that will be appropriate for the learners. The bibliography contains recommended sources for stories on many topics for various age groups. Equally important, the educator must feel comfortable with the specific selection of story or stories for the lesson. Students respond well when the material excites and/or inspires the teacher, too.

Teachers have the opportunity to create a culture in which stories are widely used in the classroom. This chapter has offered some guidelines for beginning to use stories as a natural, rich enhancement for almost any lesson. Stories have been uti-

---

[4]"The Treasure," in *Miriam's Tambourine*, edited by Howard Schwartz (New York: Oxford University Press, 1988).

lized throughout our history as a vehicle for learning and appreciating our traditions. Whether the topic is ethics, Jewish holidays, *mitzvot*, or history, stories can fill a strong role in the teaching. Teachers can encourage one another by sharing their own "best practices" at staff meetings throughout the year.

In our transient, fast paced society, the transmission of our people's stories is challenging, but perhaps critical. As educators, we can do our part to continue the rich tradition of passing our values on to the next generation through the art of stories and storytelling.

APPENDIX A

My Bubbe and Zayde Told Me . . .

Note: Use this in a teacher or family workshop to introduce participants to storytelling.

Recall a story your grandmother or grandfather told you about the way that they celebrated [insert holiday] "in the old country" or during their youth in the U.S. or Canada.

Where were you when he/she told you the story?

How did you feel as the memory was shared with you?

Before today, have you ever shared this story with anyone else? If yes, when? If no, why do you suppose you didn't?

APPENDIX B

When I Was Growing Up, I Remember . . .

Recall a favorite [insert holiday] celebration from childhood, in your home or at a relative's house.

How old were you, and who was there?

What made it so special for you?

Have you ever shared this memory before? If yes, when? If no, why do you suppose you didn't?

APPENDIX C

In My Home Today, We . . .

Describe one holiday custom you have incorporated into your home ritual.

Was this tradition passed on to you from a previous generation?

Is there a new ritual you have created and chosen to add to the holiday that you had never experienced as a child? Describe.

Have you discussed with your children the importance to you of the old or new ritual and/or its history?

BIBLIOGRAPHY

Collections of Stories

Bogot, Howard, and Mary Bogot. *Seven Animal Stories for Children.* New York and Jerusalem: Pitspopany Publishers, 1998.

> Stories of courage, friendship, compassion, respect, and loyalty, told through the adventures of animal characters. Enchanting to read or tell.

Frankel, Ellen. *The Classic Tales: Four Thousand Years of Jewish Lore.* Northvale, NJ: Jason Aronson Inc., 1993.

> Almost 300 stories are included here, in language appropriate for children and adults.

Freehof, Lillian S. *Bible Legends: An Introduction To Midrash (Genesis & Exodus).* New York: UAHC Press, 1988.

> A collection of *midrashim* focusing on the first books of the Torah.

Kadden, Barbara Binder, and Bruce Kadden. *Ethical Wills: Handing Down Our Jewish Heritage.* Denver, CO: A.R.E. Publishing, Inc., 1990.

> This is a fine source when developing a course for high school students on Jewish values passed down through the family.

Reimer, Jack, and Nathaniel Stampfer. *Ethical Wills: A Modern Jewish Treasury.* New York: Schocken Books, Inc., 1983.

> A large collection of ethical wills.

Rouss, Sylvia. *Fun with Jewish Holiday Rhymes.* New York, UAHC Press, 1982.

> Great fun for PK through Grade 1. The book includes many easy rhyming poems and simple finger plays.

Rush, Barbara, and Howard Schwartz. *The Diamond Tree.* New York: HarperCollins Publishers, 1991.

> Terrific tales for PK through Grade 3. Each story is short, colorful, and perfect for the telling, especially in Tot Shabbat or services for young families. All ages respond to the magic in some of these tales, and the sweetness and humor of others.

———. *The Sabbath Lion.* New York: Harper Collins Publishers, l992.

> A bit long for one sitting, unless told during a relaxed 15-minute quiet time (during snack, or just after a lunch). Best suited for first grade and up. Magnificent illustrations.

Schmidt, Gary. *Mara's Stories: Glimmers in the Darkness.* New York: Henry Holt & Co, 2001.

> Mara tells over 20 traditional Jewish stories to women and children in the dark of her concentration camp barracks. Schmidt includes detailed notes in the back of the book on the history of the tales within Jewish tradition and lore.

Schram, Peninnah. *Chosen Tales: Stories Told by Jewish Storytellers.* Northvale, NJ: Jason Aronson Inc., 1995.

> An intimate glimpse into the lives of some of our greatest living storytellers. A directory in the back offers contact information for each featured storyteller. An amazing, rich resource for all teachers of all ages.

———. *Jewish Stories One Generation Tells Another.* Northvale, NJ: Jason Aronson Inc., 1993.

> Not only is this a wonderful collection, but the author shares with us why she has selected these particular stories. Very personal and insightful.

Schwartz, Howard. *The Day the Rabbi Disappeared: Jewish Holiday Tales of Magic.* New York: Viking Children's Books, 2000.

> Stories not of magic, but of miracles from God, written for upper elementary school students.

———. *The Dream Assembly: Tales of Rabbi Zalman Schachter-Shalomi.* New York: Amity House Publishing, 1988.

> These stories are for mature middle school students through adults. It is useful for students to have familiarity with the four levels of story interpretation in order to appreciate fully the depth and texture of these remarkable stories.

———. *Elijah's Violin.* New York: Oxford University Press, 1994.

> Because of its more complicated themes and sophisticated language this collection is appropriate for Grade 3 to adult. There is a teacher's guide with advice on helping students find meaning in the stories.

———. *Gabriel's Palace: Jewish Mystical Tales.* New York: Oxford University Press, 1999.

> These are mystical, short tales best suited for Grade 5 and up.

———. *Miriam's Tambourine: Jewish Folktales from around the World.* New York: Oxford University Press, 1988.

> An extraordinary selection of tales from different countries and centuries. (I have often used this book to introduce Jewish folklore to my adult learning classes.)

———. *Next Year in Jerusalem.* New York: Puffin Press, 1998.

> A beautiful assortment of stories from the Middle East for second grade to adult.

Singer, Isaac Bashevis. *The Power of Light.* New York: Farrar, Straus & Giroux. 1990.

> Chanukah stories for Grade 3 and up. Many of the stories are quite intense, some dealing with Holocaust experiences.

Weiss, Stewart. *The Shammas.* Southfield, MI: Targum Press, 1992.

> Very poignant and powerful stories for junior high students and older.

Zusman, Evelyn. *The Passover Parrot.* Minneapolis, MN: Kar-Ben Copies, Inc., 1988.

> A delightful story to read or to tell. For Kindergarten and up.

Newsletter

The Jewish Storytelling Center
The 92nd Street "Y" Library
1395 Lexington Avenue
New York, NY 10128
212-427-6000

An excellent newsletter that puts you in touch with programs, courses, and Storytellers.

Internet Resources

City Lore/Center for Folk Arts
www.carts.org

> The Center for Folk Arts advocates for inclusion of folk and traditional arts and culture in education. It offers teacher training through web sites and all day workshops in folk arts, folk life and oral history. This web site offers a full calendar of educational resources for teachers, including films, lectures by professional folklorists, organizational meetings, and discussions on new cultural heritage projects.

The Art of Storytelling
www.eldrbarry.net/roos/art.htm

> The subtitle of this site, "The Art of Storytelling," gives us a good sense of its primary focus. It is designed to help teachers find resources for fine stories, as well as techniques for good storytelling. It lists many associations and storytellers to contact for more information and networking.

Library of Congress, the American Folk Life Center
http://lcweb.loc.gov/folklife

> This web site has a few links worth noting: The "Ethnographic Resources" source leads educators to a *Teacher's Guide To Folklife: Resources for K-12 Classrooms* by Peter Barlis. Another link is to the Smithsonian Center for Folklife Programming and Cultural Heritage. There is also a section on Mythology and Narrative.

Enriching Instruction with Games

Susan Arias Weinman

Only the lesson which is enjoyed can be learned well. (*Avodah Zarah* 19a)

Games are an important teaching tool. When utilized properly, they become interactive, engaging, and successful learning activities. Good games are both fun and effective. This chapter is about how to determine what games students like to play, how to utilize games for community building, learning and review, and strategies for creating and constructing your own games. In each section, sample games are presented for your use.

WHAT YOU NEED TO KNOW BEFORE PLAYING GAMES

Games People Play

How do you find out what games your students enjoy playing? Ask the parents; ask the children. Send home a brightly colored "Family Questionnaire" (see Appendix for an example) to be completed and returned the first week of school. Ask the parents and students what games they like to play as a family and ask what games they play alone or with friends. Share these lists in class, and have students discuss the reasons why they like certain games. You will now have a broad base of card games, board games, and others from which to create your own classroom "tried and true" games. Student favorites (board games, ball games) played at some point during the year will greatly enhance your chances for successful learning and community building. However, be creative. Your own game ideas, and those listed in this chapter, will add a surprise element to your classroom. Who knows; you may create a new "school family" favorite!

Parents are the first teachers in a child's life to utilize games to teach. By playing games such as *Peek-a-boo, Sort the Socks, Finger Plays, I Spy with My Eye, Candyland, Chutes and Ladders, Dominoes*, etc., children learn about colors, objects, counting, letters, and the sheer joy of learning. These family games teach, enrich lives, and build lifelong family bonds and memories. Weekends still mean family *Monopoly* sessions to me. To continue this familial enrichment, you could invite the parents into your classroom for at least one "family games" session. Games discussed throughout this chapter can easily be used (or modified) for such use.

Learning Styles of Students

There are three major learning styles that people exhibit — visual (looking, reading, watching), auditory (listening and talking), and tactile/kinesthetic (touch, movement, doing). The variety of games should reflect the variety of student learning styles. In this way, the joy and involvement of each child is maximized in the classroom.

How do you determine your students' learning styles? Some school registration forms will have a section asking parents to describe their child's: (1) learning style, (2) strengths, (3) weaknesses, and (4) after school activities. If this information has not yet been sought by your school office, send home a questionnaire/survey asking parents to describe these four items (see Appendix). This information gives you great insight into the children with whom you will be working, and can help you decide which types of games would be appropriate for each student.

Follow up this knowledge by playing a variety of games during the school year that are inclusive of all students' learning styles. Three categories of games, with examples, are listed below:

1. Visual Games

   • Hebrew vocabulary games using picture cards and word cards

   • "Dress the Torah" (also tactile) - student teams "dress" a foam board Torah as quickly as possible with a *hagorah* (cardboard belt), *tzitz* (mantle), *choshen* (breastplate), *yad* (pointer), and *rimonim* or *keter* (finials or crown).

2. Auditory Games

- A circle game - Children complete the following sentence aloud: "I'm walking through the synagogue and I see ____." Each child adds another item to the list until the circle is complete.

- "Name that Tune" - Students have to guess the holiday song or prayer to which they are listening.

3. Tactile/Kinesthetic Games

- *Holiday Bag* - Students touch an object inside a bag and guess what it is and what it is used for.

- *Holiday Pick-up Race* - Two teams of students run to the end of the room and pick up a Jewish object used for a certain holiday (called aloud by the teacher), run back to their team, and put the object in their team's pile.

- *Shimon Omer (Simon Says)* - Students are asked to touch different body parts using Hebrew names for the parts. Or, they can be asked to hop while singing songs such as *"David Melech Yisrael."*

- *Jericho Jenga* - Students use building blocks (wooden or cardboard) to build the wall of Jericho. Then, one by one, they take away blocks (but not from the top) until the wall falls down.

Learning Abilities/Disabilities of Students

Take into account the learning abilities/disabilities of students. Games should be a positive, fun experience for all involved. Refer to the student registration forms (school, camp) to get an idea of what difficulties (or strengths) some students may have. Again, if not covered in registration forms, this can be covered in your own parent questionnaire (see Appendix).

There should always be a place in your game for varied abilities. Maybe those students identified as taking longer to "process" information should

become the game show host when playing *Jeopardy* — they will learn the material without feeling embarrassed as a slow or poor player on the team. The student with artistic abilities could be the one drawing the word/phrase clues in the game *Pictionary* for their teammates to guess. (In *Pictionary*, students are given a word or phrase to draw on a white board, which their team members need to guess. Drawings can also be done with yarn on a felt board. No verbal clues are given. Points are awarded for correct guesses.) Individual games on tape (tape recorded directions that students follow for pre-printed games such as word finds and puzzles) can be created for those children who need one-on-one help or when you don't have the time or additional classroom aides to give them this individualized attention. Those with visual impairments could become a classroom magician. The magician gives students clues as to what's in a bag he/she is holding. The students have to guess what the item is, and finally the magician makes it appear. Those with a hearing loss can be the guest actor, or successful guesser, for a game of *Charades*. Tailor your games to your students' needs, and you will have created a classroom full of possibilities.

Energy Level and Attention Span

The time of day you are working with students (morning, afternoon, evening) should be taken into consideration. Are you with them when they are ready for the day to begin or when they are tired at the end of a school day? Games help create the atmosphere you desire, whether you want the youngsters to be physically active or calm. Choose the type of activity accordingly.

Always be aware of the attention span of learners, whether they are of preschool or high school age. No matter the age, students need activities to shift during the course of the day. Younger children can be engaged in one activity for shorter time periods (15 minutes) before needing to move onto another activity, while older students can remain on task for a half hour. Games can be easily interspersed during the day to create this learning environment shift.

Choosing Teams Can Be Stressful

Have you ever been on the playground and watched how children choose teammates for a game, and then seen the look on the face of the child who was chosen last? What should be a fun experience for all often begins with hurt feelings for some. A sensitive teacher can change that. Be creative when separating students into classroom teams. Several successful approaches to make this task more positive and fun for the students follow. Try these methods when playing any games:

1. Use craft sticks with students' full names (Hebrew or English) written on them. At the beginning of the school year, either the teacher or students can make name sticks that are then kept in a special can or box. Let the students know the sticks will be used throughout the year for choosing game partners, activity partners, project groupings, etc. How are these craft name sticks used?

    a. Separate the sticks at random into the different number of teams you need for a game.

    b. As teacher, choose two* craft sticks (*the number corresponds to the number of teams needed for this game). Those two students become the team captains. Without looking at the names on the sticks, have the team captains alternate choosing craft sticks from the can/box until their teams are complete.

    c. Choose two* craft sticks (*the number corresponds to the number of teams needed for this game). Those two students become the team captains. Have the team captains choose the next craft stick (without looking at the names on the sticks) and call the name aloud. That new person stands and then chooses the next stick. Continue this process until all teammates are chosen.

2. Puzzle pieces - At the beginning of the school year, draw or glue two different Jewish-themed pictures onto two pieces of heavy card stock and laminate. Divide the number of students you will have in your class by two, and then cut each card stock into that many pieces. (Example: 14 students divided by two. Cut each card stock into seven puzzle pieces. There will now be one puzzle piece per child.) Keep all of the puzzle pieces in one bag. Before playing, tell students what the two completed puzzle pictures are. Students take a puzzle piece from the bag, and then try to find other students with pieces to complete their puzzle. Two teams for the game will thus have been chosen. This idea can also be used with two or more "real" Jewish puzzles already in the classroom. Be creative.

3. Cut slips of white paper into small squares, equaling the number of students in your class. Using Hebrew letters and their corresponding numbers, "number" the squares, starting with "alef-1" and counting up to half the number of students, with two pieces sharing the same Hebrew letter and number. For example: For 16 students, cut 16 squares "numbering" two of them "alef-1" through "chet-8." Place the squares in a bag. Have students take turns picking a slip of paper from the bag. Odd numbers are one team; even numbers are a second team. Alternatively, keep those with the same numbers on the same team — you choose how many pairs make up each team.

4. Jewish stickers can easily be found. Cut up stickers (keep the backing on) with two different pictures (Jewish stars, Israeli flags) or holiday themes (Passover, Chanukah). Place in a bag and have students pick a sticker. Students who draw the same picture or holiday theme are teammates.

5. Don't forget the ever popular way to choose teams — boys versus girls.

INCLUDE GAMES IN CLASSROOM ROUTINES

Students work well when routines are established in the classroom. They have a clear sense of what to expect, and what is expected of them during the course of the day.

My Hebrew students know to come into the classroom and go to our voting box and "vote" for one of three prayers we will sing at the end of our class. They sit down and begin the review work they find written on the white board. When all are seated, I take attendance. Next, we tackle new material, have discussions, and play a game. Finally, five minutes before the end of our session, we sing our voted upon closing prayer. To my students, the act of using a ballot box to choose the final song for the session is a game in itself. This provides them with an activity over which they have control.

Choose a game to play at a given time during the day, or build a unit review game into your schedule, which students know will always be played at the end of each unit.

A game could routinely start your day. As students enter the classroom, have them take a game sheet they can immediately play independently, such as a word search, crossword puzzle, maze, connect the dots, word scramble, cryptogram, etc. When students are done, they may check their own work by using an answer sheet on the teacher's desk. Prizes, such as stickers or candy, are optional. The web site www.discoveryschool.com/puzzlemaker is an excellent resource to use to create (and recreate) these games. Plug in the curriculum-specific information you want to use, and this web site creates the game for you.

Additional games to play at the beginning of a session include *Beat the Clock* (choose material students should be able to read within one minute and use a minute timer for the reading) and small group trivia questions.

> The game *Jewish Jeopardy*, during which students supply the question for an answer, is a popular way to review content at my religious school. However, I try to "glitz" it up. Library card pockets on tag board are for the answers, but I frame it in dazzling lights! Punch holes all around the edge of the board and insert a small holiday light in each hole, taping it on to the back. Plug it in and you're in Hollywood!
>
> *(Sheila Lepkin, Denver, Colorado)*

COMMUNITY BUILDING GAMES

Communal activity is as meritorious as studying Torah.
(Jerusalem Talmud: *Brachot* 5.1)

It is important to play games together for the sake of forming friendships and building commu-

nity. Our values speak to the idea that what is important is how we treat and interact with others in our daily lives. To this end, "getting to know you" and "working together for a common goal" should be important themes for community building games.

"Getting to Know You" Friendship Games

1. *"Shalom, koreem li _____."* (Hello, my name is _____.) - Students stand or sit in a circle. Throw a lightweight ball (nerf, wiffle) to a student saying, *"Shalom, Sarah, koreem li Morah[1] _____."* Sarah replies, *"Shalom, Morah _____, koreem li Sarah."* Sarah then throws the ball to a second student. The second student says, *"Shalom Sarah, koreem li Rachel."* Rachel throws the ball to a third student. The third student says, *"Shalom Rachel, koreem li Aharon."* The game continues until all have had a chance to introduce themselves to the group, and the last student throws the ball back to the teacher.

2. *Boker Tov* (Good morning), *I Like _____.* - Students stand or sit in a circle. Give students a topic for the game (Jewish holidays, Jewish objects, Jewish heroes, etc.). If the topic chosen is Jewish objects, you start the game by saying, *"Boker tov, I like Shabbat candlesticks"* and then pass the ball to the student to your right. The student says, *"Boker tov, I like Shabbat candlesticks and _____,"* filling in the blank with a Jewish object he/she likes. Continue passing the ball to the right, with each student repeating what the student before said, plus adding something he or she likes. The game is over when everyone in the circle has had a chance to contribute a sentence. This game reinforces course content, while allowing students to find out more about each other. It is also a lot of fun.

3. *Same Sound* - Give each student a name tag and ask everyone to stand or sit in a circle.

   a. Start the circle game with, "My name is Sarah and I like . . . singing the 'Shema.'" Go around the circle and ask

---

[1]*Morah* is Hebrew for "teacher." In some schools, female teachers are called "*Morah* (their first name)"; male teachers are called *Moreh* (their first name).

students to fill in their own name and something Jewish they like that begins with the first letter of their name. David might say, "My name is David and I like *davening*," or "My name is David and I like dancing the *Hora*." Continue this until the circle is complete.

b. For the second part of the game, ask students to look to the person on their right and say, "Your name is Sarah and you like _____." Continue this until the circle is complete. See how much students remember about each other. The alliterative sounds should help.

4. *I Did a Mitzvah: Circle Clapping Game* - Have students sit in a circle cross-legged, and in a singsong fashion pat their thighs four times in cadence to the words, "Who did a *mitzvah*?" While everyone continues to clap their hands four times in rhythm, the student to your right replies, "I did a *mitzvah*." Everyone in the circle pats their thighs four times and rhythmically says, "What was your *mitzvah*?" The group stops patting the beat to listen to that same student's reply, "I _____." (A sample response might be: "I visited my friend in the hospital.") Everyone in the circle claps their hands six times in cadence and says *Tov me'od*, very good!" This cycle is repeated until everyone in the circle has a chance to reply. Other thoughtful topics are: Who is kind? Who is patient? Who likes to share? and Who gave *tzedakah*?

5. *I Believe* - This is an extraordinary way for teenagers to get to know one another, while respecting each other's beliefs without judgment or ridicule. This non-team game can be used for groups studying Bible texts, ethics, and theology in school, camp, or retreat settings, either indoors or out. Place yourself in front of a wide-open area, with the students facing you in a side-by-side line, halfway back. In this game, students respond to statements by moving closer to or further away from the teacher. The closer to you, the more they agree with the statement; the further away from you, the less they agree with the statement. Once they have moved, students take turns explaining their opinions (though "passing" in this

discussion is an option). Sample statements include: God wrote the Torah; The stories told in the Bible are true; In order to be an observant Jew, you must keep kosher; If someone gambles at a casino and donates his winnings to a synagogue, the leadership must not accept the money. The conversations this game brings up are personal and should stay within the class.

An easy to make game I have used with students of all ages has a single, simple picture (a Torah, a *Siddur*, a rainbow, etc.) or a word (Moses, Israel, birthright, prophet, etc.) on each of the many cards I've made. Played either with all cards face up or as a game of *Concentration* with them all face down, the object remains the same. Find two that go together. The catch is that the player must be able to provide a reason why they go together.

For example, a picture of a Torah can be matched with any of the following: an *Aron Kodesh* (that's where it's kept); Moses (God gave him the Torah to give to us); a *Siddur* (they're both found in synagogue); a *tallit* (one wears a *tallit* when reading Torah, or one uses a *tallit* to touch the Torah during its *hakafah*, or when reciting the Torah blessings); a picture of Mount Sinai (where we got the Torah); Shavuot (when we got the Torah); Simchat Torah (when we finish reading Torah and start again); or a picture of the Tablets of the Law (The Ten Commandments are found in the Torah).

(Carol Cohn, Orlando, Florida)

Working Together for a Common Goal

A community is too heavy for any one to carry alone.
(*Deuteronomy Rabbah* 1:10)

The students had just finished their unit on Shabbat when I was invited to join them for their special Shabbat meal. The long classroom table was beautifully set with a tablecloth, place settings, Shabbat candlesticks and candles, challah and cover, jam and butter, and juice. We sang the blessings, ate, drank, and shared some special time together. They were so happy to share their knowledge of this won-

derful weekly holiday with me. Sitting around the table together, we felt like a family.

How did this community bonding come to be? Their teacher began the morning playing *Shabbat Hide and Seek* with them. Before the students came to school, the teacher hid the Shabbat items, (tablecloth, candlesticks, candles, wine cup, *challah* cover, *challah*, etc.) around the classroom. When class began, she had each student choose a Shabbat card (with name and picture on it) from a bag and then asked each to look for the matching item that was hidden somewhere in the classroom. When they found their item, they were to bring it to the table. When all found what they were looking for, they shared the name of their item and what it was used for. As a class, they then properly set the Shabbat dinner table and we enjoyed our Shabbat together. This was a game with a purpose — a wonderful review of a lesson learned, a "real" experience using their knowledge, and the understanding that a community is made up of people working together for a common goal. Scavenger hunts and hide and seek games provide excellent opportunities for engaging students in working toward a community goal. Which part of your curriculum can you use to play these games?

Other games in which the whole community must work together to accomplish its goals are:

1. *Brainstorm* - This is an ongoing class game that can last weeks or months. The object of this game is for the class to collect 180 points (ten times *chai*) to receive a class party, or some other coveted class prize. This game is played on a weekly or daily basis until the students reach their goal. The teacher develops questions with multiple answers. The class brainstorms aloud the answers, and for each correct answer they receive one point. For example, you might ask the class to name Jewish objects that would be used on Shabbat. Immediately, students start naming objects aloud. Each correct object named earns the class a point. To add a twist, and to make certain that all of the students participate, one day you can have one row of students answer the first question, a second row the second question, etc. On a second day, the boys and girls alternate answering the questions. On the third day, all students answer at the

same time. On the fourth day, students with birthdays from January through June and June through December answer alternating questions. Keep a running tally of the total points earned each time students play. The game is over when the class reaches 180 cumulative points. Besides serving as an enjoyable class review, this game builds community while students work for a common goal and cheer each other on.

2. *Family Feud* - Based on the television show, this game needs the cooperation of the entire group of campers and counselors (or students and teachers). The game can be played as an all-camp activity or between smaller groups. How is this game developed? The camp director creates a camper questionnaire form with questions such as: (1) My three favorite camp foods are ____. (2) My three favorite Jewish foods are ____. (3) My three favorite camp activities are ____. (4) My three favorite Jewish activities are ____. (5) My favorite sound that I hear at camp is ____. (6) My favorite Jewish sound to hear is ____. (7) My favorite Jewish song to sing is ____. (8) My favorite Jewish holiday is ____. (9) My favorite Bible story is ____. (10) My favorite Jewish object is ____. Have the counselors give a copy to each camper to complete in his/her tent/cabin. The counselor collects and tabulates the top three answers of his/her campers (including the number of campers that used each of the top answers) on a master form (blank questionnaire form) and hands in the master form to the camp director. The totals of all collected master forms are then tabulated by the camp director to form the official "top three answers" to the game's ten questions. The camp director (or the counselors) acts as the game show host. There are ten questions, with the top three answers (one point each) for each question used as the correct answers. Two teams take turns answering one question at a time. To earn all three points per question, the teammates must guess all three correct answers before guessing three incorrect answers. If they get three incorrect answers, however, the other team may guess one answer to receive one point. Play switches when a

team either earns all three points or guesses three incorrect answers. The game ends when all ten questions have been answered. The team with the highest score wins. Remind the campers, though, that it took the whole community to create the game and play it together. An ice cream cone for all!

3. *Noah's Ark* - Preschool/Kindergarten students are each given a picture of an animal. They each act out their animals at the same time and they go around the room trying to find their "partner." Once they find their partner they can enter "Noah's Ark" (be creative — use blocks, chairs, playhouse, etc.) to hear a story of Noah.

4. *Light the Chanukiyah* - Use a felt *chanukiyah* with a candles wall hanging as the game board and movable yellow felt flames as the game pieces. The object is to "light" all the candles on the *chanukiyah* after singing eight songs (three Chanukah candle lighting blessings and five other Jewish songs, not all of them necessarily Chanukah related). You will need to prepare song sheets ahead of time for those songs not known by heart. Students sit on the floor in a half circle, facing the *chanukiyah* wall hanging. The teacher sits in front of the students. Tell students that the object is to light all the candles, but they must solve clues/riddles to discover which song they need to sing before a new candle can be lit. (If your clue is, "I'm so dizzy I think I'm going to fall down," they need to guess that the song is "I Have a Little Dreidel.") Students answer clues/riddles as a class. The student who answers the riddle correctly gets to light that candle and the group sings the song. If that person has already lit a candle, he or she chooses someone else that has not yet had a turn to light. For the last candle, all the students that have not yet lit a candle do so together.

5. *Seder Plate Thesaurus* - This Passover game has the students work together to express their feelings about the symbolism of the *Seder* plate items and create a class mural. Separate the class into two groups, giving each an oak tag poster with "Seder Plate Thesaurus" written at the top as the title in outline form. Below it place a huge round *Seder* plate with five circles on which are written in outline form the following words: egg (*baytzah*), shank bone (*zeroa*), bitter herbs (*maror*), *charoset*, and greens/parsley (*karpas*). Do a separate circle for salt water on the board, as well. Each group tries to come up with as many words as possible to fit within each circle to explain what the meaning/feeling of the item is. For example: salt water = tears for Israel, heartbroken, plagues, sea, tears of sadness, hard times, ocean, crying. Give students a certain amount of time to complete each circle, then count the number of ideas they brainstormed. In sharing the ideas with the class, one point is granted for each answer, and two points for each answer that the other team did *not* consider. At the end of the game, the team with the most points is the Thesaurus Winner. Students then decorate the outlined forms for the words on the oak tag and sign the names of their teammates. Hang their posters on the walls of the classroom as a Passover mural.

I use games for both reinforcement and review (and of course the students often think of them as a reward). I like to use a *Jeopardy* board with changing categories. For a Bible class, categories can be Books, Personalities, Grammar, Rashi, and *Parashiot* (Torah portions). Or, we can use more general categories like *Chumash*, *Nevi'im* (Prophets), *Megillot, and Tefilah* in the Tanach (Bible). Sometimes I ask students to create questions and sometimes I create my own.

(Cheryl Birkner Mack, Cleveland, Ohio)

GAMES AS PART OF THE LEARNING PROCESS

One who learns by finding out has sevenfold the skill of one who learns by being told. (Arthur Guiterman, *A Poet's Proverbs*)

One of the most significant learning tools, which includes using games, is a three-part student process:

1. Students are given separate portions of a curriculum unit to study individually or in

small student groups consisting of no more than four students. This can include textbook chapter study or student research into a specific topic. At least some classroom time should be used for this portion so that the teacher is available to answer questions students might have.

2. Students formally present (teach) the material they learned to the class.

3. Students create a stand-alone game or a portion of a curriculum unit game to be played by their classmates as a review for the unit just studied. Stand-alone games can take any game format students choose. These can be board games, card games, puzzles, word finds, television game show formats, etc. The teacher chooses the specific format for a curriculum unit game and gives specific instructions to students as to what they need to contribute to the game. For example, if it's a *Jeopardy* game format, students write a set of 15 questions per category based on their studies.

Prayer Book Monopoly, Jeopardy, and Hollywood Squares

How to Create These Three Games

In this section, the prayers of the Shabbat worship service are used to demonstrate the process of creating learning versions of three popular games: *Prayer Book Monopoly, Seder [Order] of the Siddur Jeopardy*, and *Holywood Squares* (misspelling intentional). Each of our games begins with the same acrostic sentence, "I See A Torah Coming." The acrostic sentence gives students an easy way to remember the service sections, and provides an easy way for the teacher to separate students into five different groups. "I" stands for "Introduction." "See" stands for "*Shema* and Its Blessings." "A" stands for "*Amidah*." "Torah" stands for "Torah Service." "Coming" stands for "Concluding Prayers." Students need to be able to identify the five different sections of the prayer service, know which prayers are in each section, and what the themes for each section are.

Step 1: Separate students into these five groups (corresponding to I See A Torah Coming). Give each student a *Siddur*. Ask the groups to read the Hebrew and English prayers in their section, write notes, and discuss the themes they discover in the section. During this process, rotate around the groups to help as needed.

Step 2: The groups decide how they want to present their findings to the class and begin working on their presentations. The work can be done in or out of class, but schedule in-class time for the final group presentations.

Step 3: After the presentations, it is time to create the unit game. Give specific instructions to each group. For *Prayer Book Monopoly*, each group writes three questions per prayer in their section — one easy, one medium, one hard. For both *Seder of the Siddur* and *Holywood Squares*, each group writes 15 questions about their section. After students accomplish this, the physical construction of the game begins.

1. *Prayer Book Monopoly* is created as a floor board game using a large 12' x 20' heavy duty clear plastic sheet (purchase from any hardware store), permanent felt markers, colored construction paper for the questions, and an 8" x 8" sturdy cardboard box cube for the game dice. Students write "Prayer Book Monopoly" in the center of the plastic sheet. The number of spaces needed for the game board has to be calculated. To get this number, the students count the number of prayers in the Shabbat service, add two to this count for "Start" and "*Oneg*." They then calculate how much space they would need per game space, and then draw the spaces around the perimeter. The prayer names have to be written in the order they are found in the prayer service, beginning after the "Start" box and ending with "*Oneg*." Each group is responsible for writing their own section of prayers onto the game board, and transferring their questions (easy, medium, hard) onto construction paper for each prayer. One student writes the numbers on the dice.

    To play *Prayer Book Monopoly*, you need a large open area. Play outside, in the gym, or in the social hall if your classes are held in a synagogue. Divide the class into two or more teams. One student per team becomes the human game piece, one person rolls the dice, and the teacher asks the questions. Teams take turns rolling dice, moving that number of spaces, and answering questions (they can choose easy, medium, or hard) for the prayers they land on. If the answer is correct, they stay on that spot. If incorrect, they move back to their original square. The first team to reach *"Oneg"* wins. When the game is over, celebrate with your own class *Oneg*!

2. *Seder of the Siddur Jeopardy* uses one poster board divided into five category columns the width of an index card: Introduction, *Shema* and its Blessings, *Amidah*, Torah Service, and Concluding Prayers. Each category has five rows. Each group writes their 15 questions on individual index cards of the color assigned to their group. These index cards are glued (using a re-stickable adhesive glue stick so they can be reused for other games) onto the poster board from easiest at the top, to the most difficult at the bottom. Write the numbers 100, 200, 300, 400, and 500 each on different restickable sticky notes the size of index cards; place these over each of the questions, starting with 100 at the top. Split the class into two teams. Either you or a student can be the game show host. Teams take turns choosing a category and numbered question. If they answer correctly, they receive those points. If incorrect, the other team can answer and add half of those points to their total. The game ends when all questions are answered. The team scoring the most points wins.

3. *Holywood Squares* is a human tic-tac-toe game based on the television game show *Hollywood Squares*. Use the same index card questions that were created for *Seder of the Siddur Jeopardy*. Make nine large cardboard cutouts each of X's and O's or have students choose two Jewish symbols and make cutouts of those instead. You need nine students to be the "squares" and any number of students in two teams to be the contestants. Either you or a student can be the game show host. Hosts keep the set of index cards. Set the "squares" up at the front of the room. Three standing in the back row, three sitting on chairs in the middle row, and three sitting on the floor in the first row. Each "square" holds onto an

X and an O. The contestants sit in two rows at their seats, with the host at the teacher's desk. Teams take turns choosing a "square." The host asks the "square" a question and the "square" answers it. The team listens to the answer and responds with either "I agree" or "I disagree." If they chose the correct response, their team wins their X or O. If incorrect, the other team wins their X or O. The "square" must then hold up their "X/O" sign for the remainder of the game. The game is over when one team gets three X's or O's in a row.

What makes such games so exciting is that students have ownership in the learning process and are deeply involved throughout. They are both successful learners and teachers, and they realize the pleasure of creating and playing teaching games that will continue to be used from year to year.

> In one fourth grade class, I had a couple of boys, Harry and Sam. They were great friends. When we played a *Jewish Jeopardy* game, the two of them practically came to blows over the rules and who had won a particular game. After that, I came up with two alternatives to the issue of competitive kids. At times, I would call upon the vast repertoire of "cooperative" games from the *New Games* books and the Project Adventure people. I've also designed games in which the class plays against the teacher. They certainly enjoy beating me more than each other (and frankly I have to *kvell* a bit when they do win!).
>
> (Michael Fixler, Syracuse, New York)

GAMES AS REVIEW/REINFORCEMENT

Reviewing a lesson a hundred times cannot be compared with reviewing it a hundred and one times.
(*Hagigah* 9a)

Games are a great way to review and reinforce lessons learned. They provide a much needed study time for students, and can demonstrate what may or may not need to be retaught before moving on in the curriculum. A variety of review games are described below.

1. *Running Relay* - Write a list of questions students should be able to answer based on the curriculum unit being studied. Have the students line up, one behind the other, at the back of the classroom. The teacher stands at the very front. Set the clock timer for five minutes. Send one student to the board to keep score of the number of correct answers given. One at a time, the students run to the teacher and each are asked a question. The student answers it, and the teacher says "correct" or "incorrect, the correct answer is ____." The runner returns to the line to tag the next person. Finally he/she goes to the end of the line while the next person runs up and gets a new question to answer. Repeat this until the time runs out. Check the score. Try this again, encouraging students to beat their score in the next relay race. Use the same set of questions in a different order. The game ends after doing as many relay races as you wish.

2. *Timed Progressive Relay Game* - Place a set of four different activity games at each of four stations (tables) located around the room. Divide the class into four groups. All teams play at the same time; each team's home base is one of the four corners of the room where they stand in line, one behind the other. Each student takes a turn going to their team's station and completing one portion of each of the activities, then going back to the group and passing the baton (pencil/pen) to the next student on his/her team who will then go to the same station and complete a portion of each activity. This continues until all students have had at least one turn and the four activities are completed. When a team finishes, its members sit down and yell out "time" and the teacher writes their relay time on the board. When all teams are finished, the teams go to their stations and correct the activities as the class reviews the answers. Teams count the number of correct answers and record these on the board next to the relay times. There will be two sets of winners: one team with the fastest time and one team with the most correct answers for the four activities. Four sample activities at each station could include: crossword puzzles with four words, sorting objects into four holiday piles, unscrambling four words, and complete four sentences about the topic studied.

3. *Israeli Foot Race* - This is an outside game using a ball. Draw two outline maps of Israel (with major cities listed) in chalk on the school playground. Split the class into two teams. The students have to dribble a basketball to each of the cities, say the name of the city aloud and one thing they know about it, and then dribble back to the team and pass the ball to the next player. The first team finished wins.

4. *Supermarket Dash* - This game can be used as a review of Hebrew names for foods, or as a review of fruits eaten for Tu B'Shevat. Set up a supermarket with plastic foods, and provide students with a Hebrew checklist of items they need to buy in an Israeli supermarket. Teams place these items in a cart and then go to the cashier to be "checked out." The group with the most correct items checked off wins.

5. *Pass the Hat* - Sit in a circle. Pass around a huge hat into which each student places his/her own written question about the lesson just learned. Pass the hat around the circle a second time so that each student may pull out a question to answer. If the student doesn't know the answer, other students may help. No teams, no points, just a circle of learners.

6. *Who Can Retell?* (or *Memory Bag* or *Do You Remember?*) - Whichever name you choose to call it, this is a highly effective review game, similar to *Pass the Hat* in #5 above, but much more involved. To play this game you will need a "memory bag" (use a tote bag or a drawstring bag), index cards cut into 1" x 5" strips, beads, necklaces (use long shoe strings, lanyard, or yarn that can be retied), empty cardboard jewelry boxes (department stores can give them to you free), and penny prizes (stickers or candy). The class helps create the questions for this review game, which can be ongoing for a month or for half the year. Add to it daily and play it weekly. At the end of each ses-

sion, ask the students to develop five questions that review the day's learning. Write each question (including the answer that the class agrees to) on a separate index card slip and place each in the class "memory bag." Let the students know that each time you will add two questions of your own to the memory bag; when you add yours, be sure to read each aloud and review the answers with students.

Every so often take out the bag to review what has been learned to date. Pull from one to five questions randomly from the "memory bag." Students can write their answers on paper individually or you can split the class into teams and they can write their answers as a team. (If played individually, each student receives his/her own "necklace of knowledge" and a jewelry box in which to store it. If played in teams, each team receives a necklace and jewelry box in which to store it.)

Each correct answer earns a bead for the necklace. Each time a student or team reaches five beads on their necklace, they receive a prize. Collect the jewelry boxes and store them in the classroom for the next time the game is played.

Camps can be creative and use this game idea as well. Place daily memories of camp or bunk happenings in a "memory bag," and for a "color war" have this as part of the games.

7. *Football Phonics* - This game can be played indoors or out, preferably during the football season. To simulate a football field, write two sets of the yard line numbers (10, 20, 30, 40, 50) and the word "Touchdown" on long strips of heavy duty white cardboard or oak tag. Place each set facing away from the other, only sharing the 50 yard line space. Create questions based on the topic you are studying in class that you want the students to be able to answer. If it is Hebrew prayers, each question can be to read a line from the prayer. If it is Bible study, each question can focus on the story or person the class is studying. This format can also be used for a Jewish trivia questions game.

Divide the class into two teams, each

starting at the 50 yard line (in the middle of the "field," facing away from each other). Toss a coin to see which team goes first. The object of the game is to have alternating team members individually answer questions, thereby physically moving one ten yard line at a time (with a correct answer) until they make a touchdown. As soon as a student makes a touchdown, he/she sits down in their team's touchdown area. The game ends when all students on one team make a touchdown. This is my son's favorite Hebrew school game.

8. *Who Wants to Be a Millionaire?* - This television type game show is extremely popular with students. Play it with a twist. Write a series of Jewish general knowledge questions that students in your grade level should know, ranging from easy to hard. Divide the students into two teams that take turns answering the questions, starting with the easiest and working their way up to the hardest. For each correct answer, the team is awarded the next dollar amount level until one team reaches one million dollars. Levels are: $100, $500, $1,000, $10,000, $100,000, $250,000, $500,000 and $1,000,000.

9. *Yesh Li [I Have] Bingo* (or *Yesh Li Shabbat Bingo*) is fun at any age. The title, theme, and number of squares should relate to the age group of students and to your curriculum. Younger grades play with a grid of nine squares, while older grades can play with a grid of 16 or 25. Preschool, kindergarten, and first graders can play *Shabbat Bingo*. The three Hebrew letters in the top columns will be "*shin-bet-tav*" (which spell Shabbat), and the nine squares on the bingo boards will have Shabbat items on them. Older grades can play "*Tefilah Bingo*. The five Hebrew letters in the top columns will be "*tav-fay-yud-lamed-hey*" (which spell *Tefilah),* and the 25 squares can have either prayer names written on them, or words from just one prayer. When someone wins the game (3, 4, or 5 in a row, depending on your game board), have them call out, "*Yesh Li Bingo!*" or substitute the title of your game for "bingo."

10. . . . *And Action!* - Split students into two teams. Hand one player from the first team a one-sentence written scene from their class studies to read (e.g., Moses bringing the Ten Commandments down from the mountain), and say "And Action!" As in *Charades*, the student acts out the scene and their teammates have to figure it out. However, unlike *Charades*, they may speak, but not use any words or names that were written on the sheet of paper they were given. Ten points are given to the team when their teammates correctly identify the scene. If the team cannot identify the scene within one minute, the other team can give one answer. If correct, they receive five points. The game ends when all scenes are played out, or one team reaches 40 points.

11. *Not Quite Twins Jeopardy* - The game board is set up and scored the same way as the *Seder of the Siddur Jeopardy* game described above (see page 628). In this case, words within each category have letters or vowels that can be confusing (i.e., *ayin/tzadee*, *shin/sin*, *hey/chet*, *tzayray/segol*). Two teams take turns choosing categories. Points are awarded for each correct pronunciation of a word. The game ends when all words on the *Jeopardy* board are uncovered.

12. *Avot v'Emahot Rummy* - Laminate a deck of cards with four sets of three *Avot* — Abraham/*Avraham*, Isaac/*Yitzchak*, Jacob/*Yaakov*; four sets of the four *Emahot* — Sarah/*Sara*, Rebecca/*Rivka*, Rachel and Leah/*Rachel v'Leah* (put Rachel and Leah on the same card, united as the wives of Jacob); and four sets of the 12 tribes of Israel — Reuben, Simeon, Judah, Dan, Naphtali, Gad, Asher, Issachar, Zebulun, Benjamin, Ephraim, Manasseh. The object of the game is to get two pairs (of any tribe of Israel), and one three-of-a-kind (one of each of the *Avot* or *Emahot*). Students are dealt eight cards. As in regular *Rummy*, they take turns taking a card from the deck of leftover cards and then discarding a card onto the discard pile. As they get a pair or three of a kind, they place it face up in front of them. The first one to get two pairs and one three-of-a-kind wins.

STEPS IN CREATING AND CONSTRUCTING GAMES

Games are constructed backwards. You must begin with your final goal first — what you want the student to achieve from playing this game. This is your outcome based objective. Knowing this, you can begin to work backwards to construct a game to fit your needs. Below are steps to follow in creating a game.

1. What is the goal of this game? Is it to build community and just to have fun together, or is it to know specific information in the curriculum?

2. Write a list of the specific outcomes you want achieved. For *community*, your specific objectives might be: students will identify each other's Hebrew names; students will enact one *mitzvah* that other students have recently performed; students will state the other students' favorite Jewish foods; students will match classmates to their favorite Jewish holiday. For *curriculum* study, write the specific learning objectives you want students to know once the game is over. For a study of the Ten Commandments, your objectives might be: Students will tell the story of how we received the Ten Commandments from God at Mount Sinai; Students will explain how God's commandments guide us to live an ethical life; Students will be able to recite the Ten Commandments; Students will be able to categorize the commandments as to those that are between God and human beings, and those that are between one person and another; Students will be able to give an example of each commandment being followed; Students will be able to give one reason why they believe each commandment is important.

3. This is the time to choose the actual format you wish your game to take. Think of your student population: age group, learning styles, abilities, attention spans, maturity levels. Which basic types of games do they most like to play, and which of those would best fit the specific objectives of this game? Would your goals best fit physical activity games, such as relay races, or those played

with a ball, a game show question/answer type game such as *Jeopardy*, a picture/word recognition game using card games such as *Memory* and *Rummy*, or a board game format such as *Monopoly*? Stretch your mind, visit a toy store for ideas, or think "games" when you look at the fun classroom teaching techniques and activities provided in the book *TNT Teaching* (see the Bibliography at the end of this chapter). Let your imagination soar.

4. Now it's time to create that game. What materials will you need? Which supplies will you have to buy? What "stuff" can be found around the house or school?

Card Games - Use heavy card stock (found in office supply stores) to create the cards for card games. Felt marker words and numbers, picture cutouts from magazines (color copy if possible), and stickers can all be used for the front of the cards. When the cards are fully decorated, make sure you laminate them so that they will last.

Board Games - For most board games, you will need: a sturdy board game surface (leftover plastic panels donated by a local home building store, cardboard sheets, thick presentation or foam boards, a smoothly cut piece of wood, or even paper if you make sure you laminate it before playing; be creative); a well thought out layout (the easiest to use is one with block spaces drawn in straight lines around the perimeter of your game board, as in *Monopoly* — so that you have an easily defined beginning and end to travel and an open space in the center for any game cards you create); craft supplies to draw the face of the game board (permanent markers, fabric, pictures, glue, scissors, stick-on letters, religious objects and *alef bet* rubber stamps (sets sold by KTAV Publishing House, Inc. and Chai Kids), theme-related children's stickers for certain spaces they will land on; game pieces (different coins, multi-colored plastic *Bingo* chips, matchbox cars (buy a set of inexpensive wooden miniatures your local crafts store painted different colors); dice or spinner to help you move your game pieces around the board (sold in toy

stores, teacher resource stores, or create your own dice by using square cube cardboard boxes, such as coffee mug boxes or larger ones); and, a set of easily understood directions for students to follow (have someone else read the directions and give you feedback on their clarity).

Ball Games - For ball games with younger children, buy plastic beach balls with the *alef bet* on them (sold by KTAV Publishing House, Inc.), plastic Matzah Ball (sold by Chai Kids), or buy single colored large plastic balls (at any toy store) and let the children help decorate them to be used as their special game ball for the year.

5. Now your game is ready for a test drive. Play it with family, friends, or children you know other than your students. If it worked well, *mazal tov*! If there are a few things that need to be adjusted, make the changes and play again. Once you are satisfied, it's time to play the game with the students.

6. When the game is over, get student feedback. Students love to let you know what they liked and did not like about the game. You will also be giving them a boost in confidence, knowing that their teacher trusts and values their opinions.

CONCLUSION

I love to engage students in learning and to teach with games! My home and office are filled with "stuff" that others might perceive as trash . . . and often do. But I see this "stuff" as opportunities for learning. Those skeins of wool, Ping-Pong balls, game pieces from games long gone, bottle caps, felt, cardboard, etc., will one day be an integral part of a classroom game.

Games are a wonderful conduit for education in our schools. They are important and effective teaching tools, student motivators, community builders, spirit builders, student engagement opportunities, and, most important, they encourage students to see that learning is fun. May the games and ideas in this chapter spark the same joy in teaching for you as they have for me. We're never too old to play! Happy gaming.

TEACHING CONSIDERATIONS

- Know your students - When planning games, take into account individual student likes, learning styles, learning abilities, strengths and weaknesses, and attention spans. This will lead you to choose a variety of games to play throughout the year that will showcase and include all of your students.

- Games as community builders - Learning about your students and becoming a community through a circle game is much more fun and effective than just hearing the roll call at the beginning of the session. Playing together for a common goal creates a strong bond.

- Games as an integral part of learning - Students who are challenged to study a unit individually or in a group, then to present their findings to the larger group, and then to create a game to play based on their studies are most likely to learn the material.

- Games as review and reinforcement - Playing a game as a class review or reinforcement of a unit taught is effective because students are fully engaged in learning. They see themselves as having a good time. You see them becoming successful learners — a win-win situation for you and your students.

- Steps for creating your own games - Define your major goal for the game. Write out the specific items (learning objectives) you want the students to know when the game is over. Choose the format the game will take that will best suit these objectives. Create the physical game. Try the game out with others (not your students) and make any necessary adjustments. Play the game with your students. Get their feedback.

APPENDIX

"Getting to Know You" Family Questionnaire

Parents: To know your child better, and to help me create a more positive, inclusive, and enjoyable classroom environment for your child, please complete the sections below with your child. Please return this questionnaire to school in the envelope provided.

Section 1: Family Games and Student Activities

A. Describe your family's favorite games to play together:

B. Describe the student's favorite games to play alone or with friends:

C. Describe the student's after school activities (organized sports, music, etc.):

Section II: Learning Styles and Classroom Environment

A. Describe the student's best learning styles (reading, listening, doing, etc.):

B. Describe the student's special strengths and weaknesses (artistic, subjects, etc.):

C. Describe any special student needs regarding classroom environment (room setup, etc.):

BIBLIOGRAPHY

Books and Articles

Barish, Shirley. *The Big Book of Great Teaching Ideas.* New York: UAHC Press, 1995.

> The title tells it all. This book has excellent ideas for instruction, activities, and games for all grade levels.

Baron, Joseph L. *A Treasury of Jewish Quotations.* Northvale, NJ: Jason Aronson Inc., 1996.

> A wonderful compilation of Jewish quotes, listed by subject and theme. All footnoted quotes in this chapter can be found in this book of quotations. An important addition to any Jewish home and school library.

Brinn, Ruth Esrig. *Jewish Holiday Games for Little Hands.* Minneapolis, MN: Kar-Ben, Publishing, 1995.

> A great assortment of fun and easy to play holiday games for younger grades. Reading and writing skills are not needed.

Isaacs, Ronald H. *The Jewish Instructional Games Book.* Cleveland, OH: Bureau of Jewish Education, 1986.

> Excellent compilation of Jewish holiday games, Hebrew language games, games for prayer and use in junior congregations, and experiential games.

McGill, Dan. *No Supplies Required: Crowdbreakers & Games.* Loveland, CO: Group Publishing Inc., 1995.

> Introductions, mixers, indoor games, outdoor games, travel games, and night games written for use with teenagers to encourage community building. Good resource for camps and youth groups. Some work needed on the part of camp directors and youth group advisors to build in a Jewish theme.

Moberg, Randy. *TNT Teaching: Over 200 Dynamite Ways to Make Your Classroom Come Alive.* Minneapolis, MN: Free Spirit Publishing Inc., 1994.

> Compilation of exciting methods for presentation of curriculum in a classroom that can be creatively modified into games. Although not written for a Jewish school, it is an excellent resource for beginning and veteran teachers, especially in a day school setting. One unit in this book is dedicated to helping students create their own review games.

Moskowitz, Nachama Skolnik. *Games, Games, and More Games.* New York: UAHC Press, 1998.

> From cover to cover, this book is filled with a rich variety of well thought out games for Hebrew language instruction, with variations for these games to include Jewish history and holiday rituals curricula. An excellent resource.

Shapiro, Chava Schild. *Learn While You Play.* Brooklyn, NY: Torah Umesorah Publications, 2000.

> 100 gaming ideas based on Hebrew language skills and Torah studies. Geared to primary grades in day schools.

Warren, Jean. *1-2-3 Games: No-Lose Group Games for Young Children.* Everett, WA: Warren Publishing House, 1986.

> Compilation of cooperative, non-competitive secular games written primarily for preschool aged children. However, many games can be played with children through age eight. Games can be adapted for use in a Jewish setting.

"Games and Other Activities." In *Time to Read Hebrew Teacher Guide, Volumes I and II* by Hillary Zana, with Orna Lenchner. rev. ed. Denver, CO: A.R.E. Publishing, Inc., 2002, pp. 141-151.

> This chapter features creative games and activities usable with any Hebrew program for reinforcing decoding.

Games and Supplies Distributors

A.R.E. Publishing, Inc.
700 N. Colorado Blvd. #356
Denver, CO 80206
800-346-7779
www.arepublish.com

Chai Kids
21346 St. Andrews Blvd.
Boca Raton, FL 33433
888-CHAI KID
www.chaikids.com

Constructive Playthings
c/o U.S. Toy Company
13201 Arrington Road
Grandview, MO 64030
800-448-7830
www.constplay.com

Davka Corporation
7074 N. Western Ave.
Chicago, IL 60645,
800-621-8227
davka.com

Judaism.com
800-Judaism
www.judaism.com

KTAV Publishing House, Inc.
900 Jefferson Street
Hoboken, NJ 07030-7205
201-963-9524
www.ktav.com

The Learning Plant
P.O. Box 17233
West Palm Beach, FL 33416,
561-686-9456
www.learningplant.com

Torah Aura Productions
4423 Fruitland Avenue
Los Angeles, CA 90058
800-BeTorah
torahaura.com

CHAPTER 52

The Teacher/Principal Relationship

Jody Rosenbloom

One of the pivotal relationships for a Jewish teacher is with the principal. The term "principal" is used in this chapter to refer to the educational leader in the school whose primary responsibility is the day-to-day running of the school in keeping with its vision. (In a supplementary school, this position is often referred to as an education director and is sometimes held by a Rabbi. In a day school, it is often referred to as the head of school.) Teachers enter a system in which each principal is unique in relation to the formation and implementation of the vision and to the school network within which he/she works.

This chapter defines the parameters of the relationship between the principal and the teacher in a Jewish school, with an emphasis on the teacher's perspective. A bit of self-reflection and exploration on the part of the teacher is a worthwhile investment in assessing this relationship. Optimally, a healthy, synergistic relationship with the principal guides a teacher to improved effectiveness in the classroom, to increased job satisfaction in the school, to enriched connections to Judaism, and to enhanced participation within the school community. At the very least, a realistic view of the teacher/principal relationship can potentially save time, energy, and aggravation.

This chapter interweaves examples from the workplace so that each teacher can reflect on the roles, motivations, and school structures that affect this pivotal relationship. Emphasis on three priorities guides the discussion of each example: (1) cohering with the school's mission, (2) building relationships (*al tifrosh min hazibur* — don't cut yourself off from the community), and (3) maintaining one's integrity as a teacher (*b'chol l'vavcha, b'chol nafshecha, uv'chol m'odecha* — with all your heart, with all your soul, with all your might). Ultimately, the focus becomes how a teacher can realistically build and maximize the relationship with his/her principal.

Coherence - Students, parents, teachers, and the principal maintain focus and clarity through the school's mission, which acts as a frame and guidepost. For example, a teacher may notice that some of the B'nai Mitzvah students sneak drinks at a synagogue *"Kiddush,"* and argue that the school should include a drugs and alcohol use and abuse curriculum. This issue may not appear to be related to the mission of a school, since at first glance it seems to lack a Jewish educational piece. Some parents and school administration may think the topic inappropriate or premature for middle school students. On the other hand, the teacher who looks at the issue and highlights the threads to Jewish values and customs, makes a stronger case for course inclusion when negotiating with the principal or education committee. Coherence with a school's mission is more apparent when teaching about *pikuach nefesh* (the precedence of saving a life), *ad lo yada* (until you don't know — the Purim custom of drinking until you don't know your friend from your enemy), while stressing responsible drinking, the spirit of ritual and celebration, and the dangers of addiction and drunk driving.

Relationships - Connections between principals, teachers, parents, and students can support and enrich a school's social and learning fabric, or it can inadvertently unravel and lead to tensions and crisis situations. Not cutting oneself off from the community emphasizes the interconnectedness of all interactions.

Integrity - *B'chol l'vavchah* is about listening with your heart, improving your skills, knowing your own needs, strengths, and weakness, and bringing your best to the classroom.

The following vignettes explore the dynamic between teacher and principal. After each vignette there are questions and comments to help the reader look at the dimensions of each issue relating to mission coherence, relationship building, and teacher integrity. In approaching each vignette, assume both the teacher and the principal have valuable insights and contributions to share.

LESSON PLANNING, A TOOL OR TORTURE

Esther fits teaching at the local Hebrew School in between her classes at the local university. She considers herself to be a fairly organized person and is trying hard to do her job. She loves working with children. She was a teaching assistant in her religious school, yet is not a trained teacher. While she grudgingly attended religious school as a child, she is more connected to her Judaism as an adult, and is interested in learning more. She spends hours reading up on the topics to teach and surfs the Internet for supplementary worksheets for her lessons. Esther puts in much time and effort, but she doesn't feel as if her students are learning. She has been hesitant to go to the principal because she doesn't want to appear incompetent.

Coherence with a Mission

- What would help Esther link her preparation with the goals of the school?

- How could she find out the learning expectations of her school?

- If Esther's expectations and preparation are realistic, does the principal need to reexamine the goals of the school?

- If Esther's expectations are unrealistic, what resources could give her perspective?

Building Relationships

- How can Esther present her concerns to the principal?

- In what ways can the principal support Esther?

- In what ways could Esther's colleagues/ fellow teachers support her?

- Is there a role for Esther in sharing her teaching goals with her students and parents as a way to strengthen their learning community?

Integrity as a Teacher

- What assessments would help Esther discern the effectiveness of her lessons?

- How can the principal help Esther focus her preparation time?

- Is Esther's time spent reading and surfing used in attaining reliable and appropriate resources?

- Does Esther have realistic expectations of herself and the "growth curve" necessary for maturing as a teacher?

Some Thoughts

Esther has a variety of resources at her disposal, but has kept her needs to herself. If she is interested in growing as a teacher, the principal and her colleagues can help with perspective, pedagogic tools, and familiarizing her with the best resources. Esther may have a time management challenge of which she is unaware that is making her anxious about her performance. Teachers, who are also students, have a rhythm of demands during the school year that necessitate a certain amount of pacing and prioritization. Esther may have unrealistic expectations given the structure of the school and the realities of the community. If her preparation is adequate, perhaps the goals of the school need to be reassessed; her concerns will provide a vehicle for change that is useful to the principal.

CONFIDENTIALITY CONFLICT

When Isaac began teaching his sixth grade class, the principal wanted to make sure he had up-to-date emergency first aid certification. He was told he had a student, Ben, with severe allergies and occasional mysterious seizures in his class. A variety of accommodations had to be made to protect Ben's health and safety. The classroom was cleaned regularly. The students could not bring any food in the class, nor could the teacher provide any treats. The teacher was not to use chalk because of the dust created and only used certain types of non-toxic markers. Ben needed to sit by the teacher so he was close to medical attention if he needed it. Students were starting to grumble that Ben was teacher's pet. During parent-teacher conferences, several parents asked for permission to send snacks for their children since they were complaining of hunger during the day.

Six weeks into the school year, Isaac is unsure of what to do. His own stress level is building because of his worries about Ben. He feels pressure to tell the students and other parents about Ben's

*needs. Frustrated, he enlists his housemates to lis-
ten to his concerns. As he details the problems, it
turns out that one of his housemates works with
Ben's mother and volunteers all kinds of information about what kind of person the mother is. Isaac
now worries he has inadvertently violated Ben's
family's confidentiality.*

Cohering with the Mission

- How does Isaac find out the school's policy regarding students with special needs and inclusion? regarding confidentiality of information and the dissemination of information to students, parents, and staff?

Building Relationships

- At what point should the teacher voice his concerns to the principal?

- When concern for one student affects the dynamics of the entire class, what information is appropriate to share with the class and the families affected?

- If a family wishes to guard information about their child, what is the teacher's role vis-à-vis the principal if issues and concerns emerge?

- What are the advantages and disadvantages with venting frustrations to non-school personnel?

Maintaining Integrity as a Teacher

- How does Isaac weigh the needs of a single student against the needs of the entire class?

- What guidance from the principal would support Isaac in this situation?

- What teachable moments could the teacher create under these circumstances? for the students? for the parents?

- When Isaac needs to discuss his frustrations, who are the appropriate people to talk to without violating confidentiality?

Some Thoughts

In this day and age, it is common to have a student with special needs in the classroom. Different schools have different philosophies and guidelines about accommodating the student and there are often legal parameters covered in the Federal Disability Guidelines.[1] Isaac is challenged by the lack of clarity about who is privy to the information about Ben, as well as by the "ripple" affects of Ben's needs on the rest of the class. A discussion with the principal would be the place to start with regard to approaching Ben's parents or Ben himself about possibly sharing information with the class. This is a potential teachable moment for the parents and students on important Jewish values that could improve the working relationship in the class.

On the other hand, Ben and his family may have tried this approach in the past and may be less open to it now. The teacher can be a useful link between the parties concerned and offer valuable insights on the maturity level of Ben and his classmates in approaching this situation. In addition, when a teacher is feeling frustrated about classroom dynamics, it is normal to need to "process" perceptions and get support, but it is important to know the appropriate venues for support.

Respecting confidentiality is safest when a teacher talks to the principal directly. Outside of school, be careful to do so only anonymously (i.e., without using names or distinguishing characteristics) or the consequences are potentially painful or libelous. Isaac's information could be misused by his housemate. Sometimes informal information "grapevines" are useful, but the political and social parameters are tricky. You never know who is related to whom.

RESPONDING TO A BEHAVIOR CHALLENGE

Samuel had been teaching several years and developed decent classroom management skills. He was content with the performance of his well behaved students. This year he was in line to teach a class with a history of behavioral challenges. He tried seating charts, awards system, and raising his voice to improve students' behavior. He was uncomfortable sending anyone to the office as punishment,

---

[1]For more information on special needs students, see Chapter 16, "Special Needs Students" by Ellen Fishman, pp. 177-186 in this Handbook.

figuring that a good teacher just needed to find the right approach to control the class. By the second month, he was particularly frustrated with the behavior of his student, Shaina, who constantly baited and teased the other children. One day, Shaina went too far and started pulling the hair of her classmate. Samuel yanked Shaina from her chair, swore at her, and made her sit in a chair facing the corner. He then continued on with the lesson. The students all seemed to pay attention after the incident, and the class went well the remainder of the day.

That night, Samuel received an icy call from the principal asking for a description of what happened in his class that day. Samuel very calmly explained his lesson and gave a brief description of Shaina's disruption, which he reported handling in a new, more effective and forceful manner. The principal then explained that he received an irate call at home from Shaina's mother about the abusive treatment of her daughter. The principal asked Samuel to write his version of what happened, to bring the description to school in the morning, and to prepare a lesson plan for the substitute teacher who would cover his class for the day.

Cohering with the Mission

- In what way are Jewish values part of intervention in discipline/supervision procedures?

- How would Samuel have better followed the school's behavior guidelines and discipline procedures listed in the teacher's handbook and described at teacher orientation?

- What is the accountability structure of the school (who "answers" to whom or to what committee)?

Building Relationships:

- What is the teacher modeling for the other students when intervening with one student in this particular way?

- Is there information the principal could have supplied the teacher that could have prevented this situation?

- What is an effective way of collecting information under such circumstances that is respectful of all involved? Who is/are the proper person(s) to do this?

- How much of the issue is the child, and how much is Samuel's handling of the situation?

- What is the school's obligation to the student, parent, teacher, and principal in this situation?

- How might a school use a peer-led *Bet Din* (Jewish court) or issues committee to mediate when difficult situations arise involving several constituencies?

- How could Samuel better understand the school's mythology/history around such issues in order to anticipate the response of the different constituencies to the situation?

- What in the local public school system or press (e.g., distress over a school shooting or the popularity of a new classroom management technique) may be influencing the response/expectation of participants?

Maintaining Integrity as a Teacher

- What classroom situations need to be shared between the principal and teacher in order to support the teacher?

- What steps of intervention would be appropriate for a teacher having difficulties in the classroom?

- If a teacher exceeds his authority in a situation, what is the best time and place to discuss the problem with the principal?

Some Thoughts

Effective discipline is a process of learning boundaries that involves the teamwork of parent, principal, child, and teacher. When discipline is viewed only as punishment, this isolates the teacher and student, and limits the interventions. An added dimension of structuring a discipline system are cultural and value differences between teachers, school culture, and parents.

The interdependence of discipline, classroom management. and building community within the framework of Jewish values can provide a rich learning experience. Often schools develop a code of behavior for students and teachers with a set of steps toward enforcement. As a general rule, a teacher is always better off keeping the principal informed since there can be legal ramifications with discipline situations. Written documentation becomes crucial when the safety of a student or the school has been breached and/or the reputation of a teacher is threatened.

In this case, the principal provided a buffer zone by immediately providing a substitute teacher and initiating a process of collecting information. Possibly, an unknown home situation (divorce in process, a sibling harrassing the child, a history of abuse) was exacerbating student behavior. Perhaps this teacher's previous experience led him to overestimate his ability to work with a group he didn't have the skills to manage. The principal could provide classroom management training and help the teacher increase his skills, as well as identify intervention strategies in difficult situations. Perhaps the teacher has anger management issues that make classroom teaching unsafe for students. No one should underestimate the legal ramification of physical contact in a school setting.

> I've had seven educational directors or principals to work with over the last 20 years. The first and the latest stand out in my mind as the two best. Why? They've treated my ideas with respect. That doesn't mean things always go the way I want them to. That doesn't matter too much to me because I feel like my voice was heard and that I was a part of the decision making process.
>
> What does that tell me about the way I should be teaching? My students want to be heard. They want their ideas to be respected. Even when things don't go their way, they can handle it if they feel like their voices are heard.
>
> (Maura Pollak, Tulsa, Oklahoma)

NEGOTIATING AN INTERSECTION WITH THE SECULAR WORLD

Halloween was coming up and Rose decorated her day school classroom in orange and black. She was the general studies teacher and had minimal contact with the Jewish studies curriculum. She had loved dressing up for Halloween when she was a child and planned to come to school as a costumed character from the students' favorite book, Harry Potter. As a treat, she would bring some candy for the students.

However, as soon as he saw her room, the principal asked her to change the décor and the colors. That afternoon at the staff meeting, he reinforced to all that Halloween was not a Jewish holiday and that teachers were to proceed as usual, not acknowledging Halloween. Rose was disappointed. She figured that since all the children went trick or treating anyway, why not share in the fun at school?

Cohering with the Mission

- What does the principal consider when assessing teachable moments that intersect the secular world and the Jewish classroom?

- When planning class treats, rewards, and events, how does the teacher verify the school food policy?

Building Relationships

- What procedures, by either the teacher or the principal, could facilitate communication in anticipation of school holiday observances?

- What school protocols help integrate non-Jewish teachers into the fabric of the Jewish school?

- In what ways can teachers and principals work to encourage teacher interests that potentially nourish the classroom environment?

- In what ways could holiday observance of the Jewish community at large affect a particular Jewish school's observance?

- In what ways could holiday observance of the secular community at large affect Jewish school observance?

Maintaining Integrity as a Teacher

- If you are not Jewish, but are teaching secular studies in a Jewish school, what do you need to know to better interface with the Judaic curriculum?

- What could be the mediation process when a teacher's interests are in ignorance of, or in conflict with, the school's curriculum or policies?

Some Thoughts

The principal and teacher need to communicate about secular holiday observance guidelines in the school and the implementation of special activities in the classroom. The principal or teacher could take the initiative to convene staff meetings in advance to clarify observance parameters, school related issues, precedents, and/or negotiate options based on teaching staff input. Compromises in this particular situation could include a unit on scary stories in Jewish literature (e.g,. "The Golem" or "The Dybbuk"), or an integrated unit on celebrations where people dress in costume (Halloween, Purim, Mardi Gras, Dia de los Muertos). In cases where significant community concern is attached to the issue, the principal may need to defer to an Education Committee or other accountable body for guidelines.

Pivotal is the reality that teachers like to take advantage of important teachable moments. Yet principals have the added responsibility of seeing that the teaching is integrated into the larger fabric of the school. In this case, curriculum parameters dictate orienting non-Jewish teachers who are working in a Jewish setting. That Rose distributed candy in the classroom without prior approval touches on a variety of issues that could have serious ramifications: complying with the school *kashrut* policies so as not to violate dietary choices of the school/children, following guidelines and prohibitions set to minimize life threatening food allergies and eating disorders, or recognizing teaching philosophies that limit food related incentives as useless or harmful.

JUST THIS ONCE, IS IT OKAY IF . . .

Simon is frustrated with trying to maintain class continuity. His Hebrew school class meets Sundays, and then students' families choose either Monday/ Wednesday or Tuesday/Thursday sessions. Each sports season, parents come to him and want to switch days of attendance for their child. On Sunday mornings he often has a "visitor" as students show up in class with a friend who "slept over." Sometimes a parent sticks his or her head in to ask if having a guest is okay, but often this is in front of the children and Simon wants to be respectful to the parents. Simon finally asks the principal for help.

Cohering with the Mission

- In this situation, in what ways does teacher-principal communication facilitate the school's mission?

- How would Simon find out the student attendance and guest policy in the school?

- Are there options for session flexibility that support the goals of the school?

- Does it make a difference if the guest is Jewish or not?

- What might be the school's reasons for welcoming guests into continuing classes?

Building Relationships

- What is the role of the teacher in protecting the boundaries of the classroom learning environment? How might he enlist the principal's help?

- When do individual needs take precedence over the needs of the class as a whole?

- What communication with parents could increase their awareness of the affects of multiple session changes or last minute guests on class viability?

- How do school professionals handle parents who advocate for their own needs, and the needs of their children, when they are in tension with the needs of the school?

Maintaining Integrity as a Teacher

- When is flexibility a useful quality?

- At what point is flexibility disruptive to the learning process of the class?

- What parental or student requests are appropriate for the teacher to honor, and which have larger ramifications in the school?

Some Thoughts

What seems like a small logistical adjustment often has ramifications related to classroom dynamics. Teachers may be inadvertently put in the middle of these decisions. It is advisable to inform the principal of a discernable pattern, or to determine how individual situations should be handled. Parents do not always think about what is best for the class, but rather what is convenient for them. Teachers and the principal help parents and students to see the whole picture and to understand boundaries. There may be options that are more or less disruptive to the student and class.

Principals need information to see overall school trends based on the information provided from the dynamics in different classrooms. Parents and students often share information with each other so that however a situation is handled, a seemingly one-time decision could become an undesirable precedent.

In this particular situation, guests might report first to the principal who then privately approaches the teacher to find out if a visitor is possible on a particular day. Likewise, if a class functions better with a critical mass of seven or more students, then the whole soccer team can't change days in a given week; someone needs to communicate that to parents. The continuity of class composition is important to the dynamics of the class. On the other hand, it is nice to have parents and students who care enough to look for attendance alternatives when they feel they need to miss a class.

JUST HOW LONG IS THE PAPER TRAIL?!

Noah has begun teaching third grade in a local supplementary school. He is feeling overwhelmed, and it is only the first month. Though the students are a bit challenging, Noah comes to this job with experience in working with children this age and can work through most issues. The curriculum materials are adequate to plan his lessons. But the principal wants more forms filled out than Noah has ever had to do in other jobs. Teacher orientation was two full days with an extensive teacher handbook distributed. He is expected to turn in lesson plans and material requests a week in advance then incorporate any feedback the principal suggests. Any phone calls to the children's parents must be documented on a phone log and copies of

any homework must be shown to the principal in advance. The principal often edits the homework before allowing it to be sent home. Attendance and tzedakah calculations must be kept and turned in weekly. Classroom behavior issues that need the principal's intervention must be documented on a special form. Only the office staff can use the copy machine, so a form must be filled out to request copies. Noah is so exhausted by all the procedures, he finds less time to plan for teaching in his classroom, and no longer enjoys going into work.

Cohering with the Mission

- In what ways might Noah be feeling that documentation facilitates or hinders the mission of the school?

- What are ways to keep the big picture of the school's mission (the forest) in mind while attending to details (the trees)?

Building Relationships

- What might be some of the reasons the principal has instituted the various forms and procedures?

- If Noah is overwhelmed, what are his options for negotiating with the principal?

- How might he find out how the other teachers and staff are affected by the forms and procedures, without being seen as subversive to the principal?

Maintaining Integrity as a Teacher

- How might Noah balance the principal's need for structure with his own desire for spontaneity?

- In what ways can Noah use paperwork as a tool for reflection and organization?

- In what ways is paperwork necessary documentation of class progress?

Some Thoughts

Documentation is a necessary accountability loop between teachers and principals, but some paperwork is more important to the process, and some is less critical. The principal and teacher are part of a larger web of community building information that has many checks and balances.

For example, the entry by the office of family information in a database can be cross-checked with a teacher's class attendance records or home communication forms. The basics of lesson plans, parent communication, and student progress are important to the reflection and monitoring of what is going on. A principal is better prepared to advocate for the needs of a teacher who attends to the communication in these areas.

For example, imagine a parent who comes to the principal with a need to discuss what is being studied in Noah's class. A principal who has current lesson plans, attendance sheets, and home communication forms is better able to have an informed conversation that includes Noah's perspective. In this case, too, the teacher has specific examples for approaching students, parents. or administration with what is going on in his or her classroom. A school's files of past paperwork could also be useful to a teacher with questions about how the curriculum has been taught or the history of a particular student.

Noah is particularly concerned with the disproportionate time he is spending on paperwork, rather than his lessons. Noah can start a conversation with the principal to determine what timesaving options can be negotiated. For example, once the principal has an idea of his planning and teaching abilities, could Noah turn in lesson plans once each month, rather than weekly? If Noah has a different system for monitoring communication with parents, he could share that with the principal and see if it is an acceptable alternative to the established system.

As to the paperwork involved with office requirements (such as time sheets, resource requests, and copy machine use), the principal may or may not have options. Each school has a system for administrative realities that often takes into account a variety of issues the teachers rarely see. For example, issues may include the time necessary to process payroll, the frustration of a principal on a tight budget checking the closets in each class only to find hoarded supplies that were not shared, or the abuses of copy machine users that have inconvenienced other personnel using the same equipment.

Some systems are inherited and some are developed in response to specific situations. Procedures are intended to minimize problems and maximize service delivery for the most people. Principals and teachers have varying influence in these systems, but can work cooperatively to facilitate paperwork that supports the healthy functioning of the school, and community building.

ROOM PARENTS AS HELP OR HINDRANCE

Nathaniel is a new teacher with a group of very energetic second graders. One of the parents is very concerned about her daughter beginning religious school and feeling comfortable in the class. This parent is a former teacher and has offered to be a teacher's helper in the class. Nathaniel would love the help, but is concerned that he would then be "watched" and critiqued.

Cohering with the Mission

- How could Nathaniel find out if the school has any precedent or policy for parents working in the classrooms?

- How could such an arrangement further the mission of the school?

Building Relationships

- How can the principal work with Nathaniel and the parent to structure a teacher's helper position so that Nathaniel gets the help he wants, the parent's child feels comfortable, and the parent feels useful?

- What kind of job description can keep clear boundaries between the parent helper and the teacher?

- What are the possible drawbacks and advantages to having a parent helper in the classroom? the advantages?

Maintaining Integrity as a Teacher

- How can Nathaniel get help that supports and nurtures his growth as a teacher?

- What skills are necessary for Nathaniel to structure tasks for a helper?

Some Thoughts

Nathaniel could use some support and guidance with his lively class, with at least one student that may need attention as they begin school, and with a parent who is interested in helping in the classroom. A general check with the principal might give Nathaniel an idea of the history of the class and individual students, a few options for helping students transition into the school, and some history of parents as helpers. Before anyone is allowed to work with students, most schools have procedures for checking into the background, references, and trustworthiness of the helper. The teacher is primarily responsible for everything that happens in a classroom and is expected to take the lead in organizing tasks for the helper. The other factor is the child's need to build her own friendships, and how that is helped or hindered with her parent in the class.

WHEN PERSONAL AND WORK COMMITMENTS COLLIDE

David was born in South Africa and grew up in an observant home. In Johannesburg, he led junior congregation services, was an active member of B'nai Akiva, and spent several summers in Israel. He moved to a rural town in Kansas and agreed to teach in the only school in his area, a very progressive Reconstructionist synagogue. While David knew he was uncomfortable teaching things that went against his Jewish convictions (such as patrilineal descent), it was very important for him to stay connected to the Jewish community, and so he agreed to teach first grade. Initially, all went well as he taught introduction to Jewish holidays, blessings, and the synagogue. Then he realized the curriculum included a Shabbat family potluck dinner, a Consecration ceremony during Saturday morning services, and programming on the second day of Sukkot. The principal has approached him with her concerns that the students lose important continuity with his absences. Yet, the principal also feels David nicely role models a different observance level for his students. The teaching assistant who was assigned to the class to soften the transitions is starting to be resentful that she is covering for the teacher. David is conflicted about continuing to teach.

Cohering with the Mission

- What are the conflicts David may face while working in this setting because of the differences in his observance level?

- What are the classroom objectives and dynamics that are not in conflict with David's observance level?

- David agreed to teach in this school because of its openness to a range of Jewish observance. What questions should David ask the principal to find out where his boundaries are? How can David clarify the "teachable moments" the principal was hoping he would bring to the setting?

Building Relationships

- Given the limits that David has as a result of his observance level impinging on a portion of his curriculum-related activities, how can he build relationships with the children and their parents?

- As David began realizing the extent of his religious conflicts, how could he better anticipate the issues, making it less problematic for the principal?

Maintaining Integrity as a Teacher

- How could David demonstrate to the principal that he was attentive to issues related to his observance?

- How could David show accountability to the students?

- What might David say to his teaching assistant, who is beginning to feel confused and resentful?

Some Thoughts

David, while aware of his observance level differences, has really enjoyed interacting with the children and their families and being exposed to a school system and an observance level very different from any he had previously experienced. In order to strengthen his teaching position and offset the concerns of the principal, he has some options. He can develop ways to build relationships with the students and their parents, with the understanding that missing some of the events has put him at a deficit. For example, he could send a weekly letter home to the parents, sharing with them what is happening in the classroom. He can do a special parent-child program, not scheduled on a holiday. He can make a conscientious effort to prepare the students before they attend the regularly scheduled events, debriefing with them afterward, and incorporating the material into the class routine. He can use the difference in observance levels as a teaching tool and work with the director how best to do this, within the mission of the school. David might talk to the teaching assistant and the director, requesting that they help him create more continuity for the students and find out from them what they need from him to make this work. In particular, David and the principal need to assess the impact of this lack of continuity on the children. Given that first graders may have trouble with transitions, is the process of building community undermined by David's schedule and ultimately unworkable? Can David find other ways to stay connected to the congregation other than teaching weekly in the school?

WHAT DID I DO WRONG NOW? WHY ARE YOU ALWAYS DOWN ON ME?"

Ruth is a Youth Advisor to a small, growing teen program, and she is a seventh grade teacher. A college junior, she was a camp counselor for a few years, and likes hanging out with junior high and high school kids. She is charismatic, and the teens think she is a lot of fun. She brings them treats, tells great stories about her friends, and is easygoing in the classroom. The principal is concerned she is not following the curriculum, but tries to be a bit flexible given that the teens like Ruth and that they have been tough to engage in the past.

A local Jewish film festival scheduled a good movie for teens, but only for a week. Ruth asked the principal if she could arrange for a group to go. The principal met with Ruth and went over her concerns and parameters. Ruth felt as if the principal was micromanaging her every move, but that he was able to address the concerns and prepare for the field trip. The evening after the program, the

principal expected to hear from Ruth. After waiting until 6 p.m., the principal called her. She said they had a good time, but only three students showed up. The following day, the principal saw one of the teens who went to the movie and asked about the event. The teen expressed disappointment at the number of students who attended, but excitedly described Ruth's cute boyfriend and what a great Chinese meal they had together after the movie.

The principal is now considering firing Ruth because of his concern that Ruth does not understand accountability and the many steps involved to ensure student safety and timely communication. Ruth feels like she can never plan anything fun and interesting without her ideas being dismissed.

Cohering with the Mission

- Who and what determines teachable moments happening outside the classroom?

Building Relationships

- What could Ruth have done to head off the principal's reactions?

- When a teacher is expected to motivate students, how does she discern the difference between being friends with students and teaching students?

- How does a teacher best work with a principal who seems to be micromanaging?

- What are the parameters that ensure safety and build the program, versus the realities of an offense that warrants dismissal?

Maintaining Integrity as a Teacher

- What steps are open to a teacher when she and the principal interpret opportunity or facts differently?

Some Thoughts

There are three issues that contribute to the potential severity of the above situation: the process of accountability, the need for ongoing communication, and the perception of omission. Accountability, can be a tricky thing to establish if the teacher regards authority as problematic. This played out in

Ruth's relationship with the students, as well as in her relationship with the principal. As a teacher, Ruth preferred to be a friend rather than teacher. Not that these are mutually exclusive, but she found friendship and being liked by her students a priority with little regard for the school structure or negotiations with the principal. And the principal's attempts at guiding her lessons were perceived as micromanaging.

Both the principal and Ruth had a series of concerns and approaches that they did not clearly discuss with each other along the way. This led to "dump trucking" of many little issues onto a particular incident. The field trip took on greater significance and then became a focus for more than the particular concern. The principal has been uncomfortable with Ruth's loose lessons and last minute arrangements. Ruth believed she was not given enough materials to plan lessons and cited the movie as having just come to town. She was simply responding to a learning opportunity. Ruth and the principal may have needed a format for discussing issues prior to the field trip, developing groundwork to facilitate teachable moments.

On the other hand, Ruth perceives the principal's need for planning and formalities as micromanaging when, in fact, principals often have procedures in place to avoid very real hazards. Ultimately, when Ruth failed to report the whole of the situation to the principal, she left the impression of hiding information.

Never underestimate the power of the grapevine. As a general policy, it is better for the principal to hear something directly from the teacher than in a round about way through a student. The principal was particularly disturbed about hearing from one of the teens about the boyfriend and Chinese food. Ruth may have avoided the perception of impropriety by asking up front about her boyfriend helping staff a program and about the use of allocated program funds for last minute programming changes. A range of issues could be at play: whether the boyfriend was Jewish or not, the suspicion of physical contact with the boyfriend while with the youth group, concern as to whether or not the boyfriend has experience working with teens, or observance of *kashrut* parameters when eating out.

With regard to personnel issues, a school often has backup people the principal can consult with, such as the education committee, personnel com-

mittee, and/or school administrator to determine different options. In this case, Ruth could be put on probation, or the principal and Ruth could agree to a series of meetings to help with lesson planning.

> Even after many years in the classroom, I still find myself going to my education directors for guidance, to bounce ideas, and yes, even at times to cry for help. I really appreciate that most of the education directors I have worked with understand that, despite my experience, I am still a work in progress, as they are.
>
> I have learned that it is really important to give an education director a heads up whenever something happens in class that could cause parental concern. Most of the time, no one comments, but I've found it helpful to be proactive, so that the director can better handle any issues arising from the class situation.
>
> *(Cheryl Cash-Linietsky, Philadelphia, Pennsylvania)*

APPROACHING A LEADERSHIP CHANGE

Miriam is a seasoned teacher in a Jewish day school that has had three directors in six years, with a fourth recently hired. She has her own children in the school, and is committed to Jewish education. She and her family are pillars in the community, having taken a variety of leadership roles in the main feeder synagogue for the day school. She feels she has more experience than the last two directors, and that the leadership of the school has been more of a drain on the teaching staff than an inspiration. The teachers interviewed the candidates for director, but generally feel out of the loop as to the direction the Board of Directors may be taking the school. She is not looking forward to "training" another director for the school, who is coming with yet another set of "new ideas."

Cohering with the Mission

- What roles are possible for Miriam and the other teachers to clarify the mission of the school with the Board of Directors?

- In order to facilitate positive growth, what roles are appropriate for Miriam in clarifying the mission with the new principal?

Building Relationships

- How can teachers help minimize the tension between a principal's new ideas and the history of the "collective angst" of the staff for short-lived changes by the previous principals?

- How can teachers be more open to — and even contribute to — a new principal's ideas and success?

- How might Miriam help support the parents in achieving a healthy relationship with the new principal?

Maintaining Integrity as a Teacher

- If teachers sit and talk about every "mistake" that the new director makes (bordering on *lashon hara* — literally, evil tongue or, figuratively, gossip or speaking ill of someone), how might Miriam help shift the negative energy in a positive direction?

Some Thoughts

Miriam has several options. She could choose to remain focused on her classroom, adopting a "wait and see" approach. Based on all the continuing changes in the school, Miriam might reflect on the toll of these changes on her personal life, and decide to leave. More complex is the option that Miriam, while aware of her frustration with the many transitions, could determine that she wants to continue in her teaching position and be hopeful about the potential of the new principal. Miriam decides to channel her energy into helping the new principal "have a chance." She doesn't know enough about her to take sides at this point. She could offer her historical perspective to the new principal, as well as to the transition team. When talking with teachers and fellow community members, she has the option of feeding into the negative perceptions, being neutral, or highlighting the potential and the positive. This is a public relations opportunity for Miriam. She could be a spokesperson and model for the school among the parents, the students, and the larger synagogue community. Given her stature, she needs to be sensitive that others may follow her lead. Directly or indirectly, she could facilitate or undermine the transition. Part of every school's mission is the strengthening

of Jewish educators, connecting with community, and maintaining the integrity of the dynamic between principals and teachers. Look for and identify the steps that led to this successful synergy.

ESTABLISH FOR YOURSELF A TEACHER, AND ACQUIRE A FRIEND (Pirke Avot)

A successful synergy occurred: Kayla went off to college thinking she wanted to be a Rabbi. She had been active in her youth group at a mid-size congregation and worked a bit in their school as a teaching assistant. The college Kayla attended was down the road from a small synagogue that often recruited college students to teach in their religious school. Kayla decided to check into a possible part-time teaching job. This would look good on her résumé. It would also give her a chance to stay connected to the Jewish community and to explore jobs in Jewish education.

The principal in this small synagogue had extensive experience mentoring high school and college students. Because Kayla had little actual teaching experience and the school had hired all teachers the previous spring, Kayla was given a job as a tutor. In this position, Kayla was able to observe each class, work with small groups of children, and occasionally substitute for a missing teacher.

By mid-year, Kayla replaced one of the teachers who had another commitment. Kayla found that she loved teaching children in the early grades. She often went to the principal looking for materials to cover the topics she was expected to teach. Kayla identified issues of concern to her students and their families, and freely shared her challenges and questions with her principal. The principal helped Kayla with lesson planning and parent communication. She tweaked Kayla's programming so that it was more age appropriate. Their working relationship inspired the principal and generated energy among the staff. The principal was impressed with Kayla's thoroughness, her planning, her immediate application of resources in an effective way. In turn, the principal continually offered Kayla new teaching challenges.

Over her four-year college career, Kayla grew into a strong teacher for mid-primary grades, became active in peer leadership at the campus Hillel, went to regional and national Jewish teacher conferences, and expanded her network within the

Jewish community. The principal provided Kayla with numerous references for summer jobs in a range of Jewish organizations (camps, Israel trips, and Jewish movement organizations). And Kayla did go on to Rabbinic school. She regularly keeps in touch with the principal as both "rav (teacher) and chavayrah (friend)."

CONCLUSION

In conclusion, while not all principal-teacher relationships have the synergy Kayla experienced, the potential is there.[2] Refer to the Appendix on the next page for a chart to use as a tool in strategizing potential intersections of strength arenas that are useful in teacher-principal relationships. The chart includes many of the traits described in the previous vignettes and allows for the individual differences of teachers and principals. The traits of specific principals and teachers may open the door to better resolutions for particular situations, in particular contexts.

The vignettes above serve to broaden the reader's view of the many approaches available to a teacher and principal in dealing with school situations that may at first appear to be simple. Often, there are formal (job descriptions, accountability loops) and informal (friendships, adjustments made to accommodate strengths) aspects of each of the strength arenas. There is also a spectrum of skills and influence.

On the other hand, given the strengths or weaknesses of the participants in any situation, a constructive synergy may never develop — or could derail at any stage. In the event that this occurs, each teacher must assess whether continuing to teach under the circumstances is in the best interest of the students or his or her own professional development. Such insights can lead to different opportunities. *"Me'at ohr docheh harbeh choshech"* (A small amount of light dispels a lot of darkness). Remember that ultimately the teacher and principal have a key relationship in the success of the school and sense of community for the students. A supportive philosophy by Rabbi Tarfon in *Pirke Avot* captures the essence of the process and offers a thoughtful summary of this chapter: *"Lo aleycha hamlachah ligmor, v'lo atah ben chorin l'hibatel mi-menah"* (It is not up to you to finish the work, but neither are you free to refrain from it).

---

[2]For more on such mentoring, see Chapter 53, "Partnering with a Mentor" by Judy Aronson, pp. 653-661 in this Handbook.

APPENDIX

Summary of Possible Strength Arenas Necessary for Teacher-Principal Relations

Strength	Teacher	Principal	Other Resource
Understands the curriculum parameters and is familiar with resources (publishers, books, videos, etc.)			
Has experience and knowledge of pedagogy (teaching methods) and classroom management			
Has a strong Judaic background (able to link the Jewish teachable moment)			
Has a strong community network			
Knows the students and their families			
Understands the accountability system of the school, including committees and staff			
Has organization and administrative skills (timely and thorough paperwork)			
Understands the culture of the school: *minhagim* (customs), sacred cows, and comfort rituals			
Is flexible and able to troubleshoot			
Knows how to be a team player and or build the team			

BIBLIOGRAPHY

Lee, Sara S., and Michael Zeldin, eds. *Touching the Future: Mentoring and the Jewish Professional*. Los Angeles, CA: Rhea Hirsch School of Education, Hebrew Union College-Jewish Institute of Religion, 1995.

This publication advises that mentoring relationships have the potential to strengthen retention of Jewish professionals in their fields. Chapters provide examples of mentoring relationships within the Jewish professional world and highlight a range of mentoring circumstances and approaches. The epilogue focuses on the connections between mentoring and the culture within Jewish institutions that facilitate or inhibit this process.

Aron, Isa; Sara Lee; and Seymour Rossel, eds. *A Congregation of Learners: Transforming the Synagogue into a Learning Community*. New York: UAHC Press, 1995.

This book focuses on the synagogue as a learning environment and on the issues that nourish and deplete that potential dynamic. It expands and challenges the model of the traditional classroom school.

Barth, Roland. *Improving Schools from Within: Teachers, Parents and Principals Can Make the Difference*. San Francisco, CA: Jossey Bass, 1990.

This book is directed at the adults who help children learn. The premise here is that a key characteristic of good schools is a healthy, collegial relationship between teachers and principal. Reflections are based on observations in the public school system. There are useful chapers on cultivating collegial relationships, a community of learners, and leaders with vision.

Grishaver, Joel Lurie, with Ron Wolfson. *Jewish Parents: A Teacher's Guide*. Los Angeles, CA: Torah Aura Productions, 1997.

A series of vignettes and examples for strengthening classroom dynamics and building relationships with parents. Gives useful perspectives for teachers that are inclusive of the principal's accountability paradigm.

Hagberg, Janet O. *Real Power: Stages of Personal Power in Organizations*. Salem, WI: Sheffield Publishing Company, 1994.

A secular view of the power in relationships that can be useful in understanding the dynamics between co-workers. This book is one of many written for the business community that attempts to link personal process with work dynamics.

Hagberg, Janet O., and Terry Donavan. *Learning Styles Inventory*. Plymouth, MN: Personal Power Products, 1996.

This book features an example of a useful tool for understanding one's own learning style and how that style affects work relationships. The learning of teachers and principals extends beyond the classroom!

Kelman, Stuart, ed. *What We Know about Jewish Education: A Handbook of Today's Research for Tomorrow's Jewish Education*. Los Angeles, CA: Torah Aura Productions, 1992.

The section "The Settings and the Community" and the Appendixes pertain to the many stakeholders in the learning process that can influence the teacher/principal dynamic in the Jewish school.

Mahrer, Lawrence, and Debi Mahrer Rowe. *A Guide To Small Congregation Religious schools*. New York: UAHC Press, 1996.

A user-friendly resource that is directly applicable. Chapters on "Organizational Structure of the School" and "Faculty" explain the general framework of the school in a small congregation.

Mandel, Scott. *Wired into Judaism: The Internet and Jewish Education*. Denver, CO: A.R.E. Publishing, Inc., 2000.

The Internet can be a tremendous support for teachers and principals. It can enrich a classroom, offer specific resources for the many issues challenging the school, and provide e-mail access for information exchange. This book tells how to log on and find information specific to Jewish education and curriculum enhancement. (There is little in the way of protocols, legal ramifications, and boundaries for online interactions as a school communication tool. So before linking teacher, principals, students, and parents for online use of classroom web sites, chat rooms, e-mail or instant messaging, check into school policies and precedents.)

The Personal DISCernment Inventory. Atlanta, GA: Team Resources Inc., 1993.

Part of the DISC Profile system. Here is a simple instrument designed to increase understanding of self and others in an effort to achieve greater personal and interpersonal effectiveness. Contains a short series of questions and answers with a guide to interpretation and implementation in the workplace.

Senge, Peter M., et al, eds. *Schools That Learn: A Fifth Discipline Fieldbook for Educators, Parents, and Everyone Who Cares about Education*. New York: Doubleday/Currency, 2000.

This book frames a dialogue about educating children in the twenty-first century based on the modified application of Senge's principles developed in *The Fifth Discipline: The Art and Practice of the Learning Organization* (New York: Doubleday/Currency, 1990). Senge challenges assumptions about how people learn and are effective in an organization. Coming from the MIT Sloan School of Management, he applies a variety of perspectives to arrive at his approach

that "to practice a discipline is to be a lifelong learner." The book includes descriptions of the disciplines and principles, case studies, practical tools for assessing school dynamics, and anecdotes from prominent educators, administrators, parents and students. While there are implications for exploring the teacher/principal relationship, the emphasis is on the larger vision of the school as an organization of many interdependent dynamics.

Tornberg, Robert, ed. *The Jewish Educational Leader's Handbook*. Denver, CO: A.R.E. Publishing, Inc., 1998.

An excellent compilation of chapters on issues in Jewish educational leadership. Each chapter has a useful, annotated bibliography. Check out the chapter by Ellen Lodgen and Lawrence Cybuch Lodgen, "Principal/Head of School and Teacher Relations." Though written for the principal to foster better understanding of his/her role in the school, teachers will also find this chapter useful.

CHAPTER 53

Partnering with a Mentor

Judy Aronson

When Dena received the phone call to substitute for six weeks in the seventh grade religious school class, she felt as if a dream had come true. In high school she was a teacher's assistant in a religious school, and in college she studied Hebrew, Judaic studies, and Child Psychology, along with her degree in American Studies. In the back of her mind she pictured herself teaching in a Jewish setting, but somehow she was sidetracked and ended up in media advertising. Her career went well, and even after she married, she sold advertising on a part-time basis. When her daughter began religious school, she started thinking about her earlier goal. She got to know the school director at her synagogue, who was always on the lookout for talent. A few months later, she was asked to be a long-term substitute in the seventh grade. Laden with lesson plans, attendance lists, tzedakah envelopes, and textbooks, she prepared for her first day of teaching with eager anticipation. It was a disaster.

In many cases, this vignette might be about the demise of a career in Jewish education. Talented people with the best intentions enter the Jewish classroom and feel completely and surprisingly inadequate. Despite Dena's deep desire to preserve and transmit the Jewish heritage, she failed to reach the students. Dena's class appeared to be bored and rude on that first day. They had no respect for the substitute and told her they didn't like their "regular" teacher either. Dena was appalled and humiliated, especially since her director had assured her that these were bright and terrific students — a really good class.

Fortunately, it was not Dena's last day. Rather it was the start of a long and satisfying career in Jewish education. What held her to her good intention was a chance meeting. After class ended, she quickly determined that even though she felt hurt, she would try to fulfill her six-week commitment. The lesson plan she had tried to follow might have worked for the teacher who had written it, but it was clearly not appropriate for her.

"I am not a quitter," Dena states, *"so I walked downstairs to the library and began to look for materials that might point me to a more interesting approach to the material. The more I looked, the more anxious I became. I did not want to talk to the director because she seemed to have such faith in me. Should I have majored in education? Did I know enough about Jewish history to even attempt to teach it to very bright seventh graders?*

I began to steam up. Who needs this? I am giving up Sunday brunch with my family to encounter disinterested kids. Just as I was about to leave my stack of books, one of the Rabbis of the congregation, who had a master's degree in Jewish education, sat down beside me. She said she noticed that I looked rather upset. Was anything wrong? I almost burst into tears and began babbling about my disappointment with the class and myself. Obviously, I told her, I was not well prepared enough to teach in the religious school. She gently touched my shoulder and said, "Better the passionate beginner than the jaded professional. May I help you find the resources you need?"

That moment of listening, caring, and reassurance was what Dena needed to give teaching a try. Those of us who have taught for many years know that the first day with any new group requires special strategies. We also know that anyone can have an off day. But without a mentoring relationship, Dena might not have learned this in time. She would not have felt supported in the challenging work of teaching our tradition effectively.

All teachers in the field can benefit from a mentor who helps them with their skills and personal commitment. And, just as important, mature and experienced teachers can benefit from the opportunity to give a piece of all that they have learned over the years to someone just starting out.

Mentoring is fast becoming a buzzword in the world of business, as well as the world of education. Major corporations and the federal government advocate the use of mentoring between adults and children, peers, business associates, and novices and veterans. In the Jewish world today, it is seen as one available way of increasing support for teachers.

Communities often sabotage their efforts to recruit and retain Jewish teachers (an endangered species) by not acknowledging and appreciating these dedicated individuals. It is essential that we invest in teacher training that encompasses best practice, observation, and support. If the popularity of mentoring accomplishes nothing more than giving greater attention to the needs of teachers, *dayenu*, it would be enough. But this chapter goes further by exploring what mentoring is or can be, how we become mentors and mentees, and what the nature of these relationships might be. The stories that frame this discussion are based on composites of people I have mentored, or been mentored by, over the past decades. If any of my former mentees and interns see themselves in these stories, each will know that he/she is cherished by me and has taught me important lessons that I now share with a wider audience.

> Having a mentor has proved to be one of the most valuable experiences in my teaching career. I met with my mentor on a weekly basis and reflected on my practice. This allowed me a safe environment to process what I had done and gain valuable feedback from a seasoned professional. Her ability to listen and her genuine investment in my growth made my work in that school one of the most positive teaching experiences I have had to date.
>
> *(Amy Appelman, West Bloomfield, Michigan)*

MENTORING IS A JEWISH THING TO DO

Pirke Avot 1:6 hints at the importance of a mentoring relationship when it states, "Provide yourself with a teacher (*rav*), get yourself a companion, and judge all favorably." Our tradition tells us to find a

"rav," to sit at the feet of a great teacher, since the transmission of learning is central to the Jewish experience. My friends who study the mystic tradition[1] look reflexively at the verb "provide." From their viewpoint, you can become your own great teacher. You can befriend yourself, validate your qualities, and judge yourself based on personal merits. Mentorship is both self-reflective and relational.

Mentoring is defined as the individualized support, assistance, guidance, and challenge that one professional provides for another. Thus, the mentoring process is *inherently* dependent on the connections of the people involved. One of my mentors taught me that a *good* relationship is one that brings out the best in us. Dr. William Cutter in his article, "Hierarchy and Mutuality: Mentor Protégé and Spirit" suggests that the authority of the mentor is inevitable. She bears more experience about the presenting problem, she carries the memory and tradition of the culture being transmitted, and she must be the net onto which the protégé's highwire act may fall if he stumbles at culture and professional practice. The mentor may, if skilled at such practice, become the guide in exercises, which lead toward mutuality and obliterate hierarchy.

The ideal that Dr. Cutter describes (i.e., "partners in reciprocity") is a precious commodity, but one that is not impossible to attain. We don't have to ask someone to cross the sea or go up to the heavens, we simply have to look for opportunities (both formal and informal) and build relationships that deepen the meaning of what we do as teachers and learners.

In her article, "Lessons from Mentoring at Sinai," Lois J. Zachary, author of *The Mentor's Guide*, has used text from Exodus 18 to provide a biblical template for mentoring. She writes, "The dynamic interaction between Jethro and Moses offers mentoring partners powerful insights about some of the qualities and characteristics necessary to build and maintain effective mentoring relationships." The core elements she describes are "respect, candor, observation, listening, communication, questioning, and feedback." We might surmise that mentoring has always been a method to transmit the tools of leadership from one generation to another. The wisdom that we receive from those who are "in the know" becomes a storehouse for the novice that

---

[1]Thanks to Dr. Bonna Devorah Haberman of the Mistabra Institute.

will reveal its riches over and over again in the course of any career — and indeed of one's life.

THE SKILLS OF MENTORS AND MENTEES

Before Dennis entered the graduate program for educators, he was anxious about the academic workload. He was embarking on his second career after holding a responsible job using his great math skills. He was in a program focusing on subject matter, particularly text study that came harder to him. He knew that he had some minor learning disabilities that slowed him down. But he was determined to be a Jewish educator with a specialty in informal education.

The academic workload was exhausting, especially paired with his 15 hours of required teaching. At first, Dennis resented the time he had to devote to his weekly mentoring session. He knew he had much to learn about classroom management and curriculum development. He wasn't prepared for the even more vexing problem that arose: his uncertainty as to whether he fit in with the expectations for his program. He felt like he just didn't belong. However, he hoped that if he could get through the first year, he might pass his courses and adjust.

"What I didn't realize," said Dennis, "was that my mentor would save my life that year. She saw my classroom skills improve and gave me lots of validation for it. My weakness in writing papers and taking tests were not her main concern. She was the only person who thought I was capable of completing the program. Maybe I would never fit in the mold, but with her help I toughed it out and matriculated in the expected time."

Parker Palmer believes that "mentoring is a mutuality that requires more than meeting the right teacher: the teacher must meet the right student. In this encounter, not only are the qualities of the mentor revealed, but the qualities of the student are drawn out in a way that is equally revealing.[2] For a student like Dennis, a supportive non-academic mentor could assist him in finding his unique qualities and encourage him to use them to best advantage.

Dennis needed to be questioned about how his teaching was improved by what he was learning in his education classes and readings. When his mentor listened to his anecdotal accounts, she validated and identified the moments during which she recognized the changes. Soon, Dennis began to recognize them, too. Rather than resisting what he was learning, he was eager to use his new information. Mentoring with the right person encouraged him to become a teacher who valued intellectual stimulation, rather than fearing he would not measure up to his peers.

WE'RE MATCHED, NOW WHAT?

Carrie is teaching for the second year in a school that has just initiated a Mentor Teacher Program. She is honored to be chosen as the novice partner, and attended a few weeks of training before the school year began. She wants nothing more than to pick Lynn's brain and talk about classroom strategies.

Lynn is a most successful classroom teacher. She has much to offer Carrie, who has all the elements for success in the field, but hasn't yet been able to have a class that "gels."

At their first meeting, as suggested in their training, they agree to tell each other a brief version of their life stories to build a base for trust and understanding. Lynn hears that Carrie is a hard worker, but that for some reason she can't get her students excited about their learning. Lynn wonders immediately if the children are aware of Carrie's passion for teaching. She knows she can be a help in this case.

As the relationship grows, these two teachers start to see each other as partners in a dance: the leader knows the steps, and the follower is eager to learn the routine. With awareness and respect for their strengths and weaknesses, the dance whirls them into new stages of their professional and personal development. Carrie learns Lynn's techniques for appropriately inspiring her students with her passion for education. She recognizes that her mentor is happy helping her because she has learned that Carrie is disciplined and follows through on her role modeling. They begin to see each other as peers, people who are vulnerable and complex.

The mentoring relationship, indeed, is like a dance that two partners, new to each other, have

---

[2]Parker J. Palmer, *The Courage to Teach* (San Francisco, CA: Jossey-Bass, 1998), 21.

to choreograph together. There are moments of awkwardness and, at times, toes get stepped on, but with commitment, the dance develops between them. Upon first meeting, a mentor and mentee have a variety of tasks to undertake. These include:

Getting to know each other - Telling each other the reasons they decided to teach, and the path taken to get there is one level of information giving. But personal information about family and passions in life is equally as important.

Setting parameters - Mentors and mentees need to decide together about when and where they will meet, and whether electronic media (phones, e-mail, instant messaging) will complement their face-to-face conversations. If either has specific times when it is more convenient to get together (or times that won't work), these, too, need to be talked about.

Discussing roles - A mentor might be a listener, supporter, cheerleader, advisor, counselor, role model, friend, nurturer, and/or a gentle nudge. A mentee might be an observer, a clarifier of needed help, someone who wants help but values autonomy, or a teacher who is so new to the field that he/she doesn't know what to ask for. Each partner should discuss initially what might be his or her preferred role in the relationship. Both mentor and mentee, however, need to realize that over time, these roles may shift.

Determining goals - While much of the mentoring relationship will grow and develop over time, the mentee must give thought to the specific goals he/she wishes from their time together. The mentor, as the experienced member of the relationship, will need to consider the ways the goals could be achieved, as well as avenues for monitoring progress.

Because mentoring work can be truly sacred, partners may want to try starting any mentoring session or meeting with a blessing, choosing from any number of prayers or blessings for study, communication, friendship, or growth. Whatever the words, we are then inviting the Divine into our meeting. Dr. Leonard Felder writes in *Seven Prayers That Can Change Your Life*, "Prayer is not about imposing your will or your ego on a situation. Rather it's about going deeply inside and connecting with a source of profound energy and support that is hard to describe or measure." With this in mind, a blessing can provide that moment of refreshment that we may crave before we go on to yet another activity in our busy day. Our collaborative work provides a renewal of energy and spirit, and we should leave it feeling newly blessed.

Listening: An Acquired Skill

Linda was an Israeli dance teacher for a religious school that met on Sunday. Helen, her supervisor, felt that although the students loved Linda's classes, they did not relate to the curriculum. She took Linda out for lunch to get to know her better. An experienced mentor, Helen first told Linda about herself as a teacher, and then asked her what Jewish teaching meant to her. As a freshman, Linda had started dancing at Hillel and found she had a flair for it. She needed tuition money, and her teacher recommended that she teach at several synagogues. Linda was surprised when Helen called her "a colleague" and listened to her ideas about improving her program. Helen recognized a yearning for meaning in Linda's life. They met several more times. The next semester, Linda enrolled in a Jewish Studies course. She said it was because Helen had heard what Linda herself did not know she felt.

We teach our lives by telling our stories. Someone once said that we think we are falling in love when someone listens to what we are saying to him or her and understands our words as we understand them ourselves. It is easy to be seduced into believing that this is true love, and sometimes it is. But even if not true love, it can be the starting point of effective communication. What gives it strength is that we know our partner has listened to us intently and heard us clearly.

Listening is an acquired skill, one that is key to a mentor-mentee relationship. If we stick to our role as a listener for even a short while, not even stopping to criticize or comment, we can be amazingly comforting and inspiring to the one who is speaking.

In a good mentoring relationship, both partners should practice listening to each other. One way to do this is to agree to a short period at the start of any meeting when each person will speak without interruption for three to five minutes. This means no questions, no comments, just maintaining a friendly demeanor and listening intently. At the end of the agreed upon time (tracked by a watch or clock to monitor the minutes), switch roles so that the speaker becomes the listener and vice-versa.

During this listening time, we might talk about what happened to us since our last meeting. We can learn what is on our mentor or mentee's mind at the moment. Without interruption or critical comment, the words flow from our mouths. A kind listener is like an aphrodisiac. We feel giddy from the attention and are much more willing to move on to the issues of our agreed upon agenda.

The mutuality builds authenticity into the dual relationship. We are appreciated for what we are and what we think. We do not have to be more like each other, but rather more like ourselves.

It is indeed rare in life that we get the kind of undivided listening that this method advocates. It sets a tone that increases trust and appreciation for this valuable exchange of mentor and mentee.

> One of my mentors made it a point never to take a phone call or accept interruptions (within reason) during our meetings. This always made me feel important and demonstrated his level of respect for our time together. Now, whenever I am meeting with someone, I do the same.
>
> (Amy Appelman, West Bloomfield, Michigan)

Shifting Relations

Kayla's training was as a kindergarten and early childhood teacher. She retired when she had her family, but after her husband went through a serious illness, she realized that she should find some meaningful work to add to their diminished income. Her children were nearing the age for religious school and a good friend suggested that she might be able to teach in that program.

Although her formal Jewish education was not extensive, Kayla thought she would like to try doing this. Her friend, Miriam, became her mentor. She began meeting with Kayla and describing the curriculum she used to teach first grade. She recommended several books that Kayla might read that would begin to prepare her for religious school teaching. She invited Kayla to visit her class and find out if she would like to assist. Kayla met with the principal of the school and volunteered to assist in Miriam's class for the second half of the year, with the understanding that if it went well, she might have a paid assistant's position in the fall and enroll her eldest child in the school.

Miriam found their meetings were moving her in new directions. She enjoyed searching the literature to help Kayla on her way. She recommended a Torah class for Kayla, and they would talk afterward about what she studied. Kayla proved to be a good assistant and was ready to substitute when Miriam was out of town for a family life cycle event.

Because the school had a growth spurt the following year that greatly enlarged the first grade, Kayla joined Miriam as a co-teacher. They realized that their meetings had become very important to them and that they enjoyed planning together and supporting each other.

It is both blessing and curse to develop a new professional colleague. The blessing is the joy of watching someone grow and prosper: the curse is that as time goes on, the mentee is less needy and may become more assertive. Should that happen, mentors might need an objective colleague to think through these shifting roles.

In almost all situations, mentors hope for loyalty and recognition from the mentoring relationship. Sometimes it is enough to see their mentee prosper. But as the mentee reaches a position of equality, she is in a position to support the mentor and help her maintain her growth in the field as well.

Mentoring does not exist in a vacuum. Both partners bring their personal and professional successes and failures with them. It is only in a trusting partnership that these are revealed and sometimes resolved. Often when people enter a mentoring session, their first utterance is a sigh. That moment of relaxing is a prelude to productive discourse that can exist only when partners feel safe and secure with each other.

In *Managers as Mentors*, Chip R. Bell teaches, "The most powerful and difficult part of mentoring is being who you are." This is not to imply that a mentor must be some kind of superhero without flaws, doubts, or the capacity for making mistakes.

INCREASING MENTORING OPPORTUNITIES

Mentoring Groups

In an article for corporate management called, "The New Corporate Ladder Is Round," the writers advocate a mentoring model to fit new ways of doing business. "Mentoring relationships have changed from traditional and hierarchical to dynamic relationships that are contemporary, open, and flexible. Individuals can now learn from each other in reciprocal partnerships where they are both the giver and receiver of wisdom and information." We in the world of education have known that the teacher involved in her own professional development heightens the potential of the students. Each of us needs to learn from both failure and success. The self-reflective practitioner who becomes a mentor has much to offer from his/her stories of personal insight. It is those experiences that can turn mentors into "learning leaders."

In addition to powerful one-on-one relationships, schools can benefit from learning groups constructed of a senior mentor and a group of mentees interested in learning from both the mentor and each other. The mentor in this case is someone with group development skills and a commitment to helping a learning team prosper. Kaye and Jacobson suggest a leader with "A sense of humor that enables the learning leader to set a lighter context when relating past experiences that may have seemed devastating at one time." With sensitivity to the awareness that each class is idiosyncratic unto itself and we all need support to maintain openness to the challenges of teaching. Within a mentored group, there is the comfort of finding an ally to support one's personal and professional growth. Through the five to seven group members, teachers "gain an understanding of different perspectives," and the dialogue "sparks creative and free-flowing thought that allows them to share insights and search for meaning."

In turn, the mentor "learns how to learn from other people's experience." While the mentor may ask the right questions that inspire dialogue, the imagination that may lead to innovation is released, particularly because this is a group that makes no decisions.

Mentoring groups thrive on developing peer relationships. Rather than a structured discussion, dialogue gives everyone the freedom "to meander, tell stories, exchange concerns, and discuss beliefs," and leads to "a higher level of thinking" about issues of common interest to the whole group. Mentoring groups can become a feature of ongoing adult learning and development. To ensure their success, mentors become facilitators, rather than gurus, and mentees take charge of their own learning.

Were schools to organize such groups in addition to other more conventional mentoring pairs, it would spread the notion that we all deserve mentoring to progress in our careers and our development as professionals.

> Like so much that we talk about, mentoring has been going on for a long time in informal ways. It has served us well when it is nurtured and successful. I feel that I have mentored people, without either of us calling it that. I strike up a relationship with another teacher and for whatever reason, mostly a willingness to give each other the time, the relationship turns into a mentoring one. Aaron and I both taught the two sections of the same class. I knew he was busy and so was I. In looking back on it, it worked because we were both respectful of each other and also respectful of each other's time. I would often think of ways to mention things to him that I thought he could use. I was also careful to accept and use his ideas. At times, we would put our classes together and we would "team teach."
>
> (Michael Fixler, Syracuse, New York)

Virtual Mentoring

College students are faced with career decisions from the time they begin their first semester, when they choose courses, majors, minors, internships and summer jobs. Travel and international study help them determine life goals. Through all of this, connection with Jewish mentors can be extremely helpful.

Mentors and mentees communicate on e-mail and by phone. Both parties need to have realistic expectations for the scope of their influence on each other. Some tips for building a virtual mentoring relationship include exchanging photos of oneself and one's environment if the participants have never met in person. Both partners must be willing to paint a full picture of their needs and concerns. This requires commitment to meeting times, if on the phone, and prompt response on e-mail. Prepare an agreed upon agenda yet, as in any good mentoring, respectfully allow for the ideas that come out of left field. Although one does not have the opportunity to observe body language and meet eye-to-eye, with experience, a long-distance virtual mentoring relationship can be an expansion of repertoire and expertise for both partners.

HOW CAN I FIND A MENTOR?

If this chapter has convinced you that a mentor could help you improve your teaching, here are some ways that you might go about finding one:

1. Think back to all of the special people who have acted as mentors for you in the past. Figure out why they were so effective in helping you. Either make contact with them again, or look for people like them.

2. Check to see if your school or institution has a formal mentoring program, or can direct you to one sponsored by a local Jewish agency.

3. Contact Jewish educational professional organizations such as the National Association of Temple Educators (NATE), the Jewish Educators Association (JEA), The Coalition for the Advancement of Jewish Education (CAJE), or the Association of Jewish Community Organization Professionals (AJCOP) Chaver Program for information on their mentoring services.

4. If none of these works, talk with colleagues and see if anyone else is interested in a mentoring partnership, or organize a mentoring group. You will need to research the mentoring literature or check out the Internet, but if you keep the expectations realistic, you will learn from the experience.

ARE YOU READY TO ACT AS A MENTOR?

If you are already a successful Jewish teacher and want to help others, yet wonder if you are ready to do so, consider the following:

1. Are you a good role model? Are you willing to celebrate what you do well and reveal when you have trouble coping?

2. Will you encourage your mentee when you recognize a problem? Are you willing to verbalize your distress? Can you encourage your mentee to take action to solve problems?

3. Do you know how to take care of yourself and still have time and energy left to nurture another person? When you can take care of your personal and professional needs you can give generously of your time and wisdom.

4. Have you the confidence to admit that Jewish education is a most challenging field and that some of our problems are not easily solved? Do you love your work and want others to enjoy it as you do despite the realities we all must face?

If you have said "yes" or "maybe," to several of these questions, you should probably give mentoring a try. The immense rewards — learning from your mentee and growing as a professional — make it worth the risk. None of us has every base covered in our lives, but if you love to teach, you will add an important new dimension to your skills.

CONCLUSION

Every stage of our teaching careers produces its own challenges. Whether we are just starting out or winding down a distinguished career, we need each other. When we become mentors or mentees, we use our experience to help our colleagues while we continue our own professional growth. This is a "win/win" situation and one that can change the world. Get started!

POSTSCRIPT: THE MENTEE WHO KNEW MORE THAN THE MENTOR

Several years after completing a master's degree in museum education, Rachel felt that she was in the wrong field. To everyone's surprise, she enrolled in a graduate program in Jewish education. Her first year's internship was as a teacher in a religious school. The mentoring relationship was a requirement for the degree. Her mentor, Ben, a Rabbi-Educator, was concerned about what he might have to offer this confident and experienced professional. His expertise was in informal education and, if he could have turned his school into a full-time camp situation, he would have. Rachel preferred that everything be highly organized and based on (excessive) advance planning.

Fortunately for Rachel, she and Ben hit it off well enough, although their styles could not have been more different. Without a tightly structured lesson plan, Rachel felt incapable of facing a class. Without spontaneity, Ben felt that children would be bored and unenthusiastic about their learning.

After a time, Ben talked Rachel into taking a class in theater improvisation that he thought would give Rachel some tools to seize the teaching moment. Rachel liked the class, and it made an impact on her style. Rachel became closer with her children. She continued to plan well structured frontal lessons, but she took Ben's suggestion and instituted cooperative learning and learning centers.

Several years later, Rachel became director of a religious school. She wrote to Ben and thanked him for the investment he had made in her future. She said in her letter, "When I walk into a sixth grade class and see the teacher sitting on the desk and the children sprawled in their chairs I still get a little uncomfortable. But then I think about what you taught me and I observe that the children are deeply engaged in a discussion and that the teacher is asking the important questions. I smile and compliment him later on his good teaching."

It is important to add that because of Rachel, Ben reorganized his teachers' center, began a children's library, and finally produced parent and teacher manuals for his school.

There are arranged mentorships that might at first glance look unworkable. In this case, what might have been a poor match turned out to be beneficial to both participants. Here are some points to think about in regard to this vignette:

- What were the qualities that made their relationship awkward?

- Should Ben have insisted or encouraged Rachel to study improvisational techniques?

- What would have happened if Rachel had balked at "loosening up"?

- Is there a right or wrong way of running a classroom?

- How much leeway should a classroom teacher have?

- Is it up to the mentor to decide the changes a teacher might make?

- Who changed more in this relationship, Ben or Rachel?

BIBLIOGRAPHY

Bell, Chip R. *Managers as Mentors: Building Partnerships for Learning.* 2d ed. San Francisco, CA: Berrett-Koehler Publishers, Inc. 2002.

This is a comprehensive description of how to initiate mentoring in the business world. Using the acronym SAGE (Surrendering, Accepting, Gifting, and Extending), Bell outlines the steps of the process for both the mentor and the "protégé."

Cutter, William. "Hierarchy and Mutuality: Mentor, Protégé, and Spirit." In *Touching the Future: Mentoring and the Jewish Professional*, edited by Michael Zeldin and Sara S. Lee. Los Angeles, CA: Hebrew Union College-Jewish Institute of Religion, 1995.

This classic anthology includes thought provoking articles under the headings of "A Vision of Mentoring" and "Mentoring in Action." In the preface, Professor Sara S. Lee says, "The papers in this volume reflect the significance of a lifelong process in which human beings can be both protégés and mentors."

Felder, Leonard. *Seven Prayers That Can Change Your Life.* Kansas City, MO: Andrews McMeel Publishing, 2001.

Dr. Felder is a therapist who encourages prayer as a means for his clients to develop more fulfilling habits and lifestyles. For example, he expands the purpose of the blessing for washing to "lifting up our hands" to do creative work. His ideas can be readily adapted to your mentoring relationship (and your classroom).

Hughy, Jane. "Creating a Circle of Many: Mentoring and the Preservice Teacher." In *Breaking the Circle of One*, edited by Carol A. Mullen, et al. New York: Peter Lang Publishing, Inc., 1997.

Each of the chapters in this collection by faculty and graduate students in a university school of education reflects on how a mentoring circle changed the dynamics of their relationships, writing, and careers. Their stories of isolation and anxiety reveal the need for trust and collegiality in the teaching professions.

Kaye, Beverly L.; Beverly Bernstein Olevin; and Mary Ammerman. "The New Corporate Ladder Is Round: A New Mentoring Model to Fit the Changing Shape of Business." *Career Planning and Adult Development Journal*, Spring 2001.

This article focuses on reciprocity in mentoring relationships in the business world.

Kaye, Beverly L., and Devon Scheef. "Mentoring." In *Info-Line*. Alexandria, VA: American Society for Training and Development, 2000, Issue #0004, pp. 1-16.

This monograph is part of a series called "Info-line Single Issues" that covers a wide range of topics from business skills to workplace Issues. A complete listing of other titles can be found at www.astd.org.

Palmer, Parker J. *The Courage to Teach.* San Francisco, CA: Jossey-Bass, 1998.

Palmer uses his personal experience as a teacher of teachers to lead a spiritual journey that deepens and expands the quality of our classrooms and institutions. Every page stands on its own as a treasure.

Zachary, Lois. "Lessons from a Mentoring at Sinai." *Jewish Education News* 22, no. 3, Summer 2001/5761.

This issue of *Jewish Education News* focuses on the struggle to recruit personnel for Jewish schools. It includes articles that describe why it is difficult to find teachers, as well as on how to solve the problem. Each article could be used as a trigger for discussion in mentoring groups. Back issues may be ordered from www.caje.org.

CHAPTER 54

Collaborative Curriculum Development[1]

Rhonda Rosenheck

INTRODUCTION

We have come to a new understanding of the life of the mind. Generative ideas emerge from joint thinking, from significant conversations, and from sustained, shared struggles to achieve new insights by partners in thought. (John-Steiner, p. 3)

We teachers are regularly asked to develop our own curricula, which often means late nights at the computer, or with a legal pad, writing outlines and lessons. You may share my recollection of homework as a solitary activity; completing it with a classmate may even have been called "cheating." That early message about working alone may have led us to assume that planning — a teacher's homework — is best done alone.

This chapter is meant to encourage you to reject that premise and to seek opportunities to plan with others. Here you will find examples and guidelines for taking the plunge into collaborative planning, with all its challenges and benefits.

ABOUT COLLABORATION

My power, my particular ability, lies in visualizing the effects, consequences and possibilities, and the bearings on present thought of the discoveries of others. I grasp things in a broad way easily. I cannot do mathematical calculations easily. (Albert Einstein, as quoted in John-Steiner, p. 42)

Today, educational theorists and expert practitioners encourage us to plan collaborative learning experiences for students. Students enter our classrooms with unique sets of strengths and challenges, understandings, and interests; it is our job to help them help each other learn and grow. New

research on the human brain confirms much of what many recent educational theorists have been suggesting: we (children and adults) learn best when we are happy, safe, supported, and challenged. For most people, fear and loneliness shut down creative processes. Cooperation, on the other hand, promotes the development and clarification of innovative ideas. Collaborative work can be intrinsically rewarding (the work itself becomes more enjoyable because of the camaraderie) and can provide its partners the courage and tools to move beyond individual limitations.

True for students, this notion holds true as well for teachers, and even for many of the intellectual giants we think of as lone geniuses. Albert Einstein, for instance, in working through his ideas about relativity, turned to a friend, mathematician Marcel Grossmann, for help. This early collaboration with Grossmann gave Einstein the tools he needed to hone and express his radically innovative ideas. When people work together, bringing their unique gifts to the venture, creative sparks can fly.

COLLABORATIVE PLANNING

The input of others who add to the "teachability" of my curriculum provides me insights into teaching that I know will help me next time around. (Adam Gregerman, teacher)

I found the collaboration process . . . to be a wonderful one. It took a lot of the pressure off of me, just knowing that there was another human being who had dedicated time to discussing ideas for my class. (Rabbi Patricia Fenton, teacher)

The beauty of successful collaborations is that everybody learns. In 1997, as director of professional development at the Rebecca and Israel Ivry

---

[1]This chapter originated as a project for the Day School Leadership Training Program.

Prozdor, the high school program of the Jewish Theological Seminary of America, I began to encourage collaboration among teachers. At first, I offered the faculty loosely structured options. They responded with great enthusiasm. Over the years, several models of collaborative curriculum development took shape, both at the Ivry Prozdor and at other schools at which I consulted. Not every effort was successful or long lasting. Teachers and I were continually refining processes together and, in so doing, we were continually learning about collaboration, curriculum development, teaching methods, our subject matter, each other, our students, and ourselves.

THREE MODELS OF COLLABORATIVE CURRICULUM DEVELOPMENT

I recommend that you start with a modest foray into collaboration so that you can find and enjoy a comfortable process within a limited commitment. The models I present here (figure 1 on page 664) vary in complexity and by no means represent the full range of possibilities. Their scope is limited to one curricular unit of a course or between one and six lessons. "Parallel teachers" teach the same material to different students. "Complementary teachers" teach different material to the same students. In the third model, the "resource person" may be a traditional member of the school community, such as the computer, art, or drama specialist, or the guidance counselor or school nurse, but he/she may also be someone from outside the school who brings a different perspective or methodology to the material. In one of my examples, you will see that a Deaf Jewish educator teamed up with teachers as the resource person, offering students entirely new ways to encounter and study Jewish texts. If I succeed in my objectives and you are "sold" on the joys of collaborative curriculum development, you may want to try each of these models — and invent more of your own.

As worthwhile and exciting as collaboration can be, each model comes with its own set of obstacles and potential frustrations, many of which revolve around that most precious commodity: time. The term "release time" might become important as you prepare to plunge into collaborative planning and face the two main scheduling challenges of teacher-collaborators: (1) deciding when to teach what material to whom and where (most poignant for complementary teachers whose schedules are often mirror images), and (2) finding unrushed opportunities for the rich conversation and joint thinking that can lead to deeply educative learning experiences for students. From an administrative perspective, granting teachers release time from teaching or other responsibilities poses legitimate problems. (Remember that problems can be solved by those motivated to do so, which is why making a compelling case for your collaboration is important.) The basic question for an administrator is, "If teachers A and B aren't going to do that teaching/lunch duty/mentoring/ etc., then who is?" This then branches into two further areas of consideration:

- *Financial* - Do we have the funds to hire someone for the tasks from which this team of teachers wants to be released? Is this expenditure the best way to use the school's limited resources? Can we commit similar expenditures to substitutes for other teachers who request release time?

  You may offer to seek a mini-grant to cover the costs of a substitute teacher or substitutes for your administrative tasks. Good sources of small grants include your local central agency (or Federation education department) and school/congregation members who have family foundations from which they can draw. You may convince a Rabbi to tap into her/his discretionary fund for an innovative project. A one-page description of the plan including a clear but simple budget of expenses is usually sufficient for such mini-grants. Ask your school director for guidance in pursuing these sources. Receipt of such a grant has the added benefits of providing the administrator a *kvelling* point for newsletter articles and press releases, and conferring status on the collaborative project — and thus, on the idea of collaboration — within the school community.

- *Equity and Morale* - If we ask teachers to cover the collaborating team's tasks, will we be able to accommodate affected teachers' release requests in the future? How do we limit the possibility that students and teachers will feel unsettled by schedule or personnel changes while allowing teachers the opportunity to collaborate?

Three Models of Collaborative Curriculum Development

PARALLEL TEACHERS	COMPLEMENTARY TEACHERS	TEACHER/RESOURCE PERSON
• Teach the same subject to different students	• Teach the same students different subject matter	• Person with specific skills/perspective collaborates with the teacher
STUDENT BENEFITS	**STUDENT BENEFITS**	**STUDENT BENEFITS**
• Opportunity to work and socialize in fresh groupings • Chance to become better acquainted with other schoolmates • Change of routine and venue • Newly energized teachers	• Opportunity to make connections between disciplines • Challenge to synthesize understanding (combine ideas anew, meaningfully) • Reinforce subject knowledge by relating it to other content areas	• View subject through a new lens • Learn through fresh multiple intelligences emphasis • Experience, and perhaps reflect on, the impact of perspective on understanding
COLLABORATOR BENEFITS	**COLLABORATOR BENEFITS**	**COLLABORATOR BENEFITS**
• Chance to view material through multiple perspectives • Can develop/try creative methods with the support of colleagues • Opportunity to work on a larger scale than when alone • Get to know more students • Personal growth and pleasure of camaraderie through the collaborative interaction	• Enhanced connection to school life and other teachers • New synthesis of subject matter • Opportunity to learn something in another discipline • Teaching repertoire infused with methods from other disciplines	• Novelty of a new and unusual partnership • Discovery of new ways to understand and convey subject matter • Strengthened areas of one's own intelligences • Opportunity to learn something in another field • Teaching repertoire infused with methods from other fields or realms of life
CHALLENGES	**CHALLENGES**	**CHALLENGES**
• Finding time to meet • Trusting collaborators to put in effort and to have good ideas • Managing a big project with complex logistics • Gaining administrative support for increased planning time and project costs, if any	• Finding time to meet • Finding organic and meaningful connections between subject matter areas • Working out the complex logistics of who teaches whom what, where, and when • Gaining administrative support for temporary scheduling and space re-allocations	• Identifying potential collaborators • Finding time to meet • Teaching in an unfamiliar manner • Gaining administrative support for increased planning time and project costs, if any

Figure 1

Collaborations should raise morale in a school, not lower it. In order to ensure that your project has only a positive impact, be sure to *request* your colleagues' and administrators' support rather than assume that it is forthcoming. Talk about the project with colleagues, and gently encourage them to try a collaboration of their own. Find ways to minimize the burden your project places on others. Be sure to offer to reciprocate their favors. And, most important, don't forget to acknowledge and thank everybody who helps you.

As for student morale, encourage all affected teachers to explain to students the reason for changes in their schedule, rooms, etc. They are likely to wish they were in on the other project. If they speak up, perhaps their teachers will agree to plan an integrated unit themselves later on!

In the following section, you will find examples and brief rationales of the three models, along with a step-by-step implementation guide, including suggested timetables and support structures. The last section will address more deeply the nature of collaborative relationships and their potential for facilitating personal and professional growth.

COLLABORATION BY PARALLEL TEACHERS

Sheryl, Tirza, and Adam (parallel teachers of three concurrent sections of the Ivry Prozdor's tenth grade seminar, Medieval Jewish Civilization) were struggling to engage students actively in material that seemed particularly foreign. The class had just finished studying the painful relations between Jews and the Christian Church, a topic with which their students did not resonate strongly. It was late winter, and everyone was getting tired. In planning the transition to the unit on the creative and intellectual dimensions of Medieval Jewish culture, Sheryl, Tirza, and Adam were concerned that the material — personality profiles, poetry, philosophy, and halachah — would feel dry as dust. In the "dust" of that concern, the seeds of collaboration were planted.

Deciding that a change of scenery and routine would reenergize them and their students, the teachers identified resources available within the curriculum and the facility, and then brainstormed ideas that would put all three classes to work on one major project. They took advantage of the Jewish Theological Seminary's extensive library to engage students in researching biographies and con-tributions of various Medieval Jewish personalities (the Rambam, Yehudah HaLevi, and others). Teams, formed across class lists to let students work with schoolmates from the other two classes, were to prepare for and hold a "wine" soiree, such as might have been held in the cosmopolitan centers of Sepharad (Iberia). Their research would result in a morning of poetry readings, declarations of philosophy, discussions of beliefs, and much festive revelry. Members of each research group were encouraged to take specific roles in the process. Some scoured the library for likely resources on their assigned personality; others perused the first groups' findings and identified the most useful sources. Teams discussed what they were learning and together decided their presentation's focus and style. Again dividing tasks among members, groups wrote fact sheets and skit scripts, created costumes, and practiced recitations, performances, and in-role responses to likely questions from the crowd.

The morning of the soiree, a lounge with low couches and coffee tables was set up in intimate groupings. Grape juice, mini-donuts, and an array of other goodies were served while Sephardic music played softly in the background. Groups made their presentations and responded to those of the other groups. Students taught each other while celebrating their learning process in a manner that itself taught them something of medieval Sephardic culture. Sheryl, Tirza, and Adam each reported feeling completely recharged by the collaboration. They taught the remaining units with increased energy, focus, and impact to students who also had shaken off their late winter fatigue.

In this collaboration, one teacher, Sheryl, took the initiative, seeking my support and inviting her colleagues to talk about the obstacles and opportunities of the curriculum. The three teachers met several times during the weeks prior to teaching the unit. In conversation together, they planned and structured the project, set a time line, and divvied up tasks. Since each knew his or her students best, they worked together on grouping the students. One teacher wrote out the research assignment, while another planned how to facilitate the differentiation of tasks within each group. Two of the teachers spent time in the library, identifying a broad (but manageable) range of resources and arranging for easy access. The third reserved the student lounge and CD player, acquired CDs of Sephardic music, and invited me to attend the soiree.

During the unit, Sheryl, Tirza, and Adam played both different and overlapping roles. One introduced the subject and the project, while another assigned students to research groups and the third provided detailed project guidelines. All three circulated among students in the library encouraging and assisting them. The teachers bought snacks, kept the groups on track, finalized presentation plans, selected music and, on the morning of the soiree, set up the lounge in an inviting manner. Finally, in the week after the concluding event, Sheryl gathered their planning notes and examples of student work and contributed them to the office so that a record of the project would be included in future versions of the curriculum's teacher's guide.

COLLABORATION BY COMPLEMENTARY TEACHERS

I very much wanted my students to understand that there are many different gates into the Talmud. Using the image of the Sea of Talmud, you could say that [this collaborative unit] touched on many shores. (Rabbi Patricia Fenton, teacher)

Virtuoso Yo-Yo Ma has been playing Bach's *Suites for Unaccompanied Cello* since he was five years old. When he felt the need to renew his appreciation for these delicate masterpieces, he chose to collaborate with artists in different disciplines. He reinterpreted one Suite with the help of two ice dancers. Another Suite was utterly transformed through his collaboration with landscape architect Julie Moir Messervy that led to plans for a music garden, "as they envisioned the joining of music and nature" (John-Steiner, p. 95).

Complementary teachers teach the same students different courses. You teach Hebrew and he teaches Bible. She teaches science and you teach the holidays. Collaboration across subjects can help students see connections among aspects of their world that course divisions, or academic disciplines, often compartmentalize. Curriculum integration is all about helping students experience new relationships among the many aspects of their world. It strengthens their synthesizing skills (making meaning by putting things together in new ways), which are at least as important in the life of

the mind as those of analysis (understanding by examining component parts of wholes), but are often less well developed in school. When you collaborate with complementary teachers, you, too, may find new relevance in your subject matter, new ways to understand its place in the whole, new meanings. Collaborations among complementary teachers can be quite exciting, and worth the logistical challenges that often arise around scheduling.

In workshops I have run for teachers at several Solomon Schechter high schools, participants begin collaborations by bringing to the table several aspects of their Jewish and general studies curricula. On the first day, teachers choose their partners and begin to brainstorm what material would integrate well: what subject matter could be more deeply or differently explored for richer learning, or what skills could be reinforced by application across courses. In one school, a team of science and Hebrew teachers created a botany/Hebrew unit in which concepts, contexts, and language were synthesized across the disciplines. The unit focused on plant life in the Land of Israel. It incorporated practice in the scientific skills of identification, sorting, and categorization, and in the active language skills of writing and presenting in Hebrew. Several Judaic studies and English literature teachers developed a unit around a Holocaust-related novel. The English teachers planned to explore the book through a literary lens, while the Judaic studies teachers would place it in its historical context and use its protagonists' experiences as a springboard to discussions of faith, courage, Jewish identity, and theodicy. Teams of students would produce extensive multimedia projects to satisfy the requirements of both courses. A middle school social studies teacher worked with her Jewish studies colleague on an integrated unit about the agricultural underpinnings of the Jewish festivals as they related to migration and sustenance patterns of the ancient Near East. In a high school, the math and science teachers developed lessons on the calculus of physics, while the French and Hebrew teachers planned a comparative linguistics unit that reinforced students' grasp of the syntactic patterns of both languages.

During the workshops in which these collaborations begin, we address logistical, pragmatic, and personal questions, along with educational considerations. Aware of the challenge teachers face in finding time to work together, I often have them review their calendars on the spot. With some difficulty, teams can succeed in carving out several collaborative meetings during their packed school days. In one case, the entire Judaic studies department identified one hour per week and set it aside for collaboration throughout the spring semester: a feat they would have bet was not possible. I ask collaborating partners to consider in whose classrooms students will learn which parts of the unit. Urged to be open about those aspects of the unit's content in which they feel less than fully knowledgeable, team members explore what they could teach each other in advance, and how far out of their personal comfort zones they are willing to stretch. Additionally, I encourage them to imagine aloud how they can best support each other as they learn and teach the new material.

One solution to teaching a mix of content is to team teach, but for complementary teachers, who teach the same students at different times of the day, team teaching can require logistical gymnastics. To effect the temporary scheduling and room changes that allow for it, the teams need to enlist their administration's support. In situations that emerge from my workshops, making the case is easier than it might otherwise be. For one thing, the administrator(s) — who, after all, have brought me in to do the workshop — approve the idea of collaboration in advance, and are forewarned that logistical requests might result. Additionally, when teachers are enthusiastic about their own integrated collaborations, they tend also to be generous about adapting their schedules to accommodate other teams' needs. Even so, I encourage collaborative partners to practice developing a clear case for their request, outlining the unit, articulating the benefits the collaboration would bring to students, and noting that in the future they would be willing to make sacrifices similar to those their adaptation imposes on other personnel. Depending on the dynamics of your school, when you follow this process, you might choose to suggest ways in which the adaptations could be made. If so, I suggest that you enlist the cooperation of affected teachers before making your suggestion to administrators so that your colleagues have the opportunity to choose to help, and can feel they are a part of something exciting, rather than feeling imposed upon.

While developing integrated units, teachers report enjoying the friendly, intellectual conversation with colleagues and appreciate being granted time to "luxuriate" (to quote one participant) in collegial conversation and planning. This first taste of collaborative planning across disciplines allows them to practice the intellectual work of integrating curricular areas and the logistical and political work of advocating for the adaptation of school structures to make room for their collaboration. Most teachers express excitement about their collaborative projects, though many of the high school teachers with whom I work are more skeptical about the impact of implementing them. With the pressure that exists in today's high schools to "cover" material, these teachers need more assurance that the occasional integrated unit can help them effectively cover the material, as long as it is carefully planned around the real learning objectives of each course. Even those most eager to get under way also express concern about being able to "pull it off" in the hectic reality of school. This is why I recommend a modest beginning. Most school schedules have a tiny amount of stretch built into them. While deep ongoing changes can emanate only from a school-wide commitment to collaborative, integrative teaching, an administrator and colleagues who share your enthusiasm can generally accommodate a few such units a year.

COLLABORATIVE UNIT BY THE TEACHER AND A RESOURCE PERSON

> The art project with Lia was fabulous. I very much wanted my students to understand that there are many gates into the Talmud. For them to express their ideas in clay was — at least for me — a fabulous experience. My least articulate student produced the most beautiful piece. (Rabbi Patricia Fenton, teacher)

So often in Jewish education, particularly in the older grades, our teaching style resembles the oral/aural methods revered and documented in our Jewish and Western traditions: reading, questioning, answering, more questioning, more reading, some writing, and so on. In programs such as the Ivry Prozdor, where courses are taught seminar-style and designed around primary source texts, teachers work hard to develop the skills of good discussion leading. They may employ a range of oral/aural strategies to help students encounter texts directly, stimulating higher order thinking and the construction of knowledge, while encouraging students to challenge and support each other.

Even in such programs grounded in the discussion method, periodically employing other strategies is crucial. Elsewhere in this volume, you may read about Howard Gardner's theory of multiple intelligences,[2] which posits that individuals best understand the world around them through one or more of a variety of intelligences: oral/aural, artistic, kinesthetic musical, interpersonal, intrapersonal, and logical/mathematical (Gardner, 1983). Expert educators developing practical applications of Gardner's theory to teaching practice suggest that students be given opportunities to work both in their areas of strength and in those areas that are less fully developed.

Teachers, too, understand the world and their subject matter most comfortably through particular intelligences and lenses, and can benefit from exposure to diverse methods and perspectives. In this rich collaborative model, the teacher invites a resource person to co-plan a unit of the curriculum. Through developing new ways for students to explore a subject, all collaborative partners learn about themselves, the students, and the content. To be clear, I am not talking about bringing a guest in to teach your class, but rather, inviting someone to plan a unit *with* you. This model is a powerful eye-opener; all the teachers whom I know to have engaged in it feel enriched, even exhilarated by, the experience.

Generally, resource people are defined as those who offer additional help or teach a particular specialty within a school: the art or music teacher, technology or drama specialist, guidance counselor or psychologist. One example is the team at a Solomon Schechter high school, which consisted of an English literature teacher and a Bible teacher (complementary pairing), and the college counselor and the school psychologist (resource people). Together, they planned a unit on personal journeys that began with familiar biblical wandering narratives, moved through contemporary fiction of personal growth, and culminated in journaling and group reflection to help students articulate their own journeys through adolescence and high school, and to imagine their futures.

Broadening the possibilities for this model, I define the term resource person to include anyone who may bring a completely different approach, perspective, or skill set to the subject matter. In one of the following examples, the collaborative partner is an art specialist; in the other she is a Deaf Jewish educator whose professional focus is increasing accessibility to Jewish life for the Deaf. (This educator taught me that many Deaf people consider themselves to be part of a Deaf community in addition to the other communities in which they dwell, and therefore prefer to capitalize Deaf as we would capitalize Jewish or American. I am happy to honor that wish.)

You may need to seek the approval and support of your school director to implement this model, as certain decisions may lie in her/his domain. For instance, outside specialists often (and reasonably) expect a modest fee or honorarium. At very least, the school should offer to reimburse travel and material expenses. On the other hand, specialists within the school may need to request scheduling allowances to team teach in your class. And, as always, finding planning opportunities may require some release time.

Example A

In 1997, students at the Ivry Prozdor were privileged to have a Deaf Jewish educator, Marla, address them in an assembly about access issues in Jewish communal and religious life for Deaf Jews. Marla's presentation was among the most well received in my time at the program: students clamored to have her come back to work with them again. At the time, I was seeking innovative models of professional development with which to tempt a very part-time faculty. Marla, at the time completing a master's degree in Jewish education, was interested in learning about what students in a high school program of this nature studied. We all agreed something more should be done.

Marla and I formulated a plan wherein teachers could sign up to collaborate with her in team teaching a brief unit. The school's primary mode of teaching and learning, oral/aural, was not suitable for a Deaf educator; Marla would therefore help my teachers invite their students to enter the subject

---

[2]See Chapter 27, "Multiple Intelligences" by Renee Holtz and Barbara Lapetina, pp. 323-333 in this Handbook.

matter through different doors. We set project parameters as follows:

- All participants must attend a group meeting about collaborative planning and team teaching.

- The collaborative unit had to be part of the class's regular curriculum.

- Each teacher agreed to meet with Marla at least twice before the unit and to share planning responsibilities.

- Each teacher actively team taught with Marla each session of the unit.

Four teachers signed up — the maximum we could accommodate. At the opening meeting, we explored together what each would want and expect from this new experience for all of us: team teaching. This is a discussion I urge you to have with anyone with whom you set out to plan and/or team teach collaboratively. We forged working agreements by addressing such questions as: How can I trust that the individual work I bring to the collaboration will be respected? What do we do if one partner has a brainstorm during a lesson and wants to switch gears? How do we communicate without breaking the flow of the lesson? Who is in charge of the lesson's pace? What is each team member's standard of student behavior and, where the standards differ, what level of expectation can we consider acceptable? How do we jump in if we want to add to what the other teacher is saying?

Over the semester, we saw rings of learning expand from this project far beyond what we imagined. Marla and the teachers — all novices at this — learned what it meant to plan and teach with a partner. They all enjoyed the initial conversations and idea development. First, the teacher would describe the students and the curriculum to Marla, giving her the full course context, then focusing on upcoming units. Marla would listen carefully. (Of course, these meetings included an ASL, American Sign Language, interpreter.) She would look for content that jumped out as material that could be explored and expressed through movement, dramatics, or the visual arts. They would study the relevant texts together, and discuss what they wanted the students to learn. Then the planning began: the teacher and Marla would brainstorm nonverbal ways to have the students encounter the ideas of the text. They might have students find movements

that express the key elements of a text or use torn paper midrash to create their own interpretations. When they were starting a unit or lesson with exploration of the students' ideas and beliefs, similar methods were employed for personal expression. For some students, these experiences brought "aha" moments about a text's meaning in the way discussion rarely did. Sometimes, people (some more than others) understand things more deeply without words. Finding alternative means of expression can help students retain those understandings, even as they move back into discussion.

Everyone involved in these collaborations also benefited by learning the pace and manners of communicating with a Deaf person with the help of an interpreter signing and vocalizing. Teachers and students learned and practiced some ASL. I, as an administrator, learned not only how to manage the logistics of multiple collaborations in one semester, but also about the powerful, uplifting effect on faculty and students of such projects. And, of course, Marla, the specialist who devoted her time to this project, learned what students study at this academic Judaic studies program.

Example B

Students in the intensive Beit Midrash program at the Ivry Prozdor study Talmud in chevruta (paired study) one period, and in a shiur (lesson) with their teacher a second period. The teacher in this example, a Rabbi completing a doctorate in Talmud whom students fondly call Talmud Pat, regularly employs strategies with her students that involve reading, translating, theorizing, applying theories, debating, and expressing personal beliefs and feelings.

I had engaged Lia, a Judaic artist completing a master's degree in art education to teach an elective and to serve as a resource for other teachers. With teachers' professional development in mind, I set parameters for collaborations with Lia: Lia may team teach a unit or may co-plan one that the teacher teaches alone. She may not, however, come in and teach a class or unit alone, even if the teacher is present.

Intrigued by my invitation to collaborate with a Judaic artist, Pat signed up. She had no idea how an artist might help her students learn Talmud, but was adventurous enough to explore the possibility. In their initial meeting, neither Pat nor Lia knew what to expect. They knew little about the other's field, and even less about teaching it. After some initial "getting to know you" conversation, talk turned to Pat's upcoming units. Listening and asking questions, Lia identified a topic that struck her as having the easiest translation into an artistic medium. Pat's students were approaching a section of text on ritual purity and impurity. Part of the discussion was about the kaylim (vessels or implements, singular: kli) used in the Holy Temple for sacrificial rituals. While Pat was thinking conceptually, Lia, with her "artistic intelligence" at full alert, heard the word "kli" and thought, clay. They talked in greater depth, Pat teaching Lia the concepts and implications of purity laws, and Lia imagining how students could learn about them through pottery work.

In a subsequent meeting, Pat and Lia planned the entire unit. Pat would engage the students in studying the sugya (topical unit of Talmudic text) in their accustomed manner: translating the text; becoming familiar with the Rabbinic concepts and vocabulary; and discussing the social, religious, and legal ramifications — then and now — of laws concerning purity. Pat and Lia together would then engage students in considering the roles of ritual objects in their own lives and in creating their own kaylim.

On the day of the team taught component, the bayt midrash (study hall) where class took place became a pottery studio, with paper covering every table, and mounds of clay at students' fingertips. Pat and Lia co-led a discussion. Students were challenged to move from considering the texts to considering their own religious lives. How can an object have the characteristics of purity or impurity? What roles do implements and objects play in ritual? In the Bible and to the Rabbis, what made an implement worthy of the highest ritual use? Today, what kaylim would enhance their religious, ritual, and/or spiritual life? What characteristics would make it worthy? Then they got to work, imagining a worthy kli, beginning to form and beautify it. Pat kept the discussion going one-on-one as she moved among tables. Lia helped students create in clay the images they formed in their minds, encouraging them to express their imagination, and suggesting methods and tools. While the finished products ranged in quality by artistic standards, the process made concrete and salient the relevance of the ancient Talmudic concepts. The collaboration transformed Talmud for the students and for their teacher, who

has since invited an environmentalist, a poet, and another visual artist to collaborate with her.

It is wonderful to have lots of time to sit around and talk through curriculum while collaborating on a new project. However, I have found that a creative environment can be created through focused e-mail discussions. In preparation for a summer children's program, I offered a piece of text for an e-mail discussion. As teachers were hired, they joined in the discussion. We began with a summer theme — a quote from *Tehillim* (Psalms) — moved into classical Rabbinic *midrash*, and ended with brainstorming art projects and cross-age pairing of groups. Catching latecomers up was as easy as forwarding previous communications. All this occurred while I was in Israel and everybody else was scattered around the east coast.

(Anne Johnston, New Haven, Connecticut)

COLLABORATIVE RELATIONSHIPS

The co-construction of ideas is helped by a listening ear. Building a resilient sense of identity is aided by a self that is stretched and strengthened in partnership. The gifts of confidence and support may outlast a creative partnership . . . (John-Steiner, p. 127).

One week, while I was struggling with how to conclude this chapter, I scheduled a series of complicated fittings that would turn the sample dress I bought on sale into the bridal gown of my dreams. Little did I suspect that while playing manikin, I would witness the unfolding of a beautiful collaboration over silk and crinoline. Carmen and Connie are the senior seamstresses of a bridal boutique in Boca Raton, Florida. Their example is the entry point I was seeking to discuss the power of collaboration to transform and strengthen the individual partners.

I first met Connie when I purchased the gown months earlier. At the shop owner's request, she worked quickly that afternoon to determine that she would, indeed, be able to remake the gown for me. When I arrived for the first fitting, she and Carmen brought it out in two parts — bodice and dress having been separated and most of the seams opened up — for me to slip into. From that moment forward, they engaged in a soft-spoken conversation in lovely Spanish that concluded, several days and much skilled work later, with happy grins all around when the dress was deemed perfect. Despite my poor Spanish comprehension and my relative ignorance of their craft, I learned a lot about the affectionate interdependent relationship of these professional women.

Carmen and Connie are each highly talented, confident artisans. Their discussions were not those of mentor and apprentice (there was also an apprentice who worked with them part of the time). Rather, these were consultations between equals, two people who set out to reach a goal together. First they developed a shared vision of the outcome: what the gown was going to look like on me when all the work was done. Only then did they discuss how they were going to achieve it. They walked around, alternately looking at me directly and from my vantage point in the mirror. They pinched seams closed and released them, lifted and lowered my arms, stood back and moved close. They looked at the skirt, and asked me about the second pair of shoes I bought for comfortable dancing. They spent nearly 15 minutes discussing the seam under my right arm, using words and hand motions that expressed the relationship they were working out between their approach to that seam and to the rest of the dress.

Connie and Carmen are the equivalent of "parallel teachers." They do the same sort of work, but as individuals with different strengths, experiences, perceptions, and personalities, they each contribute uniquely to the partnership. If one were a specialist in beading while the other did all the lace work, they would be more like "complementary teachers," those with different areas of specialty working with the same students/gown. In that case, their specific areas of knowledge would differ as well as all the rest. (Their ongoing interdependence makes it difficult to imagine them as "teacher and resource person," which by definition is a partnership of limited scope.)

Collaborations develop a unique rhythm and flow. In this team, sewing was actually done by one seamstress at a time. I was not privy to how they decided who did what tasks, but there seemed to be little to no tension about it. Sometimes one woman did pinning sometimes; at other times they did it together. They made all major decisions together. Connie seemed to be "point person" on my dress — the project initiator and primary contact in discussions involving my mother, the boutique owner, and me. One day, another bride came in for a final fitting concurrent with mine. Carmen seemed to be point person on that project. During the hours that this other bride and I coincided, Connie and Carmen worked across the room from each other, calling each other over for consultations whenever new decisions had to be made. My guess is that they would not normally schedule two brides at once.

What are some characteristics of a successful collaborative relationship? Manifested in the easy flow of ideas between these women, I noticed the combination of self-confidence, openness, and trust that I believe to be essential. Connie and Carmen construct a shared vision and plan: to do this, each partner has hear the other. They are kind but honest. Each takes creative risks, knowing full well that the other will challenge her thinking, raise issues to be resolved and, perhaps, propose alternatives for consideration. They engage in a dialogic creative process: ideas are formulated, honed, improved, and ultimately, crystallized and implemented jointly. Neither partner is shy about proposing new ideas or critiquing ones under discussion. Each trusts that the other shares her focus on, and commitment to, the end result. They have confidence in their own abilities and in the abilities of the other. They are willing to learn and grow from the interaction. They have fun.

Over the length of their partnership, collaborators like Connie and Carmen amass a bank of shared experiences on which to draw. Not only do they learn *from* each other, they learn new things *with* each other. The partnership strengthens each one's individual identity and confidence, as it enables both to stretch, producing work better than they may have done alone. Finally, I can say with confidence that Connie and Carmen enjoy working together. Sewing, an easily isolating craft, has been transformed for them into a shared practice filled with personally satisfying camaraderie and professionally enriching conversation.

Collaboration can elevate the work of teaching, a field in which creativity is essential, and enrich the partners both professionally and personally. Yet, while it offers extensive creative, cognitive, and emotional value, there are also risks and costs involved in collaborating. As in all interpersonal relationships, collaborators risk unmet expectations, frustration. and disappointment. Not every colleague is the right collaborative partner for you. Vera John-Steiner notes that the successful collaborators she studied were mostly dialogic thinkers, people who think best in conversation with others. People who think best alone and bring fully completed thoughts to the table may not work as well in collaborative teams. Some, like Einstein, think well both ways, at times working alone and at other times needing dialogue with colleagues to go beyond their own limitations. In a short-lived collaboration at the Ivry Prozdor, one partner reported that she was uncomfortable with the work habits of the other. This teacher did not feel confident that her partner was putting equal effort in, or that the important tasks would get done in time. In fact, this issue was more a matter of mismatched styles than lack of commitment: one preferred to prepare meticulously and far in advance while the other felt more inspired by spontaneous, in-the-moment decisions.

I do not need to tell teachers that the biggest obstacle to and cost of collaboration is time. Thinking jointly often takes more time than thinking in isolation. How do you carve out the time to work together? If collaboration is not already part of your school's culture, start with a modest strategy. Plan to collaborate on one unit, as I suggest above, and spend your first meeting structuring your working relationship. Decide how many meetings you will plan, and put them in your calendars that day. A collaborative team in a school where I consulted sought their supervisor's support in freeing up the partners' time and finding a meeting place. The head of school reassigned some of their non-teaching tasks to others during the length of the collaborative project, and dedicated to them the one room that was free on the morning each week that the team could convene. Exam periods and special program days often provide opportunities for flexible staffing during which a team might carve out time to meet. For extensive collaborations, funds might be made available by school leadership for substitute teachers to step in while the team meets. As mentioned above, you might apply for mini-grants to provide funds for class release coverage. I urge you to make the effort at least once this year. While collaborating is not always as easy as working alone, it is almost always more energizing, stimulating, and confidence

building. When you collaborate, you can stretch beyond the limitations of your own knowledge and skills; you can become a better, more creative teacher.

TEACHING CONSIDERATIONS

A Step-by-Step Guide To Collaborative Curriculum Planning

1. Decide with whom you want to work: a parallel teacher, complementary teacher, or a resource person from within or outside the school.

2. Invite that person to collaborate with you. You may want to share this chapter with him or her. Talk about shared students or subject matter, as well as how your work differs. Discuss what is coming up in your (or both of your) curriculum, looking for aspects of your subject matter that lend themselves to collaboration between you. It should also look like fun for both partners.

3. Bring your administrator in on the project. Make the case for your collaboration and enlist his/her support.

4. Don't expect to meet on the fly. Schedule two or three additional meetings up front, clarifying their length and purpose as much as possible. You can schedule more if you need them.

5. Brainstorm ways to approach the collaborative unit in innovative ways. Be creative, even wild. Don't judge, critique, or debate the relative worth of ideas at this stage. Remember, this is your chance to break out of your usual constraints. Brainstorming means getting all the ideas out there between you. Write them down!

6. Focus in on one set of ideas that works well: it should promote each partner's goals for students and result in an extraordinary learning experience. It should also be stimulating, challenging, and fun for the partners, as well as realistic within the parameters of one unit at school.

7. Here's where you deepen the significant conversations and joint thinking. Talk your idea through, envisioning the whole unit, planning every step together. What are the unit objectives? What activities will you employ? How will you meet the logistical challenges? How

many sessions do you need? What do you each need to learn about your partner's respective subject matter or approach? How will you build in a demonstration of mastery or other form(s) of assessment? How can you support each other during the collaboration? Chal-lenge each other's assumptions. Hone each other's ideas. Be courageous. Enjoy learning something new and approaching your own material with fresh eyes.

8. Will you be team teaching or simply co-planning? If you choose to team teach, work out scheduling issues now. If not, carefully plan unit components for each class that link together thematically, through skill development, and/or by leading to a final project in which students demonstrate mastery/understanding in both areas. Pay attention to sequencing: does X need to happen in classroom A before Y can happen in classroom B?

9. Generate a To Do list with timetables and deadlines. Decide and note which team member will take responsibility for which tasks. (Some tasks, like enlisting the administration's help, might be done collaboratively. Others, like buying supplies, photocopying pages, making worksheets, or cutting out templates might be assigned to one person or the other.)

10. Meet before the unit begins for a status check of preparations. Reflect on and hone the plan one more time, and if you are team teaching as well, establish your plan for joint presentation and facilitation.

11. Teach well and have fun!

12. Meet again to celebrate and reflect on the collaboration. Consolidate notes on the idea, the collaborative process, and students' responses for future reference. If you choose, you may want to submit a write-up of the unit and samples of student work to your school's curriculum bank. In addition, if you received a minigrant, you may be obligated to submit a brief write-up in fulfillment of that agreement.

BIBLIOGRAPHY

Gardner, Howard. *Frames of Mind: The Theory of Multiple Intelligences*. New York: Basic Books. 1983.

This book sets forth Gardner's theory of multiple intelligences. If you prefer a wonderful application-oriented work around Gardner's theory, try Robin Fogarty's book, *Problem-based Learning & Other Curriculum Models for the Multiple Intelligences Classroom* (Arlington Heights, IL: SkyLight Professional Development, 1997).

———. *Creating Minds: An Anatomy of Creativity Seen through the Lives of Freud, Einstein, Picasso, Stravinsky, Eliot, Graham, and Gandhi*. New York: Basic Books, 1993.

This book contains rich examples of creativity in action, embedded in Gardner's analysis of the creative process. Notice especially how many people's creativity is influenced by their work with others.

John-Steiner, Vera. *Creative Collaboration*. New York: Oxford University Press, 2000.

This is the scholarly work from which I borrow so many of the quotations and ideas in this chapter. I recommend it highly; it is an easy read and profoundly enlightening.

CHAPTER 55

Working with Teen Assistants

Patti Kroll

*I*t was the first day of religious school classes and Morah Devorah scanned the classroom to make sure everything was ready for the 12 active kindergarten students who would soon be coming into the room. She had been preparing for opening day for several weeks and was satisfied that there would be a number of activities to keep the students occupied while she collected their supply boxes and introduced herself to their anxious parents. The first student to enter her room was a good deal taller than any kindergartner; Morah Devorah recognized him as an eighth grader whose name was David. (They had actually met the week before when David was introduced to her at a teachers' meeting as her teaching assistant for the year.) Great timing! They had about ten minutes to talk before the first students would come bounding through the classroom door.

In the room next door, Morah Karen was getting ready for the 14 first grade students who would soon arrive. An experienced teacher, Morah Karen has a special needs student in her class this year, Katie, who requires a full-time paraprofessional to assist with all areas of the curriculum. Morah Karen has already met with the school director, the inclusion specialist, Katie's teacher from last year, and Jamie, a teen who would be working as a paraprofessional. Jamie is an eleventh grader who completed her synagogue's Confirmation Program last year and now needs community service hours for public school. When the school director suggested she might like to work as a paraprofessional, the idea appealed to her. She likes children and has even thought about becoming a teacher. Jamie felt that this would be good experience that could offer some career direction.

Down the hall, there are two second grade classes that for the first time have two teen assistants working with them. One assistant in each class has experience, and the other assistant is new to the program. Both of the second grade teachers are experienced; they have worked with teen assistants before and welcome the additional help with hands-on projects. The teachers know they will need to provide direction, even though they hope that the experienced assistants will be positive role models for the "first timers." However, there is also a concern that two assistants in the classroom may become too "chummy" and give their attention to each other rather than to the students. The teachers are aware of this and will be watching out for this situation.

This was just the beginning of what was to be a wonderful experience for Morah Devorah, David, Morah Karen, Jamie, the second grade teachers and assistants, the students in the classroom, the congregation, and the community. Teen assistants, (*madrichim*[1]), enrich the scope of Jewish education and bring an inquisitiveness and youthful enthusiasm to both formal and informal educational programs. They are a valuable resource and willing learners, given the right guidance and learning environment.

Teens who work as assistants see education from the inside out. They begin to have a new appreciation for the educational process as they recognize how much work goes into planning a good lesson and all that is involved with running a classroom or program. With proper guidance, teen assistants can become involved in the educational process and become active rather than passive learners.

In many settings, teen assistants mainly serve in a support role. They are there to assist the teacher and students in any aspect of the learning process and the educational program. For some, this may mean working in a classroom or with an educational specialist, working with individual students or small groups of students, teaching a lesson or assisting with other school programs. Teen assistants help in the school office, lead services, provide child care

---

[1] The word *"madrich"* means guide. The plural is *madrichim.*

for the younger children of the faculty during school hours, tutor B'nai Mitzvah students, work one-on-one as a paraprofessional with special needs students, or partner with specialists such as the music teacher or art teacher. This is a unique learning opportunity for teenagers and provides a chance to work closely with a skilled teaching professional.

From the onset, teens need to sense that they are needed and that they must be responsible. For some, it is their first real job, and as with any employee, there are certain expectations that need to be clearly understood. These students are developing work skills and work ethics, and when treated as valued "employees," they acquire skills they will use throughout their lives. Their insights and questions open up new educational perspectives. Working with a teaching assistant is a commitment that takes time and patience, but the benefits are immense.

This chapter offers some suggestions for training, supervision, expectations, and teacher-to-teen interactions. Throughout this chapter, for ease of language, references will be mostly to a school setting; however, these situations may be applied to an informal setting as well. At the end of the chapter, informal educational programs such as camps and retreats will be addressed briefly.

A thoughtful, supportive teacher can enhance the teen's participation in his or her classroom by:

- explaining the content, philosophy, and structure of the class to the assistant before the school year begins.

- providing information about available resources and how to access those resources.

- maintaining positive classroom control and helping the assistant learn how to support a climate of respect.

- encouraging the teen assistant's creativity and providing opportunities for that creativity.

- involving (when possible) the teen assistant in the development of lessons.

- helping the teen assistant identify the skills and areas he/she feels are strengths.

- guiding gently a teen assistant to take on more responsibility as he or she is ready to do so.

An assistant must clearly understand his or her responsibilities to the school and to the classroom teacher. The teen is usually asked to:

- enroll as a student in a Jewish day school or in the congregational religious school (this may vary as some congregations no longer have formal programs past tenth or eleventh grade).

- remember the teacher is the one who has ultimate responsibility for the class.

- dress and behave appropriately (standards are set by each school and teacher or supervisor).

- view him or herself as a "professional," working at a real job.

- notify his or her teacher and coordinator/ school director if he/she is going to be absent.

- maintain open communications with his or her teacher.

- interact with students one-on-one or in small groups.

- maintain the confidentiality of a teaching situation.

- demonstrate a desire to understand teaching strategies by asking questions.

- learn to take initiative, not waiting to be told to do something, but seeing a need and acting on it.

- participate in workshops and other sessions designed to enhance classroom skills.

- discuss concerns or other issues with the teacher, the coordinator, and/or the school director.

It is reasonable to have teen assistants run short errands in the building, set up the class snack, pick up supplies, take children to the office, get things ready for art projects, prepare materials for the next lesson, go to the library to get resource materials, and perform other non-teaching tasks. While some might see these as busy work, they are vital to the functioning of the class and the work of the teacher with the students. However, assistants should not be limited to doing only these tasks.

Elizabeth has been an assistant in the school for the past three years. Based on her previous evaluations, it was decided that Elizabeth has the skills and experience to plan and teach some of the lessons. This year, she will co-teach with Morah Stephanie, an experienced third grade teacher, with the intention that Elizabeth will have some solo teaching time under the watchful eye of her "lead" teacher. Due to her positive experiences as a teen assistant, Elizabeth has indicated she is interested in pursuing education as a career choice. It is hoped that she will also see the potential for combining her love of Judaism with her emerging teaching skills and consider the field of Jewish education.

Questions to Consider:

- If you were Morah Stephanie, how might you help Elizabeth plan a lesson? How will you prepare for your initial meeting with her? What criteria would you use to help her evaluate her experience?

- If you were part of the teaching staff of this school, how might you support Elizabeth's thoughts about entering the field of Jewish education?

My teen assistant, or *ozeret*, is awesome, and I didn't want to lose her for our second year together. So when Sasha told me that school and youth group commitments might keep her away once a month, I said, "No problem." I work around it with subs. We also exchange e-mails, and I keep her up to date on what is going on in class. Our commitment to making it work has been great for both of us. Hey, I might be training a future Rabbi or religious school teacher!

(Sheila Lepkin, Denver, Colorado)

THE TEACHER–ASSISTANT RELATIONSHIP

When working with teen assistants in a formal educational program, or an informal program such as a camp or retreat setting, it is important to establish clear expectations for the teachers and the teen participants. Both must understand their complementary roles and that everyone benefits from this kind of relationship. A good and supportive teacher is a positive role model, and has the poten-

tial to influence the development of a possible future Jewish educator. When teaching assistants have a positive classroom experience, we increase the chances that in a couple of years they may be teaching in the classroom next to yours.

Getting Started

Teachers and their teen assistants need to have some contact prior to the start of a school year. This should be a time for the teacher to share the goals for the class and a general overview of the curriculum, talk through the daily routine, and set out expectations. It is helpful for the assistant to review a copy of the curriculum, textbook, teacher guide, materials, and resources. This is also a time to find out about the assistant and to consider where he or she will work best. Often assistants have skills, talents and training that complement the teacher's skill set, perhaps Hebrew, musical ability, or art talent. They may have traveled to Israel or have some other interest that can enhance the educational program. The teacher often finds out these things through ongoing conversations and communication with the assistant.

The Teacher-Assistant Relationship

Establishing a good working relationship with a teen assistant takes time, effort, and a commitment, but it is well worth it. This is an ongoing process and as the relationship grows, ideally, teaching skills will improve. Teachers know they have been successful role models when, without being told to do something, their assistant takes the initiative, offers an idea for a lesson, or plans and teaches a lesson. Teen assistants are creative and genuinely happy to be working in a classroom. With a little encouragement, they can bring new ideas to the teaching environment. They do not just want to sit and watch; they want to be involved.

The role of a teacher is to help the assistant learn the proper behaviors and how to use their skills appropriately in the educational setting. One way this is done is by modeling: the teacher presents the lesson and then engages in dialogue with the assistant about what occurred. It is the conversation between the teacher and the assistant that reinforces the educational skills, and it is important for teachers to be honest with teen assistants, beginning with an atmosphere of mutual respect.

Criticism should never take place in front of other teen assistants, students, or staff. Suggestions are best given in private. At the end of class, the teacher and the assistant may take some time to go over the session and begin planning for the next class. Teen assistants thrive on positive feedback; a little praise will go a long way. Teachers need both to praise and encourage the teen assistant, offering suggestions for improvement and initiating planning for another lesson.

Teachers and their teen assistants need to work compatibly because students in a class sense if there is tension. When the teacher and the teaching assistant do not have a good working relationship, it is important to resolve the situation by working together or, if necessary, through the help of the school director or coordinator. Sometimes, in spite of all a teacher does, it may not be a good match and, for the benefit of all involved, a new placement may need to be found for the teen assistant.

> Some teen aides are good, and some aren't, but I generally find that all need a lot of guidance. Since they are usually very willing, but not really prepared, I find that it works best to give them a specific task. If they are doing Hebrew reading with a child, I have them read the prayer to me first to make sure that they are reading it correctly, and that they know it well enough to correct a child's mistakes.
>
> (Nancy Hersh, Chatham, New Jersey)

"GROWING" TEEN ASSISTANTS

Understanding adolescent development can be most helpful, especially for teachers who have not had much contact with older students. Generally, teens at this age are beginning to search for their philosophy of life and are in the process of their own faith development and concepts of God. Teens are becoming more confident with their emerging leadership skills and find that there is a sense of achievement in taking on responsibility. They are beginning to be able to take guidance from adults and respond positively to criticism when framed

constructively. This is the age when they want to take on the responsibility of a job, begin considering what college to attend, and begin considering accomplishments for a college résumé.

Most teen assistants make the time to become involved in our programs because they truly want to be a part of the school. They have a natural curiosity and believe that as they are searching for a personal religious philosophy, they may be able to find answers to their questions by being involved in the school setting. When they are in a position of importance, they take their own learning more seriously, synthesize their experiences, and develop relationships with adults on a different level. As teachers, we know that our best learning is when we teach, and the same holds true for teen assistants. When encouraged to "stretch" intellectually, they will take on the task with seriousness and commitment. Teens thrive on positive reinforcement; they want to be appreciated and to feel important.

Time management is an important consideration when working with teen assistants. As educators, we know how much time it takes to plan an effective lesson, and it is necessary to communicate this expectation to your assistant. At no time should assistants come into the class unprepared to teach a lesson they agreed to teach. It is their responsibility to find the time to prepare their lesson, including collecting all materials they will need when they teach. It is the teacher's responsibility to make sure they have the necessary skills to teach the lesson. There are several ways this communication can be facilitated, and it is best established between the teacher and the assistant early on in the relationship. Often, this may be done at the end of class, or through a phone conference or e-mail,[2] well in advance of when the teen assistant will be teaching a lesson. Utilizing the time prior to class is another possibility, and it is a good idea to go over the lesson just to make sure everything has been planned for and is in place. If there is a *madrichim* coordinator, he or she can be of assistance, and may want to observe the lesson. Open lines of communication include feedback on a lesson the teen assistant has presented, as well as positive and constructive comments on performance and suggestions for future lessons.

---

[2]One of the best ways to communicate is through e-mail. Teens are online, and are inclined to read their e-mails and respond to them.

Teen assistants of all ages need the guidance and support of the teacher in understanding the curriculum and the social, emotional structure of the class. Teachers can be most effective when they model expected behavior or techniques and then discuss this with their assistant. This is reflective practice, and it helps the teen assistant understand the philosophy of the teacher, the most effective strategies, and ways to anticipate the needs of the class and individual students.

The following are commonly seen student behaviors and situations in which teaching assistants may be of special help:

- If a student is off task, teen assistants can sit close to the child and remind the student of what he/she should be doing. A student may not understand the task or may not be able to begin it because the materials are not immediately available or direction and guidance on what to do is not clear. Teen assistants should not do the work, but guide the student to understand what is expected and provide encouragement so the student can complete the task.

- When a class works in small groups, a teen assistant is most effective going to each group and listening for progress toward task completion. The assistant's role should be one of keeping students on task and guiding with suggestions. The assistant might remind students to take turns; they might restate the objectives, or divide up tasks. Teen assistants should acquire the skills in these areas.

- It is the responsibility of the classroom teacher, not the assistant, to handle any behavior issues. However, the teen is sometimes asked to bring a student or students to the principal's office. This is not a time for the teen assistant to reprimand the student, but rather respect the child's dignity and the seriousness of the situation. In situations in which a student is loud or dangerous or if there is a medical emergency, it is prudent for the assistant to go to the office for help, leaving the teacher to deal with the immediate situation.

When planning for a class, the teacher needs to consider what he or she wants the assistant to accomplish and clearly communicate this to the teen. At no time should an assistant sit with nothing to do. This is not a good use of time, nor is it a productive experience.

Teen assistants should be encouraged to think proactively, to respond to the needs of the students, anticipate materials needed for an upcoming project, and know the best place to be situated in the classroom (for example, next to a child who may need assistance or settling down). As a general rule, teen assistants should not be expected to monitor the children in the class when the teacher is not present. An exception may be with an experienced assistant or a mature eleventh or twelfth grader. However, this will vary from assistant to assistant and from school to school, depending on school policy. Teachers need to know beforehand if their teen can manage the class if they are out of the room, even for a few minutes. In some cases, teens may be so familiar with the class routine that they may be of great assistance to a substitute. While assistants can take on a great deal of classroom responsibility, they do need to be aware of school policy and should not pass on information to parents, such as comments on academic progress or concerns about a child's behavior. These are areas that should be handled only by the classroom teacher.

Special Situations

Some classroom situations will necessitate additional support from the teacher or coordinator for their teen assistant. For example, a special needs child in the class can present challenges and may necessitate additional training for a teen assistant. If the teacher knows the class will include a special needs child, this information should be communicated to the teaching assistant, with the understanding that it is confidential and not to be discussed with their friends, parents of the students in the class, or any other students or adult. This is a trust issue between the school, the special needs students, and their parents. Teens need to understand their role with the special needs student and have specific strategies for assistance. Some teens are uncomfortable with special needs students, while others truly enjoy working with them.

There are times when a parent is upset over something and may try to discuss the situation with the teen assistant. Teens should not be put in this position. They should calmly respond, saying that they understand the concern, but that this really is a matter for the parent to discuss with the teacher.

Teens often show their emotions, either through their tone of voice in verbal communications or by withdrawing. A change in teen behavior is a good indicator that something is of concern. A supportive teacher who has developed a close relationship with the teen assistant at the start of the year may be able to discover if this behavior is a result of something from outside the teaching situation or if it is an issue related to school. A teacher who senses a change in performance might say, "You have been so helpful with the students, but in the last couple of weeks you seem withdrawn and uninvolved or unhappy. Is their something we need to talk about?" Teens want to know an adult is concerned, but if after gentle probing there is no response, stop questioning and wait to see if there is a change in the behavior. If, however, the behavior continues and you sense something is wrong with your working relationship, or that the teen is troubled, ask the school director or coordinator for help. He or she may have some additional insights as to what is going on in this teen's life at this time.

While most teens like to visit with friends while working, they do not realize that socializing during class time disrupts the program. When a situation such as this occurs, gently remind the assistant that she is really needed in class. Make a point of limiting out of class errands, and if such errands are necessary, remind him/her to come right back. A helpful statement is, "When you leave class on an errand and are gone for 20 minutes, I have no one helping me with the project. I really need your help and need you to be in the class with the students." When teachers set expectations at the start of the year, they minimize this behavior.

If a teen assistant demonstrates behavior that is not acceptable, it is important to deal quickly and fairly with the situation. Often when a teen realizes that his/her actions have an effect on others, he/she will alter their behavior. Most teens really want to please adults. If this does not happen and the problem continues, it would seem that this assistant might not be appropriate for the program.

The Assistant-Student Relationship

Maintaining professional distance is an issue that has ramifications in this day and age. Generally, we do not place a younger teaching assistant with a group of older students as there is not enough disparity in their ages. Teens working with students beyond the early primary grades should discourage children from sitting on their lap and limit any physical contact. In this day and age, we must be very careful regarding the physical contact that takes place between the teens and their students. It is very important for teachers to monitor this, to alert their assistant to any behavior that might be misunderstood by a student, and to limit the physical contact between opposite sex assistants and students. Teen assistants should not ask students to share their personal belongings, nor should a teen share any aspect of their private life with the students. Younger students do not need to know where the teens went the night before, or who they are dating.

There are times when the activity in class is so much fun that teen assistants want to participate and act like they are one of the students. This may happen during art, drama, a game, or any other less formal activity. This is one reason why it is necessary to set expectations for their role during the activity. It may be possible to provide the teen with an extra set of art materials to take home in advance to create a sample for the class, or to take home after the activity is completed. Teens respond positively to being the expert and taking the lead role in explaining an activity to others.

The above examples demonstrate the importance for a supportive teacher and the school director to set expectations and deal directly with any unacceptable behaviors. There are times when a teen does better in a different placement, or should not be invited back to the program. Having a teen assistant should be enjoyable to all involved, and the teen should also be seen by the students as a positive Jewish role model.

DEALING WITH SITUATIONS THAT ARISE

The following situations were introduced briefly at the beginning of this chapter. Analyze each based on the questions that follow it. Decide which actions you agree with, and which you would approach differently.

Situation A

Morah Devorah and David started out well in their

kindergarten classroom. David had lots of energy and a wonderful manner with the students. He was patient and worked well with children one-on-one and in small groups. David wanted all the children to like him, so saying "no" and setting limits was difficult for him to do. After the first few weeks, the students got a little wild with David, and he didn't know how to change this.

Questions to Consider:

- What concerns do you see developing?

- What could Morah Devorah do or say to be helpful to David?

David and Morah Devorah talked about the situation and decided that it would be best for David to supervise a small group of students in a quiet activity that was highly structured and to limit the amount of unstructured time he spent with them. Morah Devorah spoke with the students about appropriate behavior. Helping David see he could engage the students in quiet activities made a difference in the behavior of the students. David also needed to learn to set boundaries and how to redirect their activity. David had an open and collegial relationship with Morah Devorah. He found her advice to be helpful as she offered new paradigms. He had always thought that he had to be "one of the kids" to be liked by them. Now David discovered that he could set limits and find appropriate activities, and that the students liked him just as much. Morah Devorah and David decided to continue to work on student behavior out on the playground. David learned to set limits by saying to the students, "I don't like it when you jump on me. Let's find something we can do that is safe and fun."

Questions to Consider:

- What other issues can develop when a teen assistant does not set clear limits?

- How can Morah Devorah anticipate these issues when beginning with a new assistant in the future?

Situation B

Jamie was a little apprehensive about working with Katie, a second grader with special needs. She had seen Katie around the building, but working with her each week in class was something she was not sure she would have the skills to do. She wanted to know exactly what was expected of her and what Katie specifically needed.

Questions to Consider:

- What are the personal characteristics that Jamie has that will contribute to her success with a special needs child?

- What kinds of things are you sure Jamie knew before starting the year?

- How can Morah Karen impart that information in a way that does not overwhelm Jamie?

It was decided that a meeting would be a good way to get Jamie started. The meeting included Morah Karen, the inclusion specialist, the teacher from last year, Jamie, and the school director. It was important for Jamie to know that she was hearing confidential information that was not to be shared outside this setting. Jamie was given an overview of what Katie could do and strategies for integrating her into the classroom. Behavior management techniques were discussed, and Jamie was given the curriculum guides and the teacher's plan for the first few sessions so she could adapt some of the curriculum to meet Katie's skills. The more support Jamie received, the more at ease she felt, and by the end of the meeting she was eagerly looking forward to the first class. Morah Karen set up a meeting with herself, Jamie, Katie and Katie's parents so that a relationship could begin to form prior to the start of class. Jamie knew that once classes started, she would have more questions and need more guidance. Her support team was already in place and ready to offer direction as she continued through the year.

Questions to Consider:

- What role should Morah Karen play in the first few sessions as Jamie is learning her role as paraprofessional?

- What issues might Morah Karen anticipate needing to deal with in the first few months of school?

- What strategies can Jamie use to keep Katie's parents informed of her progress or to share any questions or concerns the school or the parents may have?

- How can Morah Karen and Jamie work together to adjust academic expectations and implement other academic strategies?

Situation C

In the second grade classes, both experienced madrichim demonstrated a clear sense of purpose. They anticipated the needs of the teacher and worked well with the students in small groups or on large group projects. However, each of the new assistants needed more supervision and direction from the teachers.

Questions to Consider:

- What could the second grade teachers do to integrate the new assistants into the classroom more effectively?

- What role(s) could the experienced assistants take on in the orientation of the new *madrichim*?

Situation D

In Morah Stephanie's third grade class, Elizabeth exceeded everyone's expectations. For the first few classes, Elizabeth was mainly an observer, watching how Morah Stephanie led services, introduced Hebrew, led discussions, and handled behavior issues. They spent many hours talking about the class. Morah Stephanie explained her rationale for certain situations, including the seating arrangement, lesson planning, and her teaching philosophy. Morah Stephanie went over the teacher's guides with Elizabeth and, by the third week of class, Elizabeth was able to lead Tefilot, work with a small group of students in Hebrew, plan and teach a Torah lesson. This class was soon characterized as one of cooperative teaching. If Morah Stephanie was teaching the lesson, Elizabeth was walking through the room making sure the students were following along, and the same thing took place when Elizabeth taught the lesson. Following a lesson taught by Elizabeth, they both spent time discussing what went well and areas Elizabeth could improve upon. Morah Stephanie always began with a positive aspect of the lesson, such as, "Your opening question certainly got their attention," and she

ended with something positive as well. They also taught in small groups and both of them checked homework or work done in class. Morah Stephanie and Elizabeth discussed some of the problems that emerged, and both were involved in the process of working out solutions. Elizabeth welcomed the opportunity to "process" and it helped her to understand Morah Stephanie's approach to behavior management, class philosophy, special programs that may have an impact on their class, and anything that might be going on in the student's lives that could affect their performance. When it was time for parent-teacher conferences, Elizabeth was an integral part of the teaching team, offering valued insight into the student's progress.

Questions to Consider:

- What factors led to Elizabeth's success as an assistant?

- How might Morah Stephanie structure their lesson planning sessions together to help Elizabeth plan effective future lessons?

- What potential problems might arise from Morah Stephanie's empowerment of Elizabeth?

- How can she make sure these do not distract from their working relationship?

Situation E

Darcy, an assistant in Moreh Aaron's class, arrived at school as part of a carpool that was often late. Moreh Aaron needed Darcy to be at school at least ten minutes before class to help get organized for the day. During class, Darcy sat with the students, as is expected. However, she had children sit on her lap, let them play with her long curly hair, and when a question was asked, she provided the answer by whispering it to the children seated around her. For Moreh Aaron, it seemed as though he had another student in class, rather than an assistant.

Questions to Consider:

- What are the potential problems if Darcy does not alter her behavior in the class?

- Does Darcy realize that what she is doing is not in the best interest of the students and the class goals?

- What solutions can you generate for Moreh Aaron and Darcy?

After discussing the situation with the madrichim supervisor, it was decided that another pair of eyes (e.g.. the madrichim coordinator, school director, teaching colleague, or Rabbi) was needed to identify specific behaviors that needed to be corrected. Following an observation by the education director, Moreh Aaron spoke to Darcy about expected behaviors and things she was doing that were positive additions to the class. They then discussed ways in which Darcy was detracting from the class. They decided to work on one or two behaviors. They discussed Darcy's late arrival and the need for her to be on time. Darcy said she would talk to her parents and work out a different carpool arrangement. As the year progressed, Moreh Aaron shared more of what he was doing in the class with Darcy. When she was included in the class preparation, the relationship with Moreh Aaron took a turn for the better. Darcy was very open and receptive to supervision and really wanted to be successful. She loved working with the children and, when given proper direction, her creative side blossomed and she became one of the success stories for the year.

Questions to Consider:

- What were the potential benefits of working on one or two of Darcy's behaviors at first, rather than all at once?

- Which behaviors would you have picked as the starting points?

- How could Moreh Aaron have been more proactive?

Situation F

Shayna was one of the assistants in Morah Lisa's second grade class. From the onset, they did not work well together. Shayna felt Morah Lisa was too strict with some of the children and that she did not offer them positive reinforcement. Shayna also knew that Morah Lisa taught some Hebrew and holiday information incorrectly. She was uncertain as to whether she should say something about this to Morah Lisa. At the same time, Morah Lisa felt a distance develop between herself and Shayna.

Questions to Consider:

- What can Morah Lisa do to gain some insight as to the change in relationship she feels with Shayna?

- What can Morah Lisa do to turn this into a positive relationship?

Morah Lisa was not sure what caused the change in both behavior and attitude, but decided there were enough signals and she needed to say something to Shayna. She met with Shayna and asked her how she felt things were going. Was there a particular area Shayna felt she wanted to become more involved with, or an area in which she felt she could take on more responsibility? Shayna indicated she would like to become more involved in lesson planning, in the areas of Hebrew and holidays. These were two areas in which she felt confident she could make a positive contribution to the class. They decided to take some time each week to talk about what was going on in class and to plan for the next week. When Shayna was given more responsibility, she felt she was a valued part of the team and began to work more cooperatively with Morah Lisa.

Questions to Consider:

- What are some ways teachers can identify the skills of teen assistants and integrate them effectively into the class?

- What are the advantages of allowing another to take the lead in teaching areas of the curriculum with which we are less confident?

Situation G

In the fourth grade class, a group of four students seemed to be working at a faster pace than the others, while another child with special needs struggled. Luckily, Sarah, a tenth grader and a teaching assistant with excellent Hebrew decoding skills, was assigned to the class. Moreh Daniel decided that he could use Sarah's skills to help students at both ends of the learning spectrum. His plan was to give Sarah some teaching materials and have her work for ten to 20 minutes of each class session with these students.

Questions to Consider:

- How do we help teen assistants access resource materials and understand and establish curricular objectives?

- How can we assist them in identifying teaching strategies and assessing student needs and progress?

Moreh Daniel and Sarah discussed the best way to handle the four students who were at an advanced level and what types of resource materials they thought would work best. They discussed what they wanted the students to accomplish, methods Sarah could use, and ways she could evaluate student progress. They also used the same process for the student who needed additional assistance. Moreh Daniel and Sarah have established a great working relationship, with open and ongoing communications. Sarah enjoyed the challenges of lesson planning and teaching, and took her responsibilities seriously. When it was time to prepare student progress reports, Sarah was able to take the lead in communicating the progress of the students she worked with directly. This gave her a great sense of accomplishment.

Questions to Consider:

- What are the advantages of establishing clear goals and teaching strategies for small groups of students?

- With the guidance of her teacher, Sarah is learning some basic teaching techniques and is directly responsible for lesson planning and student progress. How can she be encouraged to expand her teaching skills and consider taking on additional responsibility next year?

WORKING IN INFORMAL SETTINGS

Teen assistants have worked successfully in informal settings, such as retreats and both day and sleep-away camp programs. In the original models for counselor training programs, one of the main objectives was to employ and train Jewish counselors who would become future Jewish leaders. These programs were amazingly successful in attaining this objective.

Day camps generally have teen assistants who are in junior high or high school, while sleep-away camps engage staff who are entering eleventh or twelfth grade, or are college or graduate students. Often, the teens who participate in the programs have a wonderful camping experience, and want others to enjoy it as much as they did. Their role models are their former counselors. Unlike in the formal school setting, the staff at a camp is most often made up of college-age students who enjoy what they are doing, but often do not have the formal skills, experience, or training to mentor or train others. In this setting, it is important for counselors to turn to more experienced staff members or adults who are responsible for the supervision and training of the teen assistants or counselors-in-training.

Many camps have a staff orientation prior to their opening. Senior counselors need to understand the purpose of having junior counselors and how to guide them in building their skills. In a camp setting, a junior counselor is quickly involved with the children. Camp sessions are short, and junior staffers often do not have the luxury of observing the staff or campers prior to the start of camp. Teen counselors begin with small responsibilities and continue to take on more and more as they gain confidence and are successful.

In a camp setting, counselors-in-training need some formal instruction on stages of child development, basic educational techniques such as how to plan and lead a *sichah* (discussion), and techniques for good communication and listening skills. Whether in a retreat or camp setting, new staff should work with a mentor, thus empowering experienced staff to train others and, in the process, to reflect on their own skill sets.

In a camp or retreat setting, teen assistants offer creative program ideas, often drawn from their own experiences. Teens are most effective when they are an integral part of the planning and are able to take on certain responsibilities. They can assume leadership roles, such as explaining or leading a small group activity. For instance, a ninth grader who has great music skills will enjoy taking over the morning opening program and sharing the fun songs he or she learned at camp. With the guidance of the senior counselor, they can work out a morning routine, and the teen will come to see this as his or her responsibility.

Another teen assistant is great at sports and makes this a focus for activity and responsibility.

There is more to sports than just playing a game, and the role of the senior staff member is to help the assistant think through the activity. How do we get the kids excited about playing? What do they need to know before they begin? How long will we do this activity? What are the expectations of the participants? How do we demonstrate qualities of playing fair and being good sports? Often, our assistants think we just play the game, and they don't consider the preparation necessary for participation. Part of their own education is learning how to break down an activity into the smaller steps needed to do it.

> I can't say that I have successfully worked with every teen aide assigned to me in 15 years of religious school. Most of my aides have worked out well, though. I usually talk to them before school begins for the year. I ask them for their ideas, and I implement them if possible. I expect them to work hard and give them teaching responsibilities that use their particular skills, whether in art, music, or storytelling. I offer constructive help after the elementary students have left the room, so that the younger students do not hear an older student corrected.
>
> At the same time, it is important to remember that teen aides are still kids. If I bring a treat for class, I make sure the aide gets a large portion. I give them small Chanukah gifts and *Mishloach Manot* baskets at Purim. I send them home to recover if they are sick or worried about getting school assignments done. I make sure the younger students treat them with respect. And when they go to Israel, I give them money to donate to the charity of their choice. They respond to this approach and feel a sense of commitment to the class.
>
> (Maura Pollak, Tulsa, Oklahoma)

COMPENSATION

In a perfect world, *madrichim* and camp staff would work in our programs because they love working with children and for the experience. However, this is not realistic, as these youth give many hours of their time in our programs. If the situation allows, teen assistants should be compensated in some way for the hours they work. This can take the form of payment according to a set scale, taking into consideration their age and years of prior experience, or allowing them to fulfill community service hours. In institutions that have a scholarship program, teen assistants may be able to "bank" their pay and withdraw it for various approved youth, camp, and Israel programs. Philosophically, we want our teen assistants to view themselves as professionals, with a professional responsibility. This means that they are valued members of the team, that they will have an opportunity to learn some real world skills, and that when they are not with their program, they are missed.

CONCLUSION

Rabbi Sam Joseph, in *The Madrikhim Handbook*, states, "experience suggests that successful *madrikhim* programs offer four elements: *Hevraschaft*, bonding/mentoring with/from Jewish educational leaders, opportunities for significant learning, and rewarding work experiences." Working with a teen assistant takes time, interest, planning, and cooperation. It is a relationship that grows from the desire of the assistant to be a part of a Jewish setting, and the realization that our future Jewish educators will come from the young people who are in our formal and informal programs. Exposure in the classroom is not sufficient; we need to have opportunities available for our teens to become actively involved in the educational process and to experience it from a teaching perspective. The best models of programs are the ones in which teen assistants become active participants and move from minor roles into areas where many of them can take on added responsibility.

Teen assistants should be challenged to use their skills, talents, and passions to become active participants in a learning environment. They have a wealth of creativity and youthful spirit. When channeled and challenged, they enrich and enhance our programs. As with other professions and acquired skills, we must never assume teen assistants innately know what to do or how it is to be done. They need to be guided, mentored, and have positive role models as they work and become successful in our formal and informal settings.

Teachers and informal program staff have an awesome responsibility. As Jewish educators, we have an obligation to teach and nourish the next generation of educators. Eligible teen assistants are eager and enthusiastic about participating in our programs. They look to educators to model and provide support for their entry into the field of education.

There is nothing more rewarding as an educator than to know you have shaped the life of another. There is immense pleasure in knowing that in some small way we have touched the life of a future Jewish educator or community leader. Use the information in this chapter, adapt it to your situation, and set out to inspire the next generation of educators.

CONSIDERATIONS WHEN WORKING WITH ASSISTANTS

- Keep your eyes open — anyone is a potential teacher.

- Make a first priority the personal education of teen assistants.

- Urge your school director to institute an effective training component, both for teachers and teens.

- In partnership, establish expectations of the teen assistant as well as classroom guidelines.

- Assess the skills of your teen workers before the program begins.

- Help assistants learn appropriate behaviors and ways to use their skills.

- Support, praise, and encourage your assistants.

- Increase your assistants' responsibilities as their skills increase.

- Reflect with your assistant on your work as a teacher to promote understanding and to communicate elements of success.

- Empower teen assistants as participants in the program, with decision making opportunities, and through direction.

- Evaluate teen assistants through the use of the Madrichim Survey in the Appendix on the next page.

APPENDIX

Madrichim Survey
January, 2003

Name: _____ Grade or Position: _____

Please complete the following survey. I would like to learn about how you "see" your position in the school. Please make comments wherever appropriate.

Please rank the following with 5 being the most positive and 1 negative. n/a= Not Applicable

1. I enjoy working with the students.   5   4   3   2   1   n/a

2. I feel I am respected by my teacher & the students in the classroom. 5   4   3   2   1   n/a

3. I enjoy working in the school.   5   4   3   2   1   n/a

4. I am focused in the classroom.   5   4   3   2   1   n/a

5. I am on time.   5   4   3   2   1   n/a

6. I would like to teach a lesson by myself.   5   4   3   2   1   n/a

7. I have a positive attitude while I am here.   5   4   3   2   1   n/a

8. I am learning how to be flexible.   5   4   3   2   1   n/a

9. I call when I am unable to work.   5   4   3   2   1   n/a

10. I would like to be more actively involved in my classroom.   5   4   3   2   1   n/a

11. I would like to work with small groups of students.   5   4   3   2   1   n/a

12. I am an asset to my classroom and teacher.   5   4   3   2   1   n/a

13. Please identify one word which describes something you have learned from participating in this

    program. _____

14. Please identify one word which describes how you feel about being a Madrich(ah).

    _____

15. Please comment on what you feel is lacking in this program.

    _____

16. What can I do to enable you to be more successful working in the school?

    _____

BIBLIOGRAPHY

Note: For additional resources on teaching that are useful for *madrichim*, see the Bibliography for Chapter 23, "Summer Camping: Teaching in Your Pajamas" by Gerard W. Kaye, p. 276.

Herman, Dorothy C. *Planning for Success*. Los Angeles, CA: Torah Aura Productions, 1991.

> This book contains many ideas and strategies for administrators of religious schools. Effective strategies for working with teachers also apply to setting up teaching assistants to be successful.

Joseph, Samuel. *How to Be a Jewish Teacher*. Los Angeles, CA: Torah Aura Productions, 1997.

> Teaching is a real commitment, and we recognize the need to encourage and promote the development of Jewish teachers. This book is a wonderful resource for anyone considering Jewish education, and the same principles apply to working with *madrichim*.

———. *The Madrikhim Handbook*. Los Angeles, CA: Torah Aura Publications, 1989.

> This is a landmark book for those working with teen assistants. It includes a philosophy and also practical ideas for developing a successful *madrichim* program.

Morgan, Jill, and Betty Y. Ashbaker. *A Teacher's Guide to Working with Paraeducators and Other Classroom Aides*. Alexandria, VA: Association for Supervision and Curriculum Development, 2001.

> This book covers such topics as leading the classroom instructional team, assigning roles and responsibilities, improving communication, monitoring the quality of the paraeducator's work, providing on the job training, creating a feedback loop, logistics, troubleshooting, and practicing what has been learned. While it is geared to teachers in secular schools, the book is a valuable resource for religious educators as well.

Rossel, Seymour. *Managing the Jewish Classroom: How to Transform Yourself into a Master Teacher*. Los Angeles, CA: Torah Aura Productions, 1998.

> The wisdom and practical ideas in this book are successful with teachers, and I have found application here for working with *madrichim*. The book contains many useful teaching techniques and strategies.

Resources for Jewish Educators

PUBLISHERS, DISTRIBUTORS, AND ORGANIZATIONS

Anti-Defamation League
823 United Nations Plaza
New York, NY 10017
212-885-7700
www.adl.org

ADL publishes and distributes materials on human relations, anti-Semitism, multi-cultural topics, Holocaust, etc. Some items in their collection contain specific lesson plans.

AOS/Greenfield
129-20 18th Ave.
College Point, NY 11356
866-888-8740
e-mail: zerach@aol.com

The largest importer of Israeli educational materials in North America — posters, puzzles, puppets, games, crafts, videos, stencils, cutouts, workshops, and more.

A.R.E. Publishing, Inc.
700 N. Colorado Blvd. #356
Denver, CO 80206
800-346-7779
www.arepublish.com

A source for innovative Jewish educational materials, including Hebrew materials, teacher and principal manuals, workbooks, mini-courses, Copy Paks, clip art, games, and certificates, as well as a full line of music CDs for use in the classroom.

ATID (Academy for Torah Initiatives and Directions)
9 HaNassi Street
Jerusalem 92188 Israel
972-2-567-1719
www.atid.org

ATID enables talented men and women, who have a rich background in Torah study, to make informed decisions about the education of the next generation. It helps shape and develop the future of Jewish educational leadership.

Attractive Land
The Yoel Amster Company
Moshav Ben-Ami, Israel, 25240 Israel
www.attractiveland.co.il

Attractive Land is an Israel education program based on a set of very colorful and versatile educational tools that teach about Israel in an "experiential" and "family" style.

Auerbach Central Agency for Jewish Education of Greater Philadelphia
Mandell Education Campus
7607 Old York Road
Melrose Park, PA 19027
212-635-8940
www.acaje.org

The Auerbach Central Agency is the educational resource and planning institution for Greater Philadelphia. Their web site has interesting information and links, especially in moral, family, Holocaust, and Israel education.

Barvaz Press
5353 N. Wayne
Chicago, IL 60640
773-419-0787
www.barvazpress.com

Hebrew texts including conversational and prayer.

Behrman House
11 Edison Place
Springfield, NJ 07081
800-221-2755
www.behrmanhouse.com

Publisher of Jewish textbooks ranging from nursery school to college level. Subjects include: Hebrew, Bible, history, holidays, Jewish thought, and ethics.

Benny's Educational Toys
140-25 69th Avenue
Flushing, NY 11367
718-520-6204
www.jewisheducationalmaterials.com

The source for Israel's educational toys, including contemporary Jewish and Hebrew related learning materials for PK to Grade 3.

Board of Jewish Education of Greater New York
426 W. 58th Street
New York, NY 10019
212-245-8200
www.bjeny.org

This BJE offers a wide range of materials for the classroom in both English and Hebrew. The web site has a number of curricula organized by holiday or topic, all available for downloading.

Bureau of Jewish Education of Greater Boston
333 Nahanton Street
Newton, MA 02159
617-965-7350
www.bje.org

Publishes and distributes print and media materials for all subject areas and grade levels, with particularly good material for junior and senior high school levels.

Bureau of Jewish Education of Los Angeles
6505 Wilshire Blvd., Suite 300
Los Angeles, CA 90048
323-761-8640
www.bjela.org

Publishes a variety of educational materials useful in school settings.

Bureau of Jewish Education of San Francisco, Marin, the Peninsula and Sonoma Counties
601 14th Avenue
San Francisco, CA 94118
415-751-6983
www.bjesf.org

A wonderful site, with special information for early childhood, family, teen, and other specialty educators. See also their Battat Educational Resource Center web page.

Central Agency for Jewish Education
4200 Biscayne Blvd.
Miami, FL 33137
305-576-4030
www.caje-miami.org

In addition to student-oriented educational materials, this agency distributes curriculum guides on a variety of topics. These guides include experiential activities for student participation.

CCAR Press
Central Conference of American Rabbis
355 Lexington Avenue
New York, NY 10017
212-972-3636
www.ccarnet.org

Publishes liturgical materials and Rabbinic manuals for the Reform Movement.

Chai Kids
21346 Street Andrews Blvd., #218
Boca Raton, FL 33433
888-242-4543
www.chaikids.com

Bible and Purim puppets and other educational material.

C.I.S. Publishers
www.virtualgeula.com/cis/c-i-s.htm

Publishers of books for children and adults, in Hebrew and English, within the Orthodox framework. (Now located in Israel.)

Coalition for the Advancement of Jewish Education
261 W. 35th Street, Floor 12A
New York, NY 10001
212-268-4210
www.caje.org

In addition to sponsoring its annual educators conference each summer, CAJE publishes a periodical, *Jewish Education News*. Through another publication, *Bikurim*, teachers can learn about materials from the CAJE Curriculum Bank. In addition, CAJE publishes units on specific topics and has branched out into day and early childhood education support.

Coalition for Jewish Learning
(The Education Program for the Jewish Federation of Milwaukee)
6401 N. Santa Monica Blvd.
Milwaukee, WI 53217
414-962-8860
www.cjlmilwaukee.org/Creativity/intro.htm

This central Jewish education agency is well-known for its creative materials and curriculum.

Cybertropes, Inc.
P.O. Box 1648
Fairfield, CT 06432
888-CHANT-80
www.cybertropes.com

An interactive learning system on CD-Rom for teaching Torah and Haftarah tropes and *Tefilot* to Bar/Bat Mitzvah students. Can be customized with your Cantor's voice.

Davka Corporation
3601 W. Devon Avenue
Chicago, IL 60659
800-621-8227
www.davka.com

The world's largest developer of Hebrew/Judaica software for computers used in homes, schools, and institutions. Encompasses reference, word processing, Hebrew language, games, and more.

Dor L'Dor
7103 Mill Run Drive
Rockville, MD 20855
888-HEBREW2
www.dorldor.com

Interactive, multi-sensory software that teaches *alef bet*, Rashi, *brachot, Tefilah*. Also carries *alef bet* activity books, mouse pads, T-shirts, jewelry.

Dreidelmaker Crafts Kits and Projects
P.O. Box 1904
Frederick, MD 21702
301-695-4375
www.dreidelmaker.com

Unique wood craft kits for all ages for creating real, usable Judaic objects.

EKS Publishing
1029A Solano Avenue
Albany, CA 94706
877-743-2739
www.ekspublishing.com

Instructional materials for students of biblical and prayer book Hebrew. Books, audiotapes, charts, flashcards, and posters for classroom use and self-study.

Enjoy-a-Book Club
555 Chestnut Street
Cedarhurst, NY 11516
516-569-0324
enjoyabook.com

Forms are distributed for this club through individual schools, enabling parents to purchase books, games, videos, and audiotapes for the home. The company also coordinates book fairs.

Feldheim Publishers
200 Airport Executive Park
Nanuet, NY 10954
845-356-2282
www.feldheim.com

Provides books with an Orthodox orientation for personal library and classroom use.

Gefen Books Ltd.
12 New Street
Hewlett, NY 11557
800-477-5257
www.genfenpublishing.com

In addition to publishing books on or about Israel, Gefen is the distributor for other Israeli publishers.

Growth Associates
212 Stuart Rd. E.
Princeton, NJ 08540
609-497-7375
www.DPElkins.com

Specializes in books for Jewish professionals, educators, youth leaders, and Rabbis that bring together spirituality, education, and psychology.

Hadassah, The Women's Zionist Organization of America
50 W. 58th Street
New York, NY 10019
212-355-7900
www.hadassah.org

Prepares and publishes topical units that can be used for adults and, with some modifications, for religious schools. They distribute *Textures* and *Bat Kol* for adult education, and *Gilgalim* for preschools.

Ikkar Publishing Inc.
43 Haran Circle
Millburn, NJ 07041
973-912-9233
e-mail: ikkarpub@aol.com

Creates and disseminates text-based non-denominational curricula for supplementary and day schools.

Israeli Poster Center
29 King George Street
Jerusalem 94261
Israel
972-2-624-0042
www.israeliposters.co.il

Huge selection of art and educational posters, religious posters, and maps.

Jason Aronson Inc.
230 Livingston Street
Northvale, NJ 07647
800-782-0015
www.aronson.com

Scholarly titles of Jewish interest, as well as reprints of classics.

JEMM Productions
P.O. Box 10023
Jerusalem 91100
Israel
www.j-central.com/jemm

Developer of Jewish media, including "Starting with Aleph," an online course in Jewish literacy.

Jewish Agency for Israel
The Department for Zionist Education
Pedagogic Center
972-2-6216059 (Israel)
www.jajz-ed.org.il

An incredible site that helps Jewish educators worldwide. Great curricular resources on current events, holidays, and Israel. Check out the links for a very complete list.

Jewish Book Council
15 E. 26th Street
New York, NY 10010
212-532-4949
www.jewishbookcouncil.org

The national clearinghouse for Jewish literature, and sponsor of Jewish Book Month and the National Jewish Book Awards. Publishes numerous thematic bibliographies for educators.

The Jewish Braille Institute of America
110 E. 30th Street
New York, NY 10016
800-433-1531
www.jewishbraille.org

Provides material in large print, talking books, and books in Braille for the visually impaired and for others with learning disabilities.

Jewish Education Center of Cleveland (JECC)
2030 S. Taylor Road
Cleveland, OH 44118
216-371-0446
www.jecc.org

The JECC is well-known for its great resources and curriculum. Check out the Immediate Response Curricula (published when world-events warrant) and the links in the Technology section to a variety of Jewish subject areas, and education related sites.

Jewish Education Commission
9901 Donna Klein Blvd
Boca Raton, FL 33428
561-852-3318
http://jewishboca.org

The JEC publishes MASORET, a binder of hands-on games and activities to reinforce Hebrew reading, decoding skills for prayer, and Judaic studies. Also has art projects for the Jewish classroom.

Jewish Educational Service of North America (JESNA)
111 8th Avenue
New York, NY 10011
212-284-6950
www.jesna.org

The planning, coordinating, and service agency for communal Jewish education organizations in the U.S. and Canada. JESNA provides consultations, has a placement service, and does research.

Jewish Lights Publishing
P.O. Box 237
Woodstock, VT 05091
800-457-4000
www.jewishlights.com

Publishes books for adults and children that reflect Jewish tradition on such subjects as spirituality, meditation, and recovery.

Jewish National Fund
Department of Education
78 Randall Avenue
Rockville Centre, NY 11570
888-JNF-0099
www.jnf.org

JNF, the caretaker of the Land of Israel, is committed to educating Jewish youth about the concepts of solidarity, responsibility, and partnership with the people of Israel and the Land.

Jewish Publication Society
2100 Arch Street, 2nd Floor
Philadelphia, PA 19103
800-234-3151
www.jewishpub.org

The oldest publisher of Judaica in the English language. Selections include Bible translations and commentaries, history, literature, philosophy, poetry, and children's books.

Jewish Reconstructionist Federation
7804 Montgomery Avenue, Suite 9
Elkins Park, PA 19027
215-782-8500
www.jrf.org

Publishes a prayer book series, Passover *Haggadah*, books on Reconstructionism, study guides and curricula for educators, and JRF position papers.

Jewish Software Center
15466 Los Gatos Blvd., Suite #109-106
Los Gatos, CA 95032
408-395-6457
http://users.aol.com/jewishsoft/jsc.html

Software programs on all aspects of Jewish life for home and school.

Jewish Theological Seminary of America
3080 Broadway
New York, NY 10027
212-678-8000
www.jtsa.edu

Distributes books, curricula, Melton mini-lessons, library exhibits, and has a growing distance learning department online.

Jewish Women's Archive
68 Harvard Street
Brookline, MA 02445
617-232-2258
www.jwa.org

The mission of the Jewish Women's Archive is to "uncover, chronicle, and transmit the rich legacy of Jewish women and their contributions to our families and communities, to our people and our world." The site includes primary sources, posters, exhibits, and teaching guides.

Judaic Art Kits
P.O. Box 10828
Rochester, NY 14610
800-862-3449
www.judaicakits.com

A source for art-based family education programs. Many choices of projects offered.

JudaiCrafts
PO BOX 978
Monsey, NY 10952
877-752-7238
www.judaicrafts.com

JudaiCrafts produces unique and creative Jewish Educational Materials, teaching aides, decorations, arts and crafts materials, and classroom kits for all Jewish holidays and subjects. Suitable for all ages.

Kabbalah Software
8 Price Drive, Dept CJ
Edison, NJ 08817
732-572-0891
www.kabsoft.com

Creators and distributors of Judaic-oriented software for home, institution, and school use.

Kar-Ben Publishing
A Division of Lerner Publishing Group
1251 Washington Avenue N.
Minneapolis, MN 55401
800-4karben
www.kar-ben.com

Story, craft, and activity books and tape sets for young children and families, including board books, family Shabbat and holiday worship services, toddler books, and Jewish calendars.

Kehot Publication Society
770 Eastern Parkway
Brooklyn, NY 11213
877-4 MERKOS
www.kehotonline.com

Produces Jewish materials from a Chabad perspective, including some teaching aids.

Kinnor Software
1415 Alberta Street
Key West, FL 33040
305-293-8801
www.kinnor.com

Trope Trainer software for both Torah and Haftarah.

KTAV Publishing House, Inc.
900 Jefferson Street, Box 6249
Hoboken, NJ 07030
201-963-9524
www.ktav.com

One of the largest and oldest distributors of texts and learning materials for both day and supplementary schools. Their catalog includes basic curriculum information for the use of their texts.

The Learning Plant
P.O. Box 17233
West Palm Beach, FL 33416
561-686-9456
www.learningplant.com

Lots of Jewish educational materials, including books, videos, CDs, audiotapes, puzzles, games, awards, flannels, and stickers.

Lookstein Center for Jewish Education in the Diaspora
Bar-Ilan University
Ramat Gan 52900, Israel
972-3-531-8199
www.lookstein.org

The Center focuses its programming for the advancement of Jewish education in the Diaspora on leadership, teacher and curriculum development. Its web site includes resources, bulletin boards, e-lists, and links.

Make Me a Story
6549 Sheltondale Avenue
Westhills, CA 91307
818-676-0342
www.makemeastory.com

Premade flannel board kits for toddlers through Kindergarten. Kits include Bible, holiday, and some contemporary themes.

Melton Research Center for Jewish Education
3080 Broadway
New York, NY 10027
212-678-8031
www.jtsa.edu/melton

This Center is dedicated to the general improvement of Jewish education through its work with Jewish educators and the develop-ment of materials for both formal and informal settings, for schools and families.

Mesorah Publications, Ltd.
4401 Second Avenue
Brooklyn, NY 11232
800-637-6724
www.artscroll.com

Publishers of the ArtScroll series, in addition to other books. Their collection includes story-books for children, as well as texts and com-mentaries for adults. Publications are based on a strict Orthodox adherence to *halachah*.

PANIM: The Institute for Jewish Leadership and Values
6101 Montrose Road, Suite 200
Rockville, MD 20852
301-770-5070
www.wijlv.org

A curriculum guide and student textbook, with complementary teen programming in Wash-ington, D.C., educating for Jewish values and leadership.

Pitome Publishing
P.O. Box 30961
Santa Barbara, CA 93130
805-898-9207
www.pitome.com

Innovative holiday-based copy packs, family education programs. *Jewish Family Times* pro-vides camera ready material on various topics to hand out to families, send as a newsletter, or send home as enrichment.

Pitspopany Press
40 E. 78th Street, Suite 16D
New York, NY 10021
800-232-2931
www.pitspopany.com

Publisher of children's books in the fields of Bible, Jewish holidays, humor, science fiction, health, self-awareness, Jewish history, life cycles.

Ruach UnLtd.
9701 Nordstrom Court
Montgomery Village, MD 20886
e-mail: ruachunltd@aol.com

Offers programs for Jewish families that include text study, interactive learning adventures, thought provoking questions, and additional resources and opportunities.

Social Studies School Service

P.O. Box 802

Culver City, CA 90232

800-421-4246

www.socialstudies.com

Distributes a variety of quality materials to secular schools and has a separate catalog of resources and materials on teaching the Holocaust, Middle East, and other areas of Jewish interest.

Sukkah Project

4 Pine Tree Lane

Chapel Hill, NC 27515

919-489-7325

www.sukkot.com

"Klutz-proof" *sukkah* kits for home, school, and *shul*. Includes instruction manual and special connecting hardware.

Tal Am and Tal Sela: Hebrew and Heritage Curricula for Jewish Schools

Bronfman Jewish Education Centre

1 Carré Cummings Square

Montreal, Quebec H3W 1M6

514-345-2610

www.talam.org

Hebrew language curricula for day school students, Grades 1-6. Comprehensive materials and support provided.

Tara Publications

8 Music Fair Road

Owings Mills, MD 21117

800-827-2400

www.jewishmusic.com

A source for Jewish music for all ages in all forms: audiocassettes, videos, CDs, sheet music, songbooks. A broad based and varied selection in English, Yiddish, and Hebrew.

Torah Aura Productions

4423 Fruitland Avenue

Los Angeles, CA 90058

800-BE-TORAH

www.torahaura.com

Publishers of materials for the classroom, including workbooks, texts, instant lessons, and media. Texts for adults on Jewish education and family education are also available.

Torah Umesorah Publications — National Society for Hebrew Day Schools

5723 Eighteenth Avenue

Brooklyn, NY 11204

718-259-1223

The organizational headquarters for Orthodox day schools across the country. Publishes texts and audiovisual materials for classroom use. Many of these are useful for adult education. They also publish the children's magazine *Olomeinu*.

Transcontinental Music Publications

633 Third Avenue

New York, NY 10017

800-455-5223

www.etranscon.com

The largest publisher of Jewish choral music, providing recordings and sheet music on Jewish themes.

UAHC Department of Jewish Education

633 Third Avenue

New York, NY 10017

212-650-4000

http://uahc.org/educate

This is the central educational resource for the Reform Movement. Their web site includes many resources for educators who teach a variety of subjects, in a variety of settings. Check the many links on the home page.

UAHC Press

633 Third Avenue

New York, NY 10017

212-650-4000

www.uahcpress.com

Publishes and distributes textbooks and materials with a Reform orientation for classroom and general use for all ages.

United Synagogue of Conservative Judaism Education Department

155 Fifth Avenue

New York, NY 10010

212-533-7800, ext. 2501

http://uscj.org/lifelong_learning.html

This is the central educational address for the Conservative Movement. Their web site includes many resources for educators who teach a variety of subjects, in a variety of settings. Check the links on the home page.

United Synagogue of America Book Service
155 Fifth Avenue
New York, NY 10010
800-594-5617
www.uscj.org/booksvc

Publishes and distributes publications and resource material for the United Synagogue, the Rabbinical Assembly, the Commission on Jewish Education, and Youth Department.

United States Holocaust Memorial Museum
100 Raoul Wallenberg Place, SW
Washington, DC 20024
202-488-0400
www.ushmm.org

This outstanding museum is an excellent source for materials on the Holocaust in both print and audiovisual formats. Members receive a newsletter about the museum and a listing of new Holocaust materials.

World Zionist Organization — American Section
110 E. 58th Street
New York, NY 10021
212-339-6001
www.wzo.org/il

As part of its mission as the Aliyah Center and the agent of the WZO in Israel that promotes Israel in North America, this organization publishes and distributes books and videos on all aspects of Israeli life. Various departments publish textbooks in English and Hebrew, e.g., The Department of Education and Culture and Herzl Press. WZO also provides options for Jewish educators to travel and study in Israel.

Yisra-ed
P.O. Box 2019
East Hampton, NY 11937
888-323-8947
www.yisraed.com

A source for Hebrew educational materials from Israel, including *alef bet* puzzles, educational software programs, posters, Hebrew crossword puzzles, etc.

JEWISH MEDIA DISTRIBUTORS

Alden Films
Box 449
Clarksburg, NJ 08510
732-462-3522
www.aldenfilms.com

Anti-Defamation League
823 United Nations Plaza
New York, NY 10019
212-885-7951
www.adl.org

Board of Jewish Education of Greater New York
426 W. 58th Street
New York, NY 10019
212-245-8200
www.bjeny.org

Bureau of Jewish Education Los Angeles
6505 Wilshire Blvd., Suite 300
Los Angeles, CA 90048
323-761-8605
http://bjela.org

Ergo Media Inc.
P.O. Box 2037
Teaneck, NJ 07666
800-695-3746
www.jewishvideo.com

Facets Multimedia, Inc.
1517 W. Fullerton Avenue
Chicago, IL 60614
800-331-6197
www.facets.org

Filmmakers Library
124 E. 40th Street
New York, NY 10016
212-808-4980
www.filmakers.com

National Center for Jewish Film
Brandeis University, Lown 102 MS053
Waltham, MA 02454
781-899-7044
www.jewishfilm.org

SISU Home Entertainment/Kol-Ami
18 West 27th Street 10th Floor
New York, NY 10001
800-223-7478
www.sisuent.com

Steven Spielberg Jewish Film Archive
The Jack Valenti Pavilion
Humanities Building, Block 8
Hebrew University of Jerusalem, Mount Scopus
972-2-5882513, 5881511
http://sites.huji.ac.il/jfa/

PERIODICALS

Jewish

Index To Jewish Periodicals
216-921-5566
www.jewishperiodicals.com

> An author and subject index to over 70 English language journals of general and scholarly interest to the Jewish community.

Jewish Book World
Jewish Book Council
212-532-4949
www.jewishbookcouncil.org/subscribe.htm

> Published three times a year, each issue includes full reviews of important new books and an annotated listing of over 150 titles of Jewish interest.

Jewish Parent Connection
Torah Umesorah — National Society for Hebrew Day Schools
212-227-1000

> Contains articles that center on the home and school.

Olomeinu/Our World
Torah Umesorah — National Society for Hebrew Day Schools
718-259-1223

> A student magazine with stories about personalities, holidays, and Jewish values.

Religious Education
Religious Education Associaton
404-527-7739
www.religiouseducation.net

> Contains articles on religious education of interest to educators of all denominations.

Secular

Childhood Education
Association for Childhood Education International
800-423-3563
www.udel.edu/bateman/acei

> Articles address a broad range of topics on the well-being of children from infancy through adolescence. Includes articles on innovative practices in the classroom and significant findings in educational research.

Early Childhood Today
Scholastic, Inc.
800-544-2917
www.teaher.scholastic.com/products/ect

> Contains articles on development, tools for teaching, home-school links, etc.

Educational Leadership
Association for Supervision and Curriculum Development
800-923-2723
www.ascd.org

> Contains articles on such subjects as curriculum, instruction, supervision, and leadership.

Instructor Magazine
Scholastic, Inc.
www.teacher.scholastic.com/products/instructor.htm

> Includes articles on classroom or all-school programs, effective teaching strategies, new ideas and teaching devices, and art projects.

Phi Delta Kappan
Phi Delta Kappan, Inc.
812-339-1156
www.pdkintl.org/kappan/kappan.htm

> A magazine for professional educators that addresses all issues in education.

Teacher
Editorial Projects in Education, Inc.
202-364-4114
www.teachermagazine.org

> Contains news stories, features, and commentaries on hot issues in education.

Young Children
National Association for the Education of Young Children
800-424-2460
www.naecy.org/resources/journal/default.asp

The practical articles in this journal are geared to teachers and others who work with children up to eight years of age.

VERY SPECIAL WEB SITES

Torah Umesorah
www.e-Chinuch.org

This is a large database of materials created by Torah (*halachic*) educators, "home of the Pinchas Hochberger Creative Learning Pavilion."

Jewish Education Center of Cleveland (JECC)
www.jecc.org

Check out the Immediate Response Curricula (published when world events warrant) and the links in the Technology section to a variety of Jewish subject areas, and education related sites.

JewishPathway.org
1127 High Ridge Road #340
Stamford, CT 06905
www.jewishpathway.org

JewishPathway.org is an internet-based educational tool for Jewish elementary and middle school students that creatively combines multimedia and traditional Judaic studies with advanced technology.

JewishPrograms.com
www.jewishprograms.com

Created by the American Jewish Joint Distribution Committee in Paris, France, this "family of web sites" includes many high quality programs for both formal and informal Jewish education. Each program has been screened before being placed on the web site. Searchers must register to use this site, but the results are well worth it!

Kathy Schrock's Guide for Educators
http://school.discovery.com/schrockguide

This is an online, highly respected, categorized list of sites useful for enhancing curriculum and professional growth. It is updated often to include the best sites for teaching and learning.

MyJewishLearning.com
http://myjewishlearning.com

This incredible web site has information about almost anything Jewish, with explanations that begin on the basic level and become more advanced.

EDUCATIONAL OPPORTUNITIES

Note the following:

- Local central Jewish education agencies (BJE's) offer short-term courses in Jewish education.

- JESNA (The Jewish Education Service of North America) provides an excellent listing of online learning opportunities at www.jesna.org/cgi-bin/resources.php3?op1=28.

- There are a number of colleges and universities that offer specialized programs in Jewish education. For an up-to-date listing see JESNA's Guide to Academic Programs in Formal and Informal Education: www.jesna.org/cgi-bin/academic.php3.

- The listing, below, contains mostly programs with distance learning opportunities.

Hebrew College
160 Herrick Road
Newton Centre, MA 02459
800-866-4814
www.hebrewcollege.edu

Hebrew College offers online courses for Jewish educators.

Gratz College
7605 Old York Road
Melrose Park ,PA 19027
800-475-4635
www.gratzcollege.edu

Online study available.

JSkyway
617-965-7700
www.JSkyway.com

Created to enhance the quality of Jewish day school faculty and professional leadership, JSkyway offers a plethora of online courses.

Kaminer Center for Distance Education
3080 Broadway
New York, NY 10027
212-78-8000
www.courses.jtsa.edu/registration

> The Distance Learning Project of the Melton Research Center at JTS offers interactive courses for credit/audit or continuing adult and teacher education.

Laura and Alvin Siegal College of Judaic Studies
26500 Shaker Blvd.
Beachwood, OH 44122
216-64-4050
www.siegalcollege.edu

> Siegal College offers a Bachelor of Judaic Studies and a Master of Arts in Judaic Studies. Provides courses in Judaic and Hebrew studies to adults, educators, and administrators, and also offers accredited interactive distance learning degree programs in Jewish studies and education using videoconferencing.

Spertus College
Spertus Institute of Jewish Studies
618 S. Michigan Avenue
Chicago, Illinois 60605
312-322-1769
www.spertus.edu/college/js/distance.html

> Distance Learning is currently available for the Master of Science in Jewish Studies (MSJS), the Master of Science in Jewish Education (MSJE), the Doctor of Jewish Studies (DJS), and the Doctor of Science in Jewish Studies (DSJS) program.

UAHC Department of Education
http://e-learning.uahc.org

> The UAHC's online learning site, geared to the improvement of teaching, and the deepening of Jewish knowledge.

BECOMING A TEACHER OR CHANGING POSITIONS

DeLeT: Day School Leadership through Teaching
601 Skokie Blvd.
Suite 2B
Northbrook, IL 60062
847-564-4515
www.delet.org

DeLeT is a 13-month fellowship program designed to increase the number of professional teacher-leaders who are prepared to teach and support Jewish families enrolled in day schools.

National Board of License
For Teachers and Principals of Jewish Schools in North America
15 East 26th Street
New York, NY 10010-1579
212-532-4949, ext. 452
www.nationalboardoflicense.org

> For more than 50 years, the National Board of License has served the Jewish community through the establishment of standards and criteria for the certification of professional educators.

ONLINE JOB PLACEMENT

The following four web sites that assist Jewish educators in finding a job:

- The Everett JewishJobFinder.com
  www.jewishjobfinder.com

- CAJE Job Board
  www.caje.org/interact/fs_job.html

- Jewishjobs.com
  www.jewishjobs.com

- The Lookstein Center Job Board
  www.lookstein.org/bulletin_board.htm

PERIODICALS

Jewish

BabagaNewz
Tel. 888-458-8535
www.babaganewz.com

> This monthly magazine encourages fourth through seventh graders to explore Jewish values from novel, thought provoking perspectives. Teacher's Guide. Jewish Book Club. Web site. Subsidized class subscriptions available now.

Jewish Education Center of Cleveland

- **Daf** - www.jecc.org (Find under Educational Resources)

The JECC publishes *Daf* six times a year, with annotated listings of educational resources around a central theme.

- **Immediate Response Curriculum** - Look to the JECC web site when national and international news breaks. An Immediate Response Curriculum is posted usually within 5-12 hours.

Union of American Hebrew Congregation.

Note: The following periodicals/newsletters may be found online.

Ganeinu: Our Garden

http://uahc.org/educate/ganeinu/index.shtml

A periodical for Jewish early childhood education issues.

The Jewish Parent Page

http://uahc.org/educate/parent

A periodical that educates parents about Jewish holidays and rituals.

Torah at the Center

http://uahc.org/educate/tatc

A quarterly for Jewish educators.

V'shinantam

http://uahc.org/educate/teacher

The UAHC's national Jewish teacher newsletter.

United Synagogue of Conservative Judaism.

Note: To order any of the following, contact the Education Department, 212-533-7800, ext. 2507.

Shibboley Schechter

Bulletin for Solomon Schechter Day Schools containing ideas for lay and professional day school leaders, including descriptions of programs, research, and resources.

Tov L'Horot

Designed for synagogue school principals and teachers, this publication includes descriptions of existing synagogue school programs, articles by educators, lesson plans, and resource information. Back issues with articles on videos, Purim costume making, professionalism, Hebrew, and the like, are available.

Your Child

Designed for parents of young children, this newsletter is published three times a year and focuses on issues, problems, and goals involved in raising and educating the young Jewish child.

Secular

The Mailbox: Where Great Teachers Find Great Ideas (There is also a link on this page to *Learning* Magazine On Line.)

The Master Teacher
(800) 669-9633
www.masterteacher.com

Contributors

Sylvia F. Abrams, Ph.D., holds a B.A., M.A., and Ph.D. from Case Western Reserve University, and a B.H.L. and M.H.L. from the Cleveland College of Jewish Studies. Her Ph.D. is in the field of Social Policy History. She is the Dean and Professor of Jewish Education at the Laura and Alvin Siegal College of Jewish Studies. She teaches courses in educational administration and in Jewish identity and Israel, is a frequent workshop presenter, and an advocate for the Jewish education profession. Previously, she was the Director of Educational Services, Office of the Executive, Jewish Education Center of Cleveland. She was Chairperson of the Coalition for the Advancement of Jewish Education (CAJE). Dr. Abram's works have appeared in numerous publications, and she is involved in Holocaust education in Ohio.

Rabbi Robert Abramson, Ed.D., holds an M.H.L. from the Jewish Theological Seminary, where he was ordained as a Rabbi. He also earned a Doctorate in Education from Teachers College, Columbia University. He is the Director of the Department of Education of the United Synagogue of Conservative Judaism. Previously, he was Headmaster of the Hillel Day School of Metropolitan Detroit and Educational Director of Kehillath Israel Hebrew School in Brookline, Massachusetts. Dr. Abramson has been a Visiting Adjunct Professor of Jewish Education. He has also served as both Director and Associate Director of Camp Ramah in New England.

Janice P. Alper, a graduate of HUC-JIR's Rhea Hirsch School of Education, is the Executive Director of Jewish Educational Services of Atlanta. She has actively implemented many professional development opportunities, among them a partnership with the Siegal College of Judaic Studies to deliver a Master's Degree in Jewish Education via synchronous video-conferencing; DOLEV, an active dialogue for congregational educators with teachers in Israel; and programs for preschool teachers. A

curriculum writer, an early pioneer in family education, a successful administrator, and a founder of CAJE, Ms. Alper is the author of numerous books and articles on Jewish education. Recently, she was selected by the National Association of Temple Educators to be a mentor as part of a national team of people who work with new educators.

Judy Aronson began her career in Jewish education as an assistant when she was in high school. At Brandeis University, she studied both Hebrew and American Studies. She holds a master's degree in Theological Studies from the Harvard Divinity School, majoring in Hebrew Scripture and History of Religion. Since 1979, Ms. Aronson has worked in Los Angeles as Director of Education in day and religious schools. The Chair of CAJE 28, she has been a member of the Clinical Faculty of the Rhea Hirsch School of Education at Hebrew Union College and is a Lecturer at the University of Judaism.

Julie Jaslow Auerbach is the Director of Family and Adult Education at Gross Solomon Schechter Day School in Cleveland, Ohio. She has worked as a Curriculum Associate at the Jewish Education Center of Cleveland and as a senior educator for Melitz, serving as the North American Coordinator for Project Numbers 2000. Ms. Auerbach has shared her songs and talents at JCC camps, preschools, BBYO Israel programs, and with families and Jewish educators in all kinds of settings around the world. Her original songs can be heard on the audiotape *Seasoned with Song,* and are published in *Jewish Every Day* (A.R.E. Publishing, Inc.). A contributor to several other books published by A.R.E., Ms. Auerbach earned her master's degree in Jewish Studies with an emphasis on Jewish Education from the Cleveland College of Jewish Studies.

Ofra Arieli Backenroth holds a B.A. in Comparative Literature, a teaching diploma from Tel Aviv University, an M.F.A. in Dance Education from

Teachers College, Columbia University, and is a doctoral student in Jewish Education at the Davidson School, Jewish Theological Seminary. She has written about, presented, and published articles on the merits and impact of using the arts in teaching Judaic subjects. Ms. Backenroth is the education director of MeltonArts.org, a web site that is co-sponsored by the Melton research centers of the Hebrew University in Jerusalem, the Ohio State University, and The Jewish Theological Seminary, and is dedicated to the promotion and the teaching of Judaic subjects through the arts. For the past 30 years, she has taught dance, Hebrew, and literature in Israel, New York, and New Jersey.

Rabbi Steven Bayar is the Rabbi of Congregation B'nai Israel of Millburn, New Jersey. He is co-author of *Teens and Trust* (Torah Aura Productions) and the Ziv/Giraffe Curriculum (Righteous Person's Foundation). Co-founder of Ikkar Publishing and author of various curricula on ethics and values, Rabbi Bayar also teaches Rabbinics at the Solomon Schechter High School at West Orange, New Jersey.

Melissa Bailin Bernstein received a Bachelor of Arts degree in Jewish Studies from American University, a Master of Science in Social Administration from Case Western Reserve University, and a Master of Judaic Studies from the Cleveland College of Jewish Studies. She has been a religious school teacher, family educator, teacher, and camp director. Ms. Bernstein is currently the Curriculum Associate of the Jewish Education Center of Cleveland, where she writes curriculum, coaches and consults with teachers, and teaches professional development classes, including active learning.

Sherry H. Blumberg, Ph.D., received both her master's and doctorate in Jewish Education from Hebrew Union College-Jewish Institute of Religion Rhea Hirsch School of Education in Los Angeles. Currently the Education Director of Congregation Shalom in Milwaukee, Wisconsin, she was formerly an Associate Professor for 14 years on the faculty of HUC-JIR in New York. A co-founder of the Jewish family education movement, Dr. Blumberg works extensively in the areas of curriculum design, teaching about God and spirituality, and informal education. She is listed in *Who's Who in the World*, and is a past president of the Religious Education Association and co-editor of *Teaching about God and*

Spirituality: A Resource for Jewish Settings (A.R.E. Publishing, Inc.).

Rivkah Dahan is an independent educational consultant and learning disabilities specialist who founded and continues to serve as the coordinator of Teaching Made Easier, a consulting service empowering teachers to enhance their own skills in producing top-level instructional aids. A materials specialist, she has developed many innovative teaching aids and hands-on materials to facilitate specialized instruction. Ms. Dahan holds an M.S.Ed from CUNY, the Jerusalem Teacher's Certificate, is a graduate of the Mandel Foundation's Teacher Educator Institute, and has taught elementary, special, and adult education.

Cynthia Dolgin is a doctoral candidate at Teachers College, Columbia University, and co-director of Curriculum Development for Project Etgar, the new middle school curriculum for synagogue schools. She is a teacher educator for the Suffolk Association of Jewish Educational Services (SAJES).

Gail Zaiman Dorph, Ph.D., is the Director of the Mandel Foundation's Teacher Education Institute (TEI), an innovative two-year professional development program for senior Jewish educators. In addition to teaching, she consults with communal organizations, universities, and schools on the creation of professional programs for principals and teachers. She is currently co-chair of the national advisory board for DeLeT (Day School Leadership through Teaching), a privately funded new teacher initiative that has two sites, Brandeis and HUC-JIR, and teaches in the program. Prior to her work with the Mandel Foundation, Dr. Dorph directed the Fingerhut School of Education at the University of Judaism. She was also a part of a national team that wrote and implemented the Melton Curriculum.

Eileen Ettinger is a religious school educator, artist, and Judaic art education specialist. She earned an M.S. in education from Queens College and her M.A. in Jewish Education from Hebrew Union College-Jewish Institute of Religion in Los Angeles. She worked at the Skirball Museum in Los Angeles, and was a religious school educator at schools in Los Angeles and New Mexico. Combining her background in Jewish education with extensive art studies, Ms. Ettinger has taught Judaic art to all ages from preschool to master teaching programs. She gives teacher training workshops on incorporating art into the Jewish classroom.

Debbie Findling, Ed.D., is a Program Officer at the Richard & Rhonda Goldman Fund in San Francisco, California. She previously served as Director of Tikea, an innovative fellowship for educators of Jewish teens in the Bay Area, and was an educator on the March of the Living for ten years. She graduated summa cum laude with a doctorate in education from the University of San Francisco, and earned graduate degrees in education and Hebrew letters from the University of Judaism. Dr. Findling, who has published and lectured widely on Jewish topics, was a fellow in the Wexner Heritage Foundation and the Teacher Educator Institute of the Mandel Foundation.

Ellen S. Fishman holds a B.A. from Ursuline College and an M.Ed. from John Carroll University. She is the Executive Director of the Learning Disabilities Association of Cuyahoga County/Cleveland. Prior to this position, she was the Director of Special Education at the Jewish Education Center of Cleveland. A former day and supplementary school teacher, Ms. Fishman has co-developed a special needs curriculum for students. She is a trained cooperative learning facilitator, a distance learning instructor, and conducts workshops locally, nationally, and internationally.

Ronna Fox earned a B.Ed. in Elementary and Special Education from the University of Toledo and an M.Ed. in Education Supervision from Cleveland State University. She is the Co-Director of the Teacher Center at the Jewish Education Center of Cleveland. Ms. Fox has worked as a special education and primary public school teacher. She has experience in informal education as a synagogue youth group advisor, as well as in storytelling with preschool and religious school students.

Shayna Friedman is the Director of Professional Development for the Jewish Educational Services in Atlanta, Georgia, and a teacher in the Atlanta Florence Melton Adult Mini-School. Before coming to Atlanta, she served as the Assistant Principal of the Ilene and Stanley P. Gold Religious School at Wilshire Boulevard Temple. She received her B.A.

from Newcomb College of Tulane University and her M.A. from the Rhea Hirsch School of Education at Hebrew Union College-Jewish Institute of Religion. She has taught in a variety of settings from camp to congregational schools.

Roberta Louis Goodman, Ph.D., resides in her hometown of Chicago, and serves as Director of Distance Learning and Assistant Professor of Jewish Education for the Laura and Alvin Siegal College of Judaic Studies in Cleveland, Ohio. She received her Master's in Jewish Education from the Rhea Hirsch School of Education at Hebrew Union College-Jewish Institute of Religion in Los Angeles, and her doctorate in Adult Education from Teacher's College of Columbia University. A former student of James Fowler, she has written extensively on faith development, God and spirituality, adult learning, research and evaluation, and other topics. She is the co-editor of *Teaching about God and Spirituality* and co-author of *Head Start on Holidays*, both published by A.R.E. Publishing, Inc.

Marilyn E. Gootman, Ed.D., is founder of Gootman Education Associates, an educational consulting company that provides workshops and seminars for parents and educators on successful strategies for raising and teaching children. She was a faculty member of the University of Georgia College of Education for 20 years, and has also taught in both day school and synagogue school settings. Dr. Gootman holds degrees in Jewish education from Boston Hebrew College and Brandeis University. She is the author of *The Caring Teacher's Guide To Discipline* (Corwin Press), *The Loving Parent's Guide To Discipline* (Berkley Publishing), and *When a Friend Dies: A Book for Teens about Grieving and Healing* (Free Spirit Publishing).

Lauren B. Granite, Ph.D. earned her doctorate in the Sociology of Religion from Drew University. In addition to teaching Jewish history at American University, Gettysburg College, and Elizabethtown College, she has taught Jewish history for the past six years to high school students, adults, and supplementary school students in a variety of Jewish educational settings. She would like to thank her mentor, Cynthia Peterman, Chair, Jewish History Department, Charles E. Smith Jewish Day School, Rockville, Maryland, for teaching her how to teach Jewish history.

Lisa D. Grant, Ph.D., Assistant Professor of Jewish Education at Hebrew Union College-Jewish Institute of Religion in New York, holds a B.A. from the University of Michigan and a Ph.D. in Jewish Education from the Jewish Theological Seminary. Her research and teaching interests include adult Jewish learning, professional development of teachers, and the roles that ritual and Israel play in American Jewish Life. Dr. Grant has published studies on adult trips to Israel, adult Bat Mitzvah, Bar and Bat Mitzvah in Israel, and the impact of professional development of education on school change. The author of *Aytz Hayim Hi/She Is a Tree of Life: A Curriculum for Adult Bat Mitzvah* (Women's League for Conservative Judaism), she has recently completed a collaborative study entitled *Meaning, Connection, and Practice: Contemporary Trends in Adult Jewish Learning,* an in-depth study of the Florence Melton Adult Mini-School, to be published in 2004.

Joel Lurie Grishaver, co-founder and co-owner of Torah Aura Productions, is a Jewish writer, teacher, and storyteller. He was a founding board member of the Coalition for the Advancement of Jewish Education, and is a consultant to the Whizin Institute for Jewish Family Life. In 1998, Mr. Grishaver was awarded the Covenant Award for outstanding contributions to Jewish life. He is the author of the *Bible People* series and *The Life Cycle Workbook* (both published by A.R.E. Publishing, Inc.); *Learning Torah: A Self-Guided Journey through the Layers of Jewish Learning* (UAHC Press); *40 Things You Can Do to Save the Jewish People; Being Torah; Learn Torah With . . . Torah Annual, Volumes 1 and 2* (all published by Torah Aura Productions). His articles have appeared in previous A.R.E. teacher handbooks.

Maxine Segal Handelman is the Director of Early Childhood Jewish Education for the Pritzker Center for Jewish Education, Jewish Community Centers of Chicago. She holds an M.A. in Early Childhood Education from Pacific Oaks College, and an M.A. in Jewish Education from Hebrew Union College-Jewish Institute of Religion. She is a graduate of the Wexner Heritage Foundation. The author of *Jewish Every Day: The Complete Handbook for Early Childhood Teachers* (A.R.E. Publishing, Inc.), Ms. Handelman is also a sought after speaker, a professional storyteller, and leader of Tot Shabbat services for young families.

Francine Hirschman is the Principal of the Ezra Academy in Forest Hills, New York. She is the co-author of *Teens & Trust* (Torah Aura Productions), *Teaching Theology through Science Fiction & Fantasy* (Ikkar Publishing), and author of *In the Beginning . . . There Was a Video, In Case of Emergency, Being Jewish Means Having to Say You're Sorry* (Ikkar Publishing), and various articles on Jewish education. A co-founder of Ikkar Publishing, Ms. Hirschman holds degrees in English, education, and Jewish education and supervision from New York University, Monmouth College, and Yeshiva University.

Renee Frank Holtz, Ph.D., is the Director of Education at Congregation Kol Ami in White Plains, New York, and an adjunct Assistant Professor at Fordham University in the Graduate School of Education. She is the author of *Hineni 1 Family Companion* (Behrman House) and various articles on Jewish education.

Rabbi Linda Holtzman was ordained from the Reconstructionist Rabbinical College. She is currently an associate professor and Director of the Department of Practical Rabbinics at RRC. Rabbi Holtzman is a native Philadelphian who received both a B.A. and M.A. in English literature from Temple University. She also received a B.H.L. from Gratz College. She has served as the Rabbinic leader of Mishkan Shalom, a Reconstructionst synagogue in Philadelphia.

Bethamie Horowitz, Ph.D., is a graduate of Harvard University, and received her doctorate in social psychology from The Graduate School of The City University of New York. She is the author of the 2000 study *Connections and Journeys: Assessing Critical Opportunities for Enhancing Jewish Identity,* commissioned by UJA-Federation of Jewish Philanthropies of New York. At UJA-Federation of New York, where she was Director of Planning and Research from 1992-96, she directed the *1991 New York Jewish Population Study.* Her monograph about the Jews of New York was published in 1993. A research consultant to the Mandel Foundation (and the Mandel School in Jerusalem), Dr. Horowitz is a member of the National Technical Advisory Committee for the 2001 National Jewish Population Study.

Carol K. Ingall, Ed.D., is the Dr. Bernard Heller Professor of Jewish Education at the William Davidson Graduate School of Jewish Education of the Jewish Theological Seminary. Her special areas of expertise include curriculum development and moral education; she also directs the Day School Teaching Program. A former consultant and curriculum writer for numerous Jewish educational organizations, Dr. Ingall served as the Executive Director of the Bureau of Jewish Education of Rhode Island, and taught in Jewish schools for more than 25 years. Her book *Transmission and Transformation: A Jewish Perspective on Moral Education* (Melton) won the 1999 National Jewish Book Award in the field of Jewish education. Dr. Ingall holds a doctorate from Boston University School of Education, where she studied moral education.

Rabbi Bruce Kadden has served as Rabbi of Temple Beth El in Salinas, California, since 1984. He is a graduate of Stanford University, and was ordained by Hebrew Union College-Jewish Institute of Religion. He is co-author, along with his wife, Barbara, of *Teaching Mitzvot: Concepts, Values, and Activities, Teaching Tefilah: Insights and Activities on Prayer, Teaching Jewish Life Cycle: Traditions and Activities,* and *Ethical Wills: Handing Down Our Jewish Heritage* (all published by A.R.E. Publishing, Inc.). Rabbi Kadden has taught interfaith Bible Study classes for more than ten years, and is a board member of the Pacific Association of Reform Rabbis. He also writes for the web site Interfaithfamily.com.

Gabrielle Kaplan-Mayer is a playwright, storyteller, and Jewish educator. She holds a B.F.A. in theater from Emerson College and an M.A. in Jewish Studies from the Reconstructionist Rabbinical College. Her books of plays include *The Magic Tanach and Other Short Plays* and *Extraordinary Jews: Staging Their Lives* (both published by A.R.E. Publishing, Inc.), and she is currently working on another book for A.R.E. She is a consultant for the Creative Arts at the Auerbach Central Agency for Jewish Education in Philadelphia, and also teaches theater at Congregation Mishkan Shalom and for the Philadelphia Young Playwrights Festival. Ms. Kaplan-Mayer conducts custom designed drama workshops across the country and writes frequently about the arts, education, health, and spiritual growth.

Betsy Dolgin Katz, Ed.D., is the North American Director of the Florence Melton Adult Mini-School, a two-year adult school located in 41 cities in North America. A former Director of Reform Education and Adult Education for the Chicago Community Foundation for Jewish Education, Dr. Katz served as Chairperson of CAJE and for the Alliance for Adult Jewish Learning. She is a member of the Board of Directors of the Covenant Foundation. She is author of many articles and curricula, as well as *Or Hadash, Let a New Light Shine* (UAHC Press), an adult curriculum on Jerusalem.

Sally Klein-Katz received her M.A. from Hebrew Union College-Jewish Institute of Religion. After serving for 12 years in Jewish education directing summer camps and religious schools, she made *aliyah* to Israel. She has been a Jerusalem Fellow, directed a four-year research/development project for Melitz Centers for Zionist Education, and was responsible for the manual *Family Israel Experiences: The Ma Nishtana of Family Education Israel Trips.* Currently, Ms. Klein-Katz teaches the graduate seminar on Jewish Education for HUC-JIR Jerusalem, is the Coordinator/Faculty for the JESNA Graduate Seminars in Israel, and serves as the Education and Strategic Planning Consultant for various Federations around the world. In addition, she has a private consulting company for groups and individual families coming to visit Israel.

Rabbi Jan Katzew, Ph.D., serves as the Director of the Department of Education of the Union of American Hebrew Congregations. Previously, he held positions of educational leadership in a congregational school, a central agency for Jewish education, and a day school. Ordained at Hebrew Union College, he earned a doctorate in Education and Jewish Thought at the Hebrew University. Rabbi Katzew has written articles for the *Hebrew Union College Annual*, the *CCAR Journal*, and *Reform Judaism* on education and ethics.

Jo Kay has an M.A. in Jewish Education from N.Y.U., and is the Director of the New York School of Education at Hebrew Union College-Jewish Institute of Religion. She served as the Director of Jewish Studies at the Rodeph Sholom Day School in New York, and most recently as Director of the congregation's religious school. Ms. Kay created the PACE (Parent and Child Education) model of family education, and is a consultant to the Whizin Institute for Jewish Family Life at the University of Judaism in Los Angeles. A recipient in 2001 of the Covenant Award for Excellence in Jewish Education, she also serves as chair of the editorial boards of *Jewish Education News*.

Gerard W. Kaye earned a master's degree in Counseling Psychology from Roosevelt University, and completed postgraduate studies at the Chicago Medical School/University of Health Sciences. He is the Director of the Olin-Sang-Ruby Union Institute in Oconomowoc, Wisconsin, a member of the Brandeis University Professional Advisory Committee on Informal Education, and a Life Fellow of the American Orthopsychiatric Association. Mr. Kaye was selected as the first recipient of the Guardian of Hope Award from Keshet, an organization of families with special needs children and, in 2000, he was awarded a Doctor of Human Letters *honoris causa* from Hebrew Union College-Jewish Institute of Religion.

Marc N. Kramer, Ed.D., is the Executive Director of RAVSAK: The Jewish Community Day School Network. He is a former Jewish Studies Director and Head of School. He holds a B.A. in Near Eastern and Judaic Studies from Brandeis University, an M.S.W. from Columbia University School of Social Work, an M.A. in Jewish Studies from the Jewish Theological Seminary of America, and both a masters and doctorate from Teachers College-Columbia University. In addition to his day school work, Dr. Kramer is a consultant to the Jewish Board of Family and Children's Services of New York, where he works as a group facilitator and develops psycho-educational programs that explore the intersection of traditional Jewish text, contemporary social issues, and normative mental health. A Wexner Graduate Fellowship alum, Dr. Kramer is the author or co-author of several studies on Jewish community day schools.

Patti Kroll is Director of Education at The Family Education Center of Conservative Judaism at Congregation Beth Shalom in Kansas City, Missouri, designated a "Framework for Excellent School" by United Synagogue. She has designed and implemented *madrichim* programs in two congregations, has worked five summers as the coordinator of a counselor-in-training program at Olin-Sang-Ruby Union Institute in Oconomowoc, Wisconsin, and participated in developing and implementing the CAJE teen experience at the CAJE conference. Ms. Kroll received a Bachelor of Science in Education from Northern Illinois University, a Master of Arts in Guidance and Counseling from Northeastern Illinois University, and a Master of Arts in Judaic Studies from the Laura and Alvin Siegal College of Jewish Studies. She is the national chairperson for youth programs for CAJE and leads a teen leadership program in Kansas City.

Enid C. Lader is a graduate of the Cleveland fellows Program, with a master's degree in Judaic Studies from the Cleveland College of Jewish Studies. She is presently the Director of Congregation and Family Education at Beth Israel-The West Temple in Cleveland, Ohio, and is the Jewish Life Coordinator for Knesseth Israel Temple in Wooster, Ohio. Ms. Lader has written many songs for children and parents and taught a number of teacher education courses, helping teachers think beyond the walls of their classroom. She has also written about the role of communication with families and Interactive Homework in *Growing Together: Resources, Programs, and Experiences for Jewish Family Education*, edited by Jeffrey Schein and Judith C. Schiller (A.R.E. Publishing, Inc.).

Barbara Lapetina, Ph.D., is an Adjunct Assistant Professor at Iona College in New Rochelle, New York. She was an elementary school teacher, and does staff development in Math and Science in Westchester County, New York. Dr. Lapetina has been part of the team of writers for the New York State Math Assessment.

Caren N. Levine is a principal at Etheoreal, a consultancy specializing in educational media and technology, and a senior consultant for media and technology at JESNA, Jewish Education Service of North America. Her face-to-face teaching includes a congregational school and Yeshiva University's Azrieli Graduate School of Jewish Education and Administration. She has also taught online through the School of Education at Hebrew Union College-Jewish Institute of Religion, the Jewish Theological Seminary Distance Learning Project, and JSkyway. Ms. Levine holds a B.A. in Ancient Studies from Barnard College and an M.A. from JTS in Jewish Studies with a concentration in Jewish Education.

A recipient of a Wexner Graduate Fellowship, she is completing her Ed.D. at Teachers College, Columbia University in educational technology.

Paul Liptz received his M.A. from the Hebrew University of Jerusalem. He was born in Zimbabwe and made *aliyah* to Israel on June 6, 1967 — one day before the Six Day War. He has been lecturing at Tel Aviv University for over 30 years in the Department of Middle Eastern and African History, where he deals with social and political history in Arab and African countries. At the Hebrew Union College-Jewish Institute of Religion in Jerusalem, he deals with modern Jewish history and contemporary issues of Israel and the Middle East. Mr. Liptz travels extensively around the world lecturing and conducting workshops. He is presently studying Jewish communities in the former Soviet Union.

Dina Maiben, Director of Religious Education at Temple Shaari Emeth in Manalapan, New Jersey, has taught Hebrew on the elementary, high school, and adult levels. Ms. Maiben is the co-author of the primer *Z'man Likro* and the prayer series *Z'man L'Tefilah* (A.R.E. Publishing, Inc.), co-author of *Abraham's Great Discovery* and *How Tzipi the Bird Got Her* Wings (NightinGale Resources), and author of the *Let's Learn Prayer Activity Masters* (KTAV), and has published extensively in *The Special Educator, Jewish Education News,* and *Shofar Magazine.* She is currently on the Editorial Board of *Jewish Education News,* is chairperson of the CAJE Writing and Publishing Network, and co-chairs Monmouth County's Commission on Jewish Education.

Rabbi Leonard A. Matanky, Ph.D., is the Associate Superintendent of Schools of the Associated Talmud Torahs of Chicago and the Director of its Morris and Rose Goldman Computer Department for Jewish Studies. For the past seven years, Rabbi Matanky has also served as the Dean of the Ida Crown Jewish Academy. In addition, he serves as the spiritual leader of Congregation K.I.N.S. of West Rogers Park in Chicago. Rabbi Matanky earned his Rabbinic ordination and a Master of Religious Education from Hebrew Theological College, a Master of Education from Loyola University, and a Ph.D. from New York University. A contributor to many journals and other educational publications, he has lectured extensively on the use

of technology in Jewish education and on the preparation of teachers for Jewish schools.

Bernice McCarthy, Ph.D., is founder of About Learning Inc., an executive and educational consulting and training company, with school, corporate, and government clients throughout the world. She received her Ph.D. from Northwestern University, and is the author of several publications, including *About Teaching* and *About Learning,* both published by About Learning Inc.

Sharon Morton has been the Director of Education at Am Shalom Congregation in Glencoe, Illinois since 1976. She was president of the National Association of Temple Educators from 1998-2000, the educational advisor to the Institute for Catholic/Jewish Education, the regional chair of social action for the Great Lakes Region of the UAHC to the Commission on Social Action for the last five years, and served on the advisory committee of the Midwest Avenue of the Righteous. Ms. Morton's congregation has won the Fain Award twice for their work in social action. She was the founder of SoJuRN — Social Justice Religious Resource Network, an organization that coordinated social action activities throughout the region. Her travels for social justice have included three trips to Russia, a trip to Poland, and a conference in Jerusalem with the international group of the Srs. of Sion.

Julia C. Phillips is the Director of Education at the Congregation of Liberal Judaism in Orlando, Florida. She received her master's degree in History Museum Studies from the Cooperstown Graduate Program, a cooperative graduate studies program administered by the State University of New York at Oneonta and the New York State Historical Association. As the Director of Education and Public Programming at a historic site in Ohio, Ms. Phillips developed special tours for children and adults, and worked with the local Board of Education to develop an interdisciplinary field trip partnership with the public schools. She returned to school to earn her Master's Degree in Jewish Education from the Rhea Hirsch School of Education at Hebrew Union College-Jewish Institute of Religion in Los Angeles. She is currently working on a forthcoming book for A.R.E. Publishing, Inc. called *Teaching Jewish History.*

Bunnie R. Piltch holds a B.A. and M.Ed. from Temple University, where she is working on a doctorate in foreign language education. Her area of research is the importance of Hebrew as a heritage language for Jewish college students. Ms. Piltch teaches Hebrew at Lehigh University and at Congregation Brith Sholom, Bethlehem, Pennsylvania. Formerly, she has taught at Muhlenberg College, and at the elementary and secondary levels in both day schools and supplementary schools. She has developed and produced formal and informal curriculum materials, and is an active member of CAJE for whom she has led Hebrew teaching workshops at annual conferences. Her article, "An Examination of Second Language Research Findings: Truth or Dare," was published in *Jewish Education News* in Fall 1997.

Rachel Raviv received a Bachelor of Arts degree in Psychology from the University of Judaism, a Master of Arts degree in Education from Tufts University, and a Master of Arts degree in Jewish Communal Service from the Hornstein Program at Brandeis University. After teaching in supplemental schools, as well as day schools, she served as the Education and Youth Director for a Conservative congregation in Connecticut. Ms. Raviv currently works with curriculum design and staff development at the Jewish Education Center of Cleveland in the Curriculum Resources Department.

Marci Rogozen is a Co-Director of the Teacher Center at the Jewish Education Center of Cleveland. She holds a Master's in Education from the University of Judaism in Los Angeles. She has worked in both day schools and supplementary schools in teaching and administrative capacities. Ms. Rogozen's current work allows her to work creatively with teachers in the creation of educational materials and professional development.

Jody Rosenbloom is currently the Education Director at the Jewish Community of Amherst, a Reconstructionist congregation in Western Massachusetts. She formerly held a variety of teaching and administrative roles at Temple Israel in Minneapolis, Minnesota. Ms. Rosenbloom began her career in Jewish education as a Hebrew school teacher of Grades 5-8. She is an active member of area Jewish educator networks, and a long-standing member of the National Association of Temple

Educators and the Coalition for the Advancement of Jewish Education. She has earned a Bachelor of Arts in Urban Studies from Antioch College and a Master's of Arts in Leadership from Augsburg College.

Rhonda Rosenheck is founding Principal of the new Schechter Regional High School, serving Bergen, Passaic, and Rockland Counties in New Jersey. She and Director Jay Dewey have structured the school's innovative program around the principle of collaboration. Prior to this, Ms. Rosenheck was Principal of the Ivry Prozdor, the high school program of the Jewish Theological Seminary, and before that was Assistant Executive Director of the Commission for Jewish Education of the Palm Beaches. She has studied Rabbinics and applied linguistics at the graduate level, holds an M.A. in Jewish Education from the Jewish Theological Seminary, and is writing her doctoral dissertation.

Rabbi Jeffrey Schein, Ed.D., is a Professor and Director of the Department of Jewish Education at the Laura and Alvin Siegal College of Judaic Studies, and the Senior Consultant for Jewish Education for the Jewish Reconstructionist Foundation. Ordained at the Reconstructionist Rabbinical College, he was awarded a doctorate in Curriculum Studies at Temple University. He is the co-editor of *Growing Together: Resources, Programs, and Experiences for Jewish Family Education* (A.R.E. Publishing, Inc.), and author of *Creative Jewish Education* (Rossel Books), *Targilon: A Guide for Charting the Course of Jewish Education* (JESNA and JRF), *Windows on the Jewish Soul, Connecting Prayer and Spirituality, The Reconstructionist Curriculum Resource Guide*, and *Lifelong Jewish Learning* (all four published by JRF). Dr. Schein is the first non-pulpit Rabbi to receive the Ira Eisenstein Award from the Reconstructionist Rabbinical Association for distinguished service.

Judith S. Schiller is the Director of the Retreat Institute of the Jewish Education Center of Cleveland, and works collaboratively with Jewish institutions in the Cleveland community to develop and implement 35-40 retreats a year for youth, families, and educators. She has held positions in administration, teaching, and family education in Jewish institutions in Cleveland. Earlier career experience was in the field of Marketing and

Corporate Training and Development. Ms. Schiller earned a B.A. at Case Western Reserve University, and is a graduate of the Cleveland Fellows Program of the Cleveland College of Jewish Studies, where she earned a master's degree of Judaic Studies in Jewish Education. She is the co-editor of *Growing Together: Resources, Programs, and Experiences for Jewish Family Education* (A.R.E. Publishing, Inc.).

Diane Tickton Schuster, Ph.D., is Director of the Institute for Teaching Jewish Adults at Hebrew Union College-Jewish Institute of Religion in Los Angeles. She also teaches there and at Brandeis University's Institute for Informal Jewish Education. Her book, *Jewish Lives, Jewish Learning,* is forthcoming from UAHC Press. Recently, with Lisa Grant, Meredith Woocher, and Steven Cohen, Dr. Schuster completed an in-depth analysis of the impact of the Florence Melton Adult Mini-School on adult learners; the study findings will be published in a forthcoming book, *Meaning, Connection, and Practice: Contemporary Issues in Adult Jewish Learning.* Dr. Schuster earned a B.A. at the University of Michigan, a Master's Degree in Social Welfare from the University of California-Berkeley, and a Ph.D. in Human Development and Education at Claremont Graduate University.

Zena W. Sulkes, Ph.D., holds a B.A. from the University of Michigan in Education, an M.Ed. in Guidance and Counseling from Wayne State University, and a Ph.D. in Curriculum and Instruction from the University of South Florida. She currently serves as the Head of School at The Hebrew Day School of Central Florida, a community day school serving Grades K through 8. She is the president of the Jewish Community Day School Network and past president of the National Association of Temple Educators. Dr. Sulkes is Adjunct Professor at Rollins College, Winter Park, Florida, where she teaches courses in Jewish Ethics and Character Development. Her publications include *Mitzvot Copy Pak™* (A.R.E. Publishing, Inc.), *Teacher's Guide* for *The Shrinking Circle: Memories of Nazi Berlin 1933-1939* (UAHC Press), and two chapters in *The Jewish Educational Leader's Handbook* (A.R.E. Publishing, Inc.)

Serene Victor was a Director of Synagogue Education at Ohabei Shalom in Brookline, Massachusetts, and then at Temple Emunah in Lexington, Massa-

chusetts. She has an M.Ed. from Boston University, and is a graduate of the Mandel Teacher Education Institute. Presently, Ms. Victor is Consultant for Synagogue Education with United Synagogue of Conservative Judaism. She is responsible for the New Director's Institute and U-Step (United Synagogue Teacher Enrichment Program). She also has an independent practice consulting with synagogues and coaching, mentoring, and teaching religious school teachers and directors.

Cantor Marcey Wagner is a graduate of the H.L. Miller Cantorial School of the Jewish Theological Seminary, and currently serves as Cantor at the Jewish Congregation of Brookville. She is Co-Director with Cynthia Dolgin of Curriculum Development for Project Etgar, a New Curriculum for Synagogue Schools sponsored by United Synagogue of Conservative Judaism and the Melton Educational Research Center of JTS. Cantor Wagner is also a liturgy instructor and teacher educator for the Morasha Teacher Training Program at the Suffolk Association of Jewish Educational Services (SAJES). She serves on the Jewish Leader's Council of MAZON: A Jewish Response To Hunger, is a member of the Executive Council of the Cantor's Assembly, and is an educational consultant for About Learning Inc.

Meryl Wassner has been in the field of education for over 25 years — as teacher, storyteller, director, mentor, and independent consultant in professional development. She holds a B.A. in Literature from the University of Judaism, where she received a full Leadership Scholarship. She is completing her final papers for her M.S.J.S. at Spertus Institute of Jewish Studies in Chicago. Ms. Wassner is an alumna of the Mandel Foundation TEI (Teacher Educator Institute). She is currently a literacy instructor, teaching a course at the University of Oklahoma, funded by the Department of Education.

Susan Arias Weinman is the Religious School Principal for Temple Beth Hillel in South Windsor, Connecticut. In her 25 years in the field of education, she has been a high school business education teacher, nursery school teacher, elementary school storyteller, and religious school teacher. Ms. Weinman has been a CAJE presenter on communications for new principals, and a workshop facilitator for Connecticut Mitnick Teacher Conferences.

Jonathan S. Woocher, Ph.D., is the President of JESNA, the Jewish Education Service of North America, North America's organization for Jewish education advocacy and excellence. He earned a B.A., summa cum laude, from Yale University, and a Ph.D. in religion from Temple University. He has served on the faculty of Carleton College in Minnesota and Brandeis University, where he taught in the Benjamin S. Hornstein Program in Jewish Communal Service and directed the continuing education program for Jewish leadership. Dr. Woocher is the author of *Sacred Survival: The Civil Religion of American Jews* (Indiana University Press), and numerous articles on Jewish education, community, and religious education. Like so many others, he began his career in Jewish education as a religious school teacher, camp counselor, and youth group advisor.

Commentators

Amy Appelman holds a Masters Degree in Jewish Education from Hebrew Union College-Jewish Institute of Religion, Rhea Hirsch School of Education. She currently is the Jewish Family Educator at Temple Israel in West Bloomfield, Michigan. She received her undergraduate degree in Jewish Studies and Religious Studies from Indiana University. Amy's diverse background includes working full-time at Hillel at the University of Cincinnati, in supplementary schools across the country, camps, and as the Judaic Studies Coordinator/HUC-JIR Postgraduate Resident at Temple Israel of Hollywood Day School in Los Angeles, California.

Cheryl Cash-Linietsky has been a Jewish educator for over 25 years in Greater Philadelphia and southern New Jersey, as well as in Omaha, Nebraska, and Canada. Her experience includes Orthodox and Conservative day schools and Reform and Conservative supplementary schools. She has also led Junior Congregation, taught at Ramah, presented at CAJE, and has been both a USY and Kadima advisor. Ms. Cash-Linietsky received the Phyllis Scheinlin Memorial Teaching Award from the Auerbach Central Agency for Jewish Education in Philadelphia. She also received an award for her curriculum "Eastern European Immigration to America, 1880-1920."

Carol Cohn earned her B.S. in Early Childhood Education from Kent State University, and spent nine years teaching primary grades, including one of Cleveland's very first multi-age classes. Ms. Cohn has been involved in Jewish education for most of the 30+ years she has been teaching, from pre-kindergarten through high school and adult Bar/Bat Mitzvah preparation. She taught Nursery School for nine years at the Jewish Community Center of Orlando, creating and teaching the Judaic Enrichment Program for children ages three and a half through pre-kindergarten. Currently, she is the Educator at Congregation Bet Chaim in Casselberry, Florida, a position held since 1991 when she was given the opportunity to create its school. Ms. Cohn also serves as the primary *shlichah tzibur* for her lay-led congregation, and as the newly-elected Secretary of the UAHC's Southeast Council.

Karen Elson is Assistant Director of Education and Family Jewish Educator of Congregation Beth Tikvah in Worthington (Columbus), Ohio. She previously served as Assistant Director and Branch Principal of the former Kol Ami Community Hebrew school in Columbus, and as Religious School Director at Temple Israel of Columbus and Temple Emanuel of McAllen, Texas. She holds an M.A. in Judaic Studies/Jewish Education from Hebrew Union College in Cincinnati, as well as teacher, principal, and R.J.E. (Reform Jewish Educator) certification from the Reform Movement.

Rabbi David Feder serves Tree of Life Congregation in Morgantown, West Virginia. He has previously served congregations in Evansville, Indiana, Davis, California, and Oak Park, Michigan.

Michael Fixler has been teaching in supplementary and public schools for over a quarter of a century, mostly in the Syracuse, New York area. He has taught first through sixth grades. Mr. Fixler also plays guitar, klezmer clarinet, and saxophone. As an educational leader, he has presented at Jewish and secular education conferences on Cooperative Learning, Reading Education, Using Humor in the Classroom, and Conflict Resolution. He is on his synagogue's Board of Trustees and has served on the National Governing Board of Educators for Social Responsibility.

Nancy Hersh is the educational director at Congregation Beth Hatikvah, a Reconstructionist synagogue in Chatham, New Jersey. She has been involved in Jewish education for over 20 years, having taught all grade levels, including adults, and a variety of Judaic courses and Hebrew prayer. Ms. Hersh does private tutoring to prepare students to become B'nai Mitzvah. Currently, she also teaches at Temple Shalom, a Reform temple in Succasunna, New Jersey, where she is a member. She is certified by the National Board of License for Teachers and Principals of Jewish Schools in North America.

Anne Johnston came to Jewish education by way of literature, alternative journalism, and special education. She spent the 2001-2002 school year in Jerusalem with her family and is an alumna of the Conservative Yeshiva there. She has taught and directed the Children's Program of the National Havurah Institute. Currently, she teaches Jewish special education in the Talmud Torah Meyuchad program of the Jewish Federation of Greater New Haven, Connecticut, as well as serving as Jewish Family Educator and as an outreach teacher to Jewish adults with special needs at Congregation Beth El-Kesher Israel in New Haven. She is in her last year homeschooling her eighth grade son.

Kim Lausin is the Director of Early Childhood at the Gross Schechter Day School of Cleveland. She has been teaching in a Jewish preschool setting for 16 years. Ms. Lausin also directs a junior show choir and the middle school drama program at Schechter. She is currently completing a Master's degree program in Curriculum and Specialized Instruction at Cleveland State University.

Sheila Lepkin began her career in Jewish education in 1969 as a teacher's assistant at Temple Emanuel in Greensboro, North Carolina. She has been a school psychologist for 24 years in North Carolina, Maryland, Virginia, and Colorado public schools. Along the way, she has been president of a cooperative preschool and principal of the religious school at Temple Beit Torah in Colorado Springs. Currently, Ms. Lepkin teaches fourth graders Torah, *Menschlichkeit*, and Hebrew at Temple Sinai in Denver. She is also a contributor to *Moment*.

Cheryl Birkner Mack is a teacher of middle School Judaics at the Gross Schechter Day School in Cleveland. She teaches Tanach and Mishnah to 6th, 7th and 8th grade students. Ms. Mack also teaches courses on *Tefilah*, holidays, and life cycle at the Siegal College of Judaic Studies in Cleveland. She holds an A.B. in education from Washington

University in St. Louis, an M.A.J.E. from the Jewish Theological Seminary of America. Ms. Mack spent the 5761 academic year as a fellow in the Melton Senior Educators' program at the Hebrew University in Jerusalem.

Maura Pollak is the director of Judaic Studies at Heritage Academy in Tulsa, Okaloma, and a Jew-by-Choice. She has been involved in Jewish education for the last 20 years, teaching religious school and day school, working on Hebrew reading skills with elementary and adult students, training teen aides, tutoring Bar/Bat Mitzvah students, and telling Judaic stories to preschoolers. She is a member of Tulsa's *Chevra Kadishah*.

Dena Salmon is a freelance writer and a religious school teacher at Bnai Keshet, a Reconstructionist synagogue in Montclair, New Jersey. She has an M.A. in Religious Studies from the University of Pennsylvania, a B.A. in Biblical Studies from SUNY College at Purchase, and a Secondary Teacher's Certificate from Tulane University.

Sally Stefano is currently the Interim Director of Education at Congregation Beth Tikvah in Worthington, Ohio. She has been a teacher for 35 years, beginning her career in the public schools in California, moving to a Jewish day school in Texas, a laboratory school in Kansas, and university settings in Kansas, Illinois, and now Ohio as a teacher educator. She has taught something, in some form, to preschool through eighth grade, and at the college and adult levels. Jewish education is just the latest endeavor!

Diane Schon Wirtschafter has taught both general and Jewish studies in kindergarten through seventh grades at Minneapolis Jewish Day School and Tehiyah Jewish Day School in Berkeley, California, where she currently works in curriculum and staff development. Ms. Wirtschafter taught Math Education Methods at Saint Benedict's College in St. Joseph, Minnesota. She is a two-time state winner of the Presidential Award in Teaching Mathematics. A founder of Mayim Rabim, a Reconstructionist synagogue in Minneapolis, she served as chair of its Youth Education Committee. She also performs Yiddish songs.

Index

A

Academic Connections (Wolf), 534-535

Active learning, 542-544
   graphic organizers, 546-547
   lesson planning with, 548-550
   stickies, fun with, 547
   techniques of, 544-548
   Think-Pair-Share, 544-545
   voting technique, 545

Activity based teaching, weakness of, 2

Adolescent learners. *See* Teenage and adolescent learners.

Adoption, 463

Adult learners, teaching
   andragogy, 170-171
   attendance and participation, 142
   B'nai Mitzvah class, 146-147
   developmentally appropriate practice, 156-159
   developmental psychology, 105-106, 152-155, 156-159
   ethical will program, 141, 147-148
   expansion of, 29
   experiential learning, 147
   growth and change dynamic, 150-152
   holidays, 478
   ideas, feelings, and actions based learning, 146-147, 155
   Jewish identity and, 153-154
   Jewish perspectives in mid-life class, 141, 143, 144, 145
   knowing-learning types, 157-158
   learner motivation types, 156
   life transitions and programming, 171
   midrash class, 140
   Rozenzweig reflection on, 146
   safety issue, 143-144
   sequentially structured curriculum for, 145
   with storytelling, 613
   teacher-class relationship, 144-145, 148
   team learning approach, 148-149
   transformative learning, 156, 171-172
   twelve principles for effective learning, 142-150
   Women in Midrash class, 149

Age appropriate teaching. *See* Developmental psychology.

Aging, 464

AIDS and communicable diseases, 197-198

America, culture clash with, 61-62

Analytic learners, 297

Andragogy, 170-171

Animal sacrifices, Reconstructionist Movement position on, 52

Anorexia Nervosa, 193-194

Application domain question, 530-531, 531

Art, teaching with, 384
   ceremonial art, 567
   collaging, 559-561
   Jerusalem mosaic, 563-564
   masks, 564-566
   micography project, 553-555
   mosaics, 563-564
   murals, 561
   painting, 562-563
   papier mâché masks, 566-567
   and process, 552-553
   and self-esteem, 553
   Seven Days of Creation, 562-563
   stenciling, 556-557
   wimpels projects, 555-558

Ascribed and chosen identities, 38

Asperger Syndrome, 180

Assimilation and intermarriage, 74-75

Association of Collaborating Educators for Instructional Technology (ACEiT), 258

At-risk children, 187-188
   AIDS and communicable diseases, 197-198
   Anorexia Nervosa, 193-194
   Bulimia, 193-194
   bullying, threats, and aggression, 188-189
   Christian missionaries, 196-197
   cults, 195-196
   death of a loved one, 198
   depression and suicide, 194-195
   drug and alcohol abuse, 190-191
   eating disorders, 193
   inappropriate relationships, 191-192
   Jews for Jesus, 196-197
   learning disabilities and, 189-190
   legal issues, 193
   parental separation and divorce, 198-199
   physical and sexual abuse, 192-193
   sexual harassment, 191-192

Attendance, 22

Attention Deficit (Hyperactive) Disorder, 180-181

Avi Chai Foundation, 64

Avot prayer, 36

Avot v'Emahot Rummy, 631

B

Babylonian community education precedent, 36-37

Backpacks, theme, 120

Baeck, R. Leo, 536

Bal Taschit/Be Not Destructive value, fostering, 222

Bar/Bat Mitzvah family *wimpel* project, 557-558

Bedtime supervision at retreats, 233

Beginning the school year. *See* Starting in a new school.

Behavior challenges, 639-641

Benjamin, Idie, 118

Ben-Peretz, Miriam, 318
Bibliodrama, 389
Big U classroom setup, 203
Bikur cholim, 111, 112, 222, 454-455, 464
Bloom, Benjamin, 529
Bodily/Kinesthetic (body smart) intelligence type, 325-327, 329
Brachot, teaching with learning centers, 342
Brain-mind learning, 4Mat model, 299-301
Brainstorm class game, 625
Brothers legend, teaching with dance and movement, 602-603
Brown, Steven M., 293
Bruner, James, 535
Bruner, Jerome, 49
B'tzelem Elohim, 113
Buber, Martin, 41
Bulimia, 193-194
Bullying, threats, and aggression, 188-189
Burial, preparing the body, 464
Business ethics, 81-82

C

Camping, summer, 269-275
Ceremonial art projects, 567
Chanukah, 330, 477
Chatimot, in prayer, 417
Chazan, Barry, 154
Chesed, 482
Chevruta learning, 93-94, 352, 381-382
Childbirth, *mitzvah* of procreation, 462-463
Chosen people status, 52-53
Christian missionaries, 196-197
Classroom environment. *See also* Classroom management.
    entropy and chaos, 210-211
    interactive displays, 207
    Jewishness, 206
    Jews around the World display, 207
    Leap into Learning student display, 207
    materials organization, 210-211
    My House student display, 206
    room arrangement, 202-205
    safety, 205
    student displays, 206-207
    teaching displays, 207-208
    traffic flow, 205
    vignettes, 211-213
    visual displays, 205-210
    What's Kosher display, 207
Classroom management, 215-216
    character development, fostering, 221-224
    communication and cooperation, 218-221
    grouping, 219-220
    Knesset, class meeting, 220-221
    misbehavior, 223-224
    repentance, three R's of, 224
    responsibility sense, fostering, 221-224
    rules, 217-218
    space and structure, 216
    time, 216-217
Classroom observation chart, 360
Classrooms, constructivist, 334-338
Clay chips, making, 564

Collaborative learning. *See* Cooperative and collaborative learning.
Collage art projects, 559-561
Common sense learners, 297
Communicable diseases, 197-198
Community building. *See also* Family education; Home-school partnerships; Retreats, community and family.
    Babylonian experience of, 36-37
    communication and cooperation, 218-221
    covenantal community, 33
    with games, 623-626
    peer relationships, importance of, 8, 10
    Reconstructionist Movement, 51
    secular world, intersection with, 641-642
    theater and drama, 576
    values, fostering, 221-224
Complementary teacher collaboration, 664, 666-667
Comprehension domain question, 530
Confidentiality, 638-639
Confirmation class memories *wimpel* project, 558
Consciousness-raising (CR) tasks, 522-524
Conservative Movement
    9/11, influence of, 47
    learning strategy, 45-46
    mitzvot, teaching, 44-45
    "not yet" posture, 46-47
    prayer and music, 581
    Project Etgar, 293
    striving Jews, 46-47
    willing identity, 44-45
Constructed knowers, 158-159
Constructivist education model, 8-10, 334-338
Conversion, 36, 464
Cooperative and collaborative learning, 351-353, 662-663
    classroom observation chart, 360
    complementary teachers, 664, 666-667
    Jewish schools application, 354=356
    jigsaw technique, 354-355
    parallel teachers, 664, 665-666
    Please Listen To Me sheet, 359
    poem writing, 355
    and Rabbinic Judaism, 357-358
    relationships, nature of, 670-672
    resource person collaboration, 664, 667-670
    Student Teams-Achievement Divisions (STAD), 354, 357
Counselor role in summer camping, 271-274
Covenantal community, 33
Cranston, Patricia, 171-172
CR (consciousness-raising) tasks, 522-524
Creative writing, teaching with, 384
Cults, 195-196
Culture clash, American, 61-62
Curricular knowledge, deepening
    importance of, 311-313
    materials, adaptation, 318-320
    teacher study groups, 313-314, 320-321
    unpacking template and evaluation, 312-318
Curriculum development. *See also* Cooperative and collaborative learning; Developmental psychology; Multiple intelligences; Understanding by Design.
    activity based teaching, weakness of, 2

big ideas centered, 3, 5-8, 10
constructivist vs traditional approach, 8-10
developmentally appropriate, 3, 5, 10, 118-119
early childhood, 110-111, 118-119
E-Learning and technology, 254-255
emergent curriculum, 118-119
emotionally engaging, 5, 8, 10
learning *vs.* teaching centered, 2, 3-4, 5, 8, 10
non-core knowledge teaching, 3
Orthodox Jewish education, 58-59
spirituality and God, 363-368
supplementary schools, 1
teacher's role, 6-7
teenage and adolescent learners, 131-132
traditional *vs.* constructivist model, 9
unit planning, importance of, 278-279
Cutter, William, 392, 654

D

Dance and movement, teaching with, 584, 592-594
Bible stories, 597-599
Brothers legend, 602-603
elements of, 594-596
ice breakers, 595-596
Jacob's dilemma, 597-599
prayer, 601-602
rituals, 604
Das Freie Juedische Lehrhaus (The Free House of Jewish Learning), 46
Day camps, working with teen assistants, 684-685
Day schools, Jewish
characteristics of, 67-69
expansion of, 29
historical perspective, 66-67
importance of, 69
non-denominational, 67
pluralism and, 71
and RAVSAK, 68, 72
St. Paul *va'ad din,* 97
teacher community presence, importance of, 71-72
working within, 69-70
Death and dying, 198, 464-465, 467-468
Deitcher, Howard, 384
Depression, 194-195
Developmentally appropriate teaching. *See* Developmental psychology.
Developmental psychology, 85-88
see also Format (4Mat) model, application of; Multiple intelligences.
Adam and Eve story, 85
adult learners, 105-106, 152-159
application of, 101-106
Erikson psychological development, 87-88, 91-94, 102, 105
four developmental theories, 87-88
four kinds of learning styles, 296-297
Fowler faith development, 87-88, 97-101, 103, 104, 105
Gilligan's feminine critique of, 96-97
Heinz Dilemma, 94
Kohlberg moral reasoning, 87-88, 94-97, 102, 104, 106
Piaget cognitive development, 87, 88-91, 101-102, 103, 105, 130

teenage and adolescent learners, 104-105 130-131
Vygotsky theory, 90
Digital world. *See* E-Learning and technology
Dignity to the Elderly, 222
Diseases, communicable, 197-198
Divorce, 165, 198-199, 464
Dorph, Gail, 398
Drama, teaching with, 570-571
bibliodrama, 389
class play, 572-574
developmentally appropriate, 574-575
games, 575
and Hebrew teaching, 576-577
and multiple intelligences, 571
playing our roots program for teens, 134-135
texts, teaching, 384
theater and community, 576
tzedakah projects, 575-576
Dress awareness professional, 23-24
Drug, alcohol abuse, and At-risk children, 190-191
Dynamic learners, 297

E

Early childhood
blessings, teaching, 117
challenges of, 122
developmental psychology, 101-102
every day Judaism, 110
family education, 119-120
God, teaching about, 112-113
holidays, 116, 117-119, 118-119, 476-477
Israel, connection, 115-116
Israel of the Imagination, 116
Jewish identity and, 109
Jewish values, 111-112
joys of, 121-122
non-Jewish teachers, 120-121
physical environment and values, 111-112
Shabbat, 116-117
Torah teaching, 113-115
unspoken curriculum, 110-111
Eating disorders, 193
Education, 21st century
community building, 33-34
critique of, 29-31
goals confusion of, 29-30
"just in time" Jewish education, 32
personalization approach, 32-33
teacher's role, 33
Elderly, honoring, 455-456
E-Learning and technology, 250-252
curricula development, 254-255
home and school connections, 260-262
Internet, 252-254
Knowledge Hunts, 255
online projects, 256-257
PDAs, use of, 259
resource centers, online, 259-260
search engines, 253
software, 254

technomenschen, developing, 262
   vignettes, 250-251, 257-258
   Webquests, 255-256
Elementary age students
   developmental psychology, 101-103
   drama activities, 574-575
   fairness issue, 103
   holidays, 477-478
   music, using, 587-588
Ellis, Rod, 522
Emergent curriculum, 118-119
Enactive, iconic, logical modes of learning, 49
Encyclopedia of Special Education, 180
Enduring understanding, teaching. *See* Understanding by
   Design.
Episodic Jews, 35
Epstein, Joyce, 241
Erikson, Erik, 87-88, 91-94
Ethical will program, 141, 147-148
Ethics. *See* Values and ethics, teaching.
Evaluation domain question, 532
Exceptions, making and living with, 642-643
Exodus dropout issue, 3-4

F
Fabric stenciling, 556-557
Family education. *see also* Community building; Home-school
   partnerships; Retreats, community and family
   activity based teaching, weakness of, 2-3
   adult program development for, 170-172
   divorce and, 165
   early childhood, 119-120
   expansion of, 29
   gay and lesbian parents, 167-168
   intermarriage and, 165-166
   interracial adoptions and, 165-166
   parent parallel education, 168-170
   Reconstructionist Movement, 51
   secular world, intersection with, 641-642
   Shabbat bag, 120
   singles with children, 166
   with storytelling, 612-613
   teenage and adolescents, 131
   transformative learning, 171-172
Family Feud class game, 625-626
Fate and free will, 599
Field trips, 432
Florence Melton Adult Mini-School, 145
Football Phonics game, 630
Footprints and New Worlds (Gezari), 552
4MAT model, application of, 292-294
   brain-mind learning, 299-301
   four kinds of learning styles, 296-297
   four quadrants, 295-296, 301-307
   learner diversity, 294-295
   left and right-mode dimensions, 300-301
   perception and processing, 297-299
   12 principles of, 294
   unit development, 307-309
Four Corners activity, 385
Fowler faith development, 87-88, 97-101, 103, 104, 105

Fox, Everett, 599
Funerals, 464

G
Games, teaching with, 620-622
   Brainstorm, 625
   constructing and creating, 631-632
   Family Feud, 625-626
   Getting to Know You, friendship game, 623-624, 634
   Hollywood Squares, 627-628
   Noah's Ark, 626
   Prayer Book Monopoly, 627-628
   Reinforcement and review, 628-631
   Seder plate thesaurus, 626
   Siddur Jeopardy, 627-628
Gardner, Howard, 323, 331, 571
Gay and lesbian parents, 167-168
Gemara Berurah, software, 258
Gemilut Chasadim, Loving-kindness, 222
Getting to Know You, friendship game, 623-624, 634
Gezari, Temina, 552
Global Jewish mall approach, 440-441
God, teaching about
   b'tzelem Elohim, 113
   conceptual approach, 367
   curricular approach, 364
   developmentally appropriate, 364-365
   discovering God's secrets, 113
   early childhood, 112-113
   emotional approach, 366-367
   fate and free will, 599
   Finding God: Ten Jewish Responses, 105
   God-talk, 113
   historical approach, 366, 367-368
   integrated approach, 368
   micography art project, 554-555
   prayer and, 418-421
   Reconstructionist Movement, 52
   social justice and, 489
   sugar water metaphor, 113
   teenage and adolescent learners, 104-105
   theologian's approach, 365-366
God-talk strategy, 113
Graphic organizers, 546-547
Greenberg, Maury, 256
Guided imagery, 421
Guided questions, 416-417

H
Hachnasat Orchim, hospitality, 222
Havdalah service, 41
Hebrew, teaching
   conversational environment, creating, 525-526
   with dance and movement, 603-604
   with drama, 576-577
   five stages of language, 520-522
   Gemara Berurah, software, 258
   grammar, 522-524
   group poem technique, 355
   jigsaw activity, 524
   language, 516-517

language play, 526
magic loom, 509-510
with multiple intelligences, 328-330
with music, 582
Nahir critique of, 511
online tutorials, 261
reading, 495-499
reading development, six stages of, 509-510
recitation, 506-509
religious program for, 517-518
script and pronunciation, 499-504
Siddur and tefilah, 519-522
survivalist-nationalist program for, 518-519
Zigzagworld's Hebrew for Me, 251
Hebrew for Me, Zigzagworld's, 251
Heinz Dilemma, 94
Heschel, Abraham Joshua, 40
History, teaching, 4, 424-425
activities, 431-436
Avot v'Emahot Rummy, 631
big ideas approach, 428-429
developmentally appropriate, 426-427
developmental psychology and, 105
history party drama, 575
masks project, 564-566
oral histories, 436
reenactments, 433-434
sacred *vs.* academic, 425-426
three elements to, 427-436
trials, 435-436
Holes (Sachar), 390
Holidays, teaching, 2
curriculum development, 473-475
developmentally appropriate, 476-478
drama and, 574
Hebrew, place of, 476
issues, 472-473, 475-478
with multiple intelligences, 330
murals for, 561
ritual objects, use of, 475, 476
year, calendaring, 478
Hollywood Squares, 627-628
Holtzman, R. Linda, 50
Home and school partnerships. *See also* Community building;
    Family education.
calendars, 245-246
car talk, 245-246
communication, 245-248
homework, interactive, 242-245
parent participation, fostering, 243
strengthening, 247-248
summer learning packets, 247
Horowitz, Bethamie, 8, 10, 92
How Jews became White Folk, 75
Hunger awareness, student, 61

I
Ice breakers, dance and movement, 595-596
Identity, Jewish, 32-33
adult learners, 153-154

ascribed and chosen identity, 38
assimilation and intermarriage, 74-75
Conservative Movement, 44
early childhood and, 109
Erikson theory and, 91-92
Horowitz findings, 92
How Jews became White Folk, 75
Jewishness, concepts of, 75-79
Jews by Choice, 37-38
meaningfulness and, 76
"not yet" Jews, 46-47
Reform movement, 36
teacher identity and, 40
willing Jews, 44
Imaginative learners, 297
Immigration chart and activities, 487
In a Different Voice (Gilligan), 96-97
Inappropriate relationships and At-risk children, 191-192
Independent Schools Association (ISACS), 14
In My Home Today, storytelling technique, 617
Instructional technology. *See* E-Learning and technology.
Interactive displays, 207
Intermarriage and family education, 165-166
Internet. *See* E-Learning and technology.
Interpersonal (people smart) intelligence type, 327, 329
Interracial adoptions and family education, 165-166
Intrapersonal (self smart) intelligence type, 327, 329
Intuitive learners, 159
(ISACS) Independent Schools Association, 14
Israel, connection to
Am and Eretz Yisrael connection, 442-443
calendar and rhythm, 444-445
culture, 447-449
early childhood, 115-116
ecology and landscape, 441-442
global Jewish mall approach, 440-441
Hebrew and, 442-444
immigration chart and activities, 487
Israel experience, 449-450
Israeli Foot Race game, 629
Israel of the Imagination, 116
Meraglim L'aretz scouting activity, 237
Reconstructionist Movement, 52-53
symbols and heroes, 445-447
Israel of the Imagination, 116

J
Jacob's dilemma, teaching with dance and movement, 597-599
Jeopardy, 627-628
Jerusalem, Four Corners activity, 385
Jerusalem mosaic project, 563-564
Jewish Community Day School Network (RAVSAK), 14, 68, 72
Jews around the World display, 207
Jews by Choice, 35
Jews for Jesus, 196-197
Jigsaw activity for Hebrew, 524
Jigsaw technique, cooperative learning, 354-355
Joseph, R. Sam, 685
Joseph, teaching with dance and movement, 599-600
"Just in time" Jewish education, 32

K

Kabbalat Shabbat music service, 588-589
Kaplan, R. Mordechai, 52
Kashrut, 45
Kaunfer, Alvin, 383
Kinesthetic (body smart) intelligence type, 325-327, 329
K'lal Yisrael, 81, 115-116
Knesset class meeting, 220-221
Knowledge domain question, 530
Knowledge Hunts, 255
Knowles, Malcolm, 170
Koch, Kenneth, 355
Kohlberg moral reasoning, 87-88, 94-97, 102, 104, 106
Kohn, Alfie, 353
Kollel study, 63
Kornhaber, Mindy, 331

L

Langer, Suzanne, 593
Large circle classroom setup, 204
Leadership changes, 647-648
Leap into Learning student display, 207
Learning and learning theory. *See* Developmental psychology;
        Multiple intelligences
Learning centers, 340-343
    classroom environment and scheduling, 343-347
    contract models, 348
    process *vs.* content based, 341
Learning disabilities and At-risk children, 189-190
Learning environment. *See* Classroom environment.
Left and right-mode dimensions, 4MAT model, 300-301
Lehadayr P'nai Zakayn, 455-456
Levine, Mel, 185
Library policy, 22-23
Life cycle, teaching, 461-462
    adoption, 463
    adulthood issues, 464, 468
    childbirth, 462-463
    childhood and adolescence, 463
    curriculum development, 465-466
    death and dying, 464-465, 467-468
    pregnancy, 463
    strategies for, 466-467
Logical/Mathematical (reasoning) intelligence type, 325
London, Perry, 154
Love Thy Neighbor as Thyself, 222-223
Loving-kindness, 222

M

Maimonides, 36, 132
Marriage, 464
Masks, 564-566
Masorah scribes micorgraphy, 553-554
MaTok curriculum, 597-599
Matrilineal vs patrilineal identity, 36
Mazon, food for the hungry, 223
McCarthy, Bernice, 293
McKenzie, Leon, 154-155
McTighe, Jay, 2
Meditation and prayer, 420

Mentoring, 653-657
    finding a mentor, 23, 659
    groups, 657-658
    importance of, 70
    virtual, 658
Meraglim L'aretz scouting activity, 237
Metaphors, similes, 383
Meyer, Michael, 38
Mezuzot, 110
Micography art project, 553-555
Middot and values. *See* Values and ethics.
Midrash, 389, 403-408, 416, 558-559
Milgrom, Jo, 558
Mitzvot, teaching, 6, 453-458, 580
    see also Social Justice, teaching; Values and ethics, teaching
    bikur cholim, 111, 112, 454-455
    Conservative Movement, 44-45
    with dance and movement, 596-597
    four types of doers, 299
    K'lal Yisrael, 111
    learning and doing, balancing, 298-299
    modeling, 456-457
    procreation, 462-463
    texts, use of, 457-458
Moonies, 195
Moral development, 87-88, 94-97
    see also Developmental psychology
    In a Different Voice (Gilligan), 96-97
    in females, 96-97
    Kohlberg moral reasoning, 87-88, 94-97
Mosaics, 563-564
Moses, teaching with dance and movement, 600-601
Mourning rituals, 465
Multiple intelligences. *See also* Developmental psychology;
        Learning centers.
    and drama, 571
    lessons design combining types, 328-331
    Schools Using Multiple Intelligences Theory (SUMIT), 323-
        324, 331
    seven types, 323-324
Murals, 561
Museum, creating your own, 432-433
Music, teaching with, 384
    dance and movement, 584
    developmentally appropriate, 584-588
    Hebrew, 582
    Israel connection, 447-448
    Kabbalat Shabbat service, 588-589
    lesson plans, sample, 586-588
    prayers, 420-421, 580-582
    Purim, 584-585
    techniques, 584-586
    text and, 583-584
Musical/rhythmic (music smart) intelligence type, 324-325, 329
My Bubbe and Zayde told me, storytelling technique, 615
Myers, John L., 353
My Exodus, video, 392
My House student display, 206

N

Nahir, Moshe, 511

Natural Cycle of Learning. *See* 4MAT model, application of.
Naturalist (nature smart) intelligence type, 328, 329
Night hike for teens, 133-134
Noah's Ark, 394
Noah's Ark game, 626
Non-Jewish teachers, 120-121
Novick, Sol, 258

O
Object reading, 434-435
Online. *See* E-Learning and technology.
Opening the school year. *See* Starting in a new school.
Oral histories, 436
Orthodox Jewish education
    administrators crisis, 64
    belief system, 55-56
    challenges facing, 61-62
    culture clash, American, 61-62
    curriculum, 58-59
    day school orientation, 55
    development of, 55
    faculty, 59-60
    financial issue, 62-63
    governance, 58
    home, role of, 59
    homework, 60
    Kollel study and, 63
    lifelong study orientation, 56-57
    personnel recruitment and retention, 63-64
    school day, 60-61
    separatist trend, 62
    student hunger, 61
    Thirteen "*Ani Ma'amins*," 55-56
    Torah m'Sinai, 56
Oxford, Rebecca, 525-526

P
Painting, 562-563
Palmer, Parker, 144, 655
Papier mâché masks project, 566-567
Paper Midrash, 558-559
Paper stenciling, 556
Parallel teachers collaboration, 664, 665-666
Parental separation and divorce, 198-199
Parent communication, 22
Parenting, 464
Parent parallel education, 168-170
Parents. *See* Family education; Home-school partnerships.
Passover, 536, 588, 626
Pass the Hat game, 629
Patrilineal *vs.* matrilineal identity, 36
PDAs, use of, 259
Pedagogy of understanding, 2
Pediatric Judaism mode, 152153
Peer relationships, importance of, 8, 10
Perception and processing, 4MAT model, 297-299
Pervasive Developmental Disorder, 181
Physical and sexual abuse, 192-193
Physical environment. *See* Classroom environment.
Piaget cognitive development, 87, 88-91, 101-102, 103, 105, 130
Pinkenson-Feldman, Ruth, 116

Planning cycles, 17-18
Playing Our Roots program for teens, 134-135
Please Listen To Me sheet, 359
Pods classroom setup, 203
Practical learners, 159
Prayer, teaching, 38
    Avot prayer, 36
    blessings, teaching, 117
    brachot, with learning centers, 342
    bringing meaning, 415-417
    with dance and movement, 601-602
    Football Phonics game, 630
    four elements, 413-414
    games and Hebrew, 414-415
    guided questions, 416-417
    meditation and, 420
    Prayer Book Monopoly, 627-628
    Rainbow *brachah* micography, 555
    Reconstructionist Movement, 52
    room parents, 644-645
    Shema, with dance and movement, 601-602
    Siddur and *tefilah,* 519-522
    Siddur Jeopardy, 627-628
    social justice and, 489
    spiritual environment, creating, 418-421
    Tefilah Bingo, 630
    theological conversations, 417-418
Prayer Book Monopoly, 627-628
Pregnancy, 463
Preparing to Teach Melton faculty handbook, 145
Principal and teacher relationship, 637-638
    behavior challenges, 639-641
    confidentiality, 638-639
    evaluation worksheet, 650
    leadership changes, 647-648
    paperwork requirements, 643-644
    personal commitments conflicts, 645-646
    rules, making exceptions, 642-643
    secular world, intersection with, 641-642
Procedural knowers, 158-159
Procreation, *mitzvah* of, 462
Programming. *See* Curriculum development.
Project Etgar, 293
Project Spectrum, 323
Project SUMIT, 323
Project Zero, 323
Puppet show, 574
Purim, 584-585

Q
Quadrants classroom setup, 203
Questions, asking and use of
    Bloom's taxonomy, 529-536
    Passover *Seder,* 536
    teacher's role, 536-337
    tricks of the trade, 537-538
    vignettes and analysis, 533-536

R
Rablab, 258
Rashi and *midrash,* 403-411

RAVSAK (Jewish Community Day School Network), 14, 68, 72
Reading. *See* Hebrew, teaching.
Received knowers, 158-159
Reconstructionist Educational Study Packet, 49, 50
Reconstructionist Movement
    animal sacrifices, position on, 52
    chosen people status, 52-53
    community building, 51
    developmentally appropriate teaching, 52
    enactive, iconic, logical modes of learning, 49
    family participation, 51
    God, teaching about, 52
    prayer, 52
    teacher development, 49
    teaching from life tradition, 50-51
Reenactments, 433-434
Reform movement
    authority of autonomy, 38-39
    Babylonian experience, 36-37
    community education, 36-37
    conversion, 36
    Havdalah service, 41
    Jewish identity, 36
    Jews by Choice, 37-38
    nature of, 35-36
    patrilineal *vs.* matrilineal identity, 36
    Tikkun Leyl Shavuot, 38-39
    tikkun middot initiatives, 39
    tikkun olam agenda, 39
Reinforcement and review games, 628-631
Religious Action Center, Washington DC, 39
Religious issues in summer camps, 275
Remorse, 224
Repentance, three R's of, 224
Resnikoff, Lauren, 258
Retreats, community and family
    bedtime supervision, 233
    community building, 228-229
    cooperative games, 232
    nature of, 227-229
    preparation, 234-235
    program facilitation, 231-233
    safety, 229
    Shabbaton sample schedule, 237-238
    staff roles and responsibilities, 229-234
    teen assistants, 684-685
Rituals, teaching with dance and movement, 604
Rodef shalom, 454-455
Room parents, 644-645
Rosenzweig, Franz, 40, 46, 146
Rules, making and living with exceptions, 642-643
Running relay game, 629
Russia, life in, 487

S
Sachar, Louis, 390
Sacred *vs.* academic history, 425-426
Scheinerman, R. Amy, 261
Scholem, Gershon, 39
Schools Using Multiple Intelligences Theory (SUMIT), 323-324, 331

Schuster, Diane Tickton, 171
Schwab, Joseph, 314-315
Schwartz, Earl, 97
Scientology, 195
Seder plate thesaurus game, 626
Seminar-style classroom setup, 204-205
Sequential learners, 158-159
Seven Days of Creation painting project, 562-563
Sexual abuse, 192-193
Sexual harassment and At-risk children, 191-192
Sha'ar'ei Tefillah, 40-41
Shabbaton sample schedule, 237-238
Shabbat, teaching, 318-319
    brachot micography, 555
    early childhood, 116-117
    Shabbat bag, 120
    work and rest, concepts, 319
    Yesh Li Shabbat Bingo, 630
Shabbat bag, 120
Shavuot, 38-39
Shema, teaching with dance and movement, 601-602
Shema, with dance and movement, 601-602
Sh'lom Bayit, 223
Sick, visiting. *See Bikur cholim.*
Siddur and *tefilah,* 519-522
Siddur Jeopardy, 627-628
Silent knowers, 158-159
Singles with children and family education, 166
Social action projects, 482-483
Social Justice, teaching, 481-482
    curriculum, 483-486
    holidays, 489
    Jewish context for, 486-490
    prayer and, 489
    social action projects, 482-483
    texts, 488
Soundscape, 574
Special needs students, 82-83
    Asperger Syndrome, 180
    Attention Deficit (Hyperactive) Disorder, 180-181
    classroom scenario for, 177-179
    cooperative learning, 184
    ethical attitudes toward, 82-83
    history of, 177
    inclusion issue, 179
    least restrictive environment, 177
    peer tutoring, 183
    Pervasive Developmental Disorder, 181
    student success, causing, 181-185
    teaching considerations, 185
Spirituality and God, teaching. *See* God, teaching about.
Spitzer, Jeff, 258
Starting school
    administrative procedures, installing, 22-23
    bulletin boards, 20
    community norms orientation, 14
    curriculum orientation, 15-16
    dress awareness, professional, 23-24
    first week, 24-25
    goals orientation, 13-15
    lesson plans, 18

library policy, 22-23
parent communication, 22
physical space, setting up, 18-20
plan development, 17-18
procedural expectations, 20-22
security and safety, 21-22
student assessment, 24-25
summer preparation checklist, 26
Stenciling, 556-557
Sternberg, Robert, 323
Stickies, fun with, 547
Stocking wire hanger masks project, 565
Storytelling, teaching with, 421, 608-617
Student empowerment, 8, 9
Student Teams-Achievement Divisions (STAD), 354, 357
Student workspace, setting up, 19-20
Stuffed Torahs technique, 114
Subjective knowers, 158-159
Sugar water metaphor for God, 113
Suicide, 194-195, 464
Sukkot, 6, 354
Summer camping, 269-275
Summer learning packets, 247
Summer preparation checklist, 26
Supermarket Dash game, 629
Supplementary schools, 1, 2-3
Survivalist-nationalist program for teaching Hebrew, 518-519
Synectics, 383, 398
Synthesis domain question, 531-532

T
Tabernacle, 394-395
Tarone, Elaine, 526
Teacher curriculum study groups, 313-314, 320-321
Teaching in the home. *See* Home-school partnerships.
Technology, use of. *See* E-Learning and technology.
Technomenschen, developing, 262
Teenage and adolescent learners
activity based teaching, weakness of, 2-3
case studies, 133-135
developmental psychology, 103-105, 130-131
family context and, 131
four programming strategies for, 135-136
God, teaching about, 104-105
holidays, 478
Jewish content, 132-133
nature of, 128-129
night hike for, 133-134
Playing Our Roots program, 134-135
programming for, 127-128
teachers of, 129-130
Torah teaching with storytelling, 612
Teen assistants, working with, 675-677
compensation issue, 685
in day camps and retreats, 684-685
growing them, 678-680
Madrichim survey sheet, 687
relationship, assistant to student, 680
relationship with, 677-678
vignettes analysis, 680-684
Tefilah Bingo, 630

Tefilah. See Prayer, teaching.
Ten Commandments, 394
Textonomy, 377
Texts, teaching, 374-375
see also Torah, teaching
activities, experiential, 384-385
chevruta learning, 381-382
developmentally appropriate, 378-379
discussion, teacher guided, 379-381
literary tools, 382-384
metaphors, similes, 383
mitzvot, 457-458
planning, 376-378
Rashi, dealing with, 408-411
Siddur and *tefilah*, 519-522
Textonomy, 377
The Bird's Nest (Bialik), 603
The Courage to Teach (Palmer), 144
The Elephants Wing (Owen and Bruner), 603-604
The Forgotten Language (Fromm), 319
The Madrikhim Handbook (Joseph), 685
Theme backpacks, 120
The Mentor's Guide (Zachary), 654-655
The Process of Education (Bruner), 535
The Teacher-Curriculum Encounter (Ben-Peretz), 318
Think-Pair-Share, 544-545
Thirteen *"Ani Ma'amins,"* 55-56
Tikkun Leyl Shavuot, 38-39
Tikkun olam, 223
Timed progressive relay game, 629
Torah, teaching. *See also* Texts, teaching.
activities, 389-391, 396-397
art and, 562
bibliodrama, 389
connections, making, 394-397
constructive arguing, 398-399
developmental psychology and, 103
early childhood, 113-115
filling in feelings approach, 388-390
holes, filling in, 390-391
Jacob's ladder, 397-398
from life and insight, 391-393
life experience approach, 40
midrash and Rashi, 403-411
with multiple intelligences, 330
with music, 583-584
Orthodox Jewish education, 56
Reconstructionist Movement, 52
with storytelling, 612
stuffed Torahs, 114
TorahQuests, 258
Torah statues, 574
torn paper *midrash*, 389
unpacking sample, 395-396
TorahQuests, 258
Torah statues, 574
Torn paper *midrash*, 389
Towards a Theory of Instruction (Bruner), 49
Trials for history teaching, 435-436
Tu B'Shevat collage, 560-561
Two-faced masks project, 565-566

Tyrell, Ronald, 357
Tzedakah, 22, 80-81, 223

U

Understanding by Design, 280-282
    assessing learning, 282-284
    calendaring, 286, 287
    curricula, 280-282
    learning activities, 284-286
    lesson preparation, 286-288
    lesson structure, 288-290
    unit specifics focus, 281-282
Understanding By Design (Wiggins and McTighe), 6
Ushpizin, 6

V

Va'ad din, court, 97
Values and ethics, teaching. *See also Mitzvot,* teaching; Social
    Justice, teaching.
    Bal Taschit/Be Not Destructive, 222
    bikur cholim, 222
    business ethics, 81-82
    chesed, 482
    children's literature, 232
    with dance and movement, 596-597
    Gemilut Chasadim, Loving-kindness, 222
    Hachnasat Orchim, hospitality, 222
    honoring the elderly, 222, 455-456
    justice, 490
    K'lal Yisrael, 81
    Lashon Hara, 83
    Lehadayr P'nai Zakayn, 455-456
    Love Thy Neighbor as Thyself, 222-223
    Mazon, food for the hungry, 223
    Sh'lom bayit, 223
    special needs students, 82-83
    summer camps, 274-275

    texts activity, 384
    tikkun olam, 223
    tzedakah, 80-81, 223
Vella, Jane, 142-150
Verbal/Linguistic (word-smart) intelligence type, 324
Virtual Field Trips Webquest (Greenberg), 256
Visual/Spatial (picture smart) intelligence type, 325, 329
Voting technique, 545
Vygotsky, Lev, 90

W

WebQuests, 255-256
What's Kosher display, 207
What to teach dilemma, 1-2, 3-4
When I Was Growing Up I Remember, storytelling technique,
    616
Who Can Retell game, 629-630
Who Wants to Be a Millionaire game, 630
Wiggins, Grant, 2
Wimpels art projects, 555-558
Wishes, Lies, and Dreams (Koch), 355
Wolf, Dennis Palmer, 534-535
Women in Midrash class, 149
Woocher, Jonathan S., 169
Word repetition in prayer, 420
Work and rest, concepts, 319

Y

Yeshivat Etz Chayyim, 55
Yeshivat Rabbi Yitzchak Elchanan, 55
Yesh Li game, 630
Youth groups, success of, 8, 10

Z

Zachary, Lois J., 654-655
Zigzagworld Hebrew for Me, 251